Principles of Microeconomics

Includes Required Online Access Code

2012-2013 University of Toledo Edition

N. Gregory Mankiw

CENGAGE
Learning·

Australia • Brazil • Japan • Korea • Mexico • Singapore • Spain • United Kingdom • United States

Principles of Microeconomics: Includes Required Online Access Code, 2012-2013 University of Toledo Edition

Sources:

Principles of Microeconomics, 6th Edition
N. Gregory Mankiw
© 2012 Cengage Learning. All rights reserved.

Global Economic Watch: Impact on Economics, 1st Edition
Global Economics Crisis Resource Center
© 2010 Cengage Learning. All rights reserved.

Executive Editors:
 Maureen Staudt
 Michael Stranz

Senior Project Development Manager:
 Linda deStefano

Marketing Specialist:
 Courtney Sheldon

Senior Production/Manufacturing Manager:
 Donna M. Brown

Production Editorial Manager:
 Kim Fry

Sr. Rights Acquisition Account Manager:
 Todd Osborne

For product information and technology assistance, contact us at
Cengage Learning Customer & Sales Support, 1-800-354-9706

For permission to use material from this text or product,
submit all requests online at **cengage.com/permissions**
Further permissions questions can be emailed to
permissionrequest@cengage.com

This book contains select works from existing Cengage Learning resources and was produced by Cengage Learning Custom Solutions for collegiate use. As such, those adopting and/or contributing to this work are responsible for editorial content accuracy, continuity and completeness.

Compilation © 2012 Cengage Learning
ISBN-13: 978-1-285-10161-3

ISBN-10: 1-285-10161-8

Cengage Learning
5191 Natorp Boulevard
Mason, Ohio 45040
USA

Cengage Learning is a leading provider of customized learning solutions with office locations around the globe, including Singapore, the United Kingdom, Australia, Mexico, Brazil, and Japan. Locate your local office at:
international.cengage.com/region.
Cengage Learning products are represented in Canada by Nelson Education, Ltd.
For your lifelong learning solutions, visit **www.cengage.com/custom.**
Visit our corporate website at **www.cengage.com.**

Printed in the United States of America

Brief Contents

STUDY GUIDE PORTION

MODULES

PART **I** Introduction

Ten Principles of Economics

The word *economy* comes from the Greek word *oikonomos*, which means "one who manages a household." At first, this origin might seem peculiar. But in fact, households and economies have much in common.

A household faces many decisions. It must decide which members of the household do which tasks and what each member gets in return: Who cooks dinner? Who does the laundry? Who gets the extra dessert at dinner? Who gets to choose what TV show to watch? In short, the household must allocate its scarce resources among its various members, taking into account each member's abilities, efforts, and desires.

Like a household, a society faces many decisions. A society must find some way to decide what jobs will be done and who will do them. It needs some people to grow food, other people to make clothing, and still others to design computer software. Once society has allocated people (as well as land, buildings, and machines) to various jobs, it must also allocate the output of goods and services they produce. It must decide who will eat caviar and who will eat potatoes. It must decide who will drive a Ferrari and who will take the bus.

The management of society's resources is important because resources are scarce. **Scarcity** means that society has limited resources and therefore cannot produce all the goods and services people wish to have. Just as each member of a household cannot get everything he or she wants, each individual in a society cannot attain the highest standard of living to which he or she might aspire.

Economics is the study of how society manages its scarce resources. In most societies, resources are allocated not by an all-powerful dictator but through the combined actions of millions of households and firms. Economists therefore study how people make decisions: how much they work, what they buy, how much they save, and how they invest their savings. Economists also study how people interact with one another. For instance, they examine how the multitude of buyers and sellers of a good together determine the price at which the good is sold and the quantity that is sold. Finally, economists analyze forces and trends that affect the economy as a whole, including the growth in average income, the fraction of the population that cannot find work, and the rate at which prices are rising.

The study of economics has many facets, but it is unified by several central ideas. In this chapter, we look at *Ten Principles of Economics*. Don't worry if you don't understand them all at first or if you aren't completely convinced. We will explore these ideas more fully in later chapters. The ten principles are introduced here to give you an overview of what economics is all about. Consider this chapter a "preview of coming attractions."

scarcity
the limited nature of society's resources

economics
the study of how society manages its scarce resources

How People Make Decisions

There is no mystery to what an economy is. Whether we are talking about the economy of Los Angeles, the United States, or the whole world, an economy is just a group of people dealing with one another as they go about their lives. Because the behavior of an economy reflects the behavior of the individuals who make up the economy, we begin our study of economics with four principles of individual decision making.

Principle 1: People Face Trade-offs

You may have heard the old saying, "There ain't no such thing as a free lunch." Grammar aside, there is much truth to this adage. To get one thing that we like, we usually have to give up another thing that we like. Making decisions requires trading off one goal against another.

Consider a student who must decide how to allocate her most valuable resource—her time. She can spend all her time studying economics, spend all of it studying psychology, or divide it between the two fields. For every hour she studies one subject, she gives up an hour she could have used studying the other. And for every hour she spends studying, she gives up an hour that she could have spent napping, bike riding, watching TV, or working at her part-time job for some extra spending money.

Or consider parents deciding how to spend their family income. They can buy food, clothing, or a family vacation. Or they can save some of the family income for retirement or the children's college education. When they choose to spend an extra dollar on one of these goods, they have one less dollar to spend on some other good.

When people are grouped into societies, they face different kinds of trade-offs. One classic trade-off is between "guns and butter." The more a society spends on national defense (guns) to protect its shores from foreign aggressors, the less it can spend on consumer goods (butter) to raise the standard of living at home. Also important in modern society is the trade-off between a clean environment and a high level of income. Laws that require firms to reduce pollution raise the cost of producing goods and services. Because of the higher costs, these firms end up earning smaller profits, paying lower wages, charging higher prices, or some combination of these three. Thus, while pollution regulations yield the benefit of a cleaner environment and the improved health that comes with it, the regulations come at the cost of reducing the incomes of the regulated firms' owners, workers, and customers.

Another trade-off society faces is between efficiency and equality. **Efficiency** means that society is getting the maximum benefits from its scarce resources. **Equality** means that those benefits are distributed uniformly among society's members. In other words, efficiency refers to the size of the economic pie, and equality refers to how the pie is divided into individual slices.

When government policies are designed, these two goals often conflict. Consider, for instance, policies aimed at equalizing the distribution of economic well-being. Some of these policies, such as the welfare system or unemployment insurance, try to help the members of society who are most in need. Others, such as the individual income tax, ask the financially successful to contribute more than others to support the government. While achieving greater equality, these policies reduce efficiency. When the government redistributes income from the rich to the poor, it reduces the reward for working hard; as a result, people work less and produce fewer goods and services. In other words, when the government tries to cut the economic pie into more equal slices, the pie gets smaller.

Recognizing that people face trade-offs does not by itself tell us what decisions they will or should make. A student should not abandon the study of psychology just because doing so would increase the time available for the study of economics. Society should not stop protecting the environment just because environmental regulations reduce our material standard of living. The poor should not be ignored just because helping them distorts work incentives. Nonetheless, people are likely to make good decisions only if they understand the options they have available. Our study of economics, therefore, starts by acknowledging life's trade-offs.

efficiency
the property of society getting the most it can from its scarce resources

equality
the property of distributing economic prosperity uniformly among the members of society

Principle 2: The Cost of Something Is What You Give Up to Get It

Because people face trade-offs, making decisions requires comparing the costs and benefits of alternative courses of action. In many cases, however, the cost of an action is not as obvious as it might first appear.

Consider the decision to go to college. The main benefits are intellectual enrichment and a lifetime of better job opportunities. But what are the costs? To answer this question, you might be tempted to add up the money you spend on tuition, books, room, and board. Yet this total does not truly represent what you give up to spend a year in college.

There are two problems with this calculation. First, it includes some things that are not really costs of going to college. Even if you quit school, you need a place to sleep and food to eat. Room and board are costs of going to college only to the extent that they are more expensive at college than elsewhere. Second, this calculation ignores the largest cost of going to college—your time. When you spend a year listening to lectures, reading textbooks, and writing papers, you cannot spend that time working at a job. For most students, the earnings given up to attend school are the largest single cost of their education.

opportunity cost

whatever must be given up to obtain some item

The **opportunity cost** of an item is what you give up to get that item. When making any decision, decision makers should be aware of the opportunity costs that accompany each possible action. In fact, they usually are. College athletes who can earn millions if they drop out of school and play professional sports are well aware that their opportunity cost of college is very high. It is not surprising that they often decide that the benefit of a college education is not worth the cost.

Principle 3: Rational People Think at the Margin

rational people

people who systematically and purposefully do the best they can to achieve their objectives

Economists normally assume that people are rational. **Rational people** systematically and purposefully do the best they can to achieve their objectives, given the available opportunities. As you study economics, you will encounter firms that decide how many workers to hire and how much of their product to manufacture and sell to maximize profits. You will also encounter individuals who decide how much time to spend working and what goods and services to buy with the resulting income to achieve the highest possible level of satisfaction.

marginal change

a small incremental adjustment to a plan of action

Rational people know that decisions in life are rarely black and white but usually involve shades of gray. At dinnertime, the decision you face is not between fasting or eating like a pig but whether to take that extra spoonful of mashed potatoes. When exams roll around, your decision is not between blowing them off or studying 24 hours a day but whether to spend an extra hour reviewing your notes instead of watching TV. Economists use the term **marginal change** to describe a small incremental adjustment to an existing plan of action. Keep in mind that *margin* means "edge," so marginal changes are adjustments around the edges of what you are doing. Rational people often make decisions by comparing *marginal benefits* and *marginal costs*.

For example, consider an airline deciding how much to charge passengers who fly standby. Suppose that flying a 200-seat plane across the United States costs the airline $100,000. In this case, the average cost of each seat is $100,000/200, which is $500. One might be tempted to conclude that the airline should never sell a ticket for less than $500. Actually, a rational airline can often find ways to raise its profits by thinking at the margin. Imagine that a plane is about to take off with ten empty seats, and a standby passenger waiting at the gate will pay $300 for a seat. Should the airline sell the ticket? Of course it should. If the plane has empty seats, the cost of adding one more passenger is tiny. Although the *average* cost of flying a passenger is $500, the *marginal* cost is merely the cost of the bag of peanuts and can of soda that the extra passenger will consume. As long as the standby passenger pays more than the marginal cost, selling the ticket is profitable.

Marginal decision making can help explain some otherwise puzzling economic phenomena. Here is a classic question: Why is water so cheap, while diamonds are so expensive? Humans need water to survive, while diamonds are unnecessary; but for some reason, people are willing to pay much more for a diamond than for a cup of water. The reason is that a person's willingness to pay for a good is based on the marginal benefit that an extra unit of the good would yield. The marginal benefit, in turn, depends on how many units a person already has. Water is essential, but the marginal benefit of an extra cup is small because water is plentiful. By contrast, no one needs diamonds to survive, but because diamonds are so rare, people consider the marginal benefit of an extra diamond to be large.

A rational decision maker takes an action if and only if the marginal benefit of the action exceeds the marginal cost. This principle can explain why airlines are willing to sell a ticket below average cost and why people are willing to pay more for diamonds than for water. It can take some time to get used to the logic of marginal thinking, but the study of economics will give you ample opportunity to practice.

Principle 4: People Respond to Incentives

An **incentive** is something that induces a person to act, such as the prospect of a punishment or a reward. Because rational people make decisions by comparing costs and benefits, they respond to incentives. You will see that incentives play a central role in the study of economics. One economist went so far as to suggest that the entire field could be summarized simply: "People respond to incentives. The rest is commentary."

incentive
something that induces a person to act

Incentives are crucial to analyzing how markets work. For example, when the price of an apple rises, people decide to eat fewer apples. At the same time, apple orchards decide to hire more workers and harvest more apples. In other words, a higher price in a market provides an incentive for buyers to consume less and an incentive for sellers to produce more. As we will see, the influence of prices on the behavior of consumers and producers is crucial for how a market economy allocates scarce resources.

Public policymakers should never forget about incentives: Many policies change the costs or benefits that people face and, therefore, alter their behavior. A tax on gasoline, for instance, encourages people to drive smaller, more fuel-efficient cars. That is one reason people drive smaller cars in Europe, where gasoline taxes are high, than in the United States, where gasoline taxes are low. A gasoline tax also encourages people to carpool, take public transportation, and live closer to where they work. If the tax were larger, more people would be driving hybrid cars, and if it were large enough, they would switch to electric cars.

When policymakers fail to consider how their policies affect incentives, they often end up with unintended consequences. For example, consider public policy regarding auto safety. Today, all cars have seat belts, but this was not true 50 years ago. In the 1960s, Ralph Nader's book *Unsafe at Any Speed* generated much public concern over auto safety. Congress responded with laws requiring seat belts as standard equipment on new cars.

How does a seat belt law affect auto safety? The direct effect is obvious: When a person wears a seat belt, the probability of surviving an auto accident rises. But that's not the end of the story because the law also affects behavior by altering incentives. The relevant behavior here is the speed and care with which drivers operate their cars. Driving slowly and carefully is costly because it uses the driver's time and energy. When deciding how safely to drive, rational people compare, perhaps unconsciously, the marginal benefit from safer driving to the marginal cost. As a result, they drive more slowly and carefully when the benefit of increased safety is high. For example, when road conditions are icy, people drive more attentively and at lower speeds than they do when road conditions are clear.

Consider how a seat belt law alters a driver's cost–benefit calculation. Seat belts make accidents less costly because they reduce the likelihood of injury or death. In other words, seat belts reduce the benefits of slow and careful driving. People respond to seat belts as they would to an improvement in road conditions—by driving faster and less carefully. The result of a seat belt law, therefore, is a larger number of accidents. The decline in safe driving has a clear, adverse impact on pedestrians, who are more likely to find themselves in an accident but (unlike the drivers) don't have the benefit of added protection.

At first, this discussion of incentives and seat belts might seem like idle speculation. Yet in a classic 1975 study, economist Sam Peltzman argued that auto-safety laws have had many of these effects. According to Peltzman's evidence, these laws produce both fewer deaths per accident and more accidents. He concluded that the net result is little change in the number of driver deaths and an increase in the number of pedestrian deaths.

Peltzman's analysis of auto safety is an offbeat and controversial example of the general principle that people respond to incentives. When analyzing any policy, we must consider not only the direct effects but also the less obvious indirect effects that work through incentives. If the policy changes incentives, it will cause people to alter their behavior.

The Incentive Effects of Gasoline Prices

From 2005 to 2008 the price of oil in world oil markets skyrocketed, the result of limited supplies together with surging demand from robust world growth, especially in China. The price of gasoline in the United States rose from about $2 to about $4 a gallon. At the time, the news was filled with stories about how people responded to the increased incentive to conserve, sometimes in obvious ways, sometimes in less obvious ways.

Here is a sampling of various stories:

- "As Gas Prices Soar, Buyers Are Flocking to Small Cars"
- "As Gas Prices Climb, So Do Scooter Sales"
- "Gas Prices Knock Bicycles Sales, Repairs into Higher Gear"
- "Gas Prices Send Surge of Riders to Mass Transit"
- "Camel Demand Up as Oil Price Soars": Farmers in the Indian state of Rajasthan are rediscovering the humble camel. As the cost of running gas-guzzling tractors soars, even-toed ungulates are making a comeback.
- "The Airlines Are Suffering, But the Order Books of Boeing and Airbus Are Bulging": Demand for new, more fuel-efficient aircraft has never been greater. The latest versions of the Airbus A320 and Boeing 737, the single-aisle workhorses for which demand is strongest, are up to 40% cheaper to run than the vintage planes some American airlines still use.
- "Home Buying Practices Adjust to High Gas Prices": In his hunt for a new home, Demetrius Stroud crunched the numbers to find out that, with gas prices climbing, moving near an Amtrak station is the best thing for his wallet.
- "Gas Prices Drive Students to Online Courses": For Christy LaBadie, a sophomore at Northampton Community College, the 30-minute drive from her home to the Bethlehem, Pa., campus has become a financial hardship now that gasoline prices have soared to more than $4 a gallon. So this semester she decided to take an online course to save herself the trip—and the money.
- "Diddy Halts Private Jet Flights Over Fuel Prices": Fuel prices have grounded an unexpected frequent-flyer: Sean "Diddy" Combs. . . . The hip-hop mogul said he is now flying on commercial airlines instead of in private jets, which Combs said had previously cost him $200,000 and up for a roundtrip between New York and Los Angeles. "I'm actually flying commercial," Diddy said before walking onto an airplane, sitting in a first-class seat and flashing his boarding pass to the camera. "That's how high gas prices are."

Hip-hop mogul Sean "Diddy" Combs responds to incentives.

Many of these developments proved transitory. The economic downturn that began in 2008 and continued into 2009 reduced the world demand for oil, and the price of gasoline declined substantially. No word yet on whether Mr. Combs has returned to his private jet. ■

QUICK QUIZ   *Describe an important trade-off you recently faced. • Give an example of some action that has both a monetary and nonmonetary opportunity cost. • Describe an incentive your parents offered to you in an effort to influence your behavior.*

· in the news

› *Incentive Pay*

As this article illustrates, how people are paid affects their incentives and the decisions they make. (The article's author, by the way, subsequently became one of the chief economic advisers to President Barack Obama.)

Where the Buses Run on Time

By Austan Goolsbee

On a summer afternoon, the drive home from the University of Chicago to the north side of the city must be one of the most beautiful commutes in the world. On the left on Lake Shore Drive you pass Grant Park, some of the world's first skyscrapers, and the Sears Tower. On the right is the intense blue of Lake Michigan. But for all the beauty, the traffic can be hell. So, if you drive the route every day, you learn the shortcuts. You know that if it backs up from the Buckingham Fountain all the way to McCormick Place, you're better off taking the surface streets and getting back onto Lake Shore Drive a few miles north.

A lot of buses, however, wait in the traffic jams. I have always wondered about that: Why don't the bus drivers use the shortcuts? Surely they know about them—they drive the same route every day, and they probably avoid the traffic when they drive their own

cars. Buses don't stop on Lake Shore Drive, so they wouldn't strand anyone by detouring around the congestion. And when buses get delayed in heavy traffic, it wreaks havoc on the scheduled service. Instead of arriving once every 10 minutes, three buses come in at the same time after half an hour. That sort of bunching is the least efficient way to run a public transportation system. So, why not take the surface streets if that would keep the schedule properly spaced and on time?

You might think at first that the problem is that the drivers aren't paid enough to strategize. But Chicago bus drivers are the seventh-highest paid in the nation; full-timers earned more than $23 an hour, according to a November 2004 survey. The problem may have to do not with how much they are paid, but how they are paid. At least, that's the implication of a new study of Chilean bus drivers by Ryan Johnson and David Reiley of the University of Arizona and Juan Carlos Muñoz of Pontificia Universidad Católica de Chile.

Companies in Chile pay bus drivers one of two ways: either by the hour or by the passenger. Paying by the passenger leads to significantly shorter delays. Give them

incentives, and drivers start acting like regular people do. They take shortcuts when the traffic is bad. They take shorter meal breaks and bathroom breaks. They want to get on the road and pick up more passengers as quickly as they can. In short, their productivity increases....

Not everything about incentive pay is perfect, of course. When bus drivers start moving from place to place more quickly, they get in more accidents (just like the rest of us). Some passengers also complain that the rides make them nauseated because the drivers stomp on the gas as soon as the last passenger gets on the bus. Yet when given the choice, people overwhelmingly choose the bus companies that get them where they're going on time. More than 95 percent of the routes in Santiago use incentive pay.

Perhaps we should have known that incentive pay could increase bus driver productivity. After all, the taxis in Chicago take the shortcuts on Lake Shore Drive to avoid the traffic that buses just sit in. Since taxi drivers earn money for every trip they make, they want to get you home as quickly as possible so they can pick up somebody else.

Source: Slate.com, March 16, 2006.

How People Interact

The first four principles discussed how individuals make decisions. As we go about our lives, many of our decisions affect not only ourselves but other people as well. The next three principles concern how people interact with one another.

Principle 5: Trade Can Make Everyone Better Off

You may have heard on the news that the Japanese are our competitors in the world economy. In some ways, this is true because American and Japanese firms produce many of the same goods. Ford and Toyota compete for the same customers in the market for automobiles. Apple and Sony compete for the same customers in the market for digital music players.

Yet it is easy to be misled when thinking about competition among countries. Trade between the United States and Japan is not like a sports contest in which one side wins and the other side loses. In fact, the opposite is true: Trade between two countries can make each country better off.

To see why, consider how trade affects your family. When a member of your family looks for a job, he or she competes against members of other families who are looking for jobs. Families also compete against one another when they go shopping because each family wants to buy the best goods at the lowest prices. In a sense, each family in the economy is competing with all other families.

Despite this competition, your family would not be better off isolating itself from all other families. If it did, your family would need to grow its own food, make its own clothes, and build its own home. Clearly, your family gains much from its ability to trade with others. Trade allows each person to specialize in the activities he or she does best, whether it is farming, sewing, or home building. By trading with others, people can buy a greater variety of goods and services at lower cost.

Countries as well as families benefit from the ability to trade with one another. Trade allows countries to specialize in what they do best and to enjoy a greater variety of goods and services. The Japanese, as well as the French and the Egyptians and the Brazilians, are as much our partners in the world economy as they are our competitors.

Principle 6: Markets Are Usually a Good Way to Organize Economic Activity

The collapse of communism in the Soviet Union and Eastern Europe in the 1980s may be the most important change in the world during the past half century. Communist countries worked on the premise that government officials were in the best position to allocate the economy's scarce resources. These central planners decided what goods and services were produced, how much was produced, and who produced and consumed these goods and services. The theory behind central planning was that only the government could organize economic activity in a way that promoted economic well-being for the country as a whole.

Most countries that once had centrally planned economies have abandoned the system and are instead developing market economies. In a **market economy**, the decisions of a central planner are replaced by the decisions of millions of firms and households. Firms decide whom to hire and what to make. Households decide which firms to work for and what to buy with their incomes. These firms

THE WALL STREET JOURNAL

ENGLEMAN

"For $5 a week you can watch baseball without being nagged to cut the grass!"

market economy

an economy that allocates resources through the decentralized decisions of many firms and households as they interact in markets for goods and services and households interact in the marketplace, where prices and self-interest guide their decisions.

At first glance, the success of market economies is puzzling. In a market economy, no one is looking out for the economic well-being of society as a whole. Free markets contain many buyers and sellers of numerous goods and services, and all of them are interested primarily in their own well-being. Yet despite decentralized decision making and self-interested decision makers, market economies have proven remarkably successful in organizing economic activity to promote overall economic well-being.

In his 1776 book *An Inquiry into the Nature and Causes of the Wealth of Nations*, economist Adam Smith made the most famous observation in all of economics: Households and firms interacting in markets act as if they are guided by an "invisible hand" that leads them to desirable market outcomes. One of our goals in this book is to understand how this invisible hand works its magic.

As you study economics, you will learn that prices are the instrument with which the invisible hand directs economic activity. In any market, buyers look at the price when determining how much to demand, and sellers look at the price when deciding how much to supply. As a result of the decisions that buyers and sellers make, market prices reflect both the value of a good to society and the cost to society of making the good. Smith's great insight was that prices adjust to guide these individual buyers and sellers to reach outcomes that, in many cases, maximize the well-being of society as a whole.

Smith's insight has an important corollary: When the government prevents prices from adjusting naturally to supply and demand, it impedes the invisible hand's ability to coordinate the decisions of the households and firms that make up the economy. This corollary explains why taxes adversely affect the allocation of resources, for they distort prices and thus the decisions of households and firms. It also explains the great harm caused by policies that directly control prices, such as rent control. And it explains the failure of communism. In communist countries, prices were not determined in the marketplace but were dictated by central planners. These planners lacked the necessary information about consumers' tastes and producers' costs, which in a market economy is reflected in prices. Central planners failed because they tried to run the economy with one hand tied behind their backs—the invisible hand of the marketplace.

Principle 7: Governments Can Sometimes Improve Market Outcomes

If the invisible hand of the market is so great, why do we need government? One purpose of studying economics is to refine your view about the proper role and scope of government policy.

One reason we need government is that the invisible hand can work its magic only if the government enforces the rules and maintains the institutions that are key to a market economy. Most important, market economies need institutions to enforce **property rights** so individuals can own and control scarce resources. A farmer won't grow food if he expects his crop to be stolen; a restaurant won't serve meals unless it is assured that customers will pay before they leave; and an entertainment company won't produce DVDs if too many potential customers avoid paying by making illegal copies. We all rely on government-provided police and courts to enforce our rights over the things we produce—and the invisible hand counts on our ability to enforce our rights.

property rights
the ability of an individual to own and exercise control over scarce resources

FYI

> ## Adam Smith and the Invisible Hand

It may be only a coincidence that Adam Smith's great book *The Wealth of Nations* was published in 1776, the exact year American revolutionaries signed the Declaration of Independence. But the two documents share a point of view that was prevalent at the time: Individuals are usually best left to their own devices, without the heavy hand of government guiding their actions. This political philosophy provides the intellectual basis for the market economy and for free society more generally.

Why do decentralized market economies work so well? Is it because people can be counted on to treat one another with love and kindness? Not at all. Here is Adam Smith's description of how people interact in a market economy:

Man has almost constant occasion for the help of his brethren, and it is in vain for him to expect it from their benevolence only. He will be more likely to prevail if he can interest their self-love in his favour, and show them that it is for their own advantage to do for him what he requires of them. . . . Give me that which I want, and you shall have this which you want, is the meaning of every such offer; and it is in this manner that we obtain from one another the far greater part of those good offices which we stand in need of.

Adam Smith

It is not from the benevolence of the butcher, the brewer, or the baker that we expect our dinner, but from their regard to their own interest. We address ourselves, not to their humanity but to their self-love, and never talk to them of our own necessities but of their advantages. Nobody but a beggar chooses to depend chiefly upon the benevolence of his fellow-citizens. . . .

Every individual . . . neither intends to promote the public interest, nor knows how much he is promoting it. . . . He intends only his own gain, and he is in this, as in many other cases, led by an invisible hand to promote an end which was no part of his intention. Nor is it always the worse for the society that it was no part of it. By pursuing his own interest he frequently promotes that of the society more effectually than when he really intends to promote it.

Smith is saying that participants in the economy are motivated by self-interest and that the "invisible hand" of the marketplace guides this self-interest into promoting general economic well-being.

Many of Smith's insights remain at the center of modern economics. Our analysis in the coming chapters will allow us to express Smith's conclusions more precisely and to analyze more fully the strengths and weaknesses of the market's invisible hand.

market failure
a situation in which a market left on its own fails to allocate resources efficiently

externality
the impact of one person's actions on the well-being of a bystander

Yet there is another reason we need government: The invisible hand is powerful, but it is not omnipotent. There are two broad reasons for a government to intervene in the economy and change the allocation of resources that people would choose on their own: to promote efficiency or to promote equality. That is, most policies aim either to enlarge the economic pie or to change how the pie is divided.

Consider first the goal of efficiency. Although the invisible hand usually leads markets to allocate resources to maximize the size of the economic pie, this is not always the case. Economists use the term **market failure** to refer to a situation in which the market on its own fails to produce an efficient allocation of resources. As we will see, one possible cause of market failure is an **externality,** which is the impact of one person's actions on the well-being of a bystander. The classic example of an externality is pollution. Another possible cause of market failure is **market power,** which refers to the ability of a single person (or small group) to unduly influence market prices. For example, if everyone in town needs water but there is only one well, the owner of the well is not subject to the rigorous competition with which the invisible hand normally keeps self-interest in check. In the presence of externalities or market power, well-designed public policy can enhance economic efficiency.

market power
the ability of a single economic actor (or small group of actors) to have a substantial influence on market prices

Now consider the goal of equality. Even when the invisible hand is yielding efficient outcomes, it can nonetheless leave sizable disparities in economic well-being. A market economy rewards people according to their ability to produce things that other people are willing to pay for. The world's best basketball player earns more than the world's best chess player simply because people are willing to pay more to watch basketball than chess. The invisible hand does not ensure that everyone has sufficient food, decent clothing, and adequate health-care. This inequality may, depending on one's political philosophy, call for government intervention. In practice, many public policies, such as the income tax and the welfare system, aim to achieve a more equal distribution of economic well-being.

To say that the government *can* improve on market outcomes at times does not mean that it always *will*. Public policy is made not by angels but by a political process that is far from perfect. Sometimes policies are designed simply to reward the politically powerful. Sometimes they are made by well-intentioned leaders who are not fully informed. As you study economics, you will become a better judge of when a government policy is justifiable because it promotes efficiency or equality and when it is not.

QUICK QUIZ *Why is a country better off not isolating itself from all other countries?* • *Why do we have markets, and, according to economists, what roles should government play in them?*

How the Economy as a Whole Works

We started by discussing how individuals make decisions and then looked at how people interact with one another. All these decisions and interactions together make up "the economy." The last three principles concern the workings of the economy as a whole.

Principle 8: A Country's Standard of Living Depends on Its Ability to Produce Goods and Services

The differences in living standards around the world are staggering. In 2008, the average American had an income of about $47,000. In the same year, the average Mexican earned about $10,000, and the average Nigerian earned only $1,400. Not surprisingly, this large variation in average income is reflected in various measures of the quality of life. Citizens of high-income countries have more TV sets, more cars, better nutrition, better healthcare, and a longer life expectancy than citizens of low-income countries.

Changes in living standards over time are also large. In the United States, incomes have historically grown about 2 percent per year (after adjusting for changes in the cost of living). At this rate, average income doubles every 35 years. Over the past century, average U.S. income has risen about eightfold.

What explains these large differences in living standards among countries and over time? The answer is surprisingly simple. Almost all variation in living standards is attributable to differences in countries' **productivity**—that is, the amount of goods and services produced from each unit of labor input. In nations where workers can produce a large quantity of goods and services per unit of time, most people enjoy a high standard of living; in nations where workers are less productive, most people endure a more meager existence. Similarly, the growth rate of a nation's productivity determines the growth rate of its average income.

The fundamental relationship between productivity and living standards is simple, but its implications are far-reaching. If productivity is the primary determinant of living standards, other explanations must be of secondary importance. For example, it might be tempting to credit labor unions or minimum-wage laws for the rise in living standards of American workers over the past century. Yet the real hero of American workers is their rising productivity. As another example, some commentators have claimed that increased competition from Japan and other countries explained the slow growth in U.S. incomes during the 1970s and 1980s. Yet the real villain was not competition from abroad but flagging productivity growth in the United States.

The relationship between productivity and living standards also has profound implications for public policy. When thinking about how any policy will affect living standards, the key question is how it will affect our ability to produce goods and services. To boost living standards, policymakers need to raise productivity by ensuring that workers are well educated, have the tools needed to produce goods and services, and have access to the best available technology.

productivity
the quantity of goods and services produced from each unit of labor input

---

· · · · · · · · · · · · · · · · · · in the **news**

> ### Why You Should Study Economics
> *In this excerpt from a commencement address, the former president of the Federal Reserve Bank of Dallas makes the case for studying economics*

The Dismal Science? Hardly!

BY ROBERT D. MCTEER, JR.

My take on training in economics is that it becomes increasingly valuable as you move up the career ladder. I can't imagine a better major for corporate CEOs, congressmen, or American presidents. You've learned a systematic, disciplined way of thinking that will serve you well. By contrast, the economically challenged must be perplexed about how it is that economies work better the fewer people they have in charge. Who does the planning? Who makes decisions? Who decides what to produce?

For my money, Adam Smith's invisible hand is the most important thing you've learned by studying economics. You understand how we can each work for our own self-interest and still produce a desirable social outcome. You know how uncoordinated activity gets coordinated by the market to enhance the wealth of nations. You understand the magic of markets and the dangers of tampering with them too much. You know better what you first learned in kindergarten: that you shouldn't kill or cripple the goose that lays the golden eggs. . . .

Economics training will help you understand fallacies and unintended consequences.

Principle 9: Prices Rise When the Government Prints Too Much Money

In January 1921, a daily newspaper in Germany cost 0.30 marks. Less than two years later, in November 1922, the same newspaper cost 70,000,000 marks. All other prices in the economy rose by similar amounts. This episode is one of history's most spectacular examples of **inflation,** an increase in the overall level of prices in the economy.

Although the United States has never experienced inflation even close to that of Germany in the 1920s, inflation has at times been an economic problem. During the 1970s, for instance, when the overall level of prices more than doubled, President Gerald Ford called inflation "public enemy number one." By contrast, inflation in the first decade of the 21st century has run about 2½ percent per year; at this rate, it would take almost 30 years for prices to double. Because high inflation imposes various costs on society, keeping inflation at a low level is a goal of economic policymakers around the world.

What causes inflation? In almost all cases of large or persistent inflation, the culprit is growth in the quantity of money. When a government creates large quantities of the nation's money, the value of the money falls. In Germany in the early 1920s, when prices were on average tripling every month, the quantity of money was also tripling every month. Although less dramatic, the economic history of the United States points to a similar conclusion: The high inflation of the 1970s was associated with rapid growth in the quantity of money, and the low inflation of more recent experience was associated with slow growth in the quantity of money.

inflation

an increase in the overall level of prices in the economy

"Well it may have been 68 cents when you got in line, but it's 74 cents now!"

In fact, I am inclined to define economics as the study of how to anticipate unintended consequences. . . .

Little in the literature seems more relevant to contemporary economic debates than what usually is called the broken window fallacy. Whenever a government program is justified not on its merits but by the jobs it will create, remember the broken window: Some teenagers, being the little beasts that they are, toss a brick through a bakery window. A crowd gathers and laments, "What a shame." But before you know it, someone suggests a silver lining to the situation: Now the baker will have to spend money to have the window repaired. This will add to the income of the repairman, who will spend his additional income, which will add to another seller's income, and so on. You know the drill. The chain of spending will multiply and generate higher income and employment. If the broken window is large enough, it might produce an economic boom! . . .

Most voters fall for the broken window fallacy, but not economics majors. They will say, "Hey, wait a minute!" If the baker hadn't spent his money on window repair, he would have spent it on the new suit he was saving to buy. Then the tailor would have the new income to spend, and so on. The broken window didn't create net new spending; it just diverted spending from somewhere else. The broken window does not create new activity, just different activity. People see the activity that takes place. They don't see the activity that *would* have taken place.

The broken window fallacy is perpetuated in many forms. Whenever job creation or retention is the primary objective I call it the job-counting fallacy. Economics majors understand the non-intuitive reality that real progress comes from job destruction. It once took 90 percent of our population to grow our food. Now it takes 3 percent. Pardon me, Willie, but are we worse off because of the job losses in agriculture? The would-have-been farmers are now college professors and computer gurus. . . .

So instead of counting jobs, we should make every job count. We will occasionally hit a soft spot when we have a mismatch of supply and demand in the labor market. But that is temporary. Don't become a Luddite and destroy the machinery, or become a protectionist and try to grow bananas in New York City.

Source: *The Wall Street Journal,* June 4, 2003.

Principle 10: Society Faces a Short-Run Trade-off between Inflation and Unemployment

Although a higher level of prices is, in the long run, the primary effect of increasing the quantity of money, the short-run story is more complex and controversial. Most economists describe the short-run effects of monetary injections as follows:

- Increasing the amount of money in the economy stimulates the overall level of spending and thus the demand for goods and services.
- Higher demand may over time cause firms to raise their prices, but in the meantime, it also encourages them to hire more workers and produce a larger quantity of goods and services.
- More hiring means lower unemployment.

This line of reasoning leads to one final economy-wide trade-off: a short-run trade-off between inflation and unemployment.

Although some economists still question these ideas, most accept that society faces a short-run trade-off between inflation and unemployment. This simply means that, over a period of a year or two, many economic policies push inflation and unemployment in opposite directions. Policymakers face this trade-off regardless of whether inflation and unemployment both start out at high levels (as they did in the early 1980s), at low levels (as they did in the late 1990s), or someplace in between. This short-run trade-off plays a key role in the analysis of the **business cycle**—the irregular and largely unpredictable fluctuations in economic activity, as measured by the production of goods and services or the number of people employed.

Policymakers can exploit the short-run trade-off between inflation and unemployment using various policy instruments. By changing the amount that the government spends, the amount it taxes, and the amount of money it prints, policymakers can influence the overall demand for goods and services. Changes in demand in turn influence the combination of inflation and unemployment that the economy experiences in the short run. Because these instruments of economic policy are potentially so powerful, how policymakers should use these instruments to control the economy, if at all, is a subject of continuing debate.

This debate heated up in the early years of Barack Obama's presidency. In 2008 and 2009, the U.S. economy, as well as many other economies around the world, experienced a deep economic downturn. Problems in the financial system, caused by bad bets on the housing market, spilled over into the rest of the economy, causing incomes to fall and unemployment to soar. Policymakers responded in various ways to increase the overall demand for goods and services. President Obama's first major initiative was a stimulus package of reduced taxes and increased government spending. At the same time, the nation's central bank, the Federal Reserve, increased the supply of money. The goal of these policies was to reduce unemployment. Some feared, however, that these policies might over time lead to an excessive level of inflation.

business cycle

fluctuations in economic activity, such as employment and production

QUICK QUIZ   *List and briefly explain the three principles that describe how the economy as a whole works.*

FYI

> ## How to Read This Book

Economics is fun, but it can also be hard to learn. My aim in writing this text is to make it as enjoyable and easy as possible. But you, the student, also have a role to play. Experience shows that if you are actively involved as you study this book, you will enjoy a better outcome both on your exams and in the years that follow. Here are a few tips about how best to read this book.

1. *Read before class.* Students do better when they read the relevant textbook chapter before attending a lecture. You will understand the lecture better, and your questions will be better focused on where you need extra help.

2. *Summarize, don't highlight.* Running a yellow marker over the text is too passive an activity to keep your mind engaged. Instead, when you come to the end of a section, take a minute and summarize what you just learned in your own words, writing your summary in the wide margins we've provided. When you've finished the chapter, compare your summaries with the one at the end of the chapter. Did you pick up the main points?

3. *Test yourself.* Throughout the book, Quick Quizzes offer instant feedback to find out if you've learned what you are supposed to. Take the opportunity to write down your answer, and then check it against the answers provided at this book's website. The quizzes are meant to test your basic comprehension. If your answer is incorrect, you probably need to review the section.

4. *Practice, practice, practice.* At the end of each chapter, Questions for Review test your understanding, and Problems and Applications ask you to apply and extend the material. Perhaps your instructor will assign some of these exercises as homework.

If so, do them. If not, do them anyway. The more you use your new knowledge, the more solid it becomes.

5. *Go online.* The publisher of this book maintains an extensive website to help you in your study of economics. It includes additional examples, applications, and problems, as well as quizzes so you can test yourself. Check it out. The website is www .cengage.com/economics/mankiw.

6. *Study in groups.* After you've read the book and worked problems on your own, get together with classmates to discuss the material. You will learn from each other—an example of the gains from trade.

7. *Teach someone.* As all teachers know, there is no better way to learn something than to teach it to someone else. Take the opportunity to teach new economic concepts to a study partner, a friend, a parent, or even a pet.

8. *Don't skip the real-world examples.* In the midst of all the numbers, graphs, and strange new words, it is easy to lose sight of what economics is all about. The Case Studies and In the News boxes sprinkled throughout this book should help remind you. They show how the theory is tied to events happening in all our lives.

9. *Apply economic thinking to your daily life.* Once you've read about how others apply economics to the real world, try it yourself! You can use economic analysis to better understand your own decisions, the economy around you, and the events you read about in the newspaper. The world may never look the same again.

Conclusion

You now have a taste of what economics is all about. In the coming chapters, we develop many specific insights about people, markets, and economies. Mastering these insights will take some effort, but it is not an overwhelming task. The field of economics is based on a few big ideas that can be applied in many different situations.

Throughout this book, we will refer back to the *Ten Principles of Economics* highlighted in this chapter and summarized in Table 1. Keep these building blocks in mind: Even the most sophisticated economic analysis is founded on the ten principles introduced here.

Table 1

Ten Principles of Economics

How People Make Decisions
1: People Face Trade-offs
2: The Cost of Something Is What You Give Up to Get It
3: Rational People Think at the Margin
4: People Respond to Incentives

How People Interact
5: Trade Can Make Everyone Better Off
6: Markets Are Usually a Good Way to Organize Economic Activity
7: Governments Can Sometimes Improve Market Outcomes

How the Economy as a Whole Works
8: A Country's Standard of Living Depends on Its Ability to Produce Goods and Services
9: Prices Rise When the Government Prints Too Much Money
10: Society Faces a Short-Run Trade-off between Inflation and Unemployment

SUMMARY

- The fundamental lessons about individual decision making are that people face trade-offs among alternative goals, that the cost of any action is measured in terms of forgone opportunities, that rational people make decisions by comparing marginal costs and marginal benefits, and that people change their behavior in response to the incentives they face.

- The fundamental lessons about interactions among people are that trade and interdependence can be mutually beneficial, that markets are usually a good way of coordinating economic activity among people, and that the government can potentially improve market outcomes by remedying a market failure or by promoting greater economic equality.

- The fundamental lessons about the economy as a whole are that productivity is the ultimate source of living standards, that growth in the quantity of money is the ultimate source of inflation, and that society faces a short-run trade-off between inflation and unemployment.

KEY CONCEPTS

scarcity, *p. 4*
economics, *p. 4*
efficiency, *p. 5*
equality, *p. 5*
opportunity cost, *p. 6*
rational people, *p. 6*

marginal change, *p. 6*
incentive, *p. 7*
market economy, *p. 10*
property rights, *p. 11*
market failure, *p. 12*
externality, *p. 12*

market power, *p. 13*
productivity, *p. 14*
inflation, *p. 15*
business cycle, *p. 16*

QUESTIONS FOR REVIEW

1. Give three examples of important trade-offs that you face in your life.
2. What is the opportunity cost of seeing a movie?
3. Water is necessary for life. Is the marginal benefit of a glass of water large or small?
4. Why should policymakers think about incentives?

5. Why isn't trade among countries like a game with some winners and some losers?
6. What does the "invisible hand" of the marketplace do?
7. Explain the two main causes of market failure and give an example of each.
8. Why is productivity important?
9. What is inflation and what causes it?
10. How are inflation and unemployment related in the short run?

PROBLEMS AND APPLICATIONS

1. Describe some of the trade-offs faced by each of the following:
   a. a family deciding whether to buy a new car
   b. a member of Congress deciding how much to spend on national parks
   c. a company president deciding whether to open a new factory
   d. a professor deciding how much to prepare for class
   e. a recent college graduate deciding whether to go to graduate school
2. You are trying to decide whether to take a vacation. Most of the costs of the vacation (airfare, hotel, and forgone wages) are measured in dollars, but the benefits of the vacation are psychological. How can you compare the benefits to the costs?
3. You were planning to spend Saturday working at your part-time job, but a friend asks you to go skiing. What is the true cost of going skiing? Now suppose you had been planning to spend the day studying at the library. What is the cost of going skiing in this case? Explain.
4. You win $100 in a basketball pool. You have a choice between spending the money now or putting it away for a year in a bank account that pays 5 percent interest. What is the opportunity cost of spending the $100 now?
5. The company that you manage has invested $5 million in developing a new product, but the development is not quite finished. At a recent meeting, your salespeople report that the introduction of competing products has reduced the expected sales of your new product to $3 million. If it would cost $1 million to finish development and make the product, should you go ahead and do so? What is the most that you should pay to complete development?
6. The Social Security system provides income for people over age 65. If a recipient of Social Security decides to work and earn some income, the amount he or she receives in Social Security benefits is typically reduced.
   a. How does the provision of Social Security affect people's incentive to save while working?
   b. How does the reduction in benefits associated with higher earnings affect people's incentive to work past age 65?
7. A 1996 bill reforming the federal government's antipoverty programs limited many welfare recipients to only two years of benefits.
   a. How does this change affect the incentives for working?
   b. How might this change represent a trade-off between equality and efficiency?
8. Your roommate is a better cook than you are, but you can clean more quickly than your roommate can. If your roommate did all the cooking and you did all the cleaning, would your chores take you more or less time than if you divided each task evenly? Give a similar example of how specialization and trade can make two countries both better off.
9. Explain whether each of the following government activities is motivated by a concern about equality or a concern about efficiency. In the case of efficiency, discuss the type of market failure involved.
   a. regulating cable TV prices
   b. providing some poor people with vouchers that can be used to buy food
   c. prohibiting smoking in public places
   d. breaking up Standard Oil (which once owned 90 percent of all oil refineries) into several smaller companies
   e. imposing higher personal income tax rates on people with higher incomes
   f. instituting laws against driving while intoxicated

10. Discuss each of the following statements from the standpoints of equality and efficiency.
    a. "Everyone in society should be guaranteed the best healthcare possible."
    b. "When workers are laid off, they should be able to collect unemployment benefits until they find a new job."
11. In what ways is your standard of living different from that of your parents or grandparents when they were your age? Why have these changes occurred?
12. Suppose Americans decide to save more of their incomes. If banks lend this extra saving to businesses, which use the funds to build new factories, how might this lead to faster growth in productivity? Who do you suppose benefits from the higher productivity? Is society getting a free lunch?
13. In 2010, President Barack Obama and Congress enacted a healthcare reform bill in the United States. Two goals of the bill were to provide more Americans with health insurance (via subsidies for lower-income households financed by taxes on higher-income households) and to reduce the cost of healthcare (via various reforms in how healthcare is provided).
    a. How do these goals relate to equality and efficiency?

b. How might healthcare reform increase productivity in the United States?
c. How might healthcare reform decrease productivity in the United States?
14. During the Revolutionary War, the American colonies could not raise enough tax revenue to fully fund the war effort; to make up this difference, the colonies decided to print more money. Printing money to cover expenditures is sometimes referred to as an "inflation tax." Who do you think is being "taxed" when more money is printed? Why?
15. Imagine that you are a policymaker trying to decide whether to reduce the rate of inflation. To make an intelligent decision, what would you need to know about inflation, unemployment, and the trade-off between them?
16. A policymaker is deciding how to finance the construction of a new airport. He can either pay for it by increasing citizens' taxes or by printing more money. What are some of the short-run and long-run consequences of each option?

For further information on topics in this chapter, additional problems, applications, examples, online quizzes, and more, please visit our website at www.cengage.com/economics/mankiw.

Thinking Like an Economist

E very field of study has its own language and its own way of thinking. Mathematicians talk about axioms, integrals, and vector spaces. Psychologists talk about ego, id, and cognitive dissonance. Lawyers talk about venue, torts, and promissory estoppel.

Economics is no different. Supply, demand, elasticity, comparative advantage, consumer surplus, deadweight loss—these terms are part of the economist's language. In the coming chapters, you will encounter many new terms and some familiar words that economists use in specialized ways. At first, this new language may seem needlessly arcane. But as you will see, its value lies in its ability to provide you with a new and useful way of thinking about the world in which you live.

The purpose of this book is to help you learn the economist's way of thinking. Just as you cannot become a mathematician, psychologist, or lawyer overnight, learning to think like an economist will take some time. Yet with a combination of theory, case studies, and examples of economics in the news, this book will give you ample opportunity to develop and practice this skill.

Before delving into the substance and details of economics, it is helpful to have an overview of how economists approach the world. This chapter discusses the field's methodology. What is distinctive about how economists confront a question? What does it mean to think like an economist?

The Economist as Scientist

Economists try to address their subject with a scientist's objectivity. They approach the study of the economy in much the same way a physicist approaches the study of matter and a biologist approaches the study of life: They devise theories, collect data, and then analyze these data in an attempt to verify or refute their theories.

To beginners, it can seem odd to claim that economics is a science. After all, economists do not work with test tubes or telescopes. The essence of science, however, is the *scientific method*—the dispassionate development and testing of theories about how the world works. This method of inquiry is as applicable to studying a nation's economy as it is to studying the earth's gravity or a species' evolution. As Albert Einstein once put it, "The whole of science is nothing more than the refinement of everyday thinking."

Although Einstein's comment is as true for social sciences such as economics as it is for natural sciences such as physics, most people are not accustomed to looking at society through the eyes of a scientist. Let's discuss some of the ways in which economists apply the logic of science to examine how an economy works.

"I'm a social scientist, Michael. That means I can't explain electricity or anything like that, but if you ever want to know about people, I'm your man."

The Scientific Method: Observation, Theory, and More Observation

Isaac Newton, the famous 17th-century scientist and mathematician, allegedly became intrigued one day when he saw an apple fall from a tree. This observation motivated Newton to develop a theory of gravity that applies not only to an apple falling to the earth but to any two objects in the universe. Subsequent testing of Newton's theory has shown that it works well in many circumstances (although, as Einstein would later emphasize, not in all circumstances). Because Newton's theory has been so successful at explaining observation, it is still taught in undergraduate physics courses around the world.

This interplay between theory and observation also occurs in the field of economics. An economist might live in a country experiencing rapidly increasing prices and be moved by this observation to develop a theory of inflation. The theory might assert that high inflation arises when the government prints too much money. To test this theory, the economist could collect and analyze data on prices and money from many different countries. If growth in the quantity of money were not at all related to the rate at which prices are rising, the economist would start to doubt the validity of this theory of inflation. If money growth and inflation were strongly correlated in international data, as in fact they are, the economist would become more confident in the theory.

Although economists use theory and observation like other scientists, they face an obstacle that makes their task especially challenging: In economics, conducting experiments is often difficult and sometimes impossible. Physicists studying gravity can drop many objects in their laboratories to generate data to test their theories. By contrast, economists studying inflation are not allowed to manipulate a nation's monetary policy simply to generate useful data. Economists, like astronomers and evolutionary biologists, usually have to make do with whatever data the world happens to give them.

To find a substitute for laboratory experiments, economists pay close attention to the natural experiments offered by history. When a war in the Middle East interrupts the flow of crude oil, for instance, oil prices skyrocket around the world. For consumers of oil and oil products, such an event depresses living standards. For economic policymakers, it poses a difficult choice about how best to respond. But for economic scientists, the event provides an opportunity to study the effects of a key natural resource on the world's economies. Throughout this book, therefore, we consider many historical episodes. These episodes are valuable to study because they give us insight into the economy of the past and, more important, because they allow us to illustrate and evaluate economic theories of the present.

The Role of Assumptions

If you ask a physicist how long it would take a marble to fall from the top of a ten-story building, she will likely answer the question by assuming that the marble falls in a vacuum. Of course, this assumption is false. In fact, the building is surrounded by air, which exerts friction on the falling marble and slows it down. Yet the physicist will point out that the friction on the marble is so small that its effect is negligible. Assuming the marble falls in a vacuum simplifies the problem without substantially affecting the answer.

Economists make assumptions for the same reason: Assumptions can simplify the complex world and make it easier to understand. To study the effects of international trade, for example, we might assume that the world consists of only two countries and that each country produces only two goods. In reality, there are numerous countries, each of which produces thousands of different types of goods. But by assuming two countries and two goods, we can focus our thinking on the essence of the problem. Once we understand international trade in this simplified imaginary world, we are in a better position to understand international trade in the more complex world in which we live.

The art in scientific thinking—whether in physics, biology, or economics—is deciding which assumptions to make. Suppose, for instance, that instead of dropping a marble from the top of the building, we were dropping a beachball of the same weight. Our physicist would realize that the assumption of no friction is less accurate in this case: Friction exerts a greater force on a beachball than on a marble because a beachball is much larger. The assumption that gravity works in a vacuum is reasonable for studying a falling marble but not for studying a falling beachball.

Similarly, economists use different assumptions to answer different questions. Suppose that we want to study what happens to the economy when the government changes the number of dollars in circulation. An important piece of this analysis, it turns out, is how prices respond. Many prices in the economy change infrequently; the newsstand prices of magazines, for instance, change only every few years. Knowing this fact may lead us to make different assumptions when studying the effects of the policy change over different time horizons. For studying the short-run effects of the policy, we may assume that prices do not change much. We may even make the extreme and artificial assumption that all prices are completely fixed. For studying the long-run effects of the policy, however, we may assume that all prices are completely flexible. Just as a physicist uses different assumptions when studying falling marbles and falling beachballs, economists use different assumptions when studying the short-run and long-run effects of a change in the quantity of money.

Economic Models

High school biology teachers teach basic anatomy with plastic replicas of the human body. These models have all the major organs: the heart, the liver, the kidneys, and so on. The models allow teachers to show their students very simply how the important parts of the body fit together. Because these plastic models are stylized and omit many details, no one would mistake one of them for a real person. Despite this lack of realism—indeed, because of this lack of realism—studying these models is useful for learning how the human body works.

Economists also use models to learn about the world, but instead of being made of plastic, they are most often composed of diagrams and equations. Like a biology teacher's plastic model, economic models omit many details to allow us to see what is truly important. Just as the biology teacher's model does not include all the body's muscles and capillaries, an economist's model does not include every feature of the economy.

As we use models to examine various economic issues throughout this book, you will see that all the models are built with assumptions. Just as a physicist begins the analysis of a falling marble by assuming away the existence of friction, economists assume away many of the details of the economy that are irrelevant for studying the question at hand. All models—in physics, biology, and economics—simplify reality to improve our understanding of it.

Our First Model: The Circular-Flow Diagram

The economy consists of millions of people engaged in many activities—buying, selling, working, hiring, manufacturing, and so on. To understand how the economy works, we must find some way to simplify our thinking about all these activities. In other words, we need a model that explains, in general terms, how the economy is organized and how participants in the economy interact with one another.

Figure 1 presents a visual model of the economy called a **circular-flow diagram.** In this model, the economy is simplified to include only two types of decision makers—firms and households. Firms produce goods and services using inputs, such as labor, land, and capital (buildings and machines). These inputs are called the *factors of production.* Households own the factors of production and consume all the goods and services that the firms produce.

Households and firms interact in two types of markets. In the *markets for goods and services,* households are buyers, and firms are sellers. In particular, households buy the output of goods and services that firms produce. In the *markets for the factors of production,* households are sellers, and firms are buyers. In these markets, households provide the inputs that firms use to produce goods and services. The circular-flow diagram offers a simple way of organizing the economic transactions that occur between households and firms in the economy.

The two loops of the circular-flow diagram are distinct but related. The inner loop represents the flows of inputs and outputs. The households sell the use of

circular-flow diagram

a visual model of the economy that shows how dollars flow through markets among households and firms

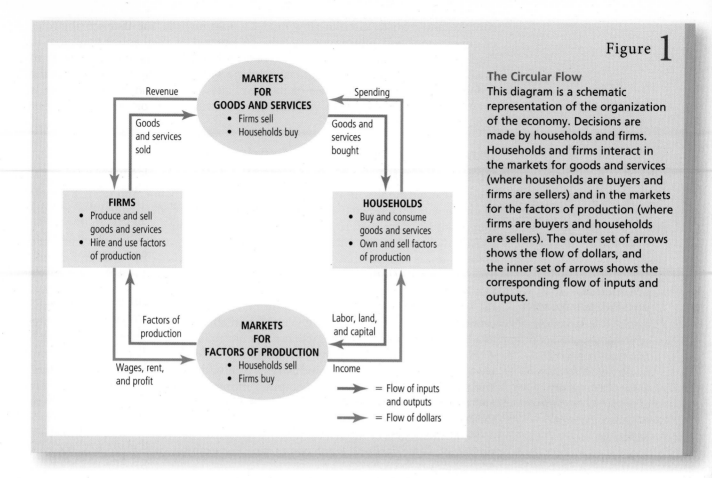

Figure **1**

The Circular Flow
This diagram is a schematic representation of the organization of the economy. Decisions are made by households and firms. Households and firms interact in the markets for goods and services (where households are buyers and firms are sellers) and in the markets for the factors of production (where firms are buyers and households are sellers). The outer set of arrows shows the flow of dollars, and the inner set of arrows shows the corresponding flow of inputs and outputs.

their labor, land, and capital to the firms in the markets for the factors of production. The firms then use these factors to produce goods and services, which in turn are sold to households in the markets for goods and services. The outer loop of the diagram represents the corresponding flow of dollars. The households spend money to buy goods and services from the firms. The firms use some of the revenue from these sales to pay for the factors of production, such as the wages of their workers. What's left is the profit of the firm owners, who themselves are members of households.

Let's take a tour of the circular flow by following a dollar bill as it makes its way from person to person through the economy. Imagine that the dollar begins at a household, say, in your wallet. If you want to buy a cup of coffee, you take the dollar to one of the economy's markets for goods and services, such as your local Starbucks coffee shop. There, you spend it on your favorite drink. When the dollar moves into the Starbucks cash register, it becomes revenue for the firm. The dollar doesn't stay at Starbucks for long, however, because the firm uses it to buy inputs in the markets for the factors of production. Starbucks might use the dollar to pay rent to its landlord for the space it occupies or to pay the wages of its workers. In either case, the dollar enters the income of some household and, once again, is back in someone's wallet. At that point, the story of the economy's circular flow starts once again.

The circular-flow diagram in Figure 1 is a very simple model of the economy. It dispenses with details that, for some purposes, are significant. A more complex and realistic circular-flow model would include, for instance, the roles of government and international trade. (A portion of that dollar you gave to Starbucks might be used to pay taxes or to buy coffee beans from a farmer in Brazil.) Yet these details are not crucial for a basic understanding of how the economy is organized. Because of its simplicity, this circular-flow diagram is useful to keep in mind when thinking about how the pieces of the economy fit together.

Our Second Model: The Production Possibilities Frontier

Most economic models, unlike the circular-flow diagram, are built using the tools of mathematics. Here we use one of the simplest such models, called the production possibilities frontier, to illustrate some basic economic ideas.

Although real economies produce thousands of goods and services, let's assume an economy that produces only two goods—cars and computers. Together, the car industry and the computer industry use all of the economy's factors of production. The **production possibilities frontier** is a graph that shows the various combinations of output—in this case, cars and computers—that the economy can possibly produce given the available factors of production and the available production technology that firms use to turn these factors into output.

Figure 2 shows this economy's production possibilities frontier. If the economy uses all its resources in the car industry, it produces 1,000 cars and no computers. If it uses all its resources in the computer industry, it produces 3,000 computers and no cars. The two endpoints of the production possibilities frontier represent these extreme possibilities.

More likely, the economy divides its resources between the two industries, producing some cars and some computers. For example, it can produce 600 cars

production possibilities frontier

a graph that shows the combinations of output that the economy can possibly produce given the available factors of production and the available production technology

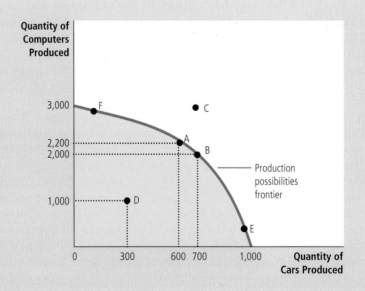

Figure **2**

The Production Possibilities Frontier
The production possibilities frontier shows the combinations of output—in this case, cars and computers—that the economy can possibly produce. The economy can produce any combination on or inside the frontier. Points outside the frontier are not feasible given the economy's resources.

and 2,200 computers, shown in the figure by point A. Or, by moving some of the factors of production to the car industry from the computer industry, the economy can produce 700 cars and 2,000 computers, represented by point B.

Because resources are scarce, not every conceivable outcome is feasible. For example, no matter how resources are allocated between the two industries, the economy cannot produce the amount of cars and computers represented by point C. Given the technology available for manufacturing cars and computers, the economy does not have enough of the factors of production to support that level of output. With the resources it has, the economy can produce at any point on or inside the production possibilities frontier, but it cannot produce at points outside the frontier.

An outcome is said to be *efficient* if the economy is getting all it can from the scarce resources it has available. Points on (rather than inside) the production possibilities frontier represent efficient levels of production. When the economy is producing at such a point, say point A, there is no way to produce more of one good without producing less of the other. Point D represents an *inefficient* outcome. For some reason, perhaps widespread unemployment, the economy is producing less than it could from the resources it has available: It is producing only 300 cars and 1,000 computers. If the source of the inefficiency is eliminated, the economy can increase its production of both goods. For example, if the economy moves from point D to point A, its production of cars increases from 300 to 600, and its production of computers increases from 1,000 to 2,200.

One of the *Ten Principles of Economics* discussed in Chapter 1 is that people face trade-offs. The production possibilities frontier shows one trade-off that society faces. Once we have reached the efficient points on the frontier, the only way of producing more of one good is to produce less of the other. When the economy moves from point A to point B, for instance, society produces 100 more cars but at the expense of producing 200 fewer computers.

This trade-off helps us understand another of the *Ten Principles of Economics:* The cost of something is what you give up to get it. This is called the *opportunity cost*. The production possibilities frontier shows the opportunity cost of one good as measured in terms of the other good. When society moves from point A to point B, it gives up 200 computers to get 100 additional cars. That is, at point A, the opportunity cost of 100 cars is 200 computers. Put another way, the opportunity cost of each car is two computers. Notice that the opportunity cost of a car equals the slope of the production possibilities frontier. (If you don't recall what slope is, you can refresh your memory with the graphing appendix to this chapter.)

The opportunity cost of a car in terms of the number of computers is not constant in this economy but depends on how many cars and computers the economy is producing. This is reflected in the shape of the production possibilities frontier. Because the production possibilities frontier in Figure 2 is bowed outward, the opportunity cost of a car is highest when the economy is producing many cars and few computers, such as at point E, where the frontier is steep. When the economy is producing few cars and many computers, such as at point F, the frontier is flatter, and the opportunity cost of a car is lower.

Economists believe that production possibilities frontiers often have this bowed shape. When the economy is using most of its resources to make computers, such as at point F, the resources best suited to car production, such as skilled autoworkers, are being used in the computer industry. Because these workers probably aren't very good at making computers, the economy won't have to lose much computer production to increase car production by one unit. The opportunity cost of a car in terms of computers is small, and the frontier is relatively flat. By contrast, when the economy is using most of its resources to make cars, such as at point E, the resources best suited to making cars are already in the car industry. Producing an additional car means moving some of the best computer technicians out of the computer industry and making them autoworkers. As a result, producing an additional car will mean a substantial loss of computer output. The opportunity cost of a car is high, and the frontier is steep.

The production possibilities frontier shows the trade-off between the outputs of different goods at a given time, but the trade-off can change over time. For example, suppose a technological advance in the computer industry raises the number of computers that a worker can produce per week. This advance expands society's set of opportunities. For any given number of cars, the economy can make more computers. If the economy does not produce any computers, it can still produce 1,000 cars, so one endpoint of the frontier stays the same. But the rest of the production possibilities frontier shifts outward, as in Figure 3.

This figure illustrates economic growth. Society can move production from a point on the old frontier to a point on the new frontier. Which point it chooses depends on its preferences for the two goods. In this example, society moves from point A to point G, enjoying more computers (2,300 instead of 2,200) and more cars (650 instead of 600).

The production possibilities frontier simplifies a complex economy to highlight some basic but powerful ideas: scarcity, efficiency, trade-offs, opportunity cost,

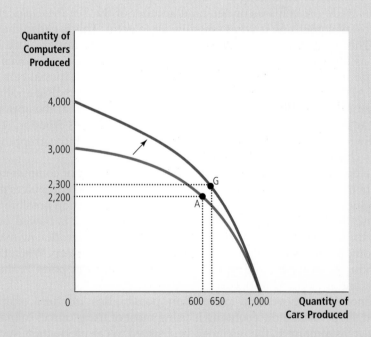

Figure 3

A Shift in the Production Possibilities Frontier
A technological advance in the computer industry enables the economy to produce more computers for any given number of cars. As a result, the production possibilities frontier shifts outward. If the economy moves from point A to point G, then the production of both cars and computers increases.

and economic growth. As you study economics, these ideas will recur in various forms. The production possibilities frontier offers one simple way of thinking about them.

Microeconomics and Macroeconomics

Many subjects are studied on various levels. Consider biology, for example. Molecular biologists study the chemical compounds that make up living things. Cellular biologists study cells, which are made up of many chemical compounds and, at the same time, are themselves the building blocks of living organisms. Evolutionary biologists study the many varieties of animals and plants and how species change gradually over the centuries.

Economics is also studied on various levels. We can study the decisions of individual households and firms. Or we can study the interaction of households and firms in markets for specific goods and services. Or we can study the operation of the economy as a whole, which is the sum of the activities of all these decision makers in all these markets.

The field of economics is traditionally divided into two broad subfields. **Microeconomics** is the study of how households and firms make decisions and how they interact in specific markets. **Macroeconomics** is the study of economywide phenomena. A microeconomist might study the effects of rent control on housing in New York City, the impact of foreign competition on the U.S. auto industry, or the effects of compulsory school attendance on workers' earnings. A macroeconomist might study the effects of borrowing by the federal government, the changes over time in the economy's rate of unemployment, or alternative policies to promote growth in national living standards.

Microeconomics and macroeconomics are closely intertwined. Because changes in the overall economy arise from the decisions of millions of individuals, it is impossible to understand macroeconomic developments without considering the associated microeconomic decisions. For example, a macroeconomist might study the effect of a federal income tax cut on the overall production of goods and services. But to analyze this issue, he or she must consider how the tax cut affects the decisions of households about how much to spend on goods and services.

Despite the inherent link between microeconomics and macroeconomics, the two fields are distinct. Because they address different questions, each field has its own set of models, which are often taught in separate courses.

microeconomics
the study of how households and firms make decisions and how they interact in markets

macroeconomics
the study of economywide phenomena, including inflation, unemployment, and economic growth

QUICK QUIZ *In what sense is economics like a science?* • *Draw a production possibilities frontier for a society that produces food and clothing. Show an efficient point, an inefficient point, and an infeasible point. Show the effects of a drought.* • *Define* microeconomics *and* macroeconomics.

The Economist as Policy Adviser

Often, economists are asked to explain the causes of economic events. Why, for example, is unemployment higher for teenagers than for older workers? Sometimes, economists are asked to recommend policies to improve economic outcomes. What, for instance, should the government do to improve the economic

····· FYI ·····

Who Studies Economics?

As a college student, you might be asking yourself: How many economics classes should I take? How useful will this stuff be to me later in life? Economics can seem abstract at first, but the field is fundamentally very practical, and the study of economics is useful in many different career paths. Here is a small sampling of some well-known people who majored in economics when they were in college.

George H. W. Bush	Former President of the United States
Donald Trump	Business and TV Mogul
Meg Whitman	Former Chief Executive Officer of eBay
Danny Glover	Actor
Barbara Boxer	U.S. Senator
John Elway	Former NFL Quarterback
Kofi Annan	Former Secretary General, United Nations
Ted Turner	Founder of CNN
Lionel Richie	Singer

Diane von Furstenberg	Fashion Designer
Michael Kinsley	Journalist
Ben Stein	Political Speechwriter, Journalist, and Actor
Cate Blanchett	Actor
Anthony Zinni	General (ret.), U.S. Marine Corps
Steve Ballmer	Chief Executive Officer, Microsoft
Arnold Schwarzenegger	Governor of California
Sandra Day-O'Connor	Former Supreme Court Justice
Scott Adams	Cartoonist for *Dilbert*
Mick Jagger	Singer for the Rolling Stones

When asked in 2005 why The Rolling Stones were going on tour again, former economics major Mick Jagger replied, "Supply and demand." Keith Richards added, "If the demand's there, we'll supply."

Having studied at the London School of Economics may not help Mick Jagger hit the high notes, but it has probably given him some insight about how to invest the substantial sums he has earned during his rock 'n' roll career.

well-being of teenagers? When economists are trying to explain the world, they are scientists. When they are trying to help improve it, they are policy advisers.

Positive versus Normative Analysis

To help clarify the two roles that economists play, let's examine the use of language. Because scientists and policy advisers have different goals, they use language in different ways.

For example, suppose that two people are discussing minimum-wage laws. Here are two statements you might hear:

> POLLY: Minimum-wage laws cause unemployment.
> NORM: The government should raise the minimum wage.

Ignoring for now whether you agree with these statements, notice that Polly and Norm differ in what they are trying to do. Polly is speaking like a scientist: She is making a claim about how the world works. Norm is speaking like a policy adviser: He is making a claim about how he would like to change the world.

In general, statements about the world come in two types. One type, such as Polly's, is positive. **Positive statements** are descriptive. They make a claim about how the world *is*. A second type of statement, such as Norm's, is normative. **Normative statements** are prescriptive. They make a claim about how the world *ought to be*.

A key difference between positive and normative statements is how we judge their validity. We can, in principle, confirm or refute positive statements by examining evidence. An economist might evaluate Polly's statement by analyzing data on changes in minimum wages and changes in unemployment over time. By contrast, evaluating normative statements involves values as well as facts. Norm's statement cannot be judged using data alone. Deciding what is good or bad policy is not just a matter of science. It also involves our views on ethics, religion, and political philosophy.

Positive and normative statements are fundamentally different, but they are often intertwined in a person's set of beliefs. In particular, positive views about how the world works affect normative views about what policies are desirable. Polly's claim that the minimum wage causes unemployment, if true, might lead her to reject Norm's conclusion that the government should raise the minimum wage. Yet normative conclusions cannot come from positive analysis alone; they involve value judgments as well.

As you study economics, keep in mind the distinction between positive and normative statements because it will help you stay focused on the task at hand. Much of economics is positive: It just tries to explain how the economy works. Yet those who use economics often have normative goals: They want to learn how to improve the economy. When you hear economists making normative statements, you know they are speaking not as scientists but as policy advisers.

Economists in Washington

President Harry Truman once said that he wanted to find a one-armed economist. When he asked his economists for advice, they always answered, "On the one hand, . . . On the other hand, . . . "

Truman was right in realizing that economists' advice is not always straightforward. This tendency is rooted in one of the *Ten Principles of Economics*: People face trade-offs. Economists are aware that trade-offs are involved in most policy decisions. A policy might increase efficiency at the cost of equality. It might help future generations but hurt current generations. An economist who says that all policy decisions are easy is an economist not to be trusted.

Truman was not the only president who relied on the advice of economists. Since 1946, the president of the United States has received guidance from the Council of Economic Advisers, which consists of three members and a staff of a few dozen economists. The council, whose offices are just a few steps from the White House, has no duty other than to advise the president and to write the annual *Economic Report of the President*, which discusses recent developments in the economy and presents the council's analysis of current policy issues.

The president also receives input from economists in many administrative departments. Economists at the Office of Management and Budget help formulate spending plans and regulatory policies. Economists at the Department of the Treasury help design tax policy. Economists at the Department of Labor analyze data on workers and those looking for work to help formulate labor-market policies. Economists at the Department of Justice help enforce the nation's antitrust laws.

Economists are also found outside the administrative branch of government. To obtain independent evaluations of policy proposals, Congress relies on the advice of the Congressional Budget Office, which is staffed by economists. The

© JAMES STEVENSON. THE NEW YORKER COLLECTION/WWW.CARTOONBANK.COM

positive statements
claims that attempt to describe the world as it is

normative statements
claims that attempt to prescribe how the world should be

"Let's switch. I'll make the policy, you implement it, and he'll explain it."

> ## The Economics of President Obama

Here is how Larry Summers, a chief economic adviser to Barack Obama, describes the president's policies.

A Vision for Innovation, Growth, and Quality Jobs

BY LAWRENCE H. SUMMERS

President Obama laid out his vision for innovation, growth, and quality jobs earlier today at Hudson Valley Community College. This President's plan is grounded not only in the American tradition of entrepreneurship, but also in the traditions of robust economic thought.

During the past two years, the ideas propounded by John Maynard Keynes have assumed greater importance than most people would have thought in the previous generation. As Keynes famously observed, during those rare times of deep financial and economic crisis, when the "invisible hand" Adam Smith talked about has temporarily ceased to function, there is a more urgent need for government to play an active role in restoring markets to their healthy function.

The wisdom of Keynesian policies has been confirmed by the performance of the economy over the past year. After the collapse of Lehman Brothers last September, government policy moved in a strongly activist direction.

As a result of those policies, our outlook today has shifted from rescue to recovery, from worrying about the very real prospect of depression to thinking about what kind of an expansion we want to have.

An important aspect of any economic expansion is the role innovation plays as

Federal Reserve, the institution that sets the nation's monetary policy, employs hundreds of economists to analyze economic developments in the United States and throughout the world.

The influence of economists on policy goes beyond their role as advisers: Their research and writings often affect policy indirectly. Economist John Maynard Keynes offered this observation:

> The ideas of economists and political philosophers, both when they are right and when they are wrong, are more powerful than is commonly understood. Indeed, the world is ruled by little else. Practical men, who believe themselves to be quite exempt from intellectual influences, are usually the slaves of some defunct economist. Madmen in authority, who hear voices in the air, are distilling their frenzy from some academic scribbler of a few years back.

Although these words were written in 1935, they remain true. Indeed, the "academic scribbler" now influencing public policy is often Keynes himself.

Why Economists' Advice Is Not Always Followed

Any economist who advises presidents or other elected leaders knows that his or her recommendations are not always heeded. Frustrating as this can be, it is easy to understand. The process by which economic policy is actually made differs in many ways from the idealized policy process assumed in economics textbooks.

an engine of economic growth. In this regard, the most important economist of the twenty-first century might actually turn out to be not Smith or Keynes, but Joseph Schumpeter.

One of Schumpeter's most important contributions was the emphasis he placed on the tremendous power of innovation and entrepreneurial initiative to drive growth through a process he famously characterized as "creative destruction." His work captured not only an economic truth, but also the particular source of America's strength and dynamism.

One of the ways to view the trajectory of economic history is through the key technologies that have reverberated across the economy. In the nineteenth century, these included the transcontinental railroad, the telegraph, and the steam engine, among others. In the twentieth, the most powerful innovations included the automobile, the jet plane, and, over the last generation, information technology.

While we can't know exactly where the next great area of American innovation will be, we already see a number of prominent sectors where American entrepreneurs are unleashing explosive, innovative energy:

- In information technology, where tremendous potential remains for a range of applications to increase for years to come;
- In life-science technologies, where developments made at the National Institutes of Health and in research facilities around the country will have profound implications not just for human health, but also for the environment, agriculture, and a range of other areas that require technological creativity; and,
- In energy, where the combination of environmental and geopolitical imperatives have created the context for an enormously productive period in developing energy technologies as well.

Looking across the breadth of the U.S. economy, the prospects for transformational innovation to occur are enormous. But to ensure that the entrepreneurial spirit that Schumpeter recognized in the early twentieth century will continue to drive the American economy in the twenty-first century requires a role for government as well: to create an environment that is conducive to generating those developments.

Source: The White House Blog, September 21, 2009. http://www.whitehouse.gov/blog/A-Vision-for-Innovation-Growth-and-Quality-Jobs/

Throughout this text, whenever we discuss economic policy, we often focus on one question: What is the best policy for the government to pursue? We act as if policy were set by a benevolent king. Once the king figures out the right policy, he has no trouble putting his ideas into action.

In the real world, figuring out the right policy is only part of a leader's job, sometimes the easiest part. After a president hears from his economic advisers about what policy is best from their perspective, he turns to other advisers for related input. His communications advisers will tell him how best to explain the proposed policy to the public, and they will try to anticipate any misunderstandings that might make the challenge more difficult. His press advisers will tell him how the news media will report on his proposal and what opinions will likely be expressed on the nation's editorial pages. His legislative affairs advisers will tell him how Congress will view the proposal, what amendments members of Congress will suggest, and the likelihood that Congress will pass some version of the president's proposal into law. His political advisers will tell him which groups will organize to support or oppose the proposed policy, how this proposal will affect his standing among different groups in the electorate, and whether it will affect support for any of the president's other policy initiatives. After hearing and weighing all this advice, the president then decides how to proceed.

Making economic policy in a representative democracy is a messy affair—and there are often good reasons presidents (and other politicians) do not advance the policies that economists advocate. Economists offer crucial input into the policy process, but their advice is only one ingredient of a complex recipe.

QUICK QUIZ *Give an example of a positive statement and an example of a normative statement that somehow relates to your daily life.* • *Name three parts of government that regularly rely on advice from economists.*

Why Economists Disagree

"If all economists were laid end to end, they would not reach a conclusion." This quip from George Bernard Shaw is revealing. Economists as a group are often criticized for giving conflicting advice to policymakers. President Ronald Reagan once joked that if the game Trivial Pursuit were designed for economists, it would have 100 questions and 3,000 answers.

Why do economists so often appear to give conflicting advice to policymakers? There are two basic reasons:

- Economists may disagree about the validity of alternative positive theories about how the world works.
- Economists may have different values and therefore different normative views about what policy should try to accomplish.

Let's discuss each of these reasons.

Differences in Scientific Judgments

Several centuries ago, astronomers debated whether the earth or the sun was at the center of the solar system. More recently, meteorologists have debated whether the earth is experiencing global warming and, if so, why. Science is a search for understanding about the world around us. It is not surprising that as the search continues, scientists can disagree about the direction in which truth lies.

Economists often disagree for the same reason. Economics is a young science, and there is still much to be learned. Economists sometimes disagree because they have different hunches about the validity of alternative theories or about the size of important parameters that measure how economic variables are related.

For example, economists disagree about whether the government should tax a household's income or its consumption (spending). Advocates of a switch from the current income tax to a consumption tax believe that the change would encourage households to save more because income that is saved would not be taxed. Higher saving, in turn, would free resources for capital accumulation, leading to more rapid growth in productivity and living standards. Advocates of the current income tax system believe that household saving would not respond much to a change in the tax laws. These two groups of economists hold different normative views about the tax system because they have different positive views about the responsiveness of saving to tax incentives.

Differences in Values

Suppose that Peter and Paula both take the same amount of water from the town well. To pay for maintaining the well, the town taxes its residents. Peter has income of $100,000 and is taxed $10,000, or 10 percent of his income. Paula has income of $20,000 and is taxed $4,000, or 20 percent of her income.

Is this policy fair? If not, who pays too much and who pays too little? Does it matter whether Paula's low income is due to a medical disability or to her decision to pursue an acting career? Does it matter whether Peter's high income is due to a large inheritance or to his willingness to work long hours at a dreary job?

These are difficult questions on which people are likely to disagree. If the town hired two experts to study how the town should tax its residents to pay for the well, we would not be surprised if they offered conflicting advice.

This simple example shows why economists sometimes disagree about public policy. As we learned earlier in our discussion of normative and positive analysis, policies cannot be judged on scientific grounds alone. Economists give conflicting advice sometimes because they have different values. Perfecting the science of economics will not tell us whether Peter or Paula pays too much.

Perception versus Reality

Because of differences in scientific judgments and differences in values, some disagreement among economists is inevitable. Yet one should not overstate the amount of disagreement. Economists agree with one another far more than is sometimes understood.

Table 1 contains 20 propositions about economic policy. In surveys of professional economists, these propositions were endorsed by an overwhelming majority of respondents. Most of these propositions would fail to command a similar consensus among the public.

The first proposition in the table is about rent control, a policy that sets a legal maximum on the amount landlords can charge for their apartments. Almost all economists believe that rent control adversely affects the availability and quality of housing and is a costly way of helping the neediest members of society. Nonetheless, many city governments ignore the advice of economists and place ceilings on the rents that landlords may charge their tenants.

The second proposition in the table concerns tariffs and import quotas, two policies that restrict trade among nations. For reasons we discuss more fully later in this text, almost all economists oppose such barriers to free trade. Nonetheless, over the years, presidents and Congress have chosen to restrict the import of certain goods.

Why do policies such as rent control and trade barriers persist if the experts are united in their opposition? It may be that the realities of the political process stand as immovable obstacles. But it also may be that economists have not yet convinced enough of the public that these policies are undesirable. One purpose of this book is to help you understand the economist's view of these and other subjects and, perhaps, to persuade you that it is the right one.

QUICK QUIZ   *Why might economic advisers to the president disagree about a question of policy?*

Let's Get Going

The first two chapters of this book have introduced you to the ideas and methods of economics. We are now ready to get to work. In the next chapter, we start learning in more detail the principles of economic behavior and economic policy.

As you proceed through this book, you will be asked to draw on many of your intellectual skills. You might find it helpful to keep in mind some advice from the great economist John Maynard Keynes:

Table 1

Propositions about Which Most Economists Agree

Proposition (and percentage of economists who agree)

1. A ceiling on rents reduces the quantity and quality of housing available. (93%)
2. Tariffs and import quotas usually reduce general economic welfare. (93%)
3. Flexible and floating exchange rates offer an effective international monetary arrangement. (90%)
4. Fiscal policy (e.g., tax cut and/or government expenditure increase) has a significant stimulative impact on a less than fully employed economy. (90%)
5. The United States should not restrict employers from outsourcing work to foreign countries. (90%)
6. Economic growth in developed countries like the United States leads to greater levels of well-being. (88%)
7. The United States should eliminate agricultural subsidies. (85%)
8. An appropriately designed fiscal policy can increase the long-run rate of capital formation. (85%)
9. Local and state governments should eliminate subsidies to professional sports franchises. (85%)
10. If the federal budget is to be balanced, it should be done over the business cycle rather than yearly. (85%)
11. The gap between Social Security funds and expenditures will become unsustainably large within the next 50 years if current policies remain unchanged. (85%)
12. Cash payments increase the welfare of recipients to a greater degree than do transfers-in-kind of equal cash value. (84%)
13. A large federal budget deficit has an adverse effect on the economy. (83%)
14. The redistribution of income in the United State is a legitimate role for the government. (83%)
15. Inflation is caused primarily by too much growth in the money supply. (83%)
16. The United States should not ban genetically modified crops. (82%)
17. A minimum wage increases unemployment among young and unskilled workers. (79%)
18. The government should restructure the welfare system along the lines of a "negative income tax." (79%)
19. Effluent taxes and marketable pollution permits represent a better approach to pollution control than imposition of pollution ceilings. (78%)
20. Government subsidies on ethanol in the United States should be reduced or eliminated. (78%)

Source: Richard M. Alston, J. R. Kearl, and Michael B. Vaughn, "Is There Consensus among Economists in the 1990s?" *American Economic Review* (May 1992): 203–209; Dan Fuller and Doris Geide-Stevenson, "Consensus among Economists Revisited," *Journal of Economics Education* (Fall 2003): 369–387; Robert Whaples, "Do Economists Agree on Anything? Yes!" *Economists' Voice* (November 2006): 1–6; Robert Whaples, "The Policy Views of American Economic Association Members: The Results of a New Survey, *Econ Journal Watch* (September 2009): 337–348.

The study of economics does not seem to require any specialized gifts of an unusually high order. Is it not . . . a very easy subject compared with the higher branches of philosophy or pure science? An easy subject, at which very few excel! The paradox finds its explanation, perhaps, in that the master-economist must possess a rare *combination* of gifts. He must be mathematician, historian, statesman, philosopher—in some degree. He must understand symbols and speak in words. He must contemplate the particular in terms of the general, and touch abstract and concrete in the same flight of thought. He must study the present in the light of the past for the purposes of the future. No part of man's nature or his institutions must lie entirely outside his regard. He must be purposeful and disinterested in a simultaneous mood; as aloof and incorruptible as an artist, yet sometimes as near the earth as a politician.

It is a tall order. But with practice, you will become more and more accustomed to thinking like an economist.

in the news

> ## Environmental Economics
> *Some economists are helping to save the planet.*

Green Groups See Potent Tool in Economics

By Jessica E. Vascellaro

Many economists dream of getting high-paying jobs on Wall Street, at prestigious think tanks and universities or at powerful government agencies like the Federal Reserve.

But a growing number are choosing to use their skills not to track inflation or interest rates but to rescue rivers and trees. These are the "green economists," more formally known as environmental economists, who use economic arguments and systems to persuade companies to clean up pollution and to help conserve natural areas.

Working at dozens of advocacy groups and a myriad of state and federal environmental agencies, they are helping to formulate the intellectual framework behind approaches to protecting endangered species, reducing pollution and preventing climate change. They also are becoming a link between left-leaning advocacy groups and the public and private sectors.

"In the past, many advocacy groups interpreted economics as how to make a profit or maximize income," says Lawrence Goulder, a professor of environmental and resource economics at Stanford University in Stanford, Calif. "More economists are

Source: *The Wall Street Journal,* August 23, 2005.

realizing that it offers a framework for resource allocation where resources are not only labor and capital but natural resources as well."

Environmental economists are on the payroll of government agencies (the Environmental Protection Agency had about 164 on staff in 2004, up 36% from 1995) and groups like the Wilderness Society, a Washington-based conservation group, which has four of them to work on projects such as assessing the economic impact of building off-road driving trails. Environmental Defense, also based in Washington, was one of the first environmental-advocacy groups to hire economists and now has about eight, who do such things as develop market incentives to address environmental problems like climate change and water shortages. . . .

"There used to be this idea that we shouldn't have to monetize the environment because it is invaluable," says Caroline Alkire, who in 1991 joined the Wilderness Society, an advocacy group in Washington, D.C., as one of the group's first economists. "But if we are going to engage in debate on the Hill about drilling in the Arctic we need to be able to combat the financial arguments. We have to play that card or we are going to lose."

The field of environmental economics began to take form in the 1960s when academics started to apply the tools of economics to the nascent green movement. The discipline grew more popular through-

out the 1980s when the Environmental Protection Agency adopted a system of tradable permits for phasing out leaded gasoline. It wasn't until the 1990 amendment to the Clean Air Act, however, that most environmentalists started to take economics seriously.

The amendment implemented a system of tradable allowances for acid rain, a program pushed by Environmental Defense. Under the law, plants that can reduce their emissions more cost-effectively may sell their allowances to more heavy polluters. Today, the program has exceeded its goal of reducing the amount of acid rain to half its 1980 level and is celebrated as evidence that markets can help achieve environmental goals.

Its success has convinced its former critics, who at the time contended that environmental regulation was a matter of ethics, not economics, and favored installing expensive acid rain removal technology in all power plants instead.

Greenpeace, the international environmental giant, was one of the leading opponents of the 1990 amendment. But Kert Davies, research director for Greenpeace USA, said its success and the lack of any significant action on climate policy throughout [the] early 1990s brought the organization around to the concept. "We now believe that [tradable permits] are the most straightforward system of reducing emissions and creating the incentives necessary for massive reductions."

SUMMARY

- Economists try to address their subject with a scientist's objectivity. Like all scientists, they make appropriate assumptions and build simplified models to understand the world around them. Two simple economic models are the circular-flow diagram and the production possibilities frontier.

- The field of economics is divided into two subfields: microeconomics and macroeconomics. Microeconomists study decision making by households and firms and the interaction among households and firms in the marketplace. Macroeconomists study the forces and trends that affect the economy as a whole.

- A positive statement is an assertion about how the world *is*. A normative statement is an assertion about how the world *ought to be*. When economists make normative statements, they are acting more as policy advisers than scientists.

- Economists who advise policymakers offer conflicting advice either because of differences in scientific judgments or because of differences in values. At other times, economists are united in the advice they offer, but policymakers may choose to ignore it.

KEY CONCEPTS

circular-flow diagram, *p. 24*
production possibilities
   frontier, *p. 26*

microeconomics, *p. 29*
macroeconomics, *p. 29*

positive statements, *p. 31*
normative statements, *p. 31*

QUESTIONS FOR REVIEW

1. How is economics a science?
2. Why do economists make assumptions?
3. Should an economic model describe reality exactly?
4. Name a way that your family interacts in the factor market and a way that it interacts in the product market.
5. Name one economic interaction that isn't covered by the simplified circular-flow diagram.
6. Draw and explain a production possibilities frontier for an economy that produces milk and cookies. What happens to this frontier if disease kills half of the economy's cows?
7. Use a production possibilities frontier to describe the idea of "efficiency."
8. What are the two subfields into which economics is divided? Explain what each subfield studies.
9. What is the difference between a positive and a normative statement? Give an example of each.
10. Why do economists sometimes offer conflicting advice to policymakers?

PROBLEMS AND APPLICATIONS

1. Draw a circular-flow diagram. Identify the parts of the model that correspond to the flow of goods and services and the flow of dollars for each of the following activities.
   a. Selena pays a storekeeper $1 for a quart of milk.
   b. Stuart earns $4.50 per hour working at a fast-food restaurant.
   c. Shanna spends $30 to get a haircut.
   d. Sally earns $10,000 from her 10 percent ownership of Acme Industrial.

2. Imagine a society that produces military goods and consumer goods, which we'll call "guns" and "butter."

    a. Draw a production possibilities frontier for guns and butter. Using the concept of opportunity cost, explain why it most likely has a bowed-out shape.

    b. Show a point that is impossible for the economy to achieve. Show a point that is feasible but inefficient.

    c. Imagine that the society has two political parties, called the Hawks (who want a strong military) and the Doves (who want a smaller military). Show a point on your production possibilities frontier that the Hawks might choose and a point the Doves might choose.

    d. Imagine that an aggressive neighboring country reduces the size of its military. As a result, both the Hawks and the Doves reduce their desired production of guns by the same amount. Which party would get the bigger "peace dividend," measured by the increase in butter production? Explain.

3. The first principle of economics discussed in Chapter 1 is that people face trade-offs. Use a production possibilities frontier to illustrate society's trade-off between two "goods"—a clean environment and the quantity of industrial output. What do you suppose determines the shape and position of the frontier? Show what happens to the frontier if engineers develop a new way of producing electricity that emits fewer pollutants.

4. An economy consists of three workers: Larry, Moe, and Curly. Each works ten hours a day and can produce two services: mowing lawns and washing cars. In an hour, Larry can either mow one lawn or wash one car; Moe can either mow one lawn or wash two cars; and Curly can either mow two lawns or wash one car.

    a. Calculate how much of each service is produced under the following circumstances, which we label A, B, C, and D:

    - All three spend all their time mowing lawns. (A)
    - All three spend all their time washing cars. (B)
    - All three spend half their time on each activity. (C)
    - Larry spends half his time on each activity, while Moe only washes cars and Curly only mows lawns. (D)

    b. Graph the production possibilities frontier for this economy. Using your answers to part (a), identify points A, B, C, and D on your graph.

    c. Explain why the production possibilities frontier has the shape it does.

    d. Are any of the allocations calculated in part (a) inefficient? Explain.

5. Classify the following topics as relating to microeconomics or macroeconomics.

    a. a family's decision about how much income to save

    b. the effect of government regulations on auto emissions

    c. the impact of higher national saving on economic growth

    d. a firm's decision about how many workers to hire

    e. the relationship between the inflation rate and changes in the quantity of money

6. Classify each of the following statements as positive or normative. Explain.

    a. Society faces a short-run trade-off between inflation and unemployment.

    b. A reduction in the rate of money growth will reduce the rate of inflation.

    c. The Federal Reserve should reduce the rate of money growth.

    d. Society ought to require welfare recipients to look for jobs.

    e. Lower tax rates encourage more work and more saving.

7. If you were president, would you be more interested in your economic advisers' positive views or their normative views? Why?

For further information on topics in this chapter, additional problems, applications, examples, online quizzes, and more, please visit our website at www.cengage.com/economics/mankiw.

Appendix

Graphing: A Brief Review

Many of the concepts that economists study can be expressed with numbers—the price of bananas, the quantity of bananas sold, the cost of growing bananas, and so on. Often, these economic variables are related to one another: When the price of bananas rises, people buy fewer bananas. One way of expressing the relationships among variables is with graphs.

Graphs serve two purposes. First, when developing economic theories, graphs offer a way to visually express ideas that might be less clear if described with equations or words. Second, when analyzing economic data, graphs provide a powerful way of finding and interpreting patterns. Whether we are working with theory or with data, graphs provide a lens through which a recognizable forest emerges from a multitude of trees.

Numerical information can be expressed graphically in many ways, just as there are many ways to express a thought in words. A good writer chooses words that will make an argument clear, a description pleasing, or a scene dramatic. An effective economist chooses the type of graph that best suits the purpose at hand.

In this appendix, we discuss how economists use graphs to study the mathematical relationships among variables. We also discuss some of the pitfalls that can arise in the use of graphical methods.

Graphs of a Single Variable

Three common graphs are shown in Figure A-1. The *pie chart* in panel (a) shows how total income in the United States is divided among the sources of income, including compensation of employees, corporate profits, and so on. A slice of the

---

Figure 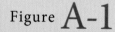 A-1

Types of Graphs

The pie chart in panel (a) shows how U.S. national income in 2008 was derived from various sources. The bar graph in panel (b) compares the 2008 average income in four countries. The time-series graph in panel (c) shows the productivity of labor in U.S. businesses from 1950 to 2000.

(a) Pie Chart

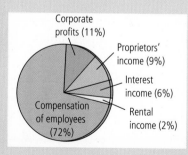

(b) Bar Graph

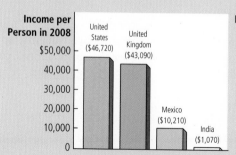

(c) Time-Series Graph

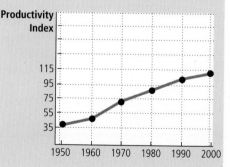

pie represents each source's share of the total. The *bar graph* in panel (b) compares income for four countries. The height of each bar represents the average income in each country. The *time-series graph* in panel (c) traces the rising productivity in the U.S. business sector over time. The height of the line shows output per hour in each year. You have probably seen similar graphs in newspapers and magazines.

Graphs of Two Variables: The Coordinate System

The three graphs in Figure A-1 are useful in showing how a variable changes over time or across individuals, but they are limited in how much they can tell us. These graphs display information only on a single variable. Economists are often concerned with the relationships between variables. Thus, they need to display two variables on a single graph. The *coordinate system* makes this possible.

Suppose you want to examine the relationship between study time and grade point average. For each student in your class, you could record a pair of numbers: hours per week spent studying and grade point average. These numbers could then be placed in parentheses as an *ordered pair* and appear as a single point on the graph. Albert E., for instance, is represented by the ordered pair (25 hours/week, 3.5 GPA), while his "what-me-worry?" classmate Alfred E. is represented by the ordered pair (5 hours/week, 2.0 GPA).

We can graph these ordered pairs on a two-dimensional grid. The first number in each ordered pair, called the *x-coordinate*, tells us the horizontal location of the point. The second number, called the *y-coordinate*, tells us the vertical location of the point. The point with both an *x*-coordinate and a *y*-coordinate of zero is known as the *origin*. The two coordinates in the ordered pair tell us where the point is located in relation to the origin: *x* units to the right of the origin and *y* units above it.

Figure A-2 graphs grade point average against study time for Albert E., Alfred E., and their classmates. This type of graph is called a *scatterplot* because it plots scattered points. Looking at this graph, we immediately notice that points farther

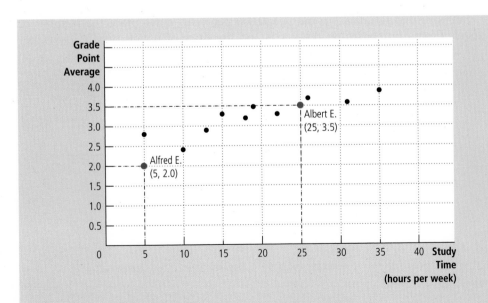

Figure **A-2**

Using the Coordinate System
Grade point average is measured on the vertical axis and study time on the horizontal axis. Albert E., Alfred E., and their classmates are represented by various points. We can see from the graph that students who study more tend to get higher grades.

to the right (indicating more study time) also tend to be higher (indicating a better grade point average). Because study time and grade point average typically move in the same direction, we say that these two variables have a *positive correlation*. By contrast, if we were to graph party time and grades, we would likely find that higher party time is associated with lower grades; because these variables typically move in opposite directions, we call this a *negative correlation*. In either case, the coordinate system makes the correlation between the two variables easy to see.

Curves in the Coordinate System

Students who study more do tend to get higher grades, but other factors also influence a student's grade. Previous preparation is an important factor, for instance, as are talent, attention from teachers, even eating a good breakfast. A scatterplot like Figure A-2 does not attempt to isolate the effect that studying has on grades from the effects of other variables. Often, however, economists prefer looking at how one variable affects another, holding everything else constant.

To see how this is done, let's consider one of the most important graphs in economics: the *demand curve*. The demand curve traces out the effect of a good's price on the quantity of the good consumers want to buy. Before showing a demand curve, however, consider Table A-1, which shows how the number of novels that Emma buys depends on her income and on the price of novels. When novels are cheap, Emma buys them in large quantities. As they become more expensive, she instead borrows books from the library or chooses to go to the movies rather than read. Similarly, at any given price, Emma buys more novels when she has a higher income. That is, when her income increases, she spends part of the additional income on novels and part on other goods.

We now have three variables—the price of novels, income, and the number of novels purchased—which are more than we can represent in two dimensions. To put the information from Table A-1 in graphical form, we need to hold one of the three variables constant and trace out the relationship between the other two. Because the demand curve represents the relationship between price and quantity demanded, we hold Emma's income constant and show how the number of novels she buys varies with the price of novels.

Suppose that Emma's income is $30,000 per year. If we place the number of novels Emma purchases on the x-axis and the price of novels on the y-axis, we

Table A-1

Novels Purchased by Emma
This table shows the number of novels Emma buys at various incomes and prices. For any given level of income, the data on price and quantity demanded can be graphed to produce Emma's demand curve for novels, as shown in Figures A-3 and A-4.

Price	For $20,000 Income:	For $30,000 Income:	For $40,000 Income:
$10	2 novels	5 novels	8 novels
9	6	9	12
8	10	13	16
7	14	17	20
6	18	21	24
5	22	25	28
	Demand curve, D_3	Demand curve, D_1	Demand curve, D_2

can graphically represent the middle column of Table A-1. When the points that represent these entries from the table—(5 novels, $10), (9 novels, $9), and so on—are connected, they form a line. This line, pictured in Figure A-3, is known as Emma's demand curve for novels; it tells us how many novels Emma purchases at any given price. The demand curve is downward sloping, indicating that a higher price reduces the quantity of novels demanded. Because the quantity of novels demanded and the price move in opposite directions, we say that the two variables are *negatively related*. (Conversely, when two variables move in the same direction, the curve relating them is upward sloping, and we say the variables are *positively related*.)

Now suppose that Emma's income rises to $40,000 per year. At any given price, Emma will purchase more novels than she did at her previous level of income. Just as earlier we drew Emma's demand curve for novels using the entries from the middle column of Table A-1, we now draw a new demand curve using the entries from the right column of the table. This new demand curve (curve D_2) is pictured alongside the old one (curve D_1) in Figure A-4; the new curve is a similar line drawn farther to the right. We therefore say that Emma's demand curve for novels *shifts* to the right when her income increases. Likewise, if Emma's income were to fall to $20,000 per year, she would buy fewer novels at any given price and her demand curve would shift to the left (to curve D_3).

In economics, it is important to distinguish between *movements along a curve* and *shifts of a curve*. As we can see from Figure A-3, if Emma earns $30,000 per year and novels cost $8 apiece, she will purchase 13 novels per year. If the price of novels falls to $7, Emma will increase her purchases of novels to 17 per year. The demand curve, however, stays fixed in the same place. Emma still buys the same

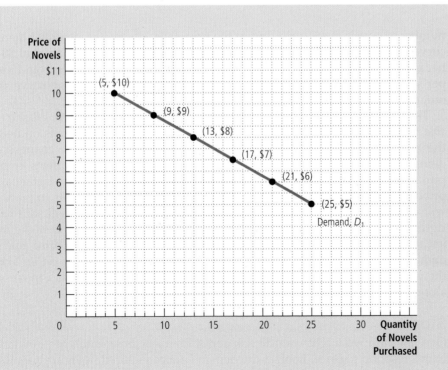

Figure A-3

Demand Curve
The line D_1 shows how Emma's purchases of novels depend on the price of novels when her income is held constant. Because the price and the quantity demanded are negatively related, the demand curve slopes downward.

Figure A-4

Shifting Demand Curves
The location of Emma's demand curve for novels depends on how much income she earns. The more she earns, the more novels she will purchase at any given price, and the farther to the right her demand curve will lie. Curve D_1 represents Emma's original demand curve when her income is $30,000 per year. If her income rises to $40,000 per year, her demand curve shifts to D_2. If her income falls to $20,000 per year, her demand curve shifts to D_3.

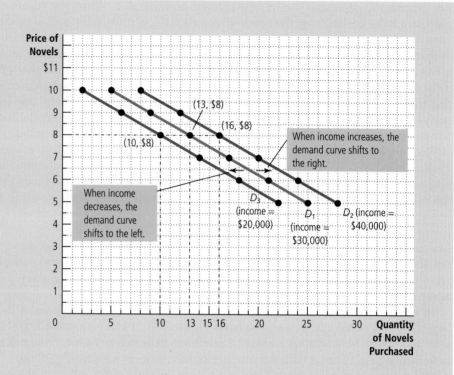

number of novels *at each price*, but as the price falls, she moves along her demand curve from left to right. By contrast, if the price of novels remains fixed at $8 but her income rises to $40,000, Emma increases her purchases of novels from 13 to 16 per year. Because Emma buys more novels *at each price*, her demand curve shifts out, as shown in Figure A-4.

There is a simple way to tell when it is necessary to shift a curve: *When a variable that is not named on either axis changes, the curve shifts.* Income is on neither the *x*-axis nor the *y*-axis of the graph, so when Emma's income changes, her demand curve must shift. The same is true for any change that affects Emma's purchasing habits besides a change in the price of novels. If, for instance, the public library closes and Emma must buy all the books she wants to read, she will demand more novels at each price, and her demand curve will shift to the right. Or if the price of movies falls and Emma spends more time at the movies and less time reading, she will demand fewer novels at each price, and her demand curve will shift to the left. By contrast, when a variable on an axis of the graph changes, the curve does not shift. We read the change as a movement along the curve.

Slope

One question we might want to ask about Emma is how much her purchasing habits respond to price. Look at the demand curve pictured in Figure A-5. If this curve is very steep, Emma purchases nearly the same number of novels regardless

Figure A-5

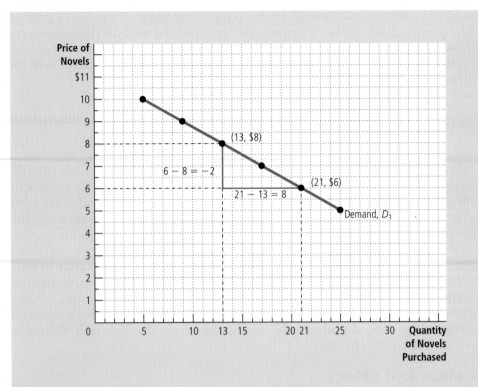

Calculating the Slope of a Line

To calculate the slope of the demand curve, we can look at the changes in the *x*- and *y*-coordinates as we move from the point (21 novels, $6) to the point (13 novels, $8). The slope of the line is the ratio of the change in the *y*-coordinate (−2) to the change in the *x*-coordinate (+8), which equals −¼

of whether they are cheap or expensive. If this curve is much flatter, the number of novels Emma purchases is more sensitive to changes in the price. To answer questions about how much one variable responds to changes in another variable, we can use the concept of *slope*.

The slope of a line is the ratio of the vertical distance covered to the horizontal distance covered as we move along the line. This definition is usually written out in mathematical symbols as follows:

$$\text{slope} = \frac{\Delta y}{\Delta x},$$

where the Greek letter Δ (delta) stands for the change in a variable. In other words, the slope of a line is equal to the "rise" (change in *y*) divided by the "run" (change in *x*). The slope will be a small positive number for a fairly flat upward-sloping line, a large positive number for a steep upward-sloping line, and a negative number for a downward-sloping line. A horizontal line has a slope of zero because in this case the *y*-variable never changes; a vertical line is said to have an infinite slope because the *y*-variable can take any value without the *x*-variable changing at all.

What is the slope of Emma's demand curve for novels? First of all, because the curve slopes down, we know the slope will be negative. To calculate a numerical value for the slope, we must choose two points on the line. With Emma's income at $30,000, she will purchase 21 novels at a price of $6 or 13 novels at a price of $8. When we apply the slope formula, we are concerned with the change between these two points; in other words, we are concerned with the difference between them, which lets us know that we will have to subtract one set of values from the other, as follows:

$$\text{slope} = \frac{\Delta y}{\Delta x} = \frac{\text{first } y\text{-coordinate} - \text{second } y\text{-coordinate}}{\text{first } x\text{-coordinate} - \text{second } x\text{-coordinate}} = \frac{6 - 8}{21 - 13} = \frac{-2}{8} = \frac{-1}{4}$$

Figure A-5 shows graphically how this calculation works. Try computing the slope of Emma's demand curve using two different points. You should get exactly the same result, $-\frac{1}{4}$. One of the properties of a straight line is that it has the same slope everywhere. This is not true of other types of curves, which are steeper in some places than in others.

The slope of Emma's demand curve tells us something about how responsive her purchases are to changes in the price. A small slope (a number close to zero) means that Emma's demand curve is relatively flat; in this case, she adjusts the number of novels she buys substantially in response to a price change. A larger slope (a number farther from zero) means that Emma's demand curve is relatively steep; in this case, she adjusts the number of novels she buys only slightly in response to a price change.

Cause and Effect

Economists often use graphs to advance an argument about how the economy works. In other words, they use graphs to argue about how one set of events *causes* another set of events. With a graph like the demand curve, there is no doubt about cause and effect. Because we are varying price and holding all other variables constant, we know that changes in the price of novels cause changes in the quantity Emma demands. Remember, however, that our demand curve came from a hypothetical example. When graphing data from the real world, it is often more difficult to establish how one variable affects another.

The first problem is that it is difficult to hold everything else constant when studying the relationship between two variables. If we are not able to hold other variables constant, we might decide that one variable on our graph is causing changes in the other variable when actually those changes are caused by a third *omitted variable* not pictured on the graph. Even if we have identified the correct

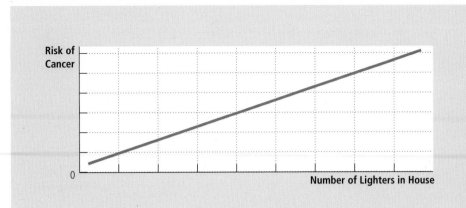

Figure A-6

Graph with an Omitted Variable
The upward-sloping curve shows
that members of households
with more cigarette lighters are
more likely to develop cancer.
Yet we should not conclude that
ownership of lighters causes
cancer because the graph does not
take into account the number of
cigarettes smoked.

two variables to look at, we might run into a second problem—*reverse causality*. In other words, we might decide that A causes B when in fact B causes A. The omitted-variable and reverse-causality traps require us to proceed with caution when using graphs to draw conclusions about causes and effects.

Omitted Variables   To see how omitting a variable can lead to a deceptive graph, let's consider an example. Imagine that the government, spurred by public concern about the large number of deaths from cancer, commissions an exhaustive study from Big Brother Statistical Services, Inc. Big Brother examines many of the items found in people's homes to see which of them are associated with the risk of cancer. Big Brother reports a strong relationship between two variables: the number of cigarette lighters that a household owns and the probability that someone in the household will develop cancer. Figure A-6 shows this relationship.

What should we make of this result? Big Brother advises a quick policy response. It recommends that the government discourage the ownership of cigarette lighters by taxing their sale. It also recommends that the government require warning labels: "Big Brother has determined that this lighter is danger-ous to your health."

In judging the validity of Big Brother's analysis, one question is paramount: Has Big Brother held constant every relevant variable except the one under consideration? If the answer is no, the results are suspect. An easy explanation for Figure A-6 is that people who own more cigarette lighters are more likely to smoke cigarettes and that cigarettes, not lighters, cause cancer. If Figure A-6 does not hold constant the amount of smoking, it does not tell us the true effect of own-ing a cigarette lighter.

This story illustrates an important principle: When you see a graph used to support an argument about cause and effect, it is important to ask whether the movements of an omitted variable could explain the results you see.

Reverse Causality   Economists can also make mistakes about causality by misreading its direction. To see how this is possible, suppose the Association of American Anarchists commissions a study of crime in America and arrives at

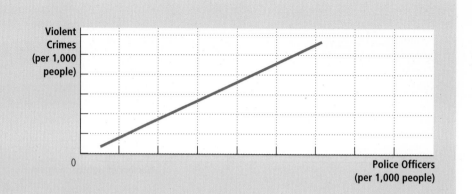

Figure A-7

Graph Suggesting Reverse Causality
The upward-sloping curve shows that cities with a higher concentration of police are more dangerous. Yet the graph does not tell us whether police cause crime or crime-plagued cities hire more police.

Figure A-7, which plots the number of violent crimes per thousand people in major cities against the number of police officers per thousand people. The anarchists note the curve's upward slope and argue that because police increase rather than decrease the amount of urban violence, law enforcement should be abolished.

If we could run a controlled experiment, we would avoid the danger of reverse causality. To run an experiment, we would set the number of police officers in different cities randomly and then examine the correlation between police and crime. Figure A-7, however, is not based on such an experiment. We simply observe that more dangerous cities have more police officers. The explanation for this may be that more dangerous cities hire more police. In other words, rather than police causing crime, crime may cause police. Nothing in the graph itself allows us to establish the direction of causality.

It might seem that an easy way to determine the direction of causality is to examine which variable moves first. If we see crime increase and then the police force expand, we reach one conclusion. If we see the police force expand and then crime increase, we reach the other. Yet there is also a flaw with this approach: Often, people change their behavior not in response to a change in their present conditions but in response to a change in their *expectations* of future conditions. A city that expects a major crime wave in the future, for instance, might hire more police now. This problem is even easier to see in the case of babies and minivans. Couples often buy a minivan in anticipation of the birth of a child. The minivan comes before the baby, but we wouldn't want to conclude that the sale of minivans causes the population to grow!

There is no complete set of rules that says when it is appropriate to draw causal conclusions from graphs. Yet just keeping in mind that cigarette lighters don't cause cancer (omitted variable) and minivans don't cause larger families (reverse causality) will keep you from falling for many faulty economic arguments.

Interdependence and the Gains from Trade

3

onsider your typical day. You wake up in the morning and pour yourself juice from oranges grown in Florida and coffee from beans grown in Brazil. Over breakfast, you watch a news program broadcast from New York on your television made in China. You get dressed in clothes made of cotton grown in Georgia and sewn in factories in Thailand. You drive to class in a car made of parts manufactured in more than a dozen countries around the world. Then you open up your economics textbook written by an author living in Massachusetts, published by a company located in Ohio, and printed on paper made from trees grown in Oregon.

Every day, you rely on many people, most of whom you have never met, to provide you with the goods and services that you enjoy. Such interdependence is possible because people trade with one another. Those people providing you goods and services are not acting out of generosity. Nor is some government agency directing them to satisfy your desires. Instead, people provide you and other consumers with the goods and services they produce because they get something in return.

In subsequent chapters, we examine how our economy coordinates the activities of millions of people with varying tastes and abilities. As a starting point for this analysis, here we consider the reasons for economic interdependence. One of the *Ten Principles of Economics* highlighted in Chapter 1 is that trade can make everyone better off. In this chapter, we examine this principle more closely. What exactly do people gain when they trade with one another? Why do people choose to become interdependent?

The answers to these questions are key to understanding the modern global economy. In most countries today, many goods and services consumed are imported from abroad, and many goods and services produced are exported to foreign customers. The analysis in this chapter explains interdependence not only among individuals but also among nations. As we will see, the gains from trade are much the same whether you are buying a haircut from your local barber or a T-shirt made by a worker on the other side of the globe.

A Parable for the Modern Economy

To understand why people choose to depend on others for goods and services and how this choice improves their lives, let's look at a simple economy. Imagine that there are two goods in the world: meat and potatoes. And there are two people in the world—a cattle rancher and a potato farmer—each of whom would like to eat both meat and potatoes.

The gains from trade are most obvious if the rancher can produce only meat and the farmer can produce only potatoes. In one scenario, the rancher and the farmer could choose to have nothing to do with each other. But after several months of eating beef roasted, boiled, broiled, and grilled, the rancher might decide that self-sufficiency is not all it's cracked up to be. The farmer, who has been eating potatoes mashed, fried, baked, and scalloped, would likely agree. It is easy to see that trade would allow them to enjoy greater variety: Each could then have a steak with a baked potato or a burger with fries.

Although this scene illustrates most simply how everyone can benefit from trade, the gains would be similar if the rancher and the farmer were each capable of producing the other good, but only at great cost. Suppose, for example, that the potato farmer is able to raise cattle and produce meat, but that he is not very good at it. Similarly, suppose that the cattle rancher is able to grow potatoes but that her land is not very well suited for it. In this case, the farmer and the rancher can each benefit by specializing in what he or she does best and then trading with the other.

The gains from trade are less obvious, however, when one person is better at producing *every* good. For example, suppose that the rancher is better at raising cattle *and* better at growing potatoes than the farmer. In this case, should the rancher choose to remain self-sufficient? Or is there still reason for her to trade with the farmer? To answer this question, we need to look more closely at the factors that affect such a decision.

Production Possibilities

Suppose that the farmer and the rancher each work 8 hours per day and can devote this time to growing potatoes, raising cattle, or a combination of the two.

The table in Figure 1 shows the amount of time each person requires to produce 1 ounce of each good. The farmer can produce an ounce of potatoes in 15 minutes and an ounce of meat in 60 minutes. The rancher, who is more productive in both activities, can produce an ounce of potatoes in 10 minutes and an ounce of meat in 20 minutes. The last two columns in the table show the amounts of meat or potatoes the farmer and rancher can produce if they work an 8-hour day producing only that good.

Panel (b) of Figure 1 illustrates the amounts of meat and potatoes that the farmer can produce. If the farmer devotes all 8 hours of his time to potatoes, he produces 32 ounces of potatoes (measured on the horizontal axis) and no meat. If he devotes all his time to meat, he produces 8 ounces of meat (measured on the vertical axis) and no potatoes. If the farmer divides his time equally between the two activities, spending 4 hours on each, he produces 16 ounces of potatoes and 4 ounces of meat. The figure shows these three possible outcomes and all others in between.

Panel (a) shows the production opportunities available to the farmer and the rancher. Panel (b) shows the combinations of meat and potatoes that the farmer can produce. Panel (c) shows the combinations of meat and potatoes that the rancher can produce. Both production possibilities frontiers are derived assuming that the farmer and rancher each work 8 hours per day. If there is no trade, each person's production possibilities frontier is also his or her consumption possibilities frontier.

Figure **1**

The Production Possibilities Frontier

(a) Production Opportunities

	Minutes Needed to Make 1 Ounce of:		Amount Produced in 8 Hours	
	Meat	**Potatoes**	**Meat**	**Potatoes**
Farmer	60 min/oz	15 min/oz	8 oz	32 oz
Rancher	20 min/oz	10 min/oz	24 oz	48 oz

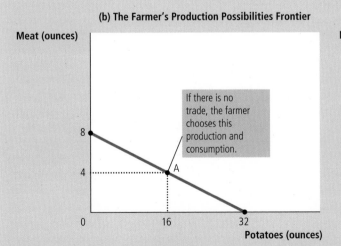

(b) The Farmer's Production Possibilities Frontier

If there is no trade, the farmer chooses this production and consumption.

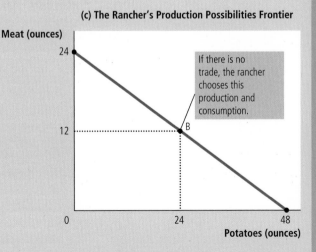

(c) The Rancher's Production Possibilities Frontier

If there is no trade, the rancher chooses this production and consumption.

This graph is the farmer's production possibilities frontier. As we discussed in Chapter 2, a production possibilities frontier shows the various mixes of output that an economy can produce. It illustrates one of the *Ten Principles of Economics* in Chapter 1: People face trade-offs. Here the farmer faces a trade-off between producing meat and producing potatoes.

You may recall that the production possibilities frontier in Chapter 2 was drawn bowed out. In that case, the rate at which society could trade one good for the other depended on the amounts that were being produced. Here, however, the farmer's technology for producing meat and potatoes (as summarized in Figure 1) allows him to switch between the two goods at a constant rate. Whenever the farmer spends 1 hour less producing meat and 1 hour more producing potatoes, he reduces his output of meat by 1 ounce and raises his output of potatoes by 4 ounces—and this is true regardless of how much he is already producing. As a result, the production possibilities frontier is a straight line.

Panel (c) of Figure 1 shows the production possibilities frontier for the rancher. If the rancher devotes all 8 hours of her time to potatoes, she produces 48 ounces of potatoes and no meat. If she devotes all her time to meat, she produces 24 ounces of meat and no potatoes. If the rancher divides her time equally, spending 4 hours on each activity, she produces 24 ounces of potatoes and 12 ounces of meat. Once again, the production possibilities frontier shows all the possible outcomes.

If the farmer and rancher choose to be self-sufficient rather than trade with each other, then each consumes exactly what he or she produces. In this case, the production possibilities frontier is also the consumption possibilities frontier. That is, without trade, Figure 1 shows the possible combinations of meat and potatoes that the farmer and rancher can each produce and then consume.

These production possibilities frontiers are useful in showing the trade-offs that the farmer and rancher face, but they do not tell us what the farmer and rancher will actually choose to do. To determine their choices, we need to know the tastes of the farmer and the rancher. Let's suppose they choose the combinations identified by points A and B in Figure 1: The farmer produces and consumes 16 ounces of potatoes and 4 ounces of meat, while the rancher produces and consumes 24 ounces of potatoes and 12 ounces of meat.

Specialization and Trade

After several years of eating combination B, the rancher gets an idea and goes to talk to the farmer:

RANCHER: Farmer, my friend, have I got a deal for you! I know how to improve life for both of us. I think you should stop producing meat altogether and devote all your time to growing potatoes. According to my calculations, if you work 8 hours a day growing potatoes, you'll produce 32 ounces of potatoes. If you give me 15 of those 32 ounces, I'll give you 5 ounces of meat in return. In the end, you'll get to eat 17 ounces of potatoes and 5 ounces of meat every day, instead of the 16 ounces of potatoes and 4 ounces of meat you now get. If you go along with my plan, you'll have more of *both* foods. [To illustrate her point, the rancher shows the farmer panel (a) of Figure 2.]

FARMER: (sounding skeptical) That seems like a good deal for me. But I don't understand why you are offering it. If the deal is so good for me, it can't be good for you too.

RANCHER: Oh, but it is! Suppose I spend 6 hours a day raising cattle and 2 hours growing potatoes. Then I can produce 18 ounces of meat

The proposed trade between the farmer and the rancher offers each of them a combination of meat and potatoes that would be impossible in the absence of trade. In panel (a), the farmer gets to consume at point A* rather than point A. In panel (b), the rancher gets to consume at point B* rather than point B. Trade allows each to consume more meat and more potatoes.

Figure 2

How Trade Expands the Set of Consumption Opportunities

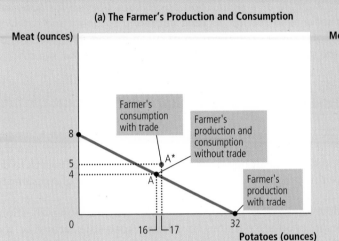

(a) The Farmer's Production and Consumption

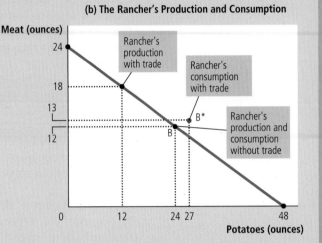

(b) The Rancher's Production and Consumption

(c) The Gains from Trade: A Summary

	Farmer		Rancher	
	Meat	**Potatoes**	**Meat**	**Potatoes**
Without Trade:				
Production and Consumption	4 oz	16 oz	12 oz	24 oz
With Trade:				
Production	0 oz	32 oz	18 oz	12 oz
Trade	Gets 5 oz	Gives 15 oz	Gives 5 oz	Gets 15 oz
Consumption	5 oz	17 oz	13 oz	27 oz
GAINS FROM TRADE:				
Increase in Consumption	+1 oz	+1 oz	+1 oz	+3 oz

and 12 ounces of potatoes. After I give you 5 ounces of my meat in exchange for 15 ounces of your potatoes, I'll end up with 13 ounces of meat and 27 ounces of potatoes, instead of the 12 ounces of meat and 24 ounces of potatoes that I now get. So I will also consume more of both foods than I do now. [She points out panel (b) of Figure 2.]

FARMER: I don't know. . . . This sounds too good to be true.

RANCHER: It's really not as complicated as it first seems. Here—I've summarized my proposal for you in a simple table. [The rancher shows the farmer a copy of the table at the bottom of Figure 2.]

FARMER: (after pausing to study the table) These calculations seem correct, but I am puzzled. How can this deal make us both better off?

RANCHER: We can both benefit because trade allows each of us to specialize in doing what we do best. You will spend more time growing potatoes and less time raising cattle. I will spend more time raising cattle and less time growing potatoes. As a result of specialization and trade, each of us can consume more meat and more potatoes without working any more hours.

QUICK QUIZ *Draw an example of a production possibilities frontier for Robinson Crusoe, a shipwrecked sailor who spends his time gathering coconuts and catching fish. Does this frontier limit Crusoe's consumption of coconuts and fish if he lives by himself? Does he face the same limits if he can trade with natives on the island?*

Comparative Advantage: The Driving Force of Specialization

The rancher's explanation of the gains from trade, though correct, poses a puzzle: If the rancher is better at both raising cattle and growing potatoes, how can the farmer ever specialize in doing what he does best? The farmer doesn't seem to do anything best. To solve this puzzle, we need to look at the principle of *comparative advantage*.

As a first step in developing this principle, consider the following question: In our example, who can produce potatoes at a lower cost—the farmer or the rancher? There are two possible answers, and in these two answers lie the solution to our puzzle and the key to understanding the gains from trade.

Absolute Advantage

absolute advantage
the ability to produce a good using fewer inputs than another producer

One way to answer the question about the cost of producing potatoes is to compare the inputs required by the two producers. Economists use the term **absolute advantage** when comparing the productivity of one person, firm, or nation to that of another. The producer that requires a smaller quantity of inputs to produce a good is said to have an absolute advantage in producing that good.

In our example, time is the only input, so we can determine absolute advantage by looking at how much time each type of production takes. The rancher has an absolute advantage both in producing meat and in producing potatoes because she requires less time than the farmer to produce a unit of either good. The rancher needs to input only 20 minutes to produce an ounce of meat, whereas the farmer needs 60 minutes. Similarly, the rancher needs only 10 minutes to produce an ounce of potatoes, whereas the farmer needs 15 minutes. Based on this information, we can conclude that the rancher has the lower cost of producing potatoes, if we measure cost by the quantity of inputs.

Opportunity Cost and Comparative Advantage

opportunity cost
whatever must be given up to obtain some item

There is another way to look at the cost of producing potatoes. Rather than comparing inputs required, we can compare the opportunity costs. Recall from Chapter 1 that the **opportunity cost** of some item is what we give up to get that item. In our example, we assumed that the farmer and the rancher each spend 8 hours a day working. Time spent producing potatoes, therefore, takes away from time available for producing meat. When reallocating time between the two goods, the rancher and farmer give up units of one good to produce units of the other, thereby moving along the production possibilities frontier. The opportunity cost measures the trade-off between the two goods that each producer faces.

Table **1**

The Opportunity Cost of Meat and Potatoes

	Opportunity Cost of:	
	1 oz of Meat	**1 oz of Potatoes**
Farmer	4 oz potatoes	¼ oz meat
Rancher	2 oz potatoes	½ oz meat

Let's first consider the rancher's opportunity cost. According to the table in panel (a) of Figure 1, producing 1 ounce of potatoes takes 10 minutes of work. When the rancher spends those 10 minutes producing potatoes, she spends 10 minutes less producing meat. Because the rancher needs 20 minutes to produce 1 ounce of meat, 10 minutes of work would yield ½ ounce of meat. Hence, the rancher's opportunity cost of producing 1 ounce of potatoes is ½ ounce of meat.

Now consider the farmer's opportunity cost. Producing 1 ounce of potatoes takes him 15 minutes. Because he needs 60 minutes to produce 1 ounce of meat, 15 minutes of work would yield ¼ ounce of meat. Hence, the farmer's opportunity cost of 1 ounce of potatoes is ¼ ounce of meat.

Table 1 shows the opportunity costs of meat and potatoes for the two producers. Notice that the opportunity cost of meat is the inverse of the opportunity cost of potatoes. Because 1 ounce of potatoes costs the rancher ½ ounce of meat, 1 ounce of meat costs the rancher 2 ounces of potatoes. Similarly, because 1 ounce of potatoes costs the farmer ¼ ounce of meat, 1 ounce of meat costs the farmer 4 ounces of potatoes.

Economists use the term **comparative advantage** when describing the opportunity cost of two producers. The producer who gives up less of other goods to produce Good X has the smaller opportunity cost of producing Good X and is said to have a comparative advantage in producing it. In our example, the farmer has a lower opportunity cost of producing potatoes than the rancher: An ounce of potatoes costs the farmer only ¼ ounce of meat, but it costs the rancher ½ ounce of meat. Conversely, the rancher has a lower opportunity cost of producing meat than the farmer: An ounce of meat costs the rancher 2 ounces of potatoes, but it costs the farmer 4 ounces of potatoes. Thus, the farmer has a comparative advantage in growing potatoes, and the rancher has a comparative advantage in producing meat.

Although it is possible for one person to have an absolute advantage in both goods (as the rancher does in our example), it is impossible for one person to have a comparative advantage in both goods. Because the opportunity cost of one good is the inverse of the opportunity cost of the other, if a person's opportunity cost of one good is relatively high, the opportunity cost of the other good must be relatively low. Comparative advantage reflects the relative opportunity cost. Unless two people have exactly the same opportunity cost, one person will have a comparative advantage in one good, and the other person will have a comparative advantage in the other good.

comparative advantage

the ability to produce a good at a lower opportunity cost than another producer

Comparative Advantage and Trade

The gains from specialization and trade are based not on absolute advantage but on comparative advantage. When each person specializes in producing the good for which he or she has a comparative advantage, total production in the economy rises. This increase in the size of the economic pie can be used to make everyone better off.

In our example, the farmer spends more time growing potatoes, and the rancher spends more time producing meat. As a result, the total production of potatoes rises from 40 to 44 ounces, and the total production of meat rises from 16 to 18 ounces. The farmer and rancher share the benefits of this increased production.

We can also look at the gains from trade in terms of the price that each party pays the other. Because the farmer and rancher have different opportunity costs, they can both get a bargain. That is, each benefits from trade by obtaining a good at a price that is lower than his or her opportunity cost of that good.

Consider the proposed deal from the viewpoint of the farmer. The farmer gets 5 ounces of meat in exchange for 15 ounces of potatoes. In other words, the farmer buys each ounce of meat for a price of 3 ounces of potatoes. This price of meat is lower than his opportunity cost for an ounce of meat, which is 4 ounces of potatoes. Thus, the farmer benefits from the deal because he gets to buy meat at a good price.

Now consider the deal from the rancher's viewpoint. The rancher buys 15 ounces of potatoes for a price of 5 ounces of meat. That is, the price of potatoes is ⅓ ounce of meat. This price of potatoes is lower than her opportunity cost of an ounce of potatoes, which is ½ ounce of meat. The rancher benefits because she gets to buy potatoes at a good price.

The moral of the story of the farmer and the rancher should now be clear: *Trade can benefit everyone in society because it allows people to specialize in activities in which they have a comparative advantage.*

The Price of the Trade

The principle of comparative advantage establishes that there are gains from specialization and trade, but it leaves open a couple of related questions: What determines the price at which trade takes place? How are the gains from trade shared between the trading parties? The precise answer to these questions is beyond the scope of this chapter, but we can state one general rule: *For both parties to gain from trade, the price at which they trade must lie between the two opportunity costs.*

In our example, the farmer and rancher agreed to trade at a rate of 3 ounces of potatoes for each ounce of meat. This price is between the rancher's opportunity cost (2 ounces of potatoes per ounce of meat) and the farmer's opportunity cost (4 ounces of potatoes per ounce of meat). The price need not be exactly in the middle for both parties to gain, but it must be somewhere between 2 and 4.

To see why the price has to be in this range, consider what would happen if it were not. If the price of meat were below 2 ounces of potatoes, both the farmer and the rancher would want to buy meat, because the price would be below their opportunity costs. Similarly, if the price of meat were above 4 ounces of potatoes, both would want to sell meat, because the price would be above their opportunity costs. But there are only two members of this economy. They cannot both be buyers of meat, nor can they both be sellers. Someone has to take the other side of the deal.

A mutually advantageous trade can be struck at a price between 2 and 4. In this price range, the rancher wants to sell meat to buy potatoes, and the farmer wants to sell potatoes to buy meat. Each party can buy a good at a price that is lower than his or her opportunity cost. In the end, both of them specialize in the good for which he or she has a comparative advantage and are, as a result, better off.

QUICK QUIZ *Robinson Crusoe can gather 10 coconuts or catch 1 fish per hour. His friend Friday can gather 30 coconuts or catch 2 fish per hour. What is Crusoe's opportunity cost of catching one fish? What is Friday's? Who has an absolute advantage in catching fish? Who has a comparative advantage in catching fish?*

FYI

> ## The Legacy of Adam Smith and David Ricardo

Economists have long understood the gains from trade. Here is how the great economist Adam Smith put the argument:

It is a maxim of every prudent master of a family, never to attempt to make at home what it will cost him more to make than to buy. The tailor does not attempt to make his own shoes, but buys them of the shoemaker. The shoemaker does not attempt to make his own clothes but employs a tailor. The farmer attempts to make neither the one nor the other, but employs those different artificers. All of them find it for their interest to employ their whole industry in a way in which they have some advantage over their neighbors, and to purchase with a part of its produce, or what is the same thing, with the price of part of it, whatever else they have occasion for.

This quotation is from Smith's 1776 book *An Inquiry into the Nature and Causes of the Wealth of Nations*, which was a landmark in the analysis of trade and economic interdependence.

Smith's book inspired David Ricardo, a millionaire stockbroker, to become an economist. In his 1817

David Ricardo

book *Principles of Political Economy and Taxation*, Ricardo developed the principle of comparative advantage as we know it today. He considered an example with two goods (wine and cloth) and two countries (England and Portugal). He showed that both countries can gain by opening up trade and specializing based on comparative advantage.

Ricardo's theory is the starting point of modern international economics, but his defense of free trade was not a mere academic exercise. Ricardo put his beliefs to work as a member of the British Parliament, where he opposed the Corn Laws, which restricted the import of grain.

The conclusions of Adam Smith and David Ricardo on the gains from trade have held up well over time. Although economists often disagree on questions of policy, they are united in their support of free trade. Moreover, the central argument for free trade has not changed much in the past two centuries. Even though the field of economics has broadened its scope and refined its theories since the time of Smith and Ricardo, economists' opposition to trade restrictions is still based largely on the principle of comparative advantage.

Applications of Comparative Advantage

The principle of comparative advantage explains interdependence and the gains from trade. Because interdependence is so prevalent in the modern world, the principle of comparative advantage has many applications. Here are two examples, one fanciful and one of great practical importance.

Should Tom Brady Mow His Own Lawn?

Tom Brady spends a lot of time running around on grass. One of the most talented football players of all time, he can throw a pass with a speed and accuracy that most casual athletes can only dream of. Most likely, he is talented at other physical activities as well. For example, let's imagine that Brady can mow his lawn faster than anyone else. But just because he *can* mow his lawn fast, does this mean he *should?*

To answer this question, we can use the concepts of opportunity cost and comparative advantage. Let's say that Brady can mow his lawn in 2 hours. In that

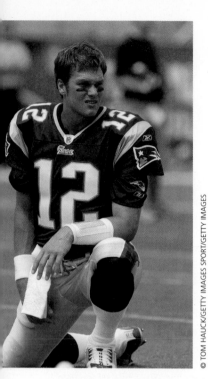

"They did a nice job mowing this grass."

imports

goods produced abroad and sold domestically

exports

goods produced domestically and sold abroad

same 2 hours, he could film a television commercial and earn $20,000. By contrast, Forrest Gump, the boy next door, can mow Brady's lawn in 4 hours. In that same 4 hours, Gump could work at McDonald's and earn $40.

In this example, Brady has an absolute advantage in mowing lawns because he can do the work with a lower input of time. Yet because Brady's opportunity cost of mowing the lawn is $20,000 and Gump's opportunity cost is only $40, Gump has a comparative advantage in mowing lawns.

The gains from trade in this example are tremendous. Rather than mowing his own lawn, Brady should make the commercial and hire Gump to mow the lawn. As long as Brady pays Gump more than $40 and less than $20,000, both of them are better off.

Should the United States Trade with Other Countries?

Just as individuals can benefit from specialization and trade with one another, as the farmer and rancher did, so can populations of people in different countries. Many of the goods that Americans enjoy are produced abroad, and many of the goods produced in the United States are sold abroad. Goods produced abroad and sold domestically are called **imports**. Goods produced domestically and sold abroad are called **exports**.

To see how countries can benefit from trade, suppose there are two countries, the United States and Japan, and two goods, food and cars. Imagine that the two countries produce cars equally well: An American worker and a Japanese worker can each produce one car per month. By contrast, because the United States has more and better land, it is better at producing food: A U.S. worker can produce 2 tons of food per month, whereas a Japanese worker can produce only 1 ton of food per month.

The principle of comparative advantage states that each good should be produced by the country that has the smaller opportunity cost of producing that good. Because the opportunity cost of a car is 2 tons of food in the United States but only 1 ton of food in Japan, Japan has a comparative advantage in producing cars. Japan should produce more cars than it wants for its own use and export some of them to the United States. Similarly, because the opportunity cost of a ton of food is 1 car in Japan but only ½ car in the United States, the United States has a comparative advantage in producing food. The United States should produce more food than it wants to consume and export some to Japan. Through specialization and trade, both countries can have more food and more cars.

In reality, of course, the issues involved in trade among nations are more complex than this example suggests. Most important among these issues is that each country has many citizens with different interests. International trade can make some individuals worse off, even as it makes the country as a whole better off. When the United States exports food and imports cars, the impact on an American farmer is not the same as the impact on an American autoworker. Yet, contrary to the opinions sometimes voiced by politicians and pundits, international trade is not like war, in which some countries win and others lose. Trade allows all countries to achieve greater prosperity.

QUICK QUIZ   *Suppose that a skilled brain surgeon also happens to be the world's fastest typist. Should she do her own typing or hire a secretary? Explain.*

in the news

> The Changing Face of International Trade

A decade ago, no one would have asked which nation has a comparative advantage in slaying ogres. But technology is rapidly changing the goods and services that are traded across national borders.

Ogre to Slay? Outsource It to Chinese

BY DAVID BARBOZA

Fuzhou, China—One of China's newest factories operates here in the basement of an old warehouse. Posters of World of Warcraft and Magic Land hang above a corps of young people glued to their computer screens, pounding away at their keyboards in the latest hustle for money.

The people working at this clandestine locale are "gold farmers." Every day, in 12-hour shifts, they "play" computer games by killing onscreen monsters and winning battles, harvesting artificial gold coins and other virtual goods as rewards that, as it turns out, can be transformed into real cash.

That is because, from Seoul to San Francisco, affluent online gamers who lack the time and patience to work their way up to the higher levels of gamedom are willing to pay the young Chinese here to play the early rounds for them.

"For 12 hours a day, 7 days a week, my colleagues and I are killing monsters," said a 23-year-old gamer who works here in this makeshift factory and goes by the online code name Wandering. "I make about $250 a month, which is pretty good compared with the other jobs I've had. And I can play games all day."

He and his comrades have created yet another new business out of cheap Chinese labor. They are tapping into the fast-growing world of "massively multi-player online games," which involve role playing and often revolve around fantasy or warfare in medieval kingdoms or distant galaxies. . . .

For the Chinese in game-playing factories like these, though, it is not all fun and games. These workers have strict quotas and are supervised by bosses who equip them with computers, software and Internet connections to thrash online trolls, gnomes and ogres.

As they grind through the games, they accumulate virtual currency that is valuable to game players around the world. The games allow players to trade currency to other players, who can then use it to buy better armor, amulets, magic spells and other accoutrements to climb to higher levels or create more powerful characters.

The Internet is now filled with classified advertisements from small companies—many of them here in China—auctioning for real money their powerful figures, called avatars. . . .

"It's unimaginable how big this is," says Chen Yu, 27, who employs 20 full-time gamers here in Fuzhou. "They say that in some of these popular games, 40 or 50 percent of the players are actually Chinese farmers."

Source: *New York Times*, December 9, 2005.

Conclusion

You should now understand more fully the benefits of living in an interdependent economy. When Americans buy tube socks from China, when residents of Maine drink orange juice from Florida, and when a homeowner hires the kid next door to mow the lawn, the same economic forces are at work. The principle of comparative advantage shows that trade can make everyone better off.

Having seen why interdependence is desirable, you might naturally ask how it is possible. How do free societies coordinate the diverse activities of all the people involved in their economies? What ensures that goods and services will get from those who should be producing them to those who should be consuming them? In a world with only two people, such as the rancher and the farmer, the answer is simple: These two people can bargain and allocate resources between themselves. In the real world with billions of people, the answer is less obvious. We take up this issue in the next chapter, where we see that free societies allocate resources through the market forces of supply and demand.

SUMMARY

- Each person consumes goods and services produced by many other people both in the United States and around the world. Interdependence and trade are desirable because they allow everyone to enjoy a greater quantity and variety of goods and services.

- There are two ways to compare the ability of two people in producing a good. The person who can produce the good with the smaller quantity of inputs is said to have an *absolute advantage* in producing the good. The person who has the smaller opportunity cost of producing the good is said to have a *comparative advantage*. The gains from trade are based on comparative advantage, not absolute advantage.

- Trade makes everyone better off because it allows people to specialize in those activities in which they have a comparative advantage.

- The principle of comparative advantage applies to countries as well as to people. Economists use the principle of comparative advantage to advocate free trade among countries.

KEY CONCEPTS

absolute advantage, *p. 54*
opportunity cost, *p. 54*

comparative advantage, *p. 55*
imports, *p. 58*

exports, *p. 58*

QUESTIONS FOR REVIEW

1. Under what conditions is the production possibilities frontier linear rather than bowed out?
2. Explain how absolute advantage and comparative advantage differ.
3. Give an example in which one person has an absolute advantage in doing something but another person has a comparative advantage.
4. Is absolute advantage or comparative advantage more important for trade? Explain your

reasoning using the example in your answer to Question 3.
5. If two parties trade based on comparative advantage and both gain, in what range must the price of the trade lie?
6. Will a nation tend to export or import goods for which it has a comparative advantage? Explain.
7. Why do economists oppose policies that restrict trade among nations?

PROBLEMS AND APPLICATIONS

1. Maria can read 20 pages of economics in an hour. She can also read 50 pages of sociology in an hour. She spends 5 hours per day studying.
   a. Draw Maria's production possibilities frontier for reading economics and sociology.
   b. What is Maria's opportunity cost of reading 100 pages of sociology?

2. American and Japanese workers can each produce 4 cars a year. An American worker can produce 10 tons of grain a year, whereas a Japanese worker can produce 5 tons of grain a year. To keep things simple, assume that each country has 100 million workers.
   a. For this situation, construct a table analogous to the table in Figure 1.
   b. Graph the production possibilities frontier of the American and Japanese economies.
   c. For the United States, what is the opportunity cost of a car? Of grain? For Japan, what is the opportunity cost of a car? Of grain? Put this information in a table analogous to Table 1.
   d. Which country has an absolute advantage in producing cars? In producing grain?
   e. Which country has a comparative advantage in producing cars? In producing grain?
   f. Without trade, half of each country's workers produce cars and half produce grain. What quantities of cars and grain does each country produce?
   g. Starting from a position without trade, give an example in which trade makes each country better off.

3. Pat and Kris are roommates. They spend most of their time studying (of course), but they leave some time for their favorite activities: making pizza and brewing root beer. Pat takes 4 hours to brew a gallon of root beer and 2 hours to make a pizza. Kris takes 6 hours to brew a gallon of root beer and 4 hours to make a pizza.
   a. What is each roommate's opportunity cost of making a pizza? Who has the absolute advantage in making pizza? Who has the comparative advantage in making pizza?
   b. If Pat and Kris trade foods with each other, who will trade away pizza in exchange for root beer?
   c. The price of pizza can be expressed in terms of gallons of root beer. What is the highest price at which pizza can be traded that would make both roommates better off? What is the lowest price? Explain.

4. Suppose that there are 10 million workers in Canada and that each of these workers can produce either 2 cars or 30 bushels of wheat in a year.
   a. What is the opportunity cost of producing a car in Canada? What is the opportunity cost of producing a bushel of wheat in Canada? Explain the relationship between the opportunity costs of the two goods.
   b. Draw Canada's production possibilities frontier. If Canada chooses to consume 10 million cars, how much wheat can it consume without trade? Label this point on the production possibilities frontier.
   c. Now suppose that the United States offers to buy 10 million cars from Canada in exchange for 20 bushels of wheat per car. If Canada continues to consume 10 million cars, how much wheat does this deal allow Canada to consume? Label this point on your diagram. Should Canada accept the deal?

5. England and Scotland both produce scones and sweaters. Suppose that an English worker can produce 50 scones per hour or 1 sweater per hour. Suppose that a Scottish worker can produce 40 scones per hour or 2 sweaters per hour.
   a. Which country has the absolute advantage in the production of each good? Which country has the comparative advantage?
   b. If England and Scotland decide to trade, which commodity will Scotland trade to England? Explain.
   c. If a Scottish worker could produce only 1 sweater per hour, would Scotland still gain from trade? Would England still gain from trade? Explain.

6. The following table describes the production possibilities of two cities in the country of Baseballia:

	Pairs of Red Socks per Worker per Hour	Pairs of White Socks per Worker per Hour
Boston	3	3
Chicago	2	1

   a. Without trade, what is the price of white socks (in terms of red socks) in Boston? What is the price in Chicago?
   b. Which city has an absolute advantage in the production of each color sock? Which city has

a comparative advantage in the production of each color sock?

c. If the cities trade with each other, which color sock will each export?

d. What is the range of prices at which trade can occur?

7. Suppose that in a year an American worker can produce 100 shirts or 20 computers, while a Chinese worker can produce 100 shirts or 10 computers.

a. Graph the production possibilities curve for the two countries. Suppose that without trade the workers in each country spend half their time producing each good. Identify this point in your graph.

b. If these countries were open to trade, which country would export shirts? Give a specific numerical example and show it on your graph. Which country would benefit from trade? Explain.

c. Explain at what price of computers (in terms of shirts) the two countries might trade.

d. Suppose that China catches up with American productivity so that a Chinese worker can produce 100 shirts or 20 computers. What pattern of trade would you predict now? How does this advance in Chinese productivity affect the economic well-being of the citizens of the two countries?

8. An average worker in Brazil can produce an ounce of soybeans in 20 minutes and an ounce of coffee in 60 minutes, while an average worker in Peru can produce an ounce of soybeans in 50 minutes and an ounce of coffee in 75 minutes.

a. Who has the absolute advantage in coffee? Explain.

b. Who has the comparative advantage in coffee? Explain.

c. If the two countries specialize and trade with each other, who will import coffee? Explain.

d. Assume that the two countries trade and that the country importing coffee trades 2 ounces of soybeans for 1 ounce of coffee. Explain why both countries will benefit from this trade.

9. Are the following statements true or false? Explain in each case.

a. "Two countries can achieve gains from trade even if one of the countries has an absolute advantage in the production of all goods."

b. "Certain very talented people have a comparative advantage in everything they do."

c. "If a certain trade is good for one person, it can't be good for the other one."

d. "If a certain trade is good for one person, it is always good for the other one."

e. "If trade is good for a country, it must be good for everyone in the country."

10. The United States exports corn and aircraft to the rest of the world, and it imports oil and clothing from the rest of the world. Do you think this pattern of trade is consistent with the principle of comparative advantage? Why or why not?

11. Bill and Hillary produce food and clothing. In an hour, Bill can produce 1 unit of food or 1 unit of clothing, while Hillary can produce 2 units of food or 3 units of clothing. They each work 10 hours a day.

a. Who has an absolute advantage in producing food? Who has an absolute advantage in producing clothing? Explain.

b. Who has a comparative advantage in producing food? Who has a comparative advantage in producing clothing? Explain.

c. Draw the production possibilities frontier for the household (that is, Bill and Hillary together) assuming that each spends the same number of hours each day as the other producing food and clothing.

d. Hillary suggests, instead, that she specialize in making clothing. That is, she will do all the clothing production for the family; however, if all her time is devoted to clothing and they still want more, then Bill can help with clothing production. What does the household production possibilities frontier look like now?

e. Bill suggests that Hillary specialize in producing food. That is, Hillary will do all the food production for the family; however, if all her time is devoted to food and they still want more, then Bill can help with food production. What does the household production possibilities frontier look like under Bill's proposal?

f. Comparing your answers to parts c, d, and e, which allocation of time makes the most sense? Relate your answer to the theory of comparative advantage.

For further information on topics in this chapter, additional problems, applications, examples, online quizzes, and more, please visit our website at <u>www</u> <u>.cengage.com/economics/mankiw</u>.

PART **II** How Markets Work

The Market Forces of Supply and Demand

4

When a cold snap hits Florida, the price of orange juice rises in supermarkets throughout the country. When the weather turns warm in New England every summer, the price of hotel rooms in the Caribbean plummets. When a war breaks out in the Middle East, the price of gasoline in the United States rises, and the price of a used Cadillac falls. What do these events have in common? They all show the workings of supply and demand.

Supply and *demand* are the two words economists use most often—and for good reason. Supply and demand are the forces that make market economies work. They determine the quantity of each good produced and the price at which it is sold. If you want to know how any event or policy will affect the economy, you must think first about how it will affect supply and demand.

This chapter introduces the theory of supply and demand. It considers how buyers and sellers behave and how they interact with one another. It shows how supply and demand determine prices in a market economy and how prices, in turn, allocate the economy's scarce resources.

Markets and Competition

The terms *supply* and *demand* refer to the behavior of people as they interact with one another in competitive markets. Before discussing how buyers and sellers behave, let's first consider more fully what we mean by the terms *market* and *competition*.

What Is a Market?

market

a group of buyers and sellers of a particular good or service

A **market** is a group of buyers and sellers of a particular good or service. The buyers as a group determine the demand for the product, and the sellers as a group determine the supply of the product.

Markets take many forms. Some markets are highly organized, such as the markets for many agricultural commodities. In these markets, buyers and sellers meet at a specific time and place, where an auctioneer helps set prices and arrange sales.

More often, markets are less organized. For example, consider the market for ice cream in a particular town. Buyers of ice cream do not meet together at any one time. The sellers of ice cream are in different locations and offer somewhat different products. There is no auctioneer calling out the price of ice cream. Each seller posts a price for an ice-cream cone, and each buyer decides how much ice cream to buy at each store. Nonetheless, these consumers and producers of ice cream are closely connected. The ice-cream buyers are choosing from the various ice-cream sellers to satisfy their cravings, and the ice-cream sellers are all trying to appeal to the same ice-cream buyers to make their businesses successful. Even though it is not as organized, the group of ice-cream buyers and ice-cream sellers forms a market.

What Is Competition?

The market for ice cream, like most markets in the economy, is highly competitive. Each buyer knows that there are several sellers from which to choose, and each seller is aware that his or her product is similar to that offered by other sellers. As a result, the price of ice cream and the quantity of ice cream sold are not determined by any single buyer or seller. Rather, price and quantity are determined by all buyers and sellers as they interact in the marketplace.

competitive market

a market in which there are many buyers and many sellers so that each has a negligible impact on the market price

Economists use the term **competitive market** to describe a market in which there are so many buyers and so many sellers that each has a negligible impact on the market price. Each seller of ice cream has limited control over the price because other sellers are offering similar products. A seller has little reason to charge less than the going price, and if he or she charges more, buyers will make their purchases elsewhere. Similarly, no single buyer of ice cream can influence the price of ice cream because each buyer purchases only a small amount.

In this chapter, we assume that markets are *perfectly competitive*. To reach this highest form of competition, a market must have two characteristics: (1) the goods offered for sale are all exactly the same, and (2) the buyers and sellers are so numerous that no single buyer or seller has any influence over the market price. Because buyers and sellers in perfectly competitive markets must accept the price the market determines, they are said to be *price takers*. At the market price, buyers can buy all they want, and sellers can sell all they want.

There are some markets in which the assumption of perfect competition applies perfectly. In the wheat market, for example, there are thousands of farmers who sell wheat and millions of consumers who use wheat and wheat products. Because no single buyer or seller can influence the price of wheat, each takes the price as given.

Not all goods and services, however, are sold in perfectly competitive markets. Some markets have only one seller, and this seller sets the price. Such a seller is called a *monopoly*. Your local cable television company, for instance, may be a monopoly. Residents of your town probably have only one cable company from which to buy this service. Still other markets fall between the extremes of perfect competition and monopoly.

Despite the diversity of market types we find in the world, assuming perfect competition is a useful simplification and, therefore, a natural place to start. Perfectly competitive markets are the easiest to analyze because everyone participating in the market takes the price as given by market conditions. Moreover, because some degree of competition is present in most markets, many of the lessons that we learn by studying supply and demand under perfect competition apply in more complicated markets as well.

QUICK QUIZ   *What is a market? • What are the characteristics of a perfectly competitive market?*

Demand

We begin our study of markets by examining the behavior of buyers. To focus our thinking, let's keep in mind a particular good—ice cream.

The Demand Curve: The Relationship between Price and Quantity Demanded

The **quantity demanded** of any good is the amount of the good that buyers are willing and able to purchase. As we will see, many things determine the quantity demanded of any good, but in our analysis of how markets work, one determinant plays a central role—the price of the good. If the price of ice cream rose to $20 per scoop, you would buy less ice cream. You might buy frozen yogurt instead. If the price of ice cream fell to $0.20 per scoop, you would buy more. This relationship between price and quantity demanded is true for most goods in the economy and, in fact, is so pervasive that economists call it the **law of demand**: Other things equal, when the price of a good rises, the quantity demanded of the good falls, and when the price falls, the quantity demanded rises.

The table in Figure 1 shows how many ice-cream cones Catherine buys each month at different prices of ice cream. If ice cream is free, Catherine eats 12 cones per month. At $0.50 per cone, Catherine buys 10 cones each month. As the price rises further, she buys fewer and fewer cones. When the price reaches $3.00, Catherine doesn't buy any ice cream at all. This table is a **demand schedule**, a table that shows the relationship between the price of a good and the quantity demanded, holding constant everything else that influences how much of the good consumers want to buy.

quantity demanded
the amount of a good that buyers are willing and able to purchase

law of demand
the claim that, other things equal, the quantity demanded of a good falls when the price of the good rises

demand schedule
a table that shows the relationship between the price of a good and the quantity demanded

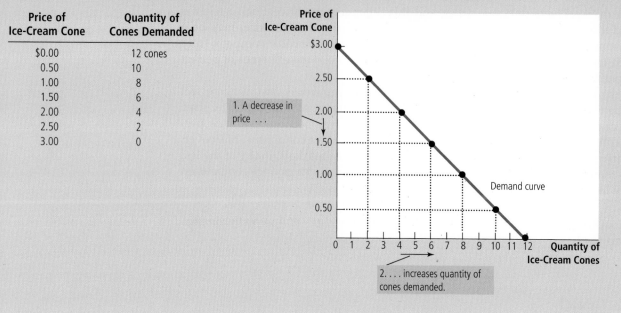

Figure 1

Catherine's Demand Schedule and Demand Curve

The demand schedule is a table that shows the quantity demanded at each price. The demand curve, which graphs the demand schedule, illustrates how the quantity demanded of the good changes as its price varies. Because a lower price increases the quantity demanded, the demand curve slopes downward.

Price of Ice-Cream Cone	Quantity of Cones Demanded
$0.00	12 cones
0.50	10
1.00	8
1.50	6
2.00	4
2.50	2
3.00	0

The graph in Figure 1 uses the numbers from the table to illustrate the law of demand. By convention, the price of ice cream is on the vertical axis, and the quantity of ice cream demanded is on the horizontal axis. The downward-sloping line relating price and quantity demanded is called the **demand curve**.

demand curve
a graph of the relationship between the price of a good and the quantity demanded

Market Demand versus Individual Demand

The demand curve in Figure 1 shows an individual's demand for a product. To analyze how markets work, we need to determine the *market demand*, the sum of all the individual demands for a particular good or service.

The table in Figure 2 shows the demand schedules for ice cream of the two individuals in this market—Catherine and Nicholas. At any price, Catherine's demand schedule tells us how much ice cream she buys, and Nicholas's demand schedule tells us how much ice cream he buys. The market demand at each price is the sum of the two individual demands.

The graph in Figure 2 shows the demand curves that correspond to these demand schedules. Notice that we sum the individual demand curves horizontally to obtain the market demand curve. That is, to find the total quantity demanded at any price, we add the individual quantities, which are found on the horizontal axis of the individual demand curves. Because we are interested in analyzing how markets function, we work most often with the market demand curve. The market demand curve shows how the total quantity demanded of a

The quantity demanded in a market is the sum of the quantities demanded by all the buyers at each price. Thus, the market demand curve is found by adding horizontally the individual demand curves. At a price of $2.00, Catherine demands 4 ice-cream cones, and Nicholas demands 3 ice-cream cones. The quantity demanded in the market at this price is 7 cones.

Figure **2**

Market Demand as the Sum of Individual Demands

Price of Ice-Cream Cone	Catherine		Nicholas		Market
$0.00	12	+	7	=	19 cones
0.50	10		6		16
1.00	8		5		13
1.50	6		4		10
2.00	4		3		7
2.50	2		2		4
3.00	0		1		1

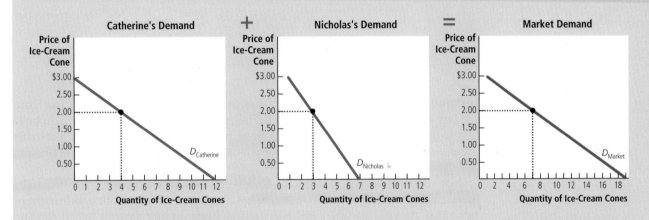

good varies as the price of the good varies, while all the other factors that affect how much consumers want to buy are held constant.

Shifts in the Demand Curve

Because the market demand curve holds other things constant, it need not be stable over time. If something happens to alter the quantity demanded at any given price, the demand curve shifts. For example, suppose the American Medical Association discovered that people who regularly eat ice cream live longer, healthier lives. The discovery would raise the demand for ice cream. At any given price, buyers would now want to purchase a larger quantity of ice cream, and the demand curve for ice cream would shift.

Figure 3 illustrates shifts in demand. Any change that increases the quantity demanded at every price, such as our imaginary discovery by the American Medical Association, shifts the demand curve to the right and is called an *increase in demand*. Any change that reduces the quantity demanded at every price shifts the demand curve to the left and is called a *decrease in demand*.

There are many variables that can shift the demand curve. Here are the most important.

Figure 3

Shifts in the Demand Curve
Any change that raises the quantity that buyers wish to purchase at any given price shifts the demand curve to the right. Any change that lowers the quantity that buyers wish to purchase at any given price shifts the demand curve to the left.

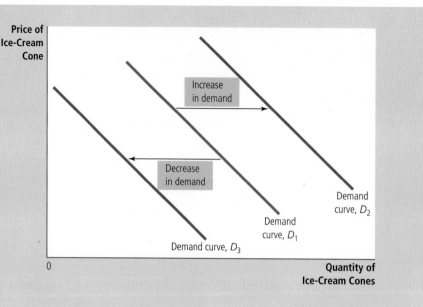

Income   What would happen to your demand for ice cream if you lost your job one summer? Most likely, it would fall. A lower income means that you have less to spend in total, so you would have to spend less on some—and probably most—goods. If the demand for a good falls when income falls, the good is called a **normal good**.

Not all goods are normal goods. If the demand for a good rises when income falls, the good is called an **inferior good**. An example of an inferior good might be bus rides. As your income falls, you are less likely to buy a car or take a cab and more likely to ride a bus.

Prices of Related Goods   Suppose that the price of frozen yogurt falls. The law of demand says that you will buy more frozen yogurt. At the same time, you will probably buy less ice cream. Because ice cream and frozen yogurt are both cold, sweet, creamy desserts, they satisfy similar desires. When a fall in the price of one good reduces the demand for another good, the two goods are called **substitutes**. Substitutes are often pairs of goods that are used in place of each other, such as hot dogs and hamburgers, sweaters and sweatshirts, and movie tickets and DVD rentals.

Now suppose that the price of hot fudge falls. According to the law of demand, you will buy more hot fudge. Yet in this case, you will buy more ice cream as well because ice cream and hot fudge are often used together. When a fall in the price of one good raises the demand for another good, the two goods are called **complements**. Complements are often pairs of goods that are used together, such as gasoline and automobiles, computers and software, and peanut butter and jelly.

Tastes   The most obvious determinant of your demand is your tastes. If you like ice cream, you buy more of it. Economists normally do not try to explain people's tastes because tastes are based on historical and psychological forces that are beyond the realm of economics. Economists do, however, examine what happens when tastes change.

normal good
a good for which, other things equal, an increase in income leads to an increase in demand

inferior good
a good for which, other things equal, an increase in income leads to a decrease in demand

substitutes
two goods for which an increase in the price of one leads to an increase in the demand for the other

complements
two goods for which an increase in the price of one leads to a decrease in the demand for the other

Expectations   Your expectations about the future may affect your demand for a good or service today. If you expect to earn a higher income next month, you may choose to save less now and spend more of your current income buying ice cream. If you expect the price of ice cream to fall tomorrow, you may be less willing to buy an ice-cream cone at today's price.

Number of Buyers   In addition to the preceding factors, which influence the behavior of individual buyers, market demand depends on the number of these buyers. If Peter were to join Catherine and Nicholas as another consumer of ice cream, the quantity demanded in the market would be higher at every price, and market demand would increase.

Summary   The demand curve shows what happens to the quantity demanded of a good when its price varies, holding constant all the other variables that influence buyers. When one of these other variables changes, the demand curve shifts. Table 1 lists the variables that influence how much consumers choose to buy of a good.

If you have trouble remembering whether you need to shift or move along the demand curve, it helps to recall a lesson from the appendix to Chapter 2. A curve shifts when there is a change in a relevant variable that is not measured on either axis. Because the price is on the vertical axis, a change in price represents a movement along the demand curve. By contrast, income, the prices of related goods, tastes, expectations, and the number of buyers are not measured on either axis, so a change in one of these variables shifts the demand curve.

 Two Ways to Reduce the Quantity of Smoking Demanded

Public policymakers often want to reduce the amount that people smoke because of smoking's adverse health effects. There are two ways that policy can attempt to achieve this goal.

One way to reduce smoking is to shift the demand curve for cigarettes and other tobacco products. Public service announcements, mandatory health warnings on cigarette packages, and the prohibition of cigarette advertising on television are all policies aimed at reducing the quantity of cigarettes demanded at any given price. If successful, these policies shift the demand curve for cigarettes to the left, as in panel (a) of Figure 4.

What is the best way to stop this?

Table 1

Variable	A Change in This Variable . . .
Price of the good itself	Represents a movement along the demand curve
Income	Shifts the demand curve
Prices of related goods	Shifts the demand curve
Tastes	Shifts the demand curve
Expectations	Shifts the demand curve
Number of buyers	Shifts the demand curve

Variables That Influence Buyers
This table lists the variables that affect how much consumers choose to buy of any good. Notice the special role that the price of the good plays: A change in the good's price represents a movement along the demand curve, whereas a change in one of the other variables shifts the demand curve.

Figure 4

Shifts in the Demand Curve versus Movements along the Demand Curve

If warnings on cigarette packages convince smokers to smoke less, the demand curve for cigarettes shifts to the left. In panel (a), the demand curve shifts from D_1 to D_2. At a price of $2.00 per pack, the quantity demanded falls from 20 to 10 cigarettes per day, as reflected by the shift from point A to point B. By contrast, if a tax raises the price of cigarettes, the demand curve does not shift. Instead, we observe a movement to a different point on the demand curve. In panel (b), when the price rises from $2.00 to $4.00, the quantity demanded falls from 20 to 12 cigarettes per day, as reflected by the movement from point A to point C.

(a) A Shift in the Demand Curve

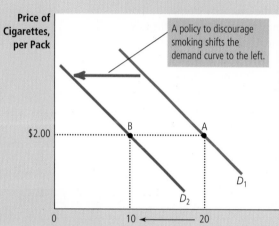

(b) A Movement along the Demand Curve

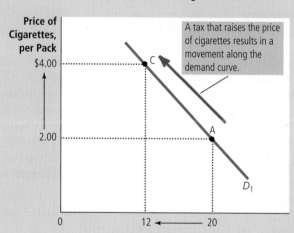

Alternatively, policymakers can try to raise the price of cigarettes. If the government taxes the manufacture of cigarettes, for example, cigarette companies pass much of this tax on to consumers in the form of higher prices. A higher price encourages smokers to reduce the numbers of cigarettes they smoke. In this case, the reduced amount of smoking does not represent a shift in the demand curve. Instead, it represents a movement along the same demand curve to a point with a higher price and lower quantity, as in panel (b) of Figure 4.

How much does the amount of smoking respond to changes in the price of cigarettes? Economists have attempted to answer this question by studying what happens when the tax on cigarettes changes. They have found that a 10 percent increase in the price causes a 4 percent reduction in the quantity demanded. Teenagers are found to be especially sensitive to the price of cigarettes: A 10 percent increase in the price causes a 12 percent drop in teenage smoking.

A related question is how the price of cigarettes affects the demand for illicit drugs, such as marijuana. Opponents of cigarette taxes often argue that tobacco and marijuana are substitutes so that high cigarette prices encourage marijuana use. By contrast, many experts on substance abuse view tobacco as a "gateway drug" leading the young to experiment with other harmful substances. Most studies of the data are consistent with this latter view: They find that lower cigarette prices are associated with greater use of marijuana. In other words, tobacco and marijuana appear to be complements rather than substitutes. ■

QUICK QUIZ   *Make up an example of a monthly demand schedule for pizza and graph the implied demand curve. • Give an example of something that would shift this demand curve, and briefly explain your reasoning. • Would a change in the price of pizza shift this demand curve?*

Supply

We now turn to the other side of the market and examine the behavior of sellers. Once again, to focus our thinking, let's consider the market for ice cream.

The Supply Curve: The Relationship between Price and Quantity Supplied

The **quantity supplied** of any good or service is the amount that sellers are willing and able to sell. There are many determinants of quantity supplied, but once again, price plays a special role in our analysis. When the price of ice cream is high, selling ice cream is profitable, and so the quantity supplied is large. Sellers of ice cream work long hours, buy many ice-cream machines, and hire many workers. By contrast, when the price of ice cream is low, the business is less profitable, so sellers produce less ice cream. At a low price, some sellers may even choose to shut down, and their quantity supplied falls to zero. This relationship between price and quantity supplied is called the **law of supply**: Other things equal, when the price of a good rises, the quantity supplied of the good also rises, and when the price falls, the quantity supplied falls as well.

The table in Figure 5 shows the quantity of ice-cream cones supplied each month by Ben, an ice-cream seller, at various prices of ice cream. At a price below $1.00, Ben does not supply any ice cream at all. As the price rises, he supplies a greater and greater quantity. This is the **supply schedule**, a table that shows the relationship between the price of a good and the quantity supplied, holding constant everything else that influences how much producers of the good want to sell.

The graph in Figure 5 uses the numbers from the table to illustrate the law of supply. The curve relating price and quantity supplied is called the **supply curve**. The supply curve slopes upward because, other things equal, a higher price means a greater quantity supplied.

Market Supply versus Individual Supply

Just as market demand is the sum of the demands of all buyers, market supply is the sum of the supplies of all sellers. The table in Figure 6 shows the supply schedules for the two ice-cream producers in the market—Ben and Jerry. At any price, Ben's supply schedule tells us the quantity of ice cream Ben supplies, and Jerry's supply schedule tells us the quantity of ice cream Jerry supplies. The market supply is the sum of the two individual supplies.

The graph in Figure 6 shows the supply curves that correspond to the supply schedules. As with demand curves, we sum the individual supply curves *horizontally* to obtain the market supply curve. That is, to find the total quantity supplied at any price, we add the individual quantities, which are found on the horizontal axis of the individual supply curves. The market supply curve shows how the

quantity supplied
the amount of a good that sellers are willing and able to sell

law of supply
the claim that, other things equal, the quantity supplied of a good rises when the price of the good rises

supply schedule
a table that shows the relationship between the price of a good and the quantity supplied

supply curve
a graph of the relationship between the price of a good and the quantity supplied

Figure 5

Ben's Supply Schedule and Supply Curve

The supply schedule is a table that shows the quantity supplied at each price. This supply curve, which graphs the supply schedule, illustrates how the quantity supplied of the good changes as its price varies. Because a higher price increases the quantity supplied, the supply curve slopes upward.

Price of Ice-Cream Cone	Quantity of Cones Supplied
$0.00	0 cones
0.50	0
1.00	1
1.50	2
2.00	3
2.50	4
3.00	5

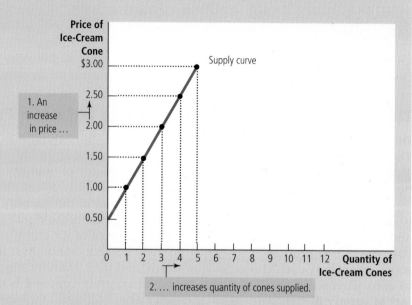

1. An increase in price …

2. … increases quantity of cones supplied.

total quantity supplied varies as the price of the good varies, holding constant all the other factors beyond price that influence producers' decisions about how much to sell.

Shifts in the Supply Curve

Because the market supply curve holds other things constant, the curve shifts when one of the factors changes. For example, suppose the price of sugar falls. Sugar is an input into producing ice cream, so the fall in the price of sugar makes selling ice cream more profitable. This raises the supply of ice cream: At any given price, sellers are now willing to produce a larger quantity. The supply curve for ice cream shifts to the right.

Figure 7 illustrates shifts in supply. Any change that raises quantity supplied at every price, such as a fall in the price of sugar, shifts the supply curve to the right and is called an *increase in supply*. Similarly, any change that reduces the quantity supplied at every price shifts the supply curve to the left and is called a *decrease in supply*.

There are many variables that can shift the supply curve. Here are some of the most important.

Input Prices   To produce their output of ice cream, sellers use various inputs: cream, sugar, flavoring, ice-cream machines, the buildings in which the ice cream is made, and the labor of workers to mix the ingredients and operate the machines. When the price of one or more of these inputs rises, producing

The quantity supplied in a market is the sum of the quantities supplied by all the sellers at each price. Thus, the market supply curve is found by adding horizontally the individual supply curves. At a price of $2.00, Ben supplies 3 ice-cream cones, and Jerry supplies 4 ice-cream cones. The quantity supplied in the market at this price is 7 cones.

Figure 6

Market Supply as the Sum of Individual Supplies

Price of Ice-Cream Cone	Ben		Jerry		Market
$0.00	0	+	0	=	0 cones
0.50	0		0		0
1.00	1		0		1
1.50	2		2		4
2.00	3		4		7
2.50	4		6		10
3.00	5		8		13

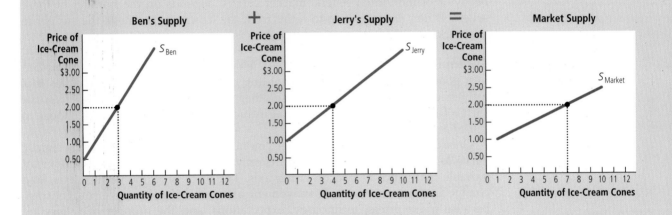

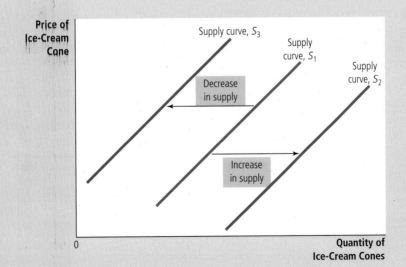

Figure 7

Shifts in the Supply Curve
Any change that raises the quantity that sellers wish to produce at any given price shifts the supply curve to the right. Any change that lowers the quantity that sellers wish to produce at any given price shifts the supply curve to the left.

ice cream is less profitable, and firms supply less ice cream. If input prices rise substantially, a firm might shut down and supply no ice cream at all. Thus, the supply of a good is negatively related to the price of the inputs used to make the good.

Technology   The technology for turning inputs into ice cream is another determinant of supply. The invention of the mechanized ice-cream machine, for example, reduced the amount of labor necessary to make ice cream. By reducing firms' costs, the advance in technology raised the supply of ice cream.

Expectations   The amount of ice cream a firm supplies today may depend on its expectations about the future. For example, if a firm expects the price of ice cream to rise in the future, it will put some of its current production into storage and supply less to the market today.

Number of Sellers   In addition to the preceding factors, which influence the behavior of individual sellers, market supply depends on the number of these sellers. If Ben or Jerry were to retire from the ice-cream business, the supply in the market would fall.

Summary   The supply curve shows what happens to the quantity supplied of a good when its price varies, holding constant all the other variables that influence sellers. When one of these other variables changes, the supply curve shifts. Table 2 lists the variables that influence how much producers choose to sell of a good.

Once again, to remember whether you need to shift or move along the supply curve, keep in mind that a curve shifts only when there is a change in a relevant variable that is not named on either axis. The price is on the vertical axis, so a change in price represents a movement along the supply curve. By contrast, because input prices, technology, expectations, and the number of sellers are not measured on either axis, a change in one of these variables shifts the supply curve.

QUICK QUIZ   *Make up an example of a monthly supply schedule for pizza and graph the implied supply curve. • Give an example of something that would shift this supply curve, and briefly explain your reasoning. • Would a change in the price of pizza shift this supply curve?*

Table 2

Variables That Influence Sellers
This table lists the variables that affect how much producers choose to sell of any good. Notice the special role that the price of the good plays: A change in the good's price represents a movement along the supply curve, whereas a change in one of the other variables shifts the supply curve.

Variable	A Change in This Variable . . .
Price of the good itself	Represents a movement along the supply curve
Input prices	Shifts the supply curve
Technology	Shifts the supply curve
Expectations	Shifts the supply curve
Number of sellers	Shifts the supply curve

Supply and Demand Together

Having analyzed supply and demand separately, we now combine them to see how they determine the price and quantity of a good sold in a market.

Equilibrium

Figure 8 shows the market supply curve and market demand curve together. Notice that there is one point at which the supply and demand curves intersect. This point is called the market's **equilibrium**. The price at this intersection is called the **equilibrium price**, and the quantity is called the **equilibrium quantity**. Here the equilibrium price is $2.00 per cone, and the equilibrium quantity is 7 ice-cream cones.

The dictionary defines the word *equilibrium* as a situation in which various forces are in balance—and this also describes a market's equilibrium. *At the equilibrium price, the quantity of the good that buyers are willing and able to buy exactly balances the quantity that sellers are willing and able to sell.* The equilibrium price is sometimes called the *market-clearing price* because, at this price, everyone in the market has been satisfied: Buyers have bought all they want to buy, and sellers have sold all they want to sell.

The actions of buyers and sellers naturally move markets toward the equilibrium of supply and demand. To see why, consider what happens when the market price is not equal to the equilibrium price.

Suppose first that the market price is above the equilibrium price, as in panel (a) of Figure 9. At a price of $2.50 per cone, the quantity of the good supplied (10 cones) exceeds the quantity demanded (4 cones). There is a **surplus** of the good: Suppliers are unable to sell all they want at the going price. A surplus is sometimes called a situation of *excess supply*. When there is a surplus in the ice-cream market, sellers of ice cream find their freezers increasingly full of ice cream they would like to sell

equilibrium
a situation in which the market price has reached the level at which quantity supplied equals quantity demanded

equilibrium price
the price that balances quantity supplied and quantity demanded

equilibrium quantity
the quantity supplied and the quantity demanded at the equilibrium price

surplus
a situation in which quantity supplied is greater than quantity demanded

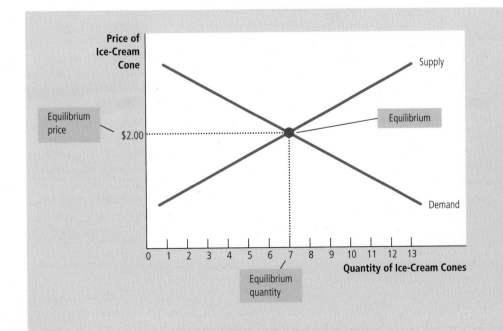

Price of Ice-Cream Cone

Equilibrium price

$2.00

Supply

Equilibrium

Demand

0 1 2 3 4 5 6 7 8 9 10 11 12 13 **Quantity of Ice-Cream Cones**

Equilibrium quantity

Figure **8**

The Equilibrium of Supply and Demand
The equilibrium is found where the supply and demand curves intersect. At the equilibrium price, the quantity supplied equals the quantity demanded. Here the equilibrium price is $2.00: At this price, 7 ice-cream cones are supplied, and 7 ice-cream cones are demanded.

Figure 9

Markets Not in Equilibrium

In panel (a), there is a surplus. Because the market price of $2.50 is above the equilibrium price, the quantity supplied (10 cones) exceeds the quantity demanded (4 cones). Suppliers try to increase sales by cutting the price of a cone, and this moves the price toward its equilibrium level. In panel (b), there is a shortage. Because the market price of $1.50 is below the equilibrium price, the quantity demanded (10 cones) exceeds the quantity supplied (4 cones). With too many buyers chasing too few goods, suppliers can take advantage of the shortage by raising the price. Hence, in both cases, the price adjustment moves the market toward the equilibrium of supply and demand.

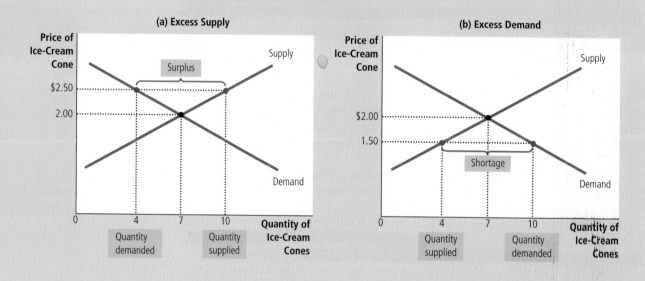

but cannot. They respond to the surplus by cutting their prices. Falling prices, in turn, increase the quantity demanded and decrease the quantity supplied. These changes represent movements *along* the supply and demand curves, not shifts in the curves. Prices continue to fall until the market reaches the equilibrium.

Suppose now that the market price is below the equilibrium price, as in panel (b) of Figure 9. In this case, the price is $1.50 per cone, and the quantity of the good demanded exceeds the quantity supplied. There is a **shortage** of the good: Demanders are unable to buy all they want at the going price. A shortage is sometimes called a situation of *excess demand*. When a shortage occurs in the ice-cream market, buyers have to wait in long lines for a chance to buy one of the few cones available. With too many buyers chasing too few goods, sellers can respond to the shortage by raising their prices without losing sales. These price increases cause the quantity demanded to fall and the quantity supplied to rise. Once again, these changes represent movements *along* the supply and demand curves, and they move the market toward the equilibrium.

Thus, regardless of whether the price starts off too high or too low, the activities of the many buyers and sellers automatically push the market price toward the equilibrium price. Once the market reaches its equilibrium, all buyers and sellers are satisfied, and there is no upward or downward pressure on the price. How quickly equilibrium is reached varies from market to market depending on how quickly prices adjust. In most free markets, surpluses and shortages are only temporary because prices eventually move toward their equilibrium levels.

shortage

a situation in which quantity demanded is greater than quantity supplied

Indeed, this phenomenon is so pervasive that it is called the **law of supply and demand**: The price of any good adjusts to bring the quantity supplied and quantity demanded for that good into balance.

Three Steps to Analyzing Changes in Equilibrium

So far, we have seen how supply and demand together determine a market's equilibrium, which in turn determines the price and quantity of the good that buyers purchase and sellers produce. The equilibrium price and quantity depend on the position of the supply and demand curves. When some event shifts one of these curves, the equilibrium in the market changes, resulting in a new price and a new quantity exchanged between buyers and sellers.

When analyzing how some event affects the equilibrium in a market, we proceed in three steps. First, we decide whether the event shifts the supply curve, the demand curve, or, in some cases, both curves. Second, we decide whether the curve shifts to the right or to the left. Third, we use the supply-and-demand diagram to compare the initial and the new equilibrium, which shows how the shift affects the equilibrium price and quantity. Table 3 summarizes these three steps. To see how this recipe is used, let's consider various events that might affect the market for ice cream.

Example: A Change in Market Equilibrium Due to a Shift in Demand

Suppose that one summer the weather is very hot. How does this event affect the market for ice cream? To answer this question, let's follow our three steps.

1. The hot weather affects the demand curve by changing people's taste for ice cream. That is, the weather changes the amount of ice cream that people want to buy at any given price. The supply curve is unchanged because the weather does not directly affect the firms that sell ice cream.
2. Because hot weather makes people want to eat more ice cream, the demand curve shifts to the right. Figure 10 shows this increase in demand as the shift in the demand curve from D_1 to D_2. This shift indicates that the quantity of ice cream demanded is higher at every price.
3. At the old price of $2, there is now an excess demand for ice cream, and this shortage induces firms to raise the price. As Figure 10 shows, the increase in demand raises the equilibrium price from $2.00 to $2.50 and the equilibrium quantity from 7 to 10 cones. In other words, the hot weather increases the price of ice cream and the quantity of ice cream sold.

Shifts in Curves versus Movements along Curves Notice that when hot weather increases the demand for ice cream and drives up the price, the quantity of ice cream that firms supply rises, even though the supply curve remains the

---

law of supply and demand

the claim that the price of any good adjusts to bring the quantity supplied and the quantity demanded for that good into balance

---

Table **3**

Three Steps for Analyzing Changes in Equilibrium

1. Decide whether the event shifts the supply or demand curve (or perhaps both).
2. Decide in which direction the curve shifts.
3. Use the supply-and-demand diagram to see how the shift changes the equilibrium price and quantity.

Figure **10**

How an Increase in Demand Affects the Equilibrium

An event that raises quantity demanded at any given price shifts the demand curve to the right. The equilibrium price and the equilibrium quantity both rise. Here an abnormally hot summer causes buyers to demand more ice cream. The demand curve shifts from D_1 to D_2, which causes the equilibrium price to rise from $2.00 to $2.50 and the equilibrium quantity to rise from 7 to 10 cones.

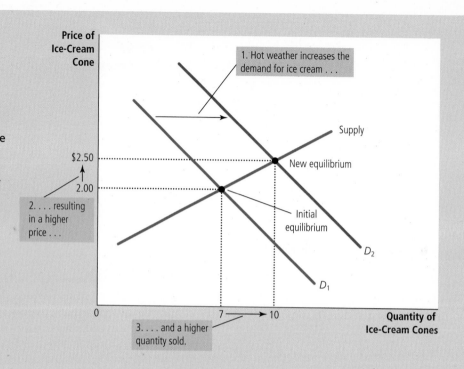

same. In this case, economists say there has been an increase in "quantity supplied" but no change in "supply."

Supply refers to the position of the supply curve, whereas the *quantity supplied* refers to the amount suppliers wish to sell. In this example, supply does not change because the weather does not alter firms' desire to sell at any given price. Instead, the hot weather alters consumers' desire to buy at any given price and thereby shifts the demand curve to the right. The increase in demand causes the equilibrium price to rise. When the price rises, the quantity supplied rises. This increase in quantity supplied is represented by the movement along the supply curve.

To summarize, a shift *in* the supply curve is called a "change in supply," and a shift *in* the demand curve is called a "change in demand." A movement *along* a fixed supply curve is called a "change in the quantity supplied," and a movement *along* a fixed demand curve is called a "change in the quantity demanded."

Example: A Change in Market Equilibrium Due to a Shift in Supply
Suppose that during another summer, a hurricane destroys part of the sugarcane crop and drives up the price of sugar. How does this event affect the market for ice cream? Once again, to answer this question, we follow our three steps.

1. The change in the price of sugar, an input for making ice cream, affects the supply curve. By raising the costs of production, it reduces the amount of ice cream that firms produce and sell at any given price. The demand curve does not change because the higher cost of inputs does not directly affect the amount of ice cream households wish to buy.
2. The supply curve shifts to the left because, at every price, the total amount that firms are willing and able to sell is reduced. Figure 11 illustrates this decrease in supply as a shift in the supply curve from S_1 to S_2.

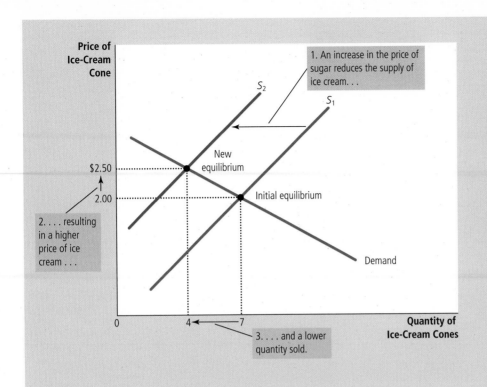

Price of Ice-Cream Cone

1. An increase in the price of sugar reduces the supply of ice cream. . .

S_2

S_1

New equilibrium

$2.50

Initial equilibrium

2.00

2. . . . resulting in a higher price of ice cream . . .

Demand

0   4←——7

3. . . . and a lower quantity sold.

Quantity of Ice-Cream Cones

Figure **11**

How a Decrease in Supply Affects the Equilibrium
An event that reduces quantity supplied at any given price shifts the supply curve to the left. The equilibrium price rises, and the equilibrium quantity falls. Here an increase in the price of sugar (an input) causes sellers to supply less ice cream. The supply curve shifts from S_1 to S_2, which causes the equilibrium price of ice cream to rise from $2.00 to $2.50 and the equilibrium quantity to fall from 7 to 4 cones.

3. At the old price of $2, there is now an excess demand for ice cream, and this shortage causes firms to raise the price. As Figure 11 shows, the shift in the supply curve raises the equilibrium price from $2.00 to $2.50 and lowers the equilibrium quantity from 7 to 4 cones. As a result of the sugar price increase, the price of ice cream rises, and the quantity of ice cream sold falls.

Example: Shifts in Both Supply and Demand   Now suppose that a heat wave and a hurricane occur during the same summer. To analyze this combination of events, we again follow our three steps.

1. We determine that both curves must shift. The hot weather affects the demand curve because it alters the amount of ice cream that households want to buy at any given price. At the same time, when the hurricane drives up sugar prices, it alters the supply curve for ice cream because it changes the amount of ice cream that firms want to sell at any given price.
2. The curves shift in the same directions as they did in our previous analysis: The demand curve shifts to the right, and the supply curve shifts to the left. Figure 12 illustrates these shifts.
3. As Figure 12 shows, two possible outcomes might result depending on the relative size of the demand and supply shifts. In both cases, the equilibrium price rises. In panel (a), where demand increases substantially while supply falls just a little, the equilibrium quantity also rises. By contrast, in panel (b), where supply falls substantially while demand rises just a little, the equilibrium quantity falls. Thus, these events certainly raise the price of ice cream, but their impact on the amount of ice cream sold is ambiguous (that is, it could go either way).

Figure 12

A Shift in Both Supply and Demand

Here we observe a simultaneous increase in demand and decrease in supply. Two outcomes are possible. In panel (a), the equilibrium price rises from P_1 to P_2, and the equilibrium quantity rises from Q_1 to Q_2. In panel (b), the equilibrium price again rises from P_1 to P_2, but the equilibrium quantity falls from Q_1 to Q_2.

(a) Price Rises, Quantity Rises

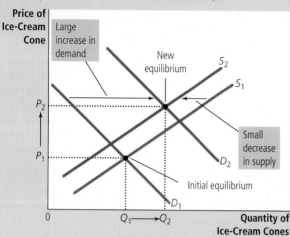

(b) Price Rises, Quantity Falls

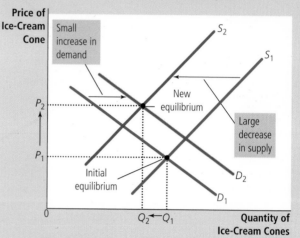

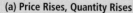

in the news

> ### Price Increases after Disasters

For several days in 2010, many towns around Boston found themselves without drinkable tap water. This increased the demand for bottled water, putting upward pressure on the price. While some policymakers cried foul, this opinion piece endorses the market's natural response.

What's Wrong with Price Gouging?

By Jeff Jacoby

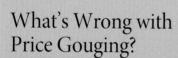

There wasn't much [Attorney General] Martha Coakley could do about the massive pipe break that left dozens of Greater Boston towns without clean drinking water over the weekend. So she kept herself busy instead lecturing vendors not to increase the price of the bottled water that tens of thousands of consumers were suddenly in a frenzy to buy.

"We have begun hearing anecdotal reports of the possible price gouging of store-bought water," Coakley announced Sunday. "Businesses and individuals cannot and should not take advantage of this public emergency to unfairly charge consumers . . . for water." Inspectors were being dispatched, "spot-checks" were being conducted, and "if we discover that businesses are engaging in price gouging," she warned, "we will take appropriate legal action."

Governor Deval Patrick got into the act, too. He ordered the state's Division of Standards to "closely monitor bottled water prices" in the area affected by the water emergency. "There is never an excuse for taking advantage of consumers," he intoned, "especially not during times like this."

It never fails. No sooner does some calamity trigger an urgent need for basic resources than self-righteous voices are raised to denounce the amazingly efficient system that stimulates suppliers to speed those resources to the people who need them. That system is the free market's price mechanism—the fluctuation of prices because of changes in supply and demand.

When the demand for bottled water goes through the roof—which is another way of saying that bottled water has become (relatively) scarce—the price of water quickly rises in response. That price spike may be annoying, but it's not nearly as annoying as being unable to find water for sale at any price.

Table **4**

	No Change in Supply	An Increase in Supply	A Decrease in Supply
No Change in Demand	P same Q same	P down Q up	P up Q down
An Increase in Demand	P up Q up	P ambiguous Q up	P up Q ambiguous
A Decrease in Demand	P down Q down	P down Q ambiguous	P ambiguous Q down

What Happens to Price and Quantity When Supply or Demand Shifts?
As a quick quiz, make sure you can explain at least a few of the entries in this table using a supply-and-demand diagram.

Summary We have just seen three examples of how to use supply and demand curves to analyze a change in equilibrium. Whenever an event shifts the supply curve, the demand curve, or perhaps both curves, you can use these tools to predict how the event will alter the price and quantity sold in equilibrium. Table 4 shows the predicted outcome for any combination of shifts in the two curves. To make sure you understand how to use the tools of supply and demand, pick a

Rising prices help keep limited quantities from vanishing today, while increasing the odds of fresh supplies arriving tomorrow.

It is easy to demonize vendors who charge what the market will bear following a catastrophe. "After storm come the vultures" *USA Today* memorably headlined a story about the price hikes that followed Hurricane Charley in Florida in 2004. Coakley hasn't called anybody a vulture, at least not yet, but her office has dedicated a telephone hotline and is encouraging the public to drop a dime on "price gougers."

Before you drop that dime, though, consider who really serves the public interest—the merchant who boosts his price during a crisis, or the merchant who refuses to?

A thought experiment: A massive pipe ruptures, tap water grows undrinkable, and consumers rush to buy bottled water from the only two vendors who sell it. Vendor A, not wanting to annoy the governor and attorney general, leaves the price of his water unchanged at 69 cents a bottle. Vendor B, who is more interested in doing business than truckling to politicians, more than quadruples his price to $2.99.

Source: *The Boston Globe*, May 4, 2010.

You don't need an economics textbook to know what happens next.

Customers descend on Vendor A in droves, loading up on his 69-cent water. Within hours his entire stock has been cleaned out, and subsequent customers are turned away empty-handed. At Vendor B's, on the other hand, sales of water are slower and there is a lot of grumbling about the high price. But even late-arriving customers are able to buy the water they need—and almost no one buys more than he truly *needs*.

A scarce resource.

When demand intensifies, prices rise. And as prices rise, suppliers work harder to meet demand. The same *Globe* story that reported yesterday on Coakley's "price-gouging" statement reported as well on the lengths to which bottlers and retailers were going to get more water into customers' hands.

"Suppliers worked overtime, pumping up production at regional bottling facilities and coordinating deliveries," reporter Erin Ailworth noted. Polar Beverages in Worcester, for example, "had emptied out its plant in the city last night and trucked in loads of water from its New York facility."

Letting prices rise freely isn't the only possible response to a sudden shortage. Government rationing is an option, and so are price controls—assuming you don't object to the inevitable corruption, long lines, and black market. Better by far to let prices rise and fall freely. That isn't "gouging," but plain good sense—and the best method yet devised for allocating goods and services among free men and women.

© GYRO PHOTOGRAPHY/AMANAIMAGESRF/JUPITER IMAGES

few entries in this table and make sure you can explain to yourself why the table contains the prediction it does.

QUICK QUIZ   *On the appropriate diagram, show what happens to the market for pizza if the price of tomatoes rises. • On a separate diagram, show what happens to the market for pizza if the price of hamburgers falls.*

Conclusion: How Prices Allocate Resources

"Two dollars"

"—and seventy-five cents."

This chapter has analyzed supply and demand in a single market. Although our discussion has centered on the market for ice cream, the lessons learned here apply in most other markets as well. Whenever you go to a store to buy something, you are contributing to the demand for that item. Whenever you look for a job, you are contributing to the supply of labor services. Because supply and demand are such pervasive economic phenomena, the model of supply and demand is a powerful tool for analysis. We will be using this model repeatedly in the following chapters.

One of the *Ten Principles of Economics* discussed in Chapter 1 is that markets are usually a good way to organize economic activity. Although it is still too early to judge whether market outcomes are good or bad, in this chapter we have begun to see how markets work. In any economic system, scarce resources have to be allocated among competing uses. Market economies harness the forces of supply and demand to serve that end. Supply and demand together determine the prices of the economy's many different goods and services; prices in turn are the signals that guide the allocation of resources.

For example, consider the allocation of beachfront land. Because the amount of this land is limited, not everyone can enjoy the luxury of living by the beach. Who gets this resource? The answer is whoever is willing and able to pay the price. The price of beachfront land adjusts until the quantity of land demanded exactly balances the quantity supplied. Thus, in market economies, prices are the mechanism for rationing scarce resources.

Similarly, prices determine who produces each good and how much is produced. For instance, consider farming. Because we need food to survive, it is crucial that some people work on farms. What determines who is a farmer and who is not? In a free society, there is no government planning agency making this decision and ensuring an adequate supply of food. Instead, the allocation of workers to farms is based on the job decisions of millions of workers. This decentralized system works well because these decisions depend on prices. The prices of food and the wages of farmworkers (the price of their labor) adjust to ensure that enough people choose to be farmers.

If a person had never seen a market economy in action, the whole idea might seem preposterous. Economies are enormous groups of people engaged in a multitude of interdependent activities. What prevents decentralized decision making from degenerating into chaos? What coordinates the actions of the millions of people with their varying abilities and desires? What ensures that what needs to be done is in fact done? The answer, in a word, is *prices*. If an invisible hand guides market economies, as Adam Smith famously suggested, then the price system is the baton that the invisible hand uses to conduct the economic orchestra.

SUMMARY

- Economists use the model of supply and demand to analyze competitive markets. In a competitive market, there are many buyers and sellers, each of whom has little or no influence on the market price.

- The demand curve shows how the quantity of a good demanded depends on the price. According to the law of demand, as the price of a good falls, the quantity demanded rises. Therefore, the demand curve slopes downward.

- In addition to price, other determinants of how much consumers want to buy include income, the prices of substitutes and complements, tastes, expectations, and the number of buyers. If one of these factors changes, the demand curve shifts.

- The supply curve shows how the quantity of a good supplied depends on the price. According to the law of supply, as the price of a good rises, the quantity supplied rises. Therefore, the supply curve slopes upward.

- In addition to price, other determinants of how much producers want to sell include input prices, technology, expectations, and the number of sellers. If one of these factors changes, the supply curve shifts.

- The intersection of the supply and demand curves determines the market equilibrium. At the equilibrium price, the quantity demanded equals the quantity supplied.

- The behavior of buyers and sellers naturally drives markets toward their equilibrium. When the market price is above the equilibrium price, there is a surplus of the good, which causes the market price to fall. When the market price is below the equilibrium price, there is a shortage, which causes the market price to rise.

- To analyze how any event influences a market, we use the supply-and-demand diagram to examine how the event affects the equilibrium price and quantity. To do this, we follow three steps. First, we decide whether the event shifts the supply curve or the demand curve (or both). Second, we decide in which direction the curve shifts. Third, we compare the new equilibrium with the initial equilibrium.

- In market economies, prices are the signals that guide economic decisions and thereby allocate scarce resources. For every good in the economy, the price ensures that supply and demand are in balance. The equilibrium price then determines how much of the good buyers choose to consume and how much sellers choose to produce.

KEY CONCEPTS

market, *p. 66*
competitive market, *p. 66*
quantity demanded, *p. 67*
law of demand, *p. 67*
demand schedule, *p. 67*
demand curve, *p. 68*
normal good, *p. 70*

inferior good, *p. 70*
substitutes, *p. 70*
complements, *p. 70*
quantity supplied, *p. 73*
law of supply, *p. 73*
supply schedule, *p. 73*
supply curve, *p. 73*

equilibrium, *p. 77*
equilibrium price, *p. 77*
equilibrium quantity, *p. 77*
surplus, *p. 77*
shortage, *p. 78*
law of supply and
    demand, *p. 79*

QUESTIONS FOR REVIEW

1. What is a competitive market? Briefly describe a type of market that is not perfectly competitive.

2. What are the demand schedule and the demand curve, and how are they related? Why does the demand curve slope downward?

3. Does a change in consumers' tastes lead to a movement along the demand curve or a shift in the demand curve? Does a change in price lead to a movement along the demand curve or a shift in the demand curve?

4. Popeye's income declines, and as a result, he buys more spinach. Is spinach an inferior or a normal good? What happens to Popeye's demand curve for spinach?

5. What are the supply schedule and the supply curve, and how are they related? Why does the supply curve slope upward?

6. Does a change in producers' technology lead to a movement along the supply curve or a shift in the supply curve? Does a change in price lead to a movement along the supply curve or a shift in the supply curve?

7. Define the equilibrium of a market. Describe the forces that move a market toward its equilibrium.

8. Beer and pizza are complements because they are often enjoyed together. When the price of beer rises, what happens to the supply, demand, quantity supplied, quantity demanded, and the price in the market for pizza?

9. Describe the role of prices in market economies.

PROBLEMS AND APPLICATIONS

1. Explain each of the following statements using supply-and-demand diagrams.
   a. "When a cold snap hits Florida, the price of orange juice rises in supermarkets throughout the country."
   b. "When the weather turns warm in New England every summer, the price of hotel rooms in Caribbean resorts plummets."
   c. "When a war breaks out in the Middle East, the price of gasoline rises, and the price of a used Cadillac falls."

2. "An increase in the demand for notebooks raises the quantity of notebooks demanded but not the quantity supplied." Is this statement true or false? Explain.

3. Consider the market for minivans. For each of the events listed here, identify which of the determinants of demand or supply are affected. Also indicate whether demand or supply increases or decreases. Then draw a diagram to show the effect on the price and quantity of minivans.
   a. People decide to have more children.
   b. A strike by steelworkers raises steel prices.
   c. Engineers develop new automated machinery for the production of minivans.
   d. The price of sports utility vehicles rises.
   e. A stock-market crash lowers people's wealth.

4. Consider the markets for DVDs, TV screens, and tickets at movie theaters.
   a. For each pair, identify whether they are complements or substitutes:
      - DVDs and TV screens
      - DVDs and movie tickets
      - TV screens and movie tickets
   b. Suppose a technological advance reduces the cost of manufacturing TV screens. Draw a diagram to show what happens in the market for TV screens.
   c. Draw two more diagrams to show how the change in the market for TV screens affects the markets for DVDs and movie tickets.

5. Over the past 30 years, technological advances have reduced the cost of computer chips. How do you think this has affected the market for computers? For computer software? For typewriters?

6. Using supply-and-demand diagrams, show the effect of the following events on the market for sweatshirts.
   a. A hurricane in South Carolina damages the cotton crop.
   b. The price of leather jackets falls.
   c. All colleges require morning exercise in appropriate attire.
   d. New knitting machines are invented.

7. A survey shows an increase in drug use by young people. In the ensuing debate, two hypotheses are proposed:
   - Reduced police efforts have increased the availability of drugs on the street.
   - Cutbacks in education efforts have decreased awareness of the dangers of drug addiction.

a   Use supply-and-demand diagrams to show how each of these hypotheses could lead to an increase in quantity of drugs consumed.

b   How could information on what has happened to the price of drugs help us to distinguish between these explanations?

8. Suppose that in the year 2015 the number of births is temporarily high. How does this baby boom affect the price of babysitting services in 2020 and 2030? (Hint: 5-year-olds need babysitters, whereas 15-year-olds can be babysitters.)

9. Ketchup is a complement (as well as a condiment) for hot dogs. If the price of hot dogs rises, what happens to the market for ketchup? For tomatoes? For tomato juice? For orange juice?

10. The market for pizza has the following demand and supply schedules:

Price	Quantity Demanded	Quantity Supplied
$4	135 pizzas	26 pizzas
5	104	53
6	81	81
7	68	98
8	53	110
9	39	121

a. Graph the demand and supply curves. What is the equilibrium price and quantity in this market?

b. If the actual price in this market were *above* the equilibrium price, what would drive the market toward the equilibrium?

c. If the actual price in this market were *below* the equilibrium price, what would drive the market toward the equilibrium?

11. Consider the following events: Scientists reveal that consumption of oranges decreases the risk of diabetes, and at the same time, farmers use a new fertilizer that makes orange trees more productive. Illustrate and explain what effect these changes have on the equilibrium price and quantity of oranges.

12. Because bagels and cream cheese are often eaten together, they are complements.

a. We observe that both the equilibrium price of cream cheese and the equilibrium quantity of bagels have risen. What could be responsible for this pattern—a fall in the price of flour or a fall in the price of milk? Illustrate and explain your answer.

b. Suppose instead that the equilibrium price of cream cheese has risen but the equilibrium quantity of bagels has fallen. What could be responsible for this pattern—a rise in the price of flour or a rise in the price of milk? Illustrate and explain your answer.

13. Suppose that the price of basketball tickets at your college is determined by market forces. Currently, the demand and supply schedules are as follows:

Price	Quantity Demanded	Quantity Supplied
$ 4	10,000 tickets	8,000 tickets
8	8,000	8,000
12	6,000	8,000
16	4,000	8,000
20	2,000	8,000

a. Draw the demand and supply curves. What is unusual about this supply curve? Why might this be true?

b. What are the equilibrium price and quantity of tickets?

c. Your college plans to increase total enrollment next year by 5,000 students. The additional students will have the following demand schedule:

Price	Quantity Demanded
$ 4	4,000 tickets
8	3,000
12	2,000
16	1,000
20	0

Now add the old demand schedule and the demand schedule for the new students to calculate the new demand schedule for the entire college. What will be the new equilibrium price and quantity?

14. Market research has revealed the following information about the market for chocolate bars: The demand schedule can be represented by the equation $Q^D = 1,600 - 300P$, where Q^D is the quantity demanded and P is the price. The supply schedule can be represented by the equation $Q^S = 1,400 + 700P$, where Q^S is the quantity supplied. Calculate the equilibrium price and quantity in the market for chocolate bars.

For further information on topics in this chapter, additional problems, applications, examples, online quizzes, and more, please visit our website at www .cengage.com/economics/mankiw.

Elasticity and Its Application

5

I magine that some event drives up the price of gasoline in the United States. It could be a war in the Middle East that disrupts the world supply of oil, a booming Chinese economy that boosts the world demand for oil, or a new tax on gasoline passed by Congress. How would U.S. consumers respond to the higher price?

It is easy to answer this question in broad fashion: Consumers would buy less. That is simply the law of demand we learned in the previous chapter But you might want a precise answer. By how much would consumption of gasoline fall? This question can be answered using a concept called *elasticity*, which we develop in this chapter.

Elasticity is a measure of how much buyers and sellers respond to changes in market conditions. When studying how some event or policy affects a market, we can discuss not only the direction of the effects but their magnitude as well. Elasticity is useful in many applications, as we see toward the end of this chapter.

Before proceeding, however, you might be curious about the answer to the gasoline question. Many studies have examined consumers' response to gasoline prices, and they typically find that the quantity demanded responds more in the long run than it does in the short run. A 10 percent increase in gasoline prices reduces gasoline consumption by about 2.5 percent after a year and about 6 percent after five years. About half of the long-run reduction in quantity demanded arises because people drive less and half arises because they switch to more fuel-efficient cars. Both responses are reflected in the demand curve and its elasticity.

The Elasticity of Demand

elasticity

a measure of the responsiveness of quantity demanded or quantity supplied to a change in one of its determinants

When we introduced demand in Chapter 4, we noted that consumers usually buy more of a good when its price is lower, when their incomes are higher, when the prices of substitutes for the good are higher, or when the prices of complements of the good are lower. Our discussion of demand was qualitative, not quantitative. That is, we discussed the direction in which quantity demanded moves but not the size of the change. To measure how much consumers respond to changes in these variables, economists use the concept of **elasticity.**

The Price Elasticity of Demand and Its Determinants

The law of demand states that a fall in the price of a good raises the quantity demanded. The **price elasticity of demand** measures how much the quantity demanded responds to a change in price. Demand for a good is said to be *elastic* if the quantity demanded responds substantially to changes in the price. Demand is said to be *inelastic* if the quantity demanded responds only slightly to changes in the price.

price elasticity of demand

a measure of how much the quantity demanded of a good responds to a change in the price of that good, computed as the percentage change in quantity demanded divided by the percentage change in price

The price elasticity of demand for any good measures how willing consumers are to buy less of the good as its price rises. Because the demand curve reflects the many economic, social, and psychological forces that shape consumer preferences, there is no simple, universal rule for what determines the demand curve's elasticity. Based on experience, however, we can state some rules-of-thumb about what influences the price elasticity of demand.

Availability of Close Substitutes Goods with close substitutes tend to have more elastic demand because it is easier for consumers to switch from that good to others. For example, butter and margarine are easily substitutable. A small increase in the price of butter, assuming the price of margarine is held fixed, causes the quantity of butter sold to fall by a large amount. By contrast, because eggs are a food without a close substitute, the demand for eggs is less elastic than the demand for butter.

Necessities versus Luxuries Necessities tend to have inelastic demands, whereas luxuries have elastic demands. When the price of a doctor's visit rises, people will not dramatically reduce the number of times they go to the doctor, although they might go somewhat less often. By contrast, when the price of sailboats rises, the quantity of sailboats demanded falls substantially. The reason is that most people view doctor visits as a necessity and sailboats as a luxury. Whether a good is a necessity or a luxury depends not on the intrinsic properties of the good but on the preferences of the buyer. For avid sailors with little concern over their health, sailboats might be a necessity with inelastic demand and doctor visits a luxury with elastic demand.

Definition of the Market The elasticity of demand in any market depends on how we draw the boundaries of the market. Narrowly defined markets tend to have more elastic demand than broadly defined markets because it is easier to find close substitutes for narrowly defined goods. For example, food, a broad category, has a fairly inelastic demand because there are no good substitutes for food. Ice cream, a narrower category, has a more elastic demand because it is easy to substitute other desserts for ice cream. Vanilla ice cream, a very narrow category, has a very elastic demand because other flavors of ice cream are almost perfect substitutes for vanilla.

Time Horizon   Goods tend to have more elastic demand over longer time horizons. When the price of gasoline rises, the quantity of gasoline demanded falls only slightly in the first few months. Over time, however, people buy more fuel-efficient cars, switch to public transportation, and move closer to where they work. Within several years, the quantity of gasoline demanded falls more substantially.

Computing the Price Elasticity of Demand

Now that we have discussed the price elasticity of demand in general terms, let's be more precise about how it is measured. Economists compute the price elasticity of demand as the percentage change in the quantity demanded divided by the percentage change in the price. That is,

$$\text{Price elasticity of demand} = \frac{\text{Percentage change in quantity demanded}}{\text{Percentage change in price}}.$$

For example, suppose that a 10 percent increase in the price of an ice-cream cone causes the amount of ice cream you buy to fall by 20 percent. We calculate your elasticity of demand as

$$\text{Price elasticity of demand} = \frac{20 \text{ percent}}{10 \text{ percent}} = 2.$$

In this example, the elasticity is 2, reflecting that the change in the quantity demanded is proportionately twice as large as the change in the price.

   Because the quantity demanded of a good is negatively related to its price, the percentage change in quantity will always have the opposite sign as the percentage change in price. In this example, the percentage change in price is a *positive* 10 percent (reflecting an increase), and the percentage change in quantity demanded is a *negative* 20 percent (reflecting a decrease). For this reason, price elasticities of demand are sometimes reported as negative numbers. In this book, we follow the common practice of dropping the minus sign and reporting all price elasticities of demand as positive numbers. (Mathematicians call this the *absolute value.*) With this convention, a larger price elasticity implies a greater responsiveness of quantity demanded to changes in price.

The Midpoint Method: A Better Way to Calculate Percentage Changes and Elasticities

If you try calculating the price elasticity of demand between two points on a demand curve, you will quickly notice an annoying problem: The elasticity from point A to point B seems different from the elasticity from point B to point A. For example, consider these numbers:

Point A:	Price = $4	Quantity = 120
Point B:	Price = $6	Quantity = 80

Going from point A to point B, the price rises by 50 percent, and the quantity falls by 33 percent, indicating that the price elasticity of demand is 33/50, or 0.66. By contrast, going from point B to point A, the price falls by 33 percent, and the quantity rises by 50 percent, indicating that the price elasticity of demand is 50/33, or 1.5. This difference arises because the percentage changes are calculated from a different base.

One way to avoid this problem is to use the *midpoint method* for calculating elasticities. The standard procedure for computing a percentage change is to divide the change by the initial level. By contrast, the midpoint method computes a percentage change by dividing the change by the midpoint (or average) of the initial and final levels. For instance, $5 is the midpoint between $4 and $6. Therefore, according to the midpoint method, a change from $4 to $6 is considered a 40 percent rise because $(6 - 4) / 5 \times 100 = 40$. Similarly, a change from $6 to $4 is considered a 40 percent fall.

Because the midpoint method gives the same answer regardless of the direction of change, it is often used when calculating the price elasticity of demand between two points. In our example, the midpoint between point A and point B is:

Midpoint: Price = $5   Quantity = 100

According to the midpoint method, when going from point A to point B, the price rises by 40 percent, and the quantity falls by 40 percent. Similarly, when going from point B to point A, the price falls by 40 percent, and the quantity rises by 40 percent. In both directions, the price elasticity of demand equals 1.

The following formula expresses the midpoint method for calculating the price elasticity of demand between two points, denoted (Q_1, P_1) and (Q_2, P_2):

$$\text{Price elasticity of demand} = \frac{(Q_2 - Q_1) / [(Q_2 + Q_1) / 2]}{(P_2 - P_1) / [(P_2 + P_1) / 2]}.$$

The numerator is the percentage change in quantity computed using the midpoint method, and the denominator is the percentage change in price computed using the midpoint method. If you ever need to calculate elasticities, you should use this formula.

In this book, however, we rarely perform such calculations. For most of our purposes, what elasticity represents—the responsiveness of quantity demanded to a change in price—is more important than how it is calculated.

The Variety of Demand Curves

Economists classify demand curves according to their elasticity. Demand is considered *elastic* when the elasticity is greater than 1, which means the quantity moves proportionately more than the price. Demand is considered *inelastic* when the elasticity is less than 1, which means the quantity moves proportionately less than the price. If the elasticity is exactly 1, the quantity moves the same amount proportionately as the price, and demand is said to have *unit elasticity*.

Because the price elasticity of demand measures how much quantity demanded responds to changes in the price, it is closely related to the slope of the demand curve. The following rule of thumb is a useful guide: The flatter the demand curve that passes through a given point, the greater the price elasticity of demand. The steeper the demand curve that passes through a given point, the smaller the price elasticity of demand.

Figure 1 shows five cases. In the extreme case of a zero elasticity, shown in panel (a), demand is *perfectly inelastic*, and the demand curve is vertical. In this case, regardless of the price, the quantity demanded stays the same. As the elasticity rises, the demand curve gets flatter and flatter, as shown in panels (b), (c), and (d). At the opposite extreme, shown in panel (e), demand is *perfectly elastic*. This

The Price Elasticity of Demand

The price elasticity of demand determines whether the demand curve is steep or flat.
Note that all percentage changes are calculated using the midpoint method.

Figure 1

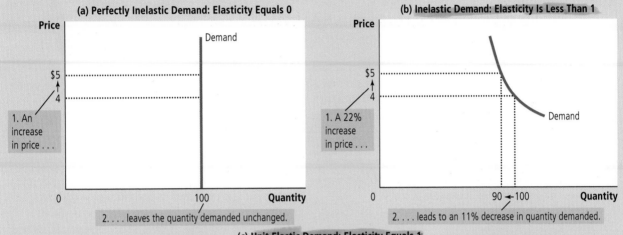

(a) Perfectly Inelastic Demand: Elasticity Equals 0

Price

Demand

$5
4

1. An increase in price . . .

0   100   Quantity

2. . . . leaves the quantity demanded unchanged.

(b) Inelastic Demand: Elasticity Is Less Than 1

Price

$5
4

1. A 22% increase in price . . .

Demand

0   90 ← 100   Quantity

2. . . . leads to an 11% decrease in quantity demanded.

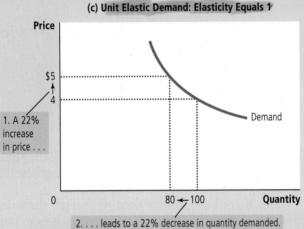

(c) Unit Elastic Demand: Elasticity Equals 1

Price

$5
4

1. A 22% increase in price . . .

Demand

0   80 ← 100   Quantity

2. . . . leads to a 22% decrease in quantity demanded.

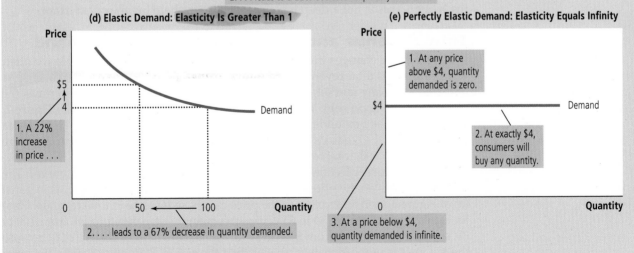

(d) Elastic Demand: Elasticity Is Greater Than 1

Price

$5
4

1. A 22% increase in price . . .

Demand

0   50 ←——— 100   Quantity

2. . . . leads to a 67% decrease in quantity demanded.

(e) Perfectly Elastic Demand: Elasticity Equals Infinity

Price

1. At any price above $4, quantity demanded is zero.

$4   Demand

2. At exactly $4, consumers will buy any quantity.

0   Quantity

3. At a price below $4, quantity demanded is infinite.

FYI

> ### A Few Elasticities from the Real World

We have talked about what elasticity means, what determines it, and how it is calculated. Beyond these general ideas, you might ask for a specific number. How much, precisely, does the price of a particular good influence the quantity demanded?

To answer such a question, economists collect data from market outcomes and apply statistical techniques to estimate the price elasticity of demand. Here are some price elasticities of demand, obtained from various studies, for a range of goods:

Eggs	0.1
Healthcare	0.2
Rice	0.5
Housing	0.7
Beef	1.6
Restaurant Meals	2.3
Mountain Dew	4.4

These kinds of numbers are fun to think about, and they can be useful when comparing markets.

Nonetheless, one should take these estimates with a grain of salt. One reason is that the statistical techniques used to obtain them require some assumptions about the world, and these assumptions might not be true in practice. (The details of these techniques are beyond the scope of this book, but you will encounter them if you take a course in econometrics.) Another reason is that the price elasticity of demand need not be the same at all points on a demand curve, as we will see shortly in the case of a linear demand curve. For both reasons, you should not be surprised if different studies report different price elasticities of demand for the same good.

occurs as the price elasticity of demand approaches infinity and the demand curve becomes horizontal, reflecting the fact that very small changes in the price lead to huge changes in the quantity demanded.

Finally, if you have trouble keeping straight the terms *elastic* and *inelastic*, here's a memory trick for you: *I*nelastic curves, such as in panel (a) of Figure 1, look like the letter I. This is not a deep insight, but it might help on your next exam.

Total Revenue and the Price Elasticity of Demand

total revenue

the amount paid by buyers and received by sellers of a good, computed as the price of the good times the quantity sold

When studying changes in supply or demand in a market, one variable we often want to study is **total revenue,** the amount paid by buyers and received by sellers of the good. In any market, total revenue is $P \times Q$, the price of the good times quantity of the good sold. We can show total revenue graphically, as in Figure 2. The height of the box under the demand curve is P, and the width is Q. The area of this box, $P \times Q$, equals the total revenue in this market. In Figure 2, where $P = \$4$ and $Q = 100$, total revenue is $\$4 \times 100$, or $\$400$.

How does total revenue change as one moves along the demand curve? The answer depends on the price elasticity of demand. If demand is inelastic, as in panel (a) of Figure 3, then an increase in the price causes an increase in total revenue. Here an increase in price from \$4 to \$5 causes the quantity demanded to fall from 100 to 90, so total revenue rises from \$400 to \$450. An increase in price raises $P \times Q$ because the fall in Q is proportionately smaller than the rise in P. In other words, the extra revenue from selling units at a higher price (represented by area A in the figure) more than offsets the decline in revenue from selling fewer units (represented by area B).

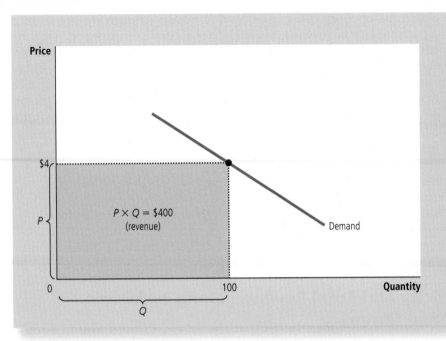

Figure **2**

Total Revenue
The total amount paid by buyers, and received as revenue by sellers, equals the area of the box under the demand curve, $P \times Q$. Here, at a price of $4, the quantity demanded is 100, and total revenue is $400.

The impact of a price change on total revenue (the product of price and quantity) depends on the elasticity of demand. In panel (a), the demand curve is inelastic. In this case, an increase in the price leads to a decrease in quantity demanded that is proportionately smaller, so total revenue increases. Here an increase in the price from $4 to $5 causes the quantity demanded to fall from 100 to 90. Total revenue rises from $400 to $450. In panel (b), the demand curve is elastic. In this case, an increase in the price leads to a decrease in quantity demanded that is proportionately larger, so total revenue decreases. Here an increase in the price from $4 to $5 causes the quantity demanded to fall from 100 to 70. Total revenue falls from $400 to $350.

Figure **3**

How Total Revenue Changes When Price Changes

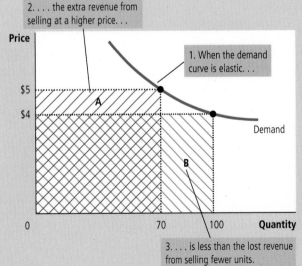
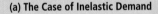

We obtain the opposite result if demand is elastic: An increase in the price causes a decrease in total revenue. In panel (b) of Figure 3, for instance, when the price rises from $4 to $5, the quantity demanded falls from 100 to 70, so total revenue falls from $400 to $350. Because demand is elastic, the reduction in the quantity demanded is so great that it more than offsets the increase in the price. That is, an increase in price reduces $P \times Q$ because the fall in Q is proportionately greater than the rise in P. In this case, the extra revenue from selling units at a higher price (area A) is smaller than the decline in revenue from selling fewer units (area B).

The examples in this figure illustrate some general rules:

- When demand is inelastic (a price elasticity less than 1), price and total revenue move in the same direction.
- When demand is elastic (a price elasticity greater than 1), price and total revenue move in opposite directions.
- If demand is unit elastic (a price elasticity exactly equal to 1), total revenue remains constant when the price changes.

Elasticity and Total Revenue along a Linear Demand Curve

Let's examine how elasticity varies along a linear demand curve, as shown in Figure 4. We know that a straight line has a constant slope. Slope is defined as

Figure 4

Elasticity of a Linear Demand Curve
The slope of a linear demand curve is constant, but its elasticity is not. The demand schedule in the table was used to calculate the price elasticity of demand by the midpoint method. At points with a low price and high quantity, the demand curve is inelastic. At points with a high price and low quantity, the demand curve is elastic.

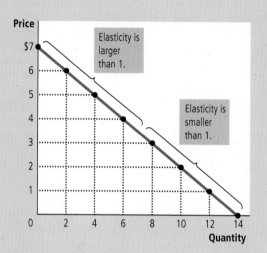

Price	Quantity	Total Revenue (Price × Quantity)	Percentage Change in Price	Percentage Change in Quantity	Elasticity	Description
$7	0	$ 0				
			15	200	13.0	Elastic
6	2	12				
			18	67	3.7	Elastic
5	4	20				
			22	40	1.8	Elastic
4	6	24				
			29	29	1.0	Unit elastic
3	8	24				
			40	22	0.6	Inelastic
2	10	20				
			67	18	0.3	Inelastic
1	12	12				
			200	15	0.1	Inelastic
0	14	0				

"rise over run," which here is the ratio of the change in price ("rise") to the change in quantity ("run"). This particular demand curve's slope is constant because each $1 increase in price causes the same two-unit decrease in the quantity demanded.

Even though the slope of a linear demand curve is constant, the elasticity is not. This is true because the slope is the ratio of *changes* in the two variables, whereas the elasticity is the ratio of *percentage changes* in the two variables. You can see this by looking at the table in Figure 4, which shows the demand schedule for the linear demand curve in the graph. The table uses the midpoint method to calculate the price elasticity of demand. At points with a low price and high quantity, the demand curve is inelastic. At points with a high price and low quantity, the demand curve is elastic.

The table also presents total revenue at each point on the demand curve. These numbers illustrate the relationship between total revenue and elasticity. When the price is $1, for instance, demand is inelastic, and a price increase to $2 raises total revenue. When the price is $5, demand is elastic, and a price increase to $6 reduces total revenue. Between $3 and $4, demand is exactly unit elastic, and total revenue is the same at these two prices.

The linear demand curve illustrates that the price elasticity of demand need not be the same at all points on a demand curve. A constant elasticity is possible, but it is not always the case.

Other Demand Elasticities

In addition to the price elasticity of demand, economists use other elasticities to describe the behavior of buyers in a market.

The Income Elasticity of Demand   The **income elasticity of demand** measures how the quantity demanded changes as consumer income changes. It is calculated as the percentage change in quantity demanded divided by the percentage change in income. That is,

$$\text{Income elasticity of demand} = \frac{\text{Percentage change in quantity demanded}}{\text{Percentage change in income}}.$$

As we discussed in Chapter 4, most goods are *normal goods:* Higher income raises the quantity demanded. Because quantity demanded and income move in the same direction, normal goods have positive income elasticities. A few goods, such as bus rides, are *inferior goods:* Higher income lowers the quantity demanded. Because quantity demanded and income move in opposite directions, inferior goods have negative income elasticities.

Even among normal goods, income elasticities vary substantially in size. Necessities, such as food and clothing, tend to have small income elasticities because consumers choose to buy some of these goods even when their incomes are low. Luxuries, such as caviar and diamonds, tend to have large income elasticities because consumers feel that they can do without these goods altogether if their incomes are too low.

The Cross-Price Elasticity of Demand   The **cross-price elasticity of demand** measures how the quantity demanded of one good responds to a change in the price of another good. It is calculated as the percentage change in quantity demanded of good 1 divided by the percentage change in the price of good 2. That is,

$$\text{Cross-price elasticity of demand} = \frac{\text{Percentage change in quantity demanded of good 1}}{\text{Percentage change in the price of good 2}}.$$

income elasticity of demand
a measure of how much the quantity demanded of a good responds to a change in consumers' income, computed as the percentage change in quantity demanded divided by the percentage change in income

cross-price elasticity of demand
a measure of how much the quantity demanded of one good responds to a change in the price of another good, computed as the percentage change in quantity demanded of the first good divided by the percentage change in the price of the second good

Whether the cross-price elasticity is a positive or negative number depends on whether the two goods are substitutes or complements. As we discussed in Chapter 4, substitutes are goods that are typically used in place of one another, such as hamburgers and hot dogs. An increase in hot dog prices induces people to grill hamburgers instead. Because the price of hot dogs and the quantity of hamburgers demanded move in the same direction, the cross-price elasticity is positive. Conversely, complements are goods that are typically used together, such as computers and software. In this case, the cross-price elasticity is negative, indicating that an increase in the price of computers reduces the quantity of software demanded.

QUICK QUIZ   *Define the price elasticity of demand. • Explain the relationship between total revenue and the price elasticity of demand.*

The Elasticity of Supply

When we introduced supply in Chapter 4, we noted that producers of a good offer to sell more of it when the price of the good rises. To turn from qualitative to quantitative statements about quantity supplied, we once again use the concept of elasticity.

The Price Elasticity of Supply and Its Determinants

price elasticity of supply

a measure of how much the quantity supplied of a good responds to a change in the price of that good, computed as the percentage change in quantity supplied divided by the percentage change in price

The law of supply states that higher prices raise the quantity supplied. The **price elasticity of supply** measures how much the quantity supplied responds to changes in the price. Supply of a good is said to be *elastic* if the quantity supplied responds substantially to changes in the price. Supply is said to be *inelastic* if the quantity supplied responds only slightly to changes in the price.

The price elasticity of supply depends on the flexibility of sellers to change the amount of the good they produce. For example, beachfront land has an inelastic supply because it is almost impossible to produce more of it. By contrast, manufactured goods, such as books, cars, and televisions, have elastic supplies because firms that produce them can run their factories longer in response to a higher price.

In most markets, a key determinant of the price elasticity of supply is the time period being considered. Supply is usually more elastic in the long run than in the short run. Over short periods of time, firms cannot easily change the size of their factories to make more or less of a good. Thus, in the short run, the quantity supplied is not very responsive to the price. By contrast, over longer periods, firms can build new factories or close old ones. In addition, new firms can enter a market, and old firms can shut down. Thus, in the long run, the quantity supplied can respond substantially to price changes.

Computing the Price Elasticity of Supply

Now that we have a general understanding about the price elasticity of supply, let's be more precise. Economists compute the price elasticity of supply as the percentage change in the quantity supplied divided by the percentage change in the price. That is,

$$\text{Price elasticity of supply} = \frac{\text{Percentage change in quantity supplied}}{\text{Percentage change in price}}.$$

For example, suppose that an increase in the price of milk from $2.85 to $3.15 a gallon raises the amount that dairy farmers produce from 9,000 to 11,000 gallons per month. Using the midpoint method, we calculate the percentage change in price as

$$\text{Percentage change in price} = (3.15 - 2.85) / 3.00 \times 100 = 10 \text{ percent.}$$

Similarly, we calculate the percentage change in quantity supplied as

$$\text{Percentage change in quantity supplied} = (11{,}000 - 9{,}000) / 10{,}000 \times 100 = 20 \text{ percent.}$$

In this case, the price elasticity of supply is

$$\text{Price elasticity of supply} = \frac{20 \text{ percent}}{10 \text{ percent}} = 2.0.$$

In this example, the elasticity of 2 indicates that the quantity supplied changes proportionately twice as much as the price.

The Variety of Supply Curves

Because the price elasticity of supply measures the responsiveness of quantity supplied to the price, it is reflected in the appearance of the supply curve. Figure 5 shows five cases. In the extreme case of a zero elasticity, as shown in panel (a), supply is *perfectly inelastic*, and the supply curve is vertical. In this case, the quantity supplied is the same regardless of the price. As the elasticity rises, the supply curve gets flatter, which shows that the quantity supplied responds more to changes in the price. At the opposite extreme, shown in panel (e), supply is *perfectly elastic*. This occurs as the price elasticity of supply approaches infinity and the supply curve becomes horizontal, meaning that very small changes in the price lead to very large changes in the quantity supplied.

In some markets, the elasticity of supply is not constant but varies over the supply curve. Figure 6 shows a typical case for an industry in which firms have factories with a limited capacity for production. For low levels of quantity supplied, the elasticity of supply is high, indicating that firms respond substantially to changes in the price. In this region, firms have capacity for production that is not being used, such as plants and equipment idle for all or part of the day. Small increases in price make it profitable for firms to begin using this idle capacity. As the quantity supplied rises, firms begin to reach capacity. Once capacity is fully used, increasing production further requires the construction of new plants. To induce firms to incur this extra expense, the price must rise substantially, so supply becomes less elastic.

Figure 6 presents a numerical example of this phenomenon. When the price rises from $3 to $4 (a 29 percent increase, according to the midpoint method), the quantity supplied rises from 100 to 200 (a 67 percent increase). Because quantity supplied changes proportionately more than the price, the supply curve has elasticity greater than 1. By contrast, when the price rises from $12 to $15 (a 22 percent increase), the quantity supplied rises from 500 to 525 (a 5 percent increase). In this case, quantity supplied moves proportionately less than the price, so the elasticity is less than 1.

QUICK QUIZ *Define the price elasticity of supply.* • *Explain why the price elasticity of supply might be different in the long run than in the short run.*

Figure

The Price Elasticity of Supply

The price elasticity of supply determines whether the supply curve is steep or flat. Note that all percentage changes are calculated using the midpoint method.

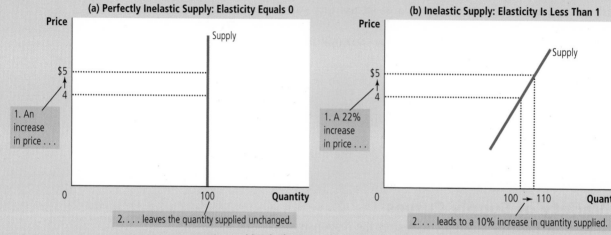

(a) Perfectly Inelastic Supply: Elasticity Equals 0

Price

Supply

$5
4

1. An increase in price . . .

0   100   **Quantity**

2. . . . leaves the quantity supplied unchanged.

(b) Inelastic Supply: Elasticity Is Less Than 1

Price

Supply

$5
4

1. A 22% increase in price . . .

0   100 → 110   **Quantity**

2. . . . leads to a 10% increase in quantity supplied.

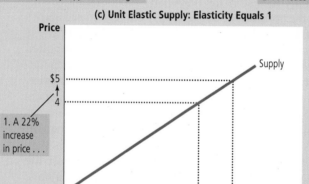

(c) Unit Elastic Supply: Elasticity Equals 1

Price

Supply

$5
4

1. A 22% increase in price . . .

0   100 → 125   **Quantity**

2. . . . leads to a 22% increase in quantity supplied.

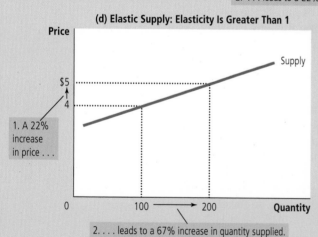

(d) Elastic Supply: Elasticity Is Greater Than 1

Price

Supply

$5
4

1. A 22% increase in price . . .

0   100 → 200   **Quantity**

2. . . . leads to a 67% increase in quantity supplied.

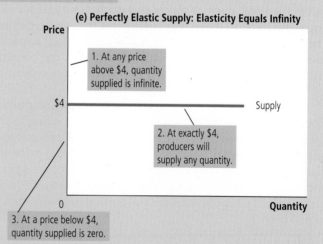

(e) Perfectly Elastic Supply: Elasticity Equals Infinity

Price

1. At any price above $4, quantity supplied is infinite.

$4   Supply

2. At exactly $4, producers will supply any quantity.

0   **Quantity**

3. At a price below $4, quantity supplied is zero.

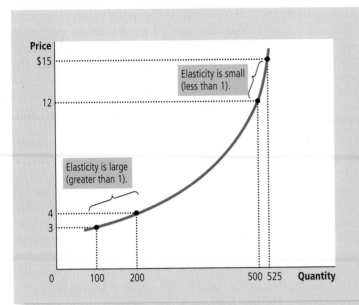

Figure **6**

Price
$15
12
4
3
0   100   200   500 525   **Quantity**

Elasticity is small
(less than 1).

Elasticity is large
(greater than 1).

How the Price Elasticity of Supply Can Vary
Because firms often have a maximum capacity for
production, the elasticity of supply may be very high
at low levels of quantity supplied and very low at high
levels of quantity supplied. Here an increase in price
from $3 to $4 increases the quantity supplied from 100
to 200. Because the 67 percent increase in quantity
supplied (computed using the midpoint method) is
larger than the 29 percent increase in price, the supply
curve is elastic in this range. By contrast, when the
price rises from $12 to $15, the quantity supplied rises
only from 500 to 525. Because the 5 percent increase in
quantity supplied is smaller than the 22 percent increase
in price, the supply curve is inelastic in this range.

Three Applications of Supply, Demand, and Elasticity

Can good news for farming be bad news for farmers? Why did OPEC fail to keep
the price of oil high? Does drug interdiction increase or decrease drug-related
crime? At first, these questions might seem to have little in common. Yet all three
questions are about markets, and all markets are subject to the forces of supply
and demand. Here we apply the versatile tools of supply, demand, and elasticity
to answer these seemingly complex questions.

Can Good News for Farming Be Bad News for Farmers?

Imagine yourself as a Kansas wheat farmer. Because you earn all your income
from selling wheat, you devote much effort to making your land as productive
as possible. You monitor weather and soil conditions, check your fields for pests
and disease, and study the latest advances in farm technology. You know that the
more wheat you grow, the more you will have to sell after the harvest, and the
higher will be your income and your standard of living.

One day, Kansas State University announces a major discovery. Researchers
in its agronomy department have devised a new hybrid of wheat that raises the
amount farmers can produce from each acre of land by 20 percent. How should
you react to this news? Does this discovery make you better off or worse off than
you were before?

Recall from Chapter 4 that we answer such questions in three steps. First, we
examine whether the supply or demand curve shifts. Second, we consider in
which direction the curve shifts. Third, we use the supply-and-demand diagram
to see how the market equilibrium changes.

In this case, the discovery of the new hybrid affects the supply curve. Because the hybrid increases the amount of wheat that can be produced on each acre of land, farmers are now willing to supply more wheat at any given price. In other words, the supply curve shifts to the right. The demand curve remains the same because consumers' desire to buy wheat products at any given price is not affected by the introduction of a new hybrid. Figure 7 shows an example of such a change. When the supply curve shifts from S_1 to S_2, the quantity of wheat sold increases from 100 to 110, and the price of wheat falls from $3 to $2.

Does this discovery make farmers better off? As a first cut to answering this question, consider what happens to the total revenue received by farmers. Farmers' total revenue is $P \times Q$, the price of the wheat times the quantity sold. The discovery affects farmers in two conflicting ways. The hybrid allows farmers to produce more wheat (Q rises), but now each bushel of wheat sells for less (P falls).

Whether total revenue rises or falls depends on the elasticity of demand. In practice, the demand for basic foodstuffs such as wheat is usually inelastic because these items are relatively inexpensive and have few good substitutes. When the demand curve is inelastic, as it is in Figure 7, a decrease in price causes total revenue to fall. You can see this in the figure: The price of wheat falls substantially, whereas the quantity of wheat sold rises only slightly. Total revenue falls from $300 to $220. Thus, the discovery of the new hybrid lowers the total revenue that farmers receive from the sale of their crops.

If farmers are made worse off by the discovery of this new hybrid, one might wonder why they adopt it. The answer goes to the heart of how competitive markets work. Because each farmer is only a small part of the market for wheat, he or she takes the price of wheat as given. For any given price of wheat, it is better to use the new hybrid to produce and sell more wheat. Yet when all farmers do this, the supply of wheat increases, the price falls, and farmers are worse off.

Although this example may at first seem hypothetical, it helps to explain a major change in the U.S. economy over the past century. Two hundred years ago, most Americans lived on farms. Knowledge about farm methods was sufficiently

Figure 7

An Increase in Supply in the Market for Wheat
When an advance in farm technology increases the supply of wheat from S_1 to S_2, the price of wheat falls. Because the demand for wheat is inelastic, the increase in the quantity sold from 100 to 110 is proportionately smaller than the decrease in the price from $3 to $2. As a result, farmers' total revenue falls from $300 ($3 × 100) to $220 ($2 × 110).

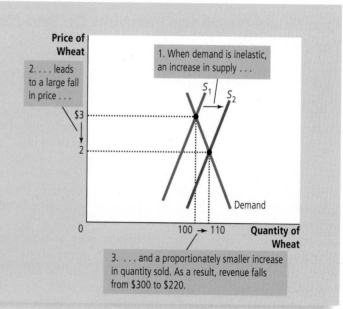

primitive that most Americans had to be farmers to produce enough food to feed the nation's population. Yet over time, advances in farm technology increased the amount of food that each farmer could produce. This increase in food supply, together with inelastic food demand, caused farm revenues to fall, which in turn encouraged people to leave farming.

A few numbers show the magnitude of this historic change. As recently as 1950, 10 million people worked on farms in the United States, representing 17 percent of the labor force. Today, fewer than 3 million people work on farms, or 2 percent of the labor force. This change coincided with tremendous advances in farm productivity: Despite the 70 percent drop in the number of farmers, U.S. farms now produce more than twice the output of crops and livestock that they did in 1950.

This analysis of the market for farm products also helps to explain a seeming paradox of public policy: Certain farm programs try to help farmers by inducing them *not* to plant crops on all of their land. The purpose of these programs is to reduce the supply of farm products and thereby raise prices. With inelastic demand for their products, farmers as a group receive greater total revenue if they supply a smaller crop to the market. No single farmer would choose to leave his land fallow on his own because each takes the market price as given. But if all farmers do so together, each of them can be better off.

When analyzing the effects of farm technology or farm policy, it is important to keep in mind that what is good for farmers is not necessarily good for society as a whole. Improvement in farm technology can be bad for farmers because it makes farmers increasingly unnecessary, but it is surely good for consumers who pay less for food. Similarly, a policy aimed at reducing the supply of farm products may raise the incomes of farmers, but it does so at the expense of consumers.

Why Did OPEC Fail to Keep the Price of Oil High?

Many of the most disruptive events for the world's economies over the past several decades have originated in the world market for oil. In the 1970s, members of the Organization of Petroleum Exporting Countries (OPEC) decided to raise the world price of oil to increase their incomes. These countries accomplished this goal by jointly reducing the amount of oil they supplied. From 1973 to 1974, the price of oil (adjusted for overall inflation) rose more than 50 percent. Then, a few years later, OPEC did the same thing again. From 1979 to 1981, the price of oil approximately doubled.

Yet OPEC found it difficult to maintain a high price. From 1982 to 1985, the price of oil steadily declined about 10 percent per year. Dissatisfaction and disarray soon prevailed among the OPEC countries. In 1986, cooperation among OPEC members completely broke down, and the price of oil plunged 45 percent. In 1990, the price of oil (adjusted for overall inflation) was back to where it began in 1970, and it stayed at that low level throughout most of the 1990s. (In the first decade of the 21st century, the price of oil fluctuated substantially once again, but the main driving force was changes in world demand rather than OPEC supply restrictions. Early in the decade, oil demand and prices spiked up, in part because of a large and rapidly growing Chinese economy. Prices plunged in 2008–2009 as the world economy fell into a deep recession and then started rising once again as the world economy started to recover.)

The OPEC episodes of the 1970s and 1980s show how supply and demand can behave differently in the short run and in the long run. In the short run, both the supply and demand for oil are relatively inelastic. Supply is inelastic because the quantity of known oil reserves and the capacity for oil extraction cannot be changed quickly. Demand is inelastic because buying habits do not respond immediately to changes in price. Thus, as panel (a) of Figure 8 shows, the short-run supply and demand curves are steep. When the supply of oil shifts from S_1 to S_2, the price increase from P_1 to P_2 is large.

The situation is very different in the long run. Over long periods of time, producers of oil outside OPEC respond to high prices by increasing oil exploration and by building new extraction capacity. Consumers respond with greater conservation, such as by replacing old inefficient cars with newer efficient ones. Thus, as panel (b) of Figure 8 shows, the long-run supply and demand curves are

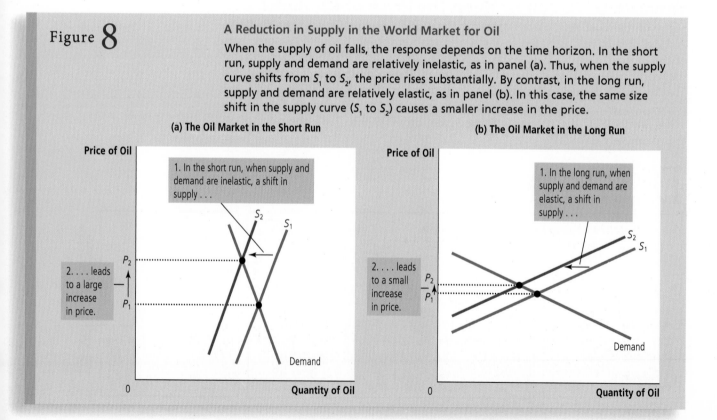

Figure **8**

A Reduction in Supply in the World Market for Oil

When the supply of oil falls, the response depends on the time horizon. In the short run, supply and demand are relatively inelastic, as in panel (a). Thus, when the supply curve shifts from S_1 to S_2, the price rises substantially. By contrast, in the long run, supply and demand are relatively elastic, as in panel (b). In this case, the same size shift in the supply curve (S_1 to S_2) causes a smaller increase in the price.

(a) The Oil Market in the Short Run

Price of Oil

1. In the short run, when supply and demand are inelastic, a shift in supply . . .

S_2 S_1

2. . . . leads to a large increase in price.

P_2

P_1

Demand

0   Quantity of Oil

(b) The Oil Market in the Long Run

Price of Oil

1. In the long run, when supply and demand are elastic, a shift in supply . . .

S_2 S_1

2. . . . leads to a small increase in price.

P_2

P_1

Demand

0   Quantity of Oil

more elastic. In the long run, the shift in the supply curve from S_1 to S_2 causes a much smaller increase in the price.

This analysis shows why OPEC succeeded in maintaining a high price of oil only in the short run. When OPEC countries agreed to reduce their production of oil, they shifted the supply curve to the left. Even though each OPEC member sold less oil, the price rose by so much in the short run that OPEC incomes rose. By contrast, in the long run, when supply and demand are more elastic, the same reduction in supply, measured by the horizontal shift in the supply curve, caused a smaller increase in the price. Thus, OPEC's coordinated reduction in supply proved less profitable in the long run. The cartel learned that raising prices is easier in the short run than in the long run.

Does Drug Interdiction Increase or Decrease Drug-Related Crime?

A persistent problem facing our society is the use of illegal drugs, such as heroin, cocaine, ecstasy, and crack. Drug use has several adverse effects. One is that drug dependence can ruin the lives of drug users and their families. Another is that drug addicts often turn to robbery and other violent crimes to obtain the money needed to support their habit. To discourage the use of illegal drugs, the U.S. government devotes billions of dollars each year to reduce the flow of drugs into the country. Let's use the tools of supply and demand to examine this policy of drug interdiction.

Suppose the government increases the number of federal agents devoted to the war on drugs. What happens in the market for illegal drugs? As is usual, we answer this question in three steps. First, we consider whether the supply or demand curve shifts. Second, we consider the direction of the shift. Third, we see how the shift affects the equilibrium price and quantity.

Although the purpose of drug interdiction is to reduce drug use, its direct impact is on the sellers of drugs rather than the buyers. When the government stops some drugs from entering the country and arrests more smugglers, it raises the cost of selling drugs and, therefore, reduces the quantity of drugs supplied at any given price. The demand for drugs—the amount buyers want at any given price—is not changed. As panel (a) of Figure 9 shows, interdiction shifts the supply curve to the left from S_1 to S_2 and leaves the demand curve the same. The equilibrium price of drugs rises from P_1 to P_2, and the equilibrium quantity falls from Q_1 to Q_2. The fall in the equilibrium quantity shows that drug interdiction does reduce drug use.

But what about the amount of drug-related crime? To answer this question, consider the total amount that drug users pay for the drugs they buy. Because few drug addicts are likely to break their destructive habits in response to a higher price, it is likely that the demand for drugs is inelastic, as it is drawn in the figure. If demand is inelastic, then an increase in price raises total revenue in the drug market. That is, because drug interdiction raises the price of drugs proportionately more than it reduces drug use, it raises the total amount of money that drug users pay for drugs. Addicts who already had to steal to support their habits would have an even greater need for quick cash. Thus, drug interdiction could increase drug-related crime.

Because of this adverse effect of drug interdiction, some analysts argue for alternative approaches to the drug problem. Rather than trying to reduce the supply of drugs, policymakers might try to reduce the demand by pursuing a policy of drug education. Successful drug education has the effects shown in panel (b) of Figure 9. The demand curve shifts to the left from D_1 to D_2. As a result, the equilibrium quantity falls from Q_1 to Q_2, and the equilibrium price falls from P_1 to P_2.

Figure **9**

Policies to Reduce the Use of Illegal Drugs

Drug interdiction reduces the supply of drugs from S_1 to S_2, as in panel (a). If the demand for drugs is inelastic, then the total amount paid by drug users rises, even as the amount of drug use falls. By contrast, drug education reduces the demand for drugs from D_1 to D_2, as in panel (b). Because both price and quantity fall, the amount paid by drug users falls.

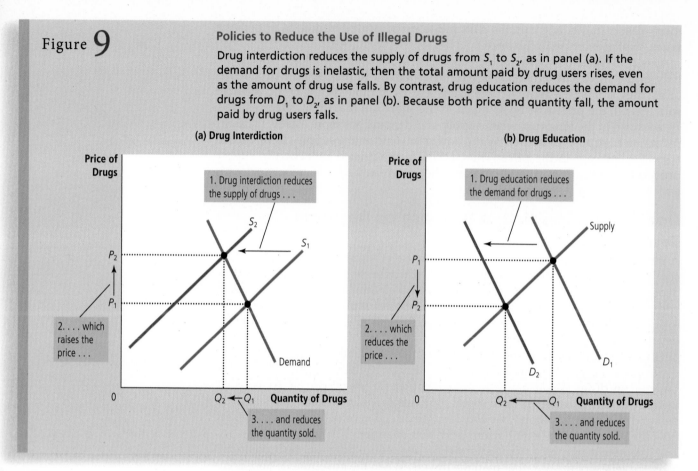

(a) Drug Interdiction

Price of Drugs

1. Drug interdiction reduces the supply of drugs . . .

S_2

S_1

P_2

P_1

2. . . . which raises the price . . .

Demand

0

$Q_2 \leftarrow Q_1$ **Quantity of Drugs**

3. . . . and reduces the quantity sold.

(b) Drug Education

Price of Drugs

1. Drug education reduces the demand for drugs . . .

Supply

P_1

P_2

2. . . . which reduces the price . . .

D_1

D_2

0

$Q_2 \leftarrow Q_1$ **Quantity of Drugs**

3. . . . and reduces the quantity sold.

Total revenue, which is price times quantity, also falls. Thus, in contrast to drug interdiction, drug education can reduce both drug use and drug-related crime.

Advocates of drug interdiction might argue that the long-run effects of this policy are different from the short-run effects because the elasticity of demand depends on the time horizon. The demand for drugs is probably inelastic over short periods because higher prices do not substantially affect drug use by established addicts. But demand may be more elastic over longer periods because higher prices would discourage experimentation with drugs among the young and, over time, lead to fewer drug addicts. In this case, drug interdiction would increase drug-related crime in the short run while decreasing it in the long run.

QUICK QUIZ   *How might a drought that destroys half of all farm crops be good for farmers? If such a drought is good for farmers, why don't farmers destroy their own crops in the absence of a drought?*

Conclusion

According to an old quip, even a parrot can become an economist simply by learning to say "supply and demand." These last two chapters should have convinced you that there is much truth in this statement. The tools of supply and demand allow you to analyze many of the most important events and policies that shape the economy. You are now well on your way to becoming an economist (or at least a well-educated parrot).

SUMMARY

- The price elasticity of demand measures how much the quantity demanded responds to changes in the price. Demand tends to be more elastic if close substitutes are available, if the good is a luxury rather than a necessity, if the market is narrowly defined, or if buyers have substantial time to react to a price change.

- The price elasticity of demand is calculated as the percentage change in quantity demanded divided by the percentage change in price. If quantity demanded moves proportionately less than the price, then the elasticity is less than 1, and demand is said to be inelastic. If quantity demanded moves proportionately more than the price, then the elasticity is greater than 1, and demand is said to be elastic.

- Total revenue, the total amount paid for a good, equals the price of the good times the quantity sold. For inelastic demand curves, total revenue moves in the same direction as the price. For elastic demand curves, total revenue moves in the opposite direction as the price.

- The income elasticity of demand measures how much the quantity demanded responds to changes in consumers' income. The cross-price elasticity of demand measures how much the quantity demanded of one good responds to changes in the price of another good.

- The price elasticity of supply measures how much the quantity supplied responds to changes in the price. This elasticity often depends on the time horizon under consideration. In most markets, supply is more elastic in the long run than in the short run.

- The price elasticity of supply is calculated as the percentage change in quantity supplied divided by the percentage change in price. If quantity supplied moves proportionately less than the price, then the elasticity is less than 1, and supply is said to be inelastic. If quantity supplied moves proportionately more than the price, then the elasticity is greater than 1, and supply is said to be elastic.

- The tools of supply and demand can be applied in many different kinds of markets. This chapter uses them to analyze the market for wheat, the market for oil, and the market for illegal drugs.

KEY CONCEPTS

elasticity, *p. 90*
price elasticity of demand, *p. 90*
total revenue, *p. 94*

income elasticity of demand, *p. 97*
cross-price elasticity of
   demand, *p. 97*

price elasticity of supply, *p. 98*

QUESTIONS FOR REVIEW

1. Define the price elasticity of demand and the income elasticity of demand.
2. List and explain the four determinants of the price elasticity of demand discussed in the chapter.
3. What is the main advantage of using the midpoint method for calculating elasticity?
4. If the elasticity is greater than 1, is demand elastic or inelastic? If the elasticity equals 0, is demand perfectly elastic or perfectly inelastic?

5. On a supply-and-demand diagram, show equilibrium price, equilibrium quantity, and the total revenue received by producers.
6. If demand is elastic, how will an increase in price change total revenue? Explain.
7. What do we call a good whose income elasticity is less than 0?
8. How is the price elasticity of supply calculated? Explain what it measures.
9. What is the price elasticity of supply of Picasso paintings?

10. Is the price elasticity of supply usually larger in the short run or in the long run? Why?

11. How can elasticity help explain why drug interdiction could reduce the supply of drugs, yet possibly increase drug-related crime?

PROBLEMS AND APPLICATIONS

1. For each of the following pairs of goods, which good would you expect to have more elastic demand and why?
   a. required textbooks or mystery novels
   b. Beethoven recordings or classical music recordings in general
   c. subway rides during the next six months or subway rides during the next five years
   d. root beer or water

2. Suppose that business travelers and vacationers have the following demand for airline tickets from New York to Boston:

Price	Quantity Demanded (business travelers)	Quantity Demanded (vacationers)
$150	2,100 tickets	1,000 tickets
200	2,000	800
250	1,900	600
300	1,800	400

   a. As the price of tickets rises from $200 to $250, what is the price elasticity of demand for (i) business travelers and (ii) vacationers? (Use the midpoint method in your calculations.)
   b. Why might vacationers have a different elasticity from business travelers?

3. Suppose the price elasticity of demand for heating oil is 0.2 in the short run and 0.7 in the long run.
   a. if the price of heating oil rises from $1.80 to $2.20 per gallon, what happens to the quantity of heating oil demanded in the short run? In the long run? (Use the midpoint method in your calculations.)
   b. Why might this elasticity depend on the time horizon?

4. A price change causes the quantity demanded of a good to decrease by 30 percent, while the total revenue of that good increases by 15 percent. Is the demand curve elastic or inelastic? Explain.

5. The equilibrium price of coffee mugs rose sharply last month, but the equilibrium quantity was the same as ever. Three people tried to explain the situation. Which explanations could be right? Explain your logic.

   BILLY: Demand increased, but supply was totally inelastic.
   MARIAN: Supply increased, but so did demand.
   VALERIE: Supply decreased, but demand was totally inelastic.

6. Suppose that your demand schedule for DVDs is as follows:

Price	Quantity Demanded (income = $10,000)	Quantity Demanded (income = $12,000)
$ 8	40 DVDs	50 DVDs
10	32	45
12	24	30
14	16	20
16	8	12

   a. Use the midpoint method to calculate your price elasticity of demand as the price of DVDs increases from $8 to $10 if (i) your income is $10,000 and (ii) your income is $12,000.
   b. Calculate your income elasticity of demand as your income increases from $10,000 to $12,000 if (i) the price is $12 and (ii) the price is $16.

7. You have the following information about good X and good Y:
   • Income elasticity of demand for good X: –3
   • Cross-price elasticity of demand for good X with respect to the price of good Y: 2

   Would an increase in income and a decrease in the price of good Y unambiguously decrease the demand for good X? Why or why not?

8. Maria has decided always to spend one-third of her income on clothing.

a. What is her income elasticity of clothing demand?

b. What is her price elasticity of clothing demand?

c. If Maria's tastes change and she decides to spend only one-fourth of her income on clothing, how does her demand curve change? What is her income elasticity and price elasticity now?

9. The *New York Times* reported (Feb. 17, 1996) that subway ridership declined after a fare increase: "There were nearly four million fewer riders in December 1995, the first full month after the price of a token increased 25 cents to $1.50, than in the previous December, a 4.3 percent decline."

a. Use these data to estimate the price elasticity of demand for subway rides.

b. According to your estimate, what happens to the Transit Authority's revenue when the fare rises?

c. Why might your estimate of the elasticity be unreliable?

10. Two drivers—Tom and Jerry—each drive up to a gas station. Before looking at the price, each places an order. Tom says, "I'd like 10 gallons of gas." Jerry says, "I'd like $10 worth of gas." What is each driver's price elasticity of demand?

11. Consider public policy aimed at smoking.

a. Studies indicate that the price elasticity of demand for cigarettes is about 0.4. If a pack of cigarettes currently costs $2 and the government wants to reduce smoking by 20 percent, by how much should it increase the price?

b. If the government permanently increases the price of cigarettes, will the policy have a larger effect on smoking one year from now or five years from now?

c. Studies also find that teenagers have a higher price elasticity than do adults. Why might this be true?

12. You are the curator of a museum. The museum is running short of funds, so you decide to increase revenue. Should you increase or decrease the price of admission? Explain.

13. Pharmaceutical drugs have an inelastic demand, and computers have an elastic demand. Suppose that technological advance doubles the supply of both products (that is, the quantity supplied at each price is twice what it was).

a. What happens to the equilibrium price and quantity in each market?

b. Which product experiences a larger change in price?

c. Which product experiences a larger change in quantity?

d. What happens to total consumer spending on each product?

14. Several years ago, flooding along the Missouri and the Mississippi rivers destroyed thousands of acres of wheat.

a. Farmers whose crops were destroyed by the floods were much worse off, but farmers whose crops were not destroyed benefited from the floods. Why?

b. What information would you need about the market for wheat to assess whether farmers as a group were hurt or helped by the floods?

15. Explain why the following might be true: A drought around the world raises the total revenue that farmers receive from the sale of grain, but a drought only in Kansas reduces the total revenue that Kansas farmers receive.

For further information on topics in this chapter, additional problems, applications, examples, online quizzes, and more, please visit our website at www .cengage.com/economics/mankiw.

Supply, Demand, and Government Policies

Economists have two roles. As scientists, they develop and test theories to explain the world around them. As policy advisers, they use their theories to help change the world for the better. The focus of the preceding two chapters has been scientific. We have seen how supply and demand determine the price of a good and the quantity of the good sold. We have also seen how various events shift supply and demand and thereby change the equilibrium price and quantity.

This chapter offers our first look at policy. Here we analyze various types of government policy using only the tools of supply and demand. As you will see, the analysis yields some surprising insights. Policies often have effects that their architects did not intend or anticipate.

We begin by considering policies that directly control prices. For example, rent-control laws dictate a maximum rent that landlords may charge tenants. Minimum-wage laws dictate the lowest wage that firms may pay workers. Price controls are usually enacted when policymakers believe that the market price of a good or service is unfair to buyers or sellers. Yet, as we will see, these policies can generate inequities of their own.

After discussing price controls, we consider the impact of taxes. Policymakers use taxes to raise revenue for public purposes and to influence market outcomes. Although the prevalence of taxes in our economy is obvious, their effects are not. For example, when the government levies a tax on the amount that firms pay their workers, do the firms or the workers bear the burden of the tax? The answer is not at all clear—until we apply the powerful tools of supply and demand.

Controls on Prices

To see how price controls affect market outcomes, let's look once again at the market for ice cream. As we saw in Chapter 4, if ice cream is sold in a competitive market free of government regulation, the price of ice cream adjusts to balance supply and demand: At the equilibrium price, the quantity of ice cream that buyers want to buy exactly equals the quantity that sellers want to sell. To be concrete, suppose the equilibrium price is $3 per cone.

Not everyone may be happy with the outcome of this free-market process. Let's say the American Association of Ice-Cream Eaters complains that the $3 price is too high for everyone to enjoy a cone a day (their recommended daily allowance). Meanwhile, the National Organization of Ice-Cream Makers complains that the $3 price—the result of "cutthroat competition"—is too low and is depressing the incomes of its members. Each of these groups lobbies the government to pass laws that alter the market outcome by directly controlling the price of an ice-cream cone.

price ceiling

a legal maximum on the price at which a good can be sold

price floor

a legal minimum on the price at which a good can be sold

Because buyers of any good always want a lower price while sellers want a higher price, the interests of the two groups conflict. If the Ice-Cream Eaters are successful in their lobbying, the government imposes a legal maximum on the price at which ice-cream cones can be sold. Because the price is not allowed to rise above this level, the legislated maximum is called a **price ceiling.** By contrast, if the Ice-Cream Makers are successful, the government imposes a legal minimum on the price. Because the price cannot fall below this level, the legislated minimum is called a **price floor.** Let us consider the effects of these policies in turn.

How Price Ceilings Affect Market Outcomes

When the government, moved by the complaints and campaign contributions of the Ice-Cream Eaters, imposes a price ceiling on the market for ice cream, two outcomes are possible. In panel (a) of Figure 1, the government imposes a price ceiling of $4 per cone. In this case, because the price that balances supply and demand ($3) is below the ceiling, the price ceiling is *not binding*. Market forces naturally move the economy to the equilibrium, and the price ceiling has no effect on the price or the quantity sold.

Panel (b) of Figure 1 shows the other, more interesting, possibility. In this case, the government imposes a price ceiling of $2 per cone. Because the equilibrium price of $3 is above the price ceiling, the ceiling is a *binding constraint* on the market. The forces of supply and demand tend to move the price toward the equilibrium price, but when the market price hits the ceiling, it can, by law, rise no further. Thus, the market price equals the price ceiling. At this price, the quantity of ice cream demanded (125 cones in the figure) exceeds the quantity supplied

In panel (a), the government imposes a price ceiling of $4. Because the price ceiling is above the equilibrium price of $3, the price ceiling has no effect, and the market can reach the equilibrium of supply and demand. In this equilibrium, quantity supplied and quantity demanded both equal 100 cones. In panel (b), the government imposes a price ceiling of $2. Because the price ceiling is below the equilibrium price of $3, the market price equals $2. At this price, 125 cones are demanded and only 75 are supplied, so there is a shortage of 50 cones.

Figure **1**

A Market with a Price Ceiling

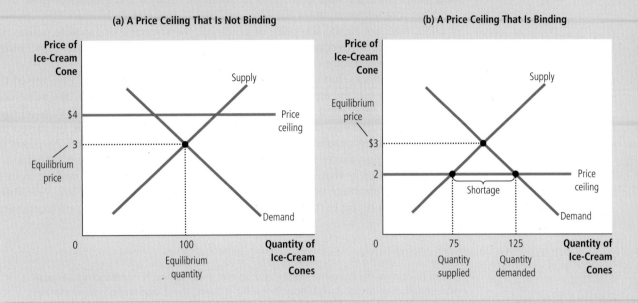

(a) A Price Ceiling That Is Not Binding

(b) A Price Ceiling That Is Binding

(75 cones). There is a shortage: 50 people who want to buy ice cream at the going price are unable to do so.

In response to this shortage, some mechanism for rationing ice cream will naturally develop. The mechanism could be long lines: Buyers who are willing to arrive early and wait in line get a cone, but those unwilling to wait do not. Alternatively, sellers could ration ice-cream cones according to their own personal biases, selling them only to friends, relatives, or members of their own racial or ethnic group. Notice that even though the price ceiling was motivated by a desire to help buyers of ice cream, not all buyers benefit from the policy. Some buyers do get to pay a lower price, although they may have to wait in line to do so, but other buyers cannot get any ice cream at all.

This example in the market for ice cream shows a general result: *When the government imposes a binding price ceiling on a competitive market, a shortage of the good arises, and sellers must ration the scarce goods among the large number of potential buyers.* The rationing mechanisms that develop under price ceilings are rarely desirable. Long lines are inefficient because they waste buyers' time. Discrimination according to seller bias is both inefficient (because the good does not necessarily go to the buyer who values it most highly) and potentially unfair. By contrast, the rationing mechanism in a free, competitive market is both efficient and impersonal. When the market for ice cream reaches its equilibrium, anyone who wants to pay the market price can get a cone. Free markets ration goods with prices.

CASE
STUDY
Lines at the Gas Pump

As we discussed in the preceding chapter, in 1973 the Organization of Petroleum Exporting Countries (OPEC) raised the price of crude oil in world oil markets. Because crude oil is the major input used to make gasoline, the higher oil prices reduced the supply of gasoline. Long lines at gas stations became commonplace, and motorists often had to wait for hours to buy only a few gallons of gas.

What was responsible for the long gas lines? Most people blame OPEC. Surely, if OPEC had not raised the price of crude oil, the shortage of gasoline would not have occurred. Yet economists blame U.S. government regulations that limited the price oil companies could charge for gasoline.

Figure 2 shows what happened. As shown in panel (a), before OPEC raised the price of crude oil, the equilibrium price of gasoline, P_1, was below the price ceiling. The price regulation, therefore, had no effect. When the price of crude oil rose, however, the situation changed. The increase in the price of crude oil raised the cost of producing gasoline, and this reduced the supply of gasoline. As panel (b) shows, the supply curve shifted to the left from S_1 to S_2. In an unregulated market, this shift in supply would have raised the equilibrium price of gasoline from P_1 to P_2, and no shortage would have resulted. Instead, the price ceiling prevented the price from rising to the equilibrium level. At the price ceiling, producers were

---

Figure **2**

The Market for Gasoline with a Price Ceiling

Panel (a) shows the gasoline market when the price ceiling is not binding because the equilibrium price, P_1, is below the ceiling. Panel (b) shows the gasoline market after an increase in the price of crude oil (an input into making gasoline) shifts the supply curve to the left from S_1 to S_2. In an unregulated market, the price would have risen from P_1 to P_2. The price ceiling, however, prevents this from happening. At the binding price ceiling, consumers are willing to buy Q_D, but producers of gasoline are willing to sell only Q_S. The difference between quantity demanded and quantity supplied, $Q_D - Q_S$, measures the gasoline shortage.

(a) The Price Ceiling on Gasoline Is Not Binding

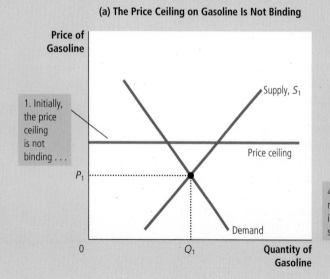

(b) The Price Ceiling on Gasoline Is Binding

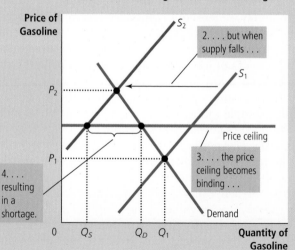

willing to sell Q_S, and consumers were willing to buy Q_D. Thus, the shift in supply caused a severe shortage at the regulated price.

Eventually, the laws regulating the price of gasoline were repealed. Lawmakers came to understand that they were partly responsible for the many hours Americans lost waiting in line to buy gasoline. Today, when the price of crude oil changes, the price of gasoline can adjust to bring supply and demand into equilibrium. ■

Rent Control in the Short Run and the Long Run

One common example of a price ceiling is rent control. In many cities, the local government places a ceiling on rents that landlords may charge their tenants. The goal of this policy is to help the poor by making housing more affordable. Economists often criticize rent control, arguing that it is a highly inefficient way to help the poor raise their standard of living. One economist called rent control "the best way to destroy a city, other than bombing."

The adverse effects of rent control are less apparent to the general population because these effects occur over many years. In the short run, landlords have a fixed number of apartments to rent, and they cannot adjust this number quickly as market conditions change. Moreover, the number of people searching for housing in a city may not be highly responsive to rents in the short run because people take time to adjust their housing arrangements. Therefore, the short-run supply and demand for housing are relatively inelastic.

Panel (a) of Figure 3 shows the short-run effects of rent control on the housing market. As with any binding price ceiling, rent control causes a shortage. Yet because

Panel (a) shows the short-run effects of rent control: Because the supply and demand curves for apartments are relatively inelastic, the price ceiling imposed by a rent-control law causes only a small shortage of housing. Panel (b) shows the long-run effects of rent control: Because the supply and demand curves for apartments are more elastic, rent control causes a large shortage.

Figure 3

Rent Control in the Short Run and in the Long Run

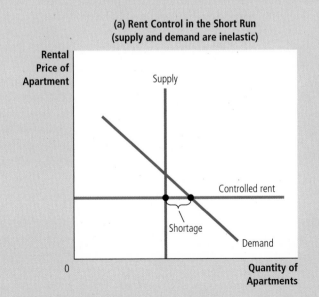

supply and demand are inelastic in the short run, the initial shortage caused by rent control is small. The primary effect in the short run is to reduce rents.

The long-run story is very different because the buyers and sellers of rental housing respond more to market conditions as time passes. On the supply side, landlords respond to low rents by not building new apartments and by failing to maintain existing ones. On the demand side, low rents encourage people to find their own apartments (rather than living with their parents or sharing apartments with roommates) and induce more people to move into a city. Therefore, both supply and demand are more elastic in the long run.

Panel (b) of Figure 3 illustrates the housing market in the long run. When rent control depresses rents below the equilibrium level, the quantity of apartments supplied falls substantially, and the quantity of apartments demanded rises substantially. The result is a large shortage of housing.

In cities with rent control, landlords use various mechanisms to ration housing. Some landlords keep long waiting lists. Others give a preference to tenants without children. Still others discriminate on the basis of race. Sometimes apartments are allocated to those willing to offer under-the-table payments to building superintendents. In essence, these bribes bring the total price of an apartment (including the bribe) closer to the equilibrium price.

To understand fully the effects of rent control, we have to remember one of the *Ten Principles of Economics* from Chapter 1: People respond to incentives. In free markets, landlords try to keep their buildings clean and safe because desirable apartments command higher prices. By contrast, when rent control creates shortages and waiting lists, landlords lose their incentive to respond to tenants' concerns. Why should a landlord spend money to maintain and improve the property when people are waiting to get in as it is? In the end, tenants get lower rents, but they also get lower-quality housing.

Policymakers often react to the effects of rent control by imposing additional regulations. For example, various laws make racial discrimination in housing illegal and require landlords to provide minimally adequate living conditions. These laws, however, are difficult and costly to enforce. By contrast, when rent control is eliminated and a market for housing is regulated by the forces of competition, such laws are less necessary. In a free market, the price of housing adjusts to eliminate the shortages that give rise to undesirable landlord behavior. ■

How Price Floors Affect Market Outcomes

To examine the effects of another kind of government price control, let's return to the market for ice cream. Imagine now that the government is persuaded by the pleas of the National Organization of Ice-Cream Makers whose members feel the $3 equilibrium price is too low. In this case, the government might institute a price floor. Price floors, like price ceilings, are an attempt by the government to maintain prices at other than equilibrium levels. Whereas a price ceiling places a legal maximum on prices, a price floor places a legal minimum.

When the government imposes a price floor on the ice-cream market, two outcomes are possible. If the government imposes a price floor of $2 per cone when the equilibrium price is $3, we obtain the outcome in panel (a) of Figure 4. In this case, because the equilibrium price is above the floor, the price floor is not binding. Market forces naturally move the economy to the equilibrium, and the price floor has no effect.

Panel (b) of Figure 4 shows what happens when the government imposes a price floor of $4 per cone. In this case, because the equilibrium price of $3 is below

In panel (a), the government imposes a price floor of $2. Because this is below the equilibrium price of $3, the price floor has no effect. The market price adjusts to balance supply and demand. At the equilibrium, quantity supplied and quantity demanded both equal 100 cones. In panel (b), the government imposes a price floor of $4, which is above the equilibrium price of $3. Therefore, the market price equals $4. Because 120 cones are supplied at this price and only 80 are demanded, there is a surplus of 40 cones.

Figure 4

A Market with a Price Floor

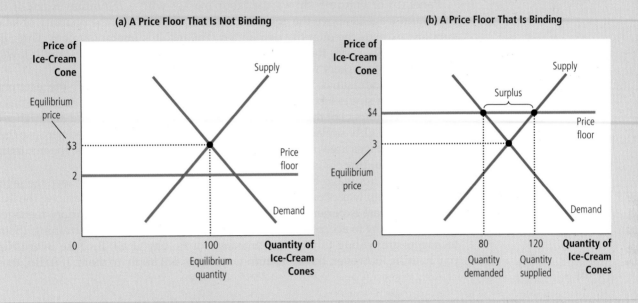

the floor, the price floor is a binding constraint on the market. The forces of supply and demand tend to move the price toward the equilibrium price, but when the market price hits the floor, it can fall no further. The market price equals the price floor. At this floor, the quantity of ice cream supplied (120 cones) exceeds the quantity demanded (80 cones). Some people who want to sell ice cream at the going price are unable to. *Thus, a binding price floor causes a surplus.*

Just as the shortages resulting from price ceilings can lead to undesirable rationing mechanisms, so can the surpluses resulting from price floors. In the case of a price floor, some sellers are unable to sell all they want at the market price. The sellers who appeal to the personal biases of the buyers, perhaps due to racial or familial ties, are better able to sell their goods than those who do not. By contrast, in a free market, the price serves as the rationing mechanism, and sellers can sell all they want at the equilibrium price.

The Minimum Wage

An important example of a price floor is the minimum wage. Minimum-wage laws dictate the lowest price for labor that any employer may pay. The U.S. Congress first instituted a minimum wage with the Fair Labor Standards Act of 1938 to ensure workers a minimally adequate standard of living. In 2009, the minimum wage according to federal law was $7.25 per hour. (Some states mandate minimum wages above the federal level.) Most European nations have minimum-wage laws as well; some, such as France and the United Kingdom, have significantly higher minimums than the United States.

To examine the effects of a minimum wage, we must consider the market for labor. Panel (a) of Figure 5 shows the labor market, which, like all markets, is subject to the forces of supply and demand. Workers determine the supply of labor, and firms determine the demand. If the government doesn't intervene, the wage normally adjusts to balance labor supply and labor demand.

Panel (b) of Figure 5 shows the labor market with a minimum wage. If the minimum wage is above the equilibrium level, as it is here, the quantity of labor supplied exceeds the quantity demanded. The result is unemployment. Thus, the minimum wage raises the incomes of those workers who have jobs, but it lowers the incomes of workers who cannot find jobs.

To fully understand the minimum wage, keep in mind that the economy contains not a single labor market but many labor markets for different types of workers. The impact of the minimum wage depends on the skill and experience of the worker. Highly skilled and experienced workers are not affected because their equilibrium wages are well above the minimum. For these workers, the minimum wage is not binding.

The minimum wage has its greatest impact on the market for teenage labor. The equilibrium wages of teenagers are low because teenagers are among the least skilled and least experienced members of the labor force. In addition, teenagers are often willing to accept a lower wage in exchange for on-the-job training. (Some teenagers are willing to work as "interns" for no pay at all. Because internships pay nothing, however, the minimum wage does not apply to them. If it did, these

Figure 5

How the Minimum Wage Affects the Labor Market

Panel (a) shows a labor market in which the wage adjusts to balance labor supply and labor demand. Panel (b) shows the impact of a binding minimum wage. Because the minimum wage is a price floor, it causes a surplus: The quantity of labor supplied exceeds the quantity demanded. The result is unemployment.

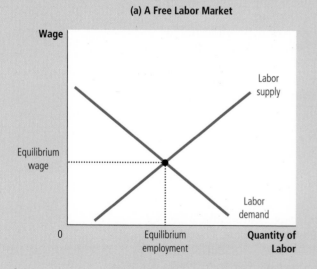

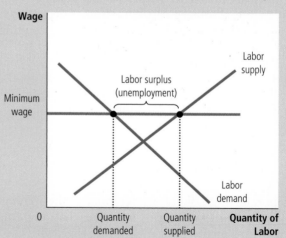

jobs might not exist.) As a result, the minimum wage is more often binding for teenagers than for other members of the labor force.

Many economists have studied how minimum-wage laws affect the teenage labor market. These researchers compare the changes in the minimum wage over time with the changes in teenage employment. Although there is some debate about how much the minimum wage affects employment, the typical study finds that a 10 percent increase in the minimum wage depresses teenage employment between 1 and 3 percent. In interpreting this estimate, note that a 10 percent increase in the minimum wage does not raise the average wage of teenagers by 10 percent. A change in the law does not directly affect those teenagers who are already paid well above the minimum, and enforcement of minimum-wage laws is not perfect. Thus, the estimated drop in employment of 1 to 3 percent is significant.

In addition to altering the quantity of labor demanded, the minimum wage alters the quantity supplied. Because the minimum wage raises the wage that teenagers can earn, it increases the number of teenagers who choose to look for jobs. Studies have found that a higher minimum wage influences which teenagers are employed. When the minimum wage rises, some teenagers who are still attending high school choose to drop out and take jobs. These new dropouts displace other teenagers who had already dropped out of school and who now become unemployed.

The minimum wage is a frequent topic of debate. Economists are about evenly divided on the issue. In a 2006 survey of Ph.D. economists, 47 percent favored eliminating the minimum wage, while 14 percent would maintain it at its current level and 38 percent would increase it.

Advocates of the minimum wage view the policy as one way to raise the income of the working poor. They correctly point out that workers who earn the minimum wage can afford only a meager standard of living. In 2009, for instance, when the minimum wage was $7.25 per hour, two adults working 40 hours a week for every week of the year at minimum-wage jobs had a total annual income of only $30,160, which was less than two-thirds of the median family income in the United States. Many advocates of the minimum wage admit that it has some adverse effects, including unemployment, but they believe that these effects are small and that, all things considered, a higher minimum wage makes the poor better off.

Opponents of the minimum wage contend that it is not the best way to combat poverty. They note that a high minimum wage causes unemployment, encourages teenagers to drop out of school, and prevents some unskilled workers from getting the on-the-job training they need. Moreover, opponents of the minimum wage point out that it is a poorly targeted policy. Not all minimum-wage workers are heads of households trying to help their families escape poverty. In fact, fewer than a third of minimum-wage earners are in families with incomes below the poverty line. Many are teenagers from middle-class homes working at part-time jobs for extra spending money. ■

Evaluating Price Controls

One of the *Ten Principles of Economics* discussed in Chapter 1 is that markets are usually a good way to organize economic activity. This principle explains why economists usually oppose price ceilings and price floors. To economists, prices are not the outcome of some haphazard process. Prices, they contend, are the

······················· in the **news**

> ## Should Unpaid Internships Be Allowed?

Some students take internships without pay to gain skills and experience. Regulators are starting to ask whether this should be legal.

The Unpaid Intern, Legal or Not

BY STEVEN GREENHOUSE

With job openings scarce for young people, the number of unpaid internships has climbed in recent years, leading federal and state regulators to worry that more employers are illegally using such internships for free labor.

Convinced that many unpaid internships violate minimum wage laws, officials in Oregon, California and other states have

begun investigations and fined employers. Last year, M. Patricia Smith, then New York's labor commissioner, ordered investigations into several firms' internships. Now, as the federal Labor Department's top law enforcement official, she and the wage and hour division are stepping up enforcement nationwide....

The Labor Department says it is cracking down on firms that fail to pay interns properly and expanding efforts to educate companies, colleges and students on the law regarding internships.

"If you're a for-profit employer or you want to pursue an internship with a

for-profit employer, there aren't going to be many circumstances where you can have an internship and not be paid and still be in compliance with the law," said Nancy J. Leppink, the acting director of the department's wage and hour division.

Note from the author: The rules discussed in this article are being applied to for-profit firms but not to government. Many government internships, including those at congressional offices, are unpaid. The Labor Department is not trying to prohibit this arrangement.

Source: *New York Times,* April 2, 2010.

result of the millions of business and consumer decisions that lie behind the supply and demand curves. Prices have the crucial job of balancing supply and demand and, thereby, coordinating economic activity. When policymakers set prices by legal decree, they obscure the signals that normally guide the allocation of society's resources.

Another one of the *Ten Principles of Economics* is that governments can sometimes improve market outcomes. Indeed, policymakers are led to control prices because they view the market's outcome as unfair. Price controls are often aimed at helping the poor. For instance, rent-control laws try to make housing affordable for everyone, and minimum-wage laws try to help people escape poverty.

Yet price controls often hurt those they are trying to help. Rent control may keep rents low, but it also discourages landlords from maintaining their buildings and makes housing hard to find. Minimum-wage laws may raise the incomes of some workers, but they also cause other workers to be unemployed.

Helping those in need can be accomplished in ways other than controlling prices. For instance, the government can make housing more affordable by paying a fraction of the rent for poor families. Unlike rent control, such rent subsidies do not reduce the quantity of housing supplied and, therefore, do not lead to housing shortages. Similarly, wage subsidies raise the living standards of the working poor without discouraging firms from hiring them. An example of a wage subsidy is the *earned income tax credit*, a government program that supplements the incomes of low-wage workers.

Although these alternative policies are often better than price controls, they are not perfect. Rent and wage subsidies cost the government money and, therefore, require higher taxes. As we see in the next section, taxation has costs of its own.

QUICK QUIZ *Define* price ceiling *and* price floor *and give an example of each. Which leads to a shortage? Which leads to a surplus? Why?*

Taxes

All governments—from the federal government in Washington, D.C., to the local governments in small towns—use taxes to raise revenue for public projects, such as roads, schools, and national defense. Because taxes are such an important policy instrument, and because they affect our lives in many ways, we return to the study of taxes several times throughout this book. In this section, we begin our study of how taxes affect the economy.

To set the stage for our analysis, imagine that a local government decides to hold an annual ice-cream celebration—with a parade, fireworks, and speeches by town officials. To raise revenue to pay for the event, the town decides to place a $0.50 tax on the sale of ice-cream cones. When the plan is announced, our two lobbying groups swing into action. The American Association of Ice-Cream Eaters claims that consumers of ice cream are having trouble making ends meet, and it argues that *sellers* of ice cream should pay the tax. The National Organization of Ice-Cream Makers claims that its members are struggling to survive in a competitive market, and it argues that *buyers* of ice cream should pay the tax. The town mayor, hoping to reach a compromise, suggests that half the tax be paid by the buyers and half be paid by the sellers.

To analyze these proposals, we need to address a simple but subtle question: When the government levies a tax on a good, who actually bears the burden of the tax? The people buying the good? The people selling the good? Or if buyers and sellers share the tax burden, what determines how the burden is divided? Can the government simply legislate the division of the burden, as the mayor is suggesting, or is the division determined by more fundamental market forces? The term **tax incidence** refers to how the burden of a tax is distributed among the various people who make up the economy. As we will see, some surprising lessons about tax incidence can be learned by applying the tools of supply and demand.

tax incidence
the manner in which the burden of a tax is shared among participants in a market

How Taxes on Sellers Affect Market Outcomes

We begin by considering a tax levied on sellers of a good. Suppose the local government passes a law requiring sellers of ice-cream cones to send $0.50 to the government for each cone they sell. How does this law affect the buyers and sellers of ice cream? To answer this question, we can follow the three steps in Chapter 4 for analyzing supply and demand: (1) We decide whether the law affects the supply curve or demand curve. (2) We decide which way the curve shifts. (3) We examine how the shift affects the equilibrium price and quantity.

Step One The immediate impact of the tax is on the sellers of ice cream. Because the tax is not levied on buyers, the quantity of ice cream demanded at any given price is the same; thus, the demand curve does not change. By contrast, the tax on sellers makes the ice-cream business less profitable at any given price, so it shifts the supply curve.

Step Two   Because the tax on sellers raises the cost of producing and selling ice cream, it reduces the quantity supplied at every price. The supply curve shifts to the left (or, equivalently, upward).

In addition to determining the direction in which the supply curve moves, we can also be precise about the size of the shift. For any market price of ice cream, the effective price to sellers—the amount they get to keep after paying the tax—is $0.50 lower. For example, if the market price of a cone happened to be $2.00, the effective price received by sellers would be $1.50. Whatever the market price, sellers will supply a quantity of ice cream as if the price were $0.50 lower than it is. Put differently, to induce sellers to supply any given quantity, the market price must now be $0.50 higher to compensate for the effect of the tax. Thus, as shown in Figure 6, the supply curve shifts *upward* from S_1 to S_2 by the exact size of the tax ($0.50).

Step Three   Having determined how the supply curve shifts, we can now compare the initial and the new equilibriums. The figure shows that the equilibrium price of ice cream rises from $3.00 to $3.30, and the equilibrium quantity falls from 100 to 90 cones. Because sellers sell less and buyers buy less in the new equilibrium, the tax reduces the size of the ice-cream market.

Implications   We can now return to the question of tax incidence: Who pays the tax? Although sellers send the entire tax to the government, buyers and sellers share the burden. Because the market price rises from $3.00 to $3.30 when the tax is introduced, buyers pay $0.30 more for each ice-cream cone than they did without the tax. Thus, the tax makes buyers worse off. Sellers get a higher price ($3.30) from buyers than they did previously, but the effective price after paying the tax falls from $3.00 before the tax to $2.80 with the tax ($3.30 − $0.50 = $2.80). Thus, the tax also makes sellers worse off.

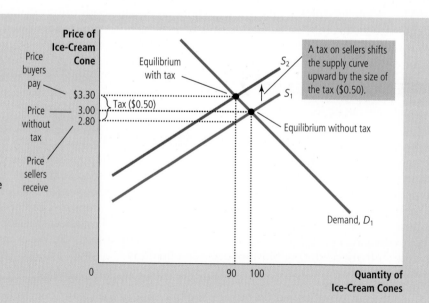

Figure **6**

A Tax on Sellers
When a tax of $0.50 is levied on sellers, the supply curve shifts up by $0.50 from S_1 to S_2. The equilibrium quantity falls from 100 to 90 cones. The price that buyers pay rises from $3.00 to $3.30. The price that sellers receive (after paying the tax) falls from $3.00 to $2.80. Even though the tax is levied on sellers, buyers and sellers share the burden of the tax.

To sum up, this analysis yields two lessons:

- Taxes discourage market activity. When a good is taxed, the quantity of the good sold is smaller in the new equilibrium.
- Buyers and sellers share the burden of taxes. In the new equilibrium, buyers pay more for the good, and sellers receive less.

How Taxes on Buyers Affect Market Outcomes

Now consider a tax levied on buyers of a good. Suppose that our local government passes a law requiring buyers of ice-cream cones to send $0.50 to the government for each ice-cream cone they buy. What are the effects of this law? Again, we apply our three steps.

Step One   The initial impact of the tax is on the demand for ice cream. The supply curve is not affected because, for any given price of ice cream, sellers have the same incentive to provide ice cream to the market. By contrast, buyers now have to pay a tax to the government (as well as the price to the sellers) whenever they buy ice cream. Thus, the tax shifts the demand curve for ice cream.

Step Two   We next determine the direction of the shift. Because the tax on buyers makes buying ice cream less attractive, buyers demand a smaller quantity of ice cream at every price. As a result, the demand curve shifts to the left (or, equivalently, downward), as shown in Figure 7.

Once again, we can be precise about the size of the shift. Because of the $0.50 tax levied on buyers, the effective price to buyers is now $0.50 higher than the market price (whatever the market price happens to be). For example, if the market price of a cone happened to be $2.00, the effective price to buyers would be $2.50. Because buyers look at their total cost including the tax, they demand a quantity of ice cream as if the market price were $0.50 higher than it actually is. In other words, to induce buyers to demand any given quantity, the market price

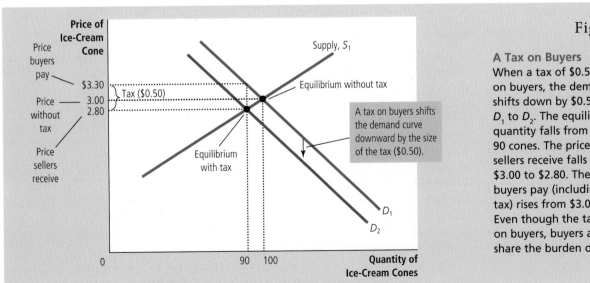

Figure 7

A Tax on Buyers
When a tax of $0.50 is levied on buyers, the demand curve shifts down by $0.50 from D_1 to D_2. The equilibrium quantity falls from 100 to 90 cones. The price that sellers receive falls from $3.00 to $2.80. The price that buyers pay (including the tax) rises from $3.00 to $3.30. Even though the tax is levied on buyers, buyers and sellers share the burden of the tax.

must now be $0.50 lower to make up for the effect of the tax. Thus, the tax shifts the demand curve *downward* from D_1 to D_2 by the exact size of the tax ($0.50).

Step Three Having determined how the demand curve shifts, we can now see the effect of the tax by comparing the initial equilibrium and the new equilibrium. You can see in the figure that the equilibrium price of ice cream falls from $3.00 to $2.80, and the equilibrium quantity falls from 100 to 90 cones. Once again, the tax on ice cream reduces the size of the ice-cream market. And once again, buyers and sellers share the burden of the tax. Sellers get a lower price for their product; buyers pay a lower market price to sellers than they did previously, but the effective price (including the tax buyers have to pay) rises from $3.00 to $3.30.

Implications If you compare Figures 6 and 7, you will notice a surprising conclusion: *Taxes levied on sellers and taxes levied on buyers are equivalent.* In both cases, the tax places a wedge between the price that buyers pay and the price that sellers receive. The wedge between the buyers' price and the sellers' price is the same, regardless of whether the tax is levied on buyers or sellers. In either case, the wedge shifts the relative position of the supply and demand curves. In the new equilibrium, buyers and sellers share the burden of the tax. The only difference between taxes on sellers and taxes on buyers is who sends the money to the government.

The equivalence of these two taxes is easy to understand if we imagine that the government collects the $0.50 ice-cream tax in a bowl on the counter of each ice-cream store. When the government levies the tax on sellers, the seller is required to place $0.50 in the bowl after the sale of each cone. When the government levies the tax on buyers, the buyer is required to place $0.50 in the bowl every time a cone is bought. Whether the $0.50 goes directly from the buyer's pocket into the bowl, or indirectly from the buyer's pocket into the seller's hand and then into the bowl, does not matter. Once the market reaches its new equilibrium, buyers and sellers share the burden, regardless of how the tax is levied.

Can Congress Distribute the Burden of a Payroll Tax?

If you have ever received a paycheck, you probably noticed that taxes were deducted from the amount you earned. One of these taxes is called FICA, an acronym for the Federal Insurance Contributions Act. The federal government uses the revenue from the FICA tax to pay for Social Security and Medicare, the income support and healthcare programs for the elderly. FICA is an example of a *payroll tax*, which is a tax on the wages that firms pay their workers. In 2010, the total FICA tax for the typical worker was 15.3 percent of earnings.

Who do you think bears the burden of this payroll tax—firms or workers? When Congress passed this legislation, it tried to mandate a division of the tax burden. According to the law, half of the tax is paid by firms, and half is paid by workers. That is, half of the tax is paid out of firms' revenues, and half is deducted from workers' paychecks. The amount that shows up as a deduction on your pay stub is the worker contribution.

Our analysis of tax incidence, however, shows that lawmakers cannot so easily dictate the distribution of a tax burden. To illustrate, we can analyze a payroll tax as merely a tax on a good, where the good is labor and the price is

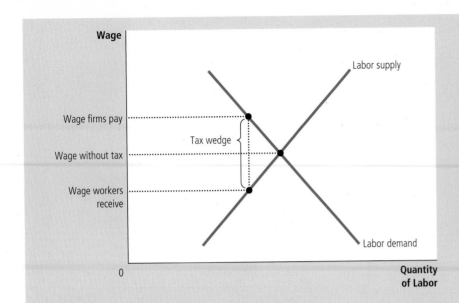

Figure 8

A Payroll Tax
A payroll tax places a wedge between the wage that workers receive and the wage that firms pay. Comparing wages with and without the tax, you can see that workers and firms share the tax burden. This division of the tax burden between workers and firms does not depend on whether the government levies the tax on workers, levies the tax on firms, or divides the tax equally between the two groups.

the wage. The key feature of the payroll tax is that it places a wedge between the wage that firms pay and the wage that workers receive. Figure 8 shows the outcome. When a payroll tax is enacted, the wage received by workers falls, and the wage paid by firms rises. In the end, workers and firms share the burden of the tax, much as the legislation requires. Yet this division of the tax burden between workers and firms has nothing to do with the legislated division: The division of the burden in Figure 8 is not necessarily fifty-fifty, and the same outcome would prevail if the law levied the entire tax on workers or if it levied the entire tax on firms.

This example shows that the most basic lesson of tax incidence is often overlooked in public debate. Lawmakers can decide whether a tax comes from the buyer's pocket or from the seller's, but they cannot legislate the true burden of a tax. Rather, tax incidence depends on the forces of supply and demand. ■

Elasticity and Tax Incidence

When a good is taxed, buyers and sellers of the good share the burden of the tax. But how exactly is the tax burden divided? Only rarely will it be shared equally. To see how the burden is divided, consider the impact of taxation in the two markets in Figure 9. In both cases, the figure shows the initial demand curve, the initial supply curve, and a tax that drives a wedge between the amount paid by buyers and the amount received by sellers. (Not drawn in either panel of the figure is the new supply or demand curve. Which curve shifts depends on whether the tax is levied on buyers or sellers. As we have seen, this is irrelevant for the incidence of the tax.) The difference in the two panels is the relative elasticity of supply and demand.

Panel (a) of Figure 9 shows a tax in a market with very elastic supply and relatively inelastic demand. That is, sellers are very responsive to changes in the price of the good (so the supply curve is relatively flat), whereas buyers are not very responsive (so the demand curve is relatively steep). When a tax is imposed on a

Figure **9**

How the Burden of a Tax Is Divided
In panel (a), the supply curve is elastic, and the demand curve is inelastic. In this case, the price received by sellers falls only slightly, while the price paid by buyers rises substantially. Thus, buyers bear most of the burden of the tax. In panel (b), the supply curve is inelastic, and the demand curve is elastic. In this case, the price received by sellers falls substantially, while the price paid by buyers rises only slightly. Thus, sellers bear most of the burden of the tax.

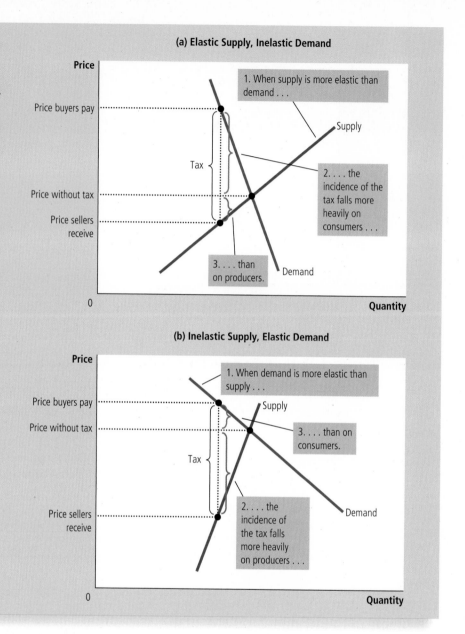

(a) Elastic Supply, Inelastic Demand

1. When supply is more elastic than demand . . .

Supply

Tax

2. . . . the incidence of the tax falls more heavily on consumers . . .

Price buyers pay

Price without tax

Price sellers receive

3. . . . than on producers.

Demand

0

Quantity

(b) Inelastic Supply, Elastic Demand

1. When demand is more elastic than supply . . .

Supply

3. . . . than on consumers.

Tax

2. . . . the incidence of the tax falls more heavily on producers . . .

Demand

Price buyers pay

Price without tax

Price sellers receive

0

Quantity

market with these elasticities, the price received by sellers does not fall much, so sellers bear only a small burden. By contrast, the price paid by buyers rises substantially, indicating that buyers bear most of the burden of the tax.

Panel (b) of Figure 9 shows a tax in a market with relatively inelastic supply and very elastic demand. In this case, sellers are not very responsive to changes in the price (so the supply curve is steeper), whereas buyers are very responsive (so the demand curve is flatter). The figure shows that when a tax is imposed, the price paid by buyers does not rise much, but the price received by sellers falls substantially. Thus, sellers bear most of the burden of the tax.

The two panels of Figure 9 show a general lesson about how the burden of a tax is divided: *A tax burden falls more heavily on the side of the market that is less elastic.* Why is this true? In essence, the elasticity measures the willingness of buyers or sellers to leave the market when conditions become unfavorable. A small elasticity of demand means that buyers do not have good alternatives to consuming this particular good. A small elasticity of supply means that sellers do not have good alternatives to producing this particular good. When the good is taxed, the side of the market with fewer good alternatives is less willing to leave the market and must, therefore, bear more of the burden of the tax.

We can apply this logic to the payroll tax discussed in the previous case study. Most labor economists believe that the supply of labor is much less elastic than the demand. This means that workers, rather than firms, bear most of the burden of the payroll tax. In other words, the distribution of the tax burden is not at all close to the fifty-fifty split that lawmakers intended.

 Who Pays the Luxury Tax?

In 1990, Congress adopted a new luxury tax on items such as yachts, private airplanes, furs, jewelry, and expensive cars. The goal of the tax was to raise revenue from those who could most easily afford to pay. Because only the rich could afford to buy such extravagances, taxing luxuries seemed a logical way of taxing the rich.

Yet, when the forces of supply and demand took over, the outcome was quite different from the one Congress intended. Consider, for example, the market for yachts. The demand for yachts is quite elastic. A millionaire can easily not buy a yacht; she can use the money to buy a bigger house, take a European vacation, or leave a larger bequest to her heirs. By contrast, the supply of yachts is relatively inelastic, at least in the short run. Yacht factories are not easily converted to alternative uses, and workers who build yachts are not eager to change careers in response to changing market conditions.

Our analysis makes a clear prediction in this case. With elastic demand and inelastic supply, the burden of a tax falls largely on the suppliers. That is, a tax on yachts places a burden largely on the firms and workers who build yachts because they end up getting a significantly lower price for their product. The workers, however, are not wealthy. Thus, the burden of a luxury tax falls more on the middle class than on the rich.

The mistaken assumptions about the incidence of the luxury tax quickly became apparent after the tax went into effect. Suppliers of luxuries made their congressional representatives well aware of the economic hardship they experienced, and Congress repealed most of the luxury tax in 1993. ■

"If this boat were any more expensive, we'd be playing golf."

QUICK QUIZ *In a supply-and-demand diagram, show how a tax on car buyers of $1,000 per car affects the quantity of cars sold and the price of cars. In another diagram, show how a tax on car sellers of $1,000 per car affects the quantity of cars sold and the price of cars. In both of your diagrams, show the change in the price paid by car buyers and the change in the price received by car sellers.*

Conclusion

The economy is governed by two kinds of laws: the laws of supply and demand and the laws enacted by governments. In this chapter, we have begun to see how these laws interact. Price controls and taxes are common in various markets in the economy, and their effects are frequently debated in the press and among policymakers. Even a little bit of economic knowledge can go a long way toward understanding and evaluating these policies.

In subsequent chapters, we analyze many government policies in greater detail. We examine the effects of taxation more fully and consider a broader range of policies than we considered here. Yet the basic lessons of this chapter will not change: When analyzing government policies, supply and demand are the first and most useful tools of analysis.

SUMMARY

- A price ceiling is a legal maximum on the price of a good or service. An example is rent control. If the price ceiling is below the equilibrium price, then the price ceiling is binding, and the quantity demanded exceeds the quantity supplied. Because of the resulting shortage, sellers must in some way ration the good or service among buyers.

- A price floor is a legal minimum on the price of a good or service. An example is the minimum wage. If the price floor is above the equilibrium price, then the price floor is binding, and the quantity supplied exceeds the quantity demanded. Because of the resulting surplus, buyers' demands for the good or service must in some way be rationed among sellers.

- When the government levies a tax on a good, the equilibrium quantity of the good falls. That is, a tax on a market shrinks the size of the market.

- A tax on a good places a wedge between the price paid by buyers and the price received by sellers. When the market moves to the new equilibrium, buyers pay more for the good and sellers receive less for it. In this sense, buyers and sellers share the tax burden. The incidence of a tax (that is, the division of the tax burden) does not depend on whether the tax is levied on buyers or sellers.

- The incidence of a tax depends on the price elasticities of supply and demand. Most of the burden falls on the side of the market that is less elastic because that side of the market can respond less easily to the tax by changing the quantity bought or sold.

KEY CONCEPTS

price ceiling, *p. 112*   price floor, *p. 112*   tax incidence, *p. 121*

QUESTIONS FOR REVIEW

1. Give an example of a price ceiling and an example of a price floor.
2. Which causes a shortage of a good—a price ceiling or a price floor? Justify your answer with a graph.
3. What mechanisms allocate resources when the price of a good is not allowed to bring supply and demand into equilibrium?
4. Explain why economists usually oppose controls on prices.

5. Suppose the government removes a tax on buyers of a good and levies a tax of the same size on sellers of the good. How does this change in tax policy affect the price that buyers pay sellers for this good, the amount buyers are out of pocket including the tax, the amount sellers receive net of the tax, and the quantity of the good sold?

6. How does a tax on a good affect the price paid by buyers, the price received by sellers, and the quantity sold?

7. What determines how the burden of a tax is divided between buyers and sellers? Why?

PROBLEMS AND APPLICATIONS

1. Lovers of classical music persuade Congress to impose a price ceiling of $40 per concert ticket. As a result of this policy, do more or fewer people attend classical music concerts?

2. The government has decided that the free-market price of cheese is too low.
   a. Suppose the government imposes a binding price floor in the cheese market. Draw a supply-and-demand diagram to show the effect of this policy on the price of cheese and the quantity of cheese sold. Is there a shortage or surplus of cheese?
   b. Farmers complain that the price floor has reduced their total revenue. Is this possible? Explain.
   c. In response to farmers' complaints, the government agrees to purchase all the surplus cheese at the price floor. Compared to the basic price floor, who benefits from this new policy? Who loses?

3. A recent study found that the demand and supply schedules for Frisbees are as follows:

Price per Frisbee	Quantity Demanded	Quantity Supplied
$11	1 million Frisbees	15 million Frisbees
10	2	12
9	4	9
8	6	6
7	8	3
6	10	1

   a. What are the equilibrium price and quantity of Frisbees?
   b. Frisbee manufacturers persuade the government that Frisbee production improves scientists' understanding of aerodynamics and thus is important for national security. A concerned Congress votes to impose a price floor $2 above the equilibrium price. What is the new market price? How many Frisbees are sold?
   c. Irate college students march on Washington and demand a reduction in the price of Frisbees. An even more concerned Congress votes to repeal the price floor and impose a price ceiling $1 below the former price floor. What is the new market price? How many Frisbees are sold?

4. Suppose the federal government requires beer drinkers to pay a $2 tax on each case of beer purchased. (In fact, both the federal and state governments impose beer taxes of some sort.)
   a. Draw a supply-and-demand diagram of the market for beer without the tax. Show the price paid by consumers, the price received by producers, and the quantity of beer sold. What is the difference between the price paid by consumers and the price received by producers?
   b. Now draw a supply-and-demand diagram for the beer market with the tax. Show the price paid by consumers, the price received by producers, and the quantity of beer sold. What is the difference between the price paid by consumers and the price received by producers? Has the quantity of beer sold increased or decreased?

5. A senator wants to raise tax revenue and make workers better off. A staff member proposes raising the payroll tax paid by firms and using part of the extra revenue to reduce the payroll

tax paid by workers. Would this accomplish the senator's goal? Explain.

6. If the government places a $500 tax on luxury cars, will the price paid by consumers rise by more than $500, less than $500, or exactly $500? Explain.

7. Congress and the president decide that the United States should reduce air pollution by reducing its use of gasoline. They impose a $0.50 tax for each gallon of gasoline sold.
   a. Should they impose this tax on producers or consumers? Explain carefully using a supply-and-demand diagram.
   b. If the demand for gasoline were more elastic, would this tax be more effective or less effective in reducing the quantity of gasoline consumed? Explain with both words and a diagram.
   c. Are consumers of gasoline helped or hurt by this tax? Why?
   d. Are workers in the oil industry helped or hurt by this tax? Why?

8. A case study in this chapter discusses the federal minimum-wage law.
   a. Suppose the minimum wage is above the equilibrium wage in the market for unskilled labor. Using a supply-and-demand diagram of the market for unskilled labor, show the market wage, the number of workers who are employed, and the number of workers who are unemployed. Also show the total wage payments to unskilled workers.
   b. Now suppose the secretary of labor proposes an increase in the minimum wage. What effect would this increase have on employment? Does the change in employment depend on the elasticity of demand, the elasticity of supply, both elasticities, or neither?
   c. What effect would this increase in the minimum wage have on unemployment? Does the change in unemployment depend on the elasticity of demand, the elasticity of supply, both elasticities, or neither?
   d. If the demand for unskilled labor were inelastic, would the proposed increase in the minimum wage raise or lower total wage payments to unskilled workers? Would your answer change if the demand for unskilled labor were elastic?

9. The U.S. government administers two programs that affect the market for cigarettes. Media campaigns and labeling requirements are aimed at making the public aware of the dangers of cigarette smoking. At the same time, the Department of Agriculture maintains a price-support program for tobacco farmers, which raises the price of tobacco above the equilibrium price.
   a. How do these two programs affect cigarette consumption? Use a graph of the cigarette market in your answer.
   b. What is the combined effect of these two programs on the price of cigarettes?
   c. Cigarettes are also heavily taxed. What effect does this tax have on cigarette consumption?

10. At Fenway Park, home of the Boston Red Sox, seating is limited to 39,000. Hence, the number of tickets issued is fixed at that figure. Seeing a golden opportunity to raise revenue, the City of Boston levies a per ticket tax of $5 to be paid by the ticket buyer. Boston sports fans, a famously civic-minded lot, dutifully send in the $5 per ticket. Draw a well-labeled graph showing the impact of the tax. On whom does the tax burden fall—the team's owners, the fans, or both? Why?

11. A subsidy is the opposite of a tax. With a $0.50 tax on the buyers of ice-cream cones, the government collects $0.50 for each cone purchased; with a $0.50 subsidy for the buyers of ice-cream cones, the government pays buyers $0.50 for each cone purchased.
    a. Show the effect of a $0.50 per cone subsidy on the demand curve for ice-cream cones, the effective price paid by consumers, the effective price received by sellers, and the quantity of cones sold.
    b. Do consumers gain or lose from this policy? Do producers gain or lose? Does the government gain or lose?

12. In the spring of 2008, Senators John McCain and Hillary Clinton (who were then running for president) proposed a temporary elimination of the federal gasoline tax, effective only during the summer of 2008, in order to help consumers deal with high gasoline prices.

a. During the summer, when gasoline demand is high because of vacation driving, gasoline refiners are operating near full capacity. What does this fact suggest about the price elasticity of supply?

b. In light of your answer to (a), who do you predict would benefit from the temporary gas tax holiday?

For further information on topics in this chapter, additional problems, examples, applications, online quizzes, and more, please visit our website at www .cengage.com/economics/mankiw.

PART III Markets and Welfare

Consumers, Producers, and the Efficiency of Markets

When consumers go to grocery stores to buy their turkeys for Thanksgiving dinner, they may be disappointed that the price of turkey is as high as it is. At the same time, when farmers bring to market the turkeys they have raised, they wish the price of turkey were even higher. These views are not surprising: Buyers always want to pay less, and sellers always want to be paid more. But is there a "right price" for turkey from the standpoint of society as a whole?

In previous chapters, we saw how, in market economies, the forces of supply and demand determine the prices of goods and services and the quantities sold. So far, however, we have described the way markets allocate scarce resources without directly addressing the question of whether these market allocations are

desirable. In other words, our analysis has been *positive* (what is) rather than *normative* (what should be). We know that the price of turkey adjusts to ensure that the quantity of turkey supplied equals the quantity of turkey demanded. But at this equilibrium, is the quantity of turkey produced and consumed too small, too large, or just right?

welfare economics

the study of how the allocation of resources affects economic well-being

In this chapter, we take up the topic of **welfare economics**, the study of how the allocation of resources affects economic well-being. We begin by examining the benefits that buyers and sellers receive from taking part in a market. We then examine how society can make these benefits as large as possible. This analysis leads to a profound conclusion: The equilibrium of supply and demand in a market maximizes the total benefits received by buyers and sellers.

As you may recall from Chapter 1, one of the *Ten Principles of Economics* is that markets are usually a good way to organize economic activity. The study of welfare economics explains this principle more fully. It also answers our question about the right price of turkey: The price that balances the supply and demand for turkey is, in a particular sense, the best one because it maximizes the total welfare of turkey consumers and turkey producers. No consumer or producer of turkeys aims to achieve this goal, but their joint action directed by market prices moves them toward a welfare-maximizing outcome, as if led by an invisible hand.

Consumer Surplus

We begin our study of welfare economics by looking at the benefits buyers receive from participating in a market.

Willingness to Pay

Imagine that you own a mint-condition recording of Elvis Presley's first album. Because you are not an Elvis Presley fan, you decide to sell it. One way to do so is to hold an auction.

Four Elvis fans show up for your auction: John, Paul, George, and Ringo. Each of them would like to own the album, but there is a limit to the amount that each is willing to pay for it. Table 1 shows the maximum price that each of the four possible buyers would pay. Each buyer's maximum is called his **willingness to pay,** and it measures how much that buyer values the good. Each buyer would be eager to buy the album at a price less than his willingness to pay, and he would refuse to buy the album at a price greater than his willingness to pay. At a price equal to his willingness to pay, the buyer would be indifferent about buying the good: If the price is exactly the same as the value he places on the album, he would be equally happy buying it or keeping his money.

willingness to pay

the maximum amount that a buyer will pay for a good

Table **1**

Four Possible Buyers' Willingness to Pay

Buyer	Willingness to Pay
John	$100
Paul	80
George	70
Ringo	50

To sell your album, you begin the bidding at a low price, say, $10. Because all four buyers are willing to pay much more, the price rises quickly. The bidding stops when John bids $80 (or slightly more). At this point, Paul, George, and Ringo have dropped out of the bidding because they are unwilling to bid any more than $80. John pays you $80 and gets the album. Note that the album has gone to the buyer who values it most highly.

What benefit does John receive from buying the Elvis Presley album? In a sense, John has found a real bargain: He is willing to pay $100 for the album but pays only $80 for it. We say that John receives *consumer surplus* of $20. **Consumer surplus** is the amount a buyer is willing to pay for a good minus the amount the buyer actually pays for it.

Consumer surplus measures the benefit buyers receive from participating in a market. In this example, John receives a $20 benefit from participating in the auction because he pays only $80 for a good he values at $100. Paul, George, and Ringo get no consumer surplus from participating in the auction because they left without the album and without paying anything.

Now consider a somewhat different example. Suppose that you had two identical Elvis Presley albums to sell. Again, you auction them off to the four possible buyers. To keep things simple, we assume that both albums are to be sold for the same price and that no buyer is interested in buying more than one album. Therefore, the price rises until two buyers are left.

In this case, the bidding stops when John and Paul bid $70 (or slightly higher). At this price, John and Paul are each happy to buy an album, and George and Ringo are not willing to bid any higher. John and Paul each receive consumer surplus equal to his willingness to pay minus the price. John's consumer surplus is $30, and Paul's is $10. John's consumer surplus is higher now than in the previous example because he gets the same album but pays less for it. The total consumer surplus in the market is $40.

Using the Demand Curve to Measure Consumer Surplus

Consumer surplus is closely related to the demand curve for a product. To see how they are related, let's continue our example and consider the demand curve for this rare Elvis Presley album.

We begin by using the willingness to pay of the four possible buyers to find the demand schedule for the album. The table in Figure 1 shows the demand schedule that corresponds to Table 1. If the price is above $100, the quantity demanded in the market is 0 because no buyer is willing to pay that much. If the price is between $80 and $100, the quantity demanded is 1 because only John is willing to pay such a high price. If the price is between $70 and $80, the quantity demanded is 2 because both John and Paul are willing to pay the price. We can continue this analysis for other prices as well. In this way, the demand schedule is derived from the willingness to pay of the four possible buyers.

The graph in Figure 1 shows the demand curve that corresponds to this demand schedule. Note the relationship between the height of the demand curve and the buyers' willingness to pay. At any quantity, the price given by the demand curve shows the willingness to pay of the *marginal buyer*, the buyer who would leave the market first if the price were any higher. At a quantity of 4 albums, for instance, the demand curve has a height of $50, the price that Ringo (the marginal buyer) is willing to pay for an album. At a quantity of 3 albums, the demand curve has a height of $70, the price that George (who is now the marginal buyer) is willing to pay.

consumer surplus
the amount a buyer is willing to pay for a good minus the amount the buyer actually pays for it

Figure 1

The table shows the demand schedule for the buyers in Table 1. The graph shows the corresponding demand curve. Note that the height of the demand curve reflects buyers' willingness to pay.

The Demand Schedule and the Demand Curve

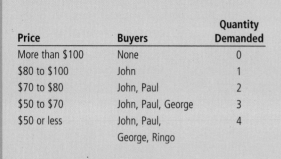

Price	Buyers	Quantity Demanded
More than $100	None	0
$80 to $100	John	1
$70 to $80	John, Paul	2
$50 to $70	John, Paul, George	3
$50 or less	John, Paul, George, Ringo	4

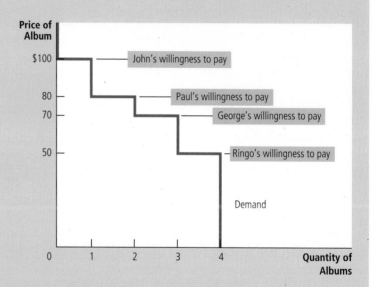

Because the demand curve reflects buyers' willingness to pay, we can also use it to measure consumer surplus. Figure 2 uses the demand curve to compute consumer surplus in our two examples. In panel (a), the price is $80 (or slightly above), and the quantity demanded is 1. Note that the area above the price and below the demand curve equals $20. This amount is exactly the consumer surplus we computed earlier when only 1 album is sold.

Panel (b) of Figure 2 shows consumer surplus when the price is $70 (or slightly above). In this case, the area above the price and below the demand curve equals the total area of the two rectangles: John's consumer surplus at this price is $30 and Paul's is $10. This area equals a total of $40. Once again, this amount is the consumer surplus we computed earlier.

The lesson from this example holds for all demand curves: *The area below the demand curve and above the price measures the consumer surplus in a market*. This is true because the height of the demand curve measures the value buyers place on the good, as measured by their willingness to pay for it. The difference between this willingness to pay and the market price is each buyer's consumer surplus. Thus, the total area below the demand curve and above the price is the sum of the consumer surplus of all buyers in the market for a good or service.

How a Lower Price Raises Consumer Surplus

Because buyers always want to pay less for the goods they buy, a lower price makes buyers of a good better off. But how much does buyers' well-being rise in

In panel (a), the price of the good is $80, and the consumer surplus is $20. In panel (b), the price of the good is $70, and the consumer surplus is $40.

Figure 2

Measuring Consumer Surplus with the Demand Curve

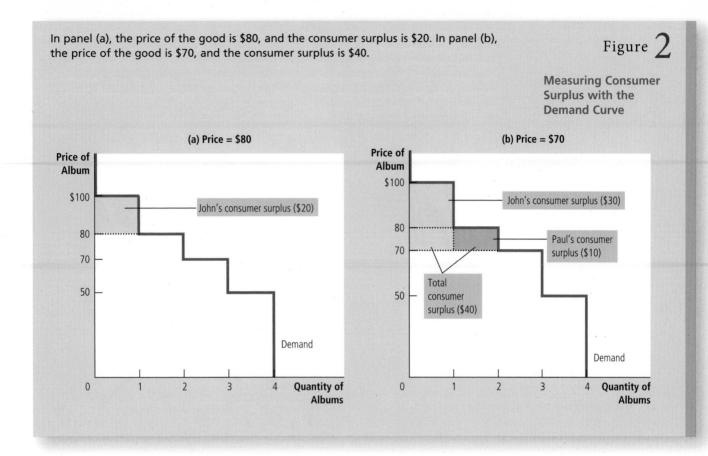

response to a lower price? We can use the concept of consumer surplus to answer this question precisely.

Figure 3 shows a typical demand curve. You may notice that this curve gradually slopes downward instead of taking discrete steps as in the previous two figures. In a market with many buyers, the resulting steps from each buyer dropping out are so small that they form, in essence, a smooth curve. Although this curve has a different shape, the ideas we have just developed still apply: Consumer surplus is the area above the price and below the demand curve. In panel (a), consumer surplus at a price of P_1 is the area of triangle ABC.

Now suppose that the price falls from P_1 to P_2, as shown in panel (b). The consumer surplus now equals area ADF. The increase in consumer surplus attributable to the lower price is the area BCFD.

This increase in consumer surplus is composed of two parts. First, those buyers who were already buying Q_1 of the good at the higher price P_1 are better off because they now pay less. The increase in consumer surplus of existing buyers is the reduction in the amount they pay; it equals the area of the rectangle BCED. Second, some new buyers enter the market because they are willing to buy the good at the lower price. As a result, the quantity demanded in the market increases from Q_1 to Q_2. The consumer surplus these newcomers receive is the area of the triangle CEF.

Figure **3**

**How the Price Affects
Consumer Surplus**

In panel (a), the price is P_1, the quantity demanded is Q_1, and consumer surplus equals the area of the triangle ABC. When the price falls from P_1 to P_2, as in panel (b), the quantity demanded rises from Q_1 to Q_2, and the consumer surplus rises to the area of the triangle ADF. The increase in consumer surplus (area BCFD) occurs in part because existing consumers now pay less (area BCED) and in part because new consumers enter the market at the lower price (area CEF).

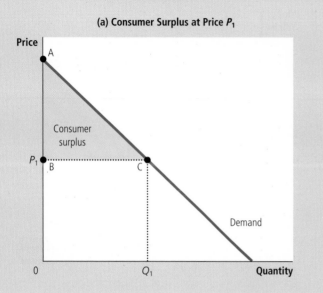

(a) Consumer Surplus at Price P_1

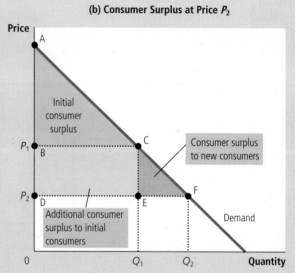

(b) Consumer Surplus at Price P_2

What Does Consumer Surplus Measure?

Our goal in developing the concept of consumer surplus is to make judgments about the desirability of market outcomes. Now that you have seen what consumer surplus is, let's consider whether it is a good measure of economic well-being.

Imagine that you are a policymaker trying to design a good economic system. Would you care about the amount of consumer surplus? Consumer surplus, the amount that buyers are willing to pay for a good minus the amount they actually pay for it, measures the benefit that buyers receive from a good *as the buyers themselves perceive it*. Thus, consumer surplus is a good measure of economic well-being if policymakers want to respect the preferences of buyers.

In some circumstances, policymakers might choose not to care about consumer surplus because they do not respect the preferences that drive buyer behavior. For example, drug addicts are willing to pay a high price for heroin. Yet we would not say that addicts get a large benefit from being able to buy heroin at a low price (even though addicts might say they do). From the standpoint of society, willingness to pay in this instance is not a good measure of the buyers' benefit, and consumer surplus is not a good measure of economic well-being, because addicts are not looking after their own best interests.

In most markets, however, consumer surplus does reflect economic well-being. Economists normally assume that buyers are rational when they make decisions. Rational people do the best they can to achieve their objectives, given their opportunities. Economists also normally assume that people's preferences should be respected. In this case, consumers are the best judges of how much benefit they receive from the goods they buy.

QUICK QUIZ *Draw a demand curve for turkey. In your diagram, show a price of turkey and the consumer surplus at that price. Explain in words what this consumer surplus measures.*

Producer Surplus

We now turn to the other side of the market and consider the benefits sellers receive from participating in a market. As you will see, our analysis of sellers' welfare is similar to our analysis of buyers' welfare.

Cost and the Willingness to Sell

Imagine now that you are a homeowner and you want to get your house painted. You turn to four sellers of painting services: Mary, Frida, Georgia, and Grandma. Each painter is willing to do the work for you if the price is right. You decide to take bids from the four painters and auction off the job to the painter who will do the work for the lowest price.

Each painter is willing to take the job if the price she would receive exceeds her cost of doing the work. Here the term **cost** should be interpreted as the painters' opportunity cost: It includes the painters' out-of-pocket expenses (for paint, brushes, and so on) as well as the value that the painters place on their own time. Table 2 shows each painter's cost. Because a painter's cost is the lowest price she would accept for her work, cost is a measure of her willingness to sell her services. Each painter would be eager to sell her services at a price greater than her cost, and she would refuse to sell her services at a price less than her cost. At a price exactly equal to her cost, she would be indifferent about selling her services: She would be equally happy getting the job or using her time and energy for another purpose.

When you take bids from the painters, the price might start high, but it quickly falls as the painters compete for the job. Once Grandma has bid $600 (or slightly less), she is the sole remaining bidder. Grandma is happy to do the job for this price because her cost is only $500. Mary, Frida, and Georgia are unwilling to do the job for less than $600. Note that the job goes to the painter who can do the work at the lowest cost.

What benefit does Grandma receive from getting the job? Because she is willing to do the work for $500 but gets $600 for doing it, we say that she receives *producer surplus* of $100. **Producer surplus** is the amount a seller is paid minus the cost of production. Producer surplus measures the benefit sellers receive from participating in a market.

cost
the value of everything a seller must give up to produce a good

producer surplus
the amount a seller is paid for a good minus the seller's cost of providing it

Seller	Cost
Mary	$900
Frida	800
Georgia	600
Grandma	500

Table 2

The Costs of Four Possible Sellers

Now consider a somewhat different example. Suppose that you have two houses that need painting. Again, you auction off the jobs to the four painters. To keep things simple, let's assume that no painter is able to paint both houses and that you will pay the same amount to paint each house. Therefore, the price falls until two painters are left.

In this case, the bidding stops when Georgia and Grandma each offer to do the job for a price of $800 (or slightly less). Georgia and Grandma are willing to do the work at this price, while Mary and Frida are not willing to bid a lower price. At a price of $800, Grandma receives producer surplus of $300, and Georgia receives producer surplus of $200. The total producer surplus in the market is $500.

Using the Supply Curve to Measure Producer Surplus

Just as consumer surplus is closely related to the demand curve, producer surplus is closely related to the supply curve. To see how, let's continue our example.

We begin by using the costs of the four painters to find the supply schedule for painting services. The table in Figure 4 shows the supply schedule that corresponds to the costs in Table 2. If the price is below $500, none of the four painters is willing to do the job, so the quantity supplied is zero. If the price is between $500 and $600, only Grandma is willing to do the job, so the quantity supplied is 1. If the price is between $600 and $800, Grandma and Georgia are willing to do the job, so the quantity supplied is 2, and so on. Thus, the supply schedule is derived from the costs of the four painters.

The graph in Figure 4 shows the supply curve that corresponds to this supply schedule. Note that the height of the supply curve is related to the sellers' costs.

Figure 4

The Supply Schedule and the Supply Curve

The table shows the supply schedule for the sellers in Table 2. The graph shows the corresponding supply curve. Note that the height of the supply curve reflects sellers' costs.

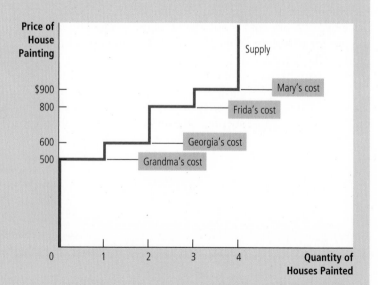

Price	Sellers	Quantity Supplied
$900 or more	Mary, Frida, Georgia, Grandma	4
$800 to $900	Frida, Georgia, Grandma	3
$600 to $800	Georgia, Grandma	2
$500 to $600	Grandma	1
Less than $500	None	0

At any quantity, the price given by the supply curve shows the cost of the *marginal seller*, the seller who would leave the market first if the price were any lower. At a quantity of 4 houses, for instance, the supply curve has a height of $900, the cost that Mary (the marginal seller) incurs to provide her painting services. At a quantity of 3 houses, the supply curve has a height of $800, the cost that Frida (who is now the marginal seller) incurs.

Because the supply curve reflects sellers' costs, we can use it to measure producer surplus. Figure 5 uses the supply curve to compute producer surplus in our two examples. In panel (a), we assume that the price is $600. In this case, the quantity supplied is 1. Note that the area below the price and above the supply curve equals $100. This amount is exactly the producer surplus we computed earlier for Grandma.

Panel (b) of Figure 5 shows producer surplus at a price of $800. In this case, the area below the price and above the supply curve equals the total area of the two rectangles. This area equals $500, the producer surplus we computed earlier for Georgia and Grandma when two houses needed painting.

The lesson from this example applies to all supply curves: *The area below the price and above the supply curve measures the producer surplus in a market*. The logic is straightforward: The height of the supply curve measures sellers' costs, and the difference between the price and the cost of production is each seller's producer surplus. Thus, the total area is the sum of the producer surplus of all sellers.

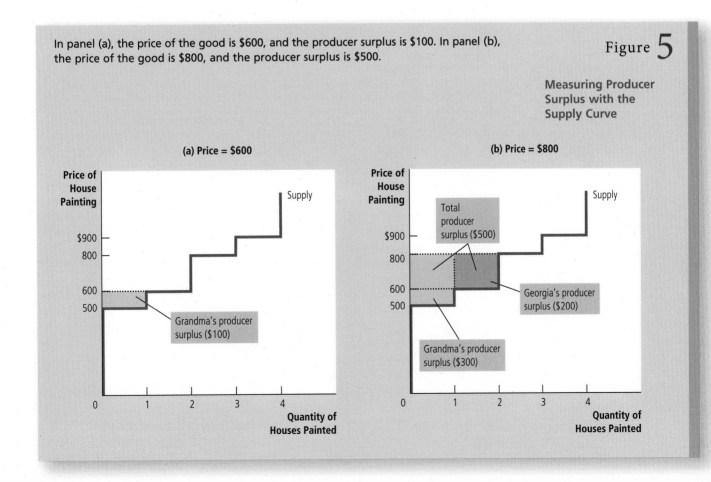

In panel (a), the price of the good is $600, and the producer surplus is $100. In panel (b), the price of the good is $800, and the producer surplus is $500.

Figure 5

Measuring Producer Surplus with the Supply Curve

How a Higher Price Raises Producer Surplus

You will not be surprised to hear that sellers always want to receive a higher price for the goods they sell. But how much does sellers' well-being rise in response to a higher price? The concept of producer surplus offers a precise answer to this question.

Figure 6 shows a typical upward-sloping supply curve that would arise in a market with many sellers. Although this supply curve differs in shape from the previous figure, we measure producer surplus in the same way: Producer surplus is the area below the price and above the supply curve. In panel (a), the price is P_1, and producer surplus is the area of triangle ABC.

Panel (b) shows what happens when the price rises from P_1 to P_2. Producer surplus now equals area ADF. This increase in producer surplus has two parts. First, those sellers who were already selling Q_1 of the good at the lower price P_1 are better off because they now get more for what they sell. The increase in producer surplus for existing sellers equals the area of the rectangle BCED. Second, some new sellers enter the market because they are willing to produce the good at the higher price, resulting in an increase in the quantity supplied from Q_1 to Q_2. The producer surplus of these newcomers is the area of the triangle CEF.

As this analysis shows, we use producer surplus to measure the well-being of sellers in much the same way as we use consumer surplus to measure the well-being of buyers. Because these two measures of economic welfare are so similar, it is natural to use them together. And indeed, that is exactly what we do in the next section.

Figure 6

How the Price Affects Producer Surplus

In panel (a), the price is P_1, the quantity demanded is Q_1, and producer surplus equals the area of the triangle ABC. When the price rises from P_1 to P_2, as in panel (b), the quantity supplied rises from Q_1 to Q_2, and the producer surplus rises to the area of the triangle ADF. The increase in producer surplus (area BCFD) occurs in part because existing producers now receive more (area BCED) and in part because new producers enter the market at the higher price (area CEF).

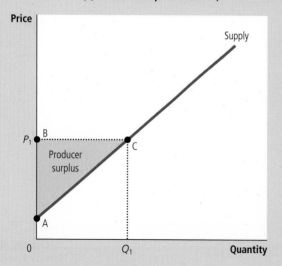

(a) Producer Surplus at Price P_1

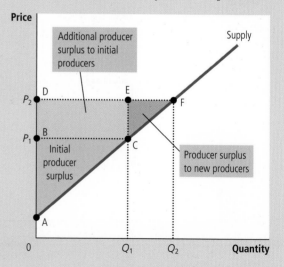

(b) Producer Surplus at Price P_2

QUICK QUIZ   *Draw a supply curve for turkey. In your diagram, show a price of turkey and the producer surplus at that price. Explain in words what this producer surplus measures.*

Market Efficiency

Consumer surplus and producer surplus are the basic tools that economists use to study the welfare of buyers and sellers in a market. These tools can help us address a fundamental economic question: Is the allocation of resources determined by free markets desirable?

The Benevolent Social Planner

To evaluate market outcomes, we introduce into our analysis a new, hypothetical character called the benevolent social planner. The benevolent social planner is an all-knowing, all-powerful, well-intentioned dictator. The planner wants to maximize the economic well-being of everyone in society. What should this planner do? Should he just leave buyers and sellers at the equilibrium that they reach naturally on their own? Or can he increase economic well-being by altering the market outcome in some way?

To answer this question, the planner must first decide how to measure the economic well-being of a society. One possible measure is the sum of consumer and producer surplus, which we call *total surplus*. Consumer surplus is the benefit that buyers receive from participating in a market, and producer surplus is the benefit that sellers receive. It is therefore natural to use total surplus as a measure of society's economic well-being.

To better understand this measure of economic well-being, recall how we measure consumer and producer surplus. We define consumer surplus as

Consumer surplus = Value to buyers − Amount paid by buyers.

Similarly, we define producer surplus as

Producer surplus = Amount received by sellers − Cost to sellers.

When we add consumer and producer surplus together, we obtain

Total surplus = (Value to buyers − Amount paid by buyers)
                + (Amount received by sellers − Cost to sellers).

The amount paid by buyers equals the amount received by sellers, so the middle two terms in this expression cancel each other. As a result, we can write total surplus as

Total surplus = Value to buyers − Cost to sellers.

Total surplus in a market is the total value to buyers of the goods, as measured by their willingness to pay, minus the total cost to sellers of providing those goods.

If an allocation of resources maximizes total surplus, we say that the allocation exhibits **efficiency.** If an allocation is not efficient, then some of the potential gains from trade among buyers and sellers are not being realized. For example,

efficiency
the property of a resource allocation of maximizing the total surplus received by all members of society

an allocation is inefficient if a good is not being produced by the sellers with low-est cost. In this case, moving production from a high-cost producer to a low-cost producer will lower the total cost to sellers and raise total surplus. Similarly, an allocation is inefficient if a good is not being consumed by the buyers who value it most highly. In this case, moving consumption of the good from a buyer with a low valuation to a buyer with a high valuation will raise total surplus.

equality

the property of distrib-uting economic prosperity uniformly among the members of society

In addition to efficiency, the social planner might also care about **equality**—that is, whether the various buyers and sellers in the market have a similar level of economic well-being. In essence, the gains from trade in a market are like a pie to be shared among the market participants. The question of efficiency concerns whether the pie is as big as possible. The question of equality concerns how the pie is sliced and how the portions are distributed among members of society. In this chapter, we concentrate on efficiency as the social planner's goal. Keep in mind, however, that real policymakers often care about equality as well.

Evaluating the Market Equilibrium

Figure 7 shows consumer and producer surplus when a market reaches the equilibrium of supply and demand. Recall that consumer surplus equals the area above the price and under the demand curve and producer surplus equals the area below the price and above the supply curve. Thus, the total area between the supply and demand curves up to the point of equilibrium represents the total surplus in this market.

Is this equilibrium allocation of resources efficient? That is, does it maximize total surplus? To answer this question, recall that when a market is in equilibrium, the price determines which buyers and sellers participate in the market. Those buyers who value the good more than the price (represented by the segment

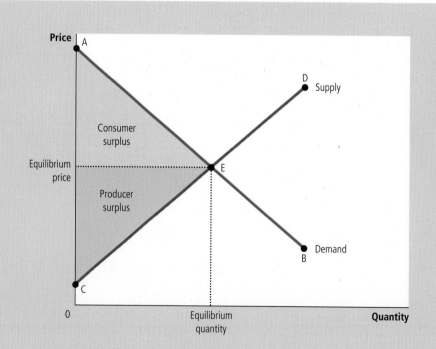

Figure 7

Consumer and Producer Surplus in the Market Equilibrium
Total surplus—the sum of consumer and producer surplus—is the area between the supply and demand curves up to the equilibrium quantity.

AE on the demand curve) choose to buy the good; buyers who value it less than the price (represented by the segment EB) do not. Similarly, those sellers whose costs are less than the price (represented by the segment CE on the supply curve) choose to produce and sell the good; sellers whose costs are greater than the price (represented by the segment ED) do not.

These observations lead to two insights about market outcomes:

1. Free markets allocate the supply of goods to the buyers who value them most highly, as measured by their willingness to pay.
2. Free markets allocate the demand for goods to the sellers who can produce them at the lowest cost.

Thus, given the quantity produced and sold in a market equilibrium, the social planner cannot increase economic well-being by changing the allocation of consumption among buyers or the allocation of production among sellers.

But can the social planner raise total economic well-being by increasing or decreasing the quantity of the good? The answer is no, as stated in this third insight about market outcomes:

3. Free markets produce the quantity of goods that maximizes the sum of consumer and producer surplus.

Figure 8 illustrates why this is true. To interpret this figure, keep in mind that the demand curve reflects the value to buyers and the supply curve reflects the cost to sellers. At any quantity below the equilibrium level, such as Q_1, the value to the marginal buyer exceeds the cost to the marginal seller. As a result, increasing the

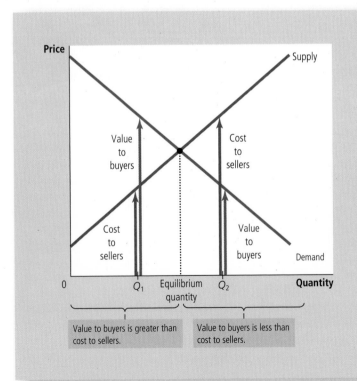

Figure **8**

The Efficiency of the Equilibrium Quantity
At quantities less than the equilibrium quantity, such as Q_1, the value to buyers exceeds the cost to sellers. At quantities greater than the equilibrium quantity, such as Q_2, the cost to sellers exceeds the value to buyers. Therefore, the market equilibrium maximizes the sum of producer and consumer surplus.

quantity produced and consumed raises total surplus. This continues to be true until the quantity reaches the equilibrium level. Similarly, at any quantity beyond the equilibrium level, such as Q_2, the value to the marginal buyer is less than the cost to the marginal seller. In this case, decreasing the quantity raises total surplus, and this continues to be true until quantity falls to the equilibrium level. To maximize total surplus, the social planner would choose the quantity where the supply and demand curves intersect.

Together, these three insights tell us that the market outcome makes the sum of consumer and producer surplus as large as it can be. In other words, the equilibrium outcome is an efficient allocation of resources. The benevolent social planner can, therefore, leave the market outcome just as he finds it. This policy of leaving well enough alone goes by the French expression *laissez faire*, which literally translates to "allow them to do."

Society is lucky that the planner doesn't need to intervene. Although it has been a useful exercise imagining what an all-knowing, all-powerful, well-intentioned dictator would do, let's face it: Such characters are hard to come by. Dictators are rarely benevolent, and even if we found someone so virtuous, he would lack crucial information.

Suppose our social planner tried to choose an efficient allocation of resources on his own, instead of relying on market forces. To do so, he would need to know

in the news

> ### Ticket Scalping

To allocate resources efficiently, an economy must get goods—including tickets to the Red Sox—to the consumers who value them most highly.

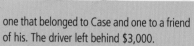

Like It or Not, Scalping Is a Force in the Free Market

BY CHARLES STEIN

Chip Case devotes a class each year to the reselling of sports tickets. He has a section in his economics textbook on the same subject.

But for Case, an economics professor at Wellesley College, the sale and scalping of sports tickets is more than an interesting theoretical pursuit. Like Margaret Mead, he

has done plenty of firsthand research in the jungle, and he has the stories to prove it.

In 1984, Case waited in line for two nights on Causeway Street to get $11 tickets to one of the classic Celtics-Lakers championship series. The night before the climactic seventh game, he was in the shower when his daughter called out to him: "Dad, there's a guy on the phone who wants to buy your Celtics tickets." Case said he wasn't selling. "But Dad," his daughter added, "he's willing to pay at least $1,000 apiece for them."

Case was selling. An hour later, a limo arrived at the house to pick up two tickets—

one that belonged to Case and one to a friend of his. The driver left behind $3,000.

To Case and other economists, tickets are a textbook case of the free market in action. When supply is limited and demand is not, prices rise and the people willing to pay more will eventually get their hands on the tickets. "As long as people can communicate, there will be trades," said Case.

In the age of the Internet, buyers and sellers can link up online, through eBay or the sites devoted solely to ticket sales. But even in the pre-Internet era, the process worked, albeit more slowly. In 1984, the man who bought Case's tickets was a rich

the value of a particular good to every potential consumer in the market and the cost of every potential producer. And he would need this information not only for this market but for every one of the many thousands of markets in the economy. The task is practically impossible, which explains why centrally planned economies never work very well.

The planner's job becomes easy, however, once he takes on a partner: Adam Smith's invisible hand of the marketplace. The invisible hand takes all the information about buyers and sellers into account and guides everyone in the market to the best outcome as judged by the standard of economic efficiency. It is, truly, a remarkable feat. That is why economists so often advocate free markets as the best way to organize economic activity.

Should There Be a Market in Organs?

Some years ago, the front page of the *Boston Globe* ran the headline "How a Mother's Love Helped Save Two Lives." The newspaper told the story of Susan Stephens, a woman whose son needed a kidney transplant. When the doctor

New Yorker whose son attended a Boston private school. The man called a friend at the school, who called someone else, who eventually called Case. Where there is a will, there is a way.

Trading happens no matter how hard teams try to suppress it. The National Football League gives some of its Super Bowl tickets to its teams, and prohibits them from reselling. Yet many of those same tickets wind up back on the secondary market. Last season the league caught Minnesota Vikings head coach Mike Tice selling his tickets to a California ticket agency. "I regret it," Tice told *Sports Illustrated* afterward. Or at least he regretted getting caught.

Like any good market, the one for tickets is remarkably sensitive to information. Case has a story about that, too. He was in Kenmore Square just before game four of last year's playoff series between the Yankees and Red Sox. The Red Sox had dropped the first three games and there was no joy in Mudville. Scalpers were

unloading tickets for the fourth game for only slightly more than face value. Tickets for a possible fifth game were going for even less.

But the Red Sox rallied to win game four in extra innings. By 2 that morning, said Case, top tickets for game five were already selling for more than $1,000 online. A bear market had become a bull market instantaneously.

As defenders of the free market, economists generally see nothing wrong with

scalping. "Consenting adults should be able to make economic trades when they think it is to their mutual advantage," said Greg Mankiw, a Harvard economics professor who recently stepped down as chairman of President Bush's Council of Economic Advisers. Mankiw has a section about scalping in his own textbook.

Teams could eliminate scalping altogether by holding their own online auctions for desirable tickets. Case doesn't expect that to happen. "People would burn down Fenway Park if the Red Sox charged $2,000 for a ticket," he said. The team would be accused of price gouging. Yet if you went online last week, you could find front-row Green Monster seats for the July 15 game against the Yankees selling for more than $2,000. Go figure.

Case will be at Fenway Park this Friday. He is taking his father-in-law to the game. He paid a small fortune for the tickets online. But he isn't complaining. It's the free market at work.

Source: *Boston Globe,* May 1, 2005.

learned that the mother's kidney was not compatible, he proposed a novel solution: If Stephens donated one of her kidneys to a stranger, her son would move to the top of the kidney waiting list. The mother accepted the deal, and soon two patients had the transplant they were waiting for.

The ingenuity of the doctor's proposal and the nobility of the mother's act cannot be doubted. But the story raises some intriguing questions. If the mother could trade a kidney for a kidney, would the hospital allow her to trade a kidney for an expensive, experimental cancer treatment that she could not otherwise afford? Should she be allowed to exchange her kidney for free tuition for her son at the hospital's medical school? Should she be able to sell her kidney so she can use the cash to trade in her old Chevy for a new Lexus?

As a matter of public policy, our society makes it illegal for people to sell their organs. In essence, in the market for organs, the government has imposed a price ceiling of zero. The result, as with any binding price ceiling, is a shortage of the good. The deal in the Stephens case did not fall under this prohibition because no cash changed hands.

Many economists believe that there would be large benefits to allowing a free market in organs. People are born with two kidneys, but they usually need only one. Meanwhile, a few people suffer from illnesses that leave them without any working kidney. Despite the obvious gains from trade, the current situation is dire: The typical patient has to wait several years for a kidney transplant, and every year thousands of people die because a compatible kidney cannot be found. If those needing a kidney were allowed to buy one from those who have two, the price would rise to balance supply and demand. Sellers would be better off with the extra cash in their pockets. Buyers would be better off with the organ they need to save their lives. The shortage of kidneys would disappear.

Such a market would lead to an efficient allocation of resources, but critics of this plan worry about fairness. A market for organs, they argue, would benefit the rich at the expense of the poor because organs would then be allocated to those most willing and able to pay. But you can also question the fairness of the current system. Now, most of us walk around with an extra organ that we don't really need, while some of our fellow citizens are dying to get one. Is that fair? ∎

QUICK QUIZ *Draw the supply and demand for turkey. In the equilibrium, show producer and consumer surplus. Explain why producing more turkeys would lower total surplus.*

Conclusion: Market Efficiency and Market Failure

This chapter introduced the basic tools of welfare economics—consumer and producer surplus—and used them to evaluate the efficiency of free markets. We showed that the forces of supply and demand allocate resources efficiently. That is, even though each buyer and seller in a market is concerned only about his or her own welfare, they are together led by an invisible hand to an equilibrium that maximizes the total benefits to buyers and sellers.

A word of warning is in order. To conclude that markets are efficient, we made several assumptions about how markets work. When these assumptions do not hold, our conclusion that the market equilibrium is efficient may no longer be true. As we close this chapter, let's consider briefly two of the most important of these assumptions.

First, our analysis assumed that markets are perfectly competitive. In the world, however, competition is sometimes far from perfect. In some markets, a single buyer or seller (or a small group of them) may be able to control market prices. This ability to influence prices is called *market power*. Market power can cause markets to be inefficient because it keeps the price and quantity away from the equilibrium of supply and demand.

Second, our analysis assumed that the outcome in a market matters only to the buyers and sellers in that market. Yet, in the world, the decisions of buyers and sellers sometimes affect people who are not participants in the market at all. Pollution is the classic example. The use of agricultural pesticides, for instance, affects not only the manufacturers who make them and the farmers who use them, but many others who breathe air or drink water that has been polluted with these pesticides. Such side effects, called *externalities*, cause welfare in a market to depend on more than just the value to the buyers and the cost to the sellers. Because buyers and sellers do not consider these side effects when deciding how much to consume and produce, the equilibrium in a market can be inefficient from the standpoint of society as a whole.

Market power and externalities are examples of a general phenomenon called *market failure*—the inability of some unregulated markets to allocate resources efficiently. When markets fail, public policy can potentially remedy the problem and increase economic efficiency. Microeconomists devote much effort to studying when market failure is likely and what sorts of policies are best at correcting market failures. As you continue your study of economics, you will see that the tools of welfare economics developed here are readily adapted to that endeavor.

Despite the possibility of market failure, the invisible hand of the marketplace is extraordinarily important. In many markets, the assumptions we made in this chapter work well, and the conclusion of market efficiency applies directly. Moreover, we can use our analysis of welfare economics and market efficiency to shed light on the effects of various government policies. In the next two chapters, we apply the tools we have just developed to study two important policy issues—the welfare effects of taxation and of international trade.

SUMMARY

- Consumer surplus equals buyers' willingness to pay for a good minus the amount they actually pay, and it measures the benefit buyers get from participating in a market. Consumer surplus can be computed by finding the area below the demand curve and above the price.

- Producer surplus equals the amount sellers receive for their goods minus their costs of production, and it measures the benefit sellers get from participating in a market. Producer surplus can be computed by finding the area below the price and above the supply curve.

- An allocation of resources that maximizes the sum of consumer and producer surplus is said to be efficient. Policymakers are often concerned with the efficiency, as well as the equality, of economic outcomes.

- The equilibrium of supply and demand maximizes the sum of consumer and producer surplus. That is, the invisible hand of the marketplace leads buyers and sellers to allocate resources efficiently.

- Markets do not allocate resources efficiently in the presence of market failures such as market power or externalities.

KEY CONCEPTS

welfare economics, *p. 136*   cost, *p. 141*   efficiency, *p. 145*
willingness to pay, *p. 136*   producer surplus, *p. 141*   equality, *p. 146*
consumer surplus, *p. 137*

QUESTIONS FOR REVIEW

1. Explain how buyers' willingness to pay, consumer surplus, and the demand curve are related.
2. Explain how sellers' costs, producer surplus, and the supply curve are related.
3. In a supply-and-demand diagram, show producer and consumer surplus in the market equilibrium.
4. What is efficiency? Is it the only goal of economic policymakers?
5. What does the invisible hand do?
6. Name two types of market failure. Explain why each may cause market outcomes to be inefficient.

PROBLEMS AND APPLICATIONS

1. Melissa buys an iPod for $120 and gets consumer surplus of $80.
   a. What is her willingness to pay?
   b. If she had bought the iPod on sale for $90, what would her consumer surplus have been?
   c. If the price of an iPod were $250, what would her consumer surplus have been?
2. An early freeze in California sours the lemon crop. Explain what happens to consumer surplus in the market for lemons. Explain what happens to consumer surplus in the market for lemonade. Illustrate your answers with diagrams.
3. Suppose the demand for French bread rises. Explain what happens to producer surplus in the market for French bread. Explain what happens to producer surplus in the market for flour. Illustrate your answers with diagrams.
4. It is a hot day, and Bert is thirsty. Here is the value he places on a bottle of water:

Value of first bottle	$7
Value of second bottle	5
Value of third bottle	3
Value of fourth bottle	1

   a. From this information, derive Bert's demand schedule. Graph his demand curve for bottled water.
   b. If the price of a bottle of water is $4, how many bottles does Bert buy? How much consumer surplus does Bert get from his purchases? Show Bert's consumer surplus in your graph.
   c. If the price falls to $2, how does quantity demanded change? How does Bert's consumer surplus change? Show these changes in your graph.
5. Ernie owns a water pump. Because pumping large amounts of water is harder than pumping small amounts, the cost of producing a bottle of water rises as he pumps more. Here is the cost he incurs to produce each bottle of water:

Cost of first bottle	$1
Cost of second bottle	3
Cost of third bottle	5
Cost of fourth bottle	7

   a. From this information, derive Ernie's supply schedule. Graph his supply curve for bottled water.
   b. If the price of a bottle of water is $4, how many bottles does Ernie produce and sell? How much producer surplus does Ernie get from these sales? Show Ernie's producer surplus in your graph.
   c. If the price rises to $6, how does quantity supplied change? How does Ernie's producer

surplus change? Show these changes in your graph.

6. Consider a market in which Bert from Problem 4 is the buyer and Ernie from Problem 5 is the seller.
   a. Use Ernie's supply schedule and Bert's demand schedule to find the quantity supplied and quantity demanded at prices of $2, $4, and $6. Which of these prices brings supply and demand into equilibrium?
   b. What are consumer surplus, producer surplus, and total surplus in this equilibrium?
   c. If Ernie produced and Bert consumed one fewer bottle of water, what would happen to total surplus?
   d. If Ernie produced and Bert consumed one additional bottle of water, what would happen to total surplus?

7. The cost of producing flat-screen TVs has fallen over the past decade. Let's consider some implications of this fact.
   a. Draw a supply-and-demand diagram to show the effect of falling production costs on the price and quantity of flat-screen TVs sold.
   b. In your diagram, show what happens to consumer surplus and producer surplus.
   c. Suppose the supply of flat-screen TVs is very elastic. Who benefits most from falling production costs—consumers or producers of these TVs?

8. There are four consumers willing to pay the following amounts for haircuts:

   Jerry: $7   Oprah: $2   Ellen: $8   Phil: $5

   There are four haircutting businesses with the following costs:

   Firm A: $3   Firm B: $6   Firm C: $4   Firm D: $2

   Each firm has the capacity to produce only one haircut. For efficiency, how many haircuts should be given? Which businesses should cut hair and which consumers should have their hair cut? How large is the maximum possible total surplus?

9. Suppose a technological advance reduces the cost of making computers.
   a. Draw a supply-and-demand diagram to show what happens to price, quantity, consumer surplus, and producer surplus in the market for computers.

b. Computers and typewriters are substitutes. Use a supply-and-demand diagram to show what happens to price, quantity, consumer surplus, and producer surplus in the market for typewriters. Should typewriter producers be happy or sad about the technological advance in computers?
c. Computers and software are complements. Draw a supply-and-demand diagram to show what happens to price, quantity, consumer surplus, and producer surplus in the market for software. Should software producers be happy or sad about the technological advance in computers?
d. Does this analysis help explain why software producer Bill Gates is one of the world's richest men?

10. A friend of yours is considering two cell phone service providers. Provider A charges $120 per month for the service regardless of the number of phone calls made. Provider B does not have a fixed service fee but instead charges $1 per minute for calls. Your friend's monthly demand for minutes of calling is given by the equation $Q^D = 150 - 50P$, where P is the price of a minute.
    a. With each provider, what is the cost to your friend of an extra minute on the phone?
    b. In light of your answer to (a), how many minutes would your friend talk on the phone with each provider?
    c. How much would he end up paying each provider every month?
    d. How much consumer surplus would he obtain with each provider? (Hint: Graph the demand curve and recall the formula for the area of a triangle.)
    e. Which provider would you recommend that your friend choose? Why?

11. Consider how health insurance affects the quantity of healthcare services performed. Suppose that the typical medical procedure has a cost of $100, yet a person with health insurance pays only $20 out of pocket. Her insurance company pays the remaining $80. (The insurance company recoups the $80 through premiums, but the premium a person pays does not depend on how many procedures that person chooses to undertake.)
    a. Draw the demand curve in the market for medical care. (In your diagram, the

horizontal axis should represent the number of medical procedures.) Show the quantity of procedures demanded if each procedure has a price of $100.

b. On your diagram, show the quantity of procedures demanded if consumers pay only $20 per procedure. If the cost of each procedure to society is truly $100, and if individuals have health insurance as just described, will the number of procedures performed maximize total surplus? Explain.

c. Economists often blame the health insurance system for excessive use of medical care. Given your analysis, why might the use of care be viewed as "excessive"?

d. What sort of policies might prevent this excessive use?

For further information on topics in this chapter, additional problems, applications, examples, online quizzes, and more, please visit our website at www .cengage.com/economics/mankiw.

Application: The Costs of Taxation

8

Taxes are often a source of heated political debate. In 1776, the anger of the American colonists over British taxes sparked the American Revolution. More than two centuries later, the American political parties continue to debate the proper size and shape of the tax system. Yet no one would deny that some level of taxation is necessary. As Oliver Wendell Holmes Jr. once said, "Taxes are what we pay for civilized society."

Because taxation has such a major impact on the modern economy, we return to the topic several times throughout this book as we expand the set of tools we have at our disposal. We began our study of taxes in Chapter 6. There we saw how a tax on a good affects its price and the quantity sold and how the forces of supply and demand divide the burden of a tax between buyers and sellers. In this chapter, we extend this analysis and look at how taxes affect welfare, the economic well-being of participants in a market. In other words, we see how high the price of civilized society can be.

The effects of taxes on welfare might at first seem obvious. The government enacts taxes to raise revenue and that revenue must come out of someone's pocket. As we saw in Chapter 6, both buyers and sellers are worse off when a good is taxed: A tax raises the price buyers pay and lowers the price sellers receive. Yet to understand more fully how taxes affect economic well-being, we must compare the reduced welfare of buyers and sellers to the amount of revenue the government raises. The tools of consumer and producer surplus allow us to make this comparison. The analysis will show that the cost of taxes to buyers and sellers exceeds the revenue raised by the government.

The Deadweight Loss of Taxation

We begin by recalling one of the surprising lessons from Chapter 6: The outcome is the same whether a tax on a good is levied on buyers or sellers of the good. When a tax is levied on buyers, the demand curve shifts downward by the size of the tax; when it is levied on sellers, the supply curve shifts upward by that amount. In either case, when the tax is enacted, the price paid by buyers rises, and the price received by sellers falls. In the end, the elasticities of supply and demand determine how the tax burden is distributed between producers and consumers. This distribution is the same regardless of how it is levied.

Figure 1 shows these effects. To simplify our discussion, this figure does not show a shift in either the supply or demand curve, although one curve must shift. Which curve shifts depends on whether the tax is levied on sellers (the supply curve shifts) or buyers (the demand curve shifts). In this chapter, we can keep the analysis general and simplify the graphs by not bothering to show the shift. The key result for our purposes here is that the tax places a wedge between the price buyers pay and the price sellers receive. Because of this tax wedge, the quantity sold falls below the level that would be sold without a tax. In other words, a tax on

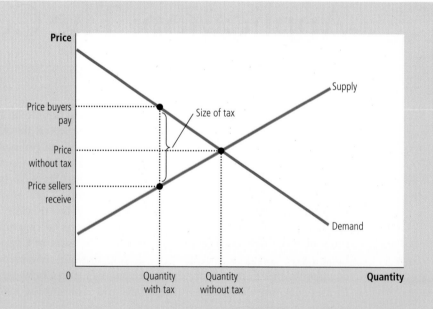

Figure **1**

The Effects of a Tax
A tax on a good places a wedge between the price that buyers pay and the price that sellers receive. The quantity of the good sold falls.

a good causes the size of the market for the good to shrink. These results should be familiar from Chapter 6.

How a Tax Affects Market Participants

Let's use the tools of welfare economics to measure the gains and losses from a tax on a good. To do this, we must take into account how the tax affects buyers, sellers, and the government. The benefit received by buyers in a market is measured by consumer surplus—the amount buyers are willing to pay for the good minus the amount they actually pay for it. The benefit received by sellers in a market is measured by producer surplus—the amount sellers receive for the good minus their costs. These are precisely the measures of economic welfare we used in Chapter 7.

What about the third interested party, the government? If T is the size of the tax and Q is the quantity of the good sold, then the government gets total tax revenue of $T \times Q$. It can use this tax revenue to provide services, such as roads, police, and public education, or to help the needy. Therefore, to analyze how taxes affect economic well-being, we use the government's tax revenue to measure the public benefit from the tax. Keep in mind, however, that this benefit actually accrues not to the government but to those on whom the revenue is spent.

Figure 2 shows that the government's tax revenue is represented by the rectangle between the supply and demand curves. The height of this rectangle is the size of the tax, T, and the width of the rectangle is the quantity of the good sold, Q. Because a rectangle's area is its height times its width, this rectangle's area is $T \times Q$, which equals the tax revenue.

Welfare without a Tax To see how a tax affects welfare, we begin by considering welfare before the government imposes a tax. Figure 3 shows the supply-and-demand diagram and marks the key areas with the letters A through F.

"You know, the idea of taxation with representation doesn't appeal to me very much, either."

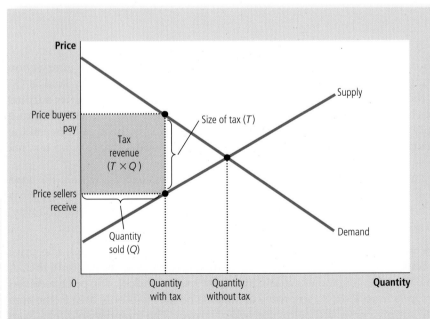

Figure **2**

Tax Revenue
The tax revenue that the government collects equals $T \times Q$, the size of the tax T times the quantity sold Q. Thus, tax revenue equals the area of the rectangle between the supply and demand curves.

Figure 3

How a Tax Affects Welfare

A tax on a good reduces consumer surplus (by the area B + C) and producer surplus (by the area D + E). Because the fall in producer and consumer surplus exceeds tax revenue (area B + D), the tax is said to impose a deadweight loss (area C + E).

	Without Tax	With Tax	Change
Consumer Surplus	A + B + C	A	−(B + C)
Producer Surplus	D + E + F	F	−(D + E)
Tax Revenue	None	B + D	+(B + D)
Total Surplus	A + B + C + D + E + F	A + B + D + F	−(C + E)

The area C + E shows the fall in total surplus and is the deadweight loss of the tax.

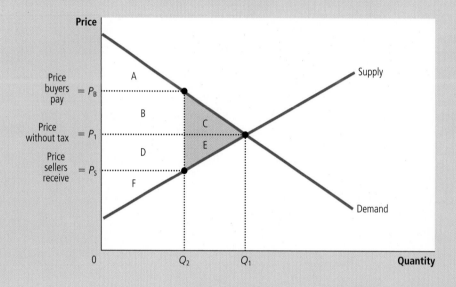

Without a tax, the equilibrium price and quantity are found at the intersection of the supply and demand curves. The price is P_1, and the quantity sold is Q_1. Because the demand curve reflects buyers' willingness to pay, consumer surplus is the area between the demand curve and the price, A + B + C. Similarly, because the supply curve reflects sellers' costs, producer surplus is the area between the supply curve and the price, D + E + F. In this case, because there is no tax, tax revenue equals zero.

Total surplus, the sum of consumer and producer surplus, equals the area A + B + C + D + E + F. In other words, as we saw in Chapter 7, total surplus is the area between the supply and demand curves up to the equilibrium quantity. The first column of the table in Figure 3 summarizes these conclusions.

Welfare with a Tax Now consider welfare after the tax is enacted. The price paid by buyers rises from P_1 to P_B, so consumer surplus now equals only area A (the area below the demand curve and above the buyer's price). The price received by sellers falls from P_1 to P_S, so producer surplus now equals only area F (the area above the supply curve and below the seller's price). The quantity sold falls from Q_1 to Q_2, and the government collects tax revenue equal to the area B + D.

To compute total surplus with the tax, we add consumer surplus, producer surplus, and tax revenue. Thus, we find that total surplus is area A + B + D + F. The second column of the table summarizes these results.

Changes in Welfare   We can now see the effects of the tax by comparing welfare before and after the tax is enacted. The third column of the table in Figure 3 shows the changes. The tax causes consumer surplus to fall by the area B + C and producer surplus to fall by the area D + E. Tax revenue rises by the area B + D. Not surprisingly, the tax makes buyers and sellers worse off and the government better off.

The change in total welfare includes the change in consumer surplus (which is negative), the change in producer surplus (which is also negative), and the change in tax revenue (which is positive). When we add these three pieces together, we find that total surplus in the market falls by the area C + E. *Thus, the losses to buyers and sellers from a tax exceed the revenue raised by the government.* The fall in total surplus that results when a tax (or some other policy) distorts a market outcome is called the **deadweight loss.** The area C + E measures the size of the deadweight loss.

To understand why taxes impose deadweight losses, recall one of the *Ten Principles of Economics* in Chapter 1: People respond to incentives. In Chapter 7, we saw that free markets normally allocate scarce resources efficiently. That is, the equilibrium of supply and demand maximizes the total surplus of buyers and sellers in a market. When a tax raises the price to buyers and lowers the price to sellers, however, it gives buyers an incentive to consume less and sellers an incentive to produce less than they would in the absence of the tax. As buyers and sellers respond to these incentives, the size of the market shrinks below its optimum (as shown in the figure by the movement from Q_1 to Q_2). Thus, because taxes distort incentives, they cause markets to allocate resources inefficiently.

deadweight loss
the fall in total surplus that results from a market distortion, such as a tax

Deadweight Losses and the Gains from Trade

To get some further insight into why taxes result in deadweight losses, consider an example. Imagine that Joe cleans Jane's house each week for $100. The opportunity cost of Joe's time is $80, and the value of a clean house to Jane is $120. Thus, Joe and Jane each receive a $20 benefit from their deal. The total surplus of $40 measures the gains from trade in this particular transaction.

Now suppose that the government levies a $50 tax on the providers of cleaning services. There is now no price that Jane can pay Joe that will leave both of them better off after paying the tax. The most Jane would be willing to pay is $120, but then Joe would be left with only $70 after paying the tax, which is less than his $80 opportunity cost. Conversely, for Joe to receive his opportunity cost of $80, Jane would need to pay $130, which is above the $120 value she places on a clean house. As a result, Jane and Joe cancel their arrangement. Joe goes without the income, and Jane lives in a dirtier house.

The tax has made Joe and Jane worse off by a total of $40 because they have each lost $20 of surplus. But note that the government collects no revenue from Joe and Jane because they decide to cancel their arrangement. The $40 is pure deadweight loss: It is a loss to buyers and sellers in a market that is not offset by an increase in government revenue. From this example, we can see the ultimate source of deadweight losses: *Taxes cause deadweight losses because they prevent buyers and sellers from realizing some of the gains from trade.*

The area of the triangle between the supply and demand curves (area C + E in Figure 3) measures these losses. This conclusion can be seen more easily in Figure 4

Figure 4

The Deadweight Loss
When the government imposes a tax on a good, the quantity sold falls from Q_1 to Q_2. At every quantity between Q_1 and Q_2, the potential gains from trade among buyers and sellers are not realized. These lost gains from trade create the deadweight loss.

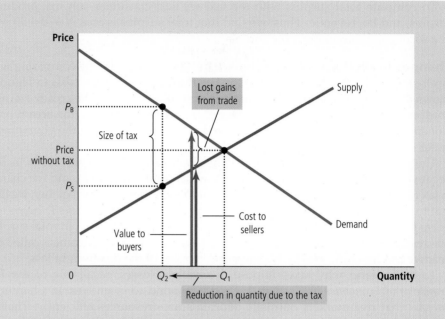

by recalling that the demand curve reflects the value of the good to consumers and that the supply curve reflects the costs of producers. When the tax raises the price to buyers to P_B and lowers the price to sellers to P_S, the marginal buyers and sellers leave the market, so the quantity sold falls from Q_1 to Q_2. Yet as the figure shows, the value of the good to these buyers still exceeds the cost to these sellers. At every quantity between Q_1 and Q_2, the situation is the same as in our example with Joe and Jane. The gains from trade—the difference between buyers' value and sellers' cost—are less than the tax. As a result, these trades are not made once the tax is imposed. The deadweight loss is the surplus lost because the tax discourages these mutually advantageous trades.

QUICK QUIZ   *Draw the supply and demand curves for cookies. If the government imposes a tax on cookies, show what happens to the price paid by buyers, the price received by sellers, and the quantity sold. In your diagram, show the deadweight loss from the tax. Explain the meaning of the deadweight loss.*

The Determinants of the Deadweight Loss

What determines whether the deadweight loss from a tax is large or small? The answer is the price elasticities of supply and demand, which measure how much the quantity supplied and quantity demanded respond to changes in the price.

Let's consider first how the elasticity of supply affects the size of the deadweight loss. In the top two panels of Figure 5, the demand curve and the size of the tax are the same. The only difference in these figures is the elasticity of the supply curve. In panel (a), the supply curve is relatively inelastic: Quantity supplied responds only slightly to changes in the price. In panel (b), the supply curve is relatively elastic: Quantity supplied responds substantially to changes in the price. Notice that the deadweight loss, the area of the triangle between the supply and demand curves, is larger when the supply curve is more elastic.

Similarly, the bottom two panels of Figure 5 show how the elasticity of demand affects the size of the deadweight loss. Here the supply curve and the size of the tax are held constant. In panel (c), the demand curve is relatively inelastic, and the

In panels (a) and (b), the demand curve and the size of the tax are the same, but the price elasticity of supply is different. Notice that the more elastic the supply curve, the larger the deadweight loss of the tax. In panels (c) and (d), the supply curve and the size of the tax are the same, but the price elasticity of demand is different. Notice that the more elastic the demand curve, the larger the deadweight loss of the tax.

Figure **5**

Tax Distortions and Elasticities

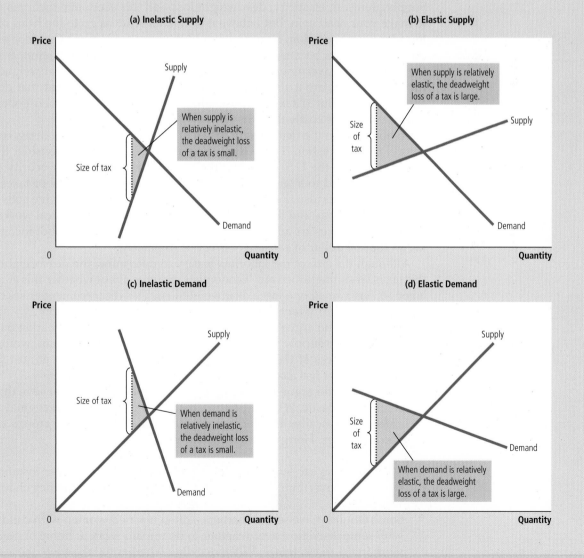

(a) Inelastic Supply

Price

Supply

When supply is relatively inelastic, the deadweight loss of a tax is small.

Size of tax

Demand

0   **Quantity**

(b) Elastic Supply

Price

When supply is relatively elastic, the deadweight loss of a tax is large.

Size of tax

Supply

Demand

0   **Quantity**

(c) Inelastic Demand

Price

Supply

Size of tax

When demand is relatively inelastic, the deadweight loss of a tax is small.

Demand

0   **Quantity**

(d) Elastic Demand

Price

Supply

Size of tax

Demand

When demand is relatively elastic, the deadweight loss of a tax is large.

0   **Quantity**

deadweight loss is small. In panel (d), the demand curve is more elastic, and the deadweight loss from the tax is larger.

The lesson from this figure is apparent. A tax has a deadweight loss because it induces buyers and sellers to change their behavior. The tax raises the price paid by buyers, so they consume less. At the same time, the tax lowers the price received by sellers, so they produce less. Because of these changes in behavior, the size of the market shrinks below the optimum. The elasticities of supply and demand measure how much sellers and buyers respond to the changes in the price and, therefore, determine how much the tax distorts the market outcome. Hence, *the greater the elasticities of supply and demand, the greater the deadweight loss of a tax.*

 ### The Deadweight Loss Debate

Supply, demand, elasticity, deadweight loss—all this economic theory is enough to make your head spin. But believe it or not, these ideas go to the heart of a profound political question: How big should the government be? The debate hinges on these concepts because the larger the deadweight loss of taxation, the larger the cost of any government program. If taxation entails large deadweight losses, then these losses are a strong argument for a leaner government that does less and taxes less. But if taxes impose small deadweight losses, then government programs are less costly than they otherwise might be.

So how big are the deadweight losses of taxation? Economists disagree on the answer to this question. To see the nature of this disagreement, consider the most important tax in the U.S. economy: the tax on labor. The Social Security tax, the Medicare tax, and to a large extent, the federal income tax are labor taxes. Many state governments also tax labor earnings. A labor tax places a wedge between the wage that firms pay and the wage that workers receive. For a typical worker, if all forms of labor taxes are added together, the *marginal tax rate* on labor income—the tax on the last dollar of earnings—is about 40 percent.

Although the size of the labor tax is easy to determine, the deadweight loss of this tax is less straightforward. Economists disagree about whether this 40 percent labor tax has a small or a large deadweight loss. This disagreement arises because economists hold different views about the elasticity of labor supply.

Economists who argue that labor taxes do not greatly distort market outcomes believe that labor supply is fairly inelastic. Most people, they claim, would work full time regardless of the wage. If so, the labor supply curve is almost vertical, and a tax on labor has a small deadweight loss.

Economists who argue that labor taxes are highly distorting believe that labor supply is more elastic. While admitting that some groups of workers may supply their labor inelastically, these economists claim that many other groups respond more to incentives. Here are some examples:

- Many workers can adjust the number of hours they work—for instance, by working overtime. The higher the wage, the more hours they choose to work.
- Some families have second earners—often married women with children—with some discretion over whether to do unpaid work at home or paid work in the marketplace. When deciding whether to take a job, these second

earners compare the benefits of being at home (including savings on the cost of child care) with the wages they could earn.

- Many of the elderly can choose when to retire, and their decisions are partly based on the wage. Once they are retired, the wage determines their incentive to work part time.
- Some people consider engaging in illegal economic activity, such as the drug trade, or working at jobs that pay "under the table" to evade taxes. Economists call this the *underground economy*. In deciding whether to work in the underground economy or at a legitimate job, these potential criminals compare what they can earn by breaking the law with the wage they can earn legally.

"What's your position on the elasticity of labor supply?"

In each of these cases, the quantity of labor supplied responds to the wage (the price of labor). Thus, these workers' decisions are distorted when their labor earnings are taxed. Labor taxes encourage workers to work fewer hours, second earners to stay at home, the elderly to retire early, and the unscrupulous to enter the underground economy.

These two views of labor taxation persist to this day. Indeed, whenever you see two political candidates debating whether the government should provide more services or reduce the tax burden, keep in mind that part of the disagreement may rest on different views about the elasticity of labor supply and the deadweight loss of taxation. ■

QUICK QUIZ   *The demand for beer is more elastic than the demand for milk. Would a tax on beer or a tax on milk have a larger deadweight loss? Why?*

Deadweight Loss and Tax Revenue as Taxes Vary

Taxes rarely stay the same for long periods of time. Policymakers in local, state, and federal governments are always considering raising one tax or lowering another. Here we consider what happens to the deadweight loss and tax revenue when the size of a tax changes.

Figure 6 shows the effects of a small, medium, and large tax, holding constant the market's supply and demand curves. The deadweight loss—the reduction in total surplus that results when the tax reduces the size of a market below the optimum—equals the area of the triangle between the supply and demand curves. For the small tax in panel (a), the area of the deadweight loss triangle is quite small. But as the size of a tax rises in panels (b) and (c), the deadweight loss grows larger and larger.

Indeed, the deadweight loss of a tax rises even more rapidly than the size of the tax. This occurs because the deadweight loss is an area of a triangle, and the area of a triangle depends on the *square* of its size. If we double the size of a tax, for instance, the base and height of the triangle double, so the deadweight loss rises by a factor of 4. If we triple the size of a tax, the base and height triple, so the deadweight loss rises by a factor of 9.

The government's tax revenue is the size of the tax times the amount of the good sold. As the first three panels of Figure 6 show, tax revenue equals the area of the rectangle between the supply and demand curves. For the small tax in panel (a), tax revenue is small. As the size of a tax increases from panel (a) to panel (b),

Figure **6**

How Deadweight Loss and Tax Revenue Vary with the Size of a Tax

The deadweight loss is the reduction in total surplus due to the tax. Tax revenue is the amount of the tax times the amount of the good sold. In panel (a), a small tax has a small deadweight loss and raises a small amount of revenue. In panel (b), a somewhat larger tax has a larger deadweight loss and raises a larger amount of revenue. In panel (c), a very large tax has a very large deadweight loss, but because it has reduced the size of the market so much, the tax raises only a small amount of revenue. Panels (d) and (e) summarize these conclusions. Panel (d) shows that as the size of a tax grows larger, the deadweight loss grows larger. Panel (e) shows that tax revenue first rises and then falls. This relationship is sometimes called the Laffer curve.

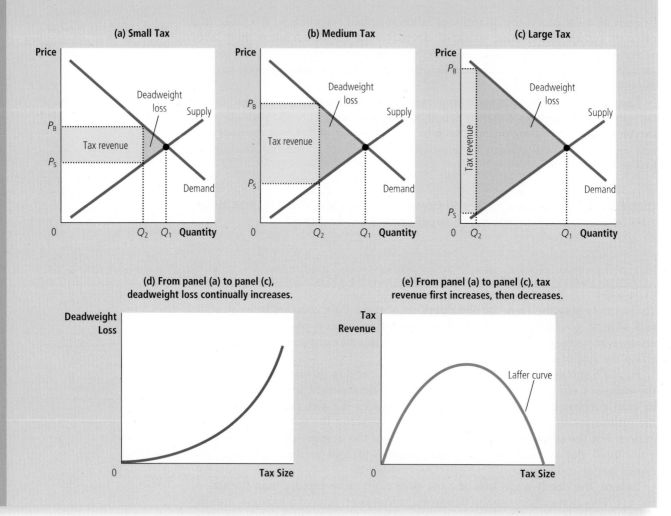

tax revenue grows. But as the size of the tax increases further from panel (b) to panel (c), tax revenue falls because the higher tax drastically reduces the size of the market. For a very large tax, no revenue would be raised because people would stop buying and selling the good altogether.

The last two panels of Figure 6 summarize these results. In panel (d), we see that as the size of a tax increases, its deadweight loss quickly gets larger. By contrast, panel (e) shows that tax revenue first rises with the size of the tax, but as the tax gets larger, the market shrinks so much that tax revenue starts to fall.

The Laffer Curve and Supply-Side Economics

One day in 1974, economist Arthur Laffer sat in a Washington restaurant with some prominent journalists and politicians. He took out a napkin and drew a figure on it to show how tax rates affect tax revenue. It looked much like panel (e) of our Figure 6. Laffer then suggested that the United States was on the downward-sloping side of this curve. Tax rates were so high, he argued, that reducing them would actually increase tax revenue.

Most economists were skeptical of Laffer's suggestion. The idea that a cut in tax rates could increase tax revenue was correct as a matter of economic theory, but there was more doubt about whether it would do so in practice. There was little evidence for Laffer's view that U.S. tax rates had in fact reached such extreme levels.

Nonetheless, the *Laffer curve* (as it became known) captured the imagination of Ronald Reagan. David Stockman, budget director in the first Reagan administration, offers the following story:

> [Reagan] had once been on the Laffer curve himself. "I came into the Big Money making pictures during World War II," he would always say. At that time the wartime income surtax hit 90 percent. "You could only make four pictures and then you were in the top bracket," he would continue. "So we all quit working after four pictures and went off to the country." High tax rates caused less work. Low tax rates caused more. His experience proved it.

When Reagan ran for president in 1980, he made cutting taxes part of his platform. Reagan argued taxes were so high that they were discouraging hard work. He argued that lower taxes would give people the proper incentive to work, which would raise economic well-being and perhaps even tax revenue. Because the cut in tax rates was intended to encourage people to increase the quantity of labor they supplied, the views of Laffer and Reagan became known as *supply-side economics*.

Economists continue to debate Laffer's argument. Many believe that subsequent history refuted Laffer's conjecture that lower tax rates would raise tax revenue. Yet because history is open to alternative interpretations, other economists view the events of the 1980s as more favorable to the supply siders. To evaluate Laffer's hypothesis definitively, we would need to rerun history without the Reagan tax cuts and see if tax revenues were higher or lower. Unfortunately, that experiment is impossible.

Some economists take an intermediate position on this issue. They believe that while an overall cut in tax rates normally reduces revenue, some taxpayers at some times may find themselves on the wrong side of the Laffer curve. Other things equal, a tax cut is more likely to raise tax revenue if the cut applies to those taxpayers facing the highest tax rates. In addition, Laffer's argument may be more compelling when considering countries with much higher tax rates than the United States. In Sweden in the early 1980s, for instance, the typical worker faced a marginal tax rate of about 80 percent. Such a high tax rate provides a substantial disincentive to work. Studies have suggested that Sweden would indeed have raised more tax revenue if it had lowered its tax rates.

in the **news**

> ## New Research on Taxation
>
> *According to the latest research, most countries are on the left side of the Laffer curve. But that is not true everywhere for all taxes.*

ECB Paper Looks at U.S., Europe Spots on the Laffer Curve

BY BRIAN BLACKSTONE

Economist Arthur Laffer's theory is that, after a certain point, tax increases become self-defeating by weakening economic growth and draining tax revenues. There are two points—zero and 100%—where the government receives no revenue. The trick is finding the peak point between the two.

The Laffer curve served as an intellectual foundation for large-scale tax cuts in the U.S. in the early 1980s. Now, the U.S. is on the "left side" of the Laffer curve even more so than Europe, especially when it comes to labor taxes, meaning higher tax rates would still bring in added revenues, a European Central Bank paper concludes.

"We find that the U.S. can increase tax revenues by 30% by raising labor taxes but only 6% by raising capital income taxes, while the same numbers for EU-14 are 8% and 1% respectively," ECB economist Mathias Trabandt and University of Chicago economist Harald Uhlig wrote. Germany could raise about another 10% in revenues by increasing labor taxes, they estimate, but just 2% via capital taxes.

Only 32% of a cut in U.S. labor taxes would be self-financed, the economists note, versus 54% self-financing in Europe. Just over 50% of a cut in U.S. capital taxes would pay for itself, the authors estimate, versus 79% in Europe.

"In terms of a 'Laffer hill', both the U.S. and the EU-14 are on the left side of the peak with respect to their capital tax rates," the authors wrote. But in the case of Denmark and Sweden, "these countries are on the 'slippery side' of the Laffer curve and can actually improve their budgetary situation by cutting capital taxes, according to our calculations," they wrote.

Source: *Wall Street Journal*, Real Time Economics blog, April 21, 2010.

Economists disagree about these issues in part because there is no consensus about the size of the relevant elasticities. The more elastic supply and demand are in any market, the more taxes in the market distort behavior, and the more likely it is that a tax cut will increase tax revenue. There is no debate, however, about the general lesson: How much revenue the government gains or loses from a tax change cannot be computed just by looking at tax rates. It also depends on how the tax change affects people's behavior. ■

QUICK QUIZ   *If the government doubles the tax on gasoline, can you be sure that revenue from the gasoline tax will rise? Can you be sure that the deadweight loss from the gasoline tax will rise? Explain.*

Conclusion

In this chapter we have used the tools developed in the previous chapter to further our understanding of taxes. One of the *Ten Principles of Economics* discussed in Chapter 1 is that markets are usually a good way to organize economic activity. In

Chapter 7, we used the concepts of producer and consumer surplus to make this principle more precise. Here we have seen that when the government imposes taxes on buyers or sellers of a good, society loses some of the benefits of market efficiency. Taxes are costly to market participants not only because taxes transfer resources from those participants to the government but also because they alter incentives and distort market outcomes.

The analysis presented here and in Chapter 6 should give you a good basis for understanding the economic impact of taxes, but this is not the end of the story. Microeconomists study how best to design a tax system, including how to strike the right balance between equality and efficiency. Macroeconomists study how taxes influence the overall economy and how policymakers can use the tax system to stabilize economic activity and to achieve more rapid economic growth. So as you continue your study of economics, don't be surprised when the subject of taxation comes up yet again.

SUMMARY

- A tax on a good reduces the welfare of buyers and sellers of the good, and the reduction in consumer and producer surplus usually exceeds the revenue raised by the government. The fall in total surplus—the sum of consumer surplus, producer surplus, and tax revenue—is called the deadweight loss of the tax.

- Taxes have deadweight losses because they cause buyers to consume less and sellers to produce less, and these changes in behavior shrink the size of the market below the level that maximizes total surplus. Because the elasticities of supply and demand measure how much market participants respond to market conditions, larger elasticities imply larger deadweight losses.

- As a tax grows larger, it distorts incentives more, and its deadweight loss grows larger. Because a tax reduces the size of the market, however, tax revenue does not continually increase. It first rises with the size of a tax, but if a tax gets large enough, tax revenue starts to fall.

KEY CONCEPT

deadweight loss, *p. 159*

QUESTIONS FOR REVIEW

1. What happens to consumer and producer surplus when the sale of a good is taxed? How does the change in consumer and producer surplus compare to the tax revenue? Explain.
2. Draw a supply-and-demand diagram with a tax on the sale of the good. Show the deadweight loss. Show the tax revenue.
3. How do the elasticities of supply and demand affect the deadweight loss of a tax? Why do they have this effect?
4. Why do experts disagree about whether labor taxes have small or large deadweight losses?
5. What happens to the deadweight loss and tax revenue when a tax is increased?

PROBLEMS AND APPLICATIONS

1. The market for pizza is characterized by a downward-sloping demand curve and an upward-sloping supply curve.
   a. Draw the competitive market equilibrium. Label the price, quantity, consumer surplus, and producer surplus. Is there any deadweight loss? Explain.
   b. Suppose that the government forces each pizzeria to pay a $1 tax on each pizza sold. Illustrate the effect of this tax on the pizza market, being sure to label the consumer surplus, producer surplus, government revenue, and deadweight loss. How does each area compare to the pre-tax case?
   c. If the tax were removed, pizza eaters and sellers would be better off, but the government would lose tax revenue. Suppose that consumers and producers voluntarily transferred some of their gains to the government. Could all parties (including the government) be better off than they were with a tax? Explain using the labeled areas in your graph.

2. Evaluate the following two statements. Do you agree? Why or why not?
   a. "A tax that has no deadweight loss cannot raise any revenue for the government."
   b. "A tax that raises no revenue for the government cannot have any deadweight loss."

3. Consider the market for rubber bands.
   a. If this market has very elastic supply and very inelastic demand, how would the burden of a tax on rubber bands be shared between consumers and producers? Use the tools of consumer surplus and producer surplus in your answer.
   b. If this market has very inelastic supply and very elastic demand, how would the burden of a tax on rubber bands be shared between consumers and producers? Contrast your answer with your answer to part (a).

4. Suppose that the government imposes a tax on heating oil.
   a. Would the deadweight loss from this tax likely be greater in the first year after it is imposed or in the fifth year? Explain.
   b. Would the revenue collected from this tax likely be greater in the first year after it is imposed or in the fifth year? Explain.

5. After economics class one day, your friend suggests that taxing food would be a good way to raise revenue because the demand for food is quite inelastic. In what sense is taxing food a "good" way to raise revenue? In what sense is it not a "good" way to raise revenue?

6. Daniel Patrick Moynihan, the late senator from New York, once introduced a bill that would levy a 10,000 percent tax on certain hollow-tipped bullets.
   a. Do you expect that this tax would raise much revenue? Why or why not?
   b. Even if the tax would raise no revenue, why might Senator Moynihan have proposed it?

7. The government places a tax on the purchase of socks.
   a. Illustrate the effect of this tax on equilibrium price and quantity in the sock market. Identify the following areas both before and after the imposition of the tax: total spending by consumers, total revenue for producers, and government tax revenue.
   b. Does the price received by producers rise or fall? Can you tell whether total receipts for producers rise or fall? Explain.
   c. Does the price paid by consumers rise or fall? Can you tell whether total spending by consumers rises or falls? Explain carefully. (Hint: Think about elasticity.) If total consumer spending falls, does consumer surplus rise? Explain.

8. Suppose the government currently raises $100 million through a 1-cent tax on widgets, and another $100 million through a 10-cent tax on gadgets. If the government doubled the tax rate on widgets and eliminated the tax on gadgets, would it raise more tax revenue than it does today, less tax revenue, or the same amount? Explain.

9. This chapter analyzed the welfare effects of a tax on a good. Consider now the opposite policy. Suppose that the government *subsidizes* a good: For each unit of the good sold, the government pays $2 to the buyer. How does the subsidy affect consumer surplus, producer surplus, tax revenue, and total surplus? Does a subsidy lead to a deadweight loss? Explain.

10. Hotel rooms in Smalltown go for $100, and 1,000 rooms are rented on a typical day.
    a. To raise revenue, the mayor decides to charge hotels a tax of $10 per rented room. After the tax is imposed, the going rate for hotel rooms rises to $108, and the number of rooms rented falls to 900. Calculate the amount of revenue this tax raises for Smalltown and the deadweight loss of the tax. (Hint: The area of a triangle is ½ × base × height.)
    b. The mayor now doubles the tax to $20. The price rises to $116, and the number of rooms rented falls to 800. Calculate tax revenue and deadweight loss with this larger tax. Do they double, more than double, or less than double? Explain.

11. Suppose that a market is described by the following supply and demand equations:

$$Q^S = 2P$$
$$Q^D = 300 - P$$

    a. Solve for the equilibrium price and the equilibrium quantity.
    b. Suppose that a tax of T is placed on buyers, so the new demand equation is

$$Q^D = 300 - (P + T).$$

    Solve for the new equilibrium. What happens to the price received by sellers, the price paid by buyers, and the quantity sold?
    c. Tax revenue is $T \times Q$. Use your answer to part (b) to solve for tax revenue as a function of T. Graph this relationship for T between 0 and 300.
    d. The deadweight loss of a tax is the area of the triangle between the supply and demand curves. Recalling that the area of a triangle is ½ × base × height, solve for deadweight loss as a function of T. Graph this relationship for T between 0 and 300. (Hint: Looking sideways, the base of the deadweight loss triangle is T, and the height is the difference between the quantity sold with the tax and the quantity sold without the tax.)
    e. The government now levies a tax on this good of $200 per unit. Is this a good policy? Why or why not? Can you propose a better policy?

For further information on topics in this chapter, additional problems, applications, examples, online quizzes, and more, please visit our website at www .cengage.com/economics/mankiw.

Application: International Trade

If you check the labels on the clothes you are now wearing, you will probably find that some of your clothes were made in another country. A century ago, the textile and clothing industry was a major part of the U.S. economy, but that is no longer the case. Faced with foreign competitors that can produce quality goods at low cost, many U.S. firms have found it increasingly difficult to produce and sell textiles and clothing at a profit. As a result, they have laid off their workers and shut down their factories. Today, much of the textiles and clothing that Americans consume are imported.

The story of the textile industry raises important questions for economic policy: How does international trade affect economic well-being? Who gains and who loses from free trade among countries, and how do the gains compare to the losses?

Chapter 3 introduced the study of international trade by applying the principle of comparative advantage. According to this principle, all countries can benefit from trading with one another because trade allows each country to specialize in doing what it does best. But the analysis in Chapter 3 was incomplete. It did not explain how the international marketplace achieves these gains from trade or how the gains are distributed among various economic participants.

We now return to the study of international trade and take up these questions. Over the past several chapters, we have developed many tools for analyzing how markets work: supply, demand, equilibrium, consumer surplus, producer surplus, and so on. With these tools, we can learn more about how international trade affects economic well-being.

The Determinants of Trade

Consider the market for textiles. The textile market is well suited to examining the gains and losses from international trade: Textiles are made in many countries around the world, and there is much world trade in textiles. Moreover, the textile market is one in which policymakers often consider (and sometimes implement) trade restrictions to protect domestic producers from foreign competitors. We examine here the textile market in the imaginary country of Isoland.

The Equilibrium without Trade

As our story begins, the Isolandian textile market is isolated from the rest of the world. By government decree, no one in Isoland is allowed to import or export textiles, and the penalty for violating the decree is so large that no one dares try.

Because there is no international trade, the market for textiles in Isoland consists solely of Isolandian buyers and sellers. As Figure 1 shows, the domestic price adjusts to balance the quantity supplied by domestic sellers and the quantity demanded by domestic buyers. The figure shows the consumer and producer surplus in the equilibrium without trade. The sum of consumer and producer surplus measures the total benefits that buyers and sellers receive from participating in the textile market.

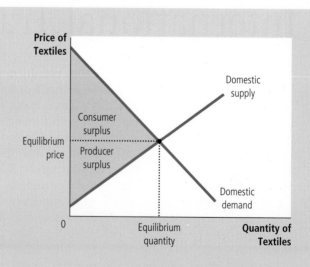

Figure **1**

The Equilibrium without International Trade
When an economy cannot trade in world markets, the price adjusts to balance domestic supply and demand. This figure shows consumer and producer surplus in an equilibrium without international trade for the textile market in the imaginary country of Isoland.

Now suppose that, in an election upset, Isoland elects a new president. The president campaigned on a platform of "change" and promised the voters bold new ideas. Her first act is to assemble a team of economists to evaluate Isolandian trade policy. She asks them to report on three questions:

- If the government allows Isolandians to import and export textiles, what will happen to the price of textiles and the quantity of textiles sold in the domestic textile market?
- Who will gain from free trade in textiles and who will lose, and will the gains exceed the losses?
- Should a tariff (a tax on textile imports) be part of the new trade policy?

After reviewing supply and demand in their favorite textbook (this one, of course), the Isolandian economics team begins its analysis.

The World Price and Comparative Advantage

The first issue our economists take up is whether Isoland is likely to become a textile importer or a textile exporter. In other words, if free trade is allowed, will Isolandians end up buying or selling textiles in world markets?

To answer this question, the economists compare the current Isolandian price of textiles to the price of textiles in other countries. We call the price prevailing in world markets the **world price.** If the world price of textiles is higher than the domestic price, then Isoland will export textiles once trade is permitted. Isolandian textile producers will be eager to receive the higher prices available abroad and will start selling their textiles to buyers in other countries. Conversely, if the world price of textiles is lower than the domestic price, then Isoland will import textiles. Because foreign sellers offer a better price, Isolandian textile consumers will quickly start buying textiles from other countries.

In essence, comparing the world price and the domestic price before trade indicates whether Isoland has a comparative advantage in producing textiles. The domestic price reflects the opportunity cost of textiles: It tells us how much an Isolandian must give up to obtain one unit of textiles. If the domestic price is low, the cost of producing textiles in Isoland is low, suggesting that Isoland has a comparative advantage in producing textiles relative to the rest of the world. If the domestic price is high, then the cost of producing textiles in Isoland is high, suggesting that foreign countries have a comparative advantage in producing textiles.

As we saw in Chapter 3, trade among nations is ultimately based on comparative advantage. That is, trade is beneficial because it allows each nation to specialize in doing what it does best. By comparing the world price and the domestic price before trade, we can determine whether Isoland is better or worse at producing textiles than the rest of the world.

world price

the price of a good that prevails in the world market for that good

QUICK QUIZ *The country Autarka does not allow international trade. In Autarka, you can buy a wool suit for 3 ounces of gold. Meanwhile, in neighboring countries, you can buy the same suit for 2 ounces of gold. If Autarka were to allow free trade, would it import or export wool suits? Why?*

The Winners and Losers from Trade

To analyze the welfare effects of free trade, the Isolandian economists begin with the assumption that Isoland is a small economy compared to the rest of the world. This small-economy assumption means that Isoland's actions have little effect on world markets. Specifically, any change in Isoland's trade policy will not affect the world price of textiles. The Isolandians are said to be *price takers* in the world economy. That is, they take the world price of textiles as given. Isoland can be an exporting country by selling textiles at this price or an importing country by buying textiles at this price.

The small-economy assumption is not necessary to analyze the gains and losses from international trade. But the Isolandian economists know from experience (and from reading Chapter 2 of this book) that making simplifying assumptions is a key part of building a useful economic model. The assumption that Isoland is a small economy simplifies the analysis, and the basic lessons do not change in the more complicated case of a large economy.

The Gains and Losses of an Exporting Country

Figure 2 shows the Isolandian textile market when the domestic equilibrium price before trade is below the world price. Once trade is allowed, the domestic price rises to equal the world price. No seller of textiles would accept less than the world price, and no buyer would pay more than the world price.

Figure 2

International Trade in an Exporting Country
Once trade is allowed, the domestic price rises to equal the world price. The supply curve shows the quantity of textiles produced domestically, and the demand curve shows the quantity consumed domestically. Exports from Isoland equal the difference between the domestic quantity supplied and the domestic quantity demanded at the world price. Sellers are better off (producer surplus rises from C to B + C + D), and buyers are worse off (consumer surplus falls from A + B to A). Total surplus rises by an amount equal to area D, indicating that trade raises the economic well-being of the country as a whole.

	Before Trade	After Trade	Change
Consumer Surplus	A + B	A	−B
Producer Surplus	C	B + C + D	+(B + D)
Total Surplus	A + B + C	A + B + C + D	+D

The area D shows the increase in total surplus and represents the gains from trade.

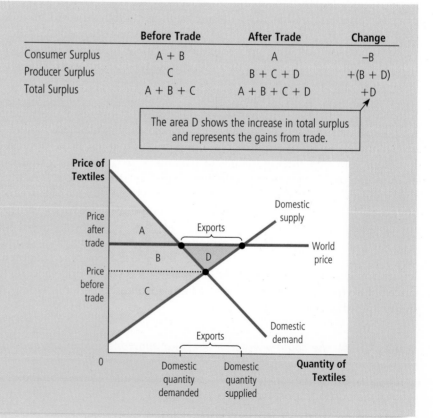

After the domestic price has risen to equal the world price, the domestic quantity supplied differs from the domestic quantity demanded. The supply curve shows the quantity of textiles supplied by Isolandian sellers. The demand curve shows the quantity of textiles demanded by Isolandian buyers. Because the domestic quantity supplied is greater than the domestic quantity demanded, Isoland sells textiles to other countries. Thus, Isoland becomes a textile exporter.

Although domestic quantity supplied and domestic quantity demanded differ, the textile market is still in equilibrium because there is now another participant in the market: the rest of the world. One can view the horizontal line at the world price as representing the rest of the world's demand for textiles. This demand curve is perfectly elastic because Isoland, as a small economy, can sell as many textiles as it wants at the world price.

Now consider the gains and losses from opening up trade. Clearly, not everyone benefits. Trade forces the domestic price to rise to the world price. Domestic producers of textiles are better off because they can now sell textiles at a higher price, but domestic consumers of textiles are worse off because they have to buy textiles at a higher price.

To measure these gains and losses, we look at the changes in consumer and producer surplus. Before trade is allowed, the price of textiles adjusts to balance domestic supply and domestic demand. Consumer surplus, the area between the demand curve and the before-trade price, is area A + B. Producer surplus, the area between the supply curve and the before-trade price, is area C. Total surplus before trade, the sum of consumer and producer surplus, is area A+ B + C.

After trade is allowed, the domestic price rises to the world price. Consumer surplus is reduced to area A (the area between the demand curve and the world price). Producer surplus is increased to area B + C + D (the area between the supply curve and the world price). Thus, total surplus with trade is area A + B + C + D.

These welfare calculations show who wins and who loses from trade in an exporting country. Sellers benefit because producer surplus increases by the area B + D. Buyers are worse off because consumer surplus decreases by the area B. Because the gains of sellers exceed the losses of buyers by the area D, total surplus in Isoland increases.

This analysis of an exporting country yields two conclusions:

- When a country allows trade and becomes an exporter of a good, domestic producers of the good are better off, and domestic consumers of the good are worse off.
- Trade raises the economic well-being of a nation in the sense that the gains of the winners exceed the losses of the losers.

The Gains and Losses of an Importing Country

Now suppose that the domestic price before trade is above the world price. Once again, after trade is allowed, the domestic price must equal the world price. As Figure 3 shows, the domestic quantity supplied is less than the domestic quantity demanded. The difference between the domestic quantity demanded and the domestic quantity supplied is bought from other countries, and Isoland becomes a textile importer.

In this case, the horizontal line at the world price represents the supply of the rest of the world. This supply curve is perfectly elastic because Isoland is a small economy and, therefore, can buy as many textiles as it wants at the world price.

Figure 3

International Trade in an Importing Country
Once trade is allowed, the domestic price falls to equal the world price. The supply curve shows the amount produced domestically, and the demand curve shows the amount consumed domestically. Imports equal the difference between the domestic quantity demanded and the domestic quantity supplied at the world price. Buyers are better off (consumer surplus rises from A to A + B + D), and sellers are worse off (producer surplus falls from B + C to C). Total surplus rises by an amount equal to area D, indicating that trade raises the economic well-being of the country as a whole.

	Before Trade	After Trade	Change
Consumer Surplus	A	A + B + D	+(B + D)
Producer Surplus	B + C	C	−B
Total Surplus	A + B + C	A + B + C + D	+D

The area D shows the increase in total surplus and represents the gains from trade.

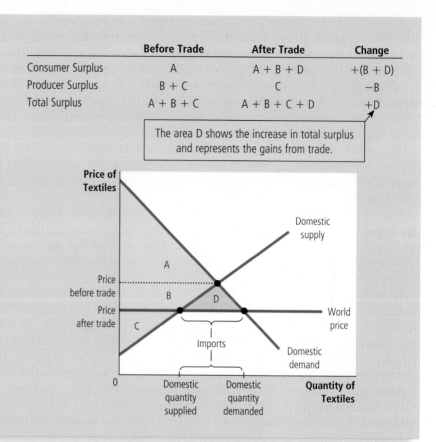

Now consider the gains and losses from trade. Once again, not everyone benefits. When trade forces the domestic price to fall, domestic consumers are better off (they can now buy textiles at a lower price), and domestic producers are worse off (they now have to sell textiles at a lower price). Changes in consumer and producer surplus measure the size of the gains and losses. Before trade, consumer surplus is area A, producer surplus is area B + C, and total surplus is area A + B + C. After trade is allowed, consumer surplus is area A + B + D, producer surplus is area C, and total surplus is area A + B + C + D.

These welfare calculations show who wins and who loses from trade in an importing country. Buyers benefit because consumer surplus increases by the area B + D. Sellers are worse off because producer surplus falls by the area B. The gains of buyers exceed the losses of sellers, and total surplus increases by the area D.

This analysis of an importing country yields two conclusions parallel to those for an exporting country:

- When a country allows trade and becomes an importer of a good, domestic consumers of the good are better off, and domestic producers of the good are worse off.
- Trade raises the economic well-being of a nation in the sense that the gains of the winners exceed the losses of the losers.

Having completed our analysis of trade, we can better understand one of the *Ten Principles of Economics* in Chapter 1: Trade can make everyone better off. If Isoland opens its textile market to international trade, the change will create winners and losers, regardless of whether Isoland ends up exporting or importing textiles. In either case, however, the gains of the winners would exceed the losses of the losers, so the winners could compensate the losers and still be better off. In this sense, trade *can* make everyone better off. But *will* trade make everyone better off? Probably not. In practice, compensation for the losers from international trade is rare. Without such compensation, opening an economy to international trade is a policy that expands the size of the economic pie, while perhaps leaving some participants in the economy with a smaller slice.

We can now see why the debate over trade policy is often contentious. Whenever a policy creates winners and losers, the stage is set for a political battle. Nations sometimes fail to enjoy the gains from trade because the losers from free trade are better organized than the winners. The losers may turn their cohesiveness into political clout, lobbying for trade restrictions such as tariffs or import quotas.

The Effects of a Tariff

The Isolandian economists next consider the effects of a **tariff**—a tax on imported goods. The economists quickly realize that a tariff on textiles will have no effect if Isoland becomes a textile exporter. If no one in Isoland is interested in importing textiles, a tax on textile imports is irrelevant. The tariff matters only if Isoland becomes a textile importer. Concentrating their attention on this case, the economists compare welfare with and without the tariff.

tariff
a tax on goods produced abroad and sold domestically

Figure 4 shows the Isolandian market for textiles. Under free trade, the domestic price equals the world price. A tariff raises the price of imported textiles above the world price by the amount of the tariff. Domestic suppliers of textiles, who compete with suppliers of imported textiles, can now sell their textiles for the world price plus the amount of the tariff. Thus, the price of textiles—both imported and domestic—rises by the amount of the tariff and is, therefore, closer to the price that would prevail without trade.

The change in price affects the behavior of domestic buyers and sellers. Because the tariff raises the price of textiles, it reduces the domestic quantity demanded from Q_1^D to Q_2^D and raises the domestic quantity supplied from Q_1^S to Q_2^S. *Thus, the tariff reduces the quantity of imports and moves the domestic market closer to its equilibrium without trade.*

Now consider the gains and losses from the tariff. Because the tariff raises the domestic price, domestic sellers are better off, and domestic buyers are worse off. In addition, the government raises revenue. To measure these gains and losses, we look at the changes in consumer surplus, producer surplus, and government revenue. These changes are summarized in the table in Figure 4.

Before the tariff, the domestic price equals the world price. Consumer surplus, the area between the demand curve and the world price, is area A + B + C + D + E + F. Producer surplus, the area between the supply curve and the world price, is area G. Government revenue equals zero. Total surplus, the sum of consumer surplus, producer surplus, and government revenue, is area A + B + C + D + E + F + G.

Once the government imposes a tariff, the domestic price exceeds the world price by the amount of the tariff. Consumer surplus is now area A + B. Producer surplus is area C + G. Government revenue, which is the quantity of after-tariff imports times the size of the tariff, is the area E. Thus, total surplus with the tariff is area A + B + C + E + G.

A tariff reduces the quantity of imports and moves a market closer to the equilibrium that would exist without trade. Total surplus falls by an amount equal to area D + F. These two triangles represent the deadweight loss from the tariff.

	Before Tariff	After Tariff	Change
Consumer Surplus	A + B + C + D + E + F	A + B	–(C + D + E + F)
Producer Surplus	G	C + G	+C
Government Revenue	None	E	+E
Total Surplus	A + B + C + D + E + F + G	A + B + C + E + G	–(D + F)

The area D + F shows the fall in total surplus and represents the deadweight loss of the tariff.

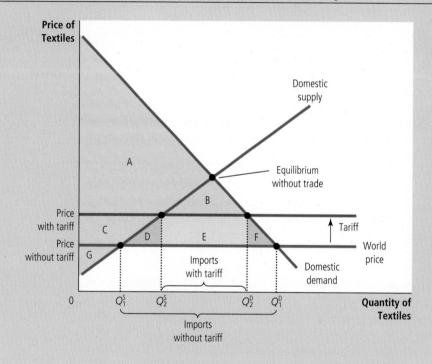

To determine the total welfare effects of the tariff, we add the change in consumer surplus (which is negative), the change in producer surplus (positive), and the change in government revenue (positive). We find that total surplus in the market decreases by the area D + F. This fall in total surplus is called the *deadweight loss* of the tariff.

A tariff causes a deadweight loss because a tariff is a type of tax. Like most taxes, it distorts incentives and pushes the allocation of scarce resources away from the optimum. In this case, we can identify two effects. First, when the tariff raises the domestic price of textiles above the world price, it encourages domestic producers to increase production from Q_1^S to Q_2^S. Even though the cost of making these incremental units exceeds the cost of buying them at the world price, the

·········· FYI ··········

> ## Import Quotas:
> ## Another Way to Restrict Trade

Beyond tariffs, another way that nations sometimes restrict international trade is by putting limits on how much of a good can be imported. In this book, we will not analyze such a policy, other than to point out the conclusion: Import quotas are much like tariffs. Both tariffs and import quotas reduce the quantity of imports, raise the domestic price of the good, decrease the welfare of domestic consumers, increase the welfare of domestic producers, and cause deadweight losses.

There is only one difference between these two types of trade restriction: A tariff raises revenue for the government, whereas an import quota creates surplus for those who obtain the licenses to import. The profit for the holder of an import license is the difference between the domestic price (at which he sells the imported good) and the world price (at which he buys it).

Tariffs and import quotas are even more similar if the government charges a fee for the import licenses. Suppose the government sets the license fee equal to the difference between the domestic price and the world price. In this case, all the profit of license holders is paid to the government in license fees, and the import quota works exactly like a tariff. Consumer surplus, producer surplus, and government revenue are precisely the same under the two policies.

In practice, however, countries that restrict trade with import quotas rarely do so by selling the import licenses. For example, the U.S. government has at times pressured Japan to "voluntarily" limit the sale of Japanese cars in the United States. In this case, the Japanese government allocates the import licenses to Japanese firms, and the surplus from these licenses accrues to those firms. From the standpoint of U.S. welfare, this kind of import quota is worse than a U.S. tariff on imported cars. Both a tariff and an import quota raise prices, restrict trade, and cause deadweight losses, but at least the tariff produces revenue for the U.S. government rather than profit for foreign producers.

tariff makes it profitable for domestic producers to manufacture them nonetheless. Second, when the tariff raises the price that domestic textile consumers have to pay, it encourages them to reduce consumption of textiles from Q_1^D to Q_2^D. Even though domestic consumers value these incremental units at more than the world price, the tariff induces them to cut back their purchases. Area D represents the deadweight loss from the overproduction of textiles, and area F represents the deadweight loss from the underconsumption of textiles. The total deadweight loss of the tariff is the sum of these two triangles.

The Lessons for Trade Policy

The team of Isolandian economists can now write to the new president:

Dear Madame President,

You asked us three questions about opening up trade. After much hard work, we have the answers.

Question: If the government allows Isolandians to import and export textiles, what will happen to the price of textiles and the quantity of textiles sold in the domestic textile market?

Answer: Once trade is allowed, the Isolandian price of textiles will be driven to equal the price prevailing around the world.

If the world price is now higher than the Isolandian price, our price will rise. The higher price will reduce the amount of textiles Isolandians consume and raise the amount of textiles that Isolandians produce. Isoland will, therefore, become a textile exporter. This occurs because, in this case, Isoland has a comparative advantage in producing textiles.

Conversely, if the world price is now lower than the Isolandian price, our price will fall. The lower price will raise the amount of textiles that Isolandians consume and lower the amount of textiles that Isolandians produce. Isoland will, therefore, become a textile importer. This occurs because, in this case, other countries have a comparative advantage in producing textiles.

Question: Who will gain from free trade in textiles and who will lose, and will the gains exceed the losses?

Answer: The answer depends on whether the price rises or falls when trade is allowed. If the price rises, producers of textiles gain, and consumers of textiles lose. If the price falls, consumers gain, and producers lose. In both cases, the gains are larger than the losses. Thus, free trade raises the total welfare of Isolandians.

Question: Should a tariff be part of the new trade policy?

Answer: A tariff has an impact only if Isoland becomes a textile importer. In this case, a tariff moves the economy closer to the no-trade equilibrium and, like most taxes, has deadweight losses. Although a tariff improves the welfare of domestic producers and raises revenue for the government, these gains are more than offset by the losses suffered by consumers. The best policy, from the standpoint of economic efficiency, would be to allow trade without a tariff.

We hope you find these answers helpful as you decide on your new policy.

Your faithful servants,
Isolandian economics team

Other Benefits of International Trade

The conclusions of the Isolandian economics team are based on the standard analysis of international trade. Their analysis uses the most fundamental tools in the economist's toolbox: supply, demand, and producer and consumer surplus. It shows that there are winners and losers when a nation opens itself up to trade, but the gains to the winners exceed the losses of the losers.

The case for free trade can be made even stronger, however, because there are several other economic benefits of trade beyond those emphasized in the standard analysis. Here, in a nutshell, are some of these other benefits:

- **Increased variety of goods.** Goods produced in different countries are not exactly the same. German beer, for instance, is not the same as American beer. Free trade gives consumers in all countries greater variety from which to choose.
- **Lower costs through economies of scale.** Some goods can be produced at low cost only if they are produced in large quantities—a phenomenon called *economies of scale*. A firm in a small country cannot take full advantage of economies of scale if it can sell only in a small domestic market. Free trade

in the news

> ### Trade Skirmishes

In recent years, trade between the United States and China has not been completely free, as the following two articles illustrate.

U.S. Adds Tariffs on Chinese Tires

BY EDMUND L. ANDREWS

Washington—In a break with the trade policies of his predecessor, President Obama announced on Friday night that he would impose a 35 percent tariff on automobile and light-truck tires imported from China.

The decision is a major victory for the United Steelworkers, the union that represents American tire workers. And Mr. Obama cannot afford to jeopardize his relationship with major unions as he pushes Congress to overhaul the nation's health care system.

A U.S. import

But China is certain to be antagonized by the decision....

The decision signals the first time that the United States has invoked a special safeguard provision that was part of its agreement to support China's entry into the World Trade Organization in 2001.

Under that safeguard provision, American companies or workers harmed by imports from China can ask the government for protection simply by demonstrating that American producers have suffered a "market disruption" or a "surge" in imports from China.

Unlike more traditional anti-dumping cases, the government does not need to determine that a country is competing unfairly or selling its products at less than their true cost.

[Three days later]

China Moves to Retaliate Against U.S. Tire Tariff

BY KEITH BRADSHER

Hong Kong—China unexpectedly increased pressure Sunday on the United States in a widening trade dispute, taking the first steps toward imposing tariffs on American exports of automotive products and chicken meat in retaliation for President Obama's decision late Friday to levy tariffs on tires from China.

The Chinese government's strong countermove followed a weekend of nationalistic

vitriol against the United States on Chinese Web sites in response to the tire tariff. "The U.S. is shameless!" said one posting, while another called on the Chinese government to sell all of its huge holdings of Treasury bonds.

The impact of the dispute extends well beyond tires, chickens and cars. Both governments are facing domestic pressure to take a tougher stand against the other on economic issues. But the trade battle increases political tensions between the two nations even as they try to work together to revive the global economy and combat mutual security threats, like the nuclear ambitions of Iran and North Korea.

A U.S. export

Source: *New York Times,* September 11 and 14, 2009.

gives firms access to larger world markets and allows them to realize economies of scale more fully.

- **Increased competition.** A company shielded from foreign competitors is more likely to have market power, which in turn gives it the ability to raise prices above competitive levels. This is a type of market failure. Opening up trade fosters competition and gives the invisible hand a better chance to work its magic.
- **Enhanced flow of ideas.** The transfer of technological advances around the world is often thought to be linked to the trading of the goods that embody those advances. The best way for a poor agricultural nation to learn about the computer revolution, for instance, is to buy some computers from abroad rather than trying to make them domestically.

Thus, free international trade increases variety for consumers, allows firms to take advantage of economies of scale, makes markets more competitive, and facilitates the spread of technology. If the Isolandian economists also took these effects into account, their advice to their president would be even more forceful.

QUICK QUIZ *Draw a supply and demand diagram for wool suits in the country of Autarka. When trade is allowed, the price of a suit falls from 3 to 2 ounces of gold. In your diagram, show the change in consumer surplus, the change in producer surplus, and the change in total surplus. How would a tariff on suit imports alter these effects?*

The Arguments for Restricting Trade

The letter from the economics team starts to persuade the new president of Isoland to consider allowing trade in textiles. She notes that the domestic price is now high compared to the world price. Free trade would, therefore, cause the price of textiles to fall and hurt domestic textiles producers. Before implementing the new policy, she asks Isolandian textile companies to comment on the economists' advice.

Not surprisingly, the textile companies oppose free trade in textiles. They believe that the government should protect the domestic textile industry from foreign competition. Let's consider some of the arguments they might give to support their position and how the economics team would respond.

The Jobs Argument

Opponents of free trade often argue that trade with other countries destroys domestic jobs. In our example, free trade in textiles would cause the price of textiles to fall, reducing the quantity of textiles produced in Isoland and thus reducing employment in the Isolandian textile industry. Some Isolandian textile workers would lose their jobs.

Yet free trade creates jobs at the same time that it destroys them. When Isolandians buy textiles from other countries, those countries obtain the resources to buy other goods from Isoland. Isolandian workers would move from the textile industry to those industries in which Isoland has a comparative advantage. The transition may impose hardship on some workers in the short run, but it allows Isolandians as a whole to enjoy a higher standard of living.

Opponents of trade are often skeptical that trade creates jobs. They might respond that *everything* can be produced more cheaply abroad. Under free trade, they might argue, Isolandians could not be profitably employed in any industry.

Berry's World

"You like protectionism as a 'working man.' How about as a consumer?"

As Chapter 3 explains, however, the gains from trade are based on comparative advantage, not absolute advantage. Even if one country is better than another country at producing everything, each country can still gain from trading with the other. Workers in each country will eventually find jobs in an industry in which that country has a comparative advantage.

in the **news**

> ### Should the Winners from Free Trade Compensate the Losers?

Politicians and pundits often say that the government should help workers made worse off by international trade by, for example, paying for their retraining. In this opinion piece, an economist makes the opposite case.

What to Expect When You're Free Trading

BY STEVEN E. LANDSBURG

All economists know that when American jobs are outsourced, Americans as a group are net winners. What we lose through lower wages is more than offset by what we gain through lower prices. In other words, the winners can more than afford to compensate the losers. Does that mean they ought to? Does it create a moral mandate for taxpayer-subsidized retraining programs?…

Um, no. Even if you've just lost your job, there's something fundamentally churlish about blaming the very phenomenon that's elevated you above the subsistence level since the day you were born. If the world owes you compensation for enduring the downside of trade, what do you owe the world for enjoying the upside?

I doubt there's a human being on earth who hasn't benefited from the opportunity to trade freely with his neighbors. Imagine what your life would be like if you had to grow your own food, make your own clothes and rely on your grandmother's home reme-

dies for health care. Access to a trained physician might reduce the demand for grandma's home remedies, but—especially at her age—she's still got plenty of reason to be thankful for having a doctor.

Some people suggest, however, that it makes sense to isolate the moral effects of a single new trading opportunity or free trade agreement. Surely we have fellow citizens who are hurt by those agreements, at least in the limited sense that they'd be better off in a world where trade flourishes, except in this one instance. What do we owe those fellow citizens?

One way to think about that is to ask what your moral instincts tell you in analogous situations. Suppose, after years of buying shampoo at your local pharmacy, you discover you can order the same shampoo for less money on the Web. Do you have an obligation to compensate your pharmacist? If you move to a cheaper apartment, should you compensate your landlord? When you eat at McDonald's, should you compensate the owners of the diner next door? Public policy should not be designed to advance moral instincts that we all reject every day of our lives.

In what morally relevant way, then, might displaced workers differ from dis-

placed pharmacists or displaced landlords? You might argue that pharmacists and landlords have always faced cutthroat competition and therefore knew what they were getting into, while decades of tariffs and quotas have led manufacturing workers to expect a modicum of protection. That expectation led them to develop certain skills, and now it's unfair to pull the rug out from under them.

Once again, that argument does not mesh with our everyday instincts. For many decades, schoolyard bullying has been a profitable occupation. All across America, bullies have built up skills so they can take advantage of that opportunity. If we toughen the rules to make bullying unprofitable, must we compensate the bullies?

Bullying and protectionism have a lot in common. They both use force (either directly or through the power of the law) to enrich someone else at your involuntary expense. If you're forced to pay $20 an hour to an American for goods you could have bought from a Mexican for $5 an hour, you're being extorted. When a free trade agreement allows you to buy from the Mexican after all, rejoice in your liberation.

Source: *New York Times*, January 16, 2008.

The National-Security Argument

When an industry is threatened with competition from other countries, opponents of free trade often argue that the industry is vital for national security. For example, if Isoland were considering free trade in steel, domestic steel companies might point out that steel is used to make guns and tanks. Free trade would allow Isoland to become dependent on foreign countries to supply steel. If a war later broke out and the foreign supply was interrupted, Isoland might be unable to produce enough steel and weapons to defend itself.

Economists acknowledge that protecting key industries may be appropriate when there are legitimate concerns over national security. Yet they fear that this argument may be used too quickly by producers eager to gain at consumers' expense.

One should be wary of the national-security argument when it is made by representatives of industry rather than the defense establishment. Companies have an incentive to exaggerate their role in national defense to obtain protection from foreign competition. A nation's generals may see things very differently. Indeed, when the military is a consumer of an industry's output, it would benefit from

in the **news**

> ### Second Thoughts about Free Trade

Some economists worry about the impact of trade on the distribution of income. Even if free trade enhances efficiency, it may reduce equality.

Trouble with Trade

By Paul Krugman

While the United States has long imported oil and other raw materials from the third world, we used to import manufactured goods mainly from other rich countries like Canada, European nations and Japan.

But recently we crossed an important watershed: we now import more manufactured goods from the third world than from other advanced economies. That is, a majority of our industrial trade is now with countries that are much poorer than we are and that pay their workers much lower wages.

For the world economy as a whole—and especially for poorer nations—growing trade between high-wage and low-wage countries is a very good thing. Above all, it offers backward economies their best hope of moving up the income ladder.

But for American workers the story is much less positive. In fact, it's hard to avoid the conclusion that growing U.S. trade with third-world countries reduces the real wages of many and perhaps most workers in this country. And that reality makes the politics of trade very difficult.

Let's talk for a moment about the economics.

Trade between high-wage countries tends to be a modest win for all, or almost

all, concerned. When a free-trade pact made it possible to integrate the U.S. and Canadian auto industries in the 1960s, each country's industry concentrated on producing a narrower range of products at larger scale. The result was an all-round, broadly shared rise in productivity and wages.

By contrast, trade between countries at very different levels of economic development tends to create large classes of losers as well as winners.

Although the outsourcing of some high-tech jobs to India has made headlines, on balance, highly educated workers in the United States benefit from higher wages and expanded job opportunities because of trade. For example, ThinkPad notebook

imports. Cheaper steel in Isoland, for example, would allow the Isolandian military to accumulate a stockpile of weapons at lower cost.

The Infant-Industry Argument

New industries sometimes argue for temporary trade restrictions to help them get started. After a period of protection, the argument goes, these industries will mature and be able to compete with foreign firms.

Similarly, older industries sometimes argue that they need temporary protection to help them adjust to new conditions. For example, in 2002, President Bush imposed temporary tariffs on imported steel. He said, "I decided that imports were severely affecting our industry, an important industry." The tariff, which lasted 20 months, offered "temporary relief so that the industry could restructure itself."

Economists are often skeptical about such claims, largely because the infant-industry argument is difficult to implement in practice. To apply protection successfully, the government would need to decide which industries will eventually be profitable and decide whether the benefits of establishing these industries exceed the costs of this protection to consumers. Yet "picking winners" is extraordinarily difficult. It is made even more difficult by the political process, which often awards protection to those industries that are politically powerful. And

computers are now made by a Chinese company, Lenovo, but a lot of Lenovo's research and development is conducted in North Carolina.

But workers with less formal education either see their jobs shipped overseas or find their wages driven down by the ripple effect as other workers with similar qualifications crowd into their industries and look for employment to replace the jobs they lost to foreign competition. And lower prices at Wal-Mart aren't sufficient compensation.

All this is textbook international economics: contrary to what people sometimes assert, economic theory says that free trade normally makes a country richer, but it doesn't say that it's normally good for everyone. Still, when the effects of third-world exports on U.S. wages first became an issue in the 1990s, a number of economists—myself included—looked at the data and concluded that any negative effects on U.S. wages were modest.

The trouble now is that these effects may no longer be as modest as they were, because imports of manufactured goods from the third world have grown dramatically—

from just 2.5 percent of G.D.P. in 1990 to 6 percent in 2006.

And the biggest growth in imports has come from countries with very low wages. The original "newly industrializing economies" exporting manufactured goods—South Korea, Taiwan, Hong Kong and Singapore—paid wages that were about 25 percent of U.S. levels in 1990. Since then, however, the sources of our imports have shifted to Mexico, where wages are only 11 percent of the U.S. level, and China, where they're only about 3 percent or 4 percent.

There are some qualifying aspects to this story. For example, many of those made-in-China goods contain components made in Japan and other high-wage economies. Still, there's little doubt that the pressure of globalization on American wages has increased.

So am I arguing for protectionism? No. Those who think that globalization is always and everywhere a bad thing are wrong. On the contrary, keeping world markets relatively open is crucial to the hopes of billions of people.

But I am arguing for an end to the finger-wagging, the accusation either of not

understanding economics or of kowtowing to special interests that tends to be the editorial response to politicians who express skepticism about the benefits of free-trade agreements.

It's often claimed that limits on trade benefit only a small number of Americans, while hurting the vast majority. That's still true of things like the import quota on sugar. But when it comes to manufactured goods, it's at least arguable that the reverse is true. The highly educated workers who clearly benefit from growing trade with third-world economies are a minority, greatly outnumbered by those who probably lose.

As I said, I'm not a protectionist. For the sake of the world as a whole, I hope that we respond to the trouble with trade not by shutting trade down, but by doing things like strengthening the social safety net. But those who are worried about trade have a point, and deserve some respect.

Source: *New York Times*, December 28, 2007.

once a powerful industry is protected from foreign competition, the "temporary" policy is sometimes hard to remove.

In addition, many economists are skeptical about the infant-industry argument in principle. Suppose, for instance, that an industry is young and unable to compete profitably against foreign rivals, but there is reason to believe that the industry can be profitable in the long run. In this case, firm owners should be willing to incur temporary losses to obtain the eventual profits. Protection is not necessary for an infant industry to grow. History shows that start-up firms often incur temporary losses and succeed in the long run, even without protection from competition.

The Unfair-Competition Argument

A common argument is that free trade is desirable only if all countries play by the same rules. If firms in different countries are subject to different laws and regulations, then it is unfair (the argument goes) to expect the firms to compete in the international marketplace. For instance, suppose that the government of Neighborland subsidizes its textile industry by giving textile companies large tax breaks. The Islandian textile industry might argue that it should be protected from this foreign competition because Neighborland is not competing fairly.

Would it, in fact, hurt Isoland to buy textiles from another country at a subsidized price? Certainly, Islandian textile producers would suffer, but Islandian textile consumers would benefit from the low price. The case for free trade is no different: The gains of the consumers from buying at the low price would exceed the losses of the producers. Neighborland's subsidy to its textile industry may be a bad policy, but it is the taxpayers of Neighborland who bear the burden. Isoland can benefit from the opportunity to buy textiles at a subsidized price.

The Protection-as-a-Bargaining-Chip Argument

Another argument for trade restrictions concerns the strategy of bargaining. Many policymakers claim to support free trade but, at the same time, argue that trade restrictions can be useful when we bargain with our trading partners. They claim that the threat of a trade restriction can help remove a trade restriction already imposed by a foreign government. For example, Isoland might threaten to impose a tariff on textiles unless Neighborland removes its tariff on wheat. If Neighborland responds to this threat by removing its tariff, the result can be freer trade.

The problem with this bargaining strategy is that the threat may not work. If it doesn't work, the country faces a choice between two bad options. It can carry out its threat and implement the trade restriction, which would reduce its own economic welfare. Or it can back down from its threat, which would cause it to lose prestige in international affairs. Faced with this choice, the country would probably wish that it had never made the threat in the first place.

Trade Agreements and the World Trade Organization

A country can take one of two approaches to achieving free trade. It can take a *unilateral* approach and remove its trade restrictions on its own. This is the approach that Great Britain took in the 19th century and that Chile and South Korea have taken in recent years. Alternatively, a country can take a *multilateral* approach and reduce its trade restrictions while other countries do the same. In other words, it can bargain with its trading partners in an attempt to reduce trade restrictions around the world.

One important example of the multilateral approach is the North American Free Trade Agreement (NAFTA), which in 1993 lowered trade barriers among the United States, Mexico, and Canada. Another is the General Agreement on Tariffs and Trade (GATT), which is a continuing series of negotiations among many of the world's countries with the goal of promoting free trade. The United States helped to found GATT after World War II in response to the high tariffs imposed during the Great Depression of the 1930s. Many economists believe that the high tariffs contributed to the worldwide economic hardship of that period. GATT has successfully reduced the average tariff among member countries from about 40 percent after World War II to about 5 percent today.

The rules established under GATT are now enforced by an international institution called the World Trade Organization (WTO). The WTO was established in 1995 and has its headquarters in Geneva, Switzerland. As of 2009, 153 countries have joined the organization, accounting for more than 97 percent of world trade. The functions of the WTO are to administer trade agreements, provide a forum for negotiations, and handle disputes among member countries.

What are the pros and cons of the multilateral approach to free trade? One advantage is that the multilateral approach has the potential to result in freer trade than a unilateral approach because it can reduce trade restrictions abroad as well as at home. If international negotiations fail, however, the result could be more restricted trade than under a unilateral approach.

In addition, the multilateral approach may have a political advantage. In most markets, producers are fewer and better organized than consumers—and thus wield greater political influence. Reducing the Isolandian tariff on textiles, for example, may be politically difficult if considered by itself. The textile companies would oppose free trade, and the buyers of textiles who would benefit are so numerous that organizing their support would be difficult. Yet suppose that Neighborland promises to reduce its tariff on wheat at the same time that Isoland reduces its tariff on textiles. In this case, the Isolandian wheat farmers, who are also politically powerful, would back the agreement. Thus, the multilateral approach to free trade can sometimes win political support when a unilateral approach cannot. ■

QUICK QUIZ *The textile industry of Autarka advocates a ban on the import of wool suits. Describe five arguments its lobbyists might make. Give a response to each of these arguments.*

Conclusion

Economists and the public often disagree about free trade. In 2008, the *Los Angeles Times* asked the American public, "Generally speaking, do you believe that free international trade has helped or hurt the economy, or hasn't it made a difference to the economy one way or the other?" Only 26 percent of those polled said free international trade helped, whereas 50 percent thought it hurt. (The rest thought it made no difference or were unsure.) By contrast, most economists support free international trade. They view free trade as a way of allocating production efficiently and raising living standards both at home and abroad.

Economists view the United States as an ongoing experiment that confirms the virtues of free trade. Throughout its history, the United States has allowed unrestricted trade among the states, and the country as a whole has benefited from the specialization that trade allows. Florida grows oranges, Alaska pumps oil, California makes wine, and so on. Americans would not enjoy the high standard of living they do today if people could consume only those goods and services produced in their own states. The world could similarly benefit from free trade among countries.

To better understand economists' view of trade, let's continue our parable. Suppose that the president of Isoland, after reading the latest poll results, ignores the advice of her economics team and decides not to allow free trade in textiles. The country remains in the equilibrium without international trade.

Then, one day, some Isolandian inventor discovers a new way to make textiles at very low cost. The process is quite mysterious, however, and the inventor insists on keeping it a secret. What is odd is that the inventor doesn't need traditional inputs such as cotton or wool. The only material input he needs is wheat. And even more oddly, to manufacture textiles from wheat, he hardly needs any labor input at all.

The inventor is hailed as a genius. Because everyone buys clothing, the lower cost of textiles allows all Isolandians to enjoy a higher standard of living. Workers who had previously produced textiles experience some hardship when their factories close, but eventually, they find work in other industries. Some become farmers and grow the wheat that the inventor turns into textiles. Others enter new industries that emerge as a result of higher Isolandian living standards. Everyone understands that the displacement of workers in outmoded industries is an inevitable part of technological progress and economic growth.

After several years, a newspaper reporter decides to investigate this mysterious new textiles process. She sneaks into the inventor's factory and learns that the inventor is a fraud. The inventor has not been making textiles at all. Instead, he has been smuggling wheat abroad in exchange for textiles from other countries. The only thing that the inventor had discovered was the gains from international trade.

When the truth is revealed, the government shuts down the inventor's operation. The price of textiles rises, and workers return to jobs in textile factories. Living standards in Isoland fall back to their former levels. The inventor is jailed and held up to public ridicule. After all, he was no inventor. He was just an economist.

SUMMARY

- The effects of free trade can be determined by comparing the domestic price without trade to the world price. A low domestic price indicates that the country has a comparative advantage in producing the good and that the country will become an exporter. A high domestic price indicates that the rest of the world has a comparative advantage in producing the good and that the country will become an importer.

- When a country allows trade and becomes an exporter of a good, producers of the good are better off, and consumers of the good are worse off. When a country allows trade and becomes an importer of a good, consumers are better off, and producers are worse off. In both cases, the gains from trade exceed the losses.

- A tariff—a tax on imports—moves a market closer to the equilibrium that would exist without trade and, therefore, reduces the gains from trade. Although domestic producers are better off and the government raises revenue, the losses to consumers exceed these gains.

- There are various arguments for restricting trade: protecting jobs, defending national security,

helping infant industries, preventing unfair competition, and responding to foreign trade restrictions. Although some of these arguments have some merit in some cases, economists believe that free trade is usually the better policy.

KEY CONCEPTS

world price, *p. 173*

tariff, *p. 177*

QUESTIONS FOR REVIEW

1. What does the domestic price that prevails without international trade tell us about a nation's comparative advantage?
2. When does a country become an exporter of a good? An importer?
3. Draw the supply-and-demand diagram for an importing country. What is consumer surplus and producer surplus before trade is allowed? What is consumer surplus and producer surplus with free trade? What is the change in total surplus?
4. Describe what a tariff is and its economic effects.
5. List five arguments often given to support trade restrictions. How do economists respond to these arguments?
6. What is the difference between the unilateral and multilateral approaches to achieving free trade? Give an example of each.

PROBLEMS AND APPLICATIONS

1. Mexico represents a small part of the world orange market.
   a. Draw a diagram depicting the equilibrium in the Mexican orange market without international trade. Identify the equilibrium price, equilibrium quantity, consumer surplus, and producer surplus.
   b. Suppose that the world orange price is below the Mexican price before trade and that the Mexican orange market is now opened to trade. Identify the new equilibrium price, quantity consumed, quantity produced domestically, and quantity imported. Also show the change in the surplus of domestic consumers and producers. Has total surplus increased or decreased?
2. The world price of wine is below the price that would prevail in Canada in the absence of trade.

   a. Assuming that Canadian imports of wine are a small part of total world wine production, draw a graph for the Canadian market for wine under free trade. Identify consumer surplus, producer surplus, and total surplus in an appropriate table.
   b. Now suppose that an unusual shift of the Gulf Stream leads to an unseasonably cold summer in Europe, destroying much of the grape harvest there. What effect does this shock have on the world price of wine? Using your graph and table from part (a), show the effect on consumer surplus, producer surplus, and total surplus in Canada. Who are the winners and losers? Is Canada as a whole better or worse off?
3. Suppose that Congress imposes a tariff on imported autos to protect the U.S. auto industry

from foreign competition. Assuming that the United States is a price taker in the world auto market, show the following on a diagram: the change in the quantity of imports, the loss to U.S. consumers, the gain to U.S. manufacturers, government revenue, and the deadweight loss associated with the tariff. The loss to consumers can be decomposed into three pieces: a gain to domestic producers, revenue for the government, and a deadweight loss. Use your diagram to identify these three pieces.

4. When China's clothing industry expands, the increase in world supply lowers the world price of clothing.

a. Draw an appropriate diagram to analyze how this change in price affects consumer surplus, producer surplus, and total surplus in a nation that imports clothing, such as the United States.

b. Now draw an appropriate diagram to show how this change in price affects consumer surplus, producer surplus, and total surplus in a nation that exports clothing, such as the Dominican Republic.

c. Compare your answers to parts (a) and (b). What are the similarities and what are the differences? Which country should be concerned about the expansion of the Chinese textile industry? Which country should be applauding it? Explain.

5. Imagine that winemakers in the state of Washington petitioned the state government to tax wines imported from California. They argue that this tax would both raise tax revenue for the state government and raise employment in the Washington state wine industry. Do you agree with these claims? Is it a good policy?

6. Consider the arguments for restricting trade.

a. Assume you are a lobbyist for timber, an established industry suffering from low-priced foreign competition. Which two or three of the five arguments do you think would be most persuasive to the average member of Congress as to why he or she should support trade restrictions? Explain your reasoning.

b. Now assume you are an astute student of economics (hopefully not a hard assumption). Although all the arguments for restricting trade have their shortcomings, name the two or three arguments that seem

to make the most economic sense to you. For each, describe the economic rationale for and against these arguments for trade restrictions.

7. Senator Ernest Hollings once wrote that "consumers *do not* benefit from lower-priced imports. Glance through some mail-order catalogs and you'll see that consumers pay exactly the same price for clothing whether it is U.S.-made or imported." Comment.

8. The nation of Textilia does not allow imports of clothing. In its equilibrium without trade, a T-shirt costs $20, and the equilibrium quantity is 3 million T-shirts. One day, after reading Adam Smith's *The Wealth of Nations* while on vacation, the president decides to open the Textilian market to international trade. The market price of a T-shirt falls to the world price of $16. The number of T-shirts consumed in Textilia rises to 4 million, while the number of T-shirts produced declines to 1 million.

a. Illustrate the situation just described in a graph. Your graph should show all the numbers.

b. Calculate the change in consumer surplus, producer surplus, and total surplus that results from opening up trade. (Hint: Recall that the area of a triangle is ½ × base × height.)

9. China is a major producer of grains, such as wheat, corn, and rice. In 2008 the Chinese government, concerned that grain exports were driving up food prices for domestic consumers, imposed a tax on grain exports.

a. Draw the graph that describes the market for grain in an exporting country. Use this graph as the starting point to answer the following questions.

b. How does an export tax affect domestic grain prices?

c. How does it affect the welfare of domestic consumers, the welfare of domestic producers, and government revenue?

d. What happens to total welfare in China, as measured by the sum of consumer surplus, producer surplus, and tax revenue?

10. Consider a country that imports a good from abroad. For each of following statements, say whether it is true or false. Explain your answer.

a. "The greater the elasticity of demand, the greater the gains from trade."

b. "If demand is perfectly inelastic, there are no gains from trade."

c. "If demand is perfectly inelastic, consumers do not benefit from trade."

11. Kawmin is a small country that produces and consumes jelly beans. The world price of jelly beans is $1 per bag, and Kawmin's domestic demand and supply for jelly beans are governed by the following equations:

Demand: $Q^D = 8 - P$
Supply: $Q^S = P$,

where P is in dollars per bag and Q is in bags of jelly beans.

a. Draw a well-labeled graph of the situation in Kawmin if the nation does not allow trade. Calculate the following (recalling that the area of a triangle is ½ × base × height): the equilibrium price and quantity, consumer surplus, producer surplus, and total surplus.

b. Kawmin then opens the market to trade. Draw another graph to describe the new situation in the jelly bean market. Calculate the equilibrium price, quantities of consumption and production, imports, consumer surplus, producer surplus, and total surplus.

c. After a while, the Czar of Kawmin responds to the pleas of jelly bean producers by placing a $1 per bag tariff on jelly bean imports. On a graph, show the effects of this tariff. Calculate the equilibrium price, quantities of consumption and production, imports, consumer surplus, producer surplus, government revenue, and total surplus.

d. What are the gains from opening up trade? What are the deadweight losses from restricting trade with the tariff? Give numerical answers.

12. Having rejected a tariff on textiles (a tax on imports), the president of Isoland is now considering the same-sized tax on textile consumption (including both imported and domestically produced textiles).

a. Using Figure 4, identify the quantity consumed and the quantity produced in Isoland under a textile consumption tax.

b. Construct a table similar to that in Figure 4 for the textile consumption tax.

c. Which raises more revenue for the government—the consumption tax or the tariff? Which has a smaller deadweight loss? Explain.

13. Assume the United States is an importer of televisions and there are no trade restrictions. U.S. consumers buy 1 million televisions per year, of which 400,000 are produced domestically and 600,000 are imported.

a. Suppose that a technological advance among Japanese television manufacturers causes the world price of televisions to fall by $100. Draw a graph to show how this change affects the welfare of U.S. consumers and U.S. producers and how it affects total surplus in the United States.

b. After the fall in price, consumers buy 1.2 million televisions, of which 200,000 are produced domestically and 1 million are imported. Calculate the change in consumer surplus, producer surplus, and total surplus from the price reduction.

c. If the government responded by putting a $100 tariff on imported televisions, what would this do? Calculate the revenue that would be raised and the deadweight loss. Would it be a good policy from the standpoint of U.S. welfare? Who might support the policy?

d. Suppose that the fall in price is attributable not to technological advance but to a $100 per television subsidy from the Japanese government to Japanese industry. How would this affect your analysis?

14. Consider a small country that exports steel. Suppose that a "pro-trade" government decides to subsidize the export of steel by paying a certain amount for each ton sold abroad. How does this export subsidy affect the domestic price of steel, the quantity of steel produced, the quantity of steel consumed, and the quantity of steel exported? How does it affect consumer surplus, producer surplus, government revenue, and total surplus? Is it a good policy from the standpoint of economic efficiency? (Hint: The analysis of an export subsidy is similar to the analysis of a tariff.)

For further information on topics in this chapter, additional problems, applications, examples, online quizzes, and more, please visit our website at www.cengage.com/economics/mankiw.

PART **IV** The Economics of
the Public Sector

Externalities

Firms that make and sell paper also create, as a by-product of the manufacturing process, a chemical called dioxin. Scientists believe that once dioxin enters the environment, it raises the population's risk of cancer, birth defects, and other health problems.

Is the production and release of dioxin a problem for society? In Chapters 4 through 9, we examined how markets allocate scarce resources with the forces of supply and demand, and we saw that the equilibrium of supply and demand is typically an efficient allocation of resources. To use Adam Smith's famous metaphor, the "invisible hand" of the marketplace leads self-interested buyers and sellers in a market to maximize the total benefit that society derives from that market. This insight is the basis for one of the *Ten Principles of Economics* in Chapter 1: Markets are usually a good way to organize economic activity. Should we conclude, therefore, that the invisible hand prevents firms in the paper market from emitting too much dioxin?

Markets do many things well, but they do not do everything well. In this chapter, we begin our study of another of the *Ten Principles of Economics*: Government action can sometimes improve upon market outcomes. We examine why markets sometimes fail to allocate resources efficiently, how government policies can potentially improve the market's allocation, and what kinds of policies are likely to work best.

The market failures examined in this chapter fall under a general category called *externalities*. An **externality** arises when a person engages in an activity that influences the well-being of a bystander but neither pays nor receives any compensation for that effect. If the impact on the bystander is adverse, it is called a *negative externality*. If it is beneficial, it is called a *positive externality*. In the presence of externalities, society's interest in a market outcome extends beyond the well-being of buyers and sellers who participate in the market to include the well-being of bystanders who are affected indirectly. Because buyers and sellers neglect the external effects of their actions when deciding how much to demand or supply, the market equilibrium is not efficient when there are externalities. That is, the equilibrium fails to maximize the total benefit to society as a whole. The release of dioxin into the environment, for instance, is a negative externality. Self-interested paper firms will not consider the full cost of the pollution they create in their production process, and consumers of paper will not consider the full cost of the pollution they contribute from their purchasing decisions. Therefore, the firms will emit too much pollution unless the government prevents or discourages them from doing so.

Externalities come in many varieties, as do the policy responses that try to deal with the market failure. Here are some examples:

- The exhaust from automobiles is a negative externality because it creates smog that other people have to breathe. As a result of this externality, drivers tend to pollute too much. The federal government attempts to solve this problem by setting emission standards for cars. It also taxes gasoline to reduce the amount that people drive.
- Restored historic buildings convey a positive externality because people who walk or ride by them can enjoy the beauty and the sense of history that these buildings provide. Building owners do not get the full benefit of restoration and, therefore, tend to discard older buildings too quickly. Many local governments respond to this problem by regulating the destruction of historic buildings and by providing tax breaks to owners who restore them.
- Barking dogs create a negative externality because neighbors are disturbed by the noise. Dog owners do not bear the full cost of the noise and, therefore, tend to take too few precautions to prevent their dogs from barking. Local governments address this problem by making it illegal to "disturb the peace."
- Research into new technologies provides a positive externality because it creates knowledge that other people can use. Because inventors cannot capture the full benefits of their inventions, they tend to devote too few resources to research. The federal government addresses this problem partially through the patent system, which gives inventors exclusive use of their inventions for a limited time.

In each of these cases, some decision maker fails to take account of the external effects of his or her behavior. The government responds by trying to influence this behavior to protect the interests of bystanders.

externality

the uncompensated impact of one person's actions on the well-being of a bystander

Externalities and Market Inefficiency

In this section, we use the tools of welfare economics developed in Chapter 7 to examine how externalities affect economic well-being. The analysis shows precisely why externalities cause markets to allocate resources inefficiently. Later in the chapter, we examine various ways in which private individuals and public policymakers may remedy this type of market failure.

Welfare Economics: A Recap

We begin by recalling the key lessons of welfare economics from Chapter 7. To make our analysis concrete, we consider a specific market—the market for aluminum. Figure 1 shows the supply and demand curves in the market for aluminum.

As you should recall from Chapter 7, the supply and demand curves contain important information about costs and benefits. The demand curve for aluminum reflects the value of aluminum to consumers, as measured by the prices they are willing to pay. At any given quantity, the height of the demand curve shows the willingness to pay of the marginal buyer. In other words, it shows the value to the consumer of the last unit of aluminum bought. Similarly, the supply curve reflects the costs of producing aluminum. At any given quantity, the height of the supply curve shows the cost to the marginal seller. In other words, it shows the cost to the producer of the last unit of aluminum sold.

In the absence of government intervention, the price adjusts to balance the supply and demand for aluminum. The quantity produced and consumed in the market equilibrium, shown as Q_{MARKET} in Figure 1, is efficient in the sense that it maximizes the sum of producer and consumer surplus. That is, the market allocates resources in a way that maximizes the total value to the consumers who buy and use aluminum minus the total costs to the producers who make and sell aluminum.

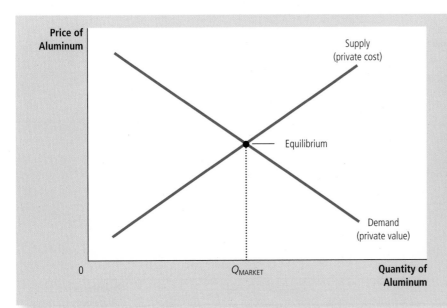

Price of Aluminum

Supply (private cost)

Equilibrium

Demand (private value)

0   Q_{MARKET} **Quantity of Aluminum**

Figure **1**

The Market for Aluminum
The demand curve reflects the value to buyers, and the supply curve reflects the costs of sellers. The equilibrium quantity, Q_{MARKET}, maximizes the total value to buyers minus the total costs of sellers. In the absence of externalities, therefore, the market equilibrium is efficient.

"All I can say is that if being a leading manufacturer means being a leading polluter, so be it."

Negative Externalities

Now let's suppose that aluminum factories emit pollution: For each unit of aluminum produced, a certain amount of smoke enters the atmosphere. Because this smoke creates a health risk for those who breathe the air, it is a negative externality. How does this externality affect the efficiency of the market outcome?

Because of the externality, the cost to *society* of producing aluminum is larger than the cost to the aluminum producers. For each unit of aluminum produced, the *social cost* includes the private costs of the aluminum producers plus the costs to those bystanders affected adversely by the pollution. Figure 2 shows the social cost of producing aluminum. The social-cost curve is above the supply curve because it takes into account the external costs imposed on society by aluminum production. The difference between these two curves reflects the cost of the pollution emitted.

What quantity of aluminum should be produced? To answer this question, we once again consider what a benevolent social planner would do. The planner wants to maximize the total surplus derived from the market—the value to consumers of aluminum minus the cost of producing aluminum. The planner understands, however, that the cost of producing aluminum includes the external costs of the pollution.

The planner would choose the level of aluminum production at which the demand curve crosses the social-cost curve. This intersection determines the optimal amount of aluminum from the standpoint of society as a whole. Below this level of production, the value of the aluminum to consumers (as measured by the height of the demand curve) exceeds the social cost of producing it (as measured by the height of the social-cost curve). The planner does not produce more than this level because the social cost of producing additional aluminum exceeds the value to consumers.

Note that the equilibrium quantity of aluminum, Q_{MARKET}, is larger than the socially optimal quantity, $Q_{OPTIMUM}$. This inefficiency occurs because the market

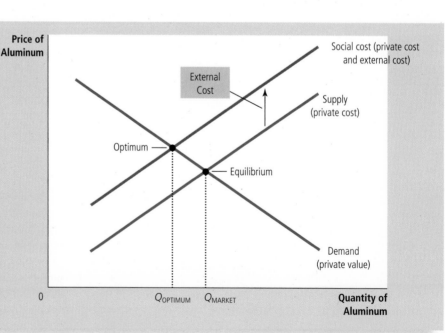

Figure 2

Pollution and the Social Optimum
In the presence of a negative externality, such as pollution, the social cost of the good exceeds the private cost. The optimal quantity, $Q_{OPTIMUM}$, is therefore smaller than the equilibrium quantity, Q_{MARKET}.

equilibrium reflects only the private costs of production. In the market equilibrium, the marginal consumer values aluminum at less than the social cost of producing it. That is, at Q_{MARKET}, the demand curve lies below the social-cost curve. Thus, reducing aluminum production and consumption below the market equilibrium level raises total economic well-being.

How can the social planner achieve the optimal outcome? One way would be to tax aluminum producers for each ton of aluminum sold. The tax would shift the supply curve for aluminum upward by the size of the tax. If the tax accurately reflected the external cost of pollutants released into the atmosphere, the new supply curve would coincide with the social-cost curve. In the new market equilibrium, aluminum producers would produce the socially optimal quantity of aluminum.

The use of such a tax is called **internalizing the externality** because it gives buyers and sellers in the market an incentive to take into account the external effects of their actions. Aluminum producers would, in essence, take the costs of pollution into account when deciding how much aluminum to supply because the tax would make them pay for these external costs. And, because the market price would reflect the tax on producers, consumers of aluminum would have an incentive to use a smaller quantity. The policy is based on one of the *Ten Principles of Economics*: People respond to incentives. Later in this chapter, we consider in more detail how policymakers can deal with externalities.

internalizing the externality
altering incentives so that people take account of the external effects of their actions

Positive Externalities

Although some activities impose costs on third parties, others yield benefits. For example, consider education. To a large extent, the benefit of education is private: The consumer of education becomes a more productive worker and thus reaps much of the benefit in the form of higher wages. Beyond these private benefits, however, education also yields positive externalities. One externality is that a more educated population leads to more informed voters, which means better government for everyone. Another externality is that a more educated population tends to mean lower crime rates. A third externality is that a more educated population may encourage the development and dissemination of technological advances, leading to higher productivity and wages for everyone. Because of these three positive externalities, a person may prefer to have neighbors who are well educated.

The analysis of positive externalities is similar to the analysis of negative externalities. As Figure 3 shows, the demand curve does not reflect the value to society of the good. Because the social value is greater than the private value, the social-value curve lies above the demand curve. The optimal quantity is found where the social-value curve and the supply curve (which represents costs) intersect. Hence, the socially optimal quantity is greater than the quantity determined by the private market.

Once again, the government can correct the market failure by inducing market participants to internalize the externality. The appropriate response in the case of positive externalities is exactly the opposite to the case of negative externalities. To move the market equilibrium closer to the social optimum, a positive externality requires a subsidy. In fact, that is exactly the policy the government follows: Education is heavily subsidized through public schools and government scholarships.

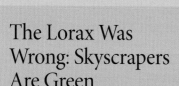

in the news

The Externalities of Country Living

Economist Ed Glaeser says urbanization gets a bum rap.

The Lorax Was Wrong: Skyscrapers Are Green

BY EDWARD L. GLAESER

In Dr. Seuss' environmentalist fable, "The Lorax," the Once-ler, a budding textile magnate, chops down Truffula to knit "Thneeds."

Over the protests of the environmentally sensitive Lorax, the Once-ler builds a great industrial town that despoils the environment, because he "had to grow bigger." Eventually, the Once-ler overdoes it, and he chops down the last Truffula tree, destroying the source of his income. Chastened, Dr. Seuss's industrialist turns green, urging a young listener to take the last Truffula seed and plant a new forest.

Some of the lessons told by this story are correct. From a purely profit-maximizing point of view, the Once-ler is pretty inept, because he kills his golden goose. Any good management consultant would have told him to manage his growth more wisely. One aspect of the story's environmentalist message, that bad things happen when we overfish a common pool, is also correct.

But the unfortunate aspect of the story is that urbanization comes off terribly. The forests are good; the factories are bad. Not only does the story disparage the remarkable benefits that came from the mass production of clothing in 19th-century textile towns, it sends exactly the wrong message on the environment. Contrary to the story's implied message, living in cities is green, while living surrounded by forests is brown.

By building taller and taller buildings, the Once-ler was proving himself to be the real environmentalist.

Matthew Kahn, a U.C.L.A. environmental economist, and I looked across America's metropolitan areas and calculated the carbon emissions associated with a new home in different parts of the country. We estimated expected energy use from driving and public transportation, for a family of fixed size and

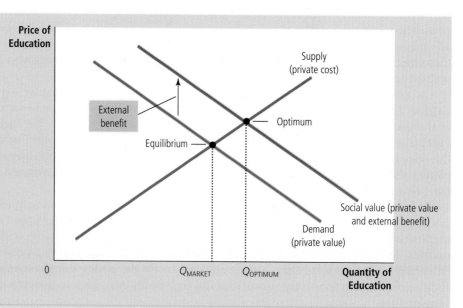

Figure 3

Education and the Social Optimum
In the presence of a positive externality, the social value of the good exceeds the private value. The optimal quantity, $Q_{OPTIMUM}$, is therefore larger than the equilibrium quantity, Q_{MARKET}.

income. We added in carbon emissions from home electricity and home heating. . . .

In almost every metropolitan area, we found the central city residents emitted less carbon than the suburban counterparts. In New York and San Francisco, the average urban family emits more than two tons less carbon annually because it drives less. In Nashville, the city-suburb carbon gap due to driving is more than three tons. After all, density is the defining characteristic of cities. All that closeness means that people need to travel shorter distances, and that shows up clearly in the data.

While public transportation certainly uses much less energy, per rider, than driving, large carbon reductions are possible without any switch to buses or rails. Higher-density suburban areas, which are still entirely car-dependent, still involve a lot less travel than the really sprawling places. This fact offers some hope for greens eager to reduce carbon emissions, since it is a lot easier to imagine Americans driving shorter distances than giving up their cars.

But cars represent only one-third of the gap in carbon emissions between New Yorkers and their suburbanites. The gap in electricity usage between New York City and its suburbs is also about two tons. The gap in emissions from home heating is almost three tons. All told, we estimate

a seven-ton difference in carbon emissions between the residents of Manhattan's urban aeries and the good burghers of Westchester County. Living surrounded by concrete is actually pretty green. Living surrounded by trees is not.

The policy prescription that follows from this is that environmentalists should be championing the growth of more and taller skyscrapers. Every new crane in New York City means less low-density development. The environmental ideal should be an apartment in downtown San Francisco, not a ranch in Marin County.

Of course, many environmentalists will still prefer to take their cue from Henry David Thoreau, who advocated living alone in the woods. They would do well to remember that Thoreau, in a sloppy chowder-cooking moment, burned down 300 acres of prime Concord woodland. Few Boston merchants did as much environmental harm, which suggests that if you want to take good care of the environment, stay away from it and live in cities.

Source: *New York Times,* Economix blog, March 10, 2009.

To summarize: *Negative externalities lead markets to produce a larger quantity than is socially desirable. Positive externalities lead markets to produce a smaller quantity than is socially desirable. To remedy the problem, the government can internalize the externality by taxing goods that have negative externalities and subsidizing goods that have positive externalities.*

CASE STUDY: Technology Spillovers, Industrial Policy, and Patent Protection

A potentially important type of positive externality is called a *technology spillover*— the impact of one firm's research and production efforts on other firms' access to technological advance. For example, consider the market for industrial robots. Robots are at the frontier of a rapidly changing technology. Whenever a firm builds a robot, there is some chance that the firm will discover a new and better design. This new design may benefit not only this firm but society as a whole because the design will enter society's pool of technological knowledge. That is, the new design may have positive externalities for other producers in the economy.

In this case, the government can internalize the externality by subsidizing the production of robots. If the government paid firms a subsidy for each robot produced, the supply curve would shift down by the amount of the subsidy, and this shift would increase the equilibrium quantity of robots. To ensure that the market equilibrium equals the social optimum, the subsidy should equal the value of the technology spillover.

How large are technology spillovers, and what do they imply for public policy? This is an important question because technological progress is the key to why living standards rise over time. Yet it is also a difficult question on which economists often disagree.

Some economists believe that technology spillovers are pervasive and that the government should encourage those industries that yield the largest spillovers. For instance, these economists argue that if making computer chips yields greater spillovers than making potato chips, then the government should encourage the production of computer chips relative to the production of potato chips. The U.S. tax code does this in a limited way by offering special tax breaks for expenditures on research and development. Some other nations go farther by subsidizing specific industries that supposedly offer large technology spillovers. Government intervention in the economy that aims to promote technology-enhancing industries is sometimes called *industrial policy*.

Other economists are skeptical about industrial policy. Even if technology spillovers are common, the success of an industrial policy requires that the government be able to measure the size of the spillovers from different markets. This measurement problem is difficult at best. Moreover, without precise measurements, the political system may end up subsidizing industries with the most political clout rather than those that yield the largest positive externalities.

Another way to deal with technology spillovers is patent protection. The patent laws protect the rights of inventors by giving them exclusive use of their inventions for a period of time. When a firm makes a technological breakthrough, it can patent the idea and capture much of the economic benefit for itself. The patent internalizes the externality by giving the firm a *property right* over its invention. If other firms want to use the new technology, they have to obtain permission from the inventing firm and pay it a royalty. Thus, the patent system gives firms a greater incentive to engage in research and other activities that advance technology. ■

QUICK QUIZ   *Give an example of a negative externality and a positive externality. Explain why market outcomes are inefficient in the presence of these externalities.*

Public Policies toward Externalities

We have discussed why externalities lead markets to allocate resources inefficiently but have mentioned only briefly how this inefficiency can be remedied. In practice, both public policymakers and private individuals respond to externalities in various ways. All of the remedies share the goal of moving the allocation of resources closer to the social optimum.

This section considers governmental solutions. As a general matter, the government can respond to externalities in one of two ways. *Command-and-control policies* regulate behavior directly. *Market-based policies* provide incentives so that private decision makers will choose to solve the problem on their own.

Command-and-Control Policies: Regulation

The government can remedy an externality by making certain behaviors either required or forbidden. For example, it is a crime to dump poisonous chemicals into the water supply. In this case, the external costs to society far exceed the benefits to the polluter. The government therefore institutes a command-and-control policy that prohibits this act altogether.

In most cases of pollution, however, the situation is not this simple. Despite the stated goals of some environmentalists, it would be impossible to prohibit all polluting activity. For example, virtually all forms of transportation—even the horse—produce some undesirable polluting by-products. But it would not be sensible for the government to ban all transportation. Thus, instead of trying to eradicate pollution entirely, society has to weigh the costs and benefits to decide the kinds and quantities of pollution it will allow. In the United States, the Environmental Protection Agency (EPA) is the government agency with the task of developing and enforcing regulations aimed at protecting the environment.

Environmental regulations can take many forms. Sometimes the EPA dictates a maximum level of pollution that a factory may emit. Other times the EPA requires that firms adopt a particular technology to reduce emissions. In all cases, to design good rules, the government regulators need to know the details about specific industries and about the alternative technologies that those industries could adopt. This information is often difficult for government regulators to obtain.

Market-Based Policy 1: Corrective Taxes and Subsidies

Instead of regulating behavior in response to an externality, the government can use market-based policies to align private incentives with social efficiency. For instance, as we saw earlier, the government can internalize the externality by taxing activities that have negative externalities and subsidizing activities that have positive externalities. Taxes enacted to deal with the effects of negative externalities are called **corrective taxes.** They are also called *Pigovian taxes* after economist Arthur Pigou (1877–1959), an early advocate of their use. An ideal corrective tax would equal the external cost from an activity with negative externalities, and an ideal corrective subsidy would equal the external benefit from an activity with positive externalities.

Economists usually prefer corrective taxes to regulations as a way to deal with pollution because they can reduce pollution at a lower cost to society. To see why, let us consider an example.

Suppose that two factories—a paper mill and a steel mill—are each dumping 500 tons of glop into a river every year. The EPA decides that it wants to reduce the amount of pollution. It considers two solutions:

- Regulation: The EPA could tell each factory to reduce its pollution to 300 tons of glop per year.
- Corrective tax: The EPA could levy a tax on each factory of $50,000 for each ton of glop it emits.

The regulation would dictate a level of pollution, whereas the tax would give factory owners an economic incentive to reduce pollution. Which solution do you think is better?

corrective tax
a tax designed to induce private decision makers to take account of the social costs that arise from a negative externality

Arthur Pigou

Most economists prefer the tax. To explain this preference, they would first point out that a tax is just as effective as a regulation in reducing the overall level of pollution. The EPA can achieve whatever level of pollution it wants by setting the tax at the appropriate level. The higher the tax, the larger the reduction in pollution. If the tax is high enough, the factories will close down altogether, reducing pollution to zero.

Although regulation and corrective taxes are both capable of reducing pollution, the tax accomplishes this goal more efficiently. The regulation requires each factory to reduce pollution by the same amount. An equal reduction, however, is not necessarily the least expensive way to clean up the water. It is possible that the paper mill can reduce pollution at lower cost than the steel mill. If so, the paper mill would respond to the tax by reducing pollution substantially to avoid the tax, whereas the steel mill would respond by reducing pollution less and paying the tax.

In essence, the corrective tax places a price on the right to pollute. Just as markets allocate goods to those buyers who value them most highly, a corrective tax allocates pollution to those factories that face the highest cost of reducing it. Whatever the level of pollution the EPA chooses, it can achieve this goal at the lowest total cost using a tax.

Economists also argue that corrective taxes are better for the environment. Under the command-and-control policy of regulation, the factories have no reason to reduce emission further once they have reached the target of 300 tons of glop. By contrast, the tax gives the factories an incentive to develop cleaner technologies because a cleaner technology would reduce the amount of tax the factory has to pay.

Corrective taxes are unlike most other taxes. As we discussed in Chapter 8, most taxes distort incentives and move the allocation of resources away from the social optimum. The reduction in economic well-being—that is, in consumer and producer surplus—exceeds the amount of revenue the government raises, resulting in a deadweight loss. By contrast, when externalities are present, society also cares about the well-being of the bystanders who are affected. Corrective taxes alter incentives to account for the presence of externalities and thereby move the allocation of resources closer to the social optimum. Thus, while corrective taxes raise revenue for the government, they also enhance economic efficiency.

Why Is Gasoline Taxed So Heavily?

In many nations, gasoline is among the most heavily taxed goods. The gas tax can be viewed as a corrective tax aimed at addressing three negative externalities associated with driving:

- *Congestion:* If you have ever been stuck in bumper-to-bumper traffic, you have probably wished that there were fewer cars on the road. A gasoline tax keeps congestion down by encouraging people to take public transportation, carpool more often, and live closer to work.
- *Accidents:* Whenever people buy large cars or sport-utility vehicles, they may make themselves safer but they certainly put their neighbors at risk. According to the National Highway Traffic Safety Administration, a person driving a typical car is five times as likely to die if hit by a sport-utility vehicle than if hit by another car. The gas tax is an indirect way of making people pay when their large, gas-guzzling vehicles impose risk on others.

It would induce them to take this risk into account when choosing what vehicle to purchase.

- *Pollution:* Cars cause smog. Moreover, the burning of fossil fuels such as gasoline is widely believed to be the primary cause of global warming. Experts disagree about how dangerous this threat is, but there is no doubt that the gas tax reduces the threat by reducing the use of gasoline.

So the gas tax, rather than causing deadweight losses like most taxes, actually makes the economy work better. It means less traffic congestion, safer roads, and a cleaner environment.

How high should the tax on gasoline be? Most European countries impose gasoline taxes that are much higher than those in the United States. Many observers have suggested that the United States also should tax gasoline more heavily. A 2007 study published in the *Journal of Economic Literature* summarized the research on the size of the various externalities associated with driving. It concluded that the optimal corrective tax on gasoline was $2.10 per gallon, compared to the actual tax in the United States of only 40 cents.

The tax revenue from a gasoline tax could be used to lower taxes that distort incentives and cause deadweight losses, such as income taxes. In addition, some of the burdensome government regulations that require automakers to produce more fuel-efficient cars would prove unnecessary. This idea, however, has never proven politically popular. ∎

Market-Based Policy 2: Tradable Pollution Permits

Returning to our example of the paper mill and the steel mill, let us suppose that, despite the advice of its economists, the EPA adopts the regulation and requires each factory to reduce its pollution to 300 tons of glop per year. Then one day, after the regulation is in place and both mills have complied, the two firms go to the EPA with a proposal. The steel mill wants to increase its emission of glop by 100 tons. The paper mill has agreed to reduce its emission by the same amount if the steel mill pays it $5 million. Should the EPA allow the two factories to make this deal?

From the standpoint of economic efficiency, allowing the deal is good policy. The deal must make the owners of the two factories better off because they are voluntarily agreeing to it. Moreover, the deal does not have any external effects because the total amount of pollution remains the same. Thus, social welfare is enhanced by allowing the paper mill to sell its pollution rights to the steel mill.

The same logic applies to any voluntary transfer of the right to pollute from one firm to another. If the EPA allows firms to make these deals, it will, in essence, have created a new scarce resource: pollution permits. A market to trade these permits will eventually develop, and that market will be governed by the forces of supply and demand. The invisible hand will ensure that this new market allocates the right to pollute efficiently. That is, the permits will end up in the hands of those firms that value them most highly, as judged by their willingness to pay. A firm's willingness to pay for the right to pollute, in turn, will depend on its cost of reducing pollution: The more costly it is for a firm to cut back on pollution, the more it will be willing to pay for a permit.

An advantage of allowing a market for pollution permits is that the initial allocation of pollution permits among firms does not matter from the standpoint of economic efficiency. Those firms that can reduce pollution at a low cost will sell whatever permits they get, and firms that can reduce pollution only at a high cost will buy whatever permits they need. As long as there is a free market for the pollution rights, the final allocation will be efficient regardless of the initial allocation.

Reducing pollution using pollution permits may seem very different from using corrective taxes, but the two policies have much in common. In both cases, firms pay for their pollution. With corrective taxes, polluting firms must pay a tax to the government. With pollution permits, polluting firms must pay to buy the permit. (Even firms that already own permits must pay to pollute: The opportunity cost of polluting is what they could have received by selling their permits on the open market.) Both corrective taxes and pollution permits internalize the externality of pollution by making it costly for firms to pollute.

The similarity of the two policies can be seen by considering the market for pollution. Both panels in Figure 4 show the demand curve for the right to pollute. This curve shows that the lower the price of polluting, the more firms will choose to pollute. In panel (a), the EPA uses a corrective tax to set a price for pollution. In this case, the supply curve for pollution rights is perfectly elastic (because firms can pollute as much as they want by paying the tax), and the position of the demand curve determines the quantity of pollution. In panel (b), the EPA sets a quantity of pollution by issuing pollution permits. In this case, the supply curve for pollution rights is perfectly inelastic (because the quantity of pollution is fixed by the number of permits), and the position of the demand curve determines the price of pollution. Hence, the EPA can achieve any point on a given demand curve either by setting a price with a corrective tax or by setting a quantity with pollution permits.

In some circumstances, however, selling pollution permits may be better than levying a corrective tax. Suppose the EPA wants no more than 600 tons of glop dumped into the river. But because the EPA does not know the demand curve

In panel (a), the EPA sets a price on pollution by levying a corrective tax, and the demand curve determines the quantity of pollution. In panel (b), the EPA limits the quantity of pollution by limiting the number of pollution permits, and the demand curve determines the price of pollution. The price and quantity of pollution are the same in the two cases.

Figure 4

The Equivalence of Corrective Taxes and Pollution Permits

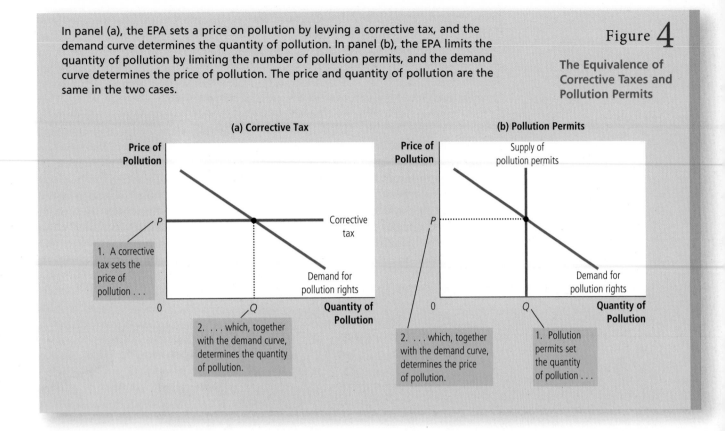

for pollution, it is not sure what size tax would achieve that goal. In this case, it can simply auction off 600 pollution permits. The auction price would yield the appropriate size of the corrective tax.

The idea of the government auctioning off the right to pollute may at first sound like a creature of some economist's imagination. And in fact, that is how the idea began. But increasingly, the EPA has used the system as a way to control pollution. A notable success story has been the case of sulfur dioxide (SO_2), a leading cause of acid rain. In 1990, amendments to the Clean Air Act required power plants to reduce SO_2 emissions substantially. At the same time, the amendments set up a system that allowed plants to trade their SO_2 allowances. Initially, both industry representatives and environmentalists were skeptical of the proposal, but over time the system has reduced pollution with minimal disruption. Pollution permits, like corrective taxes, are now widely viewed as a cost-effective way to keep the environment clean.

Objections to the Economic Analysis of Pollution

"We cannot give anyone the option of polluting for a fee." This comment by the late Senator Edmund Muskie reflects the view of some environmentalists. Clean air and clean water, they argue, are fundamental human rights that should not be debased by considering them in economic terms. How can you put a price on clean air and clean water? The environment is so important, they claim, that we should protect it as much as possible, regardless of the cost.

Economists have little sympathy for this type of argument. To economists, good environmental policy begins by acknowledging the first of the *Ten Principles of Economics* in Chapter 1: People face trade-offs. Certainly, clean air and clean water have value. But their value must be compared to their opportunity cost—that is, to what one must give up to obtain them. Eliminating all pollution is impossible. Trying to eliminate all pollution would reverse many of the technological advances that allow us to enjoy a high standard of living. Few people would be willing to accept poor nutrition, inadequate medical care, or shoddy housing to make the environment as clean as possible.

Economists argue that some environmental activists hurt their own cause by not thinking in economic terms. A clean environment can be viewed as simply another good. Like all normal goods, it has a positive income elasticity: Rich countries can afford a cleaner environment than poor ones and, therefore, usually have more rigorous environmental protection. In addition, like most other goods, clean air

in the news

> ### Cap and Trade

President Obama has proposed a policy to deal with the externalities from carbon emissions.

A Missed Opportunity on Climate Change

BY N. GREGORY MANKIW

During the presidential campaign of 2008, Barack Obama distinguished himself on the economics of climate change, speaking far more sensibly about the issue than most of his rivals. Unfortunately, now that he is president, Mr. Obama may sign a climate bill that falls far short of his aspirations. Indeed, the legislation making its way to his desk could well be worse than nothing at all.

Let's start with the basics. The essential problem of climate change, scientists tell us, is that humans are emitting too much carbon into the atmosphere, which tends to raise world temperatures. Emitting carbon is what economists call a "negative externality"—an adverse side effect of certain market activities on bystanders.

The textbook solution for dealing with negative externalities is to use the tax system to align private incentives with social costs and benefits. Suppose the government imposed a tax on carbon-based products and used the proceeds to cut other taxes. People would have an incentive to shift their consumption toward less carbon-intensive products. A carbon tax is the remedy for climate change that wins overwhelming support among economists and policy wonks.

When he was still a candidate, Mr. Obama did not exactly endorse a carbon tax. He wanted to be elected, and embracing any tax that hits millions of middle-class voters is not a recipe for electoral success. But he did come tantalizingly close.

What Mr. Obama proposed was a cap-and-trade system for carbon, with all the allowances sold at auction. In short, the system would put a ceiling on the amount of carbon released, and companies would bid on the right to emit carbon into the atmosphere.

Such a system is tantamount to a carbon tax. The auction price of an emission right is effectively a tax on carbon. The revenue raised by the auction gives the government the resources to cut other taxes that distort behavior, like income or payroll taxes.

So far, so good. The problem occurred as this sensible idea made the trip from the campaign trail through the legislative process. Rather than auctioning the carbon and clean water obey the law of demand: The lower the price of environmental protection, the more the public will want. The economic approach of using pollution permits and corrective taxes reduces the cost of environmental protection and should, therefore, increase the public's demand for a clean environment.

QUICK QUIZ   *A glue factory and a steel mill emit smoke containing a chemical that is harmful if inhaled in large amounts. Describe three ways the town government might respond to this externality. What are the pros and cons of each solution?*

Private Solutions to Externalities

Although externalities tend to cause markets to be inefficient, government action is not always needed to solve the problem. In some circumstances, people can develop private solutions.

allowances, the bill that recently passed the House would give most of them away to powerful special interests.

The numbers involved are not trivial. From Congressional Budget Office estimates, one can calculate that if all the allowances were auctioned, the government could raise $989 billion in proceeds over 10 years. But in the bill as written, the auction proceeds are only $276 billion.

Mr. Obama understood these risks. When asked about a carbon tax in an interview in July 2007, he said: "I believe that, depending on how it is designed, a carbon tax accomplishes much of the same thing that a cap-and-trade program accomplishes. The danger in a cap-and-trade system is that the permits to emit greenhouse gases are given away for free as opposed to priced at auction. One of the mistakes the Europeans made in setting up a cap-and-trade system was to give too many of those permits away."

Congress is now in the process of sending President Obama a bill that makes exactly this mistake.

How much does it matter? For the purpose of efficiently allocating the carbon rights, it doesn't. Even if these rights are handed out on political rather than economic

grounds, the "trade" part of "cap and trade" will take care of the rest. Those companies with the most need to emit carbon will buy carbon allowances on newly formed exchanges. Those without such pressing needs will sell whatever allowances they are given and enjoy the profits that resulted from Congress's largess.

The problem arises in how the climate policy interacts with the overall tax system. As the president pointed out, a cap-and-trade system is like a carbon tax. The price of carbon allowances will eventually be passed on to consumers in the form of higher prices for carbon-intensive products. But if most of those allowances are handed out rather than auctioned, the government won't have the resources to cut other taxes and offset that price increase. The result is an increase in the effective tax rates facing most Americans, leading to lower real take-home wages, reduced work incentives, and depressed economic activity.

The hard question is whether, on net, such a policy is good or bad. Here you can find policy wonks on both sides. To those who view climate change as an impending catastrophe and the distorting effects of the tax system as a mere annoyance, an

imperfect bill is better than none at all. To those not fully convinced of the enormity of global warming but deeply worried about the adverse effects of high current and prospective tax rates, the bill is a step in the wrong direction.

What everyone should agree on is that the legislation making its way through Congress is a missed opportunity. President Obama knows what a good climate bill would look like. But despite his immense popularity and personal charisma, he appears unable to persuade Congress to go along.

Source: *New York Times,* August 9, 2009.

The Types of Private Solutions

Sometimes the problem of externalities is solved with moral codes and social sanctions. Consider, for instance, why most people do not litter. Although there are laws against littering, these laws are not vigorously enforced. Most people do not litter just because it is the wrong thing to do. The Golden Rule taught to most children says, "Do unto others as you would have them do unto you." This moral injunction tells us to take account of how our actions affect other people. In economic terms, it tells us to internalize externalities.

Another private solution to externalities is charities, many of which are established to deal with externalities. For example, the Sierra Club, whose goal is to protect the environment, is a nonprofit organization funded with private donations. As another example, colleges and universities receive gifts from alumni, corporations, and foundations in part because education has positive externalities for society. The government encourages this private solution to externalities through the tax system by allowing an income tax deduction for charitable donations.

The private market can often solve the problem of externalities by relying on the self-interest of the relevant parties. Sometimes the solution takes the form of integrating different types of businesses. For example, consider an apple grower and a beekeeper who are located next to each other. Each business confers a positive externality on the other: By pollinating the flowers on the trees, the bees help the orchard produce apples. At the same time, the bees use the nectar they get from the apple trees to produce honey. Nonetheless, when the apple grower is deciding how many trees to plant and the beekeeper is deciding how many bees to keep, they neglect the positive externality. As a result, the apple grower plants too few trees and the beekeeper keeps too few bees. These externalities could be internalized if the beekeeper bought the apple orchard or if the apple grower bought the beehives: Both activities would then take place within the same firm, and this single firm could choose the optimal number of trees and bees. Internalizing externalities is one reason that some firms are involved in different types of businesses.

Another way for the private market to deal with external effects is for the interested parties to enter into a contract. In the foregoing example, a contract between the apple grower and the beekeeper can solve the problem of too few trees and too few bees. The contract can specify the number of trees, the number of bees, and perhaps a payment from one party to the other. By setting the right number of trees and bees, the contract can solve the inefficiency that normally arises from these externalities and make both parties better off.

The Coase Theorem

Coase theorem

the proposition that if private parties can bargain without cost over the allocation of resources, they can solve the problem of externalities on their own

How effective is the private market in dealing with externalities? A famous result, called the **Coase theorem** after economist Ronald Coase, suggests that it can be very effective in some circumstances. According to the Coase theorem, if private parties can bargain over the allocation of resources at no cost, then the private market will always solve the problem of externalities and allocate resources efficiently.

To see how the Coase theorem works, consider an example. Suppose that Dick owns a dog named Spot. Spot barks and disturbs Jane, Dick's neighbor. Dick gets a benefit from owning the dog, but the dog confers a negative externality on Jane. Should Dick be forced to send Spot to the pound, or should Jane have to suffer sleepless nights because of Spot's barking?

Consider first what outcome is socially efficient. A social planner, considering the two alternatives, would compare the benefit that Dick gets from the dog to the cost that Jane bears from the barking. If the benefit exceeds the cost, it is efficient for Dick to keep the dog and for Jane to live with the barking. Yet if the cost exceeds the benefit, then Dick should get rid of the dog.

According to the Coase theorem, the private market will reach the efficient outcome on its own. How? Jane can simply offer to pay Dick to get rid of the dog. Dick will accept the deal if the amount of money Jane offers is greater than the benefit of keeping the dog.

By bargaining over the price, Dick and Jane can always reach the efficient outcome. For instance, suppose that Dick gets a $500 benefit from the dog and Jane bears an $800 cost from the barking. In this case, Jane can offer Dick $600 to get rid of the dog, and Dick will gladly accept. Both parties are better off than they were before, and the efficient outcome is reached.

It is possible, of course, that Jane would not be willing to offer any price that Dick would accept. For instance, suppose that Dick gets a $1,000 benefit from the dog and Jane bears an $800 cost from the barking. In this case, Dick would turn down any offer below $1,000, while Jane would not offer any amount above $800. Therefore, Dick ends up keeping the dog. Given these costs and benefits, however, this outcome is efficient.

So far, we have assumed that Dick has the legal right to keep a barking dog. In other words, we have assumed that Dick can keep Spot unless Jane pays him enough to induce him to give up the dog voluntarily. But how different would the outcome be if Jane had the legal right to peace and quiet?

According to the Coase theorem, the initial distribution of rights does not matter for the market's ability to reach the efficient outcome. For instance, suppose that Jane can legally compel Dick to get rid of the dog. Having this right works to Jane's advantage, but it probably will not change the outcome. In this case, Dick can offer to pay Jane to allow him to keep the dog. If the benefit of the dog to Dick exceeds the cost of the barking to Jane, then Dick and Jane will strike a bargain in which Dick keeps the dog.

Although Dick and Jane can reach the efficient outcome regardless of how rights are initially distributed, the distribution of rights is not irrelevant: It determines the distribution of economic well-being. Whether Dick has the right to a barking dog or Jane the right to peace and quiet determines who pays whom in the final bargain. But in either case, the two parties can bargain with each other and solve the externality problem. Dick will end up keeping the dog only if the benefit exceeds the cost.

To sum up: *The Coase theorem says that private economic actors can potentially solve the problem of externalities among themselves. Whatever the initial distribution of rights, the interested parties can reach a bargain in which everyone is better off and the outcome is efficient.*

Why Private Solutions Do Not Always Work

Despite the appealing logic of the Coase theorem, private individuals on their own often fail to resolve the problems caused by externalities. The Coase theorem applies only when the interested parties have no trouble reaching and enforcing an agreement. In the real world, however, bargaining does not always work, even when a mutually beneficial agreement is possible.

transaction costs

the costs that parties incur in the process of agreeing to and following through on a bargain

Sometimes the interested parties fail to solve an externality problem because of **transaction costs,** the costs that parties incur in the process of agreeing to and following through on a bargain. In our example, imagine that Dick and Jane speak different languages so that, to reach an agreement, they need to hire a translator. If the benefit of solving the barking problem is less than the cost of the translator, Dick and Jane might choose to leave the problem unsolved. In more realistic examples, the transaction costs are the expenses not of translators but of the lawyers required to draft and enforce contracts.

At other times, bargaining simply breaks down. The recurrence of wars and labor strikes shows that reaching agreement can be difficult and that failing to reach agreement can be costly. The problem is often that each party tries to hold out for a better deal. For example, suppose that Dick gets a $500 benefit from the dog, and Jane bears an $800 cost from the barking. Although it is efficient for Jane to pay Dick to get rid of the dog, there are many prices that could lead to this outcome. Dick might demand $750, and Jane might offer only $550. As they haggle over the price, the inefficient outcome with the barking dog persists.

Reaching an efficient bargain is especially difficult when the number of interested parties is large because coordinating everyone is costly. For example, consider a factory that pollutes the water of a nearby lake. The pollution confers a negative externality on the local fishermen. According to the Coase theorem, if the pollution is inefficient, then the factory and the fishermen could reach a bargain in which the fishermen pay the factory not to pollute. If there are many fishermen, however, trying to coordinate them all to bargain with the factory may be almost impossible.

When private bargaining does not work, the government can sometimes play a role. The government is an institution designed for collective action. In this example, the government can act on behalf of the fishermen, even when it is impractical for the fishermen to act for themselves.

QUICK QUIZ   *Give an example of a private solution to an externality.* • *What is the Coase theorem?* • *Why are private economic participants sometimes unable to solve the problems caused by an externality?*

Conclusion

The invisible hand is powerful but not omnipotent. A market's equilibrium maximizes the sum of producer and consumer surplus. When the buyers and sellers in the market are the only interested parties, this outcome is efficient from the standpoint of society as a whole. But when there are external effects, such as pollution, evaluating a market outcome requires taking into account the well-being of third parties as well. In this case, the invisible hand of the marketplace may fail to allocate resources efficiently.

In some cases, people can solve the problem of externalities on their own. The Coase theorem suggests that the interested parties can bargain among themselves and agree on an efficient solution. Sometimes, however, an efficient outcome cannot be reached, perhaps because the large number of interested parties makes bargaining difficult.

When people cannot solve the problem of externalities privately, the government often steps in. Yet even with government intervention, society should not abandon market forces entirely. Rather, the government can address the problem by requiring decision makers to bear the full costs of their actions. Corrective taxes on emissions and pollution permits, for instance, are designed to internalize the externality of pollution. More and more, these are the policies of choice for those interested in protecting the environment. Market forces, properly redirected, are often the best remedy for market failure.

SUMMARY

- When a transaction between a buyer and seller directly affects a third party, the effect is called an externality. If an activity yields negative externalities, such as pollution, the socially optimal quantity in a market is less than the equilibrium quantity. If an activity yields positive externalities, such as technology spillovers, the socially optimal quantity is greater than the equilibrium quantity.

- Governments pursue various policies to remedy the inefficiencies caused by externalities. Sometimes the government prevents socially inefficient activity by regulating behavior. Other times it internalizes an externality using corrective taxes. Another public policy is to issue permits. For example, the government could protect the environment by issuing a limited number of

pollution permits. The result of this policy is largely the same as imposing corrective taxes on polluters.

- Those affected by externalities can sometimes solve the problem privately. For instance, when one business imposes an externality on another business, the two businesses can internalize the externality by merging. Alternatively, the interested parties can solve the problem by negotiating a contract. According to the Coase theorem, if people can bargain without cost, then they can always reach an agreement in which resources are allocated efficiently. In many cases, however, reaching a bargain among the many interested parties is difficult, so the Coase theorem does not apply.

KEY CONCEPTS

externality, *p. 196*
internalizing the externality, *p. 199*

corrective tax, *p. 203*
Coase theorem, *p. 210*

transaction costs, *p. 212*

QUESTIONS FOR REVIEW

1. Give an example of a negative externality and an example of a positive externality.
2. Draw a supply-and-demand diagram to explain the effect of a negative externality that occurs as a result of a firm's production process.
3. In what way does the patent system help society solve an externality problem?
4. What are corrective taxes? Why do economists prefer them to regulations as a way to protect the environment from pollution?
5. List some of the ways that the problems caused by externalities can be solved without government intervention.
6. Imagine that you are a nonsmoker sharing a room with a smoker. According to the Coase theorem, what determines whether your roommate smokes in the room? Is this outcome efficient? How do you and your roommate reach this solution?

PROBLEMS AND APPLICATIONS

1. Consider two ways to protect your car from theft. The Club (a steering wheel lock) makes it difficult for a car thief to take your car. Lojack (a tracking system) makes it easier for the police to catch the car thief who has stolen it. Which of these types of protection conveys a negative externality on other car owners? Which conveys a positive externality? Do you think there are any policy implications of your analysis?

2. Do you agree with the following statements? Why or why not?
   a. "The benefits of corrective taxes as a way to reduce pollution have to be weighed against the deadweight losses that these taxes cause."
   b. "When deciding whether to levy a corrective tax on consumers or producers, the government should be careful to levy the tax on the side of the market generating the externality."

3. Consider the market for fire extinguishers.
   a. Why might fire extinguishers exhibit positive externalities?
   b. Draw a graph of the market for fire extinguishers, labeling the demand curve, the social-value curve, the supply curve, and the social-cost curve.
   c. Indicate the market equilibrium level of output and the efficient level of output. Give an intuitive explanation for why these quantities differ.
   d. If the external benefit is $10 per extinguisher, describe a government policy that would yield the efficient outcome.

4. A local drama company proposes a new neighborhood theater in San Francisco. Before approving the building permit, the city planner completes a study of the theater's impact on the surrounding community.
   a. One finding of the study is that theaters attract traffic, which adversely affects the community. The city planner estimates that the cost to the community from the extra traffic is $5 per ticket. What kind of an externality is this? Why?
   b. Graph the market for theater tickets, labeling the demand curve, the social-value curve, the supply curve, the social-cost curve, the market equilibrium level of output, and the efficient level of output. Also show the per-unit amount of the externality.
   c. Upon further review, the city planner uncovers a second externality. Rehearsals for the plays tend to run until late at night, with actors, stagehands, and other theater members coming and going at various hours. The planner has found that the increased foot traffic improves the safety of the surrounding streets, an estimated benefit to the community of $2 per ticket. What kind of externality is this? Why?
   d. On a new graph, illustrate the market for theater tickets in the case of these two externalities. Again, label the demand curve, the social-value curve, the supply curve, the social-cost curve, the market equilibrium level of output, the efficient level of output, and the per-unit amount of both externalities.
   e. Describe a government policy that would result in an efficient outcome.

5. Greater consumption of alcohol leads to more motor vehicle accidents and, thus, imposes costs on people who do not drink and drive.
   a. Illustrate the market for alcohol, labeling the demand curve, the social-value curve, the supply curve, the social-cost curve, the market equilibrium level of output, and the efficient level of output.
   b. On your graph, shade the area corresponding to the deadweight loss of the market equilibrium. (Hint: The deadweight loss occurs because some units of alcohol are consumed for which the social cost exceeds the social value.) Explain.

6. Many observers believe that the levels of pollution in our society are too high.
   a. If society wishes to reduce overall pollution by a certain amount, why is it efficient to have different amounts of reduction at different firms?
   b. Command-and-control approaches often rely on uniform reductions among firms. Why are these approaches generally unable to target the firms that should undertake bigger reductions?
   c. Economists argue that appropriate corrective taxes or tradable pollution rights will result

in efficient pollution reduction. How do these approaches target the firms that should undertake bigger reductions?

7. The many identical residents of Whoville love drinking Zlurp. Each resident has the following willingness to pay for the tasty refreshment:

First bottle	$5
Second bottle	4
Third bottle	3
Fourth bottle	2
Fifth bottle	1
Further bottles	0

a. The cost of producing Zlurp is $1.50, and the competitive suppliers sell it at this price. (The supply curve is horizontal.) How many bottles will each Whovillian consume? What is each person's consumer surplus?

b. Producing Zlurp creates pollution. Each bottle has an external cost of $1. Taking this additional cost into account, what is total surplus per person in the allocation you described in part (a)?

c. Cindy Lou Who, one of the residents of Whoville, decides on her own to reduce her consumption of Zlurp by one bottle. What happens to Cindy's welfare (her consumer surplus minus the cost of pollution she experiences)? How does Cindy's decision affect total surplus in Whoville?

d. Mayor Grinch imposes a $1 tax on Zlurp. What is consumption per person now? Calculate consumer surplus, the external cost, government revenue, and total surplus per person.

e. Based on your calculations, would you support the mayor's policy? Why or why not?

8. Ringo loves playing rock 'n' roll music at high volume. Luciano loves opera and hates rock 'n' roll. Unfortunately, they are next-door neighbors in an apartment building with paper-thin walls.

a. What is the externality here?

b. What command-and-control policy might the landlord impose? Could such a policy lead to an inefficient outcome?

c. Suppose the landlord lets the tenants do whatever they want. According to the Coase theorem, how might Ringo and Luciano reach an efficient outcome on their own?

What might prevent them from reaching an efficient outcome?

9. Figure 4 shows that for any given demand curve for the right to pollute, the government can achieve the same outcome either by setting a price with a corrective tax or by setting a quantity with pollution permits. Suppose there is a sharp improvement in the technology for controlling pollution.

a. Using graphs similar to those in Figure 4, illustrate the effect of this development on the demand for pollution rights.

b. What is the effect on the price and quantity of pollution under each regulatory system? Explain.

10. Suppose that the government decides to issue tradable permits for a certain form of pollution.

a. Does it matter for economic efficiency whether the government distributes or auctions the permits? Why or why not?

b. If the government chooses to distribute the permits, does the allocation of permits among firms matter for efficiency? Explain.

11. There are three industrial firms in Happy Valley.

Firm	Initial Pollution Level	Cost of Reducing Pollution by 1 Unit
A	70 units	$20
B	80 units	$25
C	50 units	$10

The government wants to reduce pollution to 120 units, so it gives each firm 40 tradable pollution permits.

a. Who sells permits and how many do they sell? Who buys permits and how many do they buy? Briefly explain why the sellers and buyers are each willing to do so. What is the total cost of pollution reduction in this situation?

b. How much higher would the costs of pollution reduction be if the permits could not be traded?

For further information on topics in this chapter, additional problems, applications, examples, online quizzes, and more, please visit our website at www .cengage.com/economics/mankiw.

Public Goods and Common Resources

11

An old song lyric maintains that "the best things in life are free." A moment's thought reveals a long list of goods that the songwriter could have had in mind. Nature provides some of them, such as rivers, mountains, beaches, lakes, and oceans. The government provides others, such as playgrounds, parks, and parades. In each case, people do not pay a fee when they choose to enjoy the benefit of the good.

Goods without prices provide a special challenge for economic analysis. Most goods in our economy are allocated in markets, in which buyers pay for what they receive and sellers are paid for what they provide. For these goods, prices are the signals that guide the decisions of buyers and sellers, and these decisions lead to an efficient allocation of resources. When goods are available free of charge, however, the market forces that normally allocate resources in our economy are absent.

In this chapter, we examine the problems that arise for the allocation of resources when there are goods without market prices. Our analysis will shed light on one of the *Ten Principles of Economics* in Chapter 1: Governments can sometimes improve market outcomes. When a good does not have a price attached to it, private markets cannot ensure that the good is produced and consumed in the proper amounts. In such cases, government policy can potentially remedy the market failure and raise economic well-being.

The Different Kinds of Goods

How well do markets work in providing the goods that people want? The answer to this question depends on the good being considered. As we discussed in Chapter 7, a market can provide the efficient number of ice-cream cones: The price of ice-cream cones adjusts to balance supply and demand, and this equilibrium maximizes the sum of producer and consumer surplus. Yet as we discussed in Chapter 10, the market cannot be counted on to prevent aluminum manufacturers from polluting the air we breathe: Buyers and sellers in a market typically do not take into account the external effects of their decisions. Thus, markets work well when the good is ice cream, but they work badly when the good is clean air.

In thinking about the various goods in the economy, it is useful to group them according to two characteristics:

excludability

the property of a good whereby a person can be prevented from using it

- Is the good **excludable**? That is, can people be prevented from using the good?
- Is the good **rival in consumption**? That is, does one person's use of the good reduce another person's ability to use it?

Using these two characteristics, Figure 1 divides goods into four categories:

rivalry in consumption

the property of a good whereby one person's use diminishes other people's use

private goods

goods that are both excludable and rival in consumption

1. **Private goods** are both excludable and rival in consumption. Consider an ice-cream cone, for example. An ice-cream cone is excludable because it is possible to prevent someone from eating an ice-cream cone—you just don't give it to him. An ice-cream cone is rival in consumption because if one person eats an ice-cream cone, another person cannot eat the same cone. Most goods in the economy are private goods like ice-cream cones: You don't get one unless you pay for it, and once you have it, you are the only person who benefits. When we analyzed supply and demand in Chapters 4, 5, and 6 and the efficiency of markets in Chapters 7, 8, and 9, we implicitly assumed that goods were both excludable and rival in consumption.

public goods

goods that are neither excludable nor rival in consumption

2. **Public goods** are neither excludable nor rival in consumption. That is, people cannot be prevented from using a public good, and one person's use of a public good does not reduce another person's ability to use it. For example, a tornado siren in a small town is a public good. Once the siren sounds, it is impossible to prevent any single person from hearing it (so it is not excludable). Moreover, when one person gets the benefit of the warning, she does not reduce the benefit to anyone else (so it is not rival in consumption).

common resources

goods that are rival in consumption but not excludable

3. **Common resources** are rival in consumption but not excludable. For example, fish in the ocean are rival in consumption: When one person catches fish, there are fewer fish for the next person to catch. Yet these fish are not an excludable good because, given the vast size of an ocean, it is difficult to stop fishermen from taking fish out of it.

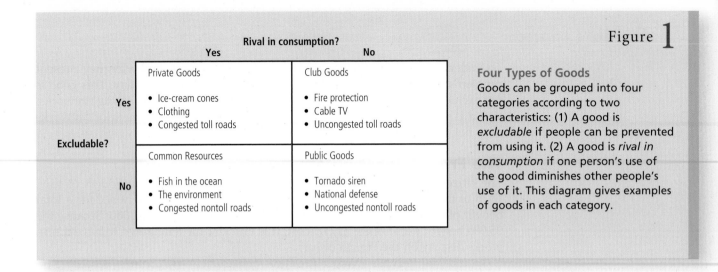

Figure 1

Four Types of Goods
Goods can be grouped into four categories according to two characteristics: (1) A good is *excludable* if people can be prevented from using it. (2) A good is *rival in consumption* if one person's use of the good diminishes other people's use of it. This diagram gives examples of goods in each category.

4. **Club goods** are excludable but not rival in consumption. For instance, consider fire protection in a small town. It is easy to exclude someone from using this good: The fire department can just let his house burn down. Yet fire protection is not rival in consumption: Once a town has paid for the fire department, the additional cost of protecting one more house is small. (We discuss club goods again in Chapter 15, where we see that they are one type of a *natural monopoly*.)

club goods
goods that are excludable but not rival in consumption

Although Figure 1 offers a clean separation of goods into four categories, the boundaries between the categories are sometimes fuzzy. Whether goods are excludable or rival in consumption is often a matter of degree. Fish in an ocean may not be excludable because monitoring fishing is so difficult, but a large enough coast guard could make fish at least partly excludable. Similarly, although fish are generally rival in consumption, this would be less true if the population of fishermen were small relative to the population of fish. (Think of North American fishing waters before the arrival of European settlers.) For purposes of our analysis, however, it will be helpful to group goods into these four categories.

In this chapter, we examine goods that are not excludable: public goods and common resources. Because people cannot be prevented from using these goods, they are available to everyone free of charge. The study of public goods and common resources is closely related to the study of externalities. For both of these types of goods, externalities arise because something of value has no price attached to it. If one person were to provide a public good, such as a tornado siren, other people would be better off. They would receive a benefit without paying for it—a positive externality. Similarly, when one person uses a common resource such as the fish in the ocean, other people are worse off because there are fewer fish to catch. They suffer a loss but are not compensated for it—a negative externality. Because of these external effects, private decisions about consumption and production can lead to an inefficient allocation of resources, and government intervention can potentially raise economic well-being.

QUICK QUIZ *Define* public goods *and* common resources *and give an example of each.*

Public Goods

To understand how public goods differ from other goods and why they present problems for society, let's consider an example: a fireworks display. This good is not excludable because it is impossible to prevent someone from seeing fireworks, and it is not rival in consumption because one person's enjoyment of fireworks does not reduce anyone else's enjoyment of them.

The Free-Rider Problem

The citizens of Smalltown, U.S.A., like seeing fireworks on the Fourth of July. Each of the town's 500 residents places a $10 value on the experience for a total benefit of $5,000. The cost of putting on a fireworks display is $1,000. Because the $5,000 benefit exceeds the $1,000 cost, it is efficient for Smalltown to have a fireworks display on the Fourth of July.

Would the private market produce the efficient outcome? Probably not. Imagine that Ellen, a Smalltown entrepreneur, decided to put on a fireworks display. Ellen would surely have trouble selling tickets to the event because her potential customers would quickly figure out that they could see the fireworks even without a ticket. Because fireworks are not excludable, people have an incentive to be free riders. A **free rider** is a person who receives the benefit of a good but does not pay for it. Because people would have an incentive to be free riders rather than ticket buyers, the market would fail to provide the efficient outcome.

free rider

a person who receives the benefit of a good but avoids paying for it

One way to view this market failure is that it arises because of an externality. If Ellen puts on the fireworks display, she confers an external benefit on those who see the display without paying for it. When deciding whether to put on the display, however, Ellen does not take the external benefits into account. Even though the fireworks display is socially desirable, it is not profitable. As a result, Ellen makes the privately rational but socially inefficient decision not to put on the display.

Although the private market fails to supply the fireworks display demanded by Smalltown residents, the solution to Smalltown's problem is obvious: The local government can sponsor a Fourth of July celebration. The town council can raise everyone's taxes by $2 and use the revenue to hire Ellen to produce the fireworks. Everyone in Smalltown is better off by $8—the $10 at which residents value the fireworks minus the $2 tax bill. Ellen can help Smalltown reach the efficient outcome as a public employee even though she could not do so as a private entrepreneur.

The story of Smalltown is simplified but realistic. In fact, many local governments in the United States pay for fireworks on the Fourth of July. Moreover, the story shows a general lesson about public goods: Because public goods are not excludable, the free-rider problem prevents the private market from supplying them. The government, however, can potentially remedy the problem. If the government decides that the total benefits of a public good exceed its costs, it can provide the public good, pay for it with tax revenue, and make everyone better off.

Some Important Public Goods

There are many examples of public goods. Here we consider three of the most important.

National Defense   The defense of a country from foreign aggressors is a classic example of a public good. Once the country is defended, it is impossible to prevent any single person from enjoying the benefit of this defense. Moreover, when one person enjoys the benefit of national defense, he does not reduce the benefit to anyone else. Thus, national defense is neither excludable nor rival in consumption.

National defense is also one of the most expensive public goods. In 2009, the U.S. federal government spent a total of $661 billion on national defense, more than $2,150 per person. People disagree about whether this amount is too small or too large, but almost no one doubts that some government spending for national defense is necessary. Even economists who advocate small government agree that the national defense is a public good the government should provide.

"I like the concept if we can do it with no new taxes."

Basic Research   Knowledge is created through research. In evaluating the appropriate public policy toward knowledge creation, it is important to distinguish general knowledge from specific technological knowledge. Specific technological knowledge, such as the invention of a longer-lasting battery, a smaller microchip, or a better digital music player, can be patented. The patent gives the inventor the exclusive right to the knowledge he or she has created for a period of time. Anyone else who wants to use the patented information must pay the inventor for the right to do so. In other words, the patent makes the knowledge created by the inventor excludable.

By contrast, general knowledge is a public good. For example, a mathematician cannot patent a theorem. Once a theorem is proven, the knowledge is not excludable: The theorem enters society's general pool of knowledge that anyone can use without charge. The theorem is also not rival in consumption: One person's use of the theorem does not prevent any other person from using the theorem.

Profit-seeking firms spend a lot on research trying to develop new products that they can patent and sell, but they do not spend much on basic research. Their incentive, instead, is to free ride on the general knowledge created by others. As a result, in the absence of any public policy, society would devote too few resources to creating new knowledge.

The government tries to provide the public good of general knowledge in various ways. Government agencies, such as the National Institutes of Health and the National Science Foundation, subsidize basic research in medicine, mathematics, physics, chemistry, biology, and even economics. Some people justify government funding of the space program on the grounds that it adds to society's pool of knowledge (although many scientists are skeptical of the scientific value of manned space travel). Determining the appropriate level of government support for these endeavors is difficult because the benefits are hard to measure. Moreover, the members of Congress who appropriate funds for research usually have little expertise in science and, therefore, are not in the best position to judge what lines of research will produce the largest benefits. So, while basic research is surely a public good, we should not be surprised if the public sector fails to pay for the right amount and the right kinds.

Fighting Poverty   Many government programs are aimed at helping the poor. The welfare system (officially called the Temporary Assistance for Needy Families program) provides a small income for some poor families. Similarly, the Food Stamp program subsidizes the purchase of food for those with low incomes, and various government housing programs make shelter more affordable. These antipoverty programs are financed by taxes paid by families that are financially more successful.

Economists disagree among themselves about what role the government should play in fighting poverty. We discuss this debate more fully in Chapter 20, but here we note one important argument: Advocates of antipoverty programs claim that fighting poverty is a public good. Even if everyone prefers living in a society without poverty, fighting poverty is not a "good" that private actions will adequately provide.

To see why, suppose someone tried to organize a group of wealthy individuals to try to eliminate poverty. They would be providing a public good. This good would not be rival in consumption: One person's enjoyment of living in a society without poverty would not reduce anyone else's enjoyment of it. The good would not be excludable: Once poverty is eliminated, no one can be prevented from taking pleasure in this fact. As a result, there would be a tendency for people to free ride on the generosity of others, enjoying the benefits of poverty elimination without contributing to the cause.

Because of the free-rider problem, eliminating poverty through private charity will probably not work. Yet government action can solve this problem. Taxing the wealthy to raise the living standards of the poor can potentially make everyone better off. The poor are better off because they now enjoy a higher standard of living, and those paying the taxes are better off because they enjoy living in a society with less poverty.

Are Lighthouses Public Goods?

Some goods can switch between being public goods and being private goods depending on the circumstances. For example, a fireworks display is a public good if performed in a town with many residents. Yet if performed at a private amusement park, such as Walt Disney World, a fireworks display is more like a private good because visitors to the park pay for admission.

Another example is a lighthouse. Economists have long used lighthouses as an example of a public good. Lighthouses mark specific locations along the coast so that passing ships can avoid treacherous waters. The benefit that the lighthouse provides to the ship captain is neither excludable nor rival in consumption, so each captain has an incentive to free ride by using the lighthouse to navigate without paying for the service. Because of this free-rider problem, private markets usually fail to provide the lighthouses that ship captains need. As a result, most lighthouses today are operated by the government.

In some cases, however, lighthouses have been closer to private goods. On the coast of England in the 19th century, for example, some lighthouses were privately owned and operated. Instead of trying to charge ship captains for the service, however, the owner of the lighthouse charged the owner of the nearby port. If the port owner did not pay, the lighthouse owner turned off the light, and ships avoided that port.

In deciding whether something is a public good, one must determine who the beneficiaries are and whether these beneficiaries can be excluded from using the good. A free-rider problem arises when the number of beneficiaries is large and exclusion of any one of them is impossible. If a lighthouse benefits many ship

What kind of good is this?

captains, it is a public good. Yet if it primarily benefits a single port owner, it is more like a private good. ■

The Difficult Job of Cost–Benefit Analysis

So far we have seen that the government provides public goods because the private market on its own will not produce an efficient quantity. Yet deciding that the government must play a role is only the first step. The government must then determine what kinds of public goods to provide and in what quantities.

Suppose that the government is considering a public project, such as building a new highway. To judge whether to build the highway, it must compare the total benefits of all those who would use it to the costs of building and maintaining it. To make this decision, the government might hire a team of economists and engineers to conduct a study, called a **cost–benefit analysis,** to estimate the total costs and benefits of the project to society as a whole.

Cost–benefit analysts have a tough job. Because the highway will be available to everyone free of charge, there is no price with which to judge the value of the highway. Simply asking people how much they would value the highway is not reliable: Quantifying benefits is difficult using the results from a questionnaire, and respondents have little incentive to tell the truth. Those who would use the highway have an incentive to exaggerate the benefit they receive to get the highway built. Those who would be harmed by the highway have an incentive to exaggerate the costs to them to prevent the highway from being built.

The efficient provision of public goods is, therefore, intrinsically more difficult than the efficient provision of private goods. When buyers of a private good enter a market, they reveal the value they place on it through the prices they are willing to pay. At the same time, sellers reveal their costs with the prices they are willing to accept. The equilibrium is an efficient allocation of resources because it reflects all this information. By contrast, cost–benefit analysts do not have any price signals to observe when evaluating whether the government should provide a public good and how much to provide. Their findings on the costs and benefits of public projects are rough approximations at best.

cost–benefit analysis

a study that compares the costs and benefits to society of providing a public good

CASE STUDY   How Much Is a Life Worth?

Imagine that you have been elected to serve as a member of your local town council. The town engineer comes to you with a proposal: The town can spend $10,000 to build and operate a traffic light at a town intersection that now has only a stop sign. The benefit of the traffic light is increased safety. The engineer estimates, based on data from similar intersections, that the traffic light would reduce the risk of a fatal traffic accident over the lifetime of the traffic light from 1.6 to 1.1 percent. Should you spend the money for the new light?

To answer this question, you turn to cost–benefit analysis. But you quickly run into an obstacle: The costs and benefits must be measured in the same units if you are to compare them meaningfully. The cost is measured in dollars, but the benefit—the possibility of saving a person's life—is not directly monetary. To make your decision, you have to put a dollar value on a human life.

At first, you may be tempted to conclude that a human life is priceless. After all, there is probably no amount of money that you could be paid to voluntarily give up your life or that of a loved one. This suggests that a human life has an infinite dollar value.

For the purposes of cost–benefit analysis, however, this answer leads to non-sensical results. If we truly placed an infinite value on human life, we should place traffic lights on every street corner, and we should all drive large cars loaded with all the latest safety features. Yet traffic lights are not at every corner, and people sometimes choose to pay less for smaller cars without safety options such as side-impact air bags or antilock brakes. In both our public and private decisions, we are at times willing to risk our lives to save some money.

Once we have accepted the idea that a person's life has an implicit dollar value, how can we determine what that value is? One approach, sometimes used by courts to award damages in wrongful-death suits, is to look at the total amount of money a person would have earned if he or she had lived. Economists are often critical of this approach because it ignores other opportunity costs of losing one's life. It thus has the bizarre implication that the life of a retired or disabled person has no value.

A better way to value human life is to look at the risks that people are voluntarily willing to take and how much they must be paid for taking them. Mortality risk varies across jobs, for example. Construction workers in high-rise buildings face greater risk of death on the job than office workers do. By comparing wages in risky and less risky occupations, controlling for education, experience, and other determinants of wages, economists can get some sense about what value people put on their own lives. Studies using this approach conclude that the value of a human life is about $10 million.

We can now return to our original example and respond to the town engineer. The traffic light reduces the risk of fatality by 0.5 percentage points. Thus, the expected benefit from installing the traffic light is 0.005 × $10 million, or $50,000. This estimate of the benefit well exceeds the cost of $10,000, so you should approve the project. ∎

QUICK QUIZ *What is the* free-rider *problem? Why does the free-rider problem induce the government to provide public goods? • How should the government decide whether to provide a public good?*

Common Resources

Tragedy of the Commons

a parable that illustrates why common resources are used more than is desirable from the standpoint of society as a whole

Common resources, like public goods, are not excludable: They are available free of charge to anyone who wants to use them. Common resources are, however, rival in consumption: One person's use of the common resource reduces other people's ability to use it. Thus, common resources give rise to a new problem. Once the good is provided, policymakers need to be concerned about how much it is used. This problem is best understood from the classic parable called the **Tragedy of the Commons**.

The Tragedy of the Commons

Consider life in a small medieval town. Of the many economic activities that take place in the town, one of the most important is raising sheep. Many of the town's families own flocks of sheep and support themselves by selling the sheep's wool, which is used to make clothing.

As our story begins, the sheep spend much of their time grazing on the land surrounding the town, called the Town Common. No family owns the land. Instead, the town residents own the land collectively, and all the residents are allowed to graze their sheep on it. Collective ownership works well because land is plentiful. As long as everyone can get all the good grazing land they want, the Town Common is not rival in consumption, and allowing residents' sheep to graze for free causes no problems. Everyone in the town is happy.

As the years pass, the population of the town grows, and so does the number of sheep grazing on the Town Common. With a growing number of sheep and a fixed amount of land, the land starts to lose its ability to replenish itself. Eventually, the land is grazed so heavily that it becomes barren. With no grass left on the Town Common, raising sheep is impossible, and the town's once prosperous wool industry disappears. Many families lose their source of livelihood.

What causes the tragedy? Why do the shepherds allow the sheep population to grow so large that it destroys the Town Common? The reason is that social and private incentives differ. Avoiding the destruction of the grazing land depends on the collective action of the shepherds. If the shepherds acted together, they could reduce the sheep population to a size that the Town Common can support. Yet no single family has an incentive to reduce the size of its own flock because each flock represents only a small part of the problem.

In essence, the Tragedy of the Commons arises because of an externality. When one family's flock grazes on the common land, it reduces the quality of the land available for other families. Because people neglect this negative externality when deciding how many sheep to own, the result is an excessive number of sheep.

If the tragedy had been foreseen, the town could have solved the problem in various ways. It could have regulated the number of sheep in each family's flock, internalized the externality by taxing sheep, or auctioned off a limited number of sheep-grazing permits. That is, the medieval town could have dealt with the problem of overgrazing in the way that modern society deals with the problem of pollution.

In the case of land, however, there is a simpler solution. The town can divide the land among town families. Each family can enclose its parcel of land with a fence and then protect it from excessive grazing. In this way, the land becomes a private good rather than a common resource. This outcome in fact occurred during the enclosure movement in England in the 17th century.

The Tragedy of the Commons is a story with a general lesson: When one person uses a common resource, he or she diminishes other people's enjoyment of it. Because of this negative externality, common resources tend to be used excessively. The government can solve the problem by using regulation or taxes to reduce consumption of the common resource. Alternatively, the government can sometimes turn the common resource into a private good.

This lesson has been known for thousands of years. The ancient Greek philosopher Aristotle pointed out the problem with common resources: "What is common to many is taken least care of, for all men have greater regard for what is their own than for what they possess in common with others."

Some Important Common Resources

There are many examples of common resources. In almost all cases, the same problem arises as in the Tragedy of the Commons: Private decision makers use the common resource too much. Governments often regulate behavior or impose fees to mitigate the problem of overuse.

Clean Air and Water   As we discussed in Chapter 10, markets do not adequately protect the environment. Pollution is a negative externality that can be remedied with regulations or with corrective taxes on polluting activities. One can view this market failure as an example of a common-resource problem. Clean air and clean water are common resources like open grazing land, and excessive pollution is like excessive grazing. Environmental degradation is a modern Tragedy of the Commons.

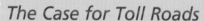

in the **news**

❯ *The Case for Toll Roads*

Many economists think drivers should be charged more for using roads. Here is why.

Why You'll Love Paying for Roads That Used to Be Free

BY ERIC A. MORRIS

To end the scourge of traffic congestion, Julius Caesar banned most carts from the streets of Rome during daylight hours. It didn't work—traffic jams just shifted to dusk. Two thousand years later, we have put a man on the moon and developed garments infinitely more practical than the toga, but we seem little nearer to solving the congestion problem.

If you live in a city, particularly a large one, you probably need little convincing that traffic congestion is frustrating and wasteful. According to the Texas Transportation Institute, the average American urban traveler lost 38 hours, nearly one full work week, to congestion in 2005. And congestion is getting worse, not better; urban travelers in 1982 were delayed only 14 hours that year.

Americans want action, but unfortunately there aren't too many great ideas about what that action might be. As Anthony Downs's excellent book *Still Stuck in Traffic: Coping With Peak-Hour Traffic Congestion* chronicles, most of the proposed solutions are too difficult to implement, won't work, or both.

Fortunately, there is one remedy which is both doable and largely guaranteed to succeed. In the space of a year or two we could have you zipping along the 405 or the LIE at the height of rush hour at a comfortable 55 miles per hour.

There's just one small problem with this silver bullet for congestion: many people seem to prefer the werewolf. Despite its merits, this policy, which is known as "congestion pricing," "value pricing," or "variable tolling," is not an easy political sell.

For decades, economists and other transportation thinkers have advocated imposing tolls that vary with congestion levels on roadways. Simply put, the more congestion, the higher the toll, until congestion goes away.

To many people, this sounds like a scheme by mustache-twirling bureaucrats and their academic apologists to fleece drivers out of their hard-earned cash. Why should drivers have to pay to use roads their tax dollars have already paid for? Won't the remaining free roads be swamped as drivers are forced off the tolled roads? Won't the working-class and poor be the victims here, as the tolled routes turn into "Lexus lanes"?

And besides, adopting this policy would mean listening to economists, and who wants to do that?

There's a real problem with this logic, which is that, on its own terms, it makes perfect sense (except for the listening to economists part). Opponents of tolls are certainly not stupid, and their arguments deserve serious consideration. But in the end, their concerns are largely overblown, and the benefits of tolling swamp the potential costs.

Unfortunately, it can be hard to convey this because the theory behind tolling is somewhat complex and counterintuitive.

Congested Roads   Roads can be either public goods or common resources. If a road is not congested, then one person's use does not affect anyone else. In this case, use is not rival in consumption, and the road is a public good. Yet if a road is congested, then use of that road yields a negative externality. When one person drives on the road, it becomes more crowded, and other people must drive more slowly. In this case, the road is a common resource.

One way for the government to address the problem of road congestion is to charge drivers a toll. A toll is, in essence, a corrective tax on the externality of congestion. Sometimes, as in the case of local roads, tolls are not a practical solution

This is too bad, because variable tolling is an excellent public policy. Here's why: the basic economic theory is that when you give out something valuable—in this case, road space—for less than its true value, shortages result.

Ultimately, there's no free lunch; instead of paying with money, you pay with the effort and time needed to acquire the good. Think of Soviet shoppers spending their lives in endless queues to purchase artificially low-priced but exceedingly scarce goods. Then think of Americans who can fulfill nearly any consumerist fantasy quickly but at a monetary cost. Free but congested roads have left us shivering on the streets of Moscow.

To consider it another way, delay is an externality imposed by drivers on their peers. By driving onto a busy road and contributing to congestion, drivers slow the speeds of others—but they never have to pay for it, at least not directly. In the end, of course, everybody pays, because as we impose congestion on others, others impose it on us. This degenerates into a game that nobody can win.

Markets work best when externalities are internalized: i.e., you pay for the hassle you inflict on others. ... Using tolls to help internalize the congestion externality would somewhat reduce the number of trips made on the most congested roads at the peak usage periods; some trips would be moved to less congested times and routes, and others would be foregone entirely. This way we

would cut down on the congestion costs we impose on each other.

Granted, tolls cannot fully cope with accidents and other incidents, which are major causes of delay. But pricing can largely eliminate chronic, recurring congestion. No matter how high the demand for a road, there is a level of toll that will keep it flowing freely.

To make tolling truly effective, the price must be right. Too high a price drives away too many cars and the road does not function at its capacity. Too low a price and congestion isn't licked.

The best solution is to vary the tolls in real time based on an analysis of current traffic conditions. Pilot toll projects on roads (like the I-394 in Minnesota and the I-15 in Southern California) use sensors embedded in the pavement to monitor the number and speeds of vehicles on the facility.

A simple computer program then determines the number of cars that should be allowed in. The computer then calculates the level of toll that will attract that number of cars—and no more. Prices are then updated every few minutes on electronic message signs. Hi-tech transponders and antenna arrays make waiting at toll booths a thing of the past.

The bottom line is that speeds are kept high (over 45 m.p.h.) so that throughput is higher than when vehicles are allowed to crowd all at once onto roadways at rush hour, slowing traffic to a crawl.

To maximize efficiency, economists would like to price all travel, starting with the freeways. But given that elected officials have no burning desire to lose their jobs, a more realistic option, for now, is to toll just some freeway lanes that are either new capacity or underused carpool lanes. The other lanes would be left free—and congested. Drivers will then have a choice: wait or pay. Granted, neither is ideal. But right now drivers have no choice at all.

What's the bottom line here? The state of Washington recently opened congestion-priced lanes on its State Route 167. The peak toll in the first month of operation (reached on the evening of Wednesday, May 21) was $5.75. I know, I know, you would never pay such an exorbitant amount when America has taught you that free roads are your birthright. But that money bought Washington drivers a 27-minute time savings. Is a half hour of your time worth $6?

I think I already know the answer, and it is "it depends." Most people's value of time varies widely depending on their activities on any given day. Late for picking the kids up from daycare? Paying $6 to save a half hour is an incredible bargain. Have to clean the house? The longer your trip home takes, the better. Tolling will introduce a new level of flexibility and freedom into your life, giving you the power to tailor your travel costs to fit your schedule.

Source: *Freakonomics blog,* January 6, 2009.

because the cost of collecting them is too high. But several major cities, including London and Stockholm, have found increasing tolls to be a very effective way to reduce congestion.

Sometimes congestion is a problem only at certain times of day. If a bridge is heavily traveled only during rush hour, for instance, the congestion externality is largest during this time. The efficient way to deal with these externalities is to charge higher tolls during rush hour. This toll would provide an incentive for drivers to alter their schedules, reducing traffic when congestion is greatest.

Another policy that responds to the problem of road congestion, discussed in a case study in the previous chapter, is the tax on gasoline. Gasoline is a complementary good to driving: An increase in the price of gasoline tends to reduce the quantity of driving demanded. Therefore, a gasoline tax reduces road congestion. A gasoline tax, however, is an imperfect solution, because it affects other decisions besides the amount of driving on congested roads. For example, the gasoline tax discourages driving on uncongested roads, even though there is no congestion externality for these roads.

Fish, Whales, and Other Wildlife Many species of animals are common resources. Fish and whales, for instance, have commercial value, and anyone can go to the ocean and catch whatever is available. Each person has little incentive to maintain the species for the next year. Just as excessive grazing can destroy the Town Common, excessive fishing and whaling can destroy commercially valuable marine populations.

Oceans remain one of the least regulated common resources. Two problems prevent an easy solution. First, many countries have access to the oceans, so any solution would require international cooperation among countries that hold different values. Second, because the oceans are so vast, enforcing any agreement is difficult. As a result, fishing rights have been a frequent source of international tension among normally friendly countries.

Within the United States, various laws aim to manage the use of fish and other wildlife. For example, the government charges for fishing and hunting licenses, and it restricts the lengths of the fishing and hunting seasons. Fishermen are often required to throw back small fish, and hunters can kill only a limited number of animals. All these laws reduce the use of a common resource and help maintain animal populations.

 Why the Cow Is Not Extinct

Throughout history, many species of animals have been threatened with extinction. When Europeans first arrived in North America, more than 60 million buffalo roamed the continent. Yet hunting the buffalo was so popular during the 19th century that by 1900 the animal's population had fallen to about 400 before the government stepped in to protect the species. In some African countries today, the elephant faces a similar challenge, as poachers kill the animals for the ivory in their tusks.

Yet not all animals with commercial value face this threat. The cow, for example, is a valuable source of food, but no one worries that the cow will soon be extinct. Indeed, the great demand for beef seems to ensure that the species will continue to thrive.

Why does the commercial value of ivory threaten the elephant, while the commercial value of beef protects the cow? The reason is that elephants are a common resource, whereas cows are a private good. Elephants roam freely without any owners. Each poacher has a strong incentive to kill as many elephants as he can find. Because poachers are numerous, each poacher has only a slight incentive to preserve the elephant population. By contrast, cattle live on ranches that are privately owned. Each rancher makes great effort to maintain the cattle population on his ranch because he reaps the benefit of these efforts.

"Will the market protect me?"

Governments have tried to solve the elephant's problem in two ways. Some countries, such as Kenya, Tanzania, and Uganda, have made it illegal to kill elephants and sell their ivory. Yet these laws have been hard to enforce, and elephant populations have continued to dwindle. By contrast, other countries, such as Botswana, Malawi, Namibia, and Zimbabwe, have made elephants a private good by allowing people to kill elephants, but only those on their own property. Landowners now have an incentive to preserve the species on their own land, and as a result, elephant populations have started to rise. With private ownership and the profit motive now on its side, the African elephant might someday be as safe from extinction as the cow. ■

QUICK QUIZ   *Why do governments try to limit the use of common resources?*

Conclusion: The Importance of Property Rights

In this and the previous chapter, we have seen there are some "goods" that the market does not provide adequately. Markets do not ensure that the air we breathe is clean or that our country is defended from foreign aggressors. Instead, societies rely on the government to protect the environment and to provide for the national defense.

The problems we considered in these chapters arise in many different markets, but they share a common theme. In all cases, the market fails to allocate resources efficiently because *property rights* are not well established. That is, some item of value does not have an owner with the legal authority to control it. For example, although no one doubts that the "good" of clean air or national defense is valuable, no one has the right to attach a price to it and profit from its use. A factory pollutes too much because no one charges the factory for the pollution it emits. The market does not provide for national defense because no one can charge those who are defended for the benefit they receive.

When the absence of property rights causes a market failure, the government can potentially solve the problem. Sometimes, as in the sale of pollution permits, the solution is for the government to help define property rights and thereby unleash market forces. Other times, as in restricted hunting seasons, the solution is for the government to regulate private behavior. Still other times, as in the provision of national defense, the solution is for the government to use tax revenue to supply a good that the market fails to supply. In all cases, if the policy is well planned and well run, it can make the allocation of resources more efficient and thus raise economic well-being.

SUMMARY

- Goods differ in whether they are excludable and whether they are rival in consumption. A good is excludable if it is possible to prevent someone from using it. A good is rival in consumption if one person's use of the good reduces others' ability to use the same unit of the good. Markets work best for private goods, which are both excludable and rival in consumption. Markets do not work as well for other types of goods.

- Public goods are neither rival in consumption nor excludable. Examples of public goods include fireworks displays, national defense, and the creation of fundamental knowledge. Because people are

not charged for their use of the public good, they have an incentive to free ride when the good is provided privately. Therefore, governments provide public goods, making their decision about the quantity of each good based on cost–benefit analysis.

- Common resources are rival in consumption but not excludable. Examples include common grazing land, clean air, and congested roads. Because people are not charged for their use of common resources, they tend to use them excessively. Therefore, governments use various methods to limit the use of common resources.

KEY CONCEPTS

excludability, *p. 218*
rivalry in consumption, *p. 218*
private goods, *p. 218*

public goods, *p. 218*
common resources, *p. 218*
club goods, *p. 219*

free rider, *p. 220*
cost–benefit analysis, *p. 223*
Tragedy of the Commons, *p. 224*

QUESTIONS FOR REVIEW

1. Explain what is meant by a good being "excludable." Explain what is meant by a good being "rival in consumption." Is a slice of pizza excludable? Is it rival in consumption?
2. Define and give an example of a public good. Can the private market provide this good on its own? Explain.

3. What is cost–benefit analysis of public goods? Why is it important? Why is it hard?
4. Define and give an example of a common resource. Without government intervention, will people use this good too much or too little? Why?

PROBLEMS AND APPLICATIONS

1. Think about the goods and services provided by your local government.
   a. Using the classification in Figure 1, explain which category each of the following goods falls into:
      - police protection
      - snow plowing
      - education
      - rural roads
      - city streets

   b. Why do you think the government provides items that are not public goods?
2. Both public goods and common resources involve externalities.
   a. Are the externalities associated with public goods generally positive or negative? Use examples in your answer. Is the free-market quantity of public goods generally greater or less than the efficient quantity?

b. Are the externalities associated with common resources generally positive or negative? Use examples in your answer. Is the free-market use of common resources generally greater or less than the efficient use?

3. Charlie loves watching *Teletubbies* on his local public TV station, but he never sends any money to support the station during its fund-raising drives.

   a. What name do economists have for people like Charlie?

   b. How can the government solve the problem caused by people like Charlie?

   c. Can you think of ways the private market can solve this problem? How does the existence of cable TV alter the situation?

4. Wireless, high-speed Internet is provided for free in the airport of the city of Communityville.

   a. At first, only a few people use the service. What type of a good is this and why?

   b. Eventually, as more people find out about the service and start using it, the speed of the connection begins to fall. Now what type of a good is the wireless Internet service?

   c. What problem might result and why? What is one possible way to correct this problem?

5. Four roommates are planning to spend the weekend in their dorm room watching old movies, and they are debating how many to watch. Here is their willingness to pay for each film:

	Judd	Joel	Gus	Tim
First film	$7	$5	$3	$2
Second film	6	4	2	1
Third film	5	3	1	0
Fourth film	4	2	0	0
Fifth film	3	1	0	0

   a. Within the dorm room, is the showing of a movie a public good? Why or why not?

   b. If it costs $8 to rent a movie, how many movies should the roommates rent to maximize total surplus?

   c. If they choose the optimal number from part (b) and then split the cost of renting the movies equally, how much surplus does each person obtain from watching the movies?

   d. Is there any way to split the cost to ensure that everyone benefits? What practical problems does this solution raise?

e. Suppose they agree in advance to choose the efficient number and to split the cost of the movies equally. When Judd is asked his willingness to pay, will he have an incentive to tell the truth? If so, why? If not, what will he be tempted to say?

   f. What does this example teach you about the optimal provision of public goods?

6. Some economists argue that private firms will not undertake the efficient amount of basic scientific research.

   a. Explain why this might be so. In your answer, classify basic research in one of the categories shown in Figure 1.

   b. What sort of policy has the United States adopted in response to this problem?

   c. It is often argued that this policy increases the technological capability of American producers relative to that of foreign firms. Is this argument consistent with your classification of basic research in part (a)? (Hint: Can excludability apply to some potential beneficiaries of a public good and not others?)

7. There is often litter along highways but rarely in people's yards. Provide an economic explanation for this fact.

8. The town of Wiknam has 5 residents whose only activity is producing and consuming fish. They produce fish in two ways. Each person who works on a fish farm raises 2 fish per day. Each person who goes fishing in the town lake catches X fish per day. X depends on N, the number of residents fishing in the lake. In particular,

$$X = 6 - N.$$

Each resident is attracted to the job that pays more fish.

   a. Why do you suppose that X, the productivity of each fisherman, falls as N, the number of fishermen, rises? What economic term would you use to describe the fish in the town lake? Would the same description apply to the fish from the farms? Explain.

   b. The town's Freedom Party thinks every individual should have the right to choose between fishing in the lake and farming without government interference. Under its policy, how many of the residents would fish in the lake and how many would work on fish farms? How many fish are produced?

c. The town's Efficiency Party thinks Wiknam should produce as many fish as it can. To achieve this goal, how many of the residents should fish in the lake and how many should work on the farms? (Hint: Create a table that shows the number of fish produced—on farms, from the lake, and in total—for each N from 0 to 5.)

d. The Efficiency Party proposes achieving its goal by taxing each person fishing in the lake by an amount equal to T fish per day. It will then distribute the proceeds equally among all Wiknam residents. (Fish are assumed to be divisible, so these rebates need not be whole numbers.) Calculate the value of T that would yield the outcome you derived in part (c).

e. Compared with the Freedom Party's hands-off policy, who benefits and who loses from the imposition of the Efficiency Party's fishing tax?

9. Many transportation systems, such as the Washington, D.C., Metro (subway), charge higher fares during rush hours than during the rest of the day. Why might they do this?

10. The federal government tests the safety of car models and provides the test results free of charge to the public. Do you think this information qualifies as a public good? Why or why not?

11. High-income people are willing to pay more than lower-income people to avoid the risk of death. For example, they are more likely to pay for safety features on cars. Do you think cost–benefit analysts should take this fact into account when evaluating public projects? Consider, for instance, a rich town and a poor town, both of which are considering the installation of a traffic light. Should the rich town use a higher dollar value for a human life in making this decision? Why or why not?

For further information on topics in this chapter, additional problems, applications, examples, online quizzes, and more, please visit our website at www .cengage.com/economics/mankiw.

The Design of the Tax System

A l "Scarface" Capone, the notorious 1920s gangster and crime boss, was never convicted for his many violent crimes. Yet eventually, he did go to jail—for tax evasion. He had neglected to heed Ben Franklin's observation that "in this world nothing is certain but death and taxes."

When Franklin made this claim in 1789, the average American paid less than 5 percent of his income in taxes, and that remained true for the next hundred years. Over the course of the 20th century, however, taxes became ever more important in the life of the typical U.S. citizen. Today, all taxes taken together—including personal income taxes, corporate income taxes, payroll taxes, sales taxes, and property taxes—use up about a third of the average American's income. In many European countries, the tax bite is even larger.

Taxes are inevitable because we as citizens expect our government to provide us with various goods and services. The previous two chapters shed light on one of the *Ten Principles of Economics* from Chapter 1: The government can sometimes improve market outcomes. When the government remedies an externality (such as air pollution), provides a public good (such as national defense), or regulates the use of a common resource (such as fish in a public lake), it can raise economic well-being. Yet these activities are costly. For the government to perform these and its many other functions, it needs to raise revenue through taxation.

We began our study of taxation in earlier chapters, where we saw how a tax on a good affects supply and demand for that good. In Chapter 6, we saw that a tax reduces the quantity sold in a market, and we examined how the burden of a tax is shared by buyers and sellers depending on the elasticities of supply and demand. In Chapter 8, we examined how taxes affect economic well-being. We learned that taxes cause *deadweight losses:* The reduction in consumer and producer surplus resulting from a tax exceeds the revenue raised by the government.

In this chapter, we build on these lessons to discuss the design of a tax system. We begin with a financial overview of the U.S. government. When thinking about the tax system, it is useful to know some basic facts about how the U.S. government raises and spends money. We then consider the fundamental principles of taxation. Most people agree that taxes should impose as small a cost on society as possible and that the burden of taxes should be distributed fairly. That is, the tax system should be both *efficient* and *equitable*. As we will see, however, stating these goals is easier than achieving them.

A Financial Overview of the U.S. Government

How much of the nation's income does the government take as taxes? Figure 1 shows government revenue, including federal, state, and local governments, as a percentage of total income for the U.S. economy. It shows that the role of

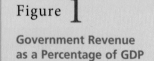

Figure 1

Government Revenue as a Percentage of GDP

This figure shows revenue of the federal government and of state and local governments as a percentage of gross domestic product (GDP), which measures total income in the economy. It shows that the government plays a large role in the U.S. economy and that its role has grown over time.

Source: *Historical Statistics of the United States;* Bureau of Economic Analysis; and author's calculations.

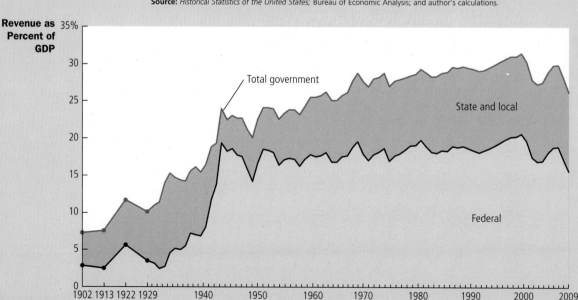

Table 1

Sweden	49%	United States	28%
France	44	Japan	28
United Kingdom	37	Mexico	21
Germany	36	Chile	20
Canada	33	China	15
Russia	32	India	14
Brazil	30		

Table 1

Total Government Tax Revenue as a Percentage of GDP

Source: OECD, United Nations. Data are for most recent year available.

government has grown substantially over the past century. In 1902, the government collected 7 percent of total income; in recent years, government has collected about 30 percent. In other words, as the economy's income has grown, the government's revenue from taxation has grown even more.

Table 1 compares the tax burden for several major countries, as measured by the government's tax revenue as a percentage of the nation's total income. The United States is in the middle of the pack. The U.S. tax burden is low compared to many European countries, but it is high compared to some other nations around the world. Less economically developed countries, such as India, often have relatively low tax burdens. This fact is consistent with the evidence in Figure 1 of a growing tax burden over time: As a nation gets richer, the government typically takes a larger share of income in taxes.

The overall size of government tells only part of the story. Behind the total dollar figures lie thousands of individual decisions about taxes and spending. To understand the government's finances more fully, let's look at how the total breaks down into some broad categories.

The Federal Government

The U.S. federal government collects about two-thirds of the taxes in our economy. It raises this money in a number of ways, and it finds even more ways to spend it.

Receipts   Table 2 shows the receipts of the federal government in 2009. Total receipts that year were $2,105 billion, a number so large that it is hard to comprehend. To bring this astronomical number down to earth, we can divide it by the size of the U.S. population, which was about 307 million in 2009. We then find that the average American paid $6,846 to the federal government.

Tax	Amount (billions)	Amount per Person	Percent of Receipts
Individual income taxes	$ 915	$2,978	43%
Social insurance taxes	891	2,899	42
Corporate income taxes	138	449	7
Other	161	524	8
Total	$2,105	$6,846	100%

Table 2

Receipts of the Federal Government: 2009

Source: *Economic Report of the President*, 2010, Table B-81. Columns may not sum to total due to rounding.

The largest source of revenue for the federal government is the individual income tax. As April 15 approaches each year, almost every American family fills out a tax form to determine how much income tax it owes the government. Each family is required to report its income from all sources: wages from working, interest on savings, dividends from corporations in which it owns shares, profits from any small businesses it operates, and so on. The family's *tax liability* (how much it owes) is then based on its total income.

A family's income tax liability is not simply proportional to its income. Instead, the law requires a more complicated calculation. Taxable income is computed as total income minus an amount based on the number of dependents (primarily children) and minus certain expenses that policymakers have deemed "deductible" (such as mortgage interest payments, state and local tax payments, and charitable giving). Then the tax liability is calculated from taxable income using a schedule such as the one shown in Table 3.

This table presents the *marginal tax rate*—the tax rate applied to each additional dollar of income. Because the marginal tax rate rises as income rises, higher-income families pay a larger percentage of their income in taxes. Note that each tax rate in the table applies only to income within the associated range, not to a person's entire income. For example, a person with an income of $1 million still pays only 10 percent of the first $8,375. (Later in this chapter we discuss the concept of marginal tax rate more fully.)

Almost as important to the federal government as the individual income tax are payroll taxes. A *payroll tax* is a tax on the wages that a firm pays its workers. Table 2 calls this revenue *social insurance taxes* because the revenue from these taxes is earmarked to pay for Social Security and Medicare. Social Security is an income-support program designed primarily to maintain the living standards of the elderly. Medicare is the government health program for the elderly. Table 2 shows that the average American paid $2,899 in social insurance taxes in 2009.

Next in magnitude, but much smaller than either individual income taxes or social insurance taxes, is the corporate income tax. A *corporation* is a business set up to have its own legal existence, distinct and separate from its owners. The government taxes each corporation based on its profit—the amount the corporation receives for the goods or services it sells minus the costs of producing those goods or services. Notice that corporate profits are, in essence, taxed twice. They are taxed once by the corporate income tax when the corporation earns the profits; they are taxed a second time by the individual income tax when the corporation

Table **3**

The Federal Income Tax Rates: 2010
This table shows the marginal tax rates for an unmarried taxpayer. The taxes owed by a taxpayer depend on all the marginal tax rates up to his or her income level. For example, a taxpayer with income of $25,000 pays 10 percent of the first $8,375 of income, and then 15 percent of the rest.

On Taxable Income . . .	The Tax Rate Is . . .
Up to $8,375	10%
From $8,375 to $34,000	15%
From $34,000 to $82,400	25%
From $82,400 to $171,850	28%
From $171,850 to $373,650	33%
Over $373,650	35%

uses its profits to pay dividends to its shareholders. In 2003, the tax rate on dividend income was reduced to 15 percent, in part to compensate for this double taxation.

The last category, labeled "other" in Table 2, makes up 8 percent of receipts. This category includes *excise taxes*, which are taxes on specific goods like gasoline, cigarettes, and alcoholic beverages. It also includes various small items, such as estate taxes and customs duties.

Spending   Table 4 shows the spending of the federal government in 2009. Total spending was $3,518 billion, or $11,441 per person. This table also shows how the federal government's spending was divided among major categories.

The largest category in Table 4 is Social Security, which represents mostly transfer payments to the elderly. A *transfer payment* is a government payment not made in exchange for a good or service. This category made up 19 percent of spending by the federal government in 2009.

The second largest category of spending is national defense. This includes both the salaries of military personnel and the purchases of military equipment such as guns, fighter jets, and warships. Spending on national defense fluctuates over time as international tensions and the political climate change. Not surprisingly, spending on national defense rises substantially during wars. In part because of the wars in Iraq and Afghanistan, defense spending rose from 17 to 19 percent of total federal spending from 2001 to 2009.

The third category in Table 4, spending on income security, includes transfer payments to poor families and the unemployed. One program is Temporary Assistance for Needy Families (TANF), often simply called "welfare." Another is the Food Stamp program, which gives poor families vouchers that they can use to buy food. A third program is unemployment compensation, which provides income to people who have recently lost their jobs. The federal government pays some of this money to state and local governments, which administer the programs under federal guidelines. Income security spending tends to rise during recessions, when people's incomes fall and the number of unemployed increases. This explains the rise in income security spending from 13 to 15 percent of total federal spending between 2006 and 2009.

Health spending looms large in the federal budget. Medicare, the fourth category in Table 4, is the government's health plan for the elderly. The fifth category

Category	Amount (billions)	Amount per Person	Percent of Spending
Social Security	$ 683	$ 2,221	19%
National defense	661	2,150	19
Income security	533	1,733	15
Medicare	430	1,398	12
Health	334	1,086	9
Net interest	187	608	5
Other	690	2,244	20
Total	$3,518	$11,441	100%

Table **4**

Spending of the Federal Government: 2009

Source: *Economic Report of the President*, 2010, Table B-81. Columns may not sum to total due to rounding.

in the table is other health spending, which includes Medicaid, the federal health program for the poor, and spending on medical research, such as that conducted through the National Institutes of Health. Total health spending makes up about a fifth of the federal budget.

Next on the list is net interest. When a person borrows from a bank, the bank requires the borrower to pay interest for the loan. The same is true when the government borrows from the public. The more indebted the government, the larger the amount it must spend in interest payments.

The "other" category in Table 4 consists of many less expensive functions of government. It includes, for example, the federal court system, the space program, farm-support programs, housing credit programs, as well as the salaries of members of Congress and the president.

budget deficit

an excess of government spending over government receipts

budget surplus

an excess of government receipts over government spending

You might have noticed that total receipts of the federal government shown in Table 2 fall short of total spending shown in Table 4 by $1,413 billion. In such a situation, the government is said to run a **budget deficit.** When receipts exceed spending, the government is said to run a **budget surplus.** The government finances a budget deficit by borrowing from the public. That is, it sells government debt to the private sector, including both investors in the United States and those abroad. When the government runs a budget surplus, it uses the excess receipts to reduce its outstanding debts.

The Fiscal Challenge Ahead

In 2009, the federal government ran a budget deficit of $1,413 billion. The magnitude of this figure represents an almost eightfold increase over the deficit in 2007. The dramatic rise in the budget deficit is due primarily to the deep recession the economy was experiencing at the time; recessions tend to increase government spending and reduce government revenue. However, this short-term increase in the deficit is only the tip of the iceberg: Long-term projections of the government's budget show that, under current law, the government will spend vastly more than it will receive in tax revenue in the decades ahead. As a percentage of gross domestic product (the total income in the economy), taxes are projected to be about constant. But government spending as a percentage of GDP is projected to rise gradually but substantially over the next several decades.

One reason for the rise in government spending is that Social Security and Medicare provide significant benefits for the elderly, who are a growing percentage of the overall population. Over the past half century, medical advances and lifestyle improvements have greatly increased life expectancy. In 1950, a man age 65 could expect to live for another 13 years; now he can expect to live another 17 years. The life expectancy of a 65-year-old woman has risen from 16 years in 1950 to 20 years today. At the same time, people are having fewer children. In 1950, the typical woman had three children. Today, the number is about two. As a result of smaller families, the labor force is growing more slowly now than it has in the past.

Panel (a) of Figure 2 shows the demographic shift that is arising from the combination of longer life expectancy and lower fertility. In 1950, the elderly population equaled about 14 percent of the working-age population. Now the elderly are about 21 percent of the working-age population, and that figure will rise to about 40 percent over the next 50 years. Turning those numbers on their head, this

Panel (a) shows the U.S. population age 65 and older as a percentage of the population age 20 to 64. The growing elderly population will put increasing pressure on the government budget. Panel (b) shows government spending on Social Security, Medicare, and Medicaid as a percentage of GDP. The projection for future years assumes no change in current law. Unless changes in benefits are enacted, government spending on these programs will rise significantly and will require large tax increases to pay for them.

Figure 2

The Demographic and Fiscal Challenge

Source: Congressional Budget Office.

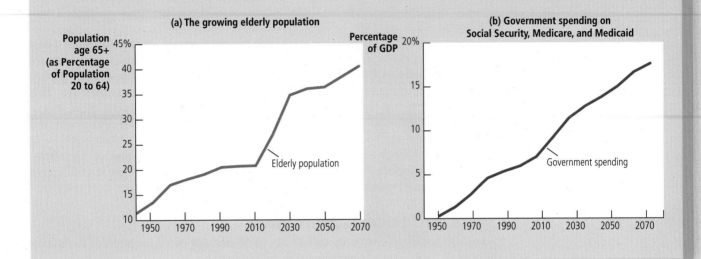

means that in 1950 there were about 7 working-age people for every elderly person, whereas in 2050 there will be only 2.5. As a result, there will be fewer workers paying taxes to support the government benefits that each elderly person receives.

A second, related trend that will affect government spending in the decades ahead is the rising cost of healthcare. The government provides healthcare to the elderly through the Medicare system and to the poor through Medicaid. As the cost of healthcare increases, government spending on these programs will increase as well.

Policymakers have proposed various ways to stem the rise in healthcare costs, such as reducing the burden of lawsuits on the healthcare system, encouraging more competition among healthcare providers, and promoting greater use of information technology. In 2010, President Obama signed a healthcare reform bill with the goal of both expanding health insurance coverage and reducing the growth of healthcare costs. Many health economists, however, believe that such measures will have only a limited impact on reducing the government's healthcare expenditures because the main reason for rising healthcare costs is medical advances that provide new, better, but often expensive ways to extend and improve our lives.

Panel (b) of Figure 2 shows government spending on Social Security, Medicare, and Medicaid as a percentage of GDP. Spending on these programs has risen from less than 1 percent in 1950 to about 10 percent today. The combination of a growing elderly population and rising healthcare costs is expected to continue and even accelerate the trend.

How our society will handle these spending increases is an open question. Simply increasing the budget deficit is not feasible. A budget deficit just pushes the cost of government spending onto a future generation of taxpayers, who will inherit a government with greater debts. In the long run, the government needs to pay for what it spends.

Some economists believe that to pay for these commitments, we will need to raise taxes substantially as a percentage of GDP. If so, the long-term trend we saw in Figure 1 will continue. Spending on Social Security, Medicare, and Medicaid is expected to rise by about 10 percentage points of GDP. Because taxes are now 30 percent of GDP, paying for these benefits would require approximately a one-third increase in all taxes.

Other economists believe that such high tax rates would impose too great a cost on younger workers. They believe that policymakers should reduce the promises now being made to the elderly of the future and that, at the same time, people should be encouraged to take a greater role caring for themselves as they age. This might entail raising the normal retirement age, while giving people more incentive to save during their working years to prepare for their own retirement and health costs.

It is likely that the final resolution will involve a combination of measures. No one can dispute that resolving this debate is one of the great challenges ahead. ■

State and Local Government

State and local governments collect about 40 percent of all taxes paid. Let's look at how they obtain tax revenue and how they spend it.

Receipts   Table 5 shows the receipts of U.S. state and local governments. Total receipts for 2007 were $2,329 billion, or $7,574 per person. The table also shows how this total is broken down into different kinds of taxes.

The two most important taxes for state and local governments are sales taxes and property taxes. Sales taxes are levied as a percentage of the total amount spent at retail stores. Every time a customer buys something, he or she pays the storekeeper an extra amount that the storekeeper remits to the government. (Some states exclude certain items that are considered necessities, such as food and clothing.) Property taxes are levied as a percentage of the estimated value of land and

Table 5

Receipts of State and Local Governments: 2007

Source: *Economic Report of the President*, 2010, Table B-86. Columns may not sum to total due to rounding.

Tax	Amount (billions)	Amount per Person	Percent of Receipts
Sales taxes	$ 439	$1,426	19%
Property taxes	383	1,246	16
Individual income taxes	289	941	12
Corporate income taxes	61	197	3
From federal government	468	1,521	20
Other	690	2,244	30
Total	$2,329	$7,574	100%

structures and are paid by property owners. Together, these two taxes make up more than a third of all receipts of state and local governments.

State and local governments also levy individual and corporate income taxes. In many cases, state and local income taxes are similar to federal income taxes. In other cases, they are quite different. For example, some states tax income from wages less heavily than income earned in the form of interest and dividends. Some states do not tax income at all.

State and local governments also receive substantial funds from the federal government. To some extent, the federal government's policy of sharing its revenue with state governments redistributes funds from high-income states (who pay more taxes) to low-income states (who receive more benefits). Often, these funds are tied to specific programs that the federal government wants to subsidize.

Finally, state and local governments receive much of their receipts from various sources included in the "other" category in Table 5. These include fees for fishing and hunting licenses, tolls from roads and bridges, and fares for public buses and subways.

Spending   Table 6 shows the total spending of state and local governments in 2007 and its breakdown among the major categories.

By far the biggest single expenditure for state and local governments is education. Local governments pay for the public schools, which educate most students from kindergarten through high school. State governments contribute to the support of public universities. In 2007, education accounted for about a third of the spending of state and local governments.

The second largest category of spending is for public welfare, which includes transfer payments to the poor. This category includes some federal programs that are administered by state and local governments. The next category is highways, which includes the building of new roads and the maintenance of existing ones. The large "other" category in Table 6 includes the many additional services provided by state and local governments, such as libraries, police, garbage removal, fire protection, park maintenance, and snow removal.

QUICK QUIZ   *What are the two most important sources of tax revenue for the federal government? • What are the two most important sources of tax revenue for state and local governments?*

Table 6

Spending of State and Local Governments: 2007

Category	Amount (billions)	Amount per Person	Percent of Spending
Education	$ 777	$2,526	34%
Public welfare	389	1,266	17
Highways	145	471	6
Other	955	3,105	42
Total	$2,265	$7,367	100%

Source: *Economic Report of the President*, 2010, Table B-86. Columns may not sum to total due to rounding.

Taxes and Efficiency

Now that we have seen how various levels of the U.S. government raise and spend money, let's consider how one might evaluate its tax policy and design a tax system. The primary aim of a tax system is to raise revenue for the government, but there are many ways to raise any given amount of money. When choosing among the many alternative tax systems, policymakers have two objectives: efficiency and equity.

One tax system is more efficient than another if it raises the same amount of revenue at a smaller cost to taxpayers. What are the costs of taxes to taxpayers? The most obvious cost is the tax payment itself. This transfer of money from the taxpayer to the government is an inevitable feature of any tax system. Yet taxes also impose two other costs, which well-designed tax policy tries to avoid or, at least, minimize:

- The deadweight losses that result when taxes distort the decisions that people make;
- The administrative burdens that taxpayers bear as they comply with the tax laws.

An efficient tax system is one that imposes small deadweight losses and small administrative burdens.

Deadweight Losses

One of the *Ten Principles of Economics* is that people respond to incentives, and this includes incentives provided by the tax system. If the government taxes ice cream, people eat less ice cream and more frozen yogurt. If the government taxes housing, people live in smaller houses and spend more of their income on other things. If the government taxes labor earnings, people work less and enjoy more leisure.

Because taxes distort incentives, they entail deadweight losses. As we first discussed in Chapter 8, the deadweight loss of a tax is the reduction in economic well-being of taxpayers in excess of the amount of revenue raised by the government. The deadweight loss is the inefficiency that a tax creates as people allocate resources according to the tax incentive rather than the true costs and benefits of the goods and services that they buy and sell.

To recall how taxes cause deadweight losses, consider an example. Suppose that Joe places an $8 value on a pizza, and Jane places a $6 value on it. If there is no tax on pizza, the price of pizza will reflect the cost of making it. Let's suppose that the price of pizza is $5, so both Joe and Jane choose to buy one. Both consumers get some surplus of value over the amount paid. Joe gets consumer surplus of $3, and Jane gets consumer surplus of $1. Total surplus is $4.

Now suppose that the government levies a $2 tax on pizza and the price of pizza rises to $7. (This occurs if supply is perfectly elastic.) Joe still buys a pizza, but now he has consumer surplus of only $1. Jane now decides not to buy a pizza because its price is higher than its value to her. The government collects tax revenue of $2 on Joe's pizza. Total consumer surplus has fallen by $3 (from $4 to $1). Because total surplus has fallen by more than the tax revenue, the tax has a deadweight loss. In this case, the deadweight loss is $1.

Notice that the deadweight loss comes not from Joe, the person who pays the tax, but from Jane, the person who doesn't. The reduction of $2 in Joe's surplus

"I was gonna fix the place up, but if I did, the city would just raise my taxes!"

exactly offsets the amount of revenue the government collects. The deadweight loss arises because the tax causes Jane to alter her behavior. When the tax raises the price of pizza, Jane is worse off, and yet there is no offsetting revenue to the government. This reduction in Jane's welfare is the deadweight loss of the tax.

Should Income or Consumption Be Taxed?

When taxes induce people to change their behavior—such as inducing Jane to buy less pizza—the taxes cause deadweight losses and make the allocation of resources less efficient. As we have already seen, much government revenue comes from the individual income tax. In a case study in Chapter 8, we discussed how this tax discourages people from working as hard as they otherwise might. Another inefficiency caused by this tax is that it discourages people from saving.

Consider a person 25 years old who is considering saving $1,000. If he puts this money in a savings account that earns 8 percent and leaves it there, he would have $21,720 when he retires at age 65. Yet if the government taxes one-fourth of his interest income each year, the effective interest rate is only 6 percent. After 40 years of earning 6 percent, the $1,000 grows to only $10,290, less than half of what it would have been without taxation. Thus, because interest income is taxed, saving is much less attractive.

Some economists advocate eliminating the current tax system's disincentive toward saving by changing the basis of taxation. Rather than taxing the amount of income that people earn, the government could tax the amount that people spend. Under this proposal, all income that is saved would not be taxed until the saving is later spent. This alternative system, called a *consumption tax,* would not distort people's saving decisions.

Various provisions of the current tax code already make the tax system a bit like a consumption tax. Taxpayers can put a limited amount of their saving into special accounts—such as Individual Retirement Accounts and 401(k) plans—that escape taxation until the money is withdrawn at retirement. For people who do most of their saving through these retirement accounts, their tax bill is, in effect, based on their consumption rather than their income.

European countries tend to rely more on consumption taxes than does the United States. Most of them raise a significant amount of government revenue through a value-added tax, or a VAT. A VAT is like the retail sales tax that many U.S. states use, but rather than collecting all of the tax at the retail level when the consumer buys the final good, the government collects the tax in stages as the good is being produced (that is, as value is added by firms along the chain of production).

Various U.S. policymakers have proposed that the tax code move further in the direction of taxing consumption rather than income. In 2005, economist Alan Greenspan, then Chairman of the Federal Reserve, offered this advice to a presidential commission on tax reform: "As you know, many economists believe that a consumption tax would be best from the perspective of promoting economic growth—particularly if one were designing a tax system from scratch—because a consumption tax is likely to encourage saving and capital formation. However, getting from the current tax system to a consumption tax raises a challenging set of transition issues." ■

· in the **news**

> ### The Temporarily Disappearing Estate Tax

In an odd twist of legislative history, the U.S. tax on large estates—bequests people leave their descendents when they die—expired in January 2010, but for one year only. That is, the tax would once again be in effect as of January 1, 2011. This article, written at the end of 2009, describes people responding to the peculiar incentives presented by the expiration and reinstatement of the estate tax.

Rich Cling to Life to Beat Tax Man

BY LAURA SAUNDERS

Nothing's certain except death and taxes—but a temporary lapse in the estate tax is causing a few wealthy Americans to try to bend those rules.

Starting Jan. 1, 2010, the estate tax—which can erase nearly half of a wealthy person's estate—goes away for a year. For families facing end-of-life decisions in the immediate future, the change is making one of life's most trying episodes only more complex.

"I have two clients on life support, and the families are struggling with whether to continue heroic measures for a few more days," says Joshua Rubenstein, a lawyer with Katten Muchin Rosenman LLP in New York. "Do they want to live for the rest of their lives having made serious medical decisions based on estate-tax law?"

Currently, the tax applies to about 5,500 taxpayers a year. So, on average, at least 15 people die every day whose estates would benefit from the tax's lapse.

The macabre situation stems from 2001, when Congress raised estate-tax exemptions, culminating with the tax's disappearance in 2010. However, due to budget constraints, lawmakers didn't make the change permanent. So the estate tax is due to come back to life in 2011—at a higher rate and lower exemption.

To make it easier on their heirs, some clients are putting provisions into their health-care proxies allowing whoever makes end-of-life medical decisions to consider changes in estate-tax law. "We have done this at least a dozen times, and have gotten more calls recently," says Andrew Katzenstein, a lawyer with Proskauer Rose LLP in Los Angeles.

Of course, plenty of taxpayers themselves are eager to live to see the new year. One wealthy, terminally ill real-estate entrepreneur has told his doctors he is determined to live until the law changes.

"Whenever he wakes up," says his lawyer, "He says: 'What day is it? Is it Jan. 1 yet?'"...

The situation is causing at least one person to add the prospect of euthanasia to his estate-planning mix, according to Mr. Katzenstein of Proskauer Rose. An elderly, infirm client of his recently asked whether undergoing euthanasia during 2010 in Holland, where it's legal, might allow his estate to dodge the tax.

His answer: Yes.

Source: *Wall Street Journal,* December 30, 2009.

Administrative Burden

If you ask the typical person on April 15 for an opinion about the tax system, you might get an earful (perhaps peppered with expletives) about the headache of filling out tax forms. The administrative burden of any tax system is part of the inefficiency it creates. This burden includes not only the time spent in early April filling out forms but also the time spent throughout the year keeping records for tax purposes and the resources the government has to use to enforce the tax laws.

Many taxpayers—especially those in higher tax brackets—hire tax lawyers and accountants to help them with their taxes. These experts in the complex tax laws fill out the tax forms for their clients and help them arrange their affairs in a way that reduces the amount of taxes owed. This behavior is legal tax avoidance, which is different from illegal tax evasion.

Critics of our tax system say that these advisers help their clients avoid taxes by abusing some of the detailed provisions of the tax code, often dubbed "loopholes." In some cases, loopholes are congressional mistakes: They arise from ambiguities or omissions in the tax laws. More often, they arise because Congress has chosen to give special treatment to specific types of behavior. For example, the U.S. federal tax code gives preferential treatment to investors in municipal bonds because Congress wanted to make it easier for state and local governments to borrow money. To some extent, this provision benefits states and localities, and to some extent, it benefits high-income taxpayers. Most loopholes are well known by those in Congress who make tax policy, but what looks like a loophole to one taxpayer may look like a justifiable tax deduction to another.

The resources devoted to complying with the tax laws are a type of deadweight loss. The government gets only the amount of taxes paid. By contrast, the taxpayer loses not only this amount but also the time and money spent documenting, computing, and avoiding taxes.

The administrative burden of the tax system could be reduced by simplifying the tax laws. Yet simplification is often politically difficult. Most people are ready to simplify the tax code by eliminating the loopholes that benefit others, but few are eager to give up the loopholes that benefit them. In the end, the complexity of the tax law results from the political process as various taxpayers with their own special interests lobby for their causes.

Marginal Tax Rates versus Average Tax Rates

When discussing the efficiency and equity of income taxes, economists distinguish between two notions of the tax rate: the average and the marginal. The **average tax rate** is total taxes paid divided by total income. The **marginal tax rate** is the extra taxes paid on an additional dollar of income.

For example, suppose that the government taxes 20 percent of the first $50,000 of income and 50 percent of all income above $50,000. Under this tax, a person who makes $60,000 pays a tax of $15,000: 20 percent of the first $50,000 (0.20 × $50,000 = $10,000) plus 50 percent of the next $10,000 (0.50 × $10,000 = $5,000). For this person, the average tax rate is $15,000/$60,000, or 25 percent. But the marginal tax rate is 50 percent. If the taxpayer earned an additional dollar of income, that dollar would be subject to the 50 percent tax rate, so the amount the taxpayer would owe to the government would rise by $0.50.

The marginal and average tax rates each contain a useful piece of information. If we are trying to gauge the sacrifice made by a taxpayer, the average tax rate is more appropriate because it measures the fraction of income paid in taxes. By contrast, if we are trying to gauge how much the tax system distorts incentives, the marginal tax rate is more meaningful. One of the *Ten Principles of Economics* in Chapter 1 is that rational people think at the margin. A corollary to this principle is that the marginal tax rate measures how much the tax system discourages people from working. If you are thinking of working an extra few hours, the marginal tax rate determines how much the government takes of your additional earnings. It is the marginal tax rate, therefore, that determines the deadweight loss of an income tax.

Lump-Sum Taxes

Suppose the government imposes a tax of $4,000 on everyone. That is, everyone owes the same amount, regardless of earnings or any actions that a person might take. Such a tax is called a **lump-sum tax.**

average tax rate
total taxes paid divided by total income

marginal tax rate
the extra taxes paid on an additional dollar of income

lump-sum tax
a tax that is the same amount for every person

A lump-sum tax shows clearly the difference between average and marginal tax rates. For a taxpayer with income of $20,000, the average tax rate of a $4,000 lump-sum tax is 20 percent; for a taxpayer with income of $40,000, the average tax rate is 10 percent. For both taxpayers, the marginal tax rate is zero because no tax is owed on an additional dollar of income.

A lump-sum tax is the most efficient tax possible. Because a person's decisions do not alter the amount owed, the tax does not distort incentives and, therefore, does not cause deadweight losses. Because everyone can easily compute the amount owed and because there is no benefit to hiring tax lawyers and accountants, the lump-sum tax imposes a minimal administrative burden on taxpayers.

If lump-sum taxes are so efficient, why do we rarely observe them in the real world? The reason is that efficiency is only one goal of the tax system. A lump-sum tax would take the same amount from the poor and the rich, an outcome most people would view as unfair. To understand the tax systems that we observe, we must therefore consider the other major goal of tax policy: equity.

QUICK QUIZ   *What is meant by the efficiency of a tax system? • What can make a tax system inefficient?*

Taxes and Equity

Ever since American colonists dumped imported tea into Boston harbor to protest high British taxes, tax policy has generated some of the most heated debates in American politics. The heat is rarely fueled by questions of efficiency. Instead, it arises from disagreements over how the tax burden should be distributed. Senator Russell Long once mimicked the public debate with this ditty:

> Don't tax you.
> Don't tax me.
> Tax that fella behind the tree.

Of course, if we are to rely on the government to provide some of the goods and services we want, taxes must fall on someone. In this section, we consider the equity of a tax system. How should the burden of taxes be divided among the population? How do we evaluate whether a tax system is fair? Everyone agrees that the tax system should be equitable, but there is much disagreement about what equity means and how the equity of a tax system can be judged.

The Benefits Principle

benefits principle
the idea that people should pay taxes based on the benefits they receive from government services

One principle of taxation, called the **benefits principle,** states that people should pay taxes based on the benefits they receive from government services. This principle tries to make public goods similar to private goods. It seems fair that a person who often goes to the movies pays more in total for movie tickets than a person who rarely goes. Similarly, a person who gets great benefit from a public good should pay more for it than a person who gets little benefit.

The gasoline tax, for instance, is sometimes justified using the benefits principle. In some states, revenues from the gasoline tax are used to build and maintain roads. Because those who buy gasoline are the same people who use the roads, the gasoline tax might be viewed as a fair way to pay for this government service.

The benefits principle can also be used to argue that wealthy citizens should pay higher taxes than poorer ones. Why? Simply because the wealthy benefit more from public services. Consider, for example, the benefits of police protection from theft. Citizens with much to protect benefit more from police than do those with less to protect. Therefore, according to the benefits principle, the wealthy should contribute more than the poor to the cost of maintaining the police force. The same argument can be used for many other public services, such as fire protection, national defense, and the court system.

It is even possible to use the benefits principle to argue for antipoverty programs funded by taxes on the wealthy. As we discussed in Chapter 11, people may prefer living in a society without poverty, suggesting that antipoverty programs are a public good. If the wealthy place a greater dollar value on this public good than members of the middle class do, perhaps just because the wealthy have more to spend, then according to the benefits principle, they should be taxed more heavily to pay for these programs.

The Ability-to-Pay Principle

Another way to evaluate the equity of a tax system is called the **ability-to-pay principle,** which states that taxes should be levied on a person according to how well that person can shoulder the burden. This principle is sometimes justified by the claim that all citizens should make an "equal sacrifice" to support the government. The magnitude of a person's sacrifice, however, depends not only on the size of his tax payment but also on his income and other circumstances. A $1,000 tax paid by a poor person may require a larger sacrifice than a $10,000 tax paid by a rich one.

The ability-to-pay principle leads to two corollary notions of equity: vertical equity and horizontal equity. **Vertical equity** states that taxpayers with a greater ability to pay taxes should contribute a larger amount. **Horizontal equity** states that taxpayers with similar abilities to pay should contribute the same amount. These notions of equity are widely accepted, but applying them to evaluate a tax system is rarely straightforward.

Vertical Equity   If taxes are based on ability to pay, then richer taxpayers should pay more than poorer taxpayers. But how much more should the rich pay? Much of the debate over tax policy concerns this question.

Consider the three tax systems in Table 7. In each case, taxpayers with higher incomes pay more. Yet the systems differ in how quickly taxes rise with income.

ability-to-pay principle
the idea that taxes should be levied on a person according to how well that person can shoulder the burden

vertical equity
the idea that taxpayers with a greater ability to pay taxes should pay larger amounts

horizontal equity
the idea that taxpayers with similar abilities to pay taxes should pay the same amount

Income	Proportional Tax		Regressive Tax		Progressive Tax	
	Amount of Tax	Percent of Income	Amount of Tax	Percent of Income	Amount of Tax	Percent of Income
$ 50,000	$12,500	25%	$15,000	30%	$10,000	20%
100,000	25,000	25	25,000	25	25,000	25
200,000	50,000	25	40,000	20	60,000	30

Table 7

Three Tax Systems

proportional tax

a tax for which
high-income and
low-income taxpayers
pay the same fraction of
income

regressive tax

a tax for which
high-income taxpayers
pay a smaller fraction
of their income than do
low-income taxpayers

progressive tax

a tax for which
high-income taxpayers
pay a larger fraction of
their income than do
low-income taxpayers

The first system is called **proportional** because all taxpayers pay the same fraction of income. The second system is called **regressive** because high-income taxpayers pay a smaller fraction of their income, even though they pay a larger amount. The third system is called **progressive** because high-income taxpayers pay a larger fraction of their income.

Which of these three tax systems is most fair? There is no obvious answer, and economic theory does not offer any help in trying to find one. Equity, like beauty, is in the eye of the beholder.

CASE STUDY

How the Tax Burden Is Distributed

Much debate over tax policy concerns whether the wealthy pay their fair share. There is no objective way to make this judgment. In evaluating the issue for yourself, however, it is useful to know how much families with different incomes pay under the current tax system.

Table 8 presents some data on how all federal taxes are distributed among income classes. To construct this table, families are ranked according to their income and placed into five groups of equal size, called *quintiles*. The table also presents data on the richest 1 percent of Americans.

The second column of the table shows the average income of each group. The poorest one-fifth of families had average income of $17,200, and the richest one-fifth had average income of $248,400. The richest 1 percent had average income of over $1.7 million.

The next column of the table shows total taxes as a percentage of income. As you can see, the U.S. federal tax system is progressive. The poorest fifth of families paid 4.3 percent of their incomes in taxes, and the richest fifth paid 25.8 percent. The top 1 percent paid 31.2 percent of their incomes.

The fourth and fifth columns compare the distribution of income and the distribution of taxes. The poorest quintile earns 3.9 percent of all income and pays 0.8 percent of all taxes. The richest quintile earns 55.7 percent of all income and pays 69.3 percent of all taxes. The richest 1 percent (which, remember, is $1/20$ the size of each quintile) earns 18.8 percent of all income and pays 28.3 percent of all taxes.

Table **8**

The Burden of Federal Taxes

Source: Congressional Budget Office.
Figures are for 2006.

Quintile	Average Income	Taxes as a Percentage of Income	Percentage of All Income	Percentage of All Taxes
Lowest	$ 17,200	4.3%	3.9%	0.8%
Second	39,400	10.2	8.4	4.1
Middle	60,700	14.2	13.2	9.1
Fourth	89,500	17.6	19.5	16.5
Highest	248,400	25.8	55.7	69.3
Top 1%	1,743,700	31.2	18.8	28.3

This table on taxes is a good starting point for understanding the burden of government, but the picture it offers is incomplete. Although it includes all the taxes that flow from households to the federal government, it fails to include the transfer payments, such as Social Security and welfare, that flow from the federal government back to households.

Studies that include both taxes and transfers show even greater progressivity. The richest group of families still pays about one-quarter of its income to the government, even after transfers are subtracted. By contrast, poor families typically receive more in transfers than they pay in taxes. The average tax rate of the poorest quintile, rather than being 4.3 percent as in the table, is approximately *negative* 30 percent. In other words, their income is about 30 percent higher than it would be without government taxes and transfers. The lesson is clear: To understand fully the progressivity of government policies, one must take account of both what people pay and what they receive. ■

Horizontal Equity   If taxes are based on ability to pay, then similar taxpayers should pay similar amounts of taxes. But what determines if two taxpayers are similar? Families differ in many ways. To evaluate whether a tax code is horizontally equitable, one must determine which differences are relevant for a family's ability to pay and which differences are not.

Suppose the Smith and Jones families each have income of $100,000. The Smiths have no children, but Mr. Smith has an illness that causes medical expenses of $40,000. The Joneses are in good health, but they have four children. Two of the Jones children are in college, generating tuition bills of $60,000. Would it be fair for these two families to pay the same tax because they have the same income? Would it be fair to give the Smiths a tax break to help them offset their high medical expenses? Would it be fair to give the Joneses a tax break to help them with their tuition expenses?

There are no easy answers to these questions. In practice, the U.S. income tax is filled with special provisions that alter a family's tax based on its specific circumstances.

Tax Incidence and Tax Equity

Tax incidence—the study of who bears the burden of taxes—is central to evaluating tax equity. As we first saw in Chapter 6, the person who bears the burden of a tax is not always the person who gets the tax bill from the government. Because taxes alter supply and demand, they alter equilibrium prices. As a result, they affect people beyond those who, according to statute, actually pay the tax. When evaluating the vertical and horizontal equity of any tax, it is important to take these indirect effects into account.

Many discussions of tax equity ignore the indirect effects of taxes and are based on what economists mockingly call the *flypaper theory* of tax incidence. According to this theory, the burden of a tax, like a fly on flypaper, sticks wherever it first lands. This assumption, however, is rarely valid.

For example, a person not trained in economics might argue that a tax on expensive fur coats is vertically equitable because most buyers of furs are wealthy. Yet if these buyers can easily substitute other luxuries for furs, then a tax on furs might only reduce the sale of furs. In the end, the burden of the tax will fall more on those who make and sell furs than on those who buy them. Because most workers who make furs are not wealthy, the equity of a fur tax could be quite different from what the flypaper theory indicates.

CASE STUDY

Who Pays the Corporate Income Tax?

The corporate income tax provides a good example of the importance of tax incidence for tax policy. The corporate tax is popular among voters. After all, corporations are not people. Voters are always eager to have their taxes reduced and have some impersonal corporation pick up the tab.

But before deciding that the corporate income tax is a good way for the government to raise revenue, we should consider who bears the burden of the corporate tax. This is a difficult question on which economists disagree, but one thing is certain: *People pay all taxes*. When the government levies a tax on a corporation, the corporation is more like a tax collector than a taxpayer. The burden of the tax ultimately falls on people—the owners, customers, or workers of the corporation.

in the **news**

❯ *The Value-Added Tax*

In 2010, as the U.S. government faced large budget deficits over a long time horizon, some policymakers started wondering whether a new source of tax revenue was needed. One widely discussed option was a value-added tax.

Much to Love, and Hate, in a VAT

BY N. GREGORY MANKIW

The policy world is abuzz with talk about whether a value-added tax should be part of the solution to our long-term fiscal problems. Most recently, Paul A. Volcker, head of President Obama's economic advisory board, said a VAT was "not as toxic an idea" as it used to be.

But is it actually a good idea? Regardless of whether your politics lean left or right, the VAT gives you some things to love and some to hate.

Let's start with the basics. Economists define a business's "value added" as the revenue it gets from the sale of goods and

services, minus the amount it pays for goods and services. So, for example, if a farmer sells wheat to a miller for $1, the miller sells flour to a baker for $2, and the baker sells bread to a customer for $3, each of the three producers has a value-added of $1.

(For simplicity, I am assuming that the farmer does not buy anything to grow the wheat.)

Now let's invoke a piece of advanced mathematics: $1 + $1 + $1 = $3. That is, the value of the final product—the $3 bread—is the sum of the value-added along the chain of production.

This leads to the first and most important insight about a value-added tax: It is essentially the same as a retail sales tax. The government could impose, say, a 10 percent retail sales tax, causing the baker to add 30

cents to the price of bread. Or it could impose a 10 percent tax on value-added. In this case, the farmer raises the price of wheat to $1.10, the miller raises the price of flour to $2.20 (reflecting both the tax and the higher price of wheat), and the baker raises the price of bread to $3.30. Either way, the consumer pays 10 percent more for the final product.

Although a value-added tax is just another form of a retail sales tax, a VAT has the advantage of being harder to evade. Tax experts believe that large retail sales taxes lead to compliance problems, which we can avoid by collecting the same tax along the chain of production.

So that's what a VAT is. What is there to love and hate about it?

For liberals, the main advantage of a VAT is that it would be a source of revenue to

Many economists believe that workers and customers bear much of the burden of the corporate income tax. To see why, consider an example. Suppose that the U.S. government decides to raise the tax on the income earned by car companies. At first, this tax hurts the owners of the car companies, who receive less profit. But over time, these owners will respond to the tax. Because producing cars is less profitable, they invest less in building new car factories. Instead, they invest their wealth in other ways—for example, by buying larger houses or by building factories in other industries or other countries. With fewer car factories, the supply of cars declines, as does the demand for autoworkers. Thus, a tax on corporations making cars causes the price of cars to rise and the wages of autoworkers to fall.

The corporate income tax shows how dangerous the flypaper theory of tax incidence can be. The corporate income tax is popular in part because it appears to be paid by rich corporations. Yet those who bear the ultimate burden of the tax—the customers and workers of corporations—are often not rich. If the true incidence of the corporate tax were more widely known, this tax might be less popular among voters. ■

This worker pays part of the corporate income tax.

fund a robust, compassionate government. Over the past century in the United States, the federal government has expanded the social safety net, including programs like Social Security, Medicare, Medicaid and, most recently, the insurance subsidies in Mr. Obama's health care overhaul. Yet Congress has been more successful promising benefits than finding the revenue to pay for them. A VAT could solve that problem.

Yet liberals balk at the distributional impact of a VAT. The tax has the same effect on rich and poor, as gauged by a proportion of their spending. But because high-income households save a higher fraction of their income, they will pay a lower fraction of their income.

Whether this distribution of the tax burden is fair is open to debate. (What is indisputable is that adding it without subtracting something else would violate Mr. Obama's campaign pledge not to raise taxes on families making less than $250,000 a year.)

Conservatives emphasize an altogether different set of concerns. For them, the main disadvantage of a VAT is that it would be a source of revenue to fund a large, intrusive government.

Western Europe is a case in point. Many nations there have large governments financed in part by value-added

taxes. Europeans also typically work less than Americans and, as a result, have lower income per person. While sorting out cause-and-effect among these international differences is hard, many conservatives agree with Edward C. Prescott, a Nobel laureate in economics whose research suggests that Europe's lower income is largely attributable to its higher tax rates.

On the other hand, conservatives have long argued that the American tax system is grossly inefficient and impedes the economy's ability to reach its full potential. They contend that taxing consumption is better than taxing income, and a value-added tax does exactly that.

Moreover, a VAT is the twin of the flat tax that conservatives sometimes advocate.

To see why, imagine that we started with a VAT. Then we add a wrinkle: We allow businesses to deduct wages, in addition to the cost of goods and services. We also require households to pay a tax on their wage income.

Other than shifting the responsibility for the tax on wages from the business to the household, it might seem that we haven't done anything significant. Indeed, we haven't. But the new tax system would no longer be a VAT. It would be the flat tax that Robert E. Hall and Alvin Rabushka first proposed back in 1981.

So why, if these two tax systems are really the same, are conservatives attracted to the flat tax and repelled by the VAT? It is because the flat tax is usually proposed as a substitute for our current tax system, whereas the VAT is often suggested as an addition to it.

The bottom line, from both political perspectives, is that a VAT is neither blessed nor evil. It is a tool. We can use it to advance a larger government, a more efficient tax system, or some combination of the two.

That will be the key issue in the coming debate.

Source: *New York Times,* April 30, 2010.

QUICK QUIZ *Explain the* benefits principle *and the* ability-to-pay principle. • *What are* vertical equity *and* horizontal equity? • *Why is studying tax incidence important for determining the equity of a tax system?*

Conclusion: The Trade-off between Equity and Efficiency

Almost everyone agrees that equity and efficiency are the two most important goals of a tax system. But these two goals often conflict, especially when equity is judged by the progressivity of the tax system. People disagree about tax policy often because they attach different weights to these goals.

The recent history of tax policy shows how political leaders differ in their views on equity and efficiency. When Ronald Reagan was elected president in 1980, the marginal tax rate on the earnings of the richest Americans was 50 percent. On interest income, the marginal tax rate was 70 percent. Reagan argued that such high tax rates greatly distorted economic incentives to work and save. In other words, he claimed that these high tax rates cost too much in terms of economic efficiency. Tax reform was, therefore, a high priority of his administration. Reagan signed into law large cuts in tax rates in 1981 and then again in 1986. When Reagan left office in 1989, the richest Americans faced a marginal tax rate of only 28 percent.

The pendulum of political debate swings both ways. When Bill Clinton ran for president in 1992, he argued that the rich were not paying their fair share of taxes. In other words, the low tax rates on the rich violated his view of vertical equity. In 1993, President Clinton signed into law a bill that raised the tax rates on the richest Americans to about 40 percent. When George W. Bush ran for president, he reprised many of Reagan's themes, and as president he reversed part of the Clinton tax increase, reducing the highest tax rate to 35 percent. Barack Obama pledged during the 2008 presidential campaign that he would raise taxes on high-income households, and it looks likely that during his presidency the top marginal tax rate will increase to levels not seen since Ronald Reagan took office.

Economics alone cannot determine the best way to balance the goals of efficiency and equity. This issue involves political philosophy as well as economics. But economists have an important role in this debate: They can shed light on the trade-offs that society inevitably faces when designing the tax system and can help us avoid policies that sacrifice efficiency without any benefit in terms of equity.

SUMMARY

- The U.S. government raises revenue using various taxes. The most important taxes for the federal government are individual income taxes and payroll taxes for social insurance. The most important taxes for state and local governments are sales taxes and property taxes.

- The efficiency of a tax system refers to the costs it imposes on taxpayers. There are two costs of taxes beyond the transfer of resources from the taxpayer to the government. The first is the deadweight loss that arises as taxes alter incentives and distort the allocation of resources. The second is the administrative burden of complying with the tax laws.

- The equity of a tax system concerns whether the tax burden is distributed fairly among the population. According to the benefits principle, it is fair for people to pay taxes based on the benefits they receive from the government. According to the ability-to-pay principle, it is fair for people to pay taxes based on their capability to handle the financial burden.

When evaluating the equity of a tax system, it is important to remember a lesson from the study of tax incidence: The distribution of tax burdens is not the same as the distribution of tax bills.

- When considering changes in the tax laws, policymakers often face a trade-off between efficiency and equity. Much of the debate over tax policy arises because people give different weights to these two goals.

KEY CONCEPTS

budget deficit, *p. 238*
budget surplus, *p. 238*
average tax rate, *p. 245*
marginal tax rate, *p. 245*
lump-sum tax, *p. 245*
benefits principle, *p. 246*

ability-to-pay principle, *p. 247*
vertical equity, *p. 247*
horizontal equity, *p. 247*
proportional tax, *p. 248*
regressive tax, *p. 248*
progressive tax, *p. 248*

QUESTIONS FOR REVIEW

1. Over the past century, has the government's tax revenue grown more or less slowly than the rest of the economy?
2. What are the two most important sources of revenue for the U.S. federal government?
3. Explain how corporate profits are taxed twice.
4. Why is the burden of a tax to taxpayers greater than the revenue received by the government?
5. Why do some economists advocate taxing consumption rather than income?

6. What is the marginal tax rate on a lump-sum tax? How is this related to the efficiency of the tax?
7. Give two arguments why wealthy taxpayers should pay more taxes than poor taxpayers.
8. What is the concept of horizontal equity and why is it hard to apply?

PROBLEMS AND APPLICATIONS

1. In a published source or on the Internet, find out whether the U.S. federal government had a budget deficit or surplus last year. What do policymakers expect to happen over the next few years? (Hint: The website of the Congressional Budget Office is http://www.cbo.gov.)
2. The information in many of the tables in this chapter can be found in the *Economic Report of the President*, which appears annually. Using a

recent issue of the report at your library or on the Internet, answer the following questions and provide some numbers to support your answers. (Hint: The website of the Government Printing Office is http://www.gpo.gov.)
   a. Figure 1 shows that government revenue as a percentage of total income has increased over time. Is this increase primarily attributable to changes in federal government revenue or in state and local government revenue?

b. Looking at the combined revenue of the federal government and state and local governments, how has the composition of total revenue changed over time? Are personal income taxes more or less important? Social insurance taxes? Corporate profits taxes?

c. Looking at the combined expenditures of the federal government and state and local governments, how have the relative shares of transfer payments and purchases of goods and services changed over time?

3. The chapter states that the elderly population in the United States is growing more rapidly than the total population. In particular, the number of workers is rising slowly, while the number of retirees is rising quickly. Concerned about the future of Social Security, some members of Congress propose a "freeze" on the program.

a. If total expenditures were frozen, what would happen to benefits per retiree? To tax payments per worker? (Assume that Social Security taxes and receipts are balanced in each year.)

b. If benefits per retiree were frozen, what would happen to total expenditures? To tax payments per worker?

c. If tax payments per worker were frozen, what would happen to total expenditures? To benefits per retiree?

d. What do your answers to parts (a), (b), and (c) imply about the difficult decisions faced by policymakers?

4. Suppose you are a typical person in the U.S. economy. You pay 4 percent of your income in a state income tax and 15.3 percent of your labor earnings in federal payroll taxes (employer and employee shares combined). You also pay federal income taxes as in Table 3. How much tax of each type do you pay if you earn $20,000 a year? Taking all taxes into account, what are your average and marginal tax rates? What happens to your tax bill and to your average and marginal tax rates if your income rises to $40,000?

5. Some states exclude necessities, such as food and clothing, from their sales tax. Other states do not. Discuss the merits of this exclusion. Consider both efficiency and equity.

6. When someone owns an asset (such as a share of stock) that rises in value, he has an "accrued" capital gain. If he sells the asset, he "realizes" the gains that have previously accrued. Under the U.S. income tax, realized capital gains are taxed, but accrued gains are not.

a. Explain how individuals' behavior is affected by this rule.

b. Some economists believe that cuts in capital gains tax rates, especially temporary ones, can raise tax revenue. How might this be so?

c. Do you think it is a good rule to tax realized but not accrued capital gains? Why or why not?

7. Suppose that your state raises its sales tax from 5 percent to 6 percent. The state revenue commissioner forecasts a 20 percent increase in sales tax revenue. Is this plausible? Explain.

8. The Tax Reform Act of 1986 eliminated the deductibility of interest payments on consumer debt (mostly credit cards and auto loans) but maintained the deductibility of interest payments on mortgages and home equity loans. What do you think happened to the relative amounts of borrowing through consumer debt and home equity debt?

9. Categorize each of the following funding schemes as examples of the benefits principle or the ability-to-pay principle.

a. Visitors to many national parks pay an entrance fee.

b. Local property taxes support elementary and secondary schools.

c. An airport trust fund collects a tax on each plane ticket sold and uses the money to improve airports and the air traffic control system.

10. Any income tax schedule embodies two types of tax rates: average tax rates and marginal tax rates.

a. The average tax rate is defined as total taxes paid divided by income. For the proportional tax system presented in Table 7, what are the average tax rates for people earning $50,000, $100,000, and $200,000? What are the corresponding average tax rates in the regressive and progressive tax systems?

b. The marginal tax rate is defined as the extra taxes paid on additional income divided by the increase in income. Calculate the marginal tax rate for the proportional tax system as income rises from $50,000 to $100,000. Calculate the marginal tax rate as income rises from $100,000 to $200,000.

Calculate the corresponding marginal tax rates for the regressive and progressive tax systems.

c. Describe the relationship between average tax rates and marginal tax rates for each of these three systems. In general, which rate is relevant for someone deciding whether to accept a job that pays slightly more than her current job? Which rate is relevant for judging the vertical equity of a tax system?

12. Each of the following expenditures is a deduction for the purposes of calculating a person's federal income tax liability:

a. Mortgage interest
b. State and local taxes
c. Charitable contributions

If the income tax base were broadened by eliminating these deductions, tax rates could be lowered, while raising the same amount of tax revenue.

For each of these deductions, what would you expect the likely effect on taxpayer behavior to be? Discuss the pros and cons of each deduction from the standpoint of efficiency, vertical equity, and horizontal equity. Would you keep or eliminate the deduction?

For further information on topics in this chapter, additional problems, applications, examples, online quizzes, and more, please visit our website at www.cengage.com/economics/mankiw.

PART **V**   Firm Behavior and the Organization of Industry

The Costs of Production

The economy is made up of thousands of firms that produce the goods and services you enjoy every day: General Motors produces automobiles, General Electric produces lightbulbs, and General Mills produces breakfast cereals. Some firms, such as these three, are large; they employ thousands of workers and have thousands of stockholders who share in the firms' profits. Other firms, such as the local barbershop or candy store, are small; they employ only a few workers and are owned by a single person or family.

In previous chapters, we used the supply curve to summarize firms' production decisions. According to the law of supply, firms are willing to produce and sell a greater quantity of a good when the price of the good is higher, and this response leads to a supply curve that slopes upward. For analyzing many questions, the law of supply is all you need to know about firm behavior.

In this chapter and the ones that follow, we examine firm behavior in more detail. This topic will give you a better understanding of the decisions behind the supply curve. In addition, it will introduce you to a part of economics called *industrial organization*—the study of how firms' decisions about prices and quantities depend on the market conditions they face. The town in which you live, for instance, may have several pizzerias but only one cable television company. This raises a key question: How does the number of firms affect the prices in a market and the efficiency of the market outcome? The field of industrial organization addresses exactly this question.

Before turning to these issues, we need to discuss the costs of production. All firms, from Delta Air Lines to your local deli, incur costs as they make the goods and services that they sell. As we will see in the coming chapters, a firm's costs are a key determinant of its production and pricing decisions. In this chapter, we define some of the variables that economists use to measure a firm's costs, and we consider the relationships among these variables.

A word of warning: This topic is dry and technical. To be honest, one might even call it boring. But this material provides a crucial foundation for the fascinating topics that follow.

What Are Costs?

We begin our discussion of costs at Caroline's Cookie Factory. Caroline, the owner of the firm, buys flour, sugar, chocolate chips, and other cookie ingredients. She also buys the mixers and ovens and hires workers to run this equipment. She then sells the cookies to consumers. By examining some of the issues that Caroline faces in her business, we can learn some lessons about costs that apply to all firms in an economy.

Total Revenue, Total Cost, and Profit

We begin with the firm's objective. To understand the decisions a firm makes, we must understand what it is trying to do. It is conceivable that Caroline started her firm because of an altruistic desire to provide the world with cookies or, perhaps, out of love for the cookie business. More likely, Caroline started her business to make money. Economists normally assume that the goal of a firm is to maximize profit, and they find that this assumption works well in most cases.

total revenue
the amount a firm receives for the sale of its output

total cost
the market value of the inputs a firm uses in production

profit
total revenue minus total cost

What is a firm's profit? The amount that the firm receives for the sale of its output (cookies) is called its **total revenue.** The amount that the firm pays to buy inputs (flour, sugar, workers, ovens, and so forth) is called its **total cost.** Caroline gets to keep any revenue that is not needed to cover costs. **Profit** is a firm's total revenue minus its total cost:

$$\text{Profit} = \text{Total revenue} - \text{Total cost}.$$

Caroline's objective is to make her firm's profit as large as possible.

To see how a firm goes about maximizing profit, we must consider fully how to measure its total revenue and its total cost. Total revenue is the easy part: It equals the quantity of output the firm produces times the price at which it sells its output. If Caroline produces 10,000 cookies and sells them at $2 a cookie, her total revenue is $20,000. By contrast, the measurement of a firm's total cost is more subtle.

Costs as Opportunity Costs

When measuring costs at Caroline's Cookie Factory or any other firm, it is important to keep in mind one of the *Ten Principles of Economics* from Chapter 1: The cost of something is what you give up to get it. Recall that the *opportunity cost* of an item refers to all those things that must be forgone to acquire that item. When economists speak of a firm's cost of production, they include all the opportunity costs of making its output of goods and services.

While some of a firm's opportunity costs of production are obvious, others are less so. When Caroline pays $1,000 for flour, that $1,000 is an opportunity cost because Caroline can no longer use that $1,000 to buy something else. Similarly, when Caroline hires workers to make the cookies, the wages she pays are part of the firm's costs. Because these opportunity costs require the firm to pay out some money, they are called **explicit costs.** By contrast, some of a firm's opportunity costs, called **implicit costs,** do not require a cash outlay. Imagine that Caroline is skilled with computers and could earn $100 per hour working as a programmer. For every hour that Caroline works at her cookie factory, she gives up $100 in income, and this forgone income is also part of her costs. The total cost of Caroline's business is the sum of the explicit costs and the implicit costs.

The distinction between explicit and implicit costs highlights an important difference between how economists and accountants analyze a business. Economists are interested in studying how firms make production and pricing decisions. Because these decisions are based on both explicit and implicit costs, economists include both when measuring a firm's costs. By contrast, accountants have the job of keeping track of the money that flows into and out of firms. As a result, they measure the explicit costs but usually ignore the implicit costs.

The difference between economists and accountants is easy to see in the case of Caroline's Cookie Factory. When Caroline gives up the opportunity to earn money as a computer programmer, her accountant will not count this as a cost of her cookie business. Because no money flows out of the business to pay for this cost, it never shows up on the accountant's financial statements. An economist, however, will count the forgone income as a cost because it will affect the decisions that Caroline makes in her cookie business. For example, if Caroline's wage as a computer programmer rises from $100 to $500 per hour, she might decide that running her cookie business is too costly and choose to shut down the factory to become a full-time computer programmer.

The Cost of Capital as an Opportunity Cost

An important implicit cost of almost every business is the opportunity cost of the financial capital that has been invested in the business. Suppose, for instance, that Caroline used $300,000 of her savings to buy her cookie factory from its previous owner. If Caroline had instead left this money deposited in a savings account that pays an interest rate of 5 percent, she would have earned $15,000 per year. To own her cookie factory, therefore, Caroline has given up $15,000 a year in interest income. This forgone $15,000 is one of the implicit opportunity costs of Caroline's business.

As we have already noted, economists and accountants treat costs differently, and this is especially true in their treatment of the cost of capital. An economist views the $15,000 in interest income that Caroline gives up every year as a cost of her business, even though it is an implicit cost. Caroline's accountant, however, will not show this $15,000 as a cost because no money flows out of the business to pay for it.

To further explore the difference between economists and accountants, let's change the example slightly. Suppose now that Caroline did not have the entire $300,000 to buy the factory but, instead, used $100,000 of her own savings and borrowed $200,000

explicit costs
input costs that require an outlay of money by the firm

implicit costs
input costs that do not require an outlay of money by the firm

from a bank at an interest rate of 5 percent. Caroline's accountant, who only measures explicit costs, will now count the $10,000 interest paid on the bank loan every year as a cost because this amount of money now flows out of the firm. By contrast, according to an economist, the opportunity cost of owning the business is still $15,000. The opportunity cost equals the interest on the bank loan (an explicit cost of $10,000) plus the forgone interest on savings (an implicit cost of $5,000).

Economic Profit versus Accounting Profit

economic profit

total revenue minus total cost, including both explicit and implicit costs

accounting profit

total revenue minus total explicit cost

Now let's return to the firm's objective: profit. Because economists and accountants measure costs differently, they also measure profit differently. An economist measures a firm's **economic profit** as the firm's total revenue minus all the opportunity costs (explicit and implicit) of producing the goods and services sold. An accountant measures the firm's **accounting profit** as the firm's total revenue minus only the firm's explicit costs.

Figure 1 summarizes this difference. Notice that because the accountant ignores the implicit costs, accounting profit is usually larger than economic profit. For a business to be profitable from an economist's standpoint, total revenue must cover all the opportunity costs, both explicit and implicit.

Economic profit is an important concept because it is what motivates the firms that supply goods and services. As we will see, a firm making positive economic profit will stay in business. It is covering all its opportunity costs and has some revenue left to reward the firm owners. When a firm is making economic losses (that is, when economic profits are negative), the business owners are failing to earn enough revenue to cover all the costs of production. Unless conditions change, the firm owners will eventually close down the business and exit the industry. To understand business decisions, we need to keep an eye on economic profit.

QUICK QUIZ   *Farmer McDonald gives banjo lessons for $20 an hour. One day, he spends 10 hours planting $100 worth of seeds on his farm. What opportunity cost has he incurred? What cost would his accountant measure? If these seeds yield $200 worth of crops, does McDonald earn an accounting profit? Does he earn an economic profit?*

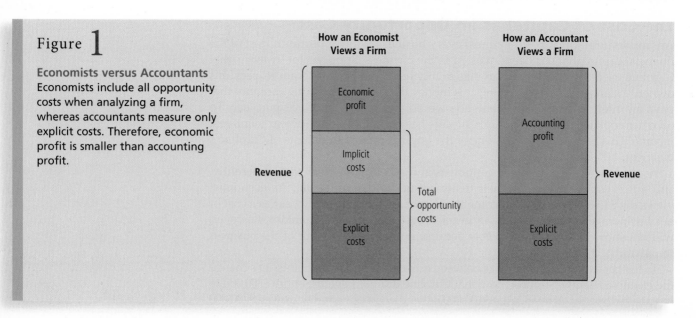

Figure 1

Economists versus Accountants
Economists include all opportunity costs when analyzing a firm, whereas accountants measure only explicit costs. Therefore, economic profit is smaller than accounting profit.

How an Economist Views a Firm

How an Accountant Views a Firm

Revenue

Economic profit

Implicit costs

Explicit costs

Total opportunity costs

Accounting profit

Explicit costs

Revenue

Production and Costs

Firms incur costs when they buy inputs to produce the goods and services that they plan to sell. In this section, we examine the link between a firm's production process and its total cost. Once again, we consider Caroline's Cookie Factory.

In the analysis that follows, we make an important simplifying assumption: We assume that the size of Caroline's factory is fixed and that Caroline can vary the quantity of cookies produced only by changing the number of workers she employs. This assumption is realistic in the short run but not in the long run. That is, Caroline cannot build a larger factory overnight, but she can do so over the next year or two. This analysis, therefore, describes the production decisions that Caroline faces in the short run. We examine the relationship between costs and time horizon more fully later in the chapter.

The Production Function

Table 1 shows how the quantity of cookies produced per hour at Caroline's factory depends on the number of workers. As you can see in the first two columns, if there are no workers in the factory, Caroline produces no cookies. When there is 1 worker, she produces 50 cookies. When there are 2 workers, she produces 90 cookies and so on. Panel (a) of Figure 2 presents a graph of these two columns of numbers. The number of workers is on the horizontal axis, and the number of cookies produced is on the vertical axis. This relationship between the quantity of inputs (workers) and quantity of output (cookies) is called the **production function.**

production function
the relationship between quantity of inputs used to make a good and the quantity of output of that good

Number of Workers	Output (quantity of cookies produced per hour)	Marginal Product of Labor	Cost of Factory	Cost of Workers	Total Cost of Inputs (cost of factory + cost of workers)
0	0		$30	$0	$30
		50			
1	50		30	10	40
		40			
2	90		30	20	50
		30			
3	120		30	30	60
		20			
4	140		30	40	70
		10			
5	150		30	50	80
		5			
6	155		30	60	90

Table 1

A Production Function and Total Cost: Caroline's Cookie Factory

Figure 2

Caroline's Production Function and Total-Cost Curve

The production function in panel (a) shows the relationship between the number of workers hired and the quantity of output produced. Here the number of workers hired (on the horizontal axis) is from the first column in Table 1, and the quantity of output produced (on the vertical axis) is from the second column. The production function gets flatter as the number of workers increases, which reflects diminishing marginal product. The total-cost curve in panel (b) shows the relationship between the quantity of output produced and total cost of production. Here the quantity of output produced (on the horizontal axis) is from the second column in Table 1, and the total cost (on the vertical axis) is from the sixth column. The total-cost curve gets steeper as the quantity of output increases because of diminishing marginal product.

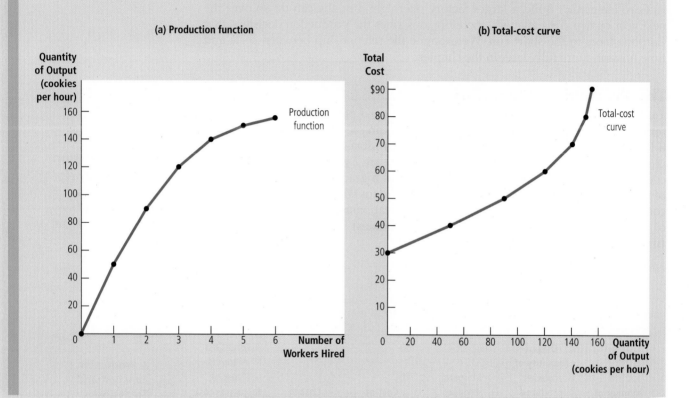

(a) Production function

(b) Total-cost curve

marginal product

the increase in output that arises from an additional unit of input

One of the *Ten Principles of Economics* introduced in Chapter 1 is that rational people think at the margin. As we will see in future chapters, this idea is the key to understanding the decisions a firm makes about how many workers to hire and how much output to produce. To take a step toward understanding these decisions, the third column in the table gives the marginal product of a worker. The **marginal product** of any input in the production process is the increase in the quantity of output obtained from one additional unit of that input. When the number of workers goes from 1 to 2, cookie production increases from 50 to 90, so the marginal product of the second worker is 40 cookies. And when the number of workers goes from 2 to 3, cookie production increases from 90 to 120, so the marginal product of the third worker is 30 cookies. In the table, the marginal product is shown halfway between two rows because it represents the change in output as the number of workers increases from one level to another.

Notice that as the number of workers increases, the marginal product declines. The second worker has a marginal product of 40 cookies, the third worker has a marginal product of 30 cookies, and the fourth worker has a marginal product of 20 cookies. This property is called **diminishing marginal product.** At first, when only a few workers are hired, they have easy access to Caroline's kitchen equipment. As the number of workers increases, additional workers have to share equipment and work in more crowded conditions. Eventually, the kitchen is so crowded that the workers start getting in each other's way. Hence, as more and more workers are hired, each additional worker contributes fewer additional cookies to total production.

Diminishing marginal product is also apparent in Figure 2. The production function's slope ("rise over run") tells us the change in Caroline's output of cookies ("rise") for each additional input of labor ("run"). That is, the slope of the production function measures the marginal product of a worker. As the number of workers increases, the marginal product declines, and the production function becomes flatter.

diminishing marginal product
the property whereby the marginal product of an input declines as the quantity of the input increases

From the Production Function to the Total-Cost Curve

The last three columns of Table 1 show Caroline's cost of producing cookies. In this example, the cost of Caroline's factory is $30 per hour, and the cost of a worker is $10 per hour. If she hires 1 worker, her total cost is $40 per hour. If she hires 2 workers, her total cost is $50 per hour, and so on. With this information, the table now shows how the number of workers Caroline hires is related to the quantity of cookies she produces and to her total cost of production.

Our goal in the next several chapters is to study firms' production and pricing decisions. For this purpose, the most important relationship in Table 1 is between quantity produced (in the second column) and total costs (in the sixth column). Panel (b) of Figure 2 graphs these two columns of data with the quantity produced on the horizontal axis and total cost on the vertical axis. This graph is called the *total-cost curve.*

Now compare the total-cost curve in panel (b) with the production function in panel (a). These two curves are opposite sides of the same coin. The total-cost curve gets steeper as the amount produced rises, whereas the production function gets flatter as production rises. These changes in slope occur for the same reason. High production of cookies means that Caroline's kitchen is crowded with many workers. Because the kitchen is crowded, each additional worker adds less to production, reflecting diminishing marginal product. Therefore, the production function is relatively flat. But now turn this logic around: When the kitchen is crowded, producing an additional cookie requires a lot of additional labor and is thus very costly. Therefore, when the quantity produced is large, the total-cost curve is relatively steep.

QUICK QUIZ   *If Farmer Jones plants no seeds on his farm, he gets no harvest. If he plants 1 bag of seeds, he gets 3 bushels of wheat. If he plants 2 bags, he gets 5 bushels. If he plants 3 bags, he gets 6 bushels. A bag of seeds costs $100, and seeds are his only cost. Use these data to graph the farmer's production function and total-cost curve. Explain their shapes.*

The Various Measures of Cost

Our analysis of Caroline's Cookie Factory demonstrated how a firm's total cost reflects its production function. From data on a firm's total cost, we can derive several related measures of cost, which will turn out to be useful when we analyze

Table 2

The Various Measures of Cost: Conrad's Coffee Shop

Quantity of Coffee (cups per hour)	Total Cost	Fixed Cost	Variable Cost	Average Fixed Cost	Average Variable Cost	Average Total Cost	Marginal Cost
0	$ 3.00	$3.00	$ 0.00	—	—	—	
							$0.30
1	3.30	3.00	0.30	$3.00	$0.30	$3.30	
							0.50
2	3.80	3.00	0.80	1.50	0.40	1.90	
							0.70
3	4.50	3.00	1.50	1.00	0.50	1.50	
							0.90
4	5.40	3.00	2.40	0.75	0.60	1.35	
							1.10
5	6.50	3.00	3.50	0.60	0.70	1.30	
							1.30
6	7.80	3.00	4.80	0.50	0.80	1.30	
							1.50
7	9.30	3.00	6.30	0.43	0.90	1.33	
							1.70
8	11.00	3.00	8.00	0.38	1.00	1.38	
							1.90
9	12.90	3.00	9.90	0.33	1.10	1.43	
							2.10
10	15.00	3.00	12.00	0.30	1.20	1.50	

production and pricing decisions in future chapters. To see how these related measures are derived, we consider the example in Table 2. This table presents cost data on Caroline's neighbor—Conrad's Coffee Shop.

The first column of the table shows the number of cups of coffee that Conrad might produce, ranging from 0 to 10 cups per hour. The second column shows Conrad's total cost of producing coffee. Figure 3 plots Conrad's total-cost curve. The quantity of coffee (from the first column) is on the horizontal axis, and total cost (from the second column) is on the vertical axis. Conrad's total-cost curve has a shape similar to Caroline's. In particular, it becomes steeper as the quantity produced rises, which (as we have discussed) reflects diminishing marginal product.

Fixed and Variable Costs

fixed costs

costs that do not vary with the quantity of output produced

variable costs

costs that vary with the quantity of output produced

Conrad's total cost can be divided into two types. Some costs, called **fixed costs,** do not vary with the quantity of output produced. They are incurred even if the firm produces nothing at all. Conrad's fixed costs include any rent he pays because this cost is the same regardless of how much coffee he produces. Similarly, if Conrad needs to hire a full-time bookkeeper to pay bills, regardless of the quantity of coffee produced, the bookkeeper's salary is a fixed cost. The third column in Table 2 shows Conrad's fixed cost, which in this example is $3.00.

Some of the firm's costs, called **variable costs,** change as the firm alters the quantity of output produced. Conrad's variable costs include the cost of coffee

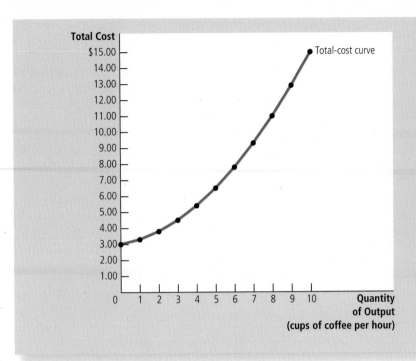

Figure **3**

Conrad's Total-Cost Curve
Here the quantity of output produced
(on the horizontal axis) is from the first
column in Table 2, and the total cost
(on the vertical axis) is from the second
column. As in Figure 2, the total-cost
curve gets steeper as the quantity of
output increases because of diminishing
marginal product.

beans, milk, sugar, and paper cups: The more cups of coffee Conrad makes, the
more of these items he needs to buy. Similarly, if Conrad has to hire more workers
to make more cups of coffee, the salaries of these workers are variable costs. The
fourth column of the table shows Conrad's variable cost. The variable cost is 0 if
he produces nothing, $0.30 if he produces 1 cup of coffee, $0.80 if he produces 2
cups, and so on.

A firm's total cost is the sum of fixed and variable costs. In Table 2, total cost
in the second column equals fixed cost in the third column plus variable cost in
the fourth column.

Average and Marginal Cost

As the owner of his firm, Conrad has to decide how much to produce. A key part
of this decision is how his costs will vary as he changes the level of production. In
making this decision, Conrad might ask his production supervisor the following
two questions about the cost of producing coffee:

- How much does it cost to make the typical cup of coffee?
- How much does it cost to increase production of coffee by 1 cup?

Although at first these two questions might seem to have the same answer, they
do not. Both answers will turn out to be important for understanding how firms
make production decisions.

To find the cost of the typical unit produced, we would divide the firm's costs
by the quantity of output it produces. For example, if the firm produces 2 cups
of coffee per hour, its total cost is $3.80, and the cost of the typical cup is $3.80/2,
or $1.90. Total cost divided by the quantity of output is called **average total cost.**
Because total cost is the sum of fixed and variable costs, average total cost can be

average total cost
total cost divided by the
quantity of output

average fixed cost
fixed cost divided by the quantity of output

average variable cost
variable cost divided by the quantity of output

marginal cost
the increase in total cost that arises from an extra unit of production

expressed as the sum of average fixed cost and average variable cost. **Average fixed cost** is the fixed cost divided by the quantity of output, and **average variable cost** is the variable cost divided by the quantity of output.

Average total cost tells us the cost of the typical unit, but it does not tell us how much total cost will change as the firm alters its level of production. The last column in Table 2 shows the amount that total cost rises when the firm increases production by 1 unit of output. This number is called **marginal cost.** For example, if Conrad increases production from 2 to 3 cups, total cost rises from $3.80 to $4.50, so the marginal cost of the third cup of coffee is $4.50 minus $3.80, or $0.70. In the table, the marginal cost appears halfway between two rows because it represents the change in total cost as quantity of output increases from one level to another.

It may be helpful to express these definitions mathematically:

$$\text{Average total cost} = \text{Total cost}/\text{Quantity}$$
$$ATC = TC/Q$$

and

$$\text{Marginal cost} = \text{Change in total cost}/\text{Change in quantity}$$
$$MC = \Delta TC/\Delta Q.$$

Here Δ, the Greek letter delta, represents the change in a variable. These equations show how average total cost and marginal cost are derived from total cost. *Average total cost tells us the cost of a typical unit of output if total cost is divided evenly over all the units produced. Marginal cost tells us the increase in total cost that arises from producing an additional unit of output.* As we will see more fully in the next chapter, business managers like Conrad need to keep in mind the concepts of average total cost and marginal cost when deciding how much of their product to supply to the market.

Cost Curves and Their Shapes

Just as in previous chapters we found graphs of supply and demand useful when analyzing the behavior of markets, we will find graphs of average and marginal cost useful when analyzing the behavior of firms. Figure 4 graphs Conrad's costs using the data from Table 2. The horizontal axis measures the quantity the firm produces, and the vertical axis measures marginal and average costs. The graph shows four curves: average total cost (*ATC*), average fixed cost (*AFC*), average variable cost (*AVC*), and marginal cost (*MC*).

The cost curves shown here for Conrad's Coffee Shop have some features that are common to the cost curves of many firms in the economy. Let's examine three features in particular: the shape of the marginal-cost curve, the shape of the average-total-cost curve, and the relationship between marginal and average total cost.

Rising Marginal Cost   Conrad's marginal cost rises with the quantity of output produced. This reflects the property of diminishing marginal product. When Conrad produces a small quantity of coffee, he has few workers, and much of his equipment is not used. Because he can easily put these idle resources to use, the marginal product of an extra worker is large, and the marginal cost of an extra cup of coffee is small. By contrast, when Conrad produces a large quantity of coffee,

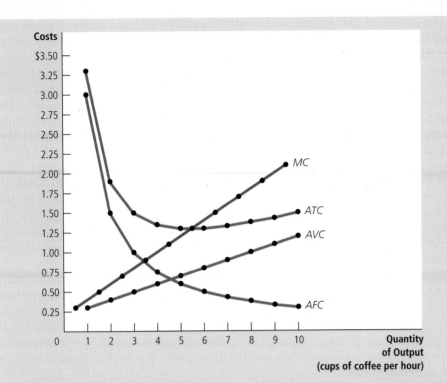

Figure 4

Conrad's Average-Cost and Marginal-Cost Curves
This figure shows the average total cost (*ATC*), average fixed cost (*AFC*), average variable cost (*AVC*), and marginal cost (*MC*) for Conrad's Coffee Shop. All of these curves are obtained by graphing the data in Table 2. These cost curves show three features that are typical of many firms: (1) Marginal cost rises with the quantity of output. (2) The average-total-cost curve is U-shaped. (3) The marginal-cost curve crosses the average-total-cost curve at the minimum of average total cost.

his shop is crowded with workers, and most of his equipment is fully utilized. Conrad can produce more coffee by adding workers, but these new workers have to work in crowded conditions and may have to wait to use the equipment. Therefore, when the quantity of coffee produced is already high, the marginal product of an extra worker is low, and the marginal cost of an extra cup of coffee is large.

U-Shaped Average Total Cost Conrad's average-total-cost curve is U-shaped, as shown in Figure 4. To understand why, remember that average total cost is the sum of average fixed cost and average variable cost. Average fixed cost always declines as output rises because the fixed cost is spread over a larger number of units. Average variable cost typically rises as output increases because of diminishing marginal product.

Average total cost reflects the shapes of both average fixed cost and average variable cost. At very low levels of output, such as 1 or 2 cups per hour, average total cost is very high. Even though average variable cost is low, average fixed cost is high because the fixed cost is spread over only a few units. As output increases, the fixed cost is spread more widely. Average fixed cost declines, rapidly at first and then more slowly. As a result, average total cost also declines until the firm's output reaches 5 cups of coffee per hour, when average total cost is $1.30 per cup. When the firm produces more than 6 cups per hour, however, the increase in average variable cost becomes the dominant force, and average total cost starts rising. The tug of war between average fixed cost and average variable cost generates the U-shape in average total cost.

efficient scale

the quantity of output that minimizes average total cost

The bottom of the U-shape occurs at the quantity that minimizes average total cost. This quantity is sometimes called the **efficient scale** of the firm. For Conrad, the efficient scale is 5 or 6 cups of coffee per hour. If he produces more or less than this amount, his average total cost rises above the minimum of $1.30. At lower levels of output, average total cost is higher than $1.30 because the fixed cost is spread over so few units. At higher levels of output, average total cost is higher than $1.30 because the marginal product of inputs has diminished significantly. At the efficient scale, these two forces are balanced to yield the lowest average total cost.

The Relationship between Marginal Cost and Average Total Cost   If you look at Figure 4 (or back at Table 2), you will see something that may be surprising at first. *Whenever marginal cost is less than average total cost, average total cost is falling. Whenever marginal cost is greater than average total cost, average total cost is rising.* This feature of Conrad's cost curves is not a coincidence from the particular numbers used in the example: It is true for all firms.

To see why, consider an analogy. Average total cost is like your cumulative grade point average. Marginal cost is like the grade in the next course you will take. If your grade in your next course is less than your grade point average, your grade point average will fall. If your grade in your next course is higher than your grade point average, your grade point average will rise. The mathematics of average and marginal costs is exactly the same as the mathematics of average and marginal grades.

This relationship between average total cost and marginal cost has an important corollary: *The marginal-cost curve crosses the average-total-cost curve at its minimum.* Why? At low levels of output, marginal cost is below average total cost, so average total cost is falling. But after the two curves cross, marginal cost rises above average total cost. For the reason we have just discussed, average total cost must start to rise at this level of output. Hence, this point of intersection is the minimum of average total cost. As you will see in the next chapter, minimum average total cost plays a key role in the analysis of competitive firms.

Typical Cost Curves

In the examples we have studied so far, the firms exhibit diminishing marginal product and, therefore, rising marginal cost at all levels of output. This simplifying assumption was useful because it allowed us to focus on the key features of cost curves that will prove useful in analyzing firm behavior. Yet actual firms are usually more complicated than this. In many firms, marginal product does not start to fall immediately after the first worker is hired. Depending on the production process, the second or third worker might have a higher marginal product than the first because a team of workers can divide tasks and work more productively than a single worker. Firms exhibiting this pattern would experience increasing marginal product for a while before diminishing marginal product set in.

Figure 5 shows the cost curves for such a firm, including average total cost (*ATC*), average fixed cost (*AFC*), average variable cost (*AVC*), and marginal cost (*MC*). At low levels of output, the firm experiences increasing marginal product, and the marginal-cost curve falls. Eventually, the firm starts to experience diminishing marginal product, and the marginal-cost curve starts to rise. This combination of increasing then diminishing marginal product also makes the average-variable-cost curve U-shaped.

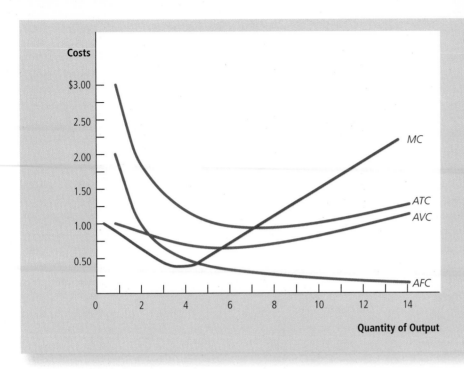

Figure **5**

Cost Curves for a Typical Firm
Many firms experience increasing marginal product before diminishing marginal product. As a result, they have cost curves shaped like those in this figure. Notice that marginal cost and average variable cost fall for a while before starting to rise.

Despite these differences from our previous example, the cost curves shown here share the three properties that are most important to remember:

- Marginal cost eventually rises with the quantity of output.
- The average-total-cost curve is U-shaped.
- The marginal-cost curve crosses the average-total-cost curve at the minimum of average total cost.

QUICK QUIZ   *Suppose Honda's total cost of producing 4 cars is $225,000 and its total cost of producing 5 cars is $250,000. What is the average total cost of producing 5 cars? What is the marginal cost of the fifth car?* • *Draw the marginal-cost curve and the average-total-cost curve for a typical firm, and explain why these curves cross where they do.*

Costs in the Short Run and in the Long Run

We noted earlier in this chapter that a firm's costs might depend on the time horizon under consideration. Let's examine more precisely why this might be the case.

The Relationship between Short-Run and Long-Run Average Total Cost

For many firms, the division of total costs between fixed and variable costs depends on the time horizon. Consider, for instance, a car manufacturer such as Ford Motor Company. Over a period of only a few months, Ford cannot adjust the number or size of its car factories. The only way it can produce additional cars is to hire more workers at the factories it already has. The cost of these factories is, therefore, a fixed cost in the short run. By contrast, over a period of several years, Ford can expand the size of its factories, build new factories, or close old ones. Thus, the cost of its factories is a variable cost in the long run.

Figure 6

Average Total Cost in the Short and Long Runs
Because fixed costs are variable in the long run, the average-total-cost curve in the short run differs from the average-total-cost curve in the long run.

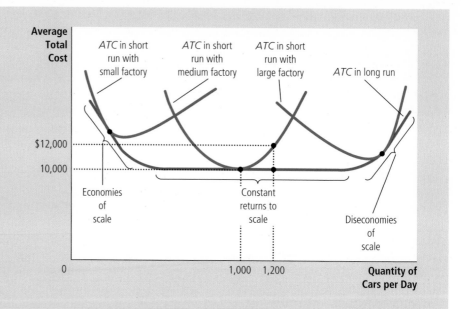

Because many decisions are fixed in the short run but variable in the long run, a firm's long-run cost curves differ from its short-run cost curves. Figure 6 shows an example. The figure presents three short-run average-total-cost curves—for a small, medium, and large factory. It also presents the long-run average-total-cost curve. As the firm moves along the long-run curve, it is adjusting the size of the factory to the quantity of production.

This graph shows how short-run and long-run costs are related. The long-run average-total-cost curve is a much flatter U-shape than the short-run average-total-cost curve. In addition, all the short-run curves lie on or above the long-run curve. These properties arise because firms have greater flexibility in the long run. In essence, in the long run, the firm gets to choose which short-run curve it wants to use. But in the short run, it has to use whatever short-run curve it has chosen in the past.

The figure shows an example of how a change in production alters costs over different time horizons. When Ford wants to increase production from 1,000 to 1,200 cars per day, it has no choice in the short run but to hire more workers at its existing medium-sized factory. Because of diminishing marginal product, average total cost rises from $10,000 to $12,000 per car. In the long run, however, Ford can expand both the size of the factory and its workforce, and average total cost returns to $10,000.

How long does it take a firm to get to the long run? The answer depends on the firm. It can take a year or more for a major manufacturing firm, such as a car company, to build a larger factory. By contrast, a person running a coffee shop can buy another coffee maker within a few days. There is, therefore, no single answer to how long it takes a firm to adjust its production facilities.

Economies and Diseconomies of Scale

economies of scale
the property whereby long-run average total cost falls as the quantity of output increases

diseconomies of scale
the property whereby long-run average total cost rises as the quantity of output increases

The shape of the long-run average-total-cost curve conveys important information about the production processes that a firm has available for manufacturing a good. In particular, it tells us how costs vary with the scale—that is, the size—of a firm's operations. When long-run average total cost declines as output increases, there are said to be **economies of scale.** When long-run average total cost rises as output increases, there are said to be **diseconomies of scale.** When long-run average total cost does not vary with the level of output, there are said to be **constant returns to scale.** In this example, Ford has economies of scale at low levels of output, constant returns to scale at intermediate levels of output, and diseconomies of scale at high levels of output.

What might cause economies or diseconomies of scale? Economies of scale often arise because higher production levels allow *specialization* among workers, which permits each worker to become better at a specific task. For instance, if Ford hires a large number of workers and produces a large number of cars, it can reduce costs with modern assembly-line production. Diseconomies of scale can arise because of *coordination problems* that are inherent in any large organization. The more cars Ford produces, the more stretched the management team becomes, and the less effective the managers become at keeping costs down.

This analysis shows why long-run average-total-cost curves are often U-shaped. At low levels of production, the firm benefits from increased size because it can take advantage of greater specialization. Coordination problems, meanwhile, are not yet acute. By contrast, at high levels of production, the benefits of specialization have already been realized, and coordination problems become more severe as the firm grows larger. Thus, long-run average total cost is falling at low levels of production because of increasing specialization and rising at high levels of production because of increasing coordination problems.

constant returns to scale
the property whereby long-run average total cost stays the same as the quantity of output changes

QUICK QUIZ   *If Boeing produces 9 jets per month, its long-run total cost is $9.0 million per month. If it produces 10 jets per month, its long-run total cost is $9.5 million per month. Does Boeing exhibit economies or diseconomies of scale?*

FYI

> ### *Lessons from a Pin Factory*

"Jack of all trades, master of none." This well-known adage helps explain why firms sometimes experience economies of scale. A person who tries to do everything usually ends up doing nothing very well. If a firm wants its workers to be as productive as they can be, it is often best to give each worker a limited task that he or she can master. But this is possible only if a firm employs many workers and produces a large quantity of output.

In his celebrated book *An Inquiry into the Nature and Causes of the Wealth of Nations*, Adam Smith described a visit he made to a pin factory. Smith was impressed by the specialization among the workers and the resulting economies of scale. He wrote,

> One man draws out the wire, another straightens it, a third cuts it, a fourth points it, a fifth grinds it at the top for receiving the head; to make the head requires two or three distinct operations; to put it on is a peculiar business; to whiten it is another; it is even a trade by itself to put them into paper.

Smith reported that because of this specialization, the pin factory produced thousands of pins per worker every day. He conjectured that if the workers had chosen to work separately, rather than as a team of specialists, "they certainly could not each of them make twenty, perhaps not one pin a day." In other words, because of specialization, a large pin factory could achieve higher output per worker and lower average cost per pin than a small pin factory.

The specialization that Smith observed in the pin factory is prevalent in the modern economy. If you want to build a house, for instance, you could try to do all the work yourself. But most people turn to a builder, who in turn hires carpenters, plumbers, electricians, painters, and many other types of workers. These workers specialize in particular jobs, and this allows them to become better at their jobs than if they were generalists. Indeed, the use of specialization to achieve economies of scale is one reason modern societies are as prosperous as they are.

Conclusion

The purpose of this chapter has been to develop some tools to study how firms make production and pricing decisions. You should now understand what economists mean by the term *costs* and how costs vary with the quantity of output a firm produces. To refresh your memory, Table 3 summarizes some of the definitions we have encountered.

By themselves, a firm's cost curves do not tell us what decisions the firm will make. But they are a key component of that decision, as we will see in the next chapter.

Table **3**

The Many Types of Cost: A Summary

Term	Definition	Mathematical Description
Explicit costs	Costs that require an outlay of money by the firm	
Implicit costs	Costs that do not require an outlay of money by the firm	
Fixed costs	Costs that do not vary with the quantity of output produced	FC
Variable costs	Costs that vary with the quantity of output produced	VC
Total cost	The market value of all the inputs that a firm uses in production	$TC = FC + VC$
Average fixed cost	Fixed cost divided by the quantity of output	$AFC = FC/Q$
Average variable cost	Variable cost divided by the quantity of output	$AVC = VC/Q$
Average total cost	Total cost divided by the quantity of output	$ATC = TC/Q$
Marginal cost	The increase in total cost that arises from an extra unit of production	$MC = \Delta TC/\Delta Q$

SUMMARY

- The goal of firms is to maximize profit, which equals total revenue minus total cost.

- When analyzing a firm's behavior, it is important to include all the opportunity costs of production. Some of the opportunity costs, such as the wages a firm pays its workers, are explicit. Other opportunity costs, such as the wages the firm owner gives up by working in the firm rather than taking another job, are implicit.

Economic profit takes both explicit and implicit costs into account, whereas accounting profits considers only explicit costs.

- A firm's costs reflect its production process. A typical firm's production function gets flatter as the quantity of an input increases, displaying the property of diminishing marginal product. As a result, a firm's total-cost curve gets steeper as the quantity produced rises.

- A firm's total costs can be divided between fixed costs and variable costs. Fixed costs are costs that do not change when the firm alters the quantity of output produced. Variable costs are costs that change when the firm alters the quantity of output produced.

- From a firm's total cost, two related measures of cost are derived. Average total cost is total cost divided by the quantity of output. Marginal cost is the amount by which total cost rises if output increases by 1 unit.

- When analyzing firm behavior, it is often useful to graph average total cost and marginal cost. For a typical firm, marginal cost rises with the quantity of output. Average total cost first falls as output increases and then rises as output increases further. The marginal-cost curve always crosses the average-total-cost curve at the minimum of average total cost.

- A firm's costs often depend on the time horizon considered. In particular, many costs are fixed in the short run but variable in the long run. As a result, when the firm changes its level of production, average total cost may rise more in the short run than in the long run.

KEY CONCEPTS

total revenue, *p. 260*
total cost, *p. 260*
profit, *p. 260*
explicit costs, *p. 261*
implicit costs, *p. 261*
economic profit, *p. 262*
accounting profit, *p. 262*

production function, *p. 263*
marginal product, *p. 264*
diminishing marginal
   product, *p. 265*
fixed costs, *p. 266*
variable costs, *p. 266*
average total cost, *p. 267*

average fixed cost, *p. 268*
average variable cost, *p. 268*
marginal cost, *p. 268*
efficient scale, *p. 270*
economies of scale, *p. 272*
diseconomies of scale, *p. 272*
constant returns to scale, *p. 273*

QUESTIONS FOR REVIEW

1. What is the relationship between a firm's total revenue, profit, and total cost?
2. Give an example of an opportunity cost that an accountant might not count as a cost. Why would the accountant ignore this cost?
3. What is marginal product, and what does it mean if it is diminishing?
4. Draw a production function that exhibits diminishing marginal product of labor. Draw the associated total-cost curve. (In both cases, be sure to label the axes.) Explain the shapes of the two curves you have drawn.

5. Define *total cost*, *average total cost*, and *marginal cost*. How are they related?
6. Draw the marginal-cost and average-total-cost curves for a typical firm. Explain why the curves have the shapes that they do and why they cross where they do.
7. How and why does a firm's average-total-cost curve differ in the short run and in the long run?
8. Define *economies of scale* and explain why they might arise. Define *diseconomies of scale* and explain why they might arise.

PROBLEMS AND APPLICATIONS

1. This chapter discusses many types of costs: opportunity cost, total cost, fixed cost, variable cost, average total cost, and marginal cost. Fill in the type of cost that best completes each sentence:
   a. What you give up for taking some action is called the _____.
   b. _____ is falling when marginal cost is below it and rising when marginal cost is above it.
   c. A cost that does not depend on the quantity produced is a(n) _____.
   d. In the ice-cream industry in the short run, _____ includes the cost of cream and sugar but not the cost of the factory.
   e. Profits equal total revenue less _____.
   f. The cost of producing an extra unit of output is the _____.

2. Your aunt is thinking about opening a hardware store. She estimates that it would cost $500,000 per year to rent the location and buy the stock. In addition, she would have to quit her $50,000 per year job as an accountant.
   a. Define *opportunity cost*.
   b. What is your aunt's opportunity cost of running a hardware store for a year? If your aunt thought she could sell $510,000 worth of merchandise in a year, should she open the store? Explain.

3. A commercial fisherman notices the following relationship between hours spent fishing and the quantity of fish caught:

Hours	Quantity of Fish (in pounds)
0 hours	0 lb.
1	10
2	18
3	24
4	28
5	30

   a. What is the marginal product of each hour spent fishing?
   b. Use these data to graph the fisherman's production function. Explain its shape.
   c. The fisherman has a fixed cost of $10 (his pole). The opportunity cost of his time is $5 per hour. Graph the fisherman's total-cost curve. Explain its shape.

4. Nimbus, Inc., makes brooms and then sells them door-to-door. Here is the relationship between the number of workers and Nimbus's output in a given day:

Workers	Output	Marginal Product	Total Cost	Average Total Cost	Marginal Cost
0	0		—	—	
		—			—
1	20		—	—	
		—			—
2	50		—	—	
		—			—
3	90		—	—	
		—			—
4	120		—	—	
		—			—
5	140		—	—	
		—			—
6	150		—	—	
		—			—
7	155		—	—	

   a. Fill in the column of marginal products. What pattern do you see? How might you explain it?
   b. A worker costs $100 a day, and the firm has fixed costs of $200. Use this information to fill in the column for total cost.
   c. Fill in the column for average total cost. (Recall that $ATC = TC/Q$.) What pattern do you see?
   d. Now fill in the column for marginal cost. (Recall that $MC = \Delta TC/\Delta Q$.) What pattern do you see?
   e. Compare the column for marginal product and the column for marginal cost. Explain the relationship.
   f. Compare the column for average total cost and the column for marginal cost. Explain the relationship.

5. You are the chief financial officer for a firm that sells digital music players. Your firm has the following average-total-cost schedule:

Quantity	Average Total Cost
600 players	$300
601	301

   Your current level of production is 600 devices, all of which have been sold. Someone calls, desperate to buy one of your music players. The caller offers you $550 for it. Should you accept the offer? Why or why not?

6. Consider the following cost information for a pizzeria:

Quantity	Total Cost	Variable Cost
0 dozen pizzas	$300	$ 0
1	350	50
2	390	90
3	420	120
4	450	150
5	490	190
6	540	240

   a. What is the pizzeria's fixed cost?
   b. Construct a table in which you calculate the marginal cost per dozen pizzas using the information on total cost. Also, calculate the marginal cost per dozen pizzas using the information on variable cost. What is the relationship between these sets of numbers? Comment.

7. You are thinking about setting up a lemonade stand. The stand itself costs $200. The ingredients for each cup of lemonade cost $0.50.
   a. What is your fixed cost of doing business? What is your variable cost per cup?
   b. Construct a table showing your total cost, average total cost, and marginal cost for output levels varying from 0 to 10 gallons. (Hint: There are 16 cups in a gallon.) Draw the three cost curves.

8. Your cousin Vinnie owns a painting company with fixed costs of $200 and the following schedule for variable costs:

Quantity of Houses Painted per Month	1	2	3	4	5	6	7
Variable Costs	$10	$20	$40	$80	$160	$320	$640

   Calculate average fixed cost, average variable cost, and average total cost for each quantity. What is the efficient scale of the painting company?

9. A firm uses two inputs in production: capital and labor. In the short run, the firm cannot adjust the amount of capital it is using, but it can adjust the size of its workforce. What happens to the firm's average total cost curve, the average variable cost curve, and the marginal cost curve when
   a. the cost of renting capital increases?
   b. the cost of hiring labor increases?

10. The city government is considering two tax proposals:

   - A lump-sum tax of $300 on each producer of hamburgers.
   - A tax of $1 per burger, paid by producers of hamburgers.

   a. Which of the following curves—average fixed cost, average variable cost, average total cost, and marginal cost—would shift as a result of the lump-sum tax? Why? Show this in a graph. Label the graph as precisely as possible.
   b. Which of these same four curves would shift as a result of the per-burger tax? Why? Show this in a new graph. Label the graph as precisely as possible.

11. Jane's Juice Bar has the following cost schedules:

Quantity	Variable Cost	Total Cost
0 vats of juice	$ 0	$ 30
1	10	40
2	25	55
3	45	75
4	70	100
5	100	130
6	135	165

   a. Calculate average variable cost, average total cost, and marginal cost for each quantity.
   b. Graph all three curves. What is the relationship between the marginal-cost curve and the average-total-cost curve? Between the marginal-cost curve and the average-variable-cost curve? Explain.

12. Consider the following table of long-run total costs for three different firms:

Quantity	1	2	3	4	5	6	7
Firm A	$60	$70	$80	$90	$100	$110	$120
Firm B	11	24	39	56	75	96	119
Firm C	21	34	49	66	85	106	129

   Does each of these firms experience economies of scale or diseconomies of scale?

For further information on topics in this chapter, additional problems, applications, examples, online quizzes, and more, please visit our website at www .cengage.com/economics/mankiw.

Firms in Competitive Markets

If your local gas station raised its price for gasoline by 20 percent, it would see a large drop in the amount of gasoline it sold. Its customers would quickly switch to buying their gasoline at other gas stations. By contrast, if your local water company raised the price of water by 20 percent, it would see only a small decrease in the amount of water it sold. People might water their lawns less often and buy more water-efficient showerheads, but they would be hard-pressed to reduce water consumption greatly and would be unlikely to find another supplier. The difference between the gasoline market and the water market is obvious: Many firms supply gasoline to the local market, but only one firm supplies water. As you might expect, this difference in market structure shapes the pricing and production decisions of the firms that operate in these markets.

In this chapter, we examine the behavior of competitive firms, such as your local gas station. You may recall that a market is competitive if each buyer and seller is small compared to the size of the market and, therefore, has little ability

279

to influence market prices. By contrast, if a firm can influence the market price of the good it sells, it is said to have *market power*. Later in the book, we examine the behavior of firms with market power, such as your local water company.

Our analysis of competitive firms in this chapter sheds light on the decisions that lie behind the supply curve in a competitive market. Not surprisingly, we will find that a market supply curve is tightly linked to firms' costs of production. Less obvious, however, is the question of which among a firm's many types of cost—fixed, variable, average, and marginal—are most relevant for its supply decisions. We will see that all these measures of cost play important and interrelated roles.

What Is a Competitive Market?

Our goal in this chapter is to examine how firms make production decisions in competitive markets. As a background for this analysis, we begin by reviewing what a competitive market is.

The Meaning of Competition

competitive market
a market with many buyers and sellers trading identical products so that each buyer and seller is a price taker

A **competitive market**, sometimes called a *perfectly competitive market*, has two characteristics:

* There are many buyers and many sellers in the market.
* The goods offered by the various sellers are largely the same.

As a result of these conditions, the actions of any single buyer or seller in the market have a negligible impact on the market price. Each buyer and seller takes the market price as given.

As an example, consider the market for milk. No single consumer of milk can influence the price of milk because each buyer purchases a small amount relative to the size of the market. Similarly, each dairy farmer has limited control over the price because many other sellers are offering milk that is essentially identical. Because each seller can sell all he wants at the going price, he has little reason to charge less, and if he charges more, buyers will go elsewhere. Buyers and sellers in competitive markets must accept the price the market determines and, therefore, are said to be *price takers*.

In addition to the foregoing two conditions for competition, there is a third condition sometimes thought to characterize perfectly competitive markets:

* Firms can freely enter or exit the market.

If, for instance, anyone can decide to start a dairy farm, and if any existing dairy farmer can decide to leave the dairy business, then the dairy industry would satisfy this condition. Much of the analysis of competitive firms does not need the assumption of free entry and exit because this condition is not necessary for firms to be price takers. Yet, as we will see later in this chapter, if there is free entry and exit in a competitive market, it is a powerful force shaping the long-run equilibrium.

The Revenue of a Competitive Firm

A firm in a competitive market, like most other firms in the economy, tries to maximize profit (total revenue minus total cost). To see how it does this, we first consider the revenue of a competitive firm. To keep matters concrete, let's consider a specific firm: the Vaca Family Dairy Farm.

The Vaca Farm produces a quantity of milk, Q, and sells each unit at the market price, P. The farm's total revenue is $P \times Q$. For example, if a gallon of milk sells for $6 and the farm sells 1,000 gallons, its total revenue is $6,000.

Because the Vaca Farm is small compared to the world market for milk, it takes the price as given by market conditions. This means, in particular, that the price of milk does not depend on the number of gallons that the Vaca Farm produces and sells. If the Vacas double the amount of milk they produce to 2,000 gallons, the price of milk remains the same, and their total revenue doubles to $12,000. As a result, total revenue is proportional to the amount of output.

Table 1 shows the revenue for the Vaca Family Dairy Farm. The first two columns show the amount of output the farm produces and the price at which it sells its output. The third column is the farm's total revenue. The table assumes that the price of milk is $6 a gallon, so total revenue is $6 times the number of gallons.

Just as the concepts of average and marginal were useful in the preceding chapter when analyzing costs, they are also useful when analyzing revenue. To see what these concepts tell us, consider these two questions:

- How much revenue does the farm receive for the typical gallon of milk?
- How much additional revenue does the farm receive if it increases production of milk by 1 gallon?

The last two columns in Table 1 answer these questions.

The fourth column in the table shows **average revenue**, which is total revenue (from the third column) divided by the amount of output (from the first column). Average revenue tells us how much revenue a firm receives for the typical unit sold. In Table 1, you can see that average revenue equals $6, the price of a gallon of milk. This illustrates a general lesson that applies not only to competitive firms but to other firms as well. Average revenue is total revenue ($P \times Q$) divided by the quantity (Q). Therefore, *for all firms, average revenue equals the price of the good.*

average revenue
total revenue divided by the quantity sold

Quantity (Q)	Price (P)	Total Revenue $(TR = P \times Q)$	Average Revenue $(AR = TR/Q)$	Marginal Revenue $(MR = \Delta TR/\Delta Q)$
1 gallon	$6	$ 6	$6	
				$6
2	6	12	6	
				6
3	6	18	6	
				6
4	6	24	6	
				6
5	6	30	6	
				6
6	6	36	6	
				6
7	6	42	6	
				6
8	6	48	6	

Table **1**

Total, Average, and Marginal Revenue for a Competitive Firm

marginal revenue

the change in total revenue from an additional unit sold

The fifth column shows **marginal revenue**, which is the change in total revenue from the sale of each additional unit of output. In Table 1, marginal revenue equals $6, the price of a gallon of milk. This result illustrates a lesson that applies only to competitive firms. Total revenue is $P \times Q$, and P is fixed for a competitive firm. Therefore, when Q rises by 1 unit, total revenue rises by P dollars. *For competitive firms, marginal revenue equals the price of the good.*

QUICK QUIZ   *When a competitive firm doubles the amount it sells, what happens to the price of its output and its total revenue?*

Profit Maximization and the Competitive Firm's Supply Curve

The goal of a competitive firm is to maximize profit, which equals total revenue minus total cost. We have just discussed the firm's revenue, and in the preceding chapter, we discussed the firm's costs. We are now ready to examine how a competitive firm maximizes profit and how that decision determines its supply curve.

A Simple Example of Profit Maximization

Let's begin our analysis of the firm's supply decision with the example in Table 2. In the first column of the table is the number of gallons of milk the Vaca Family Dairy Farm produces. The second column shows the farm's total revenue, which is $6 times the number of gallons. The third column shows the farm's total cost. Total cost includes fixed costs, which are $3 in this example, and variable costs, which depend on the quantity produced.

The fourth column shows the farm's profit, which is computed by subtracting total cost from total revenue. If the farm produces nothing, it has a loss of $3 (its fixed cost). If it produces 1 gallon, it has a profit of $1. If it produces 2 gallons, it has a profit of $4 and so on. Because the Vaca family's goal is to maximize profit, it chooses to produce the quantity of milk that makes profit as large as possible. In this example, profit is maximized when the farm produces either 4 or 5 gallons of milk, for a profit of $7.

There is another way to look at the Vaca Farm's decision: The Vacas can find the profit-maximizing quantity by comparing the marginal revenue and marginal cost from each unit produced. The fifth and sixth columns in Table 2 compute marginal revenue and marginal cost from the changes in total revenue and total cost, and the last column shows the change in profit for each additional gallon produced. The first gallon of milk the farm produces has a marginal revenue of $6 and a marginal cost of $2; hence, producing that gallon increases profit by $4 (from -$3 to $1). The second gallon produced has a marginal revenue of $6 and a marginal cost of $3, so that gallon increases profit by $3 (from $1 to $4). As long as marginal revenue exceeds marginal cost, increasing the quantity produced raises profit. Once the Vaca Farm has reached 5 gallons of milk, however, the situation changes. The sixth gallon would have a marginal revenue of $6 and a marginal cost of $7, so producing it would reduce profit by $1 (from $7 to $6). As a result, the Vacas would not produce beyond 5 gallons.

One of the *Ten Principles of Economics* in Chapter 1 is that rational people think at the margin. We now see how the Vaca Family Dairy Farm can apply this principle. If marginal revenue is greater than marginal cost—as it is at 1, 2, or 3 gallons—the Vacas should increase the production of milk because it will put more money in their pockets (marginal revenue) than it takes out (marginal cost).

Table 2

Profit Maximization: A Numerical Example

Quantity (Q)	Total Revenue (TR)	Total Cost (TC)	Profit (TR − TC)	Marginal Revenue (MR = ΔTR/ΔQ)	Marginal Cost (MC = ΔTC/ΔQ)	Change in Profit (MR − MC)
0 gallons	$ 0	$ 3	−$3			
				$6	$2	$4
1	6	5	1			
				6	3	3
2	12	8	4			
				6	4	2
3	18	12	6			
				6	5	1
4	24	17	7			
				6	6	0
5	30	23	7			
				6	7	−1
6	36	30	6			
				6	8	−2
7	42	38	4			
				6	9	−3
8	48	47	1			

If marginal revenue is less than marginal cost—as it is at 6, 7, or 8 gallons—the Vacas should decrease production. If the Vacas think at the margin and make incremental adjustments to the level of production, they are naturally led to produce the profit-maximizing quantity.

The Marginal-Cost Curve and the Firm's Supply Decision

To extend this analysis of profit maximization, consider the cost curves in Figure 1. These cost curves have the three features that, as we discussed in the previous chapter, are thought to describe most firms: The marginal-cost curve (MC) is upward sloping. The average-total-cost curve (ATC) is U-shaped. And the marginal-cost curve crosses the average-total-cost curve at the minimum of average total cost. The figure also shows a horizontal line at the market price (P). The price line is horizontal because the firm is a price taker: The price of the firm's output is the same regardless of the quantity that the firm decides to produce. Keep in mind that, for a competitive firm, the firm's price equals both its average revenue (AR) and its marginal revenue (MR).

We can use Figure 1 to find the quantity of output that maximizes profit. Imagine that the firm is producing at Q_1. At this level of output, marginal revenue is greater than marginal cost. That is, if the firm raised its level of production and sales by 1 unit, the additional revenue (MR_1) would exceed the additional cost (MC_1). Profit, which equals total revenue minus total cost, would increase. Hence, if marginal revenue is greater than marginal cost, as it is at Q_1, the firm can increase profit by increasing production.

Figure 1

Profit Maximization for a Competitive Firm

This figure shows the marginal-cost curve (*MC*), the average-total-cost curve (*ATC*), and the average-variable-cost curve (*AVC*). It also shows the market price (*P*), which equals marginal revenue (*MR*) and average revenue (*AR*). At the quantity Q_1, marginal revenue MR_1 exceeds marginal cost MC_1, so raising production increases profit. At the quantity Q_2, marginal cost MC_2 is above marginal revenue MR_2, so reducing production increases profit. The profit-maximizing quantity Q_{MAX} is found where the horizontal price line intersects the marginal-cost curve.

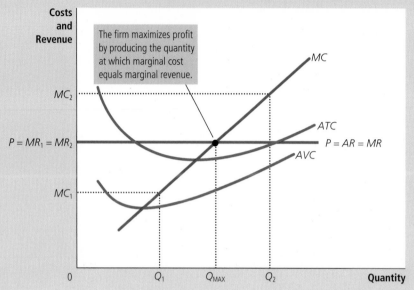

A similar argument applies when output is at Q_2. In this case, marginal cost is greater than marginal revenue. If the firm reduced production by 1 unit, the costs saved (MC_2) would exceed the revenue lost (MR_2). Therefore, if marginal revenue is less than marginal cost, as it is at Q_2, the firm can increase profit by reducing production.

Where do these marginal adjustments to production end? Regardless of whether the firm begins with production at a low level (such as Q_1) or at a high level (such as Q_2), the firm will eventually adjust production until the quantity produced reaches Q_{MAX}. This analysis yields three general rules for profit maximization:

- If marginal revenue is greater than marginal cost, the firm should increase its output.
- If marginal cost is greater than marginal revenue, the firm should decrease its output.
- At the profit-maximizing level of output, marginal revenue and marginal cost are exactly equal.

These rules are the key to rational decision making by a profit-maximizing firm. They apply not only to competitive firms but, as we will see in the next chapter, to other types of firms as well.

We can now see how the competitive firm decides the quantity of its good to supply to the market. Because a competitive firm is a price taker, its marginal revenue equals the market price. For any given price, the competitive firm's profit-maximizing quantity of output is found by looking at the intersection of the price with the marginal-cost curve. In Figure 1, that quantity of output is Q_{MAX}.

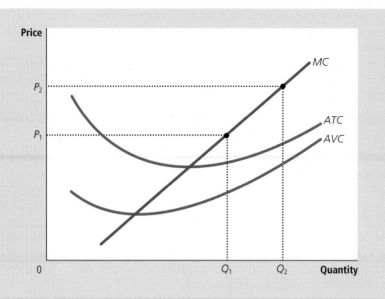

Figure **2**

Marginal Cost as the Competitive Firm's Supply Curve
An increase in the price from P_1 to P_2 leads to an increase in the firm's profit-maximizing quantity from Q_1 to Q_2. Because the marginal-cost curve shows the quantity supplied by the firm at any given price, it is the firm's supply curve.

Suppose that the price prevailing in this market rises, perhaps because of an increase in market demand. Figure 2 shows how a competitive firm responds to the price increase. When the price is P_1, the firm produces quantity Q_1, the quantity that equates marginal cost to the price. When the price rises to P_2, the firm finds that marginal revenue is now higher than marginal cost at the previous level of output, so the firm increases production. The new profit-maximizing quantity is Q_2, at which marginal cost equals the new higher price. *In essence, because the firm's marginal-cost curve determines the quantity of the good the firm is willing to supply at any price, the marginal-cost curve is also the competitive firm's supply curve.* There are, however, some caveats to that conclusion, which we examine next.

The Firm's Short-Run Decision to Shut Down

So far, we have been analyzing the question of how much a competitive firm will produce. In certain circumstances, however, the firm will decide to shut down and not produce anything at all.

Here we need to distinguish between a temporary shutdown of a firm and the permanent exit of a firm from the market. A *shutdown* refers to a short-run decision not to produce anything during a specific period of time because of current market conditions. *Exit* refers to a long-run decision to leave the market. The short-run and long-run decisions differ because most firms cannot avoid their fixed costs in the short run but can do so in the long run. That is, a firm that shuts down temporarily still has to pay its fixed costs, whereas a firm that exits the market does not have to pay any costs at all, fixed or variable.

For example, consider the production decision that a farmer faces. The cost of the land is one of the farmer's fixed costs. If the farmer decides not to produce any crops one season, the land lies fallow, and he cannot recover this cost. When making the short-run decision whether to shut down for a season, the fixed cost of land is said to be a *sunk cost*. By contrast, if the farmer decides to leave farming altogether, he can sell the land. When making the long-run decision whether to exit the market, the cost of land is not sunk. (We return to the issue of sunk costs shortly.)

Now let's consider what determines a firm's shutdown decision. If the firm shuts down, it loses all revenue from the sale of its product. At the same time, it saves the variable costs of making its product (but must still pay the fixed costs). Thus, *the firm shuts down if the revenue that it would earn from producing is less than its variable costs of production.*

A bit of mathematics can make this shutdown criterion more useful. If *TR* stands for total revenue and *VC* stands for variable costs, then the firm's decision can be written as

$$\text{Shut down if } TR < VC.$$

The firm shuts down if total revenue is less than variable cost. By dividing both sides of this inequality by the quantity *Q*, we can write it as

$$\text{Shut down if } TR/Q < VC/Q.$$

The left side of the inequality, *TR/Q*, is total revenue *P × Q* divided by quantity *Q*, which is average revenue, most simply expressed as the good's price, *P*. The right side of the inequality, *VC/Q*, is average variable cost, *AVC*. Therefore, the firm's shutdown criterion can be restated as

$$\text{Shut down if } P < AVC.$$

That is, a firm chooses to shut down if the price of the good is less than the average variable cost of production. This criterion is intuitive: When choosing to produce, the firm compares the price it receives for the typical unit to the average variable cost that it must incur to produce the typical unit. If the price doesn't cover the average variable cost, the firm is better off stopping production altogether. The firm still loses money (because it has to pay fixed costs), but it would lose even more money by staying open. The firm can reopen in the future if conditions change so that price exceeds average variable cost.

We now have a full description of a competitive firm's profit-maximizing strategy. If the firm produces anything, it produces the quantity at which marginal cost equals the price of the good. Yet if the price is less than average variable cost at that quantity, the firm is better off shutting down and not producing anything. These results are illustrated in Figure 3. *The competitive firm's short-run supply curve is the portion of its marginal-cost curve that lies above average variable cost.*

Spilt Milk and Other Sunk Costs

sunk cost

a cost that has already been committed and cannot be recovered

Sometime in your life you may have been told, "Don't cry over spilt milk," or "Let bygones be bygones." These adages hold a deep truth about rational decision making. Economists say that a cost is a **sunk cost** when it has already been committed and cannot be recovered. Because nothing can be done about sunk costs, you can ignore them when making decisions about various aspects of life, including business strategy.

Our analysis of the firm's shutdown decision is one example of the irrelevance of sunk costs. We assume that the firm cannot recover its fixed costs by temporarily stopping production. That is, regardless of the quantity of output supplied (even if it is zero), the firm still has to pay its fixed costs. As a result, the fixed costs are sunk in the short run, and the firm can ignore them when deciding how much to produce. The firm's short-run supply curve is the part of the marginal-cost curve that lies above average variable cost, and the size of the fixed cost does not matter for this supply decision.

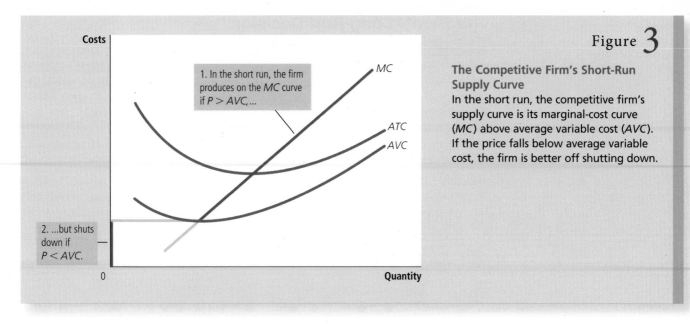

Costs

1. In the short run, the firm produces on the *MC* curve if *P* > *AVC*,...

MC

ATC

AVC

2. ...but shuts down if *P* < *AVC*.

0

Quantity

Figure **3**

The Competitive Firm's Short-Run Supply Curve
In the short run, the competitive firm's supply curve is its marginal-cost curve (*MC*) above average variable cost (*AVC*). If the price falls below average variable cost, the firm is better off shutting down.

The irrelevance of sunk costs is also important when making personal decisions. Imagine, for instance, that you place a $15 value on seeing a newly released movie. You buy a ticket for $10, but before entering the theater, you lose the ticket. Should you buy another ticket? Or should you now go home and refuse to pay a total of $20 to see the movie? The answer is that you should buy another ticket. The benefit of seeing the movie ($15) still exceeds the opportunity cost (the $10 for the second ticket). The $10 you paid for the lost ticket is a sunk cost. As with spilt milk, there is no point in crying about it.

 Near-Empty Restaurants and Off-Season Miniature Golf

Have you ever walked into a restaurant for lunch and found it almost empty? Why, you might have asked, does the restaurant even bother to stay open? It might seem that the revenue from so few customers could not possibly cover the cost of running the restaurant.

In making the decision whether to open for lunch, a restaurant owner must keep in mind the distinction between fixed and variable costs. Many of a restaurant's costs—the rent, kitchen equipment, tables, plates, silverware, and so on—are fixed. Shutting down during lunch would not reduce these costs. In other words, these costs are sunk in the short run. When the owner is deciding whether to serve lunch, only the variable costs—the price of the additional food and the wages of the extra staff—are relevant. The owner shuts down the restaurant at lunchtime only if the revenue from the few lunchtime customers fails to cover the restaurant's variable costs.

An operator of a miniature-golf course in a summer resort community faces a similar decision. Because revenue varies substantially from season to season, the firm must decide when to open and when to close. Once again, the fixed costs—the costs of buying the land and building the course—are irrelevant in making this decision. The miniature-golf course should be open for business only during those times of year when its revenue exceeds its variable costs. ∎

Staying open can be profitable, even with many tables empty.

The Firm's Long-Run Decision to Exit or Enter a Market

A firm's long-run decision to exit a market is similar to its shutdown decision. If the firm exits, it will again lose all revenue from the sale of its product, but now it will save not only its variable costs of production but also its fixed costs. Thus, *the firm exits the market if the revenue it would get from producing is less than its total costs.*

We can again make this criterion more useful by writing it mathematically. If *TR* stands for total revenue, and *TC* stands for total cost, then the firm's exit criterion can be written as

$$\text{Exit if } TR < TC.$$

The firm exits if total revenue is less than total cost. By dividing both sides of this inequality by quantity *Q*, we can write it as

$$\text{Exit if } TR/Q < TC/Q.$$

We can simplify this further by noting that *TR/Q* is average revenue, which equals the price *P*, and that *TC/Q* is average total cost, *ATC*. Therefore, the firm's exit criterion is

$$\text{Exit if } P < ATC.$$

That is, a firm chooses to exit if the price of its good is less than the average total cost of production.

A parallel analysis applies to an entrepreneur who is considering starting a firm. The firm will enter the market if such an action would be profitable, which occurs if the price of the good exceeds the average total cost of production. The entry criterion is

$$\text{Enter if } P > ATC.$$

The criterion for entry is exactly the opposite of the criterion for exit.

We can now describe a competitive firm's long-run profit-maximizing strategy. If the firm is in the market, it produces the quantity at which marginal cost equals the price of the good. Yet if the price is less than the average total cost at that quantity, the firm chooses to exit (or not enter) the market. These results are illustrated in Figure 4. *The competitive firm's long-run supply curve is the portion of its marginal-cost curve that lies above average total cost.*

Measuring Profit in Our Graph for the Competitive Firm

As we study exit and entry, it is useful to analyze the firm's profit in more detail. Recall that profit equals total revenue (*TR*) minus total cost (*TC*):

$$\text{Profit} = TR - TC.$$

We can rewrite this definition by multiplying and dividing the right side by *Q*:

$$\text{Profit} = (TR/Q - TC/Q) \times Q.$$

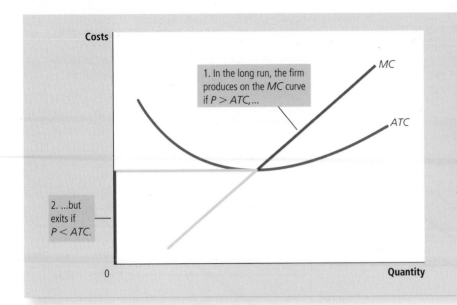

Costs

1. In the long run, the firm produces on the *MC* curve if *P* > *ATC*,...

MC

ATC

2. ...but exits if *P* < *ATC*.

0

Quantity

Figure **4**

The Competitive Firm's Long-Run Supply Curve
In the long run, the competitive firm's supply curve is its marginal-cost curve (*MC*) above average total cost (*ATC*). If the price falls below average total cost, the firm is better off exiting the market.

But note that TR/Q is average revenue, which is the price, P, and TC/Q is average total cost, ATC. Therefore,

$$\text{Profit} = (P - ATC) \times Q.$$

This way of expressing the firm's profit allows us to measure profit in our graphs.

Panel (a) of Figure 5 shows a firm earning positive profit. As we have already discussed, the firm maximizes profit by producing the quantity at which price equals marginal cost. Now look at the shaded rectangle. The height of the rectangle is $P - ATC$, the difference between price and average total cost. The width of the rectangle is Q, the quantity produced. Therefore, the area of the rectangle is $(P - ATC) \times Q$, which is the firm's profit.

Similarly, panel (b) of this figure shows a firm with losses (negative profit). In this case, maximizing profit means minimizing losses, a task accomplished once again by producing the quantity at which price equals marginal cost. Now consider the shaded rectangle. The height of the rectangle is $ATC - P$, and the width is Q. The area is $(ATC - P) \times Q$, which is the firm's loss. Because a firm in this situation is not making enough revenue to cover its average total cost, the firm would choose in the long run to exit the market.

QUICK QUIZ *How does a competitive firm determine its profit-maximizing level of output? Explain • When does a profit-maximizing competitive firm decide to shut down? When does it decide to exit a market?*

The Supply Curve in a Competitive Market

Now that we have examined the supply decision of a single firm, we can discuss the supply curve for a market. There are two cases to consider. First, we examine a market with a fixed number of firms. Second, we examine a market in which the number of firms can change as old firms exit the market and new firms enter.

Figure 5

Profit as the Area between Price and Average Total Cost

The area of the shaded box between price and average total cost represents the firm's profit. The height of this box is price minus average total cost (P – ATC), and the width of the box is the quantity of output (Q). In panel (a), price is above average total cost, so the firm has positive profit. In panel (b), price is less than average total cost, so the firm has losses.

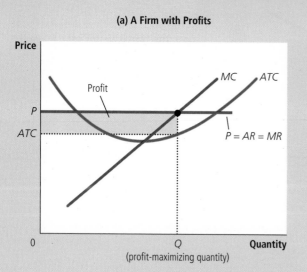

(a) A Firm with Profits

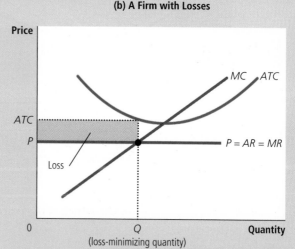

(b) A Firm with Losses

Both cases are important, for each applies over a specific time horizon. Over short periods of time, it is often difficult for firms to enter and exit, so the assumption of a fixed number of firms is appropriate. But over long periods of time, the number of firms can adjust to changing market conditions.

The Short Run: Market Supply with a Fixed Number of Firms

Consider first a market with 1,000 identical firms. For any given price, each firm supplies a quantity of output so that its marginal cost equals the price, as shown in panel (a) of Figure 6. That is, as long as price is above average variable cost, each firm's marginal-cost curve is its supply curve. The quantity of output supplied to the market equals the sum of the quantities supplied by each of the 1,000 individual firms. Thus, to derive the market supply curve, we add the quantity supplied by each firm in the market. As panel (b) of Figure 6 shows, because the firms are identical, the quantity supplied to the market is 1,000 times the quantity supplied by each firm.

The Long Run: Market Supply with Entry and Exit

Now consider what happens if firms are able to enter or exit the market. Let's suppose that everyone has access to the same technology for producing the good and access to the same markets to buy the inputs into production. Therefore, all current and potential firms have the same cost curves.

Decisions about entry and exit in a market of this type depend on the incentives facing the owners of existing firms and the entrepreneurs who could start new firms. If firms already in the market are profitable, then new firms will have an incentive to enter the market. This entry will expand the number of firms, increase

In the short run, the number of firms in the market is fixed. As a result, the market supply curve, shown in panel (b), reflects the individual firms' marginal-cost curves, shown in panel (a). Here, in a market of 1,000 firms, the quantity of output supplied to the market is 1,000 times the quantity supplied by each firm.

Figure 6

Short-Run Market Supply

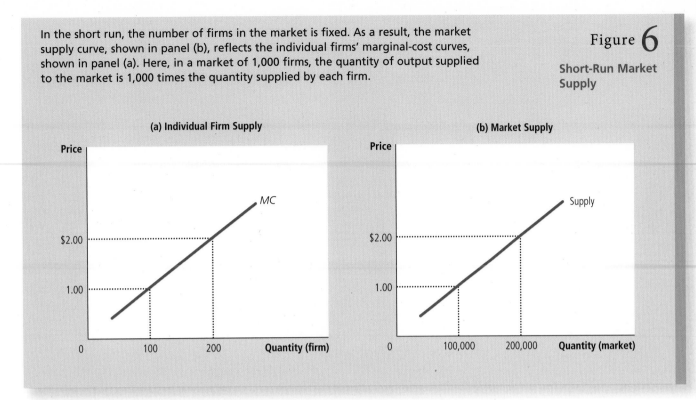

the quantity of the good supplied, and drive down prices and profits. Conversely, if firms in the market are making losses, then some existing firms will exit the market. Their exit will reduce the number of firms, decrease the quantity of the good supplied, and drive up prices and profits. *At the end of this process of entry and exit, firms that remain in the market must be making zero economic profit.*

Recall that we can write a firm's profit as

$$\text{Profit} = (P - ATC) \times Q.$$

This equation shows that an operating firm has zero profit if and only if the price of the good equals the average total cost of producing that good. If price is above average total cost, profit is positive, which encourages new firms to enter. If price is less than average total cost, profit is negative, which encourages some firms to exit. *The process of entry and exit ends only when price and average total cost are driven to equality.*

This analysis has a surprising implication. We noted earlier in the chapter that competitive firms maximize profits by choosing a quantity at which price equals marginal cost. We just noted that free entry and exit force price to equal average total cost. But if price is to equal both marginal cost and average total cost, these two measures of cost must equal each other. Marginal cost and average total cost are equal, however, only when the firm is operating at the minimum of average total cost. Recall from the preceding chapter that the level of production with lowest average total cost is called the firm's *efficient scale*. Therefore, *in the long-run equilibrium of a competitive market with free entry and exit, firms must be operating at their efficient scale.*

Panel (a) of Figure 7 shows a firm in such a long-run equilibrium. In this figure, price *P* equals marginal cost *MC*, so the firm is maximizing profits. Price also equals average total cost *ATC*, so profits are zero. New firms have no incentive to enter the market, and existing firms have no incentive to leave the market.

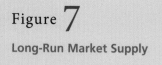

Figure 7

Long-Run Market Supply

In the long run, firms will enter or exit the market until profit is driven to zero. As a result, price equals the minimum of average total cost, as shown in panel (a). The number of firms adjusts to ensure that all demand is satisfied at this price. The long-run market supply curve is horizontal at this price, as shown in panel (b).

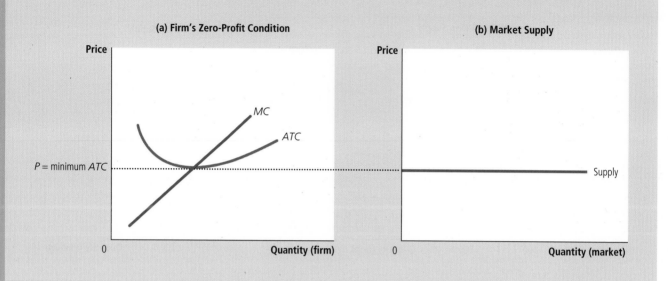

(a) Firm's Zero-Profit Condition

(b) Market Supply

From this analysis of firm behavior, we can determine the long-run supply curve for the market. In a market with free entry and exit, there is only one price consistent with zero profit—the minimum of average total cost. As a result, the long-run market supply curve must be horizontal at this price, as illustrated by the perfectly elastic supply curve in panel (b) of Figure 7. Any price above this level would generate profit, leading to entry and an increase in the total quantity supplied. Any price below this level would generate losses, leading to exit and a decrease in the total quantity supplied. Eventually, the number of firms in the market adjusts so that price equals the minimum of average total cost, and there are enough firms to satisfy all the demand at this price.

Why Do Competitive Firms Stay in Business If They Make Zero Profit?

At first, it might seem odd that competitive firms earn zero profit in the long run. After all, people start businesses to make a profit. If entry eventually drives profit to zero, there might seem to be little reason to stay in business.

To understand the zero-profit condition more fully, recall that profit equals total revenue minus total cost and that total cost includes all the opportunity costs of the firm. In particular, total cost includes the time and money that the firm owners devote to the business. In the zero-profit equilibrium, the firm's revenue must compensate the owners for these opportunity costs.

Consider an example. Suppose that, to start his farm, a farmer had to invest $1 million, which otherwise he could have deposited in a bank and earned $50,000 a year in interest. In addition, he had to give up another job that would have paid him $30,000 a year. Then the farmer's opportunity cost of farming includes both the interest he could have earned and the forgone wages—a total of $80,000. Even if his profit is driven to zero, his revenue from farming compensates him for these opportunity costs.

Keep in mind that accountants and economists measure costs differently. As we discussed in the previous chapter, accountants keep track of explicit costs but not implicit costs. That is, they measure costs that require an outflow of money from the firm, but they do not include the opportunity costs of production that do not involve an outflow of money. As a result, in the zero-profit equilibrium, economic profit is zero, but accounting profit is positive. Our farmer's accountant, for instance, would conclude that the farmer earned an accounting profit of $80,000, which is enough to keep the farmer in business.

"We're a nonprofit organization—we don't intend to be, but we are!"

A Shift in Demand in the Short Run and Long Run

Now that we have a more complete understanding of how firms make supply decisions, we can better explain how markets respond to changes in demand. Because firms can enter and exit in the long run but not in the short run, the response of a market to a change in demand depends on the time horizon. To see this, let's trace the effects of a shift in demand over time.

Suppose the market for milk begins in a long-run equilibrium. Firms are earning zero profit, so price equals the minimum of average total cost. Panel (a) of Figure 8 shows this situation. The long-run equilibrium is point A, the quantity sold in the market is Q_1, and the price is P_1.

Now suppose scientists discover that milk has miraculous health benefits. As a result, the demand curve for milk shifts outward from D_1 to D_2, as in panel (b). The short-run equilibrium moves from point A to point B; as a result, the quantity rises from Q_1 to Q_2, and the price rises from P_1 to P_2. All of the existing firms respond to the higher price by raising the amount produced. Because each firm's supply curve reflects its marginal-cost curve, how much they each increase production is determined by the marginal-cost curve. In the new short-run equilibrium, the price of milk exceeds average total cost, so the firms are making positive profit.

Over time, the profit generated in this market encourages new firms to enter. Some farmers may switch to milk from other farm products, for example. As the number of firms grows, the short-run supply curve shifts to the right from S_1 to S_2, as in panel (c), and this shift causes the price of milk to fall. Eventually, the price is driven back down to the minimum of average total cost, profits are zero, and firms stop entering. Thus, the market reaches a new long-run equilibrium, point C. The price of milk has returned to P_1, but the quantity produced has risen to Q_3. Each firm is again producing at its efficient scale, but because more firms are in the dairy business, the quantity of milk produced and sold is higher.

Why the Long-Run Supply Curve Might Slope Upward

So far, we have seen that entry and exit can cause the long-run market supply curve to be perfectly elastic. The essence of our analysis is that there are a large number of potential entrants, each of which faces the same costs. As a result, the long-run market supply curve is horizontal at the minimum of average total cost. When the demand for the good increases, the long-run result is an increase in the number of firms and in the total quantity supplied, without any change in the price.

There are, however, two reasons that the long-run market supply curve might slope upward. The first is that some resources used in production may be available only in limited quantities. For example, consider the market for farm products.

Figure 8

An Increase in Demand in the Short Run and Long Run

The market starts in a long-run equilibrium, shown as point A in panel (a). In this equilibrium, each firm makes zero profit, and the price equals the minimum average total cost. Panel (b) shows what happens in the short run when demand rises from D_1 to D_2. The equilibrium goes from point A to point B, price rises from P_1 to P_2, and the quantity sold in the market rises from Q_1 to Q_2. Because price now exceeds average total cost, firms make profits, which over time encourage new firms to enter the market. This entry shifts the short-run supply curve to the right from S_1 to S_2, as shown in panel (c). In the new long-run equilibrium, point C, price has returned to P_1 but the quantity sold has increased to Q_3. Profits are again zero, price is back to the minimum of average total cost, but the market has more firms to satisfy the greater demand.

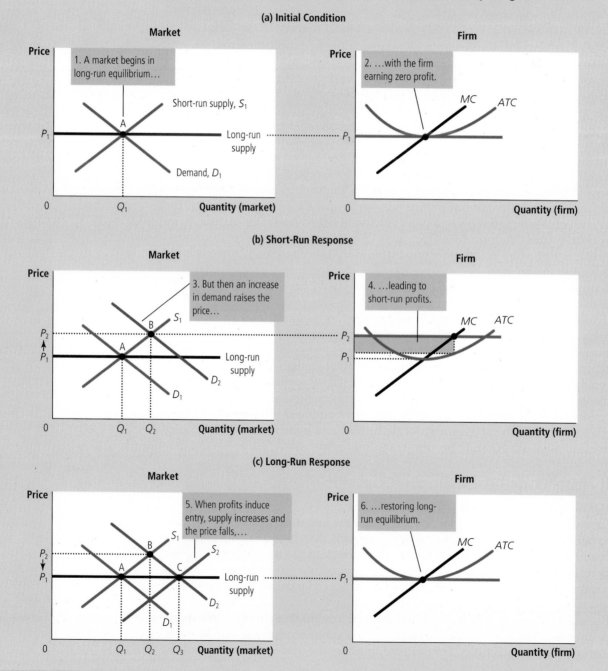

(a) Initial Condition

Market

Price

1. A market begins in long-run equilibrium...

Short-run supply, S_1

A

P_1

Long-run supply

Demand, D_1

0   Q_1 Quantity (market)

Firm

Price

2. ...with the firm earning zero profit.

MC   ATC

P_1

0   Quantity (firm)

(b) Short-Run Response

Market

Price

3. But then an increase in demand raises the price...

S_1

B

P_2

A

P_1

Long-run supply

D_2

D_1

0   Q_1 Q_2 Quantity (market)

Firm

Price

4. ...leading to short-run profits.

MC   ATC

P_2

P_1

0   Quantity (firm)

(c) Long-Run Response

Market

Price

5. When profits induce entry, supply increases and the price falls,...

S_1

B S_2

P_2

A   C

P_1

Long-run supply

D_2

D_1

0   Q_1 Q_2 Q_3 Quantity (market)

Firm

Price

6. ...restoring long-run equilibrium.

MC   ATC

P_1

0   Quantity (firm)

Anyone can choose to buy land and start a farm, but the quantity of land is limited. As more people become farmers, the price of farmland is bid up, which raises the costs of all farmers in the market. Thus, an increase in demand for farm products cannot induce an increase in quantity supplied without also inducing a rise in farmers' costs, which in turn means a rise in price. The result is a long-run market supply curve that is upward sloping, even with free entry into farming.

A second reason for an upward-sloping supply curve is that firms may have different costs. For example, consider the market for painters. Anyone can enter the market for painting services, but not everyone has the same costs. Costs vary in part because some people work faster than others and in part because some people have better alternative uses of their time than others. For any given price, those with lower costs are more likely to enter than those with higher costs. To increase the quantity of painting services supplied, additional entrants must be encouraged to enter the market. Because these new entrants have higher costs, the price must rise to make entry profitable for them. Thus, the long-run market supply curve for painting services slopes upward even with free entry into the market.

Notice that if firms have different costs, some firms earn profit even in the long run. In this case, the price in the market reflects the average total cost of the *marginal firm*—the firm that would exit the market if the price were any lower. This firm earns zero profit, but firms with lower costs earn positive profit. Entry does not eliminate this profit because would-be entrants have higher costs than firms already in the market. Higher-cost firms will enter only if the price rises, making the market profitable for them.

Thus, for these two reasons, a higher price may be necessary to induce a larger quantity supplied, in which case the long-run supply curve is upward sloping rather than horizontal. Nonetheless, the basic lesson about entry and exit remains true. *Because firms can enter and exit more easily in the long run than in the short run, the long-run supply curve is typically more elastic than the short-run supply curve.*

QUICK QUIZ   *In the long run with free entry and exit, is the price in a market equal to marginal cost, average total cost, both, or neither? Explain with a diagram.*

Conclusion: Behind the Supply Curve

We have been discussing the behavior of profit-maximizing firms that supply goods in perfectly competitive markets. You may recall from Chapter 1 that one of the *Ten Principles of Economics* is that rational people think at the margin. This chapter has applied this idea to the competitive firm. Marginal analysis has given us a theory of the supply curve in a competitive market and, as a result, a deeper understanding of market outcomes.

We have learned that when you buy a good from a firm in a competitive market, you can be assured that the price you pay is close to the cost of producing that good. In particular, if firms are competitive and profit maximizing, the price of a good equals the marginal cost of making that good. In addition, if firms can freely enter and exit the market, the price also equals the lowest possible average total cost of production.

Although we have assumed throughout this chapter that firms are price takers, many of the tools developed here are also useful for studying firms in less competitive markets. We now turn to an examination of the behavior of firms with market power. Marginal analysis will again be useful, but it will have quite different implications.

SUMMARY

- Because a competitive firm is a price taker, its revenue is proportional to the amount of output it produces. The price of the good equals both the firm's average revenue and its marginal revenue.

- To maximize profit, a firm chooses a quantity of output such that marginal revenue equals marginal cost. Because marginal revenue for a competitive firm equals the market price, the firm chooses quantity so that price equals marginal cost. Thus, the firm's marginal-cost curve is its supply curve.

- In the short run when a firm cannot recover its fixed costs, the firm will choose to shut down temporarily if the price of the good is less than average variable cost. In the long run when the firm can recover both fixed and variable costs, it will choose to exit if the price is less than average total cost.

- In a market with free entry and exit, profits are driven to zero in the long run. In this long-run equilibrium, all firms produce at the efficient scale, price equals the minimum of average total cost, and the number of firms adjusts to satisfy the quantity demanded at this price.

- Changes in demand have different effects over different time horizons. In the short run, an increase in demand raises prices and leads to profits, and a decrease in demand lowers prices and leads to losses. But if firms can freely enter and exit the market, then in the long run, the number of firms adjusts to drive the market back to the zero-profit equilibrium.

KEY CONCEPTS

competitive market, *p. 280*
average revenue, *p. 281*

marginal revenue, *p. 282*
sunk cost, *p. 286*

QUESTION FOR REVIEW

1. What is meant by a competitive firm?
2. Explain the difference between a firm's revenue and its profit. Which do firms maximize?
3. Draw the cost curves for a typical firm. For a given price, explain how the firm chooses the level of output that maximizes profit. At that level of output, show on your graph the firm's total revenue and total costs.
4. Under what conditions will a firm shut down temporarily? Explain.

5. Under what conditions will a firm exit a market? Explain.
6. Does a firm's price equal marginal cost in the short run, in the long run, or both? Explain.
7. Does a firm's price equal the minimum of average total cost in the short run, in the long run, or both? Explain.
8. Are market supply curves typically more elastic in the short run or in the long run? Explain.

PROBLEMS AND APPLICATIONS

1. Many small boats are made of fiberglass, which is derived from crude oil. Suppose that the price of oil rises.
   a. Using diagrams, show what happens to the cost curves of an individual boat-making firm and to the market supply curve.
   b. What happens to the profits of boat makers in the short run? What happens to the number of boat makers in the long run?
2. You go out to the best restaurant in town and order a lobster dinner for $40. After eating half

of the lobster, you realize that you are quite full. Your date wants you to finish your dinner because you can't take it home and because "you've already paid for it." What should you do? Relate your answer to the material in this chapter.
3. Bob's lawn-mowing service is a profit-maximizing, competitive firm. Bob mows lawns for $27 each. His total cost each day is $280, of which $30 is a fixed cost. He mows 10 lawns a day. What can you say about Bob's short-run decision regarding shutdown and his long-run decision regarding exit?

4. Consider total cost and total revenue given in the following table:

Quantity	0	1	2	3	4	5	6	7
Total cost	$8	9	10	11	13	19	27	37
Total revenue	$0	8	16	24	32	40	48	56

a. Calculate profit for each quantity. How much should the firm produce to maximize profit?

b. Calculate marginal revenue and marginal cost for each quantity. Graph them. (Hint: Put the points between whole numbers. For example, the marginal cost between 2 and 3 should be graphed at 2½.) At what quantity do these curves cross? How does this relate to your answer to part (a)?

c. Can you tell whether this firm is in a competitive industry? If so, can you tell whether the industry is in a long-run equilibrium?

5. Ball Bearings, Inc. faces costs of production as follows:

Quantity	Total Fixed Costs	Total Variable Costs
0	$100	$ 0
1	100	50
2	100	70
3	100	90
4	100	140
5	100	200
6	100	360

a. Calculate the company's average fixed costs, average variable costs, average total costs, and marginal costs at each level of production.

b. The price of a case of ball bearings is $50. Seeing that she can't make a profit, the Chief Executive Officer (CEO) decides to shut down operations. What are the firm's profits/losses? Was this a wise decision? Explain.

c. Vaguely remembering his introductory economics course, the Chief Financial Officer tells the CEO it is better to produce 1 case of ball bearings, because marginal revenue equals marginal cost at that quantity. What are the firm's profits/losses at that level of production? Was this the best decision? Explain.

6. Suppose the book-printing industry is competitive and begins in a long-run equilibrium.

a. Draw a diagram describing the typical firm in the industry.

b. Hi-Tech Printing Company invents a new process that sharply reduces the cost of printing books. What happens to Hi-Tech's profits and the price of books in the short run when Hi-Tech's patent prevents other firms from using the new technology?

c. What happens in the long run when the patent expires and other firms are free to use the technology?

7. A firm in a competitive market receives $500 in total revenue and has marginal revenue of $10. What is the average revenue, and how many units were sold?

8. A profit-maximizing firm in a competitive market is currently producing 100 units of output. It has average revenue of $10, average total cost of $8, and fixed costs of $200.

a. What is its profit?

b. What is its marginal cost?

c. What is its average variable cost?

d. Is the efficient scale of the firm more than, less than, or exactly 100 units?

9. The market for fertilizer is perfectly competitive. Firms in the market are producing output, but are currently making economic losses.

a. How does the price of fertilizer compare to the average total cost, the average variable cost, and the marginal cost of producing fertilizer?

b. Draw two graphs, side by side, illustrating the present situation for the typical firm and in the market.

c. Assuming there is no change in either demand or the firms' cost curves, explain what will happen in the long run to the price of fertilizer, marginal cost, average total cost, the quantity supplied by each firm, and the total quantity supplied to the market.

10. The market for apple pies in the city of Ectenia is competitive and has the following demand schedule:

Price	Quantity Demanded
$ 1	1,200 pies
2	1,100
3	1,000
4	900
5	800
6	700
7	600
8	500
9	400
10	300
11	200
12	100
13	0

Each producer in the market has fixed costs of $9 and the following marginal cost:

Quantity	Marginal Cost
1 pie	$ 2
2	4
3	6
4	8
5	10
6	12

a. Compute each producer's total cost and average total cost for 1 to 6 pies.
b. The price of a pie is now $11. How many pies are sold? How many pies does each producer make? How many producers are there? How much profit does each producer earn?
c. Is the situation described in part (b) a long-run equilibrium? Why or why not?
d. Suppose that in the long run there is free entry and exit. How much profit does each producer earn in the long-run equilibrium? What is the market price and number of pies each producer makes? How many pies are sold? How many pie producers are operating?

11. Suppose that the U.S. textile industry is competitive, and there is no international trade in textiles. In long-run equilibrium, the price per unit of cloth is $30.
a. Describe the equilibrium using graphs for the entire market and for an individual producer.

Now suppose that textile producers in other countries are willing to sell large quantities of cloth in the United States for only $25 per unit.

b. Assuming that U.S. textile producers have large fixed costs, what is the short-run effect of these imports on the quantity produced by an individual producer? What is the short-run effect on profits? Illustrate your answer with a graph.
c. What is the long-run effect on the number of U.S. firms in the industry?

12. An industry currently has 100 firms, all of which have fixed costs of $16 and average variable cost as follows:

Quantity	Average Variable Cost
1	$1
2	2
3	3
4	4
5	5
6	6

a. Compute marginal cost and average total cost.
b. The price is currently $10. What is the total quantity supplied in the market?
c. As this market makes the transition to its long-run equilibrium, will the price rise or fall? Will the quantity demanded rise or fall? Will the quantity supplied by each firm rise or fall?
d. Graph the long-run supply curve for this market.

13. Suppose there are 1,000 hot pretzel stands operating in New York City. Each stand has the usual U-shaped average-total-cost curve. The market demand curve for pretzels slopes downward, and the market for pretzels is in long-run competitive equilibrium.
a. Draw the current equilibrium, using graphs for the entire market and for an individual pretzel stand.
b. The city decides to restrict the number of pretzel-stand licenses, reducing the number of stands to only 800. What effect will this action have on the market and on an individual stand that is still operating? Draw graphs to illustrate your answer.
c. Suppose that the city decides to charge a fee for the 800 licenses, all of which are quickly sold. How will the size of the fee affect the number of pretzels sold by an individual stand? How will it affect the price of pretzels in the city?
d. The city wants to raise as much revenue as possible, while ensuring that all 800 licenses are sold. How high should the city set the license fee? Show the answer on your graph.

For further information on topics in this chapter, additional problems, applications, examples, online quizzes, and more, please visit our website at www .cengage.com/economics/mankiw.

Monopoly

15

I f you own a personal computer, it probably uses some version of Windows, the operating system sold by the Microsoft Corporation. When Microsoft first designed Windows many years ago, it applied for and received a copyright from the government. The copyright gives Microsoft the exclusive right to make and sell copies of the Windows operating system. If a person wants to buy a copy of Windows, he or she has little choice but to give Microsoft the approximately $100 that the firm has decided to charge for its product. Microsoft is said to have a *monopoly* in the market for Windows.

Microsoft's business decisions are not well described by the model of firm behavior we developed in the previous chapter. In that chapter, we analyzed competitive markets, in which there are many firms offering essentially identical products, so each firm has little influence over the price it receives. By contrast, a monopoly such as Microsoft has no close competitors and, therefore, has the power to influence the market price of its product. While a competitive firm is a *price taker*, a monopoly firm is a *price maker*.

In this chapter, we examine the implications of this market power. We will see that market power alters the relationship between a firm's costs and the price at which it sells its product. A competitive firm takes the price of its output as given by the market and then chooses the quantity it will supply so that price equals marginal cost. By contrast, a monopoly charges a price that exceeds marginal cost. This result is clearly true in the case of Microsoft's Windows. The marginal cost of Windows—the extra cost that Microsoft incurs by printing one more copy of the program onto a CD—is only a few dollars. The market price of Windows is many times its marginal cost.

It is not surprising that monopolies charge high prices for their products. Customers of monopolies might seem to have little choice but to pay whatever the monopoly charges. But if so, why does a copy of Windows not cost $1,000? Or $10,000? The reason is that if Microsoft sets the price that high, fewer people would buy the product. People would buy fewer computers, switch to other operating systems, or make illegal copies. A monopoly firm can control the price of the good it sells, but because a high price reduces the quantity that its customers buy, the monopoly's profits are not unlimited.

As we examine the production and pricing decisions of monopolies, we also consider the implications of monopoly for society as a whole. Monopoly firms, like competitive firms, aim to maximize profit. But this goal has very different ramifications for competitive and monopoly firms. In competitive markets, self-interested consumers and producers behave as if they are guided by an invisible hand to promote general economic well-being. By contrast, because monopoly firms are unchecked by competition, the outcome in a market with a monopoly is often not in the best interest of society.

One of the *Ten Principles of Economics* in Chapter 1 is that governments can sometimes improve market outcomes. The analysis in this chapter sheds more light on this principle. As we examine the problems that monopolies raise for society, we discuss the various ways in which government policymakers might respond to these problems. The U.S. government, for example, keeps a close eye on Microsoft's business decisions. In 1994, it blocked Microsoft from buying Intuit, a leading seller of personal finance software, on the grounds that combining the two firms would concentrate too much market power. Similarly, in 1998, the U.S. Department of Justice objected when Microsoft started integrating its Internet browser into its Windows operating system, claiming that this addition would extend the firm's market power into new areas. To this day, Microsoft continues to wrangle with antitrust regulators in the United States and abroad.

Why Monopolies Arise

monopoly
a firm that is the sole seller of a product without close substitutes

A firm is a **monopoly** if it is the sole seller of its product and if its product does not have close substitutes. The fundamental cause of monopoly is *barriers to entry*: A monopoly remains the only seller in its market because other firms cannot enter the market and compete with it. Barriers to entry, in turn, have three main sources:

- *Monopoly resources:* A key resource required for production is owned by a single firm.
- *Government regulation:* The government gives a single firm the exclusive right to produce some good or service.

- *The production process:* A single firm can produce output at a lower cost than can a larger number of producers.

Let's briefly discuss each of these.

Monopoly Resources

The simplest way for a monopoly to arise is for a single firm to own a key resource. For example, consider the market for water in a small town in the Old West. If dozens of town residents have working wells, the competitive model discussed in the preceding chapter describes the behavior of sellers. As a result of the competition among water suppliers, the price of a gallon is driven to equal the marginal cost of pumping an extra gallon. But if there is only one well in town and it is impossible to get water from anywhere else, then the owner of the well has a monopoly on water. Not surprisingly, the monopolist has much greater market power than any single firm in a competitive market. In the case of a necessity like water, the monopolist could command quite a high price, even if the marginal cost of pumping an extra gallon is low.

A classic example of market power arising from the ownership of a key resource is DeBeers, the South African diamond company. Founded in 1888 by Cecil Rhodes, an English businessman (and benefactor for the Rhodes scholarship), DeBeers has at times controlled up to 80 percent of the production from the world's diamond mines. Because its market share is less than 100 percent, DeBeers is not exactly a monopoly, but the company has nonetheless exerted substantial influence over the market price of diamonds.

Although exclusive ownership of a key resource is a potential cause of monopoly, in practice monopolies rarely arise for this reason. Economies are large, and resources are owned by many people. Indeed, because many goods are traded internationally, the natural scope of their markets is often worldwide. There are, therefore, few examples of firms that own a resource for which there are no close substitutes.

"Rather than a monopoly, we like to consider ourselves 'the only game in town.'"

Government-Created Monopolies

In many cases, monopolies arise because the government has given one person or firm the exclusive right to sell some good or service. Sometimes the monopoly arises from the sheer political clout of the would-be monopolist. Kings, for example, once granted exclusive business licenses to their friends and allies. At other times, the government grants a monopoly because doing so is viewed to be in the public interest.

The patent and copyright laws are two important examples. When a pharmaceutical company discovers a new drug, it can apply to the government for a patent. If the government deems the drug to be truly original, it approves the patent, which gives the company the exclusive right to manufacture and sell the drug for twenty years. Similarly, when a novelist finishes a book, she can copyright it. The copyright is a government guarantee that no one can print and sell the work without the author's permission. The copyright makes the novelist a monopolist in the sale of her novel.

The effects of patent and copyright laws are easy to see. Because these laws give one producer a monopoly, they lead to higher prices than would occur under competition. But by allowing these monopoly producers to charge higher prices and earn higher profits, the laws also encourage some desirable behavior.

Drug companies are allowed to be monopolists in the drugs they discover to encourage research. Authors are allowed to be monopolists in the sale of their books to encourage them to write more and better books.

Thus, the laws governing patents and copyrights have benefits and costs. The benefits of the patent and copyright laws are the increased incentives for creative activity. These benefits are offset, to some extent, by the costs of monopoly pricing, which we examine fully later in this chapter.

Natural Monopolies

natural monopoly

a monopoly that arises because a single firm can supply a good or service to an entire market at a smaller cost than could two or more firms

An industry is a **natural monopoly** when a single firm can supply a good or service to an entire market at a lower cost than could two or more firms. A natural monopoly arises when there are economies of scale over the relevant range of output. Figure 1 shows the average total costs of a firm with economies of scale. In this case, a single firm can produce any amount of output at least cost. That is, for any given amount of output, a larger number of firms leads to less output per firm and higher average total cost.

An example of a natural monopoly is the distribution of water. To provide water to residents of a town, a firm must build a network of pipes throughout the town. If two or more firms were to compete in the provision of this service, each firm would have to pay the fixed cost of building a network. Thus, the average total cost of water is lowest if a single firm serves the entire market.

We saw other examples of natural monopolies when we discussed public goods and common resources in Chapter 11. We noted that *club goods* are excludable but not rival in consumption. An example is a bridge used so infrequently that it is never congested. The bridge is excludable because a toll collector can prevent someone from using it. The bridge is not rival in consumption because use of the bridge by one person does not diminish the ability of others to use it. Because there is a fixed cost of building the bridge and a negligible marginal cost of additional users, the average total cost of a trip across the bridge (the total cost divided by the number of trips) falls as the number of trips rises. Hence, the bridge is a natural monopoly.

When a firm is a natural monopoly, it is less concerned about new entrants eroding its monopoly power. Normally, a firm has trouble maintaining a monopoly

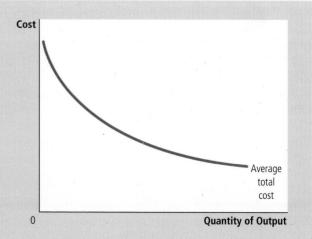

Figure **1**

Economies of Scale as a Cause of Monopoly
When a firm's average-total-cost curve continually declines, the firm has what is called a natural monopoly. In this case, when production is divided among more firms, each firm produces less, and average total cost rises. As a result, a single firm can produce any given amount at the smallest cost.

position without ownership of a key resource or protection from the government. The monopolist's profit attracts entrants into the market, and these entrants make the market more competitive. By contrast, entering a market in which another firm has a natural monopoly is unattractive. Would-be entrants know that they cannot achieve the same low costs that the monopolist enjoys because, after entry, each firm would have a smaller piece of the market.

In some cases, the size of the market is one determinant of whether an industry is a natural monopoly. Again, consider a bridge across a river. When the population is small, the bridge may be a natural monopoly. A single bridge can satisfy the entire demand for trips across the river at lowest cost. Yet as the population grows and the bridge becomes congested, satisfying the entire demand may require two or more bridges across the same river. Thus, as a market expands, a natural monopoly can evolve into a more competitive market.

QUICK QUIZ   *What are the three reasons that a market might have a monopoly?*
• Give two examples of monopolies and explain the reason for each.

How Monopolies Make Production and Pricing Decisions

Now that we know how monopolies arise, we can consider how a monopoly firm decides how much of its product to make and what price to charge for it. The analysis of monopoly behavior in this section is the starting point for evaluating whether monopolies are desirable and what policies the government might pursue in monopoly markets.

Monopoly versus Competition

The key difference between a competitive firm and a monopoly is the monopoly's ability to influence the price of its output. A competitive firm is small relative to the market in which it operates and, therefore, has no power to influence the price of its output. It takes the price as given by market conditions. By contrast, because a monopoly is the sole producer in its market, it can alter the price of its good by adjusting the quantity it supplies to the market.

One way to view this difference between a competitive firm and a monopoly is to consider the demand curve that each firm faces. When we analyzed profit maximization by competitive firms in the preceding chapter, we drew the market price as a horizontal line. Because a competitive firm can sell as much or as little as it wants at this price, the competitive firm faces a horizontal demand curve, as in panel (a) of Figure 2. In effect, because the competitive firm sells a product with many perfect substitutes (the products of all the other firms in its market), the demand curve that any one firm faces is perfectly elastic.

By contrast, because a monopoly is the sole producer in its market, its demand curve is the market demand curve. Thus, the monopolist's demand curve slopes downward for all the usual reasons, as in panel (b) of Figure 2. If the monopolist raises the price of its good, consumers buy less of it. Looked at another way, if the monopolist reduces the quantity of output it produces and sells, the price of its output increases.

The market demand curve provides a constraint on a monopoly's ability to profit from its market power. A monopolist would prefer, if it were possible, to charge a high price and sell a large quantity at that high price. The market

Figure 2

Demand Curves for Competitive and Monopoly Firms

Because competitive firms are price takers, they in effect face horizontal demand curves, as in panel (a). Because a monopoly firm is the sole producer in its market, it faces the downward-sloping market demand curve, as in panel (b). As a result, the monopoly has to accept a lower price if it wants to sell more output.

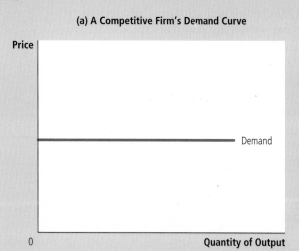

(a) A Competitive Firm's Demand Curve

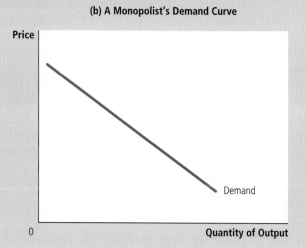

(b) A Monopolist's Demand Curve

demand curve makes that outcome impossible. In particular, the market demand curve describes the combinations of price and quantity that are available to a monopoly firm. By adjusting the quantity produced (or equivalently, the price charged), the monopolist can choose any point on the demand curve, but it cannot choose a point off the demand curve.

What price and quantity of output will the monopolist choose? As with competitive firms, we assume that the monopolist's goal is to maximize profit. Because the firm's profit is total revenue minus total costs, our next task in explaining monopoly behavior is to examine a monopolist's revenue.

A Monopoly's Revenue

Consider a town with a single producer of water. Table 1 shows how the monopoly's revenue might depend on the amount of water produced.

The first two columns show the monopolist's demand schedule. If the monopolist produces 1 gallon of water, it can sell that gallon for $10. If it produces 2 gallons, it must lower the price to $9 to sell both gallons. If it produces 3 gallons, it must lower the price to $8. And so on. If you graphed these two columns of numbers, you would get a typical downward-sloping demand curve.

The third column of the table presents the monopolist's *total revenue*. It equals the quantity sold (from the first column) times the price (from the second column). The fourth column computes the firm's *average revenue*, the amount of revenue the firm receives per unit sold. We compute average revenue by taking the number for total revenue in the third column and dividing it by the quantity of output in the first column. As we discussed in the previous chapter, average revenue always equals the price of the good. This is true for monopolists as well as for competitive firms.

The last column of Table 1 computes the firm's *marginal revenue*, the amount of revenue that the firm receives for each additional unit of output. We compute

Table 1

A Monopoly's
Total, Average,
and Marginal
Revenue

Quantity of Water (Q)	Price (P)	Total Revenue (TR = P × Q)	Average Revenue (AR = TR/Q)	Marginal Revenue (MR = ΔTR/ΔQ)
0 gallons	$11	$ 0	—	
				$10
1	10	10	$10	
				8
2	9	18	9	
				6
3	8	24	8	
				4
4	7	28	7	
				2
5	6	30	6	
				0
6	5	30	5	
				−2
7	4	28	4	
				−4
8	3	24	3	

marginal revenue by taking the change in total revenue when output increases by 1 unit. For example, when the firm is producing 3 gallons of water, it receives total revenue of $24. Raising production to 4 gallons increases total revenue to $28. Thus, marginal revenue from the sale of the fourth gallon is $28 minus $24, or $4.

Table 1 shows a result that is important for understanding monopoly behavior: *A monopolist's marginal revenue is always less than the price of its good.* For example, if the firm raises production of water from 3 to 4 gallons, it will increase total revenue by only $4, even though it will be able to sell each gallon for $7. For a monopoly, marginal revenue is lower than price because a monopoly faces a downward-sloping demand curve. To increase the amount sold, a monopoly firm must lower the price it charges to all customers. Hence, to sell the fourth gallon of water, the monopolist will get $1 less revenue for each of the first three gallons. This $3 loss accounts for the difference between the price of the fourth gallon ($7) and the marginal revenue of that fourth gallon ($4).

Marginal revenue for monopolies is very different from marginal revenue for competitive firms. When a monopoly increases the amount it sells, this action has two effects on total revenue (P × Q):

- *The output effect:* More output is sold, so Q is higher, which tends to increase total revenue.
- *The price effect:* The price falls, so P is lower, which tends to decrease total revenue.

Because a competitive firm can sell all it wants at the market price, there is no price effect. When it increases production by 1 unit, it receives the market price for that unit, and it does not receive any less for the units it was already selling. That is, because the competitive firm is a price taker, its marginal revenue equals the price of its good. By contrast, when a monopoly increases production by 1 unit, it

Figure 3

Demand and Marginal-Revenue Curves for a Monopoly
The demand curve shows how the quantity affects the price of the good. The marginal-revenue curve shows how the firm's revenue changes when the quantity increases by 1 unit. Because the price on *all* units sold must fall if the monopoly increases production, marginal revenue is always less than the price.

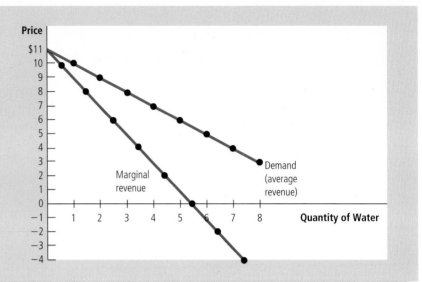

must reduce the price it charges for every unit it sells, and this cut in price reduces revenue on the units it was already selling. As a result, a monopoly's marginal revenue is less than its price.

Figure 3 graphs the demand curve and the marginal-revenue curve for a monopoly firm. (Because the firm's price equals its average revenue, the demand curve is also the average-revenue curve.) These two curves always start at the same point on the vertical axis because the marginal revenue of the first unit sold equals the price of the good. But for the reason we just discussed, the monopolist's marginal revenue on all units after the first is less than the price of the good. Thus, a monopoly's marginal-revenue curve lies below its demand curve.

You can see in the figure (as well as in Table 1) that marginal revenue can even become negative. Marginal revenue is negative when the price effect on revenue is greater than the output effect. In this case, when the firm produces an extra unit of output, the price falls by enough to cause the firm's total revenue to decline, even though the firm is selling more units.

Profit Maximization

Now that we have considered the revenue of a monopoly firm, we are ready to examine how such a firm maximizes profit. Recall from Chapter 1 that one of the *Ten Principles of Economics* is that rational people think at the margin. This lesson is as true for monopolists as it is for competitive firms. Here we apply the logic of marginal analysis to the monopolist's decision about how much to produce.

Figure 4 graphs the demand curve, the marginal-revenue curve, and the cost curves for a monopoly firm. All these curves should seem familiar: The demand and marginal-revenue curves are like those in Figure 3, and the cost curves are like those we encountered in the last two chapters. These curves contain all the

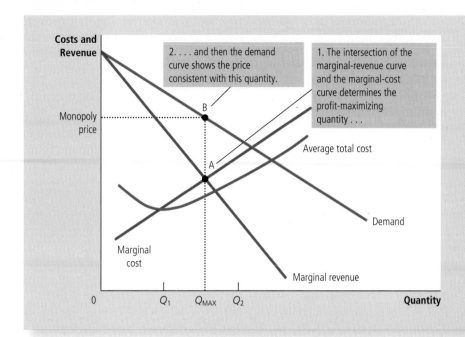

Figure 4

Profit Maximization for a Monopoly
A monopoly maximizes profit by choosing the quantity at which marginal revenue equals marginal cost (point A). It then uses the demand curve to find the price that will induce consumers to buy that quantity (point B).

information we need to determine the level of output that a profit-maximizing monopolist will choose.

Suppose, first, that the firm is producing at a low level of output, such as Q_1. In this case, marginal cost is less than marginal revenue. If the firm increased production by 1 unit, the additional revenue would exceed the additional costs, and profit would rise. Thus, when marginal cost is less than marginal revenue, the firm can increase profit by producing more units.

A similar argument applies at high levels of output, such as Q_2. In this case, marginal cost is greater than marginal revenue. If the firm reduced production by 1 unit, the costs saved would exceed the revenue lost. Thus, if marginal cost is greater than marginal revenue, the firm can raise profit by reducing production.

In the end, the firm adjusts its level of production until the quantity reaches Q_{MAX}, at which marginal revenue equals marginal cost. Thus, *the monopolist's profit-maximizing quantity of output is determined by the intersection of the marginal-revenue curve and the marginal-cost curve.* In Figure 4, this intersection occurs at point A.

You might recall from the previous chapter that competitive firms also choose the quantity of output at which marginal revenue equals marginal cost. In following this rule for profit maximization, competitive firms and monopolies are alike. But there is also an important difference between these types of firms: The marginal revenue of a competitive firm equals its price, whereas the marginal revenue of a monopoly is less than its price. That is,

For a competitive firm: $P = MR = MC$.
For a monopoly firm: $P > MR = MC$.

The equality of marginal revenue and marginal cost determines the profit-maximizing quantity for both types of firm. What differs is how the price is related to marginal revenue and marginal cost.

How does the monopoly find the profit-maximizing price for its product? The demand curve answers this question because the demand curve relates the amount that customers are willing to pay to the quantity sold. Thus, after the monopoly firm chooses the quantity of output that equates marginal revenue and marginal cost, it uses the demand curve to find the highest price it can charge for that quantity. In Figure 4, the profit-maximizing price is found at point B.

We can now see a key difference between markets with competitive firms and markets with a monopoly firm: *In competitive markets, price equals marginal cost. In monopolized markets, price exceeds marginal cost.* As we will see in a moment, this finding is crucial to understanding the social cost of monopoly.

A Monopoly's Profit

How much profit does a monopoly make? To see a monopoly firm's profit in a graph, recall that profit equals total revenue (*TR*) minus total costs (*TC*):

$$\text{Profit} = TR - TC.$$

We can rewrite this as

$$\text{Profit} = (TR/Q - TC/Q) \times Q.$$

TR/Q is average revenue, which equals the price, P, and TC/Q is average total cost, ATC. Therefore,

$$\text{Profit} = (P - ATC) \times Q.$$

FYI

Why a Monopoly Does Not Have a Supply Curve

You may have noticed that we have analyzed the price in a monopoly market using the market demand curve and the firm's cost curves. We have not made any mention of the market supply curve. By contrast, when we analyzed prices in competitive markets beginning in Chapter 4, the two most important words were always *supply* and *demand*.

What happened to the supply curve? Although monopoly firms make decisions about what quantity to supply (in the way described in this chapter), a monopoly does not have a supply curve. A supply curve tells us the quantity that firms choose to supply at any given price. This concept makes sense when we are analyzing competitive firms, which are price takers. But a monopoly firm is a price maker, not a price taker. It is not meaningful to ask what amount such a firm would produce at any price because the firm sets the price at the same time as it chooses the quantity to supply.

Indeed, the monopolist's decision about how much to supply is impossible to separate from the demand curve it faces. The shape of the demand curve determines the shape of the marginal-revenue curve, which in turn determines the monopolist's profit-maximizing quantity. In a competitive market, supply decisions can be analyzed without knowing the demand curve, but that is not true in a monopoly market. Therefore, we never talk about a monopoly's supply curve.

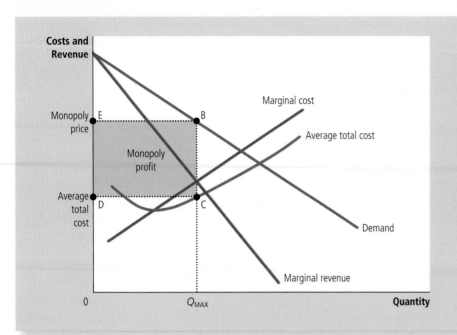

Figure **5**

The Monopolist's Profit
The area of the box BCDE equals the profit of the monopoly firm. The height of the box (BC) is price minus average total cost, which equals profit per unit sold. The width of the box (DC) is the number of units sold.

This equation for profit (which also holds for competitive firms) allows us to measure the monopolist's profit in our graph.

Consider the shaded box in Figure 5. The height of the box (the segment BC) is price minus average total cost, $P - ATC$, which is the profit on the typical unit sold. The width of the box (the segment DC) is the quantity sold, Q_{MAX}. Therefore, the area of this box is the monopoly firm's total profit.

Monopoly Drugs versus Generic Drugs

According to our analysis, prices are determined differently in monopolized markets and competitive markets. A natural place to test this theory is the market for pharmaceutical drugs because this market takes on both market structures. When a firm discovers a new drug, patent laws give the firm a monopoly on the sale of that drug. But eventually, the firm's patent runs out, and any company can make and sell the drug. At that time, the market switches from being monopolistic to being competitive.

What should happen to the price of a drug when the patent runs out? Figure 6 shows the market for a typical drug. In this figure, the marginal cost of producing the drug is constant. (This is approximately true for many drugs.) During the life of the patent, the monopoly firm maximizes profit by producing the quantity at which marginal revenue equals marginal cost and charging a price well above marginal cost. But when the patent runs out, the profit from making the drug should encourage new firms to enter the market. As the market becomes more competitive, the price should fall to equal marginal cost.

Experience is, in fact, consistent with our theory. When the patent on a drug expires, other companies quickly enter and begin selling so-called generic products that are chemically identical to the former monopolist's brand-name product. And just as our analysis predicts, the price of the competitively produced generic drug is well below the price that the monopolist was charging.

Figure **6**

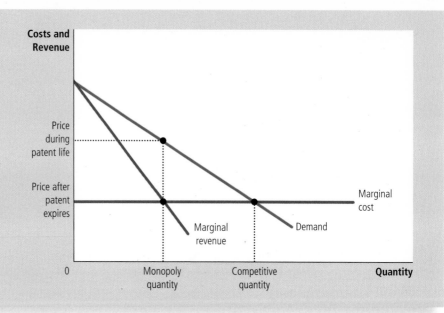

The Market for Drugs
When a patent gives a firm a monopoly over the sale of a drug, the firm charges the monopoly price, which is well above the marginal cost of making the drug. When the patent on a drug runs out, new firms enter the market, making it more competitive. As a result, the price falls from the monopoly price to marginal cost.

The expiration of a patent, however, does not cause the monopolist to lose all its market power. Some consumers remain loyal to the brand-name drug, perhaps out of fear that the new generic drugs are not actually the same as the drug they have been using for years. As a result, the former monopolist can continue to charge a price above the price charged by its new competitors.

For example, one of the most widely used antidepressants is the drug fluoxetine, which is taken by millions of Americans. Because the patent on this drug expired in 2001, a consumer today has the choice between the original drug, sold under the brand name Prozac, and a generic version of the same medicine. Prozac sells for about three times the price of generic fluoxetine. This price differential can persist because some consumers are not convinced that the two pills are perfect substitutes. ■

QUICK QUIZ *Explain how a monopolist chooses the quantity of output to produce and the price to charge.*

The Welfare Cost of Monopolies

Is monopoly a good way to organize a market? We have seen that a monopoly, in contrast to a competitive firm, charges a price above marginal cost. From the standpoint of consumers, this high price makes monopoly undesirable. At the same time, however, the monopoly is earning profit from charging this high price. From the standpoint of the owners of the firm, the high price makes monopoly very desirable. Is it possible that the benefits to the firm's owners exceed the costs imposed on consumers, making monopoly desirable from the standpoint of society as a whole?

We can answer this question using the tools of welfare economics. Recall from Chapter 7 that total surplus measures the economic well-being of buyers and sellers in a market. Total surplus is the sum of consumer surplus and producer surplus. Consumer surplus is consumers' willingness to pay for a good minus the amount they actually pay for it. Producer surplus is the amount producers receive for a good minus their costs of producing it. In this case, there is a single producer—the monopolist.

You can probably guess the result of this analysis. In Chapter 7, we concluded that the equilibrium of supply and demand in a competitive market is not only a natural outcome but also a desirable one. The invisible hand of the market leads to an allocation of resources that makes total surplus as large as it can be. Because a monopoly leads to an allocation of resources different from that in a competitive market, the outcome must, in some way, fail to maximize total economic well-being.

The Deadweight Loss

We begin by considering what the monopoly firm would do if it were run by a benevolent social planner. The social planner cares not only about the profit earned by the firm's owners but also about the benefits received by the firm's consumers. The planner tries to maximize total surplus, which equals producer surplus (profit) plus consumer surplus. Keep in mind that total surplus equals the value of the good to consumers minus the costs of making the good incurred by the monopoly producer.

Figure 7 analyzes how a benevolent social planner would choose the monopoly's level of output. The demand curve reflects the value of the good to consumers, as measured by their willingness to pay for it. The marginal-cost curve reflects the costs of the monopolist. Thus, *the socially efficient quantity is found where the demand curve and the marginal-cost curve intersect.* Below this quantity, the value of

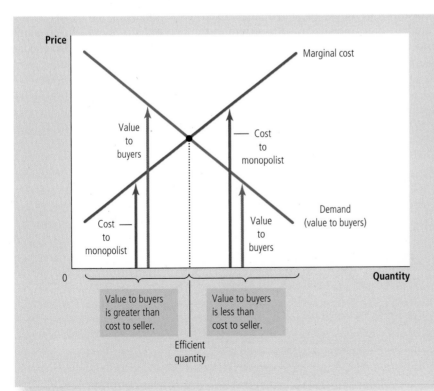

Figure 7

The Efficient Level of Output
A benevolent social planner who wanted to maximize total surplus in the market would choose the level of output where the demand curve and marginal-cost curve intersect. Below this level, the value of the good to the marginal buyer (as reflected in the demand curve) exceeds the marginal cost of making the good. Above this level, the value to the marginal buyer is less than marginal cost.

an extra unit to consumers exceeds the cost of providing it, so increasing output would raise total surplus. Above this quantity, the cost of producing an extra unit exceeds the value of that unit to consumers, so decreasing output would raise total surplus. At the optimal quantity, the value of an extra unit to consumers exactly equals the marginal cost of production.

If the social planner were running the monopoly, the firm could achieve this efficient outcome by charging the price found at the intersection of the demand and marginal-cost curves. Thus, like a competitive firm and unlike a profit-maximizing monopoly, a social planner would charge a price equal to marginal cost. Because this price would give consumers an accurate signal about the cost of producing the good, consumers would buy the efficient quantity.

We can evaluate the welfare effects of monopoly by comparing the level of output that the monopolist chooses to the level of output that a social planner would choose. As we have seen, the monopolist chooses to produce and sell the quantity of output at which the marginal-revenue and marginal-cost curves intersect; the social planner would choose the quantity at which the demand and marginal-cost curves intersect. Figure 8 shows the comparison. *The monopolist produces less than the socially efficient quantity of output.*

We can also view the inefficiency of monopoly in terms of the monopolist's price. Because the market demand curve describes a negative relationship between the price and quantity of the good, a quantity that is inefficiently low is equivalent to a price that is inefficiently high. When a monopolist charges a price above marginal cost, some potential consumers value the good at more than its marginal cost but less than the monopolist's price. These consumers do not buy the good. Because the value these consumers place on the good is greater than the cost of providing it to them, this result is inefficient. Thus, monopoly pricing prevents some mutually beneficial trades from taking place.

The inefficiency of monopoly can be measured with a deadweight loss triangle, as illustrated in Figure 8. Because the demand curve reflects the value to consumers and the marginal-cost curve reflects the costs to the monopoly producer,

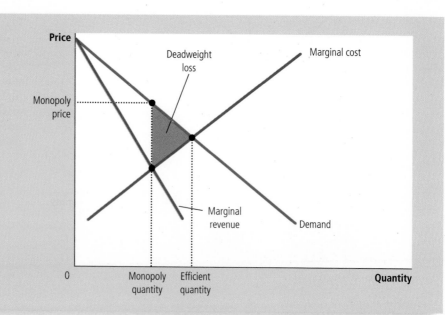

Figure **8**

The Inefficiency of Monopoly
Because a monopoly charges a price above marginal cost, not all consumers who value the good at more than its cost buy it. Thus, the quantity produced and sold by a monopoly is below the socially efficient level. The deadweight loss is represented by the area of the triangle between the demand curve (which reflects the value of the good to consumers) and the marginal-cost curve (which reflects the costs of the monopoly producer).

the area of the deadweight loss triangle between the demand curve and the marginal-cost curve equals the total surplus lost because of monopoly pricing. It is the reduction in economic well-being that results from the monopoly's use of its market power.

The deadweight loss caused by monopoly is similar to the deadweight loss caused by a tax. Indeed, a monopolist is like a private tax collector. As we saw in Chapter 8, a tax on a good places a wedge between consumers' willingness to pay (as reflected by the demand curve) and producers' costs (as reflected by the supply curve). Because a monopoly exerts its market power by charging a price above marginal cost, it creates a similar wedge. In both cases, the wedge causes the quantity sold to fall short of the social optimum. The difference between the two cases is that the government gets the revenue from a tax, whereas a private firm gets the monopoly profit.

The Monopoly's Profit: A Social Cost?

It is tempting to decry monopolies for "profiteering" at the expense of the public. And indeed, a monopoly firm does earn a higher profit by virtue of its market power. According to the economic analysis of monopoly, however, the firm's profit is not in itself necessarily a problem for society.

Welfare in a monopolized market, like all markets, includes the welfare of both consumers and producers. Whenever a consumer pays an extra dollar to a producer because of a monopoly price, the consumer is worse off by a dollar, and the producer is better off by the same amount. This transfer from the consumers of the good to the owners of the monopoly does not affect the market's total surplus—the sum of consumer and producer surplus. In other words, the monopoly profit itself represents not a reduction in the size of the economic pie but merely a bigger slice for producers and a smaller slice for consumers. Unless consumers are for some reason more deserving than producers—a normative judgment about equity that goes beyond the realm of economic efficiency—the monopoly profit is not a social problem.

The problem in a monopolized market arises because the firm produces and sells a quantity of output below the level that maximizes total surplus. The deadweight loss measures how much the economic pie shrinks as a result. This inefficiency is connected to the monopoly's high price: Consumers buy fewer units when the firm raises its price above marginal cost. But keep in mind that the profit earned on the units that continue to be sold is not the problem. The problem stems from the inefficiently low quantity of output. Put differently, if the high monopoly price did not discourage some consumers from buying the good, it would raise producer surplus by exactly the amount it reduced consumer surplus, leaving total surplus the same as could be achieved by a benevolent social planner.

There is, however, a possible exception to this conclusion. Suppose that a monopoly firm has to incur additional costs to maintain its monopoly position. For example, a firm with a government-created monopoly might need to hire lobbyists to convince lawmakers to continue its monopoly. In this case, the monopoly may use up some of its monopoly profits paying for these additional costs. If so, the social loss from monopoly includes both these costs and the deadweight loss resulting from a price above marginal cost.

QUICK QUIZ *How does a monopolist's quantity of output compare to the quantity of output that maximizes total surplus? How does this difference relate to the concept of deadweight loss?*

Price Discrimination

So far, we have been assuming that the monopoly firm charges the same price to all customers. Yet in many cases, firms sell the same good to different customers for different prices, even though the costs of producing for the two customers are the same. This practice is called **price discrimination.**

price discrimination

the business practice of selling the same good at different prices to different customers

Before discussing the behavior of a price-discriminating monopolist, we should note that price discrimination is not possible when a good is sold in a competitive market. In a competitive market, many firms are selling the same good at the market price. No firm is willing to charge a lower price to any customer because the firm can sell all it wants at the market price. And if any firm tried to charge a higher price to a customer, that customer would buy from another firm. For a firm to price discriminate, it must have some market power.

A Parable about Pricing

To understand why a monopolist would price discriminate, let's consider an example. Imagine that you are the president of Readalot Publishing Company. Readalot's best-selling author has just written a new novel. To keep things simple, let's imagine that you pay the author a flat $2 million for the exclusive rights to publish the book. Let's also assume that the cost of printing the book is zero. Readalot's profit, therefore, is the revenue from selling the book minus the $2 million it has paid to the author. Given these assumptions, how would you, as Readalot's president, decide the book's price?

Your first step is to estimate the demand for the book. Readalot's marketing department tells you that the book will attract two types of readers. The book will appeal to the author's 100,000 die-hard fans who are willing to pay as much as $30. In addition, the book will appeal to about 400,000 less enthusiastic readers who will pay up to $5.

If Readalot charges a single price to all customers, what price maximizes profit? There are two natural prices to consider: $30 is the highest price Readalot can charge and still get the 100,000 die-hard fans, and $5 is the highest price it can charge and still get the entire market of 500,000 potential readers. Solving Readalot's problem is a matter of simple arithmetic. At a price of $30, Readalot sells 100,000 copies, has revenue of $3 million, and makes profit of $1 million. At a price of $5, it sells 500,000 copies, has revenue of $2.5 million, and makes profit of $500,000. Thus, Readalot maximizes profit by charging $30 and forgoing the opportunity to sell to the 400,000 less enthusiastic readers.

Notice that Readalot's decision causes a deadweight loss. There are 400,000 readers willing to pay $5 for the book, and the marginal cost of providing it to them is zero. Thus, $2 million of total surplus is lost when Readalot charges the higher price. This deadweight loss is the inefficiency that arises whenever a monopolist charges a price above marginal cost.

Now suppose that Readalot's marketing department makes a discovery: These two groups of readers are in separate markets. The die-hard fans live in Australia, and the other readers live in the United States. Moreover, it is hard for readers in one country to buy books in the other.

In response to this discovery, Readalot can change its marketing strategy and increase profits. To the 100,000 Australian readers, it can charge $30 for the book. To the 400,000 American readers, it can charge $5 for the book. In this case, revenue is $3 million in Australia and $2 million in the United States, for a total of

$5 million. Profit is then $3 million, which is substantially greater than the $1 million the company could earn charging the same $30 price to all customers. Not surprisingly, Readalot chooses to follow this strategy of price discrimination.

The story of Readalot Publishing is hypothetical, but it describes accurately the business practice of many publishing companies. Textbooks, for example, are often sold at a lower price in Europe than in the United States. Even more important is the price differential between hardcover books and paperbacks. When a publisher has a new novel, it initially releases an expensive hardcover edition and later releases a cheaper paperback edition. The difference in price between these two editions far exceeds the difference in printing costs. The publisher's goal is just as in our example. By selling the hardcover to die-hard fans and the paperback to less enthusiastic readers, the publisher price discriminates and raises its profit.

The Moral of the Story

Like any parable, the story of Readalot Publishing is stylized. Yet also like any parable, it teaches some general lessons. In this case, three lessons can be learned about price discrimination.

The first and most obvious lesson is that price discrimination is a rational strategy for a profit-maximizing monopolist. That is, by charging different prices to different customers, a monopolist can increase its profit. In essence, a price-discriminating monopolist charges each customer a price closer to his or her willingness to pay than is possible with a single price.

The second lesson is that price discrimination requires the ability to separate customers according to their willingness to pay. In our example, customers were separated geographically. But sometimes monopolists choose other differences, such as age or income, to distinguish among customers.

A corollary to this second lesson is that certain market forces can prevent firms from price discriminating. In particular, one such force is *arbitrage*, the process of buying a good in one market at a low price and selling it in another market at a higher price to profit from the price difference. In our example, if Australian bookstores could buy the book in the United States and resell it to Australian readers, the arbitrage would prevent Readalot from price discriminating, because no Australian would buy the book at the higher price.

The third lesson from our parable is the most surprising: Price discrimination can raise economic welfare. Recall that a deadweight loss arises when Readalot charges a single $30 price because the 400,000 less enthusiastic readers do not end up with the book, even though they value it at more than its marginal cost of production. By contrast, when Readalot price discriminates, all readers get the book, and the outcome is efficient. Thus, price discrimination can eliminate the inefficiency inherent in monopoly pricing.

Note that in this example the increase in welfare from price discrimination shows up as higher producer surplus rather than higher consumer surplus. Consumers are no better off for having bought the book: The price they pay exactly equals the value they place on the book, so they receive no consumer surplus. The entire increase in total surplus from price discrimination accrues to Readalot Publishing in the form of higher profit.

The Analytics of Price Discrimination

Let's consider a bit more formally how price discrimination affects economic welfare. We begin by assuming that the monopolist can price discriminate perfectly. *Perfect price discrimination* describes a situation in which the monopolist knows exactly each customer's willingness to pay and can charge each customer a different price. In this case, the monopolist charges each customer exactly his or her willingness to pay, and the monopolist gets the entire surplus in every transaction.

Figure 9 illustrates producer and consumer surplus with and without price discrimination. To keep things simple, this figure is drawn assuming constant per unit costs—that is, marginal cost and average total cost are constant and equal. Without price discrimination, the firm charges a single price above marginal cost, as shown in panel (a). Because some potential customers who value the good at more than marginal cost do not buy it at this high price, the monopoly causes a deadweight loss. Yet when a firm can perfectly price discriminate, as shown in panel (b), each customer who values the good at more than marginal cost buys the good and is charged his or her willingness to pay. All mutually beneficial trades take place, no deadweight loss occurs, and the entire surplus derived from the market goes to the monopoly producer in the form of profit.

In reality, of course, price discrimination is not perfect. Customers do not walk into stores with signs displaying their willingness to pay. Instead, firms price discriminate by dividing customers into groups: young versus old, weekday versus weekend shoppers, Americans versus Australians, and so on. Unlike those in our parable of Readalot Publishing, customers within each group differ in their willingness to pay for the product, making perfect price discrimination impossible.

Figure **9**

Welfare with and without Price Discrimination

Panel (a) shows a monopolist that charges the same price to all customers. Total surplus in this market equals the sum of profit (producer surplus) and consumer surplus. Panel (b) shows a monopolist that can perfectly price discriminate. Because consumer surplus equals zero, total surplus now equals the firm's profit. Comparing these two panels, you can see that perfect price discrimination raises profit, raises total surplus, and lowers consumer surplus.

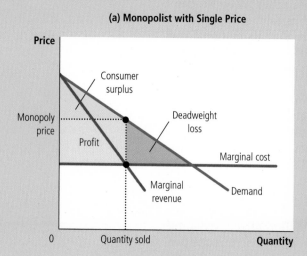

(a) Monopolist with Single Price

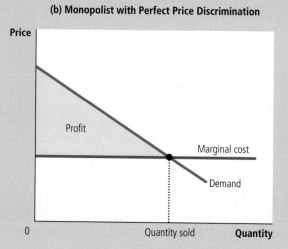

(b) Monopolist with Perfect Price Discrimination

How does this imperfect price discrimination affect welfare? The analysis of these pricing schemes is quite complicated, and it turns out that there is no general answer to this question. Compared to the monopoly outcome with a single price, imperfect price discrimination can raise, lower, or leave unchanged total surplus in a market. The only certain conclusion is that price discrimination raises the monopoly's profit; otherwise, the firm would choose to charge all customers the same price.

Examples of Price Discrimination

Firms in our economy use various business strategies aimed at charging different prices to different customers. Now that we understand the economics of price discrimination, let's consider some examples.

Movie Tickets   Many movie theaters charge a lower price for children and senior citizens than for other patrons. This fact is hard to explain in a competitive market. In a competitive market, price equals marginal cost, and the marginal cost of providing a seat for a child or senior citizen is the same as the marginal cost of providing a seat for anyone else. Yet the differential pricing is easily explained if movie theaters have some local monopoly power and if children and senior citizens have a lower willingness to pay for a ticket. In this case, movie theaters raise their profit by price discriminating.

Airline Prices   Seats on airplanes are sold at many different prices. Most airlines charge a lower price for a round-trip ticket between two cities if the traveler stays over a Saturday night. At first, this seems odd. Why should it matter to the airline whether a passenger stays over a Saturday night? The reason is that this rule provides a way to separate business travelers and leisure travelers. A passenger on a business trip has a high willingness to pay and, most likely, does not want to stay over a Saturday night. By contrast, a passenger traveling for personal reasons has a lower willingness to pay and is more likely to be willing to stay over a Saturday night. Thus, the airlines can successfully price discriminate by charging a lower price for passengers who stay over a Saturday night.

"Would it bother you to hear how little I paid for this flight?"

Discount Coupons   Many companies offer discount coupons to the public in newspapers, magazines, or online. A buyer simply has to clip the coupon to get $0.50 off his or her next purchase. Why do companies offer these coupons? Why don't they just cut the price of the product by $0.50?

The answer is that coupons allow companies to price discriminate. Companies know that not all customers are willing to spend time clipping coupons. Moreover, the willingness to clip coupons is related to the customer's willingness to pay for the good. A rich and busy executive is unlikely to spend her time clipping discount coupons out of the newspaper, and she is probably willing to pay a higher price for many goods. A person who is unemployed is more likely to clip coupons and to have a lower willingness to pay. Thus, by charging a lower price only to those customers who clip coupons, firms can successfully price discriminate.

Financial Aid   Many colleges and universities give financial aid to needy students. One can view this policy as a type of price discrimination. Wealthy students have greater financial resources and, therefore, a higher willingness to pay than needy students. By charging high tuition and selectively offering financial aid, schools in effect charge prices to customers based on the value they place on going to that school. This behavior is similar to that of any price-discriminating monopolist.

Quantity Discounts So far in our examples of price discrimination, the monopolist charges different prices to different customers. Sometimes, however, monopolists price discriminate by charging different prices to the same customer for different units that the customer buys. For example, many firms offer lower prices to customers who buy large quantities. A bakery might charge $0.50 for each donut but $5 for a dozen. This is a form of price discrimination because the customer pays a higher price for the first unit bought than for the twelfth. Quantity discounts are often a successful way of price discriminating because a customer's willingness to pay for an additional unit declines as the customer buys more units.

QUICK QUIZ *Give two examples of price discrimination.* • *How does perfect price discrimination affect consumer surplus, producer surplus, and total surplus?*

Public Policy toward Monopolies

We have seen that monopolies, in contrast to competitive markets, fail to allocate resources efficiently. Monopolies produce less than the socially desirable quantity

······ in the news

> **TKTS and Other Schemes**

Economist Hal Varian discusses a dramatic example of price discrimination.

The Dynamics of Pricing Tickets for Broadway Shows

BY HAL R. VARIAN

Every night in New York, about 25,000 people, on average, attend Broadway shows.

As avid theatergoers know, ticket prices have been rising inexorably. The top ticket price for Broadway shows has risen 31 percent since 1998. But the actual price paid has gone up by only 24 percent.

Bargain hunters

The difference is a result of discounting. Savvy fans know that there are deals available for even the most popular shows, with the most popular discounts being offered

through coupons, two-for-one deals, special prices for students, and through the TKTS booth in Times Square.

Why so much discounting? The value of a seat in a theater, like a seat on an airplane, is highly perishable. Once the show starts or the plane takes off, a seat is worth next to nothing.

In both industries, sellers use a variety of strategies to try to ensure that the seats are sold to those who are willing to pay the most.

This phenomenon was examined recently by a Stanford economist, Phillip Leslie, in an article, "Price Discrimination in Broadway

of output and, as a result, charge prices above marginal cost. Policymakers in the government can respond to the problem of monopoly in one of four ways:

- By trying to make monopolized industries more competitive.
- By regulating the behavior of the monopolies.
- By turning some private monopolies into public enterprises.
- By doing nothing at all.

Increasing Competition with Antitrust Laws

If Coca-Cola and PepsiCo wanted to merge, the deal would be closely examined by the federal government before it went into effect. The lawyers and economists in the Department of Justice might well decide that a merger between these two large soft drink companies would make the U.S. soft drink market substantially less competitive and, as a result, would reduce the economic well-being of the country as a whole. If so, the Department of Justice would challenge the merger in court, and if the judge agreed, the two companies would not be allowed to merge. It is precisely this kind of challenge that prevented software giant Microsoft from buying Intuit in 1994.

The government derives this power over private industry from the antitrust laws, a collection of statutes aimed at curbing monopoly power. The first and most important of these laws was the Sherman Antitrust Act, which Congress passed in 1890 to reduce the market power of the large and powerful "trusts" that

"But if we do merge with Amalgamated, we'll have enough resources to fight the anti-trust violation caused by the merger."

Theater," published in the autumn 2004 issue of the *RAND Journal of Economics*.

Mr. Leslie was able to collect detailed data on a 1996 Broadway play, "Seven Guitars." Over 140,000 people saw this play, and they bought tickets in 17 price categories. Some price variation was due to the quality of the seats—orchestra, mezzanine, balcony and so on—while other price differences were a result of various forms of discounting.

The combination of quality variation and discounts led to widely varying ticket prices. The average difference of two tickets chosen at random on a given night was about 40 percent of the average price. This is comparable to the price variation in airline tickets. . . .

The ticket promotions also varied over the 199 performances of the show. Targeted direct mail was used early on, while two-for-one tickets were not introduced until about halfway through the run.

The tickets offered for sale at the TKTS booth in Times Square are typically orchestra seats, the best category of seats available.

But the discounted tickets at TKTS tend to be the lower-quality orchestra seats. They sell at a fixed discount of 50 percent, but are offered only for performances that day.

Mr. Leslie's goal was primarily to model the behavior of the theatergoer. The audience for Broadway shows is highly diverse. About 10 percent, according to a 1991 survey conducted by Broadway producers, had household incomes of $25,000 or $35,000 while an equal number had incomes over $150,000 (in 1990 dollars).

The prices and discounting policy set by the producers of Broadway shows try to use this heterogeneity to get people to sort themselves by their willingness to pay for tickets.

You probably will not see Donald Trump waiting in line at TKTS; presumably, those in his income class do not mind paying full price. But a lot of students, unemployed actors and tourists do use TKTS.

Yes, it is inconvenient to wait in line at TKTS. But that is the point. If it weren't inconvenient, everyone would do it, and this

would result in substantially lower revenues for Broadway shows.

Mr. Leslie uses some advanced econometric techniques to estimate the values that different income groups put on the various categories of tickets. He finds that Broadway producers do a pretty good job, in general, at maximizing revenue. . . .

We are likely to see more and more goods and services sold using the same sort of differential pricing. As more and more transactions become computer-mediated, it becomes easier for sellers to collect data, to experiment with pricing and to analyze the results of those experiments.

This, of course, makes life more complicated for us consumers. The flip side is that pricing variations make those good deals more likely.

Last time I was in New York, I was pleased that I managed to get a ticket to "The Producers" for half price. It almost made up for the fact that I had to book my airline ticket two weeks in advance and stay over a Saturday night.

Source: *New York Times*, January 13, 2005.

were viewed as dominating the economy at the time. The Clayton Antitrust Act, passed in 1914, strengthened the government's powers and authorized private lawsuits. As the U.S. Supreme Court once put it, the antitrust laws are "a comprehensive charter of economic liberty aimed at preserving free and unfettered competition as the rule of trade."

The antitrust laws give the government various ways to promote competition. They allow the government to prevent mergers, such as our hypothetical merger between Coca-Cola and PepsiCo. They also allow the government to break up companies. For example, in 1984, the government split up AT&T, the large telecommunications company, into eight smaller companies. Finally, the antitrust laws prevent companies from coordinating their activities in ways that make markets less competitive.

Antitrust laws have costs as well as benefits. Sometimes companies merge not to reduce competition but to lower costs through more efficient joint production. These benefits from mergers are sometimes called *synergies*. For example, many

· · · · · · · · · · · · in the news

❯ President Obama's Antitrust Policy

When President Obama was elected, he promised a more vigorous application of the laws aimed at firms with monopoly power.

Trustbusters Try to Reclaim Decades of Lost Ground

BY THOMAS CATAN

WASHINGTON—If populism is emerging as a potent new force in American politics, then government trustbusters and sympathetic Democrats in Congress stand ready to offer a new outlet. But first, they'll have to overcome a major hurdle: the judges.

Over the past three decades, U.S. courts have sharply limited the scope of the 120-year-old Sherman Antitrust Act, which has been used to target companies from Standard Oil to Microsoft Corp. In so doing, judges have clipped the wings of two agencies charged with policing anticompetitive behavior: the Justice Department and the Federal Trade Commission.

Now Democrats on Capitol Hill are joining forces with antitrust cops to push back against the judicial tide. Congress is preparing measures to reverse the effect of court rulings that have made it harder for the government to win antitrust cases and break up monopolies, while the FTC and Justice Department are trying out new legal tactics to reclaim lost powers

If successful, the efforts could presage an upswing in antitrust cases against America's leading companies and reverse the legal trends of recent years.

Sensing a shift in the political landscape, big business is girding for a fight. "Voters are demanding jobs and growth, but Washington is moving in the opposite direction by advancing an agenda focused on increased litigation against business," said Lisa Rickard, president of the U.S. Chamber Institute for Legal Reform, an offshoot of the Chamber of Commerce that seeks to ease the burden of civil litigation for businesses.

Antitrust enforcers since the 1980s have had an increasingly hard time winning cases against accused monopolists. Judges have largely agreed with the reasoning of the so-called Chicago School of economists, which holds that big companies aren't necessarily bad and that the market—not government—is best placed to promote competition.

The administration of George W. Bush largely agreed. Its Justice Department didn't accuse a single company of improperly

U.S. banks have merged in recent years and, by combining operations, have been able to reduce administrative staff. If antitrust laws are to raise social welfare, the government must be able to determine which mergers are desirable and which are not. That is, it must be able to measure and compare the social benefit from synergies with the social costs of reduced competition. Critics of the antitrust laws are skeptical that the government can perform the necessary cost–benefit analysis with sufficient accuracy.

Regulation

Another way the government deals with the problem of monopoly is by regulating the behavior of monopolists. This solution is common in the case of natural monopolies, such as water and electric companies. These companies are not allowed to charge any price they want. Instead, government agencies regulate their prices.

acquiring or maintaining a monopoly in a case not involving a merger. In 2008, it enshrined its thinking in official guidelines that significantly raised the bar for bringing such a monopolization case.

The new administration is taking a different tack. President Barack Obama vowed to "reinvigorate" antitrust enforcement, and his antitrust chief, Christine Varney, ripped up the Bush-era guidelines last spring.

So far, the talk hasn't been matched by action. The Justice Department in the Obama administration has yet to bring a monopolization case. And the only FTC case brought so far—against microchip giant Intel Corp.—was already being built when it came to power.

In part, that's because the Supreme Court has embraced many antitrust principles that the Bush administration advocated, said Joseph Angland, an antitrust lawyer at White & Case. "Those changes are now law of the land and they do constrain the ability of the Obama administration to bring certain types of actions," he said.

Congressional Democrats want to show they can protect consumers. They say they want to aid family farmers squeezed by giant seed manufacturers and distributors.

They want to free up Internet retailers to discount products below manufacturers' minimum price. And they want to stop pharmaceutical companies from paying generic-drug makers to delay cheap copies of medicines. But in each of these areas they are blocked by recent Supreme Court decisions, so Congress is considering a series of legislative fixes. One would be in response to a 2007 Supreme Court decision, Leegin Creative Leather Products v. PSKS.

In that 5-4 ruling, the court overturned nearly a century of jurisprudence that had declared a practice known as retail price maintenance to be an automatic crime. That might involve, for instance, a jeans manufacturer that forbids a department store from selling its pants below its desired level. A bill sponsored by Sen. Herb Kohl (D., Wisc.) would restore the absolute ban.

Another bill sponsored by Sen. Arlen Specter (D., Pa.), with a matching version pending in the House, would try to counter a different 2007 Supreme Court decision—Bell Atlantic Corp. v. Twombly—that made it easier for defendants to get antitrust claims dismissed.

Trial lawyers, who as a group are among the top financial donors to the Democratic Party, have declared passing

the bill among their top legislative priorities. AT&T Inc., Procter & Gamble Co., Verizon Communications Inc. and other big companies oppose the bills, saying they would trigger a flood of frivolous and costly cases.

"Every business group I've spoken to regards this as a very serious issue, especially given the economy and the expense of dealing with frivolous litigation," said John Thorne, Verizon's deputy general counsel.

Antitrust enforcers are taking parallel action. The Justice Department is looking for test cases to expand its antitrust authority. And the FTC wants to circumvent the courts' narrow interpretation of the Sherman Act by reclaiming a legal tool it has hardly used in more than two decades—Section 5 of the 1914 law that created the agency.

Invoked in the FTC's Intel suit, that law allows the FTC to act against a company that engages in "unfair methods of competition." The law largely fell into disuse after courts repeatedly slapped down the FTC for using it too broadly.

"Antitrust law is far more restrictive than it was 30 years ago and if we want to accomplish our mission of protecting consumers in an age of judicial conservatism, we need to use every tool in our arsenal," FTC Chairman Jon Leibowitz said last fall.

Source: *The Wall Street Journal*, January 31, 2010.

What price should the government set for a natural monopoly? This question is not as easy as it might at first appear. One might conclude that the price should equal the monopolist's marginal cost. If price equals marginal cost, customers will buy the quantity of the monopolist's output that maximizes total surplus, and the allocation of resources will be efficient.

There are, however, two practical problems with marginal-cost pricing as a regulatory system. The first arises from the logic of cost curves. By definition, natural monopolies have declining average total cost. As we first discussed in Chapter 13, when average total cost is declining, marginal cost is less than average total cost. This situation is illustrated in Figure 10, which shows a firm with a large fixed cost and then constant marginal cost thereafter. If regulators were to set price equal to marginal cost, that price must be less than the firm's average total cost, and the firm would lose money. Instead of charging such a low price, the monopoly firm would just exit the industry.

Regulators can respond to this problem in various ways, none of which is perfect. One way is to subsidize the monopolist. In essence, the government picks up the losses inherent in marginal-cost pricing. Yet to pay for the subsidy, the government needs to raise money through taxation, which involves its own deadweight losses. Alternatively, the regulators can allow the monopolist to charge a price higher than marginal cost. If the regulated price equals average total cost, the monopolist earns exactly zero economic profit. Yet average-cost pricing leads to deadweight losses because the monopolist's price no longer reflects the marginal cost of producing the good. In essence, average-cost pricing is like a tax on the good the monopolist is selling.

The second problem with marginal-cost pricing as a regulatory system (and with average-cost pricing as well) is that it gives the monopolist no incentive to reduce costs. Each firm in a competitive market tries to reduce its costs because lower costs mean higher profits. But if a regulated monopolist knows that regulators will reduce prices whenever costs fall, the monopolist will not benefit from lower costs. In practice, regulators deal with this problem by allowing monopolists to keep some of the benefits from lower costs in the form of higher profit, a practice that requires some departure from marginal-cost pricing.

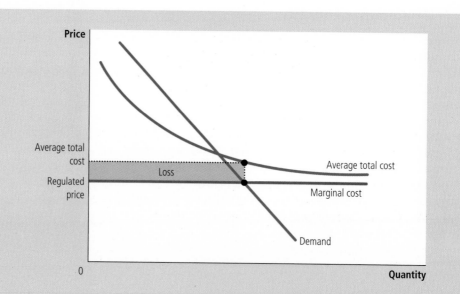

Figure **10**

Marginal-Cost Pricing for a Natural Monopoly
Because a natural monopoly has declining average total cost, marginal cost is less than average total cost. Therefore, if regulators require a natural monopoly to charge a price equal to marginal cost, price will be below average total cost, and the monopoly will lose money.

Public Ownership

The third policy used by the government to deal with monopoly is public ownership. That is, rather than regulating a natural monopoly that is run by a private firm, the government can run the monopoly itself. This solution is common in many European countries, where the government owns and operates utilities such as telephone, water, and electric companies. In the United States, the government runs the Postal Service. The delivery of ordinary first-class mail is often thought to be a natural monopoly.

Economists usually prefer private to public ownership of natural monopolies. The key issue is how the ownership of the firm affects the costs of production. Private owners have an incentive to minimize costs as long as they reap part of the benefit in the form of higher profit. If the firm's managers are doing a bad job of keeping costs down, the firm's owners will fire them. By contrast, if the government bureaucrats who run a monopoly do a bad job, the losers are the customers and taxpayers, whose only recourse is the political system. The bureaucrats may become a special-interest group and attempt to block cost-reducing reforms. Put simply, as a way of ensuring that firms are well run, the voting booth is less reliable than the profit motive.

Doing Nothing

Each of the foregoing policies aimed at reducing the problem of monopoly has drawbacks. As a result, some economists argue that it is often best for the government not to try to remedy the inefficiencies of monopoly pricing. Here is the assessment of economist George Stigler, who won the Nobel Prize for his work in industrial organization:

> A famous theorem in economics states that a competitive enterprise economy will produce the largest possible income from a given stock of resources. No real economy meets the exact conditions of the theorem, and all real economies will fall short of the ideal economy—a difference called "market failure." In my view, however, the degree of "market failure" for the American economy is much smaller than the "political failure" arising from the imperfections of economic policies found in real political systems.

As this quotation makes clear, determining the proper role of the government in the economy requires judgments about politics as well as economics.

QUICK QUIZ *Describe the ways policymakers can respond to the inefficiencies caused by monopolies. List a potential problem with each of these policy responses.*

Conclusion: The Prevalence of Monopolies

This chapter has discussed the behavior of firms that have control over the prices they charge. We have seen that these firms behave very differently from the competitive firms studied in the previous chapter. Table 2 summarizes some of the key similarities and differences between competitive and monopoly markets.

From the standpoint of public policy, a crucial result is that a monopolist produces less than the socially efficient quantity and charges a price above marginal cost. As a result, a monopoly causes deadweight losses. In some cases, these inefficiencies can be mitigated through price discrimination by the monopolist, but other times, they call for policymakers to take an active role.

How prevalent are the problems of monopoly? There are two answers to this question.

In one sense, monopolies are common. Most firms have some control over the prices they charge. They are not forced to charge the market price for their goods

Table **2**

Competition versus Monopoly: A Summary Comparison

	Competition	Monopoly
Similarities		
Goal of firms	Maximize profits	Maximize profits
Rule for maximizing	$MR = MC$	$MR = MC$
Can earn economic profits in the short run?	Yes	Yes
Differences		
Number of firms	Many	One
Marginal revenue	$MR = P$	$MR < P$
Price	$P = MC$	$P > MC$
Produces welfare-maximizing level of output?	Yes	No
Entry in long run?	Yes	No
Can earn economic profits in long run?	No	Yes
Price discrimination possible?	No	Yes

because their goods are not exactly the same as those offered by other firms. A Ford Taurus is not the same as a Toyota Camry. Ben and Jerry's ice cream is not the same as Breyer's. Each of these goods has a downward-sloping demand curve, which gives each producer some degree of monopoly power.

Yet firms with substantial monopoly power are rare. Few goods are truly unique. Most have substitutes that, even if not exactly the same, are similar. Ben and Jerry can raise the price of their ice cream a little without losing all their sales, but if they raise it a lot, sales will fall substantially as their customers switch to another brand.

In the end, monopoly power is a matter of degree. It is true that many firms have some monopoly power. It is also true that their monopoly power is usually limited. In such a situation, we will not go far wrong assuming that firms operate in competitive markets, even if that is not precisely the case.

SUMMARY

- A monopoly is a firm that is the sole seller in its market. A monopoly arises when a single firm owns a key resource, when the government gives a firm the exclusive right to produce a good, or when a single firm can supply the entire market at a lower cost than many firms could.

- Because a monopoly is the sole producer in its market, it faces a downward-sloping demand curve for its product. When a monopoly increases production by 1 unit, it causes the price of its good to fall, which reduces the amount of revenue earned on all units produced. As a result, a monopoly's marginal revenue is always below the price of its good.

- Like a competitive firm, a monopoly firm maximizes profit by producing the quantity at which marginal revenue equals marginal cost. The monopoly then chooses the price at which that quantity is demanded. Unlike a competitive firm, a monopoly firm's price exceeds its marginal revenue, so its price exceeds marginal cost.

- A monopolist's profit-maximizing level of output is below the level that maximizes the sum of consumer and producer surplus. That is, when the monopoly charges a price above marginal cost, some consumers who value the good more than its cost of production do not buy it. As a result, monopoly causes deadweight losses similar to those caused by taxes.

- A monopolist often can raise its profits by charging different prices for the same good based on a buyer's willingness to pay. This practice of price discrimination can raise economic welfare by getting the good to some consumers who otherwise would not buy it. In the extreme case of perfect price discrimination, the deadweight loss of monopoly is completely eliminated, and the entire surplus in the market goes to the monopoly producer. More generally, when price discrimination is imperfect, it can either raise or lower welfare compared to the outcome with a single monopoly price.

- Policymakers can respond to the inefficiency of monopoly behavior in four ways. They can use the antitrust laws to try to make the industry more competitive. They can regulate the prices that the monopoly charges. They can turn the monopolist into a government-run enterprise. Or if the market failure is deemed small compared to the inevitable imperfections of policies, they can do nothing at all.

KEY CONCEPTS

monopoly, *p. 300*   natural monopoly, *p. 302*   price discrimination, *p. 314*

QUESTIONS FOR REVIEW

1. Give an example of a government-created monopoly. Is creating this monopoly necessarily bad public policy? Explain.
2. Define *natural monopoly*. What does the size of a market have to do with whether an industry is a natural monopoly?
3. Why is a monopolist's marginal revenue less than the price of its good? Can marginal revenue ever be negative? Explain.
4. Draw the demand, marginal-revenue, average-total-cost, and marginal-cost curves for a monopolist. Show the profit-maximizing level of output, the profit-maximizing price, and the amount of profit.
5. In your diagram from the previous question, show the level of output that maximizes total surplus. Show the deadweight loss from the monopoly. Explain your answer.
6. Give two examples of price discrimination. In each case, explain why the monopolist chooses to follow this business strategy.
7. What gives the government the power to regulate mergers between firms? From the standpoint of the welfare of society, give a good reason and a bad reason that two firms might want to merge.
8. Describe the two problems that arise when regulators tell a natural monopoly that it must set a price equal to marginal cost.

PROBLEMS AND APPLICATIONS

1. A publisher faces the following demand schedule for the next novel from one of its popular authors:

Price	Quantity Demanded
$100	0 novels
90	100,000
80	200,000
70	300,000
60	400,000
50	500,000
40	600,000
30	700,000
20	800,000
10	900,000
0	1,000,000

The author is paid $2 million to write the book, and the marginal cost of publishing the book is a constant $10 per book.
   a. Compute total revenue, total cost, and profit at each quantity. What quantity would a profit-maximizing publisher choose? What price would it charge?
   b. Compute marginal revenue. (Recall that $MR = \Delta TR/\Delta Q$.) How does marginal revenue compare to the price? Explain.
   c. Graph the marginal-revenue, marginal-cost, and demand curves. At what quantity do the marginal-revenue and marginal-cost curves cross? What does this signify?

d. In your graph, shade in the deadweight loss. Explain in words what this means.

e. If the author were paid $3 million instead of $2 million to write the book, how would this affect the publisher's decision regarding what price to charge? Explain.

f. Suppose the publisher was not profit-maximizing but was concerned with maximizing economic efficiency. What price would it charge for the book? How much profit would it make at this price?

2. A small town is served by many competing supermarkets, which have the same constant marginal cost.

a. Using a diagram of the market for groceries, show the consumer surplus, producer surplus, and total surplus.

b. Now suppose that the independent supermarkets combine into one chain. Using a new diagram, show the new consumer surplus, producer surplus, and total surplus. Relative to the competitive market, what is the transfer from consumers to producers? What is the deadweight loss?

3. Johnny Rockabilly has just finished recording his latest CD. His record company's marketing department determines that the demand for the CD is as follows:

Price	Number of CDs
$24	10,000
22	20,000
20	30,000
18	40,000
16	50,000
14	60,000

The company can produce the CD with no fixed cost and a variable cost of $5 per CD.

a. Find total revenue for quantity equal to 10,000, 20,000, and so on. What is the marginal revenue for each 10,000 increase in the quantity sold?

b. What quantity of CDs would maximize profit? What would the price be? What would the profit be?

c. If you were Johnny's agent, what recording fee would you advise Johnny to demand from the record company? Why?

4. A company is considering building a bridge across a river. The bridge would cost $2 million to build and nothing to maintain. The following table shows the company's anticipated demand over the lifetime of the bridge:

Price per Crossing	Number of Crossings, in Thousands
$8	0
7	100
6	200
5	300
4	400
3	500
2	600
1	700
0	800

a. If the company were to build the bridge, what would be its profit-maximizing price? Would that be the efficient level of output? Why or why not?

b. If the company is interested in maximizing profit, should it build the bridge? What would be its profit or loss?

c. If the government were to build the bridge, what price should it charge?

d. Should the government build the bridge? Explain.

5. Larry, Curly, and Moe run the only saloon in town. Larry wants to sell as many drinks as possible without losing money. Curly wants the saloon to bring in as much revenue as possible. Moe wants to make the largest possible profits. Using a single diagram of the saloon's demand curve and its cost curves, show the price and quantity combinations favored by each of the three partners. Explain.

6. The residents of the town Ectenia all love economics, and the mayor proposes building an economics museum. The museum has a fixed cost of $2,400,000 and no variable costs. There are 100,000 town residents, and each has the same demand for museum visits: $Q^D = 10 - P$, where P is the price of admission.

a. Graph the museum's average-total-cost curve and its marginal-cost curve. What kind of market would describe the museum?

b. The mayor proposes financing the museum with a lump-sum tax of $24 and then opening the museum free to the public. How many times would each person visit? Calculate the benefit each person would get from the museum, measured as consumer surplus minus the new tax.

c. The mayor's anti-tax opponent says the museum should finance itself by charging an admission fee. What is the lowest price the museum can charge without incurring losses? (Hint: Find the number of visits and museum profits for prices of $2, $3, $4, and $5.)

d. For the break-even price you found in part (c), calculate each resident's consumer surplus. Compared with the mayor's plan, who is better off with this admission fee, and who is worse off? Explain.

e. What real-world considerations absent in the above problem might argue in favor of an admission fee?

7. For many years, AT&T was a regulated monopoly, providing both local and long-distance telephone service.

a. Explain why long-distance phone service was originally a natural monopoly.

b. Over the past two decades, many companies have launched communication satellites, each of which can transmit a limited number of calls. How did the growing role of satellites change the cost structure of long-distance phone service?

After a lengthy legal battle with the government, AT&T agreed to compete with other companies in the long-distance market. It also agreed to spin off its local phone service into the "Baby Bells," which remain highly regulated.

c. Why might it be efficient to have competition in long-distance phone service and regulated monopolies in local phone service?

8. Consider the relationship between monopoly pricing and price elasticity of demand:

a. Explain why a monopolist will never produce a quantity at which the demand curve is inelastic. (Hint: If demand is inelastic and the firm raises its price, what happens to total revenue and total costs?)

b. Draw a diagram for a monopolist, precisely labeling the portion of the demand curve that is inelastic. (Hint: The answer is related to the marginal-revenue curve.)

c. On your diagram, show the quantity and price that maximizes total revenue.

9. If the government wanted to encourage a monopoly to produce the socially efficient quantity, should it use a per-unit tax or a per-unit subsidy? Explain how this tax or subsidy would achieve the socially efficient level of output. Among the various interested parties—the monopoly firm, the monopoly's consumers, and other taxpayers—who would support the policy and who would oppose it?

10. You live in a town with 300 adults and 200 children, and you are thinking about putting on a play to entertain your neighbors and make some money. A play has a fixed cost of $2,000, but selling an extra ticket has zero marginal cost. Here are the demand schedules for your two types of customer:

Price	Adults	Children
$10	0	0
9	100	0
8	200	0
7	300	0
6	300	0
5	300	100
4	300	200
3	300	200
2	300	200
1	300	200
0	300	200

a. To maximize profit, what price would you charge for an adult ticket? For a child's ticket? How much profit do you make?

b. The city council passes a law prohibiting you from charging different prices to different customers. What price do you set for a ticket now? How much profit do you make?

c. Who is worse off because of the law prohibiting price discrimination? Who is better off? (If you can, quantify the changes in welfare.)

d. If the fixed cost of the play were $2,500 rather than $2,000, how would your answers to parts (a), (b), and (c) change?

11. Only one firm produces and sells soccer balls in the country of Wiknam, and as the story begins, international trade in soccer balls is prohibited. The following equations describe the monopolist's demand, marginal revenue, total cost, and marginal cost:

$$\text{Demand: } P = 10 - Q$$
$$\text{Marginal Revenue: } MR = 10 - 2Q$$
$$\text{Total Cost: } TC = 3 + Q + 0.5Q^2$$
$$\text{Marginal Cost: } MC = 1 + Q$$

where Q is quantity and P is the price measured in Wiknamian dollars.

a. How many soccer balls does the monopolist produce? At what price are they sold? What is the monopolist's profit?

b. One day, the King of Wiknam decrees that henceforth there will be free trade—either imports or exports— of soccer balls at the world price of $6. The firm is now a price taker in a competitive market. What happens to domestic production of soccer balls? To domestic consumption? Does Wiknam export or import soccer balls?

c. In our analysis of international trade in Chapter 9, a country becomes an exporter when the price without trade is below the world price and an importer when the price without trade is above the world price. Does that conclusion hold in your answers to parts (a) and (b)? Explain.

d. Suppose that the world price was not $6 but, instead, happened to be exactly the same as the domestic price without trade as determined in part (a). Would allowing trade have changed anything in the Wiknamian economy? Explain. How does the result here compare with the analysis in Chapter 9?

12. Based on market research, a film production company in Ectenia obtains the following information about the demand and production costs of its new DVD:

$$\text{Demand: } P = 1,000 - 10Q$$
$$\text{Total Revenue: } TR = 1,000Q - 10Q^2$$
$$\text{Marginal Revenue: } MR = 1,000 - 20Q$$
$$\text{Marginal Cost: } MC = 100 + 10Q$$

where Q indicates the number of copies sold and P is the price in Ectenian dollars.

a. Find the price and quantity that maximizes the company's profit.

b. Find the price and quantity that would maximize social welfare.

c. Calculate the deadweight loss from monopoly.

d. Suppose, in addition to the costs above, the director of the film has to be paid. The company is considering four options:
   i.   A flat fee of 2,000 Ectenian dollars
   ii. 50 percent of the profits
   iii. 150 Ectenian dollars per unit sold
   iv. 50 percent of the revenue
   For each option, calculate the profit-maximizing price and quantity. Which, if any, of these compensation schemes would alter the deadweight loss from monopoly? Explain.

13. Many schemes for price discriminating involve some cost. For example, discount coupons take up the time and resources of both the buyer and the seller. This question considers the implications of costly price discrimination. To keep things simple, let's assume that our monopolist's production costs are simply proportional to output so that average total cost and marginal cost are constant and equal to each other.

a. Draw the cost, demand, and marginal-revenue curves for the monopolist. Show the price the monopolist would charge without price discrimination.

b. In your diagram, mark the area equal to the monopolist's profit and call it X. Mark the area equal to consumer surplus and call it Y. Mark the area equal to the deadweight loss and call it Z.

c. Now suppose that the monopolist can perfectly price discriminate. What is the monopolist's profit? (Give your answer in terms of X, Y, and Z.)

d. What is the change in the monopolist's profit from price discrimination? What is the change in total surplus from price discrimination? Which change is larger? Explain. (Give your answer in terms of X, Y, and Z.)

e. Now suppose that there is some cost of price discrimination. To model this cost, let's assume that the monopolist has to pay a fixed cost C to price discriminate. How would a monopolist make the decision whether to pay this fixed cost? (Give your answer in terms of X, Y, Z, and C.)

f. How would a benevolent social planner, who cares about total surplus, decide whether the monopolist should price discriminate? (Give your answer in terms of X, Y, Z, and C.)

g. Compare your answers to parts (e) and (f). How does the monopolist's incentive to price discriminate differ from the social planner's? Is it possible that the monopolist will price discriminate even though it is not socially desirable?

For further information on topics in this chapter, additional problems, applications, examples, online quizzes, and more, please visit our website at www.cengage.com/economics/mankiw.

Monopolistic Competition

16

Y ou walk into a bookstore to buy a book to read during your next vacation. On the store's shelves you find a Sue Grafton mystery, a Stephen King thriller, a David McCullough history, a Stephenie Meyer vampire romance, and many other choices. When you pick out a book and buy it, what kind of market are you participating in?

On the one hand, the market for books seems competitive. As you look over the shelves at your bookstore, you find many authors and many publishers vying for your attention. A buyer in this market has thousands of competing products from which to choose. And because anyone can enter the industry by writing and publishing a book, the book business is not very profitable. For every highly paid novelist, there are hundreds of struggling ones.

On the other hand, the market for books seems monopolistic. Because each book is unique, publishers have some latitude in choosing what price to charge. The sellers in this market are price makers rather than price takers. And indeed, the price of books greatly exceeds marginal cost. The price of a typical hardcover novel, for instance, is about $25, whereas the cost of printing one additional copy of the novel is less than $5.

The market for novels fits neither the competitive nor the monopoly model. Instead, it is best described by the model of *monopolistic competition*, the subject of this chapter. The term "monopolistic competition" might at first seem to be an oxymoron, like "jumbo shrimp." But as we will see, monopolistically competitive industries are monopolistic in some ways and competitive in others. The model describes not only the publishing industry but also the market for many other goods and services.

Between Monopoly and Perfect Competition

The previous two chapters analyzed markets with many competitive firms and markets with a single monopoly firm. In Chapter 14, we saw that the price in a perfectly competitive market always equals the marginal cost of production. We also saw that, in the long run, entry and exit drive economic profit to zero, so the price also equals average total cost. In Chapter 15, we saw how monopoly firms can use their market power to keep prices above marginal cost, leading to a positive economic profit for the firm and a deadweight loss for society. Competition and monopoly are extreme forms of market structure. Competition occurs when there are many firms in a market offering essentially identical products; monopoly occurs when there is only one firm in a market.

Although the cases of perfect competition and monopoly illustrate some important ideas about how markets work, most markets in the economy include elements of both these cases and, therefore, are not completely described by either of them. The typical firm in the economy faces competition, but the competition is not so rigorous as to make the firm a price taker like the firms analyzed in Chapter 14. The typical firm also has some degree of market power, but its market power is not so great that the firm can be described exactly by the monopoly model presented in Chapter 15. In other words, many industries fall somewhere between the polar cases of perfect competition and monopoly. Economists call this situation *imperfect competition*.

oligopoly

a market structure in which only a few sellers offer similar or identical products

One type of imperfectly competitive market is an **oligopoly**, which is a market with only a few sellers, each offering a product that is similar or identical to the products offered by other sellers. Economists measure a market's domination by a small number of firms with a statistic called the *concentration ratio*, which is the percentage of total output in the market supplied by the four largest firms. In the U.S. economy, most industries have a four-firm concentration ratio under 50 percent, but in some industries, the biggest firms play a more dominant role. Highly concentrated industries include breakfast cereal (which has a concentration ratio of 78 percent), aircraft manufacturing (81 percent), electric lamp bulbs (89 percent), household laundry equipment (93 percent), and cigarettes (95 percent). These industries are best described as oligopolies.

monopolistic competition

a market structure in which many firms sell products that are similar but not identical

A second type of imperfectly competitive market is called **monopolistic competition.** This describes a market structure in which there are many firms selling products that are similar but not identical. In a monopolistically competitive market, each firm has a monopoly over the product it makes, but many other firms make similar products that compete for the same customers.

To be more precise, monopolistic competition describes a market with the following attributes:

- *Many sellers:* There are many firms competing for the same group of customers.
- *Product differentiation:* Each firm produces a product that is at least slightly different from those of other firms. Thus, rather than being a price taker, each firm faces a downward-sloping demand curve.
- *Free entry and exit*: Firms can enter or exit the market without restriction. Thus, the number of firms in the market adjusts until economic profits are driven to zero.

A moment's thought reveals a long list of markets with these attributes: books, DVDs, computer games, restaurants, piano lessons, cookies, clothing, and so on.

Monopolistic competition, like oligopoly, is a market structure that lies between the extreme cases of competition and monopoly. But oligopoly and monopolistic competition are quite different. Oligopoly departs from the perfectly competitive ideal of Chapter 14 because there are only a few sellers in the market. The small number of sellers makes rigorous competition less likely and strategic interactions among them vitally important. By contrast, under monopolistic competition, there are many sellers, each of which is small compared to the market. A monopolistically competitive market departs from the perfectly competitive ideal because each of the sellers offers a somewhat different product.

Figure 1 summarizes the four types of market structure. The first question to ask about any market is how many firms there are. If there is only one firm, the market is a monopoly. If there are only a few firms, the market is an oligopoly. If there are many firms, we need to ask another question: Do the firms sell identical or differentiated products? If the many firms sell differentiated products, the market is monopolistically competitive. If the many firms sell identical products, the market is perfectly competitive.

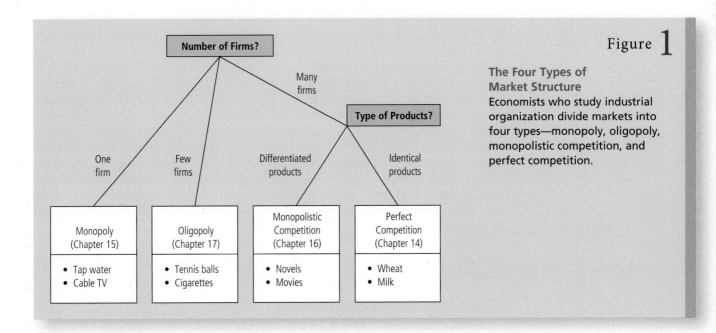

Figure 1

The Four Types of Market Structure
Economists who study industrial organization divide markets into four types—monopoly, oligopoly, monopolistic competition, and perfect competition.

Because reality is never as clear-cut as theory, at times you may find it hard to decide what structure best describes a market. There is, for instance, no magic number that separates "few" from "many" when counting the number of firms. (Do the approximately dozen companies that now sell cars in the United States make this market an oligopoly or more competitive? The answer is open to debate.) Similarly, there is no sure way to determine when products are differentiated and when they are identical. (Are different brands of milk really the same? Again, the answer is debatable.) When analyzing actual markets, economists have to keep in mind the lessons learned from studying all types of market structure and then apply each lesson as it seems appropriate.

Now that we understand how economists define the various types of market structure, we can continue our analysis of each of them. In the next chapter we analyze oligopoly. In this chapter we examine monopolistic competition.

QUICK QUIZ *Define* oligopoly *and* monopolistic competition *and give an example of each.*

Competition with Differentiated Products

To understand monopolistically competitive markets, we first consider the decisions facing an individual firm. We then examine what happens in the long run as firms enter and exit the industry. Next, we compare the equilibrium under monopolistic competition to the equilibrium under perfect competition that we examined in Chapter 14. Finally, we consider whether the outcome in a monopolistically competitive market is desirable from the standpoint of society as a whole.

The Monopolistically Competitive Firm in the Short Run

Each firm in a monopolistically competitive market is, in many ways, like a monopoly. Because its product is different from those offered by other firms, it faces a downward-sloping demand curve. (By contrast, a perfectly competitive firm faces a horizontal demand curve at the market price.) Thus, the monopolistically competitive firm follows a monopolist's rule for profit maximization: It chooses to produce the quantity at which marginal revenue equals marginal cost and then uses its demand curve to find the price at which it can sell that quantity.

Figure 2 shows the cost, demand, and marginal-revenue curves for two typical firms, each in a different monopolistically competitive industry. In both panels of this figure, the profit-maximizing quantity is found at the intersection of the marginal-revenue and marginal-cost curves. The two panels in this figure show different outcomes for the firm's profit. In panel (a), price exceeds average total cost, so the firm makes a profit. In panel (b), price is below average total cost. In this case, the firm is unable to make a positive profit, so the best the firm can do is to minimize its losses.

All this should seem familiar. A monopolistically competitive firm chooses its quantity and price just as a monopoly does. In the short run, these two types of market structure are similar.

The Long-Run Equilibrium

The situations depicted in Figure 2 do not last long. When firms are making profits, as in panel (a), new firms have an incentive to enter the market. This

Monopolistic competitors, like monopolists, maximize profit by producing the quantity at which marginal revenue equals marginal cost. The firm in panel (a) makes a profit because, at this quantity, price is above average total cost. The firm in panel (b) makes losses because, at this quantity, price is less than average total cost.

Figure 2

Monopolistic Competitors in the Short Run

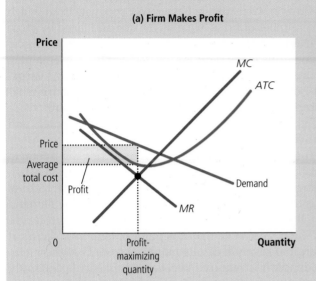

(a) Firm Makes Profit

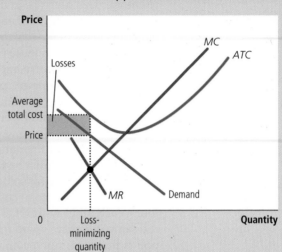

(b) Firm Makes Losses

"GIVEN THE DOWNWARD SLOPE OF OUR DEMAND CURVE, AND THE EASE WITH WHICH OTHER FIRMS CAN ENTER THE INDUSTRY, WE CAN STRENGTHEN OUR PROFIT POSITION ONLY BY EQUATING MARGINAL COST AND MARGINAL REVENUE. ORDER MORE JELLY BEANS."

entry increases the number of products from which customers can choose and, therefore, reduces the demand faced by each firm already in the market. In other words, profit encourages entry, and entry shifts the demand curves faced by the incumbent firms to the left. As the demand for incumbent firms' products falls, these firms experience declining profit.

Conversely, when firms are making losses, as in panel (b), firms in the market have an incentive to exit. As firms exit, customers have fewer products from which to choose. This decrease in the number of firms expands the demand faced by those firms that stay in the market. In other words, losses encourage exit, and exit shifts the demand curves of the remaining firms to the right. As the demand for the remaining firms' products rises, these firms experience rising profits (that is, declining losses).

This process of entry and exit continues until the firms in the market are making exactly zero economic profit. Figure 3 depicts the long-run equilibrium. Once the market reaches this equilibrium, new firms have no incentive to enter, and existing firms have no incentive to exit.

Notice that the demand curve in this figure just barely touches the average-total-cost curve. Mathematically, we say the two curves are *tangent* to each other. These two curves must be tangent once entry and exit have driven profit to zero. Because profit per unit sold is the difference between price (found on the demand curve) and average total cost, the maximum profit is zero only if these two curves touch each other without crossing. Also note that this point of tangency occurs at the same quantity where marginal revenue equals marginal cost. That these two points line up is not a coincidence: It is required because this particular quantity maximizes profit and the maximum profit is exactly zero in the long run.

To sum up, two characteristics describe the long-run equilibrium in a monopolistically competitive market:

- As in a monopoly market, price exceeds marginal cost. This conclusion arises because profit maximization requires marginal revenue to equal

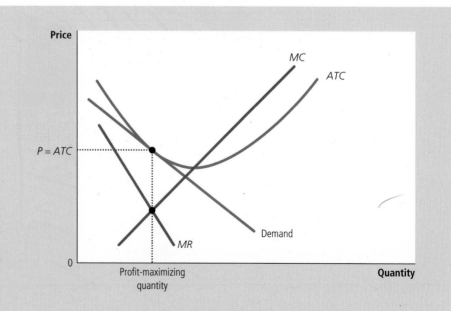

Figure 3

A Monopolistic Competitor in the Long Run
In a monopolistically competitive market, if firms are making profit, new firms enter, and the demand curves for the incumbent firms shift to the left. Similarly, if firms are making losses, old firms exit, and the demand curves of the remaining firms shift to the right. Because of these shifts in demand, a monopolistically competitive firm eventually finds itself in the long-run equilibrium shown here. In this long-run equilibrium, price equals average total cost, and the firm earns zero profit.

marginal cost and because the downward-sloping demand curve makes marginal revenue less than the price.

- As in a competitive market, price equals average total cost. This conclusion arises because free entry and exit drive economic profit to zero.

The second characteristic shows how monopolistic competition differs from monopoly. Because a monopoly is the sole seller of a product without close substitutes, it can earn positive economic profit, even in the long run. By contrast, because there is free entry into a monopolistically competitive market, the economic profit of a firm in this type of market is driven to zero.

Monopolistic versus Perfect Competition

Figure 4 compares the long-run equilibrium under monopolistic competition to the long-run equilibrium under perfect competition. (Chapter 14 discussed the equilibrium with perfect competition.) There are two noteworthy differences between monopolistic and perfect competition: excess capacity and the markup.

Excess Capacity As we have just seen, entry and exit drive each firm in a monopolistically competitive market to a point of tangency between its demand and average-total-cost curves. Panel (a) of Figure 4 shows that the quantity of output at this point is smaller than the quantity that minimizes average total cost. Thus, under monopolistic competition, firms produce on the downward-sloping

Panel (a) shows the long-run equilibrium in a monopolistically competitive market, and panel (b) shows the long-run equilibrium in a perfectly competitive market. Two differences are notable. (1) The perfectly competitive firm produces at the efficient scale, where average total cost is minimized. By contrast, the monopolistically competitive firm produces at less than the efficient scale. (2) Price equals marginal cost under perfect competition, but price is above marginal cost under monopolistic competition.

Figure 4

Monopolistic versus Perfect Competition

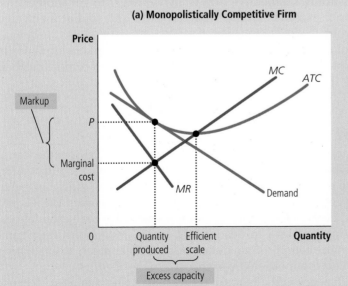

(a) Monopolistically Competitive Firm

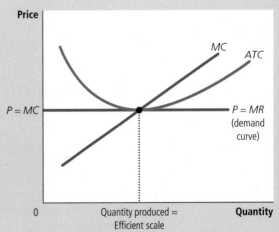

(b) Perfectly Competitive Firm

portion of their average-total-cost curves. In this way, monopolistic competition contrasts starkly with perfect competition. As panel (b) of Figure 4 shows, free entry in competitive markets drives firms to produce at the minimum of average total cost.

The quantity that minimizes average total cost is called the *efficient scale* of the firm. In the long run, perfectly competitive firms produce at the efficient scale, whereas monopolistically competitive firms produce below this level. Firms are said to have *excess capacity* under monopolistic competition. In other words, a monopolistically competitive firm, unlike a perfectly competitive firm, could increase the quantity it produces and lower the average total cost of production. The firm forgoes this opportunity because it would need to cut its price to sell the additional output. It is more profitable for a monopolistic competitor to continue operating with excess capacity.

Markup over Marginal Cost   A second difference between perfect competition and monopolistic competition is the relationship between price and marginal cost. For a competitive firm, such as that shown in panel (b) of Figure 4, price equals marginal cost. For a monopolistically competitive firm, such as that shown in panel (a), price exceeds marginal cost because the firm always has some market power.

How is this markup over marginal cost consistent with free entry and zero profit? The zero-profit condition ensures only that price equals average total cost. It does *not* ensure that price equals marginal cost. Indeed, in the long-run equilibrium, monopolistically competitive firms operate on the declining portion of their average-total-cost curves, so marginal cost is below average total cost. Thus, for price to equal average total cost, price must be above marginal cost.

In this relationship between price and marginal cost, we see a key behavioral difference between perfect competitors and monopolistic competitors. Imagine that you were to ask a firm the following question: "Would you like to see another customer come through your door ready to buy from you at your current price?" A perfectly competitive firm would answer that it didn't care. Because price exactly equals marginal cost, the profit from an extra unit sold is zero. By contrast, a monopolistically competitive firm is always eager to get another customer. Because its price exceeds marginal cost, an extra unit sold at the posted price means more profit.

According to an old quip, monopolistically competitive markets are those in which sellers send Christmas cards to the buyers. Trying to attract more customers makes sense only if price exceeds marginal cost.

Monopolistic Competition and the Welfare of Society

Is the outcome in a monopolistically competitive market desirable from the standpoint of society as a whole? Can policymakers improve on the market outcome? In previous chapters we evaluated markets from the standpoint of efficiency—that is, whether society is getting the most it can out of its scarce resources. We learned that competitive markets lead to efficient outcomes, unless there are externalities, and that monopoly markets lead to deadweight losses. Monopolistically competitive markets are more complex than either of these polar cases, so evaluating welfare in these markets is a more subtle exercise.

One source of inefficiency is the markup of price over marginal cost. Because of the markup, some consumers who value the good at more than the marginal cost of production (but less than the price) will be deterred from buying it. Thus, a monopolistically competitive market has the normal deadweight loss of monopoly pricing.

Although this outcome is undesirable compared to the first-best outcome of price equal to marginal cost, there is no easy way for policymakers to fix the problem. To enforce marginal-cost pricing, policymakers would need to regulate all firms that produce differentiated products. Because such products are so common in the economy, the administrative burden of such regulation would be overwhelming.

Moreover, regulating monopolistic competitors would entail all the problems of regulating natural monopolies. In particular, because monopolistic competitors are making zero profits already, requiring them to lower their prices to equal marginal cost would cause them to make losses. To keep these firms in business, the government would need to help them cover these losses. Rather than raise taxes to pay for these subsidies, policymakers may decide it is better to live with the inefficiency of monopolistic pricing.

Another way in which monopolistic competition may be socially inefficient is that the number of firms in the market may not be "ideal." That is, there may be too much or too little entry. One way to think about this problem is in terms of the externalities associated with entry. Whenever a new firm considers entering the market with a new product, it takes into account only the profit it would make. Yet its entry would also have two effects that are external to the firm:

- *The product-variety externality:* Because consumers get some consumer surplus from the introduction of a new product, entry of a new firm conveys a positive externality on consumers.
- *The business-stealing externality:* Because other firms lose customers and profits from the entry of a new competitor, entry of a new firm imposes a negative externality on existing firms.

Thus, in a monopolistically competitive market, there are positive and negative externalities associated with the entry of new firms. Depending on which externality is larger, a monopolistically competitive market could have either too few or too many products.

Both of these externalities are closely related to the conditions for monopolistic competition. The product-variety externality arises because a new firm would offer a product different from those of the existing firms. The business-stealing externality arises because firms post a price above marginal cost and, therefore, are always eager to sell additional units. Conversely, because perfectly competitive firms produce identical goods and charge a price equal to marginal cost, neither of these externalities exists under perfect competition.

In the end, we can conclude only that monopolistically competitive markets do not have all the desirable welfare properties of perfectly competitive markets. That is, the invisible hand does not ensure that total surplus is maximized under monopolistic competition. Yet because the inefficiencies are subtle, hard to measure, and hard to fix, there is no easy way for public policy to improve the market outcome.

QUICK QUIZ   *List the three key attributes of monopolistic competition. • Draw and explain a diagram to show the long-run equilibrium in a monopolistically competitive market. How does this equilibrium differ from that in a perfectly competitive market?*

· · · · · · · · · · · · · in the news

> ## *Insufficient Variety as a Market Failure*

University of Pennsylvania economist Joel Waldfogel argues that, in the presence of large fixed costs, the market may insufficiently service customers with unusual preferences.

If the Shoe Doesn't Fit

BY JOEL WALDFOGEL

Last week, Nike unveiled a shoe designed specifically for American Indians. The sneaker has both a native-theme design and—more importantly—a wider shape to accommodate the distinctly shaped feet of American Indians. With diabetes and related conditions near epidemic levels in some tribes, American Indian leaders were happy to welcome this comfortable product. If anything, what seems odd is that it took so long. After all, free-market economists have told us for decades that we should rely on market decisions, not the government, to meet our needs, because it's the market that satisfies everyone's every desire.

And yet it turns out that it's the Indians' long wait for a good sneaker that's typical. For small groups with preferences outside the norm, the market often fails to deliver,

as I argue in my new book, *The Tyranny of the Market: Why You Can't Always Get What You Want.*

John Stuart Mill pointed out that voting gives rise to a tyranny of the majority. If we vote on what color shirts to make—or whether to make wide or narrow shoes— then the majority gets what it prefers, and the minority does not. The market, on the other hand, is supposed to work differently.

As Milton Friedman eloquently put it in 1962, "the characteristic feature of action through political channels is that it tends to require or enforce substantial conformity. The great advantage of the market is that it permits wide diversity. Each man can vote, as it were, for the color of tie he wants and get it; he does not have to see what color the majority wants and then, if he is in the minority, submit." This is a wonderful argument. Except that for many products and for many people, it's wrong.

Two simple conditions that prevail in many markets mean that individual taste alone doesn't determine individual satisfaction. These conditions are (1) big setup costs and (2) preferences that differ across groups; when they're present, an individual's satisfaction is a function of how many people share his or her tastes. In other words, in these cases, markets share some of the objectionable features of government. They give bigger groups more and better options.

Advertising

It is nearly impossible to go through a typical day in a modern economy without being bombarded with advertising. Whether you are reading a newspaper, watching television, surfing the Internet, or driving down the highway, some firm will try to convince you to buy its product. Such behavior is a natural feature of monopolistic competition (as well as some oligopolistic industries). When firms sell differentiated products and charge prices above marginal cost, each firm has an incentive to advertise to attract more buyers to its particular product.

In my research, I've discovered that this phenomenon is widespread. Ten years ago, I started studying radio-station listening patterns. I noticed that people listened to the radio more in metro areas of the United States with relatively large populations. This is not terribly surprising. In larger cities, more stations can attract enough listeners and advertising revenue to cover their costs and stay on the air. With more to choose from on the dial, residents tune in more. So, in this situation of high fixed costs (each station needs a following to keep broadcasting), people help one another by making more options viable.

But who benefits whom? When I looked at black and white listeners separately, I noticed something surprising. Blacks listen more in cities with larger black populations, and whites listen more in cities with larger white populations. Black listening does *not* increase where there's a higher white population, and white listening does not increase with a higher black population. Which means that while overall people help each other by increasing the number of stations on the dial, blacks do not help whites, and whites do not help blacks. Similar patterns arise for Hispanics and non-Hispanics.

A closer look at the data—necessary only because I'm a middle-aged white economist—showed why this was happening. Blacks and whites don't listen to the same radio stations. The black-targeted formats account for about two-thirds of black listening and only 3 percent of white listening. Similarly, the formats that attract the largest white audiences, like country, attract almost no blacks. This means that if you dropped Larry the Cable Guy and a few thousand of his friends from a helicopter (with parachutes) into a metro area, you'd create more demand for country and perhaps album-rock stations, which would be nice for white listeners. But the influx wouldn't help black listeners at all.

In this example, different population groups don't help each other, but they don't hurt each other, either. Sometimes, though, the effect that groups have on each other through the market is actually negative. Industries like daily newspapers offer essentially one product per market. Because the paper can be pitched to appeal to one group or another, the larger one group is, the less the product is tailored to anyone else. This is the tyranny of the majority translated almost literally from politics into markets.

This brings us back to Nike's new shoe. Foot Locker is full of options that fit me and most other Americans. But American Indians make up just 1.5 percent of the U.S. population, and with feet on average three sizes wider, they need different-sized shoes.

If we had all voted in a national election on whether the Ministry of Shoes should make wide or typical-width shoes, we surely would have chosen the latter. That's why Friedman condemned government allocation. And yet the market made the same choice. If Nike's announcement looks like a solution to this problem of ignored minority preference, it really isn't. The company took too many years to bring the shoe on line, and according to the Associated Press, the new sneaker "represents less of a financial opportunity than a goodwill and branding effort."

The tyranny of the market arises elsewhere. With drug development costs $1 billion, if you are going to that your disease is con attract the interest of drug want to fly from your town to hope that your city is big enough to plane every day.

When you're not so lucky, you benefit when the government steps in on your behalf, with subsidies for research on drugs for rare diseases or for air service to small locales. For a generation, influential economists have argued for letting the market decide a wide array of questions, to protect your freedom to choose whatever you want. This is true—if everyone agrees with you.

Source: *Slate,* Thursday, October 4, 2007.

The amount of advertising varies substantially across products. Firms that sell highly differentiated consumer goods, such as over-the-counter drugs, perfumes, soft drinks, razor blades, breakfast cereals, and dog food, typically spend between 10 and 20 percent of revenue for advertising. Firms that sell industrial products, such as drill presses and communications satellites, typically spend very little on advertising. And firms that sell homogeneous products, such as wheat, peanuts, or crude oil, spend nothing at all.

For the economy as a whole, about 2 percent of total firm revenue is spent on advertising. This spending takes many forms, including commercials on television and radio, space in newspapers and magazines, direct mail, the yellow pages, billboards, and ads on websites.

The Debate over Advertising

Is society wasting the resources it devotes to advertising? Or does advertising serve a valuable purpose? Assessing the social value of advertising is difficult and often generates heated argument among economists. Let's consider both sides of the debate.

The Critique of Advertising   Critics of advertising argue that firms advertise to manipulate people's tastes. Much advertising is psychological rather than informational. Consider, for example, the typical television commercial for some brand of soft drink. The commercial most likely does not tell the viewer about the product's price or quality. Instead, it might show a group of happy people at a party on a beach on a beautiful sunny day. In their hands are cans of the soft drink. The goal of the commercial is to convey a subconscious (if not subtle) message: "You too can have many friends and be happy, if only you drink our product." Critics of advertising argue that such a commercial creates a desire that otherwise might not exist.

Critics also argue that advertising impedes competition. Advertising often tries to convince consumers that products are more different than they truly are. By increasing the perception of product differentiation and fostering brand loyalty, advertising makes buyers less concerned with price differences among similar goods. With a less elastic demand curve, each firm charges a larger markup over marginal cost.

The Defense of Advertising   Defenders of advertising argue that firms use advertising to provide information to customers. Advertising conveys the prices of the goods offered for sale, the existence of new products, and the locations of retail outlets. This information allows customers to make better choices about what to buy and, thus, enhances the ability of markets to allocate resources efficiently.

Defenders also argue that advertising fosters competition. Because advertising allows customers to be more fully informed about all the firms in the market, customers can more easily take advantage of price differences. Thus, each firm has less market power. In addition, advertising allows new firms to enter more easily because it gives entrants a means to attract customers from existing firms.

Over time, policymakers have come to accept the view that advertising can make markets more competitive. One important example is the regulation of advertising for certain professions, such as lawyers, doctors, and pharmacists. In the past, these groups succeeded in getting state governments to prohibit advertising in their fields on the grounds that advertising was "unprofessional." In recent years, however, the courts have concluded that the primary effect of these restrictions on advertising was to curtail competition. They have, therefore, overturned many of the laws that prohibit advertising by members of these professions.

 CASE STUDY

Advertising and the Price of Eyeglasses

What effect does advertising have on the price of a good? On the one hand, advertising might make consumers view products as being more different than they otherwise would. If so, it would make markets less competitive and firms' demand curves less elastic, and this would lead firms to charge higher prices. On the other hand, advertising might make it easier for consumers to find the firms offering the best prices. In this case, it would make markets more competitive and firms' demand curves more elastic, which would lead to lower prices.

In an article published in the *Journal of Law and Economics* in 1972, economist Lee Benham tested these two views of advertising. In the United States during the 1960s, the various state governments had vastly different rules about advertising by optometrists. Some states allowed advertising for eyeglasses and eye examinations. Many states, however, prohibited it. For example, the Florida law read as follows:

> It is unlawful for any person, firm, or corporation to . . . advertise either directly or indirectly by any means whatsoever any definite or indefinite price or credit terms on prescriptive or corrective lens, frames, complete prescriptive or corrective glasses, or any optometric service. . . . This section is passed in the interest of public health, safety, and welfare, and its provisions shall be liberally construed to carry out its objects and purposes.

Professional optometrists enthusiastically endorsed these restrictions on advertising.

Benham used the differences in state law as a natural experiment to test the two views of advertising. The results were striking. In those states that prohibited advertising, the average price paid for a pair of eyeglasses was $33. (This number is not as low as it seems, for this price is from 1963, when all prices were much lower than they are today. To convert 1963 prices into today's dollars, you can multiply them by about 7.) In states that did not restrict advertising, the average price was $26. Thus, advertising reduced average prices by more than 20 percent. In the market for eyeglasses, and probably in many other markets as well, advertising fosters competition and leads to lower prices for consumers. ∎

Advertising as a Signal of Quality

Many types of advertising contain little apparent information about the product being advertised. Consider a firm introducing a new breakfast cereal. A typical advertisement might have some highly paid actor eating the cereal and exclaiming how wonderful it tastes. How much information does the advertisement really provide?

The answer is more than you might think. Defenders of advertising argue that even advertising that appears to contain little hard information may in fact tell consumers something about product quality. The willingness of the firm to spend a large amount of money on advertising can itself be a *signal* to consumers about the quality of the product being offered.

Consider the problem facing two firms—Post and Kellogg. Each company has just come up with a recipe for a new cereal, which it would sell for $3 a box. To keep things simple, let's assume that the marginal cost of making cereal is zero, so the $3 is all profit. Each company knows that if it spends $10 million on advertising, it will get 1 million consumers to try its new cereal. And each company knows that if consumers like the cereal, they will buy it not once but many times.

First consider Post's decision. Based on market research, Post knows that its cereal is only mediocre. Although advertising would sell one box to each of 1 million consumers, the consumers would quickly learn that the cereal is not very good and stop buying it. Post decides it is not worth paying $10 million in advertising to get only $3 million in sales. So it does not bother to advertise. It sends its cooks back to the test kitchen to find another recipe.

Kellogg, on the other hand, knows that its cereal is great. Each person who tries it will buy a box a month for the next year. Thus, the $10 million in advertising will bring in $36 million in sales. Advertising is profitable here because Kellogg

FYI

> ## Galbraith versus Hayek

Two great economists of the 20th century were John Kenneth Galbraith and Friedrich Hayek. They held very different views about advertising, which reflected their views about the capitalist system more broadly.

John Kenneth Galbraith's most famous book was *The Affluent Society*, published in 1958. In it, he argued that corporations use advertising to create demand for products that people otherwise do not want or need. The market system should not be applauded, he believed, for satisfying desires that it has itself created. Galbraith was skeptical that economic growth was leading to higher levels of well-being, because people's aspirations were being made to keep pace with their increased material prosperity. He worried that as advertising and salesmanship artificially enhanced the desire for private goods, public spending on such items as better schools and better parks suffered. The result, according to Galbraith, was "private opulence and public squalor." Galbraith's policy recommendation was clear: Increase the size of government.

Friedrich Hayek's most famous book was *The Road to Serfdom*, published in 1944. It argued that an expansive government inevitably means a sacrifice of personal freedoms. Hayek also

John Kenneth Galbraith

Friedrich Hayek

wrote a well-known critique of Galbraith in 1961, addressing specifically Galbraith's view of advertising. Hayek observed that advertising was merely one example of a larger phenomenon: Our social environment creates many of our preferences. Literature, art, and music are all acquired tastes. A person's demand for hearing a Mozart concerto may have been created in a music appreciation class, but this fact does not make the desire less legitimate or the music professor a sinister influence. Hayek concluded, "It is because each individual producer thinks that the consumers can be persuaded to like his products that he endeavors to influence them. But though this effort is part of the influences which shape consumers' taste, no producer can in any real sense 'determine' them."

These two economists disagreed about the roles of advertising, markets, and government, but they did have one thing in common: great acclaim. In 1974, Hayek won the Nobel Prize in economics. In 2000, President Clinton awarded Galbraith the National Medal of Freedom. And even though their books are now many decades old, they are still well worth reading. The issues that Hayek and Galbraith addressed are timeless, and their insights apply as well to our economy as to their own.

has a good product that consumers will buy repeatedly. Thus, Kellogg chooses to advertise.

Now that we have considered the behavior of the two firms, let's consider the behavior of consumers. We began by asserting that consumers are inclined to try a new cereal that they see advertised. But is this behavior rational? Should a consumer try a new cereal just because the seller has chosen to advertise it?

In fact, it may be completely rational for consumers to try new products that they see advertised. In our story, consumers decide to try Kellogg's new cereal because Kellogg advertises. Kellogg chooses to advertise because it knows that its cereal is quite good, while Post chooses not to advertise because it knows that its cereal is mediocre. By its willingness to spend money on advertising,

Kellogg signals to consumers the quality of its cereal. Each consumer thinks, quite sensibly, "Boy, if the Kellogg Company is willing to spend so much money advertising this new cereal, it must be really good."

What is most surprising about this theory of advertising is that the content of the advertisement is irrelevant. Kellogg signals the quality of its product by its willingness to spend money on advertising. What the advertisements say is not as important as the fact that consumers know ads are expensive. By contrast, cheap advertising cannot be effective at signaling quality to consumers. In our example, if an advertising campaign cost less than $3 million, both Post and Kellogg would use it to market their new cereals. Because both good and mediocre cereals would be advertised, consumers could not infer the quality of a new cereal from the fact that it is advertised. Over time, consumers would learn to ignore such cheap advertising.

This theory can explain why firms pay famous actors large amounts of money to make advertisements that, on the surface, appear to convey no information at all. The information is not in the advertisement's content but simply in its existence and expense.

Brand Names

Advertising is closely related to the existence of brand names. In many markets, there are two types of firms. Some firms sell products with widely recognized brand names, while other firms sell generic substitutes. For example, in a typical drugstore, you can find Bayer aspirin on the shelf next to generic aspirin. In a typical grocery store, you can find Pepsi next to less familiar colas. Most often, the firm with the brand name spends more on advertising and charges a higher price for its product.

Just as there is disagreement about the economics of advertising, there is disagreement about the economics of brand names. Let's consider both sides of the debate.

Critics argue that brand names cause consumers to perceive differences that do not really exist. In many cases, the generic good is almost indistinguishable from the brand-name good. Consumers' willingness to pay more for the brand-name good, these critics assert, is a form of irrationality fostered by advertising. Economist Edward Chamberlin, one of the early developers of the theory of monopolistic competition, concluded from this argument that brand names were bad for the economy. He proposed that the government discourage their use by refusing to enforce the exclusive trademarks that companies use to identify their products.

More recently, economists have defended brand names as a useful way for consumers to ensure that the goods they buy are of high quality. There are two related arguments. First, brand names provide consumers with *information* about quality when quality cannot be easily judged in advance of purchase. Second, brand names give firms an *incentive* to maintain high quality because firms have a financial stake in maintaining the reputation of their brand names.

To see how these arguments work in practice, consider a famous brand name: McDonald's hamburgers. Imagine that you are driving through an unfamiliar town and want to stop for lunch. You see a McDonald's and a local restaurant next to it. Which do you choose? The local restaurant may in fact offer better food at lower prices, but you have no way of knowing that. By contrast, McDonald's offers a consistent product across many cities. Its brand name is useful to you as a way of judging the quality of what you are about to buy.

The McDonald's brand name also ensures that the company has an incentive to maintain quality. For example, if some customers were to become ill from

bad food sold at a McDonald's, the news would be disastrous for the company. McDonald's would lose much of the valuable reputation that it has built up with years of expensive advertising. As a result, it would lose sales and profit not just in the outlet that sold the bad food but in its many outlets throughout the country. By contrast, if some customers were to become ill from bad food at a local restaurant, that restaurant might have to close down, but the lost profits would be much smaller. Hence, McDonald's has a greater incentive to ensure that its food is safe.

The debate over brand names thus centers on the question of whether consumers are rational in preferring brand names to generic substitutes. Critics argue that brand names are the result of an irrational consumer response to advertising. Defenders argue that consumers have good reason to pay more for brand-name products because they can be more confident in the quality of these products.

QUICK QUIZ   *How might advertising make markets less competitive? How might it make markets more competitive? • Give the arguments for and against brand names.*

Conclusion

Monopolistic competition is true to its name: It is a hybrid of monopoly and competition. Like a monopoly, each monopolistic competitor faces a downward-sloping demand curve and, as a result, charges a price above marginal cost. As in a perfectly competitive market, there are many firms, and entry and exit drive the profit of each monopolistic competitor toward zero in the long run. Table 1 summarizes these lessons.

Because monopolistically competitive firms produce differentiated products, each firm advertises to attract customers to its own brand. To some extent, advertising manipulates consumers' tastes, promotes irrational brand loyalty, and impedes competition. To a larger extent, advertising provides information, establishes brand names of reliable quality, and fosters competition.

The theory of monopolistic competition seems to describe many markets in the economy. It is somewhat disappointing, therefore, that the theory does not yield simple and compelling advice for public policy. From the standpoint of the economic theorist, the allocation of resources in monopolistically competitive markets is not perfect. Yet from the standpoint of a practical policymaker, there may be little that can be done to improve it.

Table 1

Monopolistic Competition: Between Perfect Competition and Monopoly

	Market Structure		
	Perfect Competition	**Monopolistic Competition**	**Monopoly**
Features that all three market structures share			
Goal of firms	Maximize profits	Maximize profits	Maximize profits
Rule for maximizing	$MR = MC$	$MR = MC$	$MR = MC$
Can earn economic profits in the short run?	Yes	Yes	Yes
Features that monopolistic competition shares with monopoly			
Price taker?	Yes	No	No
Price	$P = MC$	$P > MC$	$P > MC$
Produces welfare-maximizing level of output?	Yes	No	No
Features that monopolistic competition shares with competition			
Number of firms	Many	Many	One
Entry in long run?	Yes	Yes	No
Can earn economic profits in long run?	No	No	Yes

SUMMARY

- A monopolistically competitive market is characterized by three attributes: many firms, differentiated products, and free entry.

- The equilibrium in a monopolistically competitive market differs from that in a perfectly competitive market in two related ways. First, each firm in a monopolistically competitive market has excess capacity. That is, it operates on the downward-sloping portion of the average-total-cost curve. Second, each firm charges a price above marginal cost.

- Monopolistic competition does not have all the desirable properties of perfect competition. There is the standard deadweight loss of monopoly caused by the markup of price over marginal cost. In addition, the number of firms (and thus the variety of products) can be too large or too small. In practice, the ability of policymakers to correct these inefficiencies is limited.

- The product differentiation inherent in monopolistic competition leads to the use of advertising and brand names. Critics of advertising and brand names argue that firms use them to manipulate consumers' tastes and to reduce competition. Defenders of advertising and brand names argue that firms use them to inform consumers and to compete more vigorously on price and product quality.

KEY CONCEPTS

oligopoly, *p. 330*

monopolistic competition, *p. 330*

QUESTIONS FOR REVIEW

1. Describe the three attributes of monopolistic competition. How is monopolistic competition like monopoly? How is it like perfect competition?
2. Draw a diagram depicting a firm that is making a profit in a monopolistically competitive market. Now show what happens to this firm as new firms enter the industry.
3. Draw a diagram of the long-run equilibrium in a monopolistically competitive market. How is price related to average total cost? How is price related to marginal cost?

4. Does a monopolistic competitor produce too much or too little output compared to the most efficient level? What practical considerations make it difficult for policymakers to solve this problem?
5. How might advertising reduce economic well-being? How might advertising increase economic well-being?
6. How might advertising with no apparent informational content in fact convey information to consumers?
7. Explain two benefits that might arise from the existence of brand names.

PROBLEMS AND APPLICATIONS

1. Among monopoly, oligopoly, monopolistic competition, and perfect competition, how would you classify the markets for each of the following drinks?
   a. tap water
   b. bottled water
   c. cola
   d. beer
2. Classify the following markets as perfectly competitive, monopolistic, or monopolistically competitive, and explain your answers.
   a. wooden no. 2 pencils
   b. copper
   c. local telephone service
   d. peanut butter
   e. lipstick
3. For each of the following characteristics, say whether it describes a perfectly competitive firm, a monopolistically competitive firm, both, or neither.
   a. Sells a product differentiated from that of its competitors
   b. Has marginal revenue less than price

   c. Earns economic profit in the long run
   d. Produces at the minimum of average total cost in the long run
   e. Equates marginal revenue and marginal cost
   f. Charges a price above marginal cost
4. For each of the following characteristics, say whether it describes a monopoly firm, a monopolistically competitive firm, both, or neither.
   a. Faces a downward-sloping demand curve
   b. Has marginal revenue less than price
   c. Faces the entry of new firms selling similar products
   d. Earns economic profit in the long run
   e. Equates marginal revenue and marginal cost
   f. Produces the socially efficient quantity of output
5. You are hired as the consultant to a monopolistically competitive firm. The firm reports the following information about its price, marginal cost, and average total cost. Can the firm possibly be maximizing profit? If not, what should it do to increase profit? If the firm is profit maximizing, is the firm in a long-run equilibrium?

If not, what will happen to restore long-run equilibrium?

a. $P < MC, P > ATC$
b. $P > MC, P < ATC$
c. $P = MC, P > ATC$
d. $P > MC, P = ATC$

6. Sparkle is one firm of many in the market for toothpaste, which is in long-run equilibrium.
   a. Draw a diagram showing Sparkle's demand curve, marginal-revenue curve, average-total-cost curve, and marginal-cost curve. Label Sparkle's profit-maximizing output and price.
   b. What is Sparkle's profit? Explain.
   c. On your diagram, show the consumer surplus derived from the purchase of Sparkle toothpaste. Also show the deadweight loss relative to the efficient level of output.
   d. If the government forced Sparkle to produce the efficient level of output, what would happen to the firm? What would happen to Sparkle's customers?

7. Consider a monopolistically competitive market with N firms. Each firm's business opportunities are described by the following equations:

$$\text{Demand: } Q = 100/N - P$$
$$\text{Marginal Revenue: } MR = 100/N - 2Q$$
$$\text{Total Cost: } TC = 50 + Q^2$$
$$\text{Marginal Cost: } MC = 2Q$$

   a. How does N, the number of firms in the market, affect each firm's demand curve? Why?
   b. How many units does each firm produce? (The answers to this and the next two questions depend on N.)
   c. What price does each firm charge?
   d. How much profit does each firm make?
   e. In the long run, how many firms will exist in this market?

8. The market for peanut butter in Nutville is monopolistically competitive and in long-run equilibrium. One day, consumer advocate Skippy Jif discovers that all brands of peanut butter in Nutville are identical. Thereafter, the market becomes perfectly competitive and again reaches its long-run equilibrium. Using an appropriate diagram, explain whether each of the following variables increases, decreases, or stays the same for a typical firm in the market.
   a. price
   b. quantity
   c. average total cost
   d. marginal cost
   e. profit

9. For each of the following pairs of firms, explain which firm would be more likely to engage in advertising.
   a. a family-owned farm or a family-owned restaurant
   b. a manufacturer of forklifts or a manufacturer of cars
   c. a company that invented a very comfortable razor or a company that invented a less comfortable razor

10. Sleek Sneakers Co. is one of many firms in the market for shoes.
    a. Assume that Sleek is currently earning short-run economic profits. On a correctly labeled diagram, show Sleek's profit-maximizing output and price, as well as the area representing profit.
    b. What happens to Sleek's price, output, and profit in the long run? Explain this change in words, and show it on a new diagram.
    c. Suppose that over time consumers become more focused on stylistic differences among shoe brands. How would this change in attitudes affect each firm's price elasticity of demand? In the long run, how will this change in demand affect Sleek's price, output, and profits?
    d. At the profit-maximizing price you identified in part (c), is Sleek's demand curve elastic or inelastic? Explain.

11. The market for chicken was once perfectly competitive. Then Frank Perdue began marketing chicken under his name.
    a. How do you suppose Perdue created a brand name for chicken? What did he gain from doing so?
    b. What did society gain from having brand-name chicken? What did society lose?

12. The makers of Tylenol pain reliever do a lot of advertising and have loyal customers. In contrast, the makers of generic acetaminophen do

no advertising, and their customers shop only for the lowest price. Assume that the marginal costs of Tylenol and generic acetaminophen are the same.

a. Draw a diagram showing Tylenol's demand, marginal-revenue, and marginal-cost curves. Label Tylenol's price and markup over marginal cost.

b. Repeat part (a) for a producer of generic acetaminophen. How do the diagrams differ? Which company has the bigger markup? Explain.

c. Which company has the bigger incentive for careful quality control? Why?

For further information on topics in this chapter, additional problems, applications, examples, online quizzes, and more, please visit our website at www .cengage.com/economics/mankiw.

Oligopoly

17

I f you go to a store to buy tennis balls, you will probably come home with one of four brands: Wilson, Penn, Dunlop, or Spalding. These four companies make almost all the tennis balls sold in the United States. Together these firms determine the quantity of tennis balls produced and, given the market demand curve, the price at which tennis balls are sold.

The market for tennis balls is an example of an **oligopoly**. The essence of an oligopolistic market is that there are only a few sellers. As a result, the actions of any one seller in the market can have a large impact on the profits of all the other sellers. Oligopolistic firms are interdependent in a way that competitive firms are not. Our goal in this chapter is to see how this interdependence shapes the firms' behavior and what problems it raises for public policy.

The analysis of oligopoly offers an opportunity to introduce **game theory**, the study of how people behave in strategic situations. By "strategic" we mean a situation in which a person, when choosing among alternative courses of action, must

oligopoly
a market structure in which only a few sellers offer similar or identical products

game theory
the study of how people behave in strategic situations

consider how others might respond to the action he takes. Strategic thinking is crucial not only in checkers, chess, and tic-tac-toe but in many business decisions. Because oligopolistic markets have only a small number of firms, each firm must act strategically. Each firm knows that its profit depends not only on how much it produces but also on how much the other firms produce. In making its production decision, each firm in an oligopoly should consider how its decision might affect the production decisions of all the other firms.

Game theory is not necessary for understanding competitive or monopoly markets. In a market that is either perfectly competitive or monopolistically competitive, each firm is so small compared to the market that strategic interactions with other firms are not important. In a monopolized market, strategic interactions are absent because the market has only one firm. But, as we will see, game theory is useful for understanding oligopolies and many other situations in which a small number of players interact with one another. Game theory helps explain the strategies that people choose, whether they are playing tennis or selling tennis balls.

Markets with Only a Few Sellers

Because an oligopolistic market has only a small group of sellers, a key feature of oligopoly is the tension between cooperation and self-interest. The oligopolists are best off when they cooperate and act like a monopolist—producing a small quantity of output and charging a price above marginal cost. Yet because each oligopolist cares only about its own profit, there are powerful incentives at work that hinder a group of firms from maintaining the cooperative outcome.

A Duopoly Example

To understand the behavior of oligopolies, let's consider an oligopoly with only two members, called a *duopoly*. Duopoly is the simplest type of oligopoly. Oligopolies with three or more members face the same problems as duopolies, so we do not lose much by starting with the simpler case.

Imagine a town in which only two residents—Jack and Jill—own wells that produce water safe for drinking. Each Saturday, Jack and Jill decide how many gallons of water to pump, bring the water to town, and sell it for whatever price the market will bear. To keep things simple, suppose that Jack and Jill can pump as much water as they want without cost. That is, the marginal cost of water equals zero.

Table 1 shows the town's demand schedule for water. The first column shows the total quantity demanded, and the second column shows the price. If the two well owners sell a total of 10 gallons of water, water goes for $110 a gallon. If they sell a total of 20 gallons, the price falls to $100 a gallon. And so on. If you graphed these two columns of numbers, you would get a standard downward-sloping demand curve.

The last column in Table 1 shows the total revenue from the sale of water. It equals the quantity sold times the price. Because there is no cost to pumping water, the total revenue of the two producers equals their total profit.

Let's now consider how the organization of the town's water industry affects the price of water and the quantity of water sold.

Table 1

The Demand Schedule for Water

Quantity	Price	Total Revenue (and total profit)
0 gallons	$120	$ 0
10	110	1,100
20	100	2,000
30	90	2,700
40	80	3,200
50	70	3,500
60	60	3,600
70	50	3,500
80	40	3,200
90	30	2,700
100	20	2,000
110	10	1,100
120	0	0

Competition, Monopolies, and Cartels

Before considering the price and quantity of water that would result from the duopoly of Jack and Jill, let's discuss briefly what the outcome would be if the water market were either perfectly competitive or monopolistic. These two polar cases are natural benchmarks.

If the market for water were perfectly competitive, the production decisions of each firm would drive price equal to marginal cost. Because we have assumed that the marginal cost of pumping additional water is zero, the equilibrium price of water under perfect competition would be zero as well. The equilibrium quantity would be 120 gallons. The price of water would reflect the cost of producing it, and the efficient quantity of water would be produced and consumed.

Now consider how a monopoly would behave. Table 1 shows that total profit is maximized at a quantity of 60 gallons and a price of $60 a gallon. A profit-maximizing monopolist, therefore, would produce this quantity and charge this price. As is standard for monopolies, price would exceed marginal cost. The result would be inefficient, because the quantity of water produced and consumed would fall short of the socially efficient level of 120 gallons.

What outcome should we expect from our duopolists? One possibility is that Jack and Jill get together and agree on the quantity of water to produce and the price to charge for it. Such an agreement among firms over production and price is called **collusion,** and the group of firms acting in unison is called a **cartel**. Once a cartel is formed, the market is in effect served by a monopoly, and we can apply our analysis from Chapter 15. That is, if Jack and Jill were to collude, they would agree on the monopoly outcome because that outcome maximizes the total profit that the producers can get from the market. Our two producers would produce a total of 60 gallons, which would be sold at a price of $60 a gallon. Once again, price exceeds marginal cost, and the outcome is socially inefficient.

A cartel must agree not only on the total level of production but also on the amount produced by each member. In our case, Jack and Jill must agree on how to

collusion
an agreement among firms in a market about quantities to produce or prices to charge

cartel
a group of firms acting in unison

split the monopoly production of 60 gallons. Each member of the cartel will want a larger share of the market because a larger market share means larger profit. If Jack and Jill agreed to split the market equally, each would produce 30 gallons, the price would be $60 a gallon, and each would get a profit of $1,800.

in the news

❯ Public Price Fixing

If a group of producers coordinates their prices in secret meetings, they can be sent to jail for criminal violations of antitrust laws. But what if they discuss the same topic in public?

Market Talk

BY ALISTAIR LINDSAY

Most companies have antitrust compliance policies. They typically—and quite rightly—identify a number of things that officers and employees should not do, on pain of criminal liability, eye-watering fines and unlimited damages actions. All make clear that companies must not agree with their competitors to fix prices. This is a bright-line rule. But it raises an important question: Can companies coordinate price increases without infringing the cartel rules?

In markets where competitors need to publish their prices to win business—for example, many retail markets—it is perfectly lawful to shadow a rival's increases, so long as each seller acts entirely independently in setting its charges. The very definition of an oligopoly is a market involving a small number of suppliers that set their own commercial strategies but take account of their competitors. One competitor may emerge as a leader, with others taking their cue on when to raise prices and by how much.

When prices are privately negotiated— as in many industrials markets—it is common for a customer to volunteer information about a rival's prices to obtain leverage: "*You've quoted £100 per ton, but X is offering £95 and I'm going to them unless you can do better.*" A company that receives this information obtains valuable intelligence about what its rivals are charging, but it does not infringe cartel rules. . . .

Companies also sometimes signal to one another in their communications with investors, whether deliberately or not. A competitor which informs the markets, say, that it expects a price war to end in February is providing relevant information to actual and potential owners of its stock. But of course its rivals read the same reports and can change their strategies accordingly. So a statement to the market can serve as just as much of a signal to competitors as a statement made during a cartel meeting. . . .

Signaling through investor communications raises difficult questions for cartel enforcement. The enforcers want to protect consumers from the adverse effects of blatant signaling, but not at the price of losing transparency in financial markets. For

example, it is highly relevant to an investor to know an airline's predicted growth of per-mile passenger revenue for the next quarter. But a rival airline might use the announced figure as a benchmark when setting its own fares for the next quarter.

As things stand, cartel authorities have focused their efforts in such situations on blocking mergers in markets where signaling is prevalent, arguing that consolidation in such markets can further dampen competition by making coordination easier or more successful. However, they have not taken high-profile action alleging cartel infringements against companies for announcements made to investors.

If there is no justification for a particular announcement other than to signal to competitors, cartel authorities should seek to intervene. For in this case the public announcement is analytically the same as a private discussion directly with the rivals, and there is scope for consumers to be seriously harmed. But most announcements do serve legitimate purposes, such as keeping investors informed. In these cases, intervention by the cartel authorities seems too complex, given the disparate policy objectives in play.

Source: *The Wall Street Journal,* December 13, 2007.

The Equilibrium for an Oligopoly

Oligopolists would like to form cartels and earn monopoly profits, but that is often impossible. Squabbling among cartel members over how to divide the profit in the market can make agreement among members difficult. In addition, antitrust laws prohibit explicit agreements among oligopolists as a matter of public policy. Even talking about pricing and production restrictions with competitors can be a criminal offense. Let's therefore consider what happens if Jack and Jill decide separately how much water to produce.

At first, one might expect Jack and Jill to reach the monopoly outcome on their own, because this outcome maximizes their joint profit. In the absence of a binding agreement, however, the monopoly outcome is unlikely. To see why, imagine that Jack expects Jill to produce only 30 gallons (half of the monopoly quantity). Jack would reason as follows:

"I could produce 30 gallons as well. In this case, a total of 60 gallons of water would be sold at a price of $60 a gallon. My profit would be $1,800 (30 gallons × $60 a gallon). Alternatively, I could produce 40 gallons. In this case, a total of 70 gallons of water would be sold at a price of $50 a gallon. My profit would be $2,000 (40 gallons × $50 a gallon). Even though total profit in the market would fall, my profit would be higher, because I would have a larger share of the market."

Of course, Jill might reason the same way. If so, Jack and Jill would each bring 40 gallons to town. Total sales would be 80 gallons, and the price would fall to $40. Thus, if the duopolists individually pursue their own self-interest when deciding how much to produce, they produce a total quantity greater than the monopoly quantity, charge a price lower than the monopoly price, and earn total profit less than the monopoly profit.

Although the logic of self-interest increases the duopoly's output above the monopoly level, it does not push the duopolists to reach the competitive allocation. Consider what happens when each duopolist is producing 40 gallons. The price is $40, and each duopolist makes a profit of $1,600. In this case, Jack's self-interested logic leads to a different conclusion:

"Right now, my profit is $1,600. Suppose I increase my production to 50 gallons. In this case, a total of 90 gallons of water would be sold, and the price would be $30 a gallon. Then my profit would be only $1,500. Rather than increasing production and driving down the price, I am better off keeping my production at 40 gallons."

The outcome in which Jack and Jill each produce 40 gallons looks like some sort of equilibrium. In fact, this outcome is called a Nash equilibrium. (It is named after economic theorist John Nash, whose life was portrayed in the book and movie *A Beautiful Mind*.) A **Nash equilibrium** is a situation in which economic actors interacting with one another each choose their best strategy given the strategies the others have chosen. In this case, given that Jill is producing 40 gallons, the best strategy for Jack is to produce 40 gallons. Similarly, given that Jack is producing 40 gallons, the best strategy for Jill is to produce 40 gallons. Once they reach this Nash equilibrium, neither Jack nor Jill has an incentive to make a different decision.

This example illustrates the tension between cooperation and self-interest. Oligopolists would be better off cooperating and reaching the monopoly outcome. Yet because they pursue their own self-interest, they do not end up reaching the monopoly outcome and maximizing their joint profit. Each oligopolist is tempted to raise production and capture a larger share of the market. As each of them tries to do this, total production rises, and the price falls.

Nash equilibrium
a situation in which economic actors interacting with one another each choose their best strategy given the strategies that all the other actors have chosen

At the same time, self-interest does not drive the market all the way to the competitive outcome. Like monopolists, oligopolists are aware that increasing the amount they produce reduces the price of their product, which in turn affects profits. Therefore, they stop short of following the competitive firm's rule of producing up to the point where price equals marginal cost.

In summary, *when firms in an oligopoly individually choose production to maximize profit, they produce a quantity of output greater than the level produced by monopoly and less than the level produced by competition. The oligopoly price is less than the monopoly price but greater than the competitive price (which equals marginal cost).*

How the Size of an Oligopoly Affects the Market Outcome

We can use the insights from this analysis of duopoly to discuss how the size of an oligopoly is likely to affect the outcome in a market. Suppose, for instance, that John and Joan suddenly discover water sources on their property and join Jack and Jill in the water oligopoly. The demand schedule in Table 1 remains the same, but now more producers are available to satisfy this demand. How would an increase in the number of sellers from two to four affect the price and quantity of water in the town?

If the sellers of water could form a cartel, they would once again try to maximize total profit by producing the monopoly quantity and charging the monopoly price. Just as when there were only two sellers, the members of the cartel would need to agree on production levels for each member and find some way to enforce the agreement. As the cartel grows larger, however, this outcome is less likely. Reaching and enforcing an agreement becomes more difficult as the size of the group increases.

If the oligopolists do not form a cartel—perhaps because the antitrust laws prohibit it—they must each decide on their own how much water to produce. To see how the increase in the number of sellers affects the outcome, consider the decision facing each seller. At any time, each well owner has the option to raise production by one gallon. In making this decision, the well owner weighs two effects:

- *The output effect:* Because price is above marginal cost, selling one more gallon of water at the going price will raise profit.
- *The price effect:* Raising production will increase the total amount sold, which will lower the price of water and lower the profit on all the other gallons sold.

If the output effect is larger than the price effect, the well owner will increase production. If the price effect is larger than the output effect, the owner will not raise production. (In fact, in this case, it is profitable to reduce production.) Each oligopolist continues to increase production until these two marginal effects exactly balance, taking the other firms' production as given.

Now consider how the number of firms in the industry affects the marginal analysis of each oligopolist. The larger the number of sellers, the less each seller is concerned about its own impact on the market price. That is, as the oligopoly grows in size, the magnitude of the price effect falls. When the oligopoly grows very large, the price effect disappears altogether. That is, the production decision of an individual firm no longer affects the market price. In this extreme case, each firm takes the market price as given when deciding how much to produce. It increases production as long as price is above marginal cost.

We can now see that a large oligopoly is essentially a group of competitive firms. A competitive firm considers only the output effect when deciding how much to produce: Because a competitive firm is a price taker, the price effect is absent. Thus, *as the number of sellers in an oligopoly grows larger, an oligopolistic market looks more and more like a competitive market. The price approaches marginal cost, and the quantity produced approaches the socially efficient level.*

This analysis of oligopoly offers a new perspective on the effects of international trade. Imagine that Toyota and Honda are the only automakers in Japan, Volkswagen and BMW are the only automakers in Germany, and Ford and General Motors are the only automakers in the United States. If these nations prohibited international trade in autos, each would have an auto oligopoly with only two members, and the market outcome would likely depart substantially from the competitive ideal. With international trade, however, the car market is a world market, and the oligopoly in this example has six members. Allowing free trade increases the number of producers from which each consumer can choose, and this increased competition keeps prices closer to marginal cost. Thus, the theory of oligopoly provides another reason, in addition to the theory of comparative advantage discussed in Chapter 3, why all countries can benefit from free trade.

QUICK QUIZ *If the members of an oligopoly could agree on a total quantity to produce, what quantity would they choose? • If the oligopolists do not act together but instead make production decisions individually, do they produce a total quantity more or less than in your answer to the previous question? Why?*

The Economics of Cooperation

As we have seen, oligopolies would like to reach the monopoly outcome, but doing so requires cooperation, which at times is difficult to establish and maintain. In this section we look more closely at the problems that arise when cooperation among actors is desirable but difficult. To analyze the economics of cooperation, we need to learn a little about game theory.

In particular, we focus on an important "game" called the **prisoners' dilemma.** This game provides insight into why cooperation is difficult. Many times in life, people fail to cooperate with one another even when cooperation would make them all better off. An oligopoly is just one example. The story of the prisoners' dilemma contains a general lesson that applies to any group trying to maintain cooperation among its members.

prisoners' dilemma
a particular "game" between two captured prisoners that illustrates why cooperation is difficult to maintain even when it is mutually beneficial

The Prisoners' Dilemma

The prisoners' dilemma is a story about two criminals who have been captured by the police. Let's call them Bonnie and Clyde. The police have enough evidence to convict Bonnie and Clyde of the minor crime of carrying an unregistered gun, so that each would spend a year in jail. The police also suspect that the two criminals have committed a bank robbery together, but they lack hard evidence to convict them of this major crime. The police question Bonnie and Clyde in separate rooms, and they offer each of them the following deal:

"Right now, we can lock you up for 1 year. If you confess to the bank robbery and implicate your partner, however, we'll give you immunity and you can go free. Your partner will get 20 years in jail. But if you both confess to the crime, we

Figure **1**

The Prisoners' Dilemma
In this game between two criminals suspected of committing a crime, the sentence that each receives depends both on his or her decision whether to confess or remain silent and on the decision made by the other.

	Bonnie's Decision	
	Confess	**Remain Silent**
Confess	Bonnie gets 8 years / Clyde gets 8 years	Bonnie gets 20 years / Clyde goes free
Remain Silent	Bonnie goes free / Clyde gets 20 years	Bonnie gets 1 year / Clyde gets 1 year

Clyde's Decision

won't need your testimony and we can avoid the cost of a trial, so you will each get an intermediate sentence of 8 years."

If Bonnie and Clyde, heartless bank robbers that they are, care only about their own sentences, what would you expect them to do? Figure 1 shows their choices. Each prisoner has two strategies: confess or remain silent. The sentence each prisoner gets depends on the strategy he or she chooses and the strategy chosen by his or her partner in crime.

Consider first Bonnie's decision. She reasons as follows: "I don't know what Clyde is going to do. If he remains silent, my best strategy is to confess, since then I'll go free rather than spending a year in jail. If he confesses, my best strategy is still to confess, since then I'll spend 8 years in jail rather than 20. So, regardless of what Clyde does, I am better off confessing."

dominant strategy
a strategy that is best for a player in a game regardless of the strategies chosen by the other players

In the language of game theory, a strategy is called a **dominant strategy** if it is the best strategy for a player to follow regardless of the strategies pursued by other players. In this case, confessing is a dominant strategy for Bonnie. She spends less time in jail if she confesses, regardless of whether Clyde confesses or remains silent.

Now consider Clyde's decision. He faces the same choices as Bonnie, and he reasons in much the same way. Regardless of what Bonnie does, Clyde can reduce his jail time by confessing. In other words, confessing is also a dominant strategy for Clyde.

In the end, both Bonnie and Clyde confess, and both spend 8 years in jail. Yet, from their standpoint, this is a terrible outcome. If they had *both* remained silent, both of them would have been better off, spending only 1 year in jail on the gun charge. Because each pursues his or her own interests, the two prisoners together reach an outcome that is worse for each of them.

You might have thought that Bonnie and Clyde would have foreseen this situation and planned ahead. But even with advanced planning, they would still run into problems. Imagine that, before the police captured Bonnie and Clyde, the two criminals had made a pact not to confess. Clearly, this agreement would make them both better off *if* they both lived up to it, because they would each spend only 1 year in jail. But would the two criminals in fact remain silent, simply because they had agreed to? Once they are being questioned separately, the logic of self-interest takes over and leads them to confess. Cooperation between the two prisoners is difficult to maintain, because cooperation is individually irrational.

Oligopolies as a Prisoners' Dilemma

What does the prisoners' dilemma have to do with markets and imperfect competition? It turns out that the game oligopolists play in trying to reach the monopoly outcome is similar to the game that the two prisoners play in the prisoners' dilemma.

Consider again the choices facing Jack and Jill. After prolonged negotiation, the two suppliers of water agree to keep production at 30 gallons, so that the price will be kept high and together they will earn the maximum profit. After they agree on production levels, however, each of them must decide whether to cooperate and live up to this agreement or to ignore it and produce at a higher level. Figure 2 shows how the profits of the two producers depend on the strategies they choose.

Suppose you are Jack. You might reason as follows: "I could keep production low at 30 gallons as we agreed, or I could raise my production and sell 40 gallons. If Jill lives up to the agreement and keeps her production at 30 gallons, then I earn profit of $2,000 with high production and $1,800 with low production. In this case, I am better off with high production. If Jill fails to live up to the agreement and produces 40 gallons, then I earn $1,600 with high production and $1,500 with low production. Once again, I am better off with high production. So, regardless of what Jill chooses to do, I am better off reneging on our agreement and producing at a high level."

Producing 40 gallons is a dominant strategy for Jack. Of course, Jill reasons in exactly the same way, and so both produce at the higher level of 40 gallons. The result is the inferior outcome (from Jack and Jill's standpoint) with low profits for each of the two producers.

This example illustrates why oligopolies have trouble maintaining monopoly profits. The monopoly outcome is jointly rational for the oligopoly, but each oligopolist has an incentive to cheat. Just as self-interest drives the prisoners in the prisoners' dilemma to confess, self-interest makes it difficult for the oligopoly to maintain the cooperative outcome with low production, high prices, and monopoly profits.

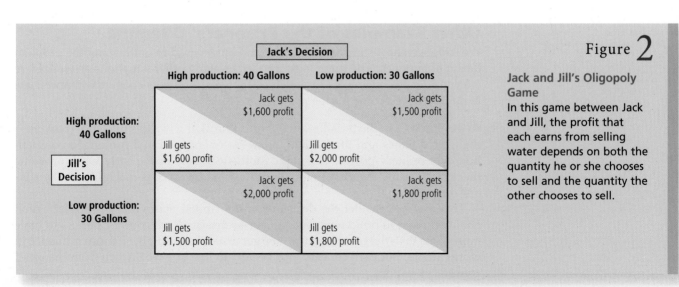

Figure 2

Jack and Jill's Oligopoly Game
In this game between Jack and Jill, the profit that each earns from selling water depends on both the quantity he or she chooses to sell and the quantity the other chooses to sell.

CASE STUDY   OPEC and the World Oil Market

Our story about the town's market for water is fictional, but if we change water to crude oil, and Jack and Jill to Iran and Iraq, the story is close to being true. Much of the world's oil is produced by a few countries, mostly in the Middle East. These countries together make up an oligopoly. Their decisions about how much oil to pump are much the same as Jack and Jill's decisions about how much water to pump.

The countries that produce most of the world's oil have formed a cartel, called the Organization of Petroleum Exporting Countries (OPEC). As originally formed in 1960, OPEC included Iran, Iraq, Kuwait, Saudi Arabia, and Venezuela. By 1973, eight other nations had joined: Qatar, Indonesia, Libya, the United Arab Emirates, Algeria, Nigeria, Ecuador, and Gabon. These countries control about three-fourths of the world's oil reserves. Like any cartel, OPEC tries to raise the price of its product through a coordinated reduction in quantity produced. OPEC tries to set production levels for each of the member countries.

The problem that OPEC faces is much the same as the problem that Jack and Jill face in our story. The OPEC countries would like to maintain a high price for oil. But each member of the cartel is tempted to increase its production to get a larger share of the total profit. OPEC members frequently agree to reduce production but then cheat on their agreements.

OPEC was most successful at maintaining cooperation and high prices in the period from 1973 to 1985. The price of crude oil rose from $3 a barrel in 1972 to $11 in 1974 and then to $35 in 1981. But in the mid-1980s, member countries began arguing about production levels, and OPEC became ineffective at maintaining cooperation. By 1986 the price of crude oil had fallen back to $13 a barrel.

In recent years, the members of OPEC have continued to meet regularly, but the cartel has been less successful at reaching and enforcing agreements. Although the price of oil rose significantly in 2007 and 2008, the primary cause was increased demand in the world oil market, in part from a booming Chinese economy, rather than restricted supply. While this lack of cooperation among OPEC nations has reduced the profits of the oil-producing nations below what they might have been, it has benefited consumers around the world. ■

Other Examples of the Prisoners' Dilemma

We have seen how the prisoners' dilemma can be used to understand the problem facing oligopolies. The same logic applies to many other situations as well. Here we consider two examples in which self-interest prevents cooperation and leads to an inferior outcome for the parties involved.

Arms Races   In the decades after World War II, the world's two superpowers—the United States and the Soviet Union—were engaged in a prolonged competition over military power. This topic motivated some of the early work on game theory. The game theorists pointed out that an arms race is much like the prisoners' dilemma.

To see why, consider the decisions of the United States and the Soviet Union about whether to build new weapons or to disarm. Each country prefers to have more arms than the other because a larger arsenal would give it more influence in world affairs. But each country also prefers to live in a world safe from the other country's weapons.

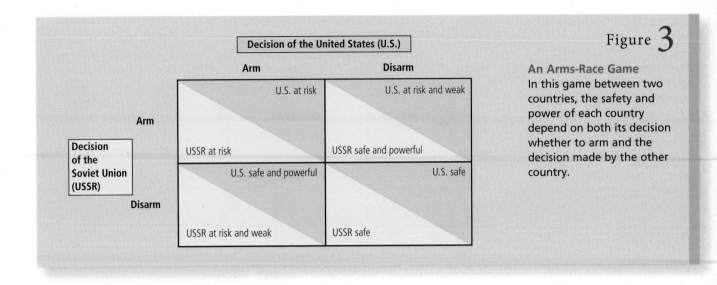

Figure **3**

An Arms-Race Game
In this game between two countries, the safety and power of each country depend on both its decision whether to arm and the decision made by the other country.

Figure 3 shows the deadly game. If the Soviet Union chooses to arm, the United States is better off doing the same to prevent the loss of power. If the Soviet Union chooses to disarm, the United States is better off arming because doing so would make it more powerful. For each country, arming is a dominant strategy. Thus, each country chooses to continue the arms race, resulting in the inferior outcome with both countries at risk.

Throughout the era of the Cold War, the United States and the Soviet Union attempted to solve this problem through negotiation and agreements over arms control. The problems that the two countries faced were similar to those that oligopolists encounter in trying to maintain a cartel. Just as oligopolists argue over production levels, the United States and the Soviet Union argued over the amount of arms that each country would be allowed. And just as cartels have trouble enforcing production levels, the United States and the Soviet Union each feared that the other country would cheat on any agreement. In both arms races and oligopolies, the relentless logic of self-interest drives the participants toward a noncooperative outcome that is worse for each party.

Common Resources   In Chapter 11 we saw that people tend to overuse common resources. One can view this problem as an example of the prisoners' dilemma.

Imagine that two oil companies—Exxon and Texaco—own adjacent oil fields. Under the fields is a common pool of oil worth $12 million. Drilling a well to recover the oil costs $1 million. If each company drills one well, each will get half of the oil and earn a $5 million profit ($6 million in revenue minus $1 million in costs).

Because the pool of oil is a common resource, the companies will not use it efficiently. Suppose that either company could drill a second well. If one company has two of the three wells, that company gets two-thirds of the oil, which yields a profit of $6 million. The other company gets one-third of the oil, for a profit of $3 million. Yet if each company drills a second well, the two companies again split the oil. In this case, each bears the cost of a second well, so profit is only $4 million for each company.

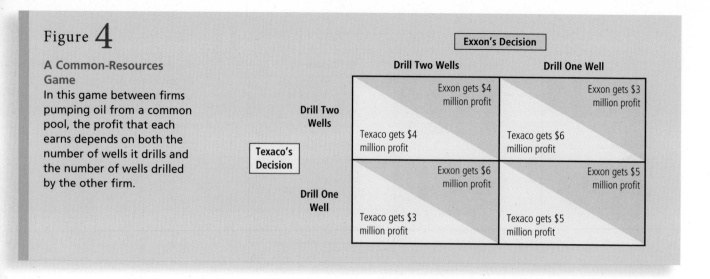

Figure 4

A Common-Resources Game
In this game between firms pumping oil from a common pool, the profit that each earns depends on both the number of wells it drills and the number of wells drilled by the other firm.

Figure 4 shows the game. Drilling two wells is a dominant strategy for each company. Once again, the self-interest of the two players leads them to an inferior outcome.

The Prisoners' Dilemma and the Welfare of Society

The prisoners' dilemma describes many of life's situations, and it shows that cooperation can be difficult to maintain, even when cooperation would make both players in the game better off. Clearly, this lack of cooperation is a problem for those involved in these situations. But is lack of cooperation a problem from the standpoint of society as a whole? The answer depends on the circumstances.

In some cases, the noncooperative equilibrium is bad for society as well as the players. In the arms-race game in Figure 3, both the United States and the Soviet Union end up at risk. In the common-resources game in Figure 4, the extra wells dug by Texaco and Exxon are pure waste. In both cases, society would be better off if the two players could reach the cooperative outcome.

By contrast, in the case of oligopolists trying to maintain monopoly profits, lack of cooperation is desirable from the standpoint of society as a whole. The monopoly outcome is good for the oligopolists, but it is bad for the consumers of the product. As we first saw in Chapter 7, the competitive outcome is best for society because it maximizes total surplus. When oligopolists fail to cooperate, the quantity they produce is closer to this optimal level. Put differently, the invisible hand guides markets to allocate resources efficiently only when markets are competitive, and markets are competitive only when firms in the market fail to cooperate with one another.

Similarly, consider the case of the police questioning two suspects. Lack of cooperation between the suspects is desirable, for it allows the police to convict more criminals. The prisoners' dilemma is a dilemma for the prisoners, but it can be a boon to everyone else.

Why People Sometimes Cooperate

The prisoners' dilemma shows that cooperation is difficult. But is it impossible? Not all prisoners, when questioned by the police, decide to turn in their partners in crime. Cartels sometimes manage to maintain collusive arrangements, despite the incentive for individual members to defect. Very often, players can solve the prisoners' dilemma because they play the game not once but many times.

To see why cooperation is easier to enforce in repeated games, let's return to our duopolists, Jack and Jill, whose choices were given in Figure 2. Jack and Jill would like to agree to maintain the monopoly outcome in which each produces 30 gallons. Yet, if Jack and Jill are to play this game only once, neither has any incentive to live up to this agreement. Self-interest drives each of them to renege and choose the dominant strategy of 40 gallons.

Now suppose that Jack and Jill know that they will play the same game every week. When they make their initial agreement to keep production low, they can also specify what happens if one party reneges. They might agree, for instance, that once one of them reneges and produces 40 gallons, both of them will produce 40 gallons forever after. This penalty is easy to enforce, for if one party is producing at a high level, the other has every reason to do the same.

The threat of this penalty may be all that is needed to maintain cooperation. Each person knows that defecting would raise his or her profit from $1,800 to $2,000. But this benefit would last for only one week. Thereafter, profit would fall to $1,600 and stay there. As long as the players care enough about future profits, they will choose to forgo the one-time gain from defection. Thus, in a game of repeated prisoners' dilemma, the two players may well be able to reach the cooperative outcome.

 The Prisoners' Dilemma Tournament

Imagine that you are playing a game of prisoners' dilemma with a person being "questioned" in a separate room. Moreover, imagine that you are going to play not once but many times. Your score at the end of the game is the total number of years in jail. You would like to make this score as small as possible. What strategy would you play? Would you begin by confessing or remaining silent? How would the other player's actions affect your subsequent decisions about confessing?

Repeated prisoners' dilemma is quite a complicated game. To encourage cooperation, players must penalize each other for not cooperating. Yet the strategy described earlier for Jack and Jill's water cartel—defect forever as soon as the other player defects—is not very forgiving. In a game repeated many times, a strategy that allows players to return to the cooperative outcome after a period of noncooperation may be preferable.

To see what strategies work best, political scientist Robert Axelrod held a tournament. People entered by sending computer programs designed to play repeated prisoners' dilemma. Each program then played the game against all the other programs. The "winner" was the program that received the fewest total years in jail.

The winner turned out to be a simple strategy called *tit-for-tat*. According to tit-for-tat, a player should start by cooperating and then do whatever the other player did last time. Thus, a tit-for-tat player cooperates until the other player defects; then she defects until the other player cooperates again. In other words, this strategy starts out friendly, penalizes unfriendly players, and forgives them if warranted. To Axelrod's surprise, this simple strategy did better than all the more complicated strategies that people had sent in.

The tit-for-tat strategy has a long history. It is essentially the biblical strategy of "an eye for an eye, a tooth for a tooth." The prisoners' dilemma tournament suggests that this may be a good rule of thumb for playing some of the games of life. ■

QUICK QUIZ   *Tell the story of the prisoners' dilemma. Write down a table showing the prisoners' choices and explain what outcome is likely.* • *What does the prisoners' dilemma teach us about oligopolies?*

Public Policy toward Oligopolies

One of the *Ten Principles of Economics* in Chapter 1 is that governments can sometimes improve market outcomes. This principle applies directly to oligopolistic markets. As we have seen, cooperation among oligopolists is undesirable from the standpoint of society as a whole, because it leads to production that is too low and prices that are too high. To move the allocation of resources closer to the social optimum, policymakers should try to induce firms in an oligopoly to compete rather than cooperate. Let's consider how policymakers do this and then examine the controversies that arise in this area of public policy.

Restraint of Trade and the Antitrust Laws

One way that policy discourages cooperation is through the common law. Normally, freedom of contract is an essential part of a market economy. Businesses and households use contracts to arrange mutually advantageous trades. In doing this, they rely on the court system to enforce contracts. Yet, for many centuries, judges in England and the United States have deemed agreements among competitors to reduce quantities and raise prices to be contrary to the public good. They have therefore refused to enforce such agreements.

The Sherman Antitrust Act of 1890 codified and reinforced this policy:

> Every contract, combination in the form of trust or otherwise, or conspiracy, in restraint of trade or commerce among the several States, or with foreign nations, is declared to be illegal. . . . Every person who shall monopolize, or attempt to monopolize, or combine or conspire with any person or persons to monopolize any part of the trade or commerce among the several States, or with foreign nations, shall be deemed guilty of a misdemeanor, and on conviction thereof, shall be punished by fine not exceeding fifty thousand dollars, or by imprisonment not exceeding one year, or by both said punishments, in the discretion of the court.

The Sherman Act elevated agreements among oligopolists from an unenforceable contract to a criminal conspiracy.

The Clayton Act of 1914 further strengthened the antitrust laws. According to this law, if a person could prove that he was damaged by an illegal arrangement to restrain trade, that person could sue and recover three times the damages he sustained. The purpose of this unusual rule of triple damages is to encourage private lawsuits against conspiring oligopolists.

Today, both the U.S. Justice Department and private parties have the authority to bring legal suits to enforce the antitrust laws. As we discussed in Chapter 15, these laws are used to prevent mergers that would lead to excessive market power in any single firm. In addition, these laws are used to prevent oligopolists from acting together in ways that would make their markets less competitive.

An Illegal Phone Call

Firms in oligopolies have a strong incentive to collude in order to reduce production, raise price, and increase profit. The great 18th-century economist Adam Smith was well aware of this potential market failure. In *The Wealth of Nations* he wrote, "People of the same trade seldom meet together, but the conversation ends in a conspiracy against the public, or in some diversion to raise prices."

To see a modern example of Smith's observation, consider the following excerpt of a phone conversation between two airline executives in the early 1980s. The call was reported in the *New York Times* on February 24, 1983. Robert Crandall was president of American Airlines, and Howard Putnam was president of Braniff Airways.

CRANDALL: I think it's dumb as hell . . . to sit here and pound the @#$% out of each other and neither one of us making a #$%& dime.
PUTNAM: Do you have a suggestion for me?
CRANDALL: Yes, I have a suggestion for you. Raise your $%*& fares 20 percent. I'll raise mine the next morning.
PUTNAM: Robert, we . . .
CRANDALL: You'll make more money, and I will, too.
PUTNAM: We can't talk about pricing!
CRANDALL: Oh @#$%, Howard. We can talk about any &*#@ thing we want to talk about.

Putnam was right: The Sherman Antitrust Act prohibits competing executives from even talking about fixing prices. When Putnam gave a tape of this conversation to the Justice Department, the Justice Department filed suit against Crandall.

Two years later, Crandall and the Justice Department reached a settlement in which Crandall agreed to various restrictions on his business activities, including his contacts with officials at other airlines. The Justice Department said that the terms of settlement would "protect competition in the airline industry, by preventing American and Crandall from any further attempts to monopolize passenger airline service on any route through discussions with competitors about the prices of airline services." ∎

Controversies over Antitrust Policy

Over time, much controversy has centered on what kinds of behavior the antitrust laws should prohibit. Most commentators agree that price-fixing agreements among competing firms should be illegal. Yet the antitrust laws have been used to condemn some business practices whose effects are not obvious. Here we consider three examples.

Resale Price Maintenance   One example of a controversial business practice is *resale price maintenance*. Imagine that Superduper Electronics sells DVD players to retail stores for $300. If Superduper requires the retailers to charge customers $350, it is said to engage in resale price maintenance. Any retailer that charged less than $350 would violate its contract with Superduper.

At first, resale price maintenance might seem anticompetitive and, therefore, detrimental to society. Like an agreement among members of a cartel, it prevents the retailers from competing on price. For this reason, the courts have at times viewed resale price maintenance as a violation of the antitrust laws.

Yet some economists defend resale price maintenance on two grounds. First, they deny that it is aimed at reducing competition. To the extent that Superduper Electronics has any market power, it can exert that power through the wholesale price, rather than through resale price maintenance. Moreover, Superduper has no incentive to discourage competition among its retailers. Indeed, because a cartel of retailers sells less than a group of competitive retailers, Superduper would be worse off if its retailers were a cartel.

Second, economists believe that resale price maintenance has a legitimate goal. Superduper may want its retailers to provide customers a pleasant showroom and a knowledgeable sales force. Yet, without resale price maintenance, some customers would take advantage of one store's service to learn about the DVD player's special features and then buy the item at a discount retailer that does not provide this service. To some extent, good service is a public good among the retailers that sell Superduper products. As we discussed in Chapter 11, when one person provides a public good, others are able to enjoy it without paying for it. In this case, discount retailers would free ride on the service provided by other retailers, leading to less service than is desirable. Resale price maintenance is one way for Superduper to solve this free-rider problem.

The example of resale price maintenance illustrates an important principle: *Business practices that appear to reduce competition may in fact have legitimate purposes.* This principle makes the application of the antitrust laws all the more difficult. The economists, lawyers, and judges in charge of enforcing these laws must determine what kinds of behavior public policy should prohibit as impeding competition and reducing economic well-being. Often that job is not easy.

Predatory Pricing   Firms with market power normally use that power to raise prices above the competitive level. But should policymakers ever be concerned that firms with market power might charge prices that are too low? This question is at the heart of a second debate over antitrust policy.

Imagine that a large airline, call it Coyote Air, has a monopoly on some route. Then Roadrunner Express enters and takes 20 percent of the market, leaving Coyote with 80 percent. In response to this competition, Coyote starts slashing its fares. Some antitrust analysts argue that Coyote's move could be anticompetitive: The price cuts may be intended to drive Roadrunner out of the market so Coyote can recapture its monopoly and raise prices again. Such behavior is called *predatory pricing*.

Although predatory pricing is a common claim in antitrust suits, some economists are skeptical of this argument and believe that predatory pricing is rarely, and perhaps never, a profitable business strategy. Why? For a price war to drive out a rival, prices have to be driven below cost. Yet if Coyote starts selling cheap tickets at a loss, it had better be ready to fly more planes, because low fares will attract more customers. Roadrunner, meanwhile, can respond to Coyote's predatory move by cutting back on flights. As a result, Coyote ends up bearing more than 80 percent of the losses, putting Roadrunner in a good position to survive the price war. As in the old Roadrunner-Coyote cartoons, the predator suffers more than the prey.

Economists continue to debate whether predatory pricing should be a concern for antitrust policymakers. Various questions remain unresolved. Is predatory pricing ever a profitable business strategy? If so, when? Are the courts capable of telling which price cuts are competitive and thus good for consumers and which are predatory? There are no simple answers.

Tying A third example of a controversial business practice is *tying*. Suppose that Makemoney Movies produces two new films—*Ironman* and *Hamlet*. If Makemoney offers theaters the two films together at a single price, rather than separately, the studio is said to be tying its two products.

When the practice of tying movies was challenged in the courts, the Supreme Court banned it. The court reasoned as follows: Imagine that *Ironman* is a blockbuster, whereas *Hamlet* is an unprofitable art film. Then the studio could use the high demand for *Ironman* to force theaters to buy *Hamlet*. It seemed that the studio could use tying as a mechanism for expanding its market power.

Many economists are skeptical of this argument. Imagine that theaters are willing to pay $20,000 for *Ironman* and nothing for *Hamlet*. Then the most that a theater would pay for the two movies together is $20,000—the same as it would pay for *Ironman* by itself. Forcing the theater to accept a worthless movie as part of the deal does not increase the theater's willingness to pay. Makemoney cannot increase its market power simply by bundling the two movies together.

Why, then, does tying exist? One possibility is that it is a form of price discrimination. Suppose there are two theaters. City Theater is willing to pay $15,000 for *Ironman* and $5,000 for *Hamlet*. Country Theater is just the opposite: It is willing to pay $5,000 for *Ironman* and $15,000 for *Hamlet*. If Makemoney charges separate prices for the two films, its best strategy is to charge $15,000 for each film, and each theater chooses to show only one film. Yet if Makemoney offers the two movies as a bundle, it can charge each theater $20,000 for the movies. Thus, if different theaters value the films differently, tying may allow the studio to increase profit by charging a combined price closer to the buyers' total willingness to pay.

Tying remains a controversial business practice. The Supreme Court's argument that tying allows a firm to extend its market power to other goods is not well founded, at least in its simplest form. Yet economists have proposed more elaborate theories for how tying can impede competition. Given our current economic knowledge, it is unclear whether tying has adverse effects for society as a whole.

The Microsoft Case

The most important and controversial antitrust case in recent years has been the U.S. government's suit against the Microsoft Corporation, filed in 1998. Certainly, the case did not lack drama. It pitted one of the world's richest men (Bill Gates) against one of the world's most powerful regulatory agencies (the U.S. Justice Department). Testifying for the government was a prominent economist (MIT professor Franklin Fisher). Testifying for Microsoft was an equally prominent economist (MIT professor Richard Schmalensee). At stake was the future of one of the world's most valuable companies (Microsoft) in one of the economy's fastest-growing industries (computer software).

A central issue in the Microsoft case involved tying—in particular, whether Microsoft should be allowed to integrate its Internet browser into its Windows operating system. The government claimed that Microsoft was bundling these two products together to expand its market power in computer operating systems into the unrelated market of Internet browsers. Allowing Microsoft to incorporate such products into its operating system, the government argued, would deter other software companies from entering the market and offering new products.

Microsoft responded by pointing out that putting new features into old products is a natural part of technological progress. Cars today include CD players and air conditioners, which were once sold separately, and cameras come with built-in flashes. The same is true with operating systems. Over time, Microsoft has added many features to Windows that were previously stand-alone products. This has made computers more reliable and easier to use because consumers can be confident that the pieces work together. The integration of Internet technology, Microsoft argued, was the natural next step.

One point of disagreement concerned the extent of Microsoft's market power. Noting that more than 80 percent of new personal computers use a Microsoft operating system, the government argued that the company had substantial monopoly power, which it was trying to expand. Microsoft replied that the software market is always changing and that Microsoft's Windows was constantly being challenged by competitors, such as the Apple Mac and Linux operating systems. It also argued that the low price it charged for Windows—about $50, or only 3 percent of the price of a typical computer—was evidence that its market power was severely limited.

Like many large antitrust suits, the Microsoft case became a legal morass. In November 1999, after a long trial, Judge Penfield Jackson ruled that Microsoft had great monopoly power and that it had illegally abused that power. In June 2000, after hearings on possible remedies, he ordered that Microsoft be broken up into two companies—one that sold the operating system and one that sold applications software. A year later, an appeals court overturned Jackson's breakup order and handed the case to a new judge. In September 2001, the Justice Department announced that it no longer sought a breakup of the company and wanted to settle the case quickly.

A settlement was finally reached in November 2002. Microsoft accepted some restrictions on its business practices, and the government accepted that a browser would remain part of the Windows operating system. But the settlement did not end Microsoft's antitrust troubles. In recent years, the company has contended with several private antitrust suits, as well as suits brought by the European Union alleging a variety of anticompetitive behaviors. ■

"*Me? A monopolist? Now just wait a minute . . .*"

QUICK QUIZ *What kind of agreement is illegal for businesses to make?* • *Why are the antitrust laws controversial?*

Conclusion

Oligopolies would like to act like monopolies, but self-interest drives them toward competition. Where oligopolies end up on this spectrum depends on the number of firms in the oligopoly and how cooperative the firms are. The story of

in the news

> ## The Next Big Antitrust Target?
>
> *Google is a widely used search engine—so widely used, in fact, that it has attracted the attention of government lawyers.*

Google Says It's Actually Quite Small

BY JEFF HORWITZ

Three times in the past month, government agencies have targeted Google for antitrust reviews. An outstanding private lawsuit alleges that Google tried to kill a business-to-business search engine with predatory pricing. And during the waning months of the Bush administration, soon-to-be Obama antitrust chief Christine Varney declared that Google "has acquired a monopoly in Internet online advertising." Last month she asserted that the Bush administration had been too lax in combating monopolistic behavior and that the Obama Justice Department would no longer "stand on the sidelines."

That should explain why Dana Wagner, a former Department of Justice antitrust lawyer hired by Google just last year, is rapidly becoming one of the company's public faces. Along with Adam Kovacevich, a company public-policy spokesman, Wagner has been talking to advertising clients, public officials, reporters and academics in an effort to diffuse the impression that Google has a competition law problem.

As might be expected, Google's presentation highlights the company's many good works and "don't be evil" corporate philosophy. But there's another element

at front and center of the presentation: According to Warner and Kovacevich, their company holds only a 2.66 percent share of its total market.

If that number seems low for the runaway success story of the Internet age, Google wants you to believe that it's just a question of market definition. Google rejects the idea that it's in the search advertising business, an industry in which it holds more than a 70 percent share of revenue. Instead, the company says that its competition is all advertising, a category broad enough to include newspaper, radio and highway billboards. Google's argument is not simply

that it's not a big bully. If you believe the company, it's not even that big....

At first glance, this seems like a tough position to defend. There's a sharp difference between how companies use mass-market tools like billboards and how they use search-based advertising, which targets consumers far closer to the point of sale. And even if you buy Google's claim that the lines between media have been blurred by technology, it's still hard to explain how the company could maintain a 30 percent operating margin, despite money-losing outlays

in a host of adjacent fields, if it faced serious competition. As Wagner himself notes, arguing that Google's market is broader than search advertising is not intuitive. When Microsoft tried to argue that it didn't have a monopoly in the 1990s, that strategy was widely seen as disingenuous.

But that raises the question: "Why bother?" There's no law against trouncing your business competitors. Ever since Judge Learned Hand's landmark decision in U.S. v. Aluminum Co. of America 64 years ago, the court has recognized that under certain circumstances a company may come to dominate its field through "superior skill, foresight, and industry."

It's hard to see Google as anything other than a model example of such a company. Moreover, nobody's come up with a particularly good case that the company has been stifling other companies....

Still, Google has reason to dread the perception of even benign dominance. Just ask Gary Reback, an attorney for Carr & Ferrell who played a big role in pinning monopoly status to Microsoft in the 1990s. Even if U.S. antitrust law allows for justly earned monopolies, it's rare that a high-profile company ever gets to enjoy that status in peace.

As Reback puts it, the government's approach has traditionally been: "We won't punish you for being successful. But if you're a monopolist and you spit on the sidewalk, we'll break up your company."

Source: *Washington Post*, June 7, 2009.

the prisoners' dilemma shows why oligopolies can fail to maintain cooperation, even when cooperation is in their best interest.

Policymakers regulate the behavior of oligopolists through the antitrust laws. The proper scope of these laws is the subject of ongoing controversy. Although price fixing among competing firms clearly reduces economic welfare and should be illegal, some business practices that appear to reduce competition may have legitimate if subtle purposes. As a result, policymakers need to be careful when they use the substantial powers of the antitrust laws to place limits on firm behavior.

SUMMARY

- Oligopolists maximize their total profits by forming a cartel and acting like a monopolist. Yet, if oligopolists make decisions about production levels individually, the result is a greater quantity and a lower price than under the monopoly outcome. The larger the number of firms in the oligopoly, the closer the quantity and price will be to the levels that would prevail under perfect competition.

- The prisoners' dilemma shows that self-interest can prevent people from maintaining cooperation, even when cooperation is in their mutual interest. The logic of the prisoners' dilemma applies in many situations, including arms races, common-resource problems, and oligopolies.

- Policymakers use the antitrust laws to prevent oligopolies from engaging in behavior that reduces competition. The application of these laws can be controversial, because some behavior that can appear to reduce competition may in fact have legitimate business purposes.

KEY CONCEPTS

oligopoly, *p. 349*
game theory, *p. 349*
collusion, *p. 351*

cartel, *p. 351*
Nash equilibrium, *p. 353*
prisoners' dilemma, *p. 355*

dominant strategy, *p. 356*

QUESTIONS FOR REVIEW

1. If a group of sellers could form a cartel, what quantity and price would they try to set?
2. Compare the quantity and price of an oligopoly to those of a monopoly.
3. Compare the quantity and price of an oligopoly to those of a competitive market.
4. How does the number of firms in an oligopoly affect the outcome in its market?

5. What is the prisoners' dilemma, and what does it have to do with oligopoly?
6. Give two examples other than oligopoly that show how the prisoners' dilemma helps to explain behavior.
7. What kinds of behavior do the antitrust laws prohibit?
8. What is resale price maintenance, and why is it controversial?

PROBLEMS AND APPLICATIONS

1. A large share of the world supply of diamonds comes from Russia and South Africa. Suppose that the marginal cost of mining diamonds is constant at $1,000 per diamond, and the demand for diamonds is described by the following schedule:

Price	Quantity
$8,000	5,000 diamonds
7,000	6,000
6,000	7,000
5,000	8,000
4,000	9,000
3,000	10,000
2,000	11,000
1,000	12,000

   a. If there were many suppliers of diamonds, what would be the price and quantity?
   b. If there were only one supplier of diamonds, what would be the price and quantity?
   c. If Russia and South Africa formed a cartel, what would be the price and quantity? If the countries split the market evenly, what would be South Africa's production and profit? What would happen to South Africa's profit if it increased its production by 1,000 while Russia stuck to the cartel agreement?
   d. Use your answers to part (c) to explain why cartel agreements are often not successful.

2. The *New York Times* (Nov. 30, 1993) reported that "the inability of OPEC to agree last week to cut production has sent the oil market into turmoil . . . [leading to] the lowest price for domestic crude oil since June 1990."
   a. Why were the members of OPEC trying to agree to cut production?
   b. Why do you suppose OPEC was unable to agree on cutting production? Why did the oil market go into "turmoil" as a result?
   c. The newspaper also noted OPEC's view "that producing nations outside the organization, like Norway and Britain, should do their share and cut production." What does the phrase "do their share" suggest about OPEC's desired relationship with Norway and Britain?

3. This chapter discusses companies that are oligopolists in the market for the goods they

sell. Many of the same ideas apply to companies that are oligopolists in the market for the inputs they buy.
   a. If sellers who are oligopolists try to increase the price of goods they sell, what is the goal of buyers who are oligopolists?
   b. Major league baseball team owners have an oligopoly in the market for baseball players. What is the owners' goal regarding players' salaries? Why is this goal difficult to achieve?
   c. Baseball players went on strike in 1994 because they would not accept the salary cap that the owners wanted to impose. If the owners were already colluding over salaries, why did the owners feel the need for a salary cap?

4. Consider trade relations between the United States and Mexico. Assume that the leaders of the two countries believe the payoffs to alternative trade policies are as follows:

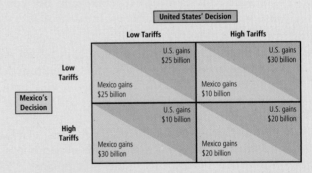

   a. What is the dominant strategy for the United States? For Mexico? Explain.
   b. Define *Nash equilibrium*. What is the Nash equilibrium for trade policy?
   c. In 1993, the U.S. Congress ratified the North American Free Trade Agreement, in which the United States and Mexico agreed to reduce trade barriers simultaneously. Do the perceived payoffs shown here justify this approach to trade policy? Explain.
   d. Based on your understanding of the gains from trade (discussed in Chapters 3 and 9), do you think that these payoffs actually reflect a nation's welfare under the four possible outcomes?

5. Synergy and Dynaco are the only two firms in a specific high-tech industry. They face the following payoff matrix as they decide upon the size of their research budget:

	Synergy's Decision	
	Large Budget	**Small Budget**
Dynaco's Decision — **Large Budget**	Synergy gains $20 million / Dynaco gains $30 million	Synergy gains zero / Dynaco gains $70 million
Dynaco's Decision — **Small Budget**	Synergy gains $30 million / Dynaco gains zero	Synergy gains $40 million / Dynaco gains $50 million

a. Does Synergy have a dominant strategy? Explain.
b. Does Dynaco have a dominant strategy? Explain.
c. Is there a Nash equilibrium for this scenario? Explain. (Hint: Look closely at the definition of Nash equilibrium.)

6. You and a classmate are assigned a project on which you will receive one combined grade. You each want to receive a good grade, but you also want to avoid hard work. In particular, here is the situation:

• If both of you work hard, you both get an A, which gives each of you 40 units of happiness.
• If only one of you works hard, you both get a B, which gives each of you 30 units of happiness.
• If neither of you works hard, you both get a D, which gives each of you 10 units of happiness.
• Working hard costs 25 units of happiness.

a. Fill in the payoffs in the following decision box:

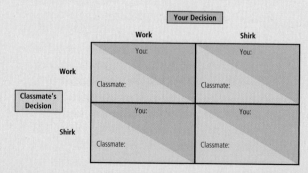

b. What is the likely outcome? Explain your answer.

c. If you get this classmate as your partner on a series of projects throughout the year, rather than only once, how might that change the outcome you predicted in part (b)?
d. Another classmate cares more about good grades: He gets 50 units of happiness for a B, and 80 units of happiness for an A. If this classmate were your partner (but your preferences were unchanged), how would your answers to parts (a) and (b) change? Which of the two classmates would you prefer as a partner? Would he also want you as a partner?

7. A case study in the chapter describes a phone conversation between the presidents of American Airlines and Braniff Airways. Let's analyze the game between the two companies. Suppose that each company can charge either a high price for tickets or a low price. If one company charges $100, it earns low profits if the other company charges $100 also and high profits if the other company charges $200. On the other hand, if the company charges $200, it earns very low profits if the other company charges $100 and medium profits if the other company charges $200 also.

a. Draw the decision box for this game.
b. What is the Nash equilibrium in this game? Explain.
c. Is there an outcome that would be better than the Nash equilibrium for both airlines? How could it be achieved? Who would lose if it were achieved?

8. Two athletes of equal ability are competing for a prize of $10,000. Each is deciding whether to take a dangerous performance-enhancing drug. If one athlete takes the drug, and the other does not, the one who takes the drug wins the prize. If both or neither take the drug, they tie and split the prize. Taking the drug imposes health risks that are equivalent to a loss of X dollars.

a. Draw a 2×2 payoff matrix describing the decisions the athletes face.
b. For what X is taking the drug the Nash equilibrium?
c. Does making the drug safer (that is, lowering X) make the athletes better or worse off? Explain.

9. Little Kona is a small coffee company that is considering entering a market dominated by Big Brew. Each company's profit depends on whether Little Kona enters and whether Big Brew sets a high price or a low price:

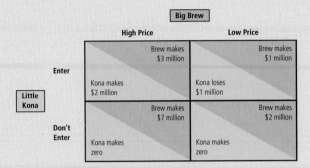

a. Does either player in this game have a dominant strategy?

b. Does your answer to part (a) help you figure out what the other player should do? What is the Nash equilibrium? Is there only one?

c. Big Brew threatens Little Kona by saying, "If you enter, we're going to set a low price, so you had better stay out." Do you think Little Kona should believe the threat? Why or why not?

d. If the two firms could collude and agree on how to split the total profits, what outcome would they pick?

10. Let's return to the chapter's discussion of Jack and Jill's water duopoly. Suppose that Jack and Jill are at the duopoly's Nash equilibrium (80 gallons) when a third person, John, discovers a water source and joins the market as a third producer.

a. Jack and Jill propose that the three of them continue to produce a total of 80 gallons, splitting the market three ways. If John agrees to this, how much profit will he make?

b. After agreeing to the proposed deal, John is considering increasing his production by 10 gallons. If he does, and Jack and Jill stick to the agreement, how much profit will John make? What does this tell you about the proposed agreement?

c. What is the Nash equilibrium for this market with three producers? How does it compare to the Nash equilibrium with two producers?

For further information on topics in this chapter, additional problems, applications, examples, online quizzes, and more, please visit our website at www .cengage.com/economics/mankiw.

PART **VI** The Economics of Labor Markets

The Markets for the Factors of Production

18

When you finish school, your income will be determined largely by what kind of job you take. If you become a computer programmer, you will earn more than if you become a gas station attendant. This fact is not surprising, but it is not obvious why it is true. No law requires that computer programmers be paid more than gas station attendants. No ethical principle says that programmers are more deserving. What then determines which job will pay you the higher wage?

Your income, of course, is a small piece of a larger economic picture. In 2010, the total income of all U.S. residents was about $15 trillion. People earned this income in various ways. Workers earned about three-fourths of it in the form of wages and fringe benefits. The rest went to landowners and to the owners of *capital*—the economy's stock of equipment and structures—in the form of rent, profit, and interest. What determines how much goes to workers? To landowners? To the owners of capital? Why do some workers earn higher wages than others, some landowners higher rental income than others, and some capital owners greater profit than others? Why, in particular, do computer programmers earn more than gas station attendants?

The answers to these questions, like most in economics, hinge on supply and demand. The supply and demand for labor, land, and capital determine the prices paid to workers, landowners, and capital owners. To understand why some people have higher incomes than others, therefore, we need to look more deeply at the markets for the services they provide. That is our job in this and the next two chapters.

This chapter provides the basic theory for the analysis of factor markets. As you may recall from Chapter 2, the **factors of production** are the inputs used to produce goods and services. Labor, land, and capital are the three most important factors of production. When a computer firm produces a new software program, it uses programmers' time (labor), the physical space on which its offices are located (land), and an office building and computer equipment (capital). Similarly, when a gas station sells gas, it uses attendants' time (labor), the physical space (land), and the gas tanks and pumps (capital).

In many ways factor markets resemble the markets for goods and services we analyzed in previous chapters, but they are different in one important way: The demand for a factor of production is a *derived demand*. That is, a firm's demand for a factor of production is derived from its decision to supply a good in another market. The demand for computer programmers is inseparably linked to the supply of computer software, and the demand for gas station attendants is inseparably linked to the supply of gasoline.

In this chapter, we analyze factor demand by considering how a competitive, profit-maximizing firm decides how much of any factor to buy. We begin our analysis by examining the demand for labor. Labor is the most important factor of production, because workers receive most of the total income earned in the U.S. economy. Later in the chapter, we will see that our analysis of the labor market also applies to the markets for the other factors of production.

The basic theory of factor markets developed in this chapter takes a large step toward explaining how the income of the U.S. economy is distributed among workers, landowners, and owners of capital. Chapter 19 builds on this analysis to examine in more detail why some workers earn more than others. Chapter 20 examines how much income inequality results from the functioning of factor markets and then considers what role the government should and does play in altering the income distribution.

factors of production

the inputs used to produce goods and services

The Demand for Labor

Labor markets, like other markets in the economy, are governed by the forces of supply and demand. This is illustrated in Figure 1. In panel (a), the supply and demand for apples determine the price of apples. In panel (b), the supply and demand for apple pickers determine the price, or wage, of apple pickers.

As we have already noted, labor markets are different from most other markets because labor demand is a derived demand. Most labor services, rather than being final goods ready to be enjoyed by consumers, are inputs into the production of other goods. To understand labor demand, we need to focus on the firms that hire the labor and use it to produce goods for sale. By examining the link between the production of goods and the demand for labor to make those goods, we gain insight into the determination of equilibrium wages.

The basic tools of supply and demand apply to goods and to labor services. Panel (a) shows how the supply and demand for apples determine the price of apples. Panel (b) shows how the supply and demand for apple pickers determine the wage of apple pickers.

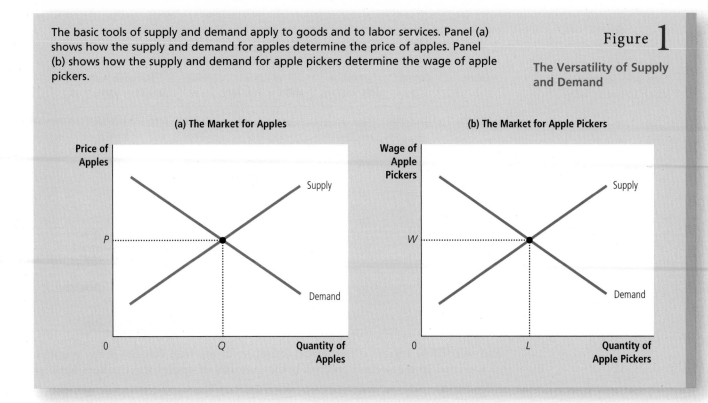

Figure 1

The Versatility of Supply and Demand

The Competitive Profit-Maximizing Firm

Let's look at how a typical firm, such as an apple producer, decides what quantity of labor to demand. The firm owns an apple orchard and each week must decide how many apple pickers to hire to harvest its crop. After the firm makes its hiring decision, the workers pick as many apples as they can. The firm then sells the apples, pays the workers, and keeps what is left as profit.

We make two assumptions about our firm. First, we assume that our firm is *competitive* both in the market for apples (where the firm is a seller) and in the market for apple pickers (where the firm is a buyer). A competitive firm is a price taker. Because there are many other firms selling apples and hiring apple pickers, a single firm has little influence over the price it gets for apples or the wage it pays apple pickers. The firm takes the price and the wage as given by market conditions. It only has to decide how many apples to sell and how many workers to hire.

Second, we assume that the firm is *profit maximizing*. Thus, the firm does not directly care about the number of workers it has or the number of apples it produces. It cares only about profit, which equals the total revenue from the sale of apples minus the total cost of producing them. The firm's supply of apples and its demand for workers are derived from its primary goal of maximizing profit.

The Production Function and the Marginal Product of Labor

To make its hiring decision, the firm must consider how the size of its workforce affects the amount of output produced. In other words, it must consider how the number of apple pickers affects the quantity of apples it can harvest

Table 1

How the Competitive Firm Decides How Much Labor to Hire

Labor L	Output Q	Marginal Product of Labor MPL $=\Delta Q/\Delta L$	Value of the Marginal Product of Labor VMPL $= P \times$ MPL	Wage W	Marginal Profit ΔProfit $=$ VMPL $-$ W
0 workers	0 bushels				
		100 bushels	$1,000	$500	$500
1	100				
		80	800	500	300
2	180				
		60	600	500	100
3	240				
		40	400	500	−100
4	280				
		20	200	500	−300
5	300				

and sell. Table 1 gives a numerical example. In the first column is the number of workers. In the second column is the quantity of apples the workers harvest each week.

These two columns of numbers describe the firm's ability to produce. Recall that economists use the term **production function** to describe the relationship between the quantity of the inputs used in production and the quantity of output from production. Here the "input" is the apple pickers and the "output" is the apples. The other inputs—the trees themselves, the land, the firm's trucks and tractors, and so on—are held fixed for now. This firm's production function shows that if the firm hires 1 worker, that worker will pick 100 bushels of apples per week. If the firm hires 2 workers, the 2 workers together will pick 180 bushels per week. And so on.

Figure 2 graphs the data on labor and output presented in Table 1. The number of workers is on the horizontal axis, and the amount of output is on the vertical axis. This figure illustrates the production function.

One of the *Ten Principles of Economics* introduced in Chapter 1 is that rational people think at the margin. This idea is the key to understanding how firms decide what quantity of labor to hire. To take a step toward this decision, the third column in Table 1 gives the **marginal product of labor**, the increase in the amount of output from an additional unit of labor. When the firm increases the number of workers from 1 to 2, for example, the amount of apples produced rises from 100 to 180 bushels. Therefore, the marginal product of the second worker is 80 bushels.

Notice that as the number of workers increases, the marginal product of labor declines. That is, the production process exhibits **diminishing marginal product**. At first, when only a few workers are hired, they can pick the low-hanging fruit. As the number of workers increases, additional workers have to climb higher up the ladders to find apples to pick. Hence, as more and more workers are hired, each additional worker contributes less to the production of apples. For this reason, the production function in Figure 2 becomes flatter as the number of workers rises.

production function
the relationship between the quantity of inputs used to make a good and the quantity of output of that good

marginal product of labor
the increase in the amount of output from an additional unit of labor

diminishing marginal product
the property whereby the marginal product of an input declines as the quantity of the input increases

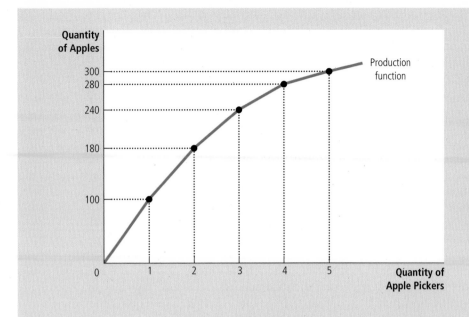

Figure *2*

The Production Function
The production function is the relationship between the inputs into production (apple pickers) and the output from production (apples). As the quantity of the input increases, the production function gets flatter, reflecting the property of diminishing marginal product.

The Value of the Marginal Product and the Demand for Labor

Our profit-maximizing firm is concerned more with money than with apples. As a result, when deciding how many workers to hire to pick apples, the firm considers how much profit each worker would bring in. Because profit is total revenue minus total cost, the profit from an additional worker is the worker's contribution to revenue minus the worker's wage.

To find the worker's contribution to revenue, we must convert the marginal product of labor (which is measured in bushels of apples) into the *value* of the marginal product (which is measured in dollars). We do this using the price of apples. To continue our example, if a bushel of apples sells for $10 and if an additional worker produces 80 bushels of apples, then the worker produces $800 of revenue.

The **value of the marginal product** of any input is the marginal product of that input multiplied by the market price of the output. The fourth column in Table 1 shows the value of the marginal product of labor in our example, assuming the price of apples is $10 per bushel. Because the market price is constant for a competitive firm while the marginal product declines with more workers, the value of the marginal product diminishes as the number of workers rises. Economists sometimes call this column of numbers the firm's *marginal revenue product:* It is the extra revenue the firm gets from hiring an additional unit of a factor of production.

Now consider how many workers the firm will hire. Suppose that the market wage for apple pickers is $500 per week. In this case, as you can see in Table 1, the first worker that the firm hires is profitable: The first worker yields $1,000 in revenue, or $500 in profit. Similarly, the second worker yields $800 in additional revenue, or $300 in profit. The third worker produces $600 in additional revenue,

value of the marginal product

the marginal product of an input times the price of the output or $100 in profit. After the third worker, however, hiring workers is unprofitable. The fourth worker would yield only $400 of additional revenue. Because the worker's wage is $500, hiring the fourth worker would mean a $100 reduction in profit. Thus, the firm hires only 3 workers.

It is instructive to consider the firm's decision graphically. Figure 3 graphs the value of the marginal product. This curve slopes downward because the marginal product of labor diminishes as the number of workers rises. The figure also includes a horizontal line at the market wage. To maximize profit, the firm hires workers up to the point where these two curves cross. Below this level of employment, the value of the marginal product exceeds the wage, so hiring another worker would increase profit. Above this level of employment, the value of the marginal product is less than the wage, so the marginal worker is unprofitable. Thus, *a competitive, profit-maximizing firm hires workers up to the point where the value of the marginal product of labor equals the wage.*

Having explained the profit-maximizing hiring strategy for a competitive firm, we can now offer a theory of labor demand. Recall that a firm's labor-demand curve tells us the quantity of labor that a firm demands at any given wage. We have just seen in Figure 3 that the firm makes that decision by choosing the quantity of labor at which the value of the marginal product equals the wage. As a result, *the value-of-marginal-product curve is the labor-demand curve for a competitive, profit-maximizing firm.*

What Causes the Labor-Demand Curve to Shift?

We now understand the labor-demand curve: It reflects the value of the marginal product of labor. With this insight in mind, let's consider a few of the things that might cause the labor-demand curve to shift.

The Output Price   The value of the marginal product is marginal product times the price of the firm's output. Thus, when the output price changes, the value of the marginal product changes, and the labor-demand curve shifts. An increase in

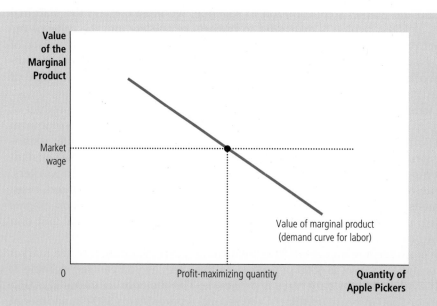

Figure **3**

The Value of the Marginal Product of Labor

This figure shows how the value of the marginal product (the marginal product times the price of the output) depends on the number of workers. The curve slopes downward because of diminishing marginal product. For a competitive, profit-maximizing firm, this value-of-marginal-product curve is also the firm's labor-demand curve.

FYI

> ### Input Demand and Output Supply: Two Sides of the Same Coin

In Chapter 14, we saw how a competitive, profit-maximizing firm decides how much of its output to sell: It chooses the quantity of output at which the price of the good equals the marginal cost of production. We have just seen how such a firm decides how much labor to hire: It chooses the quantity of labor at which the wage equals the value of the marginal product. Because the production function links the quantity of inputs to the quantity of output, you should not be surprised to learn that the firm's decision about input demand is closely linked to its decision about output supply. In fact, these two decisions are two sides of the same coin.

To see this relationship more fully, let's consider how the marginal product of labor (*MPL*) and marginal cost (*MC*) are related. Suppose an additional worker costs $500 and has a marginal product of 50 bushels of apples. In this case, producing 50 more bushels costs $500; the marginal cost of a bushel is $500/50, or $10. More generally, if *W* is the wage, and an extra unit of labor produces *MPL* units of output, then the marginal cost of a unit of output is $MC = W/MPL$.

This analysis shows that diminishing marginal product is closely related to increasing marginal cost. When our apple orchard grows crowded with workers, each additional worker adds less to the production of apples (*MPL* falls). Similarly, when the apple firm is producing a large quantity of apples, the orchard is already crowded

with workers, so it is more costly to produce an additional bushel of apples (*MC* rises).

Now consider our criterion for profit maximization. We determined earlier that a profit-maximizing firm chooses the quantity of labor so that the value of the marginal product ($P \times MPL$) equals the wage (*W*). We can write this mathematically as

$$P \times MPL = W.$$

If we divide both sides of this equation by *MPL*, we obtain

$$P = W/MPL.$$

We just noted that *W/MPL* equals marginal cost, *MC*. Therefore, we can substitute to obtain

$$P = MC.$$

This equation states that the price of the firm's output is equal to the marginal cost of producing a unit of output. Thus, *when a competitive firm hires labor up to the point at which the value of the marginal product equals the wage, it also produces up to the point at which the price equals marginal cost.* Our analysis of labor demand in this chapter is just another way of looking at the production decision we first saw in Chapter 14.

the price of apples, for instance, raises the value of the marginal product of each worker who picks apples and, therefore, increases labor demand from the firms that supply apples. Conversely, a decrease in the price of apples reduces the value of the marginal product and decreases labor demand.

Technological Change   Between 1960 and 2009, the output a typical U.S. worker produced in an hour rose by 183 percent. Why? The most important reason is technological progress: Scientists and engineers are constantly figuring out new and better ways of doing things. This has profound implications for the labor market. Technological advance typically raises the marginal product of labor, which in turn increases the demand for labor and shifts the labor-demand curve to the right.

It is also possible for technological change to reduce labor demand. The invention of a cheap industrial robot, for instance, could conceivably reduce the marginal product of labor, shifting the labor-demand curve to the left. Economists call this *labor-saving* technological change. History suggests, however, that most

FYI

The Luddite Revolt

Over the long span of history, technological progress has been the worker's friend. It has increased productivity, labor demand, and wages. Yet there is no doubt that workers sometimes see technological progress as a threat to their standard of living.

One famous example occurred in England in the early 19th century, when skilled knitters saw their jobs threatened by the invention and spread of machines that could produce textiles using less skilled workers and at much lower cost. The displaced workers organized violent revolts against the new technology. They smashed the weaving machines used in the wool and cotton mills and, in some cases, set the homes of the mill owners on fire. Because the workers claimed to be led by General Ned Ludd (who may have been a legendary figure rather than a real person), they were called Luddites.

The Luddites wanted the British government to save their jobs by restricting the spread of the new technology. Instead, the Parliament took action to stop the Luddites. Thousands of troops were sent to suppress the Luddite riots, and the Parliament eventually made destroying machines a capital crime. After a trial in York in 1813, seventeen men were hanged for the offense. Many others were convicted and sent to Australia as prisoners.

Today, the term *Luddite* refers to anyone who opposes technological progress.

The Luddites.

technological progress is instead *labor-augmenting*. Such technological advance explains persistently rising employment in the face of rising wages: Even though wages (adjusted for inflation) increased by 150 percent during the last half century, firms nonetheless increased the amount of labor they employed by 87 percent.

The Supply of Other Factors   The quantity available of one factor of production can affect the marginal product of other factors. A fall in the supply of ladders, for instance, will reduce the marginal product of apple pickers and thus the demand for apple pickers. We consider this linkage among the factors of production more fully later in the chapter.

QUICK QUIZ   *Define* marginal product of labor *and* value of the marginal product of labor. • *Describe how a competitive, profit-maximizing firm decides how many workers to hire.*

The Supply of Labor

Having analyzed labor demand in detail, let's turn to the other side of the market and consider labor supply. A formal model of labor supply is included in Chapter 21, where we develop the theory of household decision making. Here we discuss briefly and informally the decisions that lie behind the labor-supply curve.

The Trade-off between Work and Leisure

One of the *Ten Principles of Economics* in Chapter 1 is that people face trade-offs. Probably no trade-off is more obvious or more important in a person's life than the trade-off between work and leisure. The more hours you spend working, the fewer hours you have to watch TV, enjoy dinner with friends, or pursue your favorite hobby. The trade-off between labor and leisure lies behind the labor-supply curve.

Another of the *Ten Principles of Economics* is that the cost of something is what you give up to get it. What do you give up to get an hour of leisure? You give up an hour of work, which in turn means an hour of wages. Thus, if your wage is $15 per hour, the opportunity cost of an hour of leisure is $15. And when you get a raise to $20 per hour, the opportunity cost of enjoying leisure goes up.

The labor-supply curve reflects how workers' decisions about the labor-leisure trade-off respond to a change in that opportunity cost. An upward-sloping labor-supply curve means that an increase in the wage induces workers to increase the quantity of labor they supply. Because time is limited, more hours of work mean that workers are enjoying less leisure. That is, workers respond to the increase in the opportunity cost of leisure by taking less of it.

It is worth noting that the labor-supply curve need not be upward sloping. Imagine you got that raise from $15 to $20 per hour. The opportunity cost of leisure is now greater, but you are also richer than you were before. You might decide that with your extra wealth you can now afford to enjoy more leisure. That is, at the higher wage, you might choose to work fewer hours. If so, your labor-supply curve would slope backward. In Chapter 21, we discuss this possibility in terms of conflicting effects on your labor-supply decision (called the income and substitution effects). For now, we ignore the possibility of backward-sloping labor supply and assume that the labor-supply curve is upward sloping.

"I really didn't enjoy working five days a week, fifty weeks a year for forty years, but I needed the money."

What Causes the Labor-Supply Curve to Shift?

The labor-supply curve shifts whenever people change the amount they want to work at a given wage. Let's now consider some of the events that might cause such a shift.

Changes in Tastes   In 1950, 34 percent of women were employed at paid jobs or looking for work. In 2009, the number had risen to 59 percent. There are many explanations for this development, but one of them is changing tastes, or attitudes toward work. A generation or two ago, it was the norm for women to stay at home and raise children. Today, family sizes are smaller, and more mothers choose to work. The result is an increase in the supply of labor.

Changes in Alternative Opportunities   The supply of labor in any one labor market depends on the opportunities available in other labor markets. If the wage earned by pear pickers suddenly rises, some apple pickers may choose to switch occupations, and the supply of labor in the market for apple pickers falls.

Immigration   Movement of workers from region to region, or country to country, is another important source of shifts in labor supply. When immigrants come to the United States, for instance, the supply of labor in the United States increases, and the supply of labor in the immigrants' home countries falls. In fact, much of the policy debate about immigration centers on its effect on labor supply and, thereby, equilibrium wages in the labor market.

QUICK QUIZ   *Who has a greater opportunity cost of enjoying leisure—a janitor or a brain surgeon? Explain. Can this help explain why doctors work such long hours?*

Equilibrium in the Labor Market

So far we have established two facts about how wages are determined in competitive labor markets:

- The wage adjusts to balance the supply and demand for labor.
- The wage equals the value of the marginal product of labor.

At first, it might seem surprising that the wage can do both of these things at once. In fact, there is no real puzzle here, but understanding why there is no puzzle is an important step to understanding wage determination.

Figure 4 shows the labor market in equilibrium. The wage and the quantity of labor have adjusted to balance supply and demand. When the market is in this equilibrium, each firm has bought as much labor as it finds profitable at the equilibrium wage. That is, each firm has followed the rule for profit

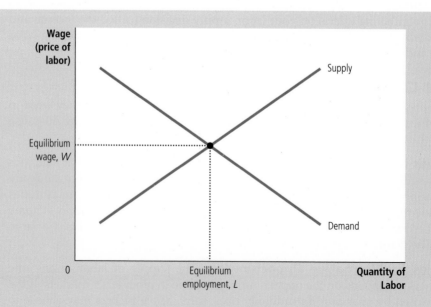

Figure **4**

Equilibrium in a Labor Market
Like all prices, the price of labor (the wage) depends on supply and demand. Because the demand curve reflects the value of the marginal product of labor, in equilibrium workers receive the value of their marginal contribution to the production of goods and services.

maximization: It has hired workers until the value of the marginal product equals the wage. Hence, the wage must equal the value of the marginal product of labor once it has brought supply and demand into equilibrium.

This brings us to an important lesson: *Any event that changes the supply or demand for labor must change the equilibrium wage and the value of the marginal product by the same amount because these must always be equal.* To see how this works, let's consider some events that shift these curves.

Shifts in Labor Supply

Suppose that immigration increases the number of workers willing to pick apples. As Figure 5 shows, the supply of labor shifts to the right from S_1 to S_2. At the initial wage W_1, the quantity of labor supplied now exceeds the quantity demanded. This surplus of labor puts downward pressure on the wage of apple pickers, and the fall in the wage from W_1 to W_2 in turn makes it profitable for firms to hire more workers. As the number of workers employed in each apple orchard rises, the marginal product of a worker falls, and so does the value of the marginal product. In the new equilibrium, both the wage and the value of the marginal product of labor are lower than they were before the influx of new workers.

An episode from Israel illustrates how a shift in labor supply can alter the equilibrium in a labor market. During most of the 1980s, many thousands of Palestinians regularly commuted from their homes in the Israeli-occupied West Bank and Gaza Strip to jobs in Israel, primarily in the construction and agriculture industries. In 1988, however, political unrest in these occupied areas induced the Israeli government to take steps that, as a by-product, reduced this supply of workers. Curfews were imposed, work permits were checked more thoroughly, and a ban on overnight stays of Palestinians in Israel was enforced more rigorously. The economic impact of these steps was exactly as theory predicts: The

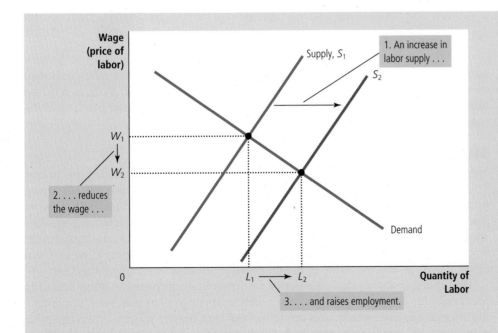

Figure 5

A Shift in Labor Supply
When labor supply increases from S_1 to S_2, perhaps because of an immigration of new workers, the equilibrium wage falls from W_1 to W_2. At this lower wage, firms hire more labor, so employment rises from L_1 to L_2. The change in the wage reflects a change in the value of the marginal product of labor: With more workers, the added output from an extra worker is smaller.

Figure labels:
Wage (price of labor) · Supply, S_1 · 1. An increase in labor supply . . . · S_2 · W_1 · W_2 · 2. . . . . reduces the wage . . . · Demand · 0 · L_1 · L_2 · Quantity of Labor · 3. . . . and raises employment.

in the news

> ### The Economics of Immigration

Here is an interview with Pia Orrenius, an economist at the Federal Reserve Bank of Dallas who studies immigration.

Pia Orrenius

Q: What can you tell us about the size of the immigrant population in the United States?

A: Immigrants make up about 12.5 percent of the overall population, which means about 38 million foreign-born live in the United States. The commonly accepted estimate for the undocumented portion of the foreign-born population is 11–12 million. Immigrants come from all parts of the world, but we've seen big changes in their origins. In the 1950s and 1960s, 75 percent of immigrants were from Europe. Today, about 80 percent are from Latin America and Asia. Inflows are also much larger today, with 1 million to 2 million newcomers entering each year.

What's interesting about the United States is how our economy has been able to absorb immigrants and put them to work. U.S. immigrants have high employment rates compared with other developed countries. This is partly because we don't set high entry-level wages or have strict hiring and firing rules. In this type of flexible system, you have more job openings. You have more opportunities. You also have lower entry-level wages, but immigrants at least get their foot in the door.

Being in the workforce allows immigrants to interact with the rest of society. They learn the language faster, pay taxes and become stakeholders.

Q: Where do immigrants fit into the U.S. economy?

A: Our immigrants are diverse in economic terms. We rely on immigrants for both high- and low-skilled jobs. Some immigrants do medium-skilled work, but more than anything else they're found on

number of Palestinians with jobs in Israel fell by half, while those who continued to work in Israel enjoyed wage increases of about 50 percent. With a reduced number of Palestinian workers in Israel, the value of the marginal product of the remaining workers was much higher.

Shifts in Labor Demand

Now suppose that an increase in the popularity of apples causes their price to rise. This price increase does not change the marginal product of labor for any given number of workers, but it does raise the *value* of the marginal product. With a higher price for apples, hiring more apple pickers is now profitable. As Figure 6 (page 388) shows, when the demand for labor shifts to the right from D_1 to D_2, the equilibrium wage rises from W_1 to W_2, and equilibrium employment rises from L_1 to L_2. Once again, the wage and the value of the marginal product of labor move together.

This analysis shows that prosperity for firms in an industry is often linked to prosperity for workers in that industry. When the price of apples rises, apple producers make greater profit, and apple pickers earn higher wages. When the price of apples falls, apple producers earn smaller profit, and apple pickers earn lower the low and the high ends of the education distribution.

The economic effects are different depending on which group you're talking about. We have an extremely important group of high-skilled immigrants. We rely on them to fill important, high-level jobs in technology, science and research. About 40 percent of our Ph.D. scientists and engineers were born in another country. We also employ many high-skilled immigrants in the health sector.

High-skilled immigration has good economic effects—it adds to GDP growth. It also has beneficial fiscal effects—the impact on government finances is large and positive. People tend to focus on illegal or low-skilled immigration when discussing immigrants and often do not recognize the tremendous contribution of high-skilled immigrants.

Q: What about the low-skilled immigration?

A: With low-skilled immigration, the economic benefits are there as well but have to be balanced against the fiscal impact, which is likely negative.

What makes the fiscal issue more difficult is the distribution of the burden. The federal government reaps much of the revenue from immigrants who work and pay employment taxes. State and local governments realize less of that benefit and have to pay more of the costs associated with low-skilled immigration—usually health care and educational expenses.

Q: Does it matter whether the immigration is legal or not?

A: If you're making value judgments about immigrants, or if you're discussing national security, you probably need to distinguish between those who come legally and those who don't. From an economic perspective, however, it makes more sense to differentiate among immigrants of various skill levels than it does to focus on legal status.

The economic benefits of low-skilled immigrants aren't typically going to depend on how they entered the United States. Illegal immigrants may pay less in taxes, but they're also eligible for fewer benefits. So being illegal doesn't mean these immigrants have a worse fiscal impact. In fact, a low-skilled illegal immigrant can create less fiscal burden than a low-skilled legal immigrant because the undocumented don't qualify for most benefits.

Q: How does immigration affect jobs and earnings for the native-born population?

A: We focus a lot on that—for example, exactly how immigration has affected the wages of Americans, particularly the low-skilled who lack a high school degree. The reason we worry about this is that real wages have been falling for low-skilled U.S. workers over the past 25 years or so.

The studies tend to show that not much of the decline is due to inflows of immigrants. The consensus seems to be that wages are about 1 to 3 percent lower today as a result of immigration. Some scholars find larger effects for low-skilled workers. Still, labor economists think it's a bit of a puzzle that they haven't been able to systematically identify larger adverse wage effects.

The reason may be the way the economy is constantly adjusting to the inflow of immigrants. On a geographical basis, for example, a large influx of immigrants into an area tends to encourage an inflow of capital to put them to use. So you have a shift out in labor supply, but you also have a shift out in labor demand, and the wage effects are ameliorated.

Source: Originally published in *Southwest Economy*, March/April 2006. Data updated for this edition by Dr. Orrenius.

wages. This lesson is well known to workers in industries with highly volatile prices. Workers in oil fields, for instance, know from experience that their earnings are closely linked to the world price of crude oil.

From these examples, you should now have a good understanding of how wages are set in competitive labor markets. Labor supply and labor demand together determine the equilibrium wage, and shifts in the supply or demand curve for labor cause the equilibrium wage to change. At the same time, profit maximization by the firms that demand labor ensures that the equilibrium wage always equals the value of the marginal product of labor.

CASE STUDY

Productivity and Wages

One of the *Ten Principles of Economics* in Chapter 1 is that our standard of living depends on our ability to produce goods and services. We can now see how this principle works in the market for labor. In particular, our analysis of labor demand shows that wages equal productivity as measured by the value of the

Figure 6

A Shift in Labor Demand
When labor demand increases from D_1 to D_2, perhaps because of an increase in the price of the firm's output, the equilibrium wage rises from W_1 to W_2, and employment rises from L_1 to L_2. Again, the change in the wage reflects a change in the value of the marginal product of labor: With a higher output price, the added output from an extra worker is more valuable.

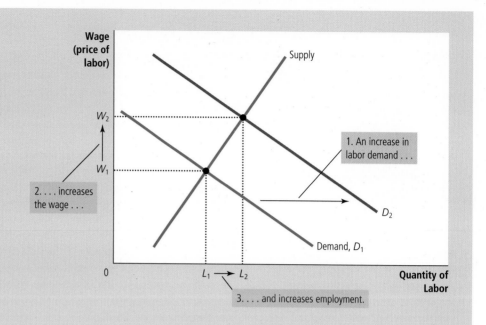

marginal product of labor. Put simply, highly productive workers are highly paid, and less productive workers are less highly paid.

This lesson is key to understanding why workers today are better off than workers in previous generations. Table 2 presents some data on growth in productivity and growth in real wages (that is, wages adjusted for inflation). From 1959 to 2009, productivity as measured by output per hour of work grew about 2.1 percent per year. Real wages grew at 1.9 percent—almost exactly the same rate. With a growth rate of 2 percent per year, productivity and real wages double about every 35 years.

Productivity growth varies over time. Table 2 also shows the data for three shorter periods that economists have identified as having very different productivity experiences. Around 1973, the U.S. economy experienced a significant slowdown in productivity growth that lasted until 1995. The cause of the productivity slowdown is not well understood, but the link between productivity and real wages is exactly as standard theory predicts. The slowdown in productivity growth from 2.8 to 1.4 percent per year coincided with a slowdown in real wage growth from 2.8 to 1.2 percent per year.

Productivity growth picked up again around 1995, and many observers hailed the arrival of the "new economy." This productivity acceleration is most often attributed to the spread of computers and information technology. As theory predicts, growth in real wages picked up as well. From 1995 to 2009, productivity grew by 2.6 percent per year, and real wages grew by 2.3 percent per year.

The bottom line: Both theory and history confirm the close connection between productivity and real wages. ■

QUICK QUIZ *How does an immigration of workers affect labor supply, labor demand, the marginal product of labor, and the equilibrium wage?*

Time Period	Growth Rate of Productivity	Growth Rate of Real Wages
1959–2009	2.1%	1.9%
1959–1973	2.8	2.8
1973–1995	1.4	1.2
1995–2009	2.6	2.3

Table 2

Productivity and Wage Growth in the United States

Source: *Economic Report of the President 2010*, Table B-49. Growth in productivity is measured here as the annualized rate of change in output per hour in the nonfarm business sector. Growth in real wages is measured as the annualized change in compensation per hour in the nonfarm business sector divided by the implicit price deflator for that sector. These productivity data measure average productivity—the quantity of output divided by the quantity of labor—rather than marginal productivity, but average and marginal productivity are thought to move closely together.

FYI

> *Monopsony*

On the preceding pages, we built our analysis of the labor market with the tools of supply and demand. In doing so, we assumed that the labor market was competitive. That is, we assumed that there were many buyers and sellers of labor, so each buyer or seller had a negligible effect on the wage.

Yet imagine the labor market in a small town dominated by a single, large employer. That employer can exert a large influence on the going wage, and it may well use that market power to alter the outcome. Such a market in which there is a single buyer is called a *monopsony*.

A monopsony (a market with one buyer) is in many ways similar to a monopoly (a market with one seller). Recall from Chapter 15 that a monopoly firm produces less of the good than would a competitive firm; by reducing the quantity offered for sale, the monopoly firm moves along the product's demand curve, raising the price and also its profits. Similarly, a monopsony firm in a labor market hires fewer workers than would a competitive firm; by reducing the number of jobs available, the monopsony firm moves along the labor supply curve, reducing the wage it pays and raising its profits. Thus, both monopolists and monopsonists reduce economic activity in a market below the socially optimal level. In both cases, the existence of market power distorts the outcome and causes deadweight losses.

This book does not present the formal model of monopsony because, in the world, monopsonies are rare. In most labor markets, workers have many possible employers, and firms compete with one another to attract workers. In this case, the model of supply and demand is the best one to use.

The Other Factors of Production: Land and Capital

We have seen how firms decide how much labor to hire and how these decisions determine workers' wages. At the same time that firms are hiring workers, they are also deciding about other inputs to production. For example, our apple-producing firm might have to choose the size of its apple orchard and the number of ladders for its apple pickers. We can think of the firm's factors of production as falling into three categories: labor, land, and capital.

capital

the equipment and structures used to produce goods and services

The meaning of the terms *labor* and *land* is clear, but the definition of *capital* is somewhat tricky. Economists use the term **capital** to refer to the stock of equipment and structures used for production. That is, the economy's capital represents the accumulation of goods produced in the past that are being used in the present to produce new goods and services. For our apple firm, the capital stock includes the ladders used to climb the trees, the trucks used to transport the apples, the buildings used to store the apples, and even the trees themselves.

Equilibrium in the Markets for Land and Capital

What determines how much the owners of land and capital earn for their contribution to the production process? Before answering this question, we need to distinguish between two prices: the purchase price and the rental price. The *purchase price* of land or capital is the price a person pays to own that factor of production indefinitely. The *rental price* is the price a person pays to use that factor for a limited period of time. It is important to keep this distinction in mind because, as we will see, these prices are determined by somewhat different economic forces.

Having defined these terms, we can now apply the theory of factor demand that we developed for the labor market to the markets for land and capital. Because the wage is the rental price of labor, much of what we have learned about wage determination applies also to the rental prices of land and capital. As Figure 7 illustrates, the rental price of land, shown in panel (a), and the rental price of capital, shown in panel (b), are determined by supply and demand. Moreover, the demand for land and capital is determined just like the demand for labor. That is, when our apple-producing firm is deciding how much land and how many ladders to rent, it follows the same logic as when deciding how many workers to hire. For both

Figure **7**

The Markets for Land and Capital

Supply and demand determine the compensation paid to the owners of land, as shown in panel (a), and the compensation paid to the owners of capital, as shown in panel (b). The demand for each factor, in turn, depends on the value of the marginal product of that factor.

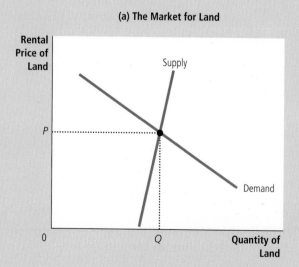

(a) The Market for Land

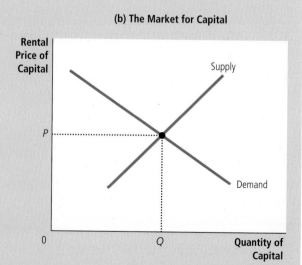

(b) The Market for Capital

FYI

› What Is Capital Income?

Labor income is an easy concept to understand: It is the paycheck that workers get from their employers. The income earned by capital, however, is less obvious.

In our analysis, we have been implicitly assuming that households own the economy's stock of capital—ladders, drill presses, warehouses, and so on—and rent it to the firms that use it. Capital income, in this case, is the rent that households receive for the use of their capital. This assumption simplified our analysis of how capital owners are compensated, but it is not entirely realistic. In fact, firms usually own the capital they use, and therefore, they receive the earnings from this capital.

These earnings from capital, however, eventually are paid to households. Some of the earnings are paid in the form of interest to those households who have lent money to firms. Bondholders and bank depositors are two examples of recipients of interest. Thus, when you receive interest on your bank account, that income is part of the economy's capital income.

In addition, some of the earnings from capital are paid to households in the form of dividends. Dividends are payments by a firm to the firm's stockholders. A stockholder is a person who has bought a share in the ownership of the firm and, therefore, is entitled to share in the firm's profits.

A firm does not have to pay out all its earnings to households in the form of interest and dividends. Instead, it can retain some earnings within the firm and use these earnings to buy additional capital. Although these retained earnings are not paid to the firm's stockholders, the stockholders benefit from them nonetheless. Because retained earnings increase the amount of capital the firm owns, they tend to increase future earnings and, thereby, the value of the firm's stock.

These institutional details are interesting and important, but they do not alter our conclusion about the income earned by the owners of capital. Capital is paid according to the value of its marginal product, regardless of whether this income is transmitted to households in the form of interest or dividends or whether it is kept within firms as retained earnings.

land and capital, the firm increases the quantity hired until the value of the factor's marginal product equals the factor's price. Thus, the demand curve for each factor reflects the marginal productivity of that factor.

We can now explain how much income goes to labor, how much goes to landowners, and how much goes to the owners of capital. As long as the firms using the factors of production are competitive and profit-maximizing, each factor's rental price must equal the value of the marginal product for that factor. *Labor, land, and capital each earn the value of their marginal contribution to the production process.*

Now consider the purchase price of land and capital. The rental price and the purchase price are related: Buyers are willing to pay more for a piece of land or capital if it produces a valuable stream of rental income. And as we have just seen, the equilibrium rental income at any point in time equals the value of that factor's marginal product. Therefore, the equilibrium purchase price of a piece of land or capital depends on both the current value of the marginal product and the value of the marginal product expected to prevail in the future.

Linkages among the Factors of Production

We have seen that the price paid to any factor of production—labor, land, or capital—equals the value of the marginal product of that factor. The marginal product of any factor, in turn, depends on the quantity of that factor that is available. Because of diminishing marginal product, a factor in abundant supply has a low marginal product and thus a low price, and a factor in scarce supply has a high marginal product and a high price. As a result, when the supply of a factor falls, its equilibrium factor price rises.

When the supply of any factor changes, however, the effects are not limited to the market for that factor. In most situations, factors of production are used together in a way that makes the productivity of each factor dependent on the quantities of the other factors available for use in the production process. As a result, a change in the supply of any one factor alters the earnings of all the factors.

For example, suppose a hurricane destroys many of the ladders that workers use to pick apples from the orchards. What happens to the earnings of the various factors of production? Most obviously, the supply of ladders falls, and therefore, the equilibrium rental price of ladders rises. Those owners who were lucky enough to avoid damage to their ladders now earn a higher return when they rent out their ladders to the firms that produce apples.

Yet the effects of this event do not stop at the ladder market. Because there are fewer ladders with which to work, the workers who pick apples have a smaller marginal product. Thus, the reduction in the supply of ladders reduces the demand for the labor of apple pickers, and this causes the equilibrium wage to fall.

This story shows a general lesson: An event that changes the supply of any factor of production can alter the earnings of all the factors. The change in earnings of any factor can be found by analyzing the impact of the event on the value of the marginal product of that factor.

 The Economics of the Black Death

In 14th-century Europe, the bubonic plague wiped out about one-third of the population within a few years. This event, called the *Black Death*, provides a grisly natural experiment to test the theory of factor markets that we have just developed. Consider the effects of the Black Death on those who were lucky enough to survive. What do you think happened to the wages earned by workers and the rents earned by landowners?

To answer this question, let's examine the effects of a reduced population on the marginal product of labor and the marginal product of land. With a smaller supply of workers, the marginal product of labor rises. (This is diminishing marginal product working in reverse.) Thus, we would expect the Black Death to raise wages.

Because land and labor are used together in production, a smaller supply of workers also affects the market for land, the other major factor of production in medieval Europe. With fewer workers available to farm the land, an additional unit of land produced less additional output. In other words, the marginal product of land fell. Thus, we would expect the Black Death to lower rents.

In fact, both predictions are consistent with the historical evidence. Wages approximately doubled during this period, and rents declined 50 percent or more. The Black Death led to economic prosperity for the peasant classes and reduced incomes for the landed classes. ■

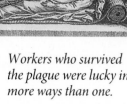

Workers who survived the plague were lucky in more ways than one.

QUICK QUIZ *What determines the income of the owners of land and capital? • How would an increase in the quantity of capital affect the incomes of those who already own capital? How would it affect the incomes of workers?*

Conclusion

This chapter explained how labor, land, and capital are compensated for the roles they play in the production process. The theory developed here is called the *neoclassical theory of distribution.* According to the neoclassical theory, the amount paid to each factor of production depends on the supply and demand for that factor. The demand, in turn, depends on that particular factor's marginal productivity. In equilibrium, each factor of production earns the value of its marginal contribution to the production of goods and services.

The neoclassical theory of distribution is widely accepted. Most economists begin with the neoclassical theory when trying to explain how the U.S. economy's $15 trillion of income is distributed among the economy's various members. In the following two chapters, we consider the distribution of income in more detail. As you will see, the neoclassical theory provides the framework for this discussion.

Even at this point, you can use the theory to answer the question that began this chapter: Why are computer programmers paid more than gas station attendants? It is because programmers can produce a good of greater market value than can gas station attendants. People are willing to pay dearly for a good computer game, but they are willing to pay little to have their gas pumped and their windshield washed. The wages of these workers reflect the market prices of the goods they produce. If people suddenly got tired of using computers and decided to spend more time driving, the prices of these goods would change, and so would the equilibrium wages of these two groups of workers.

SUMMARY

- The economy's income is distributed in the markets for the factors of production. The three most important factors of production are labor, land, and capital.

- The demand for factors, such as labor, is a derived demand that comes from firms that use the factors to produce goods and services. Competitive, profit-maximizing firms hire each factor up to the point at which the value of the marginal product of the factor equals its price.

- The supply of labor arises from individuals' trade-off between work and leisure. An upward-sloping labor-supply curve means that people respond to an increase in the wage by working more hours and enjoying less leisure.

- The price paid to each factor adjusts to balance the supply and demand for that factor. Because factor demand reflects the value of the marginal product of that factor, in equilibrium each factor is compensated according to its marginal contribution to the production of goods and services.

- Because factors of production are used together, the marginal product of any one factor depends on the quantities of all factors that are available. As a result, a change in the supply of one factor alters the equilibrium earnings of all the factors.

KEY CONCEPTS

factors of production, *p. 376*
production function, *p. 378*
marginal product of labor, *p. 378*

diminishing marginal
    product, *p. 378*

value of the marginal
    product, *p. 379*
capital, *p. 390*

QUESTIONS FOR REVIEW

1. Explain how a firm's production function is related to its marginal product of labor, how a firm's marginal product of labor is related to the value of its marginal product, and how a firm's value of marginal product is related to its demand for labor.
2. Give two examples of events that could shift the demand for labor, and explain why they do so.
3. Give two examples of events that could shift the supply of labor, and explain why they do so.

4. Explain how the wage can adjust to balance the supply and demand for labor while simultaneously equaling the value of the marginal product of labor.
5. If the population of the United States suddenly grew because of a large immigration, what would happen to wages? What would happen to the rents earned by the owners of land and capital?

PROBLEMS AND APPLICATIONS

1. Suppose that the president proposes a new law aimed at reducing healthcare costs: All Americans are required to eat one apple daily.
   a. How would this apple-a-day law affect the demand and equilibrium price of apples?
   b. How would the law affect the marginal product and the value of the marginal product of apple pickers?
   c. How would the law affect the demand and equilibrium wage for apple pickers?
2. Show the effect of each of the following events on the market for labor in the computer manufacturing industry.
   a. Congress buys personal computers for all U.S. college students.
   b. More college students major in engineering and computer science.
   c. Computer firms build new manufacturing plants.
3. Suppose that labor is the only input used by a perfectly competitive firm. The firm's production function is as follows:

Days of Labor	Units of Output
0 days	0 units
1	7
2	13
3	19
4	25
5	28
6	29
7	29

   a. Calculate the marginal product for each additional worker.
   b. Each unit of output sells for $10. Calculate the value of the marginal product of each worker.
   c. Compute the demand schedule showing the number of workers hired for all wages from zero to $100 a day.
   d. Graph the firm's demand curve.
   e. What happens to this demand curve if the price of output rises from $10 to $12 per unit?
4. Smiling Cow Dairy can sell all the milk it wants for $4 a gallon, and it can rent all the robots it wants to milk the cows at a capital rental price of $100 a day. It faces the following production schedule:

Number of Robots	Total Product
0	0 gallons
1	50
2	85
3	115
4	140
5	150
6	155

   a. In what kind of market structure does the firm sell its output? How can you tell?
   b. In what kind of market structure does the firm rent robots? How can you tell?

c. Calculate the marginal product and the value of the marginal product for each additional robot.

d. How many robots should the firm rent? Explain.

5. The nation of Ectenia has 20 competitive apple orchards, which sell apples at the world price of $2. The following equations describe the production function and the marginal product of labor in each orchard:

$$Q = 100L - L^2.$$
$$MPL = 100 - 2L$$

where Q is the number of apples produced in a day, L is the number of workers, and MPL is the marginal product of labor.

a. What is each orchard's labor demand as a function of the daily wage W? What is the market's labor demand?

b. Ectenia has 200 workers who supply their labor inelastically. Solve for the wage W. How many workers does each orchard hire? How much profit does each orchard owner make?

c. Calculate what happens to the income of workers and orchard owners if the world price of apples doubles to $4.

d. Now suppose the price of apples is back at $2, but a hurricane destroys half the orchards. Calculate how the hurricane affects the income of each worker and of each remaining orchard owner. What happens to the income of Ectenia as a whole?

6. Your enterprising uncle opens a sandwich shop that employs 7 people. The employees are paid $6 per hour, and a sandwich sells for $3. If your uncle is maximizing his profit, what is the value of the marginal product of the last worker he hired? What is that worker's marginal product?

7. Suppose a freeze destroys part of the Florida orange crop.

a. Explain what happens to the price of oranges and the marginal product of orange pickers as a result of the freeze. Can you say what happens to the demand for orange pickers? Why or why not?

b. Suppose the price of oranges doubles and the marginal product falls by 30 percent. What happens to the equilibrium wage of orange pickers?

c. Suppose the price of oranges rises by 30 percent and the marginal product falls by 50 percent. What happens to the equilibrium wage of orange pickers?

8. Leadbelly Co. sells pencils in a perfectly competitive product market and hires workers in a perfectly competitive labor market. Assume that the market wage rate for workers is $150 per day.

a. What rule should Leadbelly follow to hire the profit-maximizing amount of labor?

b. At the profit-maximizing level of output, the marginal product of the last worker hired is 30 boxes of pencils per day. Calculate the price of a box of pencils.

c. Draw a diagram of the labor market for pencil workers (as in Figure 4 of this chapter) next to a diagram of the labor supply and demand for Leadbelly Co. (as in Figure 3). Label the equilibrium wage and quantity of labor for both the market and the firm. How are these diagrams related?

d. Suppose some pencil workers switch to jobs in the growing computer industry. On the side-by-side diagrams from part (c), show how this change affects the equilibrium wage and quantity of labor for both the pencil market and for Leadbelly. How does this change affect the marginal product of labor at Leadbelly?

9. During the 1980s, 1990s, and the first decade of the 20th century, the United States experienced a significant inflow of capital from abroad. For example, Toyota, BMW, and other foreign car companies built auto plants in the United States.

a. Using a diagram of the U.S. capital market, show the effect of this inflow on the rental price of capital in the United States and on the quantity of capital in use.

b. Using a diagram of the U.S. labor market, show the effect of the capital inflow on the average wage paid to U.S. workers.

10. In recent years, some policymakers have proposed requiring firms to give workers certain fringe benefits, such as health insurance. Let's consider the effects of such a policy on the labor market.

a. Suppose that a law required firms to give each worker $3 of fringe benefits for every hour that the worker is employed by the firm. How does this law affect the marginal profit that a firm earns from each worker? How does the law affect the demand curve for labor? Draw your answer on a graph with the cash wage on the vertical axis.

b. If there is no change in labor supply, how would this law affect employment and wages?

c. Why might the labor-supply curve shift in response to this law? Would this shift in labor supply raise or lower the impact of the law on wages and employment?

d. As Chapter 6 discussed, the wages of some workers, particularly the unskilled and inexperienced, are kept above the equilibrium level by minimum-wage laws. What effect would a fringe-benefit mandate have for these workers?

11. This chapter has assumed that labor is supplied by individual workers acting competitively. In some markets, however, the supply of labor is determined by a union of workers.

a. Explain why the situation faced by a labor union may resemble the situation faced by a monopoly firm.

b. The goal of a monopoly firm is to maximize profits. Is there an analogous goal for labor unions?

c. Now extend the analogy between monopoly firms and unions. How do you suppose that the wage set by a union compares to the wage in a competitive market? How do you suppose employment differs in the two cases?

d. What other goals might unions have that make unions different from monopoly firms?

For further information on topics in this chapter, additional problems, applications, examples, online quizzes, and more, please visit our website at www .cengage.com/economics/mankiw.

Earnings and Discrimination

I n the United States today, the typical physician earns about $200,000 a year, the typical police officer about $50,000, and the typical farmworker about $20,000. These examples illustrate the large differences in earnings that are so common in our economy. The differences explain why some people live in mansions, ride in limousines, and vacation on the French Riviera, while other people live in small apartments, ride a bus, and vacation in their own backyards.

Why do earnings vary so much from person to person? Chapter 18, which developed the basic neoclassical theory of the labor market, offers an answer to this question. There we saw that wages are governed by labor supply and labor demand. Labor demand, in turn, reflects the marginal productivity of labor. In equilibrium, each worker is paid the value of his or her marginal contribution to the economy's production of goods and services.

This theory of the labor market, though widely accepted by economists, is only the beginning of the story. To understand the wide variation in earnings that we observe, we must go beyond this general framework and examine more precisely what determines the supply and demand for different types of labor. That is our goal in this chapter.

Some Determinants of Equilibrium Wages

Workers differ from one another in many ways. Jobs also have differing characteristics—both in terms of the wage they pay and in terms of their nonmonetary attributes. In this section, we consider how the characteristics of jobs and workers affect labor supply, labor demand, and equilibrium wages.

Compensating Differentials

When a worker is deciding whether to take a job, the wage is only one of many job attributes that the worker takes into account. Some jobs are easy, fun, and safe, while others are hard, dull, and dangerous. The better the job as gauged by these nonmonetary characteristics, the more people there are who are willing to do the job at any given wage. In other words, the supply of labor for easy, fun, and safe jobs is greater than the supply of labor for hard, dull, and dangerous jobs. As a result, "good" jobs will tend to have lower equilibrium wages than "bad" jobs.

For example, imagine you are looking for a summer job in a local beach community. Two kinds of jobs are available. You can take a job as a beach-badge checker, or you can take a job as a garbage collector. The beach-badge checkers take leisurely strolls along the beach during the day and check to make sure the tourists have bought the required beach permits. The garbage collectors wake up before dawn to drive dirty, noisy trucks around town to pick up garbage. Which job would you want? Most people would prefer the beach job if the wages were the same. To induce people to become garbage collectors, the town has to offer higher wages to garbage collectors than to beach-badge checkers.

compensating differential

a difference in wages that arises to offset the nonmonetary characteristics of different jobs

Economists use the term **compensating differential** to refer to a difference in wages that arises from nonmonetary characteristics of different jobs. Compensating differentials are prevalent in the economy. Here are some examples:

- Coal miners are paid more than other workers with similar levels of education. Their higher wage compensates them for the dirty and dangerous nature of coal mining, as well as the long-term health problems that coal miners experience.
- Workers who work the night shift at factories are paid more than similar workers who work the day shift. The higher wage compensates them for having to work at night and sleep during the day, a lifestyle that most people find undesirable.
- Professors are paid less than lawyers and doctors, who have similar amounts of education. Professors' lower wages compensate them for the great intellectual and personal satisfaction that their jobs offer. (Indeed, teaching economics is so much fun that it is surprising that economics professors are paid anything at all!)

"On the one hand, I know I could make more money if I left public service for the private sector, but, on the other hand, I couldn't chop off heads."

Human Capital

As we discussed in the previous chapter, the word *capital* usually refers to the economy's stock of equipment and structures. The capital stock includes the farmer's tractor, the manufacturer's factory, and the teacher's chalkboard. The essence of capital is that it is a factor of production that itself has been produced.

There is another type of capital that, while less tangible than physical capital, is just as important to the economy's production. **Human capital** is the accumulation of investments in people. The most important type of human capital is education. Like all forms of capital, education represents an expenditure of resources at one time to raise productivity in the future. But unlike an investment in other forms of capital, an investment in education is tied to a specific person, and this linkage is what makes it human capital.

Not surprisingly, workers with more human capital on average earn more than those with less human capital. College graduates in the United States, for example, earn almost twice as much as those workers who end their education with a high school diploma. This large difference has been documented in many countries around the world. It tends to be even larger in less developed countries, where educated workers are in scarce supply.

It is easy to see why education raises wages from the perspective of supply and demand. Firms—the demanders of labor—are willing to pay more for the highly educated because highly educated workers have higher marginal products. Workers—the suppliers of labor—are willing to pay the cost of becoming educated only if there is a reward for doing so. In essence, the difference in wages between highly educated workers and less educated workers may be considered a compensating differential for the cost of becoming educated.

human capital

the accumulation of investments in people, such as education and on-the-job training

CASE STUDY The Increasing Value of Skills

"The rich get richer, and the poor get poorer." Like many adages, this one is not always true, but it has been in recent years. Many studies have documented that the earnings gap between workers with high skills and workers with low skills has increased over the past two decades.

Table 1 presents data on the average earnings of college graduates and of high school graduates without any additional education. These data show the increase in the financial reward from education. In 1980, a man on average earned 44 percent more with a college degree than without one; by 2008, this figure had risen to 88 percent. For a woman, the reward for attending college rose from a 35 percent increase in earnings to a 71 percent increase. The incentive to stay in school is as great today as it has ever been.

Why has the gap in earnings between skilled and unskilled workers widened in recent years? No one knows for sure, but economists have proposed two hypotheses to explain this trend. Both hypotheses suggest that the demand for skilled labor has risen over time relative to the demand for unskilled labor. The shift in demand has led to a corresponding change in wages, which in turn has led to greater inequality.

The first hypothesis is that international trade has altered the relative demand for skilled and unskilled labor. In recent years, the amount of trade with other countries has increased substantially. As a percentage of total U.S. production of goods and services, imports have risen from 5 percent in 1970 to 14 percent in 2009, and exports have risen from 6 percent in 1970 to 11 percent in 2009. Because unskilled labor is plentiful and cheap in many foreign countries, the United States tends to import goods produced with unskilled labor and export goods produced

Table 1

Average Annual Earnings by Educational Attainment College graduates have always earned more than workers without the benefit of college, but the salary gap has grown even larger over the past few decades.

	1980	2008
Men		
High school, no college	$45,310	$43,493
College graduates	$65,287	$81,975
Percent extra for college grads	+44%	+88%
Women		
High school, no college	$27,324	$31,666
College graduates	$36,894	$54,207
Percent extra for college grads	+35%	+71%

Note: Earnings data are adjusted for inflation and are expressed in 2008 dollars. Data apply to full-time, year-round workers age 18 and over. Data for college graduates exclude workers with additional schooling beyond college, such as a master's degree or Ph.D.

Source: U.S. Census Bureau and author's calculations.

with skilled labor. Thus, when international trade expands, the domestic demand for skilled labor rises, and the domestic demand for unskilled labor falls.

The second hypothesis is that changes in technology have altered the relative demand for skilled and unskilled labor. Consider, for instance, the introduction of computers. Computers raise the demand for skilled workers who can use the new machines and reduce the demand for the unskilled workers whose jobs are replaced by the computers. For example, many companies now rely more on computer databases, and less on filing cabinets, to keep business records. This change raises the demand for computer programmers and reduces the demand for filing clerks. Thus, as more firms use computers, the demand for skilled labor rises, and the demand for unskilled labor falls.

Economists have found it difficult to gauge the validity of these two hypotheses. It is possible that both are true: Increasing international trade and technological change may share responsibility for the increasing income inequality we have observed in recent decades. ■

Ability, Effort, and Chance

Why do major league baseball players get paid more than minor league players? Certainly, the higher wage is not a compensating differential. Playing in the major leagues is not a less pleasant job than playing in the minor leagues; in fact, the opposite is true. The major leagues do not require more years of schooling or more experience. To a large extent, players in the major leagues earn more just because they have greater natural ability.

Natural ability is important for workers in all occupations. Because of heredity and upbringing, people differ in their physical and mental attributes. Some people are strong, others weak. Some people are smart, others less so. Some people are outgoing, others awkward in social situations. These and many other personal characteristics determine how productive workers are and, therefore, play a role in determining the wages they earn.

Closely related to ability is effort. Some people work hard; others are lazy. We should not be surprised to find that those who work hard are more productive and earn higher wages. To some extent, firms reward workers directly by paying people based on what they produce. Salespeople, for instance, are often paid a percentage of the sales they make. At other times, hard work is rewarded less directly in the form of a higher annual salary or a bonus.

Chance also plays a role in determining wages. If a person attended a trade school to learn how to repair televisions with vacuum tubes and then found this skill made obsolete by the invention of solid-state electronics, he or she would end up earning a low wage compared to others with similar years of training. The low wage of this worker is due to chance—a phenomenon that economists recognize but do not shed much light on.

How important are ability, effort, and chance in determining wages? It is hard to say because these factors are difficult to measure. But indirect evidence suggests that they are very important. When labor economists study wages, they relate a worker's wage to those variables that can be measured, such as years of schooling, years of experience, age, and job characteristics. All these measured variables affect a worker's wage as theory predicts, but they account for less than half of the variation in wages in our economy. Because so much of the variation in wages is left unexplained, omitted variables, including ability, effort, and chance, must play an important role.

The Benefits of Beauty

People differ in many ways. One difference is in how attractive they are. The actress Keira Knightley, for instance, is a beautiful woman. In part for this reason, her movies attract large audiences. Not surprisingly, the large audiences mean a large income for Ms. Knightley.

How prevalent are the economic benefits of beauty? Labor economists Daniel Hamermesh and Jeff Biddle tried to answer this question in a study published in the December 1994 issue of the *American Economic Review*. Hamermesh and Biddle examined data from surveys of individuals in the United States and Canada. The interviewers who conducted the survey were asked to rate each respondent's physical appearance. Hamermesh and Biddle then examined how much the wages of the respondents depended on the standard determinants—education, experience, and so on—and how much they depended on physical appearance.

Hamermesh and Biddle found that beauty pays. People who are deemed more attractive than average earn 5 percent more than people of average looks, and people of average looks earn 5 to 10 percent more than people considered less attractive than average. Similar results were found for men and women.

What explains these differences in wages? There are several ways to interpret the "beauty premium."

One interpretation is that good looks are themselves a type of innate ability determining productivity and wages. Some people are born with the physical attributes of a movie star; other people are not. Good looks are useful in any job in which workers present themselves to the public—such as acting, sales, and waiting on tables. In this case, an attractive worker is more valuable to the firm than an unattractive worker. The firm's willingness to pay more to attractive workers reflects its customers' preferences.

Good looks pay.

A second interpretation is that reported beauty is an indirect measure of other types of ability. How attractive a person appears depends on more than just heredity. It also depends on dress, hairstyle, personal demeanor, and other attributes that a person can control. Perhaps a person who successfully projects an attractive image in a survey interview is more likely to be an intelligent person who succeeds at other tasks as well.

A third interpretation is that the beauty premium is a type of discrimination, a topic to which we return later. ■

An Alternative View of Education: Signaling

Earlier we discussed the human-capital view of education, according to which schooling raises workers' wages because it makes them more productive. Although this view is widely accepted, some economists have proposed an alternative theory, which emphasizes that firms use educational attainment as a way of sorting between high-ability and low-ability workers. According to this alternative view, when people earn a college degree, for instance, they do not become more productive, but they do *signal* their high ability to prospective employers. Because it is easier for high-ability people to earn a college degree than it is for low-ability people, more high-ability people get college degrees. As a result, it is rational for firms to interpret a college degree as a signal of ability.

The signaling theory of education is similar to the signaling theory of advertising discussed in Chapter 16. In the signaling theory of advertising, the advertisement itself contains no real information, but the firm signals the quality of its product to consumers by its willingness to spend money on advertising. In the signaling theory of education, schooling has no real productivity benefit, but the worker signals his innate productivity to employers by his willingness to spend years at school. In both cases, an action is being taken not for its intrinsic benefit but because the willingness to take that action conveys private information to someone observing it.

Thus, we now have two views of education: the human-capital theory and the signaling theory. Both views can explain why more educated workers tend to earn more than less educated workers. According to the human-capital view, education makes workers more productive; according to the signaling view, education is correlated with natural ability. But the two views have radically different predictions for the effects of policies that aim to increase educational attainment. According to the human-capital view, increasing educational levels for all workers would raise all workers' productivity and thereby their wages. According to the signaling view, education does not enhance productivity, so raising all workers' educational levels would not affect wages.

Most likely, the truth lies somewhere between these two extremes. The benefits to education are probably a combination of the productivity-enhancing effects of human capital and the productivity-revealing effects of signaling. The open question is the relative size of these two effects.

The Superstar Phenomenon

Although most actors earn little and often take jobs as waiters to support themselves, Johnny Depp earns millions of dollars for each film he makes. Similarly, while most people who play tennis do it for free as a hobby, Serena Williams earns millions on the pro tour. Depp and Williams are superstars in their fields, and their great public appeal is reflected in astronomical incomes.

in the news

> ### The Human Capital of Terrorists
> *Workers with more education are better at all kinds of tasks, even those aimed at destruction.*

Even for Shoe Bombers, Education and Success Are Linked

BY AUSTAN GOOLSBEE

The fifth anniversary of 9/11 passed with a great deal of hand-wringing over all the people who want to kill Americans. Especially worrisome is the apparent rise of terrorists whose origins seem far from fanatical.

These terrorists are not desperately poor uneducated people from the Middle East. A surprisingly large share of them have college and even graduate degrees. Increasingly, they seem to be from Britain, like the shoe bomber Richard C. Reid and most of the suspects in the London Underground bombings and the liquid explosives plot.

This has left the public wondering, Why are some educated people from Western countries so prone to fanaticism?

Before trying to answer that question, though, some economists argue that we need to think about what makes a successful terrorist and they warn against extrapolating from the terrorists we catch. It is a problem economists typically refer to as "selection bias."

In their new study, "Attack Assignments in Terror Organizations and the Productivity of Suicide Bombers," two economists, Efraim Benmelech of Harvard University and

Claude Berrebi of the RAND Corporation, set out to analyze the productivity of terrorists in the same way they might analyze the auto industry. But they defined the "success" of terrorists by their ability to kill.

They gathered data on Palestinian suicide bombers in Israel from 2000 to 2005 and found that for terrorists, just like for regular workers, experience and education improve productivity. Suicide bombers who are older—in their late 20's and early 30's—and better educated are less likely to be caught on their missions and are more likely to kill large numbers of people at bigger, more difficult targets than younger and more poorly educated bombers.

Professor Benmelech and Dr. Berrebi compare a Who's Who of the biggest suicide bombers to more typical bombers. Whereas typical bombers were younger than 21 and about 18 percent of them had at least some college education, the average age of the most successful bombers was almost 26 and 60 percent of them were college educated.

Experience and education also affect the chances of being caught. Every additional year of age reduces the chance by 12 percent. Having more than a high school education cuts the chance by more than half.

There are many examples where young or uneducated terrorists made stupid mistakes that foiled them. Professor Benmelech recounts the case last April of a teenager from Nablus apprehended by Israeli soldiers

before carrying out his bombing because he was wearing an overcoat on a 95-degree day. Mr. Reid, the failed shoe bomber, had only a high school degree. Would an older terrorist with more education have tried to light a match on his shoe (as Mr. Reid did) in plain view of the flight attendant and other passengers who proceeded to thwart his plan? Would a better-educated terrorist have been more discreet? We will never know.

The research suggests, however, that there may be a reason that the average age of the 9/11 hijackers (at least the ones for whom we have a birth date) was close to 26 and that the supposed leader, Mohammed Atta, was 33 with a graduate degree.

As Professor Benmelech put it in an interview: "It's clear that there are some terrorist missions that require a certain level of skill to accomplish. The older terrorists with better educations seem to be less likely to fail them. Perhaps it is not surprising, then, that terrorist organizers assign them to these more difficult missions."

Among Palestinian suicide bombers, the older and better-educated bombers are assigned to targets in bigger cities where they can potentially kill greater numbers of people. That same idea means that the terrorists assigned to attack the United States are probably different from the typical terrorist. They will be drawn from people whose skills make them better at evading security.

Source: *New York Times,* September 14, 2006.

Why do Depp and Williams earn so much? It is not surprising that incomes differ within occupations. Good carpenters earn more than mediocre carpenters, and good plumbers earn more than mediocre plumbers. People vary in ability and effort, and these differences lead to differences in income. Yet the best carpenters and plumbers do not earn the many millions that are common among the best actors and athletes. What explains the difference?

To understand the tremendous incomes of Depp and Williams, we must examine the special features of the markets in which they sell their services. Superstars arise in markets that have two characteristics:

- Every customer in the market wants to enjoy the good supplied by the best producer.
- The good is produced with a technology that makes it possible for the best producer to supply every customer at low cost.

If Johnny Depp is the best actor around, then everyone will want to see his next movie; seeing twice as many movies by an actor half as talented is not a good substitute. Moreover, it is *possible* for everyone to enjoy a performance by Johnny Depp. Because it is easy to make multiple copies of a film, Depp can provide his service to millions of people simultaneously. Similarly, because tennis games are broadcast on television, millions of fans can enjoy the extraordinary athletic skills of Serena Williams.

We can now see why there are no superstar carpenters and plumbers. Other things equal, everyone prefers to employ the best carpenter, but a carpenter, unlike a movie actor, can provide his services to only a limited number of customers. Although the best carpenter will be able to command a somewhat higher wage than the average carpenter, the average carpenter will still be able to earn a good living.

Above-Equilibrium Wages: Minimum-Wage Laws, Unions, and Efficiency Wages

Most analyses of wage differences among workers are based on the equilibrium model of the labor market—that is, wages are assumed to adjust to balance labor supply and labor demand. But this assumption does not always apply. For some workers, wages are set above the level that brings supply and demand into equilibrium. Let's consider three reasons this might be so.

One reason for above-equilibrium wages is minimum-wage laws, as we first saw in Chapter 6. Most workers in the economy are not affected by these laws because their equilibrium wages are well above the legal minimum. But for some workers, especially the least skilled and experienced, minimum-wage laws raise wages above the level they would earn in an unregulated labor market.

A second reason that wages might rise above their equilibrium level is the market power of labor unions. A **union** is a worker association that bargains with employers over wages and working conditions. Unions often raise wages above the level that would prevail without a union, perhaps because they can threaten to withhold labor from the firm by calling a **strike**. Studies suggest that union workers earn about 10 to 20 percent more than similar nonunion workers.

A third reason for above-equilibrium wages is suggested by the theory of **efficiency wages**. This theory holds that a firm can find it profitable to pay high wages because doing so increases the productivity of its workers. In particular,

union
a worker association that bargains with employers over wages and working conditions

strike
the organized withdrawal of labor from a firm by a union

efficiency wages
above-equilibrium wages paid by firms to increase worker productivity

high wages may reduce worker turnover, increase worker effort, and raise the quality of workers who apply for jobs at the firm. If this theory is correct, then some firms may choose to pay their workers more than they would normally earn.

Above-equilibrium wages, whether caused by minimum-wage laws, unions, or efficiency wages, have similar effects on the labor market. In particular, pushing a wage above the equilibrium level raises the quantity of labor supplied and reduces the quantity of labor demanded. The result is a surplus of labor, or unemployment. The study of unemployment and the public policies aimed to deal with it is usually considered a topic within macroeconomics, so it goes beyond the scope of this chapter. But it would be a mistake to ignore these issues completely when analyzing earnings. Although most wage differences can be understood while maintaining the assumption of equilibrium in the labor market, above-equilibrium wages play a role in some cases.

QUICK QUIZ *Define* compensating differential *and give an example.* • *Give two reasons more educated workers earn more than less educated workers.*

The Economics of Discrimination

Another source of differences in wages is discrimination. **Discrimination** occurs when the marketplace offers different opportunities to similar individuals who differ only by race, ethnic group, sex, age, or other personal characteristics. Discrimination reflects some people's prejudice against certain groups in society. Discrimination is an emotionally charged topic that often generates heated debate, but economists try to study the topic objectively to separate myth from reality.

discrimination
the offering of different opportunities to similar individuals who differ only by race, ethnic group, sex, age, or other personal characteristics

Measuring Labor-Market Discrimination

How much does discrimination in labor markets affect the earnings of different groups of workers? This question is important, but answering it is not easy.

There is no doubt that different groups of workers earn substantially different wages, as Table 2 demonstrates. The median black man in the United States is paid 21 percent less than the median white man, and the median black woman is paid 13 percent less than the median white woman. The differences by sex are also significant. The median white woman is paid 24 percent less than the median

	White	Black	Percent Earnings Are Lower for Black Workers
Men	$47,370	$37,253	21%
Women	$36,198	$31,509	13%
Percent Earnings Are Lower for Women Workers	24%	15%	

Table 2

Median Annual Earnings by Race and Sex

Note: Earnings data are for the year 2008 and apply to full-time, year-round workers over age 14.

Source: U.S. Census Bureau.

white man, and the median black woman is paid 15 percent less than the median black man. Taken at face value, these differentials look like evidence that employers discriminate against blacks and women.

Yet there is a potential problem with this inference. Even in a labor market free of discrimination, different people have different wages. People differ in the amount of human capital they have and in the kinds of work they are able and willing to do. The wage differences we observe in the economy are, to some extent, attributable to the determinants of equilibrium wages we discussed in the preceding section. Simply observing differences in wages among broad groups—whites and blacks, men and women—does not prove that employers discriminate.

Consider, for example, the role of human capital. Among male workers, whites are about 75 percent more likely to have a college degree than blacks. Thus, at least some of the difference between the wages of whites and the wages of blacks can be traced to differences in educational attainment. Among white workers, men and women are now about equally likely to have a college degree, but men are about 11 percent more likely to earn a graduate or professional degree after college, indicating that some of the wage differential between men and women is also attributable to educational attainment.

Moreover, human capital may be more important in explaining wage differentials than measures of years of schooling suggest. Historically, public schools in predominantly black areas have been of lower quality—as measured by expenditure, class size, and so on—than public schools in predominantly white areas. Similarly, for many years, schools directed girls away from science and math courses, even though these subjects may have had greater value in the marketplace than some of the alternatives. If we could measure the quality as well as the quantity of education, the differences in human capital among these groups would seem even larger.

Human capital acquired in the form of job experience can also help explain wage differences. In particular, women tend to have less job experience on average compared to men. One reason is that female labor-force participation has increased over the past several decades. Because of this historic change, the average female worker today is younger than the average male worker. In addition, women are more likely to interrupt their careers to raise children. For both reasons, the average female worker has less job experience than the average male worker.

Yet another source of wage differences is compensating differentials. Men and women do not always choose the same type of work, and this fact may help explain some of the earnings differential between men and women. For example, women are more likely to be secretaries, and men are more likely to be truck drivers. The relative wages of secretaries and truck drivers depend in part on the working conditions of each job. Because these nonmonetary aspects are hard to measure, it is difficult to gauge the practical importance of compensating differentials in explaining the wage differences that we observe.

In the end, the study of wage differences among groups does not establish any clear conclusion about the prevalence of discrimination in U.S. labor markets. Most economists believe that some of the observed wage differentials are attributable to discrimination, but there is no consensus about how much. The only conclusion about which economists are in consensus is a negative one: Because the differences in average wages among groups in part reflect differences in human capital and job characteristics, they do not by themselves say anything about how much discrimination there is in the labor market.

Of course, differences in human capital among groups of workers may themselves reflect discrimination. The less rigorous curriculums historically offered to female students, for instance, can be considered a discriminatory practice. Similarly, the inferior schools historically available to black students may be traced to prejudice on the part of city councils and school boards. But this kind of discrimination occurs long before the worker enters the labor market. In this case, the disease is political, even if the symptom is economic.

Is Emily More Employable than Lakisha?

Although measuring the extent of discrimination from labor-market outcomes is hard, some compelling evidence for the existence of such discrimination comes from a creative "field experiment." Economists Marianne Bertrand and Sendhil Mullainathan answered more than 1,300 help-wanted ads run in Boston and Chicago newspapers by sending in nearly 5,000 fake résumés. Half of the résumés had names that were common in the African-American community, such as Lakisha Washington or Jamal Jones. The other half had names that were more common among the white population, such as Emily Walsh and Greg Baker. Otherwise, the résumés were similar. The results of this experiment were published in the *American Economic Review* in September 2004.

The researchers found large differences in how employers responded to the two groups of résumés. Job applicants with white names received about 50 percent more calls from interested employers than applicants with African-American names. The study found that this discrimination occurred for all types of employers, including those who claimed to be an "Equal Opportunity Employer" in their help-wanted ads. The researchers concluded that "racial discrimination is still a prominent feature of the labor market." ∎

Discrimination by Employers

Let's now turn from measurement to the economic forces that lie behind discrimination in labor markets. If one group in society receives a lower wage than another group, even after controlling for human capital and job characteristics, who is to blame for this differential?

The answer is not obvious. It might seem natural to blame employers for discriminatory wage differences. After all, employers make the hiring decisions that determine labor demand and wages. If some groups of workers earn lower wages than they should, then it seems that employers are responsible. Yet many economists are skeptical of this easy answer. They believe that competitive, market economies provide a natural antidote to employer discrimination. That antidote is called the profit motive.

Imagine an economy in which workers are differentiated by their hair color. Blondes and brunettes have the same skills, experience, and work ethic. Yet because of discrimination, employers prefer not to hire workers with blonde hair. Thus, the demand for blondes is lower than it otherwise would be. As a result, blondes earn a lower wage than brunettes.

How long can this wage differential persist? In this economy, there is an easy way for a firm to beat out its competitors: It can hire blonde workers. By hiring blondes, a firm pays lower wages and thus has lower costs than firms that hire brunettes. Over time, more and more "blonde" firms enter the market to take advantage of this cost advantage. The existing "brunette" firms have higher costs and, therefore, begin to lose money when faced with the new competitors. These losses induce the brunette firms to go out of business. Eventually, the entry of blonde firms and the exit of brunette firms cause the demand for blonde workers to rise and the demand for brunette workers to fall. This process continues until the wage differential disappears.

Put simply, business owners who care only about making money are at an advantage when competing against those who also care about discriminating. As a result, firms that do not discriminate tend to replace those that do. In this way, competitive markets have a natural remedy for employer discrimination.

Segregated Streetcars and the Profit Motive

In the early 20th century, streetcars in many southern cities were segregated by race. White passengers sat in the front of the streetcars, and black passengers sat in the back. What do you suppose caused and maintained this discriminatory practice? And how was this practice viewed by the firms that ran the streetcars?

In a 1986 article in the *Journal of Economic History*, economic historian Jennifer Roback looked at these questions. Roback found that the segregation of races on streetcars was the result of laws that required such segregation. Before these laws were passed, racial discrimination in seating was rare. It was far more common to segregate smokers and nonsmokers.

Moreover, the firms that ran the streetcars often opposed the laws requiring racial segregation. Providing separate seating for different races raised the firms' costs and reduced their profit. One railroad company manager complained to the city council that, under the segregation laws, "the company has to haul around a good deal of empty space."

Here is how Roback describes the situation in one southern city:

> The railroad company did not initiate the segregation policy and was not at all eager to abide by it. State legislation, public agitation, and a threat to arrest the president of the railroad were all required to induce them to separate the races on their cars. . . . There is no indication that the management was motivated by belief in civil rights or racial equality. The evidence indicates their primary motives were economic; separation was costly. . . . Officials of the company may or may not have disliked blacks, but they were not willing to forgo the profits necessary to indulge such prejudice.

The story of southern streetcars illustrates a general lesson: Business owners are usually more interested in making profit than in discriminating against a particular group. When firms engage in discriminatory practices, the ultimate source of the discrimination often lies not with the firms themselves but elsewhere. In this particular case, the streetcar companies segregated whites and blacks because discriminatory laws, which the companies opposed, required them to do so. ■

Discrimination by Customers and Governments

The profit motive is a strong force acting to eliminate discriminatory wage differentials, but there are limits to its corrective abilities. Two important limiting factors are customer preferences and government policies.

To see how customer preferences for discrimination can affect wages, consider again our imaginary economy with blondes and brunettes. Suppose that restaurant owners discriminate against blondes when hiring waiters. As a result, blonde waiters earn lower wages than brunette waiters. In this case, a restaurant can open up with blonde waiters and charge lower prices. If customers care only about the quality and price of their meals, the discriminatory firms will be driven out of business, and the wage differential will disappear.

On the other hand, it is possible that customers prefer being served by brunette waiters. If this preference for discrimination is strong, the entry of blonde restaurants need not succeed in eliminating the wage differential between brunettes and blondes. That is, if customers have discriminatory preferences, a competitive market is consistent with a discriminatory wage differential. An economy with such discrimination would contain two types of restaurants. Blonde restaurants hire blondes, have lower costs, and charge lower prices. Brunette restaurants hire brunettes, have higher costs, and charge higher prices. Customers who did not care about the hair color of their waiters would be attracted to the lower prices at the blonde restaurants. Bigoted customers would go to the brunette restaurants and would pay for their discriminatory preference in the form of higher prices.

Another way for discrimination to persist in competitive markets is for the government to mandate discriminatory practices. If, for instance, the government passed a law stating that blondes could wash dishes in restaurants but could not work as waiters, then a wage differential could persist in a competitive market. The example of segregated streetcars in the foregoing case study is one example of government-mandated discrimination. More recently, before South Africa abandoned its system of apartheid, blacks were prohibited from working in some jobs. Discriminatory governments pass such laws to suppress the normal equalizing force of free and competitive markets.

To sum up: *Competitive markets contain a natural remedy for employer discrimination. The entry into the market of firms that care only about profit tends to eliminate discriminatory wage differentials. These wage differentials persist in competitive markets only when customers are willing to pay to maintain the discriminatory practice or when the government mandates it.*

 ## Discrimination in Sports

As we have seen, measuring discrimination is often difficult. To determine whether one group of workers is discriminated against, a researcher must correct for differences in the productivity between that group and other workers in the economy. Yet in most firms, it is difficult to measure a particular worker's contribution to the production of goods and services.

One type of firm in which such corrections are easier is the sports team. Professional teams have many objective measures of productivity. In baseball, for instance, we can measure a player's batting average, the frequency of home runs, the number of stolen bases, and so on.

Studies of sports teams suggest that racial discrimination is, in fact, common and that much of the blame lies with customers. One study, published in the *Journal of Labor Economics* in 1988, examined the salaries of basketball players and found that black players earned 20 percent less than white players of comparable ability. The study also found that attendance at basketball games was larger for teams with a greater proportion of white players. One interpretation of these facts is that, at least at the time of the study, customer discrimination made black players less profitable than white players for team owners. In the presence of such customer discrimination, a discriminatory wage gap can persist, even if team owners care only about profit.

A similar situation once existed for baseball players. A study using data from the late 1960s showed that black players earned less than comparable white players. Moreover, fewer fans attended games pitched by blacks than games pitched by whites, even though black pitchers had better records than white pitchers. Studies of more recent salaries in baseball, however, have found no evidence of discriminatory wage differentials.

Another study, published in the *Quarterly Journal of Economics* in 1990, examined the market prices of old baseball cards. This study found similar evidence of discrimination. The cards of black hitters sold for 10 percent less than the cards of comparable white hitters, and the cards of black pitchers sold for 13 percent less than the cards of comparable white pitchers. These results suggest customer discrimination among baseball fans. ■

QUICK QUIZ *Why is it hard to establish whether a group of workers is being discriminated against? • Explain how profit-maximizing firms tend to eliminate discriminatory wage differentials. • How might a discriminatory wage differential persist?*

· · · · · · · · · · · · · · · · in the **news**

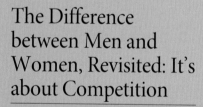

> ### Gender Differences

Recent economic research is shedding light on why men and women choose different career paths.

The Difference between Men and Women, Revisited: It's about Competition

BY HAL R. VARIAN

Gender differences are a topic of endless discussion for parents, teachers and social scientists. . . . A noteworthy case in point is a recent National Bureau of Economic Research working paper by a Stanford economist, Muriel Niederle, and Lise Vesterlund, a University of Pittsburgh economist, titled, "Do Women Shy Away

From Competition? Do Men Compete Too Much?"

It is widely noted that women are not well represented in high-paying corporate jobs, or in mathematics, science and engineering jobs. As the authors observe, the "standard economic explanations for such occupational differences include preferences, ability and discrimination."

To this list the authors add a new factor: attitudes toward competitive environments. If men prefer more competitive environments than women, then there will be more men represented in areas where competition is intense.

Of course, discussions of gender differences of any sort can only be statements about

averages; it is clear that there are women who thrive in competitive environments and men who do not. Furthermore, attitudes toward competition may be ingrained or a result of factors like social stereotyping.

Is there any evidence that the hypothesis is true? Do men really prefer more competitive environments than women? One could cite anecdote after anecdote, but the authors took a much more direct approach: they ran an experiment.

By using an experiment, the authors were able to determine not only whether men and women differ in their willingness to compete, but more important, whether they differ in their willingness to compete conditioned on their actual performance.

Conclusion

In competitive markets, workers earn a wage equal to the value of their marginal contribution to the production of goods and services. There are, however, many things that affect the value of the marginal product. Firms pay more for workers who are more talented, more diligent, more experienced, and more educated because these workers are more productive. Firms pay less to those workers against whom customers discriminate because these workers contribute less to revenue.

The theory of the labor market we have developed in the last two chapters explains why some workers earn higher wages than other workers. The theory does not say that the resulting distribution of income is equal, fair, or desirable in any way. That is the topic we take up in Chapter 20.

The economists asked 80 subjects, divided into groups of two women and two men, to add up sets of five two-digit numbers for five minutes. The subjects performed the task first on a piece-rate basis (50 cents for each correct answer) and then as a tournament (the person with the most correct answers in each group received $2 per correct answer, while other participants received nothing). Note that a subject with a 25 percent chance of being a winner in the tournament received the same average payment as in the piece-rate system.

All participants were told how many problems they got right, but not their relative performance. After completing the two tasks, the subjects were asked to choose whether they preferred a piece-rate system or a tournament for the third set of problems.

There were several interesting findings in this experiment. First, there were no differences between men and women in their performance under either compensation system. Despite this, twice as many men selected the tournament as women (75 percent versus 35 percent).

Even if one accounts for performance by comparing only men and women with the same number of correct answers, the women have a 38 percent lower probability of choosing the tournament compensation.

Why were the men much more likely to choose the tournament? Perhaps it was because they felt more confident about their abilities. The data support this hypothesis, with 75 percent of the men believing that they won their four-player tournament, while 43 percent of the women thought they were best in their group.

Though both groups were overconfident about their performance, the men were much more so. . . . The results of this experiment are consistent with the finding by a Berkeley finance professor, Terry Odean, that men trade stocks excessively, apparently because they (wrongly) feel that they have exceptional ability to pick winners. Women trade less, but do better on average, because they are more likely to follow a buy-and-hold strategy.

The authors summarized their experimental results by saying, "From a payoff-maximizing perspective, high-performing women enter the tournament too rarely, and low-performing men enter the tournament too often." The low-performing men and the high-performing women are both hurt by this behavior but, in this experiment at least, the costs to the women who did not choose the tournament when they should have exceeded the costs to the men who should have avoided the tournament.

One should not read too much into one study. But if it is really true that women choose occupations that involve less competition, then one may well ask why. Sociobiologists may suggest that such differences come from genetic propensities; sociologists may argue for differences in social roles and expectations; developmental psychologists may emphasize child-rearing practices. Whatever the cause, Ms. Niederle and Ms. Vesterlund have certainly raised a host of interesting and important questions.

Source: *New York Times*, March 9, 2006.

SUMMARY

- Workers earn different wages for many reasons. To some extent, wage differentials compensate workers for job attributes. Other things equal, workers in hard, unpleasant jobs are paid more than workers in easy, pleasant jobs.

- Workers with more human capital are paid more than workers with less human capital. The return to accumulating human capital is high and has increased over the past two decades.

- Although years of education, experience, and job characteristics affect earnings as theory predicts, there is much variation in earnings that cannot be explained by things that economists can measure. The unexplained variation in earnings is largely attributable to natural ability, effort, and chance.

- Some economists have suggested that more educated workers earn higher wages not because education raises productivity but because workers with high natural ability use education as a way to signal their high ability to employers. If this signaling theory is correct, then increasing the educational attainment of all workers would not raise the overall level of wages.

- Wages are sometimes pushed above the level that brings supply and demand into balance. Three reasons for above-equilibrium wages are minimum-wage laws, unions, and efficiency wages.

- Some differences in earnings are attributable to discrimination based on race, sex, or other factors. Measuring the amount of discrimination is difficult, however, because one must correct for differences in human capital and job characteristics.

- Competitive markets tend to limit the impact of discrimination on wages. If the wages of a group of workers are lower than those of another group for reasons not related to marginal productivity, then nondiscriminatory firms will be more profitable than discriminatory firms. Profit-maximizing behavior, therefore, can reduce discriminatory wage differentials. Discrimination persists in competitive markets, however, if customers are willing to pay more to discriminatory firms or if the government passes laws requiring firms to discriminate.

KEY CONCEPTS

compensating differential, *p. 398*
human capital, *p. 399*

union, *p. 404*
strike, *p. 404*

efficiency wages, *p. 404*
discrimination, *p. 405*

QUESTIONS FOR REVIEW

1. Why are coal miners paid more than other workers with similar amounts of education?
2. In what sense is education a type of capital?
3. How might education raise a worker's wage without raising the worker's productivity?
4. What conditions lead to economic superstars? Would you expect to see superstars in dentistry? In music? Explain.
5. Give three reasons a worker's wage might be above the level that balances supply and demand.
6. What difficulties arise in deciding whether a group of workers has a lower wage because of discrimination?
7. Do the forces of economic competition tend to exacerbate or ameliorate discrimination based on race?
8. Give an example of how discrimination might persist in a competitive market.

PROBLEMS AND APPLICATIONS

1. College students sometimes work as summer interns for private firms or the government. Many of these positions pay little or nothing.
   a. What is the opportunity cost of taking such a job?
   b. Explain why students are willing to take these jobs.
   c. If you were to compare the earnings later in life of workers who had worked as interns and those who had taken summer jobs that paid more, what would you expect to find?

2. As explained in Chapter 6, a minimum-wage law distorts the market for low-wage labor. To reduce this distortion, some economists advocate a two-tiered minimum-wage system, with a regular minimum wage for adult workers and a lower, "subminimum" wage for teenage workers. Give two reasons a single minimum wage might distort the labor market for teenage workers more than it would the market for adult workers.

3. A basic finding of labor economics is that workers who have more experience in the labor force are paid more than workers who have less experience (holding constant the amount of formal education). Why might this be so? Some studies have also found that experience at the same job (called *job tenure*) has an extra positive influence on wages. Explain.

4. At some colleges and universities, economics professors receive higher salaries than professors in some other fields.
   a. Why might this be true?
   b. Some other colleges and universities have a policy of paying equal salaries to professors in all fields. At some of these schools, economics professors have lighter teaching loads than professors in some other fields. What role do the differences in teaching loads play?

5. Imagine that someone offered you a choice: You could spend four years studying at the world's best university, but you would have to keep your attendance there a secret. Or you could be awarded an official degree from the world's best university, but you couldn't actually attend. Which choice do you think would enhance your future earnings more? What does your answer say about the debate over signaling versus human capital in the role of education?

6. When recording devices were first invented almost 100 years ago, musicians could suddenly supply their music to large audiences at low cost. How do you suppose this development affected the income of the best musicians? How do you suppose it affected the income of average musicians?

7. A current debate in education is whether teachers should be paid on a standard pay scale based solely upon their years of training and teaching experience, or whether part of their salary should be based upon their performance (called "merit pay").
   a. Why might merit pay be desirable?
   b. Who might be opposed to a system of merit pay?
   c. What is a potential challenge of merit pay?
   d. A related issue: Why might a school district decide to pay teachers significantly more than the salaries offered by surrounding districts?

8. When Alan Greenspan (who would later become chairman of the Federal Reserve) ran an economic consulting firm in the 1960s, he primarily hired female economists. He once told the *New York Times*, "I always valued men and women equally, and I found that because others did not, good women economists were cheaper than men." Is Greenspan's behavior profit-maximizing? Is it admirable or despicable? If more employers were like Greenspan, what would happen to the wage differential between men and women? Why might other economic consulting firms at the time not have followed Greenspan's business strategy?

9. Suppose that all young women were channeled into careers as secretaries, nurses, and teachers; at the same time, young men were encouraged to consider these three careers and many others as well.
   a. Draw a diagram showing the combined labor market for secretaries, nurses, and teachers.

Draw a diagram showing the combined labor market for all other fields. In which market is the wage higher? Do men or women receive higher wages on average?

b. Now suppose that society changed and encouraged both young women and young men to consider a wide range of careers. Over time, what effect would this change have on the wages in the two markets you illustrated in part (a)? What effect would the change have on the average wages of men and women?

10. This chapter considers the economics of discrimination by employers, customers, and governments. Now consider discrimination by workers. Suppose that some brunette workers did not like working with blonde workers. Do you think this worker discrimination could explain lower wages for blonde workers? If such a wage differential existed, what would a profit-maximizing entrepreneur do? If there were many such entrepreneurs, what would happen over time?

For further information on topics in this chapter, additional problems, applications, examples, online quizzes, and more, please visit our website at www .cengage.com/economics/mankiw.

Income Inequality
and Poverty

20

"The only difference between the rich and other people," Mary Colum once said to Ernest Hemingway, "is that the rich have more money." Maybe so. But this claim leaves many questions unanswered. The gap between rich and poor is a fascinating and important topic of study—for the comfortable rich, for the struggling poor, and for the aspiring and worried middle class.

From the previous two chapters, you should have some understanding about why different people have different incomes. A person's earnings depend on the supply and demand for that person's labor, which in turn depend on natural ability, human capital, compensating differentials, discrimination, and so on. Because labor earnings make up about three-fourths of the total income in the U.S. economy, the factors that determine wages are also largely responsible for determining how the economy's total income is distributed among the various members of society. In other words, they determine who is rich and who is poor.

In this chapter, we discuss the distribution of income—a topic that raises some fundamental questions about the role of economic policy. One of the *Ten Principles of Economics* in Chapter 1 is that governments can sometimes improve market outcomes. This possibility is particularly important when considering the distribution of income. The invisible hand of the marketplace acts to allocate resources efficiently, but it does not necessarily ensure that resources are allocated fairly. As a result, many economists—though not all—believe that the government should redistribute income to achieve greater equality. In doing so, however, the government runs into another of the *Ten Principles of Economics*: People face trade-offs. When the government enacts policies to make the distribution of income more equal, it distorts incentives, alters behavior, and makes the allocation of resources less efficient.

Our discussion of the distribution of income proceeds in three steps. First, we assess how much inequality there is in our society. Second, we consider some different views about what role the government should play in altering the distribution of income. Third, we discuss various public policies aimed at helping society's poorest members.

The Measurement of Inequality

We begin our study of the distribution of income by addressing four questions of measurement:

- How much inequality is there in our society?
- How many people live in poverty?
- What problems arise in measuring the amount of inequality?
- How often do people move among income classes?

These measurement questions are the natural starting point from which to discuss public policies aimed at changing the distribution of income.

U.S. Income Inequality

Imagine that you lined up all the families in the economy according to their annual income. Then you divided the families into five equal groups: the bottom fifth, the second fifth, the middle fifth, the fourth fifth, and the top fifth. Table 1

Table **1**

The Distribution of Income in the United States: 2008

Group	Annual Family Income
Bottom Fifth	Under $27,800
Second Fifth	$27,800–$49,325
Middle Fifth	$49,325–$75,000
Fourth Fifth	$75,000–$113,205
Top Fifth	$113,205 and over
Top 5 percent	$200,000 and over

Source: U.S. Bureau of the Census.

Year	Bottom Fifth	Second Fifth	Middle Fifth	Fourth Fifth	Top Fifth	Top 5%
2008	4.0%	9.6%	15.5%	23.1%	47.8%	20.5%
2000	4.3	9.8	15.5	22.8	47.4	20.8
1990	4.6	10.8	16.6	23.8	44.3	17.4
1980	5.2	11.5	17.5	24.3	41.5	15.3
1970	5.5	12.2	17.6	23.8	40.9	15.6
1960	4.8	12.2	17.8	24.0	41.3	15.9
1950	4.5	12.0	17.4	23.4	42.7	17.3
1935	4.1	9.2	14.1	20.9	51.7	26.5

Source: U.S. Bureau of the Census.

Table **2**

Income Inequality in the United States
This table shows the percentage of total before-tax income received by families in each fifth of the income distribution and by those families in the top 5 percent.

shows the income ranges for each of these groups, as well as for the top 5 percent. You can use this table to find where your family lies in the income distribution.

For examining differences in the income distribution over time, economists find it useful to present the income data as in Table 2. This table shows the share of total income that each group of families received in selected years. In 2008, the bottom fifth of all families received 4.0 percent of all income, and the top fifth of all families received 47.8 percent of all income. In other words, even though the top and bottom fifths include the same number of families, the top fifth has about twelve times as much income as the bottom fifth.

The last column in the table shows the share of total income received by the very richest families. In 2008, the top 5 percent of families received 20.5 percent of total income, which was greater than the total income of the poorest 40 percent.

Table 2 also shows the distribution of income in various years beginning in 1935. At first glance, the distribution of income appears to have been remarkably stable over time. Throughout the past several decades, the bottom fifth of families has received about 4 to 5 percent of income, while the top fifth has received about 40 to 50 percent of income. Closer inspection of the table reveals some trends in the degree of inequality. From 1935 to 1970, the distribution gradually became more equal. The share of the bottom fifth rose from 4.1 to 5.5 percent, and the share of the top fifth fell from 51.7 percent to 40.9 percent. In more recent years, this trend has reversed itself. From 1970 to 2008, the share of the bottom fifth fell from 5.5 percent to 4.0 percent, and the share of the top fifth rose from 40.9 to 47.8 percent.

In Chapter 19, we discussed some explanations for this recent rise in inequality. Increases in international trade with low-wage countries and changes in technology have tended to reduce the demand for unskilled labor and raise the demand for skilled labor. As a result, the wages of unskilled workers have fallen relative to the wages of skilled workers, and this change in relative wages has increased inequality in family incomes.

"As far as I'm concerned, they can do what they want with the minimum wage, just as long as they keep their hands off the maximum wage."

Inequality around the World

How does the amount of inequality in the United States compare to that in other countries? This question is interesting, but answering it is problematic. For some countries, data are not available. Even when they are, not every country collects data in the same way; for example, some countries collect data on individual incomes, whereas other countries collect data on family incomes, and still others collect data on expenditure rather than income. As a result, whenever we find a difference between two countries, we can never be sure whether it reflects a true difference in the economies or merely a difference in the way data are collected.

With this warning in mind, consider Figure 1, which compares inequality in twelve countries. The inequality measure is the ratio of the income received by the richest tenth of the population to the income of the poorest tenth. The most equality is found in Japan, where the top tenth receives 4.5 times as much income as the bottom tenth. The least equality is found in Brazil, where the top group receives 40.6 times as much income as the bottom group. Although all countries have significant disparities between rich and poor, the degree of inequality varies substantially around the world.

When countries are ranked by inequality, the United States ends up around the middle of the pack. The United States has more income inequality than other economically advanced countries, such as Japan, Germany, and Canada. But the United States has a more equal income distribution than many developing countries, such as South Africa, Brazil, and Mexico.

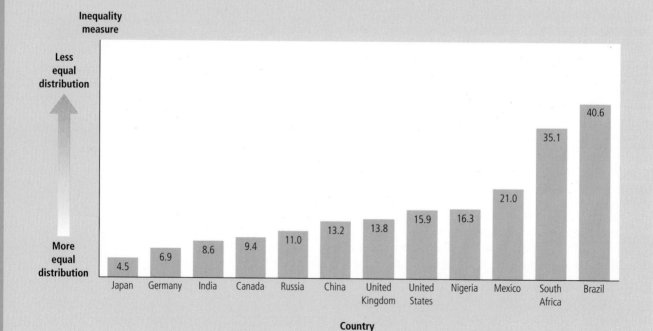

Figure **1**

Inequality around the World

Source: *Human Development Report 2009.*

This figure shows a measure of inequality: the income (or expenditure) of the richest 10 percent of the population divided by the income (or expenditure) of the poorest 10 percent. Among these nations, Japan and Germany have the most equal distribution of economic well-being, while South Africa and Brazil have the least equal.

The Poverty Rate

A commonly used gauge of the distribution of income is the poverty rate. The **poverty rate** is the percentage of the population whose family income falls below an absolute level called the **poverty line**. The poverty line is set by the federal government at roughly three times the cost of providing an adequate diet. This line is adjusted every year to account for changes in the level of prices, and it depends on family size.

To get some idea about what the poverty rate tells us, consider the data for 2008. In that year, the median family had an income of $61,521, and the poverty line for a family of four was $22,025. The poverty rate was 13.2 percent. In other words, 13.2 percent of the population were members of families with incomes below the poverty line for their family size.

Figure 2 shows the poverty rate since 1959, when the official data begin. You can see that the poverty rate fell from 22.4 percent in 1959 to a low of 11.1 percent in 1973. This decline is not surprising, because average income in the economy (adjusted for inflation) rose more than 50 percent during this period. Because the poverty line is an absolute rather than a relative standard, more families are pushed above the poverty line as economic growth pushes the entire income distribution upward. As John F. Kennedy once put it, a rising tide lifts all boats.

Since the early 1970s, however, the economy's rising tide has left some boats behind. Despite continued growth in average income, the poverty rate has not declined below the level reached in 1973. This lack of progress in reducing poverty in recent decades is closely related to the increasing inequality we saw in Table 2. Although economic growth has raised the income of the typical family, the increase in inequality has prevented the poorest families from sharing in this greater economic prosperity.

poverty rate

the percentage of the population whose family income falls below an absolute level called the poverty line

poverty line

an absolute level of income set by the federal government for each family size below which a family is deemed to be in poverty

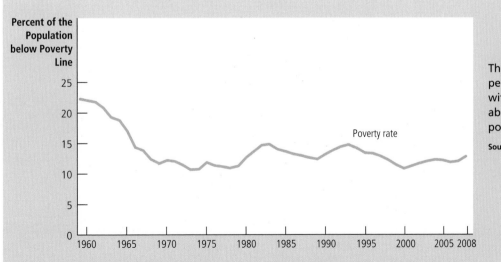

Figure **2**

The Poverty Rate

The poverty rate shows the percentage of the population with incomes below an absolute level called the poverty line.

Source: U.S. Bureau of the Census.

Table **3**

Who Is Poor?
This table shows that the poverty rate varies greatly among different groups within the population.

Group	Poverty Rate
All persons	13.2%
White, not Hispanic	8.6
Black	24.7
Hispanic	23.2
Asian	11.8
Children (under age 18)	19.0
Elderly (over age 64)	9.7
Married-couple families	5.5
Female household, no spouse present	31.4

Source: U.S. Bureau of the Census. Data are for 2008.

Poverty is an economic malady that affects all groups within the population, but it does not affect all groups with equal frequency. Table 3 shows the poverty rates for several groups, and it reveals three striking facts:

- Poverty is correlated with race. Blacks and Hispanics are about three times more likely to live in poverty than are whites.
- Poverty is correlated with age. Children are more likely than average to be members of poor families, and the elderly are less likely than average to be poor.
- Poverty is correlated with family composition. Families headed by a female adult and without a spouse present are almost six times as likely to live in poverty as a family headed by a married couple.

These three facts have described U.S. society for many years, and they show which people are most likely to be poor. These effects also work together: Among black and Hispanic children in female-headed households, about half live in poverty.

Problems in Measuring Inequality

Although data on the income distribution and the poverty rate help to give us some idea about the degree of inequality in our society, interpreting these data is not always straightforward. The data are based on households' annual incomes. What people care about, however, is not their incomes but their ability to maintain a good standard of living. For at least three reasons, data on the income distribution and the poverty rate give an incomplete picture of inequality in living standards.

in-kind transfers

transfers to the poor given in the form of goods and services rather than cash

In-Kind Transfers Measurements of the distribution of income and the poverty rate are based on families' *money* income. Through various government programs, however, the poor receive many nonmonetary items, including food stamps, housing vouchers, and medical services. Transfers to the poor given in the form of goods and services rather than cash are called **in-kind transfers**. Standard measurements of the degree of inequality do not take account of these in-kind transfers.

Because in-kind transfers are received mostly by the poorest members of society, the failure to include in-kind transfers as part of income greatly affects the measured poverty rate. According to a study by the Census Bureau, if in-kind transfers were included in income at their market value, the number of families in poverty would be about 10 percent lower than the standard data indicate.

The Economic Life Cycle Incomes vary predictably over people's lives. A young worker, especially one in school, has a low income. Income rises as the worker gains maturity and experience, peaks at around age 50, and then falls sharply when the worker retires at around age 65. This regular pattern of income variation is called the **life cycle**.

Because people can borrow and save to smooth out life cycle changes in income, their standard of living in any year depends more on lifetime income than on that year's income. The young often borrow, perhaps to go to school or to buy a house, and then repay these loans later when their incomes rise. People have their highest saving rates when they are middle-aged. Because people can save in anticipation of retirement, the large declines in incomes at retirement need not lead to similar declines in the standard of living. This normal life cycle pattern causes inequality in the distribution of annual income, but it does not necessarily represent true inequality in living standards.

life cycle
the regular pattern of income variation over a person's life

Transitory versus Permanent Income Incomes vary over people's lives not only because of predictable life cycle variation but also because of random and transitory forces. One year a frost kills off the Florida orange crop, and Florida orange growers see their incomes fall temporarily. At the same time, the Florida frost drives up the price of oranges, and California orange growers see their incomes temporarily rise. The next year the reverse might happen.

Just as people can borrow and lend to smooth out life cycle variation in income, they can also borrow and lend to smooth out transitory variation in income. To the extent that a family saves in good years and borrows (or depletes its savings) in bad years, transitory changes in income need not affect its standard of living. A family's ability to buy goods and services depends largely on its **permanent income**, which is its normal, or average, income.

permanent income
a person's normal income

To gauge inequality of living standards, the distribution of permanent income is more relevant than the distribution of annual income. Many economists believe that people base their consumption on their permanent income; as a result, inequality in consumption is one gauge of inequality of permanent income. Because permanent income and consumption are less affected by transitory changes in income, they are more equally distributed than is current income.

 Alternative Measures of Inequality

A 2008 study by Michael Cox and Richard Alm of the Federal Reserve Bank of Dallas shows how different measures of inequality lead to dramatically different results. Cox and Alm compared American households in the top fifth of the income distribution to those in the bottom fifth to see how far apart they are.

According to Cox and Alm, the richest fifth of U.S. households in 2006 had an average income of $149,963, while the poorest fifth had an average income of $9,974. Thus, the top group had about 15 times as much income as the bottom group.

The gap between rich and poor shrinks a bit if taxes are taken into account. Because the tax system is progressive, the top group paid a higher percentage of its income in taxes than did the bottom group. Cox and Alm found that the richest fifth had 14 times as much after-tax income as the poorest fifth.

The gap shrinks more substantially if one looks at consumption rather than income. Households having an unusually good year are more likely to be in the top group and are likely to save a high fraction out of their incomes. Households having an unusually bad year are more likely to be in the bottom group and are more likely to consume out of their savings. According to Cox and Alms, the consumption of the richest fifth was only 3.9 times as much as the consumption of the poorest fifth.

The consumption gap becomes smaller still if one corrects for differences in the number of people in the household. Because larger families are more likely to have two earners, they are more likely to find themselves near the top of the income distribution. But they also have more mouths to feed. Cox and Alms

in the news

> ### What's Wrong with the Poverty Rate?

The author of this article (later appointed by President Obama to be Under Secretary of Commerce for Economic Affairs) says we need better statistics.

How We Measure Poverty

BY REBECCA M. BLANK

Who is poor in America? It turns out that's a hard question to answer.

The federal government's badly outdated method of measuring poverty provides an inaccurate picture. New York found the official numbers so useless that the city recently developed its own poverty measure. Other cities, including Los Angeles, are considering doing the same thing....

But what's most needed is an overhaul of the nation's poverty measurement statistics. The good news is that legislation is being drafted in both the House and Senate. A change is long overdue.

Why does it matter if we have a good measure of poverty? In the last four decades,

the U.S. has greatly expanded programs for lower-income families, including food stamps, housing vouchers, medical care assistance, and tax credits. But the poverty rate doesn't take any of these resources into account because it doesn't account for taxes or noncash income. At the same time, Americans' medical expenses have increased, and more single parents work and pay child-care expenses. The current poverty measure is unaffected by these changes too.

The result? Poverty statistics that make it depressingly easy to claim that public spending on the poor has had little effect. Indeed, most programs to help the needy would never budge the U.S. poverty rate the way we measure it now.

The current measure of poverty was established in 1964 by a Social Security Administration economist named Mollie

Orshansky. Looking at data from 1955—the best available in the early 1960s—she found that a family spent, on average, one-third of its income on food. Hence, three-times-food became the official poverty line. That line has ticked upward only by being adjusted for inflation each year.

No other regularly reported economic statistic has been unchanged for four decades. Food prices have fallen; today, food constitutes less than one-seventh of the average family's budget. But people pay substantially more for housing and energy.

Still, the old poverty measure continues to be used by all sorts of government programs. Some use it for eligibility limits; most families below 130% of the poverty line, for instance, are eligible for food stamps. Some federal block grants to states are partly based on state poverty levels.

reported that households in the top fifth had an average of 3.1 people, while those in the bottom fifth had an average of 1.7 people. As a result, consumption per person in the richest fifth of households was only 2.1 times consumption per person in the poorest fifth.

These data show that inequality in material standards of living is much smaller than inequality in annual income. ■

Economic Mobility

People sometimes speak of "the rich" and "the poor" as if these groups consisted of the same families year after year. In fact, this is not at all the case. Economic mobility, the movement of people among income classes, is substantial in the U.S. economy. Movements up the income ladder can be due to good luck or hard work, and movements down the ladder can be due to bad luck or laziness. Some of this mobility reflects transitory variation in income, while some reflects more persistent changes in income.

In 1995, I participated in a panel of scholars at the National Academy of Sciences (NAS), a group that advises the federal government on scientific issues. We recommended a far more effective way to establish a poverty threshold, based on expenditures for a bundle of necessities, including food, shelter, clothing and utilities. Furthermore, this threshold would vary geographically, based on differences in housing costs.

This would mean that families in Los Angeles have a different poverty line from families in rural Wyoming. When New York calculated a new threshold with this methodology, officials found that it was $21,818 for a family of four, not far from the official U.S. figure of $20,444. But when they adjusted for New York's high housing costs, it rose to $26,138.

But the poverty measure also needs to recognize that the resources in low-income families extend beyond wages and cash income. The NAS panel recommended a much broader definition, including cash income adjusted for tax payments, plus the value of government benefits such as food stamps or Section 8 rental vouchers. Unavoidable costs were subtracted from income, as well, because working requires

spending money on transportation and, often, child care. Similarly, out-of-pocket medical expenses also were deducted.

Why weren't these changes made years ago? That's a story of politics getting in the way of good statistics. Back in the 1960s, the poverty measure was placed under the control of the White House. This is in contrast to all of our other national statistics, which are defined and updated by agencies with a long history of nonpolitical decision making.

Unfortunately, no president (Democrat or Republican) has wanted to touch this political hot potato. If a new measure shows higher poverty, the president looks bad, but if a new measure shows lower poverty, he'll be accused of dismissing the problem.

And the numbers will change. In New York, where the official U.S. poverty measure finds 18% of the city is poor, the new measure (largely because of housing costs) finds 23%. But the picture will be more accurate. New York found rates differed little for children but were much higher for the elderly because of out-of-pocket medical expenditures.

That's why Congress needs to pass legislation to direct one of the statistical agencies to calculate a new federal poverty

measure, guided by the NAS recommendations. Under a new measure, single-mother families receiving food stamps and in subsidized housing would appear a little better off; disabled individuals with high medical expenses, a little worse. Families in big cities with high housing costs, such as in California, would be poorer, and families that receive working tax credits less poor.

But that is just as it should be. If we want to debate new policies to help the poor, we first need a poverty measure that shows us who they really are.

Rebecca Blank

Source: *Los Angeles Times*, September 15, 2008.

Because economic mobility is so great, many of those below the poverty line are there only temporarily. Poverty is a long-term problem for relatively few families. In a typical 10-year period, about one in four families falls below the poverty line in at least one year. Yet fewer than 3 percent of families are poor for eight or more years. Because it is likely that the temporarily poor and the persistently poor face different problems, policies that aim to combat poverty need to distinguish between these groups.

Another way to gauge economic mobility is the persistence of economic success from generation to generation. Economists who have studied this topic find that having an above-average income carries over from parents to children, but the persistence is far from perfect, indicating substantial mobility among income classes. If a father earns 20 percent above his generation's average income, his son will most likely earn 8 percent above his generation's average income. There is only a small correlation between the income of a grandfather and the income of a grandson.

One result of this great economic mobility is that the U.S. economy is filled with self-made millionaires (as well as with heirs who have squandered the fortunes they inherited). According to one study, about four out of five millionaires made their money on their own, often by starting and building a business or by climbing the corporate ladder. Only one in five millionaires inherited his or her fortune.

QUICK QUIZ *What does the poverty rate measure? • Describe three potential problems in interpreting the measured poverty rate.*

The Political Philosophy of Redistributing Income

We have just seen how the economy's income is distributed and have considered some of the problems in interpreting measured inequality. This discussion was *positive* in the sense that it merely described the world as it is. We now turn to the *normative* question facing policymakers: What should the government do about economic inequality?

This question is not just about economics. Economic analysis alone cannot tell us whether policymakers should try to make our society more egalitarian. Our views on this question are, to a large extent, a matter of political philosophy. Yet because the government's role in redistributing income is central to so many debates over economic policy, here we digress from economic science to consider a bit of political philosophy.

utilitarianism

the political philosophy according to which the government should choose policies to maximize the total utility of everyone in society

utility

a measure of happiness or satisfaction

Utilitarianism

A prominent school of thought in political philosophy is **utilitarianism**. The founders of utilitarianism are the English philosophers Jeremy Bentham (1748–1832) and John Stuart Mill (1806–1873). To a large extent, the goal of utilitarians is to apply the logic of individual decision making to questions concerning morality and public policy.

The starting point of utilitarianism is the notion of **utility**—the level of happiness or satisfaction that a person receives from his or her circumstances. Utility is a measure of well-being and, according to utilitarians, is the ultimate objective of all public and private actions. The proper goal of the government, they claim, is to maximize the sum of utility achieved by everyone in society.

The utilitarian case for redistributing income is based on the assumption of *diminishing marginal utility*. It seems reasonable that an extra dollar of income provides a poor person with more additional utility than an extra dollar would provide to a rich person. In other words, as a person's income rises, the extra well-being derived from an additional dollar of income falls. This plausible assumption, together with the utilitarian goal of maximizing total utility, implies that the government should try to achieve a more equal distribution of income.

The argument is simple. Imagine that Peter and Paul are the same, except that Peter earns $80,000 and Paul earns $20,000. In this case, taking a dollar from Peter to pay Paul will reduce Peter's utility and raise Paul's utility. But because of diminishing marginal utility, Peter's utility falls by less than Paul's utility rises. Thus, this redistribution of income raises total utility, which is the utilitarian's objective.

At first, this utilitarian argument might seem to imply that the government should continue to redistribute income until everyone in society has exactly the same income. Indeed, that would be the case if the total amount of income—$100,000 in our example—were fixed. But in fact, it is not. Utilitarians reject complete equalization of incomes because they accept one of the *Ten Principles of Economics* presented in Chapter 1: People respond to incentives.

To take from Peter to pay Paul, the government must pursue policies that redistribute income. The U.S. federal income tax and welfare system are examples. Under these policies, people with high incomes pay high taxes, and people with low incomes receive income transfers. Yet if the government uses higher income taxes or phased-out transfers to take away additional income a person might earn, both Peter and Paul have less incentive to work hard. As they work less, society's income falls, and so does total utility. The utilitarian government has to balance the gains from greater equality against the losses from distorted incentives. To maximize total utility, therefore, the government stops short of making society fully egalitarian.

A famous parable sheds light on the utilitarian's logic. Imagine that Peter and Paul are thirsty travelers trapped at different places in the desert. Peter's oasis has a lot of water; Paul's has only a little. If the government could transfer water from one oasis to the other without cost, it would maximize total utility from water by equalizing the amount in the two places. But suppose that the government has only a leaky bucket. As it tries to move water from one place to the other, some of the water is lost in transit. In this case, a utilitarian government might still try to move some water from Peter to Paul, depending on the size of Paul's thirst and the size of the bucket's leak. But with only a leaky bucket at its disposal, a utilitarian government will stop short of trying to reach complete equality.

Liberalism

A second way of thinking about inequality might be called **liberalism**. Philosopher John Rawls develops this view in his book *A Theory of Justice*. This book was first published in 1971, and it quickly became a classic in political philosophy.

Rawls begins with the premise that a society's institutions, laws, and policies should be just. He then takes up the natural question: How can we, the members of society, ever agree on what justice means? It might seem that every person's point of view is inevitably based on his or her particular circumstances—whether he or she is talented or less talented, diligent or lazy, educated or less educated, born to a wealthy family or a poor one. Could we ever *objectively* determine what a just society would be?

liberalism

the political philosophy according to which the government should choose policies deemed just, as evaluated by an impartial observer behind a "veil of ignorance"

To answer this question, Rawls proposes the following thought experiment. Imagine that before any of us is born, we all get together in the beforelife (the pre-birth version of the afterlife) for a meeting to design the rules that will govern society. At this point, we are all ignorant about the station in life each of us will end up filling. In Rawls's words, we are sitting in an "original position" behind a "veil of ignorance." In this original position, Rawls argues, we can choose a just set of rules for society because we must consider how those rules will affect every person. As Rawls puts it, "Since all are similarly situated and no one is able to design principles to favor his particular conditions, the principles of justice are the result of fair agreement or bargain." Designing public policies and institutions in this way allows us to be objective about what policies are just.

Rawls then considers what public policy designed behind this veil of ignorance would try to achieve. In particular, he considers what income distribution a person would consider fair if that person did not know whether he or she would end up at the top, bottom, or middle of the distribution. Rawls argues that a person in the original position would be especially concerned about the possibility of being at the *bottom* of the income distribution. In designing public policies, therefore, we should aim to raise the welfare of the worst-off person in society. That is, rather than maximizing the sum of everyone's utility, as a utilitarian would do, Rawls would maximize the minimum utility. Rawls's rule is called the **maximin criterion**.

maximin criterion

the claim that the government should aim to maximize the well-being of the worst-off person in society

Because the maximin criterion emphasizes the least fortunate person in society, it justifies public policies aimed at equalizing the distribution of income. By transferring income from the rich to the poor, society raises the well-being of the least fortunate. The maximin criterion would not, however, lead to a completely egalitarian society. If the government promised to equalize incomes completely, people would have no incentive to work hard, society's total income would fall substantially, and the least fortunate person would be worse off. Thus, the maximin criterion still allows disparities in income because such disparities can improve incentives and thereby raise society's ability to help the poor. Nonetheless, because Rawls's philosophy puts weight on only the least fortunate members of society, it calls for more income redistribution than does utilitarianism.

social insurance

government policy aimed at protecting people against the risk of adverse events

Rawls's views are controversial, but the thought experiment he proposes has much appeal. In particular, this thought experiment allows us to consider the redistribution of income as a form of **social insurance**. That is, from the perspective of the original position behind the veil of ignorance, income redistribution is like an insurance policy. Homeowners buy fire insurance to protect themselves from the risk of their house burning down. Similarly, when we as a society choose policies that tax the rich to supplement the incomes of the poor, we are all insuring ourselves against the possibility that we might have been a member of a poor family. Because people dislike risk, we should be happy to have been born into a society that provides us this insurance.

It is not at all clear, however, that rational people behind the veil of ignorance would truly be so averse to risk as to follow the maximin criterion. Indeed, because a person in the original position might end up anywhere in the distribution of outcomes, he or she might treat all possible outcomes equally when designing public policies. In this case, the best policy behind the veil of ignorance would be to maximize the average utility of members of society, and the resulting notion of justice would be more utilitarian than Rawlsian.

Libertarianism

A third view of inequality is called **libertarianism**. The two views we have considered so far—utilitarianism and liberalism—both view the total income of society as a shared resource that a social planner can freely redistribute to achieve some social goal. By contrast, libertarians argue that society itself earns no income—only individual members of society earn income. According to libertarians, the government should not take from some individuals and give to others to achieve any particular distribution of income.

For instance, philosopher Robert Nozick writes the following in his famous 1974 book *Anarchy, State, and Utopia*:

> We are not in the position of children who have been given portions of pie by someone who now makes last minute adjustments to rectify careless cutting. There is no *central* distribution, no person or group entitled to control all the resources, jointly deciding how they are to be doled out. What each person gets, he gets from others who give to him in exchange for something, or as a gift. In a free society, diverse persons control different resources, and new holdings arise out of the voluntary exchanges and actions of persons.

Whereas utilitarians and liberals try to judge what amount of inequality is desirable in a society, Nozick denies the validity of this very question.

The libertarian alternative to evaluating economic *outcomes* is to evaluate the *process* by which these outcomes arise. When the distribution of income is achieved unfairly—for instance, when one person steals from another—the government has the right and duty to remedy the problem. But as long as the process determining the distribution of income is just, the resulting distribution is fair, no matter how unequal.

Nozick criticizes Rawls's liberalism by drawing an analogy between the distribution of income in society and the distribution of grades in a course. Suppose you were asked to judge the fairness of the grades in the economics course you are now taking. Would you imagine yourself behind a veil of ignorance and choose a grade distribution without knowing the talents and efforts of each student? Or would you ensure that the process of assigning grades to students is fair without regard for whether the resulting distribution is equal or unequal? For the case of grades at least, the libertarian emphasis on process over outcomes is compelling.

Libertarians conclude that equality of opportunities is more important than equality of incomes. They believe that the government should enforce individual rights to ensure that everyone has the same opportunity to use his or her talents and achieve success. Once these rules of the game are established, the government has no reason to alter the resulting distribution of income.

QUICK QUIZ *Pam earns more than Pauline. Someone proposes taxing Pam to supplement Pauline's income. How would a utilitarian, a liberal, and a libertarian evaluate this proposal?*

libertarianism
the political philosophy according to which the government should punish crimes and enforce voluntary agreements but not redistribute income

Policies to Reduce Poverty

As we have just seen, political philosophers hold various views about what role the government should take in altering the distribution of income. Political debate among the larger population of voters reflects a similar disagreement. Despite these continuing debates, most people believe that, at the very least, the government should try to help those most in need. According to a popular metaphor, the government should provide a "safety net" to prevent any citizen from falling too far.

Poverty is one of the most difficult problems that policymakers face. Poor families are more likely than the overall population to experience homelessness, drug dependence, health problems, teenage pregnancy, illiteracy, unemployment, and low educational attainment. Members of poor families are both more likely to commit crimes and more likely to be victims of crimes. Although it is hard to separate the causes of poverty from the effects, there is no doubt that poverty is associated with various economic and social ills.

Suppose that you were a policymaker in the government, and your goal was to reduce the number of people living in poverty. How would you achieve this goal? Here we examine some of the policy options that you might consider. Each of these options helps some people escape poverty, but none of them is perfect, and deciding upon the best combination to use is not easy.

Minimum-Wage Laws

Laws setting a minimum wage that employers can pay workers are a perennial source of debate. Advocates view the minimum wage as a way of helping the working poor without any cost to the government. Critics view it as hurting those it is intended to help.

The minimum wage is easily understood using the tools of supply and demand, as we first saw in Chapter 6. For workers with low levels of skill and experience, a high minimum wage forces the wage above the level that balances supply and demand. It therefore raises the cost of labor to firms and reduces the quantity of labor that those firms demand. The result is higher unemployment among those groups of workers affected by the minimum wage. Those workers who remain employed benefit from a higher wage, but those who might have been employed at a lower wage are worse off.

The magnitude of these effects depends crucially on the elasticity of demand. Advocates of a high minimum wage argue that the demand for unskilled labor is relatively inelastic so that a high minimum wage depresses employment only slightly. Critics of the minimum wage argue that labor demand is more elastic, especially in the long run when firms can adjust employment and production more fully. They also note that many minimum-wage workers are teenagers from middle-class families so that a high minimum wage is imperfectly targeted as a policy for helping the poor.

Welfare

welfare

government programs that supplement the incomes of the needy

One way for the government to raise the living standards of the poor is to supplement their incomes. The primary way the government does this is through the welfare system. **Welfare** is a broad term that encompasses various government programs. Temporary Assistance for Needy Families (TANF) is a program that assists families with children and no adult able to support the family. In a typical family receiving such assistance, the father is absent, and the mother is at home raising small children. Another welfare program is Supplemental Security Income (SSI), which provides assistance to the poor who are sick or disabled. Note that for both of these welfare programs, a poor person cannot qualify for assistance simply by having a low income. He or she must also establish some additional "need," such as small children or a disability.

A common criticism of welfare programs is that they create incentives for people to become "needy." For example, these programs may encourage families to break up, for many families qualify for financial assistance only if the father is absent. The programs may also encourage illegitimate births, for many poor, single women qualify for assistance only if they have children. Because poor, single mothers are such a large part of the poverty problem and because welfare programs seem to raise the number of poor, single mothers, critics of the welfare system assert that these policies exacerbate the very problems they are supposed to cure. As a result of these arguments, the welfare system was revised in a 1996 law that limited the amount of time recipients could stay on welfare.

How severe are these potential problems with the welfare system? No one knows for sure. Proponents of the welfare system point out that being a poor, single mother on welfare is a difficult existence at best, and they are skeptical that many people would be encouraged to pursue such a life if it were not thrust upon them. Moreover, trends over time do not support the view that the decline of the two-parent family is largely a symptom of the welfare system, as the system's critics sometimes claim. Since the early 1970s, welfare benefits (adjusted for inflation) have declined, yet the percentage of children living with only one parent has risen.

Negative Income Tax

Whenever the government chooses a system to collect taxes, it affects the distribution of income. This is clearly true in the case of a progressive income tax, whereby high-income families pay a larger percentage of their income in taxes than do low-income families. As we discussed in Chapter 12, equity across income groups is an important criterion in the design of a tax system.

Many economists have advocated supplementing the income of the poor using a **negative income tax**. According to this policy, every family would report its income to the government. High-income families would pay a tax based on their incomes. Low-income families would receive a subsidy. In other words, they would "pay" a "negative tax."

For example, suppose the government used the following formula to compute a family's tax liability:

$$\text{Taxes owed} = (\tfrac{1}{3} \text{ of income}) - \$10,000.$$

In this case, a family that earned $60,000 would pay $10,000 in taxes, and a family that earned $90,000 would pay $20,000 in taxes. A family that earned $30,000 would owe nothing. And a family that earned $15,000 would "owe" −$5,000. In other words, the government would send this family a check for $5,000.

Under a negative income tax, poor families would receive financial assistance without having to demonstrate need. The only qualification required to receive assistance would be a low income. Depending on one's point of view, this feature can be either an advantage or a disadvantage. On the one hand, a negative income tax does not encourage illegitimate births and the breakup of families, as critics of the welfare system believe current policy does. On the other hand, a negative income tax would subsidize not only the unfortunate but also those who are simply lazy and, in some people's eyes, undeserving of government support.

One actual tax provision that works much like a negative income tax is the Earned Income Tax Credit (EITC). This credit allows poor working families to

negative income tax
a tax system that collects revenue from high-income households and gives subsidies to low-income households

receive income tax refunds greater than the taxes they paid during the year. Because the Earned Income Tax Credit applies only to the working poor, it does not discourage recipients from working, as other antipoverty programs are claimed to do. For the same reason, however, it also does not help alleviate poverty due to unemployment, sickness, or other inability to work.

In-Kind Transfers

Another way to help the poor is to provide them directly with some of the goods and services they need to raise their living standards. For example, charities provide the needy with food, clothing, shelter, and toys at Christmas. The government gives poor families *food stamps,* which are government vouchers that can be used to buy food at stores; the stores then redeem the vouchers for money. The government also gives many poor people healthcare through a program called *Medicaid.*

Is it better to help the poor with these in-kind transfers or with direct cash payments? There is no clear answer.

Advocates of in-kind transfers argue that such transfers ensure that the poor get what they need most. Among the poorest members of society, alcohol and

· · · · · · · · · · · · · · · · · in the news

> ### The Root Cause of a Financial Crisis

In 2008 and 2009, the U.S. economy experienced a financial crisis and a deep economic downturn. In this opinion piece, an economist suggests that these events can be traced back to the changing distribution of income.

How Inequality Fueled the Crisis

By Raghuram Rajan

Before the recent financial crisis, politicians on both sides of the aisle in the United States egged on Fannie Mae and Freddie Mac, the giant government-backed mortgage agencies, to support low-income lending in their constituencies. There was a deeper concern behind this newly discovered passion for housing for the poor: growing income inequality.

Since the 1970's, wages for workers at the 90th percentile of the wage distribution in the U.S.—such as office managers— have grown much faster than wages for the median worker (at the 50th percentile), such as factory workers and office assistants. A number of factors are responsible for the growth in the 90/50 differential.

Perhaps the most important is that technological progress in the U.S. requires the labor force to have ever greater skills. A high school diploma was sufficient for office workers 40 years ago, whereas an undergraduate degree is barely sufficient today. But the education system has been unable to provide enough of the labor force with the necessary education. The reasons range from indifferent nutrition, socialization, and early-childhood learning to dysfunctional primary and secondary schools that leave too many Americans unprepared for college.

The everyday consequence for the middle class is a stagnant paycheck and growing job insecurity. Politicians feel their constituents' pain, but it is hard to improve the quality of education, for improvement requires real and effective policy change in an area where too many vested interests favor the status quo.

Moreover, any change will require years to take effect, and therefore will not address the electorate's current anxiety.

drug addiction is more common than it is in society as a whole. By providing the poor with food and shelter, society can be more confident that it is not helping to support such addictions. This is one reason in-kind transfers are more politically popular than cash payments to the poor.

Advocates of cash payments, on the other hand, argue that in-kind transfers are inefficient and disrespectful. The government does not know what goods and services the poor need most. Many of the poor are ordinary people down on their luck. Despite their misfortune, they are in the best position to decide how to raise their own living standards. Rather than giving the poor in-kind transfers of goods and services that they may not want, it may be better to give them cash and allow them to buy what they think they need most.

Antipoverty Programs and Work Incentives

Many policies aimed at helping the poor can have the unintended effect of discouraging the poor from escaping poverty on their own. To see why, consider the following example. Suppose that a family needs an income of $20,000 to maintain a reasonable standard of living. And suppose that, out of concern for the poor, the government promises to guarantee every family that income. Whatever a family

Thus, politicians have looked for other, quicker ways to mollify their constituents. We have long understood that it is not income that matters, but consumption. A smart or cynical politician would see that if somehow middle-class households' consumption kept up, if they could afford a new car every few years and the occasional exotic holiday, perhaps they would pay less attention to their stagnant paychecks.

Therefore, the political response to rising inequality—whether carefully planned or the path of least resistance—was to expand lending to households, especially low-income households. The benefits—growing consumption and more jobs—were immediate, whereas paying the inevitable bill could be postponed into the future. Cynical as it might seem, easy credit has been used throughout history as a palliative by governments that are unable to address the deeper anxieties of the middle class directly.

Politicians, however, prefer to couch the objective in more uplifting and persuasive terms than that of crassly increasing consumption. In the U.S., the expansion of home ownership—a key element of the American dream—to low- and middle-income households was the defensible linchpin for the broader aims of expanding credit and consumption....

In the end, though, the misguided attempt to push home ownership through credit has left the U.S. with houses that no one can afford and households drowning in debt. Ironically, since 2004, the homeownership rate has been in decline.

The problem, as often is the case with government policies, was not intent. It rarely is. But when lots of easy money pushed by a deep-pocketed government comes into contact with the profit motive of a sophisticated, competitive, and amoral financial sector, matters get taken far beyond the government's intent.

This is not, of course, the first time in history that credit expansion has been used to assuage the concerns of a group that is being left behind, nor will it be the last.

In fact, one does not even need to look outside the U.S. for examples. The deregulation and rapid expansion of banking in the U.S. in the early years of the twentieth century was in many ways a response to the Populist movement, backed by small and medium-sized farmers who found themselves falling behind the growing numbers of industrial workers, and demanded easier credit. Excessive rural credit was one of the important causes of bank failures during the Great Depression.

The broader implication is that we need to look beyond greedy bankers and spineless regulators (and there were plenty of both) for the root causes of this crisis. And the problems are not solved with a financial regulatory bill entrusting more powers to those regulators. America needs to tackle inequality at its root, by giving more Americans the ability to compete in the global marketplace. This is much harder than doling out credit, but more effective in the long run.

Source: Project Syndicate, July 9, 2010.

earns, the government makes up the difference between that income and $20,000. What effect would you expect this policy to have?

The incentive effects of this policy are obvious: Any person who would make under $20,000 by working has little incentive to find and keep a job. For every dollar that the person would earn, the government would reduce the income supplement by a dollar. In effect, the government taxes 100 percent of additional earnings. An effective marginal tax rate of 100 percent is surely a policy with a large deadweight loss.

The adverse effects of this high effective tax rate can persist over time. A person discouraged from working loses the on-the-job training that a job might offer. In addition, his or her children miss the lessons learned by observing a parent with a full-time job, and this may adversely affect their own ability to find and hold a job.

Although the antipoverty program we have been discussing is hypothetical, it is not as unrealistic as might first appear. Welfare, Medicaid, food stamps, and the Earned Income Tax Credit are all programs aimed at helping the poor, and they are all tied to family income. As a family's income rises, the family becomes ineligible for these programs. When all these programs are taken together, it is common for families to face effective marginal tax rates that are very high. Sometimes the effective marginal tax rates even exceed 100 percent so that poor families are worse off when they earn more. By trying to help the poor, the government discourages those families from working. According to critics of antipoverty programs, these programs alter work attitudes and create a "culture of poverty."

It might seem that there is an easy solution to this problem: Reduce benefits to poor families more gradually as their incomes rise. For example, if a poor family loses 30 cents of benefits for every dollar it earns, then it faces an effective marginal tax rate of 30 percent. Although this effective tax reduces work effort to some extent, it does not eliminate the incentive to work completely.

The problem with this solution is that it greatly increases the cost of programs to combat poverty. If benefits are phased out gradually as a poor family's income rises, then families just above the poverty level will also be eligible for substantial benefits. The more gradual the phase-out, the more families are eligible, and the more the program costs. Thus, policymakers face a trade-off between burdening the poor with high effective marginal tax rates and burdening taxpayers with costly programs to reduce poverty.

There are various other ways to reduce the work disincentive of antipoverty programs. One is to require any person collecting benefits to accept a government-provided job—a system sometimes called *workfare*. Another possibility is to provide benefits for only a limited period of time. This route was taken in the 1996 welfare reform bill, which imposed a five-year lifetime limit on welfare recipients. When President Clinton signed the bill, he explained his policy as follows: "Welfare should be a second chance, not a way of life."

QUICK QUIZ   *List three policies aimed at helping the poor, and discuss the pros and cons of each.*

Conclusion

People have long reflected on the distribution of income in society. Plato, the ancient Greek philosopher, concluded that in an ideal society the income of the richest person would be no more than four times the income of the poorest person.

Although the measurement of inequality is difficult, it is clear that our society has much more inequality than Plato recommended.

One of the *Ten Principles of Economics* discussed in Chapter 1 is that governments can sometimes improve market outcomes. There is little consensus, however, about how this principle should be applied to the distribution of income. Philosophers and policymakers today do not agree on how much income inequality is desirable, or even whether public policy should aim to alter the distribution of income. Much of public debate reflects this disagreement. Whenever taxes are raised, for instance, lawmakers argue over how much of the tax hike should fall on the rich, the middle class, and the poor.

Another of the *Ten Principles of Economics* is that people face trade-offs. This principle is important to keep in mind when thinking about economic inequality. Policies that penalize the successful and reward the unsuccessful reduce the incentive to succeed. Thus, policymakers face a trade-off between equality and efficiency. The more equally the pie is divided, the smaller the pie becomes. This is the one lesson concerning the distribution of income about which almost everyone agrees.

SUMMARY

- Data on the distribution of income show a wide disparity in U.S. society. The richest fifth of families earns more than ten times as much income as the poorest fifth.

- Because in-kind transfers, the economic life cycle, transitory income, and economic mobility are so important for understanding variation in income, it is difficult to gauge the degree of inequality in our society using data on the distribution of income in a single year. When these other factors are taken into account, they tend to suggest that economic well-being is more equally distributed than is annual income.

- Political philosophers differ in their views about the role of government in altering the distribution of income. Utilitarians (such as John Stuart Mill) would choose the distribution of income

to maximize the sum of utility of everyone in society. Liberals (such as John Rawls) would determine the distribution of income as if we were behind a "veil of ignorance" that prevented us from knowing our stations in life. Libertarians (such as Robert Nozick) would have the government enforce individual rights to ensure a fair process but then not be concerned about inequality in the resulting distribution of income.

- Various policies aim to help the poor—minimum-wage laws, welfare, negative income taxes, and in-kind transfers. While these policies help some families escape poverty, they also have unintended side effects. Because financial assistance declines as income rises, the poor often face very high effective marginal tax rates, which discourage poor families from escaping poverty on their own.

KEY CONCEPTS

poverty rate, *p. 419*
poverty line, *p. 419*
in-kind transfers, *p. 420*
life cycle, *p. 421*
permanent income, *p. 421*

utilitarianism, *p. 424*
utility, *p. 424*
liberalism, *p. 425*
maximin criterion, *p. 426*
social insurance, *p. 426*

libertarianism, *p. 427*
welfare, *p. 428*
negative income tax, *p. 429*

QUESTIONS FOR REVIEW

1. Does the richest fifth of the U.S. population earn closer to two, four, or ten times the income of the poorest fifth?
2. How does the extent of income inequality in the United States compare to that of other nations around the world?
3. What groups in the U.S. population are most likely to live in poverty?
4. When gauging the amount of inequality, why do transitory and life cycle variations in income cause difficulties?
5. How would a utilitarian, a liberal, and a libertarian determine how much income inequality is permissible?
6. What are the pros and cons of in-kind (rather than cash) transfers to the poor?
7. Describe how antipoverty programs can discourage the poor from working. How might you reduce this disincentive? What are the disadvantages of your proposed policy?

PROBLEMS AND APPLICATIONS

1. Table 2 shows that income inequality in the United States has increased since 1970. Some factors contributing to this increase were discussed in Chapter 19. What are they?
2. Table 3 shows that the percentage of children in families with income below the poverty line far exceeds the percentage of the elderly in such families. How might the allocation of government money across different social programs have contributed to this phenomenon? (Hint: See Chapter 12.)
3. Economists often view life cycle variation in income as one form of transitory variation in income around people's lifetime, or permanent, income. In this sense, how does your current income compare to your permanent income? Do you think your current income accurately reflects your standard of living?
4. The chapter discusses the importance of economic mobility.
   a. What policies might the government pursue to increase economic mobility *within* a generation?
   b. What policies might the government pursue to increase economic mobility *across* generations?
   c. Do you think we should reduce spending on current welfare programs to increase spending on programs that enhance economic mobility? What are some of the advantages and disadvantages of doing so?

5. Consider two communities. In one community, ten families have incomes of $100,000 each and ten families have incomes of $20,000 each. In the other community, ten families have incomes of $200,000 each and ten families have incomes of $22,000 each.
   a. In which community is the distribution of income more unequal? In which community is the problem of poverty likely to be worse?
   b. Which distribution of income would Rawls prefer? Explain.
   c. Which distribution of income do you prefer? Explain.
   d. Why might someone have the opposite preference?
6. This chapter uses the analogy of a "leaky bucket" to explain one constraint on the redistribution of income.
   a. What elements of the U.S. system for redistributing income create the leaks in the bucket? Be specific.
   b. Do you think that Republicans or Democrats generally believe that the bucket used for redistributing income is leakier? How does that belief affect their views about the amount of income redistribution that the government should undertake?
7. Suppose there are two possible income distributions in a society of ten people. In the first distribution, nine people have incomes of $30,000 and one person has an income of

$10,000. In the second distribution, all ten people have incomes of $25,000.

a. If the society had the first income distribution, what would be the utilitarian argument for redistributing income?

b. Which income distribution would Rawls consider more equitable? Explain.

c. Which income distribution would Nozick consider more equitable? Explain.

8. The poverty rate would be substantially lower if the market value of in-kind transfers were added to family income. The largest in-kind transfer is Medicaid, the government health program for the poor. Let's say the program costs $7,000 per recipient family.

a. If the government gave each recipient family a $7,000 check instead of enrolling them in the Medicaid program, do you think that most of these families would spend that money to purchase health insurance? Why? (Recall that the poverty level for a family of four is about $20,000.)

b. How does your answer to part (a) affect your view about whether we should determine the poverty rate by valuing in-kind transfers at the price the government pays for them? Explain.

c. How does your answer to part (a) affect your view about whether we should provide assistance to the poor in the form of cash transfers or in-kind transfers? Explain.

9. Consider two of the income security programs in the United States: Temporary Assistance for Needy Families (TANF) and the Earned Income Tax Credit (EITC).

a. When a woman with children and very low income earns an extra dollar, she receives less in TANF benefits. What do you think is the effect of this feature of TANF on the labor supply of low-income women? Explain.

b. The EITC provides greater benefits as low-income workers earn more income (up to a point). What do you think is the effect of this program on the labor supply of low-income individuals? Explain.

c. What are the disadvantages of eliminating TANF and allocating the savings to the EITC?

10. In the spring of 2010, President Barack Obama signed sweeping healthcare legislation with the aim of providing healthcare to most Americans, financed in part by increasing taxes on those with high incomes. Which of the political philosophers discussed in this chapter do you think would most likely support this legislation and why? Would any of them be against it?

For further information on topics in this chapter, additional problems, applications, examples, online quizzes, and more, please visit our website at www .cengage.com/economics/mankiw.

PART **VII** Topics for
Further Study

The Theory of Consumer Choice

When you walk into a store, you are confronted with thousands of goods that you might buy. Because your financial resources are limited, however, you cannot buy everything that you want. You therefore consider the prices of the various goods offered for sale and buy a bundle of goods that, given your resources, best suits your needs and desires.

In this chapter, we develop a theory that describes how consumers make decisions about what to buy. Thus far in this book, we have summarized consumers' decisions with the demand curve. As we have seen, the demand curve for a good reflects consumers' willingness to pay for it. When the price of a good rises, consumers are willing to pay for fewer units, so the quantity demanded falls. We now look more deeply at the decisions that lie behind the demand curve. The theory of consumer choice presented in this chapter provides a more complete understanding of demand, just as the theory of the competitive firm in Chapter 14 provides a more complete understanding of supply.

One of the *Ten Principles of Economics* discussed in Chapter 1 is that people face trade-offs. The theory of consumer choice examines the trade-offs that people face in their role as consumers. When a consumer buys more of one good, he can afford less of other goods. When he spends more time enjoying leisure and less time working, he has lower income and can afford less consumption. When he spends more of his income in the present and saves less of it, he must accept a lower level of consumption in the future. The theory of consumer choice examines how consumers facing these trade-offs make decisions and how they respond to changes in their environment.

After developing the basic theory of consumer choice, we apply it to three questions about household decisions. In particular, we ask:

- Do all demand curves slope downward?
- How do wages affect labor supply?
- How do interest rates affect household saving?

At first, these questions might seem unrelated. But as we will see, we can use the theory of consumer choice to address each of them.

The Budget Constraint: What the Consumer Can Afford

Most people would like to increase the quantity or quality of the goods they consume—to take longer vacations, drive fancier cars, or eat at better restaurants. People consume less than they desire because their spending is *constrained*, or limited, by their income. We begin our study of consumer choice by examining this link between income and spending.

To keep things simple, we examine the decision facing a consumer who buys only two goods: pizza and Pepsi. Of course, real people buy thousands of different kinds of goods. Assuming there are only two goods greatly simplifies the problem without altering the basic insights about consumer choice.

We first consider how the consumer's income constrains the amount he spends on pizza and Pepsi. Suppose the consumer has an income of $1,000 per month and he spends his entire income on pizza and Pepsi. The price of a pizza is $10, and the price of a pint of Pepsi is $2.

The table in Figure 1 shows some of the many combinations of pizza and Pepsi that the consumer can buy. The first row in the table shows that if the consumer spends all his income on pizza, he can eat 100 pizzas during the month, but he would not be able to buy any Pepsi at all. The second row shows another possible consumption bundle: 90 pizzas and 50 pints of Pepsi. And so on. Each consumption bundle in the table costs exactly $1,000.

The graph in Figure 1 illustrates the consumption bundles that the consumer can choose. The vertical axis measures the number of pints of Pepsi, and the horizontal axis measures the number of pizzas. Three points are marked on this figure. At point A, the consumer buys no Pepsi and consumes 100 pizzas. At point B, the consumer buys no pizza and consumes 500 pints of Pepsi. At point C, the consumer buys 50 pizzas and 250 pints of Pepsi. Point C, which is exactly at the middle of the line from A to B, is the point at which the consumer spends an equal amount ($500) on pizza and Pepsi. These are only three of the many combinations of pizza and Pepsi that the consumer can choose. All the points on the line from A to B are possible. This line, called the **budget constraint,** shows the consumption

budget constraint

the limit on the consumption bundles that a consumer can afford

The budget constraint shows the various bundles of goods that the consumer can buy for a given income. Here the consumer buys bundles of pizza and Pepsi. The table and graph show what the consumer can afford if his income is $1,000, the price of pizza is $10, and the price of Pepsi is $2.

Figure **1**

The Consumer's Budget Constraint

Number of Pizzas	Pints of Pepsi	Spending on Pizza	Spending on Pepsi	Total Spending
100	0	$1,000	$ 0	$1,000
90	50	900	100	1,000
80	100	800	200	1,000
70	150	700	300	1,000
60	200	600	400	1,000
50	250	500	500	1,000
40	300	400	600	1,000
30	350	300	700	1,000
20	400	200	800	1,000
10	450	100	900	1,000
0	500	0	1,000	1,000

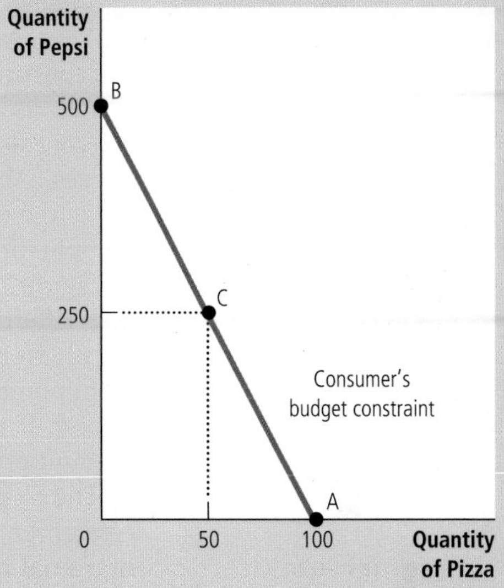

bundles that the consumer can afford. In this case, it shows the trade-off between pizza and Pepsi that the consumer faces.

The slope of the budget constraint measures the rate at which the consumer can trade one good for the other. Recall that the slope between two points is calculated as the change in the vertical distance divided by the change in the horizontal distance ("rise over run"). From point A to point B, the vertical distance is 500 pints, and the horizontal distance is 100 pizzas. Thus, the slope is 5 pints per pizza. (Actually, because the budget constraint slopes downward, the slope is a negative number. But for our purposes, we can ignore the minus sign.)

Notice that the slope of the budget constraint equals the *relative price* of the two goods—the price of one good compared to the price of the other. A pizza costs five times as much as a pint of Pepsi, so the opportunity cost of a pizza is 5 pints of Pepsi. The budget constraint's slope of 5 reflects the trade-off the market is offering the consumer: 1 pizza for 5 pints of Pepsi.

QUICK QUIZ   *Draw the budget constraint for a person with income of $1,000 if the price of Pepsi is $5 and the price of pizza is $10. What is the slope of this budget constraint?*

Preferences: What the Consumer Wants

Our goal in this chapter is to see how consumers make choices. The budget constraint is one piece of the analysis: It shows the combinations of goods the consumer can afford given his income and the prices of the goods. The consumer's choices, however, depend not only on his budget constraint but also on his preferences regarding the two goods. Therefore, the consumer's preferences are the next piece of our analysis.

Representing Preferences with Indifference Curves

The consumer's preferences allow him to choose among different bundles of pizza and Pepsi. If you offer the consumer two different bundles, he chooses the bundle that best suits his tastes. If the two bundles suit his tastes equally well, we say that the consumer is *indifferent* between the two bundles.

Just as we have represented the consumer's budget constraint graphically, we can also represent his preferences graphically. We do this with indifference curves. An **indifference curve** shows the various bundles of consumption that make the consumer equally happy. In this case, the indifference curves show the combinations of pizza and Pepsi with which the consumer is equally satisfied.

Figure 2 shows two of the consumer's many indifference curves. The consumer is indifferent among combinations A, B, and C because they are all on the same curve. Not surprisingly, if the consumer's consumption of pizza is reduced, say, from point A to point B, consumption of Pepsi must increase to keep him equally happy. If consumption of pizza is reduced again, from point B to point C, the amount of Pepsi consumed must increase yet again.

The slope at any point on an indifference curve equals the rate at which the consumer is willing to substitute one good for the other. This rate is called the **marginal rate of substitution** (*MRS*). In this case, the marginal rate of substitution measures how much Pepsi the consumer requires to be compensated for a one-unit reduction in pizza consumption. Notice that because the indifference curves are not straight lines, the marginal rate of substitution is not the same at all points on a given indifference curve. The rate at which a consumer is willing to trade one good for the other depends on the amounts of the goods he is already consuming. That is, the rate at which a consumer is willing to trade pizza for Pepsi depends on whether he is hungrier or thirstier, which in turn depends on how much pizza and Pepsi he is consuming.

The consumer is equally happy at all points on any given indifference curve, but he prefers some indifference curves to others. Because he prefers more

indifference curve

a curve that shows consumption bundles that give the consumer the same level of satisfaction

marginal rate of substitution

the rate at which a consumer is willing to trade one good for another

---

Figure **2**

The Consumer's Preferences
The consumer's preferences are represented with indifference curves, which show the combinations of pizza and Pepsi that make the consumer equally satisfied. Because the consumer prefers more of a good, points on a higher indifference curve (I_2 here) are preferred to points on a lower indifference curve (I_1). The marginal rate of substitution (*MRS*) shows the rate at which the consumer is willing to trade Pepsi for pizza. It measures the quantity of Pepsi the consumer must be given in exchange for 1 pizza.

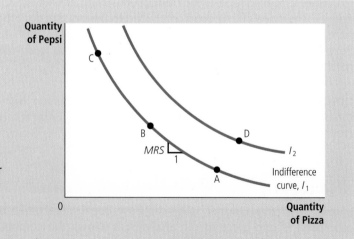

consumption to less, higher indifference curves are preferred to lower ones. In Figure 2, any point on curve I_2 is preferred to any point on curve I_1.

A consumer's set of indifference curves gives a complete ranking of the consumer's preferences. That is, we can use the indifference curves to rank any two bundles of goods. For example, the indifference curves tell us that point D is preferred to point A because point D is on a higher indifference curve than point A. (That conclusion may be obvious, however, because point D offers the consumer both more pizza and more Pepsi.) The indifference curves also tell us that point D is preferred to point C because point D is on a higher indifference curve. Even though point D has less Pepsi than point C, it has more than enough extra pizza to make the consumer prefer it. By seeing which point is on the higher indifference curve, we can use the set of indifference curves to rank any combination of pizza and Pepsi.

Four Properties of Indifference Curves

Because indifference curves represent a consumer's preferences, they have certain properties that reflect those preferences. Here we consider four properties that describe most indifference curves:

- *Property 1: Higher indifference curves are preferred to lower ones.* People usually prefer to consume more goods rather than less. This preference for greater quantities is reflected in the indifference curves. As Figure 2 shows, higher indifference curves represent larger quantities of goods than lower indifference curves. Thus, the consumer prefers being on higher indifference curves.
- *Property 2: Indifference curves are downward sloping.* The slope of an indifference curve reflects the rate at which the consumer is willing to substitute one good for the other. In most cases, the consumer likes both goods. Therefore, if the quantity of one good is reduced, the quantity of the other good must increase for the consumer to be equally happy. For this reason, most indifference curves slope downward.
- *Property 3: Indifference curves do not cross.* To see why this is true, suppose that two indifference curves did cross, as in Figure 3. Then, because point A is on the same indifference curve as point B, the two points would make

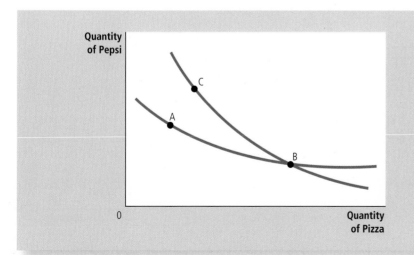

Quantity of Pepsi

Quantity of Pizza

0

Figure **3**

The Impossibility of Intersecting Indifference Curves
A situation like this can never happen. According to these indifference curves, the consumer would be equally satisfied at points A, B, and C, even though point C has more of both goods than point A.

the consumer equally happy. In addition, because point B is on the same indifference curve as point C, these two points would make the consumer equally happy. But these conclusions imply that points A and C would also make the consumer equally happy, even though point C has more of both goods. This contradicts our assumption that the consumer always prefers more of both goods to less. Thus, indifference curves cannot cross.

- *Property 4: Indifference curves are bowed inward.* The slope of an indifference curve is the marginal rate of substitution—the rate at which the consumer is willing to trade off one good for the other. The marginal rate of substitution (*MRS*) usually depends on the amount of each good the consumer is currently consuming. In particular, because people are more willing to trade away goods that they have in abundance and less willing to trade away goods of which they have little, the indifference curves are bowed inward. As an example, consider Figure 4. At point A, because the consumer has a lot of Pepsi and only a little pizza, he is very hungry but not very thirsty. To induce the consumer to give up 1 pizza, he has to be given 6 pints of Pepsi: The marginal rate of substitution is 6 pints per pizza. By contrast, at point B, the consumer has little Pepsi and a lot of pizza, so he is very thirsty but not very hungry. At this point, he would be willing to give up 1 pizza to get 1 pint of Pepsi: The marginal rate of substitution is 1 pint per pizza. Thus, the bowed shape of the indifference curve reflects the consumer's greater willingness to give up a good that he already has in large quantity.

Two Extreme Examples of Indifference Curves

The shape of an indifference curve tells us about the consumer's willingness to trade one good for the other. When the goods are easy to substitute for each other, the indifference curves are less bowed; when the goods are hard to substitute, the indifference curves are very bowed. To see why this is true, let's consider the extreme cases.

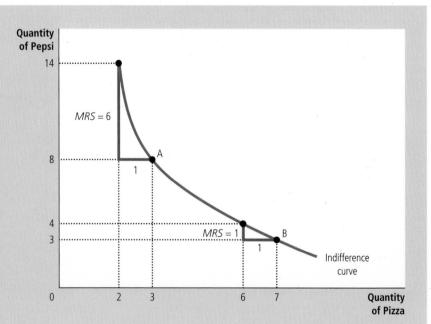

Figure 4

Bowed Indifference Curves
Indifference curves are usually bowed inward. This shape implies that the marginal rate of substitution (*MRS*) depends on the quantity of the two goods the consumer is consuming. At point A, the consumer has little pizza and much Pepsi, so he requires a lot of extra Pepsi to induce him to give up one of the pizzas: The marginal rate of substitution is 6 pints of Pepsi per pizza. At point B, the consumer has much pizza and little Pepsi, so he requires only a little extra Pepsi to induce him to give up one of the pizzas: The marginal rate of substitution is 1 pint of Pepsi per pizza.

Perfect Substitutes Suppose that someone offered you bundles of nickels and dimes. How would you rank the different bundles?

Most likely, you would care only about the total monetary value of each bundle. If so, you would always be willing to trade 2 nickels for 1 dime, regardless of the number of nickels and dimes in the bundle. Your marginal rate of substitution between nickels and dimes would be a fixed number—2.

We can represent your preferences over nickels and dimes with the indifference curves in panel (a) of Figure 5. Because the marginal rate of substitution is constant, the indifference curves are straight lines. In this extreme case of straight indifference curves, we say that the two goods are **perfect substitutes.**

perfect substitutes
two goods with straight-line indifference curves

Perfect Complements Suppose now that someone offered you bundles of shoes. Some of the shoes fit your left foot, others your right foot. How would you rank these different bundles?

In this case, you might care only about the number of pairs of shoes. In other words, you would judge a bundle based on the number of pairs you could assemble from it. A bundle of 5 left shoes and 7 right shoes yields only 5 pairs. Getting 1 more right shoe has no value if there is no left shoe to go with it.

We can represent your preferences for right and left shoes with the indifference curves in panel (b) of Figure 5. In this case, a bundle with 5 left shoes and 5 right shoes is just as good as a bundle with 5 left shoes and 7 right shoes. It is also just as good as a bundle with 7 left shoes and 5 right shoes. The indifference curves, therefore, are right angles. In this extreme case of right-angle indifference curves, we say that the two goods are **perfect complements.**

perfect complements
two goods with right-angle indifference curves

In the real world, of course, most goods are neither perfect substitutes (like nickels and dimes) nor perfect complements (like right shoes and left shoes). More typically, the indifference curves are bowed inward, but not so bowed as to become right angles.

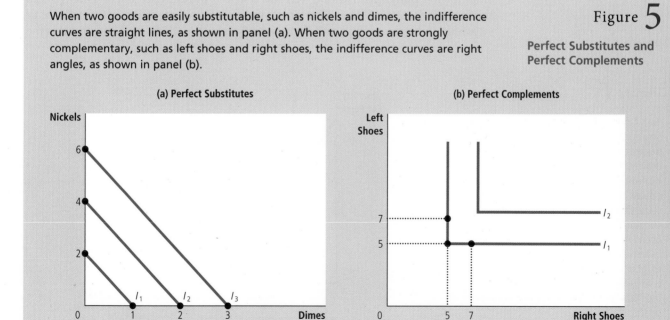

When two goods are easily substitutable, such as nickels and dimes, the indifference curves are straight lines, as shown in panel (a). When two goods are strongly complementary, such as left shoes and right shoes, the indifference curves are right angles, as shown in panel (b).

Figure 5

Perfect Substitutes and Perfect Complements

QUICK QUIZ   *Draw some indifference curves for pizza and Pepsi. Explain the four properties of these indifference curves.*

Optimization: What the Consumer Chooses

The goal of this chapter is to understand how a consumer makes choices. We have the two pieces necessary for this analysis: the consumer's budget constraint (how much he can afford to spend) and the consumer's preferences (what he wants to spend it on). Now we put these two pieces together and consider the consumer's decision about what to buy.

The Consumer's Optimal Choices

Consider once again our pizza and Pepsi example. The consumer would like to end up with the best possible combination of pizza and Pepsi for him—that is, the combination on his highest possible indifference curve. But the consumer must also end up on or below his budget constraint, which measures the total resources available to him.

Figure 6 shows the consumer's budget constraint and three of his many indifference curves. The highest indifference curve that the consumer can reach (I_2 in the figure) is the one that just barely touches his budget constraint. The point at which this indifference curve and the budget constraint touch is called the *optimum*. The consumer would prefer point A, but he cannot afford that point because it lies above his budget constraint. The consumer can afford point B, but that point is on a lower indifference curve and, therefore, provides the consumer less satisfaction. The optimum represents the best combination of pizza and Pepsi available to the consumer.

Notice that, at the optimum, the slope of the indifference curve equals the slope of the budget constraint. We say that the indifference curve is *tangent* to the budget constraint. The slope of the indifference curve is the marginal rate of substitution between pizza and Pepsi, and the slope of the budget constraint is the

Figure **6**

The Consumer's Optimum
The consumer chooses the point on his budget constraint that lies on the highest indifference curve. At this point, called the optimum, the marginal rate of substitution equals the relative price of the two goods. Here the highest indifference curve the consumer can reach is I_2. The consumer prefers point A, which lies on indifference curve I_3, but the consumer cannot afford this bundle of pizza and Pepsi. By contrast, point B is affordable, but because it lies on a lower indifference curve, the consumer does not prefer it.

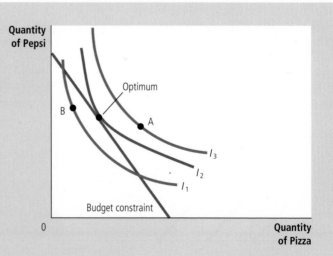

relative price of pizza and Pepsi. Thus, *the consumer chooses consumption of the two goods so that the marginal rate of substitution equals the relative price.*

In Chapter 7, we saw how market prices reflect the marginal value that consumers place on goods. This analysis of consumer choice shows the same result in another way. In making his consumption choices, the consumer takes as given the relative price of the two goods and then chooses an optimum at which his marginal rate of substitution equals this relative price. The relative price is the rate at which the *market* is willing to trade one good for the other, whereas the marginal rate of substitution is the rate at which the *consumer* is willing to trade one good for the other. At the consumer's optimum, the consumer's valuation of the two goods (as measured by the marginal rate of substitution) equals the market's valuation (as measured by the relative price). As a result of this consumer optimization, market prices of different goods reflect the value that consumers place on those goods.

FYI

Utility: An Alternative Way to Describe Preferences and Optimization

We have used indifference curves to represent the consumer's preferences. Another common way to represent preferences is with the concept of *utility*. Utility is an abstract measure of the satisfaction or happiness that a consumer receives from a bundle of goods. Economists say that a consumer prefers one bundle of goods to another if one provides more utility than the other.

Indifference curves and utility are closely related. Because the consumer prefers points on higher indifference curves, bundles of goods on higher indifference curves provide higher utility. Because the consumer is equally happy with all points on the same indifference curve, all these bundles provide the same utility. You can think of an indifference curve as an "equal-utility" curve.

The *marginal utility* of any good is the increase in utility that the consumer gets from an additional unit of that good. Most goods are assumed to exhibit *diminishing marginal utility:* The more of the good the consumer already has, the lower the marginal utility provided by an extra unit of that good.

The marginal rate of substitution between two goods depends on their marginal utilities. For example, if the marginal utility of good X is twice the marginal utility of good Y, then a person would need 2 units of good Y to compensate for losing 1 unit of good X, and the marginal rate of substitution equals 2. More generally, the marginal rate of substitution (and thus the slope of the indifference curve) equals the marginal utility of one good divided by the marginal utility of the other good.

Utility analysis provides another way to describe consumer optimization. Recall that at the consumer's optimum, the marginal rate of substitution equals the ratio of prices. That is,

$$MRS = P_X / P_Y.$$

Because the marginal rate of substitution equals the ratio of marginal utilities, we can write this condition for optimization as

$$MU_X / MU_Y = P_X / P_Y.$$

Now rearrange this expression to become

$$MU_X / P_X = MU_Y / P_Y.$$

This equation has a simple interpretation: At the optimum, the marginal utility per dollar spent on good X equals the marginal utility per dollar spent on good Y. (Why? If this equality did not hold, the consumer could increase utility by spending less on the good that provided lower marginal utility per dollar and more on the good that provided higher marginal utility per dollar.)

When economists discuss the theory of consumer choice, they might express the theory using different words. One economist might say that the goal of the consumer is to maximize utility. Another economist might say that the goal of the consumer is to end up on the highest possible indifference curve. The first economist would conclude that at the consumer's optimum, the marginal utility per dollar is the same for all goods, whereas the second would conclude that the indifference curve is tangent to the budget constraint. In essence, these are two ways of saying the same thing.

How Changes in Income Affect the Consumer's Choices

Now that we have seen how the consumer makes a consumption decision, let's examine how this decision responds to changes in the consumer's income. To be specific, suppose that income increases. With higher income, the consumer can afford more of both goods. The increase in income, therefore, shifts the budget constraint outward, as in Figure 7. Because the relative price of the two goods has not changed, the slope of the new budget constraint is the same as the slope of the initial budget constraint. That is, an increase in income leads to a parallel shift in the budget constraint.

The expanded budget constraint allows the consumer to choose a better combination of pizza and Pepsi, one that is on a higher indifference curve. Given the shift in the budget constraint and the consumer's preferences as represented by his indifference curves, the consumer's optimum moves from the point labeled "initial optimum" to the point labeled "new optimum."

Notice that, in Figure 7, the consumer chooses to consume more Pepsi and more pizza. Although the logic of the model does not require increased consumption of both goods in response to increased income, this situation is the most common one. As you may recall from Chapter 4, if a consumer wants more of a good when his income rises, economists call it a **normal good.** The indifference curves in Figure 7 are drawn under the assumption that both pizza and Pepsi are normal goods.

Figure 8 shows an example in which an increase in income induces the consumer to buy more pizza but less Pepsi. If a consumer buys less of a good when his income rises, economists call it an **inferior good.** Figure 8 is drawn under the assumption that pizza is a normal good and Pepsi is an inferior good.

normal good

a good for which an increase in income raises the quantity demanded

inferior good

a good for which an increase in income reduces the quantity demanded

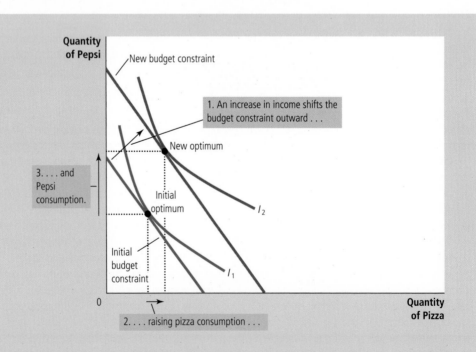

Figure **7**

An Increase in Income
When the consumer's income rises, the budget constraint shifts out. If both goods are normal goods, the consumer responds to the increase in income by buying more of both of them. Here the consumer buys more pizza and more Pepsi.

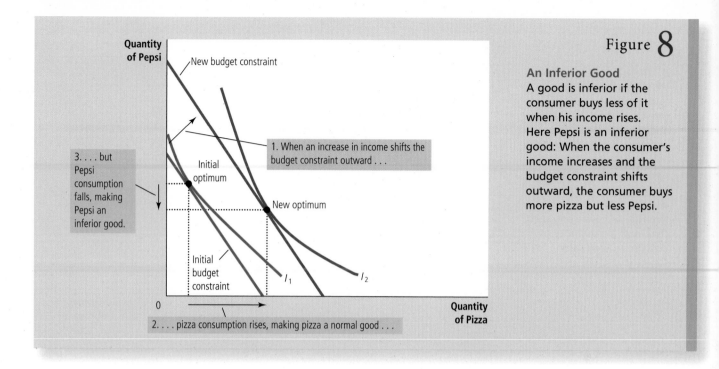

Figure **8**

An Inferior Good
A good is inferior if the consumer buys less of it when his income rises. Here Pepsi is an inferior good: When the consumer's income increases and the budget constraint shifts outward, the consumer buys more pizza but less Pepsi.

Although most goods are normal goods, there are some inferior goods in the world. One example is bus rides. As income increases, consumers are more likely to own cars or take a taxi and less likely to ride a bus. Bus rides, therefore, are an inferior good.

How Changes in Prices Affect the Consumer's Choices

Let's now use this model of consumer choice to consider how a change in the price of one of the goods alters the consumer's choices. Suppose, in particular, that the price of Pepsi falls from $2 to $1 per pint. It is no surprise that the lower price expands the consumer's set of buying opportunities. In other words, a fall in the price of any good shifts the budget constraint outward.

Figure 9 considers more specifically how the fall in price affects the budget constraint. If the consumer spends his entire $1,000 income on pizza, then the price of Pepsi is irrelevant. Thus, point A in the figure stays the same. Yet if the consumer spends his entire income of $1,000 on Pepsi, he can now buy 1,000 rather than only 500 pints. Thus, the end point of the budget constraint moves from point B to point D.

Notice that in this case the outward shift in the budget constraint changes its slope. (This differs from what happened previously when prices stayed the same but the consumer's income changed.) As we have discussed, the slope of the budget constraint reflects the relative price of pizza and Pepsi. Because the price of Pepsi has fallen to $1 from $2, while the price of pizza has remained $10, the consumer can now trade a pizza for 10 rather than 5 pints of Pepsi. As a result, the new budget constraint has a steeper slope.

Figure 9

A Change in Price
When the price of Pepsi falls, the consumer's budget constraint shifts outward and changes slope. The consumer moves from the initial optimum to the new optimum, which changes his purchases of both pizza and Pepsi. In this case, the quantity of Pepsi consumed rises, and the quantity of pizza consumed falls.

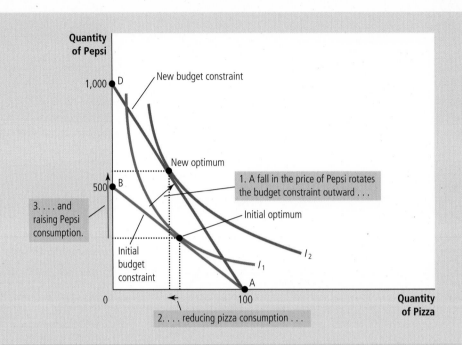

How such a change in the budget constraint alters the consumption of both goods depends on the consumer's preferences. For the indifference curves drawn in this figure, the consumer buys more Pepsi and less pizza.

Income and Substitution Effects

The impact of a change in the price of a good on consumption can be decomposed into two effects: an **income effect** and a **substitution effect.** To see what these two effects are, consider how our consumer might respond when he learns that the price of Pepsi has fallen. He might reason in the following ways:

income effect

the change in consumption that results when a price change moves the consumer to a higher or lower indifference curve

substitution effect

the change in consumption that results when a price change moves the consumer along a given indifference curve to a point with a new marginal rate of substitution

- "Great news! Now that Pepsi is cheaper, my income has greater purchasing power. I am, in effect, richer than I was. Because I am richer, I can buy both more pizza and more Pepsi." (This is the income effect.)
- "Now that the price of Pepsi has fallen, I get more pints of Pepsi for every pizza that I give up. Because pizza is now relatively more expensive, I should buy less pizza and more Pepsi." (This is the substitution effect.)

Which statement do you find more compelling?

In fact, both of these statements make sense. The decrease in the price of Pepsi makes the consumer better off. If pizza and Pepsi are both normal goods, the consumer will want to spread this improvement in his purchasing power over both goods. This income effect tends to make the consumer buy more pizza and more Pepsi. Yet at the same time, consumption of Pepsi has become less expensive relative to consumption of pizza. This substitution effect tends to make the consumer choose less pizza and more Pepsi.

Now consider the result of these two effects working at the same time. The consumer certainly buys more Pepsi because the income and substitution effects both act to raise purchases of Pepsi. But it is ambiguous whether the consumer buys more pizza because the income and substitution effects work in opposite directions. This conclusion is summarized in Table 1.

Table **1**

Income and Substitution Effects When the Price of Pepsi Falls

Good	Income Effect	Substitution Effect	Total Effect
Pepsi	Consumer is richer, so he buys more Pepsi.	Pepsi is relatively cheaper, so consumer buys more Pepsi.	Income and substitution effects act in same direction, so consumer buys more Pepsi.
Pizza	Consumer is richer, so he buys more pizza.	Pizza is relatively more expensive, so consumer buys less pizza.	Income and substitution effects act in opposite directions, so the total effect on pizza consumption is ambiguous.

We can interpret the income and substitution effects using indifference curves. *The income effect is the change in consumption that results from the movement to a higher indifference curve. The substitution effect is the change in consumption that results from being at a point on an indifference curve with a different marginal rate of substitution.*

Figure 10 shows graphically how to decompose the change in the consumer's decision into the income effect and the substitution effect. When the price of Pepsi falls, the consumer moves from the initial optimum, point A, to the new optimum, point C. We can view this change as occurring in two steps. First, the consumer moves *along* the initial indifference curve, I_1, from point A to point B. The consumer is equally happy at these two points, but at point B, the marginal rate

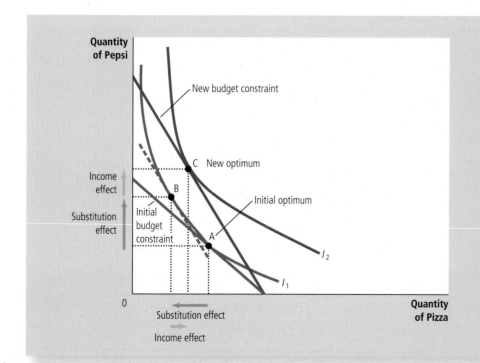

Figure **10**

Income and Substitution Effects
The effect of a change in price can be broken down into an income effect and a substitution effect. The substitution effect—the movement along an indifference curve to a point with a different marginal rate of substitution—is shown here as the change from point A to point B along indifference curve I_1. The income effect—the shift to a higher indifference curve—is shown here as the change from point B on indifference curve I_1 to point C on indifference curve I_2.

of substitution reflects the new relative price. (The dashed line through point B reflects the new relative price by being parallel to the new budget constraint.) Next, the consumer *shifts* to the higher indifference curve, I_2, by moving from point B to point C. Even though point B and point C are on different indifference curves, they have the same marginal rate of substitution. That is, the slope of the indifference curve I_1 at point B equals the slope of the indifference curve I_2 at point C.

Although the consumer never actually chooses point B, this hypothetical point is useful to clarify the two effects that determine the consumer's decision. Notice that the change from point A to point B represents a pure change in the marginal rate of substitution without any change in the consumer's welfare. Similarly, the change from point B to point C represents a pure change in welfare without any change in the marginal rate of substitution. Thus, the movement from A to B shows the substitution effect, and the movement from B to C shows the income effect.

Deriving the Demand Curve

We have just seen how changes in the price of a good alter the consumer's budget constraint and, therefore, the quantities of the two goods that he chooses to buy. The demand curve for any good reflects these consumption decisions. Recall that a demand curve shows the quantity demanded of a good for any given price. We can view a consumer's demand curve as a summary of the optimal decisions that arise from his budget constraint and indifference curves.

For example, Figure 11 considers the demand for Pepsi. Panel (a) shows that when the price of a pint falls from $2 to $1, the consumer's budget constraint shifts outward. Because of both income and substitution effects, the consumer increases

Figure **11**

Deriving the Demand Curve

Panel (a) shows that when the price of Pepsi falls from $2 to $1, the consumer's optimum moves from point A to point B, and the quantity of Pepsi consumed rises from 250 to 750 pints. The demand curve in panel (b) reflects this relationship between the price and the quantity demanded.

(a) The Consumer's Optimum

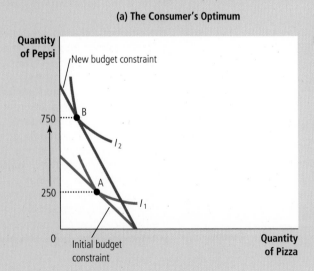

(b) The Demand Curve for Pepsi

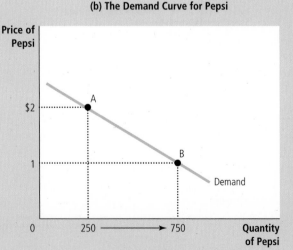

his purchases of Pepsi from 250 to 750 pints. Panel (b) shows the demand curve that results from this consumer's decisions. In this way, the theory of consumer choice provides the theoretical foundation for the consumer's demand curve.

It may be comforting to know that the demand curve arises naturally from the theory of consumer choice, but this exercise by itself does not justify developing the theory. There is no need for a rigorous, analytic framework just to establish that people respond to changes in prices. The theory of consumer choice is, however, useful in studying various decisions that people make as they go about their lives, as we see in the next section.

QUICK QUIZ *Draw a budget constraint and indifference curves for pizza and Pepsi. Show what happens to the budget constraint and the consumer's optimum when the price of pizza rises. In your diagram, decompose the change into an income effect and a substitution effect.*

Three Applications

Now that we have developed the basic theory of consumer choice, let's use it to shed light on three questions about how the economy works. These three questions might at first seem unrelated. But because each question involves household decision making, we can address it with the model of consumer behavior we have just developed.

Do All Demand Curves Slope Downward?

Normally, when the price of a good rises, people buy less of it. This usual behavior, called the *law of demand,* is reflected in the downward slope of the demand curve.

As a matter of economic theory, however, demand curves can sometimes slope upward. In other words, consumers can sometimes violate the law of demand and buy *more* of a good when the price rises. To see how this can happen, consider Figure 12. In this example, the consumer buys two goods—meat and potatoes. Initially, the consumer's budget constraint is the line from point A to point B. The optimum is point C. When the price of potatoes rises, the budget constraint shifts inward and is now the line from point A to point D. The optimum is now point E. Notice that a rise in the price of potatoes has led the consumer to buy a larger quantity of potatoes.

Why is the consumer responding in a seemingly perverse way? In this example, potatoes are a strongly inferior good. When the price of potatoes rises, the consumer is poorer. The income effect makes the consumer want to buy less meat and more potatoes. At the same time, because the potatoes have become more expensive relative to meat, the substitution effect makes the consumer want to buy more meat and fewer potatoes. In this particular case, however, the income effect is so strong that it exceeds the substitution effect. In the end, the consumer responds to the higher price of potatoes by buying less meat and more potatoes.

Economists use the term **Giffen good** to describe a good that violates the law of demand. (The term is named for economist Robert Giffen, who first noted this possibility.) In this example, potatoes are a Giffen good. Giffen goods are inferior goods for which the income effect dominates the substitution effect. Therefore, they have demand curves that slope upward.

Giffen good

a good for which an increase in the price raises the quantity demanded

Figure 12

A Giffen Good
In this example, when the price of potatoes rises, the consumer's optimum shifts from point C to point E. In this case, the consumer responds to a higher price of potatoes by buying less meat and more potatoes.

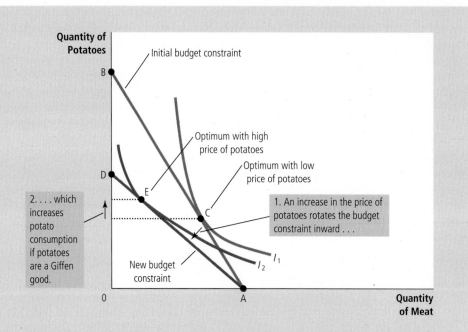

The Search for Giffen Goods

Have any actual Giffen goods ever been observed? Some historians suggest that potatoes were a Giffen good during the Irish potato famine of the 19th century. Potatoes were such a large part of people's diet that when the price of potatoes rose, it had a large income effect. People responded to their reduced living standard by cutting back on the luxury of meat and buying more of the staple food of potatoes. Thus, it is argued that a higher price of potatoes actually raised the quantity of potatoes demanded.

A recent study by Robert Jensen and Nolan Miller has produced similar but more concrete evidence for the existence of Giffen goods. These two economists conducted a field experiment for five months in the Chinese province of Hunan. They gave randomly selected households vouchers that subsidized the purchase of rice, a staple in local diets, and used surveys to measure how consumption of rice responded to changes in the price. They found strong evidence that poor households exhibited Giffen behavior. Lowering the price of rice with the subsidy voucher caused households to reduce their consumption of rice, and removing the subsidy had the opposite effect. Jensen and Miller wrote, "To the best of our knowledge, this is the first rigorous empirical evidence of Giffen behavior."

Thus, the theory of consumer choice allows demand curves to slope upward, and sometimes that strange phenomenon actually occurs. As a result, the law of demand we first saw in Chapter 4 is not completely reliable. It is safe to say, however, that Giffen goods are very rare. ∎

How Do Wages Affect Labor Supply?

So far, we have used the theory of consumer choice to analyze how a person allocates income between two goods. We can use the same theory to analyze how a person allocates time. People spend some of their time enjoying leisure and some

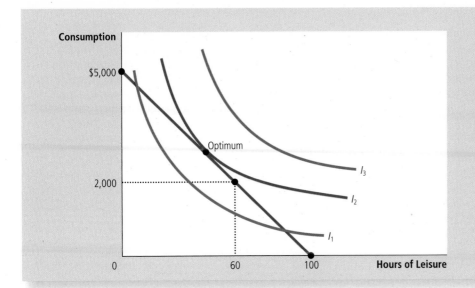

Figure **13**

The Work-Leisure Decision
This figure shows Sally's budget constraint for deciding how much to work, her indifference curves for consumption and leisure, and her optimum.

of it working so they can afford to buy consumption goods. The essence of the time-allocation problem is the trade-off between leisure and consumption.

Consider the decision facing Sally, a freelance software designer. Sally is awake for 100 hours per week. She spends some of this time enjoying leisure—riding her bike, watching television, and studying economics. She spends the rest of this time at her computer developing software. For every hour she works developing software, she earns $50, which she spends on consumption goods—food, clothing, and music downloads. Her wage ($50) reflects the trade-off Sally faces between leisure and consumption. For every hour of leisure she gives up, she works one more hour and gets $50 of consumption.

Figure 13 shows Sally's budget constraint. If she spends all 100 hours enjoying leisure, she has no consumption. If she spends all 100 hours working, she earns a weekly consumption of $5,000 but has no time for leisure. If she works a normal 40-hour week, she enjoys 60 hours of leisure and has weekly consumption of $2,000.

Figure 13 uses indifference curves to represent Sally's preferences for consumption and leisure. Here consumption and leisure are the two "goods" between which Sally is choosing. Because Sally always prefers more leisure and more consumption, she prefers points on higher indifference curves to points on lower ones. At a wage of $50 per hour, Sally chooses a combination of consumption and leisure represented by the point labeled "optimum." This is the point on the budget constraint that is on the highest possible indifference curve, I_2.

Now consider what happens when Sally's wage increases from $50 to $60 per hour. Figure 14 shows two possible outcomes. In each case, the budget constraint, shown in the left graphs, shifts outward from BC_1 to BC_2. In the process, the budget constraint becomes steeper, reflecting the change in relative price: At the higher wage, Sally earns more consumption for every hour of leisure that she gives up.

Sally's preferences, as represented by her indifference curves, determine how her choice regarding consumption and leisure responds to the higher wage. In both panels, consumption rises. Yet the response of leisure to the change in the wage is different in the two cases. In panel (a), Sally responds to the higher wage by enjoying less leisure. In panel (b), Sally responds by enjoying more leisure.

Sally's decision between leisure and consumption determines her supply of labor because the more leisure she enjoys, the less time she has left to work. In each panel

Figure 14

An Increase in the Wage

The two panels of this figure show how a person might respond to an increase in the wage. The graphs on the left show the consumer's initial budget constraint, BC_1, and new budget constraint, BC_2, as well as the consumer's optimal choices over consumption and leisure. The graphs on the right show the resulting labor-supply curve. Because hours worked equal total hours available minus hours of leisure, any change in leisure implies an opposite change in the quantity of labor supplied. In panel (a), when the wage rises, consumption rises and leisure falls, resulting in a labor-supply curve that slopes upward. In panel (b), when the wage rises, both consumption and leisure rise, resulting in a labor-supply curve that slopes backward.

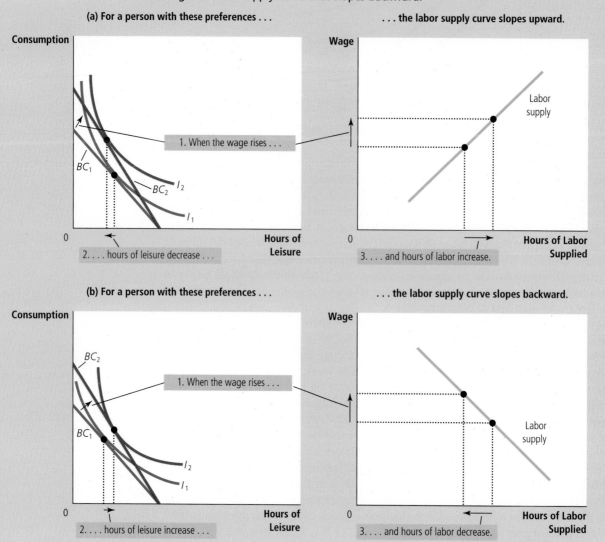

(a) For a person with these preferences . . .   **. . . the labor supply curve slopes upward.**

1. When the wage rises . . .

2. . . . hours of leisure decrease . . .

3. . . . and hours of labor increase.

(b) For a person with these preferences . . .   **. . . the labor supply curve slopes backward.**

1. When the wage rises . . .

2. . . . hours of leisure increase . . .

3. . . . and hours of labor decrease.

of Figure 14, the right graph shows the labor-supply curve implied by Sally's decision. In panel (a), a higher wage induces Sally to enjoy less leisure and work more, so the labor-supply curve slopes upward. In panel (b), a higher wage induces Sally to enjoy more leisure and work less, so the labor-supply curve slopes "backward."

At first, the backward-sloping labor-supply curve is puzzling. Why would a person respond to a higher wage by working less? The answer comes from considering the income and substitution effects of a higher wage.

Consider first the substitution effect. When Sally's wage rises, leisure becomes more costly relative to consumption, and this encourages Sally to substitute away from leisure and toward consumption. In other words, the substitution effect induces Sally to work harder in response to higher wages, which tends to make the labor-supply curve slope upward.

Now consider the income effect. When Sally's wage rises, she moves to a higher indifference curve. She is now better off than she was. As long as consumption and leisure are both normal goods, she tends to want to use this increase in well-being to enjoy both higher consumption and greater leisure. In other words, the income effect induces her to work less, which tends to make the labor-supply curve slope backward.

In the end, economic theory does not give a clear prediction about whether an increase in the wage induces Sally to work more or less. If the substitution effect is greater than the income effect for Sally, she works more. If the income effect is greater than the substitution effect, she works less. The labor-supply curve, therefore, could be either upward or backward sloping.

CASE STUDY   Income Effects on Labor Supply: Historical Trends, Lottery Winners, and the Carnegie Conjecture

The idea of a backward-sloping labor-supply curve might at first seem like a mere theoretical curiosity, but in fact, it is not. Evidence indicates that the labor-supply curve, considered over long periods, does in fact slope backward. A hundred years ago, many people worked six days a week. Today, five-day workweeks are the norm. At the same time that the length of the workweek has been falling, the wage of the typical worker (adjusted for inflation) has been rising.

Here is how economists explain this historical pattern: Over time, advances in technology raise workers' productivity and, thereby, the demand for labor. This increase in labor demand raises equilibrium wages. As wages rise, so does the reward for working. Yet rather than responding to this increased incentive by working more, most workers choose to take part of their greater prosperity in the form of more leisure. In other words, the income effect of higher wages dominates the substitution effect.

Further evidence that the income effect on labor supply is strong comes from a very different kind of data: winners of lotteries. Winners of large prizes in the lottery see large increases in their incomes and, as a result, large outward shifts in their budget constraints. Because the winners' wages have not changed, however, the *slopes* of their budget constraints remain the same. There is, therefore, no substitution effect. By examining the behavior of lottery winners, we can isolate the income effect on labor supply.

The results from studies of lottery winners are striking. Of those winners who win more than $50,000, almost 25 percent quit working within a year, and another 9 percent reduce the number of hours they work. Of those winners who win more than $1 million, almost 40 percent stop working. The income effect on labor supply of winning such a large prize is substantial.

Similar results were found in a 1993 study, published in the *Quarterly Journal of Economics,* of how receiving a bequest affects a person's labor supply. The study found that a single person who inherits more than $150,000 is four times as likely to stop working as a single person who inherits less than $25,000. This finding would not have surprised the 19th-century industrialist Andrew Carnegie. Carnegie warned that "the parent who leaves his son enormous wealth generally deadens the talents and energies of the son, and tempts him to lead a less useful and less worthy

"No more 9 to 5 for me."

life than he otherwise would." That is, Carnegie viewed the income effect on labor supply to be substantial and, from his paternalistic perspective, regrettable. During his life and at his death, Carnegie gave much of his vast fortune to charity. ■

in the news

❯ Backward-sloping Labor Supply in Kiribati

In the island nation of Kiribati, when the coconut industry pays more, people spend less time working (picking coconuts) and more time enjoying leisure (fishing).

Reef Conservation Strategy Backfires

BY RICHARD HARRIS

Aid organizations concerned about overfishing on tropical reefs often try to encourage fishermen out of their boats by offering them better-paying jobs on shore. But this strategy actually may make matters worse.

Take, for example, the story of Kiribati, an island nation in the central Pacific. Kiribati (pronounced KIR-a-bahs) has a simple economy. People either catch fish, or they pick coconuts from their trees and produce coconut oil. Sheila Walsh, a postdoctoral researcher at Brown University, says most people do a bit of each.

The Kiribati government was concerned about overfishing. So it came up with a plan: It would subsidize the coconut oil industry.

"The thought was that by paying people more to do coconut agriculture, they would do less fishing," says Walsh. "And this would fulfill two goals: One, they would reduce overfishing; and two, people would be better off. They would have higher incomes."

Walsh wanted to know whether this plan was working, and the government invited her to study the issue. So, as part of her graduate work at the Scripps Institution of

Fishing versus coconuts: The Kiribati tradeoff

Oceanography, she flew to Kiribati to interview fishermen.

"And it turned out that, actually, the result of paying people more to do coconut agriculture was to increase fishing," she says. In fact, fishing increased by a startling 33 percent. The reef fish population dropped by an estimated 17 percent, putting the whole ecosystem at risk.

"It was a bit of a surprise, and we were wondering: What's going on here?"

The answer was simplicity itself. Walsh's study concludes that people earned more money making coconut oil, which meant they could work less to support themselves. And they spent their new leisure time fishing.

"It hit us like a bumper sticker saying — a bad day fishing is better than a good day working. And that's sort of the story here," Walsh says.

It turns out she had stumbled into a universal truth about fishing. Fishermen aren't just in it for the money. Anthropologist Richard Pollnac of the University of Rhode Island says, just think of those snazzy sport-fishing excursions.

"People pay big money to go sportsfishing," he notes. There aren't very many occupations that people will actually pay money to do in their leisure time, he says.

So fishing as an occupation provides psychic benefits, as well as money. Pollnac argues that not just individuals but whole cultures get hooked on the thrill of being out on the water, and the gamble of coming back with either a boatload or empty-handed. . . .

Walsh says she's trying to help the government figure out how to fix the problem of overfishing, which they'd accidentally made worse. Maybe, she says, the government can create new jobs out on the water by hiring the fishermen to patrol newly created nature preserves.

Source: National Public Radio, November 18, 2009.

How Do Interest Rates Affect Household Saving?

An important decision that every person faces is how much income to consume today and how much to save for the future. We can use the theory of consumer choice to analyze how people make this decision and how the amount they save depends on the interest rate their savings will earn.

Consider the decision facing Sam, a worker planning for retirement. To keep things simple, let's divide Sam's life into two periods. In the first period, Sam is young and working. In the second period, he is old and retired. When young, Sam earns $100,000. He divides this income between current consumption and saving. When he is old, Sam will consume what he has saved, including the interest that his savings have earned.

Suppose the interest rate is 10 percent. Then for every dollar that Sam saves when young, he can consume $1.10 when old. We can view "consumption when young" and "consumption when old" as the two goods that Sam must choose between. The interest rate determines the relative price of these two goods.

Figure 15 shows Sam's budget constraint. If he saves nothing, he consumes $100,000 when young and nothing when old. If he saves everything, he consumes nothing when young and $110,000 when old. The budget constraint shows these and all the intermediate possibilities.

Figure 15 uses indifference curves to represent Sam's preferences for consumption in the two periods. Because Sam prefers more consumption in both periods, he prefers points on higher indifference curves to points on lower ones. Given his preferences, Sam chooses the optimal combination of consumption in both periods of life, which is the point on the budget constraint that is on the highest possible indifference curve. At this optimum, Sam consumes $50,000 when young and $55,000 when old.

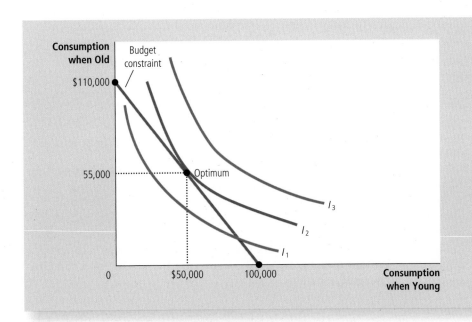

Figure **15**

The Consumption-Saving Decision
This figure shows the budget constraint for a person deciding how much to consume in the two periods of his life, the indifference curves representing his preferences, and the optimum.

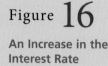

Figure 16

An Increase in the Interest Rate

In both panels, an increase in the interest rate shifts the budget constraint outward. In panel (a), consumption when young falls, and consumption when old rises. The result is an increase in saving when young. In panel (b), consumption in both periods rises. The result is a decrease in saving when young.

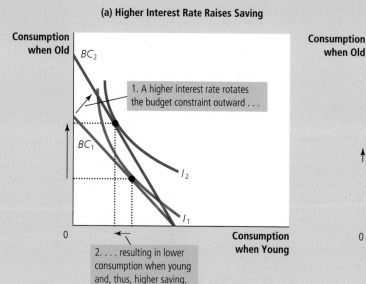

(a) Higher Interest Rate Raises Saving
Consumption when Old
BC_2
1. A higher interest rate rotates the budget constraint outward . . .
BC_1
I_2
I_1
0
Consumption when Young
2. . . . resulting in lower consumption when young and, thus, higher saving.
(b) Higher Interest Rate Lowers Saving
Consumption when Old
BC_2
1. A higher interest rate rotates the budget constraint outward . . .
BC_1
I_2
I_1
0
Consumption when Young
2. . . . resulting in higher consumption when young and, thus, lower saving.

Now consider what happens when the interest rate increases from 10 percent to 20 percent. Figure 16 shows two possible outcomes. In both cases, the budget constraint shifts outward and becomes steeper. At the new higher interest rate, Sam gets more consumption when old for every dollar of consumption that he gives up when young.

The two panels show the results given different preferences by Sam. In both cases, consumption when old rises. Yet the response of consumption when young to the change in the interest rate is different in the two cases. In panel (a), Sam responds to the higher interest rate by consuming less when young. In panel (b), Sam responds by consuming more when young.

Sam's saving is his income when young minus the amount he consumes when young. In panel (a), consumption when young falls when the interest rate rises, so saving must rise. In panel (b), Sam consumes more when young, so saving must fall.

The case shown in panel (b) might at first seem odd: Sam responds to an increase in the return to saving by saving less. Yet this behavior is not as peculiar as it might seem. We can understand it by considering the income and substitution effects of a higher interest rate.

Consider first the substitution effect. When the interest rate rises, consumption when old becomes less costly relative to consumption when young. Therefore, the substitution effect induces Sam to consume more when old and less when young. In other words, the substitution effect induces Sam to save more.

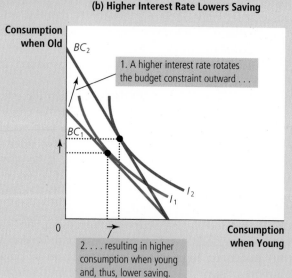

Now consider the income effect. When the interest rate rises, Sam moves to a higher indifference curve. He is now better off than he was. As long as consumption in both periods consists of normal goods, he tends to want to use this increase in well-being to enjoy higher consumption in both periods. In other words, the income effect induces him to save less.

The result depends on both the income and substitution effects. If the substitution effect of a higher interest rate is greater than the income effect, Sam saves more. If the income effect is greater than the substitution effect, Sam saves less. Thus, the theory of consumer choice says that an increase in the interest rate could either encourage or discourage saving.

This ambiguous result is interesting from the standpoint of economic theory, but it is disappointing from the standpoint of economic policy. It turns out that an important issue in tax policy hinges in part on how saving responds to interest rates. Some economists have advocated reducing the taxation of interest and other capital income, arguing that such a policy change would raise the after-tax interest rate that savers can earn and would thereby encourage people to save more. Other economists have argued that because of offsetting income and substitution effects, such a tax change might not increase saving and could even reduce it. Unfortunately, research has not led to a consensus about how interest rates affect saving. As a result, there remains disagreement among economists about whether changes in tax policy aimed to encourage saving would, in fact, have the intended effect.

QUICK QUIZ   *Explain how an increase in the wage can potentially decrease the amount that a person wants to work.*

Conclusion: Do People Really Think This Way?

The theory of consumer choice describes how people make decisions. As we have seen, it has broad applicability. It can explain how a person chooses between pizza and Pepsi, work and leisure, consumption and saving, and on and on.

At this point, however, you might be tempted to treat the theory of consumer choice with some skepticism. After all, you are a consumer. You decide what to buy every time you walk into a store. And you know that you do not decide by writing down budget constraints and indifference curves. Doesn't this knowledge about your own decision making provide evidence against the theory?

The answer is no. The theory of consumer choice does not try to present a literal account of how people make decisions. It is a model. And as we first discussed in Chapter 2, models are not intended to be completely realistic.

The best way to view the theory of consumer choice is as a metaphor for how consumers make decisions. No consumer (except an occasional economist) goes through the explicit optimization envisioned in the theory. Yet consumers are aware that their choices are constrained by their financial resources. And given those constraints, they do the best they can to achieve the highest level of satisfaction. The theory of consumer choice tries to describe this implicit, psychological process in a way that permits explicit, economic analysis.

Just as the proof of the pudding is in the eating, the test of a theory is in its applications. In the last section of this chapter, we applied the theory of consumer choice to three practical issues about the economy. If you take more advanced courses in economics, you will see that this theory provides the framework for much additional analysis.

SUMMARY

- A consumer's budget constraint shows the possible combinations of different goods he can buy given his income and the prices of the goods. The slope of the budget constraint equals the relative price of the goods.

- The consumer's indifference curves represent his preferences. An indifference curve shows the various bundles of goods that make the consumer equally happy. Points on higher indifference curves are preferred to points on lower indifference curves. The slope of an indifference curve at any point is the consumer's marginal rate of substitution—the rate at which the consumer is willing to trade one good for the other.

- The consumer optimizes by choosing the point on his budget constraint that lies on the highest indifference curve. At this point, the slope of the indifference curve (the marginal rate of substitution between the goods) equals the slope of the budget constraint (the relative price of the goods).

- When the price of a good falls, the impact on the consumer's choices can be broken down into an income effect and a substitution effect. The income effect is the change in consumption that arises because a lower price makes the consumer better off. The substitution effect is the change in consumption that arises because a price change encourages greater consumption of the good that has become relatively cheaper. The income effect is reflected in the movement from a lower to a higher indifference curve, whereas the substitution effect is reflected by a movement along an indifference curve to a point with a different slope.

- The theory of consumer choice can be applied in many situations. It explains why demand curves can potentially slope upward, why higher wages could either increase or decrease the quantity of labor supplied, and why higher interest rates could either increase or decrease saving.

KEY CONCEPTS

budget constraint, *p. 440*
indifference curve, *p. 442*
marginal rate of
   substitution, *p. 442*

perfect substitutes, *p. 445*
perfect complements, *p. 445*
normal good, *p. 448*
inferior good, *p. 448*

income effect, *p. 450*
substitution effect, *p. 450*
Giffen good, *p. 453*

QUESTIONS FOR REVIEW

1. A consumer has income of $3,000. Wine costs $3 per glass, and cheese costs $6 per pound. Draw the consumer's budget constraint. What is the slope of this budget constraint?

2. Draw a consumer's indifference curves for wine and cheese. Describe and explain four properties of these indifference curves.

3. Pick a point on an indifference curve for wine and cheese and show the marginal rate of substitution. What does the marginal rate of substitution tell us?

4. Show a consumer's budget constraint and indifference curves for wine and cheese. Show the optimal consumption choice. If the price of

wine is $3 per glass and the price of cheese is $6 per pound, what is the marginal rate of substitution at this optimum?

5. A person who consumes wine and cheese gets a raise, so his income increases from $3,000 to $4,000. Show what happens if both wine and cheese are normal goods. Now show what happens if cheese is an inferior good.

6. The price of cheese rises from $6 to $10 per pound, while the price of wine remains $3 per glass. For a consumer with a constant income of $3,000, show what happens to consumption of wine and cheese. Decompose the change into income and substitution effects.

7. Can an increase in the price of cheese possibly induce a consumer to buy more cheese? Explain.

PROBLEMS AND APPLICATIONS

1. Jennifer divides her income between coffee and croissants (both of which are normal goods). An early frost in Brazil causes a large increase in the price of coffee in the United States.
   a. Show the effect of the frost on Jennifer's budget constraint.
   b. Show the effect of the frost on Jennifer's optimal consumption bundle assuming that the substitution effect outweighs the income effect for croissants.
   c. Show the effect of the frost on Jennifer's optimal consumption bundle assuming that the income effect outweighs the substitution effect for croissants.

2. Compare the following two pairs of goods:
   • Coke and Pepsi
   • Skis and ski bindings
   a. In which case are the two goods complements? In which case are they substitutes?
   b. In which case do you expect the indifference curves to be fairly straight? In which case do you expect the indifference curves to be very bowed?
   c. In which case will the consumer respond more to a change in the relative price of the two goods?

3. You consume only soda and pizza. One day, the price of soda goes up, the price of pizza goes down, and you are just as happy as you were before the price changes.
   a. Illustrate this situation on a graph.
   b. How does your consumption of the two goods change? How does your response depend on income and substitution effects?
   c. Can you afford the bundle of soda and pizza you consumed before the price changes?

4. Mario consumes only cheese and crackers.
   a. Could cheese and crackers both be inferior goods for Mario? Explain.

   b. Suppose that cheese is a normal good for Mario while crackers are an inferior good. If the price of cheese falls, what happens to Mario's consumption of crackers? What happens to his consumption of cheese? Explain.

5. Jim buys only milk and cookies.
   a. In year 1, Jim earns $100, milk costs $2 per quart, and cookies cost $4 per dozen. Draw Jim's budget constraint.
   b. Now suppose that all prices increase by 10 percent in year 2 and that Jim's salary increases by 10 percent as well. Draw Jim's new budget constraint. How would Jim's optimal combination of milk and cookies in year 2 compare to his optimal combination in year 1?

6. State whether each of the following statements is true or false. Explain your answers.
   a. "All Giffen goods are inferior goods."
   b. "All inferior goods are Giffen goods."

7. A college student has two options for meals: eating at the dining hall for $6 per meal, or eating a Cup O' Soup for $1.50 per meal. His weekly food budget is $60.
   a. Draw the budget constraint showing the trade-off between dining hall meals and Cups O' Soup. Assuming that he spends equal amounts on both goods, draw an indifference curve showing the optimum choice. Label the optimum as point A.
   b. Suppose the price of a Cup O' Soup now rises to $2. Using your diagram from part (a), show the consequences of this change in price. Assume that our student now spends only 30 percent of his income on dining hall meals. Label the new optimum as point B.
   c. What happened to the quantity of Cups O' Soup consumed as a result of this price change? What does this result say about the income and substitution effects? Explain.

d. Use points A and B to draw a demand curve for Cup O' Soup. What is this type of good called?

8. Consider your decision about how many hours to work.

   a. Draw your budget constraint assuming that you pay no taxes on your income. On the same diagram, draw another budget constraint assuming that you pay 15 percent tax.

   b. Show how the tax might lead to more hours of work, fewer hours, or the same number of hours. Explain.

9. Sarah is awake for 100 hours per week. Using one diagram, show Sarah's budget constraints if she earns $6 per hour, $8 per hour, and $10 per hour. Now draw indifference curves such that Sarah's labor-supply curve is upward sloping when the wage is between $6 and $8 per hour, and backward sloping when the wage is between $8 and $10 per hour.

10. Draw the indifference curve for someone deciding how to allocate time between work and leisure. Suppose the wage increases. Is it possible that the person's consumption would fall? Is this plausible? Discuss. (Hint: Think about income and substitution effects.)

11. Daniel is a diligent student who loves getting As, but he also loves watching movies. Daniel is awake for 100 hours each week, and studying and watching movies are his only two activities. Daniel must study for 20 hours per week for each A he earns. Each movie is 2 hours long.

   a. Draw Daniel's budget constraint that shows the trade-off between the number of As he can receive and the number of movies he can watch. Assuming that he is happiest when he earns three As, draw an indifference curve that marks his optimal choice of studying and movie watching. How many movies does he watch each week?

   With a new semester beginning, Daniel decides to get his difficult requirements out of the way. Each class now requires him to study for 25 hours per week to get an A.

   b. Draw the new budget constraint on your graph. Show one possible outcome on your diagram. How will the relative strengths of the income and substitution effects

determine whether Daniel makes better or worse grades and whether he watches more or fewer movies?

12. Consider a couple's decision about how many children to have. Assume that over a lifetime a couple has 200,000 hours of time to either work or raise children. The wage is $10 per hour. Raising a child takes 20,000 hours of time.

   a. Draw the budget constraint showing the trade-off between lifetime consumption and number of children. (Ignore the fact that children come only in whole numbers!) Show indifference curves and an optimum choice.

   b. Suppose the wage increases to $12 per hour. Show how the budget constraint shifts. Using income and substitution effects, discuss the impact of the change on number of children and lifetime consumption.

   c. We observe that, as societies get richer and wages rise, people typically have fewer children. Is this fact consistent with this model? Explain.

13. Economist George Stigler once wrote that, according to consumer theory, "if consumers do not buy less of a commodity when their incomes rise, they will surely buy less when the price of the commodity rises." Explain this statement using the concepts of income and substitution effects.

14. The welfare system provides income to some needy families. Typically, the maximum payment goes to families that earn no income; then, as families begin to earn income, the welfare payment declines gradually and eventually disappears. Let's consider the possible effects of this program on a family's labor supply.

   a. Draw a budget constraint for a family assuming that the welfare system did not exist. On the same diagram, draw a budget constraint that reflects the existence of the welfare system.

   b. Adding indifference curves to your diagram, show how the welfare system could reduce the number of hours worked by the family. Explain, with reference to both the income and substitution effects.

   c. Using your diagram from part (b), show the effect of the welfare system on the well-being of the family.

15. Five consumers have the following marginal utility of apples and pears:

	Marginal Utility of Apples	Marginal Utility of Pears
Jerry	12	6
George	6	6
Elaine	6	3
Kramer	3	6
Newman	12	3

The price of an apple is $2, and the price of a pear is $1. Which, if any, of these consumers are optimizing over their choice of fruit? For those who are not, how should they change their spending?

For further information on topics in this chapter, additional problems, applications, examples, online quizzes, and more, please visit our website at www .cengage.com/economics/mankiw.

Frontiers of Microeconomics

22

Economics is a study of the choices that people make and the resulting interactions they have with one another. This study has many facets, as we have seen in the preceding chapters. Yet it would be a mistake to think that all the facets we have seen make up a finished jewel, perfect and unchanging. Like all scientists, economists are always on the lookout for new areas to study and new phenomena to explain. This final chapter on microeconomics offers an assortment of three topics at the discipline's frontier to see how economists are trying to expand their understanding of human behavior and society.

The first topic is the economics of *asymmetric information*. In many different situations, some people are better informed than others, and the imbalance in information affects the choices they make and how they deal with one another. Thinking about this asymmetry can shed light on many aspects of the world, from the market for used cars to the custom of gift giving.

The second topic we examine in this chapter is *political economy*. Throughout this book, we have seen many examples in which markets fail and government policy can potentially improve matters. But "potentially" is a necessary qualifier: Whether this potential is realized depends on how well our political institutions work. The field of political economy uses the tools of economics to understand the functioning of government.

The third topic in this chapter is *behavioral economics*. This field brings some of the insights from psychology into the study of economic issues. It offers a view of human behavior that is more subtle and complex than that found in conventional economic theory, a view that may be more realistic.

This chapter covers a lot of ground. To do so, it offers not a full helping of these three topics but, instead, a taste of each. One goal is to show a few of the directions economists are heading in their effort to expand knowledge of how the economy works. Another goal is to whet your appetite for more courses in economics.

Asymmetric Information

"I know something you don't know." This statement is a common taunt among children, but it also conveys a deep truth about how people sometimes interact with one another. Many times in life, one person knows more about what is going on than another. A difference in access to relevant knowledge is called an *information asymmetry*.

Examples abound. A worker knows more than his employer about how much effort he puts into his job. A seller of a used car knows more than the buyer about the car's condition. The first is an example of a *hidden action*, whereas the second is an example of a *hidden characteristic*. In each case, the uninformed party (the employer, the car buyer) would like to know the relevant information, but the informed party (the worker, the car seller) may have an incentive to conceal it.

Because asymmetric information is so prevalent, economists have devoted much effort in recent decades to studying its effects. And indeed, the 2001 Nobel Prize in Economics was awarded to three economists (George Akerlof, Michael Spence, and Joseph Stiglitz) for their pioneering work on this topic. Let's discuss some of the insights that this study has revealed.

Hidden Actions: Principals, Agents, and Moral Hazard

moral hazard
the tendency of a person who is imperfectly monitored to engage in dishonest or otherwise undesirable behavior

agent
a person who is performing an act for another person, called the principal

principal
a person for whom another person, called the agent, is performing some act

Moral hazard is a problem that arises when one person, called the **agent**, is performing some task on behalf of another person, called the **principal**. If the principal cannot perfectly monitor the agent's behavior, the agent tends to undertake less effort than the principal considers desirable. The phrase *moral hazard* refers to the risk, or "hazard," of inappropriate or otherwise "immoral" behavior by the agent. In such a situation, the principal tries various ways to encourage the agent to act more responsibly.

The employment relationship is the classic example. The employer is the principal, and the worker is the agent. The moral-hazard problem is the temptation of imperfectly monitored workers to shirk their responsibilities. Employers can respond to this problem in various ways:

- *Better monitoring.* Parents hiring nannies have been known to plant hidden video cameras in their homes to record the nanny's behavior when the parents are away. The aim is to catch irresponsible behavior.

- *High wages.* According to *efficiency-wage theories* (discussed in Chapter 19), some employers may choose to pay their workers a wage above the level that balances supply and demand in the labor market. A worker who earns an above-equilibrium wage is less likely to shirk because, if he is caught and fired, he might not be able to find another high-paying job.
- *Delayed payment.* Firms can delay part of a worker's compensation, so if the worker is caught shirking and is fired, he suffers a larger penalty. One example of delayed compensation is the year-end bonus. Similarly, a firm may choose to pay its workers more later in their lives. Thus, the wage increases that workers get as they age may reflect not just the benefits of experience but also a response to moral hazard.

FYI

Corporate Management

Much production in the modern economy takes place within corporations. Like other firms, corporations buy inputs in markets for the factors of production and sell their output in markets for goods and services. Also like other firms, they are guided in their decisions by the objective of profit maximization. But a large corporation has to deal with some issues that do not arise in, say, a small family-owned business.

What is distinctive about a corporation? From a legal standpoint, a corporation is an organization that is granted a charter recognizing it as a separate legal entity, with its own rights and responsibilities distinct from those of its owners and employees. From an economic standpoint, the most important feature of the corporate form of organization is the separation of ownership and control. One group of people, called the shareholders, own the corporation and share in its profits. Another group of people, called the managers, are employed by the corporation to make decisions about how to deploy the corporation's resources.

The separation of ownership and control creates a principal-agent problem. In this case, the shareholders are the principals, and the managers are the agents. The chief executive officer and other managers, who are in the best position to know the available business opportunities, are charged with the task of maximizing profits for the shareholders. But ensuring that they carry out this task is not always easy. The managers may have goals of their own, such as taking life easy, having a plush office and a private jet, throwing lavish parties, or presiding over a large business empire. The managers' goals may not always coincide with the goal of profit maximization.

The corporation's board of directors is responsible for hiring and firing the top management. The board monitors the managers' performance, and it designs their compensation packages. These packages often include incentives aimed at aligning the interests of shareholders with the interests of management. Managers might be given bonuses based on performance or options to buy the company's stock, which are more valuable if the company performs well.

Note, however, that the directors are themselves agents of the shareholders. The existence of a board overseeing management only shifts the principal-agent problem. The issue then becomes how to ensure that the board of directors fulfills its own legal obligation of acting in the best interest of the shareholders. If the directors become too friendly with management, they may not provide the required oversight.

The corporation's principal-agent problem became big news around 2005. The top managers of several prominent companies, such as Enron, Tyco, and WorldCom, were found to be engaging in activities that enriched themselves at the expense of their shareholders. In these cases, the actions were so extreme as to be criminal, and the corporate managers were not just fired but also sent to prison. Some shareholders sued directors for failing to monitor management sufficiently.

Fortunately, criminal activity by corporate managers is rare. But in some ways, it is only the tip of the iceberg. Whenever ownership and control are separated, as they are in most large corporations, there is an inevitable tension between the interests of shareholders and the interests of management.

Employers can use any combination of these various mechanisms to reduce the problem of moral hazard.

There are also many examples of moral hazard beyond the workplace. A homeowner with fire insurance will likely buy too few fire extinguishers because the homeowner bears the cost of the extinguisher while the insurance company receives much of the benefit. A family may live near a river with a high risk of flooding because the family enjoys the scenic views, while the government bears the cost of disaster relief after a flood. Many regulations are aimed at addressing the problem: An insurance company may require homeowners to buy fire extinguishers, and the government may prohibit building homes on land with high risk of flooding. But the insurance company does not have perfect information about how cautious homeowners are, and the government does not have perfect information about the risk that families undertake when choosing where to live. As a result, the problem of moral hazard persists.

Hidden Characteristics: Adverse Selection and the Lemons Problem

adverse selection

the tendency for the mix of unobserved attributes to become undesirable from the standpoint of an uninformed party

Adverse selection is a problem that arises in markets in which the seller knows more about the attributes of the good being sold than the buyer does. In such a situation, the buyer runs the risk of being sold a good of low quality. That is, the "selection" of goods sold may be "adverse" from the standpoint of the uninformed buyer.

The classic example of adverse selection is the market for used cars. Sellers of used cars know their vehicles' defects while buyers often do not. Because owners of the worst cars are more likely to sell them than are the owners of the best cars, buyers are apprehensive about getting a "lemon." As a result, many people avoid buying vehicles in the used car market. This lemons problem can explain why a used car only a few weeks old sells for thousands of dollars less than a new car of the same type. A buyer of the used car might surmise that the seller is getting rid of the car quickly because the seller knows something about it that the buyer does not.

A second example of adverse selection occurs in the labor market. According to another efficiency-wage theory, workers vary in their abilities, and they may know their own abilities better than do the firms that hire them. When a firm cuts the wage it pays, the more talented workers are more likely to quit, knowing they are better able to find other employment. Conversely, a firm may choose to pay an above-equilibrium wage to attract a better mix of workers.

A third example of adverse selection occurs in markets for insurance. For example, buyers of health insurance know more about their own health problems than do insurance companies. Because people with greater hidden health problems are more likely to buy health insurance than are other people, the price of health insurance reflects the costs of a sicker-than-average person. As a result, people in average health may observe the high price of insurance and decide not to buy it.

When markets suffer from adverse selection, the invisible hand does not necessarily work its magic. In the used car market, owners of good cars may choose to keep them rather than sell them at the low price that skeptical buyers are willing to pay. In the labor market, wages may be stuck above the level that balances supply and demand, resulting in unemployment. In insurance markets, buyers with low risk may choose to remain uninsured because the policies they are offered fail to reflect their true characteristics. Advocates of government-provided health insurance sometimes point to the problem of adverse selection as one reason not to trust the private market to provide the right amount of health insurance on its own.

Signaling to Convey Private Information

Although asymmetric information is sometimes a motivation for public policy, it also motivates some individual behavior that otherwise might be hard to explain. Markets respond to problems of asymmetric information in many ways. One of them is **signaling**, which refers to actions taken by an informed party for the sole purpose of credibly revealing his private information.

We have seen examples of signaling in previous chapters. As we saw in Chapter 16, firms may spend money on advertising to signal to potential customers that they have high-quality products. As we saw in Chapter 20, students may earn college degrees to signal to potential employers that they are high-ability individuals. Recall that the signaling theory of education contrasts with the human-capital theory, which asserts that education increases a person's productivity, rather than merely conveying information about innate talent. These two examples of signaling (advertising, education) may seem very different, but below the surface, they are much the same: In both cases, the informed party (the firm, the student) uses the signal to convince the uninformed party (the customer, the employer) that the informed party is offering something of high quality.

What does it take for an action to be an effective signal? Obviously, it must be costly. If a signal were free, everyone would use it, and it would convey no information. For the same reason, there is another requirement: The signal must be less costly, or more beneficial, to the person with the higher-quality product. Otherwise, everyone would have the same incentive to use the signal, and the signal would reveal nothing.

Consider again our two examples. In the advertising case, a firm with a good product reaps a larger benefit from advertising because customers who try the product once are more likely to become repeat customers. Thus, it is rational for the firm with a good product to pay for the cost of the signal (advertising), and it is rational for the customer to use the signal as a piece of information about the product's quality. In the education case, a talented person can get through school more easily than a less talented one. Thus, it is rational for the talented person to pay for the cost of the signal (education), and it is rational for the employer to use the signal as a piece of information about the person's talent.

The world is replete with instances of signaling. Magazine ads sometimes include the phrase "as seen on TV." Why does a firm selling a product in a magazine choose to stress this fact? One possibility is that the firm is trying to convey its willingness to pay for an expensive signal (a spot on television) in the hope that you will infer that its product is of high quality. For the same reason, graduates of elite schools are always sure to put that fact on their résumés.

signaling

an action taken by an informed party to reveal private information to an uninformed party

Gifts as Signals

A man is debating what to give his girlfriend for her birthday. "I know," he says to himself, "I'll give her cash. After all, I don't know her tastes as well as she does, and with cash, she can buy anything she wants." But when he hands her

"Now we'll see how much he loves me."

© TONY METAXAS/ASIA IMAGES/GETTY IMAGES

the money, she is offended. Convinced he doesn't really love her, she breaks off the relationship.

What's the economics behind this story?

In some ways, gift giving is a strange custom. As the man in our story suggests, people typically know their own preferences better than others do, so we might expect everyone to prefer cash to in-kind transfers. If your employer substituted merchandise of his choosing for your paycheck, you would likely object to this means of payment. But your reaction is very different when someone who (you hope) loves you does the same thing.

One interpretation of gift giving is that it reflects asymmetric information and signaling. The man in our story has private information that the girlfriend would like to know: Does he really love her? Choosing a good gift for her is a signal of his love. Certainly, the act of picking out a gift, rather than giving cash, has the right characteristics to be a signal. It is costly (it takes time), and its cost depends on private information (how much he loves her). If he really loves her, choosing a good gift is easy because he is thinking about her all the time. If he doesn't love her, finding the right gift is more difficult. Thus, giving a gift that suits the girlfriend is one way for him to convey the private information of his love for her. Giving cash shows that he isn't even bothering to try.

The signaling theory of gift giving is consistent with another observation: People care most about the custom when the strength of affection is most in question. Thus, giving cash to a girlfriend or boyfriend is usually a bad move. But when college students receive a check from their parents, they are less often offended. The parents' love is less likely to be in doubt, so the recipient probably won't interpret the cash gift as a signal of lack of affection. ∎

Screening to Uncover Private Information

When an informed party takes actions to reveal private information, the phenomenon is called signaling. When an uninformed party takes actions to induce the informed party to reveal private information, the phenomenon is called **screening**.

screening

an action taken by an uninformed party to induce an informed party to reveal information

Some screening is common sense. A person buying a used car may ask that it be checked by an auto mechanic before the sale. A seller who refuses this request reveals his private information that the car is a lemon. The buyer may decide to offer a lower price or to look for another car.

Other examples of screening are more subtle. For example, consider a firm that sells car insurance. The firm would like to charge a low premium to safe drivers and a high premium to risky drivers. But how can it tell them apart? Drivers know whether they are safe or risky, but the risky ones won't admit it. A driver's history is one piece of information (which insurance companies in fact use), but because of the intrinsic randomness of car accidents, history is an imperfect indicator of future risks.

The insurance company might be able to sort out the two kinds of drivers by offering different insurance policies that would induce them to separate themselves. One policy would have a high premium and cover the full cost of any accidents that occur. Another policy would have low premiums but would have, say, a $1,000 deductible. (That is, the driver would be responsible for the first $1,000 of damage, and the insurance company would cover the remaining risk.) Notice that the deductible is more of a burden for risky drivers because they are more likely to have an accident. Thus, with a large enough deductible, the low-premium policy with a deductible would attract the safe drivers, while the high-premium policy without a deductible would attract the risky drivers. Faced with these two policies, the two kinds of drivers would reveal their private information by choosing different insurance policies.

Asymmetric Information and Public Policy

We have examined two kinds of asymmetric information: moral hazard and adverse selection. And we have seen how individuals may respond to the problem with signaling or screening. Now let's consider what the study of asymmetric information suggests about the proper scope of public policy.

The tension between market success and market failure is central in microeconomics. We learned in Chapter 7 that the equilibrium of supply and demand is efficient in the sense that it maximizes the total surplus that society can obtain in a market. Adam Smith's invisible hand seemed to reign supreme. This conclusion was then tempered with the study of externalities (Chapter 10), public goods (Chapter 11), imperfect competition (Chapters 15 through 17), and poverty (Chapter 20). These examples of market failure showed that government can sometimes improve market outcomes.

The study of asymmetric information gives us a new reason to be wary of markets. When some people know more than others, the market may fail to put resources to their best use. People with high-quality used cars may have trouble selling them because buyers will be afraid of getting a lemon. People with few health problems may have trouble getting low-cost health insurance because insurance companies lump them together with those who have significant (but hidden) health problems.

Asymmetric information may call for government action in some cases, but three facts complicate the issue. First, as we have seen, the private market can sometimes deal with information asymmetries on its own using a combination of signaling and screening. Second, the government rarely has more information than the private parties. Even if the market's allocation of resources is not first-best, it may be second-best. That is, when there are information asymmetries, policymakers may find it hard to improve upon the market's admittedly imperfect outcome. Third, the government is itself an imperfect institution—a topic we take up in the next section.

QUICK QUIZ *A person who buys a life insurance policy pays a certain amount per year and receives for his family a much larger payment in the event of his death. Would you expect buyers of life insurance to have higher or lower death rates than the average person? How might this be an example of moral hazard? Of adverse selection? How might a life insurance company deal with these problems?*

Political Economy

As we have seen, markets left on their own do not always reach a desirable allocation of resources. When we judge the market's outcome to be either inefficient or inequitable, there may be a role for the government to step in and improve the situation. Yet before we embrace an activist government, we need to consider one more fact: The government is also an imperfect institution. The field of **political economy** (sometimes called the field of *public choice*) applies the methods of economics to study how government works.

political economy
the study of government using the analytic methods of economics

The Condorcet Voting Paradox

Most advanced societies rely on democratic principles to set government policy. When a city is deciding between two locations to build a new park, for example, we have a simple way to choose: The majority gets its way. Yet for most policy issues, the number of possible outcomes far exceeds two. A new park, for instance, could be placed in many possible locations. In this case, as the 18th-century French political theorist Marquis de Condorcet famously noted, democracy might run into some problems trying to choose the best outcome.

For example, suppose there are three possible outcomes, labeled A, B, and C, and there are three voter types with the preferences shown in Table 1. The mayor of our town wants to aggregate these individual preferences into preferences for society as a whole. How should she do it?

At first, she might try some pairwise votes. If she asks voters to choose first between B and C, voter types 1 and 2 will vote for B, giving B the majority. If she then asks voters to choose between A and B, voter types 1 and 3 will vote for A, giving A the majority. Observing that A beats B, and B beats C, the mayor might conclude that A is the voters' clear choice.

But wait: Suppose the mayor then asks voters to choose between A and C. In this case, voter types 2 and 3 vote for C, giving C the majority. That is, under pairwise majority voting, A beats B, B beats C, and C beats A. Normally, we expect preferences to exhibit a property called *transitivity*: If A is preferred to B, and B is preferred to C, then we would expect A to be preferred to C. The **Condorcet paradox** is that democratic outcomes do not always obey this property. Pairwise voting might produce transitive preferences for society in some cases, but as our example in the table shows, it cannot be counted on to do so.

One implication of the Condorcet paradox is that the order in which things are voted on can affect the result. If the mayor suggests choosing first between A and B and then comparing the winner to C, the town ends up choosing C. But if the voters choose first between B and C and then compare the winner to A, the town ends up with A. And if the voters choose first between A and C and then compare the winner to B, the town ends up with B.

The Condorcet paradox teaches two lessons. The narrow lesson is that when there are more than two options, setting the agenda (that is, deciding the order which items are voted on) can have a powerful influence over the outcome of a democratic election. The broad lesson is that majority voting by itself does not tell us what outcome a society really wants.

Condorcet paradox
the failure of majority rule to produce transitive preferences for society

Table 1

The Condorcet Paradox
If voters have these preferences over outcomes A, B, and C,
then in pairwise majority voting,
A beats B, B beats C, and
C beats A.

	Voter Type		
	Type 1	Type 2	Type 3
Percent of Electorate	35	45	20
First choice	A	B	C
Second choice	B	C	A
Third choice	C	A	B

Arrow's Impossibility Theorem

Since political theorists first noticed Condorcet's paradox, they have spent much energy studying existing voting systems and proposing new ones. For example, as an alternative to pairwise majority voting, the mayor of our town could ask each voter to rank the possible outcomes. For each voter, we could give 1 point for last place, 2 points for second to last, 3 points for third to last, and so on. The outcome that receives the most total points wins. With the preferences in Table 1, outcome B is the winner. (You can do the arithmetic yourself.) This voting method is called a *Borda count* for the 18th-century French mathematician and political theorist who devised it. It is often used in polls that rank sports teams.

Is there a perfect voting system? Economist Kenneth Arrow took up this question in his 1951 book *Social Choice and Individual Values*. Arrow started by defining what a perfect voting system would be. He assumes that individuals in society have preferences over the various possible outcomes: A, B, C, and so on. He then assumes that society wants a voting system to choose among these outcomes that satisfies several properties:

- *Unanimity:* If everyone prefers A to B, then A should beat B.
- *Transitivity:* If A beats B, and B beats C, then A should beat C.
- *Independence of irrelevant alternatives:* The ranking between any two outcomes A and B should not depend on whether some third outcome C is also available.
- *No dictators:* There is no person who always gets his way, regardless of everyone else's preferences.

These all seem like desirable properties of a voting system. Yet Arrow proved, mathematically and incontrovertibly, that *no voting system can satisfy all these properties*. This amazing result is called **Arrow's impossibility theorem**.

The mathematics needed to prove Arrow's theorem is beyond the scope of this book, but we can get some sense of why the theorem is true from a couple of examples. We have already seen the problem with the method of majority rule. The Condorcet paradox shows that majority rule fails to produce a ranking of outcomes that always satisfies transitivity.

As another example, the Borda count fails to satisfy the independence of irrelevant alternatives. Recall that, using the preferences in Table 1, outcome B wins with a Borda count. But suppose that suddenly C disappears as an alternative. If the Borda count method is applied only to outcomes A and B, then A wins. (Once again, you can do the arithmetic on your own.) Thus, eliminating alternative C changes the ranking between A and B. This change occurs because the result of the Borda count depends on the number of points that A and B receive, and the number of points depends on whether the irrelevant alternative, C, is also available.

Arrow's impossibility theorem is a deep and disturbing result. It doesn't say that we should abandon democracy as a form of government. But it does say that, no matter what voting system society adopts for aggregating the preferences of its members, in some way it will be flawed as a mechanism for social choice.

Arrow's impossibility theorem

a mathematical result showing that, under certain assumed conditions, there is no scheme for aggregating individual preferences into a valid set of social preferences

in the news

> ### Arrow's Problem in Practice

Voting systems matter not only for choosing political leaders but also for awarding prizes.

And the Oscar Goes to ... Not Its Voting System

By Carl Bialik

Academy Award nominees and winners are selected using two different voting systems that are, according to some political mathematicians, the worst way to convert voters' preferences into an election outcome.

The nominees are selected using a system called instant runoff, which has been adopted in some municipal and state elections. Out of last year's 281 eligible films, each voter selects five nominees in order of preference for, say, best picture. All movies without any first-place votes are eliminated. The votes for those films with the least first-place votes are re-assigned until five nominees have enough.

One problem with that system is a kind of squeaky-wheel phenomenon: A movie that is second place on every ballot will lose out to one that ranks first on only 20% of ballots but is hated by everyone else. Then, in another upside-down outcome, a movie can win for best picture even if 79% of voters hated it so long as they split their votes evenly among the losing films. This isn't as unfamiliar as it sounds: Some people think Al Gore would have won the Electoral

College in 2000 if Ralph Nader hadn't diverted more votes from him than he took from former President George W. Bush.

"It's crazy," says Michel Balinski, professor of research at École Polytechnique in Palaiseau, France. The nomination system's properties are "truly perverse and antithetical to the idea of democracy," says Steven Brams, professor of politics at New York University. He thinks the final vote for the Oscar winner may be even worse than the selection of nominees.

The big problem: If voting systems themselves were put to a vote, prominent scholars would each produce a different ballot, then disagree about which system should be used to select the winner. So it's no surprise that advocates of alternate voting systems, which range from simple yes/no approval ratings to assigning numerical scores to each candidate, have had little more luck reforming political elections than they have with entertainment awards.

Consider two systems that, on the surface, seem similar. Prof. Balinski and mathematician Rida Laraki have devised a system they call majority judgment that requires voters to rank each candidate on a scale from 1 to 6. The votes are lined up in order, and each candidate is assigned the middle, or median, score. The highest median score wins. Another system, range voting, isn't

that different: The candidate with the highest average, or mean, score wins.

Yet the second system's leading advocate, Temple University mathematician Warren D. Smith, has devoted a Web page to the Balinksi-Laraki system's "numerous disadvantages."

Brace yourselves for "Ishtar" defeating "The Godfather." Suppose 49 voters award "The Godfather" six points and "Ishtar" only four. One voter grants the desert debacle four points and the mafia masterpiece three, and the remaining 49 award "The Godfather" three points and "Ishtar" only one point. "Ishtar" actually wins with a median score of four points compared to "The Godfather's" three points. Prof. Balinski, in turn, calls range voting a "ridiculous method," because it can be manipulated by strategic voters.

Despite the flaws in Oscars voting, the system remains as it has since 1936. Every 15 years or so, the Academy re-examines its voting and has decided to stick with it, says the Academy of Motion Picture Arts and Sciences' executive director, Bruce Davis. "It is a very effective method of reflecting the will of the entire electorate," Mr. Davis says.

But many voting theorists aren't so keen on the system. It's called instant runoff because it is used in political elections in lieu of a two-stage vote in which top candidates compete again if none receives a majority of the vote. Among the potential problems, showing up to vote for your favorite candidate may create a worse outcome than not showing up at all. For example, your vote could change the order in which candidates are eliminated, and the next-in-line candidate on the ballot for the newly eliminated film may be a film you loathe.

To choose Oscar winners, voters simply choose their favorite from the nominees, and the contender with the most votes wins. That could favor a film that has a devoted faction of fans, and sink films with overlapping followings who split their vote. Even most critics of instant runoff say it beats this plurality system that led to the Gore-Nader-Bush result. In the film realm, Prof. Brams of NYU blames the current system for the best-picture victory of "Rocky" over films such as "Network" and "Taxi Driver"

that he speculates would have won head to head.

How this works out in reality is hard to know, because the Academy doesn't release any details about the balloting, even after the telecast, in part to avoid shaming fifth-place films. Mr. Davis says even he never learns the numbers from his accountants: "Are there years when I'm curious as to what the order of finish was? Absolutely. But I recognize it as a vulgar curiosity in myself."

Such secrecy frustrates voting theorists who are anxious for experimental data about voter behavior that may help them choose from among different voting systems. Without such evidence, they are left to devise their own studies, to dream up examples that sink rival systems or to create computer simulations to study how easily different systems can be manipulated.

Sports fans cry manipulation when votes don't go as they'd hoped. Many sports awards and rankings are derived from what is known as a Borda count, which asks voters to rank candidates and then assigns points on a sliding scale, with the most for first-place votes and the least for last-place ones.

Critics of these systems fear that strategic voters will assign their top choice the highest possible score, and everyone else zero, thereby seizing more power than voters who approach the system earnestly; or, in the case of rankings, bury or omit a preferred candidate's top rival. Boston Red Sox fans will tell you to this day that such strategic voting by a New York beat writer cost Pedro Martinez the American League Most Valuable Player award a decade ago.

Says Prof. Balinksi, "Not everyone will do it, but enough will do it to manipulate the results."

Choosing a Winner | Conducting and deciding a vote using an instant runoff

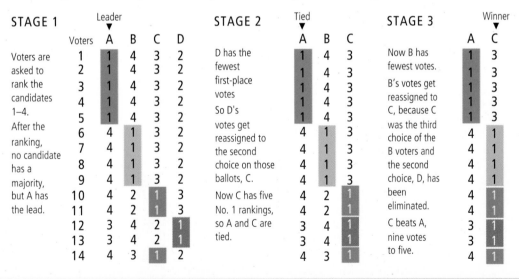

Source: *The Wall Street Journal*, February 6, 2009.

The Median Voter Is King

Despite Arrow's theorem, voting is how most societies choose their leaders and public policies, often by majority rule. The next step in studying government is to examine how governments run by majority rule work. That is, in a democratic society, who determines what policy is chosen? In some cases, the theory of democratic government yields a surprisingly simple answer.

Let's consider an example. Imagine that society is deciding how much money to spend on some public good, such as the army or the national parks. Each voter has his own most preferred budget, and he always prefers outcomes closer to his most preferred value to outcomes farther away. Thus, we can line up voters from those who prefer the smallest budget to those who prefer the largest. Figure 1 is an example. Here there are 100 voters, and the budget size varies from zero to $20 billion. Given these preferences, what outcome would you expect democracy to produce?

median voter theorem

a mathematical result showing that if voters are choosing a point along a line and each voter wants the point closest to his most preferred point, then majority rule will pick the most preferred point of the median voter

According to a famous result called the **median voter theorem**, majority rule will produce the outcome most preferred by the median voter. The *median voter* is the voter exactly in the middle of the distribution. In this example, if you take the line of voters ordered by their preferred budgets and count 50 voters from either end of the line, you will find that the median voter wants a budget of $10 billion. By contrast, the average preferred outcome (calculated by adding the preferred outcomes and dividing by the number of voters) is $9 billion, and the modal outcome (the one preferred by the greatest number of voters) is $15 billion.

The median voter rules the day because his preferred outcome beats any other proposal in a two-way race. In our example, more than half the voters want $10 billion or more, and more than half want $10 billion or less. If someone proposes, say, $8 billion instead of $10 billion, everyone who prefers $10 billion or more will vote with the median voter. Similarly, if someone proposes $12 billion instead of $10 billion, everyone who wants $10 billion or less will vote with the median voter. In either case, the median voter has more than half the voters on his side.

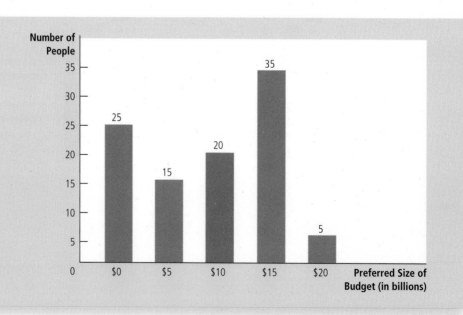

Figure **1**

The Median Voter Theorem: An Example
This bar chart shows how 100 voters' most preferred budgets are distributed over five options, ranging from zero to $20 billion. If society makes its choice by majority rule, the median voter (who here prefers $10 billion) determines the outcome.

What about the Condorcet voting paradox? It turns out that when the voters are picking a point along a line and each voter aims for his own most preferred point, the Condorcet paradox cannot arise. The median voter's most preferred outcome beats all challengers.

One implication of the median voter theorem is that if two political parties are each trying to maximize their chance of election, they will both move their positions toward the median voter. Suppose, for example, that the Democratic Party advocates a budget of $15 billion, while the Republican Party advocates a budget of $10 billion. The Democratic position is more popular in the sense that $15 billion has more proponents than any other single choice. Nonetheless, the Republicans get more than 50 percent of the vote: They will attract the 20 voters who want $10 billion, the 15 voters who want $5 billion, and the 25 voters who want zero. If the Democrats want to win, they will move their platform toward the median voter. Thus, this theory can explain why the parties in a two-party system are similar to each other: They are both moving toward the median voter.

Another implication of the median voter theorem is that minority views are not given much weight. Imagine that 40 percent of the population want a lot of money spent on the national parks, and 60 percent want nothing spent. In this case, the median voter's preference is zero, regardless of the intensity of the minority's view. Such is the logic of democracy. Rather than reaching a compromise that takes into account everyone's preferences, majority rule looks only to the person in the exact middle of the distribution.

Politicians Are People Too

When economists study consumer behavior, they assume that consumers buy the bundle of goods and services that gives them the greatest level of satisfaction. When economists study firm behavior, they assume that firms produce the quantity of goods and services that yields the greatest level of profits. What should they assume when they study people involved in the practice of politics?

Politicians also have objectives. It would be nice to assume that political leaders are always looking out for the well-being of society as a whole, that they are aiming for an optimal combination of efficiency and equality. Nice, perhaps, but not realistic. Self-interest is as powerful a motive for political actors as it is for consumers and firm owners. Some politicians, motivated by a desire for reelection, are willing to sacrifice the national interest to solidify their base of voters. Others are motivated by simple greed. If you have any doubt, you should look at the world's poor nations, where corruption among government officials is a common impediment to economic development.

This book is not the place to develop a theory of political behavior. But when thinking about economic policy, remember that this policy is made not by a benevolent king but by real people with their own all-too-human desires. Sometimes they are motivated to further the national interest, but sometimes they are motivated by their own political and financial ambitions. We shouldn't be surprised when economic policy fails to resemble the ideals derived in economics textbooks.

"Isn't that the real genius of democracy? ... The VOTERS are ultimately to blame."

QUICK QUIZ   *A public school district is voting on the school budget and the resulting student-teacher ratio. A poll finds that 20 percent of the voters want a ratio of 9:1, 25 percent want a ratio of 10:1, 15 percent want a ratio of 11:1, and 40 percent want a ratio of 12:1. What outcome would you expect the district to end up with? Explain.*

Behavioral Economics

Economics is a study of human behavior, but it is not the only field that can make that claim. The social science of psychology also sheds light on the choices that people make in their lives. The fields of economics and psychology usually proceed independently, in part because they address a different range of questions. But recently, a field called **behavioral economics** has emerged in which economists are making use of basic psychological insights. Let's consider some of these insights here.

behavioral economics
the subfield of economics that integrates the insights of psychology

People Aren't Always Rational

Economic theory is populated by a particular species of organism, sometimes called *Homo economicus*. Members of this species are always rational. As firm managers, they maximize profits. As consumers, they maximize utility (or equivalently, pick the point on the highest indifference curve). Given the constraints they face, they rationally weigh all the costs and benefits and always choose the best possible course of action.

Real people, however, are *Homo sapiens*. Although in many ways they resemble the rational, calculating people assumed in economic theory, they are far more complex. They can be forgetful, impulsive, confused, emotional, and shortsighted. These imperfections of human reasoning are the bread and butter of psychologists, but until recently, economists have neglected them.

Herbert Simon, one of the first social scientists to work at the boundary of economics and psychology, suggested that humans should be viewed not as rational maximizers but as *satisficers*. Rather than always choosing the best course of action, they make decisions that are merely good enough. Similarly, other economists have suggested that humans are only "near rational" or that they exhibit "bounded rationality."

Studies of human decision making have tried to detect systematic mistakes that people make. Here are a few of the findings:

- *People are overconfident.* Imagine that you were asked some numerical questions, such as the number of African countries in the United Nations, the height of the tallest mountain in North America, and so on. Instead of being asked for a single estimate, however, you were asked to give a 90 percent confidence interval—a range such that you were 90 percent confident the true number falls within it. When psychologists run experiments like this, they find that most people give ranges that are too small: The true number falls within their intervals far less than 90 percent of the time. That is, most people are too sure of their own abilities.
- *People give too much weight to a small number of vivid observations.* Imagine that you are thinking about buying a car of brand X. To learn about its reliability, you read *Consumer Reports*, which has surveyed 1,000 owners of car X. Then you run into a friend who owns car X, and she tells you that her car is a lemon. How do you treat your friend's observation? If you think rationally, you will realize that she has only increased your sample size from 1,000 to 1,001, which does not provide much new information. But because your friend's story is so vivid, you may be tempted to give it more weight in your decision making than you should.

- *People are reluctant to change their minds.* People tend to interpret evidence to confirm beliefs they already hold. In one study, subjects were asked to read and evaluate a research report on whether capital punishment deters crime. After reading the report, those who initially favored the death penalty said they were surer in their view, and those who initially opposed the death penalty also said they were surer in their view. The two groups interpreted the same evidence in exactly opposite ways.

Think about decisions you have made in your own life. Do you exhibit some of these traits?

A hotly debated issue is whether deviations from rationality are important for understanding economic phenomena. An intriguing example arises in the study of 401(k) plans, the tax-advantaged retirement savings accounts that some firms offer their workers. In some firms, workers can choose to participate in the plan by filling out a simple form. In other firms, workers are automatically enrolled and can opt out of the plan by filling out a simple form. It turns out many more workers participate in the second case than in the first. If workers were perfectly rational maximizers, they would choose the optimal amount of retirement saving, regardless of the default offered by their employer. In fact, workers' behavior appears to exhibit substantial inertia. Understanding their behavior seems easier once we abandon the model of rational man.

Why, you might ask, is economics built on the rationality assumption when psychology and common sense cast doubt on it? One answer is that the assumption, even if not exactly true, may be true enough that it yields reasonably accurate models of behavior. For example, when we studied the differences between competitive and monopoly firms, the assumption that firms rationally maximize profit yielded many important and valid insights. Incorporating complex psychological deviations from rationality into the story might have added realism, but it also would have muddied the waters and made those insights harder to find. Recall from Chapter 2 that economic models are not meant to replicate reality but are supposed to show the essence of the problem at hand as an aid to understanding.

Another reason economists so often assume rationality may be that economists are themselves not rational maximizers. Like most people, they are overconfident, and they are reluctant to change their minds. Their choice among alternative theories of human behavior may exhibit excessive inertia. Moreover, economists may be content with a theory that is not perfect but is good enough. The model of rational man may be the theory of choice for a satisficing social scientist.

People Care about Fairness

Another insight about human behavior is best illustrated with an experiment called the *ultimatum game.* The game works like this: Two volunteers (who are otherwise strangers to each other) are told that they are going to play a game and could win a total of $100. Before they play, they learn the rules. The game begins with a coin toss, which is used to assign the volunteers to the roles of player A and player B. Player A's job is to propose a division of the $100 prize between himself and the other player. After player A makes his proposal, player B decides whether to accept or reject it. If he accepts it, both players are paid according to the proposal. If player B rejects the proposal, both players walk away with nothing. In either case, the game then ends.

Before proceeding, stop and think about what you would do in this situation. If you were player A, what division of the $100 would you propose? If you were player B, what proposals would you accept?

Conventional economic theory assumes in this situation that people are rational wealth-maximizers. This assumption leads to a simple prediction: Player A should propose that he gets $99 and player B gets $1, and player B should accept the proposal. After all, once the proposal is made, player B is better off accepting it as long as he gets something out of it. Moreover, because player A knows that accepting the proposal is in player B's interest, player A has no reason to offer him more than $1. In the language of game theory (discussed in Chapter 17), the 99-1 split is the Nash equilibrium.

Yet when experimental economists ask real people to play the ultimatum game, the results differ from this prediction. People in player B's role usually reject

in the news

Sin Taxes

If people are inconsistent over time, as behavioral economists contend, perhaps tax policy should try to address the problem.

Can a Soda Tax Protect Us from Ourselves?

BY N. GREGORY MANKIW

As governments large and small face sizable budget shortfalls, policy makers are looking for ways to raise tax revenue that will do the least harm and, perhaps, even a bit of good. One idea keeps popping up: a tax on soda and other sugary drinks.

The city council in Washington recently passed such a tax. Gov. David A. Paterson has proposed one for New York. And a national soda tax was even briefly considered by the Senate Finance Committee as a way to help pay for President Obama's health care overhaul.

But is a soda tax a good idea?

Economists have often advocated taxing consumption rather than income, on the grounds that consumption taxes do less to discourage saving, investment, and economic growth. Hence the case for broad-based consumption taxes, like a value-added tax. The main issue for the soda tax, however, is whether certain forms of consumption should be singled out for particularly high levels of taxation.

One argument for specific taxes is that consuming certain products has an adverse impact on bystanders. Economists call these effects negative externalities.

Taxes on gasoline can be justified along these lines. Whenever you go out for a drive, you are to some degree committing an antisocial act. You make the roads more congested, increasing the commuting time of your neighbors. You increase the likelihood that other drivers will end up in

accidents. And the gasoline you burn adds to pollution, including the greenhouse gases thought to cause global climate change.

Many economists advocate gasoline taxes so that drivers will internalize these negative externalities. That is, by raising the price of gasoline, a tax would induce consumers to take into account the harm they cause after making their purchases. One prominent study added up all the externalities associated with driving and concluded that the optimal gasoline tax is over $2 a gallon, about five times the current level (combining the federal and a typical state's levies) and about the tax rate in many European countries.

Applying that logic to other consumer goods, however, is not as straightforward. Consider cigarettes. They are among the most heavily taxed products in the economy, as governments have tried to discourage

proposals that give them only $1 or a similarly small amount. Anticipating this, people in the role of player A usually propose giving player B much more than $1. Some people will offer a 50-50 split, but it is more common for player A to propose giving player B an amount such as $30 or $40, keeping the larger share for himself. In this case, player B usually accepts the proposal.

What's going on here? The natural interpretation is that people are driven in part by some innate sense of fairness. A 99-1 split seems so wildly unfair to many people that they reject it, even to their own detriment. By contrast, a 70-30 split is still unfair, but it is not so unfair that it induces people to abandon their normal self-interest.

Throughout our study of household and firm behavior, the innate sense of fairness has not played any role. But the results of the ultimatum game suggest that

people from smoking. Yet the case for such a policy cannot rely on a conventional externality argument.

When a person sits at home and smokes two packs a day, the main adverse impact is on his or her own health. And even if second-hand smoke is a concern, that problem is most naturally addressed within the household, not at the state or federal level.

Sometimes, advocates of "sin" taxes contend that consumers of certain products impose adverse budgetary externalities on the rest of us—that if the consumption induces, say, smoking- or obesity-related illness, it raises the cost of health care, which we all pay for through higher taxes or insurance premiums.

Yet this argument also has a flip side: If consumers of these products die earlier, they will also collect less in pension payments, including Social Security. Economists have run the numbers for smoking and often find that these savings may more than offset the budgetary costs. In other words, there is little net financial impact of smokers on the rest of us.

It may seem grisly to consider the budgetary savings of an early death as a "benefit" to society. But when analyzing policy, economists are nothing if not cold-blooded. If one uses budgetary costs to justify taxing

particular consumption goods, the accounting needs to be honest and complete.

There is, however, an altogether different argument for these taxes: that when someone consumes such goods, he does impose a negative externality—on the future version of himself. In other words, the person today enjoys the consumption, but the person tomorrow and every day after pays the price of increased risk of illness.

This raises an intriguing question: To what extent should we view the future versions of ourselves as different people from ourselves today?

To be sure, most parents have no trouble restricting a child's decisions on the grounds that doing so is in the young person's best interest. Few teenagers are farsighted enough to fully incorporate the interests of

their future selves when making decisions. As parents, we hope that someday our grown-up children will be grateful for our current restrictions on their behavior.

But people do not suddenly mature at the age of 18, when society deems us "adults." There is always an adolescent lurking inside us, feeling the pull of instant gratification and too easily ignoring the long-run effects of our decisions. Taxes on items with short-run benefits and long-run costs tell our current selves to take into account the welfare of our future selves.

If this is indeed the best argument for "sin" taxes, as I believe it is, we are led to vexing questions of political philosophy: To what extent should we use the power of the state to protect us from ourselves? If we go down that route, where do we stop?

Taxing soda may encourage better nutrition and benefit our future selves. But so could taxing candy, ice cream, and fried foods. Subsidizing broccoli, gym memberships, and dental floss comes next. Taxing mindless television shows and subsidizing serious literature cannot be far behind.

Even as adults, we sometimes wish for parents to be looking over our shoulders and guiding us to the right decisions. The question is, do you trust the government enough to appoint it your guardian?

© DAVID G. KLEIN

Source: *New York Times,* June 6, 2010.

perhaps it should. For example, in Chapters 18 and 19, we discussed how wages were determined by labor supply and labor demand. Some economists have suggested that the perceived fairness of what a firm pays its workers should also enter the picture. Thus, when a firm has an especially profitable year, workers (like player B) may expect to be paid a fair share of the prize, even if the standard equilibrium does not dictate it. The firm (like player A) might well decide to give workers more than the equilibrium wage for fear that the workers might otherwise try to punish the firm with reduced effort, strikes, or even vandalism.

People Are Inconsistent over Time

Imagine some dreary task, such as doing your laundry, shoveling snow off your driveway, or filling out your income tax forms. Now consider the following questions:

1. Would you prefer (A) to spend 50 minutes doing the task right now or (B) to spend 60 minutes doing the task tomorrow?
2. Would you prefer (A) to spend 50 minutes doing the task in 90 days or (B) to spend 60 minutes doing the task in 91 days?

When asked questions like these, many people choose B to question 1 and A to question 2. When looking ahead to the future (as in question 2), they minimize the amount of time spent on the dreary task. But faced with the prospect of doing the task immediately (as in question 1), they choose to put it off.

In some ways, this behavior is not surprising: Everyone procrastinates from time to time. But from the standpoint of the theory of rational man, it is puzzling. Suppose that, in response to question 2, a person chooses to spend 50 minutes in 90 days. Then, when the 90th day arrives, we allow him to change his mind. In effect, he then faces question 1, so he opts for doing the task the next day. But why should the mere passage of time affect the choices he makes?

Many times in life, people make plans for themselves, but then they fail to follow through. A smoker promises himself that he will quit, but within a few hours of smoking his last cigarette, he craves another and breaks his promise. A person trying to lose weight promises that he will stop eating dessert, but when the waiter brings the dessert cart, the promise is forgotten. In both cases, the desire for instant gratification induces the decision maker to abandon his past plans.

Some economists believe that the consumption-saving decision is an important instance in which people exhibit this inconsistency over time. For many people, spending provides a type of instant gratification. Saving, like passing up the cigarette or the dessert, requires a sacrifice in the present for a reward in the distant future. And just as many smokers wish they could quit and many overweight individuals wish they ate less, many consumers wish they saved more of their income. According to one survey, 76 percent of Americans said they were not saving enough for retirement.

An implication of this inconsistency over time is that people should try to find ways to commit their future selves to following through on their plans. A smoker trying to quit may throw away his cigarettes, and a person on a diet may put a lock on the refrigerator. What can a person who saves too little do? He should find some way to lock up his money before he spends it. Some retirement accounts, such as 401(k) plans, do exactly that. A worker can agree to have some money taken out of his paycheck before he ever sees it. The money is deposited in an account that can be used before retirement only with a penalty. Perhaps that is one reason these retirement accounts are so popular: They protect people from their own desires for instant gratification.

QUICK QUIZ   *Describe at least three ways in which human decision making differs from that of the rational individual of conventional economic theory.*

Conclusion

This chapter has examined the frontier of microeconomics. You may have noticed that we have sketched out ideas rather than fully developing them. This is no accident. One reason is that you might study these topics in more detail in advanced courses. Another reason is that these topics remain active areas of research and, therefore, are still being fleshed out.

To see how these topics fit into the broader picture, recall the *Ten Principles of Economics* from Chapter 1. One principle states that markets are usually a good way to organize economic activity. Another principle states that governments can sometimes improve market outcomes. As you study economics, you can more fully appreciate the truth of these principles as well as the caveats that go with them. The study of asymmetric information should make you more wary of market outcomes. The study of political economy should make you more wary of government solutions. And the study of behavioral economics should make you wary of any institution that relies on human decision making, including both the market and the government.

If there is a unifying theme to these topics, it is that life is messy. Information is imperfect, government is imperfect, and people are imperfect. Of course, you knew this long before you started studying economics, but economists need to understand these imperfections as precisely as they can if they are to explain, and perhaps even improve, the world around them.

SUMMARY

- In many economic transactions, information is asymmetric. When there are hidden actions, principals may be concerned that agents suffer from the problem of moral hazard. When there are hidden characteristics, buyers may be concerned about the problem of adverse selection among the sellers. Private markets sometimes deal with asymmetric information with signaling and screening.

- Although government policy can sometimes improve market outcomes, governments are themselves imperfect institutions. The Condorcet paradox shows that majority rule fails to produce transitive preferences for society, and Arrow's impossibility theorem shows that no

voting system will be perfect. In many situations, democratic institutions will produce the outcome desired by the median voter, regardless of the preferences of the rest of the electorate. Moreover, the individuals who set government policy may be motivated by self-interest rather than the national interest.

- The study of psychology and economics reveals that human decision making is more complex than is assumed in conventional economic theory. People are not always rational, they care about the fairness of economic outcomes (even to their own detriment), and they can be inconsistent over time.

KEY CONCEPTS

moral hazard, *p. 468*
agent, *p. 468*
principal, *p. 468*
adverse selection, *p. 470*

signaling, *p. 471*
screening, *p. 472*
political economy, *p. 473*
Condorcet paradox, *p. 474*

Arrow's impossibility
  theorem, *p. 475*
median voter theorem, *p. 478*
behavioral economics, *p. 480*

QUESTIONS FOR REVIEW

1. What is moral hazard? List three things an employer might do to reduce the severity of this problem.
2. What is adverse selection? Give an example of a market in which adverse selection might be a problem.
3. Define *signaling* and *screening* and give an example of each.
4. What unusual property of voting did Condorcet notice?
5. Explain why majority rule respects the preferences of the median voter rather than the average voter.
6. Describe the ultimatum game. What outcome from this game would conventional economic theory predict? Do experiments confirm this prediction? Explain.

PROBLEMS AND APPLICATIONS

1. Each of the following situations involves moral hazard. In each case, identify the principal and the agent, and explain why there is asymmetric information. How does the action described reduce the problem of moral hazard?
   a. Landlords require tenants to pay security deposits.
   b. Firms compensate top executives with options to buy company stock at a given price in the future.
   c. Car insurance companies offer discounts to customers who install antitheft devices in their cars.
2. Suppose that the Live-Long-and-Prosper Health Insurance Company charges $5,000 annually for a family insurance policy. The company's president suggests that the company raise the annual price to $6,000 to increase its profits. If the firm followed this suggestion, what economic problem might arise? Would the firm's pool of customers tend to become more or less healthy on average? Would the company's profits necessarily increase?

3. A case study in this chapter describes how a boyfriend can signal to a girlfriend that he loves her by giving an appropriate gift. Do you think saying "I love you" can also serve as a signal? Why or why not?
4. Some AIDS activists believe that health insurance companies should not be allowed to ask applicants if they are infected with the HIV virus that causes AIDS. Would this rule help or hurt those who are HIV-positive? Would it help or hurt those who are not HIV-positive? Would it exacerbate or mitigate the problem of adverse selection in the market for health insurance? Do you think it would increase or decrease the number of people without health insurance? In your opinion, would this be a good policy? Explain your answers to each question.
5. The government is considering two ways to help the needy: giving them cash or giving them free meals at soup kitchens. Give an argument for giving cash. Give an argument, based on asymmetric information, for why the soup kitchen may be better than the cash handout.

6. Ken walks into an ice-cream parlor.

WAITER: "We have vanilla and chocolate today."
    KEN: "I'll take vanilla."
WAITER: "I almost forgot. We also have strawberry."
    KEN: "In that case, I'll take chocolate."

What standard property of decision making is Ken violating? (Hint: Reread the section on Arrow's impossibility theorem.)

7. Three friends are choosing a restaurant for dinner. Here are their preferences:

	Rachel	Ross	Joey
First choice	Italian	Italian	Chinese
Second choice	Chinese	Chinese	Mexican
Third choice	Mexican	Mexican	French
Fourth choice	French	French	Italian

a. If the three friends use a Borda count to make their decision, where do they go to eat?
b. On their way to their chosen restaurant, they see that the Mexican and French restaurants are closed, so they use a Borda count again to decide between the remaining two restaurants. Where do they decide to go now?
c. How do your answers to parts (a) and (b) relate to Arrow's impossibility theorem?

8. Three friends are choosing a TV show to watch. Here are their preferences:

	Chandler	Phoebe	Monica
First choice	Dexter	Glee	House
Second choice	Glee	House	Dexter
Third choice	House	Dexter	Glee

a. If the three friends try using a Borda count to make their choice, what would happen?
b. Monica suggests a vote by majority rule. She proposes that first they choose between Dexter and Glee, and then they choose between the winner of the first vote and House. If they all vote their preferences honestly, what outcome would occur?
c. Should Chandler agree to Monica's suggestion? What voting system would he prefer?
d. Phoebe and Monica convince Chandler to go along with Monica's proposal. In round one, Chandler dishonestly says he prefers Glee over Dexter. Why might he do this?

9. Five roommates are planning to spend the weekend in their dorm room watching movies, and they are debating how many movies to watch. Here is their willingness to pay:

	Quentin	Spike	Ridley	Martin	Steven
First film	$14	$10	$8	$4	$2
Second film	12	8	4	2	0
Third film	10	6	2	0	0
Fourth film	6	2	0	0	0
Fifth film	2	0	0	0	0

Buying a DVD costs $15, which the roommates split equally, so each pays $3 per movie.
a. What is the efficient number of movies to watch (that is, the number that maximizes total surplus)?
b. From the standpoint of each roommate, what is the preferred number of movies?
c. What is the preference of the median roommate?
d. If the roommates held a vote on the efficient outcome versus the median voter's preference, how would each person vote? Which outcome would get a majority?
e. If one of the roommates proposed a different number of movies, could his proposal beat the winner from part (d) in a vote?
f. Can majority rule be counted on to reach efficient outcomes in the provision of public goods?

10. A group of athletes are competing in a multi-day triathlon. They have a running race on day one, a swimming race on day two, and a biking race on day three. You know the order in which the eligible contestants finish each of the three components. From this information, you are asked to rank them in the overall competition. You are given the following conditions:

• The ordering of athletes should be transitive: If athlete A is ranked above athlete B, and athlete B is ranked above athlete C, then athlete A must rank above athlete C.
• If athlete A beats athlete B in all three races, athlete A should rank higher than athlete B.
• The rank ordering of any two athletes should not depend on whether a third athlete drops out of the competition just before the final ranking.

According to Arrow's impossibility theorem, there are only three ways to rank the athletes that satisfy these properties. What are they? Are these desirable? Why or why not? Can you think of a better ranking scheme? Which of the three properties above does your scheme not satisfy?

11. Two ice-cream stands are deciding where to set up along a 1-mile beach. The people are uniformly located along the beach, and each person sitting on the beach buys exactly 1 ice-cream cone per day from the nearest stand. Each ice-cream seller wants the maximum number of customers. Where along the beach will the two stands locate? Of which result in this chapter does this outcome remind you?

12. Explain why the following reactions might reflect some deviation from rationality.
    a. After a widely reported earthquake in California, many people call their insurance company to apply for earthquake insurance.
    b. In January, many fitness clubs offer special annual membership fees to attract customers who have made New Year's resolutions to exercise more. Even when these memberships are costly, many of these new customers seldom visit the gym to work out.

For further information on topics in this chapter, additional problems, applications, examples, online quizzes, and more, please visit our website at www .cengage.com/economics/mankiw.

glossary

a

ability-to-pay principle the idea that taxes should be levied on a person according to how well that person can shoulder the burden

absolute advantage the ability to produce a good using fewer inputs than another producer

accounting profit total revenue minus total explicit cost

adverse selection the tendency for the mix of unobserved attributes to become undesirable from the standpoint of an uninformed party

agent a person who is performing an act for another person, called the principal

Arrow's impossibility theorem a mathematical result showing that, under certain assumed conditions, there is no scheme for aggregating individual preferences into a valid set of social preferences

average fixed cost fixed cost divided by the quantity of output

average revenue total revenue divided by the quantity sold

average tax rate total taxes paid divided by total income

average total cost total cost divided by the quantity of output

average variable cost variable cost divided by the quantity of output

b

behavioral economics the subfield of economics that integrates the insights of psychology

benefits principle the idea that people should pay taxes based on the benefits they receive from government services

budget constraint the limit on the consumption bundles that a consumer can afford

business cycle fluctuations in economic activity, such as employment and production

c

capital the equipment and structures used to produce goods and services

cartel a group of firms acting in unison

circular-flow diagram a visual model of the economy that shows how dollars flow through markets among households and firms

club goods goods that are excludable but not rival in consumption

Coase theorem the proposition that if private parties can bargain without cost over the allocation of resources, they can solve the problem of externalities on their own

collusion an agreement among firms in a market about quantities to produce or prices to charge

commodity money money that takes the form of a commodity with intrinsic value

common resources goods that are rival in consumption but not excludable

comparative advantage the ability to produce a good at a lower opportunity cost than another producer

compensating differential a difference in wages that arises to offset the non-monetary characteristics of different jobs

competitive market a market with many buyers and sellers trading identical products so that each buyer and seller is a price taker

complements two goods for which an increase in the price of one leads to a decrease in the demand for the other

Condorcet paradox the failure of majority rule to produce transitive preferences for society

constant returns to scale the property whereby long-run average total cost stays the same as the quantity of output changes

consumer surplus the amount a buyer is willing to pay for a good minus the amount the buyer actually pays for it

corrective tax a tax designed to induce private decision makers to take account of the social costs that arise from a negative externality

cost the value of everything a seller must give up to produce a good

cost–benefit analysis a study that compares the costs and benefits to society of providing a public good

cross-price elasticity of demand a measure of how much the quantity demanded of one good responds to a change in the price of another good, computed as the percentage change in quantity demanded of the first good divided by the percentage change in the price of the second good

d

deadweight loss the fall in total surplus that results from a market distortion, such as a tax

demand curve a graph of the relationship between the price of a good and the quantity demanded

demand schedule a table that shows the relationship between the price of a good and the quantity demanded

diminishing marginal product the property whereby the marginal product of an input declines as the quantity of the input increases

discrimination the offering of different opportunities to similar individuals who differ only by race, ethnic group, sex, age, or other personal characteristics

diseconomies of scale the property whereby long-run average total cost rises as the quantity of output increases

dominant strategy a strategy that is best for a player in a game regardless of the strategies chosen by the other players

e

economic profit total revenue minus total cost, including both explicit and implicit costs

economics the study of how society manages its scarce resources

economies of scale the property whereby long-run average total cost falls as the quantity of output increases

efficiency the property of society getting the most it can from its scarce resources

efficient scale the quantity of output that minimizes average total cost

elasticity a measure of the responsiveness of quantity demanded or quantity supplied to one of its determinants

equality the property of distributing economic prosperity uniformly among the members of society

equilibrium a situation in which the market price has reached the level at which quantity supplied equals quantity demanded

equilibrium price the price that balances quantity supplied and quantity demanded

equilibrium quantity the quantity supplied and the quantity demanded at the equilibrium price

excludability the property of a good whereby a person can be prevented from using it

explicit costs input costs that require an outlay of money by the firm

externality the uncompensated impact of one person's actions on the well-being of a bystander

f

factors of production the inputs used to produce goods and services

fixed costs costs that do not vary with the quantity of output produced

free rider a person who receives the benefit of a good but avoids paying for it

g

game theory the study of how people behave in strategic situations

Giffen good a good for which an increase in the price raises the quantity demanded

h

horizontal equity the idea that taxpayers with similar abilities to pay taxes should pay the same amount

i

implicit costs input costs that do not require an outlay of money by the firm

incentive something that induces a person to act

income effect the change in consumption that results when a price change moves the consumer to a higher or lower indifference curve

income elasticity of demand a measure of how much the quantity demanded of a good responds to a change in consumers' income, computed as the percentage change in quantity demanded divided by the percentage change in income

indifference curve a curve that shows consumption bundles that give the consumer the same level of satisfaction

inferior good a good for which, other things equal, an increase in income leads to a decrease in demand

inflation an increase in the overall level of prices in the economy

in-kind transfers transfers to the poor given in the form of goods and services rather than cash

internalizing the externality altering incentives so that people take account of the external effects of their actions

l

law of demand the claim that, other things equal, the quantity demanded of a good falls when the price of the good rises

law of supply the claim that, other things equal, the quantity supplied of a good rises when the price of the good rises

law of supply and demand the claim that the price of any good adjusts to bring the quantity supplied and the quantity demanded for that good into balance

liberalism the political philosophy according to which the government should choose policies deemed just, as evaluated by an impartial observer behind a "veil of ignorance"

libertarianism the political philosophy according to which the government should punish crimes and enforce voluntary agreements but not redistribute income

life cycle the regular pattern of income variation over a person's life

lump-sum tax a tax that is the same amount for every person

m

macroeconomics the study of economy-wide phenomena, including inflation, unemployment, and economic growth

marginal changes small incremental adjustments to a plan of action

marginal cost the increase in total cost that arises from an extra unit of production

marginal product the increase in output that arises from an additional unit of input

marginal product of labor the increase in the amount of output from an additional unit of labor

marginal rate of substitution the rate at which a consumer is willing to trade one good for another

marginal revenue the change in total revenue from an additional unit sold

marginal tax rate the extra taxes paid on an additional dollar of income

market a group of buyers and sellers of a particular good or service

market economy an economy that allocates resources through the decentralized decisions of many firms and households as they interact in markets for goods and services

market failure a situation in which a market left on its own fails to allocate resources efficiently

market power the ability of a single economic actor (or small group of actors) to have a substantial influence on market prices

maximin criterion the claim that the government should aim to maximize the well-being of the worst-off person in society

median voter theorem a mathematical result showing that if voters are choosing a point along a line and each voter wants the point closest to his most preferred point, then majority rule will pick the most preferred point of the median voter

microeconomics the study of how households and firms make decisions and how they interact in markets

monopolistic competition a market structure in which many firms sell products that are similar but not identical

monopoly a firm that is the sole seller of a product without close substitutes

moral hazard the tendency of a person who is imperfectly monitored to engage in dishonest or otherwise undesirable behavior

n

Nash equilibrium a situation in which economic actors interacting with one another each choose their best strategy given the strategies that all the other actors have chosen

natural monopoly a monopoly that arises because a single firm can supply a good or service to an entire market at a smaller cost than could two or more firms

negative income tax a tax system that collects revenue from high-income households and gives subsidies to low-income households

normal good a good for which, other things equal, an increase in income leads to an increase in demand

normative statements claims that attempt to prescribe how the world should be

o

oligopoly a market structure in which only a few sellers offer similar or identical products

opportunity cost whatever must be given up to obtain some item

p

perfect complements two goods with right-angle indifference curves

perfect substitutes two goods with straight-line indifference curves

permanent income a person's normal income

political economy the study of government using the analytic methods of economics

positive statements claims that attempt to describe the world as it is

poverty line an absolute level of income set by the federal government for each family size below which a family is deemed to be in poverty

poverty rate the percentage of the population whose family income falls below an absolute level called the poverty line

price ceiling a legal maximum on the price at which a good can be sold

price discrimination the business practice of selling the same good at different prices to different customers

price elasticity of demand a measure of how much the quantity demanded of a good responds to a change in the price of that good, computed as the percentage change in quantity demanded divided by the percentage change in price

price elasticity of supply a measure of how much the quantity supplied of a good responds to a change in the price of that good, computed as the percentage change in quantity supplied divided by the percentage change in price

price floor a legal minimum on the price at which a good can be sold

principal a person for whom another person, called the agent, is performing some act

prisoners' dilemma a particular "game" between two captured prisoners that illustrates why cooperation is difficult to maintain even when it is mutually beneficial

private goods goods that are both excludable and rival in consumption

producer surplus the amount a seller is paid for a good minus the seller's cost of providing it

production function the relationship between the quantity of inputs used to make a good and the quantity of output of that good

production possibilities frontier a graph that shows the combinations of output that the economy can possibly produce given the available factors of production and the available production technology

profit total revenue minus total cost

progressive tax a tax for which high-income taxpayers pay a larger fraction of their income than do low-income taxpayers

property rights the ability of an individual to own and exercise control over scarce resources

proportional tax a tax for which high-income and low-income taxpayers pay the same fraction of income

public goods goods that are neither excludable nor rival in consumption

q

quantity demanded the amount of a good that buyers are willing and able to purchase

quantity supplied the amount of a good that sellers are willing and able to sell

r

rational people people who systematically and purposefully do the best they can to achieve their objectives

regressive tax a tax for which high-income taxpayers pay a smaller fraction of their income than do low-income taxpayers

rivalry in consumption the property of a good whereby one person's use diminishes other people's use

S

scarcity the limited nature of society's resources

screening an action taken by an uninformed party to induce an informed party to reveal information

shortage a situation in which quantity demanded is greater than quantity supplied

signaling an action taken by an informed party to reveal private information to an uninformed party

social insurance government policy aimed at protecting people against the risk of adverse events

substitutes two goods for which an increase in the price of one leads to an increase in the demand for the other

substitution effect the change in consumption that results when a price change moves the consumer along a given indifference curve to a point with a new marginal rate of substitution

sunk cost a cost that has already been committed and cannot be recovered

supply curve a graph of the relationship between the price of a good and the quantity supplied

supply schedule a table that shows the relationship between the price of a good and the quantity supplied

surplus a situation in which quantity supplied is greater than quantity demanded

t

tariff a tax on goods produced abroad and sold domestically

tax incidence the manner in which the burden of a tax is shared among participants in a market

total cost the market value of the inputs a firm uses in production

total revenue (for firm) the amount a firm receives for the sale of its output

total revenue (in a market) the amount paid by buyers and received by sellers of a good, computed as the price of the good times the quantity sold

Tragedy of the Commons a parable that illustrates why common resources are used more than is desirable from the standpoint of society as a whole

transaction costs the costs that parties incur in the process of agreeing to and following through on a bargain

u

utilitarianism the political philosophy according to which the government should choose policies to maximize the total utility of everyone in society

utility a measure of happiness or satisfaction

v

value of the marginal product the marginal product of an input times the price of the output

variable costs costs that vary with the quantity of output produced

vertical equity the idea that taxpayers with a greater ability to pay taxes should pay larger amounts

w

welfare government programs that supplement the incomes of the needy

welfare economics the study of how the allocation of resources affects economic well-being

willingness to pay the maximum amount that a buyer will pay for a good

world price the price of a good that prevails in the world market for that good

index

Chapter 1
Ten Principles of Economics

Goals
In this chapter you will

- Learn that economics is about the allocation of scarce resources
- Examine some of the trade-offs that people face
- Learn the meaning of opportunity cost
- See how to use marginal reasoning when making decisions
- Discuss how incentives affect people's behavior
- Consider why trade among people or nations can be good for everyone
- Discuss why markets are a good, but not perfect, way to allocate resources
- Learn what determines some trends in the overall economy

Outcomes
After accomplishing these goals, you should be able to

- Define scarcity
- Explain the classic trade-off between "guns and butter"
- Add up your particular opportunity cost of attending college
- Compare the marginal costs and marginal benefits of continuing to attend school indefinitely
- Consider how a quadrupling of your tuition payments would affect your decision to educate yourself
- Explain why specialization and trade improve people's choices
- Give an example of an externality
- Explain the source of large and persistent inflation

Chapter Overview

Context and Purpose

Chapter 1 is the first chapter in a three-chapter section that serves as the introduction to the text. Chapter 1 introduces ten fundamental principles on which the study of economics is based. In a broad sense, the rest of the text is an elaboration on these ten principles. Chapter 2 will develop how economists approach problems, while Chapter 3 will explain how individuals and countries gain from trade.

The purpose of Chapter 1 is to lay out ten economic principles that will serve as building blocks for the rest of the text. The ten principles can be grouped into three categories: how people make decisions, how people interact, and how the economy works as a whole. Throughout the text, references will be made repeatedly to these ten principles.

Chapter Review

Introduction   Households and society face decisions about how to allocate scarce resources. Resources are scarce in that we have fewer resources than we wish. Economics is the study of how society manages its scarce resources. Economists study how people make decisions about buying and selling, and saving and investing. We study how people interact with one another in markets where prices are determined and quantities are exchanged. We also study the economy as a whole when we concern ourselves with total income, unemployment, and inflation.

This chapter addresses ten principles of economics. The text will refer to these principles throughout. The ten principles are grouped into three categories: how people make decisions, how people interact, and how the economy works as a whole.

How People Make Decisions

- **People face trade-offs**   Economists often say, "There ain't no such thing as a free lunch." This means that there are always trade-offs—to get more of something we like, we have to give up something else that we like. For example, if you spend money on dinner and a movie, you won't be able to spend it on new clothes. Socially, we face trade-offs as a group. For example, there is the classic trade-off between "guns and butter." That is, if society spends more on national defense (guns), then it will have less to spend on social programs (butter). There is also a social trade-off between efficiency (getting the most from our scarce resources) and equality (benefits being distributed uniformly across society). Policies such as taxes and welfare make incomes more equal, but these policies reduce returns to hard work, and thus, the economy doesn't produce as much. As a result, when the government tries to cut the pie into more equal pieces, the pie gets smaller.

- **The cost of something is what you give up to get it**   The opportunity cost of an item is what you give up to get that item. It is the true cost of the item. The opportunity cost of going to college obviously includes your tuition payment. It also includes the value of your time that you could have spent working, valued at your potential earnings. It would exclude your room and board payment because you have to eat and sleep whether you are in school or not.

- **Rational people think at the margin**   Rational people systematically do the best they can to achieve their objectives. A marginal change is an incremental change to an existing plan. Rational decision makers only proceed with an action if the marginal benefit exceeds the marginal cost. For example, you should only attend school for another year if the benefits from that year of schooling exceed the cost of attending that year. A farmer should produce another bushel of corn only if the benefit (price received) exceeds the cost of producing it.

- **People respond to incentives**   An incentive is something that induces a person to act. Because rational people weigh marginal costs and marginal benefits of activities, they will respond when these costs or benefits change. For example, when the price of automobiles rises, buyers have an incentive to buy fewer cars while automobile producers have an incentive to hire more workers and produce more autos. An increase in the price of gasoline causes people to buy smaller cars, ride mass transit, and ride bicycles. Public policy can alter the costs or benefits of activities. For example, a tax on gasoline raises the price and discourages the purchase of gasoline. Some policies have unintended consequences because they alter behavior in a manner that was not predicted.

How People Interact

- **Trade can make everyone better off**   Trade is not a contest in which one wins and one loses. Trade can make each trader better off. Trade allows each trader to specialize in what he or she does best, whether it be farming, building, or manufacturing, and trade their output for the output of other efficient producers. This is as true for countries as it is for individuals.

- **Markets are usually a good way to organize economic activity**   In a market economy, the decisions about what goods and services to produce, how much to produce, and who gets to consume them are made by millions of firms and households. Firms and households, guided by self-interest, interact in the marketplace where prices and quantities are determined. Although this may appear to be chaos, Adam Smith made the famous observation in the *Wealth of Nations* in 1776 that self-interested households and firms interact in markets and generate desirable social outcomes as if guided by an "invisible hand." These optimal social outcomes were not their original intent. The prices generated by their competitive activity signal the value of costs and benefits to producers and consumers, whose activities usually maximize the well-being of society. Alternatively, the prices dictated by central planners contain no information on costs and benefits, and therefore, these prices fail to guide economic activity efficiently. Prices also fail to guide economic activity efficiently when governments distort prices with taxes or restrict price movements with price controls.

- **Governments can sometimes improve market outcomes**   Government must first protect property rights in order for markets to work. In addition, government can sometimes intervene in the market to improve efficiency or equality. When markets fail to allocate resources efficiently, there has been market failure. There are many different sources of market failure. An externality is when the actions of one person affect the well-being of a bystander. Pollution is a standard example. Market power is when a single person or group can influence the price. In these cases, the government may be able to intervene and improve economic efficiency. The government may also intervene to improve equality with income taxes and welfare. Sometimes well-intentioned policy intervention has unintended consequences. Some economists are concerned that President Obama's stimulus package which is intended to reduce unemployment may lead to inflation.

How the Economy as a Whole Works

- **A country's standard of living depends on its ability to produce goods and services**   There is great variation in average incomes across countries at a point in time and within the same country over time. These differences in incomes and standards of living are largely attributable to differences in productivity. Productivity is the amount of goods and services produced from each unit of labor input. As a result, public policy intended to improve standards of living should improve education, generate more and better tools, and improve access to current technology.

- **Prices rise when the government prints too much money**   Inflation is an increase in the overall level of prices in the economy. High inflation is costly to the economy. Large and persistent inflation is caused by rapid growth in the quantity of money. Policymakers wishing to keep inflation low should maintain slow growth in the quantity of money.

- **Society faces a short-run trade-off between inflation and unemployment** In the short run, an increase in the quantity of money stimulates spending, which raises both prices and production. The increase in production requires more hiring, which reduces unemployment. Thus, in the short run, an increase in inflation tends to reduce unemployment, causing a trade-off between inflation and unemployment. The trade-off is temporary but can last for a year or two. Understanding this trade-off is important for understanding the fluctuations in economic activity known as the business cycle. In the short run, policymakers may be able to affect the mix of inflation and unemployment by changing government spending, taxes, and the quantity of money.

Helpful Hints

1. Place yourself in the story. Throughout the text, most economic situations will be composed of economic actors—buyers and sellers, borrowers and lenders, firms and workers, and so on. When you are asked to address how any economic actor would respond to economic incentives, place yourself in the story as the buyer or the seller, the borrower or the lender, the producer or the consumer. Don't think of yourself always as the buyer (a natural tendency) or always as the seller. You will find that your role-playing will usually produce the right response once you learn to think like an economist—which is the topic of the next chapter.

2. Trade is not a zero-sum game. Some people see an exchange in terms of winners and losers. Their reaction to trade is that, after the sale, if the seller is happy, the buyer must be sad because the seller must have taken something from the buyer. That is, they view trade as a zero-sum game where what one gains the other must have lost. They fail to see that both parties to a voluntary transaction gain because each party is allowed to specialize in what it can produce most efficiently and then trade for items that are produced more efficiently by others. Nobody loses, because trade is voluntary. Therefore, a government policy that limits trade reduces the potential gains from trade.

3. An externality can be positive. Because the classic example of an externality is pollution, it is easy to think of an externality as a cost that lands on a bystander. However, an externality can be positive in that it can be a benefit that lands on a bystander. For example, education is often cited as a product that emits a positive externality because when your neighbor educates herself, she is likely to be more reasonable, responsible, productive, and politically astute. In short, she is a better neighbor. Positive externalities, just as much as negative externalities, may be a reason for the government to intervene to promote efficiency.

Terms and Definitions

Choose a definition for each key term.

Key Terms	Definitions
_____ Scarcity	1. The property of distributing economic prosperity uniformly among society's members
_____ Economics	2. A situation in which the market fails to allocate resources efficiently
_____ Efficiency	3. Limited resources and unlimited wants
_____ Equality	4. The amount of goods and services produced from each unit of labor input
_____ Rational	5. The case in which there is only one seller in the market
_____ Opportunity cost	6. The principle that self-interested market participants may unknowingly maximize the welfare of society as a whole
_____ Marginal change	
_____ Incentive	7. The property of society getting the most from its scarce resources
_____ Market economy	8. An economic system where interaction of households and firms in markets determines the allocation of resources
_____ Property rights	
_____ "Invisible hand"	9. Fluctuations in economic activity
_____ Market failure	10. When one person's actions have an impact on a bystander
_____ Externality	11. An increase in the overall level of prices
_____ Market power	12. An incremental adjustment to an existing plan
_____ Monopoly	13. Study of how society manages its scarce resources
_____ Productivity	14. Whatever is given up to get something else
_____ Inflation	15. The ability of an individual or group to substantially influence market prices
_____ Business cycle	
	16. Something that induces a person to act
	17. The ability of an individual to own and exercise control over scarce resources
	18. Systematically and purposefully doing the best you can to achieve your objectives

Problems and Short-Answer Questions

Practice Problems

1. People respond to incentives. Governments can alter incentives and, hence, behavior with public policy. However, sometimes public policy generates unintended consequences by producing results that were not anticipated. For each of the following public policies, determine which result was likely the intended result and which was the unintended consequence.

   a. The government raises the minimum wage to $10 per hour. Some workers find jobs at the higher wage making these workers better off. Some workers find no job at all because few firms want to hire low-productivity workers at this high wage.

   _____

   _____

b. The government places rent controls on apartments restricting rent to $300 per month. Few landlords are willing to produce an apartment at this price causing more homelessness. Some low-income renters are able to rent an apartment more cheaply.

_____

_____

c. The government raises the tax on gasoline by $2 per gallon. The deficit is reduced, and people economize on their use of gasoline. There is a boom in bicycle sales.

_____

_____

d. The government declares marijuana and cocaine illegal. The price of illegal drugs increases, creating more gangs and gang warfare. Due to the high price of illegal drugs, fewer street drugs are consumed.

_____

_____

e. The government prohibits the killing of wolves. The wolf population increases. Sheep and cattle herds suffer losses.

_____

_____

f. The government bans imports of sugar from South America. South American sugar beet growers can't repay their loans to U.S. banks and turn to more profitable crops such as coca leaves and marijuana. U.S. sugar beet growers avoid a financial crisis.

_____

_____

2. Opportunity cost is what you give up to get an item. Because there is no such thing as a free lunch, what would likely be given up to obtain each of the items listed below?

a. Susan can work full time or go to college. She chooses college.

_____

b. Susan can work full time or go to college. She chooses work.

_____

c. Farmer Jones has 100 acres of land. He can plant corn, which yields 100 bushels per acre, or he can plant beans, which yield 40 bushels per acre. He chooses to plant corn.

_____

d. Farmer Jones has 100 acres of land. He can plant corn, which yields 100 bushels per acre, or he can plant beans, which yield 40 bushels per acre. He chooses to plant beans.

_____

e.   In *a* and *b* above and *c* and *d* above, which is the opportunity cost of which—college for work or work for college? corn for beans or beans for corn?

Short-Answer Questions

1. Is air scarce? Is clean air scarce?

2. What is the opportunity cost of saving some of your paycheck?

3. Why is there a trade-off between equality and efficiency?

4. Water is necessary for life. Diamonds are not. Is the marginal benefit of an additional glass of water greater or lesser than an additional one-carat diamond? Why?

5. Your car needs to be repaired. You have already paid $500 to have the transmission fixed, but it still doesn't work properly. You can sell your car "as is" for $2,000. If your car were fixed, you could sell it for $2,500. Your car can be fixed with a guarantee for another $300. Should you repair your car? Why?

6. Why do you think air bags have reduced deaths from auto crashes less than we had hoped?

7. Suppose one country is better at producing agricultural products (because they have land that is more fertile), while another country is better at producing manufactured goods (because they have a better educational system and more engineers). If each country produced their specialty and traded, would there be more or less total output than if each country produced all of their agricultural and manufacturing needs? Why?

_____

_____

_____

8. In the *Wealth of Nations,* Adam Smith said, "It is not from the benevolence of the butcher, the brewer, or the baker that we expect our dinner, but from their regard to their own interest." What do you think he meant?

_____

_____

_____

_____

9. If we save more and use it to build more physical capital, productivity will rise and we will have rising standards of living in the future. What is the opportunity cost of future growth?

_____

10. If the government printed twice as much money, what do you think would happen to prices and output if the economy were already producing at maximum capacity?

_____

_____

_____

11. A goal for a society is to distribute resources more equally and fairly. How might you distribute resources if everyone were equally talented and worked equally hard? What if people had different talents and some people worked hard, while others did not?

_____

_____

_____

_____

12. Who is more self-interested, the buyer or the seller?

_____

_____

_____

_____

Self-Test

True/False Questions

_____ 1. When the government redistributes income with taxes and welfare, the economy becomes more efficient.

_____ 2. When economists say, "There ain't no such thing as a free lunch," they mean that all economic decisions involve trade-offs.

_____ 3. Adam Smith's "invisible hand" concept describes how corporate business reaches into the pockets of consumers like an "invisible hand."

_____ 4. Rational people act only when the marginal benefit of the action exceeds the marginal cost.

_____ 5. The United States will benefit economically if we eliminate trade with Asian countries because we will be forced to produce more of our own cars and clothes.

_____ 6. When a jet flies overhead, the noise it generates is an externality.

_____ 7. A tax on liquor raises the price of liquor and provides an incentive for consumers to drink more.

_____ 8. An unintended consequence of public support for higher education is that low tuition provides an incentive for many people to attend state universities even if they have no desire to learn anything.

_____ 9. Sue is better at cleaning, and Bob is better at cooking. It will take fewer hours to eat and clean if Bob specializes in cooking and Sue specializes in cleaning than if they share the household duties evenly.

_____ 10. High and persistent inflation is caused by excessive growth in the quantity of money in the economy.

_____ 11. In the short run, a reduction in inflation tends to cause a reduction in unemployment.

_____ 12. An auto manufacturer should continue to produce additional autos as long as the firm is profitable, even if the cost of the additional units exceeds the price received.

_____ 13. An individual farmer is likely to have market power in the market for wheat.

_____ 14. To a student, the opportunity cost of going to a basketball game would include the price of the ticket and the value of the time that could have been spent studying.

_____ 15. Workers in the United States have a relatively high standard of living because the United States has a relatively high minimum wage.

Multiple-Choice Questions

1. Which of the following involve a trade-off?
    a. buying a new car
    b. going to college
    c. watching a football game on Saturday afternoon
    d. taking a nap
    e. All of the above involve trade-offs.

2. Trade-offs are required because wants are unlimited and resources are
   a. efficient.
   b. economical.
   c. scarce.
   d. unlimited.
   e. marginal.

3. Economics is the study of how
   a. to fully satisfy our unlimited wants.
   b. society manages its scarce resources.
   c. to reduce our wants until we are satisfied.
   d. to avoid having to make trade-offs.
   e. society manages its unlimited resources.

4. A rational person does not act unless
   a. the action makes money for the person.
   b. the action is ethical.
   c. the action produces marginal costs that exceed marginal benefits.
   d. the action produces marginal benefits that exceed marginal costs.
   e. None of the above is true.

5. Raising taxes and increasing welfare payments
   a. proves that there is such a thing as a free lunch.
   b. reduces market power.
   c. improves efficiency at the expense of equality.
   d. improves equality at the expense of efficiency.
   e. does none of the above.

6. Suppose you find $20. If you choose to use the $20 to go to the football game, your opportunity cost of going to the game is
   a. nothing, because you found the money.
   b. $20 (because you could have used the $20 to buy other things).
   c. $20 (because you could have used the $20 to buy other things) plus the value of your time spent at the game.
   d. $20 (because you could have used the $20 to buy other things) plus the value of your time spent at the game, plus the cost of the dinner you purchased at the game.
   e. none of the above.

7. Foreign trade
   a. allows a country to have a greater variety of products at a lower cost than if it tried to produce everything at home.
   b. allows a country to avoid trade-offs.
   c. makes the members of a country more equal.
   d. increases the scarcity of resources.
   e. is none of the above.

8. Because people respond to incentives, we would expect that if the average salary of accountants increases by 50 percent while the average salary of teachers increases by 20 percent,
   a. students will shift majors from education to accounting.
   b. students will shift majors from accounting to education.
   c. fewer students will attend college.
   d. None of the above is true.

9. Which of the following activities is most likely to produce an externality?
   a. A student sits at home and watches television.
   b. A student has a party in her dorm room.
   c. A student reads a novel for pleasure.
   d. A student eats a hamburger in the student union.

10. Which of the following products would be least capable of producing an externality?
    a. cigarettes
    b. stereo equipment
    c. inoculations against disease
    d. education
    e. food

11. Which of the following situations describes the greatest market power?
    a. a farmer's impact on the price of corn
    b. Volvo's impact on the price of autos
    c. Microsoft's impact on the price of desktop operating systems
    d. a student's impact on college tuition

12. Which of the following statements is true about a market economy?
    a. Market participants act as if guided by an "invisible hand" to produce outcomes that promote general economic well-being.
    b. Taxes help prices communicate costs and benefits to producers and consumers.
    c. With a large enough computer, central planners could guide production more efficiently than markets.
    d. The strength of a market system is that it tends to distribute resources evenly across consumers.

13. Workers in the United States enjoy a high standard of living because
    a. unions in the United States keep the wage high.
    b. we have protected our industry from foreign competition.
    c. the United States has a high minimum wage.
    d. workers in the United States are highly productive.
    e. None of the above is true.

14. High and persistent inflation is caused by
    a. unions increasing wages too much.
    b. OPEC raising the price of oil too much.
    c. governments increasing the quantity of money too much.
    d. regulations raising the cost of production too much.

15. In the short run,
    a. an increase in inflation temporarily increases unemployment.
    b. a decrease in inflation temporarily increases unemployment.
    c. inflation and unemployment are unrelated.
    d. the business cycle has been eliminated.
    e. None of the above is true.

16. An increase in the price of beef provides
    a. information that tells consumers to buy more beef.
    b. information that tells consumers to buy less pork.
    c. information that tells producers to produce more beef.
    d. no information because prices in a market system are managed by planning boards.

17. You have spent $1,000 building a hot-dog stand based on estimates of sales of $2,000. The hot-dog stand is nearly completed, but now you estimate total sales to be only $800. You can complete the hot-dog stand for another $300. Should you complete the hot-dog stand? (Assume that the hot dogs cost you nothing.)
    a. Yes.
    b. No.
    c. There is not enough information to answer this question.

18. Referring to question 17, your decision rule should be to complete the hot-dog stand as long as the cost to complete the stand is less than
    a. $100.
    b. $300.
    c. $500.
    d. $800.
    e. none of the above.

19. Which of the following is not part of the opportunity cost of going on vacation?
    a.   the money you could have made if you had stayed home and worked
    b.   the money you spent on food
    c.   the money you spent on airline tickets
    d.   the money you spent on a Broadway show

20. Productivity can be increased by
    a.   raising minimum wages.
    b.   raising union wages.
    c.   improving the education of workers.
    d.   restricting trade with foreign countries.

Advanced Critical Thinking

Suppose your university decides to lower the cost of parking on campus by reducing the price of a parking permit from $200 per semester to $5 per semester.

1. What do you think would happen to the number of students desiring to park their cars on campus?

    _____

    _____

2. What do you think would happen to the amount of time it would take to find a parking place?

    _____

    _____

3. Thinking in terms of opportunity cost, would the lower price of a parking permit necessarily lower the true cost of parking?

    _____

    _____

4. Would the opportunity cost of parking be the same for students with no outside employment and students with jobs earning $15 per hour?

    _____

    _____

    _____

    _____

Solutions

Terms and Definitions

_3_ Scarcity
13 Economics
_7_ Efficiency
_1_ Equality
18 Rational
14 Opportunity cost
12 Marginal change
16 Incentive
_8_ Market economy
17 Property rights
_6_ "Invisible hand"
_2_ Market failure
10 Externality
15 Market power
_5_ Monopoly
_4_ Productivity
11 Inflation
_9_ Business cycle

Practice Problems

1. a. Intended: Raise the wage of low-productivity workers. Unintended: Some workers are unemployed at the higher wage.

   b. Intended: Low-income renters get a cheap apartment. Unintended: Some people find no apartment at all causing more homelessness.

   c. Intended: Reduce the deficit and use less gasoline. Unintended: Bicycle sales increase.

   d. Intended: Fewer street drugs are consumed. Unintended: More gangs and gang warfare.

   e. Intended: Increase the wolf population. Unintended: Damage to sheep and cattle herds.

   f. Intended: Improve the financial condition of U.S. sugar beet growers. Unintended: Cause South American growers to grow marijuana and coca leaves.

2. a. Susan gives up income from work (and must pay tuition).

   b. Susan gives up a college degree and the increase in income through life that it would have brought her (but doesn't have to pay tuition).

   c. Farmer Jones gives up 4,000 bushels of beans.

   d. Farmer Jones gives up 10,000 bushels of corn.

   e. Each is the opportunity cost of the other, because each decision requires giving something up.

Short-Answer Questions

1. No, you don't have to give up anything to get air. Yes, you can't have as much clean air as you want without giving up something to get it (pollution equipment on cars, etc.).

2. The items you could have enjoyed had you spent that portion of your paycheck (current consumption).

3. Taxes and welfare make us more equal but reduce incentives for hard work, lowering total output.

4. The marginal benefit of another glass of water is generally lower because we have so much water that one more glass is of little value. The opposite is true for diamonds.

5. Yes, because the marginal benefit of fixing the car is $2,500 – $2,000 = $500, and the marginal cost is $300. The original repair payment is not relevant.

6. The cost of an accident was lowered. This changed incentives, so people drive faster and have more accidents.

7. There would be more total output if the two countries specialize and trade because each is doing what it does most efficiently.

8. The butcher, brewer, and baker produce the best food possible, not out of kindness, but because it is in their best interest to do so. Self-interest can maximize general economic well-being.

9. We must give up consumption today.

10. Spending would double, but since the quantity of output would remain the same, prices would double.

11. Fairness might require that everyone get an equal share because they were equally talented and worked equally hard. Fairness might require that people not get an equal share because they were not equally talented and did not work equally hard.

12. They are equally self-interested. The seller will sell to the highest bidder, and the buyer will buy from the lowest offer.

True/False Questions

1. F; the economy becomes less efficient because it decreases the incentive to work hard.

2. T

3. F; the "invisible hand" refers to how markets guide self-interested people to create desirable social outcomes.

4. T

5. F; all countries gain from voluntary trade.

6. T

7. F; higher prices reduce the quantity demanded.

8. T

9. T

10. T

11. F; a reduction in inflation tends to raise unemployment.

12. F; a manufacturer should produce as long as the marginal benefit exceeds the marginal cost.

13. F; a single farmer is too small to influence the market.
14. T
15. F; workers in the United States have a high standard of living because they are productive.

Multiple-Choice Questions

1. e
2. c
3. b
4. d
5. d
6. c
7. a
8. a
9. b
10. e
11. c
12. a
13. d
14. c
15. b
16. c
17. a
18. d
19. b
20. c

Advanced Critical Thinking

1. More students would wish to park on campus.
2. It would take much longer to find a parking place.
3. No, because we would have to factor in the value of our time spent looking for a parking place.
4. No. Students that could be earning money working are giving up more while looking for a parking place. Therefore, their opportunity cost is higher.

Chapter 2
Thinking Like an Economist

Goals
In this chapter you will

- See how economists apply the methods of science
- Consider how assumptions and models can shed light on the world
- Learn two simple models—the circular-flow diagram and the production possibilities frontier
- Distinguish between microeconomics and macroeconomics
- Learn the difference between positive and normative statements
- Examine the role of economists in making policy
- Consider why economists sometimes disagree with one another

Outcomes
After accomplishing these goals, you should be able to

- Describe the scientific method
- Understand the art of making useful assumptions
- Explain the slope of a production possibilities frontier
- Place economic issues into the categories of microeconomics or macroeconomics
- Place economic statements into the categories of normative or positive
- See the link between policymaking and normative statements
- List two reasons why economists disagree

Chapter Overview

Context and Purpose

Chapter 2 is the second chapter in a three-chapter section that serves as the introduction of the text. Chapter 1 introduced ten principles of economics that will be revisited throughout the text. Chapter 2 develops how economists approach problems, while Chapter 3 will explain how individuals and countries gain from trade.

The purpose of Chapter 2 is to familiarize you with how economists approach economic problems. With practice, you will learn how to approach similar problems in this dispassionate, systematic way. You will see how economists employ the scientific method, the role of assumptions in model building, and the application of two specific economic models. You will also learn the important distinction between two roles economists can play: as scientists when we try to explain the economic world, and as policymakers when we try to improve it.

Chapter Review

Introduction   Like other fields of study, economics has its own jargon and way of thinking. It is necessary to learn the special language of economics, because knowledge of the economic vocabulary will help you communicate with precision to others about economic issues. This chapter will also provide an overview of how economists look at the world.

The Economist as Scientist

Although economists don't use test tubes or telescopes, they are scientists because they employ the scientific method—the dispassionate and objective development and testing of theories.

- **The Scientific Method: Observation, Theory, and More Observation**   Just as in other sciences, an economist observes an event, develops a theory, and collects data to test the theory. An economist observes inflation, creates a theory that excessive growth in money causes inflation, and then collects data on money growth and inflation to see if there is a relationship. Collecting data to test economic theories is difficult, however, because economists usually cannot create data from experiments. That is, economists cannot manipulate the economy just to test a theory. Therefore, economists often use data gathered from historical economic events.

- **The Role of Assumptions**   Assumptions are made to make the world easier to understand. A physicist assumes an object is falling in a vacuum when measuring acceleration due to gravity. This assumption is reasonably accurate for a marble but not for a beach ball. An economist may assume that prices are fixed (can't be changed) or may assume that prices are flexible (can move up or down in response to market pressures). Because prices often cannot be changed quickly (the menu in a restaurant is expensive to change) but can be changed easily over time, it is reasonable for economists to assume that prices are fixed in the short run but flexible in the long run. The art of scientific thinking is deciding which assumptions to make.

- **Economic Models**   Biology teachers employ plastic models of the human body. They are simpler than the actual human body but that is what makes them useful. Economists use economic models that are composed of diagrams and equations. Economic models are based on assumptions and are simplifications of economic reality.

- **Our First Model: The Circular-Flow Diagram**   The circular-flow diagram shows the flow of goods and services, factors of production, and monetary payments between households and firms. Households sell the factors of production, such as land, labor, and capital to firms, in the market for factors of production. In exchange, the households receive wages, rent, and profit. Households use these dollars to buy goods and services from firms in the market for goods and services. The firms use this revenue to pay for the factors of production, and so on. This is a simplified model of the entire economy. This version of the circular-flow diagram has been simplified because it excludes international trade and the government.

- **Our Second Model: The Production Possibilities Frontier**   A production possibilities frontier is a graph that shows the combinations of output the economy can possibly produce given the available factors of production and the available production technology. It is drawn assuming the economy produces only two goods. This model demonstrates the following economic principles:

- If the economy is operating on the production possibilities frontier, it is operating *efficiently* because it is producing a mix of output that is the maximum possible from the resources available.

- Points inside the curve are, therefore, *inefficient*. Points outside the curve are currently unattainable.

- If the economy is operating on the production possibilities frontier, we can see the *trade-offs* society faces. To produce more of one good, it must produce less of the other. The amount of one good given up when producing more of another good is the *opportunity cost* of the additional production.

- The production possibilities frontier is bowed outward because the opportunity cost of producing more of a good increases as we near maximum production of that good. This is because we use resources better suited toward production of the other good in order to continue to expand production of the first good.

- A technological advance in production shifts the production possibilities frontier outward. This is a demonstration of *economic growth.*

- **Microeconomics and Macroeconomics** Economics is studied on various levels. Microeconomics is the study of how households and firms make decisions and how they interact in specific markets. Macroeconomics is the study of economy-wide phenomena such as the federal deficit, the rate of unemployment, and policies to improve our standard of living. Microeconomics and macroeconomics are related because changes in the overall economy arise from decisions of millions of individuals. Although related, the methods employed in microeconomics and macroeconomics differ enough that they are often taught in separate courses.

The Economist as Policy Adviser

When economists attempt to explain the world as it is, they act as scientists. When economists attempt to improve the world, they act as policy advisers. Correspondingly, positive statements describe the world *as it is,* while normative statements prescribe how the world *ought to be.* Positive statements can be confirmed or refuted with evidence. Normative statements involve values (ethics, religion, political philosophy) as well as facts.

For example, "Money growth causes inflation" is a positive statement (of a scientist). "The government ought to reduce inflation" is a normative statement (of a policy adviser). The two statements are related because evidence about whether money causes inflation might help us decide what tool the government should use if it chooses to reduce inflation.

Economists act as policy advisers to the government in many different areas. The president is advised by economists on the Council of Economic Advisers, the Department of the Treasury, the Department of Labor, and the Department of Justice. Congress is advised by economists from the Congressional Budget Office and the Federal Reserve. For a variety of reasons, presidents (and other politicians) do not necessarily advance policies that economists advocate.

Why Economists Disagree

There are two reasons why economists have a reputation for giving conflicting advice to policymakers.

- Economists may have different scientific judgments. That is, economists may disagree about the validity of alternative positive theories regarding how the world works. For example, economists differ in their views of the sensitivity of household saving to changes in the after-tax return to saving.

- Economists may have different values. That is, economists may have different normative views about what policy should try to accomplish. For example, economists differ in their views of whether taxes should be used to redistribute income.

In reality, although there are legitimate disagreements among economists on many issues, there is tremendous agreement on many basic principles of economics.

Let's Get Going

In the next chapter, we will begin to apply the ideas and methods of economics. As you begin to think like an economist, you will use a variety of skills—mathematics, history, politics, philosophy—with the objectivity of a scientist.

Helpful Hints

1. Opportunity costs are usually not constant along a production possibilities frontier. Notice that the production possibilities frontier shown in Exhibit 1 is bowed outward. It shows the production trade-offs for an economy that produces only paper and pencils.

   If we start at the point where the economy is using all of its resources to produce paper, producing 100 units of pencils only requires a trade-off or an opportunity cost of 25 units of paper (point A to point B). This is because when we move resources from paper to pencil production, we first move those resources best suited for pencil production and poorly suited for paper production.

   Therefore, pencil production increases with very little decrease in paper production. However, if the economy were operating at point C, the opportunity cost of an additional 100 pencils (point C to D) is 200 units of paper. This is because we now move resources toward pencil production that were extremely well suited for paper production and are poorly suited for pencil production. Therefore, as we produce more and more of any particular good, the opportunity cost per unit tends to rise because resources are specialized. That is, resources are not equally well suited for producing each output.

   The argument here applies when moving either direction on the production possibilities frontier. For example, if we start at point D (maximum production of pencils), a small reduction in pencil production (100 units) releases enough resources to increase production of paper by a large amount (200 units). However, moving from point B to point A only increases paper production by 25 units.

2. A production possibilities frontier only shows the choices available—not which point of production is best. A common mistake made by students when using production possibilities frontiers is to look at a production possibilities frontier and suggest that a point somewhere near the middle "looks best." Students make this subjective judgment because the middle point appears to provide the biggest total number of units of production of the two goods. However, ask yourself the following question. Using the production possibilities frontier in Exhibit 1, what production point would be best if paper were worth $10 per sheet and pencils were worth 1 cent per dozen? We would move our resources toward paper production. What if paper were worth 1 cent per sheet and pencils were worth $50 each? We would move our resources toward pencil production. Clearly, what we actually choose to produce depends on the price of each good. Therefore, a production possibilities frontier only provides the choices available; it alone cannot determine which choice is best.

3. Economic disagreement is interesting but economic consensus is more important. Economists have a reputation for disagreeing with one another because we tend to highlight our differences. While our disagreements are interesting to us, the matters on which we agree are more important to you. There are a great number of economic principles for which there is near unanimous support within the economics profession. The aim of this text is to concentrate on the areas of agreement within the profession as opposed to the areas of disagreement.

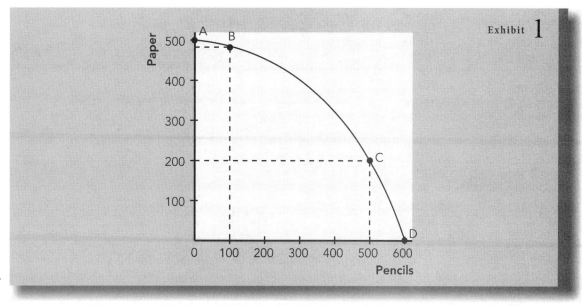

Exhibit 1

Terms and Definitions

Choose a definition for each key term.

Key Terms

_____ Scientific method

_____ Economic models

_____ Circular-flow diagram

_____ Factors of production

_____ Production possibilities frontier

_____ Opportunity cost

_____ Efficiency

_____ Microeconomics

_____ Macroeconomics

_____ Positive statements

_____ Normative statements

Definitions

1. Inputs such as land, labor, and capital

2. The study of economy-wide phenomena

3. Objective development and testing of theories

4. Whatever is given up to get something else

5. Prescription for how the world ought to be

6. Getting maximum output from the resources available

7. Descriptions of the world as it is

8. Simplifications of reality based on assumptions

9. A graph that shows the combinations of output the economy can possibly produce given the available factors of production and the available production technology

10. The study of how households and firms make decisions and how they interact in markets

11. A diagram of the economy that shows the flow of goods and services, factors of production, and monetary payments between households and firms

Problems and Short-Answer Questions

Practice Problems

1. Identify the parts of the circular-flow diagram immediately involved in the following transactions.
   a. Mary buys a car from General Motors for $20,000.

   _____

   _____

   _____

   _____

   b. General Motors pays Joe $5,000 per month for work on the assembly line.

   _____

   _____

   _____

   _____

   c. Joe gets a $15 haircut.

   _____

   _____

   _____

   _____

   d. Mary receives $10,000 of dividends on her General Motors stock.

   _____

   _____

   _____

   _____

2. The following table provides information about the production possibilities frontier of Athletic Country.

Bats	Rackets
0	420
100	400
200	360
300	300
400	200
500	0

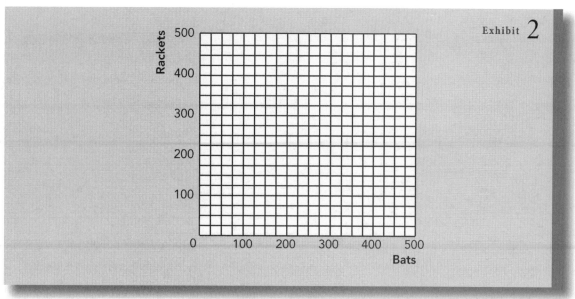

Exhibit 2

a. In Exhibit 2, plot and connect these points to create Athletic Country's production possibilities frontier.

b. If Athletic Country currently produces 100 bats and 400 rackets, what is the opportunity cost of an additional 100 bats?

_____

c. If Athletic Country currently produces 300 bats and 300 rackets, what is the opportunity cost of an additional 100 bats?

_____

d. Why does the additional production of 100 bats in part *c* cause a greater trade-off than the additional production of 100 bats in part *b*?

_____

_____

_____

e. Suppose Athletic Country is currently producing 200 bats and 200 rackets. How many additional bats could they produce without giving up any rackets? How many additional rackets could they produce without giving up any bats?

_____

f. Is the production of 200 bats and 200 rackets efficient? Explain.

_____

_____

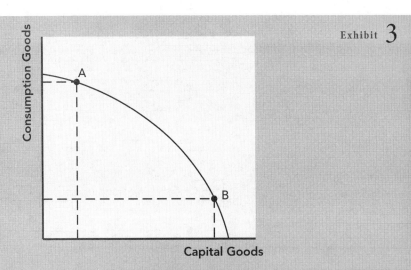

Exhibit 3

3. The production possibilities frontier in Exhibit 3 shows the available trade-offs between consumption goods and capital goods. Suppose two countries face this identical production possibilities frontier.

   a. Suppose Party Country chooses to produce at point A, while Parsimonious Country chooses to produce at point B. Which country will experience more growth in the future? Why?

   _____

   _____

   b. In this model, what is the opportunity cost of future growth?

   _____

   _____

   c. Demonstrate in Exhibit 4 the impact of growth on a production possibilities frontier such as the one shown here. Would the production possibilities frontier for Parsimonious Country shift more or less than that for Party Country? Why?

   _____

   _____

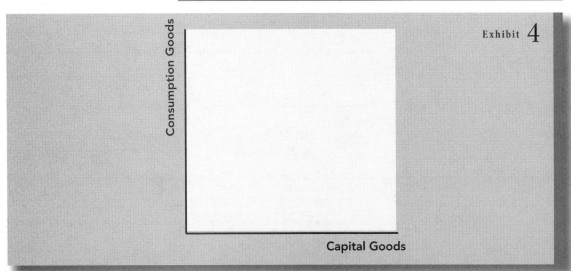

Exhibit 4

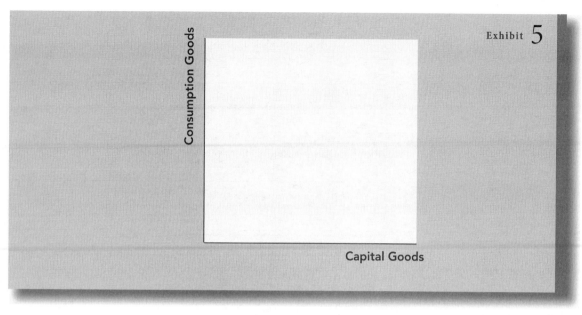

Exhibit 5

(y-axis: Consumption Goods; x-axis: Capital Goods)

d. On the graph in Exhibit 5, show the shift in the production possibilities curve if there was an increase in technology that only affected the production of capital goods.

e. Does the shift in part d imply that all additional production must be in the form of capital goods? Why?

_____

_____

Short-Answer Questions

1. Describe the scientific method.

_____

_____

_____

2. What is the role of assumptions in any science?

_____

_____

_____

3. Is a more realistic model always better?

_____

_____

_____

_____

4. Why does a production possibilities frontier have a negative slope (slope down and to the right)?

_____

_____

_____

_____

5. Why is the production possibilities frontier bowed outward?

_____

_____

_____

6. What are the two subfields within economics? Which is more likely to be a building block of the other? Why?

_____

_____

_____

_____

7. When an economist makes a normative statement, is she more likely to be acting as a scientist or a policy adviser? Why?

_____

_____

_____

_____

8. Which statements are testable: positive statements or normative statements? Why?

_____

_____

_____

9. Name two reasons why economists disagree.

_____

_____

10. Name two economic propositions for which more than 90 percent of economists agree.

_____

_____

_____

Self-Test

True/False Questions

_____ 1. Economic models must mirror reality or they are of no value.

_____ 2. Assumptions make the world easier to understand because they simplify reality and focus our attention.

_____ 3. It is reasonable to assume that the world is composed of only one person when modeling international trade.

_____ 4. When people act as scientists, they must try to be objective.

_____ 5. If an economy is operating on its production possibilities frontier, it must be using its resources efficiently.

_____ 6. If an economy is operating on its production possibilities frontier, it must produce less of one good if it produces more of another.

_____ 7. Points outside the production possibilities frontier are attainable but inefficient.

_____ 8. If an economy were experiencing substantial unemployment, the economy is producing inside the production possibilities frontier.

_____ 9. The production possibilities frontier is bowed outward because the trade-off between the production of any two goods is constant.

_____ 10. An advance in production technology would cause the production possibilities curve to shift outward.

_____ 11. Macroeconomics is concerned with the study of how households and firms make decisions and how they interact in specific markets.

_____ 12. The statement, "An increase in inflation tends to cause unemployment to fall in the short run" is normative.

_____ 13. When economists make positive statements, they are more likely to be acting as scientists.

_____ 14. Normative statements can be refuted with evidence.

_____ 15. Most economists believe that tariffs and import quotas usually reduce general economic welfare.

Multiple-Choice Questions

1. The scientific method requires that
   a. scientists use test tubes and have clean labs.
   b. scientists be objective.
   c. scientists use precision equipment.
   d. only incorrect theories are tested.
   e. only correct theories are tested.

2. Which of the following is most likely to produce scientific evidence about a theory?
   a. an economist employed by the AFL/CIO doing research on the impact of trade restrictions on workers' wages
   b. a radio talk show host collecting data on how capital markets respond to taxation
   c. a tenured economist employed at a leading university analyzing the impact of bank regulations on rural lending
   d. a lawyer employed by General Motors addressing the impact of air bags on passenger safety

3. Which of the following statements regarding the circular-flow diagram is true?
   a.   The factors of production are owned by households.
   b.   If Susan works for IBM and receives a paycheck, the transaction takes place in the market for goods and services.
   c.   If IBM sells a computer, the transaction takes place in the market for factors of production.
   d.   The factors of production are owned by firms.
   e.   None of the above is true.

4. In which of the following cases is the assumption most reasonable?
   a.   To estimate the speed at which a beach ball falls, a physicist assumes that it falls in a vacuum.
   b.   To address the impact of money growth on inflation, an economist assumes that money is strictly coins.
   c.   To address the impact of taxes on income distribution, an economist assumes that everyone earns the same income.
   d.   To address the benefits of trade, an economist assumes that there are two people and two goods.

5. Economic models are
   a.   created to duplicate reality.
   b.   built with assumptions.
   c.   usually made of wood and plastic.
   d.   useless if they are simple.

6. Which of the following is *not* a factor of production?
   a.   land
   b.   labor
   c.   capital
   d.   money
   e.   All of the above are factors of production.

7. Points on the production possibilities frontier are
   a.   efficient.
   b.   inefficient.
   c.   unattainable.
   d.   normative.
   e.   none of the above.

8. Which of the following will not shift a country's production possibilities frontier outward?
   a.   an increase in the capital stock
   b.   an advance in technology
   c.   a reduction in unemployment
   d.   an increase in the labor force

9. Economic growth is depicted by
   a.   a movement along a production possibilities frontier toward capital goods.
   b.   a shift in the production possibilities frontier outward.
   c.   a shift in the production possibilities frontier inward.
   d.   a movement from inside the curve toward the curve.

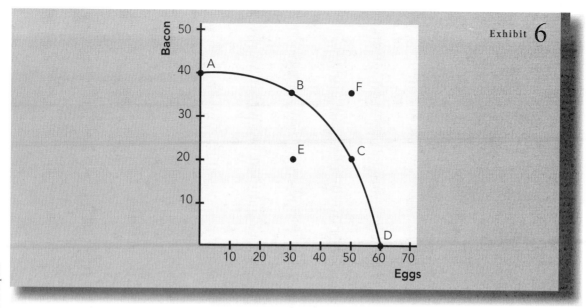

Use Exhibit 6 to answer questions 10 through 13.

10. If the economy is operating at point C, the opportunity cost of producing an additional 15 units of bacon is
   a.   10 units of eggs.
   b.   20 units of eggs.
   c.   30 units of eggs.
   d.   40 units of eggs.
   e.   50 units of eggs.

11. If the economy were operating at point E,
   a.   the opportunity cost of 20 additional units of eggs is 10 units of bacon.
   b.   the opportunity cost of 20 additional units of eggs is 20 units of bacon.
   c.   the opportunity cost of 20 additional units of eggs is 30 units of bacon.
   d.   20 additional units of eggs can be produced with no impact on bacon production.

12. Point F represents
   a.   a combination of production that can be reached if we reduce the production of eggs by 20 units.
   b.   a combination of production that is inefficient because there are unemployed resources.
   c.   a combination of production that can be reached if there is a sufficient advance in technology.
   d.   none of the above.

13. As we move from point A to point D,
   a.   the opportunity cost of eggs in terms of bacon is constant.
   b.   the opportunity cost of eggs in terms of bacon falls.
   c.   the opportunity cost of eggs in terms of bacon rises.
   d.   the economy becomes more efficient.
   e.   the economy becomes less efficient.

14. Which of the following issues is related to microeconomics?
   a.   the impact of money on inflation
   b.   the impact of technology on economic growth
   c.   the impact of the deficit on saving
   d.   the impact of oil prices on auto production

15. Which of the following statements about microeconomics and macroeconomics is *not* true?
    a. The study of very large industries is a topic within macroeconomics.
    b. Macroeconomics is concerned with economy-wide phenomena.
    c. Microeconomics is a building block for macroeconomics.
    d. Microeconomics and macroeconomics cannot be entirely separated.

16. Which of the following statements is normative?
    a. Printing too much money causes inflation.
    b. People work harder if the wage is higher.
    c. The unemployment rate should be lower.
    d. Large government deficits cause an economy to grow more slowly.

17. In making which of the following statements is an economist acting more like a scientist?
    a. A reduction in unemployment benefits will reduce the unemployment rate.
    b. The unemployment rate should be reduced because unemployment robs individuals of their dignity.
    c. The rate of inflation should be reduced because it robs the elderly of their savings.
    d. The state should increase subsidies to universities because the future of our country depends on education.

18. Positive statements are
    a. microeconomic.
    b. macroeconomic.
    c. statements of prescription that involve value judgments.
    d. statements of description that can be tested.

19. Suppose two economists are arguing about policies that deal with unemployment. One economist says, "The government should fight unemployment because it is the greatest social evil." The other economist responds, "Hogwash. Inflation is the greatest social evil." These economists
    a. disagree because they have different scientific judgments.
    b. disagree because they have different values.
    c. really don't disagree at all. It just looks that way.
    d. do none of the above.

20. Suppose two economists are arguing about policies that deal with unemployment. One economist says, "The government could lower unemployment by one percentage point if it would just increase government spending by 50 billion dollars." The other economist responds, "Hogwash. If the government spent an additional 50 billion dollars, it would reduce unemployment by only one-tenth of 1 percent, and that effect would only be temporary!" These economists
    a. disagree because they have different scientific judgments.
    b. disagree because they have different values.
    c. really don't disagree at all. It just looks that way.
    d. do none of the above.

Advanced Critical Thinking

You are watching *NewsHour with Jim Lehrer* on public television. The first focus segment is a discussion of the pros and cons of free trade (lack of obstructions to international trade). For balance, there are two economists present—one in support of free trade and one opposed. Your roommate says, "Those economists have no idea what's going on. They can't agree on anything. One says free trade makes us rich. The other says it will drive us into poverty. If the experts don't know, how is the average person ever going to know whether free trade is best?"

1. Can you give your roommate any insight into why economists might disagree on this issue?

_____

_____

_____

_____

2. Suppose you discover that 93 percent of economists believe that free trade is generally best (which is the greatest agreement on any single issue). Could you now give a more precise answer as to why economists might disagree on this issue?

_____

_____

_____

_____

3. What if you later discovered that the economist opposed to free trade worked for a labor union. Would that help you explain why there appears to be a difference of opinion on this issue?

_____

_____

_____

_____

Solutions

Terms and Definitions

 _3_ Scientific method

 _8_ Economic models

 _11_ Circular-flow diagram

 _1_ Factors of production

 _9_ Production possibilities frontier

 _4_ Opportunity cost

 _6_ Efficiency

 _10_ Microeconomics

 _2_ Macroeconomics

 _7_ Positive statements

 _5_ Normative statements

Practice Problems

1. a. $20,000 of spending from households to market for goods and services. $20,000 of revenue from market for goods and services to firms. Car moves from firm to market for goods and services. Car moves from market for goods and services to household.

   b. $5,000 of wages from firms to market for factors of production. $5,000 of income from market for factors of production to households. Labor from households to market for factors of production. Inputs from market for factors of production to firms.

   c. $15 of spending from households to market for goods and services. $15 of revenue from market for goods and services to firms. Services from firms to market for goods and services. Services from market for goods and services to households.

   d. $10,000 of profit from firms to market for factors of production. $10,000 income from market for factors of production to households. Capital services from households to market for factors of production. Inputs from market for factors of production to firms.

2. a. See Exhibit 7.

Exhibit 7

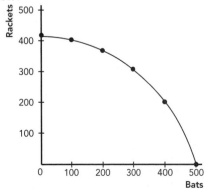

b. 40 rackets

c. 100 rackets

d. Because as we produce more bats, the resources best suited for making bats are already being used. Therefore, it takes even more resources to produce 100 bats and greater reductions in racket production.

e. 200 bats; 160 rackets

f. No. Resources were not used efficiently if production can be increased with no opportunity cost.

3. a. Parsimonious Country. Capital (plant and equipment) is a factor of production and producing more of it now will increase future production.

   b. Fewer consumption goods are produced now.

   c. See Exhibit 8. The production possibilities curve will shift more for Parsimonious Country because they have experienced a greater increase in factors of production (capital).

Exhibit 8

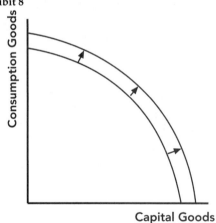

d. See Exhibit 9.

Exhibit 9

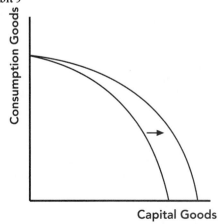

e. No, the outward shift improves choices available for both consumption and capital goods.

Short-Answer Questions

1. The dispassionate development and testing of theory by observing, testing, and observing again.

2. To simplify reality so that we can focus our thinking on what is actually important.

3. Not necessarily. Realistic models are more complex. They may be confusing and they may fail to focus on what is important.

4. Because if an economy is operating efficiently, production choices have opportunity costs. If we want more of one thing, we must have less of another.

5. Because resources are specialized and, thus, are not equally well suited for producing different outputs.

6. Microeconomics and macroeconomics. Microeconomics is more of a building block of macro because when we address macro issues (for example, unemployment) we have to consider how individuals respond to work incentives such as wages and welfare.

7. As a policy adviser because normative statements are prescriptions about what ought to be and are somewhat based on value judgments.

8. Positive statements are statements of fact and are refutable by examining evidence.

9. Economists may have different scientific judgments. Economists may have different values.

10. A ceiling on rents reduces the quantity and quality of housing available. Tariffs and import quotas usually reduce general economic welfare.

True/False Questions

1. F; economic models are simplifications of reality.
2. T
3. F; there must be at least two individuals for trade.
4. T
5. T
6. T
7. F; points outside the production possibilities frontier cannot yet be attained.
8. T
9. F; it is bowed outward because the trade-offs are not constant.
10. T
11. F; macroeconomics is the study of economy-wide phenomena.
12. F; this statement is positive.
13. T
14. F; normative statements cannot be refuted.
15. T

Multiple-Choice Questions

1. b
2. c
3. a
4. d
5. b
6. d
7. a
8. c
9. b
10. b
11. d
12. c
13. c
14. d
15. a
16. c
17. a
18. d
19. b
20. a

Advanced Critical Thinking

1. Economists may have different scientific judgments. Economists may have different values. There may not really be any real disagreement because the majority of economists may actually agree.

2. Those opposed to free trade are likely to have different values than the majority of economists. There is not much disagreement on this issue among the mainstream economics profession.

3. Yes. It suggests that impediments to international trade may benefit some groups (organized labor) but these impediments are unlikely to benefit the public in general. Supporters of these policies are promoting their own interests.

Appendix

Practice Problems

1. The following ordered pairs of price and quantity demanded describe Joe's demand for cups of gourmet coffee.

Price per cup of coffee	Quantity demanded of coffee
$5	2 cups
4	4 cups
3	6 cups
2	8 cups
1	10 cups

a. Plot and connect the ordered pairs on the graph in Exhibit 10.
b. What is the slope of Joe's demand curve for coffee in the price range of $5 and $4?

_____

c. What is the slope of Joe's demand curve for coffee in the price range of $2 and $1?

_____

d. Are the price of coffee and Joe's quantity demanded of coffee positively correlated or negatively correlated? How can you tell?

_____

_____

e. If the price of coffee moves from $2 per cup to $4 per cup, what happens to the quantity demanded? Is this a movement along a curve or a shift in the curve?

_____

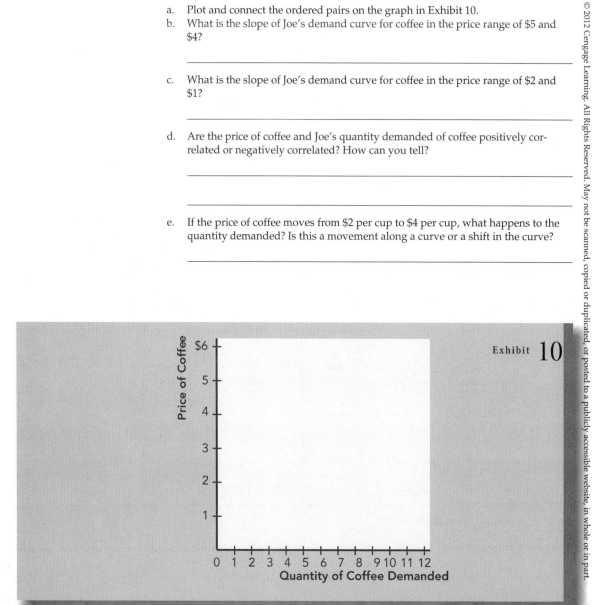

Exhibit 10

f. Suppose Joe's income doubles from $20,000 per year to $40,000 per year. Now the following ordered pairs describe Joe's demand for gourmet coffee. Plot these ordered pairs on the graph provided in part *a* above.

Price per cup of coffee	Quantity demanded of coffee
$5	4 cups
4	6 cups
3	8 cups
2	10 cups
1	12 cups

g. Did the doubling of Joe's income cause a movement along his demand curve or a shift in his demand curve? Why?

_____

_____

2. An alien lands on earth and observes the following: on mornings when people carry umbrellas, it tends to rain later in the day. The alien concludes that umbrellas cause rain.

a. What error has the alien committed?

_____

b. What role did expectations play in the alien's error?

_____

_____

c. If rain is truly caused by humidity, temperature, wind currents, and so on, what additional type of error has the alien committed when it decided that umbrellas cause rain?

_____

True/False Questions

_____   1. When graphing in the coordinate system, the x-coordinate tells us the horizontal location while the y-coordinate tells us the vertical location of the point.

_____   2. When a line slopes upward in the x-, y-coordinate system, the two variables measured on each axis are positively correlated.

_____   3. Price and quantity demanded for most goods are positively related.

_____   4. If three variables are related, one of them must be held constant when graphing the other two in the x-, y-coordinate system.

_____   5. If three variables are related, a change in the variable not represented on the x-, y-coordinate system will cause a movement along the curve drawn in the x-, y-coordinate system.

_____   6. The slope of a line is equal to the change in y divided by the change in x along the line.

_____   7. When a line has negative slope, the two variables measured on each axis are positively correlated.

_____ 8. There is a positive correlation between lying down and death. If we conclude from this evidence that it is unsafe to lie down, we have an omitted variable problem because critically ill people tend to lie down.

_____ 9. Reverse causality means that while we think A causes B, B may actually cause A.

_____ 10. Because people carry umbrellas to work in the morning and it rains later in the afternoon, carrying umbrellas must cause rain.

Solutions

Practice Problems

1. a. See Exhibit 11.

Exhibit 11

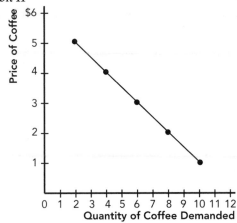

b. –1/2

c. –1/2

d. Negatively correlated, because an increase in price is associated with a decrease in quantity demanded. That is, the demand curve slopes negatively.

e. Decrease by four cups. Movement along curve.

f. See Exhibit 12.

Exhibit 12

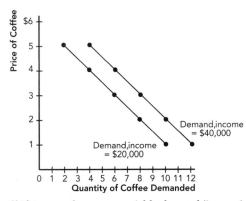

g. Shift in curve because a variable changed (income) that is not measured on either axis.

2. a. Reverse causality.

b. Because rain can be predicted, people's expectation of rain causes them to carry umbrellas before it rains, making it appear as if umbrellas cause rain.

c. Omitted variables.

True/False Questions

1. T
2. T
3. F; they are negatively correlated.
4. T
5. F; a change in a variable not represented on the graph will cause a shift in the curve.
6. T
7. F; negative slope implies negative correlation.
8. T
9. T
10. F; this is an example of reverse causation.

Chapter 3
Interdependence and the Gains from Trade

Goals
In this chapter you will

- Consider how everyone can benefit when people trade with one another
- Learn the meaning of absolute advantage and comparative advantage
- See how comparative advantage explains the gains from trade
- Apply the theory of comparative advantage to everyday life and national policy

Outcomes
After accomplishing these goals, you should be able to

- Show how total production rises when individuals specialize in the production of goods for which they have a comparative advantage
- Explain why all people have a comparative advantage even if they have no absolute advantage
- Demonstrate the link between comparative advantage and opportunity cost
- Explain why people who are good at everything still tend to specialize

Chapter Overview

Context and Purpose

Chapter 3 is the third chapter in the three-chapter section that serves as the introduction of the text. The first chapter introduced ten fundamental principles of economics. The second chapter developed how economists approach problems. This chapter shows how people and countries gain from trade (which is one of the ten principles discussed in Chapter 1).

The purpose of Chapter 3 is to demonstrate how everyone can gain from trade. Trade allows people to specialize in the production of goods for which they have a comparative advantage and then trade for goods that other people produce. Because of specialization, total output rises, and through trade, we are all able to share in the bounty. This is as true for countries as it is for individuals. Because everyone can gain from trade, restrictions on trade tend to reduce welfare.

Chapter Review

Introduction   Each of us consumes products every day that were produced in a number of different countries. Complex products contain components that were produced in many different countries, therefore these products have no single country of origin. Those who produce are neither generous nor ordered by government to produce. People produce because they wish to trade and get something in return. Hence, trade makes us interdependent.

A Parable for the Modern Economy

Imagine a simple economy. There are two people—a cattle rancher and a potato farmer. There are two goods—meat and potatoes.

- If each can produce only one product (the rancher can produce only meat and the farmer potatoes), they will trade just to increase the variety of products they consume. Each benefits because of increased variety.

- If each can produce both goods, but each is more efficient than the other at producing one good, then each will specialize in what he or she does best (again the rancher produces meat and the farmer produces potatoes), total output will rise, and they will trade. Trade allows each to benefit because trade allows for specialization, and specialization increases the total production available to share.

- If one producer is better than the other at producing both meat and potatoes, there are the same advantages to trade but it is more difficult to see. Again, trade allows each to benefit because trade allows for specialization, and specialization increases the total production available to share. To understand the source of the gains from trade when one producer is better at producing both products, we must understand the concept of comparative advantage.

Comparative Advantage: The Driving Force of Specialization

To understand comparative advantage, we begin with the concept of absolute advantage. Absolute advantage compares the quantity of inputs required to produce a good. The producer that requires fewer resources (say fewer hours worked) to produce a good is said to have an absolute advantage in the production of that good. That is, the most efficient producer (the one with the highest productivity) has an absolute advantage.

While absolute advantage compares the actual cost of production for each producer, comparative advantage compares opportunity costs of production for each producer. The producer with the lower opportunity cost of production is said to have a comparative advantage. Regardless of absolute advantage, if producers have different opportunity costs of production for each good, each should specialize in the production of the good for which their opportunity cost of production is lower. That is, each producer should produce the item for which he or she has a comparative advantage. They can then trade some of their output for the other good. Trade makes both producers better off because trade allows for specialization, and specialization increases the total production available to be shared. Both producers gain when they trade at a price that lies between their domestic opportunity costs.

The decision to specialize and the resulting gains from trade are based on comparative advantage, not absolute advantage. Although a single producer can have an absolute advantage in the production of both goods, he cannot have a comparative advantage in the production of both goods because a low opportunity cost of producing one good implies a high opportunity cost of producing the other good.

In summary, trade allows producers to exploit the differences in their opportunity costs of production. Each specializes in the production of the good for which they have the lower opportunity cost of production and, thus, a comparative advantage. This increases total production and makes the economic pie larger. Everyone can benefit. The additional production generated by specialization is the gain from trade.

Adam Smith in his 1776 book *An Inquiry into the Nature and Causes of the Wealth of Nations* and David Ricardo in his 1817 book *Principles of Political Economy and Taxation* both recognized the gains from trade through specialization and the principle of comparative advantage. Current arguments for free trade are still based on their work.

Applications of Comparative Advantage

The principle of comparative advantage applies to individuals as well as countries. Absolute advantage does not determine specialization in production. For example, suppose Tom Brady is the best football player and the best lawn mower in the world, and thus he has an absolute advantage in the production of both goods. If he can earn $20,000 filming a commercial in the time it takes him to mow his own lawn, he gains from trade as long as he pays a lawn service less than $20,000 to mow his lawn. This is because the opportunity cost of mowing for Brady is $20,000. Brady will likely specialize in football and trade for other services. He does this because he has a comparative advantage in football and a comparative disadvantage in lawn mowing (his opportunity cost of mowing is very high) even though he has an absolute advantage in both.

Trade between countries is subject to the same principle of comparative advantage. Goods produced abroad and sold domestically are called imports. Goods produced domestically and sold abroad are called exports. Even if the United States has an absolute advantage in the production of both cars and food, it should specialize in the production of the item for which it has a comparative advantage. Because the opportunity cost of food is low in the United States (better land) and high in Japan, the United States should produce more food and export it to Japan in exchange for imports of autos from Japan. Although the United States gains from trade, the impact of trade on U.S. autoworkers is different from the impact of trade on U.S. farmers.

A reduction in barriers to free trade improves the welfare of the importing country as a whole, but it does not improve the welfare of the domestic producers in the importing country. For this reason, domestic producers lobby their governments to maintain (or increase) barriers to free trade.

Helpful Hints

1. A step-by-step example of comparative advantage will demonstrate most of the concepts discussed in Chapter 3. It will give you a pattern to follow when answering questions at the end of the chapter in your text and for the problems that follow in this Study Guide.

   Suppose we have the following information about the productivity of industry in Japan and Korea. The data are the units of output per hour of work.

	Steel	Televisions
Japan	6	3
Korea	8	2

   A Japanese worker can produce 6 units of steel or 3 televisions per hour. A Korean worker can produce 8 units of steel or 2 televisions per hour.

   We can plot the production possibilities frontier for each country, assuming each country has only one worker and the worker works only one hour. To plot the frontier, plot the end points and connect them with a line. For example, Japan can produce 6 units of steel with its worker or 3 televisions. It can also allocate 1/2 hour to the production of each and get 3 units of steel and 1 1/2 televisions. Any

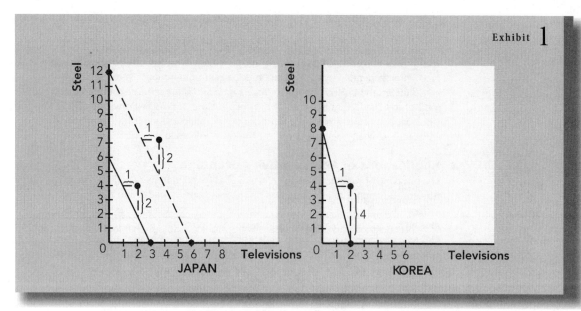

Exhibit 1

other proportion of the hour can be allocated to the two productive activities. The production possibilities frontier is linear in these cases because the labor resource can be moved from the production of one good to the other at a constant rate. We can do the same for Korea. Without trade, the production possibilities frontier is also the consumption possibilities frontier.

Comparative advantage determines specialization and trade. The opportunity cost of a television in Japan is 2 units of steel, which is shown by the slope of the production possibilities frontier in Exhibit 1. Alternatively, the opportunity cost of 1 unit of steel in Japan is 1/2 of a television. In Korea, the opportunity cost of a television is 4 units of steel and the cost of a unit of steel is 1/4 of a television. Because the opportunity cost of a television is lower in Japan, Japan has a comparative advantage in television production and should specialize in televisions. Because the opportunity cost of steel is lower in Korea, Korea has a comparative advantage in steel production and should specialize in steel.

What is the range of prices at which each country would be willing to exchange? If Japan specializes in television production, it would be willing to trade televisions for steel as long as it receives at least 2 units of steel for 1 TV because that was the rate at which it could convert TVs into steel prior to trade. Korea would be willing to specialize in steel production and trade for televisions as long as it gives less than 4 units of steel for 1 TV because that was the Korean trade-off prior to trade. In short, the final price must be between the original trade-offs each faced in the absence of trade. One television will cost between 2 and 4 units of steel, and therefore, 1 unit of steel will cost between 1/2 and 1/4 of a television.

2. Trade allows countries to consume outside their original production possibilities frontier. Suppose that Japan and Korea settle on a trading price of 3 units of steel for 1 television (or 1/3 of a television for 1 unit of steel). (I am giving you this price. There is nothing in the problem that would let you calculate the final trading price. You can only calculate the range in which it must lie.) This price is halfway between the two prices that each faces in the absence of trade. The range for the trading price is 4 units of steel for 1 television to 2 units of steel for 1 television.

If Japan specializes in television production, produces 3 televisions, and exports 1 television for 3 units of steel, Japan will be able to consume 2 televisions and 3 units of steel. If we plot this point (2 televisions and 3 steel) on Japan's graph, we see that it lies outside its production possibilities frontier. If Korea specializes, produces 8 units of steel, and exports 3 units for 1 television, Korea will be able to consume 5 units of steel and 1 television. If we plot this point (5 steel and 1 television) on Korea's graph, we see that it also lies outside its production possibilities frontier.

This is the gain from trade. Trade allows countries (and people) to specialize. Specialization increases world output. After trading, countries consume outside their individual production possibilities frontiers. In this way, trade is like an improvement in technology. It allows countries to move beyond their current production possibilities frontiers.

3. Only comparative advantage matters—absolute advantage is irrelevant. In the previous example, Japan had an absolute advantage in the production of televisions because it could produce 3 per hour whereas Korea could only produce 2. Korea had an absolute advantage in the production of steel because it could produce 8 units per hour compared to 6 for Japan.

To demonstrate that comparative advantage, not absolute advantage, determines specialization and trade, we alter the previous example so that Japan has an absolute advantage in the production of both goods. To this end, suppose Japan becomes twice as productive as in the previous table. That is, a worker can now produce 12 units of steel or 6 televisions per hour.

	Steel	Televisions
Japan	12	6
Korea	8	2

Now Japan has an absolute advantage in the production of both goods. Japan's new production possibilities frontier is the dashed line in Exhibit 1. Will this change the analysis? Not at all. The opportunity cost of each good within Japan is the same—2 units of steel per television or 1/2 television per unit of steel (and Korea is unaffected). For this reason, Japan still has the identical comparative advantage as before, and it will specialize in television production while Korea will specialize in steel. However, because productivity has doubled in Japan, its entire set of choices has improved, and thus, its material welfare has improved.

Terms and Definitions

Choose a definition for each key term.

Key Terms	Definitions
_____Absolute advantage	1. Whatever is given up to obtain some item
_____Comparative advantage	2. The ability to produce a good at a lower opportunity cost than another producer
_____Gains from trade	3. Goods produced domestically and sold abroad
_____Opportunity cost	4. Goods produced abroad and sold domestically
_____Imports	5. The ability to produce a good using fewer inputs than another producer
_____Exports	6. The increase in total production due to specialization allowed by trade

Problems and Short-Answer Questions

Practice Problems

1. Angela is a college student. She takes a full load of classes and has only 5 hours per week for her hobby. Angela is artistic and can make 2 clay pots per hour or 4 coffee mugs per hour.
   a. Draw Angela's production possibilities frontier for pots and mugs in Exhibit 2.

   b. What is Angela's opportunity cost of 1 pot? 10 pots?

   _____

   c. What is Angela's opportunity cost of 1 mug? 10 mugs?

   _____

   d. Why is her production possibilities frontier a straight line instead of bowed out like those presented in Chapter 2?

   _____

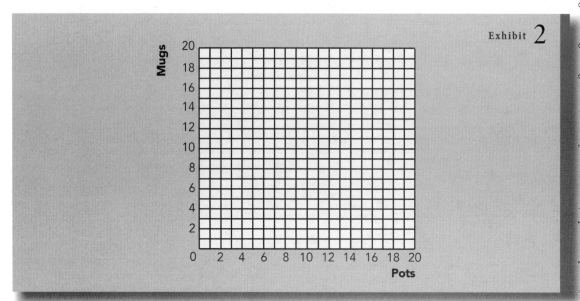

Exhibit 2

2. Suppose a worker in Germany can produce 15 computers or 5 tons of grain per month. Suppose a worker in Poland can produce 4 computers or 4 tons of grain per month. For simplicity, assume that each country has only one worker.
   a. Fill out the following table:

	Computers	Grain
Germany	_____	_____
Poland	_____	_____

   b. Graph the production possibilities frontier for each country in Exhibit 3.

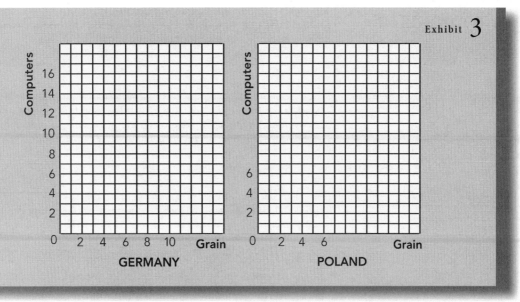

Exhibit 3

GERMANY

POLAND

c. What is the opportunity cost of 1 computer in Germany? What is the opportunity cost of 1 ton of grain in Germany?

_____

d. What is the opportunity cost of 1 computer in Poland? What is the opportunity cost of 1 ton of grain in Poland?

_____

e. Which country has the absolute advantage in producing computers? grain?

_____

_____

f. Which country has the comparative advantage in producing computers? grain?

_____

_____

g. Each country should tend toward specialization in the production of which good? Why?

_____

_____

h. What is the range of prices for computers and grain for which both countries would benefit?

_____

_____

i. Suppose Germany and Poland settle on a price of 2 computers for 1 ton of grain or 1/2 ton of grain for a computer. Suppose each country specializes in production and they trade 4 computers for 2 tons of grain. Plot the final consumption points on the graphs you made in part *b* above. Are these countries consuming inside or outside of their production possibilities frontier?

_____

j. Suppose the productivity of a worker in Poland doubles so that a worker can produce 8 computers or 8 tons of grain per month. Which country has the absolute advantage in producing computers? grain?

k. After the doubling of productivity in Poland, which country has a comparative advantage in producing computers? grain? Has the comparative advantage changed? Has the material welfare of either country changed?

l. How would your analysis change if you assumed, more realistically, that each country had 10 million workers?

3. Suppose a worker in the United States can produce 4 cars or 20 computers per month whereas a worker in Russia can produce 1 car or 5 computers per month. Again, for simplicity, assume each country has only one worker.
   a. Fill out the following table:

	Cars	Computers
United States	_____	_____
Russia	_____	_____

   b. Which country has the absolute advantage in the production of cars? computers?

   c. Which country has the comparative advantage in the production of cars? computers?

   d. Are there any gains to be made from trade? Why?

   e. Does your answer in part *d* above help you pinpoint a source for gains from trade?

   f. What might make two countries have different opportunity costs of production? (Use your imagination. This was not directly discussed in Chapter 3.)

Short-Answer Questions

1. Why do people choose to become interdependent as opposed to self-sufficient?

   _____

   _____

   _____

2. Why is comparative advantage important in determining trade instead of absolute advantage?

   _____

   _____

   _____

3. What are the gains from trade?

   _____

   _____

   _____

   _____

4. Why is a restriction of trade likely to reduce material welfare?

   _____

   _____

5. Suppose a lawyer that earns $200 per hour can also type 200 words per minute. Should the lawyer hire a secretary who can only type 50 words per minute? Why?

   _____

   _____

6. Evaluate this statement: A technologically advanced country, which is better than its neighbor at producing everything, would be better off if it closed its borders to trade because the less productive country is a burden to the advanced country.

   _____

   _____

   _____

   _____

Self-Test

True/False Questions

_____ 1. If Japan has an absolute advantage in the production of an item, it must also have a comparative advantage in the production of that item.

_____ 2. Comparative advantage, not absolute advantage, determines the decision to specialize in production.

_____ 3. Absolute advantage is a comparison among producers based on productivity.

_____ 4. Self-sufficiency is the best way to increase one's material welfare.

_____ 5. Comparative advantage is a comparison among producers based on opportunity cost.

_____ 6. If a producer is self-sufficient, the production possibilities frontier is also the consumption possibilities frontier.

_____ 7. If a country's workers can produce 5 hamburgers per hour or 10 bags of French fries per hour, absent trade, the price of 1 bag of fries is 2 hamburgers.

_____ 8. If producers have different opportunity costs of production, trade will allow them to consume outside their production possibilities frontiers.

_____ 9. If trade benefits one country, its trading partner must be worse off due to trade.

_____ 10. Talented people that are the best at everything have a comparative advantage in the production of everything.

_____ 11. The gains from trade can be measured by the increase in total production that comes from specialization.

_____ 12. When a country removes a specific import restriction, it always benefits every worker in that country.

_____ 13. If Germany's productivity doubles for everything it produces, this will not alter its prior pattern of specialization because it has not altered its comparative advantage.

_____ 14. If an advanced country has an absolute advantage in the production of everything, it will benefit if it eliminates trade with less-developed countries and becomes completely self-sufficient.

_____ 15. If gains from trade are based solely on comparative advantage, and if all countries have the same opportunity costs of production, then there are no gains from trade.

Multiple-Choice Questions

1. If a nation has an absolute advantage in the production of a good,
   a. it can produce that good at a lower opportunity cost than its trading partner.
   b. it can produce that good using fewer resources than its trading partner.
   c. it can benefit by restricting imports of that good.
   d. it will specialize in the production of that good and export it.
   e. none of the above is true.

2. If a nation has a comparative advantage in the production of a good,
   a. it can produce that good at a lower opportunity cost than its trading partner.
   b. it can produce that good using fewer resources than its trading partner.
   c. it can benefit by restricting imports of that good.
   d. it must be the only country with the ability to produce that good.
   e. none of the above is true.

3. Which of the following statements about trade is true?
    a. Unrestricted international trade benefits every person in a country equally.
    b. People that are skilled at all activities cannot benefit from trade.
    c. Trade can benefit everyone in society because it allows people to specialize in activities in which they have an absolute advantage.
    d. Trade can benefit everyone in society because it allows people to specialize in activities in which they have a comparative advantage.

4. According to the principle of comparative advantage,
    a. countries with a comparative advantage in the production of every good need not specialize.
    b. countries should specialize in the production of goods that they enjoy consuming.
    c. countries should specialize in the production of goods for which they use fewer resources in production than their trading partners.
    d. countries should specialize in the production of goods for which they have a lower opportunity cost of production than their trading partners.

5. Which of the following statements is true?
    a. Self-sufficiency is the road to prosperity for most countries.
    b. A self-sufficient country consumes outside its production possibilities frontier.
    c. A self-sufficient country at best can consume on its production possibilities frontier.
    d. Only countries with an absolute advantage in the production of every good should strive to be self-sufficient.

6. Suppose a country's workers can produce 4 watches per hour or 12 rings per hour. If there is no trade,
    a. the domestic price of 1 ring is 3 watches.
    b. the domestic price of 1 ring is 1/3 of a watch.
    c. the domestic price of 1 ring is 4 watches.
    d. the domestic price of 1 ring is 1/4 of a watch.
    e. the domestic price of 1 ring is 12 watches.

7. Suppose a country's workers can produce 4 watches per hour or 12 rings per hour. If there is no trade,
    a. the opportunity cost of 1 watch is 3 rings.
    b. the opportunity cost of 1 watch is 1/3 of a ring.
    c. the opportunity cost of 1 watch is 4 rings.
    d. the opportunity cost of 1 watch is 1/4 of a ring.
    e. the opportunity cost of 1 watch is 12 rings.

The following table shows the units of output a worker can produce per month in Australia and Korea. Use this table to answer questions 8 through 15.

	Food	Electronics
Australia	20	5
Korea	8	4

8. Which of the following statements about absolute advantage is true?
    a. Australia has an absolute advantage in the production of food while Korea has an absolute advantage in the production of electronics.
    b. Korea has an absolute advantage in the production of food while Australia has an absolute advantage in the production of electronics.
    c. Australia has an absolute advantage in the production of both food and electronics.
    d. Korea has an absolute advantage in the production of both food and electronics.

9. The opportunity cost of 1 unit of electronics in Australia is
   a. 5 units of food.
   b. 1/5 of a unit of food.
   c. 4 units of food.
   d. 1/4 of a unit of food.

10. The opportunity cost of 1 unit of electronics in Korea is
    a. 2 units of food.
    b. 1/2 of a unit of food.
    c. 4 units of food.
    d. 1/4 of a unit of food.

11. The opportunity cost of 1 unit of food in Australia is
    a. 5 units of electronics.
    b. 1/5 of a unit of electronics.
    c. 4 units of electronics.
    d. 1/4 of a unit of electronics.

12. The opportunity cost of 1 unit of food in Korea is
    a. 2 units of electronics.
    b. 1/2 of a unit of electronics.
    c. 4 units of electronics.
    d. 1/4 of a unit of electronics.

13. Which of the following statements about comparative advantage is true?
    a. Australia has a comparative advantage in the production of food while Korea has a comparative advantage in the production of electronics.
    b. Korea has a comparative advantage in the production of food while Australia has a comparative advantage in the production of electronics.
    c. Australia has a comparative advantage in the production of both food and electronics.
    d. Korea has a comparative advantage in the production of both food and electronics.
    e. Neither country has a comparative advantage.

14. Korea should
    a. specialize in food production, export food, and import electronics.
    b. specialize in electronics production, export electronics, and import food.
    c. produce both goods because neither country has a comparative advantage.
    d. produce neither good because it has an absolute disadvantage in the production of both goods.

15. Prices of electronics can be stated in terms of units of food. What is the range of prices of electronics for which both countries could gain from trade?
    a. The price must be greater than 1/5 of a unit of food but less than 1/4 of a unit of food.
    b. The price must be greater than 4 units of food but less than 5 units of food.
    c. The price must be greater than 1/4 of a unit of food but less than 1/2 of a unit of food.
    d. The price must be greater than 2 units of food but less than 4 units of food.

16. Suppose the world consists of two countries—the United States and Mexico. Furthermore, suppose there are only two goods—food and clothing. Which of the following statements is true?
    a. If the United States has an absolute advantage in the production of food, then Mexico must have an absolute advantage in the production of clothing.
    b. If the United States has a comparative advantage in the production of food, then Mexico must have a comparative advantage in the production of clothing.
    c. If the United States has a comparative advantage in the production of food, it must also have a comparative advantage in the production of clothing.
    d. If the United States has a comparative advantage in the production of food, Mexico might also have a comparative advantage in the production of food.
    e. None of the above is true.

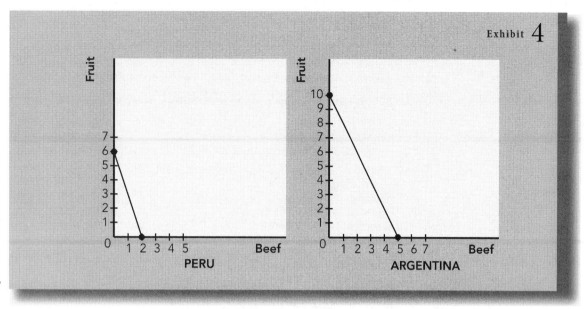

Exhibit 4

Use the production possibilities frontiers in Exhibit 4 to answer questions 17 through 19. Assume each country has the same number of workers, say 20 million, and that each axis is measured in metric tons per month.

17. Argentina has a comparative advantage in the production of
    a. both fruit and beef.
    b. fruit.
    c. beef.
    d. neither fruit nor beef.

18. Peru will export
    a. both fruit and beef.
    b. fruit.
    c. beef.
    d. neither fruit nor beef.

19. The opportunity cost of producing 1 metric ton of beef in Peru is
    a. 1/3 ton of fruit.
    b. 1 ton of fruit.
    c. 2 tons of fruit.
    d. 3 tons of fruit.
    e. 6 tons of fruit.

20. Joe is a tax accountant. He receives $100 per hour doing tax returns. He can type 10,000 characters per hour into spreadsheets. He can hire an assistant who types 2,500 characters per hour into spreadsheets. Which of the following statements is true?
    a. Joe should not hire an assistant because the assistant cannot type as fast as he can.
    b. Joe should hire the assistant as long as he pays the assistant less than $100 per hour.
    c. Joe should hire the assistant as long as he pays the assistant less than $25 per hour.
    d. None of the above is true.

Advanced Critical Thinking

You are watching an election debate on television. A candidate says, "We need to stop the flow of foreign automobiles into our country. If we limit the importation of autos, our domestic auto production will rise and the United States will be better off."

1. Is it likely that the United States will be better off if we limit auto imports? Explain.

   _____

   _____

   _____

   _____

2. Will anyone in the United States be better off if we limit auto imports? Explain.

   _____

   _____

   _____

   _____

3. In the real world, does every person in the country gain when restrictions on imports are reduced? Explain.

   _____

   _____

   _____

   _____

Solutions

Terms and Definitions

__5__ Absolute advantage

__2__ Comparative advantage

__6__ Gains from trade

__1__ Opportunity cost

__4__ Imports

__3__ Exports

Practice Problems

1. a. See Exhibit 5.

Exhibit 5

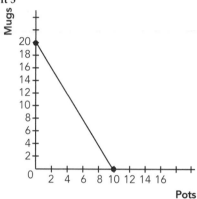

b. 2 mugs. 20 mugs.

c. 1/2 pot. 5 pots.

d. Because here resources can be moved from the production of one good to another at a constant rate.

2. a.

	Computers	Grain
Germany	15	5
Poland	4	4

b. See Exhibit 6.

Exhibit 6

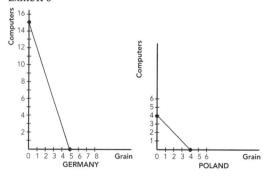

c. 1/3 ton grain. 3 computers.

d. 1 ton grain. 1 computer.

e. Germany because one worker can produce 15 computers compared to 4. Germany because one worker can produce 5 tons of grain compared to 4.

f. Germany because a computer has the opportunity cost of only 1/3 ton of grain compared to 1 ton of grain in Poland. Poland because a ton of grain has the opportunity cost of only 1 computer compared to 3 computers in Germany.

g. Germany should produce computers while Poland should produce grain because the opportunity cost of computers is lower in Germany and the opportunity cost of grain is lower in Poland. That is, each has a comparative advantage in those goods.

h. Grain must cost less than 3 computers to Germany. Computers must cost less than 1 ton of grain to Poland.

i. See Exhibit 7. They are consuming outside their production possibilities frontier.

Exhibit 7

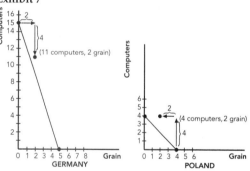

j. Germany because one worker can produce 15 compared to 8. Poland because one worker can produce 8 compared to 5.

k. Germany has comparative advantage in computers. Poland has comparative advantage in grain. No change in comparative advantage. Poland is better off, however, because it now has a larger set of choices.

l. It would not change absolute advantage or comparative advantage. It would change the scale in the previous two graphs by a factor of 10 million.

3. a.

	Cars	Computers
United States	4	20
Russia	1	5

b. United States because one worker can produce 4 cars compared to 1. The United States because one worker can produce 20 computers compared to 5.

c. In both, the opportunity cost of 1 car is 5 computers. In both, the opportunity cost of 1 computer is 1/5 of a car. Therefore, neither has a comparative advantage in either good.

d. No. Each can get the same trade-off between goods domestically.

e. Yes. There needs to be differences in opportunity costs of producing goods across countries for there to be gains from trade.

f. The availability of resources or technology might be different across countries. That is, workers could have different levels of education, land could be of different quality, capital could be of different quality, or the available technology might be different.

Short-Answer Questions

1. Because a consumer gets a greater variety of goods at a much lower cost than they could produce by themselves. That is, there are gains from trade.

2. What is important in trade is how a country's costs without trade differ from each other. This is determined by the relative opportunity costs across countries.

3. The additional output that comes from countries with different opportunity costs of production specializing in the production of the item for which they have the lower domestic opportunity cost.

4. Because it forces people to produce at a higher cost than they pay when they trade.

5. Yes, as long as the secretary earns less than $50 per hour, the lawyer is ahead.

6. This is not true. All countries can gain from trade if their opportunity costs of production differ. Even the least productive country will have a comparative advantage at producing something, and it can trade this good to the advanced country for less than the advanced country's opportunity cost.

True/False Questions

1. F; absolute advantage compares the quantities of inputs used in production while comparative advantage compares the opportunity costs.

2. T

3. T

4. F; restricting trade eliminates gains from trade.

5. T

6. T

7. F; the price of 1 bag of fries is 1/2 of a hamburger.

8. T

9. F; voluntary trade benefits both traders.

10. F; a low opportunity cost of producing one good implies a high opportunity cost of producing the other good.

11. T

12. F; it may harm those involved in that industry.

13. T

14. F; voluntary trade benefits all traders.

15. T

Multiple-Choice Questions

1. b
2. a
3. d
4. d
5. c
6. b
7. a
8. c
9. c
10. a
11. d
12. b
13. a
14. b
15. d
16. b
17. c
18. b
19. d
20. c

Advanced Critical Thinking

1. No. If we import autos, it is because the opportunity cost of producing them elsewhere is lower than in the United States.

2. Yes. Those associated with the domestic auto industry—stockholders of domestic auto producers and autoworkers.

3. No. When we reduce restrictions on imports, the country gains from the increased trade but individuals in the affected domestic industry may lose.

Chapter 4
The Market Forces of Supply and Demand

Goals
In this chapter
you will

- Learn what a competitive market is
- Examine what determines the demand for a good in a competitive market
- Examine what determines the supply of a good in a competitive market
- See how supply and demand together set the price of a good and the quantity sold
- Consider the key role of prices in allocating scarce resources in market economies

Outcomes
After accomplishing
these goals, you
should be able to

- List the two characteristics of a competitive market
- List the factors that affect the amount that consumers wish to buy in a market
- List the factors that affect the amount that producers wish to sell in a market
- Draw a graph of supply and demand in a market and find the equilibrium price and quantity
- Shift supply and demand in response to an economic event and find the new equilibrium price and quantity

Chapter Overview

Context and Purpose

Chapter 4 is the first chapter in a three-chapter sequence that deals with supply and demand and how markets work. Chapter 4 shows how supply and demand for a good determine both the quantity produced and the price at which the good sells. Chapter 5 will add precision to our discussion of supply and demand by addressing the concept of elasticity—the sensitivity of the quantity supplied and quantity demanded to changes in economic variables. Chapter 6 will address the impact of government policies on prices and quantities in markets.

The purpose of Chapter 4 is to establish the model of supply and demand. The model of supply and demand is the foundation for our discussion for the remainder of this text. For this reason, time spent studying the concepts in this chapter will return benefits to you throughout your study of economics. Many instructors would argue that this chapter is the most important chapter in the text.

Chapter Review

Introduction In a market economy, supply and demand determine both the quantity of each good produced and the price at which each good is sold. In this chapter, we develop the determinants of supply and demand. We also address how changes in supply and demand alter prices and change the allocation of the economy's resources.

Markets and Competition

A market is a group of buyers and sellers of a particular good or service. It can be highly organized like a stock market or less organized like the market for ice cream. A competitive market is a market in which there are many buyers and sellers so that each has a negligible impact on the market price.

A *perfectly competitive* market has two main characteristics:

- The goods offered for sale are all exactly the same.

- The buyers and sellers are so numerous that no one buyer or seller can influence the price.

If a market is perfectly competitive, both buyers and sellers are said to be *price takers* because they cannot influence the price. The assumption of perfect competition applies well to agricultural markets because the product is similar and no individual buyer or seller can influence the price.

If a market has only one seller, the market is known as a *monopoly*. Other types of markets fall between the extremes of perfect competition and monopoly.

Demand

The behavior of buyers is captured by the concept of demand. The quantity demanded is the amount of a good that buyers are willing and able to purchase. Although many things determine the quantity demanded of a good, the *price* of the good plays a central role. The law of demand states that, other things equal, an increase in the price of a good reduces the quantity demanded of the good, while a decrease in the price of a good increases the quantity demanded of the good.

The demand schedule is a table that shows the relationship between the price of a good and the quantity demanded. The demand curve is a graph of this relationship with the price on the vertical axis and the quantity demanded on the horizontal axis. The demand curve is downward sloping due to the law of demand.

Market demand is the sum of the quantities demanded for each individual buyer at each price. That is, the market demand curve is the horizontal sum of the individual demand curves. The market demand curve shows the total quantity demanded of a good at each price, while all other factors that affect how much buyers wish to buy are held constant.

- **Shifts in the Demand Curve**   When people change how much they wish to buy at each price, the demand curve shifts. If buyers increase the quantity demanded at each price, the demand curve shifts to the right, which is called an *increase in demand*. Alternatively, if buyers decrease the quantity demanded at each price, the demand curve shifts to the left, which is called a *decrease in demand*. The most important factors that shift demand curves are:

    - *Income:* A normal good is a good for which an increase in income leads to an increase in demand. An inferior good is a good for which an increase in income leads to a decrease in demand.

◆ *Prices of Related Goods:* If two goods can be used in place of one another, they are known as substitutes. When two goods are substitutes, an increase in the price of one good leads to an increase in the demand for the other good. If two goods are used together, they are known as complements. When two goods are complements, an increase in the price of one good leads to a decrease in the demand for the other good.

◆ *Tastes:* If your preferences shift toward a good, it will lead to an increase in the demand for that good.

◆ *Expectations:* Expectations about future income or prices will affect the demand for a good today.

◆ *Number of Buyers:* An increase in the number of buyers will lead to an increase in the market demand for a good because there are more individual demand curves to horizontally sum.

A demand curve is drawn with price on the vertical axis and quantity demanded on the horizontal axis while holding other things equal. Therefore, a change in the price of a good represents a movement along the demand curve while a change in income, prices of related goods, tastes, expectations, and the number of buyers causes a shift in the demand curve.

Supply

The behavior of sellers is captured by the concept of supply. The quantity supplied is the amount of a good that sellers are willing and able to sell. Although many things determine the quantity supplied of a good, the *price* of the good is central. An increase in the price of a good makes production of the good more profitable. Therefore, the law of supply states that, other things equal, an increase in the price of a good increases the quantity supplied of the good, while a decrease in the price of a good reduces the quantity supplied of the good.

The supply schedule is a table that shows the relationship between the price of a good and the quantity supplied. The supply curve is a graph of this relationship with the price on the vertical axis and the quantity supplied on the horizontal axis. The supply curve is upward sloping due to the law of supply.

Market supply is the sum of the quantity supplied for each individual seller at each price. That is, the market supply curve is the horizontal sum of the individual supply curves. The market supply curve shows the total quantity supplied of a good at each price, while all other factors that affect how much producers wish to sell are held constant.

• **Shifts in the Supply Curve**   When producers change how much they wish to sell at each price, the supply curve shifts. If producers increase the quantity supplied at each price, the supply curve shifts right, which is called an *increase in supply*. Alternatively, if producers decrease the quantity supplied at each price, the supply curve shifts left, which is called a *decrease in supply*. The most important factors that shift supply curves are:

◆ *Input Prices:* A decrease in the price of an input makes production more profitable and increases supply.

◆ *Technology:* An improvement in technology reduces costs, makes production more profitable, and increases supply.

◆ *Expectations:* Expectations about the future will affect the supply of a good today.

◆ *Number of Sellers:* An increase in the number of sellers will lead to an increase in the market supply for a good because there are more individual supply curves to horizontally sum.

A supply curve is drawn with price on the vertical axis and quantity supplied on the horizontal axis while holding other things equal. Therefore, a change in the price of a good represents a movement along the supply curve while a change in input prices, technology, expectations, and the number of sellers causes a shift in the supply curve.

Supply and Demand Together

When placed on the same graph, the intersection of supply and demand is called the market's equilibrium. Equilibrium is a situation in which the price has reached the level where quantity supplied equals quantity demanded. The equilibrium price, or the market-clearing price, is the price that balances the quantity demanded and the quantity supplied. When the quantity supplied equals the quantity demanded at the equilibrium price, we have determined the equilibrium quantity.

The market naturally moves toward its equilibrium. If the price is above the equilibrium price, the quantity supplied exceeds the quantity demanded and there is a surplus, or an excess supply, of the good. A surplus causes the price to fall until it reaches equilibrium. If the price is below the equilibrium price, the quantity demanded exceeds the quantity supplied and there is a shortage, or an excess demand for the good. A shortage causes the price to rise until it reaches equilibrium. This natural adjustment of the price to bring the quantity supplied and the quantity demanded into balance is known as the law of supply and demand.

When an economic event shifts the supply or the demand curve, the equilibrium in the market changes, resulting in a new equilibrium price and quantity. When analyzing the impact of some event on the market equilibrium, employ the following three steps:

- Decide whether the event shifts the supply curve or demand curve or both.
- Decide which direction the curve shifts.
- Use the supply-and-demand diagram to see how the shift changes the equilibrium price and quantity.

A shift in the demand curve is called a "change in demand." It is caused by a change in a variable that affects the amount people wish to purchase of a good *other than the price of the good*. A change in the price of a good causes a movement along a given demand curve and is called a "change in the quantity demanded." Likewise, a shift in the supply curve is called a "change in supply." It is caused by a change in a variable that affects the amount producers wish to supply of a good *other than the price of the good*. A change in the price of a good causes a movement along a supply curve and is called a "change in the quantity supplied."

For example, a frost that destroys much of the orange crop causes a decrease in the supply of oranges (supply of oranges shifts to the left). This increases the price of oranges and decreases the quantity demanded of oranges. In other words, a decrease in the supply of oranges increases the price of oranges and decreases the quantity of oranges purchased.

If both supply and demand shift at the same time, there may be more than one possible outcome for the changes in the equilibrium price and quantity. For example, if demand were to increase (shift right) while supply were to decrease (shift left), the price will certainly rise but the impact on the equilibrium quantity is ambiguous. In this case, the change in the equilibrium quantity depends on the magnitudes of the shifts in supply and demand.

Conclusion: How Prices Allocate Resources

Markets generate equilibrium prices. These prices are the signals that guide the allocation of scarce resources. Prices of products rise to the level necessary to allocate the products to those who are willing to pay for them. Prices of inputs (such as labor) rise to the level necessary to induce people to do the jobs that need to be done. Prices coordinate decentralized decision making so that no jobs go undone, and there is no shortage of goods and services for those willing and able to pay for them.

Helpful Hints

1. By far, the greatest difficulty students have when studying supply and demand is distinguishing between a "change in demand" and a "change in the quantity demanded" and between a "change in supply" and a "change in the quantity supplied." It helps to remember that "demand" is the entire relationship between price and quantity demanded. That is, demand is the entire demand curve, not a point on a demand curve. Therefore, a change in demand is a shift in the entire demand curve, which can only be caused by a change in a determinant of demand other than the price of the good. A change in the quantity demanded is a movement along the demand curve and is caused by a change in the price of the good. Likewise, "supply" refers to the entire supply curve, not a point on the supply curve. Therefore, a change in supply is a shift in the entire supply curve, which can only be caused by a change in a determinant of supply other than the price of the good. A change in the quantity supplied is a movement along the supply curve and is caused by a change in the price of the good.

2. If both supply and demand shift at the same time and we do not know the magnitude of each shift, then the change in either the price or the quantity must be ambiguous. For example, if there is an increase in supply (supply shifts right) and an increase in demand (demand shifts right), the equilibrium quantity must certainly rise, but the change in the equilibrium price is ambiguous. Do this for all four possible combinations of changes in supply and demand. You will find that if you know the impact on the equilibrium price with certainty, then the impact on the equilibrium quantity must be ambiguous. If you know the impact on the equilibrium quantity with certainty, then the impact on the equilibrium price must be ambiguous.

Terms and Definitions

Choose a definition for each key term.

Key Terms	Definitions
Key Terms	**Definitions**

Key Terms

_____ Market

_____ Competitive market

_____ Monopoly

_____ Quantity demanded

_____ Law of demand

_____ Demand schedule

_____ Demand curve

_____ Normal good

_____ Inferior good

_____ Substitutes

_____ Complements

_____ Quantity supplied

_____ Law of supply

_____ Supply schedule

_____ Supply curve

_____ Equilibrium

_____ Equilibrium price

_____ Equilibrium quantity

_____ Surplus

_____ Shortage

_____ Law of supply and demand

Definitions

1. The quantity supplied and the quantity demanded at the equilibrium price

2. A table that shows the relationship between the price of a good and the quantity demanded

3. A table that shows the relationship between the price of a good and the quantity supplied

4. Two goods for which an increase in the price of one leads to an increase in the demand for the other

5. A group of buyers and sellers of a particular good or service

6. Market with only one seller

7. A good for which, other things equal, an increase in income leads to a decrease in demand

8. A situation in which quantity demanded is greater than quantity supplied

9. A situation in which quantity supplied is greater than quantity demanded

10. The amount of a good that buyers are willing and able to purchase

11. A situation in which the price has reached the level where quantity supplied equals quantity demanded

12. A market in which there are many buyers and sellers so that each has a negligible impact on the market price

13. The claim that, other things equal, the quantity demanded of a good falls when the price of the good rises

14. A graph of the relationship between the price of a good and the quantity demanded

15. The price that balances quantity supplied and quantity demanded

16. The amount of a good that sellers are willing and able to sell

17. The claim that, other things equal, the quantity supplied of a good rises when the price of the good rises

18. The claim that the price of any good adjusts to bring the quantity supplied and quantity demanded for that good into balance

19. Two goods for which an increase in the price of one leads to a decrease in the demand for the other

20. A good for which, other things equal, an increase in income leads to an increase in demand

21. A graph of the relationship between the price of a good and the quantity supplied

Problems and Short-Answer Questions

Practice Problems

1. Suppose we have the following market supply and demand schedules for bicycles:

Price	Quantity Demanded	Quantity Supplied
$100	70	30
200	60	40
300	50	50
400	40	60
500	30	70
600	20	80

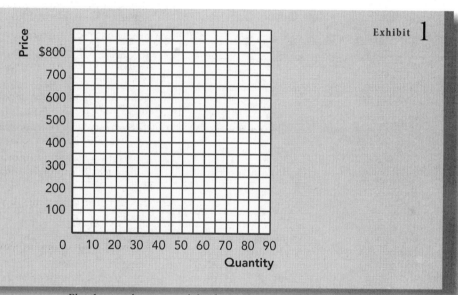

Exhibit 1

a. Plot the supply curve and the demand curve for bicycles in Exhibit 1.
b. What is the equilibrium price of bicycles?

_____

c. What is the equilibrium quantity of bicycles?

_____

d. If the price of bicycles were $100, is there a surplus or a shortage? How many units of surplus or shortage are there? Will this cause the price to rise or fall?

_____

e. If the price of bicycles were $400, is there a surplus or a shortage? How many units of surplus or shortage are there? Will this cause the price to rise or fall?

_____

_____

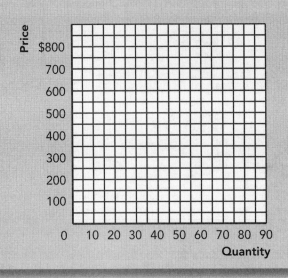

Exhibit 2

f. Suppose that the bicycle maker's labor union bargains for an increase in its wages. Furthermore, suppose this event raises the cost of production, makes bicycle manufacturing less profitable, and reduces the quantity supplied of bicycles by 20 units at each price of bicycles. Plot the new supply curve and the original supply and demand curves in Exhibit 2. What is the new equilibrium price and quantity in the market for bicycles?

_____

_____

2. Each of the events listed below has an impact on the market for bicycles. For each event, which curve is affected (supply or demand for bicycles), what direction is it shifted, and what is the resulting impact on the equilibrium price and quantity of bicycles?

a. The price of automobiles increases.

_____

b. Consumers' incomes decrease, and bicycles are a normal good.

_____

c. The price of steel used to make bicycle frames increases.

_____

d. An environmental movement shifts tastes toward bicycling.

_____

e. Consumers expect the price of bicycles to fall in the future.

_____

f. A technological advance in the manufacture of bicycles occurs.

_____

g. The prices of bicycle helmets and shoes are reduced.

_____

h. Consumers' incomes decrease, and bicycles are an inferior good.

_____

3. The following questions address a market when both supply and demand shift.
   a. What would happen to the equilibrium price and quantity in the bicycle market if there were an increase in both the supply and the demand for bicycles?

   _____

   b. What would happen to the equilibrium price and quantity in the bicycle market if the demand for bicycles increases more than the increase in the supply of bicycles?

   _____

Short-Answer Questions

1. What are the two main characteristics of a perfectly competitive market?

   _____

   _____

2. Explain the law of demand.

   _____

   _____

3. What are the variables that should affect the amount of a good that consumers wish to buy, other than its price?

   _____

   _____

4. What is the difference between a normal good and an inferior good?

   _____

   _____

5. Explain the law of supply.

   _____

   _____

6. What are the variables that should affect the amount of a good that producers wish to sell, other than its price?

   _____

   _____

7. Suppose *suppliers* of corn expect the price of corn to rise in the future. How would this affect the supply and demand for corn and the equilibrium price and quantity of corn?

   _____

   _____

   _____

   _____

8. If there is a surplus of a good, is the price above or below the equilibrium price for that good?

    _____

9. Suppose there is an increase in consumers' incomes. In the market for automobiles (a normal good), does this event cause an increase in demand or an increase in quantity demanded? Does this cause an increase in supply or an increase in quantity supplied? Explain.

    _____

    _____

    _____

    _____

    _____

    _____

10. Suppose there is an advance in the technology employed to produce automobiles. In the market for automobiles, does this event cause an increase in supply or an increase in the quantity supplied? Does this cause an increase in demand or an increase in the quantity demanded? Explain.

    _____

    _____

    _____

    _____

    _____

    _____

Self-Test

True/False Questions

_____   1. A perfectly competitive market consists of products that are all slightly different from one another.

_____   2. A monopolistic market has only one seller.

_____   3. The law of demand states that an increase in the price of a good decreases the demand for that good.

_____   4. If apples and oranges are substitutes, an increase in the price of apples will decrease the demand for oranges.

_____   5. If golf clubs and golf balls are complements, an increase in the price of golf clubs will decrease the demand for golf balls.

_____   6. If consumers expect the price of shoes to rise, there will be an increase in the demand for shoes today.

_____   7. The law of supply states that an increase in the price of a good increases the quantity supplied of that good.

_____ 8. An increase in the price of steel will shift the supply of automobiles to the right.

_____ 9. When the price of a good is below the equilibrium price, it causes a surplus.

_____ 10. The market supply curve is the horizontal summation of the individual supply curves.

_____ 11. If there is a shortage of a good, then the price of that good tends to fall.

_____ 12. If pencils and paper are complements, an increase in the price of pencils causes the demand for paper to decrease or shift to the left.

_____ 13. If Coca-Cola and Pepsi are substitutes, an increase in the price of Coca-Cola will cause an increase in the equilibrium price and quantity in the market for Pepsi.

_____ 14. An advance in the technology employed to manufacture Rollerblades™ will result in a decrease in the equilibrium price and an increase in the equilibrium quantity in the market for Rollerblades™.

_____ 15. If there is an increase in supply accompanied by a decrease in demand for coffee, then there will be a decrease in both the equilibrium price and quantity in the market for coffee.

Multiple-Choice Questions

1. A perfectly competitive market has
   a. only one seller.
   b. at least a few sellers.
   c. many buyers and sellers.
   d. firms that set their own prices.
   e. none of the above.

2. If an increase in the price of blue jeans leads to an increase in the demand for tennis shoes, then blue jeans and tennis shoes are
   a. substitutes.
   b. complements.
   c. normal goods.
   d. inferior goods.
   e. none of the above.

3. The *law of demand* states that an increase in the price of a good
   a. decreases the demand for that good.
   b. decreases the quantity demanded for that good.
   c. increases the supply of that good.
   d. increases the quantity supplied of that good.
   e. does none of the above.

4. The *law of supply* states that an increase in the price of a good
   a. decreases the demand for that good.
   b. decreases the quantity demanded for that good.
   c. increases the supply of that good.
   d. increases the quantity supplied of that good.
   e. does none of the above.

5. If an increase in consumer incomes leads to a decrease in the demand for camping equipment, then camping equipment is
   a. a complementary good.
   b. a substitute good.
   c. a normal good.
   d. an inferior good.
   e. none of the above.

6. A monopolistic market has
   a. only one seller.
   b. at least a few sellers.
   c. many buyers and sellers.
   d. firms that are price takers.
   e. none of the above.

7. Which of the following shifts the demand for watches to the right?
   a. a decrease in the price of watches
   b. a decrease in consumer incomes if watches are a normal good
   c. a decrease in the price of watch batteries if watch batteries and watches are complements
   d. an increase in the price of watches
   e. none of the above

8. All of the following shift the supply of watches to the right except
   a. an increase in the price of watches.
   b. an advance in the technology used to manufacture watches.
   c. a decrease in the wage of workers employed to manufacture watches.
   d. manufacturers' expectations of lower watch prices in the future.
   e. All of the above cause an increase in the supply of watches.

9. If the price of a good is above the equilibrium price,
   a. there is a surplus and the price will rise.
   b. there is a surplus and the price will fall.
   c. there is a shortage and the price will rise.
   d. there is a shortage and the price will fall.
   e. the quantity demanded is equal to the quantity supplied and the price remains unchanged.

10. If the price of a good is below the equilibrium price,
    a. there is a surplus and the price will rise.
    b. there is a surplus and the price will fall.
    c. there is a shortage and the price will rise.
    d. there is a shortage and the price will fall.
    e. the quantity demanded is equal to the quantity supplied and the price remains unchanged.

11. If the price of a good is equal to the equilibrium price,
    a. there is a surplus and the price will rise.
    b. there is a surplus and the price will fall.
    c. there is a shortage and the price will rise.
    d. there is a shortage and the price will fall.
    e. the quantity demanded is equal to the quantity supplied and the price remains unchanged.

12. An increase (rightward shift) in the demand for a good will tend to cause
    a. an increase in the equilibrium price and quantity.
    b. a decrease in the equilibrium price and quantity.
    c. an increase in the equilibrium price and a decrease in the equilibrium quantity.
    d. a decrease in the equilibrium price and an increase in the equilibrium quantity.
    e. none of the above.

13. A decrease (leftward shift) in the supply for a good will tend to cause
    a. an increase in the equilibrium price and quantity.
    b. a decrease in the equilibrium price and quantity.
    c. an increase in the equilibrium price and a decrease in the equilibrium quantity.
    d. a decrease in the equilibrium price and an increase in the equilibrium quantity.
    e. none of the above.

14. Suppose there is an increase in both the supply and demand for personal computers. In the market for personal computers, we would expect the
    a.   equilibrium quantity to rise and the equilibrium price to rise.
    b.   equilibrium quantity to rise and the equilibrium price to fall.
    c.   equilibrium quantity to rise and the equilibrium price to remain constant.
    d.   equilibrium quantity to rise and the change in the equilibrium price to be ambiguous.
    e.   change in the equilibrium quantity to be ambiguous and the equilibrium price to rise.

15. Suppose there is an increase in both the supply and demand for personal computers. Furthermore, suppose the supply of personal computers increases more than demand for personal computers. In the market for personal computers, we would expect the
    a.   equilibrium quantity to rise and the equilibrium price to rise.
    b.   equilibrium quantity to rise and the equilibrium price to fall.
    c.   equilibrium quantity to rise and the equilibrium price to remain constant.
    d.   equilibrium quantity to rise and the change in the equilibrium price to be ambiguous.
    e.   change in the equilibrium quantity to be ambiguous and the equilibrium price to fall.

16. Which of the following statements is true about the impact of an increase in the price of lettuce?
    a.   The demand for lettuce will decrease.
    b.   The supply of lettuce will decrease.
    c.   The equilibrium price and quantity of salad dressing will rise.
    d.   The equilibrium price and quantity of salad dressing will fall.
    e.   Both *a* and *d* are true.

17. Suppose a frost destroys much of the Florida orange crop. At the same time, suppose consumer tastes shift toward orange juice. What would we expect to happen to the equilibrium price and quantity in the market for orange juice?
    a.   Price will increase; quantity is ambiguous.
    b.   Price will increase; quantity will increase.
    c.   Price will increase; quantity will decrease.
    d.   Price will decrease; quantity is ambiguous.
    e.   The impact on both price and quantity is ambiguous.

18. Suppose consumer tastes shift toward the consumption of apples. Which of the following statements is an accurate description of the impact of this event on the market for apples?
    a.   There is an increase in the demand for apples and an increase in the quantity supplied of apples.
    b.   There is an increase in the demand and supply of apples.
    c.   There is an increase in the quantity demanded of apples and in the supply for apples.
    d.   There is an increase in the demand for apples and a decrease in the supply of apples.
    e.   There is a decrease in the quantity demanded of apples and an increase in the supply for apples.

19. Suppose both buyers and sellers of wheat expect the price of wheat to rise in the near future. What would we expect to happen to the equilibrium price and quantity in the market for wheat today?
    a.   The impact on both price and quantity is ambiguous.
    b.   Price will increase; quantity is ambiguous.
    c.   Price will increase; quantity will increase.
    d.   Price will increase; quantity will decrease.
    e.   Price will decrease; quantity is ambiguous.

20. An inferior good is one for which an increase in income causes a(n)
    a. increase in supply.
    b. decrease in supply.
    c. increase in demand.
    d. decrease in demand.

Advanced Critical Thinking

You are watching a national news broadcast. It is reported that a typhoon is heading for the Washington coast and that it will likely destroy much of this year's apple crop. Your roommate says, "If there are going to be fewer apples available, I'll bet that apple prices will rise. We should buy enormous quantities of apples now and put them in storage. Later we will sell them and make a killing."

1. If this information about the storm is publicly available so that all buyers and sellers in the apple market expect the price of apples to rise in the future, what will happen immediately to the supply and demand for apples and the equilibrium price and quantity of apples?

    _____

    _____

    _____

    _____

2. Can you "beat the market" with public information? That is, can you use publicly available information to help you buy something cheap and quickly sell it at a higher price? Why or why not?

    _____

    _____

    _____

    _____

3. Suppose a friend of yours works for the U.S. Weather Bureau. She calls you and provides you with inside information about the approaching storm—information not available to the public. Can you "beat the market" with inside information? Why or why not?

    _____

    _____

    _____

    _____

Solutions

Terms and Definitions

 5 Market
12 Competitive market
 6 Monopoly
10 Quantity demanded
13 Law of demand
 2 Demand schedule
14 Demand curve
20 Normal good
 7 Inferior good
 4 Substitutes
19 Complements
16 Quantity supplied
17 Law of supply
 3 Supply schedule
21 Supply curve
11 Equilibrium
15 Equilibrium price
 1 Equilibrium quantity
 9 Surplus
 8 Shortage
18 Law of supply and demand

Practice Problems

1. a. See Exhibit 3.

Exhibit 3

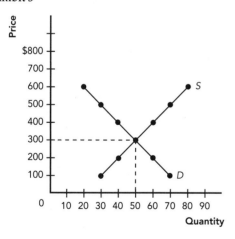

b. $300
c. 50 bicycles
d. ˙Shortage, 70 – 30 = 40 units, the price will rise
e. Surplus, 60 – 40 = 20 units, the price will fall
f. See Exhibit 4. equilibrium price = $400, equi-
    librium quantity = 40 bicycles

Exhibit 4

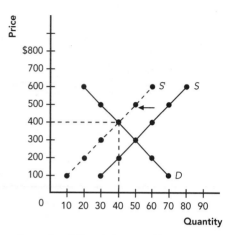

2. a. demand, shifts right, equilibrium price and
    quantity rise
b. demand, shifts left, equilibrium price and
    quantity fall
c. supply, shifts left, equilibrium price rises and
    equilibrium quantity falls
d. demand, shifts right, equilibrium price and
    quantity rise
e. demand, shifts left, equilibrium price and
    quantity fall
f. supply, shifts right, equilibrium price falls and
    equilibrium quantity rises
g. demand, shifts right, equilibrium price and
    quantity rise
h. demand, shifts right, equilibrium price and
    quantity rise

3. a. equilibrium quantity will rise, equilibrium price
    is ambiguous
b. equilibrium price and quantity will rise

Short-Answer Questions

1. The goods offered for sale are all the same, and
    the buyers and sellers are so numerous that no one
    buyer or seller can influence the price.
2. Other things equal, price and quantity demanded
    of a good are negatively related.
3. Income, prices of related goods, tastes, expecta-
    tions, and number of buyers in the market.
4. When income rises, demand for a normal good
    increases or shifts right. When income rises, de-
    mand for an inferior good decreases or shifts left.
5. Other things equal, price and quantity supplied of
    a good are positively related.
6. The variables are input prices, technology,
    expectations, and number of sellers in the market.
7. The supply of corn in today's market would
    decrease (shift left) as sellers hold back their of-
    ferings in anticipation of greater profits if the

price rises in the future. If only suppliers expect higher prices, demand would be unaffected. The equilibrium price would rise and the equilibrium quantity would fall.

8. The price must be above the equilibrium price.

9. There would be an *increase in the demand* for automobiles, which means that the entire demand curve shifts to the right. This implies a movement along the fixed supply curve as the price rises. The increase in price causes an *increase in the quantity supplied* of automobiles, but there is no increase in the supply of automobiles.

10. There would be an *increase in the supply* of automobiles, which means that the entire supply curve shifts to the right. This implies a movement along the fixed demand curve as the price falls. The decrease in price causes an *increase in the quantity demanded* of automobiles, but there is no increase in the demand for automobiles.

True/False Questions

1. F; a perfectly competitive market consists of goods offered for sale that are all exactly the same.
2. T
3. F; the law of demand states that an increase in the price of a good decreases the *quantity demanded* of that good (a movement along the demand curve).
4. F; it will increase the demand for oranges.
5. T
6. T
7. T
8. F; an increase in the price of an input shifts the supply curve for the output to the left.
9. F; it causes an excess demand.
10. T
11. F; an excess demand causes the price to rise.
12. T
13. T
14. T
15. F; there will be a decrease in the equilibrium price, but the impact on the equilibrium quantity is ambiguous.

Multiple-Choice Questions

1. c
2. a
3. b
4. d
5. d
6. a
7. c
8. a
9. b
10. c
11. e
12. a

13. c
14. d
15. b
16. d
17. a
18. a
19. b
20. d

Advanced Critical Thinking

1. Sellers reduce supply (supply shifts left) in the hope of selling apples later at a higher price, and buyers increase demand (demand shifts right) in the hope of buying apples now before the price goes up. The price will immediately rise and the quantity exchanged is ambiguous.

2. No. Usually the market immediately adjusts so that the price has already moved to its new equilibrium value before the amateur speculator can make his or her purchase.

3. Yes. In this case, you can make your purchase before the market responds to the information about the storm.

Chapter 5
Elasticity and Its Application

Goals
In this chapter you will

- Learn the meaning of the elasticity of demand

- Examine what determines the elasticity of demand

- Learn the meaning of the elasticity of supply

- Examine what determines the elasticity of supply

- Apply the concept of elasticity in three very different markets

Outcomes
After accomplishing these goals, you should be able to

- Calculate the price and income elasticity of demand

- Distinguish between the price elasticity of demand for necessities and luxuries

- Calculate the price elasticity of supply

- Distinguish between an inelastic and elastic supply curve

- Demonstrate the impact of the price elasticity of demand on total revenue

Chapter Overview

Context and Purpose

Chapter 5 is the second chapter of a three-chapter sequence that deals with supply and demand and how markets work. Chapter 4 introduced supply and demand. Chapter 5 shows how much buyers and sellers respond to changes in market conditions. Chapter 6 will address the impact of government policies on competitive markets.

The purpose of Chapter 5 is to add precision to our supply and demand model. We introduce the concept of elasticity, which measures the responsiveness of buyers and sellers to changes in economic variables such as prices and income. The concept of elasticity allows us to make quantitative observations about the impact of changes in supply and demand on equilibrium prices and quantities.

Chapter Review

Introduction   In Chapter 4, we learned that an increase in price reduces the quantity demanded and increases the quantity supplied in a market. In this chapter, we will develop the concept of elasticity so that we can address how much the quantity demanded and the quantity supplied responds to changes in market conditions such as price.

The Elasticity of Demand

To measure the response of demand to changes in its determinants, we use the concept of elasticity. Price elasticity of demand measures how much the quantity demanded responds to a change in the price of that good, computed as the percentage change in quantity demanded divided by the percentage change in price.

If the quantity demanded changes substantially from a change in price, demand is *elastic*. If the quantity demanded changes little from a change in price, demand is *inelastic*. Whether a demand curve tends to be price elastic or inelastic depends on the following:

- *Availability of close substitutes:* The demand for goods with close substitutes is more sensitive to changes in prices and, thus, is more price elastic.

- *Necessities versus luxuries:* The demand for necessities is inelastic while the demand for luxuries is elastic. Because one cannot do without a necessity, an increase in the price has little impact on the quantity demanded. However, an increase in price greatly reduces the quantity demanded of a luxury.

- *Definition of the market:* The more narrowly we define the market, the more likely there are to be close substitutes and the more price elastic the demand curve.

- *Time horizon:* The longer the time period considered, the greater the availability of close substitutes and the more price elastic the demand curve.

The formula for computing the price elasticity of demand is:

$$\text{Price elasticity of demand} = \frac{\text{Percentage change in quantity demanded}}{\text{Percentage change in price}}$$

Because price elasticity of demand is always negative, it is customary to drop the negative sign.

When we compute price elasticity between any two points on a demand curve, we get a different answer depending on our chosen starting point and our chosen finishing point if we take the change in price and quantity as a percent of the starting value for each. To avoid this problem, economists often employ the *midpoint method* to calculate elasticities. With this method, the percentage changes in quantity and price are calculated by dividing the change in the variable by the *average* or midpoint value of the two points on the curve, not the starting point on the curve. Thus, the formula for the price elasticity of demand using the midpoint method is:

$$\text{Price elasticity of demand} = \frac{(Q_2 - Q_1)/\left[(Q_2 + Q_1)/2\right]}{(P_2 - P_1)/\left[(P_2 + P_1)/2\right]}.$$

If price elasticity of demand is greater than one, demand is elastic. If elasticity is less than one, demand is inelastic. If elasticity is equal to one, demand is said to have unit elasticity. If elasticity is zero, demand is perfectly inelastic (vertical). If elasticity is infinite, demand is perfectly elastic (horizontal). In general, the flatter the demand curve, the more elastic. The steeper the demand curve, the more inelastic.

Total revenue is the amount paid by buyers and received by sellers, computed simply as price times quantity. The elasticity of demand determines the impact of a change in price on total revenue:

- If demand is price inelastic (less than one), an increase in price increases total revenue because the price increase is proportionately larger than the reduction in quantity demanded.

- If demand is price elastic (greater than one), an increase in price decreases total revenue because the decrease in the quantity demanded is proportionately larger than the increase in price.

- If demand is unit price elastic (exactly equal to one), a change in price has no impact on total revenue because the increase in price is proportionately equal to the decrease in quantity.

Along a linear demand curve, price elasticity is not constant. When price is high and quantity low, price elasticity is large because a change in price causes a larger *percentage* change in quantity. When price is low and quantity high, price elasticity is small because a change in price causes a smaller *percentage* change in quantity.

There are additional demand elasticities. The income elasticity of demand is a measure of how much the quantity demanded responds to a change in consumers' income, computed as the percentage change in quantity demanded divided by the percentage change in income or:

$$\text{Income elasticity of demand} = \frac{\text{Percentage change in quantity demanded}}{\text{Percentage change in income}}$$

For *normal goods*, income elasticity is positive. For *inferior goods*, income elasticity is negative. Within the group of normal goods, necessities like food have small income elasticities because the quantity demanded changes little when income changes. Luxuries have larger income elasticities.

The cross-price elasticity of demand is a measure of the response of the quantity demanded of one good to a change in the price of another good, computed as the percentage change in the quantity demanded of one good divided by the percentage change in the price of another good or:

$$\text{Cross-price elasticity of demand} = \frac{\text{Percentage change in quantity demanded of good 1}}{\text{Percentage change in the price of good 2}}$$

The cross-price elasticity of demand is positive for *substitutes* and negative for *complements*.

The Elasticity of Supply

Price elasticity of supply measures how much the quantity supplied responds to a change in the price of that good, computed as the percentage change in quantity supplied divided by the percentage change in price.

If the quantity supplied changes substantially from a change in price, supply is *elastic*. If the quantity supplied changes little from a change in price, supply is *inelastic*. Supply is more elastic when the sellers have greater flexibility to change the amount of a good they produce in response to a change in price. Generally, the shorter the time period considered, the less flexibility the seller has in choosing how much to produce and the more inelastic the supply curve.

The formula for computing the price elasticity of supply is:

$$\text{Price elasticity of supply} = \frac{\text{Percentage change in quantity supplied}}{\text{Percentage change in price}}$$

If price elasticity of supply is greater than one, supply is elastic. If elasticity is less than one, supply is inelastic. If elasticity is equal to one, supply is said to have unit elasticity. If elasticity is zero, supply is perfectly inelastic (vertical). If elasticity is infinite, supply is perfectly elastic (horizontal). In general, the flatter the supply curve, the more elastic. The steeper the supply curve, the more inelastic.

Price elasticity of supply may not be constant along a given supply curve. At low quantities, a small increase in price may stimulate a large increase in quantity supplied because there is excess capacity in the production facility. Therefore, price elasticity is large. At high quantities, a large increase in price may cause only a small increase in quantity supplied because the production facility is at full capacity. Therefore, price elasticity is small.

Three Applications of Supply, Demand, and Elasticity

- *The market for agricultural products:* Advances in technology have shifted the supply curve for agricultural products to the right. The demand for food, however, is generally inelastic (steep) because food is inexpensive and a necessity. As a result, the rightward shift in supply has caused a great reduction in the equilibrium price and a small increase in the equilibrium quantity. Thus, ironically, technological advances in agriculture reduce total revenue paid to farmers as a group.

- *The market for oil:* In the 1970s and early 1980s, the Organization of Petroleum Exporting Countries (OPEC) reduced the supply of oil in order to raise its price. In the short run, the demand for oil tends to be inelastic (steep) because consumers cannot easily find substitutes. Thus, the decrease in supply raised the price substantially and increased total revenue to the producers. In the long run, however, consumers found substitutes and drove more fuel-efficient cars causing the demand for oil to become more elastic, and producers searched for more oil causing supply to become more elastic. As a result, while the price of oil rose a great deal in the short run, it did not rise much in the long run.

- *The market for illegal drugs:* In the short run, the demand for illegal addictive drugs is relatively inelastic. As a result, drug interdiction policies that reduce the supply of drugs tend to greatly increase the price of drugs while reducing the quantity consumed very little, and thus, total revenue paid by drug users increases. This need for additional funds by drug users may cause drug-related crime to rise. This increase in total revenue and in crime is likely to be smaller in the long run because the demand for illegal drugs becomes more elastic as time passes. Alternatively, policies aimed at reducing the demand for drugs reduce total revenue in the drug market and reduce drug-related crime.

Conclusion

The tools of supply and demand allow you to analyze the most important events and policies that shape the economy.

Helpful Hints

1. An easy way to remember the difference between the terms elastic and inelastic is to substitute the word *sensitivity* for elasticity. For example, price elasticity of demand becomes price *sensitivity* of demand. If the quantity demanded is sensitive to a change in price (demand is relatively flat), demand is elastic. If the quantity demanded is insensitive to a change in price (demand is relatively steep), demand is inelastic. The same is true for the price elasticity of supply. If the quantity supplied is sensitive to a change in price, supply is elastic. If the quantity supplied is insensitive to a change in price, supply is inelastic.

2. Although elasticity and slope are similar, they are not the same. Along a straight line, slope is constant. Slope (rise over run) is the same anywhere on the line and is measured as the change in the dependent variable divided by the change in the independent variable. Elasticity, however, is measured as the *percent* change in the dependent variable divided by the *percent* change in the independent variable. This value changes as we move along a line, because a one-unit change in a variable is a larger percentage change when the initial values are small as opposed to when they are large. In practice, however, it is still reasonable to suggest that flatter curves tend to be more elastic and steeper curves tend to be more inelastic.

3. The term "elasticity" is used to describe how much the quantity stretches (or changes) in response to some economic event such as a change in price or income. If the quantity stretches a great deal in response to a change in price or income, it is considered elastic. This mental picture should also help you remember how to

calculate an elasticity—in the numerator, you will always find the percent change in quantity, and in the denominator, you will always find the percent change in the variable that is the source of the change in quantity.

Terms and Definitions

Choose a definition for each key term.

Key Terms

_____ Elasticity

_____ Price elasticity of demand

_____ Elastic

_____ Inelastic

_____ Total revenue

_____ Income elasticity of demand

_____ Cross-price elasticity of demand

_____ Price elasticity of supply

_____ Normal good

_____ Inferior good

Definitions

1. A measure of how much the quantity demanded of a good responds to a change in consumers' income.

2. When the quantity demanded or supplied responds substantially to a change in one of its determinants.

3. A good characterized by a negative income elasticity.

4. A measure of the responsiveness of the quantity demanded or quantity supplied to a change in one of its determinants.

5. A good characterized by a positive income elasticity.

6. A measure of how much the quantity supplied of a good responds to a change in the price of that good.

7. When the quantity demanded or supplied responds only slightly to a change in one of its determinants.

8. The amount paid by buyers and received by sellers of a good computed as $P \times Q$.

9. A measure of how much the quantity demanded of a good responds to a change in the price of that good.

10. A measure of how much the quantity demanded of one good responds to a change in the price of another good.

Problems and Short-Answer Questions

Practice Problems

1. For each pair of goods listed below, which good would you expect to have the more elastic demand? Why?
   a. cigarettes; a trip to Florida over spring break

   _____

   _____

b.   an AIDS vaccine over the next month; an AIDS vaccine over the next five years

_____

_____

_____

c.   beer; Budweiser

_____

_____

d.   insulin; aspirin

_____

_____

2.   Suppose the *Daily Newspaper* estimates that if it raises the price of its newspaper from $1.00 to $1.50 then the number of subscribers will fall from 50,000 to 40,000.
     a.   What is the price elasticity of demand for the *Daily Newspaper* when elasticity is calculated using the midpoint method?

     _____

     b.   What is the advantage of using the midpoint method?

     _____

     _____

     c.   If the *Daily Newspaper*'s only concern is to maximize total revenue, should it raise the price of a newspaper from $1.00 to $1.50? Why or why not?

     _____

     _____

3.   The table below provides the demand schedule for motel rooms at Small Town Motel. Use the information provided to complete the table. Answer the following questions based on your responses in the table. Use the midpoint method to calculate the percentage changes used to generate the elasticities.

Price	Quantity Demanded	Total Revenue	% Change in Price	% Change in Quantity	Elasticity
$ 20	24	_____			
40	20	_____	_____	_____	_____
60	16	_____	_____	_____	_____
80	12	_____	_____	_____	_____
100	8	_____	_____	_____	_____
120	4	_____	_____	_____	_____

a. Over what range of prices is the demand for motel rooms elastic? To maximize total revenue, should Small Town Motel raise or lower the price within this range?

_____

b. Over what range of prices is the demand for motel rooms inelastic? To maximize total revenue, should Small Town Motel raise or lower the price within this range?

_____

c. Over what range of prices is the demand for motel rooms unit elastic? To maximize total revenue, should Small Town Motel raise or lower the price within this range?

_____

_____

4. The demand schedule from question 3 above is reproduced below along with another demand schedule when consumer incomes have risen to $60,000 from $50,000. Use this information to answer the following questions. Use the midpoint method to calculate the percentage changes used to generate the elasticities.

Price	Quantity Demanded When Income Is $50,000	Quantity Demanded When Income Is $60,000
$ 20	24	34
40	20	30
60	16	26
80	12	22
100	8	18
120	4	14

a. What is the income elasticity of demand when motel rooms rent for $40?

_____

b. What is the income elasticity of demand when motel rooms rent for $100?

_____

c. Are motel rooms normal or inferior goods? Why?

_____

_____

d. Are motel rooms likely to be necessities or luxuries? Why?

_____

_____

5. For each pair of goods listed below, which good would you expect to have the more elastic supply? Why?
   a. televisions; beachfront property

   _____

   _____

   _____

   b. crude oil over the next week; crude oil over the next year

   _____

   _____

   _____

   c. a painting by van Gogh; a print of the same painting by van Gogh

   _____

   _____

   _____

Short-Answer Questions

1. What are the four major determinants of the price elasticity of demand?

   _____

   _____

   _____

   _____

2. If demand is inelastic, will an increase in price raise or lower total revenue? Why?

   _____

   _____

   _____

   _____

3. If the price of soda doubles from $1.00 per can to $2.00 per can and you buy the same amount, what is your price elasticity of demand for soda, and is it considered elastic or inelastic?

   _____

4. If the price of Pepsi increases by one cent and this induces you to stop buying Pepsi altogether and switch to Coca-Cola, what is your price elasticity of demand for Pepsi, and is it considered elastic or inelastic?

   _____

5. Suppose your income rises by 20 percent and your quantity demanded of eggs falls by 10 percent. What is the value of your income elasticity of demand for eggs? Are eggs normal or inferior goods to you?

   _____

6. Suppose a firm is operating at half capacity. Is its supply curve for output likely to be relatively elastic or inelastic? Why?

   _____

   _____

   _____

   _____

7. Is the price elasticity of supply for fresh fish likely to be elastic or inelastic when measured over the time period of one day? Why?

   _____

   _____

   _____

   _____

8. If a demand curve is linear, is the elasticity constant along the demand curve? Which part tends to be elastic and which part tends to be inelastic? Why?

   _____

   _____

   _____

   _____

9. Suppose that at a price of $2.00 per bushel, the quantity supplied of corn is 25 million metric tons. At a price of $3.00 per bushel, the quantity supplied is 30 million metric tons. What is the elasticity of supply for corn? Is supply elastic or inelastic?

   _____

10. Suppose that when the price of apples rises by 20 percent, the quantity demanded of oranges rises by 6 percent. What is the cross-price elasticity of demand between apples and oranges? Are these two goods substitutes or complements?

   _____

   _____

   _____

   _____

Self-Test

True/False Questions

_____ 1. If the quantity demanded of a good is sensitive to a change in the price of that good, demand is said to be price inelastic.

_____ 2. Using the midpoint method to calculate elasticity, if an increase in the price of pencils from 10 cents to 20 cents reduces the quantity demanded from 1,000 pencils to 500 pencils, then the demand for pencils is unit price elastic.

_____ 3. The demand for tires should be more inelastic than the demand for Goodyear brand tires.

_____ 4. The demand for aspirin this month should be more elastic than the demand for aspirin this year.

_____ 5. The price elasticity of demand is defined as the percentage change in the price of that good divided by the percentage change in quantity demanded of that good.

_____ 6. If the cross-price elasticity of demand between two goods is positive, the goods are likely to be complements.

_____ 7. If the demand for a good is price inelastic, an increase in its price will increase total revenue in that market.

_____ 8. The demand for a necessity such as insulin tends to be elastic.

_____ 9. If a demand curve is linear, the price elasticity of demand is constant along it.

_____ 10. If the income elasticity of demand for a bus ride is negative, then a bus ride is an inferior good.

_____ 11. The supply of automobiles for this week is likely to be more price inelastic than the supply of automobiles for this year.

_____ 12. If the price elasticity of supply for blue jeans is 1.3, an increase of 10 percent in the price of blue jeans would increase the quantity supplied of blue jeans by 13 percent.

_____ 13. The price elasticity of supply tends to be more inelastic as the firm's production facility reaches maximum capacity.

_____ 14. An advance in technology that shifts the market supply curve to the right always increases total revenue received by producers.

_____ 15. The income elasticity of demand for luxury items, such as diamonds, tends to be large (greater than 1).

Multiple-Choice Questions

1. If a small percentage increase in the price of a good greatly reduces the quantity demanded for that good, the demand for that good is
   a. price inelastic.
   b. price elastic.
   c. unit price elastic.
   d. income inelastic.
   e. income elastic.

2. The price elasticity of demand is defined as
   a. the percentage change in price of a good divided by the percentage change in the quantity demanded of that good.
   b. the percentage change in income divided by the percentage change in the quantity demanded.
   c. the percentage change in the quantity demanded of a good divided by the percentage change in the price of that good.
   d. the percentage change in the quantity demanded divided by the percentage change in income.
   e. none of the above.

3. In general, a flatter demand curve is more likely to be
   a. price elastic.
   b. price inelastic.
   c. unit price elastic.
   d. none of the above.

4. In general, a steeper supply curve is more likely to be
   a. price elastic.
   b. price inelastic.
   c. unit price elastic.
   d. none of the above.

5. Which of the following would cause a demand curve for a good to be price inelastic?
   a. There are a great number of substitutes for the good.
   b. The good is inferior.
   c. The good is a luxury.
   d. The good is a necessity.

6. The demand for which of the following is likely to be the most price inelastic?
   a. airline tickets
   b. bus tickets
   c. taxi rides
   d. transportation

7. If the cross-price elasticity between two goods is negative, the two goods are likely to be
   a. luxuries.
   b. necessities.
   c. complements.
   d. substitutes.

8. If a supply curve for a good is price elastic, then
   a. the quantity supplied is sensitive to changes in the price of that good.
   b. the quantity supplied is insensitive to changes in the price of that good.
   c. the quantity demanded is sensitive to changes in the price of that good.
   d. the quantity demanded is insensitive to changes in the price of that good.
   e. none of the above.

9. If a fisherman must sell all of his daily catch before it spoils for whatever price he is offered, once the fish are caught, the fisherman's price elasticity of supply for fresh fish is
    a. zero.
    b. one.
    c. infinite.
    d. unable to be determined from this information.

10. A decrease in supply (shift to the left) will increase total revenue in that market if
    a. supply is price elastic.
    b. supply is price inelastic.
    c. demand is price elastic.
    d. demand is price inelastic.

11. If an increase in the price of a good has no impact on the total revenue in that market, demand must be
    a. price inelastic.
    b. price elastic.
    c. unit price elastic.
    d. all of the above.

12. If consumers always spend 15 percent of their income on food, then the income elasticity of demand for food is
    a. 0.15.
    b. 1.00.
    c. 1.15.
    d. 1.50.
    e. none of the above.

13. Technological improvements in agriculture that shift the supply of agricultural commodities to the right tend to
    a. reduce total revenue to farmers as a whole because the demand for food is inelastic.
    b. reduce total revenue to farmers as a whole because the demand for food is elastic.
    c. increase total revenue to farmers as a whole because the demand for food is inelastic.
    d. increase total revenue to farmers as a whole because the demand for food is elastic.

14. If supply is price inelastic, the value of the price elasticity of supply must be
    a. zero.
    b. less than 1.
    c. greater than 1.
    d. infinite.
    e. none of the above.

15. If there is excess capacity in a production facility, it is likely that the firm's supply curve is
    a. price inelastic.
    b. price elastic.
    c. unit price elastic.
    d. none of the above.

Use the following information to answer questions 16 and 17. Suppose that at a price of $30 per month, there are 30,000 subscribers to cable television in Small Town. If Small Town Cablevision raises its price to $40 per month, the number of subscribers will fall to 20,000.

16. Using the midpoint method for calculating the elasticity, what is the price elasticity of demand for cable television in Small Town?
    a. 0.66
    b. 0.75
    c. 1.0
    d. 1.4
    e. 2.0

17. At which of the following prices does Small Town Cablevision earn the greatest total revenue?
    a. either $30 or $40 per month because the price elasticity of demand is 1.0
    b. $30 per month
    c. $40 per month
    d. $0 per month

18. If demand is linear (a straight line), then price elasticity of demand is
    a. constant along the demand curve.
    b. inelastic in the upper portion and elastic in the lower portion.
    c. elastic in the upper portion and inelastic in the lower portion.
    d. elastic throughout.
    e. inelastic throughout.

19. If the income elasticity of demand for a good is negative, it must be
    a. a luxury good.
    b. a normal good.
    c. an inferior good.
    d. an elastic good.

20. If consumers think that there are very few substitutes for a good, then
    a. supply would tend to be price elastic.
    b. supply would tend to be price inelastic.
    c. demand would tend to be price elastic.
    d. demand would tend to be price inelastic.
    e. none of the above is true.

Advanced Critical Thinking

In order to reduce teen smoking, the government places a $2 per pack tax on cigarettes. After one month, while the price to the consumer has increased a great deal, the quantity demanded of cigarettes has been reduced only slightly.

1. Is the demand for cigarettes over the period of one month elastic or inelastic?

_____

2. Suppose you are in charge of pricing for a tobacco firm. The president of your firm suggests that the evidence received over the last month demonstrates that the cigarette industry should get together and raise the price of cigarettes further because total revenue to the tobacco industry will certainly rise. Is the president of your firm correct? Why or why not?

_____

_____

_____

_____

3. As an alternative, suppose the president of your tobacco firm suggests that your firm raise the price of your cigarettes independent of the other tobacco firms because the evidence clearly shows that smokers are insensitive to changes in the price of cigarettes. Is the president of your firm correct if it is his desire to maximize total revenue? Why or why not?

_____

_____

_____

_____

Solutions

Terms and Definitions

__4__ Elasticity

__9__ Price elasticity of demand

__2__ Elastic

__7__ Inelastic

__8__ Total revenue

__1__ Income elasticity of demand

__10__ Cross-price elasticity of demand

__6__ Price elasticity of supply

__5__ Normal good

__3__ Inferior good

Practice Problems

1. a. a trip to Florida because it is a luxury whereas cigarettes are a necessity (to smokers)

   b. an AIDS vaccine over the next five years because there are likely to be more substitutes (alternative medications) developed over this time period and consumers' behavior may be modified over longer time periods

   c. Budweiser because it is a more narrowly defined market than beer so there are more substitutes for Budweiser than for beer

   d. aspirin because there are many substitutes for aspirin but few substitutes for insulin

2. a. $(10,000/45,000)/($0.50/$1.25) = 0.56$

   b. With the midpoint method, the value of the elasticity is the same whether you begin at a price of $1.00 and raise it to $1.50 or begin at a price of $1.50 and reduce it to $1.00.

   c. Yes. Because the price elasticity of demand is less than one (inelastic), an increase in price will increase total revenue.

3. See table below.

   a. $80 to $120; lower its prices

Table for problem #3.

Price	Quantity Demanded	Total Revenue	% Change in Price	% Change in Quantity	Elasticity
$20	24	480			
			0.67	0.18	0.27
40	20	800			
			0.40	0.22	0.55
60	16	960			
			0.29	0.29	1.00
80	12	960			
			0.22	0.40	1.82
100	8	800			
			0.18	0.67	3.72
120	4	480			

   b. $20 to $60; raise its prices

   c. $60 to $80; it doesn't matter. For these prices, a change in price proportionately changes the quantity demanded, so total revenue is unchanged.

4. a. $(10/25)/($10,000/$55,000) = 2.2$

   b. $(10/13)/($10,000/$55,000) = 4.2$

   c. Normal goods, because the income elasticity of demand is positive.

   d. Luxuries, because the income elasticity of demand is large (greater than one). In each case, an 18 percent increase in income caused a much larger increase in quantity demanded.

5. a. Televisions, because the production of televisions can be increased in response to an increase in the price of televisions whereas the quantity of beachfront property is fixed.

   b. Crude oil over the next year, because production of oil over the next year can more easily be increased than the production of oil over the next week.

   c. A van Gogh print, because more of them can be created in response to an increase in price whereas the quantity of an original work is fixed.

Short-Answer Questions

1. Whether the good is a necessity or a luxury, the availability of close substitutes, the definition of the market, and the time horizon over which demand is measured.

2. It will increase total revenue, because a large increase in price will be accompanied by only a small reduction in the quantity demanded if demand is inelastic.

3. Zero, therefore it is considered perfectly inelastic.

4. Infinite, therefore it is considered perfectly elastic.

5. $-0.10/0.20 = -1/2$. Eggs are inferior goods.

6. Elastic, because a small increase in price will induce the firm to increase production by a large amount.

7. Inelastic (nearly vertical), because once the fish are caught, the quantity offered for sale is fixed and must be sold before it spoils, regardless of the price.

8. No. The upper part tends to be elastic while the lower part tends to be inelastic. This is because on the upper part, for example, a one-unit change in the price is a small percentage change while a one-unit change in quantity is a large percentage change. This effect is reversed on the lower part of the demand curve.

9. $\dfrac{(30-25)/[(25+30)/2]}{(3-2)/[(2+3)/2]} = 0.45$, therefore supply is inelastic.

10. $0.06/0.20 = 0.30$, apples and oranges are substitutes, because the cross-price elasticity is positive (an increase in the price of apples increases the quantity demanded of oranges).

True/False Questions

1. F; demand would be price elastic.
2. T
3. T
4. F; the longer the time period considered, the more price elastic the demand curve because consumers have an opportunity to substitute or change their behavior.
5. F; the price elasticity of demand is defined as the percentage change in the quantity demanded of a good divided by the percentage change in the price of that good.
6. F; the two goods are likely to be substitutes.
7. T
8. F; the demand for necessities tends to be inelastic.
9. F; demand will be price elastic in its upper portion and price inelastic in its lower portion.
10. T
11. T
12. T
13. T
14. F; it will increase total revenue only if demand is price elastic.
15. T

Multiple-Choice Questions

1. b
2. c
3. a
4. b
5. d
6. d
7. c
8. a
9. a
10. d
11. c
12. b
13. a
14. b
15. b
16. d
17. b
18. c
19. c
20. d

Advanced Critical Thinking

1. Inelastic.

2. Not necessarily. Demand tends to be more elastic over longer periods. In the case of cigarettes, some consumers will substitute toward cigars and pipes. Others may quit or never start to smoke.

3. No. While the demand for cigarettes (the market broadly defined) may be inelastic, the demand for any one brand (market narrowly defined) is likely to be much more elastic because consumers can substitute toward other lower priced brands.

Chapter 6
Supply, Demand, and Government Policies

Goals
In this chapter you will

- Examine the effects of government policies that place a ceiling on prices

- Examine the effects of government policies that put a floor under prices

- Consider how a tax on a good affects the price of the good and the quantity sold

- Learn that taxes levied on sellers and taxes levied on buyers are equivalent

- See how the burden of a tax is split between buyers and sellers

Outcomes
After accomplishing these goals, you should be able to

- Describe the conditions necessary for a price ceiling to be a binding constraint

- Explain why a binding price floor creates a surplus

- Demonstrate why a tax placed on a good generally reduces the quantity of the good sold

- Demonstrate why the results are the same when a tax is placed on the sellers or buyers of a good

- Show whether the buyers or sellers of a good bear the burden of the tax when demand is inelastic and supply is elastic

Chapter Overview

Context and Purpose

Chapter 6 is the third chapter in a three-chapter sequence that deals with supply and demand and how markets work. Chapter 4 developed the model of supply and demand. Chapter 5 added precision to the model of supply and demand by developing the concept of elasticity—the sensitivity of the quantity supplied and quantity demanded to changes in economic conditions. Chapter 6 addresses the impact of government policies on competitive markets using the tools of supply and demand that you learned in Chapters 4 and 5.

The purpose of Chapter 6 is to consider two types of government policies: price controls and taxes. Price controls set the maximum or minimum price at which a good can be sold while a tax creates a wedge between what the buyer pays and the seller receives. These policies can be analyzed within the model of supply and demand. We will find that government policies sometimes produce unintended consequences.

Chapter Review

Introduction   In Chapters 4 and 5, we acted as scientists because we built the model of supply and demand to describe the world as it is. In Chapter 6, we act as policy advisers because we address how government policies are used to try to improve the world. We address two policies: price controls and taxes. Sometimes these policies produce unintended consequences.

Controls on Prices

There are two types of controls on prices: price ceilings and price floors. A price ceiling sets a legal maximum on the price at which a good can be sold. A price floor sets a legal minimum on the price at which a good can be sold.

- **Price Ceilings**   Suppose the government is persuaded by buyers to set a price ceiling. If the price ceiling is set above the equilibrium price, it is not binding. That is, it has no impact on the market because the price can move to equilibrium without restriction. If the price ceiling is set below the equilibrium price, it is a binding constraint because it does not allow the market to reach equilibrium. A binding price ceiling causes the quantity demanded to exceed the quantity supplied, or a shortage. Because there is a shortage, methods develop to ration the small quantity supplied across a large number of buyers. Buyers willing to wait in long lines might get the good, or sellers could sell only to their friends, family, or members of the same race. Lines are inefficient, and discrimination is both inefficient and unfair. Free markets are impersonal and ration goods with prices.

  Price ceilings are commonly found in the markets for gasoline and apartments. When OPEC restricted the quantity of petroleum in 1973, the supply of gasoline was reduced and the equilibrium price rose above the price ceiling and the price ceiling became binding. This caused a shortage of gas and long lines at the pump. In response, the price ceilings were later repealed. Price ceilings on apartments are known as rent controls. Binding rent controls create a shortage of housing. Both the demand and supply of housing are inelastic in the short run, so the initial shortage is small. In the long run, however, the supply and demand for housing become more elastic, and the shortage is more apparent. This causes waiting lists for apartments, bribes to landlords, unclean and unsafe buildings, and lower quality housing. Once established, however, rent controls are politically difficult to remove.

- **Price Floors**   Suppose the government is persuaded by sellers to set a price floor. If the price floor is set below the equilibrium price, it is *not binding*. That is, it has no impact on the market because the price can move to equilibrium without restriction. If the price floor is set above the equilibrium price, it is a *binding constraint* because it does not allow the market to reach equilibrium. A binding price floor causes the quantity supplied to exceed the quantity demanded, or a surplus. In order to eliminate the surplus, sellers may appeal to the biases of the buyers and sell to buyers that are family, friends, or members of the same race. Free markets are impersonal and ration goods with prices.

  An important example of a price floor is the minimum wage. The minimum wage is a binding constraint in the market for young and unskilled workers. When the wage is set above the market equilibrium wage, the quantity supplied of labor exceeds the quantity demanded. The result is unemployment. Studies show that a 10 percent increase in the minimum wage depresses teenage employment by 1 to 3 percent. The minimum wage also causes teenagers to look for work and drop out of school.

Price controls often hurt those they are trying to help—usually the poor. The minimum wage may help those who find work at the minimum wage but harm those who become unemployed because of the minimum wage. Rent controls reduce the quality and availability of housing.

Taxes

Governments use taxes to raise revenue. A tax on a good will affect the quantity sold and both the price paid by buyers and the price received by sellers. If the tax is collected from the sellers, supply shifts upward by the size of the tax per unit. As a result of the decrease in supply, the quantity sold decreases, the price paid by the buyer increases, and the price received by the seller decreases. If the tax is collected from the buyers, demand shifts downward by the size of the tax per unit. Because of the decrease in demand, the quantity sold decreases, the price paid by the buyer increases, and the price received by the seller decreases. Therefore, a tax levied on buyers has the same effect as a tax levied on sellers. After a tax has been placed on a good, the difference between what the buyer pays and the seller receives is the tax per unit and is known as the *tax wedge*. In summary:

- A tax discourages market activity. That is, the quantity sold is reduced.
- Buyers and sellers share the burden of a tax because the price paid by the buyers increases while the price received by the sellers decreases.
- The effect of a tax collected from buyers is equivalent to a tax collected from sellers.
- The government cannot legislate the relative burden of the tax between buyers and sellers. The relative burden of a tax is determined by the elasticity of supply and demand in that market.

Tax incidence is the manner in which the burden of a tax is shared among participants in a market. That is, it is the division of the tax burden. When a tax wedge is placed between buyers and sellers, the tax burden falls more heavily on the side of the market that is less elastic. That is, the tax burden falls more heavily on the side of the market that is less willing to leave the market when price movements are unfavorable to them. For example, in the market for cigarettes, because cigarettes are addictive, demand is likely to be less elastic than supply. Therefore, a tax on cigarettes tends to raise the price paid by buyers more than it reduces the price received by sellers, and as a result, the burden of a cigarette tax falls more heavily on the buyers of cigarettes. With regard to the payroll tax (Social Security and Medicare tax), because labor supply is less elastic than labor demand, most of the tax burden is borne by the workers as opposed to the 50–50 split intended by lawmakers.

Helpful Hints

1. Price ceilings and price floors only matter if they are binding constraints. Price ceilings do not automatically cause a shortage. A price ceiling only causes a shortage if the price ceiling is set below the equilibrium price. In a similar manner, a price floor only causes a surplus if the price floor is set above the equilibrium price.

2. It is useful to think of taxes as causing vertical shifts in demand and supply. Because demand is the maximum buyers are willing to pay for each quantity, a tax imposed on the buyers in a market reduces or shifts downward the demand faced by sellers by precisely the size of the tax per unit. That is, the buyers now offer the sellers an amount that has been reduced by precisely the size of the tax per unit. Alternatively, because supply is the minimum sellers are willing to accept for each quantity, a tax imposed on the sellers in a market reduces or shifts upward the supply faced by buyers by precisely the size of the tax per unit. This is because the sellers now require an additional amount from the buyers that is precisely the size of the tax per unit.

Terms and Definitions

Choose a definition for each key term.

Key Terms

_____ Price ceiling

_____ Price floor

_____ Tax incidence

_____ Tax wedge

Definitions

1. The manner in which the burden of a tax is shared among participants in a market

2. A legal maximum on the price at which a good can be sold

3. The difference between what the buyer pays and the seller receives after a tax has been imposed

4. A legal minimum on the price at which a good can be sold

Problems and Short-Answer Questions

Practice Problems

1. Use the following supply and demand schedules for bicycles to answer the questions below.

Price	Quantity Demanded	Quantity Supplied
$300	60	30
400	55	40
500	50	50
600	45	60
700	40	70
800	35	80

a. In response to lobbying by the Bicycle Riders Association, Congress places a price ceiling of $700 on bicycles. What effect will this have on the market for bicycles? Why?

b. In response to lobbying by the Bicycle Riders Association, Congress places a price ceiling of $400 on bicycles. Use the information provided above to plot the supply and demand curves for bicycles in Exhibit 1. Impose the price ceiling. What is the result of a price ceiling of $400 on bicycles?

c. Does a price ceiling of $400 on bicycles make all bicycle buyers better off? Why or why not?

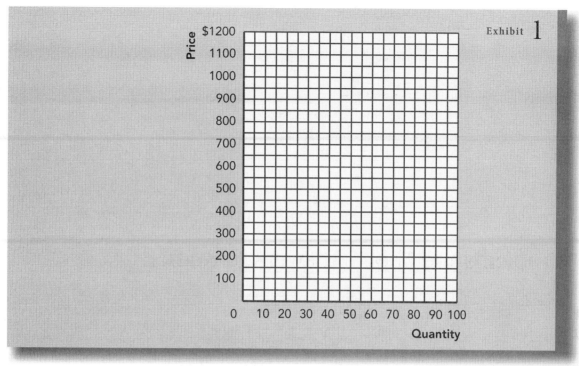

Exhibit 1

d. Suppose instead, in response to lobbying by the Bicycle Manufacturers As-
    sociation, Congress imposes a price floor on bicycles of $700. Use the information
    provided above to plot the supply and demand curves for bicycles in Exhibit 2.
    Impose the $700 price floor. What is the result of the $700 price floor?

_____

_____

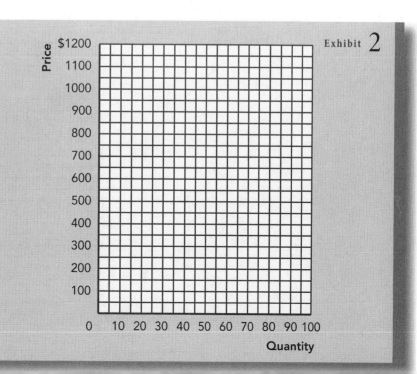

Exhibit 2

2. Use the following supply and demand schedules for bicycles to answer the questions below.

Price	Quantity Demanded	Quantity Supplied
$300	60	30
400	55	40
500	50	50
600	45	60
700	40	70
800	35	80

a. Plot the supply and demand curves for bicycles in Exhibit 3. On the graph, impose a tax of $300 per bicycle to be collected from the sellers. After the tax, what has happened to the price paid by the buyers, the price received by the sellers, and the quantity sold when compared to the free market equilibrium?

_____

_____

b. Again, plot the supply and demand curves for bicycles in Exhibit 4. On the graph, impose a tax of $300 per bicycle to be collected from the buyers. After the tax, what has happened to the price paid by the buyers, the price received by the sellers, and the quantity sold when compared to the free market equilibrium?

_____

_____

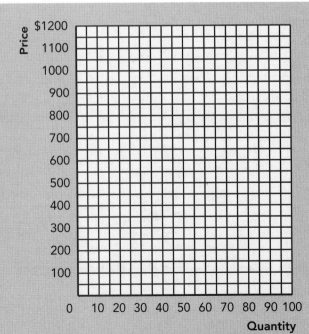

Exhibit **3**

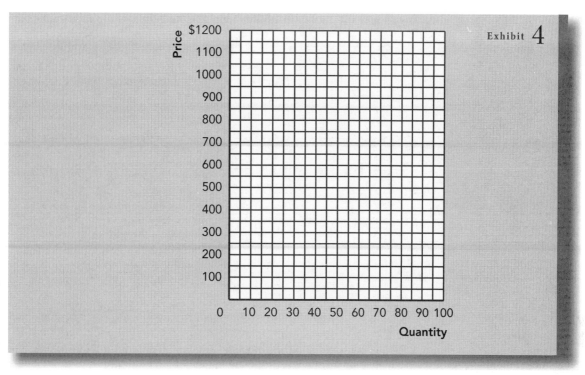

Exhibit 4

c. Compare your answers to questions *a* and *b* above. What conclusion do you draw from this comparison?

_____

_____

d. Who bears the greater burden of this tax, the buyers or the sellers? Why?

_____

_____

_____

_____

Short-Answer Questions

1. What is the impact on the price and quantity in a market if a price ceiling is set above the equilibrium price? Why?

_____

_____

_____

2. What is the impact on the price and quantity in a market if a price ceiling is set below the equilibrium price?

_____

_____

3. What are some of the problems created by a binding price ceiling?

   _____

   _____

   _____

   _____

4. Is the impact of a binding price ceiling greater in the short run or the long run? Why?

   _____

   _____

   _____

   _____

5. What is the impact on the price and quantity in a market if a price floor is set below the equilibrium price? Why?

   _____

   _____

6. What is the impact on the price and quantity in a market if a price floor is set above the equilibrium price?

   _____

   _____

7. When we use the model of supply and demand to analyze a tax that is collected from the sellers, which way do we shift the supply curve? Why?

   _____

   _____

   _____

   _____

8. When we use the model of supply and demand to analyze a tax that is collected from the buyers, which way do we shift the demand curve? Why?

   _____

   _____

   _____

   _____

9. Why is a tax collected from the buyers equivalent to a tax collected from the sellers?

   _____

   _____

   _____

   _____

10. Suppose a gas-guzzler tax is placed on luxury automobiles. Who will likely bear the greater burden of the tax, the buyers of luxury autos or the sellers? Why?

_____

_____

_____

_____

_____

_____

Self-Test

True/False Questions

____ 1. If the equilibrium price of gasoline is $1.00 per gallon and the government places a price ceiling on gasoline of $1.50 per gallon, the result will be a shortage of gasoline.

____ 2. A price ceiling set below the equilibrium price causes a surplus.

____ 3. A price floor set above the equilibrium price is a binding constraint.

____ 4. The shortage of housing caused by a binding rent control is likely to be more severe in the long run when compared to the short run.

____ 5. The minimum wage helps all teenagers because they receive higher wages than they would otherwise.

____ 6. A 10 percent increase in the minimum wage causes a 10 percent reduction in teenage employment.

____ 7. A price ceiling that is not a binding constraint today could cause a shortage in the future if demand were to increase and raise the equilibrium price above the fixed price ceiling.

____ 8. A price floor in a market always creates a surplus in that market.

____ 9. A $10 tax on baseball gloves will always raise the price that the buyers pay for baseball gloves by $10.

____ 10. The ultimate burden of a tax lands most heavily on the side of the market that is less elastic.

____ 11. If medicine is a necessity, the burden of a tax on medicine will likely land more heavily on the buyers of medicine.

____ 12. When we use the model of supply and demand to analyze a tax collected from the buyers, we shift the demand curve upward by the size of the tax.

____ 13. A tax collected from buyers has an equivalent impact to a same size tax collected from sellers.

____ 14. A tax creates a tax wedge between a buyer and a seller. This causes the price paid by the buyer to rise, the price received by the seller to fall, and the quantity sold to fall.

____ 15. The government can choose to place the burden of a tax on the buyers in a market by collecting the tax from the buyers rather than the sellers.

Multiple-Choice Questions

1. For a price ceiling to be a binding constraint on the market, the government must set it
   a. above the equilibrium price.
   b. below the equilibrium price.
   c. precisely at the equilibrium price.
   d. at any price because all price ceilings are binding constraints.

2. A binding price ceiling creates
   a. a shortage.
   b. a surplus.
   c. an equilibrium.
   d. a shortage or a surplus depending on whether the price ceiling is set above or below the equilibrium price.

3. Suppose the equilibrium price for apartments is $500 per month and the government imposes rent controls of $250. Which of the following is *unlikely* to occur as a result of the rent controls?
   a. There will be a shortage of housing.
   b. Landlords may discriminate among apartment renters.
   c. Landlords may be offered bribes to rent apartments.
   d. The quality of apartments will improve.
   e. There may be long lines of buyers waiting for apartments.

4. A price floor
   a. sets a legal maximum on the price at which a good can be sold.
   b. sets a legal minimum on the price at which a good can be sold.
   c. always determines the price at which a good must be sold.
   d. is not a binding constraint if it is set above the equilibrium price.

5. Which of the following statements about a binding price ceiling is true?
   a. The surplus created by the price ceiling is greater in the short run than in the long run.
   b. The surplus created by the price ceiling is greater in the long run than in the short run.
   c. The shortage created by the price ceiling is greater in the short run than in the long run.
   d. The shortage created by the price ceiling is greater in the long run than in the short run.

6. Which side of the market is more likely to lobby government for a price floor?
   a. Neither buyers nor sellers desire a price floor.
   b. Both buyers and sellers desire a price floor.
   c. the sellers
   d. the buyers

7. The surplus caused by a binding price floor will be greatest if
   a. both supply and demand are elastic.
   b. both supply and demand are inelastic.
   c. supply is inelastic and demand is elastic.
   d. demand is inelastic and supply is elastic.

8. Which of the following is an example of a price floor?
   a. rent controls
   b. restricting gasoline prices to $1.00 per gallon when the equilibrium price is $1.50 per gallon
   c. the minimum wage
   d. All of the above are price floors.

9. Which of the following statements is true if the government places a price ceiling on gasoline at $1.50 per gallon and the equilibrium price is $1.00 per gallon?
    a. There will be a shortage of gasoline.
    b. There will be a surplus of gasoline.
    c. A significant increase in the supply of gasoline could cause the price ceiling to become a binding constraint.
    d. A significant increase in the demand for gasoline could cause the price ceiling to become a binding constraint.

10. Studies show that a 10 percent increase in the minimum wage
    a. decreases teenage employment by about 10 to 15 percent.
    b. increases teenage employment by about 10 to 15 percent.
    c. decreases teenage employment by about 1 to 3 percent.
    d. increases teenage employment by about 1 to 3 percent.

11. Within the supply-and-demand model, a tax collected from the buyers of a good shifts the
    a. demand curve upward by the size of the tax per unit.
    b. demand curve downward by the size of the tax per unit.
    c. supply curve upward by the size of the tax per unit.
    d. supply curve downward by the size of the tax per unit.

12. Within the supply-and-demand model, a tax collected from the sellers of a good shifts the
    a. demand curve upward by the size of the tax per unit.
    b. demand curve downward by the size of the tax per unit.
    c. supply curve upward by the size of the tax per unit.
    d. supply curve downward by the size of the tax per unit.

13. Which of the following takes place when a tax is placed on a good?
    a. an increase in the price buyers pay, a decrease in the price sellers receive, and a decrease in the quantity sold
    b. an increase in the price buyers pay, a decrease in the price sellers receive, and an increase in the quantity sold
    c. a decrease in the price buyers pay, an increase in the price sellers receive, and a decrease in the quantity sold
    d. a decrease in the price buyers pay, an increase in the price sellers receive, and an increase in the quantity sold

14. When a tax is collected from the buyers in a market,
    a. the buyers bear the burden of the tax.
    b. the sellers bear the burden of the tax.
    c. the tax burden on the buyers and sellers is the same as an equivalent tax collected from the sellers.
    d. the tax burden falls most heavily on the buyers.

15. A tax of $1.00 per gallon on gasoline
    a. increases the price the buyers pay by $1.00 per gallon.
    b. decreases the price the sellers receive by $1.00 per gallon.
    c. increases the price the buyers pay by precisely $0.50 and reduces the price received by sellers by precisely $0.50.
    d. places a tax wedge of $1.00 between the price the buyers pay and the price the sellers receive.

16. The burden of a tax falls more heavily on the sellers in a market when
    a. demand is inelastic and supply is elastic.
    b. demand is elastic and supply is inelastic.
    c. both supply and demand are elastic.
    d. both supply and demand are inelastic.

17. A tax placed on a good that is a necessity for consumers will likely generate a tax burden that
    a. falls more heavily on buyers.
    b. falls more heavily on sellers.
    c. is evenly distributed between buyers and sellers.
    d. falls entirely on sellers.

18. The burden of a tax falls more heavily on the buyers in a market when
    a. demand is inelastic and supply is elastic.
    b. demand is elastic and supply is inelastic.
    c. both supply and demand are elastic.
    d. both supply and demand are inelastic.

19. Which of the following statements about the burden of a tax is correct?
    a. The tax burden generated from a tax placed on a good consumers perceive to be a necessity will fall most heavily on the sellers of the good.
    b. The tax burden falls most heavily on the side of the market (buyers or sellers) that is most willing to leave the market when price movements are unfavorable to them.
    c. The burden of a tax lands on the side of the market (buyers or sellers) from which it is collected.
    d. The distribution of the burden of a tax is determined by the relative elasticities of supply and demand and is not determined by legislation.

20. For which of the following products would the burden of a tax likely fall more heavily on the sellers?
    a. food
    b. entertainment
    c. clothing
    d. housing

Advanced Critical Thinking

Suppose that the government needs to raise tax revenue. A politician suggests that the government place a tax on food because everyone must eat and, thus, a food tax would surely raise a great deal of tax revenue. However, because the poor spend a large proportion of their income on food, the tax should be collected only from the sellers of food (grocery stores) and not from the buyers of food. The politician argues that this type of tax would place the burden of the tax on corporate grocery store chains and not on poor consumers.

1. Can the government legislate that the burden of a food tax will fall only on the sellers of food? Why or why not?

   _____

   _____

   _____

   _____

   _____

   _____

2. Do you think the burden of a food tax will tend to fall on the sellers of food or the buyers of food? Why?

   _____

   _____

   _____

   _____

   _____

   _____

Solutions

Terms and Definitions

  2   Price ceiling
  4   Price floor
  1   Tax incidence
  3   Tax wedge

Practice Problems

1. a. It will have no effect. The price ceiling is not binding because the equilibrium price is $500 and the price ceiling is set at $700.

   b. See Exhibit 5. The quantity demanded rises to 55 units, the quantity supplied falls to 40 units, and there is a shortage of 15 units.

Exhibit 5

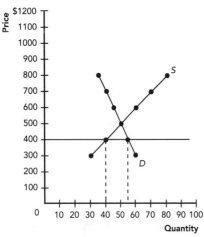

   c. No. It may make those bicycle buyers better off that actually get a bicycle. However, some buyers are unable to get a bike, must wait in line, pay a bribe, or accept a lower quality bicycle.

   d. See Exhibit 6. The quantity supplied rises to 70 units, the quantity demanded falls to 40 units, and there is a surplus of 30 units.

Exhibit 6

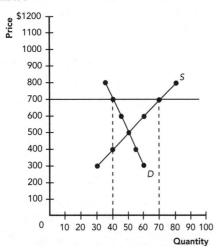

2. a. See Exhibit 7. The price paid by the buyers rises to $700, the price received by the sellers falls to $400, and the quantity sold falls to 40 units.

Exhibit 7

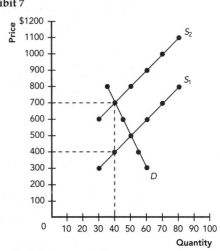

   b. See Exhibit 8. The price paid by the buyers rises to $700, the price received by the sellers falls to $400, and the quantity sold falls to 40 units.

Exhibit 8

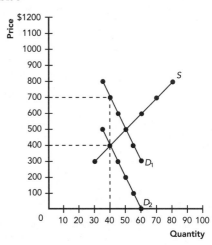

   c. The impact of a tax collected from sellers is equivalent to the impact of a tax collected from buyers.

   d. The greater burden of the tax has fallen on the buyers. The free market equilibrium price was $500. After the tax, the price the buyers pay has risen $200 while the price the sellers receive has fallen $100. This is because demand is less elastic than supply.

Short-Answer Questions

1. There is no impact because the price can move to equilibrium without restriction. That is, the price ceiling is not a binding constraint.

2. The quantity supplied decreases and the quantity demanded increases, causing a shortage.

3. There will be a shortage, buyers may wait in lines, sellers may be able to discriminate among buyers, the quality of the product may be reduced, and bribes may be paid to sellers.

4. The impact is greater in the long run because both supply and demand tend to be more elastic in the long run. As a result, the shortage becomes more severe in the long run.

5. There is no impact because the price can move to equilibrium without restriction. That is, the price floor is not a binding constraint.

6. The quantity supplied increases and the quantity demanded decreases, causing a surplus.

7. The supply curve is shifted upward by the size of the tax because the amount the seller requires from the buyer has been increased by precisely the size of the tax.

8. The demand curve is shifted downward by the size of the tax because the amount the buyer is willing to offer the seller has been reduced precisely by the size of the tax.

9. A tax places a wedge between what the buyer pays and the seller receives. Whether the buyer or the seller actually hands the tax to the government makes no difference whatsoever.

10. The sellers will bear the greater burden because the demand for luxuries tends to be highly elastic. That is, when the price buyers pay rises due to the tax, wealthy buyers can easily shift their purchases toward alternative items while producers cannot quickly reduce production when the price they receive falls. The burden falls on the side of the market that is less elastic.

True/False Questions

1. F; a price ceiling set above the equilibrium price is not binding.

2. F; it causes a shortage.

3. T

4. T

5. F; some may be helped but others become unemployed and still others quit school to earn what appears to a teenager to be a good wage.

6. F; it causes a 1 to 3 percent reduction in employment.

7. T

8. F; it creates a surplus only if the floor is set above the equilibrium price.

9. F; the difference between what the sellers receive and the buyers pay will be $10, but the price received by the sellers usually will fall some so the price paid by the buyers will rise by less than $10.

10. T

11. T

12. F; we shift the demand curve downward by the size of the tax.

13. T

14. T

15. F; the burden of a tax is determined by the relative elasticities of supply and demand.

Multiple-Choice Questions

1. b
2. a
3. d
4. b
5. d
6. c
7. a
8. c
9. d
10. c
11. b
12. c
13. a
14. c
15. d
16. b
17. a
18. a
19. d
20. b

Advanced Critical Thinking

1. No. The tax burden is determined by the elasticity of supply and demand. The burden of a tax falls most heavily on the side of the market that is less elastic. That is, the burden is on the side of the market least willing to leave the market when the price moves unfavorably.

2. The burden will fall most heavily on the buyers of food regardless of whether the tax is collected from the buyers or the sellers. Food is a necessity, and therefore, the demand for food is relatively inelastic. When the price rises due to the tax, people still must eat. Grocery chains can sell another product lines when the price they receive for food falls due to the tax.

Chapter 7
Consumers, Producers, and the Efficiency of Markets

Goals
In this chapter you will

- Examine the link between buyers' willingness to pay for a good and the demand curve

- Learn how to define and measure consumer surplus

- Examine the link between sellers' costs of producing a good and the supply curve

- Learn how to define and measure producer surplus

- See that the equilibrium of supply and demand maximizes total surplus in a market

Outcomes
After accomplishing these goals, you should be able to

- Derive a demand curve from a group of individual buyers' willingness to pay schedules

- Locate consumer surplus on a supply and demand graph

- Derive a supply curve from a group of individual sellers' cost of production schedules

- Locate producer surplus on a supply-and-demand graph

- Demonstrate why all quantities other than the equilibrium quantity fail to maximize total surplus in a market

Chapter Overview

Context and Purpose

Chapter 7 is the first chapter in a three-chapter sequence on welfare economics and market efficiency. Chapter 7 employs the supply-and-demand model to develop consumer surplus and producer surplus as a measure of welfare and market efficiency. These concepts are then utilized in Chapters 8 and 9 to determine the winners and losers from taxation and restrictions on international trade.

The purpose of Chapter 7 is to develop *welfare economics*—the study of how the allocation of resources affects economic well-being.

Chapters 4 through 6 employed supply and demand in a positive framework when we asked the question, "What is the equilibrium price and quantity in a market?" We now address the normative question, "Is the equilibrium price and quantity in a market the best possible solution to the resource allocation problem or is it simply the price and quantity that balances supply and demand?" We will discover that under most circumstances the equilibrium price and quantity is also the one that maximizes welfare.

Chapter Review

Introduction   In this chapter, we address welfare economics—the study of how the allocation of resources affects economic well-being. We measure the benefits that buyers and sellers receive from taking part in a market, and we discover that the equilibrium price and quantity in a market maximizes the total benefits received by buyers and sellers.

Consumer Surplus

Consumer surplus measures the benefits received by buyers from participating in a market. Each potential buyer in a market has some willingness to pay for a good. This willingness to pay is the maximum amount that a buyer will pay for the good. If we plot the value of the greatest willingness to pay for the first unit followed by the next greatest willingness to pay for the second unit and so on (on a price and quantity graph), we have plotted the market demand curve for the good. That is, the height of the demand curve is the marginal buyers' willingness to pay. Because some buyers value a good more than other buyers, the demand curve is downward sloping.

Consumer surplus is the amount a buyer is willing to pay for a good minus the amount the buyer actually pays for it. For example, if you are willing to pay $20 for a new CD by your favorite music artist and you are able to purchase it for $15, you receive consumer surplus on that CD of $5. In general, because the height of the demand curve measures the value buyers place on a good measured by the buyers' willingness to pay, *consumer surplus in a market is the area below the demand curve and above the price.*

When the price of a good falls, consumer surplus increases for two reasons. First, existing buyers receive greater surplus because they are allowed to pay less for the quantities they were already going to purchase, and second, new buyers are brought into the market because the price is now lower than their willingness to pay.

Note that because the height of the demand curve is the value buyers place on a good measured by their willingness to pay, consumer surplus measures the benefits received by buyers *as the buyers themselves perceive it.* Therefore, consumer surplus is an appropriate measure of buyers' benefits if policymakers respect the preferences of buyers. Economists generally believe that buyers are rational and that buyer preferences should be respected except possibly in cases of drug addiction and so on.

Producer Surplus

Producer surplus measures the benefits received by sellers from participating in a market. Each potential seller in a market has some *cost* of production. This cost is the value of everything a seller must give up to produce a good, and it should be interpreted as the producers' opportunity cost of production—actual out-of-pocket expenses plus the value of the producers' time. The cost of production is the minimum amount a seller is willing to accept in order to produce the good. If we plot the cost of the least cost producer of the first unit, then the next least cost producer of the second unit, and so on (on a price and quantity graph), we have plotted the market supply curve for the good. That is, the height of the supply curve is the marginal sellers' cost of production. Because some sellers have a lower cost than other sellers, the supply curve is upward sloping.

Producer surplus is the amount a seller is paid for a good minus the seller's cost of providing it. For example, if a musician can produce a CD for a cost of $10 and sell it for $15, the musician receives a producer surplus of $5 on that CD. In general, because the height of the supply curve measures the sellers' costs, *producer surplus in a market is the area below the price and above the supply curve.*

When the price of a good rises, producer surplus increases for two reasons. First, existing sellers receive greater surplus because they receive more for the quantities they were already going to sell, and second, new sellers are brought into the market because the price is now higher than their cost.

Market Efficiency

We measure economic well-being with *total surplus*—the sum of consumer and producer surplus.

$$\text{Total surplus} = \left(\begin{array}{c} \text{value to} \\ \text{buyers} \end{array} - \begin{array}{c} \text{amount paid} \\ \text{by buyers} \end{array} \right) + \left(\begin{array}{c} \text{amount received} \\ \text{by sellers} \end{array} - \begin{array}{c} \text{cost to} \\ \text{sellers} \end{array} \right)$$

$$\text{Total surplus} = \text{value to buyers} - \text{cost to sellers}$$

Graphically, total surplus is the area below the demand curve and above the supply curve. Resource allocation is said to exhibit efficiency if it maximizes the total surplus received by all members of society. Free market equilibrium is efficient because it maximizes total surplus. This efficiency is demonstrated by the following observations:

- Free markets allocate output to the buyers who value it the most—those with a willingness to pay greater than or equal to the equilibrium price. Therefore, consumer surplus cannot be increased by moving consumption from a current buyer to any other nonbuyer.

- Free markets allocate buyers for goods to the sellers who can produce at the lowest cost—those with a cost of production less than or equal to the equilibrium price. Therefore, producer surplus cannot be increased by moving production from a current seller to any other nonseller.

- Free markets produce the quantity of goods that maximizes the sum of consumer and producer surplus or total surplus. If we produce less than the equilibrium quantity, we fail to produce units where the value to the marginal buyer exceeds the cost to the marginal seller. If we produce more than the equilibrium quantity, we produce units where the cost to the marginal seller exceeds the value to the marginal buyer.

Economists generally advocate free markets because they are efficient. Because markets are efficient, many believe that government policy should be *laissez-faire*, which means "allow them to do." Adam Smith's "invisible hand" of the marketplace guides buyers and sellers to an allocation of resources that maximizes total surplus. The efficient outcome cannot be improved upon by a benevolent social planner. Many economists argue that free markets for scalped tickets (and possibly even markets for organs for transplant) maximize total surplus. In addition to efficiency, policymakers may also be concerned with equality—the uniformity of the distribution of well-being among the members of society.

Conclusion: Market Efficiency and Market Failure

There are two main reasons a free market may not be efficient:

- A market may not be perfectly competitive. If individual buyers or sellers (or small groups of them) can influence the price, they have *market power* and they may be able to keep the price and quantity away from equilibrium.

- A market may generate side effects, or *externalities*, which affect people who are not participants in the market at all. These side effects, such as pollution, are not taken into account by buyers and sellers in a market, so the market equilibrium may not be efficient for society as a whole.

Market power and externalities are the two main types of *market failure*—the inability of some unregulated markets to allocate resources efficiently.

Helpful Hints

1. To better understand "willingness to pay" for the buyer and "cost" to seller, read both demand and supply "backward." That is, read both demand and supply from the quantity axis to the price or dollar axis. When we read demand from quantity to price, we find that the potential buyer for the first unit has a very high willingness to pay because that buyer places a great value on the good. As we move farther out along the quantity axis, the buyers for those quantities have a somewhat lower willingness to pay, and thus, the demand curve slopes negatively. When we read supply from quantity to price, we find that the potential seller for the first unit is extremely efficient and, accordingly, has a very low cost of production. As we move farther out along the quantity axis, the sellers for those quantities have somewhat higher costs, and thus, the supply curve slopes upward. At equilibrium between supply and demand, only those units are produced that generate a value to buyers which exceeds the cost to the sellers.

2. Consumer surplus exists, in part, because in a competitive market, there is one price and all participants are price takers. With a single market price determined by the interactions of many buyers and sellers, individual buyers may have a willingness to pay that exceeds the price, and as a result, some buyers receive consumer surplus. If, however, sellers are aware of the buyers' willingness to pay and the sellers engage in price discrimination, that is, charge each buyer their willingness to pay, there would be no consumer surplus. Each buyer would be forced to pay his individual willingness to pay. This issue will be addressed in later chapters.

Terms and Definitions

Choose a definition for each key term.

Key Terms

_____ Welfare economics

_____ Willingness to pay

_____ Consumer surplus

_____ Cost

_____ Producer surplus

_____ Efficiency

_____ Equality

_____ Market failure

Definitions

1. The amount a buyer is willing to pay for a good minus the amount the buyer actually pays for it
2. The property of a resource allocation of maximizing the total surplus received by all members of society
3. The study of how the allocation of resources affects economic well-being
4. The inability of some unregulated markets to allocate resources efficiently
5. The property of distributing prosperity uniformly among the members of society
6. The amount a seller is paid for a good minus the seller's cost of providing it
7. The maximum amount that a buyer will pay for a good
8. The value of everything a seller must give up to produce a good

Problems and Short-Answer Questions

Practice Problems

1. The following information describes the value Lori Landlord places on having her five apartment houses repainted. She values the repainting of each apartment house at a different amount depending on how badly it needs repainting.

Value of new paint on first apartment house	$5,000
Value of new paint on second apartment house	4,000
Value of new paint on third apartment house	3,000
Value of new paint on fourth apartment house	2,000
Value of new paint on fifth apartment house	1,000

    a. Plot Lori Landlord's willingness to pay in Exhibit 1.
    b. If the price to repaint her apartments is $5,000 each, how many will she repaint? What is the value of her consumer surplus?

    _____

    c. Suppose the price to repaint her apartments falls to $2,000 each. How many apartments will Lori choose to have repainted? What is the value of her consumer surplus?

    _____

    _____

    d. What happened to Ms. Landlord's consumer surplus when the price of having her apartments repainted fell? Why?

    _____

    _____

    _____

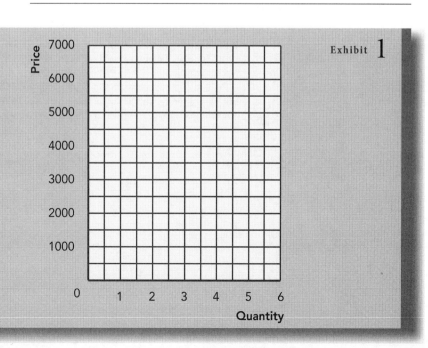

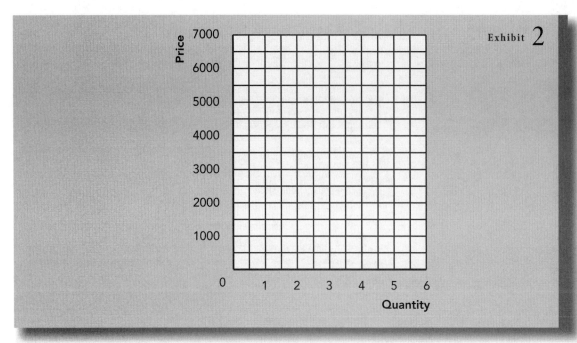

2. The following information shows the costs incurred by Peter Painter when he paints apartments. Because painting is backbreaking work, the more he paints, the higher the costs he incurs in both pain and chiropractic bills.

Cost of painting first apartment house	$1,000
Cost of painting second apartment house	2,000
Cost of painting third apartment house	3,000
Cost of painting fourth apartment house	4,000
Cost of painting fifth apartment house	5,000

a. Plot Peter Painter's cost in Exhibit 2.
b. If the price of painting apartment houses is $2,000 each, how many will he paint? What is the value of his producer surplus?

_____

c. Suppose the price to paint apartments rises to $4,000 each. How many apartments will Peter choose to repaint? What is the value of his producer surplus?

_____

_____

d. What happened to Mr. Painter's producer surplus when the price to paint apartments rose? Why?

_____

_____

_____

3. Use the information about willingness to pay and cost from questions 1 and 2 above to answer the following questions.

a. If a benevolent social planner sets the price for painting apartment houses at $5,000, what is the value of consumer surplus? producer surplus? total surplus?

_____

_____

_____

b. If a benevolent social planner sets the price for painting apartment houses at $1,000, what is the value of consumer surplus? producer surplus? total surplus?

_____

_____

_____

c. If the price for painting apartment houses is allowed to move to its free market equilibrium price of $3,000, what is the value of consumer surplus, producer surplus, and total surplus in the market? How does total surplus in the free market compare to the total surplus generated by the social planner?

_____

_____

_____

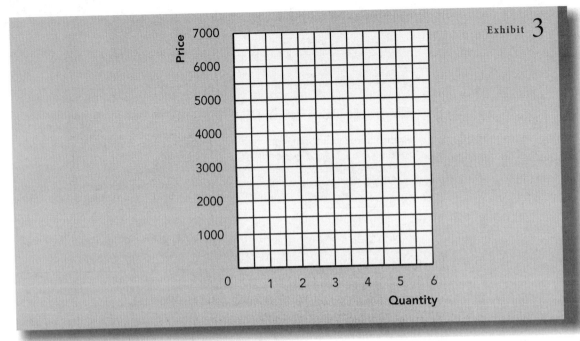

Exhibit 3

4. In Exhibit 3, plot the linear supply and demand curves for painting apartments implied by the information in questions 1 and 2 above (draw them so that they contact the vertical axis). Show consumer and producer surplus for the free market equilibrium price and quantity. Is this allocation of resources efficient? Why or why not?

_____

_____

_____

_____

_____

_____

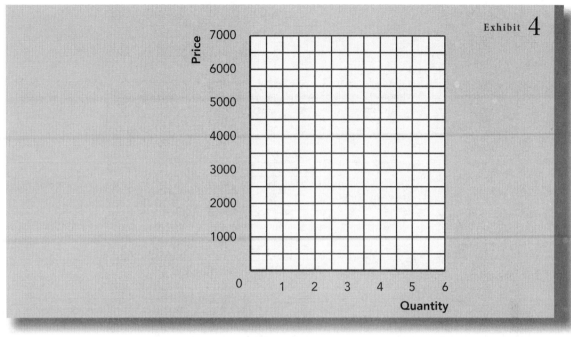

Exhibit 4

5. Suppose Lori Landlord has difficulty renting her dilapidated apartments so she increases her willingness to pay for painting by $2,000 per apartment. Plot Lori's new willingness to pay along with Peter's cost in Exhibit 4. If the equilibrium price rises to $4,000, what is the value of consumer surplus, producer surplus, and total surplus? Show consumer and producer surplus on the graph. Compare your answer to the answer you found in 3c above.

_____

_____

_____

_____

Short-Answer Questions

1. What is the relationship between the buyers' willingness to pay for a good and the demand curve for that good?

_____

_____

2. What is consumer surplus, and how is it measured?

_____

_____

3. What is the value of consumer surplus for the marginal buyer? Why?

    _____

    _____

4. If the cost for Moe to mow a lawn is $5, for Larry to mow a lawn is $7, and for Curly to mow a lawn is $9, what is the value of their producer surplus if each mows a lawn and the price for lawn mowing is $10?

    _____

    _____

5. What is the relationship between the sellers' cost to produce a good and the supply curve for that good?

    _____

    _____

6. What is producer surplus, and how is it measured?

    _____

    _____

7. When the price of a good rises, what happens to producer surplus? Why?

    _____

    _____

8. Can a benevolent social planner choose a quantity that provides greater economic welfare than the equilibrium quantity generated in a competitive market? Why?

    _____

    _____

9. What does an economist mean by "efficiency"?

    _____

    _____

10. Is a competitive market efficient? Why or why not?

    _____

    _____

11. How does a competitive market choose which producers will produce and sell a product?

    _____

    _____

Self-Test

True/False Questions

_____ 1. Consumer surplus is the amount a buyer is willing to pay for a good minus the seller's cost.

_____ 2. If the demand curve in a market is stationary, consumer surplus decreases when the price in that market increases.

_____ 3. If your willingness to pay for a hamburger is $3.00 and the price is $2.00, your consumer surplus is $5.00.

_____ 4. Producer surplus is a measure of the unsold inventories of suppliers in a market.

_____ 5. Consumer surplus is a good measure of buyers' benefits if buyers are rational.

_____ 6. Cost to the seller includes the opportunity cost of the seller's time.

_____ 7. The height of the supply curve is the marginal seller's cost.

_____ 8. Total surplus is the cost to sellers minus the value to buyers.

_____ 9. Free markets are efficient because they allocate output to buyers who have a willingness to pay that is below the price.

_____ 10. Producer surplus is the area above the supply curve and below the price.

_____ 11. The major advantage of allowing free markets to allocate resources is that the outcome of the allocation is efficient.

_____ 12. Equilibrium in a competitive market maximizes total surplus.

_____ 13. The two main types of market failure are market power and externalities.

_____ 14. Externalities are side effects, such as pollution, that are not taken into account by the buyers and sellers in a market.

_____ 15. Producing more of a product always adds to total surplus.

Multiple-Choice Questions

1. Consumer surplus is the area
   a. above the supply curve and below the price.
   b. below the supply curve and above the price.
   c. above the demand curve and below the price.
   d. below the demand curve and above the price.
   e. below the demand curve and above the supply curve.

2. A buyer's willingness to pay is
   a. that buyer's consumer surplus.
   b. that buyer's producer surplus.
   c. that buyer's maximum amount he is willing to pay for a good.
   d. that buyer's minimum amount he is willing to pay for a good.
   e. none of the above.

3. If a buyer's willingness to pay for a new Honda is $20,000 and she is able to actually buy it for $18,000, her consumer surplus is
   a. $0.
   b. $2,000.
   c. $18,000.
   d. $20,000.
   e. $38,000.

4. An increase in the price of a good along a stationary demand curve
   a.   increases consumer surplus.
   b.   decreases consumer surplus.
   c.   improves the material welfare of the buyers.
   d.   improves market efficiency.

5. Suppose there are three identical vases available to be purchased. Buyer 1 is willing to pay $30 for one, buyer 2 is willing to pay $25 for one, and buyer 3 is willing to pay $20 for one. If the price is $25, how many vases will be sold and what is the value of consumer surplus in this market?
   a.   One vase will be sold, and consumer surplus is $30.
   b.   One vase will be sold, and consumer surplus is $5.
   c.   Two vases will be sold, and consumer surplus is $5.
   d.   Three vases will be sold, and consumer surplus is $0.
   e.   Three vases will be sold, and consumer surplus is $80.

6. Producer surplus is the area
   a.   above the supply curve and below the price.
   b.   below the supply curve and above the price.
   c.   above the demand curve and below the price.
   d.   below the demand curve and above the price.
   e.   below the demand curve and above the supply curve.

7. If a benevolent social planner chooses to produce less than the equilibrium quantity of a good, then
   a.   producer surplus is maximized.
   b.   consumer surplus is maximized.
   c.   total surplus is maximized.
   d.   the value placed on the last unit of production by buyers exceeds the cost of production.
   e.   the cost of production on the last unit produced exceeds the value placed on it by buyers.

8. If a benevolent social planner chooses to produce more than the equilibrium quantity of a good, then
   a.   producer surplus is maximized.
   b.   consumer surplus is maximized.
   c.   total surplus is maximized.
   d.   the value placed on the last unit of production by buyers exceeds the cost of production.
   e.   the cost of production on the last unit produced exceeds the value placed on it by buyers.

9. The seller's cost of production is
   a.   the seller's consumer surplus.
   b.   the seller's producer surplus.
   c.   the maximum amount the seller is willing to accept for a good.
   d.   the minimum amount the seller is willing to accept for a good.
   e.   none of the above.

10. Total surplus is the area
   a.   above the supply curve and below the price.
   b.   below the supply curve and above the price.
   c.   above the demand curve and below the price.
   d.   below the demand curve and above the price.
   e.   below the demand curve and above the supply curve.

11. An increase in the price of a good along a stationary supply curve
   a. increases producer surplus.
   b. decreases producer surplus.
   c. improves market equity.
   d. does all of the above.

12. Adam Smith's "invisible hand" concept suggests that a competitive market outcome
   a. minimizes total surplus.
   b. maximizes total surplus.
   c. generates equality among the members of society.
   d. does both *b* and *c*.

13. In general, if a benevolent social planner wanted to maximize the total benefits received by buyers and sellers in a market, the planner should
   a. choose a price above the market equilibrium price.
   b. choose a price below the market equilibrium price.
   c. allow the market to seek equilibrium on its own.
   d. choose any price the planner wants because the losses to the sellers (buyers) from any change in price are exactly offset by the gains to the buyers (sellers).

14. If buyers are rational and there is no market failure,
   a. free market solutions are efficient.
   b. free market solutions generate equality.
   c. free market solutions maximize total surplus.
   d. all of the above are true.
   e. *a* and *c* are correct.

15. If a producer has market power (can influence the price of the product in the market) then free market solutions
   a. generate equality.
   b. are efficient.
   c. are inefficient.
   d. maximize consumer surplus.

16. If a market is efficient, then
   a. the market allocates output to the buyers who value it the most.
   b. the market allocates buyers to the sellers who can produce the good at least cost.
   c. the quantity produced in the market maximizes the sum of consumer and producer surplus.
   d. all of the above are true.
   e. none of the above is true.

17. If a market generates a side effect or externality, then free market solutions
   a. generate equality.
   b. are efficient.
   c. are inefficient.
   d. maximize producer surplus.

18. Medical care clearly enhances people's lives. Therefore, we should consume medical care until
   a. everyone has as much as they would like.
   b. the benefit buyers place on medical care is equal to the cost of producing it.
   c. buyers receive no benefit from another unit of medical care.
   d. we must cut back on the consumption of other goods.

19. Joe has ten baseball gloves and Sue has none. A baseball glove costs $50 to produce. If Joe values an additional baseball glove at $100 and Sue values a baseball glove at $40, then to maximize
   a. efficiency, Joe should receive the glove.
   b. efficiency, Sue should receive the glove.
   c. consumer surplus, both should receive a glove.
   d. equity, Joe should receive the glove.

20. Suppose that the price of a new bicycle is $300. Sue values a new bicycle at $400. It costs $200 for the seller to produce the new bicycle. What is the value of total surplus if Sue buys a new bike?
    a. $100
    b. $200
    c. $300
    d. $400
    e. $500

Advanced Critical Thinking

Suppose you are having an argument with your roommate about whether the federal government should subsidize the production of food. Your roommate argues that because food is something that is unambiguously good (unlike liquor, guns, and drugs, which may be considered inherently evil by some members of society), we simply cannot have too much of it. That is, because food is clearly good, having more of it must always improve our economic well-being.

1. Is it true that you cannot have too much of a good thing? Conversely, is it possible to overproduce unambiguously good things such as food, clothing, and shelter? Why or why not?

    _____

    _____

    _____

    _____

2. In Exhibit 5, demonstrate your answer to question 1 above with a supply-and-demand graph for food by showing the impact on economic well-being of producing quantities in excess of the equilibrium quantity.

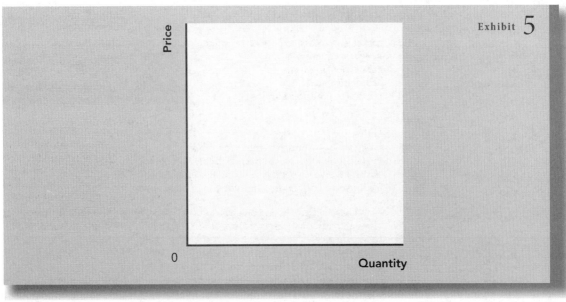

Solutions

Terms and Definitions

__3__ Welfare economics

__7__ Willingness to pay

__1__ Consumer surplus

__8__ Cost

__6__ Producer surplus

__2__ Efficiency

__5__ Equality

__4__ Market failure

Practice Problems

1. a. See Exhibit 6.

Exhibit 6

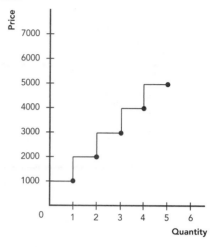

b. One apartment painted. $5,000 − $5,000 = $0, therefore she has no consumer surplus.

c. Four apartments painted. ($5,000 − $2,000) + ($4,000 − $2,000) + ($3,000 − $2,000) + ($2,000 − $2,000) = $6,000 of consumer surplus.

d. Her consumer surplus rose because she gains surplus on the unit she would have already purchased at the old price plus she gains surplus on the new units she now purchases due to the lower price.

2. a. See Exhibit 7.

Exhibit 7

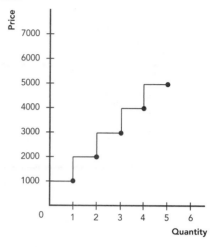

b. Two. ($2,000 − $1,000) + ($2,000 − $2,000) = $1,000 of producer surplus.

c. Four apartments. ($4,000 − $1,000) + ($4,000 − $2,000) + ($4,000 − $3,000) + ($4,000 − $4,000) = $6,000 of producer surplus.

d. He received greater producer surplus on the unit he would have produced anyway plus additional surplus on the units he now chooses to produce due to the increase in price.

3. a. Only one unit will be purchased, so consumer surplus = ($5,000 − $5,000) = $0, producer surplus = ($5,000 − $1,000) = $4,000, and total surplus = $0 + $4,000 = $4,000.

b. Only one unit will be produced, so consumer surplus = ($5,000 − $1,000) = $4,000, producer surplus = ($1,000 − $1,000) = $0, and total surplus = $4,000 + $0 = $4,000.

c. Consumer surplus = ($5,000 − $3,000) + ($4,000 − $3,000) + ($3,000 − $3,000) = $3,000. Producer surplus = ($3,000 − $1,000) + ($3,000 − $2,000) + ($3,000 − $3,000) = $3,000. Total surplus = $3,000 + $3,000 = $6,000. Free market total surplus is greater than social planner total surplus.

4. See Exhibit 8. Yes, it is efficient because at a quantity that is less than the equilibrium quantity, we fail to produce units that buyers value more than their cost. At a quantity above the equilibrium quantity, we produce units that cost more than the buyers value them. At equilibrium, we produce all possible units that are valued in excess of what they cost, which maximizes total surplus.

Exhibit 8

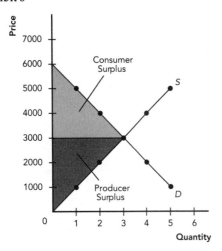

5. See Exhibit 9.

Consumer surplus = $3,000 + $2,000 + $1,000 + $0 = $6,000.

Producer surplus = $3,000 + $2,000 + $1,000 + $0 = $6,000.

Total surplus = $6,000 + $6,000 = $12,000.

Consumer surplus, producer surplus, and total surplus have all increased.

Exhibit 9

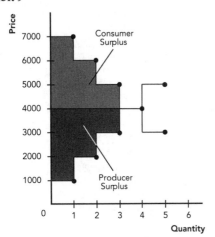

Short-Answer Questions

1. The height of the demand curve at any quantity is the marginal buyer's willingness to pay. Therefore, a plot of buyers' willingness to pay for each quantity is a plot of the demand curve.

2. Consumer surplus is the amount a buyer is willing to pay for a good minus the amount the buyer actually pays. It is measured as the area below the demand curve and above the price.

3. Zero, because the marginal buyer is the buyer who would leave the market if the price were any higher. Therefore, they are paying their willingness to pay and are receiving no surplus.

4. ($10 − $5) + ($10 − $7) + ($10 − $9) = $9

5. The height of the supply curve at any quantity is the marginal seller's cost. Therefore, a plot of the sellers' cost for each quantity is a plot of the supply curve.

6. Producer surplus is the amount a seller is paid for a good minus the seller's cost of providing it. It is measured as the area below the price and above the supply curve.

7. Producer surplus increases because existing sellers receive a greater surplus on the units they were already going to sell and new sellers enter the market because the price is now above their cost.

8. Generally, no. At any quantity below the equilibrium quantity, the market fails to produce units where the value to the marginal buyer exceeds the cost. At any quantity above the equilibrium quantity, the market produces units where the cost to the marginal producer exceeds the value to the buyers.

9. It is a resource allocation that maximizes the total surplus received by all members of society.

10. Yes, because it maximizes the area below the demand curve and above the supply curve, or total surplus.

11. Only those producers who have costs at or below the market price will be able to produce and sell that good.

True/False Questions

1. F; consumer surplus is the amount a buyer is willing to pay for a good minus the amount the buyer actually pays.

2. T

3. F; $3.00 − $2.00 = $1.00.

4. F; it is a measure of the benefits of market participation to the sellers in a market.

5. T

6. T

7. T

8. F; total surplus is the value to buyers minus the cost to sellers.

9. F; free markets allocate output to buyers who have a willingness to pay that is above the price.

10. T

11. T

12. T

13. T

14. T

15. F; producing above the equilibrium quantity reduces total surplus because units are produced for which cost exceeds the value to buyers.

Multiple-Choice Questions

1. d

2. c

3. b
4. b
5. c
6. a
7. d
8. e
9. d
10. e
11. a
12. b
13. c
14. e
15. c
16. d
17. c
18. b
19. a
20. b

Advanced Critical Thinking

1. You can have too much of a good thing. Yes, any good with a positive cost and a declining willingness to pay from the consumer can be overproduced. This is because at some point of production, the cost per unit will exceed the value to the buyer and there will be a loss to total surplus associated with additional production.

2. See Exhibit 10.

Exhibit 10

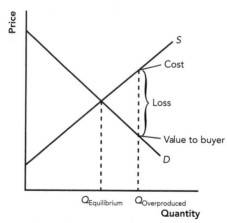

Chapter 8
Application: The Costs of Taxation

Goals
In this chapter you will

- Examine how taxes reduce consumer and producer surplus

- Learn the meaning and causes of the deadweight loss of a tax

- Consider why some taxes have larger deadweight losses than others

- Examine how tax revenue and deadweight loss vary with the size of a tax

Outcomes
After accomplishing these goals, you should be able to

- Place a tax wedge in a supply-and-demand graph and determine the tax revenue and the levels of consumer and producer surplus

- Place a tax wedge in a supply-and-demand graph and determine the value of the deadweight loss

- Show why a given tax will generate a greater deadweight loss if supply and demand are elastic than if they are inelastic

- Demonstrate why some very large taxes generate little tax revenue but a great deal of deadweight loss

Chapter Overview

Context and Purpose

Chapter 8 is the second chapter in a three-chapter sequence dealing with welfare economics. In the previous section on supply and demand, Chapter 6 introduced taxes and demonstrated how a tax affects the price and quantity sold in a market. Chapter 6 also described the factors that determine how the burden of the tax is divided between the buyers and sellers in a market. Chapter 7 developed welfare economics—the study of how the allocation of resources affects economic well-being. Chapter 8 combines the lessons learned in Chapters 6 and 7 and addresses the effects of taxation on welfare. Chapter 9 will address the effects of trade restrictions on welfare.

The purpose of Chapter 8 is to apply the lessons learned about welfare economics in Chapter 7 to the issue of taxation, which we addressed in Chapter 6. We will learn that the cost of a tax to buyers and sellers in a market exceeds the revenue collected by the government. We will also learn about the factors that determine the degree by which the cost of a tax exceeds the revenue collected by the government.

Chapter Review

Introduction   Taxes raise the price buyers pay, reduce the price sellers receive, and reduce the quantity exchanged. Clearly, the welfare of the buyers and sellers is reduced, and the welfare of the government is increased. However, overall welfare is reduced because the cost of a tax to buyers and sellers exceeds the revenue raised by the government.

The Deadweight Loss of Taxation

Recall from Chapter 6 that a tax places a wedge between what a buyer pays and a seller receives and reduces the quantity sold regardless of whether the tax is collected from the buyer or the seller. With regard to welfare, recall from Chapter 7 that consumer surplus is the amount buyers are willing to pay minus the price they actually pay, whereas producer surplus is the price sellers actually receive minus their costs. The welfare or benefit to the government from a tax is the revenue it collects from the tax, which is the quantity of the good sold *after the tax is placed on the good* multiplied by the tax per unit. This benefit actually accrues to those on whom the tax revenue is spent.

Referring to Exhibit 1, without a tax the price is P_0 and the quantity is Q_0. Thus, consumer surplus is the area A + B + C and producer surplus is D + E + F. Tax revenue is zero. Total surplus is A + B + C + D + E + F.

With a tax, the price to buyers rises to P_B, the price to sellers falls to P_S, and the quantity falls to Q_1. Consumer surplus is now A, producer surplus is now F, and tax revenue is B + D. Total surplus is now A + B + D + F. Consumer surplus and producer surplus have both been reduced and tax revenue has been increased. However, consumer surplus and producer surplus have been reduced by B + C + D + E, and government revenue has been increased by only B + D. Therefore, losses to buyers and sellers from a tax exceed the revenue raised by the government. The reduction in total surplus that results from a tax is known as deadweight loss and is equal to C + E.

Taxes cause deadweight losses because taxes prevent buyers and sellers from realizing some of the gains from trade. That is, taxes distort incentives because taxes raise the price paid by buyers, which reduces the quantity demanded and lowers the price received by sellers, which reduces the quantity supplied. The size of the market is reduced below its optimum, and sellers fail to produce and sell goods for which the benefits to buyers exceed the costs of the producers. Deadweight loss is a loss of potential gains from trade.

The Determinants of the Deadweight Loss

The size of the deadweight loss from a tax depends on the elasticities of supply and demand. Deadweight loss from a tax is caused by the distortion in the price faced by buyers and sellers. The more buyers are sensitive to an increase in the price of the good (more elastic demand), the more they reduce their quantity demanded when a tax is placed on a good. The more sellers are sensitive to a decrease in the price of a good (more elastic supply), the more they reduce their quantity supplied when a tax is placed on a good. A greater reduction in the quantity exchanged in the market causes a greater deadweight loss. As a result, *the greater the elasticities of supply and demand, the greater the deadweight loss of a tax.*

The most important tax in the U.S. economy is the tax on labor—federal and state income taxes and Social Security taxes. Taxes on labor encourage workers to work fewer hours, second earners to stay home, the elderly to retire early, and the unscrupulous to enter the underground economy. The more elastic the supply of labor, the greater the deadweight loss of taxation and, thus, the greater the cost of any government program

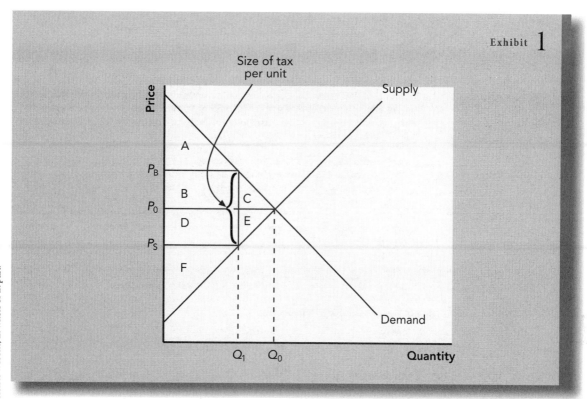

Exhibit 1

that relies on income tax revenue for funding. Economists and politicians argue about how elastic the supply of labor is and, thus, how large these effects are.

Deadweight Loss and Tax Revenue as Taxes Vary

Deadweight loss increases as a tax increases. Indeed, deadweight loss increases at an increasing rate as a tax increases. It increases as the square of the factor of increase in the tax. For example, if a tax is doubled, the deadweight loss rises by a factor of four. If a tax is tripled, the deadweight loss rises by a factor of nine, and so on.

Tax revenue first increases and then decreases as a tax increases. This is because, at first, an increase in a tax increases the taxes collected per unit more than it reduces the units sold. At some point, however, an ever-increasing tax reduces the size of the market (the quantity sold and taxed) to such a degree that the government begins to collect a large tax on such a small quantity that tax revenue begins to fall.

The idea that a high tax rate could so shrink the market that it reduces tax revenue was expressed by Arthur Laffer in 1974. The *Laffer curve* is a diagram that shows as the size of a tax on a good is increased, revenue first rises and then falls. The implication is that if tax rates are already extremely high, a reduction in tax rates could increase tax revenue. This is a part of what has come to be called supply-side economics. Evidence has shown that this may be true for individuals who are taxed at extremely high rates, but it is less likely to be true for an entire economy. A possible exception is Sweden in the 1980s because its tax rates were about 80 percent for the typical worker.

Conclusion

Taxes place a cost on market participants in two ways:

- Resources are diverted from buyers and sellers to the government.

- Taxes distort incentives so fewer goods are produced and sold than otherwise. That is, taxes cause society to lose some of the benefits of efficient markets.

Helpful Hints

1. As a tax increases, it reduces the size of the market more and more. At some point, the tax is so high that it is greater than or equal to the potential surplus even from the first unit. At that point, the tax has become a *prohibitive tax* because it eliminates the market altogether. Note that when a tax is prohibitive, the government collects no revenue at all from the tax because no units are sold. The market has reached the far side of the Laffer curve.

2. As a tax increases, the deadweight loss increases *at an increasing rate* because there are two sources to the deadweight loss and both sources are generating an increase in deadweight loss as a tax increases. First, an increase in a tax reduces the quantity exchanged and that increases deadweight loss. Second, as quantity exchanged decreases due to the tax, each successive unit that is not produced and sold *has a higher total surplus associated with it*. This further increases the deadweight loss from a tax.

Terms and Definitions

Choose a definition for each key term.

Key Terms	Definitions
_____ Tax wedge	1. The reduction in total surplus that results from a tax
_____ Deadweight loss	2. A graph showing the relationship between the size of a tax and the tax revenue collected
_____ Laffer curve	3. The difference between what the buyer pays and the seller receives when a tax is placed in a market

Problems and Short-Answer Questions

Practice Problems

1. Exhibit 2 shows the market for tires. Suppose that a $12 road-use tax is placed on each tire sold.
    a.   In Exhibit 2, locate consumer surplus, producer surplus, tax revenue, and the deadweight loss.
    b.   Why is there a deadweight loss in the market for tires after the tax is imposed?

    _____

    _____

    _____

    c.   What is the value of the tax revenue collected by the government? Why wasn't the government able to collect $12 per tire on 60 tires sold (the original equilibrium quantity)?

    _____

    _____

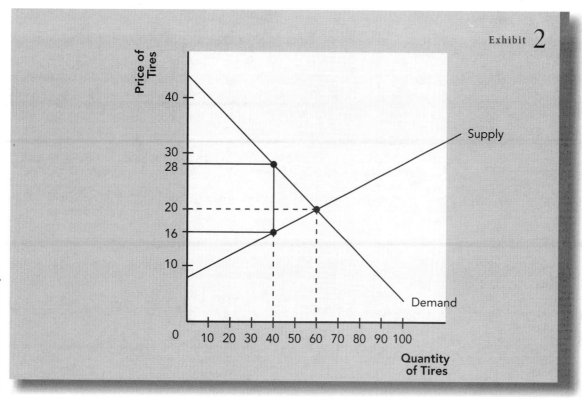

Exhibit 2

d. What is the value of the tax revenue collected from the buyers? What is the value of the tax revenue collected from the sellers? Did the burden of the tax fall more heavily on the buyers or the sellers? Why?

_____

_____

e. Suppose over time, buyers of tires are able to substitute away from auto tires (they walk or ride bicycles). Because of this, their demand for tires becomes more elastic. What will happen to the size of the deadweight loss in the market for tires? Why?

_____

_____

_____

_____

_____

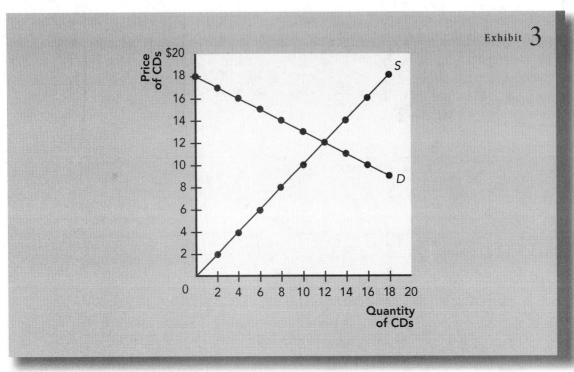

Exhibit 3

2. Use Exhibit 3, which shows the market for music CDs, to answer the following questions.

a. Complete the table. (Note: To calculate deadweight loss, the area of a triangle is 1/2 base × height).

Tax per unit	Tax revenue collected	Deadweight loss
$ 0	_____	_____
3	_____	_____
6	_____	_____
9	_____	_____
12	_____	_____
15	_____	_____
18	_____	_____

b. As the tax is increased, what happens to the amount of tax revenue collected? Why?

_____

_____

_____

c. At a tax of $18 per CD, how much tax revenue is collected? Why?

_____

_____

_____

d.   If the government wanted to maximize tax revenue, what tax per unit should it impose?

_____

e.   If the government wanted to maximize efficiency (total surplus), what tax per unit should it impose?

_____

f.   What happens to the deadweight loss due to the tax as the tax is increased? Why?

_____

_____

Short-Answer Questions

1.   Why does a tax reduce consumer surplus?

_____

_____

_____

2.   Why does a tax reduce producer surplus?

_____

_____

_____

3.   Why does a tax generally produce a deadweight loss?

_____

_____

_____

_____

4.   Under what conditions would a tax fail to produce a deadweight loss?

_____

_____

_____

5.   When a tax is placed on a good, does the government collect revenue equal to the loss in total surplus due to the tax? Why or why not?

_____

_____

_____

_____

_____

6. Suppose Rachel values having her house painted at $1,000. The cost for Paul to paint her house is $700. What is the value of the total surplus or the gains from trade on this transaction? What is the size of the tax that would eliminate this trade? What is the deadweight loss from this tax? What generalization can you make from this exercise?

_____

_____

_____

_____

7. Would you expect a tax on gasoline to have a greater deadweight loss in the short run or the long run? Why?

_____

_____

_____

_____

_____

8. Suppose the supply of oil is relatively inelastic. Would a tax on oil generate a large deadweight loss? Why or why not? Who would bear the burden of the tax, the buyer or the seller of oil? Why?

_____

_____

_____

_____

9. As a tax on a good increases, what happens to tax revenue? Why?

_____

_____

_____

_____

10. As a tax on a good increases, what happens to the deadweight loss from the tax? Why?

_____

_____

_____

_____

Self-Test

True/False Questions

_____ 1. In general, a tax raises the price the buyers pay, lowers the price the sellers receive, and reduces the quantity sold.

_____ 2. If a tax is placed on a good and it reduces the quantity sold, there must be a deadweight loss from the tax.

_____ 3. Deadweight loss is the reduction in consumer surplus that results from a tax.

_____ 4. When a tax is placed on a good, the revenue the government collects is exactly equal to the loss of consumer and producer surplus from the tax.

_____ 5. If John values having his hair cut at $20 and Mary's cost of providing the haircut is $10, any tax on haircuts larger than $10 will eliminate the gains from trade and cause a $20 loss of total surplus.

_____ 6. If a tax is placed on a good in a market where supply is perfectly inelastic, there is no deadweight loss and the sellers bear the entire burden of the tax.

_____ 7. A tax on cigarettes would likely generate a larger deadweight loss than a tax on luxury boats.

_____ 8. A tax will generate a greater deadweight loss if supply and demand are inelastic.

_____ 9. A tax causes a deadweight loss because it eliminates some of the potential gains from trade.

_____ 10. A larger tax always generates more tax revenue.

_____ 11. A larger tax always generates a larger deadweight loss.

_____ 12. If an income tax rate is high enough, a reduction in the tax rate could increase tax revenue.

_____ 13. A tax collected from buyers generates a smaller deadweight loss than a tax collected from sellers.

_____ 14. If a tax is doubled, the deadweight loss from the tax more than doubles.

_____ 15. A deadweight loss results when a tax causes market participants to fail to produce and consume units on which the benefits to the buyers exceed the costs to the sellers.

Multiple-Choice Questions

Use Exhibit 4 to answer questions 1 through 10.

1. If there is no tax placed on the product in this market, consumer surplus is the area
    a.   A + B + C.
    b.   D + C + B.
    c.   A + B + E.
    d.   C + D + F.
    e.   A.

2. If there is no tax placed on the product in this market, producer surplus is the area
    a.   A + B + C + D.
    b.   C + D + F.
    c.   D.
    d.   C + F.
    e.   A + B + E.

3. If a tax is placed on the product in this market, consumer surplus is the area
    a.   A.
    b.   A + B.
    c.   A + B + E.
    d.   A + B + C + D.
    e.   D.

4. If a tax is placed on the product in this market, producer surplus is the area
    a.   A.
    b.   A + B + E.
    c.   C + D + F.
    d.   D.
    e.   A + B + C + D.

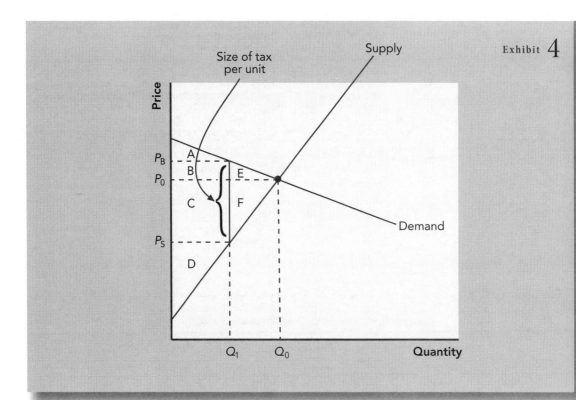

Exhibit 4

5. If a tax is placed on the product in this market, tax revenue paid by the buyers is the area
   a.   A.
   b.   B.
   c.   C.
   d.   B + C.
   e.   B + C + E + F.

6. If a tax is placed on the product in this market, tax revenue paid by the sellers is the area
   a.   A.
   b.   B.
   c.   C.
   d.   C + F.
   e.   B + C + E + F.

7. If there is no tax placed on the product in this market, total surplus is the area
   a.   A + B + C + D.
   b.   A + B + C + D + E + F.
   c.   B + C + E + F.
   d.   E + F.
   e.   A + D + E + F.

8. If a tax is placed on the product in this market, total surplus is the area
   a.   A + B + C + D.
   b.   A + B + C + D + E + F.
   c.   B + C + E + F.
   d.   E + F.
   e.   A + D.

9. If a tax is placed on the product in this market, deadweight loss is the area
   a.   B + C.
   b.   B + C + E + F.
   c.   A + B + C + D.
   d.   E + F.
   e.   A + D.

10. Which of the following is true with regard to the burden of the tax in Exhibit 4?
    a.   The buyers pay a larger portion of the tax because demand is more inelastic than supply.
    b.   The buyers pay a larger portion of the tax because demand is more elastic than supply.
    c.   The sellers pay a larger portion of the tax because supply is more elastic than demand.
    d.   The sellers pay a larger portion of the tax because supply is more inelastic than demand.

11. Which of the following would likely cause the greatest deadweight loss?
    a.   a tax on cigarettes
    b.   a tax on salt
    c.   a tax on cruise line tickets
    d.   a tax on gasoline

12. A tax on gasoline is likely to
    a.   cause a greater deadweight loss in the long run when compared to the short run.
    b.   cause a greater deadweight loss in the short run when compared to the long run.
    c.   generate a deadweight loss that is unaffected by the time period over which it is measured.
    d.   None of the above is correct.

13. Deadweight loss is greatest when
    a. both supply and demand are relatively inelastic.
    b. both supply and demand are relatively elastic.
    c. supply is elastic and demand is perfectly inelastic.
    d. demand is elastic and supply is perfectly inelastic.

14. Suppose the supply of diamonds is relatively inelastic. A tax on diamonds would generate a
    a. large deadweight loss and the burden of the tax would fall on the buyer of diamonds.
    b. small deadweight loss and the burden of the tax would fall on the buyer of diamonds.
    c. large deadweight loss and the burden of the tax would fall on the seller of diamonds.
    d. small deadweight loss and the burden of the tax would fall on the seller of diamonds.

15. Taxes on labor income tend to encourage
    a. workers to work fewer hours.
    b. second earners to stay home.
    c. the elderly to retire early.
    d. the unscrupulous to enter the underground economy.
    e. all of the above.

16. When a tax on a good starts small and is gradually increased, tax revenue will
    a. rise.
    b. fall.
    c. first rise and then fall.
    d. first fall and then rise.
    e. do none of the above.

17. The graph that shows the relationship between the size of a tax and the tax revenue collected by the government is known as a
    a. deadweight curve.
    b. tax revenue curve.
    c. Laffer curve.
    d. Reagan curve.
    e. None of the above is correct.

18. If a tax on a good is doubled, the deadweight loss from the tax
    a. stays the same.
    b. doubles.
    c. increases by a factor of four.
    d. could rise or fall.

19. The reduction of a tax
    a. could increase tax revenue if the tax had been extremely high.
    b. will always reduce tax revenue regardless of the prior size of the tax.
    c. will have no impact on tax revenue.
    d. causes a market to become less efficient.

20. When a tax distorts incentives to buyers and sellers so that fewer goods are produced and sold, the tax has
    a. increased efficiency.
    b. reduced the price buyers pay.
    c. generated no tax revenue.
    d. caused a deadweight loss.

Advanced Critical Thinking

You are watching the local news report on television with your roommate. The news anchor reports that the state budget has a deficit of $100 million. Because the state currently collects exactly $100 million from its 5 percent sales tax, your roommate says, "I can tell them how to fix their deficit. They should simply double the sales tax to 10 percent. That will double their tax revenue from $100 million to $200 million and provide the needed $100 million."

1. Is it true that doubling a tax will always double tax revenue? Why or why not?

   _____

   _____

   _____

   _____

   _____

   _____

2. Will doubling the sales tax affect the tax revenue and the deadweight loss in all markets to the same degree? Explain.

   _____

   _____

   _____

   _____

   _____

   _____

   _____

   _____

Solutions

Terms and Definitions

  _3_ Tax wedge
  _1_ Deadweight loss
  _2_ Laffer curve

Practice Problems

1. a. See Exhibit 5.

Exhibit 5

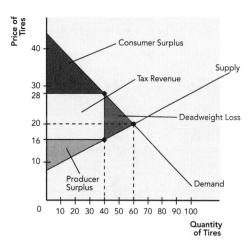

b. The tax raises the price paid by buyers and lowers the price received by sellers causing them to reduce their quantities demanded and supplied. Therefore, they fail to produce and exchange units where the value to buyers exceeds the cost to sellers.

c. $12 × 40 = $480. The tax distorted prices to the buyers and sellers so that the quantity supplied and demanded with the tax is reduced to 40 units from 60 units.

d. $8 × 40 = $320 from buyers. $4 × 40 = $160 from sellers. The burden fell more heavily on the buyers because the demand for tires was less elastic than the supply of tires.

e. Deadweight loss will increase because when buyers are more sensitive to an increase in price (due to the tax), they will reduce their quantity demanded even more and shrink the market more. Thus, even fewer units that are valued by buyers in excess of their cost will be sold.

2. a.

Tax per unit	Tax revenue collected	Deadweight loss
$ 0	$ 0	$0
3	30	($3 × 2)/2 = $3
6	48	($6 × 4)/2 = $12
9	54	($9 × 6)/2 = $27
12	48	($12 × 8)/2 = $48
15	30	($15 × 10)/2 = $75
18	0	($18 × 12)/2 = $108

b. It first rises, then falls. At first, as the tax is increased tax revenue rises. At some point, the tax reduces the size of the market to such a degree that the government is collecting a large tax on such a small quantity that tax revenue begins to fall.

c. No tax revenue is collected because the tax is as large as the total surplus on the first unit. Therefore, there is no incentive to produce and consume even one unit and the entire market is eliminated.

d. $9 per unit.

e. $0 per unit, which causes the market to return to its free market equilibrium.

f. It increases. Indeed, it increases at an increasing rate. This is because as the tax increases, it causes the quantity exchanged to be reduced on units that have an ever larger potential surplus attached to them.

Short-Answer Questions

1. Consumer surplus is what the buyer is willing to pay for a good minus what the buyer actually pays and a tax raises the price the buyer actually pays.

2. Producer surplus is the amount the seller receives for a good minus the seller's cost and a tax reduces what the seller receives for a good.

3. A tax raises the price buyers pay and lowers the price sellers receive. This price distortion reduces the quantity demanded and supplied so we fail to produce and consume units where the benefits to the buyers exceed the costs to the sellers.

4. If either supply or demand were perfectly inelastic (insensitive to a change in price), then a tax would fail to reduce the quantity exchanged and the market would not shrink.

5. No. The tax distorts prices to buyers and sellers and causes them to reduce their quantities demanded and supplied. Taxes are collected only on the units sold after the tax is imposed. Those units that are no longer produced and sold generate no tax revenue but those units would have added to total surplus because they were valued by buyers in excess of their cost to sellers. The reduction in total surplus is the deadweight loss.

6. Total surplus = $300. Any tax larger than $300. Deadweight loss would be $300. A tax that is greater than the potential gains from trade will eliminate trade and create a deadweight loss equal to the lost gains from trade.

7. There would be a greater deadweight loss in the long run. This is because both demand and supply tend to be more elastic in the long run as consumers and producers are able to substitute away from this market when prices move in an adverse direction. The more a market shrinks from a tax, the greater the deadweight loss.

8. No. Because the supply of oil is highly inelastic, the quantity supplied is not responsive to a decrease in the price received by the seller. The seller would bear the burden of the tax for the same reason—supply of oil is highly inelastic.

9. First tax revenue increases. At some point tax revenue decreases as the distortion in prices to buyers and sellers causes the market to shrink and large taxes are collected on a small number of units exchanged.

10. Deadweight loss increases continuously because as a tax increases, the distortion in prices caused by the tax causes the market to shrink continuously. Thus, we fail to produce more and more units where the benefits to buyers exceed the costs to sellers.

True/False Questions

1. T
2. T
3. F; deadweight loss is the reduction in *total surplus* that results from a tax.
4. F; the loss of producer and consumer surplus exceeds the revenue from the tax. The difference is deadweight loss.
5. F; the loss in total surplus is the buyer's value minus the seller's cost or $20 − $10 = $10.
6. T
7. F; the more elastic the demand curve, the greater the deadweight loss, and the demand for cigarettes (a necessity) should be more inelastic than the demand for luxury boats (a luxury).
8. F; a tax generates a greater deadweight loss when supply and demand are more elastic.
9. T
10. F; as a tax increases, revenue first rises and then falls as the tax shrinks the market to a point where all trades are eliminated and tax revenue is zero.
11. T
12. T
13. F; taxes collected from either the buyers or the sellers are equivalent. That is why economists simply use a tax wedge when analyzing a tax and avoid the issue altogether.
14. T
15. T

Multiple-Choice Questions

1. c
2. b
3. a
4. d
5. b
6. c
7. b
8. a
9. d
10. d
11. c
12. a
13. b
14. d
15. e
16. c
17. c
18. c
19. a
20. d

Advanced Critical Thinking

1. No. Usually an increase in a tax will reduce the size of the market because the tax will increase the price to buyers, causing them to reduce their quantity demanded and will decrease the price to sellers, causing them to reduce their quantity supplied. Therefore, when taxes double, the government collects twice as much per unit on many fewer units, so tax revenue will increase by less than double and could, in some extreme cases, even go down.

2. No. Some markets may have extremely elastic supply-and-demand curves. In these markets, an increase in a tax causes market participants to leave the market, and little revenue is generated from the tax increase but deadweight loss increases a great deal. Other markets may have inelastic supply-and-demand curves. In these markets, an increase in a tax fails to cause market participants to leave the market and a great deal of additional tax revenue is generated with little increase in deadweight loss.

Chapter 9
Application: International Trade

Goals
In this chapter you will

- Consider what determines whether a country imports or exports a good
- Examine who wins and who loses from international trade
- Learn that the gains to winners from international trade exceed the losses to losers
- Analyze the welfare effects of tariffs
- Examine the arguments people use to advocate trade restrictions

Outcomes
After accomplishing these goals, you should be able to

- Determine whether a country imports or exports a good if the world price is greater than the before-trade domestic price
- Show that the consumer wins and the producer loses when a country imports a good
- Use consumer and producer surplus to show that the gains of the consumer exceed the losses of the producer when a country imports a good
- Show the deadweight loss associated with a tariff
- Defeat the arguments made in support of trade restrictions

Chapter Overview

Context and Purpose

Chapter 9 is the third chapter in a three-chapter sequence dealing with welfare economics. Chapter 7 introduced welfare economics—the study of how the allocation of resources affects economic well-being. Chapter 8 applied the lessons of welfare economics to taxation.

Chapter 9 applies the tools of welfare economics from Chapter 7 to the study of international trade, a topic that was first introduced in Chapter 3.

The purpose of Chapter 9 is to use our knowledge of welfare economics to address the gains from trade more precisely than we did in Chapter 3 when we studied comparative advantage and the gains from trade. We will develop the conditions that determine whether a country imports or exports a good and discover who wins and who loses when a country imports or exports a good. We will find that when free trade is allowed, the gains of the winners exceed the losses of the losers. Because there are gains from trade, we will see that restrictions on free trade reduce the gains from trade and cause deadweight losses similar to those generated by a tax.

Chapter Review

Introduction   This chapter employs welfare economics to address the following questions:

- How does international trade affect economic well-being?
- Who gains and who loses from free international trade?
- How do the gains from trade compare to the losses from trade?

The Determinants of Trade

In the absence of international trade, a market generates a domestic price that equates the domestic quantity supplied and domestic quantity demanded in that market. The world price is the price of the good that prevails in the world market for that good. Prices represent opportunity costs. Therefore, comparing the world price and the domestic price of a good before trade indicates whether a country has the lower opportunity cost of production and, thus, a comparative advantage in the production of a good or if other countries have a comparative advantage in the production of the good.

- If the world price is above the domestic price for a good, the country has a comparative advantage in the production of that good and that good should be exported if trade is allowed.

- If the world price is below the domestic price for a good, foreign countries have a comparative advantage in the production of that good and that good should be imported if trade is allowed.

The Winners and Losers from Trade

Assume that the country being analyzed is a small country and is, therefore, a *price taker* on world markets. This means that the country takes the world price as given and cannot influence the world price.

Exhibit 1 depicts a situation where the world price is higher than the before-trade domestic price. This country has a comparative advantage in the production of this good. If free trade is allowed, the domestic price will rise to the world price and it will export the difference between the domestic quantity supplied and the domestic quantity demanded.

With regard to gains and losses to an exporting country from trade, before-trade consumer surplus was A + B and producer surplus was C, so total surplus was A + B + C. After trade, consumer surplus is A and producer surplus is B + C + D (the area below the price and above the supply curve). Total surplus is now A + B + C + D for a gain of area D. This analysis generates two conclusions:

- When a country allows trade and becomes an exporter of a good, domestic producers are better off and domestic consumers are worse off.

- Trade increases the economic well-being of a nation because the gains of the winners exceed the losses of the losers.

Exhibit 2 depicts a situation where the world price is lower than the before-trade domestic price. Other countries have a comparative advantage in the production of this good. If free trade is allowed, the domestic price will fall to the world price, and it will import the difference between the domestic quantity supplied and the domestic quantity demanded.

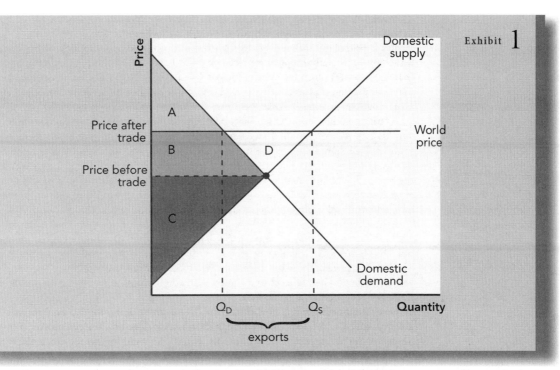

With regard to gains and losses to an importing country from trade, before-trade consumer surplus was A and producer surplus was B + C, so total surplus was A + B + C. After trade, consumer surplus is A + B + D (the area below the demand curve and above the price) and producer surplus is C. Total surplus is now A + B + C + D for a gain of area D. This analysis generates two conclusions:

- When a country allows trade and becomes an importer of a good, domestic consumers are better off and domestic producers are worse off.

- Trade increases the economic well-being of a nation because the gains of the winners exceed the losses of the losers.

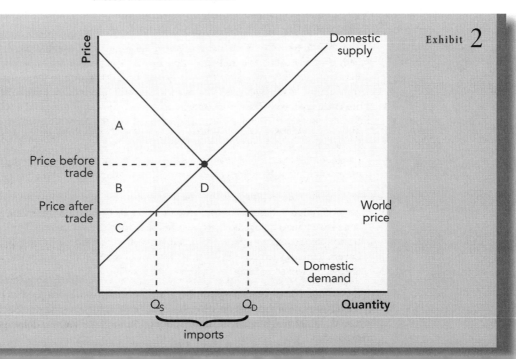

Trade can make everyone better off if the winners compensate the losers. Compensation is rarely paid, so the losers lobby for trade restrictions, such as tariffs.

Tariffs restrict international trade. A tariff is a tax on goods produced abroad and sold domestically. Therefore, a tariff is placed on a good only if the country is an importer of that good. A tariff raises the price of the good, reduces the domestic quantity demanded, increases the domestic quantity supplied, and, thus, reduces the quantity of imports. A tariff moves the market closer to the no-trade equilibrium.

A tariff increases producer surplus and government revenue but reduces consumer surplus by a greater amount than the increase in producer surplus and government revenue. Therefore, a tariff creates a deadweight loss because total surplus is reduced. The deadweight loss comes from two sources. The increase in the price due to the tariff causes the production of units that cost more to produce than the world price (overproduction) and causes consumers to fail to consume units where the value to the consumer is greater than the world price (underconsumption).

An import quota sets a limit on the quantity of a good that can be produced abroad and sold domestically. To accomplish this, a government can distribute a limited number of import licenses. As with a tariff, an import quota reduces the quantity of imports, raises the domestic price of the good, decreases the welfare of domestic consumers, increases the welfare of domestic producers, and causes deadweight losses. It moves the market closer to the no-trade equilibrium.

Note that the results of a tariff and an import quota are nearly the same except that the government collects revenue from a tariff. If the import licenses are given away, the license holders earn the surplus generated from the world price being below the domestic price. If the government sells the import licenses for the maximum possible amount, it will collect revenue equal to the tariff revenue and a tariff and a quota become identical. If quotas are "voluntary" in the sense that they are imposed by the exporting country, the revenue from the quota accrues to the foreign firms or governments.

Tariffs cause deadweight losses. Therefore, if economic efficiency is a policy goal, countries should allow free trade and avoid using tariffs.

Free trade offers benefits beyond efficiency. Free trade increases variety for consumers, allows firms to take advantage of economies of scale, makes markets more competitive, and facilitates the spread of technology.

The Arguments for Restricting Trade

Opponents of free trade (often producers hurt by free trade) offer the following arguments in support of trade restrictions:

- **The Jobs Argument**   Opponents of free trade argue that trade destroys domestic jobs. However, while free trade does destroy inefficient jobs in the importing sector, it creates more efficient jobs in the export sector, industries where the country has a comparative advantage. This is always true because each country has a comparative advantage in the production of something.

- **The National-Security Argument**   Some industries argue that their product is vital for national security, so it should be protected from international competition. The danger of this argument is that it runs the risk of being overused, particularly when the argument is made by representatives of industry rather than the defense establishment.

- **The Infant-Industry Argument**   New industries argue that they need temporary protection from international competition until they become mature enough to compete. However, there is a problem choosing which new industries to protect, and once protected, temporary protection often becomes permanent. In addition, industries government truly expects to be competitive in the future don't need protection because the owners will accept short-term losses.

- **The Unfair-Competition Argument**   Opponents of free trade argue that other countries provide their industries with unfair advantages such as subsidies, tax breaks, and lower environmental restrictions. However, the gains of consumers in the importing country will exceed the losses of the producers in that country, and the country will gain when importing subsidized production.

- **The Protection-as-a-Bargaining-Chip Argument**   Opponents of free trade argue that the threat of trade restrictions may result in other countries lowering their trade restrictions. However, if this does not work, the threatening country must back down or reduce trade—neither of which is desirable.

When countries choose to reduce trade restrictions, they can take a *unilateral* approach and remove trade restrictions on their own. Alternatively, they can take a *multilateral* approach and reduce trade restrictions along with other countries. Examples of the multilateral approach are NAFTA and GATT. The rules of GATT are enforced by the WTO. The multilateral approach has advantages in that it provides freer overall trade because many countries do it together, and thus, it is sometimes more easily accomplished politically. However, it may fail if negotiations between countries break down. Many economists suggest a unilateral approach because there will be gains to the domestic economy and this will cause other countries to emulate it.

Conclusion

Economists overwhelmingly support free trade. Free trade between states in the United States improves welfare by allowing each area of the country to specialize in the production of goods for which they have a comparative advantage. In the same manner, free trade between countries allows each country to enjoy the benefits of comparative advantage and the gains from trade.

Helpful Hints

1. Countries that restrict trade usually restrict imports rather than exports. This is because producers lose from imports and gain from exports, and producers are better organized to lobby the government to protect their interests. For example, when a country imports a product, consumers win and producers lose. Consumers are less likely to organize and lobby the government than the affected producers so imports may be restricted. When a country exports a product, producers win and consumers lose. Yet again, consumers are less likely to organize and lobby the government to restrict exports so exports are rarely restricted.

2. The overwhelming majority of economists find no sound *economic* argument in opposition to free trade. The only argument against free trade that may not be defeated on economic grounds is the "national-security argument." This is because it is the only argument against free trade that is not based on economics but rather is based on other strategic objectives.

3. A *prohibitive* tariff or import quota is one that is so restrictive that it returns the domestic market to its original no-trade equilibrium. This occurs if the tariff is greater than or equal to the difference between the world price and the no-trade domestic price or if the import quota is set at zero.

Terms and Definitions

Choose a definition for each key term.

Key Terms

_____ World price

_____ Price takers

_____ Tariff

Definitions

1. Market participants that cannot influence the price so they view the price as given

2. The price of a good that prevails in the world market for that good

3. A tax on goods produced abroad and sold domestically

Problems and Short-Answer Questions

Practice Problems

1. Use Exhibit 3 to answer the following questions.
   a. If trade is not allowed, what is the equilibrium price and quantity in this market?

   _____

   b. If trade is allowed, will this country import or export this commodity? Why?

   _____

   _____

   c. If trade is allowed, what is the price at which the good is sold, the domestic quantity supplied and demanded, and the quantity imported or exported?

   _____

   _____

   d. What area corresponds to consumer surplus if no trade is allowed?

   _____

   e. What area corresponds to consumer surplus if trade is allowed?

   _____

   f. What area corresponds to producer surplus if no trade is allowed?

   _____

   g. What area corresponds to producer surplus if trade is allowed?

   _____

   h. If free trade is allowed, who gains and who loses, the consumers or the producers, and what area corresponds to their gain or loss?

   _____

   i. What area corresponds to the gains from trade?

   _____

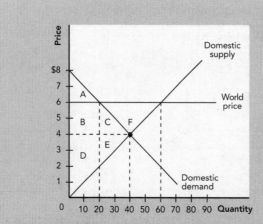

Exhibit **3**

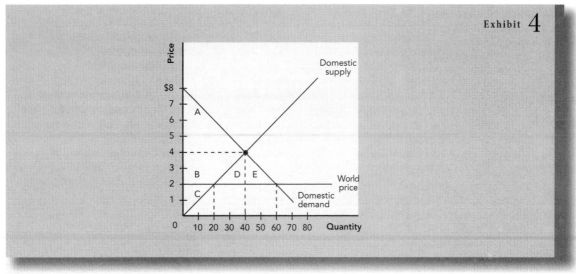

Exhibit 4

2. Use Exhibit 4 to answer the following questions.
    a. If trade is not allowed, what is the equilibrium price and quantity in this market?

    _____

    b. If trade is allowed, will this country import or export this commodity? Why?

    _____

    _____

    c. If trade is allowed, what is the price at which the good is sold, the domestic quantity supplied and demanded, and the quantity imported or exported?

    _____

    _____

    d. What area corresponds to consumer surplus if no trade is allowed?

    _____

    e. What area corresponds to consumer surplus if trade is allowed?

    _____

    f. What area corresponds to producer surplus if no trade is allowed?

    _____

    g. What area corresponds to producer surplus if trade is allowed?

    _____

    h. If free trade is allowed, who gains and who loses, the consumers or the producers, and what area corresponds to their gain or loss?

    _____

    i. What area corresponds to the gains from trade?

    _____

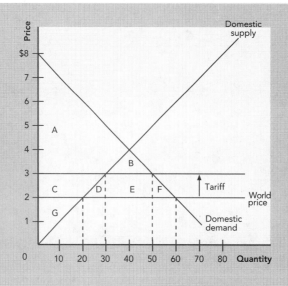

Exhibit 5

3. Use Exhibit 5 to answer the following questions.

   a. If free trade is allowed, what are the domestic quantity supplied, domestic quantity demanded, and the quantity imported?

   _____

   _____

   b. If a $1 tariff is placed on this good, what are the domestic quantity supplied, domestic quantity demanded, and the quantity imported?

   _____

   _____

   c. What area corresponds to consumer and producer surplus before the tariff is applied?

   _____

   _____

   d. What area corresponds to consumer surplus, producer surplus, and government revenue after the tariff is applied?

   _____

   _____

   e. What area corresponds to the deadweight loss associated with the tariff?

   _____

   f. Describe in words the sources of the deadweight loss from a tariff.

   _____

   _____

   _____

g. What is the size of the tariff that would eliminate trade altogether (i.e., that would return the market to its no-trade domestic solution)?

_____

Short-Answer Questions

The following table shows the amount of output a worker can produce per hour in Partyland and Laborland.

	Beer	Pizza
Partyland	2	4
Laborland	4	12

1. If free trade is allowed, which good will each country export to the other? Why? (Explain in terms of each country's opportunity cost of production.)

_____

_____

_____

_____

2. If the world price for a good is above a country's before-trade domestic price, will this country import or export this good? Why?

_____

_____

3. If residents of a country are allowed to import a good, who gains and who loses when compared to the before-trade equilibrium, the producers or the consumers? Why?

_____

_____

4. Describe in words the source of the gains from trade (the additional total surplus) received by an exporting country.

_____

_____

5. Describe in words the source of the gains from trade (the additional total surplus) received by an importing country.

_____

_____

6. Describe in words the source of the deadweight loss from restricting trade.

_____

_____

7. For every tariff there is an import quota that will generate a similar result. What are the shortcomings of using an import quota to restrict trade versus using a tariff?

_____

_____

8. What arguments are made to support trade restrictions?

_____

_____

9. Present the free-trade response to the argument that imports should be restricted on goods that a country needs for national security.

_____

_____

10. If tariffs reduce total surplus and, therefore, total economic well-being, why do governments employ them?

_____

_____

11. List other benefits of free trade beyond those suggested by our standard analysis.

_____

_____

Self-Test
True/False Questions

_____   1. If the world price for a good exceeds a country's before-trade domestic price for that good, the country should import that good.

_____   2. Countries should import products for which they have a comparative advantage in production.

_____   3. If a worker in Brazil can produce 6 oranges or 2 apples in an hour while a worker in Mexico can produce 2 oranges or 1 apple in an hour, then Brazil should export oranges and Mexico should export apples.

_____   4. If free trade is allowed and a country imports wheat, domestic buyers of bread are better off and domestic farmers are worse off when compared to the before-trade domestic equilibrium.

_____   5. If free trade is allowed and a country exports a good, domestic producers of the good are worse off and domestic consumers of the good are better off when compared to the before-trade domestic equilibrium.

_____   6. If free trade is allowed and a country exports a good, the gains of domestic producers exceed the losses of domestic consumers and total surplus rises.

_____   7. Trade makes everyone better off.

_____   8. Trade can make everyone better off if the winners from trade compensate the losers from trade.

_____   9.   Trade increases the economic well-being of a nation because the gains of the winners exceed the losses of the losers.

_____   10.   Tariffs tend to benefit consumers.

_____   11.   A tariff raises the price of a good, reduces the domestic quantity demanded, increases the domestic quantity supplied, and increases the quantity imported.

_____   12.   An import quota that restricts imports to the same degree as an equivalent tariff raises the same amount of government revenue as the equivalent tariff, even if the government gives away the import licenses.

_____   13.   Opponents of free trade often argue that free trade destroys domestic jobs.

_____   14.   If a foreign country subsidizes its export industries, its taxpayers are paying to improve the welfare of consumers in the importing countries.

_____   15.   Tariffs cause deadweight losses because they raise the price of the imported good and cause overproduction and underconsumption of the good in the importing country.

Multiple-Choice Questions

1.   If free trade is allowed, a country will export a good if the world price is
  a.   below the before-trade domestic price of the good.
  b.   above the before-trade domestic price of the good.
  c.   equal to the before-trade domestic price of the good.
  d.   none of the above.

2.   Suppose the world price is below the before-trade domestic price for a good. If a country allows free trade in this good,
  a.   consumers will gain and producers will lose.
  b.   producers will gain and consumers will lose.
  c.   both producers and consumers will gain.
  d.   both producers and consumers will lose.

The following table shows the amount of output a worker can produce per hour in the United States and Canada.

	Pens	Pencils
United States	8	4
Canada	8	2

3.   Which of the following statements about free trade between the United States and Canada is true?
  a.   The United States will export pencils, but there will be no trade in pens because neither country has a comparative advantage in the production of pens.
  b.   The United States will export pens, and Canada will export pencils.
  c.   The United States will export pencils, and Canada will export pens.
  d.   The United States will export both pens and pencils.

4.   If the world price for a good exceeds the before-trade domestic price for a good, then that country must have
  a.   an absolute advantage in the production of the good.
  b.   an absolute disadvantage in the production of the good.
  c.   a comparative advantage in the production of the good.
  d.   a comparative disadvantage in the production of the good.

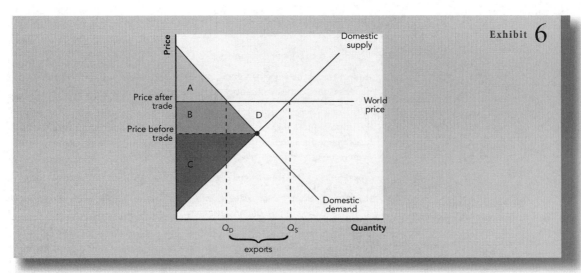

Use Exhibit 6 to answer questions 5 through 9.

5. If trade is not allowed, consumer surplus is the area
   a. A.
   b. A + B.
   c. A + B + C.
   d. A + B + D.
   e. A + B + C + D.

6. If free trade is allowed, consumer surplus is the area
   a. A.
   b. A + B.
   c. A + B + C.
   d. A + B + D.
   e. A + B + C + D.

7. If trade is not allowed, producer surplus is the area
   a. C.
   b. B + C.
   c. B + C + D.
   d. A + B + C.
   e. A + B + C + D.

8. If free trade is allowed, producer surplus is the area
   a. C.
   b. B + C.
   c. B + C + D.
   d. A + B + C.
   e. A + B + C + D.

9. The gains from trade correspond to the area
   a. A.
   b. B.
   c. C.
   d. D.
   e. B + D.

10. When a country allows trade and exports a good,
    a. domestic consumers are better off, domestic producers are worse off, and the nation is worse off because the losses of the losers exceed the gains of the winners.
    b. domestic consumers are better off, domestic producers are worse off, and the nation is better off because the gains of the winners exceed the losses of the losers.
    c. domestic producers are better off, domestic consumers are worse off, and the nation is worse off because the losses of the losers exceed the gains of the winners.
    d. domestic producers are better off, domestic consumers are worse off, and the nation is better off because the gains of the winners exceed the losses of the losers.

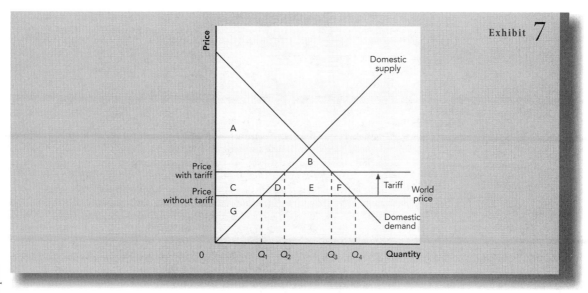

Exhibit 7

Use Exhibit 7 to answer questions 11 through 15.

11. If free trade is allowed, consumer surplus is the area
    a. A.
    b. A + B.
    c. A + B + C.
    d. A + B + C + D + E + F.
    e. A + B + C + D + E + F + G.

12. If a tariff is placed on this good, consumer surplus is the area
    a. A.
    b. A + B.
    c. A + B + C.
    d. A + B + C + D + E + F.
    e. A + B + C + D + E + F + G.

13. Government revenue from the tariff is the area
    a. C + D + E + F.
    b. D + E + F.
    c. D + F.
    d. G.
    e. E.

14. If a tariff is placed on this good, producer surplus is the area
    a. G.
    b. G + C.
    c. G + C + D + E + F.
    d. G + C + D + E + F + B.
    e. G + C + E.

15. The deadweight loss from the tariff is the area
    a. B + D + E + F.
    b. B.
    c. D + E + F.
    d. D + F.
    e. E.

16. When politicians argue that outsourcing or offshoring of technical support to India by Dell Computer Corporation is harmful to the U.S. economy, they are employing which of the following arguments for restricting trade?
    a.   the infant-industry argument
    b.   the jobs argument
    c.   the national-security argument
    d.   the deadweight-loss argument

17. Which of the following statements about a tariff is true?
    a.   A tariff increases producer surplus, decreases consumer surplus, increases revenue to the government, and reduces total surplus.
    b.   A tariff increases consumer surplus, decreases producer surplus, increases revenue to the government, and reduces total surplus.
    c.   A tariff increases producer surplus, decreases consumer surplus, increases revenue to the government, and increases total surplus.
    d.   A tariff increases consumer surplus, decreases producer surplus, increases revenue to the government, and increases total surplus.

18. Which of the following statements about import quotas is true?
    a.   Import quotas are preferred to tariffs because they raise more revenue for the imposing government.
    b.   Voluntary quotas established by the exporting country generate no deadweight loss for the importing country.
    c.   For every tariff, there is an import quota that could have generated a similar result.
    d.   An import quota reduces the price to the domestic consumers.

19. Which of the following is *not* employed as an argument in support of trade restrictions?
    a.   Free trade destroys domestic jobs.
    b.   Free trade harms the national security if vital products are imported.
    c.   Free trade is harmful to importing countries if foreign countries subsidize their exporting industries.
    d.   Free trade harms both domestic producers and domestic consumers and therefore reduces total surplus.
    e.   Free trade harms infant industries in an importing country.

20. Because producers are better able to organize than consumers are, we would expect there to be political pressure to create
    a.   free trade.
    b.   import restrictions.
    c.   export restrictions.
    d.   none of the above.

Advanced Critical Thinking

You are watching the nightly news. A political candidate being interviewed says, "I'm for free trade, but it must be fair trade. If our foreign competitors will not raise their environmental regulations, reduce subsidies to their export industries, and lower tariffs on their imports of our goods, we should retaliate with tariffs and import quotas on their goods to show them that we won't be played for fools!"

1. If a foreign country artificially lowers the cost of production for its producers with lax environmental regulations and direct subsidies and then exports the products to us, who gains and who loses in our country, producers or consumers?

_____

_____

_____

2. Continuing from question 1 above, does our country gain or lose? Why?

_____

_____

_____

3. If a foreign country subsidizes the production of a good exported to the United States, who bears the burden of their mistaken policy?

_____

_____

_____

4. What happens to our overall economic well-being if we restrict trade with a country that subsidizes its export industries? Explain.

_____

_____

_____

5. Is there any difference in the analysis of our importation of a good sold at the cost of production or sold at a subsidized price? Why?

_____

_____

_____

6. Is it a good policy to threaten trade restrictions in the hope that foreign governments will reduce their trade restrictions? Explain.

_____

_____

_____

Solutions

Terms and Definitions

  _2_   World price

  _1_   Price takers

  _3_   Tariff

Practice Problems

1. a. Price = $4, quantity = 40 units.

   b. Export because the world price is above the domestic price, which implies that this country has a comparative advantage in the production of this good.

   c. Price = $6, quantity supplied = 60 units, quantity demanded = 20 units, quantity exported = 40 units.

   d. A + B + C

   e. A

   f. D + E

   g. B + C + D + E + F

   h. Consumers lose B + C, producers gain B + C + F.

   i. F

2. a. Price = $4, quantity = 40 units.

   b. Import because the world price is below the domestic price, which implies that other countries have a comparative advantage in the production of this good.

   c. Price = $2, quantity supplied = 20 units, quantity demanded = 60 units, quantity imported = 40 units.

   d. A

   e. A + B + D + E

   f. B + C

   g. C

   h. Consumers gain B + D + E, producers lose B.

   i. D + E

3. a. Quantity supplied = 20 units, quantity demanded = 60 units, quantity imported = 40 units.

   b. Quantity supplied = 30 units, quantity demanded = 50 units, quantity imported = 20 units.

   c. Consumer surplus = A + B + C + D + E + F, producer surplus = G.

   d. Consumer surplus = A + B, producer surplus = C + G, government revenue = E.

   e. D + F

   f. First, the rise in the price due to the tariff causes *overproduction* because units are produced that cost more than the world price. Second, the rise in price causes *underconsumption* because consumers fail to consume units where the value to consumers is greater than the world price.

   g. A $2 tariff would raise the price to $4 (the no-trade domestic price) and eliminate trade.

Short-Answer Questions

1. In Partyland, the opportunity cost of 1 beer is 2 pizzas. In Laborland, the opportunity cost of 1 beer is 3 pizzas. Partyland has the lower opportunity cost of beer and, thus, a comparative advantage in beer production, and it will export beer. In Laborland, the opportunity cost of 1 pizza is 1/3 of a beer. In Partyland, the opportunity cost of 1 pizza is 1/2 of a beer. Laborland has the lower opportunity cost of pizza and, thus, a comparative advantage in pizza production, and it will export pizza. The fact that Laborland is more efficient at both is irrelevant.

2. Export, because the domestic opportunity cost of production is lower than the opportunity cost of production in other countries.

3. Consumers gain and producers lose because, if trade is allowed, the domestic price falls to the world price.

4. The gains are the additional value placed on the exported units by buyers in the rest of the world in excess of the domestic cost of production.

5. The gains are the additional value placed by domestic buyers on the imported units in excess of their cost of production in the rest of the world.

6. The rise in price from restricting trade causes overproduction of the good (production of units that cost more than the world price) and underconsumption of the good (failure to consume units valued more than the world price).

7. The revenue from an import quota will accrue to the license holders or foreign firms and governments unless the domestic government sells the import licenses for the maximum possible amount.

8. Free trade will destroy domestic jobs, reduce national security, harm infant industries, force domestic producers to compete with foreign companies that have unfair advantages, and allow other countries to have trade restrictions while our country does not.

9. The danger is that nearly any good (far beyond standard military items) can be argued by representatives of industry to be necessary for national security.

10. Tariffs harm domestic consumers while helping domestic producers. Producers are better able to organize than are consumers, and thus, they are better able to lobby the government on their behalf.

11. Free trade increases the variety of goods for consumers, allows firms to take advantage of economies of scale, makes markets more competitive, and facilitates the spread of technology.

True/False Questions

1. F; the country should *export* that good.
2. F; countries should export goods for which they have a comparative advantage in production.
3. T
4. T
5. F; producers gain, consumers lose.
6. T
7. F; some gain and some lose but the gains of the winners outweigh the losses of the losers.
8. T
9. T
10. F; tariffs benefit producers.
11. F; tariffs decrease imports.
12. F; at most, a quota can raise the same revenue if the government sells the import licenses for the maximum amount possible (the difference between the world price and the domestic price).
13. T
14. T
15. T

Multiple-Choice Questions

1. b
2. a
3. c
4. c
5. b
6. a
7. a
8. c
9. d
10. d
11. d
12. b
13. e
14. b
15. d
16. b
17. a
18. c
19. d
20. b

Advanced Critical Thinking

1. Consumers gain, producers lose.
2. Our country gains because the gains of the consumers exceed the losses of the producers.
3. The taxpayers of the foreign country.
4. Producers gain, consumers lose, but consumers lose more than producers gain so total surplus is reduced and there is a deadweight loss. The result is no different than restricting trade when the foreign producer has no unfair advantage.

5. No. In either case, the world price is lower than the before-trade domestic price, causing consumers to gain and producers to lose from trade. Also, restrictions on trade cause consumers to lose more than producers gain whether the production of the good was subsidized or not.
6. Usually not. If the other country fails to give in to the threat, the threatening country has to choose between backing down and reducing trade—neither of which is desirable.

Chapter 10
Externalities

Goals
In this chapter you will

- Learn what an externality is
- See why externalities can make market outcomes inefficient
- Examine the various government policies aimed at solving the problem of externalities
- Examine how people can sometimes solve the problem of externalities on their own
- Consider why private solutions to externalities sometimes do not work

Outcomes
After accomplishing these goals, you should be able to

- Distinguish between a positive and a negative externality
- Demonstrate why the optimal quantity and the market quantity differ in the presence of an externality
- Demonstrate the potential equality of a corrective tax and pollution permits
- Define the Coase theorem
- Explain how transaction costs may impede a private solution to an externality

Chapter Overview

Context and Purpose

Chapter 10 is the first chapter in the microeconomic section of the text. It is the first chapter in a three-chapter sequence on the economics of the public sector. Chapter 10 addresses externalities—the uncompensated impact of one person's actions on the well-being of a bystander. Chapter 11 will address public goods and common resources (goods that will be defined in Chapter 11), and Chapter 12 will address the tax system.

In Chapter 10, we address different sources of externalities and a variety of potential cures for externalities. Markets maximize total surplus to buyers and sellers in a market. However, if a market generates an externality (a cost or benefit to someone external to the market), the market equilibrium may not maximize the total benefit to society. Thus, in Chapter 10 we will see that while markets are usually a good way to organize economic activity, governments can sometimes improve market outcomes.

Chapter Review

Introduction   An externality is the uncompensated impact of one person's actions on the well-being of a bystander. If the effect is beneficial, it is called a *positive externality*. If the effect is adverse, it is called a *negative externality*. Markets maximize total surplus to buyers and sellers in a market, and this is usually efficient. However, if a market generates an externality, the market equilibrium may not maximize the total benefit to society as a whole, and thus, the market is inefficient. Government policy may be needed to improve efficiency. Examples of negative externalities are pollution from exhaust and noise. Examples of positive externalities are historic building restorations and research into new technologies.

Externalities and Market Inefficiency

The height of the demand curve measures the value of the good to the marginal consumer. The height of the supply curve measures the cost to the marginal producer. If there is no government intervention, the price adjusts to balance supply and demand. The quantity produced maximizes consumer and producer surplus. If there is no externality, the market solution is efficient because it maximizes the well-being of buyers and sellers in the market and their well-being is all that matters. However, if there is an externality and bystanders are affected by this market, the market does not maximize the total benefit to society as a whole because others beyond just the buyers and sellers in the market are affected.

There are two types of externalities:

- Negative externality: When the production of a good generates pollution, costs accrue to society beyond those that accrue to the producing firm. Thus, the social cost exceeds the private cost of production, and graphically, the social cost curve is above the supply curve (private cost curve). Total surplus is the value to the consumers minus the true social cost of production. Therefore, the optimal quantity that maximizes total surplus is less than the equilibrium quantity generated by the market.

- Positive externality: A good such as education generates benefits to people beyond just the buyers of education. As a result, the social value of education exceeds the private value. Graphically, the social value curve is above the demand curve (private value curve). Total surplus is the true social value minus the cost to producers. Therefore, the optimal quantity that maximizes total surplus is greater than the equilibrium quantity generated by the market.

Internalizing an externality is the altering of incentives so that people take into account the external effects of their actions. To internalize externalities, the government can create taxes and subsidies to shift the supply and demand curves until they are the same as the true social cost and social value curves. This will make the equilibrium quantity and the optimal quantity the same, and the market becomes efficient. Negative externalities can be internalized with taxes while positive externalities can be internalized with subsidies.

High technology production (robotics, etc.) generates a positive externality for other producers known as a *technology spillover*. Some economists consider this spillover effect to be so pervasive that they believe the government should have an industrial policy— government intervention to promote technology-enhancing industries. Other economists are skeptical. At present, the U.S. government provides a property right for new ideas in the form of patent protection, and offers special tax breaks for expenditures on research and development.

Public Policies Toward Externalities

The government can sometimes improve the outcome by responding in one of two ways: command-and-control policies or market-based policies.

- Command-and-control policies are regulations that require or prohibit (or limit) certain behaviors. The problem here is that the regulator must know all of the details of an industry and alternative technologies in order to create the efficient rules. Prohibiting a behavior altogether can be best if the cost of a particular type of pollution is enormous.

- Market-based policies align private incentives with social efficiency. There are two types of market-based policies: corrective taxes and subsidies, and tradable pollution permits.

A tax enacted to correct the effects of a negative externality is known as a corrective tax or Pigovian tax. An ideal corrective tax or subsidy would equal the external cost or benefit from the activity generating the externality. Corrective taxes can reduce negative externalities at a lower cost than regulations because the tax essentially places a price on a negative externality, say pollution. Those firms that can reduce their pollution with the least cost reduce their pollution a great deal while other firms that have higher costs of reducing their pollution reduce their pollution very little. The same amount of total reduction in pollution can be achieved with the tax as with regulation but at lower cost. In addition, with the tax firms have incentive to develop cleaner technologies and reduce pollution even further than the regulation would have required. Unlike other taxes, corrective taxes enhance efficiency rather than reduce efficiency. For example, the tax on gasoline is a corrective tax because, rather than causing a deadweight loss, it causes there to be less traffic congestion, safer roads, and a cleaner environment. Gasoline taxes are politically unpopular.

Tradable pollution permits allow the holder of the permit to pollute a certain amount. Those firms that have a high cost of reducing their pollution will be willing to pay a high price for the permits, and those firms that can reduce pollution at a low cost will sell their permits and will instead reduce their pollution. The initial allocation of the permits among industries does not affect the efficient outcome. This method is similar to a corrective tax. While a corrective tax sets the price of pollution (the tax), tradable pollution permits set the quantity of pollution permitted. In the market for pollution, either method can reach the efficient solution. Tradable pollution permits may be superior because the regulator does not need to know the demand to pollute in order to restrict pollution to a particular quantity. The EPA is increasingly and successfully using pollution permits to reduce pollution. At present, to reduce carbon emissions and global warming, the U.S. is moving toward a cap-and-trade system for carbon, which is very similar to a tax on carbon.

Some people object to an economic analysis of pollution. They feel that any pollution is too much and that putting a price on pollution is immoral. Because all economic activity creates pollution to some degree and all activities involve trade-offs, economists have little sympathy for this argument. Rich productive countries demand a cleaner environment, and market-based policies reduce pollution at a lower cost than alternatives, further increasing the demand for a clean environment.

Private Solutions to Externalities

Government action is not always needed to solve the externality problem. Some private solutions to the externality problem are as follows:

- Moral codes and social sanctions: People "do the right thing" and do not litter.

- Charities: People give tax-deductible gifts to environmental groups and private colleges and universities.

- Private markets that harness self-interest and cause efficient mergers: The beekeeper merges with the apple orchard, and the resulting firm produces more apples and more honey.

- Private markets that harness self-interest and create contracts among affected parties: The apple orchard and the beekeeper can agree to produce the optimal combined quantity of apples and honey.

The Coase theorem is the proposition that if private parties can bargain without cost over the allocation of resources, they can solve the problem of externalities on their own. In other words, regardless of the initial distribution of rights, the interested parties can always reach a bargain in which everyone is better off and the outcome is efficient. For example, if the value of peace and quiet exceeds the value of owning a barking dog, the party desiring quiet will buy the right to quiet from the dog owner and remove the dog, or the dog owner will fail to buy the right to own a barking dog from the owner of quiet space. Regardless of whether one has the property right to peace and quiet or the other has the right to make noise, there is no barking dog, which, in this case, is efficient. The result is the opposite and is also efficient if the value of owning a dog exceeds the value of peace and quiet.

Private parties often fail to reach efficient agreements, however, due to transaction costs. Transaction costs are the costs that parties incur in the process of agreeing and following through on a bargain. If transaction costs exceed the potential gains from the agreement, no private solution will occur. Some sources of high transaction costs are:

- lawyers' fees to write the agreement
- costs of enforcing the agreement
- a breakdown in bargaining when there is a range of prices that would create efficiency
- a large number of interested parties.

Conclusion

Markets maximize total surplus to buyers and sellers in a market and this is usually efficient. However, if a market generates an externality, the market equilibrium may not maximize the total benefit to society as a whole, and thus, the market is inefficient. The Coase theorem says that people can bargain among themselves and reach an efficient solution. If transaction costs are high, however, government policy may be needed to improve efficiency. Corrective taxes and pollution permits are preferred to command-and-control policies because they reduce pollution at a lower cost and, therefore, increase the quantity demanded of a clean environment.

Helpful Hints

1. Why do we use the word "externality" to refer to the uncompensated impact of one person's actions on the well-being of a bystander? An easy way to remember is to know that the word externality refers to the "external effects" of a market transaction or to costs and benefits that land on a bystander who is "external to the market."

2. Negative externalities cause the socially optimal quantity of a good to be less than the quantity produced by the market. Positive externalities cause the socially optimal quantity of a good to be greater than the quantity produced by the market. To remedy the problem, the government can tax goods that produce negative externalities by the size of the external cost, and subsidize goods that produce positive externalities by the size of the external benefit.

Terms and Definitions

Choose a definition for each key term.

Key Terms

_____ Externality

_____ Positive externality

_____ Negative externality

_____ Social cost

_____ Internalizing an externality

_____ Corrective tax

_____ Coase theorem

_____ Transaction costs

Definitions

1. The proposition that if private parties can bargain without cost over the allocation of resources, they can solve the problem of externalities on their own

2. The costs that parties incur in the process of agreeing and following through on a bargain

3. A situation when a person's actions have an adverse impact on a bystander

4. A tax designed to induce private decision makers to take into account the social costs that arise from a negative externality

5. The uncompensated impact of one person's actions on the well-being of a bystander

6. Altering incentives so that people take into account the external effects of their actions

7. The sum of private costs and external costs

8. A situation when a person's actions have a beneficial impact on a bystander

Problems and Short-Answer Questions

Practice Problems

1. The information below provides the prices and quantities in a hypothetical market for automobile antifreeze.

Price per gallon	Quantity demanded	Quantity supplied
$1	700	300
2	600	400
3	500	500
4	400	600
5	300	700
6	200	800
7	100	900
8	0	1,000

   a. Plot the supply and demand curves for antifreeze in Exhibit 1.
   b. What is the equilibrium price and quantity generated by buyers and sellers in the market?

   _____

   _____

   c. Suppose that the production of antifreeze generates pollution in the form of chemical runoff and that the pollution imposes a $2 cost on society for each gallon of antifreeze produced. Plot the social cost curve in Exhibit 1.
   d. What is the optimal quantity of antifreeze production? Does the market overproduce or underproduce antifreeze?

   _____

   _____

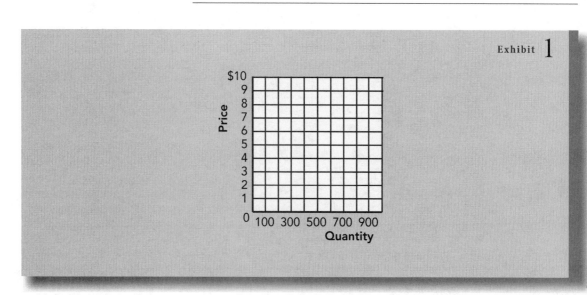

Exhibit 1

e. If the government were to intervene to make this market efficient, should it impose a corrective tax or a subsidy? What is the value of the appropriate tax or subsidy?

_____

_____

2. Suppose citizens living around Metropolitan Airport value peace and quiet at a value of $3 billion.

a. If it costs the airlines $4 billion to make their planes quieter (the airlines value noise at $4 billion), is it efficient for the government to require that the planes be muffled? Why or why not?

_____

_____

b. If it costs the airlines $2 billion to make their planes quieter, is it efficient for the government to require that the planes be muffled? Why or why not?

_____

_____

c. Suppose there are no transaction costs and suppose that people have the right to peace and quiet. If it costs the airlines $2 billion to make their planes quieter, what is the private solution to the problem?

_____

_____

d. Suppose there are no transaction costs and suppose that airlines have the right to make as much noise as they please. If it costs the airlines $2 billion to make their planes quieter, what is the private solution to the problem?

_____

_____

e. Compare your answers to c and d above. What are the similarities, and what are the differences? What general rule can you make from the comparison?

_____

_____

_____

f. Suppose it costs the airlines $2 billion to make their planes quieter. If a private solution to the noise problem requires an additional $2 billion of transaction costs (due to legal fees, the large number of affected parties, and enforcement costs), can there be a private solution to the problem? Why or why not?

_____

_____

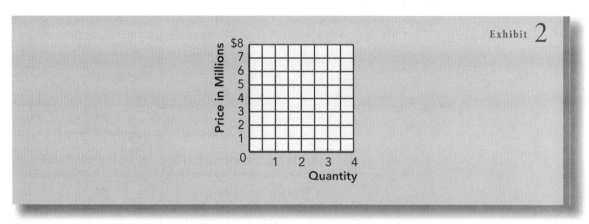

Exhibit 2

3. Suppose there are four firms that each wish to dump one barrel of waste chemicals into the river. Firm 1 produces a product that is so valued by society and sells for such a high price that it is willing to pay $8 million to dump a barrel. Firm 2 produces a somewhat less valuable product and is only willing to pay $6 million to dump a barrel. In similar fashion, suppose firm 3 is willing to pay $4 million to dump a barrel and firm 4 will pay $2 million.

   a. Draw the demand for the right to pollute in Exhibit 2.

   b. Suppose the EPA estimates that the safe level of pollutants in the river is 3 barrels. At what value should they set a corrective tax?

_____

_____

   c. Suppose the EPA estimates that the safe level of pollutants in the river is 3 barrels. How many tradable pollution permits should they allocate? At what price will the permits trade?

_____

_____

   d. Compare parts *b* and *c* above. How many barrels are dumped in each case? What is the price paid to pollute in each case? Is there an advantage to one method of internalizing the externality compared to the other?

_____

_____

_____

Short-Answer Questions

Use the following information for questions 1 through 3:

Suppose that a commercial apple orchard uses pesticides in the production of apples. In the process, dangerous fumes drift across a nearby neighborhood.

1. Is this an example of a positive or a negative externality? Explain.

_____

_____

_____

2. If this externality is not internalized, does the market overproduce or underproduce apples? What does it mean to overproduce or underproduce a product?

_____

_____

_____

3. To internalize this externality, should the government tax or subsidize apples? Why or why not?

_____

_____

_____

4. What are the two types of public policies toward externalities? Describe them. Which one do economists prefer? Why?

_____

_____

_____

5. Does a corrective tax reduce or increase efficiency? Why?

_____

_____

_____

6. Why are tradable pollution permits considered superior to corrective taxes at reducing pollution?

_____

_____

_____

7. Suppose an individual enjoys lawn care and gardening a great deal. He uses pesticides to control insects and the harmful residue drifts across the neighborhood. He values the use of the pesticides at $10,000 and the neighborhood values clean air at $15,000. What does the Coase theorem suggest will take place?

_____

_____

_____

8. In question 7 above, how large would the transaction costs need to be in order to ensure that no private solution to the problem can be found?

_____

_____

_____

9. What are the sources of transaction costs when affected parties try to eliminate an externality?

_____

_____

_____

10. What are some types of private solutions to externalities?

_____

_____

_____

Self-Test

True/False Questions

_____ 1. A positive externality is an external benefit that accrues to the buyers in a market while a negative externality is an external cost that accrues to the sellers in a market.

_____ 2. If a market generates a negative externality, the social cost curve is above the supply curve (private cost curve).

_____ 3. If a market generates a positive externality, the social value curve is above the demand curve (private value curve).

_____ 4. A market that generates a negative externality that has not been internalized generates an equilibrium quantity that is less than the optimal quantity.

_____ 5. If a market generates a negative externality, a corrective tax will move the market toward a more efficient outcome.

_____ 6. According to the Coase theorem, an externality always requires government intervention in order to internalize the externality.

_____ 7. To reduce pollution by some targeted amount, it is most efficient if each firm that pollutes reduces its pollution by an equal amount.

_____ 8. When Smokey the Bear says, "Only you can prevent forest fires," society is attempting to use moral codes and social sanctions to internalize the externality associated with using fire while camping.

_____ 9. A tax always makes a market less efficient.

_____ 10. If Bob values smoking in a restaurant at $10 and Sue values clean air while she eats at $15, according to the Coase theorem, Bob will not smoke in the restaurant only if Sue owns the right to clean air.

_____ 11. If transaction costs exceed the potential gains from an agreement between affected parties to an externality, there will be no private solution to the externality.

_____ 12. A corrective tax sets the price of pollution while tradable pollution permits set the quantity of pollution.

_____ 13. An advantage of using tradable pollution permits to reduce pollution is that the regulator need not know anything about the demand for pollution rights.

_____ 14. The majority of economists do not like the idea of putting a price on polluting the environment.

_____ 15. For any given demand curve for pollution, a regulator can achieve the same level of pollution with either a corrective tax or by allocating tradable pollution permits.

Multiple-Choice Questions

1. An externality is
    a. the benefit that accrues to the buyer in a market.
    b. the cost that accrues to the seller in a market.
    c. the uncompensated impact of one person's actions on the well-being of a bystander.
    d. the compensation paid to a firm's external consultants.
    e. none of the above.

2. A negative externality generates
    a. a social cost curve that is above the supply curve (private cost curve) for a good.
    b. a social cost curve that is below the supply curve (private cost curve) for a good.
    c. a social value curve that is above the demand curve (private value curve) for a good.
    d. none of the above.

3. A positive externality generates
    a. a social cost curve that is above the supply curve (private cost curve) for a good.
    b. a social value curve that is above the demand curve (private value curve) for a good.
    c. a social value curve that is below the demand curve (private value curve) for a good.
    d. none of the above.

4. A negative externality (that has not been internalized) causes the
    a. optimal quantity to exceed the equilibrium quantity.
    b. equilibrium quantity to exceed the optimal quantity.
    c. equilibrium quantity to equal the optimal quantity.
    d. equilibrium quantity to be either above or below the optimal quantity.

5. A positive externality (that has not been internalized) causes the
    a. optimal quantity to exceed the equilibrium quantity.
    b. equilibrium quantity to exceed the optimal quantity.
    c. equilibrium quantity to equal the optimal quantity.
    d. equilibrium quantity to be either above or below the optimal quantity.

6. To internalize a negative externality, an appropriate public policy response would be to
    a. ban the production of all goods creating negative externalities.
    b. have the government take over the production of the good causing the externality.
    c. subsidize the good.
    d. tax the good.

7. The government engages in an industrial policy
    a. to internalize the negative externality associated with industrial pollution.
    b. to internalize the positive externality associated with technology-enhancing industries.
    c. to help stimulate private solutions to the technology externality.
    d. by allocating tradable technology permits to high technology industry.

8. When an individual buys a car in a congested urban area, it generates
   a. an efficient market outcome.
   b. a technology spillover.
   c. a positive externality.
   d. a negative externality.

9. The most efficient pollution control system would ensure that
   a. each polluter reduce its pollution an equal amount.
   b. the polluters with the lowest cost of reducing pollution reduce their pollution the greatest amount.
   c. no pollution of the environment is tolerated.
   d. the regulators decide how much each polluter should reduce its pollution.

10. According to the Coase theorem, private parties can solve the problem of externalities if
    a. each affected party has equal power in the negotiations.
    b. the party affected by the externality has the initial property right to be left alone.
    c. there are no transaction costs.
    d. the government requires them to negotiate with each other.
    e. there are a large number of affected parties.

11. To internalize a positive externality, an appropriate public policy response would be to
    a. ban the good creating the externality.
    b. have the government produce the good until the value of an additional unit is zero.
    c. subsidize the good.
    d. tax the good.

12. Which of the following is not considered a transaction cost incurred by parties in the process of contracting to eliminate a pollution externality?
    a. costs incurred to reduce the pollution
    b. costs incurred due to lawyers' fees
    c. costs incurred to enforce the agreement
    d. costs incurred due to a large number of parties affected by the externality
    e. All of the above are considered transaction costs.

13. Bob and Tom live in a university dorm. Bob values playing loud music at a value of $100. Tom values peace and quiet at a value of $150. Which of the following statements is *true*?
    a. It is efficient for Bob to continue to play loud music.
    b. It is efficient for Bob to stop playing loud music only if Tom has the property right to peace and quiet.
    c. It is efficient for Bob to stop playing loud music only if Bob has the property right to play loud music.
    d. It is efficient for Bob to stop playing loud music regardless of who has the property right to the level of sound.

14. Bob and Tom live in a university dorm. Bob values playing loud music at a value of $100. Tom values peace and quiet at a value of $150. Which of the following statements is *true* about an efficient solution to this externality problem if Bob has the right to play loud music and if there are no transaction costs?
    a. Bob will pay Tom $100 and Bob will stop playing loud music.
    b. Tom will pay Bob between $100 and $150 and Bob will stop playing loud music.
    c. Bob will pay Tom $150 and Bob will continue to play loud music.
    d. Tom will pay Bob between $100 and $150 and Bob will continue to play loud music.

15. Which of the following is *true* regarding tradable pollution permits and corrective taxes?
    a.   Corrective taxes are more likely to reduce pollution to a targeted amount than tradable pollution permits.
    b.   Tradable pollution permits efficiently reduce pollution only if they are initially distributed to the firms that can reduce pollution at the lowest cost.
    c.   To set the quantity of pollution with tradable pollution permits, the regulator must know everything about the demand for pollution rights.
    d.   Corrective taxes and tradable pollution permits create an efficient market for pollution.
    e.   All of the above are true.

16. The gas-guzzler tax that is placed on new vehicles that get very poor mileage is an example of
    a.   a tradable pollution permit.
    b.   an application of the Coase theorem.
    c.   an attempt to internalize a positive externality.
    d.   an attempt to internalize a negative externality.

17. A corrective tax on pollution
    a.   sets the price of pollution.
    b.   sets the quantity of pollution.
    c.   determines the demand for pollution rights.
    d.   reduces the incentive for technological innovations to further reduce pollution.

18. Tradable pollution permits
    a.   set the price of pollution.
    b.   set the quantity of pollution.
    c.   determine the demand for pollution rights.
    d.   reduce the incentive for technological innovations to further reduce pollution.

19. When wealthy alumni provide charitable contributions to their alma mater to reduce the tuition payments of current students, it is an example of
    a.   an attempt to internalize a positive externality.
    b.   an attempt to internalize a negative externality.
    c.   a corrective tax.
    d.   a command-and-control policy.

20. Suppose an industry emits a negative externality such as pollution, and the possible methods to internalize the externality are command-and-control policies, corrective taxes, and tradable pollution permits. If economists were to rank these methods for internalizing a negative externality based on efficiency, ease of implementation, and the incentive for the industry to further reduce pollution in the future, they would likely rank them in the following order (from most favored to least favored):
    a.   corrective taxes, command-and-control policies, tradable pollution permits.
    b.   command-and-control policies, tradable pollution permits, corrective taxes.
    c.   tradable pollution permits, corrective taxes, command-and-control policies.
    d.   tradable pollution permits, command-and-control policies, corrective taxes.
    e.   They would all rank equally high because the same result can be obtained from any one of the policies.

Advanced Critical Thinking

You are home for semester break. Your father opens the mail. One of the letters is your parents' property tax bill. On the property tax bill, there is a deduction if the property owner has done anything to beautify his property. The property owner can deduct 50 percent of any expenditure on things such as landscaping from his property taxes. For example, if your parents spent $2,000 on landscaping, they can reduce their tax bill by $0.50 \times \$2,000 = \$1,000$ so that the true cost of the landscaping was only $1,000. Your father announces, "This is an outrage. If someone wants to improve his house, it is no one's business but his own. I remember some of my college economics and I know that taxes and subsidies are always inefficient."

1. What is the city government trying to subsidize with this tax break?

   _____

   _____

2. What is the externality that this subsidy is trying to internalize?

   _____

   _____

   _____

   _____

3. Although taxes and subsidies usually create inefficiencies, are taxes and subsidies always inefficient? Why or why not?

   _____

   _____

   _____

   _____

Solutions

Terms and Definitions

_5_ Externality
_8_ Positive externality
_3_ Negative externality
_7_ Social cost
_6_ Internalizing an externality
_4_ Corrective tax
_1_ Coase theorem
_2_ Transaction costs

Practice Problems

1. a. See Exhibit 3.

Exhibit 3

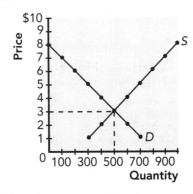

b. Price = $3, quantity = 500 units.

c. See Exhibit 4.

Exhibit 4

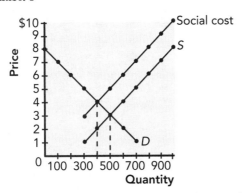

d. 400 units. The market overproduces because the market quantity is 500 while the optimal quantity is 400 units.

e. The government should impose a corrective tax of $2 per unit.

2. a. No, because the cost of correcting the externality exceeds the value placed on it by the affected parties.

b. Yes, because the value placed on peace and quiet exceeds the cost of muffling the planes.

c. The airlines could spend $2 billion and make their planes quieter or buy the right to make noise for

$3 billion, so they will choose to make the planes quieter for $2 billion.

d. The affected citizens must pay at least $2 billion and are willing to pay up to $3 billion to the airlines to have the planes made quieter.

e. Similarities: The planes will be made quieter regardless of the original property rights because it is efficient. Differences: If the citizens have the right to quiet, citizens gain and airlines lose. If the airlines have the right to make noise, airlines gain and citizens lose.

f. No, because the transaction costs exceed the potential gains from trade. (The potential gains are the $3 billion value of quiet minus the $2 billion cost to quiet the planes, or $1 billion.)

3. a. See Exhibit 5.

Exhibit 5

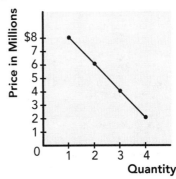

b. $4 million per barrel

c. Three permits should be sold. They will trade at a price of $4 million per permit.

d. Three barrels. $4 million per barrel. Yes, with the tradable pollution permits, the regulator does not need to know anything about the demand for pollution in this market in order to target pollution at 3 barrels and the initial allocation of pollution permits will not have an impact on the efficient solution.

Short-Answer Questions

1. Negative externality, because the social cost of producing apples exceeds the private cost of producing apples.

2. Overproduce. To overproduce is to produce units where the true cost exceeds the true value. To underproduce is to fail to produce units where the true value exceeds the true cost.

3. Tax apples because to internalize this externality, it requires that the supply curve for apples be shifted upward until it equals the true social cost curve.

4. Command-and-control policies are regulations that prohibit certain behaviors. Market-based policies align private incentives with social efficiency. Economists prefer market-based policies

because they are more efficient and they provide incentives for even further reduction in, say, pollution through advances in technology.

5. It increases efficiency by shifting the supply or demand curve toward the true social cost or value curve, thereby making the market solution equal to the optimal or efficient solution.

6. The regulator doesn't need to know anything about the demand to pollute in order to arrive at the targeted amount of pollution.

7. No pesticides will be used and the air will be clean, regardless of whether the individual owns the right to use pesticides or the neighborhood residents own the right to clean air. Either the individual will fail to buy the right to pollute or the neighborhood residents will pay the individual not to pollute.

8. There are $15,000 − $10,000 = $5,000 of potential benefits. If transaction costs exceed this amount, there will be no private solution.

9. Lawyers' fees, costs of enforcement, a breakdown in bargaining when there is a range of prices that would create efficiency, and a large number of interested parties.

10. Moral codes and social sanctions, charities, mergers between affected firms, contracts between affected firms.

True/False Questions

1. F; a positive externality is a benefit that accrues to a bystander, and a negative externality is a cost that accrues to a bystander.
2. T
3. T
4. F; the equilibrium quantity is greater than the optimal quantity.
5. T
6. F; the Coase theorem suggests that private parties can solve the problem of an externality on their own if there are no transaction costs.
7. F; firms that can reduce pollution at a lower cost should reduce their pollution more than firms that can reduce pollution at a greater cost.
8. T
9. F; corrective taxes can make a market more efficient.
10. F; the original distribution of property rights to the air will not affect the efficient solution.
11. T
12. T
13. T
14. F; economists generally think that a market for pollution will reduce pollution most efficiently.
15. T

Multiple-Choice Questions

1. c
2. a
3. b
4. b
5. a
6. d
7. b
8. d
9. b
10. c
11. c
12. a
13. d
14. b
15. d
16. d
17. a
18. b
19. a
20. c

Advanced Critical Thinking

1. Expenditures on home improvement.
2. When a house is well maintained, it raises the value (or fails to reduce the value) of the nearby property. Individual buyers and sellers in the market for home repair do not consider this when choosing the quantity of home repair, and thus, the optimal quantity exceeds the equilibrium quantity.
3. No. Appropriate corrective taxes and subsidies move a market closer to efficiency because the market equilibrium is inefficient to begin with.

Chapter 11
Public Goods and Common Resources

Goals
In this chapter you will

- Learn the defining characteristics of public goods and common resources

- Examine why private markets fail to provide public goods

- Consider some of the important public goods in our economy

- See why the cost–benefit analysis of public goods is both necessary and difficult

- Examine why people tend to use common resources too much

- Consider some of the important common resources in our economy

Outcomes
After accomplishing these goals, you should be able to

- Classify goods into the categories of public goods, private goods, common resources, or club goods

- Explain why production of public goods is unprofitable to private industry

- Explain the public good nature of national defense

- Explain why surveys to determine the benefits of public goods are a less precise valuation of benefits than prices of private goods

- Tell the story of the Tragedy of the Commons

- Explain why fish and wildlife are common resources

Chapter Overview

Context and Purpose

Chapter 11 is the second chapter in a three-chapter sequence on the economics of the public sector. Chapter 10 addressed externalities. Chapter 11 addresses public goods and common resources—goods for which it is difficult to charge prices to users. Chapter 12 will address the tax system.

The purpose of Chapter 11 is to address a group of goods that are free to the consumer. When goods are free, market forces that normally allocate resources are absent. Therefore, free goods, such as playgrounds and public parks, may not be produced and consumed in the proper amounts. Government can potentially remedy this market failure and improve economic well-being.

Chapter Review

Introduction   Some goods are free to the consumer—beaches, lakes, playgrounds. When goods are available without prices, market forces that normally allocate resources are absent. Therefore, free goods, such as playgrounds and public parks, may not be produced and consumed in the proper amounts. Government can potentially remedy this market failure and improve economic well-being.

The Different Kinds of Goods

There are two characteristics of goods that are useful when defining types of goods:

- Excludability: the property of a good whereby a person can be prevented from using it. A good is excludable if a seller can exclude nonpayers from using it (food in the grocery store) and not excludable if a seller cannot exclude nonpayers from using it (broadcast television or radio signal).

- Rivalry in consumption: the property of a good whereby one person's use of a good diminishes other people's use. A good is rival in consumption if only one person can consume the good (food) and not rival if the good can be consumed by more than one at the same time (streetlight).

With these characteristics, goods can be divided into four categories:

1.   Private goods: Goods that are both excludable and rival in consumption. Most goods like bread and blue jeans are private goods and are allocated efficiently by supply and demand in markets.

2.   Public goods: Goods that are neither excludable nor rival in consumption, such as national defense and streetlights.

3.   Common resources: Goods that are rival in consumption but not excludable, such as fish in the ocean.

4.   Club goods: Goods that are excludable but not rival in consumption, such as fire protection and cable television. Club goods are one type of natural monopoly.

This chapter examines the two types of goods that are not excludable and, thus, are free: public goods and common resources.

Public Goods

Public goods are difficult for a private market to provide because of the *free-rider problem*. A free rider is a person who receives the benefit of a good but avoids paying for it. Because public goods are not excludable, firms cannot prevent nonpayers from consuming the good, and thus, there is no incentive for a firm to produce a public good. The outcome of a public good is similar to that of a positive externality because consumers of a good fail to consume the efficient quantity of the good because they do not take into account the benefit to others.

For example, a streetlight may be valued at $1,000 by each of ten homeowners in a neighborhood. If the cost is $5,000, no individual will buy a streetlight because no one can sell the right to use the light to their neighbors for $1,000 each. This is because after the streetlight is in place, their neighbors can consume the light whether they pay or not. Even though the neighborhood values the streetlight at a total value of $10,000 and the cost of a streetlight is only $5,000, the private market will not be able to provide it. Public goods are related to positive externalities in that each neighbor ignores the external benefit provided to others when deciding whether to buy a streetlight. Often government steps in, provides goods, such as streetlights, where benefits exceed the costs, and pays for them with tax revenue. In this case, the government could provide the streetlight and tax each resident $500 and everyone would be better off.

Some important public goods are national defense, basic research that produces general knowledge, and programs to fight poverty.

Some goods can switch between being public goods and private goods depending on the circumstances. A lighthouse is a public good if the owner cannot charge each ship as it passes the light. A lighthouse becomes a private good if the owner can charge the port to which the ships are traveling.

When a private market cannot produce a public good, governments must decide whether to produce the good. Their decision tool is often cost–benefit analysis: a study that compares the costs and benefits to society of providing a public good. There are two problems with cost–benefit analysis:

- Quantifying benefits is difficult using the results of a questionnaire.

- Respondents have little incentive to tell the truth.

When governments decide whether to spend money on additional safety measures such as stoplights and stop signs, they must consider the value of a human life because the benefit of such an expenditure is the probability of saving a life times the value of a life. Studies suggest that the value of a human life is about $10 million.

Common Resources

Common resources are not excludable but are rival in consumption (say fish in the ocean). Therefore, common resources are free, but when one person uses it, it diminishes other people's enjoyment of it. The outcome of a common resource is similar to that of a negative externality because consumers of a good do not take into account the negative impact on others from their consumption. The result is that common resources are used excessively.

The Tragedy of the Commons is a parable that illustrates why common resources get used more than is desirable from the standpoint of society as a whole. The town common (open land to be grazed) will be overgrazed to the point where it becomes barren because, since it is free, private incentives suggest that each individual should graze as many sheep as possible, yet this is overgrazing from a social perspective. Possible solutions are to regulate the number of sheep grazed, tax sheep, auction off sheep-grazing permits, or divide the land and sell it to individual sheep herders, making grazing land a private good.

Some important common resources are clean air and water, congested nontoll roads, and fish, whales, and other wildlife. Private decision makers use a common resource too much, so governments regulate behavior or impose fees to reduce the problem of overuse. For example, imposing tolls on congested roads reduces congestion and shortens travel times.

Conclusion: The Importance of Property Rights

In the case of public goods and common resources, markets fail to allocate resources efficiently because property rights are not clearly established. In a private market, no one owns the clean air so no one can charge people when they pollute. The result is that people pollute too much (externality example) or use too much clean air (common resource example). Furthermore, no one can charge those who are protected by national defense for the benefit they receive so people produce too little national defense (public good example).

The government can potentially solve these problems by selling pollution permits, regulating private behavior, or providing the public good.

Helpful Hints

1. In general, public goods are underproduced and common resources are overconsumed. This is because they are both free. Because public goods are free, it is not profitable to produce them (streetlights and national defense). Because common resources are free, people overconsume them (clean air and fish in the ocean).

2. Public goods are defined by their characteristics, not by who provides them. A streetlight is a public good because it is not excludable and not rival in consumption. This is true even if, as an individual, I choose to buy one and put it in my front yard. Once in my front yard, I cannot charge you for standing near it, and when you do, it does not reduce my benefits from using it. Therefore, a streetlight is a public good whether I buy it or the city government buys it. Further, if the city government sets up a food stand and sells hot dogs, the hot dogs are private goods even though they are provided by the government because the hot dogs are both excludable and rival in consumption.

3. When governments use cost–benefit analysis as a tool to help them decide whether to produce a public good, we noted that it is difficult to collect data on the true benefits that people would receive from a public good. This is because they have an incentive to exaggerate their benefit if they would use the public good and underreport their benefit if they don't plan to use the public good very much. This is sometimes called the *liars problem*.

Terms and Definitions

Choose a definition for each key term.

Key Terms

_____ Excludability

_____ Rivalry in consumption

_____ Private goods

_____ Public goods

_____ Common resources

_____ Club goods

_____ Free rider

_____ Cost–benefit analysis

_____ Tragedy of the Commons

Definitions

1. Goods that are both excludable and rival in consumption

2. The property of a good whereby one person's use diminishes other people's use

3. A person who receives the benefit of a good but avoids paying for it

4. A study that compares the costs and benefits to society of providing a public good

5. Goods that are rival in consumption but not excludable

6. The property of a good whereby a person can be prevented from using it

7. A parable that illustrates why common resources get used more than is desirable from the standpoint of society as a whole

8. Goods that are neither excludable nor rival in consumption

9. Goods that are excludable but not rival in consumption

Problems and Short-Answer Questions

1. Consider the rivalry in consumption and excludability of each of the following goods. Use this information to determine whether the goods are public goods, private goods, common resources, or club goods. Explain.

   a. Fish in a private pond

   _____

   _____

   b. Fish in the ocean

   _____

   _____

   c. Broadcast television signals

   _____

   _____

   d. Cable television signals

   _____

   _____

   e. Basic research on lifestyle and cholesterol levels

   _____

   _____

   f. Specific research on a cholesterol-lowering drug for which a patent can be obtained

   _____

   _____

   g. An uncongested highway (no tolls)

   _____

   _____

   h. A congested highway (no tolls)

   _____

   _____

   i. An uncongested toll road

   _____

   _____

   j. A hot dog served at a private party

   _____

k. A hot dog sold at a stand owned by the city government

_____

_____

2. Suppose the city of Roadville is debating whether to build a new highway from its
    airport to the downtown area. The city surveys its citizens and finds that, on average,
    each of the one million residents values the new highway at a value of $50 and the
    highway costs $40 million to construct.
    a. Assuming the survey was accurate, is building a new highway efficient? Why or
        why not?

        _____

        _____

    b. Under what conditions would private industry build the road?

        _____

        _____

    c. Is it likely that private industry will build the road? Why or why not?

        _____

        _____

        _____

    d. Should the city build the road? On average, how much should it increase each
        resident's tax bill to pay for the road?

        _____

        _____

    e. Is it certain that building the highway is efficient? That is, what are the problems
        associated with using cost–benefit analysis as a tool for deciding whether to
        provide a public good?

        _____

        _____

        _____

Short-Answer Questions

1. What does it mean to say that a good is excludable?

    _____

    _____

2. Why is it difficult for private industry to provide public goods?

    _____

    _____

3. How is a streetlight (a public good) related to a positive externality?

_____

_____

4. Suppose the value of a human life is $10 million. Suppose the use of airbags in cars reduces the probability of dying in a car accident over one's lifetime from 0.2 percent to 0.1 percent. Further, suppose that a lifetime supply of airbags will cost the average consumer $12,000. If these numbers were accurate, would it be efficient for the government to require airbags in cars? Why or why not?

_____

_____

5. What type of problem are hunting and fishing licenses intended to relieve? Explain.

_____

_____

_____

6. How are fish in the ocean (a common resource) related to a negative externality?

_____

_____

_____

7. How can the establishment of individual property rights eliminate the problems associated with a common resource?

_____

_____

8. Food is more important than roads to the public, yet the government provides roads for the public and rarely provides food. Why?

_____

_____

_____

9. Why did buffalo almost become extinct while cows (a similar animal) are unlikely to ever become extinct?

_____

_____

10. Were the buffalo hunters that almost made the buffalo extinct behaving irrationally? Explain.

_____

_____

_____

Self-Test

True/False Questions

_____ 1. A public good is both rival in consumption and excludable.

_____ 2. A common resource is neither rival in consumption nor excludable.

_____ 3. An apple sold in a grocery store is a private good.

_____ 4. Club goods are free to the consumer of the good.

_____ 5. Private markets have difficulty providing public goods due to the free-rider problem.

_____ 6. If the city government sells apples at a roadside stand, the apples are public goods because they are provided by the government.

_____ 7. Public goods are related to positive externalities because the potential buyers of public goods ignore the external benefits those goods provide to other consumers when they make their decision about whether to purchase public goods.

_____ 8. Common resources are overused because common resources are free to the consumer.

_____ 9. The socially optimal price for a fishing license is zero.

_____ 10. The government should continue to spend to improve the safety of our highways until there are no deaths from auto accidents.

_____ 11. Common resources are related to negative externalities because consumers of common resources ignore the negative impact of their consumption on other consumers of the common resource.

_____ 12. If someone owned the property rights to clean air, that person could charge for the use of the clean air in a market for clean air, and thus, air pollution could be reduced to the optimal level.

_____ 13. A fireworks display at a private amusement park is a good provided by a natural monopoly.

_____ 14. When the government uses cost–benefit analysis to decide whether to provide a public good, the potential benefit of the public good can easily be established by surveying the potential consumers of the public good.

_____ 15. National defense is a classic example of a common resource.

Multiple-Choice Questions

1. If one person's consumption of a good diminishes other people's use of the good, the good is said to be
   a. a common resource.
   b. a club good.
   c. rival in consumption.
   d. excludable.

2. A public good is
   a. both rival in consumption and excludable.
   b. neither rival in consumption nor excludable.
   c. rival in consumption but not excludable.
   d. not rival in consumption but excludable.

3. A private good is
   a. both rival in consumption and excludable.
   b. neither rival in consumption nor excludable.
   c. rival in consumption but not excludable.
   d. not rival in consumption but excludable.

4. A club good is
   a. both rival in consumption and excludable.
   b. neither rival in consumption nor excludable.
   c. rival in consumption but not excludable.
   d. not rival in consumption but excludable.

5. A common resource is
   a. both rival in consumption and excludable.
   b. neither rival in consumption nor excludable.
   c. rival in consumption but not excludable.
   d. not rival in consumption but excludable.

6. Public goods are difficult for a private market to provide due to
   a. the public goods problem.
   b. the rivalness problem.
   c. the Tragedy of the Commons.
   d. the free-rider problem.

7. Suppose each of 20 neighbors on a street values street repairs at $3,000. The cost of the street repair is $40,000. Which of the following statements is *true*?
   a. It is not efficient to have the street repaired.
   b. It is efficient for each neighbor to pay $3,000 to repair the section of street in front of his home.
   c. It is efficient for the government to tax the residents $2,000 each and repair the road.
   d. None of the above is true.

8. A free rider is a person who
   a. receives the benefit of a good but avoids paying for it.
   b. produces a good but fails to receive payment for the good.
   c. pays for a good but fails to receive any benefit from the good.
   d. fails to produce goods but is allowed to consume goods.

9. Which of the following is an example of a public good?
   a. whales in the ocean
   b. apples on a tree in a public park
   c. hot dogs at a picnic
   d. national defense

10. A positive externality affects market efficiency in a manner similar to a
    a. private good.
    b. public good.
    c. common resource.
    d. rival good.

11. Suppose that requiring motorcycle riders to wear helmets reduces the probability of a motorcycle fatality from 0.3 percent to 0.2 percent over the lifetime of a motorcycle rider and that the cost of a lifetime supply of helmets is $500. It is efficient for the government to require riders to wear helmets if human life is valued at
    a. $100 or more.
    b. $150 or more.
    c. $500 or more.
    d. $50,000 or more.
    e. $500,000 or more.

12. A negative externality affects market efficiency in a manner similar to
    a. a private good.
    b. a public good.
    c. a common resource.
    d. an excludable good.

13. When governments employ cost–benefit analysis to help them decide whether to provide a public good, measuring benefits is difficult because
    a. one can never place a value on human life or the environment.
    b. respondents to questionnaires have little incentive to tell the truth.
    c. there are no benefits to the public because a public good is not excludable.
    d. the benefits are infinite because a public good is not rival in consumption and an infinite amount of people can consume it at the same time.

14. Which of the following is an example of a common resource?
    a. a national park
    b. a fireworks display
    c. national defense
    d. iron ore

15. The Tragedy of the Commons is a parable that illustrates why
    a. public goods are underproduced.
    b. private goods are underconsumed.
    c. common resources are overconsumed.
    d. club goods are overconsumed.

16. Which of the following are potential solutions to the problem of air pollution?
    a. auction off pollution permits
    b. grant rights of the clean air to citizens so that firms must purchase the right to pollute
    c. regulate the amount of pollutants that firms can put in the air
    d. all of the above

17. When markets fail to allocate resources efficiently, the ultimate source of the problem is usually
    a. that prices are not high enough so people overconsume.
    b. that prices are not low enough so firms overproduce.
    c. that property rights have not been well established.
    d. government regulation.

18. If a person can be prevented from using a good, the good is said to be
    a. a common resource.
    b. a public good.
    c. rival in consumption.
    d. excludable.

19. A congested toll road is
    a. a private good.
    b. a public good.
    c. a common resource.
    d. a club good.

20. A person who regularly watches public television but fails to contribute to public television's fund-raising drives is known as
    a. a common resource.
    b. a costly rider.
    c. a free rider.
    d. an unwelcome rider.
    e. excess baggage.

Advanced Critical Thinking

Broadcast television and broadcast radio send out signals that can be received by an infinite number of receivers without reducing the quality of the reception of other consumers of the signal and it is not possible to charge any of the consumers of the signal.

1. What type of good (private, public, common resource, club good) is a broadcast television or broadcast radio signal? Explain.

   _____

   _____

   _____

2. Is this type of good normally provided by private industry? Why or why not?

   _____

   _____

   _____

3. Private companies have been providing broadcast television and radio since the invention of the medium. How do they make it profitable if they cannot charge the recipient of the signal?

   _____

   _____

   _____

4. What are the "recent" alternatives to traditional commercial television and commercial radio?

   _____

   _____

   _____

5. What type of good (private, public, common resource, club good) is this newer type of television and music provision?

   _____

   _____

Solutions

Terms and Definitions

_6_ Excludability

_2_ Rivalry in consumption

_1_ Private goods

_8_ Public goods

_5_ Common resources

_9_ Club good

_3_ Free rider

_4_ Cost–benefit analysis

_7_ Tragedy of the Commons

Practice Problems

1. a. Rival in consumption and excludable, private good. Only one can eat a fish. Because it is private, nonpayers can be excluded from fishing.

   b. Rival in consumption but not excludable, common resource. Only one can eat a fish but the ocean is not privately owned so nonpayers cannot be excluded.

   c. Not rival in consumption and not excludable, public good. Additional viewers can turn on their televisions without reducing the benefits to other consumers and nonpayers cannot be excluded.

   d. Not rival in consumption but excludable, club good. More houses can be wired without reducing the benefit to other consumers and the cable company can exclude nonpayers.

   e. Not rival in consumption and not excludable, public good. Once discovered, additional people can benefit from the knowledge without reducing the benefit to other consumers of the knowledge, and once in the public domain, nonpayers cannot be excluded.

   f. Not rival in consumption but excludable, club good. Additional users of the knowledge could use it without reducing the benefit to other consumers; therefore, it is not rival. If a patent can be obtained, no one else can produce the anti-cholesterol pill so it is excludable.

   g. Not rival in consumption and not excludable, public good. Additional cars can travel the road without reducing the benefit to other consumers, and the additional cars cannot be forced to pay for the road.

   h. Rival in consumption but not excludable, common resource. Additional cars reduce the benefits of current users but they cannot be forced to pay for the use of the highway.

   i. Not rival in consumption but excludable, club good. Additional cars do not reduce the benefits to current users but they can be excluded if they don't pay the toll.

   j. Rival in consumption but not excludable, common resource. If one eats the hot dog, another cannot. However, once provided, partygoers cannot be charged for eating the hot dogs.

   k. Rival in consumption and excludable, private good. If one eats the hot dog, another cannot. Even though it is supplied by the government, it is being sold so nonpayers can be excluded.

2. a. Yes, because the total benefit is $50 × 1,000,000 = $50 million while the cost is $40 million.

   b. If the road could be built as a toll road, then private industry could make the road excludable and the project could be profitable.

   c. No. Toll roads are usually in rural areas where they can be made as limited-access roads and, therefore, excludable. It would be very difficult to make a downtown urban road limited access or excludable.

   d. Yes. $40.

   e. No. Quantifying benefits is difficult using the results from a questionnaire and respondents have little incentive to tell the truth. Therefore, those who would use the road exaggerate their benefit, and those that would rarely use it understate their benefit.

Short-Answer Questions

1. It means that those who do not pay for the good can be excluded from consuming it.

2. Because public goods are not excludable, the free-rider problem makes it unprofitable for private industry to produce public goods.

3. When people consider buying a streetlight, they fail to consider the external benefit it would provide to others and only consider their personal benefit. Thus, there is an underproduction and consumption of both public goods and goods that generate positive externalities.

4. No, because the expected benefit from airbags is $(0.2 − 0.1) × $10,000,000 = $10,000$ while the cost is $12,000.

5. The overconsumption of common resources. Because common resources are free, people use them excessively. Selling a limited number of hunting or fishing licenses restricts the number of users.

6. A common resource is free so it is overconsumed. Each consumer of fish fails to take into account the negative impact on others of their consumption causing overuse of the resource from a social perspective.

7. People overuse common resources because their benefit is positive and their cost is zero. If ownership over the resource exists, the cost of using the resource is realized and a socially optimal price is generated.

8. Food is both rival in consumption and excludable so it can be efficiently provided by the private market. Roads are often neither rival in consumption nor excludable so they will not be provided by private markets and may be most efficiently provided by government.

9. Buffalo were a common resource and over-consumed. Cows are private goods and are produced and sold at the socially efficient price and quantity.

10. No. Because the buffalo were a common property resource, the buffalo were free. Each hunter pursued his own best interest but failed to take into account the impact of his actions on other people.

True/False Questions

1. F; it is neither rival in consumption nor excludable.
2. F; it is rival in consumption but not excludable.
3. T
4. F; they are excludable so a price must be paid to receive them but they are not rival in consumption so they can be enjoyed by many at the same time.
5. T
6. F; goods are categorized as public or private based on their characteristics, not who provided them, so an apple sold to a consumer is private regardless of who provided the apple.
7. T
8. T
9. F; a positive price is optimal so that the price reduces the quantity demanded of fish to the socially optimal level.
10. F; at some point, the cost of increasing safety (reducing highway deaths) exceeds the value of a life.
11. T
12. T
13. T
14. F; quantifying benefits is difficult and respondents have little incentive to tell the truth.
15. F; national defense is an example of a public good.

Multiple-Choice Questions

1. c
2. b
3. a
4. d
5. c
6. d
7. c
8. a
9. d
10. b
11. e
12. c
13. b
14. a
15. c
16. d
17. c
18. d
19. a
20. c

Advanced Critical Thinking

1. Public good. A broadcast signal is not rival in consumption and not excludable.
2. No, because it is not profitable to produce a good for which nonpayers cannot be excluded from consuming it.
3. Broadcasters charge advertisers for the commercials they show during the broadcasters' programming. That is why it is called commercial television or commercial radio.
4. Cable television, pay-per-view television, and cable music included with cable television.
5. Club good because it is not rival in consumption but is excludable.

Chapter 12
The Design of the Tax System

Goals
In this chapter you will

- Get an overview of how the U.S. government raises and spends money
- Examine the efficiency costs of taxes
- Learn alternative ways to judge the equity of a tax system
- See why studying tax incidence is crucial for evaluating tax equity
- Consider the trade-off between efficiency and equity in the design of a tax system

Outcomes
After accomplishing these goals, you should be able to

- List the four largest sources of tax revenue to the U.S. government from the largest to the smallest source
- Describe the administrative burdens of a tax
- Compare the benefits principle to the ability-to-pay principle of allocating a tax burden
- Explain why the burden of a tax often lands on someone other than the person from whom the tax is collected
- Discuss the efficiency and equity of a lump-sum tax

Chapter Overview

Context and Purpose

Chapter 12 is the third chapter in a three-chapter sequence on the economics of the public sector. Chapter 10 addressed externalities. Chapter 11 addressed public goods and common resources. Chapter 12 addresses the tax system. Taxes are inevitable because when the government remedies an externality, provides a public good, or regulates the use of a common resource, it needs tax revenue to perform these functions.

The purpose of Chapter 12 is to build on the lessons learned about taxes in previous chapters. We have seen that a tax reduces the quantity sold in a market, that the distribution of the burden of a tax depends on the relative elasticities of supply and demand, and that taxes cause deadweight losses. We expand our study of taxes in Chapter 12 by addressing how the U.S. government raises and spends money. We then address the difficulty of making a tax system both efficient and equitable.

Chapter Review

Introduction   Taxes are inevitable because when the government remedies an externality, provides a public good, or regulates the use of a common resource, it needs tax revenue to perform these functions. In previous chapters that dealt with taxation, we learned that a tax reduces the quantity sold in a market, that the distribution of the burden of a tax depends on the relative elasticities of supply and demand, and that taxes cause deadweight losses. We now address how the U.S. government raises and spends money and how difficult it is to make a tax system both efficient and equitable.

A Financial Overview of the U.S. Government

The government is composed of federal, state, and local governments. Over time, the government has taken a larger share of total income in taxes—from 7 percent in 1902 to around 30 percent in recent years. The tax burden in the United States as measured by the government's tax revenue as a percent of GDP is 28 percent. The U.S. tax burden is about average when compared to other countries. European countries have a higher tax burden, and less-developed countries have a lower tax burden than the United States. As countries become wealthier, the tax burden tends to increase.

The U.S. federal government collects about two-thirds of the taxes in our economy. In 2009, the average American paid $6,846 in taxes to the federal government. The largest source of tax revenue for the federal government is individual income taxes (43 percent), followed by social insurance taxes or payroll taxes (42 percent), corporate income taxes (7 percent), and all other taxes (8 percent). A family's tax liability is a percentage of income after deductions for the number of dependents and deductions for certain expenses (mortgage interest payments, state and local tax payments, and charitable giving). Corporate profits are taxed twice—once as corporate income and once as individual income when profits are paid out as dividends. The category of "other taxes" includes excise taxes (taxes on specific goods), estate taxes, and customs duties.

In 2009, the federal government's greatest spending was on Social Security (19 percent) followed by national defense (19 percent), income security or welfare (15 percent), Medicare (12 percent), health (mostly Medicaid, 9 percent), net interest (5 percent), and all others that included the federal court system, space program, farm-support programs, housing credit programs, and congressional salaries (20 percent). Social Security and income security are *transfer payments*—payments for which the government does not receive a good or service in return.

A budget deficit is an excess of government spending over government receipts. A budget surplus is an excess of government receipts over government spending. Under current law, the budget deficit will continue to grow because of rising Social Security and Medicare payments to the elderly and a reduction in the number of taxpayers.

State and local governments collect about 40 percent of all taxes paid. Their greatest source of revenue is sales taxes (19 percent), followed by property taxes (16 percent), individual income taxes (12 percent), corporate income taxes (3 percent), from the federal government (20 percent), and all others that include license fees, tolls, and fares for public transportation (30 percent).

State and local governments spend the greatest share of their funds on education (34 percent), public welfare (17 percent), highways (6 percent), and all others that include libraries, police, trash and snow removal, fire protection, and park maintenance (42 percent).

Taxes and Efficiency

A tax system should be both *efficient* and *equitable*. Here we address efficiency. A tax is more efficient than another if it raises the same amount of revenue at a smaller cost to taxpayers. The cost of a tax includes the actual tax payment itself plus the following:

- the deadweight loss that results when taxes distort private decisions
- the administrative burden taxpayers bear when they comply with the tax laws.

Recall from Chapter 8 that the deadweight loss from a tax is the reduction in economic well-being of taxpayers in excess of the amount of revenue raised by the government. The loss is generated when buyers and sellers allocate resources according to the prices they face after the tax rather than the true costs and benefits of the goods. As a result of a tax, we fail to produce and consume goods on which the benefits exceed the cost of production.

Many European countries employ a value-added tax (VAT), which is a consumption tax collected at various stages of production.

Income taxes place a tax on interest income and, therefore, discourage saving. A consumption tax would not distort people's saving decisions.

The administrative burden of a tax includes the time spent filling out tax forms, the time spent throughout the year keeping records for tax purposes, and the resources the government uses to enforce the tax laws. Simplifying the tax laws would reduce the administrative burden but would require the elimination of many favorite loopholes of taxpayers.

The average tax rate is total taxes paid divided by total income. The marginal tax rate is the extra taxes paid on an additional dollar of income. The average tax rate is most appropriate for gauging the sacrifice made by a taxpayer. The marginal tax rate, however, is most appropriate for gauging how much the tax system distorts incentives and, thus, how inefficient the tax is. Since people think at the margin, a high marginal tax rate discourages hard work and causes a large deadweight loss.

A lump-sum tax is a tax that is the same amount for every person, regardless of income. A lump-sum tax is the most efficient tax because a lump-sum tax does the following:

- generates a marginal tax rate of zero so it does not distort decision making and thus creates no deadweight loss;
- imposes the minimum administrative burden.

We rarely see lump-sum taxes, however, because many perceive them as unfair or not equitable since rich and poor pay the same amount.

Taxes and Equity

There are different principles on which taxes can be based to generate fairness or equity. The benefits principle states that people should pay taxes based on the benefits they receive from government services. This principle can be used to justify gasoline taxes to pay for roads and to justify that the rich should pay more taxes than the poor because the rich benefit more from fire and police protection, national defense, and the court system. This principle can also be used to justify antipoverty programs paid for by the rich because the rich may benefit more than the middle class from not living in a society with poverty.

The ability-to-pay principle states that taxes should be levied on a person according to how well that person can shoulder the burden. This principle suggests that all taxpayers should make an "equal sacrifice" to support the government. The concept of "equal sacrifice" leads to two notions of equity: vertical equity and horizontal equity. *Vertical equity* states that taxpayers with a greater ability to pay taxes should pay larger amounts, and *horizontal equity* states that taxpayers with similar abilities to pay taxes should pay the same amount.

A proportional tax is a tax for which high-income and low-income taxpayers pay the same fraction of income. A regressive tax is a tax for which high-income taxpayers pay a smaller fraction of their income than do low-income taxpayers. A progressive tax is a tax for which high-income taxpayers pay a larger fraction of their income than do low-income taxpayers. If taxes are based on the ability-to-pay principle, then vertical equity requires that the rich pay more taxes than the poor, and thus, taxes should be progressive. The U.S. tax system is progressive because the highest income quintile of American families pays 25.8 percent of their income in taxes while the lowest income quintile pays 4.3 percent. After taking account of government transfers, the poorest quintile pays a negative 30 percent in taxes (they receive more than they pay).

It is necessary to address tax incidence in order to evaluate tax equity. This is because the person from whom the tax is collected often is not the person who bears the burden of the tax. The *flypaper theory* of tax incidence ignores the true burden of the tax and mistakenly assumes that the person from whom the tax is collected is also the one who bears the burden of the tax. For example, the corporate income tax is collected from corporations but it is actually paid by the owners, customers, and workers of the corporation.

A value-added tax is similar to a retail sales tax except that it is collected along the chain of production.

Conclusion: The Trade-Off between Equity and Efficiency

The goals of equity and efficiency for the tax system often conflict, and people attach different weights to these two goals. President Reagan was concerned with the efficiency of the tax system so he proposed lowering marginal tax rates. President Clinton was more concerned with equity of the tax system so he proposed raising marginal tax rates. George W. Bush reduced the highest rate to 35 percent. Obama has pledged to raise the top marginal tax rates.

Helpful Hints

1. The benefits principle of taxation suggests that people should pay taxes based on the benefits they receive from government services. This is similar to having the government utilize a *user fee* (a price charged by the government for using a public good) when it supplies a public good. For example, the government can charge people a direct user fee when they use a government-owned toll road. Alternatively, the government can utilize a gasoline tax as an indirect user fee to pay for the entire road system. Either way, the people who benefit from the road pay for the road.

2. Remember, only people pay taxes. When we tax a business such as a corporation, the corporation is a tax collector, not a taxpayer. The burden of the tax will be shifted to the owners, customers, and workers of the corporation based on the elasticities of supply and demand in the relevant markets for the corporation's labor, capital, and products.

Terms and Definitions

Choose a definition for each key term.

Key Terms	Definitions
_____ Budget deficit	1. A tax for which high-income and low-income taxpayers pay the same fraction of income
_____ Budget surplus	2. The idea that taxes should be levied on a person according to how well that person can shoulder the burden
_____ Average tax rate	
_____ Marginal tax rate	3. The extra taxes paid on an additional dollar of income
_____ Lump-sum tax	4. A tax that is the same amount for every person
_____ Benefits principle	5. An excess of government receipts over government spending
_____ Ability-to-pay principle	6. The idea that taxpayers with a greater ability to pay taxes should pay larger amounts
_____ Vertical equity	7. A tax for which high-income taxpayers pay a larger fraction of their income than do low-income taxpayers
_____ Horizontal equity	
_____ Proportional tax	8. An excess of government spending over government receipts
_____ Regressive tax	9. The idea that taxpayers with similar abilities to pay taxes should pay the same amount
_____ Progressive tax	10. The idea that people should pay taxes based on the benefits they receive from government services
	11. Total taxes paid divided by total income
	12. A tax for which high-income taxpayers pay a smaller fraction of their income than do low-income taxpayers

Problems and Short-Answer Questions

Practice Problems

1. a. Fill out the table below assuming that the government taxes 20 percent of the first $30,000 of income and 50 percent of all income above $30,000.

Income	Taxes Paid	Average Tax Rate	Marginal Tax Rate
$10,000	_____	_____	_____
20,000	_____	_____	_____
30,000	_____	_____	_____
40,000	_____	_____	_____
50,000	_____	_____	_____

b. Compare the taxes for someone making $10,000 to those of someone making $50,000 in part *a* above. Is this tax system progressive, regressive, or proportional? Explain.

_____

_____

_____

2. a.   Fill out the table below assuming that the government imposes a lump-sum tax of $6,000 on all individuals.

Income	Taxes Paid	Average Tax Rate	Marginal Tax Rate
$10,000	_____	_____	_____
20,000	_____	_____	_____
30,000	_____	_____	_____
40,000	_____	_____	_____
50,000	_____	_____	_____

b.   Compare the taxes for someone making $10,000 to those of someone making $50,000 in part *a* above. Is this tax system progressive, regressive, or proportional? Explain.

_____

_____

_____

_____

3. a.   Fill out the table below assuming that the government taxes 20 percent of all income.

Income	Taxes Paid	Average Tax Rate	Marginal Tax Rate
$10,000	_____	_____	_____
20,000	_____	_____	_____
30,000	_____	_____	_____
40,000	_____	_____	_____
50,000	_____	_____	_____

b.   Compare the taxes for someone making $10,000 to those of someone making $50,000 in part *a* above. Is this tax system progressive, regressive, or proportional? Explain.

_____

_____

_____

_____

4. a.   Fill out the table below assuming that the government taxes 40 percent of the first $10,000 of income and 10 percent of all income above $10,000.

Income	Taxes Paid	Average Tax Rate	Marginal Tax Rate
$10,000	_____	_____	_____
20,000	_____	_____	_____
30,000	_____	_____	_____
40,000	_____	_____	_____
50,000	_____	_____	_____

   b.   Compare the taxes for someone making $10,000 to those of someone making $50,000 in part *a* above. Is this tax system progressive, regressive, or proportional? Explain.

   _____

   _____

   _____

   _____

5. a.   Suppose the only objective of the tax system is to collect $6,000 from people who make $30,000. Which of the tax systems described in questions 1 through 4 is best? Why?

   _____

   _____

   _____

   b.   Suppose the only objective of the tax system is to be efficient. Which of the tax systems described in questions 1 through 4 is best? Why?

   _____

   _____

   _____

   _____

   c.   Suppose the only objective of the tax system is to be vertically equitable based on the ability-to-pay principle. Which of the tax systems described in questions 1 through 4 is best? Why?

   _____

   _____

Short-Answer Questions

1. List the sources of revenue for the federal government from the largest source to the smallest.

   _____

   _____

   _____

   _____

2. List the categories of spending by the federal government from the largest to the smallest.

   _____

   _____

   _____

   _____

3. List the sources of revenue for state and local governments from the largest source to the smallest.

   _____

   _____

   _____

   _____

4. List the categories of spending by state and local governments from the largest to the smallest.

   _____

   _____

   _____

   _____

5. What does it mean to say that a tax is *efficient?* What makes a tax efficient?

   _____

   _____

   _____

   _____

6. Is a consumption tax efficient? Explain.

   _____

   _____

   _____

   _____

7. Is a lump-sum tax efficient? Explain. Why do we rarely see lump-sum taxes in the real world?

_____

_____

_____

_____

8. Explain the difference between the benefits principle and the ability-to-pay principle of taxation. Which principle of taxation stresses vertical equity? Explain.

_____

_____

_____

_____

9. Are corporate income taxes truly paid by the corporation? That is, is the burden of the tax on the corporation? Explain.

_____

_____

_____

_____

10. In the United States, what is the income tax rate for the lowest income quintile? What is the income tax rate for the highest income quintile? Are income taxes in the United States progressive?

_____

Self-Test

True/False Questions

_____ 1. The largest source of revenue for the federal government is the individual income tax.

_____ 2. An excise tax is a tax on income.

_____ 3. Expenditures on national defense are an example of a government transfer payment.

_____ 4. To judge the vertical equity of a tax system, one should look at the average tax rate of taxpayers of differing income levels.

_____ 5. The marginal tax rate is the appropriate tax rate to judge how much a particular tax system distorts economic decision making.

_____ 6. A lump-sum tax is a progressive tax.

_____ 7. Lump-sum taxes are equitable but not efficient.

_____ 8. More taxes are collected by state and local governments than by the federal government.

_____ 9. An efficient tax is one that generates minimal deadweight losses and minimal administrative burdens.

_____ 10. The federal income tax system in the United States is regressive.

_____ 11. A tax system is horizontally equitable if taxpayers with similar abilities to pay actually pay the same amount of taxes.

_____ 12. Corporations bear the burden of the corporate income tax.

_____ 13. A tax system with a low marginal tax rate generates less deadweight loss and is more efficient than a similar tax system with a higher marginal tax rate.

_____ 14. If the government runs a budget deficit, it means that there is an excess of government spending over government receipts.

_____ 15. The marginal tax rate is total taxes paid divided by total income.

Multiple-Choice Questions

1. Which of the following lists the sources of tax revenue to the federal government from the largest source to the smallest source?
   a. individual income taxes, corporate income taxes, social insurance taxes
   b. corporate income taxes, individual income taxes, social insurance taxes
   c. individual income taxes, social insurance taxes, corporate income taxes
   d. social insurance taxes, individual income taxes, corporate income taxes
   e. None of the above is correct.

2. In the United States, the tax system is
   a. progressive.
   b. regressive.
   c. proportional.
   d. lump sum.

3. In 2009, the average American paid federal taxes of about
   a. $2,850.
   b. $3,850.
   c. $4,850.
   d. $5,850.
   e. $6,850.

4. Which of the following lists the spending by the federal government from the largest category to the smallest category?
   a. Social Security, national defense, income security, Medicare, health, net interest
   b. national defense, net interest, Social Security, income security, health, Medicare
   c. health, national defense, net interest, Social Security, income security, Medicare
   d. net interest, Social Security, national defense, health, Medicare, income security
   e. None of the above is correct.

5. Which one of the following statements regarding the taxes and spending of state and local governments is *true?*
   a. State and local governments collect more tax revenue than the federal government.
   b. The greatest expenditure of state and local governments is on education.
   c. Corporate income taxes are a greater source of tax revenue to state and local governments than individual income taxes.
   d. The greatest source of tax revenue to state and local governments is property taxes.

6. If the federal government runs a budget surplus, there is a(n)
   a. excess of government spending over government receipts.
   b. excess of government receipts over government spending.
   c. equality of government spending and receipts.
   d. surplus of government workers.

7. Susan values a pair of blue jeans at $40. If the price is $35, Susan buys the jeans and generates consumer surplus of $5. Suppose a tax is placed on blue jeans that causes the price of blue jeans to rise to $45. Now Susan fails to buy a pair of jeans. This example has demonstrated
   a. the administrative burden of a tax.
   b. horizontal equity.
   c. the ability-to-pay principle.
   d. the benefits principle.
   e. the deadweight loss from a tax.

8. A tax for which high-income taxpayers pay a smaller fraction of their income than do low-income taxpayers is known as a(n)
   a. proportional tax.
   b. progressive tax.
   c. regressive tax.
   d. equitable tax.

9. An efficient tax
   a. raises revenue at the smallest possible cost to taxpayers.
   b. minimizes the deadweight loss from the tax.
   c. minimizes the administrative burden from the tax.
   d. does all of the above.

10. The marginal tax rate is
    a. total taxes paid divided by total income.
    b. the taxes paid by the marginal worker.
    c. the extra taxes paid on an additional dollar of income.
    d. total income divided by total taxes paid.

11. The appropriate tax rate to employ to judge the vertical equity of a tax system is the
    a. marginal tax rate.
    b. average tax rate.
    c. proportional tax rate.
    d. horizontal tax rate.

12. The average tax rate is
    a. total taxes paid divided by total income.
    b. the taxes paid by the marginal worker.
    c. the extra taxes paid on an additional dollar of income.
    d. total income divided by total taxes paid.

13. Which of the following taxes is the most efficient tax?
    a. a proportional income tax
    b. a progressive income tax
    c. a consumption tax
    d. a lump-sum tax

14. A progressive tax system is one where
    a. marginal tax rates are low.
    b. marginal tax rates are high.
    c. higher income taxpayers pay more taxes than do lower income taxpayers.
    d. higher income taxpayers pay a greater percentage of their income in taxes than do lower income taxpayers.

Use the following information about a tax system to answer questions 15 through 17.

Income	Amount of Tax
$10,000	$1,000
20,000	2,000
30,000	5,000
40,000	15,000

15. The average tax rate for a taxpayer earning $20,000 is
    a.   0 percent.
    b.   5 percent.
    c.   10 percent.
    d.   20 percent.
    e.   none of the above.

16. This tax system is
    a.   progressive.
    b.   lump-sum.
    c.   regressive.
    d.   proportional.

17. The marginal tax rate for a taxpayer whose earnings rise from $30,000 to $40,000 is
    a.   0 percent.
    b.   16.7 percent.
    c.   37.5 percent.
    d.   100 percent.
    e.   none of the above.

18. The ability-to-pay principle of taxation suggests that if a tax system is to be vertically equitable, it should be
    a.   regressive.
    b.   proportional.
    c.   progressive.
    d.   efficient.
    e.   lump-sum.

19. Which of the following taxes can be supported by the benefits principle of taxation?
    a.   gasoline taxes used to pay for roads
    b.   progressive income taxes used to pay for national defense
    c.   property taxes used to pay for police and the court system
    d.   progressive income taxes used to pay for antipoverty programs
    e.   All of the above can be supported by the benefits principle of taxation.

20. The appropriate tax rate to employ to gauge how much the tax system distorts incentives and decision making is the
    a.   marginal tax rate.
    b.   average tax rate.
    c.   proportional tax rate.
    d.   horizontal tax rate.
    e.   vertical tax rate.

Advanced Critical Thinking

You are having a political debate with a friend. The discussion centers on taxation. You show your friend some data from your economics textbook that suggests that the average American paid about $7,000 in federal income tax in 2009. Your friend says, "If $7,000 per person is what it takes to run this country, then I think that it would be much simpler if we just billed each American $7,000 and eliminated the complex tax code."

1. What type of tax is your friend suggesting? What is its appeal?

   _____

   _____

   _____

   _____

2. Is this type of tax supported by the "benefits principle" of tax equity? Explain.

   _____

   _____

   _____

   _____

3. Is this type of tax supported by the "ability-to-pay" principle of tax equity? Is it vertically equitable? Is it horizontally equitable?

   _____

   _____

   _____

   _____

4. Since your friend agrees that the tax she suggested is not equitable, she now suggests that we simply tax rich corporations since they can clearly afford it and then people wouldn't have to pay any taxes. Is she correct? Who would actually pay the taxes? Explain how she mistakenly employed the *flypaper theory* of taxation.

   _____

   _____

   _____

   _____

Solutions

Terms and Definitions

- _8_ Budget deficit
- _5_ Budget surplus
- _11_ Average tax rate
- _3_ Marginal tax rate
- _4_ Lump-sum tax
- _10_ Benefits principle
- _2_ Ability-to-pay principle
- _6_ Vertical equity
- _9_ Horizontal equity
- _1_ Proportional tax
- _12_ Regressive tax
- _7_ Progressive tax

Practice Problems

1. a.

Income	Taxes Paid	Average Tax Rate	Marginal Tax Rate
$10,000	$2,000	20%	20%
20,000	4,000	20	20
30,000	6,000	20	20
40,000	11,000	27.5	50
50,000	16,000	32	50

   b. Progressive, because the average tax rate for a person making $50,000 exceeds the average tax rate for a person making $10,000. That is, the rich pay a larger fraction of their income than do poor people.

2. a.

Income	Taxes Paid	Average Tax Rate	Marginal Tax Rate
$10,000	$6,000	60%	0%
20,000	6,000	30	0
30,000	6,000	20	0
40,000	6,000	15	0
50,000	6,000	12	0

   b. Regressive, because the average tax rate for a person making $10,000 exceeds the average tax rate for a person making $50,000. That is, the poor pay a larger fraction of their income than do rich people.

3. a.

Income	Taxes Paid	Average Tax Rate	Marginal Tax Rate
$10,000	$2,000	20%	20%
20,000	4,000	20	20
30,000	6,000	20	20
40,000	8,000	20	20
50,000	10,000	20	20

   b. Proportional, because the average tax rate for a person making $10,000 is equal to that of a person making $50,000.

4. a.

Income	Taxes Paid	Average Tax Rate	Marginal Tax Rate
$10,000	$4,000	40%	10%
20,000	5,000	25	10
30,000	6,000	20	10
40,000	7,000	17.5	10
50,000	8,000	16	10

   b. Regressive, because the average tax rate for a person making $10,000 is greater than that of a person making $50,000.

5. a. They are all equally suitable because each system generates $6,000 tax revenue from people making $30,000.

   b. Taxes are more efficient if they generate smaller deadweight losses and smaller administrative burdens. The lump-sum tax in question 2 has a zero marginal rate, so it does not distort economic decision making (no deadweight loss) and is simple (small administrative burden), therefore, it is most efficient. However, it is regressive.

   c. The tax system in question 1, because it is the only one that is progressive.

Short-Answer Questions

1. individual income taxes, social insurance taxes, corporate income taxes
2. Social Security, national defense, income security, Medicare, health, net interest, and other spending
3. sales taxes, property taxes, individual income taxes, and corporate income taxes; they also receive money from the federal government and other fees (license fees, tolls, fares, etc.).
4. education, public welfare, highways, and other spending (libraries, police, trash and snow removal, fire protection, park maintenance)

5. A tax is efficient if it raises the same amount of revenue at a smaller cost to taxpayers. It should generate a small deadweight loss and a small administrative burden.

6. Yes. It is more efficient than an income tax because a consumption tax does not tax saving and, thus, does not distort the saving decision. An income tax does tax saving, so it does distort the saving decision and causes a deadweight loss.

7. Yes. The marginal tax rate associated with a lump-sum tax is zero, so a lump-sum tax does not distort decision making at the margin and, thus, generates no deadweight loss. It is rarely used because it is regressive.

8. The benefits principle argues that people should pay taxes based on the benefits they receive while the ability-to-pay principle argues that taxes should be based on how well a person can shoulder the burden. The ability-to-pay principle stresses vertical equity because vertical equity requires that taxpayers with a greater ability to pay should pay larger taxes.

9. No. Corporate income taxes are collected from the corporation but only people pay taxes. The tax burden is actually divided between the shareholders, the workers, and customers of the corporation.

10. 4.3%. 25.8%. Yes.

True/False Questions

1. T
2. F; an excise tax is a tax on a specific good such as gasoline or liquor.
3. F; a transfer payment is an expenditure for which no good or service is received in return.
4. T
5. T
6. F; a lump-sum tax is regressive.
7. F; lump-sum taxes are efficient but not equitable.
8. F; state and local governments collect about 40 percent of the taxes.
9. T
10. F; it is progressive because higher income people pay a larger percentage of their income in taxes.
11. T
12. F; the corporation's shareholders, workers, and purchasers of the corporation's products bear the burden of the corporate income tax.
13. T
14. T
15. F; the marginal tax rate is the extra taxes paid on an additional dollar of income.

Multiple-Choice Questions

1. c
2. a
3. e
4. a
5. b
6. b
7. e
8. c
9. d
10. c
11. b
12. a
13. d
14. d
15. c
16. a
17. d
18. c
19. e
20. a

Advanced Critical Thinking

1. Lump-sum tax. It is the most efficient tax—its marginal rate is zero so it does not distort incentives, and it imposes the minimum administrative burden.

2. No, if wealthy people benefit more from public services such as police and national defense, they should pay more in taxes.

3. No, wealthy people have a greater ability to pay. Therefore, it is not vertically equitable. However, it is horizontally equitable in that people with the same ability to pay are paying the same amount because all pay the same amount.

4. No, only people pay taxes—corporations collect taxes. The taxes are paid by the owners, workers, and customers of the corporations. The flypaper theory of taxation mistakenly says that the burden of a tax is on the person or company from whom the taxes are collected.

Chapter 13
The Costs of Production

Goals
In this chapter you will

- Examine what items are included in a firm's costs of production
- Analyze the link between a firm's production process and its total costs
- Learn the meaning of average total cost and marginal cost and how they are related
- Consider the shape of a typical firm's cost curves
- Examine the relationship between short-run and long-run costs

Outcomes
After accomplishing these goals, you should be able to

- Explain the difference between economic profit and accounting profit
- Utilize a production function to derive a total-cost curve
- Explain why the marginal-cost curve must intersect the average total-cost curve at the minimum point of the average total-cost curve
- Explain why a production function might exhibit increasing marginal product at low levels of output and decreasing marginal product at high levels of output
- Explain why, as a firm expands its scale of operation, it tends to first exhibit economies of scale, then constant returns to scale, then diseconomies of scale

Chapter Overview

Context and Purpose

Chapter 13 is the first chapter in a five-chapter sequence dealing with firm behavior and the organization of industry. It is important that you become comfortable with the material in Chapter 13 because Chapters 14 through 17 are based on the concepts developed in

Chapter 13. To be more specific, Chapter 13 develops the cost curves on which firm behavior is based. The remaining chapters in this section (Chapters 14 through 17) utilize these cost curves to develop the behavior of firms in a variety of different market structures—competitive, monopolistic, monopolistically competitive, and oligopolistic.

The purpose of Chapter 13 is to address the costs of production and develop the firm's cost curves. These cost curves underlie the firm's supply curve. In previous chapters, we summarized the firm's production decisions by starting with the supply curve. Although this is suitable for answering many questions, it is now necessary to address the costs that underlie the supply curve in order to address the part of economics known as *industrial organization*—the study of how firms' decisions about prices and quantities depend on the market conditions they face.

Chapter Review

Introduction   In previous chapters, we summarized the firm's production decisions by starting with the supply curve. Although this is suitable for answering many questions, it is now necessary to address the costs that underlie the supply curve in order to address the part of economics known as *industrial organization*—the study of how firms' decisions about prices and quantities depend on the market conditions they face.

What Are Costs?

Economists generally assume that the goal of a firm is to maximize profits.

Profit = total revenue – total cost.

Total revenue is the quantity of output the firm produces times the price at which it sells the output. Total cost is more complex. An economist considers the firm's cost of production to include all of the opportunity costs of producing its output. The total opportunity cost of production is the sum of the explicit and implicit costs of production. Explicit costs are input costs that require an outlay of money by the firm, such as when money flows out of a firm to pay for raw materials, workers' wages, rent, and so on. Implicit costs are input costs that do not require an outlay of money by the firm. Implicit costs include the value of the income forgone by the owner of the firm had the owner worked for someone else plus the forgone interest on the financial capital that the owner invested in the firm.

Accountants are usually only concerned with the firm's flow of money so they record only explicit costs. Economists are concerned with the firm's decision making, so they are concerned with total opportunity costs, which are the sum of explicit costs and implicit costs. Because accountants and economists view costs differently, they view profits differently:

- Economic profit = total revenue – (explicit costs + implicit costs)

- Accounting profit = total revenue – explicit costs

Because an accountant ignores implicit costs, accounting profit is greater than economic profit. A firm's decision about supplying goods and services is motivated by *economic* profits.

Production and Costs

For the following discussion, we assume that the size of the production facility (factory) is fixed in the short run. Therefore, this analysis describes production decisions in the short run.

A firm's costs reflect its production process. A production function shows the relationship between the quantity of inputs used to make a good (horizontal axis) and the quantity of output of that good (vertical axis). The marginal product of any input is the increase in output that arises from an additional unit of that input. The marginal product of an input can be measured as the slope of the production function or "rise over run." Production functions exhibit diminishing marginal product—the property whereby the marginal product of an input declines as the quantity of the input increases. Hence, the slope of a production function gets flatter as more and more inputs are added to the production process.

The *total-cost curve* shows the relationship between the quantity of output produced and the total cost of production. Because the production process exhibits diminishing marginal product, the quantity of inputs necessary to produce equal increments of output rises as we produce more output, and thus, the total-cost curve rises at an increasing rate or gets steeper as the amount produced increases.

The Various Measures of Cost

Several measures of cost can be derived from data on the firm's total cost. Costs can be divided into fixed costs and variable costs. Fixed costs are costs that do not vary with the quantity of output produced—for example, rent. Variable costs are costs that do vary with the quantity of output produced—for example, expenditures on raw materials and temporary workers. The sum of fixed and variable costs equals total costs.

In order to choose the optimal amount of output to produce, the producer needs to know the cost of the typical unit of output and the cost of producing one additional unit. The cost of the typical unit of output is measured by average total cost, which is total cost divided by the quantity of output. Average total cost is the sum of average fixed cost (fixed costs divided by the quantity of output) and average variable cost (variable costs divided by the quantity of output). Marginal cost is the cost of producing one additional unit. It is measured as the increase in total costs that arises from an extra unit of production. In symbols, if Q = quantity, TC = total cost, ATC = average total cost, FC = fixed costs, AFC = average fixed costs, VC = variable costs, AVC = average variable costs, and MC = marginal cost, then:

$$ATC = TC/Q,$$

$$AVC = VC/Q,$$

$$AFC = FC/Q,$$

$$MC = \Delta TC/\Delta Q.$$

When these cost curves are plotted on a graph with cost on the vertical axis and quantity produced on the horizontal axis, these cost curves will have predictable shapes. At low levels of production, the marginal product of an extra worker is large so the marginal cost of another unit of output is small. At high levels of production, the marginal product of a worker is small so the marginal cost of another unit is large. Therefore, because of diminishing marginal product, the marginal-cost curve is increasing or upward sloping. The average-total-cost curve is U-shaped because at low levels of output, average total costs are high due to high average fixed costs. As output increases, average total costs fall because fixed costs are spread across additional units of output. However, at some point, diminishing returns cause an increase in average variable costs, which in turn begins to increase average costs. The efficient scale of the firm is the quantity of output that minimizes average total cost. Whenever marginal cost is less than average total cost, average total cost is falling. Whenever marginal cost is greater than average total cost, average total cost is rising. Therefore, the marginal-cost curve crosses the average-total-cost curve at the efficient scale.

To this point, we have assumed that the production function exhibits diminishing marginal product at all levels of output, and therefore, there are rising marginal costs at all levels of output. Often, however, production first exhibits increasing marginal product and decreasing marginal costs at very low levels of output as the addition of workers allows for specialization of skills. At higher levels of output, diminishing returns eventually set in and marginal costs begin to rise, causing all cost-curve relationships previously described to continue to hold. In particular:

- Marginal cost eventually rises with the quantity of output.

- The average-total-cost curve is U-shaped.

- The marginal-cost curve crosses the average-total-cost curve at the minimum of average total cost.

Costs in the Short Run and in the Long Run

The division of costs between fixed and variable depends on the time horizon. In the short run, the size of the factory is fixed, and for many firms, the only way to vary output is hiring or firing workers. In the long run, the firm can change the size of the factory and all costs are variable. The long-run average-total-cost curve, although flatter than the short-run average-total-cost curves, is still U-shaped. For each particular factory size, there is a short-run average-total-cost curve that lies on or above the long-run average-total-cost curve. In the long run, the firm gets to choose on which short-run curve it wants to operate. In the short run, it must operate on the short-run curve it chose in the past. Some firms reach the long run faster than do others because some firms can change the size of their factory relatively easily.

At low levels of output, firms tend to have economies of scale—the property whereby long-run average total cost falls as the quantity of output increases. At high levels of output, firms tend to have diseconomies of scale—the property whereby long-run average total cost rises as the quantity of output increases. At intermediate levels of output, firms tend to have constant returns to scale—the property whereby long-run average total cost stays the same as the quantity of output changes. Economies of scale may be caused by increased *specialization* among workers as the factory gets larger while diseconomies of scale may be caused by *coordination problems* inherent in extremely large organizations. Adam Smith, 200 years ago, recognized the efficiencies captured by large factories that allowed workers to specialize in particular jobs.

Conclusion

This chapter developed a typical firm's cost curves. These cost curves will be used in the following chapters to see how firms make production and pricing decisions.

Helpful Hints

1. Because accountants and economists view costs and, thus, profits differently, it is possible for a firm that appears profitable according to an accountant to be unprofitable according to an economist. For example, suppose a firm incurs $20,000 in explicit costs to produce output that is sold for total revenue of $30,000. According to the accountant, the firm's profit is $10,000. However, suppose that the owner/manager of the firm could have worked for another firm and earned $15,000 during this period. Although the accountant would still record the firm's profits at $30,000 − $20,000 = $10,000, the economist would argue that the firm is not profitable because the total explicit and implicit costs are $20,000 + $15,000 = $35,000, which exceeds the $30,000 of total revenue.

2. In the case of discrete numerical examples, marginal values are determined over a range of a variable rather than at a point. Therefore, when we plot a marginal value, we plot it halfway between the two end points of the range of the variable of concern. For example, if we are plotting the marginal cost of production as we move from the fifth unit to the sixth unit of production, we calculate the change in cost as we move from producing five units to producing six units, and then we plot this marginal cost as if it is for the fifth and a half unit. Notice the marginal-cost curves in your text. Each marginal-cost curve is plotted in this manner. Similarly, if we were plotting the marginal cost of production as we move from producing 50 units to producing 60 units, we would plot the marginal cost of that change in production as if it were for the 55th unit.

3. The long run is usually defined as the period of time necessary for all inputs to become variable. That is, the long run is the period of time necessary for the firm to be able to change the size of the production facility or factory. Note that this period of time differs across industries. For example, it may take many years for all of the inputs of a railroad to become variable because the railroad tracks are quite permanent and the right-of-way for new track is difficult to obtain. However, an ice cream shop could add on to its production facility in just a matter of months. Thus, it takes longer for a railroad to reach the long run than it does for an ice cream shop.

Terms and Definitions

Choose a definition for each key term.

Key Terms

_____ Total revenue

_____ Total cost

_____ Profit

_____ Explicit costs

_____ Implicit costs

_____ Economic profit

_____ Accounting profit

_____ Production function

_____ Marginal product

_____ Diminishing marginal product

_____ Fixed costs

_____ Variable costs

_____ Average total cost

_____ Average fixed cost

_____ Average variable cost

_____ Marginal cost

_____ Efficient scale

_____ Economies of scale

_____ Diseconomies of scale

_____ Constant returns to scale

Definitions

1. Costs that do not vary with the quantity of output produced
2. Total revenue minus total cost
3. The increase in total cost that arises from an extra unit of production
4. The property whereby long-run average total cost falls as the quantity of output increases
5. The property whereby long-run average total cost stays the same as the quantity of output changes
6. Input costs that do not require an outlay of money by the firm
7. The increase in output that arises from an additional unit of input
8. The market value of the inputs a firm uses in production
9. The property whereby long-run average total cost rises as the quantity of output increases
10. Fixed costs divided by the quantity of output
11. Costs that vary with the quantity of output produced
12. The quantity of output that minimizes average total cost
13. The amount a firm receives for the sale of its output
14. The relationship between quantity of inputs used to make a good and the quantity of output of that good
15. Variable costs divided by the quantity of output
16. Total cost divided by the quantity of output
17. The property whereby the marginal product of an input declines as the quantity of the input increases
18. Total revenue minus total cost, including both explicit and implicit costs
19. Total revenue minus total explicit cost
20. Input costs that require an outlay of money by the firm

Problems and Short-Answer Questions

1. Joe runs a small boat factory. He can make ten boats per year and sell them for $35,000 each. It costs Joe $250,000 for the raw materials (fiberglass, wood, paint, and so on) to build the ten boats. Joe has invested $500,000 in the factory and equipment needed to produce the boats: $200,000 from his own savings and $300,000 borrowed at 10 percent interest (assume that Joe could have loaned his money out at 10 percent, too). Joe can work at a competing boat factory for $60,000 per year.

   a.   What is the total revenue Joe can earn in a year?

   _____

   _____

   b.   What are the explicit costs Joe incurs while producing ten boats?

   _____

   _____

   c.   What are the total opportunity costs of producing ten boats (explicit and implicit)?

   _____

   _____

   d.   What is the value of Joe's accounting profit?

   _____

   _____

   e.   What is the value of Joe's economic profit?

   _____

   _____

   f.   Is it truly profitable for Joe to operate his boat factory? Explain.

   _____

   _____

   _____

   _____

2. a. Complete the following table. It describes the production and cost of hamburgers at a roadside stand. All figures are measured per hour.

Number of Workers	Output	Marginal Product of Labor	Cost of Factory	Cost of Workers	Total Cost
0	0		$25	$0	_____
		_____			
1	6		25	5	_____
		_____			
2	11		25	10	_____
		_____			
3	15		25	15	_____
		_____			
4	18		25	20	_____
		_____			
5	20		25	25	_____

b. Plot the production function in Exhibit 1.

c. What happens to the marginal product of labor as more workers are added to the production facility? Why? Use this information about the marginal product of labor to explain the slope of the production function you plotted above.

_____

_____

_____

d. Plot the total-cost curve in Exhibit 2.

e. Explain the shape of the total-cost curve.

_____

_____

_____

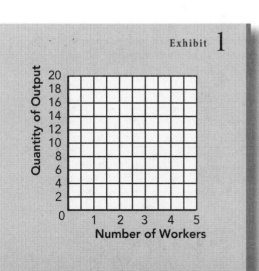

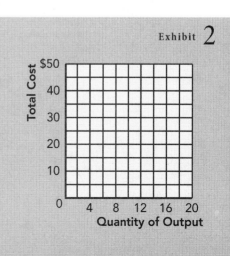

3. a.   The information below is for Bob's blue jeans manufacturing plant. All data are per hour. Complete the table. Note the following abbreviations: *FC* (fixed cost), *VC* (variable cost), *TC* (total cost), *AFC* (average fixed cost), *AVC* (average variable cost), *ATC* (average total cost), *MC* (marginal cost).

Quantity	FC	VC	TC	AFC	AVC	ATC	MC
0	$16	$0	____	____	____	____	
							____
1	16	18	____	____	____	____	
							____
2	16	31	____	____	____	____	
							____
3	16	41	____	____	____	____	
							____
4	16	49	____	____	____	____	
							____
5	16	59	____	____	____	____	
							____
6	16	72	____	____	____	____	
							____
7	16	90	____	____	____	____	
							____
8	16	114	____	____	____	____	
							____
9	16	145	____	____	____	____	
							____
10	16	184	____	____	____	____	

b.   Plot *AFC, AVC, ATC,* and *MC* in Exhibit 3. (Note: Read Helpful Hint 2 above before plotting *MC*).

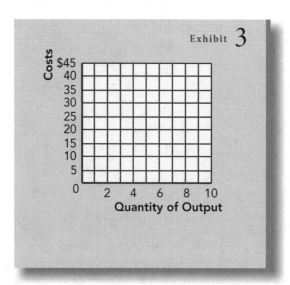

c. Explain the shape of each of the curves you plotted in part *b* above.

_____

_____

_____

_____

_____

d. Explain the relationship between *ATC* and *MC*.

_____

_____

_____

e. Explain the relationship among *ATC*, *AFC*, and *AVC*.

_____

f. What is Bob's efficient scale? How do you find the efficient scale? Explain.

_____

_____

_____

Short-Answer Questions

1. What is profit?

_____

_____

2. How does economic profit differ from accounting profit?

_____

_____

_____

3. Suppose you own and operate your own business. Furthermore, suppose that interest rates rise and another firm offers you a job paying twice what you thought you were worth in the labor market. What has happened to your accounting profit? What has happened to your economic profit? Are you more or less likely to continue to operate your own firm?

_____

_____

_____

_____

4. Explain the relationship between the production function and the total-cost curve.

_____

_____

_____

_____

5. Is the salary of management in a firm a fixed cost or a variable cost? Why?

_____

_____

_____

_____

6. What is the efficient scale of a firm?

_____

_____

_____

7. Explain the relationship between marginal cost and average total cost.

_____

_____

_____

_____

8. What is the shape of the marginal-cost curve in the typical firm? Why is it shaped this way?

_____

_____

_____

_____

9. If a firm is operating in the area of constant returns to scale, what will happen to average total costs in the short run if the firm expands production? Why? What will happen to average total costs in the long run? Why?

_____

_____

_____

_____

10. When a small firm expands the scale of its operation, why does it usually first experience increasing returns to scale? When the same firm grows to be extremely large, why might a further expansion of the scale of operation generate decreasing returns to scale?

_____

_____

_____

_____

Self-Test

True/False Questions

_____ 1. Total revenue equals the quantity of output the firm produces times the price at which it sells its output.

_____ 2. Wages and salaries paid to workers are an example of implicit costs of production.

_____ 3. If total revenue is $100, explicit costs are $50, and implicit costs are $30, then accounting profit equals $50.

_____ 4. If there are implicit costs of production, accounting profits will exceed economic profits.

_____ 5. When a production function gets flatter, the marginal product is increasing.

_____ 6. If a firm continues to employ more workers within the same size factory, it will eventually experience diminishing marginal product.

_____ 7. If the production function for a firm exhibits diminishing marginal product, the corresponding total-cost curve for the firm will become flatter as the quantity of output expands.

_____ 8. Fixed costs plus variable costs equal total costs.

_____ 9. Average total costs are total costs divided by marginal costs.

_____ 10. When marginal costs are below average total costs, average total costs must be falling.

_____ 11. If, as the quantity produced increases, a production function first exhibits increasing marginal product and later diminishing marginal product, the corresponding marginal-cost curve will be U-shaped.

_____ 12. The average-total-cost curve crosses the marginal-cost curve at the minimum of the marginal-cost curve.

_____ 13. The average-total-cost curve in the long run is flatter than the average-total-cost curve in the short run.

_____ 14. The efficient scale for a firm is the quantity of output that minimizes marginal cost.

_____ 15. In the long run, as a firm expands its production facilities, it generally first experiences diseconomies of scale, then constant returns to scale, and finally economies of scale.

Multiple-Choice Questions

1. Accounting profit is equal to total revenue minus
    a. implicit costs.
    b. explicit costs.
    c. the sum of implicit and explicit costs.
    d. marginal costs.
    e. variable costs.

2. Economic profit is equal to total revenue minus
    a. implicit costs.
    b. explicit costs.
    c. the sum of implicit and explicit costs.
    d. marginal costs.
    e. variable costs.

Use the following information to answer questions 3 and 4. Madelyn owns a small pottery factory. She can make 1,000 pieces of pottery per year and sell them for $100 each. It costs Madelyn $20,000 for the raw materials to produce the 1,000 pieces of pottery. She has invested $100,000 in her factory and equipment: $50,000 from her savings and $50,000 borrowed at 10 percent (assume that she could have loaned her money out at 10 percent, too). Madelyn can work at a competing pottery factory for $40,000 per year.

3. The accounting profit at Madelyn's pottery factory is
    a. $30,000.
    b. $35,000.
    c. $70,000.
    d. $75,000.
    e. $80,000.

4. The economic profit at Madelyn's pottery factory is
    a. $30,000.
    b. $35,000.
    c. $70,000.
    d. $75,000.
    e. $80,000.

5. If there are implicit costs of production,
    a. economic profit will exceed accounting profit.
    b. accounting profit will exceed economic profit.
    c. economic profit and accounting profit will be equal.
    d. economic profit will always be zero.
    e. accounting profit will always be zero.

6. If a production function exhibits diminishing marginal product, its slope
    a. becomes flatter as the quantity of the input increases.
    b. becomes steeper as the quantity of the input increases.
    c. is linear (a straight line).
    d. could be any of the above.

7. If a production function exhibits diminishing marginal product, the slope of the corresponding total-cost curve
    a. becomes flatter as the quantity of output increases.
    b. becomes steeper as the quantity of output increases.
    c. is linear (a straight line).
    d. could be any of the above.

Use the following information to answer questions 8 and 9.

Number of Workers	Output
0	0
1	23
2	40
3	50

8. The marginal product of labor as production moves from employing one worker to employing two workers is
    a. 0.
    b. 10.
    c. 17.
    d. 23.
    e. 40.

9. The production process described above exhibits
    a. constant marginal product of labor.
    b. increasing marginal product of labor.
    c. diminishing marginal product of labor.
    d. increasing returns to scale.
    e. decreasing returns to scale.

10. Which of the following is a variable cost in the short run?
    a. wages paid to factory labor
    b. payment on the lease for factory equipment
    c. rent on the factory
    d. interest payments on borrowed financial capital
    e. salaries paid to upper management

Use the following information to answer questions 11 through 14.

Quantity of Output	Fixed Costs	Variable Costs	Total Costs	Marginal Costs
0	$10	$0	_____	
				_____
1	10	5	_____	
				_____
2	10	11	_____	
				_____
3	10	18	_____	
				_____
4	10	26	_____	
				_____
5	10	36	_____	

11. The average fixed cost of producing four units is
    a. $26.
    b. $10.
    c. $5.
    d. $2.50.
    e. none of the above.

12. The average total cost of producing three units is
    a. $3.33.
    b. $6.
    c. $9.33.
    d. $18.
    e. $28.

13. The marginal cost of changing production from three units to four units is
    a. $5.
    b. $6.
    c. $7.
    d. $8.
    e. $9.

14. The efficient scale of production is
    a. one unit.
    b. two units.
    c. three units.
    d. four units.
    e. five units.

15. When marginal costs are below average total costs,
    a. average fixed costs are rising.
    b. average total costs are falling.
    c. average total costs are rising.
    d. average total costs are minimized.

16. If marginal costs equal average total costs,
    a. average total costs are rising.
    b. average total costs are falling.
    c. average total costs are minimized.
    d. average total costs are maximized.

17. If, as the quantity produced increases, a production function first exhibits increasing marginal product and later diminishing marginal product, the corresponding marginal-cost curve will
    a. slope upward.
    b. be U-shaped.
    c. slope downward.
    d. be flat (horizontal).

18. In the long run, if a very small factory were to expand its scale of operations, it is likely that it would initially experience
    a. economies of scale.
    b. constant returns to scale.
    c. diseconomies of scale.
    d. an increase in average total costs.

19. The efficient scale of production is the quantity of output that minimizes
    a. average total cost.
    b. marginal cost.
    c. average fixed cost.
    d. average variable cost.

20. Which of the following statements is *true?*
    a. All costs are fixed in the long run.
    b. All costs are variable in the long run.
    c. All costs are fixed in the short run.
    d. All costs are variable in the short run.

Advanced Critical Thinking

Your friend has a large garden and grows fresh fruit and vegetables to be sold at a local "farmer's market." Your friend comments, "I hired a college student who was on summer vacation to help me this summer and my production more than doubled. Next summer, I think I'll hire two or maybe three helpers and my output should go up more than three- or fourfold."

1. If all production processes eventually exhibit diminishing marginal product of the variable inputs, could it be true that your friend hired a helper (doubled the labor) and more than doubled his production? Why or why not?

    _____

    _____

    _____

    _____

    _____

2. Is it likely that he could hire more workers and continue to reap greater than proportional increases in production? Why or why not?

    _____

    _____

    _____

    _____

    _____

    _____

3. In the long run, what must your friend do to the scale of his operation if he wants to continue to hire workers and have those workers generate proportional increases in production? Explain. Even in the long run, could your friend expand his scale of operation forever and continue to keep average total costs at a minimum? Explain.

_____

_____

_____

_____

_____

_____

_____

Solutions

Terms and Definitions

_13_	Total revenue
_8_	Total cost
_2_	Profit
_20_	Explicit costs
_6_	Implicit costs
_18_	Economic profit
_19_	Accounting profit
_14_	Production function
_7_	Marginal product
_17_	Diminishing marginal product
_1_	Fixed costs
_11_	Variable costs
_16_	Average total cost
_10_	Average fixed cost
_15_	Average variable cost
_3_	Marginal cost
_12_	Efficient scale
_4_	Economies of scale
_9_	Diseconomies of scale
_5_	Constant returns to scale

Practice Problems

1. a. $10 \times \$35,000 = \$350,000$

   b. $\$250,000 + (\$300,000 \times 0.10) = \$280,000$

   c. $\$250,000 + (\$500,000 \times 0.10) + \$60,000 = \$360,000$

   d. $\$350,000 - \$280,000 = \$70,000$

   e. $\$350,000 - \$360,000 = -\$10,000$

   f. No. Joe could make $60,000 plus 10 percent interest on his $200,000 financial capital for a total of $80,000 if he worked for the competition instead of running his own factory. His factory makes an accounting profit of only $70,000 per year, so it costs him $10,000 to run his own factory (the size of the economic loss).

2. a.

Number of Workers	Output	Marginal Product of Labor	Cost of Factory	Cost of Workers	Total Cost
0	0		$25	$0	$25
		6			
1	6		25	5	30
		5			
2	11		25	10	35
		4			
3	15		25	15	40
		3			
4	18		25	20	45
		2			
5	20		25	25	50

b. See Exhibit 4.

Exhibit 4

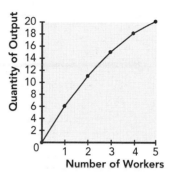

c. It diminishes because additional workers have to share the production equipment and the work area becomes more crowded. The slope of the production function is the change in output from a change in a unit of input, which is the marginal product of labor. Because it is diminishing, the slope of the production function gets flatter as a greater number of inputs are used.

d. See Exhibit 5.

Exhibit 5

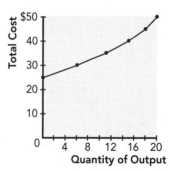

e. The total-cost curve gets steeper as the quantity produced rises due to the diminishing marginal product of labor. That is, in order to produce additional equal increments of output, the firm must employ ever greater amounts of inputs and costs rise at an increasing rate.

3. a.

Quantity	FC	VC	TC	AFC	AVC	ATC	MC
0	$16	$0	$16	—	—	—	
							$18
1	16	18	34	$16.00	$18.00	$34.00	
							13
2	16	31	47	8.00	15.50	23.50	
							10
3	16	41	57	5.33	13.67	19.00	
							8
4	16	49	65	4.00	12.25	16.25	
							10
5	16	59	75	3.20	11.80	15.00	
							13
6	16	72	88	2.67	12.00	14.67	
							18
7	16	90	106	2.29	12.86	15.14	
							24
8	16	114	130	2.00	14.25	16.25	
							31
9	16	145	161	1.78	16.11	17.88	
							39
10	16	184	200	1.60	18.40	20.00	

b. See Exhibit 6.

Exhibit 6

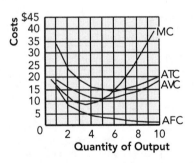

c. *AFC* declines as the quantity goes up because a fixed cost is spread across a greater number of units. *MC* declines for the first four units due to an increasing marginal product of the variable input. *MC* rises thereafter due to decreasing marginal product. *AVC* is U-shaped for the same reason as *MC*. *ATC* declines due to falling *AFC* and increasing marginal product. *ATC* rises at higher levels of production due to decreasing marginal product.

d. When *MC* is below *ATC*, *ATC* must be declining. When *MC* is above *ATC*, *ATC* must be rising. Therefore, *MC* crosses *ATC* at the minimum of *ATC*.

e. *AFC* plus *AVC* equals *ATC*.

f. Six pairs of blue jeans. Efficient scale is the output that minimizes *ATC*. It is also the place where *MC* crosses the average-total-cost curve.

Short-Answer Questions

1. Profit = total revenue – total cost.

2. Economic profit is total revenue minus explicit costs and implicit costs. Accounting profit is total revenue minus explicit costs.

3. Accounting profit is unchanged. Economic profit is reduced because implicit costs have risen—the opportunity cost of your invested money and of your time both went up. You are less likely to continue to operate your own firm because it is less profitable.

4. The total-cost curve reflects the production function. When an input exhibits diminishing marginal product, the production function gets flatter because additional increments of inputs increase output by ever smaller amounts. Correspondingly, the total-cost curve gets steeper as the amount produced rises.

5. It is a fixed cost because the salary paid to management doesn't vary with the quantity produced.

6. It is the quantity of production that minimizes average total cost.

7. When marginal cost is below average total cost, the average-total-cost curve must be falling. When marginal cost is above average total cost, the average-total-cost curve must be rising. Thus, the marginal-cost curve crosses the average-total-cost curve at the minimum of average total cost.

8. Typically, the marginal-cost curve is U-shaped. The firm often experiences increasing marginal product at very small levels of output as workers are allowed to specialize in their activities. Thus, marginal cost falls. At some point, the firm will experience diminishing marginal product and the marginal-cost curve will begin to rise.

9. In the short run, the size of the production facility is fixed so the firm will experience diminishing returns and increasing average total costs when adding additional workers. In the long run, the firm will expand the size of the factory and the number of workers together, and if the firm experiences constant returns to scale, average total costs will remain fixed at the minimum.

10. As a small firm expands the scale of operation, the higher production level allows for greater specialization of the workers and long-run average total costs fall. As an enormous firm continues to expand, it will likely develop coordination problems and long-run average total costs begin to increase.

True/False Questions

1. T

2. F; wages and salaries are explicit costs of production because dollars flow out of the firm.

3. T
4. T
5. F; marginal product is the slope of the production function, so marginal product is decreasing when the production function gets flatter.
6. T
7. F; diminishing marginal product means that it requires ever greater amounts of an input to produce equal increments of output so total costs rise at an increasing rate.
8. T
9. F; average total costs are total costs divided by the quantity of output.
10. T
11. T
12. F; the marginal-cost curve crosses the average-total-cost curve at the minimum of the average-total-cost curve.
13. T
14. F; efficient scale minimizes average total costs.
15. F; a firm generally experiences economies of scale, constant returns to scale, and diseconomies of scale as the scale of production expands.

Multiple-Choice Questions

1. b
2. c
3. d
4. a
5. b
6. a
7. b
8. c
9. c
10. a
11. d
12. c
13. d
14. d
15. b
16. c
17. b
18. a
19. a
20. b

Advanced Critical Thinking

1. Yes. Many production processes first exhibit increasing marginal product of the variable inputs (in this case, workers). This result may occur due to specialization of labor. After the second worker is hired, one worker specializes in weeding while the other specializes in watering.

2. No. At some point, if any input is fixed (say, the size of the garden), the firm will experience diminishing marginal product of the variable inputs. That is, at some point, the garden will become crowded and additional workers will add smaller and smaller amounts to output.

3. It is likely that the garden is small enough that the firm would experience economies of scale if it increased its scale of operation by expanding the size of the garden and hiring more workers. No, your friend cannot expand his scale of operation forever because, at some point, the firm becomes so large that it develops coordination problems and the firm experiences diseconomies of scale.

Chapter 14
Firms in Competitive Markets

Goals
In this chapter you will

- Learn what characteristics make a market competitive
- Examine how competitive firms decide how much output to produce
- Examine how competitive firms decide when to shut down production temporarily
- Examine how competitive firms decide whether to exit or enter a market
- See how firm behavior determines a market's short-run and long-run supply curves

Outcomes
After accomplishing these goals, you should be able to

- List up to three conditions that characterize a competitive market
- Locate the supply curve for a competitive firm on a graph of its cost curves
- Demonstrate why firms temporarily shut down if the price they receive for their output is less than average variable cost
- Demonstrate why firms exit a market permanently if the price they receive for their output is less than average total cost
- Show why the long-run supply curve in a competitive market is more elastic than the short-run supply curve

Chapter Overview

Context and Purpose

Chapter 14 is the second chapter in a five-chapter sequence dealing with firm behavior and the organization of industry. Chapter 13 developed the cost curves on which firm behavior is based. These cost curves are employed in Chapter 14 to show how a competitive firm responds to changes in market conditions. Chapters 15 through 17 will employ these cost curves to see how firms with market power (monopolistic, monopolistically competitive, and oligopolistic firms) respond to changes in market conditions.

The purpose of Chapter 14 is to examine the behavior of competitive firms—firms that do not have market power. The cost curves developed in the previous chapter shed light on the decisions that lie behind the supply curve in a competitive market.

Chapter Review

Introduction   In this chapter, we examine the behavior of competitive firms—firms that do not have *market power*. Firms that have market power can influence the market price of the goods they sell. The cost curves developed in the previous chapter shed light on the decisions that lie behind the supply curve in a competitive market.

What Is a Competitive Market?

A competitive market has two main characteristics:

- There are many buyers and sellers in the market.
- The goods offered for sale are largely the same.

The result of these two conditions is that each buyer and seller is a *price taker*. A third condition sometimes thought to characterize perfectly competitive markets is:

- Firms can freely enter or exit the market.

Firms in competitive markets try to maximize profit, which equals total revenue minus total cost. Total revenue (TR) is $P \times Q$. Because a competitive firm is small compared to the market, it takes the price as given. Thus, total revenue is proportional to the amount of output sold—doubling output sold doubles total revenue.

Average revenue (AR) equals total revenue (TR) divided by the quantity of output (Q) or $AR = TR/Q$. Because $TR = P \times Q$, then $AR = (P \times Q) / Q = P$. That is, for all firms, *average revenue equals the price of the good*.

Marginal revenue (MR) equals the change in total revenue from the sale of an additional unit of output or $MR = \Delta TR/\Delta Q$. When Q rises by one unit, total revenue rises by P dollars. Therefore, for competitive firms, *marginal revenue equals the price of the good*.

Profit Maximization and the Competitive Firm's Supply Curve

Firms maximize profit by comparing marginal revenue and marginal cost. For the competitive firm, marginal revenue is fixed at the price of the good and marginal cost is increasing as output rises. There are three general rules for profit maximization:

- If marginal revenue exceeds marginal cost, the firm should increase output to increase profit.
- If marginal cost exceeds marginal revenue, the firm should decrease output to increase profit.
- At the profit-maximizing level of output, marginal revenue and marginal cost are exactly equal.

Assume that we have a firm with typical cost curves. Graphically, marginal cost (MC) is upward sloping, average total cost (ATC) is U-shaped, and MC crosses ATC at the minimum of ATC. If we draw $P = AR = MR$ on this graph, we can see that the firm will choose to produce a quantity that will maximize profit based on the intersection of MR and MC. That is, the firm will choose to produce the quantity where $MR = MC$. At any quantity lower than the optimal quantity, $MR > MC$ and profit is increased if output is increased. At any quantity above the optimal quantity, $MC > MR$ and profit is increased if output is reduced.

If the price were to increase, the firm would respond by increasing production to the point where the new higher $P = AR = MR$ is equal to MC. That is, the firm moves up its MC curve until $MR = MC$ again. Therefore, *because the firm's marginal-cost curve determines how much the firm is willing to supply at any price, it is the competitive firm's supply curve.*

A firm will temporarily *shut down* (produce nothing) *if the revenue that it would get from producing is less than the variable costs (VC) of production.* Examples of temporary shutdowns are farmers leaving land idle for a season and restaurants closing for lunch. For the temporary shutdown decision, the firm ignores fixed costs because these are considered to be sunk costs, or costs that are not recoverable because the firm must pay them whether they produce output or not. Mathematically, the firm should temporarily shut down if $TR < VC$. Divide by Q and get $TR/Q < VC/Q$, which is $AR = MR = P < AVC$. That is, the firm should shut down if $P < AVC$. Therefore, *the competitive firm's short-run supply curve is the portion of its marginal-cost curve that lies above the average-variable-cost curve.*

In general, beyond the example of a competitive firm, all rational decision makers think at the margin and ignore sunk costs when making economic decisions. Rational decision makers undertake activities where the marginal benefit exceeds the marginal cost.

In the long run, a firm will *exit the market* (permanently cease operations) *if the revenue it would get from producing is less than its total costs.* If the firm exits the industry, it avoids both its fixed and variable costs, or total costs. Mathematically, the firm should exit if $TR < TC$. Divide by Q and get $TR/Q = TC/Q$, which is $AR = MR = P < ATC$. That is, the firm should exit if $P < ATC$. Therefore, *the competitive firm's long-run supply curve is the portion of its marginal-cost curve that lies above the average-total-cost curve.*

A competitive firm's profit $= TR - TC$. Divide and multiply by Q and get profit $= (TR/Q - TC/Q) \times Q$ or profit $= (P - ATC) \times Q$. If price is above ATC, the firm is profitable. If price is below ATC, the firm generates losses and would choose in the long run to exit the market.

The Supply Curve in a Competitive Market

In the short run, the number of firms in the market is fixed because firms cannot quickly enter or exit the market. Therefore, in the short run, the market supply curve is the horizontal sum of the portion of the individual firm's marginal-cost curves that lie above their average-variable-cost curves. That is, the market supply curve is simply the sum of the quantities supplied by each firm in the market at each price. Because the individual marginal-cost curves are upward sloping, *the short-run market supply curve is also upward sloping*.

In the long run, firms are able to enter and exit the market. Suppose all firms have the same cost curves. If firms in the market are making profits, new firms will enter the market, increasing the quantity supplied and causing the price to fall until economic profits are zero. If firms in the market are making losses, some existing firms will exit the market, decreasing the quantity supplied and causing the price to rise until economic profits are zero. In the long run, *firms that remain in the market must be making zero economic profit*. Because profit $= (P - ATC) \times Q$, *profit equals zero only when P = ATC.* For the competitive firm, $P = MC$ and MC intersects ATC at the minimum of ATC. Thus, *in the long-run equilibrium of a competitive market with free entry and exit, firms must be operating at their efficient scale.* Also, because firms enter or exit the market if the price is above or below minimum ATC, the price always returns to the minimum of ATC for each firm but the total quantity supplied in the market rises and falls with the number of firms. Thus, there is only one price consistent with zero profits, and *the long-run market supply curve must be horizontal* (perfectly elastic) at that price.

Competitive firms stay in business even though they are making zero economic profits in the long run. Recall that economists define total costs to include all the opportunity costs of the firm, so the zero-profit equilibrium is compensating the owners of the firm for their time and their money invested.

In the short run, an increase in demand increases the price of a good and existing firms make economic profits. In the long run, this attracts new firms to enter the market causing a corresponding increase in the market supply. This increase in supply reduces the price to its original level consistent with zero profits but the quantity sold in the market is now higher. Thus, if at present firms are earning high profits in a competitive industry, they can expect new firms to enter the market and prices and profits to fall in the future.

Although the standard case is one where the long-run market supply curve is perfectly elastic, the long-run market supply curve might be upward sloping for two reasons:

- If an input necessary for production is in limited supply, an expansion of firms in that industry will raise the costs for all existing firms and increase the price as output supplied increases.

- If firms have different costs (some are more efficient than others) in order to induce new less efficient firms to enter the market, the price must increase to cover the less efficient firm's costs. In this case, only the marginal firm earns zero economic profits while more efficient firms earn profits in the long run.

Regardless, because firms can enter and exit more easily in the long run than in the short run, *the long-run market supply curve is more elastic than the short-run market supply curve.*

Conclusion: Behind the Supply Curve

The supply decision is based on marginal analysis. Profit-maximizing firms that supply goods in competitive markets produce where marginal cost equals price equals minimum average total cost.

Helpful Hints

1. We have determined that, in the short run, the firm will produce the quantity of output where $P = MC$ as long as the price equals or exceeds average variable cost. An additional way to see the logic of this behavior is to recognize that because fixed costs must be paid regardless of the level of production, any time the firm can at least cover its variable costs, any additional revenue beyond its variable costs can be applied to its fixed costs. Therefore, in the short run, the firm loses less money than it would if it shut down if the price exceeds its average variable costs. As a result, the short-run supply curve for the firm is the portion of the marginal-cost curve that is above the average-variable-cost curve.

2. Recall that rational decision makers think at the margin. The decision rule for any action is that we should do things for which the marginal benefit exceeds the marginal cost and continue to do that thing until the marginal benefit equals the marginal cost. This decision rule translates directly to the firm's production decision in that the firm should continue to produce additional output until marginal revenue (the marginal benefit to the firm) equals marginal cost.

3. In this chapter, we derived the equation for profit as profit = $(P - ATC) \times Q$. It helps to remember that, in words, this formula says that profit simply equals the average profit per unit times the number of units sold. This holds true even in the case of losses. If the price is less than average total cost, then we have the average loss per unit times the number of units sold.

Terms and Definitions

Choose a definition for each key term.

Key Terms

_____ Price takers

_____ Competitive market

_____ Average revenue

_____ Marginal revenue

_____ Shut down

_____ Exit

_____ Sunk cost

Definitions

1. A short-run decision to temporarily cease production during a specific period of time due to current market conditions

2. A market with many buyers and sellers trading identical products so that each buyer and seller is a price taker

3. Total revenue divided by the quantity sold

4. A cost to which one is already committed and is not recoverable

5. The change in total revenue from an additional unit sold

6. Buyers and sellers in a competitive market that must accept the price that the market determines

7. A long-run decision to permanently cease production and leave the market

Problems and Short-Answer Questions

Practice Problems

1. Are the following markets likely to be perfectly competitive? Explain.
   a. The market for gasoline

   b. The market for blue jeans

   c. The market for agricultural products such as corn and beans

   d. The market for the common stock of IBM

   e. The market for electricity

f.   The market for cable television

_____

_____

2.   a.
The following table contains information about the revenues and costs for Barry's Baseball Manufacturing. All data are per hour. Complete the first group of columns that correspond to Barry's production if $P = \$3$. ($TR$ = total revenue, TC = total cost, MR = marginal revenue, MC = marginal cost)

Q	TR, P = \$3	TC	Profit	MR	MC	TR, P = \$2	Profit	MR
0	_____	\$1	_____			_____	_____	
				_____	_____			_____
1	_____	\$2	_____			_____	_____	
				_____	_____			_____
2	_____	\$4	_____			_____	_____	
				_____	_____			_____
3	_____	\$7	_____			_____	_____	
				_____	_____			_____
4	_____	\$11	_____			_____	_____	
				_____	_____			_____
5	_____	\$16	_____			_____	_____	

b.   If the price is \$3 per baseball, what is Barry's optimal level of production? What criteria did you use to determine the optimal level of production?

_____

_____

_____

c.   Is \$3 per baseball a long-run equilibrium price in the market for baseballs? Explain. What adjustment will take place in the market for baseballs, and what will happen to the price in the long run?

_____

_____

_____

d.   Suppose the price of baseballs falls to \$2. Fill out the remaining three columns of the table above. What is the profit-maximizing level of output when the price is \$2 per baseball? How much profit does Barry's Baseball Manufacturing earn when the price of baseballs is \$2?

_____

_____

_____

e.   Is $2 per baseball a long-run equilibrium price in the market for baseballs? Explain. Why would Barry continue to produce at this level of profit?

_____

_____

_____

f.   Describe the slope of the short-run supply curve for the market for baseballs. Describe the slope of the long-run supply curve in the market for baseballs.

_____

_____

_____

3.   a.   In Exhibit 1, show the cost curves of a representative firm in long-run equilibrium alongside the corresponding market equilibrium for an industry that has a perfectly elastic long-run market supply curve.

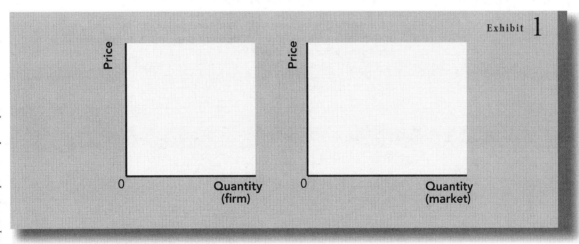

Exhibit 1

b.   Suppose there is a *decrease* in the demand for this product. In Exhibit 2, show the shift in demand in the market for this product and the corresponding profit or loss on the cost curves of the representative firm.

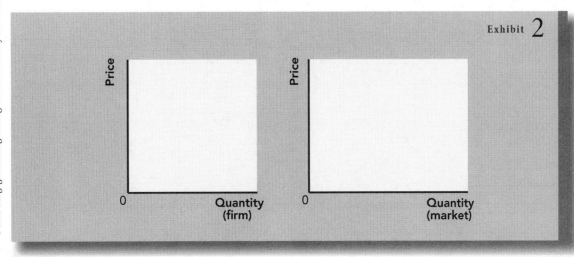

Exhibit 2

c. In Exhibit 3, show the adjustment that takes place in order to return the market and firm to long-run equilibrium.

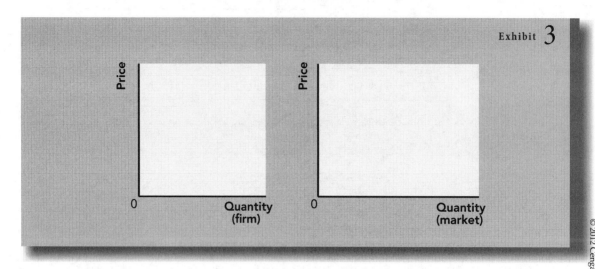

Exhibit 3

d. After the market has returned to long-run equilibrium, is the price higher, lower, or the same as the initial price? Are there more, fewer, or the same number of firms producing in the market?

_____

_____

Short-Answer Questions

1. What are the three conditions that characterize a competitive market?

_____

_____

_____

_____

2. If a firm is in a competitive market, what happens to its total revenue if it doubles its output? Why?

_____

_____

_____

_____

3. If a firm is producing a level of output where marginal revenue exceeds marginal cost, would it improve profits by increasing output, decreasing output, or keeping output unchanged? Why?

_____

_____

_____

_____

4. What constitutes a competitive firm's short-run supply curve? Explain.

_____

_____

_____

_____

5. What constitutes a competitive firm's long-run supply curve? Explain.

_____

_____

_____

_____

6. You go to your campus bookstore and see a coffee mug emblazoned with your university's shield. It costs $5 and you value it at $8, so you buy it. On the way to your car, you drop it and it breaks into pieces. Should you buy another one or should you go home because the total expenditure of $10 now exceeds the $8 value that you place on it? Why?

_____

_____

_____

_____

7. Suppose the price for a firm's output is above the average variable cost of production but below the average total cost of production. Will the firm shut down in the short run? Explain. Will the firm exit the market in the long run? Explain.

_____

_____

_____

_____

8. Why must the long-run equilibrium in a competitive market (with free entry and exit) have all firms operating at their efficient scale?

_____

_____

_____

_____

9. Why is the short-run market supply curve upward sloping while the standard long-run market supply curve is perfectly elastic?

_____

_____

_____

_____

10. Under what conditions would the long-run market supply curve be upward sloping?

_____

_____

_____

Self-Test

True/False Questions

_____ 1. The only requirement for a market to be perfectly competitive is for the market to have many buyers and sellers.

_____ 2. For a competitive firm, marginal revenue equals the price of the good it sells.

_____ 3. If a competitive firm sells three times the amount of output, its total revenue also increases by a factor of three.

_____ 4. A firm maximizes profit when it produces output up to the point where marginal cost equals marginal revenue.

_____ 5. If marginal cost exceeds marginal revenue at a firm's current level of output, the firm can increase profit if it increases its level of output.

_____ 6. A competitive firm's short-run supply curve is the portion of its marginal-cost curve that lies above its average-total-cost curve.

_____ 7. A competitive firm's long-run supply curve is the portion of its marginal-cost curve that lies above its average-variable-cost curve.

_____ 8. In the short run, if the price a firm receives for a good is above its average variable costs but below its average total costs of production, the firm will temporarily shut down.

_____ 9. In a competitive market, both buyers and sellers are price takers.

_____ 10. In the long run, if the price firms receive for their output is below their average total costs of production, some firms will exit the market.

_____ 11. In the short run, the market supply curve for a good is the sum of the quantities supplied by each firm at each price.

_____ 12. The short-run market supply curve is more elastic than the long-run market supply curve.

_____ 13. In the long run, perfectly competitive firms earn small but positive economic profits.

_____ 14. In the long run, if firms are identical and there is free entry and exit in the market, all firms in the market operate at their efficient scale.

_____ 15. If the price of a good rises above the minimum average total cost of production, positive economic profits will cause new firms to enter the market, which drives the price back down to the minimum average total cost of production.

Multiple-Choice Questions

1. Which of the following is *not* a characteristic of a competitive market?
   a. There are many buyers and sellers in the market.
   b. The goods offered for sale are largely the same.
   c. Firms can freely enter or exit the market.
   d. Firms generate small but positive economic profits in the long run.
   e. All of the above are characteristics of a competitive market.

2. Which of the following markets would most closely satisfy the requirements for a competitive market?
   a. gold bullion
   b. electricity
   c. cable television
   d. soda
   e. All of the above represent competitive markets.

3. If a competitive firm doubles its output, its total revenue
   a. more than doubles.
   b. doubles.
   c. less than doubles.
   d. cannot be determined because the price of the good may rise or fall.

4. For a competitive firm, marginal revenue is
   a. equal to the price of the good sold.
   b. average revenue divided by the quantity sold.
   c. total revenue divided by the price.
   d. equal to the quantity of the good sold.

5. The competitive firm maximizes profit when it produces output up to the point where
   a. marginal cost equals total revenue.
   b. marginal revenue equals average revenue.
   c. marginal cost equals marginal revenue.
   d. price equals average variable cost.

6. If a competitive firm is producing a level of output where marginal revenue exceeds marginal cost, the firm could increase profits if it
   a. increased production.
   b. decreased production.
   c. maintained production at the current level.
   d. temporarily shut down.

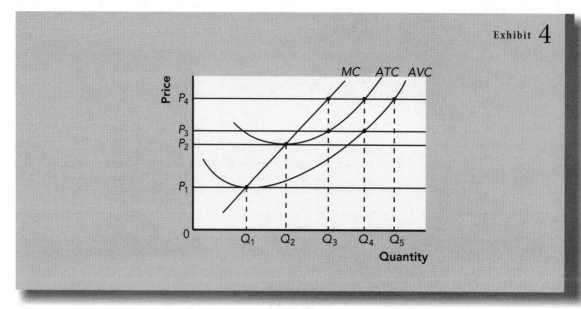

Exhibit 4

Use Exhibit 4 to answer questions 7 through 11.

7. If the price is P_4, a competitive firm will maximize profits if it produces
   a. Q_1.
   b. Q_2.
   c. Q_3.
   d. Q_4.
   e. Q_5.

8. If the price is P_4, the firm will earn profits equal to the area
   a. $(P_2 - P_1) \times Q_2$.
   b. $(P_3 - P_2) \times Q_3$.
   c. $(P_4 - P_2) \times Q_4$.
   d. $(P_4 - P_3) \times Q_3$.
   e. None of the above is correct.

9. In the short run, competitive firms will temporarily shut down production if the price falls below
   a. P_1.
   b. P_2.
   c. P_3.
   d. P_4.

10. In the long run, some competitive firms will exit the market if the price is below
   a. P_1.
   b. P_2.
   c. P_3.
   d. P_4.

11. In the long run, the competitive equilibrium is
   a. P_1, Q_1.
   b. P_2, Q_2.
   c. P_4, Q_3.
   d. P_4, Q_4.
   e. P_4, Q_5.

12. In the short run, the competitive firm's supply curve is the
    a. entire marginal-cost curve.
    b. portion of the marginal-cost curve that lies above the average-total-cost curve.
    c. portion of the marginal-cost curve that lies above the average-variable-cost curve.
    d. upward-sloping portion of the average-total-cost curve.
    e. upward-sloping portion of the average-variable-cost curve.

13. In the long run, the competitive firm's supply curve is the
    a. entire marginal-cost curve.
    b. portion of the marginal-cost curve that lies above the average-total-cost curve.
    c. portion of the marginal-cost curve that lies above the average-variable-cost curve.
    d. upward-sloping portion of the average-total-cost curve.
    e. upward-sloping portion of the average-variable-cost curve.

14. A grocery store should close at night if the
    a. total costs of staying open are greater than the total revenue due to staying open.
    b. total costs of staying open are less than the total revenue due to staying open.
    c. variable costs of staying open are greater than the total revenue due to staying open.
    d. variable costs of staying open are less than the total revenue due to staying open.

15. The long-run market supply curve
    a. is always more elastic than the short-run market supply curve.
    b. is always less elastic than the short-run market supply curve.
    c. has the same elasticity as the short-run market supply curve.
    d. is always perfectly elastic.

16. In the long run, some firms will exit the market if the price of the good offered for sale is less than
    a. marginal revenue.
    b. marginal cost.
    c. average revenue.
    d. average total cost.

17. If all firms in a market have identical cost structures and if inputs used in the production of the good in that market are readily available, then the long-run market supply curve for that good should be
    a. perfectly elastic.
    b. downward sloping.
    c. upward sloping.
    d. perfectly inelastic.

18. If an input necessary for production is in limited supply so that an expansion of the industry raises costs for all existing firms in the market, then the long-run market supply curve for a good could be
    a. perfectly elastic.
    b. downward sloping.
    c. upward sloping.
    d. perfectly inelastic.

19. If the long-run market supply curve for a good is perfectly elastic, an increase in the demand for that good will, in the long run, cause
    a. an increase in the price of the good and an increase in the number of firms in the market.
    b. an increase in the price of the good but no increase in the number of firms in the market.
    c. an increase in the number of firms in the market but no increase in the price of the good.
    d. no impact on either the price of the good or the number of firms in the market.

20. In long-run equilibrium in a competitive market, firms are operating at
    a.   the minimum of their average-total-cost curves.
    b.   the intersection of marginal cost and marginal revenue.
    c.   their efficient scale.
    d.   zero economic profit.
    e.   all of the above.

Advanced Critical Thinking

In some regions of the country, it is common for Walmart stores and large supermarkets to stay open 24 hours a day, 365 days a year.

1. You walk into a Walmart store at 2:00 a.m. with a friend to buy some VCR tapes. Your friend says, "I can't believe that these stores stay open all night. Only one out of fifteen checkout lines is open. There can't be more than ten shoppers in this store. It just doesn't make any sense for this store to be open all night." Explain to your friend what conditions must be true for it to be to the advantage of Walmart to stay open all night.

    _____

    _____

    _____

    _____

2. Are the costs of rent, equipment, fixtures, salaries of management, and so on relevant when Walmart makes the decision whether to stay open all night? Why or why not?

    _____

    _____

    _____

    _____

3. If Walmart had the same number of customers during its daytime hours as you observed during its nighttime hours, do you think it would continue to operate? Explain.

    _____

    _____

    _____

    _____

Solutions

Terms and Definitions

_6_ Price takers

_2_ Competitive market

_3_ Average revenue

_5_ Marginal revenue

_1_ Shut down

_7_ Exit

_4_ Sunk cost

Practice Problems

1. a. Yes, many buyers and sellers and the product of different sellers is nearly identical.

   b. Probably not, many buyers and sellers but the product is not identical (Levi's vs. Lee), so each seller is not a price taker.

   c. Yes, many buyers and sellers and the product of different sellers is identical.

   d. Yes, many buyers and sellers and the product of different sellers is identical.

   e. No, few sellers (often only one). If there were multiple sellers, the product would be identical.

   f. No, few sellers (often only one). If there were multiple sellers, the product would be nearly identical.

2. a.

Q	TR, P = $3	TC	Profit	MR	MC	TR, P = $2	Profit	MR
0	$0	$1	−$1			$0	−$1	
				$3	$1			$2
1	3	2	1			2	0	
				3	2			2
2	6	4	2			4	0	
				3	3			2
3	9	7	2			6	−1	
				3	4			2
4	12	11	1			8	−3	
				3	5			2
5	15	16	−1			10	−6	

   b. Optimal production is either two or three baseballs per hour. This level of production maximizes profit (at $2) and it is the level of output where MC = MR (at $3).

   c. No, because Barry is earning positive economic profits of $2. These profits will attract new firms to enter the market for baseballs, the market supply will increase, and the price will fall until economic profits are zero.

   d. See answers for the table in part a above. Optimal production is either one or two baseballs per hour. Zero economic profit is earned by Barry.

e. Yes. Economic profits are zero and firms neither enter nor exit the industry. Zero economic profits means that Barry doesn't earn anything beyond his opportunity costs of production but his revenues do cover the cost of his inputs and the value of his time and money.

f. The slope of the short-run supply curve is positive because when P = $2, quantity supplied is one or two units per firm and when P = $3, quantity supplied is two or three units per firm. In the long run, supply is horizontal (perfectly elastic) at P = $2 because any price above $2 causes firms to enter and drives the price back to $2.

3. a. See Exhibit 5.

Exhibit 5

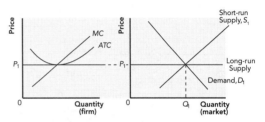

b. See Exhibit 6.

Exhibit 6

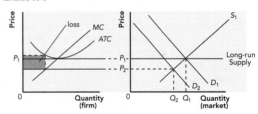

c. See Exhibit 7.

Exhibit 7

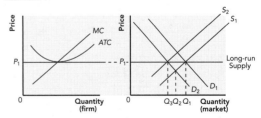

d. The price has returned to its initial level. There are fewer firms producing in this market.

Short-Answer Questions

1. There are many buyers and sellers, the goods offered for sale are largely the same, and firms can freely enter or exit the market.

2. Total revenue doubles. This is because, in a competitive market, the price is unaffected by the amount sold by any individual firm.

3.   If $MR > MC$, increasing output will increase profits because an additional unit of production increases revenue more than it increases costs.

4.   It is the portion of the firm's marginal-cost curve that lies above its average-variable-cost curve because the firm maximizes profit where $P = MC$, and in the short run, fixed or sunk costs are irrelevant and the firm must only cover its variable costs.

5.   It is the portion of the firm's marginal-cost curve that lies above its average-total-cost curve because the firm maximizes profit where $P = MC$, and in the long run, the firm must cover its total costs or it should exit the market.

6.   You should buy another mug because the marginal benefit ($8) still exceeds the marginal cost ($5). The broken mug is a sunk cost and is not recoverable. Therefore, it is irrelevant.

7.   No. In the short run, the firm's fixed costs are sunk costs so the firm will not shut down because it only needs to cover its variable costs. Yes. In the long run, the firm must cover total costs, and if $P < ATC$, the firm generates losses in the long run and it will exit the market.

8.   In the long-run equilibrium, firms must be making zero economic profits so that firms are not entering or exiting the industry. Zero profits occur when $P = ATC$ and for the competitive firm $P = MC$ determines the production level. $P = ATC = MC$ only at the minimum of ATC.

9.   In the short run, firms cannot exit or enter the market so the market supply curve is the horizontal sum of the upward-sloping MC curves of the existing firms. However, in the long run, if the price is above or below minimum ATC, firms will enter or exit the market causing the price to always return to minimum ATC for each firm, but the total quantity supplied in the market rises and falls with the number of firms. Thus, the market supply curve is horizontal.

10.   If an input necessary for production is in limited supply or if firms have different costs.

True/False Questions

1.   F; the goods offered for sale are largely the same and (possibly) firms can freely enter or exit the market.

2.   T

3.   T

4.   T

5.   F; the firm increases profits if it reduces output.

6.   F; it is the portion of the MC curve that lies above its average-variable-cost curve.

7.   F; it is the portion of the MC curve that lies above its average-total-cost curve.

8.   F; the firm will continue to operate in the short run as long as price exceeds average variable costs.

9.   T

10.   T

11.   T

12.   F; the long-run market supply curve is more elastic than the short-run market supply curve.

13.   F; they earn zero economic profits in the long run.

14.   T

15.   T

Multiple-Choice Questions

1.	d	11.	b
2.	a	12.	c
3.	b	13.	b
4.	a	14.	c
5.	c	15.	a
6.	a	16.	d
7.	c	17.	a
8.	d	18.	c
9.	a	19.	c
10.	b	20.	e

Advanced Critical Thinking

1.   For Walmart to stay open all night (and not undertake a temporary shutdown), it must be true that its total revenue at night must equal or exceed its variable costs incurred from staying open the additional hours (electricity, wages of night shift workers, etc.).

2.   No. These costs are fixed costs or sunk costs— costs that cannot be recovered even if Walmart chooses not to operate at night.

3.   It is unlikely. This is because the temporary shutdown decision (staying open additional hours at night) depends on whether total revenue equals or exceeds variable costs, but the decision to remain in the market in the long-run depends on whether total revenue equals or exceeds total costs. It is unlikely that the revenue earned at night covers total costs (both fixed and variable costs).

Chapter 15
Monopoly

Goals
In this chapter you will

- Learn why some markets have only one seller
- Analyze how a monopoly determines the quantity to produce and the price to charge
- See how the monopoly's decisions affect economic well-being
- See why monopolies try to charge different prices to different customers
- Consider the various public policies aimed at solving the problem of monopoly

Outcomes
After accomplishing these goals, you should be able to

- List three reasons why a monopoly can remain the sole seller of a product in a market
- Use a monopolist's cost curves and the demand curve it faces to show the profit earned by a monopolist
- Show the deadweight loss from a monopolist's production decision
- Demonstrate the surprising result that price discrimination by a monopolist can raise economic welfare above that generated by standard monopoly pricing
- Show why forcing a natural monopoly to charge its marginal cost of production creates losses for the monopolist

Chapter Overview

Context and Purpose

Chapter 15 is the third chapter in a five-chapter sequence dealing with firm behavior and the organization of industry. Chapter 13 developed the cost curves on which firm behavior is based. These cost curves were employed in Chapter 14 to show how a competitive firm responds to changes in market conditions. In Chapter 15, these cost curves are again employed, this time to show how a monopolistic firm chooses the quantity to produce and the price to charge. Chapters 16 and 17 will address the decisions made by monopolistically competitive and oligopolistic firms.

A monopolist is the sole seller of a product without close substitutes. As such, it has market power because it can influence the price of its output. That is, a monopolist is a price maker as opposed to a price taker. The purpose of Chapter 15 is to examine the production and pricing decisions of monopolists, the social implications of their market power, and the ways in which governments might respond to the problems caused by monopolists.

Chapter Review

Introduction   Monopolists have market power because they can influence the price of their output. That is, monopolists are *price makers* as opposed to *price takers*. While competitive firms choose to produce a quantity of output such that the given market price equals the marginal cost of production, monopolists charge prices that exceed marginal costs. In this chapter, we examine the production and pricing decisions of monopolists, the social implications of their market power, and the ways in which governments might respond to the problems caused by monopolists.

Why Monopolies Arise

A monopoly is a firm that is the sole seller of a product without close substitutes. A monopoly is able to remain the only seller in a market only if there are *barriers to entry*. That is, other firms are unable to enter the market and compete with it. There are three sources of barriers to entry:

- *Monopoly resources:* A key resource required for production is owned by a single firm. For example, if a firm owns the only well in town, it has a monopoly for the sale of water. DeBeers essentially has a monopoly in the market for diamonds because it controls 80 percent of the world's production of diamonds. This source of monopoly is somewhat rare.

- *Government created monopolies:* The government gives a single firm the exclusive right to produce some good. When the government grants patents (which last for twenty years) to inventors and copyrights to authors, it is giving someone the right to be the sole producer of that good. The benefit is that it increases incentives for creative activity. The costs will be discussed later in this chapter.

- *Natural monopolies:* The costs of production make a single producer more efficient than a large number of producers. A natural monopoly arises when a single firm can supply a good to an entire market at a smaller cost than could two or more firms. This happens when there are economies of scale over the relevant range of output. That is, the average-total-cost curve for an individual firm continually declines at least to the quantity that could supply the entire market. This cost advantage is a natural barrier to entry because firms with higher costs find it undesirable to enter the market. Common examples are utilities such as water and electricity distribution. Club goods are generally produced by natural monopolies.

How Monopolies Make Production and Pricing Decisions

A competitive firm is small relative to the market, so it takes the price of the good it produces as given. Because it can sell as much as it chooses at the given market price, the competitive firm faces a demand curve that is perfectly elastic at the market price. A monopoly is the sole producer in its market, so it faces the entire downward-sloping market demand curve. The monopolist can choose any price/quantity combination on the demand curve by choosing the quantity and seeing what price buyers will pay. As with competitive firms, monopolies choose a quantity of output that maximizes profit (total revenue minus total cost).

Because the monopolist faces a downward-sloping demand curve, it must lower the price of the good if it wishes to sell a greater quantity. Therefore, when it sells an additional unit, the sale of the additional unit has two effects on total revenue ($P \times Q$):

- The output effect: Q is higher.
- The price effect: P is lower (on the marginal unit and on the units it was already selling).

Because the monopolist must reduce the price on every unit it sells when it expands output by one unit, marginal revenue ($\Delta TR / \Delta Q$) for the monopolist declines as Q increases and marginal revenue is always less than the price of the good.

As with a competitive firm, the monopolist maximizes profit at the level of output where marginal revenue (MR) equals marginal cost (MC). As Q increases, MR decreases and MC increases. Therefore, at low levels of output, $MR > MC$ and an increase in Q increases profit. At high levels of output, $MC > MR$ and a decrease in output increases profit. The monopolist, therefore, should produce up to the point where $MR = MC$. That is, the profit-maximizing level of output is determined by the intersection of the marginal-revenue and marginal-cost curves. Because the MR curve lies below the demand curve, the price the monopolist charges is found by reading up to the demand curve from the $MR = MC$ intersection. That is, it charges the highest price consistent with that quantity.

Recall that for the competitive firm, because the demand curve facing the firm is perfectly elastic so that $P = MR$, the profit-maximizing equilibrium requires that $P = MR = MC$. However, for the monopoly firm, $MR < P$, so the profit-maximizing equilibrium requires that $P > MR = MC$. As a result, *in competitive markets, price equals marginal cost while in monopolized markets, price exceeds marginal cost.*

Evidence from the pharmaceutical drug market is consistent with our theory. While the patent is enforced, the price of a drug is high. When the patent expires and generic drugs become available, the price falls substantially.

As with the competitive firm, profit = $(P - ATC) \times Q$, or profit equals the average profit per unit times the number of units sold.

The Welfare Cost of Monopolies

Does a monopoly market maximize economic well-being as measured by total surplus? Recall that total surplus is the sum of consumer surplus and producer surplus. Equilibrium of supply and demand in a competitive market naturally maximizes total surplus because all units are produced where the value to buyers is greater than or equal to the cost of production to the sellers.

For a monopolist to produce the socially efficient quantity (maximize total surplus by producing all units where the value to buyers exceeds or equals the cost of production), it would have to produce the level of output where the marginal-cost curve intersects the demand curve. However, the monopolist chooses to produce the level of output where the marginal-revenue curve intersects the marginal-cost curve. Because for the monopolist the marginal-revenue curve is always below the demand curve, *the monopolist produces less than the socially efficient quantity of output.*

The small quantity produced by the monopolist allows the monopolist to charge a price that exceeds the marginal cost of production. Therefore, the monopolist generates a *deadweight loss* because, at the high monopoly price, consumers fail to buy units of output where the value to them exceeds the cost to the monopolist.

The deadweight loss from a monopoly is similar to the deadweight loss from a tax, and the monopolist's profit is similar to tax revenue except that the revenue is received by a private firm. Because the profit earned by a monopolist is simply a transfer of consumer surplus to producer surplus, a monopoly's profit is not a social cost. The social cost of a monopoly is the deadweight loss generated when the monopolist produces a quantity of output below that which is efficient.

Price Discrimination

Price discrimination is the business practice of selling the same good at different prices to different customers. Price discrimination can only be practiced by a firm with market power such as a monopolist. There are three lessons to note about price discrimination:

- Price discrimination is a rational strategy for a profit-maximizing monopolist because a monopolist's profits are increased when it charges each customer a price closer to his individual willingness to pay.

- Price discrimination is only possible if the monopolist is able to separate customers according to their willingness to pay—by age, income, location, etc. If there is *arbitrage*—the process of buying a good in one market at a low price and selling it in another market at a higher price—price discrimination is not possible.

- Price discrimination can raise economic welfare because output increases beyond that which would result under monopoly pricing. However, the additional surplus (reduced deadweight loss) is received by the producer, not the consumer.

Perfect price discrimination occurs when a monopolist charges each customer her exact willingness to pay. In this case, the efficient quantity is produced and consumed and there is no deadweight loss. However, total surplus goes to the monopolist in the form of profit. In reality, perfect price discrimination cannot be accomplished. Imperfect price discrimination may raise, lower, or leave unchanged total surplus in a market.

Examples of price discrimination include movie tickets, airline tickets, discount coupons, financial aid for college tuition, quantity discounts, and tickets for Broadway shows.

Public Policy Toward Monopolies

Monopolies fail to allocate resources efficiently because they produce less than the socially optimal quantity of output and charge prices that exceed marginal cost. Policymakers can respond to the problem of monopoly in one of four ways:

- *By trying to make monopolized industries more competitive.* The Justice Department can employ antitrust laws (statutes aimed at reducing monopoly power) to prevent mergers that reduce competition, break up extremely large companies to increase competition, and prevent companies from colluding. However, some mergers result in synergies that reduce costs and raise efficiency. Therefore, it is difficult for government to know which mergers to block and which ones to allow. The Obama administration has promised to enforce antitrust laws more vigorously.

- *By regulating the behavior of the monopolies.* The prices charged by natural monopolies such as utilities are often regulated by government. If a natural monopoly is required to set its price equal to its marginal cost, the efficient quantity will be consumed but the monopoly will lose money because marginal cost must be below average variable cost if average variable cost is declining. Thus, the monopolist will exit the industry. In response, regulators can subsidize a natural monopoly with tax revenue (which creates its own deadweight loss) or allow average-total-cost pricing, which is an improvement over monopoly pricing but it is not as efficient as marginal-cost pricing. Another problem with regulating prices is that monopolists have no incentive to reduce costs because their prices are reduced when their costs are reduced.

- *By turning some private monopolies into public enterprises.* Instead of regulating the prices charged by a natural monopoly, the government can run the monopoly itself. The Postal Service is an example. Economists generally prefer private ownership to government ownership because private owners have a greater incentive to minimize costs.

- *By doing nothing at all.* Because each of the previously listed solutions has its own shortcomings, some economists urge that monopolies be left alone. They believe that the "political failure" in the real world is more costly than the "market failure" caused by monopoly pricing.

Conclusion: The Prevalence of Monopolies

In one sense, monopolies are common because most firms have some control over the prices they charge. On the other hand, firms with substantial monopoly power are rare. Monopoly power is a matter of degree.

Helpful Hints

1. A monopolist can choose the quantity and see what price buyers will pay or can choose the price and see what quantity buyers will purchase. That is, a monopolist is still subject to the demand curve for its product. The monopolist cannot choose both a high price and a large quantity if that combination does not lie on the demand curve facing the monopolist.

2. A monopolist is not guaranteed to earn profits. Any one of us can be the monopolist in the production of gold-plated textbook covers (because there is currently no producer of such a product), but the demand for such a product is likely to be too low to cover the costs of production. In like manner, gaining a patent on a product does not guarantee the holder of the patent future profits.

Terms and Definitions

Choose a definition for each key term.

Key Terms

_____ Monopoly

_____ Natural monopoly

_____ Price discrimination

_____ Arbitrage

_____ Perfect price discrimination

Definitions

1. A monopoly that arises because a single firm can supply a good or service to an entire market at a smaller cost than could two or more firms

2. A firm that is the sole seller of a product without close substitutes

3. A situation in which the monopolist is able to charge each customer precisely his willingness to pay

4. The business practice of selling the same good at different prices to different customers

5. The process of buying a good in one market at a low price and selling it in another market at a higher price

Problems and Short-Answer Questions

Practice Problems

1. a. What are the three sources of the barriers to entry that allow a monopoly to remain the sole seller of a product?

   _____

   _____

   _____

   b. What is the entry barrier that is the source of the monopoly power for the following products or producers? List some competitors that keep these products or producers from having absolute monopoly power.
   (1) United States Postal Service

   _____

   _____

(2) Perrier Spring Water

_____

_____

(3) Prozac (a brand-name drug)

_____

_____

(4) DeBeers Diamonds

_____

_____

(5) *Principles of Economics* by N. Gregory Mankiw (your textbook)

_____

_____

(6) Edison Power Company

_____

_____

2. Suppose a firm has a patent on a special process to make a unique smoked salmon. The following table provides information about the demand facing this firm for this unique product.

Pounds of Salmon	Price	(P × Q) Total Revenue	(ΔTR/ΔQ) Marginal Revenue
0	$20	_____	
			_____
1	18	_____	
			_____
2	16	_____	
			_____
3	14	_____	
			_____
4	12	_____	
			_____
5	10	_____	
			_____
6	8	_____	
			_____
7	6	_____	

a. Complete the table above.
b. Plot the demand curve and the marginal-revenue curve in Exhibit 1. (Read Helpful Hint 2 in Chapter 13 of this study guide for a reminder on how to plot marginal values.)

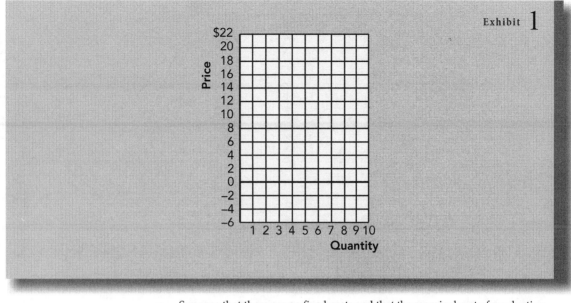

Exhibit 1

c. Suppose that there are no fixed costs and that the marginal cost of production of smoked salmon is constant at $6 per pound. (Thus, the average total cost is also constant at $6 per pound.) What is the quantity and price chosen by the monopolist? What is the profit earned by the monopolist? Show your solution on the graph you created in part *b* above.

_____

_____

_____

d. What is the price and quantity that maximizes total surplus?

_____

_____

e. Compare the monopoly solution and the efficient solution. That is, is the monopolist's price too high or too low? Is the monopolist's quantity too high or too low? Why?

_____

_____

_____

f. Is there a deadweight loss in this market if the monopolist charges the monopoly price? Explain.

_____

_____

_____

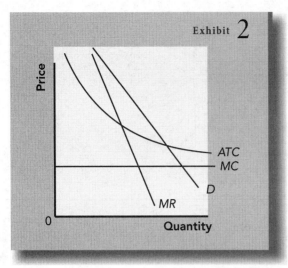

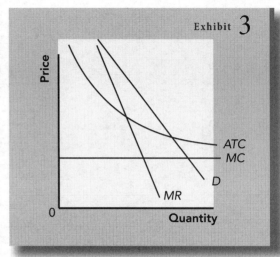

g. If the monopolist is able to costlessly and perfectly price discriminate, is the outcome efficient? Explain. What is the value of consumer surplus, producer surplus, and total surplus? Explain.

_____

_____

_____

3. a. What type of market is represented in Exhibit 2: perfect competition, monopoly, or natural monopoly? Explain.

_____

_____

_____

b. Show the profit or loss generated by this firm in Exhibit 2 assuming that the firm maximizes profit.

c. Suppose government regulators force this firm to set the price equal to its marginal cost in order to improve efficiency in this market. In Exhibit 3, show the profit or loss generated by this firm.

d. In the long run, will forcing this firm to charge a price equal to its marginal cost improve efficiency? Explain.

_____

_____

_____

Short-Answer Questions

1. What is a *barrier to entry?* What are the three sources of barriers to entry that allow a monopoly to remain the sole seller in a market?

   _____

   _____

   _____

   _____

   _____

   _____

2. If a natural monopoly is forced through regulation to charge a price equal to its marginal cost, will the outcome be efficient? Why or why not?

   _____

   _____

3. Does a monopolist charge the highest possible price for its output? Why or why not? How does a monopolist choose the price it will charge for its product?

   _____

   _____

   _____

   _____

4. Why does a monopolist produce less than the socially efficient quantity of output?

   _____

   _____

   _____

   _____

5. Are the monopolist's profits part of the social cost of monopoly? Explain.

   _____

   _____

   _____

   _____

6. Is perfect price discrimination efficient? Explain. Who receives the surplus?

   _____

   _____

   _____

   _____

7. What is the necessary condition for a monopolist to be able to price discriminate?

_____

_____

_____

_____

8. What are the four ways that policymakers can respond to the problem of monopoly?

_____

_____

_____

_____

9. Should antitrust laws be utilized to stop all mergers? Why or why not?

_____

_____

_____

_____

10. What are some of the problems associated with regulating the price charged by a natural monopoly?

_____

_____

Self-Test

True/False Questions

_____ 1. Monopolists are price takers.

_____ 2. The most common source of a barrier to entry into a monopolist's market is that the monopolist owns a key resource necessary for production of that good.

_____ 3. A monopoly is the sole seller of a product with no close substitutes.

_____ 4. A natural monopoly is a monopoly that uses its ownership of natural resources as a barrier to entry into its market.

_____ 5. The demand curve facing a monopolist is the market demand curve for its product.

_____ 6. For the monopolist, marginal revenue is always less than the price of the good.

_____ 7. The monopolist chooses the quantity of output at which marginal revenue equals marginal cost and then uses the demand curve to find the price that will induce consumers to buy that quantity.

_____ 8. The supply curve for a monopolist is always positively sloped.

_____ 9. A monopolist produces an efficient quantity of output but it is still inefficient because it charges a price that exceeds marginal cost and the resulting profit is a social cost.

_____ 10. Price discrimination is only possible if there is no arbitrage.

_____ 11. Price discrimination can raise economic welfare because output increases beyond that which would result under monopoly pricing.

_____ 12. Perfect price discrimination is efficient but all of the surplus is received by the consumer.

_____ 13. Universities are engaging in price discrimination when they charge different levels of tuition to poor and wealthy students.

_____ 14. Using regulations to force a natural monopoly to charge a price equal to its marginal cost of production will cause the monopoly to lose money and exit the industry.

_____ 15. Most economists argue that the most efficient solution to the problem of monopoly is that the monopoly should be publicly owned.

Multiple-Choice Questions

1. Which of the following is *not* a barrier to entry in a monopolized market?
   a. The government gives a single firm the exclusive right to produce some good.
   b. The costs of production make a single producer more efficient than a large number of producers.
   c. A key resource is owned by a single firm.
   d. A single firm is very large.

2. A firm whose average total cost continually declines at least to the quantity that could supply the entire market is known as a
   a. perfect competitor.
   b. natural monopoly.
   c. government monopoly.
   d. regulated monopoly.

3. When a monopolist produces an additional unit, the marginal revenue generated by that unit must be
   a. above the price because the output effect outweighs the price effect.
   b. above the price because the price effect outweighs the output effect.
   c. below the price because the output effect outweighs the price effect.
   d. below the price because the price effect outweighs the output effect.

4. A monopolist maximizes profit by producing the quantity at which
   a. marginal revenue equals marginal cost.
   b. marginal revenue equals price.
   c. marginal cost equals price.
   d. marginal cost equals demand.
   e. none of the above occurs.

5. Which of the following statements about price and marginal cost in competitive and monopolized markets is *true*?
   a. In competitive markets, price equals marginal cost; in monopolized markets, price equals marginal cost.
   b. In competitive markets, price exceeds marginal cost; in monopolized markets, price exceeds marginal cost.
   c. In competitive markets, price equals marginal cost; in monopolized markets, price exceeds marginal cost.
   d. In competitive markets, price exceeds marginal cost; in monopolized markets, price equals marginal cost.

6. South-Western is a monopolist in the production of your textbook because
   a. South-Western owns a key resource in the production of textbooks.
   b. South-Western is a natural monopoly.
   c. the government has granted South-Western exclusive rights to produce this textbook.
   d. South-Western is a very large company.

Use Exhibit 4 to answer questions 7 through 10.

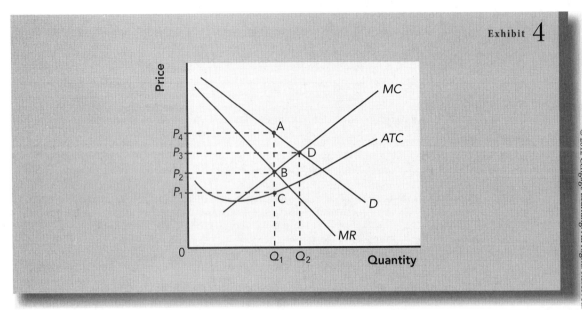

7. The profit-maximizing monopolist will choose the price and quantity represented by point
   a. A.
   b. B.
   c. C.
   d. D.
   e. None of the above is correct.

8. The profit earned by the profit-maximizing monopolist is represented by the area
   a. P_4ABP_2.
   b. P_4ACP_1.
   c. P_4AQ_10.
   d. P_3DQ_20.
   e. None of the above is correct.

9. The deadweight loss associated with monopoly pricing is represented by the area
   a. P_4ABP_2.
   b. P_4ACP_1.
   c. ABD.
   d. P_2BCP_1.
   e. None of the above is correct.

10. The efficient price and quantity are represented by point
    a. A.
    b. B.
    c. C.
    d. D.
    e. None of the above is correct.

11. The inefficiency associated with monopoly is due to
    a. the monopoly's profits.
    b. the monopoly's losses.
    c. overproduction of the good.
    d. underproduction of the good.

12. Compared to a perfectly competitive market, a monopoly market will usually generate
    a. higher prices and higher output.
    b. higher prices and lower output.
    c. lower prices and lower output.
    d. lower prices and higher output.

13. The monopolist's supply curve
    a. is the marginal-cost curve above average variable cost.
    b. is the marginal-cost curve above average total cost.
    c. is the upward-sloping portion of the average-total-cost curve.
    d. is the upward-sloping portion of the average variable cost.
    e. does not exist.

14. Using government regulations to force a natural monopoly to charge a price equal to its marginal cost will
    a. improve efficiency.
    b. raise the price of the good.
    c. attract additional firms to enter the market.
    d. cause the monopolist to exit the market.

15. The purpose of antitrust laws is to
    a. regulate the prices charged by a monopoly.
    b. increase competition in an industry by preventing mergers and breaking up large firms.
    c. increase merger activity to help generate synergies that reduce costs and raise efficiency.
    d. create public ownership of natural monopolies.
    e. do all of the above.

16. Public ownership of natural monopolies
    a. tends to be inefficient.
    b. usually lowers the cost of production dramatically.
    c. creates synergies between the newly acquired firm and other government-owned companies.
    d. does none of the above.

17. Which of the following statements about price discrimination is *not* true?
    a. Price discrimination can raise economic welfare.
    b. Price discrimination requires that the seller be able to separate buyers according to their willingness to pay.
    c. Perfect price discrimination generates a deadweight loss.
    d. Price discrimination increases a monopolist's profits.
    e. For a monopolist to engage in price discrimination, buyers must be unable to engage in arbitrage.

18. If regulators break up a natural monopoly into many smaller firms, the cost of production
    a. will fall.
    b. will rise.
    c. will remain the same.
    d. could either rise or fall depending on the elasticity of the monopolist's supply curve.

19. A monopoly is able to continue to generate economic profits in the long run because
   a. potential competitors sometimes don't notice the profits.
   b. there is some barrier to entry to that market.
   c. the monopolist is financially powerful.
   d. antitrust laws eliminate competitors for a specified number of years.
   e. of all of the above.

20. If marginal revenue exceeds marginal cost, a monopolist should
   a. increase output.
   b. decrease output.
   c. keep output the same because profits are maximized when marginal revenue exceeds marginal cost.
   d. raise the price.

Advanced Critical Thinking

You are watching a television news show. A consumer advocate is discussing the airline industry. He says, "There are so many rates offered by airlines that it is technically possible for a 747 to be carrying a full load of passengers where no two of them paid the same price for their tickets. This is clearly unfair and inefficient." He continues, "In addition, the profits of the airlines have doubled in the last few years since they began this practice, and these additional profits are clearly a social burden. We need legislation that requires airlines to charge all passengers on an airplane the same price for their travel."

1. List some of the ways airlines divide their customers according to their willingness to pay.

   _____

   _____

   _____

   _____

2. Is it necessarily inefficient for airlines to charge different prices to different customers? Why or why not?

   _____

   _____

   _____

   _____

3. Is the increase in profits generated by this type of price discrimination a social cost? Explain.

   _____

   _____

   _____

   _____

Solutions

Terms and Definitions

  2 Monopoly

  1 Natural monopoly

  4 Price discrimination

  5 Arbitrage

  3 Perfect price discrimination

Practice Problems

1. a. A key resource is owned by a single firm (monopoly resource), the government gives a single firm the exclusive right to produce a good (government-created monopoly), the costs of production make a single producer more efficient (natural monopoly).

   b. (1) Natural monopoly. E-mail, fax machines, telephone, private delivery such as FedEx.

     (2) Monopoly resource. Other bottled water, soft drinks.

     (3) Government-created monopoly due to a patent. Other drugs for depression, generic drugs when the patent expires.

     (4) Monopoly resource. Other gems such as emeralds, rubies, sapphires.

     (5) Government-created monopoly due to copyright. Other principles of economics texts.

     (6) Natural monopoly. Wood-burning stoves, gas lanterns, home generators.

2. a.

Pounds of Salmon	Price	$(P \times Q)$ Total Revenue	$(\Delta TR/\Delta Q)$ Marginal Revenue
0	$20	0	
			18
1	18	18	
			14
2	16	32	
			10
3	14	42	
			6
4	12	48	
			2
5	10	50	
			−2
6	8	48	
			−6
7	6	42	

  b. See Exhibit 5.

Exhibit 5

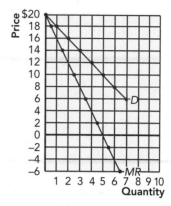

  c. $Q =$ between 3 and 4 units (say 3.5), $P =$ between $12 and $14 (say $13). Profit $= TR - TC$ or profit $= (3.5 \times \$13) - (3.5 \times \$6) = \$45.50 - \$21.00 = \$24.50$. (Or profit $= (P - ATC) \times Q = (\$13 - \$6) \times 3.5 = \$24.50$.) See Exhibit 6.

Exhibit 6

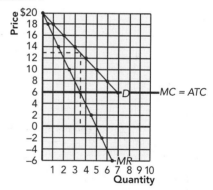

  d. Seven units at $6 each. (The efficient solution is where the market produces all units where benefits exceed or equal costs of production, which is where demand intersects MC.)

  e. The monopolist's price is too high and quantity produced too low because the monopolist faces a downward-sloping demand curve that makes $MR < P$. Therefore, when the profit-maximizing monopolist sets $MR = MC$ and the MR curve is below the demand curve, the quantity is less than optimal and the price charged exceeds the MC of production.

  f. Yes. Units from 3.5 to 7, or an additional 3.5 pounds of salmon are valued by the consumer at values in excess of the $6 per pound MC of production and these units are not produced and consumed when the price is $13. (Deadweight loss = the deadweight loss triangle $= 1/2 \, (7 - 3.5) \times (\$13 - \$6) = \$12.25$.)

g. Yes, all units are produced where the value to buyers is greater than or is equal to the cost of production (7 units). Total surplus is now producer surplus, and there is no consumer surplus. Total surplus and producer surplus is the area under the demand curve and above the price or 1/2($20 − $6) × 7 = $49. Consumer surplus = $0.

3. a. Natural monopoly because *ATC* is still declining at the quantity that could satisfy the entire market.

   b. See Exhibit 7.

Exhibit 7

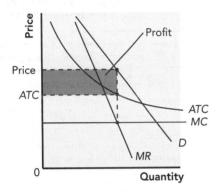

   c. See Exhibit 8.

Exhibit 8

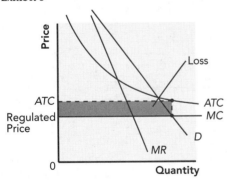

   d. No. Because marginal cost must be below average total cost if average total cost is declining, this firm will generate losses if forced to charge a price equal to marginal cost. It will simply exit the market, which eliminates all surplus associated with this market.

Short-Answer Questions

1. Anything that restricts new firms from entering a market. A key resource is owned by a single firm, the government gives a single firm the exclusive right to produce a good, or the costs of production make a single producer more efficient than a large number of producers.

2. No. The monopolist will generate losses and will exit the market.

3. No. Even a monopolist is subject to the demand for its product, so a high price would cause buyers to buy very little of the good. The monopolist chooses its price by first choosing the optimal quantity based on the intersection of *MR* and *MC* and then charging the price consistent with that quantity.

4. For a monopolist, *P* > *MR* because for a monopolist to sell another unit, it must reduce the price on the marginal unit and all of its previous units. Therefore, while a monopolist equates *MR* and *MC*, it charges a price that is greater than *MC*, which causes consumers to buy less than the efficient amount of the good.

5. No. The monopolist's profits are a redistribution of consumer surplus to producer surplus. The social cost of monopoly is the deadweight loss associated with the reduced production of output.

6. Yes, because every unit is produced where the value to buyers is greater than or equal to the cost to the producer. However, the entire total surplus is received by the producer (the monopolist).

7. The monopolist must be able to separate buyers according to their willingness to pay.

8. Try to make monopolized industries more competitive, regulate the behavior of the monopolies, turn private monopolies into public enterprises, or do nothing at all.

9. No, many mergers capture synergies between the merging firms that reduce costs and increase efficiency.

10. The monopolist may lose money and exit the market. Subsidies to prevent this require taxes that also generate deadweight losses. Regulated monopolists have little incentive to reduce costs.

True/False Questions

1. F; monopolists are price makers.

2. F; owning a key resource is the rarest source of barriers to entry.

3. T

4. F; a natural monopoly is a firm with an average total cost curve that continually declines at least to the quantity that satisfies the entire market.

5. T

6. T

7. T

8. F; monopolists have no supply curve.

9. F; the inefficiency generated by a monopoly results from the failure of the monopolist to produce units of output where the value to consumers equals or exceeds the cost of production. The monopolist's profits are not a cost to society but are just a redistribution from consumer surplus to producer surplus.

10. T

11. T

12. F; all of the surplus is received by the producer.
13. T
14. T
15. F; economists usually prefer private ownership to public ownership because private owners have a greater incentive to reduce costs.

Multiple-Choice Questions

1. d
2. b
3. d
4. a
5. c
6. c
7. a
8. b
9. c
10. d
11. d
12. b
13. e
14. d
15. b
16. a
17. c
18. b
19. b
20. a

Advanced Critical Thinking

1. Airlines segment people by age (young and old fly cheaper), by location (more competitive routes are cheaper), by length of time between leaving and returning (tourists fly cheaper than business travelers), by length of time of advance booking (later bookings can be more expensive until the very last minute when it may become cheaper again), and so on.

2. No. Price discrimination can improve efficiency. By charging buyers their willingness to pay, the monopolist increases production to the point where all units are produced where the value to buyers is greater than or equal to the cost of production.

3. No. Some of the additional profits are from the creation of additional surplus that accrues entirely to the producer, and some of the profits are a redistribution of surplus from consumer surplus to producer surplus.

Chapter 16
Monopolistic Competition

Goals
In this chapter you will

- See what market structures lie between monopoly and competition
- Analyze competition among firms that sell differentiated products
- Compare the outcome under monopolistic competition and under perfect competition
- Consider the desirability of outcomes in monopolistically competitive markets
- Examine the debate over the effects of advertising
- Examine the debate over the role of brand names

Outcomes
After accomplishing these goals, you should be able to

- Describe the characteristics of oligopoly and monopolistic competition
- Show the long-run adjustment that takes place in a monopolistically competitive market when a firm generates economic profits
- Show why monopolistically competitive firms produce at less than efficient scale in the long run
- Discuss the inefficiencies of monopolistically competitive markets
- Provide an argument in support of and in opposition to the use of advertising
- Provide an argument in support of and in opposition to the use of brand names

Chapter Overview

Context and Purpose

Chapter 16 is the fourth chapter in a five-chapter sequence dealing with firm behavior and the organization of industry. The previous two chapters developed the two extreme forms of market structure—competition and monopoly. The market structure that lies between competition and monopoly is known as *imperfect competition*. There are two types of imperfect competition—monopolistic competition and oligopoly. This chapter addresses monopolistic competition while the final chapter in the sequence addresses oligopoly. The analysis in this chapter is again based on the cost curves developed in Chapter 13.

The purpose of Chapter 16 is to address *monopolistic competition*—a market structure in which many firms sell products that are similar but not identical. Monopolistic competition differs from perfect competition because each of the many sellers offers a somewhat different product. As a result, monopolistically competitive firms face a downward-sloping demand curve whereas competitive firms face a horizontal demand curve at the market price. Monopolistic competition is common.

Chapter Review

Introduction   Monopolistic competition shares some features of competition and monopoly. Monopolistic competition is common.

Between Monopoly and Perfect Competition

Competitive firms charge a price equal to marginal cost, and in the long run, this is equal to average total cost, causing each firm to earn no economic profits. A monopolist charges a price that exceeds marginal cost. This reduces output and causes a deadweight loss. The market structure that lies between the extremes of competition and monopoly and contains elements of both is known as *imperfect competition*. There are two types of imperfect competition—oligopoly and monopolistic competition. Oligopoly is a market structure in which only a few sellers offer similar or identical products. Firms in markets with four-firm concentration ratios in excess of 50 percent are often oligopolies because four firms supply more than 50 percent of the output of the entire industry.

Monopolistic competition is a market structure in which many firms sell products that are similar but not identical. Monopolistic competition has the following characteristics:

- *Many sellers:* This is in common with competition.

- *Product differentiation:* This is in common with monopoly—each firm's product is slightly different, so each firm is a price maker and faces a downward-sloping demand for its product.

- *Free entry:* This is in common with competition—firms can enter or exit without restriction so economic profits are driven to zero.

Examples of monopolistically competitive markets are the market for books, DVDs, restaurants, and so on. Monopolistically competitive markets are common.

Oligopoly differs from perfect competition because there are only a few sellers in the market. Monopolistic competition differs from perfect competition because each of the many sellers offers a somewhat different product. As a result, monopolistically competitive firms face a downward-sloping demand curve while competitive firms face a horizontal demand curve at the market price.

To summarize the distinguishing characteristics of the various market structures:

- Monopoly has only one firm.

- Oligopoly has a few firms selling similar or identical products.

- Perfect competition has many firms selling identical products.

- Monopolistic competition has many firms selling differentiated products.

It is often difficult to decide which structure best describes a particular market.

Competition with Differentiated Products

Similar to a monopolist, a monopolistically competitive firm faces a downward-sloping demand curve for its product. Therefore, it follows the same rule for profit maximization as a monopolist—it produces the quantity at which marginal cost equals marginal revenue and then uses the demand curve to determine the price consistent with this quantity. In the short run, if the price exceeds average total cost, the firm makes economic profits. If the price is below average total cost, the firm generates losses.

As in a competitive market, if the firm is making profits, new firms have incentive to enter the market. Entry reduces the demand faced by each firm already in the market (shifts their demand curves to the left) and reduces their profits in the long run. If the firm is generating losses, incumbent firms have incentive to exit the market. Exit increases the demand faced by each firm that remains in the market (shifts their demand curves to the right) and reduces their losses. Entry and exit continue until the firms in the market are making zero economic profits. In long-run equilibrium, the demand curve facing the firm must be tangent to the average-total-cost curve so that $P = ATC$ and profits are zero.

The long-run equilibrium for a monopolistically competitive firm exhibits the following:

- As in monopoly, price exceeds marginal cost because profit maximization requires that $MR = MC$, and MR is always less than demand if demand is downward sloping.

- As in competition, price equals average total cost so economic profits equal zero because, unlike in monopoly, free entry drives profits to zero.

The long-run equilibrium under monopolistic competition differs from the long-run equilibrium under perfect competition in two ways:

- *Excess capacity:* Monopolistically competitive firms produce in the downward-sloping portion of their average-total-cost curve. Therefore, they produce a quantity that is less than that which would be produced at the *efficient scale* (minimum ATC) of the firm. As a result, they are said to have *excess capacity*. Competitive firms produce at the efficient scale.

- *Markup over marginal cost:* A monopolistically competitive firm charges a price that exceeds its marginal cost. A competitive firm charges a price that equals its marginal cost. As a result, if a monopolistically competitive firm could attract another customer, it would increase its profits.

Monopolistic competition may be inefficient for two reasons:

- Because price exceeds marginal cost, some units that buyers valued in excess of the cost of production are not produced and consumed. This is the standard deadweight loss associated with monopoly. Regulating a monopolistically competitive firm in order to reduce the deadweight loss is not easily accomplished—the task is similar to regulating a natural monopoly.

- The number of firms in the market may not be "ideal" because the entering firm only considers its own profits but its entry generates two external effects:

    (1) *The product-variety externality:* Entry creates consumer surplus in the new market, which is a positive externality.

    (2) *The business-stealing externality:* Entry causes other firms to lose customers and profits and reduces existing surplus, which is a negative externality.

Therefore, the entry of new firms into a monopolistically competitive market can raise or lower social surplus.

Monopolistically competitive markets do not ensure the maximization of total surplus. However, there is no easy way for public policy to improve the market outcome.

Advertising

Because monopolistically competitive firms sell differentiated products at prices above marginal cost, each firm has incentive to advertise to attract more buyers. Firms that sell highly differentiated consumer products spend 10 to 20 percent of revenue on advertising; firms that sell industrial products spend little; and firms that sell undifferentiated products spend nothing at all. About 2 percent of firm revenue is spent on advertising. That spending is largely on commercials on television and radio, space in newspapers and magazines, direct mail, the yellow pages, billboards, and the Internet.

Economists debate the social value of advertising. Critics argue that advertising manipulates people's tastes to create a desire that otherwise would not exist and that advertising impedes competition by increasing the perception of product differentiation, which increases brand loyalty, causes demand to be more inelastic, and allows the firm to charge a greater markup over marginal cost. Defenders of advertising argue that advertising provides information to customers about prices, the existence of new products, and the location of retail outlets. This information increases competition because consumers are aware of price differentials and it provides new firms with the means to attract customers from existing firms. Evidence suggests that advertising increases competition and reduces prices for consumers.

Advertising that appears to contain little information may be useful because it provides a *signal* of product quality. Firms are likely to spend a great deal on advertising only if they think their product is of high quality. Therefore, consumers may be rational to try new products that are expensively advertised because it signals that the product is of high quality. The content of the ad is irrelevant. What is important is that the ad is expensive.

Advertising is related to *brand names*. Critics of brand names argue that brand names cause consumers to perceive differences between goods that do not exist. Defenders of brand names argue that brand names ensure that the product is of high quality because (1) brand names provide *information* about the quality of a product and (2) brand names give firms the *incentive* to maintain high quality.

Conclusion

Monopolistic competition contains characteristics of both monopoly and competition. Like monopoly, firms face downward-sloping demand curves and charge prices above marginal cost. Like competition, entry and exit drive profits to zero in the long run. Many markets are monopolistically competitive. The allocation of resources under monopolistic competition is not perfect, but policymakers may not be able to improve on it.

Helpful Hints

1. A source of inefficiency in monopolistic competition is underproduction. That is, some units are not produced that buyers value in excess of the cost of production. The monopolistically competitive firm charges a price that exceeds marginal cost while the competitive firm charges a price equal to marginal cost. However, the higher price charged by the monopolistically competitive firm is not the source of inefficiency. As with monopoly, it is the lower quantity demanded that results from the higher price that is the source of inefficiency. By itself, the higher price simply redistributes surplus from the buyer to the seller but it does not reduce total surplus.

Terms and Definitions

Choose a definition for each key term.

Key Terms

_____ Oligopoly

_____ Monopolistic competition

_____ Free entry

_____ Efficient scale

Definitions

1. A situation where firms can enter the market without restriction

2. The quantity that minimizes average total cost

3. A market structure in which many firms sell products that are similar but not identical

4. A market structure in which only a few sellers offer similar or identical products

Problems and Short-Answer Questions

Practice Problems

1. In which market structure—monopoly, oligopoly, monopolistic competition, or perfect competition—would you place each of the following products? Why?

   a. Retail market for electricity

   _____

   b. Principles of economics textbooks

   _____

   c. *Principles of Economics* by N. Gregory Mankiw

   _____

   d. Photographic film

   _____

   e. Retail market for gasoline

   _____

   f. Restaurants in a large city

   _____

   g. Auto tires

   _____

   h. Trash collection

   _____

   i. Legal services in a metropolitan area

   _____

   j. Breakfast cereal

   _____

   k. Gold bullion

   _____

   l. Air travel from any one airport

   _____

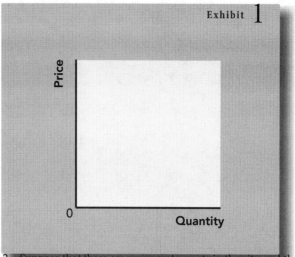

Exhibit 1

2. Suppose that there are many restaurants in the city and that each has a somewhat different menu.

a. In Exhibit 1, draw the diagram of the cost curves (average total cost and marginal cost), demand curve, and marginal-revenue curve for Mario's Pizza when it is in long-run equilibrium.

b. Is Mario's Pizza profitable in the long run? Explain.

_____

_____

_____

c. Is Mario's Pizza producing at the efficient scale? Explain. Why doesn't Mario's expand its output if it has excess capacity?

_____

_____

_____

d. In Exhibit 1, show the deadweight loss associated with Mario's level of output. Does this deadweight loss occur because the price is higher than a competitive firm would charge or because the quantity is smaller than a competitive firm would produce? Explain.

_____

_____

_____

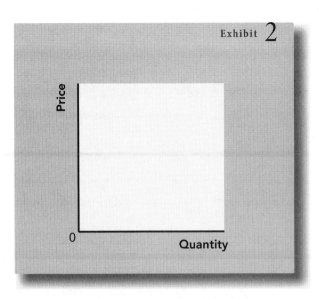

Exhibit 2

e.   Suppose that Mario's engages in an advertising campaign that is a huge suc-
     cess. In Exhibit 2, draw the diagram of Mario's cost curves, demand curve,
     and marginal-revenue curve and show Mario's profit in the short run. Can this
     situation be maintained in the long run? Explain.

     _____

     _____

3.   For each of the following pairs of firms, which firm would likely spend a higher
     proportion of its revenue on advertising? Explain.
     a.   the maker of Bayer Aspirin or the maker of generic aspirin

          _____

     b.   a firm introducing a low-quality ice cream or a firm introducing a high-quality
          ice cream that each cost about the same to make

          _____

     c.   John Deere farm tractor division or John Deere lawn mower division

          _____

     d.   the bakery that bakes Old Home Wheat Bread or a wheat farmer

          _____

Short-Answer Questions

1.   What are the two types of imperfect competition? Describe them.

     _____

     _____

2.   The market for vitamins and dietary supplements is dominated by five firms. What
     type of market structure does it represent? Explain.

     _____

     _____

3. What characteristics does monopolistic competition have in common with a monopoly?

_____

4. What characteristics does monopolistic competition have in common with perfect competition?

_____

_____

_____

5. How does a monopolistically competitive firm choose the quantity and price that maximizes its profits?

_____

_____

6. Is it possible for a monopolistically competitive firm to generate economic profits in the long run? Why or why not?

_____

_____

_____

_____

7. How does the long-run equilibrium in monopolistic competition differ from the long-run equilibrium in perfect competition?

_____

_____

_____

8. Is the long-run equilibrium in monopolistic competition efficient? Explain.

_____

_____

_____

9. Summarize the arguments in support of advertising and brand names.

_____

_____

_____

10. Summarize the arguments in opposition to advertising and brand names.

_____

_____

_____

Self-Test

True/False Questions

_____ 1. Monopolistic competition is a market structure in which few firms sell similar products.

_____ 2. Similar to firms in perfectly competitive markets, firms in monopolistically competitive markets can enter and exit the market without restriction so profits are driven to zero in the long run.

_____ 3. In the long run, firms in monopolistically competitive markets produce at the minimum of their average-total-cost curves.

_____ 4. Similar to a monopolist, a monopolistically competitive firm faces a downward-sloping demand curve for its product.

_____ 5. Both monopolists and monopolistically competitive firms produce the quantity at which marginal revenue equals marginal cost and then use the demand curve facing the firm to determine the price consistent with that quantity.

_____ 6. Because a monopolistically competitive firm charges a price that exceeds marginal cost, the firm fails to produce some units that the buyers value in excess of the cost of production, and thus, monopolistic competition is inefficient.

_____ 7. In the long run, a monopolistically competitive firm charges a price that exceeds average total cost.

_____ 8. Economists generally agree that monopolistically competitive firms should be regulated in order to increase economic efficiency.

_____ 9. Firms that sell highly differentiated consumer products are more likely to spend a large percentage of their revenue on advertising.

_____ 10. Advertising must be socially wasteful because advertising simply adds to the cost of producing a product.

_____ 11. Critics of advertising argue that advertising decreases competition while defenders of advertising argue that advertising increases competition and reduces prices to consumers.

_____ 12. Even advertising that appears to contain little information about the product may be useful because it provides a signal about the quality of the product.

_____ 13. Brand names allow firms to make economic profits in the long run because they are able to sell inferior products based on the apparent connection of those products to the firm's unrelated high-quality products.

_____ 14. Policymakers are starting to view restrictions on advertising by professionals such as doctors, lawyers, and pharmacists as anticompetitive.

_____ 15. In the long run, a monopolistically competitive firm produces at the efficient scale while a competitive firm has excess capacity.

Multiple-Choice Questions

1. Which of the following is not a characteristic of a monopolistically competitive market?
   a. many sellers
   b. differentiated products
   c. long-run economic profits
   d. free entry and exit

2. Which of the following products is least likely to be sold in a monopolistically competitive market?
   a. video games
   b. breakfast cereal
   c. beer
   d. cotton

3. Which of the following is true regarding the similarities and differences in monopolistic competition and monopoly?
   a. The monopolist faces a downward-sloping demand curve while the monopolistic competitor faces an elastic demand curve.
   b. The monopolist makes economic profits in the long run while the monopolistic competitor makes zero economic profits in the long run.
   c. Both the monopolist and the monopolistic competitor operate at the efficient scale.
   d. The monopolist charges a price above marginal cost while the monopolistic competitor charges a price equal to marginal cost.

4. In the short run, if the price is above average total cost in a monopolistically competitive market, the firm makes
   a. losses and firms enter the market.
   b. losses and firms exit the market.
   c. profits and firms enter the market.
   d. profits and firms exit the market.

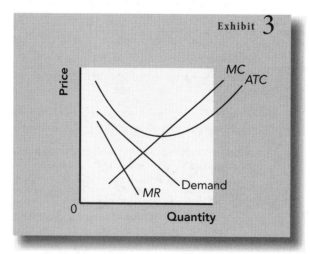

Exhibit 3

5. If the monopolistic competitor described by Exhibit 3 is producing at the profit-maximizing (loss-minimizing) level of output, it
   a. is generating losses.
   b. is generating profits.
   c. is generating zero profits.
   d. could be generating either profits or losses depending on what quantity it chooses to produce.

6. The monopolistically competitive market shown in Exhibit 3 will, in the long run,
    a. attract new producers into the market, which will shift the demand faced by incumbent firms to the right.
    b. attract new producers into the market, which will shift the demand faced by incumbent firms to the left.
    c. cause producers to exit the market, which will shift the demand faced by incumbent firms to the right.
    d. cause producers to exit the market, which will shift the demand faced by incumbent firms to the left.

7. Which of the following is true regarding the production and pricing decisions of monopolistically competitive firms? Monopolistically competitive firms choose the quantity at which marginal cost equals
    a. average total cost and then use the demand curve to determine the price consistent with this quantity.
    b. marginal revenue and then use the demand curve to determine the price consistent with this quantity.
    c. average total cost and then use the supply curve to determine the price consistent with this quantity.
    d. marginal revenue and then use the supply curve to determine the price consistent with this quantity.

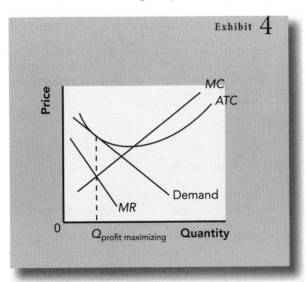

Exhibit 4

8. Exhibit 4 depicts a monopolistically competitive firm
    a. generating profits in the short run.
    b. generating losses in the short run.
    c. generating zero profits in the long run.
    d. It is impossible to determine from this graph whether the firm is generating profits or losses.

9. Which of the following is *true* with regard to monopolistically competitive firms' scale of production and pricing decisions? Monopolistically competitive firms produce
    a. at the efficient scale and charge a price equal to marginal cost.
    b. at the efficient scale and charge a price above marginal cost.
    c. with excess capacity and charge a price equal to marginal cost.
    d. with excess capacity and charge a price above marginal cost.

10. One source of inefficiency in monopolistic competition is that
    a. because price is above marginal cost, surplus is redistributed from buyers to sellers.
    b. because price is above marginal cost, some units are not produced that buyers value in excess of the cost of production and this causes a deadweight loss.
    c. monopolistically competitive firms produce beyond their efficient scale.
    d. monopolistically competitive firms earn economic profits in the long run.

11. When firms enter a monopolistically competitive market and the business-stealing externality is larger than the product-variety externality, then
     a. there are too many firms in the market and market efficiency could be increased if firms exited the market.
     b. there are too few firms in the market and market efficiency could be increased with additional entry.
     c. the number of firms in the market is optimal and the market is efficient.
     d. the only way to improve efficiency in this market is for the government to regulate it like a natural monopoly.

12. The use of the word "competition" in the name of the market structure called "monopolistic competition" refers to the fact that
     a. monopolistically competitive firms charge prices equal to the minimum of their average total cost just like competitive firms.
     b. monopolistically competitive firms face a downward-sloping demand curve just like competitive firms.
     c. the products are differentiated in a monopolistically competitive market just like in a competitive market.
     d. there are many sellers in a monopolistically competitive market and there is free entry and exit in the market just like a competitive market.

13. The use of the word "monopoly" in the name of the market structure called "monopolistic competition" refers to the fact that
     a. a monopolistically competitive firm faces a downward-sloping demand curve for its differentiated product and so does a monopolist.
     b. monopolistically competitive markets have free entry and exit just like a monopolistic market.
     c. monopolistically competitive firms charge prices equal to their marginal costs just like monopolists.
     d. monopolistically competitive firms produce beyond their efficient scale and so do monopolists.

14. Which of the following firms is most likely to spend a large percentage of their revenue on advertising?
     a. the manufacturer of an undifferentiated commodity
     b. a perfect competitor
     c. the manufacturer of an industrial product
     d. the producer of a highly differentiated consumer product
     e. the producer of a low-quality product that costs the same to produce as a similar high-quality product.

15. For the economy as a whole, what percentage of firm revenue is spent on advertising?
     a. 1 percent
     b. 2 percent
     c. 4 percent
     d. 6 percent
     e. 10 percent

16. Which of the following is *not* put forth as a criticism of advertising and brand names?
     a. Advertising manipulates people's tastes to create a desire that otherwise would not exist.
     b. Advertising increases competition, which causes unnecessary bankruptcies and layoffs.
     c. Advertising increases brand loyalty, causes demand to be more inelastic, and thus, increases markup over marginal cost.
     d. Brand names cause consumers to perceive differences that do not exist between goods.
     e. All of the above are criticisms of advertising and brand names.

17. Expensive television commercials that appear to provide no specific information about the product being advertised
     a. are most likely used by firms that are perfect competitors.
     b. should be banned by regulators because they add to the cost of the product without providing the consumer with any useful information about the product.
     c. may be useful because they provide a signal to the consumer about the quality of the product.
     d. only affect the buying habits of irrational consumers.

18. Which of the following is *not* an argument put forth by economists in support of the use of advertising?
    a. Advertising provides information to customers about prices, new products, and location of retail outlets.
    b. Advertising provides a creative outlet for artists and writers.
    c. Advertising increases competition.
    d. Advertising provides new firms with the means to attract customers from existing firms.

19. Defenders of the use of brand names argue that brand names
    a. provide information about the quality of the product.
    b. give firms incentive to maintain high quality.
    c. are useful even in socialist economies such as the former Soviet Union.
    d. do all of the above.

20. Which of the following firms has the least incentive to advertise?
    a. a manufacturer of home heating and air conditioning
    b. a manufacturer of breakfast cereal
    c. a wholesaler of crude oil
    d. a restaurant

Advanced Critical Thinking

You are watching a sporting event on television. An advertisement featuring LaBron James (a famous basketball player) is broadcast during a commercial break. In the ad, LaBron James does nothing but shoot basketballs. He never speaks. There is no written copy. At the end of the advertisement, the Nike "swoosh" appears on the screen along with the words "Nike" and "LaBron James Signature Basketball Shoes." A short time earlier, you read in a newspaper that LaBron James received $40 million to be the spokesperson for Nike basketball shoes.

1. A friend watches the Nike advertisement with you and says, "What a waste of society's resources. I didn't learn anything about Nike basketball shoes from that ad. I think there should be government regulations requiring ads to be informative in some way." Explain to your friend what you did learn from LaBron James' presence in this ad.

   _____

   _____

   _____

   _____

   _____

2. Did the use of the Nike name and the Nike "swoosh" provide any information? Explain.

   _____

   _____

   _____

   _____

3. In general, does advertising tend to decrease competition and raise prices to consumers or increase competition and reduce prices to consumers? Why?

   _____

   _____

   _____

Solutions

Terms and Definitions

__4__ Oligopoly

__3__ Monopolistic competition

__1__ Free entry

__2__ Efficient scale

Practice Problems

1. a. Monopoly, only one firm from which to purchase.

   b. Monopolistic competition, many firms each selling differentiated products.

   c. Monopoly, only one firm can produce it due to copyright laws.

   d. Oligopoly, few firms (Fuji, Kodak) selling similar products.

   e. Perfect competition, many firms selling identical products.

   f. Monopolistic competition, many firms each selling differentiated products.

   g. Oligopoly, few firms (Goodyear, Firestone, Michelin) selling very similar products.

   h. Monopoly, only one firm from which to purchase.

   i. Monopolistic competition, many firms each selling differentiated products.

   j. Oligopoly, few firms (Kellogg Company, Post, General Mills, Quaker Oats) selling similar products.

   k. Perfect competition, many firms selling identical products.

   l. Oligopoly, few airlines from which to choose at any one airport, similar product.

   Note: Although monopoly and competition are more easily distinguished, the line between oligopoly and monopolistic competition is not as sharp. For example, *b* might be considered to be an oligopoly because there are relatively few publishers and economic textbooks may be considered to be very similar, and *j* might be considered to be monopolistic competition if the products are considered to be differentiated, and so on.

2. a. See Exhibit 5.

Exhibit 5

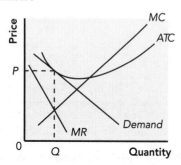

b. No. Because there is free entry, profit causes firms to enter the industry, which reduces the existing demand faced by profitable firms until $P = ATC$ and profit is zero.

c. No. Profits attract new firms, which reduce the demand for an incumbent firm's product to the point where its demand is tangent to its ATC curve causing $P = ATC$ and profits equal zero. Because the tangency of demand and ATC is in the negatively sloping portion of ATC, the firm is operating at less than the efficient scale. If Mario's expanded output, MC would exceed MR and $P < ATC$ so profits would be negative.

d. See Exhibit 6. The deadweight loss occurs because firms fail to produce units that the buyer values in excess of the cost of production. That is, the loss is due to the reduced quantity in monopolistic competition.

Exhibit 6

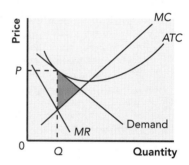

e. See Exhibit 7. No. Profits attract entry, which reduces the demand faced by each firm to the point where it is again tangent to its ATC curve.

Exhibit 7

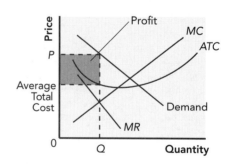

3. a. Bayer Aspirin, because it is a branded or differentiated consumer good.

   b. The firm generating high-quality ice cream because advertising is more profitable if there are repeat buyers.

   c. John Deere lawn mower division because lawn mowers are sold to consumers as opposed to industry.

d. The bakery of Old Home Wheat Bread because it is differentiated. Wheat is not differentiated.

Short-Answer Questions

1. Oligopoly and monopolistic competition. Oligopoly is a market structure in which only a few sellers offer similar or identical products. Monopolistic competition is when many firms sell products that are similar but not identical.

2. Oligopoly, because there are few firms and the products are similar or identical.

3. Both market structures involve a differentiated product so firms face downward-sloping demand curves, equate *MC* and *MR*, and charge a price above *MC*.

4. Both market structures have many sellers and free entry and exit. Thus, profits are driven to zero in the long run.

5. It chooses the quantity by equating *MC* and *MR* and then uses the demand curve to find the price that is consistent with this quantity (just like a monopolist).

6. No. Profits attract new firms to the market, which reduces the demand faced by each of the incumbent firms until the demand faced by each firm is tangent to its *ATC* curve and profits are zero.

7. Monopolistic competition has excess capacity because monopolistically competitive firms produce at less than efficient scale and they charge prices in excess of marginal cost. Competitive firms produce at the efficient scale and charge prices equal to marginal cost.

8. No. Because price exceeds marginal cost, there is underproduction—some units that buyers value in excess of marginal cost are not produced. Also, the number of firms in the market may not be ideal because entry into the industry creates the positive product-variety externality and the negative business-stealing externality.

9. Advertising provides information about prices, new products, and the location of retail outlets; provides new firms with the means to attract customers from existing firms; and can be a signal of high quality. Brand names provide information about the quality of the product and provide incentive for the producer to maintain high quality.

10. The use of advertising and brand names manipulates people's tastes, impedes competition, and creates brand loyalty when there is no difference among goods. This allows for a higher markup over marginal cost and increases inefficiency.

True/False Questions

1. F; monopolistic competition is a market structure in which many firms sell differentiated products.

2. T

3. F; monopolistic competitors produce in the downward-sloping portion of their *ATC* curve where the *ATC* curve is tangent to the demand curve faced by the firm.

4. T

5. T

6. T

7. F; monopolistically competitive firms charge a price equal to *ATC*.

8. F; it is not clear how one would regulate a monopolistically competitive firm in order to increase efficiency.

9. T

10. F; advertising may increase competition, which could increase social welfare.

11. T

12. T

13. F; brand names give the firm incentive to maintain high quality.

14. T

15. F; monopolistically competitive firms have excess capacity while competitive firms produce at the efficient scale.

Multiple-Choice Questions

1. c
2. d
3. b
4. c
5. a
6. c
7. b
8. c
9. d
10. b
11. a
12. d
13. a
14. d
15. b
16. b
17. c
18. b
19. d
20. c

Advanced Critical Thinking

1. Viewers learned that Nike was willing to spend an enormous amount of money to promote its new line of LaBron James basketball shoes. This signals that their market research suggests that they have a high-quality product that will generate repeat sales.

2. Yes. The use of the brand name provides information that the product is of high quality and that the firm has incentive to maintain high quality.

Nike is a multibillion-dollar company that would not want to risk losing existing sales of shoes and sportswear by marketing poor-quality basketball shoes marked with the Nike brand name.

3. Advertising tends to increase competition and decrease prices to consumers because it often provides information about prices, the existence of new products, and the location of retail outlets and it provides new firms with the means to attract customers from existing firms.

Chapter 17
Oligopoly

Goals
In this chapter you will

- Examine what outcomes are possible when a market is an oligopoly
- Learn about the prisoners' dilemma and how it applies to oligopoly and other issues
- Consider how the antitrust laws try to foster competition in oligopolistic markets

Outcomes
After accomplishing these goals, you should be able to

- Describe the conditions under which an oligopolistic market generates the same outcome as a monopolistic market
- Show why the outcome of the prisoners' dilemma may change if the game is repeated
- Show why some business practices that appear to reduce competition may have a legitimate business purpose

Chapter Overview

Context and Purpose

Chapter 17 is the final chapter in a five-chapter sequence dealing with firm behavior and the organization of industry. Chapters 14 and 15 discussed the two extreme forms of market structure—competition and monopoly. The market structure that lies between competition and monopoly is known as *imperfect competition*. There are two types of imperfect competition—monopolistic competition, which we addressed in the previous chapter, and oligopoly, which is the topic of the current chapter.

The purpose of Chapter 17 is to address *oligopoly*—a market structure in which only a few sellers offer similar or identical products. Because there are only a few sellers in an oligopolistic market, oligopolistic firms are interdependent while competitive firms are not. That is, in a competitive market, the decisions of one firm have no impact on the other firms in the market while in an oligopolistic market, the decisions of any one firm may affect the pricing and production decisions of the other firms in the market.

Chapter Review

Introduction   The market structure that lies between competition and monopoly is known as imperfect competition. One type of imperfectly competitive market is oligopoly—a market structure in which only a few sellers offer similar or identical products. Oligopoly differs from competition because in a competitive market, the decisions of one firm have no impact on the other firms in the market while in an oligopolistic market, the decisions of any one firm may affect the pricing and production decisions of other firms in the market. Oligopolistic firms are interdependent. Game theory is the study of how people behave in strategic situations. Strategic situations are when decision makers must consider how others might respond to their actions.

Markets with Only a Few Sellers

A *duopoly* is an oligopoly with only two firms. If a market were perfectly competitive, the price of output would equal marginal cost. If a market were monopolistic, the profit-maximizing price would exceed marginal cost and the result would be inefficient.

Collusion is an agreement among firms in a market about quantities to produce or prices to charge. A cartel is a group of firms acting in unison. If duopolists collude and form a cartel, the market solution is the same as if it were served by a monopolist and the two firms divide the monopoly profits.

Oligopolists may fail to cooperate because self-interest makes it difficult to agree on how to divide the profits or because antitrust laws prohibit collusion. Without a binding agreement, each oligopolist will maximize its profit given the production levels of the other firms. A Nash equilibrium is a situation in which economic actors interacting with one another each choose their best strategy given the strategies that all the other actors have chosen. A Nash equilibrium is a type of oligopolistic equilibrium. When oligopolists individually choose production levels to maximize individual profits, they produce a quantity that is greater than the level produced by monopoly but less than that produced by competition and they will charge a price that is less than the monopoly price but greater than the competitive price.

The larger the oligopoly (more firms), the more difficult it is for them to form a cartel and behave as a monopolist. If they each choose their own level of production to maximize individual profits, they will make the marginal decision of whether to produce an additional unit based on the following:

- *The output effect*: Because price is above marginal cost, selling one more unit at the going price will raise profit.
- *The price effect*: Raising production one unit will increase the total sold, but it will lower the price and the profit on all of the other units sold.

If the output effect exceeds the price effect, the oligopolist will produce another unit, and it will continue to expand output until these two effects balance. The greater the number of sellers in an oligopoly, the smaller the price effect because each individual firm's impact on the price is small. Thus, the level of output increases. As the number of sellers in an oligopoly grows larger, the price approaches marginal cost and the quantity approaches the socially efficient level. When there are a large number of firms, the price effect disappears altogether, and the market becomes competitive.

Unrestricted international trade increases the number of firms in domestic oligopolies and moves the outcome of the market closer to the competitive solution where prices are equal to marginal cost.

An example of a cartel is OPEC (Organization of Petroleum Exporting Countries), which limits the production of oil.

The Economics of Cooperation

Within the area of economic study known as game theory, the prisoners' dilemma is a particular "game" between two captured prisoners that illustrates why cooperation is difficult to maintain even when it is mutually beneficial. The game applies to oligopoly because oligopolistic firms would always be better off to cooperate yet they often do not.

An example of a prisoners' dilemma is the following: Two criminals are captured. If one confesses and the other does not, the confessor goes free while the other receives a long sentence. If both confess, they both receive an intermediate term. If neither confesses, they both receive a very short term. If the two could cooperate, the best strategy is for both of them to keep quiet. However, because they cannot guarantee cooperation after they are caught, the best strategy for each is to confess. That is, confessing is a dominant strategy—a strategy that is best for a player in a game regardless of the strategies chosen by the other players.

The prisoners' dilemma applies to oligopoly in the following manner: Two oligopolists are better off if they cooperate by keeping production low and sharing the monopoly profits. However, after the agreement is made, the dominant strategy for each is to cheat and produce more than they agreed to produce to enhance their individual profits. The result is that profits fall for both. Self-interest makes it difficult to maintain cooperation.

The prisoners' dilemma applies to the following:

- *Arms races:* Each country prefers to live in a safe world, but the dominant strategy is to increase armaments and the world is less safe.

- *Common resources:* Users of a common resource would find it more profitable to jointly limit their use of the resource, but the dominant strategy is to overuse the resource and joint profits fall.

Lack of cooperation in the cases previously described is harmful to society. However, lack of cooperation between oligopolists regarding the level of production may be bad for the oligopolists but it is good from the standpoint of society as a whole.

Although cooperation is difficult to maintain, it is not impossible. If the game is repeated, the prisoners' dilemma can be solved and agreements can be maintained. For example, oligopolies may include a penalty for violation of the agreement. If the penalty is that they all maintain high production forever if someone cheats, then all should maintain low production levels and share monopoly profits. If the game is played on a periodic basis (each week, month, or year new production levels are chosen), then a simple strategy of tit-for-tat generates the greatest likelihood of cooperation. *Tit-for-tat* is when a player in a game starts by cooperating and then does whatever the other player did last period. If the first player cooperated last period, then the second player should cooperate the next period. If the first player defected (cheated) last period, then the second player should cheat the next period, and so on.

Public Policy Toward Oligopolies

Because cooperating oligopolists reduce output and raise prices, policymakers try to induce firms in an oligopoly market to compete rather than cooperate. The Sherman Antitrust Act of 1890 makes agreements to not compete (to reduce quantities or raise prices) a criminal conspiracy. The Clayton Act of 1914 allows individuals harmed by such agreements the right to sue for triple damages. Price fixing clearly reduces economic welfare and is illegal.

There is some disagreement over the use of antitrust laws against some business practices that appear like price fixing. For example:

- *Resale price maintenance* is when a manufacturer requires retailers to charge a certain price. This appears to prevent retailers from competing on price. However, some economists defend the practice as legitimate because (1) if the manufacturer has market power, it is at wholesale not retail, and the manufacturer would not gain from eliminating competition at the retail level, and (2) resale price maintenance stops discount retailers from free riding on the services provided by full-service retailers.

- *Predatory pricing* occurs when a firm cuts prices with the intention of driving competitors out of the market so that the firm can become a monopolist and later raise prices. Some economists think that this behavior is unlikely because it hurts the firm that is engaged in predatory pricing the most.

- *Tying* occurs when a manufacturer bundles two products together and sells them for one price. Courts argue that tying gives the firm more market power by connecting a weak product with a strong product. Some economists disagree. They suggest that it allows the firm to price discriminate, which may actually increase efficiency. Tying remains controversial.

Conclusion

Oligopolies will look more like a competitive market if there are a large number of firms and more like a monopoly if there are a small number of firms. The prisoners' dilemma shows why cooperation is difficult to maintain even when it is in the best interest of the oligopolists. The use of antitrust laws against price fixing improves economic efficiency but their use in other areas is more controversial.

Helpful Hints

1. Oligopoly lies between monopoly and perfect competition. If oligopolists are able to collude and form a cartel, the market solution is the same as that for a monopoly. If oligopolists are unable to collude and form a cartel, the production and pricing in the market depend on the number of firms. The fewer the number of firms, the more the result appears like monopoly where the price exceeds marginal cost and the quantity is below the efficient level. The greater the number of firms, the more the result appears like competition where the price equals marginal cost and the quantity is efficient.

Terms and Definitions

Choose a definition for each key term.

Key Terms	Definitions
_____ Oligopoly	1. The study of how people behave in strategic situations
_____ Game theory	2. A group of firms acting in unison
_____ Duopoly	3. An agreement among firms in a market about quantities to produce or prices to charge
_____ Collusion	4. A strategy that is best for a player in a game regardless of the strategies chosen by the other players
_____ Cartel	
_____ Nash equilibrium	5. A situation in which economic actors interacting with one another each choose their best strategy given the strategies that all the other actors have chosen
_____ Prisoners' dilemma	
_____ Dominant strategy	6. An oligopoly with only two firms
	7. A market structure in which only a few sellers offer similar or identical products
	8. A particular "game" between two captured prisoners that illustrates why cooperation is difficult to maintain even when it is mutually beneficial

Problems and Short-Answer Questions

1. The following information describes the demand schedule for a unique type of apple. This type of apple can only be produced by two firms because they own the land on which these unique trees spontaneously grow. As a result, the marginal cost of production is zero for these duopolists, causing total revenue to equal profit.

   a. Complete the following table.

Price per Bushel	Quantity (in bushels)	Total Revenue (profit)
$12	0	_____
11	5	_____
10	10	_____
9	15	_____
8	20	_____
7	25	_____
6	30	_____
5	35	_____
4	40	_____
3	45	_____
2	50	_____
1	55	_____
0	60	_____

   b. If the market were perfectly competitive, what price and quantity would be generated by this market? Explain.

   _____

   _____

   c. If these two firms colluded and formed a cartel, what price and quantity would be generated by this market, what is the level of profit generated by the market, and what is the level of profit generated by each firm?

   _____

   _____

   d. If one firm cheats and produces one additional increment (five units) of production, what is the level of profit generated by each firm?

   _____

   e. If both firms cheat and each produces one additional increment (five units) of production (compared to the cooperative solution), what is the level of profit generated by each firm?

   _____

f. If both firms are cheating and producing one additional increment of output (five additional units compared to the cooperative solution), will either firm choose to produce an additional increment (five more units)? Why or why not? What is the value of the Nash equilibrium in this duopoly market?

_____

_____

g. Compare the competitive equilibrium to the Nash equilibrium. In which situation is society better off? Explain.

_____

_____

_____

h. What would happen to the price and quantity in this market (qualitatively) if an additional firm were able to grow these unique apples?

_____

_____

i. Use the data from the duopoly example presented here to fill in the boxes of the prisoners' dilemma. Place the value of the profits earned by each duopolist in the appropriate box in Exhibit 1.

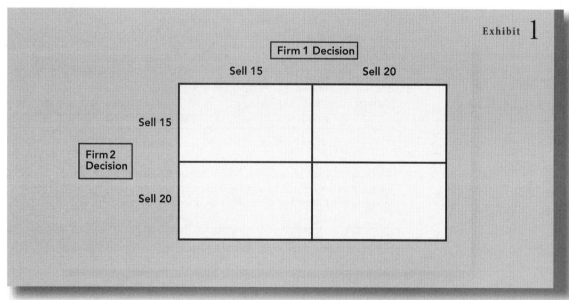

Exhibit **1**

Firm 1 Decision

Sell 15   Sell 20

Firm 2 Decision

Sell 15

Sell 20

j. What is the solution to this prisoners' dilemma? Explain.

_____

_____

k. What might the solution be if the participants were able to repeat the "game"? Why? What simple strategy might they use to maintain their cartel?

_____

_____

2. Suppose High-Tech Software sells two products—a word-processing package and a spreadsheet package. Suppose that the business community values the word-processing package at $100 per unit and the spreadsheet package at $250 per unit while the university community values the word-processing package at $125 and the spreadsheet at $200. (Assume that the marginal cost of each unit is zero.)

   a. What are the profit-maximizing prices that High-Tech should charge if they sell each product separately and what is the total price of the two goods?

_____

_____

   b. If High-Tech is able to engage in tying, what is the profit-maximizing price for the two products as a bundle?

_____

   c. Should this be legal?

_____

_____

Short-Answer Questions

1. What is the outcome in an oligopolistic market if the oligopolists collude and form a cartel? Explain.

_____

_____

2. Suppose a group of oligopolists does not collude but instead reaches a Nash equilibrium. What price and quantity will result in this oligopolist market when compared to the monopolistic or competitive result?

_____

_____

3. Referring to question 2 above, what would happen to the price and quantity in the Nash equilibrium if an additional firm were to join the oligopoly? Why?

_____

_____

4. If oligopolists would be better off if they collude, why do they so often fail to cooperate?

_____

_____

5. Is it better for society as a whole if oligopolists cooperate? Explain. What measures do we take to try to prevent cooperation between oligopolists?

_____

_____

6. What is predatory pricing? Do economists think that predatory pricing is commonly employed as a profitable business strategy? Why or why not?

_____

_____

Self-Test

True/False Questions

_____ 1. An oligopoly is a market structure in which many firms sell products that are similar but not identical.

_____ 2. The market for crude oil is an example of an oligopolistic market.

_____ 3. The unique feature of an oligopoly market is that the actions of one seller have a significant impact on the profits of all of the other sellers in the market.

_____ 4. When firms cooperate with one another, it is generally good for society as a whole.

_____ 5. When firms cooperate with one another, it is generally good for the cooperating firms.

_____ 6. When oligopolists collude and form a cartel, the outcome in the market is similar to that generated by a perfectly competitive market.

_____ 7. The price and quantity generated by a Nash equilibrium is closer to the competitive solution than the price and quantity generated by a cartel.

_____ 8. The greater the number of firms in the oligopoly, the more the outcome of the market looks like that generated by a monopoly.

_____ 9. Cooperation is easily maintained in an oligopoly because cooperation maximizes each individual firm's profits.

_____ 10. The prisoners' dilemma demonstrates why it is difficult to maintain cooperation even when cooperation is mutually beneficial.

_____ 11. There is a constant tension in an oligopoly between cooperation and self-interest because after an agreement to reduce production is reached, it is profitable for each individual firm to cheat and produce more.

_____ 12. The dominant strategy for an oligopolist is to cooperate with the group and maintain low production regardless of what the other oligopolists do.

_____ 13. Antitrust laws require manufacturers to engage in resale price maintenance.

_____ 14. Predatory pricing occurs when a firm cuts prices with the intention of driving competitors out of the market so that the firm can become a monopolist and later raise prices.

_____ 15. If a prisoners' dilemma game is repeated, the participants are more likely to independently maximize their profits and reach a Nash equilibrium.

Multiple-Choice Questions

1. The market for hand tools (such as hammers and screwdrivers) is dominated by Black & Decker, Stanley, and Craftsman. This market is best described as
   a. competitive.
   b. a monopoly.
   c. an oligopoly.
   d. a duopoly.

2. A market structure in which many firms sell products that are similar but not identical is known as
   a. perfect competition.
   b. monopoly.
   c. oligopoly.
   d. none of the above.

3. If oligopolists engage in collusion and successfully form a cartel, the market outcome is
   a. the same as if it were served by a monopoly.
   b. the same as if it were served by competitive firms.
   c. efficient because cooperation improves efficiency.
   d. known as a Nash equilibrium.

4. Suppose an oligopolist individually maximizes its profits. When calculating profits, if the output effect exceeds the price effect on the marginal unit of production, then the oligopolist
   a. has maximized profits.
   b. should produce more units.
   c. should produce fewer units.
   d. should exit the industry.
   e. is in a Nash equilibrium.

5. As the number of sellers in an oligopoly grows larger, an oligopolistic market looks more like
   a. a monopoly.
   b. a duopoly.
   c. a competitive market.
   d. a collusion solution.

6. When an oligopolist individually chooses its level of production to maximize its profits, it produces an output that is
   a. more than the level produced by a monopoly and less than the level produced by a competitive market.
   b. less than the level produced by a monopoly and more than the level produced by a competitive market.
   c. more than the level produced by either a monopoly or a competitive market.
   d. less than the level produced by either a monopoly or a competitive market.

7. When an oligopolist individually chooses its level of production to maximize its profits, it charges a price that is
   a. more than the price charged by a monopoly and less than the price charged by a competitive market.
   b. less than the price charged by a monopoly and more than the price charged by a competitive market.
   c. more than the price charged by either a monopoly or a competitive market.
   d. less than the price charged by either a monopoly or a competitive market.

8. As the number of sellers in an oligopoly increases,
    a. collusion is more likely to occur because a larger number of firms can place pressure on any firm that defects.
    b. output in the market tends to fall because each firm must cut back on production.
    c. the price in the market moves further from marginal cost.
    d. the price in the market moves closer to marginal cost.

9. A situation in which oligopolists interacting with one another each choose their best strategy given the strategies that all the other oligopolists have chosen is known as a
    a. collusion solution.
    b. cartel.
    c. Nash equilibrium.
    d. dominant strategy.

Use the table below to answer questions 10 through 13. The table shows the demand schedule for tickets to watch amateur baseball games in a medium-sized town. The city provides the ballparks, and the players play for free, so the marginal cost of providing the games is zero. The city has authorized two companies to provide baseball games in two stadiums, and the public considers the games in each stadium to be equivalent.

Price	Quantity
$12	0
11	200
10	400
9	600
8	800
7	1,000
6	1,200
5	1,400
4	1,600
3	1,800
2	2,000
1	2,200
0	2,400

10. Under competition, the price and quantity in this market would be
    a. $8; 800.
    b. $6; 1,200.
    c. $4; 1,600.
    d. $2; 2,000.
    e. $0; 2,400.

11. If the duopolists in this baseball market collude and successfully form a cartel, what is the price that each should charge in order to maximize profits?
    a. $8
    b. $7
    c. $6
    d. $5
    e. $4

12. If the duopolists in this baseball market collude and successfully form a cartel, how much profit will *each* earn?
    a. $2,700
    b. $3,200
    c. $3,500
    d. $3,600
    e. $7,200

13. Suppose that the duopolists are unable to collude. How much profit will *each* earn when the market reaches a Nash equilibrium?
    a. $2,700
    b. $3,200
    c. $3,500
    d. $3,600
    e. $7,200

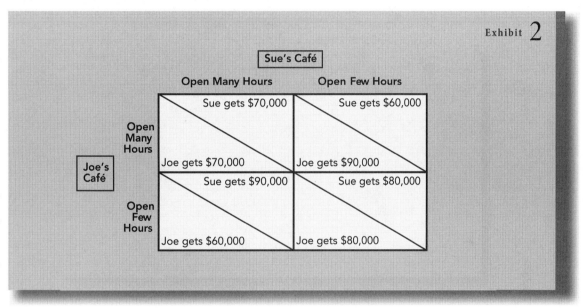

Use the prisoners' dilemma game in Exhibit 2 to answer questions 14 and 15. It shows the possible profits for duopolists that are the only two restaurants in town. Each firm can choose how many hours to be open for business.

14. The dominant strategy for Sue and Joe is for
    a. both to be open for many hours.
    b. both to be open for a few hours.
    c. Sue to be open for many hours while Joe is open for few hours.
    d. Sue to be open for few hours while Joe is open for many hours.
    e. There is no dominant strategy in this prisoners' dilemma game.

15. Suppose Sue and Joe agreed to collude and jointly maximize their profits. If Sue and Joe were to be able to repeatedly play the game shown earlier and they agreed on a penalty for defecting from their agreement, what is the likely outcome of the game?
    a. Both are open for many hours.
    b. Both are open for a few hours.
    c. Sue is open for many hours while Joe is open for few hours.
    d. Sue is open for few hours while Joe is open for many hours.

16. Many economists argue that resale price maintenance
    a. is price fixing and, therefore, is prohibited by law.
    b. enhances the market power of the producer.
    c. has a legitimate purpose of stopping discount retailers from free riding on the services provided by full-service retailers.
    d. is both *a* and *b*.

17. Collusion is difficult for an oligopoly to maintain
    a. because antitrust laws make collusion illegal.
    b. because, in the case of oligopoly, self-interest is in conflict with cooperation.
    c. if additional firms enter of the oligopoly.
    d. for all of the above reasons.

Use the following information to answer questions 18 and 19: Suppose that ABC Publishing sells an economics textbook and an accompanying study guide. Bob is willing to pay $75 for the text and $15 for the study guide. Mary is willing to spend $60 for the text and $25 for the study guide. Suppose both the book and study guide have a zero marginal cost of production.

18. If ABC Publishing charges separate prices for both products, its best strategy is to charge prices that, when combined, total
    a. $60.
    b. $75.
    c. $80.
    d. $85.
    e. $90.

19. If ABC Publishing engages in tying, its best strategy is to charge a combined price of
    a. $60.
    b. $75.
    c. $80.
    d. $85.
    e. $90.

20. Laws that make it illegal for firms to conspire to raise prices or reduce production are known as
    a. pro-competition laws.
    b. antitrust laws.
    c. antimonopoly laws.
    d. anticollusion laws.
    e. all of the above.

Advanced Critical Thinking

You are watching television. An advertisement begins, "Come on down to Warehouse Electronics. We've got deals so great you won't believe it! National brand 13-inch color television sets for $99. The price is so low that we can't tell you the name of the manufacturer!"

1. Why would Warehouse Electronics be unable to reveal the name of the manufacturer when it advertises its television sets for an unusually low price?

   _____

   _____

   _____

2. Although this activity appears like price fixing, is the objective of this practice to reduce competition? Why?

   _____

   _____

   _____

3. Why would the manufacturer place this type of restriction on the retailers that sell its products?

   _____

   _____

   _____

Solutions

Terms and Definitions

_7_ Oligopoly

_1_ Game theory

_6_ Duopoly

_3_ Collusion

_2_ Cartel

_5_ Nash equilibrium

_8_ Prisoners' dilemma

_4_ Dominant strategy

Practice Problems

1. a.

Price per Bushel	Quantity (in bushels)	Total Revenue (profit)
$12	0	$0
11	5	55
10	10	100
9	15	135
8	20	160
7	25	175
6	30	180
5	35	175
4	40	160
3	45	135
2	50	100
1	55	55
0	60	0

b. In a competitive market, competition reduces the price until it equals marginal cost (which is zero in this case), therefore $P = \$0$ and $Q = 60$.

c. These duopolists would behave as a monopolist, produce at the level that maximizes profit, and agree to divide the production levels and profit. Therefore, $P = \$6$, $Q = 30$ for the market. Profit = $\$6 \times 30 = \$180$. Each firm produces 15 units at $6 and receives profit of $90 (half of the $180).

d. Cheating firm: $20 \times \$5 = \$100$, other firm: $15 \times \$5 = \$75$.

e. Each firm: $20 \times \$4 = \$80$.

f. No, because the profit would fall for the cheater to $25 \times \$3 = \$75$, which is below $80 profit from part *e* above. Therefore, the Nash equilibrium is each firm producing 20 units (40 for the market) at a price of $4, creating $160 of profit for the market, and each duopolist receives $80 profit.

g. The Nash equilibrium has a higher price ($4 compared to $0) and a smaller quantity (40 units compared to 60 units). Society is better off with competitive equilibrium.

h. The new Nash equilibrium would have a lower price and a larger quantity. It would move toward the competitive solution.

i. See Exhibit 3.

Exhibit 3

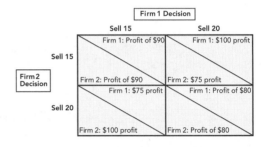

j. The dominant strategy for each is to cheat and sell 20 units because each firm's profit is greater when it sells 20 units regardless of whether the other firm sells 15 or 20 units.

k. They might be able to maintain the cooperative (monopoly) production level of 30 units and each produce 15 units because if the game is repeated, the participants can devise a penalty for cheating. The simplest penalty is "tit-for-tat."

2. a. Word-processing price = $100, spreadsheet price = $200, total = $300.

b. If tying the two together, price = $325.

c. Maybe, because it may be just a method of price discrimination that, recall, increases total surplus (is more efficient) but it moves surplus from the consumer to the producer.

Short-Answer Questions

1. The outcome is the same as if the market were served by a monopolist. Monopoly profits are divided among the firms, and production levels are limited by agreement to the level that a monopoly would produce.

2. The price will be lower than monopoly but higher than competition. The quantity sold will be greater than monopoly but less than competition.

3. The price would fall and the quantity sold would rise. This is because with the addition of another firm, the individual firm's impact on the price is reduced, which causes the output effect to exceed the price effect and the profit-maximizing output level of the group is increased. As members are added, the outcome approaches a competitive solution.

4. Once an agreement to reduce production is made, it is always profitable for the individual firm to cheat and produce in excess of the agreement regardless of whether the others cheat or maintain the agreement. Cheating is a dominant strategy. This is the prisoners' dilemma.

5. It is better if they do not cooperate because the Nash equilibrium is closer to the efficient competitive solution than the monopoly solution would have been. Antitrust laws make it illegal for firms to make agreements not to compete.

6. It is a cut in prices intended to drive competitors out of the market in order to establish a monopoly. No, because it tends to hurt the predatory pricer more than the firm being attacked.

True/False Questions

1. F; an oligopoly is where a few sellers offer similar or identical products.

2. T

3. T

4. F; it raises prices above marginal cost and reduces output below the socially optimal level.

5. T

6. F; it is the same as that generated by a monopoly.

7. T

8. F; the greater the number of firms, the more the market approaches the competitive solution.

9. F; cooperation maximizes the profits of the group and the individual firms if none of the oligopolists violates the agreement. However, once the agreement is made, an individual firm will increase its profits if it cheats and produces more.

10. T

11. T

12. F; the dominant strategy is to increase production regardless of the choices of the other firms.

13. F; sometimes courts view retail price maintenance as price fixing and declare it illegal.

14. T

15. F; repeated games are more likely to generate cooperation because a penalty for cheating can be enforced.

Multiple-Choice Questions

1. c
2. d
3. a
4. b
5. c
6. a
7. b
8. d
9. c
10. e
11. c
12. d
13. b
14. a
15. b
16. c
17. d
18. b
19. d
20. b

Advanced Critical Thinking

1. The manufacturer may be engaging in "resale price maintenance" with its retailers (including Warehouse Electronics). This may restrict the retailer's right to advertise a price below the suggested retail price for the product.

2. No, because any reduction in competition at the retail level generates market power for the retailer and fewer units will be sold. This is not in the interest of the manufacturer.

3. The purpose is to stop discount retailers from free riding on the services provided by full-service retailers—retailers with a knowledgeable sales force, a repair shop, and so on.

Chapter 18
The Markets for the Factors of Production

Goals
In this chapter you will

- Analyze the labor demand of competitive, profit-maximizing firms

- Consider the household decisions that lie behind labor supply

- Learn why equilibrium wages equal the value of the marginal product of labor

- Consider how the other factors of production— land and capital—are compensated

- Examine how a change in the supply of one factor alters the earnings of all the factors

Outcomes
After accomplishing these goals, you should be able to

- Explain why the labor-demand curve is the value-of-the-marginal-product curve for labor

- Explain why the labor-supply curve is usually upward sloping

- Explain why a competitive firm maximizes profit when it hires labor to the point where the wage equals the value of the marginal product of labor

- Demonstrate the similarity between the labor market and the market for other factors of production

- Explain why the change in the supply of one factor alters the value of the marginal product of the other factors

Chapter Overview

Context and Purpose

Chapter 18 is the first chapter in a three-chapter sequence that addresses the economics of labor markets. Chapter 18 develops and analyzes the markets for the factors of production—labor, land, and capital. Chapter 19 builds on Chapter 18 and explains in more detail why some workers earn more than others do. Chapter 20 addresses the distribution of income and the role the government can play in altering the distribution of income.

The purpose of Chapter 18 is to provide the basic theory for the analysis of factor markets—the markets for labor, land, and capital. As you might expect, we find that the wages earned by the factors of production depend on the supply and demand for the factor. What is new in our analysis is that the demand for a factor is a *derived demand*. That is, a firm's demand for a factor is determined by its decision to supply a good in another market.

Chapter Review

Introduction   The factors of production are the inputs used to produce goods and services. The most important inputs are labor, land, and capital. This chapter provides the basic theory for the analysis of factor markets. We will find that the supply and demand for a factor determine the wage earned by that factor. What is new in our analysis is that the demand for a factor is a *derived demand*. That is, a firm's demand for a factor is determined by its decision to supply a good in another market. In this chapter, we analyze the factor demand of competitive profit-maximizing firms.

The Demand for Labor

The wage of labor is determined by the supply and demand for labor. The demand for labor is a derived demand in that it depends on the firm's decision to supply output in another market. Suppose that a firm is *competitive* in both its output market and in the market for labor. Also, suppose that the firm is *profit-maximizing*. In order to derive the demand for labor, we first have to determine how the use of labor affects the amount of output the firm produces. A production function shows the relationship between the quantity of inputs used to make a good and the quantity of output of that good. Because rational decision makers think at the margin, we derive the marginal product of labor—the increase in the amount of output from an additional unit of labor holding all other inputs fixed—from the production function. Production functions exhibit diminishing marginal product, which is the property whereby the marginal product of an input declines as the quantity of the input increases.

The firm is concerned with the *value* of the output generated by each worker rather than the output itself. Thus, we calculate the value of the marginal product, which is the marginal product of an input times the price of the output. Another name for the value of the marginal product is *marginal revenue product*. Because the output is sold in a competitive market, the price is constant regardless of the amount produced and sold, and therefore, the *value* of the marginal product declines in concert with the decline in the marginal product as the quantity of the input increases.

Because the firm is also a competitor in the market for labor, it takes the wage as given. It is profitable for the firm to hire a worker if the value of the marginal product of that worker is greater than the wage. This analysis implies that:

- a competitive, profit-maximizing firm hires workers up to the point where the value of the marginal product of labor equals the wage, and

- the value-of-marginal-product curve *is* the labor-demand curve for a competitive, profit-maximizing firm.

Because the demand for labor is the value-of-marginal-product curve, the demand for labor shifts when the value of the marginal product of labor changes due to changes in the following:

- *The output price*: An increase in the price of output increases the value of the marginal product and shifts labor demand right.

- *Technological change*: An advance in technology typically raises the marginal product of labor and shifts labor demand right. *Labor-saving* technological change could shift labor demand left, but the evidence shows that most technological change is *labor-augmenting*, which shifts labor demand right. "Luddites" oppose technological progress because they mistakenly think it destroys jobs.

- *The supply of other factors*: An increase in the supply of a factor used with labor in production increases the marginal product of labor and shifts labor demand to the right.

For a competitive, profit-maximizing firm, the demand for a factor is closely related to its supply of output because the production function links inputs and output. If W is the wage, MC is marginal cost, and MPL is the marginal product of labor, then $MC = W/MPL$. Thus, diminishing marginal product is associated with increasing marginal cost. In terms of inputs, a profit-maximizing firm hires until the value of the marginal product of labor equals the wage or $P \times MPL = W$. Rearranging, we get $P = W/MPL$. Substituting MC for W/MPL from above, we get $P = MC$. Thus, when a competitive firm hires labor up to the point at which the value of the marginal product equals the wage, it also produces up to the point at which the price equals marginal cost.

The Supply of Labor

The supply of labor arises from individuals' trade-off between work and leisure. An upward-sloping labor-supply curve means that people respond to an increase in the wage by enjoying less leisure and working more hours. Although labor supply need not be upward sloping in all cases, for now we will assume that it is upward sloping.

The following events will cause the labor-supply curve to shift:

- *Changes in tastes*: Changes in attitudes toward working such that women are more likely to work outside the home will shift the supply of labor to the right.

- *Changes in alternative opportunities*: If better opportunities arise in alternative labor markets, labor supply will decrease in the market under consideration.

- *Immigration*: When immigrants come to the United States, the U.S. supply of labor shifts to the right.

Equilibrium in the Labor Market

In competitive labor markets:

- The wage adjusts to balance the supply and demand for labor, and
- The wage equals the value of the marginal product of labor.

As a result, any event that changes the supply or demand for labor must change the equilibrium wage and the value of the marginal product by the same amount because these must always be equal.

For example, suppose that immigration causes an increase in the supply of labor (supply of labor shifts right). This reduces the equilibrium wage, increases the quantity demanded of labor because it is profitable for firms to hire additional workers, and reduces the marginal product of labor (and the value of the marginal product of labor) as the number of workers employed rises. In the new equilibrium, both the wage and the value of the marginal product of labor have fallen.

Alternatively, suppose there is an increase in the demand for the output produced by firms in an industry. This causes an increase in the price of the good and increases the *value* of the marginal product of labor. This event increases the demand for labor (rightward shift in the labor-demand curve), increases the equilibrium wage, and increases employment. Again, the value of the marginal product of labor and the wage move together (both increase in this case). When there is a change in the demand for a firm's output, the prosperity of firms and their workers moves together.

Our analysis of labor demand shows that the wage equals the value of the marginal product of labor. Therefore, highly productive workers should earn more than less-productive workers. In addition, real wages should increase in relation to the increase in productivity. Statistics support this conclusion. When productivity grows quickly, real wages grow quickly. Since 1959, productivity has grown at 2.1 percent per year and real wages at 1.9 percent per year. Since 1995, productivity has grown at 2.6 percent per year and real wages have grown at 2.3 percent per year. The surge in productivity in the United States since 1995 may be due to the spread of computers and information technology.

A market with only a single buyer is called a *monopsony*. When a firm is a monopsonist in a labor market, the firm uses its market power to reduce the number of workers hired, reduce the wage it pays, and increase its profits. As in monopoly, the market is smaller than is socially optimal, which causes deadweight losses.

The Other Factors of Production: Land and Capital

A firm's factors of production fall into three categories—labor, land, and capital. Capital is the stock of equipment and structures used to produce goods and services. The *rental price* of a factor is the price one pays to use the factor for a limited period of time while the *purchase price* of a factor is the price one pays to own that factor indefinitely.

Because the wage is the rental price of labor, we can apply the theory of factor demand we used for the labor market to the markets for land and capital. For both land and capital, the firm increases the quantity hired until the value of the factor's marginal product equals the factor's price, and thus, the demand curve for each factor is the factor's value-of-marginal-product curve. As a result, labor, land, and capital each earn the value of their marginal contribution to the production process because each factor's rental price is equal to the value of its marginal product.

Capital is often owned by firms as opposed to being owned directly by households. Therefore, capital income is often paid first to a firm. Capital income is later paid to those households that have lent money to the firm in the form of *interest* and to those households that own stock in the firm in the form of *dividends*. Alternatively, the firm retains some of its capital income to buy more capital. This portion of capital income is known as *retained earnings*. Regardless of how capital income is allocated, its total value equals the value of the marginal product of capital.

The purchase price of land and capital is based on the stream of rental income it generates. Thus, the purchase price of land or capital depends on both the current and expected future value of the marginal product of that factor.

Because of diminishing returns, a factor in abundant supply has a low marginal product and a low price while a factor in scarce supply has a high marginal product and a high price. When the supply of a factor changes, however, it has an effect on other factor markets because factors are used together in production. For example, the destruction of capital in an industry increases the rental price of the remaining capital. In the labor market, the workers are now working with less capital, which reduces their marginal product. This reduces the demand for labor and reduces the wage of workers. In a real-world example, the bubonic plague reduced the labor force by one-third and increased the wage of the remaining scarce workers. This event decreased the rental price of land because the marginal product of land fell due to the reduction in workers available to farm the land.

Conclusion

The theory developed in this chapter of how labor, land, and capital are compensated is known as the *neoclassical theory of distribution*. It suggests that the amount earned by a factor depends on supply and demand and that the demand for a factor depends on its marginal productivity. In equilibrium, each factor earns the value of its marginal product. This theory is widely accepted.

Helpful Hints

1. Your text provides examples of the impact of an increase in the supply of labor and an increase in the demand for labor on the marginal product of labor and the wage. The same logic used in those examples can be applied to the cases of a decrease in the supply of labor or a decrease in the demand for labor. For example, a decrease in the supply of labor (leftward shift in the labor-supply curve) increases the equilibrium wage, decreases the quantity demanded of labor because it is profitable for firms to hire fewer workers, and increases the marginal product of labor (and the value of the marginal product of labor) as the number of workers employed decreases. In the new equilibrium, both the wage and the value of the marginal product of labor have risen. Alternatively, suppose there is a decrease in the demand for the output produced by firms in an industry. This causes a decrease in the price of the good and decreases the value of the marginal product of labor. This event decreases the demand for labor (leftward shift in the labor-demand curve), decreases the equilibrium wage, and decreases employment.

2. The categories of the factors of production are labor, land, and capital. In this context, land is more than just the land on which one might grow crops. Land is generally considered to be "nature's bounty" and is all forms of natural resources that have not yet been altered by people. This would include rivers, oil reserves, minerals, and land itself.

3. To see the impact of a change in the quantity employed of one factor on the earnings of a second factor, always look at the impact on the marginal product of the second factor. For example, an increase in the available capital will reduce the marginal product of capital and its rental rate. The increase in capital, however, will increase the marginal product of labor because workers have additional capital with which to work and their wages will rise accordingly.

Terms and Definitions

Choose a definition for each key term.

Key Terms

_____ Factors of production

_____ Derived demand

_____ Production function

_____ Marginal product of labor

_____ Diminishing marginal product

_____ Value of the marginal product

_____ Capital

_____ Rental price (of a factor)

Definitions

1. The property whereby the marginal product of an input declines as the quantity of the input increases

2. The equipment and structures used to produce goods and services

3. The inputs used to produce goods and services

4. The increase in the amount of output from an additional unit of labor

5. The relationship between the quantity of inputs used to make a good and the quantity of output of that good

6. The price a person pays to use a factor for a limited period of time

7. The marginal product of an input times the price of the output

8. The demand for a factor of production, which is derived from the firm's decision to supply another good

Problems and Short-Answer Questions

Practice Problems

1. Suppose that labor is the only variable input in the production process for a competitive profit-maximizing firm that produces coffee mugs. The firm's production function is shown below.

Labor (number of workers)	Output per Hour	Marginal Product of Labor	Value of *MPL* when *P* = $3	Value of *MPL* when *P* = $5
0	0			
1	9			
2	17			
3	24			
4	30			
5	35			
6	39			
7	42			
8	44			

a. Fill out columns three and four of the table above (the marginal product of labor and the value of the marginal product of labor when the price of output equals $3 per mug).

b. Suppose that the competitive wage for workers who can make coffee mugs is $19 per hour. How many workers should this firm hire? Why?

_____

_____

c. Suppose that schools that teach pottery skills increase the supply of workers who can make coffee mugs and that this event lowers the competitive wage for coffee mug workers to $13 per hour. How many workers should this firm hire? Why? Does this represent a shift in the firm's demand for labor or a movement along the firm's demand for labor? Explain.

_____

_____

_____

_____

d. Suppose there is an increase in the demand for coffee mugs and that the price of coffee mugs rises to $5 per mug. Fill out the last column of the table above to show the value of the marginal product of labor when the price of mugs is $5 per mug.

e. Suppose that the competitive wage for coffee mug workers remains at $13 per hour and the price of mugs is $5 per mug. How many workers should this firm now hire? Why? Does this represent a shift in the firm's demand for labor or a movement along the firm's demand for labor? Explain.

_____

_____

_____

_____

2. Suppose there is an increase in the demand for lumber, which raises the price of lumber.

a. Show the impact of the increase in the price of lumber on the market for lumberjacks in Exhibit 1.

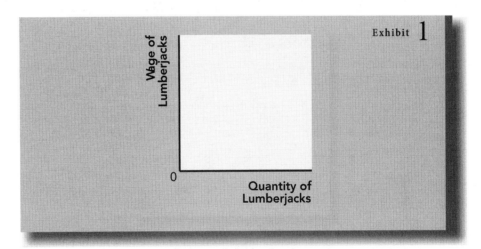

b. What did the increase in the price of lumber do to the value of the marginal product of lumberjacks and the wage of lumberjacks? Explain.

_____

_____

c. What will happen to the value of the marginal product and the rental rate for timberland and for capital that is used for cutting and shipping timber? Explain.

_____

_____

d. How has this event affected the prosperity of the firm and the owners of the factors of production employed by the firm? Explain.

_____

_____

3. Suppose that an enormous amount of forestland is cleared for agricultural use in Brazil.

a. Show the impact of this event on the market for agricultural land in Brazil in Exhibit 2. What has happened to the marginal product of land and the rental price of land in Brazil?

_____

_____

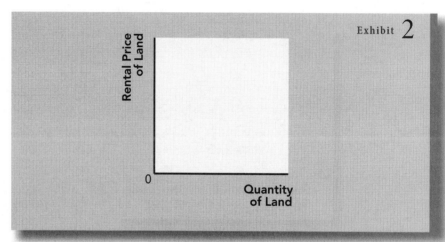

Exhibit 2

b. Show the impact of this event on the market for Brazilian farmworkers in Exhibit 3. What has happened to the marginal product of farm labor and the wage of farm labor?

_____

_____

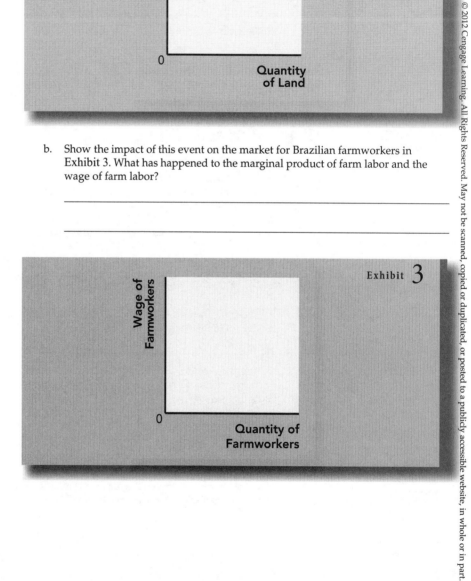

Exhibit 3

4. Describe the impact of the following events on the market for autoworkers in Tennessee. (Note that Honda operates a factory in Tennessee.)

a. Honda adds on to its factory in Tennessee.

_____

_____

b. *Consumer Reports* declares Honda to be the best-made automobile in its class.

_____

_____

_____

c. Refugees with manufacturing skills from war-torn Bosnia and Kosovo are relocated to Tennessee.

_____

_____

Short-Answer Questions

1. Why is the firm's demand curve for labor the value of the marginal product of labor?

_____

_____

_____

2. Why does the firm's demand curve for labor slope downward (that is, why does it slope negatively)?

_____

_____

_____

3. Prove that when a competitive firm hires up to the point at which the value of the marginal product equals the wage, it also produces up to the point at which price equals marginal cost.

_____

_____

_____

4. Why must the equilibrium wage in the market for labor equal the value of the marginal product of labor for each firm?

_____

_____

_____

5. Suppose there is an increase in college enrollments, which causes an increase in the demand for textbooks. What should happen in the markets for labor and capital employed in the manufacturing of textbooks? Explain.

_____

_____

_____

6. Why does an increase in the amount of capital reduce the rental rate of capital? Why does this same event increase the wage of labor?

_____

_____

_____

7. Explain the difference between the rental price of a factor and the purchase price of a factor. How are they related?

_____

_____

_____

8. When households own capital directly, capital income is in the form of rental payments to households. In what form is capital income paid when businesses own capital?

_____

_____

9. What events will shift the demand for labor to the right?

_____

_____

_____

10. What events will shift the supply of labor to the right?

_____

_____

_____

Self-Test

True/False Questions

_____ 1. The factors of production are labor, land, and money.

_____ 2. The demand for a factor is considered to be a derived demand because it is derived from the firm's decision to supply output in another market.

_____ 3. For a competitive profit-maximizing firm, the demand curve for a factor is the value-of-the-marginal-product curve for that factor.

_____ 4. A factor exhibits diminishing marginal productivity if employing additional units of the factor reduces output.

_____ 5. If there is an increase in the equilibrium wage, there must have been an increase in the value of the marginal product of labor.

_____ 6. An increase in the demand for textbooks will increase the value of the marginal product of textbook writers.

_____ 7. A decrease in the supply of labor reduces the value of the marginal product of labor, decreases the wage, and decreases employment.

_____ 8. The only way for the value of the marginal product of a factor to rise is for the price of the output produced by the factor to rise.

_____ 9. An increase in the demand for pencils will likely improve the fortunes of both the pencil factory and the workers in the pencil factory.

_____ 10. The demand for labor is downward sloping because the production function exhibits diminishing marginal productivity of labor.

_____ 11. In equilibrium, when a competitive firm hires labor up to the point at which the value of the marginal product of labor equals the wage, it also produces up to the point at which the price equals marginal cost.

_____ 12. An increase in the supply of capital will increase the marginal product of capital and the rental rate of capital.

_____ 13. If capital is owned by firms as opposed to being owned directly by households, then capital income will be in the form of stocks, bonds, and retained interest.

_____ 14. The value of the marginal product of land is the marginal product of land multiplied by the price of the output produced on the land.

_____ 15. An increase in the supply of capital decreases the value of the marginal product of capital, reduces the rental rate of capital, and decreases the value of the marginal product of labor, which reduces the wage of labor.

Multiple-Choice Questions

1. The most important factors of production are
   a. money, stocks, and bonds.
   b. water, earth, and knowledge.
   c. management, finance, and marketing.
   d. labor, land, and capital.

2. If a factor exhibits diminishing marginal product, hiring additional units of the factor will
   a. generate ever smaller amounts of output.
   b. cause a reduction in output.
   c. have no effect on output.
   d. increase the marginal product of the factor.

Use the following table to answer questions 3 through 5.

Labor (number of workers)	Output per Hour	Marginal Product of Labor	Value of the MPL
0	0		
1	5	_____	_____
2	9	_____	_____
3	12	_____	_____
4	14	_____	_____
5	15	_____	_____

3. What is the marginal product of labor as the firm moves from using three workers to using four workers?
   a. 0
   b. 2
   c. 12
   d. 14
   e. None of the above is correct.

4. If the price of output is $4 per unit, what is the value of the marginal product of labor as the firm moves from using four workers to using five workers?
   a. $4
   b. $8
   c. $12
   d. $56
   e. $60

5. If this profit-maximizing firm sells its output in a competitive market for $3 per unit and hires labor in a competitive market for $8 per hour, then this firm should hire
   a. one worker.
   b. two workers.
   c. three workers.
   d. four workers.
   e. five workers.

6. The value of the marginal product of labor is
   a. the price of the output times the wage of labor.
   b. the wage of labor times the quantity of labor.
   c. the price of the output times the marginal product of labor.
   d. the wage of labor times the marginal product of labor.
   e. none of the above.

7. For a competitive, profit-maximizing firm, the value-of-the-marginal-product curve for capital is the firm's
   a. production function.
   b. marginal-cost curve.
   c. supply curve of capital.
   d. demand curve for capital.

8. An increase in the supply of labor
   a. increases the value of the marginal product of labor and increases the wage.
   b. decreases the value of the marginal product of labor and decreases the wage.
   c. increases the value of the marginal product of labor and decreases the wage.
   d. decreases the value of the marginal product of labor and increases the wage.

9. A decrease in the demand for fish
    a. decreases the value of the marginal product of fishermen, reduces their wage, and reduces employment in the fishing industry.
    b. increases the value of the marginal product of fishermen, increases their wage, and increases employment in the fishing industry.
    c. decreases the value of the marginal product of fishermen, reduces their wage, and increases employment in the fishing industry.
    d. increases the value of the marginal product of fishermen, increases their wage, and decreases employment in the fishing industry.

10. What will a decrease in the supply of fishermen do to the market for capital employed in the fishing industry?
    a. increase the demand for fishing boats and increase rental rates on fishing boats
    b. decrease the demand for fishing boats and decrease rental rates on fishing boats
    c. increase the demand for fishing boats and decrease rental rates on fishing boats
    d. decrease the demand for fishing boats and increase rental rates on fishing boats

11. An increase in the demand for apples will cause all but which of the following?
    a. an increase in the price of apples
    b. an increase in the value of the marginal product of apple pickers
    c. an increase in the wage of apple pickers
    d. a decrease in the number of apple pickers employed

12. A decrease in the supply of farm tractors will cause all but which of the following?
    a. an increase in the rental rate for tractors
    b. an increase in the value of the marginal product of tractors
    c. an increase in the wage of farmworkers
    d. a decrease in the rental rate of farmland

13. If both input and output markets are competitive and firms are profit maximizing, then in equilibrium, each factor of production earns
    a. an equal share of output.
    b. the value of its marginal product.
    c. the amount allocated by the political process.
    d. an amount equal to the price of output times total output.

14. An individual firm's demand for a factor of production
    a. slopes downward due to the factor's diminishing marginal product.
    b. slopes downward because an increase in the production of output reduces the price at which the output can be sold in a competitive market, thereby reducing the value of the marginal product as more of the factor is used.
    c. slopes upward due to the factor's increasing marginal product.
    d. is perfectly elastic (horizontal) if the factor market is perfectly competitive.

15. An increase in the demand for a firm's output
    a. increases the prosperity of the firm but decreases the prosperity of the factors hired by the firm.
    b. decreases the prosperity of the firm but increases the prosperity of the factors hired by the firm.
    c. increases the prosperity of both the firm and the factors hired by the firm.
    d. decreases the prosperity of both the firm and the factors hired by the firm.

16. A competitive, profit-maximizing firm should hire workers up to the point where
    a. the wage, the rental price of capital, and the rental price of land are all equal.
    b. the marginal product of labor equals zero and the production function is maximized.
    c. the marginal product of labor equals the wage.
    d. the value of the marginal product of labor equals the wage.

17. Which of the following is *not* true with regard to workers who have a high value of marginal product? These workers
    a. are usually highly paid.
    b. usually have little capital with which to work.
    c. have skills that are in relatively scarce supply.
    d. produce output for which there is great demand.

18. An increase in the price of automobiles shifts the demand for autoworkers to the
    a. right and increases the wage.
    b. left and decreases the wage.
    c. right and decreases the wage.
    d. left and increases the wage.

19. When capital is owned by the firm as opposed to being directly owned by households, capital income may take any of the following forms except
    a. retained earnings.
    b. interest.
    c. dividends.
    d. stock.

20. Suppose that a war is fought with biological weapons. The weapons destroy people but not capital. What is likely to happen to equilibrium wages and rental rates after the war when compared to their values before the war?
    a. Wages rise and rental rates rise.
    b. Wages fall and rental rates fall.
    c. Wages rise and rental rates fall.
    d. Wages fall and rental rates rise.

Advanced Critical Thinking

You are watching a debate about immigration on public television with a friend. The participants represent two camps—organized labor and corporate industry. Organized labor argues against open immigration while U.S. industry argues in favor of more open immigration. Your friend says, "I can't believe that these two groups can't get together on this issue. Both firms and workers join forces to produce our industrial output. I would think that their interests would be similar. Maybe a better arbitrator could help these groups find a position on immigration that would satisfy both groups."

1. If there were open immigration, what would happen to the value of the marginal product of labor and the wage?

   _____

   _____

2. If there were open immigration, what would happen to the value of the marginal product of capital and land and their rental rates?

   _____

   _____

   _____

3. Are the positions that each group takes on immigration consistent with their interests? Explain. Is there likely to be a solution that satisfies both? Why or why not?

   _____

   _____

   _____

   _____

Solutions

Terms and Definitions

<u>3</u>   Factors of production

<u>8</u>   Derived demand

<u>5</u>   Production function

<u>4</u>   Marginal product of labor

<u>1</u>   Diminishing marginal product

<u>7</u>   Value of the marginal product

<u>2</u>   Capital

<u>6</u>   Rental price (of a factor)

Practice Problems

1. a.

Labor (number of workers)	Output per Hour	Marginal Product of Labor	Value of MPL when P = $3	Value of MPL when P = $5
0	0			
		9	$27	$45
1	9			
		8	24	40
2	17			
		7	21	35
3	24			
		6	18	30
4	30			
		5	15	25
5	35			
		4	12	20
6	39			
		3	9	15
7	42			
		2	6	10
8	44			

b. Three workers because the value of the marginal product of each of the first three workers exceeds the $19 wage, so each worker adds to profits but the fourth worker only has a value of marginal product of $18 so hiring the fourth worker would reduce profits.

c. Five workers because the value of the marginal product of each of the first five workers now exceeds the $13 wage, but the sixth worker only has a value of marginal product of $12 so hiring the sixth worker would reduce profits. This is a movement along the firm's demand curve for labor because the value of the marginal product of labor for each worker is remaining the same but the wage facing the firm has changed.

d. See the fifth column in the table in part *a* above.

e. Seven workers because the value of the marginal product of each of the first seven workers exceeds the $13 wage, but the eighth worker only has a value of marginal product of $10 so it would be unprofitable to hire that worker. This is a shift in the demand curve for labor because the value of the marginal product of labor has increased for each worker because the price of output rose. Thus, the firm demands more workers at the same $13 wage.

2. a. See Exhibit 4.

Exhibit 4

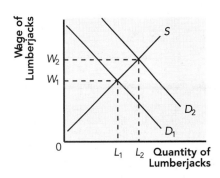

b. Increase the value of the marginal product of labor and the wage.

c. When the price of output rises, the value of the marginal product of all of the inputs increases accordingly. Thus, the value of the marginal product of both land and capital will rise and so will their rental rates.

d. When the price of output changes, the prosperity of the firm and the inputs move together. In this case, the prosperity of the firm and the inputs are increased.

3. a. See Exhibit 5. This event increases the supply of agricultural land and decreases the marginal product of land and the rental price of land.

Exhibit 5

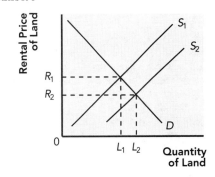

b. See Exhibit 6. The increase in the supply of agricultural land increases the marginal product of labor and shifts the demand for farm labor to the right, which increases the wage.

Exhibit 6

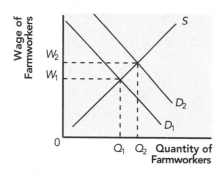

4. a. The increase in capital available for workers increases the marginal product of labor, shifts the demand for labor to the right, and increases the wage.

   b. This event increases the demand for Hondas and increases the price of Hondas. The increase in the price of Hondas increases the value of the marginal product of labor, shifts the demand for labor to the right, and increases the wage.

   c. This event increases the supply of labor, decreases the marginal product of labor, and decreases the wage.

Short-Answer Questions

1. The profit-maximizing firm will hire workers up to the point where the value of the marginal product of labor is equal to the wage. Beyond that point, additional workers cost more than the value of their marginal product and their employment would reduce profit. Because the value-of-the-marginal-product curve determines how many workers the firm will hire at each wage, it is the demand curve for labor.

2. The marginal product of labor is diminishing as more labor is added to the production process. Because the price of output is given in a competitive market, it follows that the value of the marginal product also declines as the quantity of labor is increased.

3. Given: $MC = W/MPL$. If the firm hires up to the point where the wage equals the value of the marginal product, then $P \times MPL = W$, or $P = W/MPL$. Substituting MC for W/MPL, we get $P = MC$.

4. The equilibrium wage is determined by supply and demand for labor in the market for labor. Each firm then hires workers up to the point where that wage equals the value of the marginal product of labor in each firm.

5. The value of the marginal product of both labor and capital employed in the production of textbooks should rise because the price of the

output produced by them has risen. Therefore, the wage and rental rate paid to each should also rise.

6. Because there is a declining marginal product of capital as more capital is used, an increase in capital reduces the marginal product of capital and its rental rate. The increase in capital, however, increases the marginal product of labor and increases its wage.

7. The rental price is the price one pays to use the factor for a limited period of time while the purchase price of a factor is the price one pays to own that factor indefinitely. The purchase price of a factor depends on the current and expected future value of the marginal product of the factor.

8. Interest, dividends, and retained earnings.

9. An increase in the price of output produced by labor, an advance in labor-augmenting technology used in production, and an increase in the supply of factors used with labor in production.

10. A shift in tastes toward working outside the home, a reduction in alternative opportunities for employment, and immigration.

True/False Questions

1. F; the factors are labor, land, and capital.
2. T
3. T
4. F; a factor exhibits diminishing marginal productivity if the increase in output generated from an additional unit of input diminishes as the quantity of the input increases.
5. T
6. T
7. F; a decrease in the supply of labor increases the value of the marginal product of labor, increases the wage, and decreases employment.
8. F; the marginal product of the factor could rise from a reduction in the supply of the factor (more scarce) or from an increase in the productivity of that factor.
9. T
10. T
11. T
12. F; an increase in the supply of capital will decrease the value of the marginal product of capital and decrease the rental rate.
13. F; capital income will be in the form of interest, dividends, and retained earnings.
14. T
15. F; it increases the value of the marginal product of labor and the wage.

Multiple-Choice Questions

1. d
2. a
3. b
4. a

5. c

6. c

7. d

8. b

9. a

10. b

11. d

12. c

13. b

14. a

15. c

16. d

17. b

18. a

19. d

20. c

Advanced Critical Thinking

1. Labor would be less scarce so the value of the marginal product of labor would decrease and so would the wage.

2. Additional labor could be applied to capital and land, which would increase the value of the marginal product of capital and land and increase their rental rates.

3. Yes. Organized labor wishes to keep the wage of labor high so they hope to restrict immigration. Corporate interests wish to raise the return to capital and land so it hopes to allow open immigration. No.

Chapter 19
Earnings and Discrimination

Goals
In this chapter you will

- Examine how wages compensate for differences in job characteristics

- Learn and compare the human-capital and signaling theories of education

- Examine why in some occupations a few superstars earn tremendous incomes

- Learn why wages rise above the level that balances supply and demand

- Consider why it is difficult to measure the impact of discrimination on wages

- See when market forces can and cannot provide a natural remedy for discrimination

Outcomes
After accomplishing these goals, you should be able to

- Explain why an economics professor earns less than a corporate economist of similar age, background, and training

- Explain the differing impact of policies aimed at increasing the educational attainment of all workers under the signaling and the human-capital view of education

- List the characteristics of a market where superstars can arise

- List three reasons why a wage can rise above the equilibrium wage

- Explain why differences in wages among groups does not by itself say anything about how much discrimination there is in the labor market

- Explain why competitive employers are unlikely to discriminate against groups of employees unless the customers or the government demands it

Chapter Overview

Context and Purpose

Chapter 19 is the second chapter in a three-chapter sequence that addresses the economics of labor markets. Chapter 18 developed the markets for the factors of production. Chapter 19 goes beyond the supply-and-demand models developed in Chapter 18 to help explain the wide variation in wages we find in the economy. Chapter 20 addresses the distribution of income and the role the government can play in altering the distribution of income.

The purpose of Chapter 19 is to extend the basic neoclassical theory of the labor market that we developed in Chapter 18. Neoclassical theory argues that wages depend on the supply and demand for labor and that labor demand depends on the value of the marginal productivity of labor. To address the wide variation in the wages that we observe, we must examine more precisely what determines the supply and demand for various types of labor.

Chapter Review

Introduction   Chapter 19 extends the basic neoclassical theory of the labor market that we developed in Chapter 18. Neoclassical theory argues that wages depend on the supply and demand for labor and that labor demand depends on the value of the marginal productivity of labor. To address the wide variation in the wages that we observe, Chapter 19 examines more precisely what determines the supply and demand for various types of labor.

Some Determinants of Equilibrium Wages

Workers differ from one another. Jobs also differ in terms of the wages they pay and their nonmonetary characteristics. These differences affect labor supply, labor demand, and equilibrium wages.

Some jobs are easy, fun, and safe while others are hard, dull, and dangerous. If the wages were the same, most people would prefer to do easy, fun, and safe jobs. Therefore, workers require a higher wage in order to be induced to do a hard, dull, and dangerous job. A compensating differential is the difference in wages that arises to offset the nonmonetary characteristics of different jobs. For example, people who work in coal mines or on the night shift receive a compensating differential to compensate for the disagreeable nature of their work.

Capital is a factor of production that itself has been produced. Capital includes the economy's accumulation of equipment and structures and also includes a less tangible form of capital known as human capital. Human capital is the accumulation of investments in people, such as education and on-the-job training. Workers with more human capital earn more than those with less for the following reasons: With regard to labor demand, educated workers have a higher marginal product, so firms are willing to pay more for them. With regard to labor supply, workers are only willing to educate themselves if they are rewarded for doing so. In effect, there is a compensating differential between educated and uneducated workers to compensate for the cost of becoming educated. In 1980, male college graduates earned 44 percent more than workers with a high school diploma. By 2008, the difference was 88 percent. For women, the differential rose from 35 percent to 71 percent. There are two hypotheses that may explain the increased differential. First, the growth in international trade has allowed the United States to import goods made by unskilled workers in foreign countries where unskilled workers are plentiful and export goods produced by skilled labor. In the domestic economy, this increases the demand for skilled workers and decreases the demand for unskilled workers. Second, increases in technology have increased the demand for skilled workers and decreased the demand for unskilled workers. Both hypotheses may be true.

Natural ability, effort, and chance help explain wages. Some people are smarter and stronger than others, and they are paid for their natural ability. Some people work harder than others and are compensated for their effort. Chance plays a role in that someone's education and experience can be made valueless if there is a change in technology that eliminates that person's job. Beauty may be a natural ability because attractiveness may make an actor or waiter more productive. It may also be a sign of an intelligent person who expends effort to successfully appear attractive and this may suggest that the individual may be successful at other things, too. Alternatively, a wage premium for beauty may simply be a type of discrimination. Attractive people do earn a premium over less attractive people.

The human-capital view of education argues that workers with more education are paid more because the education made them more productive. As an alternative, the *signaling* view of education argues that firms use education as a method of sorting high-ability workers from low-ability workers. Educational attainment signals high ability because it is easier for high-ability people to earn a college degree than it is for low-ability people, and firms are willing to pay more for high-ability people. Just as with the signaling theory of advertising where the advertisement itself contains no real information, the signaling theory of education suggests that schooling has no real productivity benefit. According to the human-capital view of education, a policy of increasing educational attainment for all workers should raise all workers' wages. According to the signaling view of education, additional education would not affect productivity or wages. The benefits of education are probably a combination of both human-capital and signaling effects.

A few superstars earn astronomical salaries. These superstars are often performers such as athletes, actors, writers, and so on. Superstars arise in markets that have two characteristics:

- Every customer in the market wants to enjoy the good supplied by the best producer.

- The good is produced with a technology that makes it possible for the best producer to supply every customer at low cost.

So far, we have addressed why workers might earn different equilibrium wages. Some workers, however, may earn higher wages because their wages are held above equilibrium due to the following:

- *Minimum-wage laws.* This mostly affects less-experienced and less-skilled workers.

- *The market power of labor unions.* A union is a worker association that bargains with employers over wages and working conditions. The union can hold wages 10 to 20 percent above equilibrium because they can threaten to strike or withhold labor from the firm.

- *Efficiency wages.* Efficiency wages occur when firms choose to hold wages above equilibrium to increase productivity because high wages reduce worker turnover, increase worker effort, and raise the quality of workers that apply for jobs at the firm.

Whenever the wage is held above equilibrium, the result is unemployment.

The Economics of Discrimination

Wages can differ due to discrimination. Discrimination is the offering of different opportunities to similar individuals who differ only by race, ethnic group, sex, age, or other personal characteristics. Discrimination is an emotional issue.

Wages differ across races and sexes for a number of reasons. Whites have more human capital on average than blacks due to more years of schooling and better schools. Men generally have more years of education and more job experience than women. In school, women may have been directed away from science and math courses. Men may also receive a compensating differential for doing more unpleasant jobs than women choose to do. While some of the wage differentials are likely to be due to discrimination, there is no agreement with regard to how much. Economists would agree that *because the differences in average wages among groups in part reflect differences in human capital and job characteristics, they do not by themselves say anything about how much discrimination there is in the labor market.*

A recent study suggests that job candidates with names common in the African-American community receive less interest from employers than candidates with names common in the white community.

Although it is difficult to measure discrimination, suppose we have evidence that there is discrimination in the labor market. If some employers discriminate against certain groups of employees, then the demand for the services of those that are discriminated against will be low and their wages will be low while the demand for those workers not discriminated against will be high and their wages will be high. In a competitive market, employers that discriminate against certain groups of employees will be at a competitive disadvantage because their labor costs will be higher. Firms that care only about profits and do not discriminate will tend to replace those that do discriminate because they will be more profitable. The firms that do not discriminate will increase the demand for the labor services of the group that was discriminated against, decrease the demand for the group not discriminated against, and the wages will be equalized across groups. Thus, competitive markets can be a cure for employer discrimination.

If customers or governments demand discrimination, however, then competition and the profit motive of firms may not correct the wage differential. If bigoted customers are willing to pay extra to be served by a certain group in a restaurant and are not willing to be served by another group, then the wage differential can persist even in a competitive market. If the government mandates discriminatory practices, then competition will again fail to equalize a discriminatory wage differential. There is evidence that, in some professional sports, white athletes are paid more than black athletes of comparable ability and that attendance is greater for teams with a greater proportion of white players. This suggests that sports fans are willing to pay a premium to watch white players. Because black players are less profitable, this wage differential can persist even if owners care only about profits. If a wage differential persists in a competitive market, it is because bigoted customers are willing to pay for it or because the government requires it. The wage differential cannot be maintained by a bigoted employer alone.

Conclusion

In competitive markets, workers earn a wage equal to the value of their marginal product. The workers' value of marginal product is higher if they are more talented, diligent, experienced, and educated. Firms pay less to those workers against whom customers discriminate because they are less profitable to the firm.

Helpful Hints

1. The wage is explained by supply and demand. Characteristics of both people and jobs affect supply, demand, and the wage for labor in each labor market. For example, education, experience, and hard work increase the value of the marginal productivity of workers, increase the demand for their services, and increase their wage. An increase in the disagreeable nature of the work, the expense of training, and the required ability to do the job reduce the pool of workers willing and able to do a particular job, reduce the supply of labor in that market, and increase the wage. Even the market for superstars can be explained with supply and demand. Because superstars can satisfy every customer at the same time through television, movies, music CDs, and so on, the value of their marginal product is enormous and so is the demand for their services.

2. Different pay for different groups of people is not, by itself, evidence of labor market discrimination because differences in pay among groups in part reflects differences in human capital and job characteristics. What seems to be discrimination may simply be a compensating differential that is paid for the disagreeable nature of a job. In addition, a wage differential could be due to a difference in the average productivity across groups of workers.

Terms and Definitions

Choose a definition for each key term.

Key Terms

_____ Compensating differential

_____ Human capital

_____ Union

_____ Strike

_____ Efficiency wages

_____ Discrimination

Definitions

1. The offering of different opportunities to similar individuals who differ only by race, ethnic group, sex, age, or other personal characteristics

2. A difference in wages that arises to offset the nonmonetary characteristics of different jobs

3. The organized withdrawal of labor from a firm by a union

4. The accumulation of investments in people, such as education and on-the-job training

5. Above-equilibrium wages paid by firms in order to increase worker productivity

6. A worker association that bargains with employers over wages and working conditions

Problems and Short-Answer Questions

Practice Problems

1. Within each of the following pairs of workers, which worker is likely to earn more and why? (It may be obvious which one is paid more. The real issue is to explain why one is paid more than the other is.)
    a. a carpenter working at the top of a 600-foot cooling tower of a nuclear power plant or a carpenter who frames houses

    _____

    _____

    b. a clerk in a grocery store or a lawyer

    _____

    _____

    c. a lawyer with one year of experience or a lawyer with six years of experience

    _____

    _____

    d. an attractive salesperson or a homely salesperson

    _____

    _____

    e. an autoworker in a factory who works the day shift or an autoworker in a factory who works the night shift

    _____

    _____

f.   an economics professor or a corporate economist

_____

_____

g.   a history professor or an economics professor

_____

_____

h.   someone trained as a keypunch operator (typist who types input commands on cards to be read by a mainframe computer prior to the existence of computer terminals) or someone trained as a personal computer specialist

_____

_____

i.   your favorite local blues band that plays regularly at a nearby campus bar or David Bowie

_____

_____

j.   a lazy, stupid plumber or a hardworking, bright plumber

_____

_____

k.   the best carpenter on the planet or the best writer on the planet

_____

_____

2. a.   Explain the human-capital view of education and the signaling view of education.

_____

_____

b.   What are the implications for education policy under each view?

_____

_____

_____

c.   Which of the above is true? Explain.

_____

_____

3. a.   How can a competitive market eliminate discrimination in the labor market?

_____

_____

_____

_____

    b.   What limits a competitive market's ability to reduce discrimination? Explain.

_____

_____

Short-Answer Questions

1. Why does someone who has a great amount of human capital that was acquired through education earn more than someone with a small amount of human capital?

_____

_____

_____

2. Name some characteristics of a job that might require a positive compensating differential.

_____

_____

_____

3. What has happened to the relative wages of skilled and unskilled workers in the United States since 1980? Why?

_____

_____

_____

4. What are the necessary conditions for a superstar to arise in a market? Explain.

_____

_____

5. Does a difference in average wages among groups, by itself, suggest that there is discrimination in the labor market? Explain.

_____

_____

_____

6. If a discriminatory wage differential persists in a competitive market, is it due to discrimination on the part of the employer or must it be from some other source? Explain.

_____

_____

_____

7. Is there discrimination in professional sports? Is the employer the source of the discrimination? Explain.

_____

_____

_____

8. List the professions of most superstars. What do these professions have in common?

_____

_____

_____

9. Why is a plumber's apprentice paid less than a master plumber?

_____

_____

_____

10. Provide three reasons why wages might be set above the equilibrium wage. Explain.

_____

_____

_____

_____

Self-Test

True/False Questions

_____ 1. A compensating differential is the difference in wages paid to workers who are discriminated against and those who are not discriminated against.

_____ 2. Workers on the night shift receive a compensating differential to offset the disagreeable nature of working at night.

_____ 3. Since 1980, the gap between the wages of unskilled workers and skilled workers in the United States has narrowed.

_____ 4. Firms are willing to pay more for workers with greater human capital because workers with greater human capital have a greater value of marginal product.

_____ 5. Human capital is increased by education and on-the-job training.

_____   6.   An apprentice will work for a relatively low wage because some of the apprentice's pay is in terms of on-the-job training.

_____   7.   Some superstars can earn astronomical salaries because, in some markets, everyone wants the good supplied by the best producer and technology has made it possible for the best producer to satisfy every customer at low cost.

_____   8.   If the signaling view of education is true, a policy of increasing the education of workers will increase the wages of all workers.

_____   9.   The evidence that attractive people are paid more than unattractive people clearly demonstrates that the labor market discriminates against unattractive people.

_____   10.   Ability, effort, and chance must play an important role in wage determination because less than half of the variation in wages can be explained by workers' education, experience, age, and job characteristics.

_____   11.   If a company in a competitive market persistently pays a discriminatory wage to a certain group, it must be because the employer is a bigot.

_____   12.   If there is a difference in wages among groups, it is evidence that there is discrimination in the labor market.

_____   13.   If it were not for minimum-wage laws, workers would always be paid the equilibrium wage.

_____   14.   Competition will tend to eliminate discrimination in the labor market if customers are not bigoted and if government does not require discrimination.

_____   15.   At least some of the differences in pay between men and women can be explained by the fact that, on average, men have attained more and better schooling, have more job experience, and may do more unpleasant jobs.

Multiple-Choice Questions

1.   If a person who works in a coal mine gets paid more than a person with a similar background and skills who works in a safer job, then
   a.   we have evidence of discrimination against workers outside the coal mine.
   b.   we have observed a compensating differential.
   c.   coal miners must have greater human capital than others.
   d.   coal miners must be more attractive than other workers.

2.   According to the human-capital view of education, education
   a.   increases human capital and the wages of workers.
   b.   only helps firms sort workers into high-ability and low-ability workers.
   c.   has no impact on the human capital of workers.
   d.   can make any worker into a superstar.

3.   Which of the following is not part of a worker's human capital?
   a.   education
   b.   on-the-job training
   c.   experience
   d.   effort
   e.   All of the above are parts of a worker's human capital.

4.   According to the signaling view of education, education
   a.   increases human capital and the wages of workers.
   b.   only helps firms sort workers into high-ability and low-ability workers.
   c.   reduces the wage gap between high-skilled and low-skilled workers.
   d.   can make any worker into a superstar.

5. All of the following would tend to increase a worker's wage except
   a. more education.
   b. working the night shift.
   c. doing a job that is fun.
   d. having a greater amount of natural ability.
   e. working harder.

6. In a competitive market, which of the following is least likely to be the source of a persistent discriminatory wage differential?
   a. the customer
   b. the government
   c. the employer
   d. All of the above could be the source of a persistent discriminatory wage differential.

7. If two jobs require the same amount of skills and experience, the job that pays the most is most likely to be the one that is
   a. unpleasant.
   b. safe.
   c. easy.
   d. fun.
   e. all of the above.

8. Since 1980, the gap between the wages of skilled and unskilled workers in the United States has
   a. decreased.
   b. increased.
   c. stayed the same.
   d. first increased and is now decreasing.

9. Which of the following is *true* regarding the earnings of attractive versus unattractive workers?
   a. Attractive people tend to earn less because attractive people are viewed as shallow and more self-absorbed and, therefore, as less productive.
   b. Attractive people tend to earn less because attractive people usually have less human capital.
   c. Attractive people tend to earn more because they may actually have a larger value of marginal product.
   d. Attractive people tend to earn more because attractive people usually have greater human capital.

10. The relative wage of unskilled workers has fallen in the United States likely as a result of a relative
    a. increase in the number of unskilled workers available because workers are more poorly educated.
    b. increase in the number of unskilled workers available due to immigration into the United States.
    c. decrease in the demand for unskilled workers because workers are more poorly educated.
    d. decrease in the demand for unskilled workers because of increases in technology and increases in international trade.

11. Which of the following professionals is most likely to be able to generate the income of a superstar?
    a. the best medical doctor
    b. the best professor
    c. the best accountant
    d. the best writer
    e. All of the above participate in markets that could generate a superstar.

12. It is *not* considered discrimination when an employer offers different opportunities to individuals that differ only by their
    a. race.
    b. sex.
    c. productivity.
    d. age.

13. In order for a market to support superstars, it must have which of the following characteristics?
    a. It must be involved in professional athletics.
    b. Every customer must want the good supplied by the best producer, and the technology must exist for the best producer to supply every customer at low cost.
    c. Every customer must be willing to pay an enormous amount for the product, and the product must be a necessity.
    d. Every customer must be indifferent to the price they pay, and the seller must be a competitor in the market for the product.

14. Which of the following statements regarding discrimination is *true?*
    a. Discrimination cannot exist in a competitive labor market.
    b. Discrimination can only persist in a competitive labor market if customers are willing to pay to maintain the discriminatory practice or the government requires discrimination.
    c. Bigoted employers are the main source of a persistent discriminatory wage differential in a competitive market.
    d. The existence of a wage differential among groups is strong evidence of discrimination in the labor market.

15. Competitive markets tend to
    a. reduce labor market discrimination because nondiscriminating firms will employ cheaper labor, earn more profits, and drive discriminating firms out of the market.
    b. have no impact on labor market discrimination.
    c. increase labor market discrimination because bigoted employers can charge any price they want in a competitive market to cover the cost of their discrimination.
    d. increase labor market discrimination because some workers can charge more for their services than other workers in a competitive market.

16. A wage differential among groups may not by itself be evidence of discrimination in the labor market because different groups have
    a. different levels of education.
    b. different preferences for the type of work they are willing to do.
    c. different levels of job experience.
    d. all of the above.

17. Which of the following is *not* a reason why some workers are paid above the equilibrium wage?
    a. minimum-wage laws
    b. beauty
    c. unions
    d. efficiency wages

18. Which of the following is likely to generate a compensating differential?
    a. One employee is more attractive than another.
    b. One employee works harder than another.
    c. One employee is willing to work the night shift while another is not.
    d. One employee is more educated than another.
    e. All of the above generate compensating differentials.

19. Which of the following explanations of wage differentials is *not* likely to be true?
    a. Men have more human capital than women.
    b. Whites have more human capital than blacks.
    c. Employers in competitive markets are bigots.
    d. Men have more job experience than women.

20. Which of the following could result in women being paid less than men?
    a. customers preferring to deal with men
    b. women preferring to work in pleasant, clean, safe, workplaces
    c. women entering and leaving the labor force to care for children
    d. women obtaining less human capital because they don't plan to work continuously to the age of retirement
    e. all of the above

Advanced Critical Thinking

You are at a political rally with some friends. A candidate for state office states that working women earn about 60 cents for each dollar that working men earn. The candidate says, "This is clearly evidence that employers discriminate against women. This gap between the earnings of men and women will never close because professions women tend to choose are traditionally low paying and the professions men choose are traditionally high paying. I propose that the government create a panel to decide what jobs should pay so that people of similar skills and education earn the same amount."

1. Suppose a secretary and a truck driver are judged to require the same level of education and skills, yet a secretary earns $30,000 while a truck driver earns $40,000. What would happen to the quantities supplied and demanded in the market for secretaries and truck drivers if the wage for these professions were set by law at $35,000?

    _____

    _____

    _____

    _____

    _____

2. What would happen to the level of effort and natural ability of the workers available in each market in question 1? What would happen to the quality of work generated in each market?

    _____

    _____

    _____

    _____

    _____

3. Suppose it is true that the skills and education required to do each job in question 1 are, in fact, nearly identical. What explanation would an economist likely propose to explain why the equilibrium wage differs by $10,000 across these markets?

    _____

    _____

    _____

    _____

    _____

Solutions

Terms and Definitions

_2_ Compensating differential

_4_ Human capital

_6_ Union

_3_ Strike

_5_ Efficiency wages

_1_ Discrimination

Practice Problems

1. a. The carpenter working at the 600-foot height because he will likely require a compensating differential for the danger of the job.

   b. A lawyer because the lawyer has greater human capital from years of education and the lawyer requires a compensating differential to compensate for the cost and effort of becoming educated.

   c. A lawyer with six years of experience because work experience is part of human capital.

   d. Attractive salespersons because they may have a higher value of marginal product due to being attractive or because they have signaled that they may be successful at a variety of things when they succeeded at the task of making themselves look attractive. Alternatively, it may be due to discrimination against homely people.

   e. The night-shift worker because the night shift is disagreeable, and the worker requires a compensating differential.

   f. The corporate economist because the corporate economist requires a compensating differential to compensate for the disagreeable nature of the work. Also, the corporate economist may have a greater value of marginal product.

   g. An economics professor because the market wage for economists is higher due to the economist's higher value of marginal product in the corporate labor market.

   h. A personal computer specialist because, through chance, technology has changed such that keypunch operators are no longer needed while PC specialists are needed.

   i. Superstar David Bowie because through technology he is able to satisfy the entire market at the same time. (He is the first rock star to have a net worth in excess of $1 billion.)

   j. The hardworking, bright plumber because the value of the marginal product is higher for people with ability and who work hard.

   k. The best writer because the writer is in a market that can support a superstar while the carpenter is not.

2. a. Education increases human capital and raises the value of the marginal product of labor and, thus, the wage. Alternatively, education is only a signal of high ability.

   b. According to the human-capital view, policies that increase educational attainment for all will increase all wages. According to the signaling view, an increase in educational attainment will not affect wages because education does not increase productivity.

   c. Probably both are true. It is unclear regarding the relative sizes of these two effects.

3. a. Firms only interested in profit will hire the group of workers that is discriminated against. Because their wages are relatively low, the firms that do not discriminate will have a competitive advantage over the discriminatory firms. As the nondiscriminating firms replace the discriminatory firms, the relative demand for workers previously discriminated against will increase, which will remove the discriminatory wage differential.

   b. If bigoted customers are willing to pay higher prices to firms that discriminate, or if the government requires discrimination, the competitive market cannot eliminate discrimination.

Short-Answer Questions

1. Because workers with greater human capital are more productive and firms are willing to pay more for workers with a greater value of marginal product. In addition, workers must be compensated for the cost of educating themselves.

2. A compensating differential is paid for the disagreeable, unpleasant nature of a job. Other things being equal, jobs will pay more if they are dirty, noisy, smelly, solitary, unsafe, hard, require travel, require working odd hours such as the night shift or swing shift, require working with unpleasant people, etc.

3. The gap between skilled and unskilled wages has risen, possibly because the growth in international trade has allowed the United States to import goods made by unskilled workers in countries where unskilled labor is plentiful and export goods made by skilled workers. This would increase the relative demand for skilled workers. Or it could be that increases in technology have increased the relative demand for skilled workers.

4. Every customer in the market wants to enjoy the good supplied by the best producer and the good is produced with a technology that makes it possible for the best producer to supply every customer at low cost.

5. No. Because average wages among groups are in part based on differences in human capital and job characteristics, a wage differential among groups alone tells us nothing about discrimination.

6. If customers are not bigoted and government does not require discrimination, competition

will ensure that employers cannot continuously discriminate. If a wage differential persists, it must be because the customers are willing to pay for it (they are bigoted) or the government requires it. It cannot simply be due to a bigoted employer.

7. Evidence suggests that in some professional sports, white players are paid more than equivalent black players. The source is likely to be the sports fan (the customer).

8. Writers, athletes, television and movie actors, movie directors, musicians, artists, software creators, motivational speakers, etc. Customers want only the best, and technology allows the seller to satisfy all customers at low cost.

9. Because the apprentice's value of marginal product is less and because the apprentice is being paid, in part, with on-the-job training that increases the apprentice's human capital and future earnings.

10. Minimum-wage laws (government-imposed wage floor), the market power of labor unions (threat of strike raises wage), and efficiency wages (firms pay above equilibrium wage to increase productivity because high wages reduce turnover, increase effort, and raise the quality of job applicants).

True/False Questions

1. F; it is the difference in wages that arises to offset the nonmonetary characteristics of different jobs.
2. T
3. F; the gap has been widening.
4. T
5. T
6. T
7. T
8. F; education would not increase productivity and would have no effect on wages.
9. F; attractive people may have a larger value of marginal product or attractive people may have signaled that because they are good at making themselves attractive they may also be good at other tasks.
10. T
11. F; it must be because the customer is willing to pay for the discrimination or because the government requires it.
12. F; the difference in wages may be due to differences in human capital or job characteristics.
13. F; unions may pressure firms to raise wages above equilibrium, and firms may choose to pay efficiency wages, which are above equilibrium.
14. T
15. T

Multiple-Choice Questions

1. b
2. a
3. d
4. b
5. c
6. c
7. a
8. b
9. c
10. d
11. d
12. c
13. b
14. b
15. a
16. d
17. b
18. c
19. c
20. e

Advanced Critical Thinking

1. There will be a surplus of secretaries and a shortage of truck drivers. That is, it will increase the quantity supplied of secretaries and decrease the quantity demanded while it will decrease the quantity supplied of truck drivers and increase the quantity demanded.

2. Hardworking, high-ability workers would avoid the truck-driving market and the quality of truck driving would be reduced. Hardworking, high-ability workers would be attracted to the secretary market and the quality of secretarial services would be increased.

3. An economist would argue that $10,000 is the compensating differential necessary to get someone to undertake the disagreeable nature of truck driving—working alone, overnight travel away from family, less clean and less safe work environment, etc.

Chapter 20
Income Inequality and Poverty

Goals In this chapter you will	• Examine the degree of economic inequality in our society
	• Consider some problems that arise when measuring economic inequality
	• See how political philosophers view the government's role in redistributing income
	• Consider the various policies aimed at helping poor families escape poverty

Outcomes After accomplishing these goals, you should be able to	• Explain why the gap in earnings between skilled and unskilled workers is growing in the United States
	• Name some factors that cause the measurement of income distribution to exaggerate the degree of income inequality
	• Compare and contrast utilitarianism, liberalism, and libertarianism
	• Explain the concept of a negative income tax

Chapter Overview

Context and Purpose

Chapter 20 is the third chapter in a three-chapter sequence that addresses the economics of labor markets. Chapter 18 developed the markets for the factors of production. Chapter 19 extended the basic supply-and-demand model to help explain the wide variation in wages we find in the economy. Chapter 20 addresses the measurement of the distribution of income and looks at the role the government plays in altering the distribution of income.

The purpose of Chapter 20 is to address income distribution. The discussion proceeds by answering three questions. First, how much inequality is there? Second, what do different political philosophies have to say about the proper role of government in altering the distribution of income? And third, what are the various government policies that are used to help the poor?

Chapter Review

Introduction   This chapter addresses the distribution of income by answering three questions. First, how much inequality is there? Second, what do different political philosophies have to say about the proper role of government in altering the distribution of income? And third, what are the various government policies that are used to help the poor? We will find that governments may be able to enact policies that make the income distribution more equal but at the expense of a distortion in incentives and a reduction in efficiency.

The Measurement of Inequality

The distribution of income can be described in a variety of ways. One way is to show what percent of total before-tax income is earned by families in each fifth and the top 5 percent of the income distribution. The top fifth earns about 47.8 percent of total income while the bottom fifth earns about 4.0 percent. That is, the top fifth earns about twelve times what the bottom fifth earns. The top 5 percent earns more than the bottom 40 percent.

The distribution of income is remarkably stable over time. Over the past 73 years, the bottom fifth has generally earned between 4 and 5 percent while the top fifth has earned between 40 and 50 percent. However, from 1935 to 1970 the income distribution narrowed slightly, and from 1970 to 2008 it has grown slightly wider, returning to levels similar to those in 1935. The increase in income inequality may be because of increases in international trade. Increases in technology have reduced the demand for unskilled workers while raising the demand for skilled workers, which has caused a change in relative wages.

When countries are ranked by inequality, the United States ranks about average. Japan, Germany, and Canada have greater income equality than the United States while Brazil, South Africa, and Mexico have greater income inequality.

Another measure of the distribution of income is the poverty rate—the percentage of the population whose family income falls below an absolute level called the poverty line. The poverty line is an absolute level of income set by the federal government for each family size below which a family is deemed to be in poverty. It is set at approximately three times the cost of providing an adequate diet. In 2008, the median family had an income of $61,521 while 13.2 percent of the population was in families with incomes below the poverty line of $22,025. The poverty rate fell from 1959 to 1973, but it has not declined since then. It has been argued that this measure of poverty, which hasn't changed in four decades, needs to be updated and based on expenditures on a bundle of necessities after receiving welfare payments. Poverty rates demonstrate three facts:

- *Poverty is correlated with race.* Blacks and Hispanics are three times more likely than whites to live in poverty.

- *Poverty is correlated with age.* Children are more likely than average and the elderly are less likely than average to live in poverty.

- *Poverty is correlated with family composition.* Families headed by females with no husband present are six times as likely to live in poverty as a family headed by a married couple.

There are problems associated with measuring inequality. Although data on the income distribution and the poverty rate are useful in measuring inequality, these measures are not perfect measures of someone's ability to maintain a standard of living for the following reasons:

- In-kind transfers are transfers to the poor given in the form of goods and services rather than cash. They are not accounted for in the standard measures of income inequality.

- The economic life cycle is the regular pattern of income variation over a person's life. Young and old may earn little income, but the young can borrow and the old can live off past savings. Standard measures of income inequality exaggerate the variation in living standards because annual income has greater variation than living standards.

- *Transitory versus permanent income.* Incomes vary due to random and transitory forces. That is, events can cause income to be unusually high or low for any given year. Again, people can borrow and lend so that they can maintain stable living standards even when there is variation in income. A family's living standard depends largely on its permanent income. Permanent income is a person's normal, or average, income.

For each of the reasons listed above, standard measures of income distribution exaggerate the inequality of living standards.

Alternative measures of inequality show dramatically different results. Standard measures of income inequality across families show the greatest inequality. Consumption per person shows much less inequality. In the United States, the top fifth of households had 15 times the income of the bottom fifth, but consumption per person was only 2.1 times higher.

Economic mobility in the United States is high. During any ten-year period, 25 percent of families fall below the poverty line in at least one year but only 3 percent of families are poor for eight or more years. At the other extreme, if a father earns income 20 percent above average, his son will earn income only 8 percent above average and his grandson will earn an average income. Furthermore, four out of five millionaires made their money on their own rather than inheriting it. These data suggest that deviations from average income tend to be somewhat temporary, and again, measures of income inequality tend to exaggerate the inequality in living standards.

The Political Philosophy of Redistributing Income

Economics alone cannot tell us whether governments *should* do anything about economic inequality. For this, we must address various schools of political philosophy:

- Utilitarianism: The political philosophy according to which the government should choose policies to maximize the total utility of everyone in society. Utility is a measure of happiness or satisfaction and is assumed to be the ultimate objective of all actions. If there is diminishing marginal utility for each additional dollar of income, then taking away a dollar from a rich person and giving it to a poor person lowers the rich person's utility less than the gain in utility received by the poor person. Utilitarians reject complete equalization of income because they realize that people respond to incentives, and thus, taxes create deadweight losses and there is less total income to be redistributed. The founders of this philosophy are the English philosophers Jeremy Bentham and John Stuart Mill.

- Liberalism: The political philosophy according to which the government should choose policies deemed to be just, as evaluated by an impartial observer behind a "veil of ignorance." This means that the only objective measure of economic justice is to set the rules for society as if every person were ignorant about the station in life each will end up filling—top, bottom, or middle. John Rawls, the originator of this theory of justice, argues that we would be concerned about being at the bottom of the income distribution so we would create a social rule known as the maximin criterion—the claim that the government should aim to maximize the well-being of the worst-off person in society. As a result, redistribution of income is a type of social insurance. Although not equalizing income completely, it would require greater redistribution than utilitarianism. Critics argue that rational people behind a veil of ignorance would not necessarily be so risk averse as to follow the maximin criterion.

- Libertarianism: The political philosophy according to which the government should punish crimes and enforce voluntary agreements but not redistribute income. Libertarians, such as Robert Nozick, argue that society earns no income—only individuals earn income. Therefore, income is not a shared resource to be distributed by a social planner. To a libertarian, if the *process* is fair, the *outcome* is fair, no matter how unequal. Thus, the government should punish stealing and cheating to make a fair playing field but should not be concerned with the final score if the rules were fair. Equality of opportunity is more important than equality of incomes.

Policies to Reduce Poverty

Regardless of political philosophy, most people think that the government should help the most needy because the poor are more likely to experience homelessness, drug dependency, domestic violence, health problems, teenage pregnancy, illiteracy, unemployment, and low educational attainment and are more likely to commit crimes and be victims of crime. Here are some policy options:

- *Minimum-wage laws:* Advocates argue that it helps the poor without any cost to government. Critics argue that it raises the wage above equilibrium for the lowest skilled workers and causes unemployment among those workers. Those that keep their jobs gain while those that become unemployed lose. The more elastic the demand for labor, the greater the job loss from a minimum wage. In addition, many minimum-wage workers are teenagers from middle-class families so the program is poorly targeted to the poor.

- *Welfare:* Welfare is a broad term that encompasses various government programs that supplement the incomes of the needy. These programs are cash assistance for people who have low incomes and have demonstrated a "need" such as having small children at home (Temporary Assistance for Needy Families, formerly known as Aid to Families with Dependent Children) or have a disability (Supplemental Security Income or SSI). Critics argue that these programs encourage the problems they hope to cure. Eligibility for assistance requires that the father not be in the household. This encourages fathers to abandon their families, causing broken homes, and may encourage unwed women to have illegitimate children. Evidence does not support the claim that welfare caused the decline in the two-parent family.

- *Negative income tax:* A negative income tax is a tax system that collects revenue from high-income households and gives transfers to low-income households. Under this tax system, a progressive income tax on the rich would be used to subsidize or provide a "negative tax" to low-income families. Poor families would not have to demonstrate need beyond simply being poor. This would not subsidize the breakup of families or subsidize illegitimate births, but it would subsidize more than the unfortunate by subsidizing those that are just lazy. The Earned Income Tax Credit is similar to a negative income tax but it only applies to the working poor, not the unemployed or sick.

- *In-kind transfers:* In-kind transfers occur when the poor are directly provided goods and services as opposed to being provided cash payments. Food stamps and Medicaid are examples. Supporters argue that this method ensures that the poor actually receive what they need as opposed to giving them money that they could spend on alcohol, drugs, and so on. Advocates of cash payments argue that in-kind transfers are inefficient because the government doesn't know what the poor need most. In addition, they argue that it is insulting to the poor to be forced to accept in-kind transfers.

Some antipoverty programs have the unintended effect of reducing the incentive for the poor to work. For example, suppose the government were to guarantee a fixed minimum level of income. If anyone below that income level were to work and earn a dollar, then the government would simply reduce that person's benefits by one dollar. As a result, the effective tax rate is 100 percent on any new income, and there is little incentive to work. Welfare, Medicaid, food stamps, and the Earned Income Tax Credit are all reduced when a recipient earns more income. This discourages work and may create a "culture of poverty." That is, welfare recipients lose their job skills, their children fail to see the benefits of work, and multiple generations of families become dependent on government. If benefits are reduced gradually as income rises, the incentive to work is not reduced as much. However, this increases the cost of fighting poverty because families above the poverty line will receive some benefits.

Work disincentives created by antipoverty programs can be reduced by *workfare*—programs requiring any person collecting benefits to accept a government-provided job. Another possibility is to limit the number of years a person can collect welfare. This method was used by the 1996 welfare reform bill that limits lifetime welfare to five years.

Conclusion

It is difficult to measure inequality, and there is little agreement about what to do about it. If we choose to do something about inequality, we should remember there is a trade-off between equity and efficiency. That is, the more equally the pie is divided, the smaller the pie becomes.

Helpful Hints

1. People in poverty are more likely to experience homelessness, drug dependency, domestic violence, health problems, teenage pregnancy, illiteracy, unemployment, and low educational attainment and are more likely to commit crimes and be victims of crime. Note, however, that while it is clear that poverty is associated with these social ills, it is unclear whether poverty causes these social ills or whether these social ills cause poverty. That is, it may be that drug dependency, health problems, having children while young and out of wedlock, illiteracy, and so on are as much a cause of poverty as they are an effect of poverty.

2. There are various reasons why an individual's current annual income can differ from his average lifetime income. The individual's income will depend on whether he is young, middle age, or old, and whether he has had an unusually productive or unproductive year. Because people can borrow and lend, standards of living are more stable than incomes, and thus, standard measures of income distribution will exaggerate the degree of economic inequality.

3. An additional reason why some people prefer the government to provide for the poor using in-kind transfers instead of cash payments is that in-kind transfers are thought to generate less fraud. This is because there is little incentive for an individual to file a fraudulent claim to receive medical benefits that the individual doesn't need but there may be a great incentive to file a fraudulent welfare claim to receive cash.

Terms and Definitions

Choose a definition for each key term.

Key Terms	Definitions

Key Terms

_____ Poverty rate

_____ Poverty line

_____ In-kind transfers

_____ Life cycle

_____ Permanent income

_____ Utilitarianism

_____ Utility

_____ Liberalism

_____ Maximin criterion

_____ Social insurance

_____ Libertarianism

_____ Welfare

_____ Negative income tax

Definitions

1. A measure of happiness or satisfaction

2. A person's normal income

3. Government programs that supplement the incomes of the needy

4. Transfers to the poor given in the form of goods and services rather than cash

5. The political philosophy according to which the government should choose policies to maximize the total utility of everyone in society

6. The percentage of the population whose family income falls below an absolute level called the poverty line

7. A tax system that collects revenue from high-income households and gives transfers to low-income households

8. The political philosophy according to which the government should choose policies deemed to be just, as evaluated by an impartial observer behind a "veil of ignorance"

9. The political philosophy according to which the government should punish crimes and enforce voluntary agreements but not redistribute income

10. An absolute level of income set by the federal government for each family size below which a family is deemed to be in poverty

11. The claim that the government should aim to maximize the well-being of the worst-off person in society

12. The regular pattern of income variation over a person's life

13. Government policy aimed at protecting people against the risk of adverse events

Problems and Short-Answer Questions

Practice Problems

1. Use Table 2 from Chapter 20 in your text to answer this question.
   a. In the most recent year available, what percent of income did the bottom fifth of the income distribution earn? What percent of income did the top fifth of the distribution earn? Roughly, what is the relationship between what the bottom fifth earns and what the top fifth earns?

   _____

   _____

b. What is the range of the percent of income earned by the bottom fifth of the income distribution over the last seventy-three years? What is the range for the top fifth? Describe the trend for each group over the last seventy-three years. Provide some explanations for the trends you described.

_____

_____

_____

_____

c. Describe three reasons why the measure of income distribution expressed in Table 2 in Chapter 20 may not truly measure someone's ability to maintain a certain standard of living. As a result, are the standard measures of income distribution likely to exaggerate or understate the true distribution of the standard of living? Explain.

_____

_____

_____

_____

d. What is permanent income? Why might we wish to use permanent income when measuring the distribution of income? If we used permanent income instead of current annual income when measuring the distribution of income, would this tend to exaggerate or understate the true distribution of the standard of living? Explain. (Hint: If you are a full-time student, can you borrow as much as you want in order to perfectly smooth out your lifetime consumption?)

_____

_____

_____

_____

2. Susan earns five times as much as Joe.
    a. What would the political philosophy of utilitarianism, liberalism, and libertarianism likely suggest should be done in this situation? Explain.

_____

_____

_____

_____

    b. Compare the degree of redistribution each suggests.

_____

3. Suppose the government has to choose between two antipoverty programs. Each program guarantees that every family has at least $15,000 of income. One scheme establishes a negative income tax where: Taxes = (0.50 of income) − $15,000. The other scheme is for the government to guarantee every family at least $15,000 to spend, and if a family falls short, the government will simply make up the difference.

a. Using the negative income tax scheme described above, fill out the following table.

Earned Income	Taxes Paid	After-Tax Income
$ 0	_____	_____
5,000	_____	_____
10,000	_____	_____
20,000	_____	_____
30,000	_____	_____
40,000	_____	_____

b. What is the value of income for which this family neither receives a subsidy nor pays any tax? (That is, how high does income have to be for the family to stop receiving a subsidy?)

_____

c. Under the second scheme where the government simply guarantees at least $15,000 to every family, what is the level of income at which a family stops receiving a subsidy? Explain.

_____

_____

d. Which plan is likely to be more expensive to the government? Explain.

_____

_____

e. Suppose a poor family that only earns $5,000 per year decides to plant a garden and sell the produce in a "farmer's market" in the city. Suppose the family earns an additional $5,000 selling the produce. What is the family's final income under each scheme? What is the effective tax rate on the $5,000 earned by the family under each scheme? Which scheme promotes a work ethic among the poor and which one discourages work? Explain.

_____

_____

_____

_____

Short-Answer Questions

1. How does the income distribution in the United States compare with the income distribution in other countries? Explain.

    _____

    _____

    _____

2. Does poverty affect all groups within the population the same? Explain.

    _____

    _____

    _____

3. If the poverty rate is 13 percent, does it mean that about 13 percent of the population live their entire lives in poverty? Explain.

    _____

    _____

    _____

4. Of the three political philosophies discussed in your text, which one differs the most from the other two and why? What does each school of thought suggest about income redistribution?

    _____

    _____

    _____

5. Why don't the political philosophies of utilitarianism and liberalism suggest that income be completely equalized across the population?

    _____

    _____

    _____

6. Suppose there is a minimum wage. Under which of the following conditions is employment of unskilled workers reduced by the greatest amount: when labor demand is relatively inelastic or when labor demand is relatively elastic? Why? Is labor demand likely to be more elastic or inelastic in the long run? Why?

    _____

    _____

    _____

7. How could welfare programs exacerbate the problems they are supposed to cure?

_____

_____

_____

8. What are some examples of in-kind transfers? Why do some people prefer that the government provide cash payments to the needy instead of in-kind transfers?

_____

_____

_____

Self-Test

True/False Questions

_____ 1. In the United States, the earnings of families in the top fifth of the income distribution are about twelve times the earnings of the bottom fifth of the income distribution.

_____ 2. The income distribution in the United States grew much wider from 1935 to 1970 but has narrowed since 1970.

_____ 3. The poverty line is set at approximately three times the cost of providing an adequate diet.

_____ 4. The distribution of income in the United States is more equal than the distribution of income in Japan.

_____ 5. Children are more likely than average and the elderly are less likely than average to live in poverty.

_____ 6. Because of in-kind transfers to the poor and because people's incomes vary from year to year and across their lifetimes, standard measures of income distribution exaggerate the degree of inequality in standards of living.

_____ 7. Because about 13 percent of families are below the poverty line, then it follows that about 13 percent of families live their entire lives in poverty.

_____ 8. The political philosophies of utilitarianism and liberalism both suggest that income should be equalized across the population.

_____ 9. Libertarians are more concerned with equal opportunity than with equal outcome.

_____ 10. Robert Nozick argues that economic justice would result if society chose a set of rules for the redistribution of income from behind a "veil of ignorance," and he argues that the set of rules would be the maximin criterion.

_____ 11. If the demand for labor is relatively inelastic, an increase in the minimum wage will increase unemployment among unskilled workers by a relatively small amount.

_____ 12. When compared to other welfare programs such as Temporary Assistance for Needy Families and SSI, a negative income tax would be more costly to the government but it would provide a greater incentive for the poor to work.

_____ 13. Critics of Temporary Assistance for Needy Families argue that because eligibility for this program requires that the father not be in the household, the program encourages families to break up.

_____ 14. It is more efficient for the government to provide in-kind transfers instead of cash payments.

_____ 15. If permanent income were utilized to measure the income distribution instead of current annual income, the income distribution would appear to be wider.

Multiple-Choice Questions

1. In the United States, the top 5 percent of the income distribution earns
   a. more than the bottom 40 percent of the income distribution.
   b. about twelve times what the bottom fifth of the income distribution earns.
   c. about the same as the bottom fifth of the income distribution.
   d. about half of all income.

2. The poverty line is set at
   a. two times the price of a new car.
   b. five times the value of average rent.
   c. three times the cost of providing an adequate diet.
   d. one-third of average family income.

3. Compared to other countries, the income distribution in the United States is
   a. about average.
   b. a little narrower than most.
   c. the most equal.
   d. the most unequal.

4. Which of the following is *not* an explanation for the slight widening of the income distribution in the United States since 1970?
   a. The increase in technology has decreased the demand for unskilled workers and increased the demand for skilled workers, causing the gap between their wages to widen.
   b. An increase in international trade has decreased the demand for unskilled workers and increased the demand for skilled workers, causing the gap between their wages to widen.
   c. An increase in discrimination against unskilled immigrant labor has reduced the demand for unskilled workers and caused an increase in the gap between the wages of unskilled and skilled workers.

5. In the United States, the top fifth of the income distribution earns about
   a. what the bottom fifth earns.
   b. two times what the bottom fifth earns.
   c. five times what the bottom fifth earns.
   d. twelve times what the bottom fifth earns.
   e. twenty times what the bottom fifth earns.

6. Which of the following statements about poverty rates is *not* true?
   a. Blacks and Hispanics are three times more likely to live in poverty than whites.
   b. Children are more likely than average to live in poverty.
   c. The elderly are more likely than average to live in poverty.
   d. Families headed by females with no husband present are six times as likely to live in poverty as a family headed by a married couple.

7. Since 1935, the income distribution in the United States has
   a. been unchanged.
   b. narrowed slightly from 1935 to 1970 and then widened slightly from 1970 to today.
   c. widened slightly from 1935 to 1970 and then narrowed slightly from 1970 to today.
   d. slowly widened.
   e. slowly narrowed.

8. Because in-kind transfers are not accounted for in standard measures of income distribution, the standard measures of income distribution
   a. exaggerate the inequality of living standards.
   b. understate the inequality of living standards.
   c. accurately represent the true inequality of living standards.
   d. could exaggerate or understate the inequality of living standards depending on whether the transfers are goods or services.

9. Permanent income is
   a. Social Security income of the elderly and disabled.
   b. equal to the minimum wage.
   c. a person's normal, or average, income.
   d. wages fixed by a union or other labor contract.
   e. none of the above.

10. Because people's incomes vary over the life cycle and because there are transitory shocks to people's incomes, the standard measures of income distribution
    a. exaggerate the inequality of living standards.
    b. understate the inequality of living standards.
    c. accurately represent the true inequality of living standards.
    d. could exaggerate or understate the inequality of living standards depending on whether the transitory shocks are positive or negative.

11. If people can borrow and lend to perfectly smooth out their lifetime living standards, then
    a. current annual income is a good measure of the distribution of living standards.
    b. permanent income is a good measure of the distribution of living standards.
    c. transitory income is a good measure of the distribution of living standards.
    d. life-cycle income is a good measure of the distribution of living standards.
    e. none of the above is true.

12. Jill earns more than Bob, and she came by her income fairly and honestly. Which of the following political philosophies would argue against the redistribution of income from Jill to Bob?
    a. utilitarianism
    b. liberalism
    c. libertarianism
    d. all of the above
    e. none of the above

13. The maximin criterion suggested by Rawls' theory of justice argues that the government should aim to
    a. minimize the difference between the rich and poor.
    b. maximize the total utility of society.
    c. minimize the well-being of the best-off person in society.
    d. maximize the well-being of the worst-off person in society.
    e. maximize the economic freedom of individuals by minimizing government interference in private decision making.

14. Rank utilitarianism, liberalism, and libertarianism in sequence from the political philosophy that would redistribute income the *greatest* to the one that would redistribute income the *least*.
    a.   utilitarianism, liberalism, libertarianism
    b.   libertarianism, liberalism, utilitarianism
    c.   liberalism, libertarianism, utilitarianism
    d.   liberalism, utilitarianism, libertarianism
    e.   All three political philosophies argue for similar degrees of income redistribution.

15. Utilitarianism suggests that the government should choose policies that maximize the total utility of everyone in society by
    a.   allowing each individual to maximize their own utility without interference from the government.
    b.   redistributing income from rich to poor because, due to the diminishing marginal utility of income, taking a dollar from the rich reduces their utility by less than the gain in utility generated by giving a dollar to the poor.
    c.   redistributing income from rich to poor because this would maximize the well-being of the worst-off person in society.
    d.   redistributing income from rich to poor because this is what the members of society would choose to do if they were behind a "veil of ignorance."

16. To which of the following policies is the Earned Income Tax Credit most closely related?
    a.   minimum-wage laws
    b.   welfare
    c.   negative income tax
    d.   in-kind transfers

17. An increase in the minimum wage will cause a relatively large increase in unemployment among
    a.   unskilled workers if the demand for labor is relatively elastic.
    b.   unskilled workers if the demand for labor is relatively inelastic.
    c.   skilled workers if the demand for labor is relatively elastic.
    d.   skilled workers if the demand for labor is relatively inelastic.

18. Current antipoverty programs discourage work because
    a.   they make recipients more comfortable than most middle-class Americans.
    b.   benefits are reduced at such a high rate when recipients earn more income that there is little or no incentive to work once one is receiving benefits.
    c.   antipoverty programs attract naturally lazy people to begin with.
    d.   in order to be eligible for benefits, a recipient cannot have a job.

19. The greatest advantage of a negative income tax is that it
    a.   reduces the cost to the government of fighting poverty.
    b.   generates a smaller disincentive to work than most alternative antipoverty programs.
    c.   would not provide benefits to lazy people.
    d.   ensures that the poor actually receive what the government thinks they need.
    e.   does all of the above.

20. Temporary Assistance for Needy Families
    a.   has eliminated poverty in the United States.
    b.   provides almost no disincentive to work because the benefits are very gradually reduced as a recipient's income from work increases.
    c.   may lead to the breakup of families because fathers may not be in the home if single mothers are receiving benefits.
    d.   provides in-kind transfers, such as food stamps and Medicaid, to single mothers and their children.
    e.   does all of the above.

Advanced Critical Thinking

Suppose a friend comments to you, "I think welfare recipients are simply lazy spendthrifts. I have a friend who receives Temporary Assistance for Needy Families and when she was offered a part-time job, she turned it down."

1. What happens to a welfare recipient's benefits if they increase their earnings?

   _____

   _____

   _____

2. What is the effective tax rate on their additional income if they were to lose $1 in benefits for each dollar of additional income?

   _____

   _____

   _____

   _____

3. How does this system affect a welfare recipient's incentive to work? Is a welfare recipient necessarily lazy if they turn down a part-time job?

   _____

   _____

   _____

   _____

Solutions

Terms and Definitions

<u> 6 </u> Poverty rate

<u>10</u> Poverty line

<u> 4 </u> In-kind transfers

<u>12</u> Life cycle

<u> 2 </u> Permanent income

<u> 5 </u> Utilitarianism

<u> 1 </u> Utility

<u> 8 </u> Liberalism

<u>11</u> Maximin criterion

<u>13</u> Social insurance

<u> 9 </u> Libertarianism

<u> 3 </u> Welfare

<u> 7 </u> Negative income tax

Practice Problems

1. a. Bottom fifth = 4.0 percent. Top fifth = 47.8 percent. The top fifth earns about twelve times what the bottom fifth earns.

   b. Bottom fifth range is from 4.0 percent to 5.5 percent. Top fifth range is from 40.9 percent to 51.7 percent. For the bottom fifth, their share grew until 1970 and fell thereafter. For the top fifth, their share fell until 1970 and grew thereafter. Since 1970, the increase in international trade and the increase in technology has decreased the demand for unskilled labor and increased the demand for skilled labor, increasing the relative wages of the already higher income workers.

   c. In-kind transfers are not included, the economic life cycle is not recognized, and transitory versus permanent income is not recognized. All three problems suggest that standard measures exaggerate economic inequality because the poor receive transfers in the form of goods and services and because the variation in income can be smoothed by borrowing and lending.

   d. Permanent income is a person's normal, or average, income. Using it removes the life-cycle effects and the transitory effects that cause any given year's income to be nonrepresentative of the person's true standard of living. This would probably tend to understate the true distribution of the standard of living because, in reality, we cannot fully smooth our living standards by borrowing when young or when we have a bad year.

2. a. Utilitarianism: Because there is diminishing marginal utility of income as income grows large, it would harm Susan less than it would help Joe if we redistributed income from Susan to Joe. Thus, to maximize total utility, redistribute from Susan to Joe. Liberalism: Both Susan and Joe would agree that if they didn't know their station in life, they would choose to socially insure each other with a maximin system in case they were to be the

one on the bottom end of the income distribution. So, redistribute from Susan to Joe. Libertarian: Because equal opportunity is more important than equal outcome, if each came by their income fairly and honestly, then no redistribution need take place.

   b. From least redistribution to most: libertarianism, utilitarianism, liberalism.

3. a.

Earned Income	Taxes Paid	After-Tax Income
$ 0	−$15,000	$15,000
5,000	−12,500	17,500
10,000	−10,000	20,000
20,000	−5,000	25,000
30,000	0	30,000
40,000	5,000	35,000

   b. $30,000

   c. $15,000. The government simply guarantees each family has $15,000, so once a family reaches that level, it fails to receive a subsidy.

   d. The negative income tax because, under this tax scheme, the government will continue to subsidize families in the $15,000 to $30,000 range.

   e. If negative income tax, final income = $10,000 earned income + $10,000 subsidy = $20,000. If $15,000 guarantee, final income = $10,000 + $5,000 subsidy = $15,000. If negative income tax, tax rate equals .50 because when income went up $5,000, take-home pay went up $2,500 or $2,500/$5,000 = .50. If $15,000 guarantee, tax rate equals 100 percent, because when income went up $5,000, final take-home pay stayed the same at $15,000 because benefits were reduced by $5,000 or $5,000/$5,000 = 100 percent. The $15,000 guarantee discourages work because there is no gain whatsoever from working when income is in the $0 to $15,000 range.

Short-Answer Questions

1. The United States ranks about average. Japan, Germany, India, Canada, Russia, China, and the United Kingdom have greater income equality than the United States while Nigeria, Mexico, South Africa, and Brazil have greater income inequality.

2. No. With regard to race, blacks and Hispanics are more likely to live in poverty. With regard to age, young are more likely than average and old are less likely than average to live in poverty. With regard to family composition, families headed by females are more likely to live in poverty.

3. No. There is a great deal of variation in a person's income from year to year and a great deal of variation in a person's income over their life

cycle. There is also variation from generation to generation within a family. As a result, a much larger portion of the population than 13 percent lives some small portion of their lives in poverty, and very few live a large portion of their lives in poverty.

4. Libertarianism differs from both utilitarianism and liberalism because libertarianism argues that income is earned only by individuals and not by society, so no social planner has the right to alter the distribution of income if it was generated by a fair playing field. Utilitarianism redistributes income because of the diminishing marginal utility of income, and liberalism redistributes income because of a maximin criterion for social insurance.

5. Because they recognize that taxes cause disincentives to work so that too much redistribution causes the pie to become so small that both rich and poor lose.

6. When labor demand is relatively elastic because an increase in the wage causes a large reduction in labor demand. More elastic in the long run because firms have time to adjust production in response to the rise in wages.

7. Welfare programs could cause families to break up and unwed mothers to have children. They can cause disincentives to work. Children fail to see the advantages of work, and multiple generations become dependent on government.

8. Food stamps and Medicaid. Some argue that in-kind transfers are inefficient because the government doesn't know what the poor need most, and they argue that in-kind transfers are insulting to the poor.

True/False Questions

1. T
2. F; it grew narrower from 1935 to 1970 and has grown wider since.
3. T
4. F; the distribution of income in Japan is more equal than in the United States.
5. T
6. T
7. F; because of the variation in incomes from year to year and across the life cycle, only 3 percent of families are below the poverty line for eight out of ten years.
8. F; both schools of thought recognize the disincentive to work and the reduction in total output caused by a tax system that would perfectly equalize income. Complete equality would cause both rich and poor to be worse off.
9. T
10. F; John Rawls has made this argument.
11. T
12. T
13. T

14. F; it is more efficient to provide cash payments but recipients may spend it on things taxpayers don't appreciate.
15. F; income distribution would appear to be narrower.

Multiple-Choice Questions

1. a
2. c
3. a
4. c
5. d
6. c
7. b
8. a
9. c
10. a
11. b
12. c
13. d
14. d
15. b
16. c
17. a
18. b
19. b
20. c

Advanced Critical Thinking

1. They tend to lose benefits at a very high rate.
2. The tax rate would be 100 percent on the additional income.
3. Once one is on welfare, there is little or no incentive to work. Once on welfare, one need not be lazy to remain on it. It may be rational to remain on welfare if every time a person makes a dollar, the person loses a dollar in benefits.

Chapter 21
The Theory of Consumer Choice

Goals
In this chapter
you will

- See how a budget constraint represents the choices a consumer can afford

- Learn how indifference curves can be used to represent a consumer's preferences

- Analyze how a consumer's optimal choices are determined

- See how a consumer responds to changes in income and changes in prices

- Decompose the impact of a price change into an income effect and a substitution effect

- Apply the theory of consumer choice to three questions about household behavior

Outcomes
After accomplishing
these goals, you
should be able to

- Draw a budget constraint on a graph if you are given the value of income and the prices of the goods

- Explain why indifference curves must slope downward if the two products considered are "goods"

- Explain the relationship between the relative prices and the marginal rate of substitution between two goods at the consumer's optimum

- Shift the budget constraint when the price of a good increases

- Demonstrate the income and substitution effect on a graph using indifference curves and budget constraints

- Show why someone's labor-supply curve might be backward sloping

Chapter Overview

Context and Purpose

Chapter 21 is the first of two unrelated chapters that introduce you to some advanced topics in microeconomics. These two chapters are intended to whet your appetite for further study in economics. Chapter 21 is devoted to an advanced topic known as the theory of consumer choice.

The purpose of Chapter 21 is to develop the theory that describes how consumers make decisions about what to buy. So far, we have summarized these decisions with the demand curve. We now look at the theory of consumer choice, which underlies the demand curve. After developing the theory, we apply the theory to a number of questions about how the economy works.

Chapter Review

Introduction   Chapter 21 develops the theory that describes how consumers make decisions about what to buy. So far, we have summarized these decisions with the demand curve. We now look at the theory of consumer choice, which underlies the demand curve. After developing the theory, we apply the theory to the following questions:

- Do all demand curves slope downward?
- How do wages affect labor supply?
- How do interest rates affect household saving?

The Budget Constraint: What the Consumer Can Afford

A budget constraint is the limit on the consumption bundles that a consumer can afford (given the consumer's income and the prices of the goods the consumer wishes to buy). On a graph that measures the quantity of a consumption good on each axis, a budget constraint is a straight line connecting the maximum amounts that could be purchased of each commodity given the prices of each commodity and the consumer's income. For example, if a consumer has income of $1,000 and the price of Pepsi is $2 per pint, the maximum amount of Pepsi that could be purchased is $1,000/$2 = 500 pints. If the price of pizza is $10, the maximum amount of pizza that could be purchased is $1,000/$10 = 100 pizzas.

The slope of the budget constraint is the *relative price* of the two goods. In this case since a pizza costs five times what a pint of Pepsi costs, the consumer can trade one pizza for five pints of Pepsi. If the quantity of Pepsi is plotted on the vertical axis and the quantity of pizza on the horizontal axis, the slope of the budget constraint (rise/run) is 5/1, which equals the price of pizza divided by the price of Pepsi or $10/$2 = 5. Since the budget constraint always slopes downward or negatively, we often ignore the negative sign.

Preferences: What the Consumer Wants

A consumer's preferences can be represented with indifference curves. If two bundles of commodities suit a consumer's tastes equally well, the consumer is indifferent between them. Graphically, an indifference curve is a curve that shows consumption bundles that give the consumer the same level of satisfaction. When drawn on a graph that measures the quantity consumed of each good on each axis, an indifference curve must be downward sloping because if consumption of one good is reduced, the consumption of the other good must be increased for the consumer to be equally happy. The slope at any point on an indifference curve is known as the marginal rate of substitution or *MRS*. The *MRS* is the rate at which a consumer is willing to trade one good for another while maintaining a constant level of satisfaction.

There are four properties of indifference curves:

- Higher indifference curves (further from the origin) are preferred to lower ones because people prefer more goods rather than fewer.
- Indifference curves are downward sloping because if consumption of one good is reduced, the consumption of the other good must be increased for the consumer to be equally happy.
- Indifference curves do not cross because it would suggest that a consumer's preferences are contradictory.
- Indifference curves are bowed inward because a consumer is willing to trade a greater amount of a good for another good if they have an abundance of the good they are trading away and they are willing to trade a lesser amount of a good for another good if they have very little of the good they are trading away.

When it is easy to substitute two goods for each other, indifference curves are bowed inward very little. When it is difficult to substitute two goods for each other, indifference curves are bowed inward a great deal. This is demonstrated by two extreme cases:

- Perfect substitutes: two goods with straight-line indifference curves. An example of perfect substitutes is nickels and dimes—two nickels for each dime.
- Perfect complements: two goods with right-angle indifference curves. An example of perfect complements is right shoes and left shoes—additional shoes that don't come in pairs do not increase satisfaction.

Optimization: What the Consumer Chooses

When we combine the budget constraint and the consumer's indifference curves, we are able to determine the amount of each commodity that the consumer will buy. The consumer will try to reach the highest indifference curve subject to remaining on the budget constraint. The point where an indifference curve just touches the budget constraint determines the *optimum* amount of purchases of each good. At the optimum, the indifference curve is *tangent* to the budget constraint and the slope of the indifference curve and the budget constraint are the same. Thus, the consumer chooses consumption of the two goods so that the marginal rate of substitution (slope of the indifference curve) equals the relative price of the two goods (slope of the budget constraint). At the optimum, the trade-off between the goods that the consumer is willing to make (slope of the indifference curve) is equal to the trade-off between the goods that the market is willing to make (slope of the budget constraint).

An alternative way to describe preferences and optimization is with the concept of utility. Utility is an abstract measure of the happiness or satisfaction a consumer receives from consuming a bundle of goods. Therefore, an indifference curve is actually an "equal-utility" curve. The *marginal utility* of a good is the increase in utility one gets from consuming an additional unit of that good. Goods exhibit *diminishing marginal utility* as more of any good is consumed. Since the marginal rate of substitution (the slope of the indifference curve) is the trade-off between two goods that the consumer is willing to make, it must also equal the marginal utility of one good divided by the marginal utility of the other good. Therefore, for two goods X and Y, at the optimum:

$$MRS = P_x/P_y = MU_x/MU_y$$

or

$$MU_x/P_x = MU_y/P_y.$$

At the optimum, the marginal utility of a dollar spent on X must be equal to the marginal utility of a dollar spent on Y. Similarly, one can say that, at the optimum, the indifference curve is tangent to the budget constraint.

Suppose the income of the consumer were to increase. Because the consumer can now consume more of both goods and because the relative price of the two goods remains unchanged, an increase in income shifts the budget constraint outward in a parallel fashion. The consumer can now reach a new optimum on a higher indifference curve. It is most common that the consumer will choose to consume more of both goods. Thus, a normal good is a good for which an increase in income raises the quantity demanded. Alternatively, an inferior good is a good for which an increase in income reduces the quantity demanded. Bus rides are an inferior good.

Suppose the price of one of the goods were to fall. If the consumer allocates all of his income to the good whose price has fallen, the consumer can buy more of that good. If the consumer allocates all of his income to the good whose price is unchanged, the maximum amount he can purchase remains unchanged. This causes the budget constraint to rotate outward. That is, the budget constraint only shifts outward on the axis of the good whose price has fallen. The consumer can now reach a new optimum on a higher indifference curve.

The impact of a change in the price of a good can be decomposed into two effects: an income effect and a substitution effect. The income effect is the change in consumption that results when a price change moves the consumer to a higher or lower indifference curve. The substitution effect is the change in consumption that results when a price change moves the consumer along a given indifference curve to a point with a new marginal rate of substitution. Graphically, the substitution effect is the change in consumption that results from the change in relative prices, which rotates the budget line along a given indifference curve. The income effect is the change in consumption that results from the parallel shift in the budget constraint to the new optimum on the new indifference curve.

A demand curve can be derived from the consumer's optimizing decisions that result from the consumer's budget constraint and indifference curves. The combined income and substitution effect shows the total change in quantity demanded from a change in the price of a good. When these values are plotted on a price/quantity graph, the points form the consumer's demand curve.

Three Applications

- *Do all demand curves slope downward?* Theoretically, demand can sometimes slope upward. If an increase in the price of an inferior good has a larger income effect than substitution effect (the good is very strongly inferior), then an increase in the price of the good would cause the quantity demanded to rise. A Giffen good is a good for which an increase in the price raises the quantity demanded. Giffen goods are extremely rare. Evidence suggests that rice in China may be a Giffen good.

- *How do wages affect labor supply?* The theory of consumer choice can be applied to the allocation decision between work (to afford consumption goods) and leisure. In this case, the two goods are consumption and leisure. The maximum amount of leisure is the number of hours available. The maximum amount of consumption is the number of hours available times the wage. The individual's indifference curves determine an optimum amount of leisure and consumption. Suppose the wage were to rise. The substitution effect induces more consumption and less leisure (more work). However, if both leisure and consumption are normal goods, the income effect suggests that the individual will wish to have both more consumption and more leisure (less work). If the substitution effect outweighs the income effect, an increase in wages will increase the quantity of labor supplied and labor supply is upward sloping. If the income effect outweighs the substitution effect, an increase in wages will decrease the quantity of labor supplied and labor supply slopes backward. Evidence that the workweek is getting shorter suggests that the income effect is very strong and the labor supply curve bends backward when measured over long periods of time. Evidence on the behavior of lottery winners and people who receive large bequests suggests that, at high-income levels, the labor-supply curve is backward sloping.

- *How do interest rates affect household saving?* The theory of consumer choice can be applied to the decision of how much income to consume today and how much to save for tomorrow. In this case, we measure consumption when young on the horizontal axis and consumption when old on the vertical axis. A person can consume all of his earnings when young and have nothing when old, or consume nothing when young, save all of his income, earn interest on the saving, and consume a greater amount when old. A person's preferences determine the optimal amounts of consumption in each period. If the interest rate rises, the budget constraint becomes steeper because the maximum possible consumption when old increases. When the interest rate rises, the substitution effect suggests that the consumer should increase consumption when old and decrease consumption when young (save more) because consumption when old has become relatively cheaper. However, if consumption in both periods is a normal good, the income effect suggests that the individual should consume more in both periods (save less). If the substitution effect outweighs the income effect, an increase in the interest rate will cause the individual to save more. If the income effect outweighs the substitution effect, an increase in the interest rate will cause the individual to save less. Evidence on this issue is mixed, so there is no clear recommendation for public policy toward the taxation of interest.

Conclusion: Do People Really Think This Way?

Although consumers may not literally make decisions in the manner suggested by the theory of consumer choice, the model of consumer choice describes a process that permits economic analysis. The theory is useful in many applications.

Helpful Hints

1. We have noted that the slope of the budget constraint is equal to the relative prices of the two goods represented on the graph. However, which price should we put in the numerator and which price should we put in the denominator of the slope? Place the price of the good represented on the horizontal axis in the numerator and the price of the good represented on the vertical axis in the denominator of the slope. For example, if the quantity of popcorn is measured on the horizontal axis and the quantity of candy bars is measured on the vertical axis, and if the price of a bag of popcorn is $2 while the price of a candy bar is $1, then two candy bars can be exchanged for one bag of popcorn. The slope of the budget constraint is $2/$1 or 2. (Again, the slope of the budget constraint is always negative so we often ignore the sign.)

2. A mapping of an individual's preferences generates an infinite set of indifference curves. Each indifference curve divides the commodity space into three areas—points preferred to those on the indifference curve (points outside the indifference curve or away from the origin), points inferior to the indifference curve (points inside the indifference curve or toward the origin), or points of equal satisfaction as those on the indifference curve (points on the indifference curve). Although there are an infinite set of indifference curves, it is customary to represent on a graph only those indifference curves that are tangent to a budget constraint, and thus, only those indifference curves that determine an optimum.

3. The slope of the indifference curve is the marginal rate of substitution, which is the marginal utility of one good compared to the marginal utility of the other good. The slope of the budget constraint is equal to the relative prices of the two goods. Because at the optimum, the indifference curve is tangent to the budget constraint, it follows that at the optimum the relative prices of the two goods equal the relative marginal utilities of the two goods. Thus, at the optimum, the additional utility gained by the consumer from an additional dollar's worth of one good is the same as the additional utility gained by the consumer from an additional dollar's worth of the other good. That is, at the optimum, the consumer cannot increase his total satisfaction by moving expenditures from one good to the other good.

Terms and Definitions

Choose a definition for each key term.

Key Terms

_____ Budget constraint

_____ Indifference curve

_____ Marginal rate of

substitution

_____ Perfect substitutes

_____ Perfect complements

_____ Normal good

_____ Inferior good

_____ Income effect

_____ Substitution effect

_____ Giffen good

Definitions

1. The change in consumption that results when a price change moves the consumer to a higher or lower indifference curve

2. The rate at which a consumer is willing to trade one good for another

3. The limit on the consumption bundles that a consumer can afford

4. A good for which an increase in income raises the quantity demanded

5. A good for which an increase in the price raises the quantity demanded

6. Two goods with right-angle indifference curves

7. A curve that shows consumption bundles that give the consumer the same level of satisfaction

8. A good for which an increase in income reduces the quantity demanded

9. Two goods with straight-line indifference curves

10. The change in consumption that results when a price change moves the consumer along a given indifference curve to a point with a new marginal rate of substitution

Problems and Short-Answer Questions

Practice Problems

1. Suppose a consumer only buys two goods—hot dogs and hamburgers. Suppose the price of hot dogs is $1, the price of hamburgers is $2, and the consumer's income is $20.

    a. Plot the consumer's budget constraint in Exhibit 1. Measure the quantity of hot dogs on the vertical axis and the quantity of hamburgers on the horizontal axis. Explicitly plot the points on the budget constraint associated with the even-numbered quantities of hamburgers (0, 2, 4, 6 . . .).

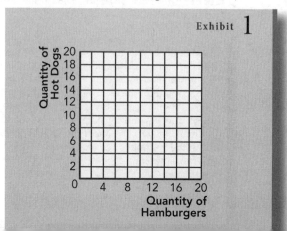

b.   Suppose the individual chooses to consume 6 hamburgers. What is the maximum amount of hot dogs that he can afford? Draw an indifference curve on the figure above that establishes this bundle of goods as the optimum.

_____

c.   What is the slope of the budget constraint? What is the slope of the consumer's indifference curve at the optimum? What is the relationship between the slope of the budget constraint and the slope of the indifference curve at the optimum? What is the economic interpretation of this relationship?

_____

_____

_____

d.   Explain why any other point on the budget constraint must be inferior to the optimum.

_____

_____

_____

_____

2. Use Exhibit 2 to answer the following questions.

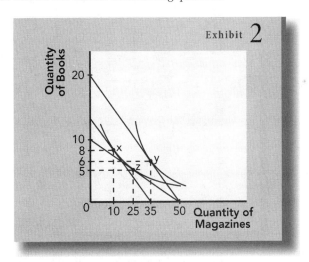

a.   Suppose the price of a magazine is $2, the price of a book is $10, and the consumer's income is $100. Which point on the graph represents the consumer's optimum—x, y, or z? What are the optimal quantities of books and magazines this individual chooses to consume?

_____

_____

b.   Suppose the price of books falls to $5. What are the two optimum points on the graph that represent the substitution effect (in sequence)? What is the change in the consumption of books due to the substitution effect?

_____

c. Again, suppose the price of books falls to $5. What are the two optimum points on the graph that represent the income effect (in sequence)? What is the change in the consumption of books due to the income effect? Is a book a normal good or an inferior good for this consumer? Explain.

_____

_____

_____

d. For this consumer, what is the total change in the quantity of books purchased when the price of books fell from $10 to $5?

_____

_____

e. Use the information in this problem to plot the consumer's demand curve for books in Exhibit 3.

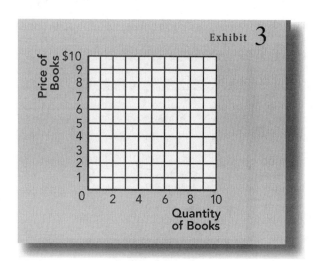

Short-Answer Questions

1. Suppose that there are two goods available to the consumer—pens and pencils. Suppose that the price of a pen is $2.00 while the price of a pencil is $0.50. If we measure the quantity of pens on the horizontal axis and the quantity of pencils on the vertical axis, what is the slope of the budget constraint? Do you need to know the income of the consumer to answer this question? Why or why not?

_____

_____

_____

_____

2. If we measure "goods" on each axis, is an indifference curve positively (upward) sloped or negatively (downward) sloped? Why? If we measure a "good" on one axis

but a "bad" (such as pollution) on the other axis, what type of slope do you think an indifference curve would have? Why?

_____

_____

_____

_____

3. Why are most indifference curves bowed inward?

_____

_____

_____

_____

4. Consider the following two pairs of goods:
    ♦ Graduation caps and graduation gowns
    ♦ Gasoline at an Exxon station and gasoline at a Shell station

    Which of the pairs of goods above is likely to be nearly perfect substitutes, and which is likely to be nearly perfect complements? Explain.

_____

_____

_____

_____

5. Referring to question 4 above, what is the shape of the indifference curves that you would expect each pair of goods to generate, straight-line or right-angle? For which pair of goods would you observe the greatest substitution effect if the relative prices of the two goods were to change? Why?

_____

_____

_____

_____

6. Suppose there are two goods available to the consumer—coffee and tea. Suppose that the price of coffee decreases. What impact will the substitution effect and income effect have on the quantity demanded of coffee if coffee is a normal good? Explain. What impact will the substitution effect and income effect have on the quantity demanded of coffee if coffee is an inferior good? Explain.

_____

_____

_____

_____

7. Suppose there are only two goods available to you, apples and oranges. Suppose that the prices of apples and oranges double and that your income also doubles. What will happen to the amount of apples and oranges that you choose to consume? Explain. (Hint: What has happened to the slope of the budget constraint? What has happened to the maximum amount of apples or oranges that you could consume if you allocated all of your income to one good or the other?)

_____

_____

_____

_____

8. Some people argue that the tax rate should be reduced on interest earned from saving because it will increase the after-tax return to saving, increase the quantity of saving supplied, and increase economic growth. Are we certain that a decrease in the tax rate on interest earned from saving will increase the quantity of saving? Explain.

_____

_____

_____

_____

Self-Test

True/False Questions

_____ 1. If we measure the quantity of French fries on the horizontal axis and the quantity of hamburgers on the vertical axis, and if the price of French fries is $0.60 and the price of a hamburger is $2.40, then the slope of the budget constraint is 1/4 (and it is negative).

_____ 2. A budget constraint is a set of commodity bundles that provide the consumer with the same level of satisfaction.

_____ 3. Indifference curves measure the consumer's willingness to trade one good for another good while maintaining a constant level of satisfaction.

_____ 4. When drawn on a graph that measures the quantity of a good on each axis, indifference curves are usually straight lines that slope downward (negatively).

_____ 5. If two goods are perfect complements, indifference curves associated with these two goods would cross each other at the optimum.

_____ 6. Indifference curves tend to be bowed inward because a consumer is willing to trade a greater amount of a good for another if they have an abundance of the good they are trading away.

_____ 7. At the consumer's optimum point, the marginal rate of substitution of apples for oranges is equal to the ratio of the price of oranges to the price of apples.

_____ 8. The more difficult it is to substitute one good for another, the more bowed inward indifference curves become.

_____ 9.   If the price of a good falls, the substitution effect always causes an increase in the quantity demanded of that good.

_____ 10.   If the price of a good falls and the good is a normal good, the income effect causes a decrease in the quantity demanded of that good.

_____ 11.   If the price of a good falls and the good is an inferior good, the income effect causes a decrease in the quantity demanded of that good.

_____ 12.   The income effect is measured as the change in consumption that results when a price change moves the consumer along a given indifference curve to a point with a new marginal rate of substitution.

_____ 13.   An increase in the interest rate will always lead to a greater amount of saving.

_____ 14.   A Giffen good is an extremely inferior good.

_____ 15.   The theory of consumer choice can be used to demonstrate that labor supply curves must be upward sloping.

Multiple-Choice Questions

1. The limit on the consumption bundles that a consumer can afford is known as
    a.   an indifference curve.
    b.   the marginal rate of substitution.
    c.   the budget constraint.
    d.   the consumption limit.

2. A change in the relative prices of which of the following pairs of goods would likely cause the smallest substitution effect?
    a.   gasoline from 7-Eleven and gasoline from Quick Stop
    b.   right shoes and left shoes
    c.   Coca-Cola and Pepsi
    d.   Bud Light and Coors Light

3. Indifference curves for perfect substitutes are
    a.   straight lines.
    b.   bowed inward.
    c.   bowed outward.
    d.   right angles.
    e.   nonexistent.

4. Suppose a consumer must choose between the consumption of sandwiches and pizza. If we measure the quantity of pizza on the horizontal axis and the quantity of sandwiches on the vertical axis, and if the price of a pizza is $10 and the price of a sandwich is $5, then the slope of the budget constraint is
    a.   5.
    b.   10.
    c.   2.
    d.   1/2.

5. The slope at any point on an indifference curve is known as
    a.   the trade-off rate.
    b.   the marginal rate of substitution.
    c.   the marginal rate of trade-off.
    d.   the marginal rate of indifference.

6. Which of the following statements is *not* true with regard to the standard properties of indifference curves?
   a.   Indifference curves are downward sloping.
   b.   Indifference curves do not cross each other.
   c.   Higher indifference curves are preferred to lower ones.
   d.   Indifference curves are bowed outward.

7. The consumer's optimal purchase of any two goods is the point where
   a.   the consumer reaches the highest indifference curve subject to remaining on the budget constraint.
   b.   the consumer has reached the highest indifference curve.
   c.   the two highest indifference curves cross.
   d.   the budget constraint crosses the indifference curve.

8. Which of the following is *true* about the consumer's optimum consumption bundle? At the optimum,
   a.   the indifference curve is tangent to the budget constraint.
   b.   the slope of the indifference curve equals the slope of the budget constraint.
   c.   the relative prices of the two goods equals the marginal rate of substitution.
   d.   all of the above are true.
   e.   none of the above is true.

9. Suppose we measure the quantity of good X on the horizontal axis and the quantity of good Y on the vertical axis. If indifference curves are bowed inward, as we move from having an abundance of good X to having an abundance of good Y, the marginal rate of substitution of good Y for good X (the slope of the indifference curve)
   a.   rises.
   b.   falls.
   c.   stays the same.
   d.   could rise or fall depending on the relative prices of the two goods.

10. If an increase in a consumer's income causes the consumer to increase his quantity demanded of a good, then the good is
    a.   an inferior good.
    b.   a normal good.
    c.   a substitute good.
    d.   a complementary good.

11. If an increase in a consumer's income causes the consumer to decrease her quantity demanded of a good, then the good is
    a.   an inferior good.
    b.   a normal good.
    c.   a substitute good.
    d.   a complementary good.

Suppose that the consumer must choose between buying socks and belts. Also, suppose that the consumer's income is $100. Use Exhibit 4 to answer questions 12 through 15.

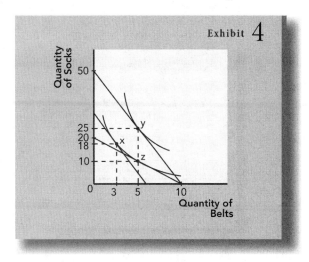

12. If the price of a belt is $10 and the price of a pair of socks is $5, the consumer will choose to buy the commodity bundle represented by point
    a. x.
    b. y.
    c. z.
    d. The optimal point cannot be determined from this graph.

13. Suppose that the price of a pair of socks falls from $5 to $2. The substitution effect is represented by the movement from point
    a. y to point x.
    b. x to point y.
    c. z to point x.
    d. x to point z.

14. Suppose that the price of a pair of socks falls from $5 to $2. The income effect is represented by the movement from point
    a. y to point x.
    b. x to point y.
    c. z to point x.
    d. x to point z.

15. A pair of socks is
    a. an inferior good.
    b. a normal good.
    c. a Giffen good.
    d. none of the above.

16. The change in consumption that results when a price change moves the consumer along a given indifference curve is known as the
    a. complementary effect.
    b. normal effect.
    c. income effect.
    d. substitution effect.
    e. inferior effect.

17. If income and prices were both to double, the budget line would
    a. shift outward in a parallel fashion.
    b. shift inward in a parallel fashion.
    c. stay the same.
    d. rotate inward.
    e. rotate outward.

18. If leisure is a normal good, an increase in the wage
    a. will always increase the quantity of labor supplied.
    b. will always decrease the amount of labor supplied.
    c. will increase the amount of labor supplied if the income effect outweighs the substitution effect.
    d. will increase the amount of labor supplied if the substitution effect outweighs the income effect.

19. If consumption when young and when old are both normal goods, an increase in the interest rate
    a. will always increase the quantity of saving.
    b. will always decrease the quantity of saving.
    c. will increase the quantity of saving if the substitution effect outweighs the income effect.
    d. will increase the quantity of saving if the income effect outweighs the substitution effect.

20. Which of the following is *not* true regarding the outcome of a consumer's optimization process?
    a. The consumer has reached his highest indifference curve subject to his budget constraint.
    b. The marginal utility per dollar spent on each good is the same.
    c. The consumer is indifferent between any two points on his budget constraint.
    d. The marginal rate of substitution between goods is equal to the ratio of the prices between goods.
    e. The consumer's indifference curve is tangent to his budget constraint.

Advanced Critical Thinking

Suppose you have a wealthy aunt. Your aunt dies and leaves you a great deal of money (potentially). When you attend the reading of the will, you discover that she has bequeathed her millions to a "family incentive trust." As the lawyer reads the will, you discover that you only get the money if you get married, have children, stay with your spouse and raise your children, don't become dependent on drugs or alcohol, and if you *continuously have a full-time job*. (Note: Family incentive trusts are real and becoming very common.)

1. Why might your aunt include the requirement that you continuously have a full-time job?

   _____

   _____

   _____

   _____

   _____

2. Does the evidence about how people behave after they receive an inheritance suggest that your aunt's concerns are well founded, or is she just a control freak who wants to control the lives of her relatives even after she is gone? Explain.

   _____

   _____

   _____

   _____

   _____

3. What does this evidence suggest about the slope of the labor-supply curve? Explain.

   _____

   _____

   _____

   _____

   _____

Solutions

Terms and Definitions

__3__   Budget constraint

__7__   Indifference curve

__2__   Marginal rate of substitution

__9__   Perfect substitutes

__6__   Perfect complements

__4__   Normal good

__8__   Inferior good

__1__   Income effect

__10__ Substitution effect

__5__   Giffen good

Practice Problems

1. a. See Exhibit 5.

Exhibit 5

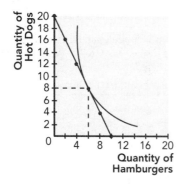

b. Eight. For the indifference curve, see Exhibit 5.

c. Rise over run = 2/1. This is also the price ratio of price of hamburgers to price of hot dogs = $2/$1. The slope of the indifference curve is also 2/1. (Note: All of these slopes are negative.) At the optimum, the indifference curve is tangent to the budget constraint so their slopes are equal. Thus, the trade-off between the goods that the individual is willing to undertake (*MRS*) is the same as the trade-off that the market requires (slope of budget constraint).

d. Because the highest indifference curve reachable is tangent to the budget constraint, any other point on the budget constraint must have an indifference curve running through it that is below the optimal indifference curve, so that point must be inferior to the optimum.

2. a. Point z. 25 magazines and 5 books.

b. From point z to point x. From 5 books to 8 books.

c. From point x to point y. From 8 books to 6 books. Books are inferior because an increase in income decreases the quantity demanded of books.

d. The quantity demanded increased from 5 books to 6 books.

e. See Exhibit 6.

Exhibit 6

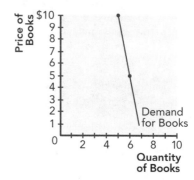

Short-Answer Questions

1. Slope = rise/run = 4/1 or 4. It is also the ratio of the price of pens to the price of pencils or $2.00/$0.50 = 4. (All slopes are negative.) No. Income simply must be any positive amount. A change in income shifts the budget constraint in or out but does not change its slope.

2. Negatively sloped because, for a consumer to be equally happy, if consumption of one good is reduced, the consumption of the other good must be increased. Positively sloped because, for a consumer to be equally happy, if consumption of the bad item is increased, the consumption of the good item must also be increased.

3. Because the marginal rate of substitution (*MRS*) is not constant along most indifference curves. A consumer is willing to trade a greater amount of a good for another if they have an abundance of the good they are trading away. They are willing to trade a lesser amount away if they have very little of the good they are trading away.

4. Exxon gas and Shell gas are nearly perfect substitutes because the marginal rate of substitution is fixed at about one—one gallon of Exxon gas for one gallon of Shell gas. Graduation caps and gowns are nearly perfect complements because additional units of caps without gowns or additional units of gowns without caps provide little or no additional satisfaction.

5. Exxon gas and Shell gas would have nearly straight-line indifference curves while graduation caps and gowns would have nearly right-angle indifference curves. A change in the relative prices of gas would cause a great substitution between gas at each station while a change in the relative prices of caps and gowns would cause little or no substitution of caps for gowns or gowns for caps.

6. The substitution effect will cause an increase in the quantity demanded of coffee regardless of whether coffee is normal or inferior. If coffee is normal, the income effect will cause an increase

in the quantity demanded of coffee. If coffee is inferior, the income effect will cause a decrease in the quantity demanded of coffee.

7. There will be no impact because the slope of the budget constraint is unaltered (relative prices are the same so the market trade-off is the same) and the position of the budget constraint is unaltered (the maximum amount of each good that can be purchased is unaltered so the end points of the budget constraint are the same).

8. No. An increase in the return to saving should increase consumption when old (substitution effect increases saving), but an increase in the return to saving increases income and should increase consumption when young and old (income effect decreases saving). If the income effect outweighs the substitution effect, a greater after-tax return on saving would decrease saving.

True/False Questions

1. T
2. F; a budget constraint is the limit on the consumption bundles that a consumer can afford.
3. T
4. F; indifference curves are negatively sloped but they are usually bowed inward.
5. F; indifference curves for perfect complements are right angles but still never cross another indifference curve.
6. T
7. T
8. T
9. T
10. F; the income effect would cause an increase in the quantity demanded.
11. T
12. F; the income effect is measured as the change in consumption that results when a change in price moves the consumer to a higher or lower indifference curve.
13. F; if the income effect from a change in interest rates outweighs the substitution effect, the individual will save less.
14. T
15. F; labor supply curves can be backward sloping if the income effect from a change in the wage outweighs the substitution effect.

Multiple-Choice Questions

1. c
2. b
3. a
4. c
5. b
6. d
7. a
8. d
9. a
10. b
11. a
12. c
13. c
14. b
15. b
16. d
17. c
18. d
19. c
20. c

Advanced Critical Thinking

1. She is probably afraid that her gift of millions would tempt you to be lazy and cause you to lead a less useful life than you would otherwise.

2. Her concerns may be well founded. People who win lotteries or receive large inheritances often quit work or reduce the hours they work.

3. This evidence suggests that the labor supply curve may be backward sloping. We generally assume that a higher wage increases the quantity supplied of labor (upward sloping labor supply), but in fact, a higher wage may decrease the quantity of labor supplied (backward sloping labor supply) if leisure is a normal good and the income effect of an increase in the wage outweighs the substitution effect.

Chapter 22
Frontiers of Microeconomics

Goals
In this chapter you will

- Examine the problems caused by asymmetric information
- Learn about market solutions to asymmetric information
- Consider why democratic voting systems may not represent the preferences of society
- Consider why people may not always behave as rational maximizers

Outcomes
After accomplishing these goals, you should be able to

- Describe the information asymmetry in the labor market
- Explain why insurance companies screen potential customers
- Generate an example of the Condorcet voting paradox
- Explain why people are willing to sign contracts that require them to contribute a portion of their paychecks to a retirement savings program

Chapter Overview

Context and Purpose

Chapter 22 is the last chapter in the microeconomics portion of the text. It is the second of two unrelated chapters that introduce you to some advanced topics in microeconomics. These two chapters are intended to whet your appetite for further study in economics.

The purpose of Chapter 22 is to give you a taste of three topics on the frontier of microeconomic research. The first topic we address is *asymmetric information*, a situation when one person in an economic relationship has more relevant knowledge than the other person. The second topic is *political economy*, the application of economic tools to the understanding of the functioning of government. The third topic we address is *behavioral economics*, the introduction of psychology into the study of economic issues.

Chapter Review

Introduction   The study of economics is always seeking to expand the understanding of human behavior and society. This chapter addresses three areas on the frontier of economic study. The first topic we address is *asymmetric information*, a situation when one person in an economic relationship has more relevant knowledge than the other person. The second topic is *political economy*, the application of economic tools to the understanding of the functioning of government. The third topic we address is *behavioral economics*, the introduction of psychology into the study of economic issues.

Asymmetric Information

A difference in access to relevant knowledge is called an *information asymmetry*. We address two types of information asymmetries: *hidden actions* and *hidden characteristics*.

- **Hidden Actions and Moral Hazard:** *Hidden actions* may occur when a person (called the agent) performs some task on behalf of another person (called the principal); generally, the agent knows more about his effort and performance than the principal. The problem of moral hazard arises if the principal cannot perfectly monitor the agent, so the agent tends to engage in dishonest or undesirable behavior (he shirks his responsibilities). In the employment relationship, the employer is the principal and the worker is the agent. Employers respond to the moral hazard problem with the following:

  - *Better monitoring:* Employers use video cameras to catch irresponsible behavior or workers.

  - *High wages:* Firms pay efficiency wages (above equilibrium wages) to raise the cost to the worker of being fired and make the worker less likely to shirk.

  - *Delayed payment:* Year-end bonuses and higher pay later in life reduce shirking today.

  - Insurance can generate moral hazard because the insured may have little incentive to reduce the risk of an accident.

  There is a principal–agent problem in the corporate structure because there is a separation of ownership (the principal) and management (the agent). Shareholders hire a board of directors to oversee management and create incentives for management to maximize profits rather than pursue their own objectives. Sometimes corporate managers are sent to prison for taking advantage of shareholders.

- **Hidden Characteristics and Adverse Selection:**   Hidden characteristics are when a seller knows more than the buyer about the good being sold. Hidden characteristics may generate a problem known as adverse selection—the buyer risks selecting goods of low quality. Adverse selection may occur in the market for the following:

  - *Used cars.* Buyers may choose not to buy even slightly used cars because they surmise that sellers know something bad about the cars. This is known as the "lemons" problem.

  - *Labor.* If a firm reduces the wage it pays, high-productivity workers tend to quit and the firm is left with low-productivity workers.

  - *Insurance.* People with hidden health problems are more likely to want to buy health insurance than people with average or good health.

  When markets suffer from adverse selection, people may continue to drive used cars they would rather sell, firms may pay wages above equilibrium and cause unemployment, and relatively healthy people may fail to purchase health insurance because it is too expensive. That is, markets may become inefficient.

Markets respond to asymmetric information in several ways:

- **Signaling** Signaling is when an informed party takes actions to reveal information to an uninformed party. Recall from previous chapters that firms spend money on expensive advertising to signal that they sell high-quality products. Students attend high-quality schools to signal that they are high-ability people. For a signal to be effective, it must be costly but less costly to the person with the higher-quality product. Signaling is rational for both the buyer and seller. A personal gift qualifies as a signal of love because it is costly (it takes time to purchase), and if someone loves another the most, they know what to buy (takes less time to buy than it would for a simple acquaintance).

- **Screening** Screening is when an uninformed party acts to induce an informed party to reveal private information. Buyers of used cars may have their mechanic check out a used car. Auto insurers may check a driver's driving history or offer different policies that have different degrees of appeal to risky and safe drivers so the two kinds of drivers will reveal their driving characteristics.

Although markets may fail to allocate resources efficiently when there is asymmetric information, it is not clear that public policy actions can improve market outcomes because of the following:

- Private markets can sometimes deal with the problem by using signaling and screening.

- The government rarely has more information than private parties, so it cannot improve upon the current imperfect allocation of resources. Thus, the market is not first-best, but is second-best.

- The government itself is an imperfect institution.

Political Economy

Political economy, also known as *public choice*, is the study of government using the analytic methods of economics. Before we choose to have the government attempt to improve market outcomes, we must recognize that government is also imperfect.

- **The Condorcet Voting Paradox** The Condorcet voting paradox is the failure of majority rule to produce transitive preferences for society. *Transitivity* is the property that if A is preferred to B, and B preferred to C, then A must be preferred to C. When society has to choose between more than two outcomes, majority rule democracy may not tell us which alternative society really wants because pair-wise voting across three or more alternatives does not guarantee transitivity, a phenomenon known as the Condorcet paradox. That is, it is possible under pair-wise voting that A is preferred to B, and B preferred to C, yet C is preferred to A. Because the property of transitivity is required for majority-rule democracy to accurately aggregate preferences, two conclusions can be drawn: (1) Majority-rule voting does not necessarily tell us what society wants, and (2) setting the order in which items are voted on can affect the outcome.

- **Arrow's Impossibility Theorem** Arrow's impossibility theorem is a mathematical result showing that, under certain assumed conditions, there is no scheme for aggregating individual preferences into a valid set of social preferences. Due to the Condorcet paradox, alternative voting systems have been proposed. A Borda count allows voters to rank and give points to possible outcomes when there are more than two outcomes—like sports team rankings. However, Arrow has shown that no voting system can satisfy the following properties required of a perfect voting scheme:

   - *Unanimity*: If everyone prefers A to B, then A should beat B.
   - *Transitivity*: If A beats B, and B beats C, then A should beat C.

♦ *Independence of irrelevant alternatives:* The rankings between any two outcomes should not depend on whether some third outcome is available.

♦ *No dictators:* There is no person who always gets his way.

For example, majority rule does not always satisfy transitivity, and the Borda count does not always satisfy the independence of irrelevant alternatives. While democracy should not be abandoned, all voting schemes are flawed mechanisms for social choice.

• **The median voter is king.**   The median voter theorem is a mathematical result showing that if voters are choosing a point along a line and each voter wants the point closest to his most preferred point, then majority rule will pick the most preferred point of the median voter. The median voter is the voter exactly in the middle of the distribution. Majority rule voting will always generate an outcome that is preferred by the median voter if each voter votes for the outcome that is closest to his most preferred outcome. This outcome will not necessarily be the average preferred outcome or the modal outcome. In addition, minority views are not given much weight.

• **Politicians may be self-interested.**   Self-interest may cause politicians to maximize their own well-being as opposed to maximizing the well-being of society. Some politicians may act out of greed, and others may sacrifice the national interest to improve their local popularity. Therefore, actual economic policy often fails to resemble the ideal policy derived in economic textbooks.

Behavioral Economics

Behavioral economics is the subfield of economics that integrates the insights of psychology.

People aren't always rational. Economists generally assume that people and firms behave rationally. But people may not act as rational maximizers but instead as *satisficers.* Or people may exhibit "near rationality" or "bounded rationality." People make the following systematic errors:

• People are overconfident.

• People give too much weight to a small number of vivid observations.

• People are reluctant to change their minds.

Regardless of these issues, economic models based on rationality may be good approximations of reality.

People care about fairness: The *ultimatum game* is a game where one player decides what portion of $100 to give to another player. The second player must either accept the split or both get nothing. Rational wealth maximizers would choose $99 and offer $1. The second player would accept this offer because $1 is better than nothing. In experiments, however, the first player tends to give much more than $1 (but less than $50) to the second player, and the second player usually rejects small offerings. People may be driven by a sense of fairness as opposed to their normal self-interest. As a result, firms may pay above equilibrium wages during profitable years to be fair or to avoid retaliation on the part of workers.

People are inconsistent over time: People tend to desire instant gratification as opposed to delayed gratification. Therefore, they fail to follow through on plans to do things that are dreary, take effort, or cause discomfort. For example, people often save less than they plan. To help follow through on a plan, people may restrict their future behavior: Smokers throw away their cigarettes, dieters put a lock on the refrigerator, and workers sign up for a retirement plan.

Conclusion

This chapter introduced areas of continuing economic research. Asymmetric information should make us more wary of market outcomes. Political economy should make us more wary of government solutions. Behavioral economics should make us more wary of human decision making.

Helpful Hints

1. The market for insurance demonstrates many of the problems and market solutions generated by asymmetric information. For auto insurance, firms first screen prospective customers to reduce adverse selection—the problem of selling insurance to worse than average drivers. After the sale of the insurance, auto insurance companies require a deductible or co-payment on collision insurance. This reduces moral hazard—the problem of insured drivers driving more recklessly once they are insured.

2. No method of economic decision making is always perfect. Markets may not maximize total surplus due to externalities, public goods, imperfect competition, and asymmetric information. In addition, people and firms may not always rationally maximize their own well-being. However, government may not be able to improve upon the situation because governments may not have any better information than markets, all voting schemes are imperfect, and politicians may choose to maximize their own well-being instead of the well-being of society.

Terms and Definitions

Choose a definition for each key term.

Key Terms

_____ Moral hazard

_____ Agent

_____ Principal

_____ Adverse selection

_____ Signaling

_____ Screening

_____ Political economy

_____ Condorcet paradox

_____ Arrow's impossibility theorem

_____ Median voter theorem

_____ Behavioral economics

Definitions

1. An action taken by an informed party to reveal private information to an uninformed party

2. The failure of majority rule to produce transitive preferences for society

3. A person for whom another person, called the agent, is performing some act

4. The tendency of a person who is imperfectly monitored to engage in dishonest or otherwise undesirable behavior

5. A mathematical result showing that if voters are choosing a point along a line and each voter wants the point closest to his most preferred point, then majority rule will pick the most preferred point of the median voter

6. A mathematical result showing that, under certain assumed conditions, there is no scheme for aggregating individual preferences into a valid set of social preferences

7. The tendency for the mix of unobserved attributes to become undesirable from the standpoint of an uninformed party

8. A person who is performing an act for another person, called the principal

9. An action taken by an uninformed party to induce an informed party to reveal information

10. The subfield of economics that integrates the insights of psychology

11. The study of government using the analytic methods of economics

Problems and Short-Answer Questions

Practice Problems

1. For each of the following situations, identify the principal and the agent, describe the information asymmetry involved, and explain how moral hazard has been reduced.

   a. Dental insurance companies offer free annual checkups

   _____

   _____

   b. Firms compensate traveling salespersons with commissions (a percentage of the value of the sales)

   _____

   _____

   c. Agricultural seed companies pay migrant workers bonuses if they work the entire summer season

   _____

   _____

   d. McDonald's pays twice the minimum wage to high school students

   _____

   _____

2. For each of the following situations, describe the information asymmetry involved, name the type of action that has been taken to reduce adverse selection (signaling or screening), and explain how adverse selection has been reduced.

   a. McDonald's only hires high school students with good grades

   _____

   _____

   b. Hyundai (a Korean auto manufacturer) provides a 100,000-mile warranty on its new cars

   _____

   _____

   c. A health insurance company requires a prospective customer to take a physical examination

   _____

   _____

   d. Budweiser sponsors the Super Bowl half-time show

   _____

   _____

3. Answer the questions regarding the Condorcet paradox for the three sets of voting preferences below.

Case 1

	Voter Type		
	Type 1	**Type 2**	**Type 3**
Percent of Electorate	15	40	45
First Choice	C	A	B
Second Choice	A	B	C
Third Choice	B	C	A

a. If voters must choose between A and B, what are the percentages of votes that each outcome receives and which outcome wins?

_____

b. If voters must choose between B and C, what are the percentages of votes that each outcome receives and which outcome wins?

_____

c. If voters must choose between C and A, what are the percentages of votes that each outcome receives and which outcome wins?

_____

d. Do these preferences exhibit transitivity? Explain.

_____

_____

e. If the voters choose between A and B and then compare to C, which outcome wins?

_____

_____

If the voters choose between B and C and then compare to A, which outcome wins?

_____

_____

If the voters choose between A and C, and then compare to B, which outcome wins?

_____

_____

Does the order in which items are voted on matter in this case? Why?

_____

_____

Case 2

	Voter Type		
	Type 1	Type 2	Type 3
Percent of Electorate	30	15	55
First Choice	A	B	C
Second Choice	B	C	A
Third Choice	C	A	B

a. If voters must choose between A and B, what are the percentages of votes that each outcome receives and which outcome wins?

_____

b. If voters must choose between B and C, what are the percentages of votes that each outcome receives and which outcome wins?

_____

c. If voters must choose between C and A, what are the percentages of votes that each outcome receives and which outcome wins?

_____

d. Do these preferences exhibit transitivity? Explain.

_____

_____

e. If the voters choose between A and B and then compare to C, which outcome wins?

_____

_____

If the voters choose between B and C and then compare to A, which outcome wins?

_____

_____

If the voters choose between A and C and then compare to B, which outcome wins?

_____

_____

Does the order in which items are voted on matter in this case? Why or why not?

_____

_____

Case 3			
	Voter Type		
	Type 1	**Type 2**	**Type 3**
Percent of Electorate	25	35	40
First Choice	A	B	C
Second Choice	B	A	A
Third Choice	C	C	B

a. If voters must choose between A and B, what are the percentages of votes that each outcome receives and which outcome wins?

_____

b. If voters must choose between B and C, what are the percentages of votes that each outcome receives and which outcome wins?

_____

c. If voters must choose between C and A, what are the percentages of votes that each outcome receives and which outcome wins?

_____

d. Do these preferences exhibit transitivity? Explain.

_____

_____

e. If the voters choose between A and B and then compare to C, which outcome wins?

_____

_____

If the voters choose between B and C and then compare to A, which outcome wins?

_____

_____

If the voters choose between A and C and then compare to B, which outcome wins?

_____

_____

Does the order in which items are voted on matter in this case? Why or why not?

_____

_____

Is the winning outcome the first choice of a large portion of the population? How can this be?

_____

_____

4. a. For Case 1 in problem 3 above, which outcome wins if you use a Borda count to determine the winner among outcomes A, B, and C, and what are the scores for each outcome?

_____

_____

   b. For Case 1 in problem 3 above, eliminate outcome C and use a Borda count to find the winner from the remaining choices of A and B. What property required of a perfect voting system has been violated? Explain.

_____

_____

   c. Compare the results of Case 1 in problem 3 under simple majority rule, a Borda count with three choices, and a Borda count with two choices. What conclusions can you draw from these results?

_____

_____

5. In each of the following situations, describe the behavior that suggests that people may not always behave as self-interested rational maximizers.
   a. Workers agree to a labor contract that gives them a 5 percent raise for each of the next three years. After one year passes, they discover that the firm's profits have increased by 100 percent. The workers go on strike and receive no income during the strike.

_____

_____

   b. A worker plans to start saving 20 percent of his income starting three months from now because he has to first pay off some overdue bills. After three months pass, the worker saves nothing and instead spends all of his monthly income.

_____

_____

   c. After a famous rock star dies in a plane crash, many people decide to ride the train rather than fly.

_____

_____

   d. Joe wants to go on a Canadian fishing trip, and his wife, Sue, wishes to take a different type of trip. The newspaper reports that the size and number of fish being caught in the area where they plan to fish is greater than normal because the temperature has become unseasonably cool. Joe is more sure about his choice of the fishing trip, and Sue is more sure about her desire to go on a different type of trip.

_____

_____

Short-Answer Questions

1. What is *moral hazard*? What steps might a firm take to avoid moral hazard in the employment relationship?

    _____

    _____

    _____

2. What is *adverse selection*? Would you pay as much for a home that is only one year old (but has been lived in by people that have since built another home in the local area) as you would for a brand new home that has yet to be lived in? Why or why not? What steps might you take to avoid adverse selection?

    _____

    _____

    _____

3. Would you expect the buyers of auto insurance to have a higher or lower than average probability of having an auto accident? Why? How does the insurance company address the adverse selection in this market? How does it address the moral hazard in this market?

    _____

    _____

    _____

4. To reduce adverse selection, firms signal high quality with expensive advertising. What are the necessary characteristics of an effective signal? Why don't firms producing low-quality goods use expensive advertising to falsely signal high quality?

    _____

    _____

    _____

5. Why does choosing a good gift qualify as a signal of love and concern to the recipient?

    _____

    _____

    _____

6. Suppose that 30 percent of the voters want to spend $10,000 on a new park, 30 percent want to spend $11,000, and 40 percent wish to spend $25,000. How much does the average voter want to spend? How much does the median voter want to spend? If each voter chooses the point closest to his most preferred choice, what will be the final choice among these three choices of a majority rule? Does the Condorcet paradox arise?

    _____

    _____

    _____

7. Use the median voter theorem to explain why the Republican presidential nominee is more conservative during the primaries than during the general election and the Democratic nominee is more liberal during the primaries than during the general election.

_____

_____

_____

8. Do politicians always choose policies that maximize the well-being of society? Why or why not?

_____

_____

_____

9. If people were rational wealth maximizers, what result would we expect from the "ultimatum game"? What results do we actually find in experiments? What does this imply about wage determination?

_____

_____

_____

10. The most popular major on campus is economics. Your best friend takes an introductory economics class and tells you that it was the worst class she has ever taken. You avoid taking any economics. Is this rational? Explain.

_____

_____

_____

Self-Test

True/False Questions

_____ 1.   Asymmetric information is a problem that occurs when one person in a transaction knows more about what is going on than the other.

_____ 2.   In the principal–agent relationship, the principal performs a task on behalf of the agent.

_____ 3.   Employers may pay higher than equilibrium wages to avoid moral hazard in the employment relationship by raising the cost of shirking.

_____ 4.   To avoid the problem of adverse selection, insurance companies screen their prospective customers to discover hidden health problems.

_____ 5.   Signals to convey high quality are most effective when they are costless to all firms in the industry.

_____ 6.   If A is preferred to B, B preferred to C, and A is preferred to C, then these preferences exhibit the property of unanimity.

_____ 7. The Condorcet paradox shows that majority-rule voting always tells us the outcome that society really wants.

_____ 8. Arrow's impossibility theorem shows that no voting system can satisfy the properties required of a perfect voting system.

_____ 9. According to the median voter theorem, majority rule will produce the average preferred outcome.

_____ 10. Politicians do not always choose the ideal economic policy because some politicians are corrupt and greedy, and others are willing to sacrifice the national interest for local popularity.

_____ 11. In the real world, people always behave rationally when making economic decisions.

_____ 12. The ultimatum game demonstrates that people will always make choices according to their self-interest.

_____ 13. Since people tend to care about fairness, firms may give bonuses during particularly profitable years to be fair and to avoid retaliation from the workers.

_____ 14. People seem to naturally engage in delayed gratification and they tend to follow through on plans made today to do something unpleasant in the future.

_____ 15. Since people are reluctant to change their minds in the face of new information, we can conclude that people do not always behave as rational maximizers.

Multiple-Choice Questions

1. John's car is in need of repair, so John decides to sell it to avoid the repair bill. Unaware of the problem, Susan buys the car. This is an example of
    a. adverse selection.
    b. moral hazard.
    c. efficiency wages.
    d. hidden actions.

2. Judy wants to avoid buying a car that is a lemon. She takes a car she would like to buy to her mechanic before she purchases it. This is known as
    a. moral hazard.
    b. adverse selection.
    c. signaling.
    d. screening.

3. Chris is a traveling salesman for an apparel company. In this employment relationship, Chris is the
    a. principal.
    b. agent.
    c. signaler.
    d. screener.

4. Which of the following must be true about a signal that is used to reveal private information in order for the signal to be effective?
    a. It must be free to the informed party.
    b. It must be costly to the informed party but less costly to the party with the higher-quality product.
    c. It must be "as seen on TV."
    d. It must be applied to an inexpensive product.

5. Which of the following is an example of a signal that is used to reveal private information?
   a. Bob carefully chooses a special gift for Carolyn.
   b. Lexus advertises its cars during the Super Bowl.
   c. Madelyn earns her MBA from the Harvard Business School.
   d. All of the above are correct.

6. Which of the following is *not* a method firms use to avoid the moral hazard problem in the employment relationship?
   a. paying above equilibrium wages
   b. putting hidden video cameras in the workplace
   c. buying life insurance on their workers
   d. paying employees with delayed compensation such as a year-end bonus

7. Which of the following best demonstrates the problem of moral hazard?
   a. Karen doesn't buy health insurance because it is too expensive and she is healthy.
   b. Rachel chooses to attend a well-respected college.
   c. Dick drives more recklessly after he buys auto insurance.
   d. A life insurance company forces Fred to have a physical prior to selling him insurance.

8. Under pair-wise majority voting, if A is preferred to B and B is preferred to C, then A should be preferred to C. This is known as the property of
   a. unanimity.
   b. transitivity.
   c. independence.
   d. impossibility.

Use the following set of voter preferences to answer questions 9 through 12.

	Voter Type		
	Type 1	Type 2	Type 3
Percent of Electorate	35	25	40
First Choice	C	A	B
Second Choice	A	B	C
Third Choice	B	C	A

9. What percent of the population votes for A when the choice is between A and B?
   a. 25 percent
   b. 35 percent
   c. 40 percent
   d. 60 percent
   e. 75 percent

10. Under pair-wise majority voting, which outcome wins?
    a. A
    b. B
    c. C
    d. These preferences suffer from the Condorcet paradox, so there is no clear winner.

11. If we first compare A to C, and then compare the winner to B, which outcome is the winner?
    a. A
    b. B
    c. C
    d. These preferences suffer from the Condorcet paradox, so there is no clear winner.

12. Using a Borda count, which outcome is preferred?
    a.   A
    b.   B
    c.   C
    d.   These preferences do not exhibit transitivity, so there is no clear winner.

13. Which of the following is *not* a property required of a perfect voting system?
    a.   The median voter always wins.
    b.   transitivity
    c.   no dictators
    d.   independence of irrelevant alternatives

14. Suppose that 40 percent of the voting population wish to spend $1,000 for artwork in City Hall, 25 percent wish to spend $20,000, and 35 percent wish to spend $22,000. What is the median preferred outcome, the average preferred outcome, and the modal preferred outcome?
    a. $1,000; $14,333; $1,000
    b. $20,000; $20,000; $22,000
    c. $20,000; $13,100; $1,000
    d. $1,000; $20,000; $22,000

15. Which of the following is true under pair-wise majority rule if people vote for the outcome closest to their most preferred outcome?
    a.   The average preferred outcome wins.
    b.   The outcome preferred by the median voter wins.
    c.   The outcome preferred by the greatest number of voters wins.
    d.   There is no clear winner due to Arrow's impossibility theorem.

16. Which of the following is *not* true about how people make decisions?
    a.   People are sometimes too sure of their own abilities.
    b.   People are reluctant to change their minds in the face of new information.
    c.   People give too much weight to a small number of vivid observations.
    d.   People are always rational maximizers.
    e.   All of the above are actually true statements about how people make decisions.

17. In the *ultimatum game*, what split would be rational for both the person proposing the split and the person who must accept or reject the split?
    a.   99/1
    b.   75/25
    c.   50/50
    d.   1/99
    e.   There is no rational solution.

18. Which of the following helps explain why firms pay bonuses to workers during particularly profitable years to prevent workers from becoming disgruntled?
    a.   People are rational maximizers.
    b.   People are inconsistent over time.
    c.   People care about fairness.
    d.   People are reluctant to change their minds.

19. John's friend dies of a sudden heart attack. John rushes to his doctor for an expensive physical examination. This response demonstrates that
    a.   people give too much weight to a small number of vivid observations.
    b.   people easily change their minds when confronted with new information.
    c.   people tend to plan ahead and follow through on their plans.
    d.   people enjoy going to the doctor.

20. Which of the following is a response to people's inconsistent behavior over time?
    a.   efficiency wages
    b.   year-end bonuses
    c.   forced contributions to a retirement plan
    d.   all of the above

Advanced Critical Thinking

You are watching a television news story about the AIDS crisis with a friend. Your friend says, "I think it is terrible that people infected with AIDS often can't buy health insurance. People who are ill are the ones that really need health insurance. Even worse, once someone gets health insurance, they often have to pay a deductible equal to 20 percent of the first $3,000 of their medical bills each year. Only then does the insurance company cover the remainder of the medical bills."

1. What problem caused by asymmetric information are insurance companies trying to avoid when they deny coverage to someone who may already be ill? What would happen if the insurance companies did not deny coverage to people who are already ill?

    _____

    _____

    _____

    _____

    _____

2. What problem does charging a deductible help solve? What might happen if insurance companies didn't require a deductible?

    _____

    _____

    _____

    _____

3. How might public policy address the problems in the market for health insurance? What are some of the shortcomings of a public policy solution?

    _____

    _____

    _____

    _____

Solutions

Terms and Definitions

_4_ Moral hazard

_8_ Agent

_3_ Principal

_7_ Adverse selection

_1_ Signaling

_9_ Screening

_11_ Political economy

_2_ Condorcet paradox

_6_ Arrow's impossibility theorem

_5_ Median voter theorem

_10_ Behavioral economics

Practice Problems

1. a. The insurance company is the principal; the insured is the agent. Only the agent knows how well he takes care of his teeth. By checking the insured's teeth each year, the insurance company can better monitor the behavior of the insured and reduce major future claims.

   b. The firm is the principal; the salesperson is the agent. The firm does not know how hard the salesperson works. By only paying the salesperson a commission, the firm is able to better monitor the salesperson's work habits, and the worker is less likely to shirk.

   c. The firm is the principal; the worker is the agent. The firm does not know how hard the migrant worker works. By paying a large bonus for completing the season, the firm raises the cost of shirking and the cost of being fired. The worker is less likely to shirk.

   d. McDonald's is the principal; the student is the agent. McDonald's does not know how hard the student works. By paying above market wages, McDonald's increases the cost of shirking and the cost of being fired. The worker is less likely to shirk.

2. a. McDonald's doesn't know the abilities of the potential workers as well as do the workers. McDonald's screens potential workers using past educational performance, and it is able to select high-ability workers.

   b. Buyers don't know the quality of Hyundai cars because they are relatively new to this market. Hyundai signals high quality with a long warranty, and buyers are able to select high-quality cars.

   c. The insurance company does not know as much about the health of the insurance buyer as does the buyer. The insurance company screens prospective customers with physical exams to find hidden health problems so its insurance pool is not sicker than average.

   d. Beer buyers don't know the quality of Budweiser as well as Budweiser. Budweiser signals high quality with expensive advertising because they could only afford to do it if they could generate repeat buyers. Customers are able to choose a high-quality beer.

3. Case 1:

   a. A = 15 + 40 = 55, B = 45. A beats B.

   b. B = 40 + 45 = 85, C = 15. B beats C.

   c. C = 15 + 45 = 60, A = 40. C beats A.

   d. No. A beats B and B beats C, so transitivity requires that A beats C but, in fact, C beats A.

   e. A beats B, so compare A to C and C wins.

   B beats C, so compare B to A and A wins.

   C beats A, so compare C to B and B wins.

   Yes, because these preferences do not exhibit transitivity.

   Case 2:

   a. A = 30 + 55 = 85, B = 15. A beats B.

   b. B = 30 + 15 = 45, C = 55. C beats B.

   c. A = 30, C = 15 + 55 = 70. C beats A.

   d. Yes. C beats A and A beats B. Transitivity requires that C beats B and it does.

   e. A beats B, so compare B to C and C wins.

   C beats B, so compare C to A and C wins.

   C beats A, so compare C to B and C wins.

   No, because these preferences exhibit transitivity.

   Case 3:

   a. A = 25 + 40 = 65, B = 35. A beats B.

   b. B = 25 + 35 = 60, C = 40. B beats C.

   c. A = 25 + 35 = 60, C = 40. A beats C.

   d. Yes. A beats B and B beats C. Transitivity requires that A beats C and it does.

   e. A beats B, so compare A to C and A wins.

   B beats C, so compare B to A and A wins.

   A beats C, so compare A to B and A wins.

   No, because these preferences exhibit transitivity. No, only 25 percent of the population chooses A as their first choice, but most of the population greatly dislikes C and none of the population greatly dislikes A.

4. a. If choosing between A, B, and C, A = 30 + 120 + 45 = 195, B = 15 + 80 + 135 = 230, C = 45 + 40 + 90 = 175 and B wins.

   b. If choosing between only A and B, A = 30 + 80 + 45 = 155, B = 15 + 40 + 90 = 145 and A wins. Independence of irrelevant alternatives: The rankings of A and B shouldn't change when C is removed, but the ranking did change.

   c. A wins, then B wins, then A wins again. Thus, majority voting does not necessarily tell us what society wants, and deciding the order on which items are voted may affect the outcome.

5. a. People care about fairness and may be willing to accept nothing so that their adversary gets nothing if they think the split was unfair.

b. People are inconsistent over time. From three months away, saving seems like a good idea, but as that date approaches, the desire for immediate gratification takes over.

c. People give too much weight to a small number of vivid observations. The probability of a plane crash has probably not changed yet people are more afraid to fly due to one highly publicized case.

d. People are reluctant to change their minds. Both Joe and Sue use the same information to defend their original opinion.

Short-Answer Questions

1. The tendency of a person who is imperfectly monitored to engage in immoral behavior. Better monitoring and paying higher wages or delaying some payment to raise the cost of shirking.

2. When unobserved attributes become undesirable from the standpoint of the uninformed party. No. Because you might assume that the sellers know something bad about the house—flooding, poor construction, bad neighbors or schools, etc. Have the house inspected and check out the neighborhood and schools.

3. Higher, because buyers of insurance know more about their probability of an accident, and those with a high probability of having accidents will need insurance. Insurance companies check a driver's driving history and offer policies that appeal differently to risky and safe drivers, and then they charge higher premiums to risky drivers. They require a deductible to avoid moral hazard.

4. It must be costly but less costly to the individual with the higher-quality product. Since low-quality firms will not generate repeat purchases from their advertising, it is not cost-effective for them to engage in expensive advertising.

5. Because it takes time (is costly), but it takes less time for someone who is knowledgeable about the recipient.

6. 0.3($10,000) + 0.3($11,000) + 0.4($25,000) = $16,300. Median voter wants to spend $11,000. $11,000 wins. No. Take any pair, find the winner, and then compare it to the remaining choice and $11,000 always wins.

7. Each candidate first must win the nomination through the primaries. To do that, they must capture the median voter within their party— conservative for the Republicans and liberal for the Democrats. After being nominated, they must capture the overall median voter, which requires each to move to the center—Republicans become more liberal and Democrats become more conservative.

8. No. Some politicians may act out of greed and others may sacrifice the national interest to improve their local popularity.

9. The first person would take $99 and give $1 to the other, and the other would accept. The first person usually offers more than $1 and the second person rejects small offers. Firms that are having particularly profitable years may pay above equilibrium wages to be fair or to avoid retaliation.

10. No. People give too much weight to a small number of vivid observations. In this case, the friend is just one additional observation out of thousands.

True/False Questions

1. T
2. F; the agent performs a task on behalf of the principal.
3. T
4. T
5. F; signals must be costly yet less costly to the person with the higher-quality product.
6. F; these preferences exhibit transitivity.
7. F; it shows that the order in which items are voted on can determine the outcome; therefore, majority-rule voting does not always tell us what society wants.
8. T
9. F; it will produce the outcome preferred by the median voter.
10. T
11. F; there is evidence that people are only "near rational."
12. F; it shows that people care about fairness.
13. T
14. F; people tend to seek instant gratification and fail to follow through on unpleasant tasks.
15. T

Multiple-Choice Questions

1. a
2. d
3. b
4. b
5. d
6. c
7. c
8. b
9. d
10. d
11. b
12. c
13. a
14. c
15. b
16. d
17. a
18. c

19. a
20. c

Advanced Critical Thinking

1. Adverse selection. People who are already ill would seek to buy insurance. Their medical bills would be far higher than average, causing premiums to rise. At the artificially high price for insurance, fewer healthy people would buy insurance because the cost would exceed their expected bills. When healthy people drop out of the market, the price rises even further for the remaining participants, further reducing the size of the insurance market.

2. Moral hazard. Without a deductible, people might go to the doctor even if they don't really need medical attention. They also have little incentive to take care of themselves to avoid illness because they bear no cost of the illness. As above, this raises the cost of insurance above the expected bills of healthy people and many will fail to buy insurance.

3. Some people advocate government-provided health insurance where everyone (sick and healthy) would be forced to participate. Majority-rule democratic institutions may not generate the amount of health care that people want. Self-interested politicians may choose to provide an amount of health care that is different from what people actually want.

Your source for turning today's challenges into tomorrow's solutions.

Impact on Economics

To get started:

❶ Go to: **academic.cengage.com/login**

❷ Click on "Create My Account."

❸ Select user type "Student."

❹ Enter account information and the access code below.

ACCESS CODE

See Inside Front Cover

www.cengage.com/login

---

❺ Record your e-mail address and password for future visits.

Tips and Troubleshooting

Keep a record of your e-mail address and password.

You will need them every time you sign in.

Your access code is NOT your password!

You will use this access code only once when you first access your eResources. Once your access code is successfully authenticated, you will not be asked for it again.

Problems with your access code? For tech support, visit our website at **www.cengage.com/support**

For tech support, visit our website at **www.cengage.com/support**

Note: All media assets accessible through this program are available to college and university students in the United States and Canada. Some restrictions may apply in other markets or countries. Please contact Cengage Learning for details.

875

Global Economic Crisis

Impact on Economics

SOUTH-WESTERN
CENGAGE Learning™

Australia • Brazil • Japan • Korea • Mexico • Singapore • Spain • United Kingdom • United States

SOUTH-WESTERN
CENGAGE Learning

Global Economic Crisis: Impact on Economics

Sr. Art Director: Michelle Kunkler

Cover Design: Rose Alcorn

Cover Images: © Jasony00 / Dreamstime.com

For product information and technology assistance, contact us at
Cengage Learning Customer & Sales Support, 1-800-354-9706

For permission to use material from this text or product,
submit all requests online at **www.cengage.com/permissions**
Further permissions questions can be emailed to
permissionrequest@cengage.com

ISBN-13: 978-1-4240-5968-3
ISBN-10: 1-4240-5968-2

South-Western Cengage Learning
5191 Natorp Boulevard
Mason, OH 45040
USA

Cengage Learning products are represented in Canada by
Nelson Education, Ltd.

For your course and learning solutions, visit www.cengage.com
Purchase any of our products at your local college store or at our
preferred online store **www.ichapters.com**

Printed in the United States of America
1 2 3 4 5 6 7 13 12 11 10 09

Building Up to the Current Crisis

Learning Objectives.

By the end of this chapter, you will be able to:

- Explain the important financial market regulation that came out of the Great Depression of the 1930s.

- Describe why the rise of American consumerism took place after World War II.

- Elaborate on why the Savings and Loan crisis took place.

- Describe why there was a drive for mortgage-backed securities during the first decade of the 21st century.

- Delineate how all of these historical events have led up to the current financial crisis.

In January 2007, everything seemed to be going right for the U.S. economy and, by extension, U.S. financial markets. On January 24, 2007, the Dow Jones Industrial Index ended the day at 12,621. This was the first time ever the Dow had climbed above 12,600[1]. As stock prices continued to increase, the Federal Reserve worried that the U.S. economy might be growing too quickly. The Federal Reserve had raised its target for the Fed Funds Rate from 5.25 percent to 5.50 percent six months earlier, in the hopes of cooling a red hot U.S. economy. Even with the higher interest rates, the economy was growing at faster than 4 percent a year, a rate many economists believed was unsustainable for an economy the size of the United States.

By the fall of 2008, things had changed drastically. By November 12, 2008, the Dow had fallen to 8,282, a 41 percent drop from its high of 14,164 on October 9, 2007. The Federal Reserve had cut its target for the Fed Funds rate to a mere 1 percent, in a desperate attempt to keep the economy from sliding into a deep recession.
What on earth happened? How could such a highly successful economy like that of the United States in January 2007 find itself on the brink of a severe recession a mere few months later? At this point, we must ask ourselves: Where is the U.S. economy headed? As the old saying goes, "If you want to know where you are going, you have to understand where you have been." To learn why the current financial crisis occurred and where the global economy is headed, we need to determine how we got here. In fact, to fully grasp how we got to where we are, we have to travel back over seventy years to the

---

1 See http://www.mdleasing.com/djia.htm.

Great Depression of the 1930s. As the American society was coming to grips with the economic catastrophe of the Great Depression, there was a call for greater regulation of our financial markets. Many of these regulations are still in place, and understanding them helps to frame the structure of the current financial crisis.

From the economic despair of the Great Depression, we moved to the post–World War II economic expansion with its boom in the housing market. One of the main players in this post-war housing boom is the Federal National Mortgage Association and later the Federal Home Loan Mortgage Corporation, or as they are better known, Fannie Mae and Freddie Mac, respectively. The financial troubles of Fannie and Freddie are a centerpiece of the current financial crisis.

The current financial crisis is not the first crisis to have centered on the American mortgage market. Over twenty years ago, the Savings & Loan crisis also focused on entities that lent money to households to buy their homes. The outfall from the Savings & Loan crisis sets the groundwork for the current global financial crisis. While our current crisis has roots dating back over seven decades ago with the Great Depression of the 1930s, the picture is by no means complete. Updates on this discussion can be found on the web page that accompanies this booklet.

THE EARLY CALL FOR REGULATION OF FINANCIAL MARKETS: THE 1930S

From Flappers to Breadlines

The 1920s was a glamorous decade. The "Roaring '20s," as they were called, saw the rise of American consumerism, with American households buying a wide range of goods and services from new automobiles and household appliances to radios and other electrical devices. Americans were able to buy these consumer goods thanks, in great part, to the booming stock market of the times. The New York Times index of 25 industrial stocks was at 110 in 1924[2]; by June 1929, it had risen to 338, and by September 1929, it stood at 452. Thus, someone buying the index in 1924 would have seen his or her investment grow by over 400 percent by September 1929.[3] The flappers with their trendy dresses, flashy zoot suits, and dancing the Charleston all night long epitomized the carefree decade. However, the good times could not last forever. By the end of the decade, the party that had been the Roaring '20s would collapse into the Great Depression of the 1930s.

---

2 Gary Walton and Hugh Rockoff, "History of the American Economy," South-Western College Publishing, 2004.

3 Charles Kindlegerger, *The World in Depression, 1929–1939*, Berkeley: University of California Press, 1973.

The Depression witnessed the once vibrant American economy seemingly imploding overnight. As the previously dynamic and ever-expanding economy contracted, unemployment across the economy increased dramatically. No sector of the economy seemed to be spared of the growing massive unemployment of the 1930s. The unemployment of unskilled workers, skilled craftsmen, farmers, businesspeople, and even executives increased rapidly. The unemployment rate that stood at only 4 percent for much of the 1920s increased to 25 percent by 1932.

The carefree dancing flappers of the 1920s were replaced with long breadlines and soup kitchens feeding the growing masses of unemployed of the 1930s. The once booming stock market seemed to evaporate and take the rest of the economy with it. The fall in the stock market was so dramatic that stocks lost 40 percent of their value in just two months. The stock market crash caused increased uncertainty over future income and employment translated into a reduction of household spending on durable goods such as automobiles and radios. [4]

The Call for Reform

As the economy contracted and unemployment rose, there were cries from the American people for their elected leaders to "do something" about the economic crisis. The election of President Franklin Delano Roosevelt in 1932 marked a dramatic change in how the federal government would approach the crisis. Roosevelt and his fellow Democrats believed that the Depression and the resulting rise in unemployment was due to the rampant speculation in the stock market and financial markets in general.

Even before Roosevelt was sworn in, Senator Ferdinand Pecora had begun hearings to examine the role the financial markets played in triggering the Depression. The Pecora Hearings, as they became known, resulted in sweeping new regulations of the financial markets. Within weeks of taking office, the Roosevelt Administration called for a bank holiday that would close all of the commercial banks in the country for seven days; passed and signed the Securities Act of 1933; and, perhaps most importantly, passed the Glass-Steagall Act or Banking Act of 1933.

The Glass-Steagall Act accomplished three key things:

- It separated commercial banks (i.e., those entities that take deposits and make loans) from investment banks (i.e., those entities involved with underwriting and selling stocks and bonds).

- It created bank deposit insurance.

- It gave the Federal Reserve the power to limit the interest rates commercial banks could pay on deposits.

The Glass-Steagall Act's separation of commercial and investment banking was based on the premise that if commercial banks were allowed to be involved in the selling of

---

4 Christina Romer, "The Great Crash and the Onset of the Depression," *Quarterly Journal of Economics,* August 1990, Vol. 105, no. 3.

stocks and bonds, a conflict of interest could exist and ultimately make commercial banks less safe.

The creation of deposit insurance was also designed to make commercial banks more stable. With the advent of government deposit insurance, depositors at insured banks could be confident that their savings were secure. Even if an insured bank failed, the government's deposit insurance would be there to ensure that savers would not lose their money. However, in order to make certain that banks were not taking on too much risk, government deposit insurance prompted the need for government regulation or oversight of the banking system.

In addition, Regulation Q of the Glass-Steagall Act was enacted to give the Federal Reserve the power to limit interest rates paid on deposits and to make the banking system more stable by limiting the amount of competition between banks. The drafters of the bill feared that if commercial banks competed for deposits, they would ultimately engage in destructive competitive behavior. Thus, to limit the amount of competition, banks were not allowed to pay interest on demand deposits (checking accounts) and had a cap on what interest rates they could pay on savings accounts.

As time went by, other legislation was passed that increased and expanded the government regulation of U.S. financial markets. The Securities Act of 1933 and the Securities Exchange Act of 1934 created the Securities and Exchange Commission, or the SEC, which is still today the main regulator of the bond and stock markets. In 1938, Congress created the Federal National Mortgage Association, or Fannie Mae, to help stabilize the home mortgage market. See the boxed feature for details.

Fannie Mae & Freddie Mac:
Government Entities to "Semi-Private" Financial Intermediaries

A mortgage loan uses real estate as collateral for the loan. Collateral is the pledge of an asset to ensure repayment by the borrower. Collateral serves as protection for the lender in case of default or nonpayment by the borrower. If a person borrows money and pledges something as collateral and does not repay as promised, the lenders allowed to take the collateral in lieu of the payment. So, a home mortgage loan, or what we will simply refer to as a home mortgage, is when the borrower pledges a house as collateral on a loan. A first mortgage is when a lender agrees to loan money to a family or an individual so that they can purchase a house.

Until the 20th century, mortgages were usually short term, lasting only about five to seven years. During those years, the borrower would have to pay interest on the money borrowed and repay the entire amount at the end of the period. Thus, at the end of the mortgage, the borrower would have to try to find someone or some entity to lend them the money again.

During the Great Depression, many people lost their jobs and could not afford to make their monthly mortgage payment, leaving the borrower to foreclose on them and have the family evicted from their home. With the federal government creation of the Federal National Mortgage Association (i.e., Fannie Mae), borrowers were encouraged to lend money to families over a period of 30 years. Over these 30 years, both interest and the loan principle would be paid. At the end of the 30-year mortgage, the borrower would own the home outright.

To entice lenders to loan money for home mortgages, Fannie Mae would agree to buy certain "qualified" mortgages from banks. Fannie Mae would then either hold the mortgages or sell them to interested investors. In doing so, Fannie Mae would free up funds for the lender to loan on new mortgages.

Due to budget constraints, President Johnson privatized Fannie Mae in 1968. In order to ensure that Fannie Mae did not have a monopoly in the mortgage securitizing business, the federal government created the Federal Home Loan Mortgage Corporation (i.e., Freddie Mac) in 1970.

Since both of these entities were created by the Federal government, many in the financial markets believed that Fannie and Freddie enjoyed a government guarantee against failure. Because of this "implied" government guarantee, Fannie and Freddie could borrow money at very low interest rates in financial markets.

The financial market regulation that came out of the Great Depression seemed to work very well. As the U.S. economy recovered from the Depression, financial markets remained stable and the number of banking failures dropped significantly. During World War II, the U.S. financial markets allowed the government to issue war bonds to finance the wars in Europe and the Pacific.

BUILDING THE AMERICAN DREAM: U.S. HOUSING BOOM IN POST-WAR AMERICA

Pent Up Consumption During World War II

The Second World War was a very hard time for American consumers. While household income increased, household spending decreased significantly. This reduction in household spending was in part necessary, as scarce consumer goods were diverted for the war effort. Many consumer goods, including sugar, meat, gasoline, tires, and even clothes, were rationed during the war. To buy these rationed goods, a family would need not only cash but a government-issued ration coupon. Even having a ration coupon did not guarantee that a consumer could find the good available for sale on store shelves. Shortages of popular goods, especially sugar, were commonplace during the war.

While consumer goods were scarce during the war, one thing was not in short supply: jobs. Workers were needed to build the tanks, ships, and arms that were critical to the war effort. The production of many consumer goods was suspended so that resources could be used for the war effort. For example, there were no new automobiles built in the United States between the end of 1942 and 1946, since the factories that built automobiles were converted into plants for making tanks, aircraft, artillery, etc., for the war. Similarly, no new farm tractors were built during the war, as those factories were likewise converted for the war effort. But these factories needed workers to produce war-related products. Because many young males had joined the military to fight in the war, workers were in short supply. For the first time in U.S. history, large numbers of women entered the labor force.

As employment increased during the war, American households saw their incomes increase. However, with the war rationing in effect, households had very few things on which to spend this new income. Instead, scores of Americans saved their money during the War, waiting and hoping for a better future.

Unleashing American Spending

The end of the Second World War saw a return of American consumerism in grand style. The long years of economic hardship of the Great Depression were behind them, as were the days of sacrifice during World War II. The American consumer had pent up spending power that was being unleashed. For military personnel who were returning from fighting the war overseas as well as those who had "fought the war on the home front," the end of the war created an opportunity to capture the "American Dream." A big part of that post-war "American Dream" was home ownership. In 1940, just 44 percent of families owned their own home; by the end of the 1950s, three out of five families owned their home (according to a U.S. Census). This remarkable increase in homeownership was due, in great part, to the expansion of the Savings and Loan industry.

Savings and Loans are depository institutions that take deposits, mostly from households, and make loans mostly to consumers; these loans are often home mortgages. While the Savings and Loan industry has a long history in the United States going back to the 19th century (the forerunners were called Building & Loans), a number of Savings and Loans failed during the depression. As a result, in 1932, Congress passed the Federal Home Loan Bank Act of 1932, which created the Federal Home Loan Bank Board to lend money to Savings and Loans that found themselves short of funds. In 1934, Congress created the Federal Savings and Loan Insurance Corporation (FSLIC), which would offer government deposit insurance to savers at Savings and Loans.[5]

Expansion of the Savings and Loan Industry

During the post–World War II era, the Savings and Loan industry thrived. The first decade after the Second World War saw the Savings & Loan industry grow at its fastest rate ever. The expansion of American suburbs during the late 1940s and 1950s increased the demand for home mortgages that the Savings and Loans were prepared to offer. In addition, the Savings and Loan trade association worked with the managers of the S&Ls

---

5 David Mason, "From Building and Loans to Bail-outs," Cambridge University Press, 2004.

showing them how to advertise their services and focus on providing a high level of consumer service. As a result, the size and reach of the Savings and Loan industry expanded greatly.

Government regulation of the Savings and Loan industry also played a large role in the industry's expansion. Thanks to Regulation Q, which the Savings and Loans became subject to in 1966, the Savings and Loans faced a cap on their cost of funds. At the same time, government regulations were changing, making it easier for the Savings and Loans to offer even more mortgages and grow even more quickly. These were very successful times for the Savings and Loans. Managers of the Savings and Loans lived by the "3-6-3 Rule," that is, pay 3 percent on deposits, lend the money at 6 percent on mortgages, and be on the golf course by 3:00 pm.

The "3-6-3 Rule" illustrates why the Savings and Loans were so profitable. When a depository institution pays 3 percent for deposits and lends the money out at 6 percent, the difference between the two is what economists call the "interest rate spread." For the Savings and Loans, the 3 percentage point interest rate spread is how they paid their expenses and generated a profit. During the decades after the Second World War, the Savings and Loans were very profitable indeed. These profits allowed existing Savings and Loans to expand and drew in a large number of new S&Ls. By 1965, the Savings and Loan industry held 26 percent of all consumer savings and provided 46 percent of the single-family mortgages in the United States. Unfortunately, the good times would not last forever.

The Savings & Loan Crisis of the 1980s

Inflation and Interest Rates

During the 1970s, the U.S. economy suffered from increased rates of inflation. Inflation is defined as the continuous increase in the general level of prices. A high rate of inflation mean the cost of living for households increases and the cost of operations for firms increase. In addition, as the rate of inflation increases, market interest rates also increase.

To see why this happens, think about how you would feel if you were a lender of money and prices increased. Suppose I ask you to lend me $2 so that I can buy a bottle of diet Coke from a vending machine and agree to repay you tomorrow. . Essentially you are lending me enough resources, the two dollars, to purchase an entire bottle of diet Coke. Now assume the person who refills the vending machine changes the price of a bottle of diet Coke from $2 to $3. Tomorrow comes and I give you $2. You say, "Wait a minute-- I gave you enough resources to buy an entire bottle of diet Coke, and yet you pay me back with resources that can now only buy two-thirds of a bottle of diet Coke!"
Notice what happened: When prices increase, or there is inflation, lenders get paid back in money that simply no longer buys as much. As a result, if lenders think there is going to be inflation, they are going to demand to be compensated for the difference and thus demand a higher interest rate before they will lend their money.

This is what happened during the 1970s. As the inflation rate in the United States increased, market interest rates also increased. Thus, interest rates on Treasury bills, corporate bonds, and other types of debt increased higher and higher as U.S. inflation got worse and worse.

The Problem of Disintermediation

One set of interest rates that did not increase during the 1970s was that paid by the Savings and Loans. Remember that during this time, the Savings and Loans were subject to Regulation Q, the law that stated the maximum interest rate that could be paid on deposits. Thus, while the market interest rates on regular passbook savings accounts could be no higher than 5.5 percent, the yield on a 1-year Treasury bill was over 12 percent by February 1980. As a result of these interest rate differences, savers started to pull their money out of the Savings and Loans in favor of higher paying money market mutual funds. The process of funds moving from one financial intermediary to another is what economists call disintermediation.

To combat disintermediation, the Savings and Loans looked for ways around Regulation Q. One "invention" was the creation of NOW, or negotiable orders of withdrawal. NOW accounts were essentially demand deposits that paid a market rate of interest. Initially the NOW accounts were of questionable legality, since they were violating the premise of Regulation Q that prohibited the paying of interest on demand deposits or checking accounts. But the operators of Savings and Loans thought they had little choice but to offer the NOW accounts. If they did not offer NOW accounts, they would see more and more deposits leave their institutions. If the disintermediation were allowed to go on unchecked, it would lead to a collapse of the Savings and Loan industry, since a depository institution with no deposits simply can not function. Clearly, something needed to change.

DIDMCA: The Solution that Did Not Work

The Savings and Loan industry turned to Washington for help with disintermediation. In response to the growing financial market difficulties, after much debate, Congress passed, and President Carter signed, the Depository Institutions Deregulation and Monetary Control Act (DIDMCA) in 1980. The DIDMCA was the Carter Administration's attempt to bring about some type of financial market reform. Four years earlier, Carter had campaigned on the promise that his administration would bring about such reform, but by 1980, little to nothing had changed in terms of financial market regulation. DIDMCA was about to change all of that.

Two of DIDMCA's major reforms were that it set up for the complete repeal of Regulation Q over six years and it would make it legal for Savings & Loans to offer NOW accounts in order to fend off the disintermediation immediately. While DIDMCA allowed the Savings and Loans to compete with the money market mutual funds for deposits, it created a whole new set of problems. Savings and Loans generated most of their income off the 30-year fixed interest rate mortgages that they had written in the past. The vast majority of these mortgages paid the Savings and Loan a 6 to 8 percent annual rate of interest. When the Savings and Loans were paying 3 to 5.5 percent on deposits, they enjoyed a positive interest rate spread. With the passage of DIDMCA, the Savings and Loans would now be paying upwards of 14 percent on their NOW accounts. That meant that the Savings and Loans would be paying 14 percent for funds while earning only 6 to 8 percent on funds. Thus, the Savings and loans were suffering from a negative interest rate spread.

Garn-St. Germain: Making a Bad Problem Worse

To get relief from their negative interest rate spread, the Savings and Loans returned to Congress in 1981 and 1982 seeking help. In response to the industry's cry for help, Congress passed the Garn-St. Germain Depository Institutions Act of 1982. Garn-St. Germain allowed the Savings and Loans to diversify their lending away from traditional 30-year fixed rate home loans and into shorter term, more profitable business loans. The Act allowed the Savings and Loans to hold up to 40 percent of their assets in commercial mortgages and up to 11 percent of their assets in secured or unsecured commercial loans. In addition, many states, including California and Texas, significantly reduced the amount of regulations on their respective state-chartered Savings and Loans.

As a result of these reduced regulations and a desire to diversify their loan portfolios, the Savings and Loans set off a business lending spree. The Savings and Loans wrote a dizzying array of commercial real estate loans, include loans for high-rise office buildings, massive suburban shopping mall developments, and retail strip mall developments. In addition, many Savings and Loans started lending money for alternative energy development such as windmill farms in the Texas panhandle. One issue with this new lending is that many Savings and Loan lenders had little to no experience in making such loans. As a result, many loans were written where risk was mispriced. Numerous office buildings were built that simply were not needed. Many shopping centers never found enough tenants because they knew shopping centers were not needed. For example, by 1986, nearly one-third of the office space in Houston, Texas, sat unoccupied. As these spaces went unrented, the real estate developers who built these buildings could not pay the loans they had taken out from the Savings and Loans.

The Zombie Savings and Loans

By the late 1980s, the Savings and Loan industry was riddled with insolvent institutions. These institutions had written so many bad loans that they simply did not have enough assets to make good on all of their deposits. These insolvent institutions, sometimes called "Zombie institutions" because they were financially "dead," should have been closed down by their regulators. These regulators, which included the Federal Home Loan Bank and FSLIC, instead chose to suspend the regulatory rules and allowed these Zombie institutions to continue to function. This suspension of the regulatory rules, called "Capital Forbearance," allowed the Zombie institutions to continue in operation and make more and more risky loans.

As the Zombie institutions were allowed to continue in operation, many of the Zombies "infected" the healthy, well run institutions. A Zombie institution would compete with a healthy institution for a loan customer by offering the customer a loan on very favorable terms with a low interest rate and/or easy repayment terms. To compete, the healthy institution would have to offer the loan customer similar terms or face being locked out of the market. Thus, the healthy institution would have to behave like the Zombie institution and essentially "become" a Zombie institution.

One question that has been raised is: why did the regulators allow the Zombie institutions to continue in operation? One answer to this question is that the regulators simply did not have the resources to close all of the Zombie institutions. Closing all of the Zombie institutions would have required perhaps hundreds of billions of dollars to pay insured depositors. Since the regulators did have the resources to close all of these Zombie institutions, they allowed them to continue in operation.

A second potential explanation to why the regulators allowed the Zombie institutions to continue in operation was the political power some of the savings and loan operators wielded. See the box below for one of the more infamous examples of political influence in the savings and loan crisis.

Charles Keating and the Keating 5

One reason many of the Savings and Loan regulators practiced capital forbearance was the political influence of the Savings and Loan operators. An example of this is what became known as the Keating 5. An Arizona real estate developer by the name of Charles Keating was allowed to buy a Savings and Loan in California called Lincoln Savings and Loan. When Lincoln Savings and Loan started to suffer from disintermediation, Keating promised depositors that he could offer them a "special account" that would pay an interest rate much above what money market mutual funds would pay.

Many of Lincoln's depositors were elderly, and they questioned Keating as to the safety of the "special accounts." Keating reassured his elderly customers that the special accounts were fully insured by the federal government. In fact, they were not. The special accounts were actual shares in his real estate development in Arizona.

The regulators of Lincoln Savings and Loan at the Federal Home Bank Board became concerned about the growing riskiness of Lincoln. But Charles Keating did not want the regulators to interfere in his operations. Keating had made large campaign contributions to five key U.S. Senators. Keating now called on these five Senators to intervene with the regulators on his behalf. The five Senators basically did what Keating requested. As a result, Keating was allowed to continue to operate Lincoln Savings and Loan as he saw fit.

In 1989, Lincoln Savings and Loan failed, costing taxpayers $1.3 billion, and more importantly, more than 22,000 depositors/bondholders at Lincoln Savings and Loan lost their savings since they were not in government-insured accounts. Charles Keating eventually was convicted of bank fraud and served four and a half years in prison. What happened to those five Senators known as the Keating 5? Basically, nothing. All were allowed to continue serving in the U.S.

Senate, and two of the Keating 5 went on to run for President of the United States despite their questionable ethical dealings with Charles Keating.

As the 1980s moved on, the Savings and Loan problem grew significantly. In 1988, the FSLIC had closed over 200 Savings and Loans that were insolvent. The problem, however, was that by the end of 1988, over 500 insolvent Savings and Loans continued to operate. Clearly, the current system had failed.

In August 1989, President George H. Bush signed the Financial Institutions Reform Recovery and Enforcement Act. FIRREA was the first dramatic step to resolve the Savings and Loan crisis. Among other things, FIRREA forced the absorption of the FSLIC into the FDIC. In addition, the Federal Home Loan Banks' independence was stripped away and it was taken over by the Office of Thrift Supervision within the Treasury Department. Perhaps most importantly, FIRREA created the Resolution Trust Corporation (RTC), which was to close the insolvent Savings and Loans and sell off their assets.

The once proud Savings and Loan industry that had helped to build the American suburbs after the Second World War was now a mere shadow of itself. The inability or unwillingness of the Savings and Loan operators to measure the riskiness of their loans problem greatly contributed to the industry's demise. The regulators such as the Federal Home Loan Bank and FSLIC arguably did not do their job correctly, and these entities were either stripped of their powers or completely eliminated.

THE SEEKING OF RETURN: 2002–2006

One of the lessons learned from the Savings and Loan crisis is that depository institutions that rely on the interest rate spread between what they earn on long-term loans and what they pay on short-term deposits can suffer greatly when market interest rates increase. The Savings and Loans suffered from negative interest rate spreads throughout the late 1970s and early 1980s, and these negative spreads triggered a series of chain reactions that ultimately led to the current financial crisis.

Banks and Fee Income

In an attempt to avoid a repeat of the Savings and Loan crisis, commercial banks in the United States during the 1990s and throughout the first decade of the 21st century attempted to end their reliance on interest rate spreads. Instead of depending on the spread as a source of profits, commercial banks envisioned themselves as providers of financial services who earned fees for their services. Since fee income was independent of changes in market interest rates, commercial banks saw it as a much more stable source of income and profits.

Commercial banks looked in a variety of places to generate fees. They charged fees for use of ATMs (automated teller machines), for use of the bank lobby, and for printing checks, and they looked at offering new services where they could generate new fees. One expanding market that caught the banks' attention was the home mortgage market. Traditionally, when a depository institution wrote a home mortgage loan, the depository institution would hold the mortgage, collect payment, or service the mortgage for 30 years until the household borrower paid off the mortgage. However, in their desire to earn fees, commercial banks were turning more and more to the securitization of home mortgages.

Securitization

Securitization is the pooling or combining of loans, such as mortgages, into one big bundle. This bundle is then used to create a new financial instrument or bond whose cash flows are the original loans in the pool. For example, the securitization of home mortgages entails the purchase of a large number of home mortgages and the creation of a mortgage-backed security, or MBS. The mortgaged-backed securities are paid the cash flow received from the households as they make their mortgage payments.

Securitization takes place with other loans in addition to home mortgages. Commercial mortgages are also securitized into their own version of securitized securities called Commercial Mortgaged-Backed Assets. Student Loans are also securitized. If you have borrowed money for a student loan, once you signed your promise to repay the loan, the bank or financial institution that lent you the money took your student loan, bundled it with other student loans, and created an Asset-Backed Security, or ABS. In 2006, $79 billion of new student-loan-backed ABS were issued, with the total market size estimated to exceed $350 billion in 2007.

Fannie Mae and Freddie Mac: Their Great Demise

Fannie Mae and Freddie Mac were originally created by Congress to provide liquidity to the mortgage market, and they were very successful. They did so by buying "qualified" mortgages and securitizing them, or bundling them and selling the bundles to investors. The two "government-sponsored entities," or GSEs, came to dominate the mortgage market. Together they hold or guarantee over $5 trillion in mortgages. By comparison, the entire U.S. economy is just over $13 trillion and the total entire outstanding mortgages in the United States amount to $12 trillion.

However, in 2007 and 2008, both Fannie Mae and Freddie Mac ran into a great deal of financial trouble. Both Fannie and Freddie had purchased mortgages without carefully examining the default risks associated with those mortgages. As a result, in 2008, the federal government had to take over both Fannie and Freddie to keep them from failing.

When a commercial bank writes a loan that will be bundled up or securitized, the bank earns a fee from the entity that does the bundling. The "bundler" or securitizer may be an investment bank, a Government-Sponsored Entity (such as Fannie Mae, Freddie Mac, or Sallie Mae--for student loans), or a Special Investment Vehicle, which is created by commercial banks. The bundler then sells the newly created asset, such as a mortgage-backed security, to an institutional investor, such as an insurance company, pension fund, or an endowment.

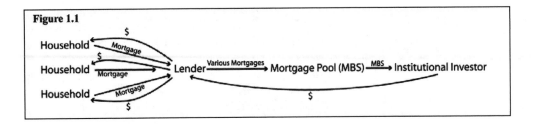

Figure 1.1

Over time, the market for mortgage-backed securities increased. The loan originators, oftentimes commercial banks, liked the process of making mortgage loans and earning a fee and then servicing the mortgage and earning more fees. They could generate fee income and move the long-term mortgages off their balance sheet, so they no longer had to worry about interest rate spreads. The process was appealing too because it enabled the mortgage bundlers to charge a fee for bundling the mortgages together and then selling them to institutional investors.

As time went on, new inventions in the mortgage market came about. One issue that arose was that not all institutional investors had the same desire for risk. Some institutional investors didn't want any risk of default. That is, they wanted to be sure that they received the payments they were expecting. At the same time, other institutional investors were more willing to take on some risk, as long as they were compensated for this increased risk by being paid a higher interest rate.

To meet the differing needs of these institutional investors, the bundlers of Mortgage-Backed Securities decided to slice the MBSs into different pieces. The first slice would be paid first, as the households made their mortgage payments. The next slice would be paid after the first slice was paid, if there was still money left over, meaning if there were only a few or no defaults. Each of the remaining slices would then be paid in descending order. These slices of the MBSs are called *tranches*, from the French word *tranch*, which means slice.

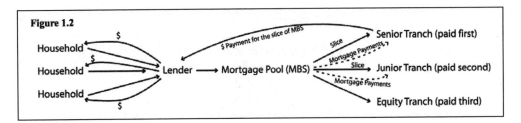

Figure 1.2

In reality, there could be more than just three tranches, but the logic remains the same: the senior tranche gets paid first and so on down the line. Some of the lower tranches, the last to be paid and thus the most risky, the lenders (including commercial banks) held onto the mortgages since they could be very difficult to sell to institutional investors. But, as long as there are no defaults on mortgages, all of the tranches get paid.

Historically, home mortgage defaults were very low, only around 2 percent, so the buyers of the Mortgage-Backed Assets felt fairly safe that they would receive their payments as promised. Thus, the securitized mortgage market grew.

Falling Market Interest Rates

In 2001, in a response to a slowing U.S. economy, the Federal Reserve set out to lower interest rates to stimulate the economy. The collapse of the dot.com boom in 2001 had brought about a significant reduction in the amount of household and business spending. To encourage more borrowing and spending by households and firms, the Federal Reserve cut interest rates throughout 2001, 2002, and 2003. By 2003, market interest rates in the United States were the lowest they had been in forty years.

In response to these falling market interest rates, institutional investors' interest rates in the home mortgage market increased significantly. While other market interest rates had dropped significantly due to the Federal Reserve's actions, the interest rates on home mortgages, and thus the return on mortgage-backed securities, had not fallen as much. Thus, there was a growing interest by institutional investors to buy these mortgage-backed securities.

The mortgage lenders, including commercial banks, were desperate to the meet the growing demand for mortgage-backed assets. But in order to create more mortgage-backed assets, these lenders needed to write more and more mortgages. The problem these lenders faced was that in order to write more mortgages, they would need to go beyond "traditional" borrowers. That is, the lenders needed to lower their lending standards so that more people could qualify for mortgages.

Traditionally, if a family wanted to borrow money to buy a house, they needed to have 20 percent of the purchase price in cash. The family could then borrow the remaining 80 percent of the purchase price of the house via a mortgage. But, as the demand for mortgage-backed assets increased, mortgage lenders began writing "zero-down" mortgages where the borrower puts no money down and borrows 100 percent of the purchase price.

One potential problem with "zero-down" mortgages is that they can result in much higher default rates. In the traditional 20-percent down mortgage, the borrower has some of their own money in the house, or as the saying goes, they have "their skin in the game." If times become financially difficult for the borrower, they would work hard to stay current on their mortgage payments, since defaulting on the mortgage or being foreclosed on would cause the borrower to lose the money they had used to purchase the house. However, with zero-down mortgages, the borrower doesn't have any "skin in the game" or any financial interest in the house. Under this setting, if financial times become difficult, the borrower is much more likely to simply walk away from the house and have the lender foreclose on the house.

Thus, the advent of the zero-down mortgage greatly increased the probability of default by the borrowers. The problem is, many in the financial markets ignored these increasing risks in the mortgage market. Instead, they continued to believe that mortgage default rates would stay exactly as they always had been. In other words, there was a major mispricing of risk occurring in the U.S. mortgage markets.

Heads I Win, Tales the Government Loses

As depository institutions such as Savings and Loans or commercial banks take on more risk, either through writing risky loans or holding risky assets, depositors usually "punish" this behavior by withdrawing their deposits. Depositors do this because if the depository institution fails due to too many of its risky assets failing to pay out as planned, the depositor will lose all of the money they have on deposit. In these cases, the depositors essentially "watch over" the depository institution and help to ensure that Savings and Loans or commercial banks do not engage in excessive risky behavior.

However, deposit insurance changes all of this. With government-sponsored deposit insurance, the depositor knows that even if the depository institution fails, the depositor will not lose any of their money. If the institution fails, all the depositor has to do is go to the government to get a check equal to the amount of the government insurance.

On the other hand, if the depository institution engages in holding risk assets and these risky assets pay off, the institution can "share" these high payoffs with the depositor in the form of higher interest rates on deposits. This is what economists call the "moral hazard" of deposit insurance. A moral hazard is the existence of a contract that can alter behavior by changing incentives.

With the creation of government deposit insurance, the incentives and behavior of depositors change. Depositors no longer "watch over" depository institutions to "keep them safe" and instead have an incentive to push lenders to hold very risky assets. If those risky assets pay off as planned, the depositor benefits, as the institution shares with them the high returns generated by the risky assets. Conversely, if the risky assets fail to pay off as planned and the depository institution fails, the depositor turns to the government to be made whole again. From the point of view of the depositor, government-sponsored deposit insurance creates a situation where the depositor can say "head I win, tails the government loses."

BRINGING IT ALL TOGETHER

The current financial crisis that centers on the home mortgage markets has its roots in the evolution of the U.S. financial markets. Many economists argue that the deposit insurance that was created during the Great Depression of the 1930s may have contributed to the excessive risk taking and the mispricing of risk in the home mortgage market during the first decade of the 21st century. What contributed to this mispricing of risk in the home mortgage market was the rapid expansion of the securitizing of home mortgages, which was an outcome of the Savings and Loan crisis of the 1980s. But this securitization would not have been possible without the rapid expansion of the U.S. housing market in the decades following the Second World War.

Building Up to the Current Crisis

But the synopsis of the current financial crisis is not complete. In the next chapter, we will examine in more depth the issues of the current crisis. Updates on the current status of the crisis can be found on the web page www.cengage.com/gec that accompanies this booklet. It will be very interesting and informative to watch this crisis unfold.

The Current Crisis

Chapter Outline

Learning Goals

After reading this chapter, you should be able to answer these questions:
1. Why is there so much uncertainty in financial markets?
2. In what ways is the current financial crisis not limited to just the United States?
3. What issues surround the Wall Street bailout package?
4. What challenges does President Obama face during his first term?

Economic slowdowns and recessions occur for a variety of reasons. Sometimes the economy slows when the central bank raises interest rates to counteract inflation. At other times, the rate of economic growth slows due to a natural disaster or a disruption in the flow of goods and services. The economic recession that began in the United States in December 2007 was triggered by a global financial crisis. Problems in the U.S. home mortgage market set off this widespread financial meltdown. In this chapter, we will examine the current global financial crisis, explain what caused it, and offer potential solutions to resolve it.

As discussed in the previous chapter, the causes of the current financial crisis go back decades. However, the specific events that led to the current financial downturn began in the summer of 2007. One recurring theme in this chapter will be the destructive role that uncertainty has played in pushing the United States into this quagmire. We will see how an entire Wall Street industry, investment banking, has been crippled by it. As policymakers continue to struggle with solutions, we will explore how their past rescue attempts have not worked as planned. Finally, we will look at the economic problems that face the Obama Administration.

The Current Crisis

The story of the current financial crisis is far from over. Updates to this compelling economic story can be found on the website www.cengage.com/gec that accompanies this chapter.

THE SUMMER OF 2007: THE CRISIS BEGINS

Summer is usually a very slow time for media events in the United States: in Washington, D.C., congress members are on their summer recess; in New York, many people who work in financial markets flee the city for long vacations; and in Europe, financial market activity slows as Europeans take advantage of month-long vacations. But during the late summer of 2007, Washington, New York, and the European financial centers were all a buzz with rumors of what appeared to be a brewing financial storm.

In July 2007, two hedge funds run by investment bank Bear Stearns collapsed, causing an estimated $1.5 billion loss to its investors.[1] The two funds—the High-Grade Structured Credit Strategies Fund and the High-Grade Structured Credit Strategies Enhanced Leveraged Fund—had borrowed huge sums of money to buy a large number of mortgage-backed securities.

In May 2007, as the first wave of mortgage defaults began to be felt, these two funds reported losses much larger than had been anticipated. As a result of these losses and growing uncertainty concerning the future value of the funds under its management, Bear Stearns announced that it would no longer allow investors to withdraw money from these two funds. Commercial banks and investment banks that had loaned money to these funds now demanded more cash as collateral on those loans. Bear Stearns announced on June 26 that it was going to lend the High-Grade Structured Credit Strategies Fund, the more conservative of the two funds, $1.6 billion in an attempt to increase investor confidence. But it was already too late. The market value of the mortgage-backed securities held by these two funds fell so dramatically that by mid-July both funds were essentially worthless.

At the end of July, Federal Reserve Chairman Ben Bernanke told Congress that the losses associated with problems in the mortgage market were "significant" and could approach $100 billion. But, Bernanke said he and the Federal Reserve (the Fed) would remain "alert" and would notify Congress if the problems in the mortgage market posed a threat to the overall economy. Mr. Bernanke did not view the mortgage crisis to be a threat to the overall U.S. economy at that time. Unfortunately for Mr. Bernanke and the Fed, the problems had only begun.

In August 2007, Countrywide Financial Corporation, the largest mortgage lender in the United States, was forced to borrow more than $11 billion from over 40 different

---

1 See Gretchen Morgenson, "Bear Stearns Says Battered Hedge Funds Are Worth Little," *The New York Times*, July 18, 2007.

creditors due to losses on mortgages it had written. Countrywide played a very important role in the U.S. mortgage market. It consistently wrote about 17 percent of all new U.S. mortgages each year; in 2007, it wrote over $400 billion of new mortgages and was servicing about 9 million loans with an estimated value of about $1.5 trillion. The financial troubles at a giant such as Countrywide sent shock waves through the financial markets. People wondered "if Countrywide and Bear Stearns can get into such deep financial troubles, who could be next?"

Who Has What Risk?

One major issue in the current financial crisis is a lack of clarity about *who* has *how much* risk exposure to *what* risk. In a "traditional" mortgage market, the risks are clear: a bank lends money to a household so that the family can purchase a house. The bank holds the mortgage and thus has default risk: the family, for whatever reason, may not be able to make their mortgage payments as promised.

However, with the creation of mortgage-backed securities and payment tranches called **collateralized debt obligations (CDOs)**, it is much more difficult to discern who is holding what portion of what mortgage. Thus, the owner of a CDO might own little slivers of thousands of different mortgages. Determining which of those mortgages is going bad at any point in time is practically impossible. Likewise, during times of financial distress, the value of CDOs can be very difficult to measure because the value of the underlying mortgages or slices of mortgages is unclear. During "good times," holders of CDOs can determine CDO value by looking at the market price of similarly traded CDOs. But when the markets are gripped by uncertainty, as they have been since the summer of 2007, it can become difficult if not impossible to place a market value on those CDOs.

Financial market participants, including bank depositors, hate such uncertainty. People and firms deposit money at commercial banks because they view those banks as safe. However, when those banks have assets, such as CDOs, that are difficult to price, depositors can become worried about their bank's safety. When depositors lose confidence in their bank's security, they can, in mass, attempt to withdrawal their funds all at once. This is called a **bank run**.

In August 2007, the commercial bank division of Countrywide Financial Corporation, called Countrywide Bank, suffered from just such a bank run. Depositors at Countrywide Bank in California feared that since the biggest U.S. mortgage company was in financial trouble that its commercial bank night run out of money.[2] Depositors lined up outside the bank and jammed its phone lines seeking to withdraw their money. Even though all deposits were insured by the FDIC up to $100,000 per account, depositors still wanted to pull their money out of Countrywide Bank "just in case." The uncertainty from the mortgage market and CDOs had now spilled over into the commercial banking market and negatively impacted the expectations and outlook of average depositors.

2 See E. Scott Reckard and Annette Haddad "A Rush to Pull out Money," *Los Angeles Times*, August 17, 2007.

The Crisis Goes Global

This inability to correctly price CDOs was also felt around the world. In August 2007, BNP Paribas, the largest bank in France and one of the largest in Europe, ran headlong into the American mortgage crisis. On August 9, BNP Paribas was forced to halt withdrawals from two of its funds because it could not "fairly value" the CDOs it held. BNP said in an August 9 statement:

"The complete evaporation of liquidity in certain market segments of the US securitisation market has made it impossible to value certain assets fairly regardless of their quality or credit rating. The situation is such that it is no longer possible to value fairly the underlying US ABS (Asset Backed Securities) assets …"[3]

The asset-backed securities to which the statement refers are CDOs and mortgaged-backed securities. Because BNP Paribas could not determine the value of these assets, it could not calculate the balance of any individual investor. Thus, it would not allow investors to sell their shares or halt withdrawals. This was very similar to the problem faced by the two American Bear Stearns' hedge funds three months earlier.

Later in August, German bank Landesbank Sachsen Girzentrale ran into financial trouble due to its exposure to the American mortgage market. Sachsen LB, as it was known, first received a $23 billion loan from a group of regional savings banks in Germany, but even that was not enough. Sachsen LB was sold to a larger rival Landesbank by the end of August.

In September 2008, Northern Rock, the United Kingdom's fifth-largest home lender, suffered a bank run. Northern Rock had borrowed money in the short-term global financial markets, called **money markets**, and then loaned that money out to UK home buyers. Consequently, Northern Rock had relatively fewer depositors than would a traditional commercial bank or an American savings & loan.[4] But, since Northern Rock had been considered stable and reliable, it had been able to borrow money in the money markets at a relatively low interest rate and relend those funds at a higher interest rate in the UK mortgage market. In addition, to support its rate of return on assets, Northern Rock had purchased U.S.-based CDOs.

By the fall of 2008, with CDOs more difficult to price and money market participants no longer willing to lend to any bank that might have exposure to the U.S. mortgage crisis, Northern Rock found it increasingly difficult to borrow money in the money markets. But Northern Rock needed these money market loans in order to have enough cash to meet its depositors' needs. Unable to secure needed funds from the money markets, Northern Rock turned to the UK government for assistance.

---

3 See http://www.bnpparibas.com/en/news/press-releases.

4 Northern Rock at the time had loans and other assets on its balance sheet of £113bn. The value of deposits placed with it by retail customers was £24bn. See http://news.bbc.co.uk/2/hi/business/6994099.stm.

On September 13, the Bank of England agreed to be the lender of last resort to Northern Rock, but it was already too late. Over the next two days, depositors lined up outside Northern Rock branches and inundated its web site, attempting to withdraw their savings. This lack of confidence in Northern Rock was simply devastating. Even though the Bank of England agreed to guarantee Northern Rock funds, depositors and financial markets had lost confidence in the institution, and its fate was sealed. Northern Rock was eventually taken over by the UK government on February 22, 2008.

The Collapse and Bailout of Wall Street

As the year 2007 drew to a close, it seemed that the fallout from the U.S. mortgage and global financial crisis might not dramatically impact the rest of the U.S. economy. The U.S. stock market was doing well in the fall of 2007, having reached a record high of 14,164 on October 9, 2007. But things were about to take a drastic turn for the worse. In December, President Bush announced a plan to help Americans who were about to lose their homes due to higher market interest rates. In presenting the housing rescue plan, President Bush described the housing downturn as a "serious challenge," but he stated: "The economy is strong, flexible and dynamic enough to weather this storm."[5] So, perhaps the worst of the financial crisis was past. Nothing could have been further from the truth.

Monday, January 21, 2008, was the Martin Luther King, Jr. holiday, which meant U.S. financial markets were closed for the day. But the financial markets across the globe were open, and investors began to panic over the growing problems in the U.S. mortgage market. Stock markets in Asia, Europe, and Latin America fell between 4 and 7 percent during the day's trading. Seemingly in response to the global stock market slide, the Federal Reserve's policymaking group, the Federal Open Market Committee, took the historically unprecedented move of holding an emergency meeting on a Monday night. They decided to drastically cut their interest rate target by 0.75 percent, where most recent changes in interest rates had been by 0.25 percent. This surprise move was thus three times the regular size interest rate change, plus it took place in an emergency meeting. One economic pundit described the Fed's move as a "once in a generation event."[6] Clearly, policymakers were worried that something had gone horribly wrong with financial markets and, by extension, the U.S. economy.

As winter gave way to spring, the problems in the financial markets seemed to get worse. In March 2008, the Federal Reserve announced its biggest move to date: it would make $200 billion of loans available to banks and other financial institutions.[7] The Fed was forced into making these funds available because banks were no longer willing to lend money to one another. Due to the uncertainty in financial markets, banks could not be sure of which other banks were connected to the growing U.S. mortgage crisis. Since banks could not evaluate the creditworthiness of other banks, they simply refused to lend money to one another.

---

5 See http://news.bbc.co.uk/2/hi/business/7129990.stm.

6 See Michael M. Grynbaum and John Holusha, "Fed Cuts Rates 0.75% and Stocks Swing," *The New York Times*, January 22, 2008.

7 See http://news.bbc.co.uk/2/hi/business/7284101.stm.

The Current Crisis

The lack of bank-to-bank lending caused major problems for other financial markets and the overall economy. If banks are unable to obtain funds from other banks, they will also be unlikely to lend money to nonbank business firms. If businesses are unable to secure loans, they cannot buy much-needed equipment or raw materials nor pay their workers. Thus, banks' refusal to lend to one another can trigger a chain reaction that can cause the entire economy to slow down. This is exactly what was happening in the spring of 2008.

Bear Stearns, JPMorgan Chase, and the Fed

The Fed's emergency lending did not resolve the problem. In March, financial market participants started to lose confidence in Bear Stearns, at the time the fifth-largest investment bank in the country. Investment banks, like commercial banks, depend on their customers' confidence for survival. For 85 years, Bear Stearns' customers had confidence in the big investment bank; it had survived the Great Depression, World War II, and the aftermath of the September 11 terrorist attacks. But it would not survive the current global financial crisis.

Bear Stearns' problems grew to a crisis level in the early days of March, and rumors of its financial distress quickly spread across Wall Street.[8] Only a year earlier, Bear Stearns had been riding a financial high with its stock trading at over $160 a share. But then came the sub-prime mortgage crisis and the failure of two of Bear Stearns' hedge funds. By March 12, the stock price had fallen to only $30 a share, and Bear Stearns' executives took to the airwaves trying in vain to convince the global financial markets that the firm was solvent. This public relations push failed. Bear Stearns needed to borrow huge amounts of money in order to keep up with investors' withdrawals. The bank's executives reportedly called officials at the Fed late in the day of March 13 and asked them to arrange a bailout of the 85-year-old company.

The Fed and Bear Stearns' officials decided to see if JPMorgan Chase would be willing to help the struggling investment bank. JPMorgan Chase had numerous business relationships with Bear Stearns and had much to lose if Bear Stearns failed. But JPMorgan Chase was reluctant to lend money without some type of guarantee of repayment from the Federal Reserve should Bear Stearns eventually fail. The Fed agreed to guarantee the loan from JPMorgan Chase to Bear Stearns, but it was already too little, too late. The financial markets had lost confidence in Bear Stearns. Virtually no one was willing to enter into trades or conduct business with Bear.

Clearly, the Fed-arranged loan was not enough to save Bear Stearns. Over the March 15–16 weekend, the Fed and Bear Stearns' executives worked around the clock to find a buyer for the beleaguered investment bank. Finally, on Sunday March 16, armed with $30 billion of Federal Reserve guarantees of Bear Stearns assets, JPMorgan Chase agreed to buy Bear Stearns at the stunning price of only $2 per share. That price represented a 93 percent discount off the price of a share of Bear Stearns stock on the close of trading on the previous Friday. But the directors of Bear Stearns had little

8 See Matthew Goldstein, "Bear Stearns' Big Bailout," *BusinessWeek*, March 14, 2008.

choice. It was either agree to the purchase by JPMorgan Chase at $2 share or face bankruptcy Monday morning at which point the shares would be essentially worthless.

A major uproar from Bear Stearns' employees, who owned one-third of the firm, as well as Bear Stearns' bondholders who would essentially be wiped out by the buyout, forced JPMorgan Chase to raise its offer to $10 per share a week later. Also, sensing a growing rage in Washington at the potential cost to taxpayers of the Fed's guarantee, JPMorgan Chase agreed that it would absorb the first $1 billion loss on Bear Stearns' assets with the Federal Reserve covering the remaining loss.

The Federal Reserve's quasi-bailout of Bear Stearns raised alarm across U.S. financial markets. Questions were being asked from one end of the country to the other: How sick was Wall Street? Who else would the Fed bail out—either indirectly like Bear Stearns or more directly?

Government Takeover of Fannie Mae and Freddie Mac

By the fall of 2008, the two mortgage market giants, Fannie Mae and Freddie Mac, were in deep financial trouble. Although both Fannie and Freddie had been created by the federal government, they were now publically traded corporations. Fannie Mae and Freddie Mac bought mortgages from lenders, repackaged some of these mortgages, and resold them to investors while holding on to other mortgages.

In order to finance this purchasing of mortgages, Fannie and Freddie issued their own bonds that were sold to a wide variety of investors around the world. Because Fannie and Freddie were both formerly part of the U.S. government, many in the financial markets believed that there was an implied government guarantee behind the bonds they issued. That is, people in financial markets believed that if Fannie and Freddie got into financial difficulty and could not repay their debt, the U.S. federal government would step in and make good on those promises to repay. With this "implicit" government guarantee, Fannie and Freddie could borrow money at a very low interest rate. They used these funds to buy mortgages, repackage them, and sell them for a price that resulted in very sizeable profits.

Although the vast majority of Fannie Mae and Freddie Mac mortgages were being repaid as planned, a small portion of them had fallen into default. What made this a significant problem is that both Fannie and Freddie held only a small amount of reserve cash in case of defaults. In other words, if the default rates on their mortgages increased even slightly, both entities would be near financial collapse.

In an attempt to reassure financial markets, Treasury Secretary Henry Paulson took the unusual step of holding a press conference on a Sunday. Standing on the front steps of the Treasury Building in Washington on July 13, Paulson proclaimed that the Treasury would stand behind both Fannie Mae and Freddie Mac.[9] This highly unusual press conference was held right before the financial markets in Asia opened and was designed

9 See "The Muddle-through Approach," *The Economist*, July 14, 2008.

The Current Crisis

to calm fears in Asia over the future of Fannie and Freddie. It was also less than a week after bank regulators had taken over the mortgage lender IndyMac Bancorp, which was the largest bank failure to date in American history. Thus, Secretary Paulson was trying to calm some pretty jittery nerves with his announcement.

Even the Treasury's backing was not enough. In fact, some economists argue[10] that the plan actually backfired. When it became clear that the federal government was taking a larger operational role and part ownership in Fannie and Freddie, no investors were willing to buy shares in Fannie and Freddie. The reason was straightforward: the bailout would essentially make the federal government the "senior" stockholder in both, meaning the government would be paid dividends before private shareholders and would have more say in running Fannie and Freddie than would private shareholders. Thus, investors basically refused to buy the shares of either Fannie or Freddie. The Treasury's plan to stand behind Fannie and Freddie was failing.

In addition, the financial markets simply did not have confidence in the financial viability of Fannie Mae and Freddie Mac. This was a major problem for the two mortgage market giants since they had issued $1.6 trillion of debt, the proceeds of which they had used to buy up mortgages. Without the confidence of financial markets, Fannie and Freddie would have a difficult time issuing new debt and thus could not continue to buy new mortgages. Unable to sell newly written mortgages to Fannie and Freddie, mortgage lenders would simply stop writing new mortgages. This would cause an already troubled housing market to spin even more out of control, and the ripple effects would be felt across the entire economy.

With the failure of the July 13 rescue plan, Secretary Paulson held yet another unprecedented Sunday news conference on September 7. This time, Paulson announced that the Treasury had placed both Fannie Mae and Freddie Mac into **conservatorship**. This basically meant that the Treasury Department, and by extension the U.S. federal government and U.S. taxpayers, were taking over Fannie and Freddie. This represented the largest involvement of the federal government in U.S. financial markets since the Great Depression of the 1930s, but it wouldn't be the last federal move. In fact, it would be the start of what news reports would call "10 days that reshaped U.S. finance."[11]

The Bailout of AIG

American International Group (AIG) is one of the world's largest insurance companies. In addition to offering traditional insurance products such as life insurance and automobile insurance, AIG was one of the biggest sellers of credit default swaps. Credit default swaps essentially provide insurance against the default of a financial asset that is tied to corporate debt or a mortgage-backed security. Since credit default swaps are a type of insurance, an insurance giant such as AIG would naturally sell them.

However, as the number of mortgages in default rose through 2007 and 2008, AIG had to pay out more on credit default swaps than it had anticipated. These huge unexpected

10 See http://freakonomics.blogs.nytimes.com/2008/09/18/diamond-and-kashyap-on-the-recent-financial-upheavals.

11 See http://online.wsj.com/article/SB122156561931242905.html.

payouts put a great deal of pressure on AIG, even though its other insurance businesses were doing fine. Things got so bad for AIG that on Monday, September 15, its credit rating was downgraded, which meant that AIG would have to come up with $14.5 billion in cash for collateral on its outstanding debt. While AIG had enough assets that it could sell to raise the $14.5 billion, it could not raise cash fast enough for the financial markets. After having been turned down by a wide variety of banks for an emergency short-term "bridge" loan, AIG turned to the U.S. government for help.

If AIG could not raise the collateral on its outstanding debt, the ripple effect through the U.S. financial markets would be severe. Many financial institutions around the world held debt issued by AIG; a collapse of the insurance giant would badly damage these financial institutions. To prevent such a financial meltdown, the Treasury Department and the Federal Reserve agreed to an $85 billion bailout for AIG. In return for this infusion of cash, the U.S. government would essentially take over the insurance giant. What made this government takeover of AIG even more unusual is that insurance companies such as AIG are not regulated by the federal government; instead, they are regulated by state governments. But the Treasury and the Federal Reserve decided AIG was "too big to fail." The government takeover of AIG represented the end of a 10-day period that saw major changes in U.S. financial markets. From September 6 to September 16, the following events occurred:

- The federal government seized control of Fannie Mae and Freddie Mac.

- Lehman Brothers, a 158-year-old major investment bank, filed for bankruptcy after the Treasury Department refused to help.

- Merrill Lynch, with 60,000 employees and on the verge of collapse, was purchased by Bank of America.

- The federal government took control of AIG.

The day after the AIG takeover—Wednesday, September 16, 2008—the U.S. stock market fell dramatically, with the Dow plummeting more than 446 points. This stock sell-off was due in part to an announcement by Washington Mutual, a major mortgage lender, that it had put itself up for sale due to staggering losses brought on by the troubled U.S. mortgage market. The two remaining investment banks, Goldman Sachs and Morgan Stanley, likewise appeared to be in significant financial trouble. Less than a week later, Goldman Sachs and Morgan Stanley announced that they would seek to become commercial banks and subject themselves to Federal Reserve oversight and regulation. With this move by Goldman Sachs and Morgan Stanley, the financial district in New York saw the end of the investment banking industry as an independent, stand-alone market on Wall Street. All of the major investment banks had failed, been merged into a commercial bank, or evolved into a commercial bank.

The $700 Billion Grasp for a Solution

With no investment banks left standing, Fannie Mae, Freddie Mac, and AIG under government control, banks unwilling to lend to one another, and mortgage default rates increasing, President Bush decided to deliver an address to the nation. On the evening of September 24, 2008, President Bush in a nationally televised speech tried to address the financial crisis by calling on Congress to swiftly pass a $700 billion bailout package for the U.S. financial markets. According to President Bush:

"Financial assets related to home mortgages have lost value during the house decline, and the banks holding these assets have restricted credit. As a result, our entire economy is in danger."

The initial $700 billion bailout bill included very few details on how or when the money would be spent. Under the original three-page plan drafted by the Treasury Department, Secretary Paulson would be given complete discretion over the funds. Paulson could use the money in any way he saw fit, and his use of the money could not be questioned by Congress, the administration, or any court. Thus, Paulson wanted complete control to give $700 billion to anyone he thought needed it in any manner he thought necessary.

Needless to say, many in Congress had serious reservations about the bailout package. To make things even more politically charged, Democrat Speaker of the House of Representatives Nancy Pelosi took to the House floor immediately before a vote on the bailout package and gave a very partisan speech. She blamed the entire financial crisis on Republicans:

"Seven hundred billion dollars, a staggering number, but only a part of the cost of the failed Bush economic policies to our country, policies that were built on budget recklessness. ... For too long this government in 8 years has followed a right-wing ideology ..."

Many Republican House members who planned to vote for the bailout bill on bipartisan terms were greatly put off by Pelosi's partisan speech. Without the Republican votes, the bill could not pass. Speaker Pelosi did little to nothing to calm the angered Republicans, and the bailout bill was rejected by a vote of 228 to 205. The stock market responded negatively to the inability of the politicians in Washington to pass a bailout bill: the Dow plunged 777 points, or 7 percent, in one day. A new bill was quickly introduced and passed by the Senate on October 1 and by the House on October 3. President Bush took the unusual step of signing the bill only two hours later. The $700 billion bailout, officially known as the Emergency Economic Stabilization Act of 2008, gave the Treasury secretary power to purchase any assets from any firm at any price. The $700 billion would be released in stages: $250 billion immediately upon passage, another $100 billion upon White House certification that the funds were necessary, and the remaining $350 billion when the Treasury secretary requested it from Congress.

With the passage of the bailout plan, the Treasury Department established **the Troubled Asset Relief Program (TARP)**, which would be administered through the newly created Office of Financial Stability. The initial purpose of TARP was to buy the difficult-to-price mortgage-backed securities that commercial banks and investment banks held. One of the hardest questions the Treasury Department faced was what price TARP should pay for the mortgage-backed assets it was about to buy from commercial banks and investment banks. This was, perhaps, the most complex finance question to be answered in over 50 years.

To answer this extremely important question, Secretary Paulson, the former CEO of investment bank Goldman Sachs, picked a 35-year-old former underling at Goldman Sachs named Neel Kashkari. In picking Kashkari to run TARP, Paulson passed over many more experienced financial experts such as former Federal Reserve Chairman Paul Volcker. Instead of seeking an experienced hand to run TARP, Paulson picked someone with only a few years of financial market experience.

Kashkari and TARP quickly found that pricing and buying the "troubled" mortgaged-backed securities was in fact very difficult to do. So instead, they decided to do something completely different: buy shares of the troubled financial institutions. In buying shares in these troubled institutions, a process called **recapitalization**, the Treasury hoped that commercial banks would start lending again. There was, of course, no guarantee that they would do so. When the government bought the shares of these banks, or recapitalized them, the banks had complete discretion over what they would do with these new funds. Instead of lending the new funds to customers, the banks could simply hold onto the new funds, pay dividends to their stockholders,[12] buy up other banks,[13] or even pay expenses including executive salaries.

Not surprisingly, a number of prominent economists raised questions about the effectiveness of the TARP program. University of Chicago economist Dr. Luigi Zingales wrote a brief article that circulated widely on the Internet, aptly named "Why Paulson Is Wrong."[14] Dr. Zingales argued that Paulson and the Treasury were going about the bailout with a failed approach. Fellow Chicago economists Anil Kashyap and Doug Diamond similarly raised troubling questions about the wisdom of the TARP.[15] Nobel Prize winner Joseph Stiglitz wrote an article very critical of the conflicts of interest in TARP and argued that the program only addressed some issues of the financial crisis.[16] Criticism of the TARP came from both liberal and conservative economists, and over 100 of them signed a letter of protest.[17]

Finally, on November 12, 2008, Secretary Paulson announced that the TARP would no longer be used to buy troubled assets from financial institutions. Instead, it will be used to offer financial assistance to banks and other firms that issue student, auto, and credit card loans.[18]

From Banks to Autos

As Paulson, Kashkari, and TARP struggled with how to best provide assistance to financial markets, the U.S. auto industry turned to the federal government for financial help. On November 18, the chief executives from the three major American automobile producers asked Congress for $25 billion in emergency loans. In testifying before Congress, Chrysler CEO Robert Nardelli, General Motors CEO Richard Wagoner, Jr.,

12 See Binyamin Applebaum, "Banks Continue to Continue Paying Dividends," *Washington Post*, October 30, 2008.

13 See Peter Whoriskey and Zachary A. Goldfarb, "Banks Weighing Other Uses for Bailout Money," *Washington Post*, October 28, 2008.

14 See http://faculty.chicagogsb.edu/luigi.zingales/Why_Paulson_is_wrong.pdf.

15 See http://freakonomics.blogs.nytimes.com/2008/09/18/diamond-and-kashyap-on-the-recent-financial-upheavals/.

16 See Joseph Stiglitz "Henry Paulson's Shell Game," *The Nation*, September 26, 2008.

17 See http://freakonomics.blogs.nytimes.com/2008/09/23/economists-on-the-bailout/.

18 See Peter Whoriskey, David Cho, and Binyamin Applebaum, "Treasury Redefines Its Rescue Program," *Washington Post*, November 12, 2008.

and Ford CEO Alan Mulally all claimed that due to the global financial crisis their companies needed emergency loans from the federal government or else they faced an almost immediate collapse.

A collapse of the U.S. auto industry could significantly impact the entire American economy. Ford, GM, and Chrysler, or The Big 3 as they are known, are the largest purchasers of U.S.-made steel, aluminum, iron, copper, plastics, rubber, and electronic computer chips. The Big 3 employ over 240,000 workers and have suppliers in every one of the 50 states. Thus, the executives argued, a collapse of the Big 3 automakers would dramatically affect the entire country in "days if not hours."

But members of Congress were skeptical about another taxpayer-funded bailout. Since the specific operation of TARP was so vague and had been so ineffective, many in Congress wanted to know, specifically, how the Big 3 would use the taxpayer money. The auto executives could not answer that question. They essentially had no specific plan on how they would use the $25 billion and could only give vague answers as to how they would split the money among the three.

Members of Congress were also upset when they learned that, shortly after receiving a government bailout, the executives at insurance giant AIG had spent $440,000 on a luxury retreat, essentially paid for by the American taxpayers. Likewise, when Congress heard that the executives of the automobile industry had flown to Washington each on their own private corporate jet to ask for taxpayer money, one member of Congress snorted:

"There's a delicious irony in seeing private luxury jets flying into D.C. and people coming off of them with tin cups in their hands … it's almost like seeing guys show up in the soup kitchen in high hat and tuxedo."

Not surprisingly, Congress voted down the auto industry bailout a few days later. Perhaps having learned their lesson, the auto executives returned to Washington two weeks later in automobiles they actually made and with a broad outline of how they would use the government funds.

The auto industry's new plea for help came after quarterly reports indicated the worst sales volume in over 25 years. The executives argued that if they did not get emergency funding within weeks, GM and Chrysler would face dire financial consequences.

PRESIDENT OBAMA'S ECONOMIC CHALLENGES

Upon being sworn in as the 44th president of the United States, Barack Obama will face some daunting economic challenges. Chief among these challenges is how he and his administration will deal with the current global financial crisis. As we have described, one of the main causes of this global downturn is the U.S. home mortgage market. The Obama Administration must find a way to stabilize the mortgage market and that, most likely, will require the stabilization of house prices.

In order to stabilize house prices, the new administration must find a way to deal with borrowers that can no longer afford to make their monthly mortgage payments. Some of these mortgage borrowers undoubtedly are caught up in circumstances beyond their control. Perhaps members of these families have lost their jobs as the economy has slowed. Others may have been duped into mortgages with low initial teaser rates that they did not understand. One could argue that the federal government should assist these types of borrowers.

Clearly, not all mortgage borrowers were innocent victims. Some borrowers sought to make "a quick buck" by purchasing a house and **flipping** the house or selling it at a much higher price in a few months. These borrowers were speculating on the mortgage market, and they lost that speculation. Offering government assistance to these types of borrowers would create what economists call a **moral hazard**.

A moral hazard exists when the creation of a financial contract alters behavior by changing incentives. If the government were to bail out real estate speculators, the government would be sending a clear signal to speculators: *go ahead, undertake risky behavior, because if your bets don't pay off, the government will be there to bail you out.* In such situations, a government bailout would be a type of financial contract that would negatively alter behavior in that it would encourage risky speculation.

Some speculation in markets is fine and even desirable. However, speculators need to suffer losses if they turn out to be wrong. If this is not done, it will encourage an excessive amount of speculation or risky behavior. Therefore, the Obama Administration has to be careful in crafting a program to stabilize house prices: it cannot and should not bail out all home buyers who cannot afford to make their mortgage payments. Arguably, the Obama Administration must find a way to delineate between those home buyers who were caught in a situation that was not of their own making and those that speculated on the housing market and perhaps should have known better.

In addition, the Obama Administration needs to find some way to get banks to start lending and increasing the flow of funds within financial markets. As described above, financial markets depend crucially on trust. If financial market participants do not trust one another, they will not lend to one another nor engage in any other type of financial transaction. The return of trust in financial markets, arguably, depends on transparency or openness. Financial markets need to be able to evaluate the riskiness of various borrowers and entities. As we have seen, the inability to correctly price mortgage-backed securities created major problems in the financial markets. Also, the lack of confidence or trust is what brought on bank runs and created the inability of long-standing firms to borrow money in financial markets.

The Obama Administration must decide what other steps will need to be taken to push the U.S. economy out of its current slowdown. Should the federal government do more to create jobs for the unemployed? As the unemployment rate increases to over 6 percent and the likelihood that firms will be able to borrow money to hire new workers remains slim, where will these unemployed people find work? Also, how will any increase in government spending be paid for? Given that the U.S. government budget deficit is already one of the largest in history, how will any new government programs be funded?

Finally, the Obama Administration will have to reconsider the extent of financial market regulation in the future. While our financial markets have changed dramatically over the past 50 years, the regulation of our markets, both domestically and internationally, has not kept pace. As new financial instruments such as mortgage-backed securities and markets that trade them are created, decisions must be made on who will regulate these markets and what form the regulations should take.

How his administration deals with these and other economic questions will have a significant impact on the success or failure of the Obama presidency. Updates on the current financial crisis and the economic challenges facing the Obama Administration can be found on the website www.cengage.com/gec that accompanies these booklets.

Discussion Questions

1. Assume that you have been appointed as an economic advisor to President Obama. What advice would you give him in terms of how to address the current financial crisis? What should he focus on first and why? Will he be able to get Congress and the American people to go along with what you suggest?

2. What steps could have been taken to prevent this crisis? How can similar crises be avoided in the future?

Key Terms

collateralized debt obligations (CDOs)
bank run
money markets
conservatorship
Troubled Asset Relief Program (TARP)
recapitalization
flipping
moral hazard

Turn Your Notes into Knowledge

You've reached a crossroads. Now that you've conscientiously taken notes, you can let all that hard work go out the window and surrender to the unforgiving power of forgetting. Or you can put in extra effort to retain all that valuable information and transform what you've read and heard into a permanent part of your knowledge. Congratulations. You've made the right choice. This chapter tells you how to:

- **Review to Cement Understanding**
- **Recite to Strengthen Memories**
- **Reflect to Add Wisdom**

Part III: Retaining Information

How do you master
your notes?

If you've taken notes thoroughly and conscientiously, you have every right to feel good about your efforts. But taking notes is not an end in itself. In fact, it is only the beginning. Far too many students jot down their notes and then forget about them until exam time rolls around. They leave them neglected in a desk drawer or repeatedly pass over their detailed textbook markings as they move on to subsequent chapters. This is a tragic mistake and a great waste of time and effort. The only way to take advantage of all the information you've jotted down or marked up and highlighted—to master information that you've worked so hard to understand—is to review it carefully, recite it regularly, and reflect on it deeply until it becomes a permanent part of your knowledge.

Review to Cement Understanding

What's wrong with
reviewing notes just
by looking them over?

Most students review their notes by reading them over and perhaps by asking themselves a question or two to see what they remember. This spot-check approach may be common, but it's also haphazard. A systematic approach not only makes your review worthwhile, but also enables you to gain a clear sense of how you're doing.

What do you gain
by conducting an
immediate review?

The purpose of the immediate review is to cement your understanding of what you've just read or heard. As you learned in Chapter 9, memory can be fleeting. Chances are that when you were taking notes, especially in a lecture, you were taking in information an idea at a time. You probably didn't have the opportunity to make sure you truly understood everything you'd marked or written down, and you almost certainly didn't have the chance to step back and see how things all fit together. That's where the immediate review comes in. By targeting key ideas with the Q System, you are able to verify that you understand your notes. And by pulling things together in summaries, you gain a valuable big-picture perspective.

Target Key Ideas with the Q System

QUESTIONING — SUMMARIZING — PLANNING

What is the Q System?

The left-hand margins of your Cornell System paper or the outside margins of your text should have remained blank up to this point. Here's your chance to put them to good use. At your earliest opportunity, move systematically through the notes you've just taken or the assignment you've just marked up, and come up with a question for each important idea. This is known as the Q System. Each question you write will provide a cue for the answer it addresses. Figure 11.1 provides a diagram of the Q System process.

How do you arrive at
Q System questions
for each important
idea?

When using the Q System, try to avoid formulating a question that can be answered with a simple yes or no. Aim instead for questions that prompt you to recall key information. Arriving at a suitable question is a little like playing the popular TV game show in which contestants are given the answers and asked to supply the questions. And it's

Turn Your Notes into Knowledge

Figure 11.1
Using the Q System to Review Your Notes
Whether you're reviewing textbook notes, lecture notes, or markings you've made directly in your textbook, the Q System is your best bet.

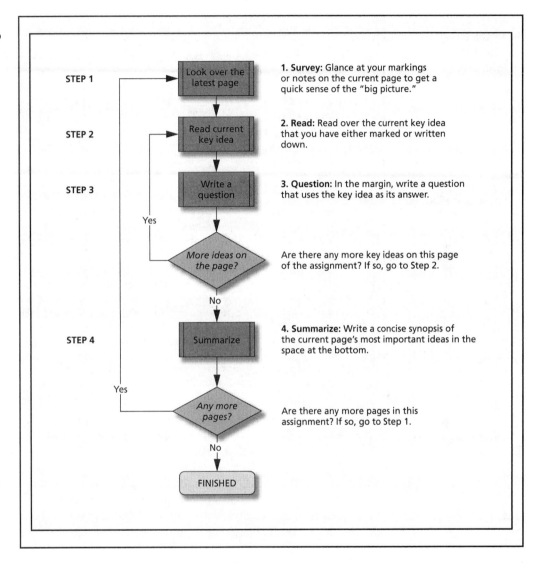

STEP 1 — Look over the latest page

1. Survey: Glance at your markings or notes on the current page to get a quick sense of the "big picture."

STEP 2 — Read current key idea

2. Read: Read over the current key idea that you have either marked or written down.

STEP 3 — Write a question

3. Question: In the margin, write a question that uses the key idea as its answer.

More ideas on the page? — Yes

Are there any more key ideas on this page of the assignment? If so, go to Step 2.

No

STEP 4 — Summarize

4. Summarize: Write a concise synopsis of the current page's most important ideas in the space at the bottom.

Any more pages? — Yes

Are there any more pages in this assignment? If so, go to Step 1.

No

FINISHED

almost identical to the process you went through as you were reading an assignment and converting the headings into questions. The only real difference is that this time you're using ideas from your notes or the lines you underlined in your textbook as the starting point. The goal is to pose a question whose answer most effectively sums up the entire key idea or paragraph. Jot (or type) the question down in the margin alongside the information it refers to. Figure 11.2 shows some marginal questions for a textbook passage.

www.cengage.com/success/Pauk/HowTOStudy10e

**Figure 11.2
Using the Q System
with a Textbook
Assignment**

WRITING GOOD PAPERS IN COLLEGE

What 2
aspects lead
to success?

The techniques of writing a good paper are easy to follow. You should remember two important aspects that lead to success. First, start work early on the paper. Second, if you have a choice, choose a subject that you are interested in or that you can develop an interest in.

What 3
elements
might make
up a paper?

Much of your work in college involves absorbing knowledge; when it comes to writing papers, you have the opportunity to put down on paper what you've learned about a subject, and perhaps your opinions and conclusions on the subject.

What's the
key in choosing
a topic?

Writing is an important form of communication. To communicate well you must have something you really want to say. So if you have a choice of topics, choose one that intrigues you. If it isn't one that everyone else is writing on, all the better.

If not sure
of a topic,
do what?

If you're not sure about your choice of topic, do a little preliminary research to see what's involved in several topics before you make a final decision. Remember the caution about allowing yourself enough time? Here's where it comes into play. Take enough time to choose a topic carefully.

**What form should
your marginal
questions take?**

Repeat the process of formulating questions and putting them in the margin as you systematically move through all the paragraphs in your text or notes from your note paper. It's OK to abbreviate your question, especially if you are short on space. (Figure 11.3 shows an excerpt from some classroom notes with abbreviated questions in the margins.) But be certain there's nothing ambiguous about what you've written down. After all, you'll want to be able to read these questions throughout the semester. A badly abbreviated question may make sense to you now, but it could leave you scratching your head later on. The same applies to your handwriting. Make sure you can read it. You may want to use the modified printing style (explained in Chapter 10) to help you write quickly and legibly.

**What should you do
if there's no space for
your questions?**

Properly ruled Cornell System note paper should provide plenty of room for your Q System questions. But if you've marked up your textbook and it has skinny margins, you have a handful of options to adjust for the limited space.

Try the Sticky Note Method

**How does the sticky
note method work?**

Jot down the same sort of question that you would have written in the margin, but put it on a "sticky note" instead (using one sticky note per question). When you've fin-

Turn Your Notes into Knowledge

Figure 11.3
Using the Q System
with Classroom Notes

	Sept. 10 (Mon.) – History 101 – Prof. A. Newhall
	A. Some facts about Alaska
Who purchased Alaska?	William H. Seward, Sec. of State –
When? Cost?	fr. Russia in 1867 – $7,200,000.
Rough dimensions of	Size – mainland: length = 1,500 mi. –
mainland?	width = 1,200 mi.
How long is the Yukon River?	Yukon River – 1,979 mi. long
Name kinds of minerals?	Minerals – oil, gold, silver, coal, chrome, iron, etc.
How are the forests?	Forests – commercial timber = 85 billion board feet
Two most numerous fish?	Fish – world's richest in salmon and halibut
Name several kinds of fur?	Furs – seal, mink, otter, beaver, fox, etc.
What's the highest mt. in No. America?	Mt. McKinley – 20,320 ft. – highest in No. America
When admitted as state?	Statehood – Jan. 3, 1959 – 49th State
Who designed the state flag?	State flag – designed by 13-year-old Benjamin Benson

ished writing the question, affix it near the paragraph it refers to. Because your sticky notes may come unstuck, it's often a good idea to put a circled number in the margin of your textbook next to the paragraph your question is intended for and to number your sticky note to match, adding the page number as well in case you renumber with each new page.

Use the Bookmark Method

What does the bookmark method involve?

One method that many students swear by is to jot their questions on slips of scrap paper that resemble extra-wide bookmarks (about two-and-a-half inches wide, the same dimension as the margin in Cornell System paper). Use one bookmark for each pair of facing pages, keeping a running list of the questions for the left-hand page on one side and putting the questions for the right-hand page on the other. Just as you did with the sticky note system, number each question and put a corresponding number in the margin alongside the paragraph it refers to. When you've written all of the questions for the two pages, you can lodge the slip in the book at just the right spot, the same way you would an ordinary bookmark.

Take Separate Notes

What is the advantage of using separate notes?

Of course, if your textbook doesn't offer an accommodating set of margins, it might be simpler to take separate notes. You'll miss some of the advantages of taking notes directly in your book (see Chapter 10), but you'll be able to carry the notes for your assignment (even stash them in a pocket or purse) without having to lug around the book.

What do you accomplish by writing marginal questions?

Regardless of the method you choose when using the Q System, you will be accomplishing something vital. The straightforward process of formulating questions should provide you with a thorough and immediate review of your material. Although it's possible to do so, it's unnecessarily difficult (not to mention pointless) to "fake" questions for each idea. Ask questions that truly get to the heart of the information. To be able to turn an idea into a meaningful question, you need to have a genuine grasp of that idea.

See the Big Picture with Summaries

SUMMARIZING — PLANNING

IT'S YOUR Q

In the same way that questions from the Q System provide you with a better grasp of the important ideas from your notes, summaries help supply the context. It's surprisingly easy to get caught up in the details of your notes and lose the grand scheme of things in the process. Writing a summary is a sure-fire way to force yourself to think about and come to grips with the broader ideas, trends, lessons, and themes that run through notes like a thread. Summaries supply a straightforward answer to the question, "What is this page about?" This cut-to-the-chase aspect of summaries should be especially handy when you're studying for an exam or doing research for a paper and want to go straight to the key information in your notes without having to read through every note on every page to find it.

The Standard Summary

What is the standard system for writing summaries?

The standard system for summaries is to write one at the bottom of every page. Figure 11.4 shows an example. If you're taking notes directly in your textbook, you may find that there's more room to write at the top of each page than at the bottom. Either place is fine. Regardless of whether you're taking notes in your textbook or on separate sheets, don't pen an epic; you probably don't have the time, and you definitely don't have the room. Just come up with a concentrated sentence or two that efficiently pulls together the key information on the page. If space permits, it's a good idea to use complete sentences for your summaries. This reinforces your goal of articulately expressing what's important on the page. It can be a little too easy to disguise your confusion in an abbreviated sentence. Now is the time to make sure you grasp what you've written down

Turn Your Notes into Knowledge

**Figure 11.4
Summarizing a Page
of Lecture Notes
in Two Sentences**

Psych. 105 – Prof. Martin – Sept. 14 (Mon.)

<u>MEMORY</u>

Memory tricky – Can recall instantly many trivial things
of childhood, yet forget things recently worked hard to
learn & retain.

Memory Trace
— Fact that we retain information means that some
 change was made in the brain.
— Change called "memory trace."
— "Trace" probably a molecular arrangement similar to
 molecular changes in a magnetic recording tape.

Three memory systems: sensory, short term, long term.
— <u>Sensory</u> (lasts one second)
 Ex. Words or numbers sent to brain by sight (visual
 image) start to disintegrate within a few tenths of
 a second & gone in one full second, unless quickly
 transferred to S-T memory by verbal repetition.
— Short-term memory [STM] (lasts 30 seconds)
 • Experiments show: a syllable of 3 letters remembered 50% of the time after 3 seconds.
 Totally forgotten end of 30 seconds.
 • S-T memory — limited capacity — holds average
 of 7 items.
 • More than 7 items — jettisons some to make room.
 • To hold items in STM, must rehearse — must hear
 <u>sound</u> of words internally or externally.
— Long-term memory [LTM] (lasts a lifetime or short time).
 • Transfer fact or idea by
 (1) <u>Associating</u> w/information already in LTM.
 (2) <u>Organizing</u> information into meaningful units.
 (3) <u>Understanding</u> by comparing & making
 relationships.
 (4) <u>Frameworking</u> – fit pieces in like in a jigsaw puzzle.
 (5) <u>Reorganizing</u> – combining new & old into a new unit.
 (6) <u>Rehearsing</u> – aloud to keep memory trace strong.

**How do psycholo-
gists account for
remembering?**

**What's a
"memory trace"?**

**What are the three
memory systems?**

**How long does
sensory memory
retain information?**

**How is information
transferred to STM?**

**What are the reten-
tion times of STM?**

**What's the capacity
of the STM?**

**How to hold
information in STM?**

**What are the reten-
tion times of LTM?**

**What are the six
ways to transfer
infomation from
STM to LTM?**

Three kinds of memory systems are sensory, which retains information for about 1
second; short-term, which retains for a maximum of 30 seconds; and long-term,
which varies from a lifetime of retention to a relatively short time.
 The six ways (activities) to transfer information to the long-term memory are
associating, organizing, understanding, frameworking, reorganizing, and rehearsing.

or read. If you don't understand things at this stage, there's a good chance that they will grow murkier with time. Make the effort right now to see clearly. If you still don't understand, you have time to get help from a tutor or instructor. If you wait, it may be too late.

The Wrap-Up Summary

What is the approach for the wrap-up summary?

Rather than summarizing each page, you may choose to write a longer summary at the very end of your lecture notes or textbook assignment. Depending on the length or importance of the assignment, this method may be enough, but in general it's not recommended, at least not in isolation. Even if you write several paragraphs for your wrap-up summary, you probably can't expect to approach the level of insight and detail that you gain from summarizing each page. However, if the lecture is especially brief or the reading assignment is a supplemental one that doesn't require a great deal of attention (see Chapter 10), a wrap-up summary may suffice.

The Split-Level Summary

Why is the split-level approach best for summarizing your notes?

The best way to review and summarize your notes is to combine the standard summaries with the wrap-up summary. Start with the standard summary, summarizing each page with a sentence or two. Then, rather than rereading all of your notes to arrive at a wrap-up summary, simply reread the summaries you've written for each page and come up with a summary of your summaries. This two-level approach makes your notes extremely useful and flexible. If you just need a reminder of what a single assignment or lecture was about, you can read the wrap-up summary. If you need more detail, you can go to the next level and read the summary on a particular page.

What else do questions and summaries provide besides an immediate review?

Formulating questions for each important idea in your notes and then coming up with summaries not only provides an extremely directed and effective means of review, but it also sets the stage for recitation, the most valuable technique you can use to help commit your notes to memory.

Recite to Strengthen Memories

What is the role of reciting?

Now that you've added Q System questions (and brief summaries) to each page and conducted a thorough review in the process, how are you going to hold on to all that valuable information? After all, forgetting never lets up. It works continuously to expel from memory what you worked so hard to put there. Luckily, you can bring forgetting almost to a standstill by using the power of recitation.

How does reciting work?

Reciting forces you to think, and this thinking leaves a neural trace in your memory. Reciting promotes concentration, forms a sound basis for understanding the next paragraph or the next chapter, provides time for consolidation, ensures that facts and ideas are remembered accurately, and supplies immediate feedback on how you're

Turn Your Notes into Knowledge

doing. Moreover, experiments have shown that the greater the proportion of reciting time to reading time, the greater the learning. Students who spent 20 percent of their time reading and 80 percent reciting did much better than students who spent less time reciting and more time reading.

What is the process for reciting?

The process of reciting is relatively straightforward. Go back to the first page and cover it with a blank sheet of paper, exposing only your Q System questions. (If you used the sticky note method, you should still be able to obscure the text while reading your questions. If you chose the bookmark method, you can use your marker to cover the text. If your notes and Q System questions are in a computer file, open the file and then open another empty file and use it as an electronic version of a blank sheet of paper to cover your text.) Read the first question, and answer it in your own words. Slide the blank sheet down to check your answer. If your answer is wrong or incomplete, try again. Do this until you get the answer right. Go through the entire assignment this way. (See Figure 11.5 for a diagram of the entire process.) Your aim is to establish an accurate, crystal-clear impression in your memory, because that's what you want to return to during an exam. If the impression in your memory is fuzzy at this time, it will be even fuzzier three or four weeks later (see Chapter 9).

Recite Out Loud

`SUMMARIZING`

IT'S YOUR Q

The traditional way to recite is out loud and in your own words. When you recite aloud, speak clearly so there's no mistake about what you are saying. Express the ideas in complete sentences, using the proper signal words. For example, when you are reciting a list of ideas or facts, enumerate them by saying *first*, *second*, and so on. Insert words such as *furthermore*, *however*, and *finally*. When you do so in oral practice, you will do so more naturally in writing during an exam. One of the best ways to recite out loud is in a group study or discussion (see Chapter 13), where there are people who can alert you right away should you answer your question incorrectly.

Recite by Writing

`SUMMARIZING`

How do you recite by writing?

If you are reluctant or unable to recite aloud, you can recite by writing out (or typing) your answers instead. This method is slower than traditional reciting, but it provides added benefits. Even more than reciting aloud, reciting by writing supplies solid proof that you can answer your questions. After all, you have a written record. And it provides excellent practice for essay and short-answer tests. To recite by writing, move through your notes a question at a time just as you would normally. But instead of speaking your answers, write them down on a separate sheet of paper. Then uncover the page and compare each answer you've just written with the one in your notes.

www.cengage.com/success/Pauk/HowTOStudy10e

**Figure 11.5
The Process of
Reciting Your Notes**

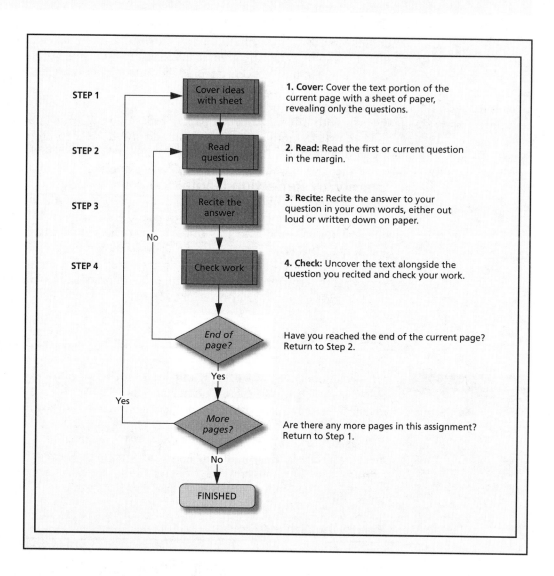

STEP 1 — Cover ideas with sheet

1. Cover: Cover the text portion of the current page with a sheet of paper, revealing only the questions.

STEP 2 — Read question

2. Read: Read the first or current question in the margin.

STEP 3 — Recite the answer

3. Recite: Recite the answer to your question in your own words, either out loud or written down on paper.

STEP 4 — Check work

4. Check: Uncover the text alongside the question you recited and check your work.

End of page?
No

Have you reached the end of the current page? Return to Step 2.

Yes

More pages?
Yes

Are there any more pages in this assignment? Return to Step 1.

No

FINISHED

ect to Add Wisdom

What is reflection?

After you learn facts and ideas through reviewing and reciting, take some time to mull them over. Use your innate sense of curiosity to speculate or play with the knowledge you've acquired. This is called *reflection*. To engage in reflection is to bring creativity to your learning. Ask yourself such questions as these: What is the significance of these

Turn Your Notes into Knowledge

facts and ideas? What principle or principles are they based on? What else could they be applied to? How do they fit in with what I already know? From these facts and ideas, what else can I learn? When you reflect, you weave new facts and ideas into your existing knowledge and create a fabric of genuine wisdom. History's greatest thinkers have relied on reflection for their breakthroughs. They make a strong case for reflection as a vital skill. With a technique or two to get you started, you can begin using reflection on your own to master your notes and gain lasting learning and genuine insight.

Learn Why Reflection Is Vital

REFRAMING

What did Bethe say about reflection?

Professor Hans Bethe, Cornell University's famous nuclear physicist and Nobel Prize winner, talked about reflection as used by a scientist:

> To become a good scientist one must live with the problem he's working on. The problem must follow the scientist wherever he goes. You can't be a good scientist working only eight hours a day. Science must be the consuming interest of your life. You must want to know. Nothing matters more than finding the answer to the question or the problem you are engaged in.[1]

What is the connection between reflection and creativity?

Professor Bethe went on to say that students who go only as far as their textbooks and lectures take them can become proficient, but never creative. Creativity comes only with reflection. That is, seeing new material in the light of what you already know is the only road to original ideas, for having an idea is nothing more than discovering a relationship not seen before. And it is impossible to have ideas without reflecting.

What was Whitehead's position on reflection?

Alfred North Whitehead, famous British philosopher and mathematician, strongly advocated reflection. He, too, spoke about the knowledge that grows out of throwing ideas "into fresh combinations." He viewed reflection as taking what one already knows and projecting one's thought beyond familiar experience—considering new knowledge and ideas in the light of the old, and the old in the light of the new.

What was Schopenhauer's point about reflection?

The famous German philosopher Arthur Schopenhauer had exceptionally strong views on the importance of reflection.

> A library may be very large, but if it is in disorder, it is not so useful as one that is small but well arranged. In the same way, a man may have a great mass of knowledge, but if he has not worked it up by thinking it over for himself, it has much less value than a far smaller amount which he has thoroughly pondered. For it is only when a man looks at his knowledge from all sides, and combines the things he knows by comparing truth with truth, that he obtains a complete hold over it and gets it into his power.

[1]Interview with Professor Hans Bethe, May 19, 1960.

www.cengage.com/success/Pauk/HowTOStudy10e

Reflections should not be left vague. Pursue the problem until ideas take definite shape. If you need more information, an encyclopedia or a standard book on the subject will often give you what you need to bring fuzzy ideas into focus.[2]

What is the connection between reflection and the subconscious?

The subconscious plays an important role in creative thinking and discovery. We have all had an exciting idea or even the solution to a problem suddenly flash upon us when we weren't consciously thinking about it. The great Hungarian physicist Leo Szilard came up with the solution to the nuclear chain reaction while crossing a London street. Archimedes arrived at the principle of displacement while sitting in his bathtub. The mind continues to work on concepts even when you aren't aware of it. The process that initiates much of this deep thinking is reflection.

Use Techniques to Help You Reflect

REFRAMING — PLANNING

What is a big advantage of reflection?

A great advantage of reflection is its flexibility. It can be molded to fit your imagination. You can take it with you wherever you go and make use of it in spare moments. You can reflect while walking from one building to another, standing in line, waiting for a friend, or riding a bus.

What is a drawback of reflection?

But reflection's flexibility can also be a disadvantage if you're unsure of how to get started. This uncertainty prompts some students to skip over the reflection step completely. Although there are no specific reflection steps like those you might find for reviewing or reciting, there are a number of strategies you can use to ease into a reflective mindset.

Use the Silver Dollar System

How does the Silver Dollar System work?

You can reflect on the information from your notes and make it more manageable by using the Silver Dollar System:

1. Read through your notes and make an *S* in the margin next to any idea that seems important. Depending on the number of pages of notes you read, you'll probably wind up with several dozen *S*'s.
2. Now read only the notes you have flagged with an *S*. As you go through these flagged notes for a second time, select the ideas that seem particularly important, and draw a vertical line through the *S*'s that are next to them. Your symbol will look like this: $.
3. Make a third and final pass through your notes, reading only those ideas that have been marked $. Out of these notes, mark the truly outstanding ideas—there will be only a handful of them—with another vertical line so your markings look like dollar signs: $.

[2]Essays of Arthur Schopenhauer, selected and translated by T. Bailey Saunders (New York: A. L. Burt, 1892), p. 321.

Turn Your Notes into Knowledge

The Silver Dollar System stimulates reflection by helping you compare the relative weights of the ideas you have noted. It shows you at a glance which ideas are crucial to remember and which are not. The $ sign alerts you to the truly important ideas, the "Silver Dollar" ideas that should receive most of your attention. Next come the $ ideas; they are worthy but shouldn't clutter up your memory if you have a lot to remember in a limited amount of time. Finally, the S ideas can be ignored. Although you flagged these as potentially important ideas, since then you've twice marked ideas that were even more important.

Rearrange Your Information

How is rearranging your information helpful?

You almost always gain insight when you *reframe* information, that is when you look at it from a different framework or perspective. If, for example, you've been studying countries geographically, you might want to consider grouping them by their systems of government or comparing them chronologically. You may want to group existing information under categories such as "pros" and "cons" or "before" and "after," depending on the nature of the information you are mastering.

Use Software

How can software be used to aid reflection?

Computer software can provide most of the benefits of manual rearranging but without the drudgery and time expense. Some computer programs can take a split second to reconfigure information that would take hours to rearrange by hand. Most word processor and spreadsheet programs allow you to sort a table of information by one or more of its columns. More sophisticated tools found in many spreadsheet programs allow you to take an existing table and turn it into a brand-new table that clusters the information in any number of ways of your choosing. Thus, if you had a table that listed all the presidents of the United States, the years they took office, their political parties, and their states of birth, you would be able to see, for example, all the presidents from Ohio, all the presidents who were members of the Whig Party, or all the presidents who took office between 1800 and 1850. These clusters could trigger any number of reflective questions: What happened to the Whig Party? What other political parties no longer exist? Why are so many presidents from Ohio? Who was the first president from Ohio? Who is the most recent president from Ohio? Which state has produced the most presidents? How does the number of presidents between 1800 and 1850 compare with the number of presidents between 1900 and 1950? And so on. Because a computer performs it, the actual rearranging teaches you nothing. But the questions you ask as a result will stimulate reflection and strengthen your memories by allowing you to remember things in a variety of ways. In a similar fashion, the increasingly popular use of tagging on blogs and other Internet sites provides an extremely helpful means of quickly and dynamically grouping information in different ways to add context, broaden understanding, and aid reflection.

**Figure 11.6
Cornell System Format
for Combining Lecture
and Textbook Notes**

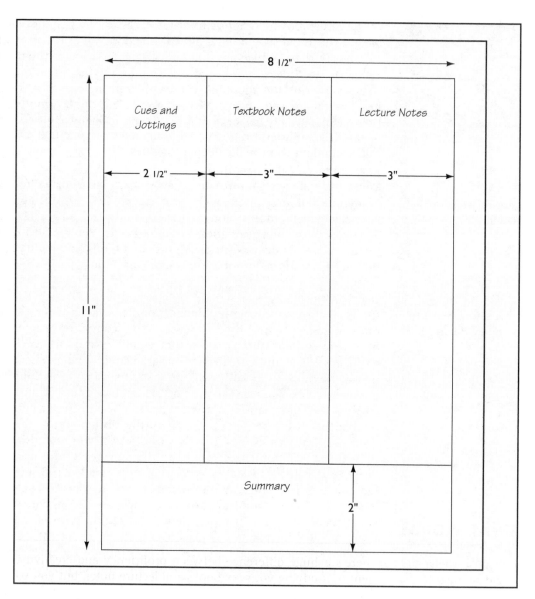

Put It in Context

Why is context an
important factor in
reflection?

Few ideas are meaningful when viewed in isolation. They need context to establish them in a realm that you can truly understand. For example, if you read about a scientific discovery from a certain time period, consider examining other events from the year the discovery was made or the place where the discovery occurred. Was this before or after the Civil War, the Second World War, the Vietnam War? Had the telephone, the radio, or the computer been invented? Were people traveling by horse, by car, or by jet? These investigations supply a basic background (see Chapter 9) that will often yield a deeper understanding.

Ask More Questions

Why is it helpful to ask additional questions?

In press conferences, the follow-up question is sometimes more insightful than the original question. If you've been using the Q System, each idea in your notes or paragraph in your reading assignment has an accompanying question. Come up with a follow-up to the original question and see if your notes or your text can provide the answer. If not, you might want to dig deeper for clues.

Think Visually

How can concept maps be used as a reflection tool?

Chapter 8 explains how concept maps can be used to work out problems, explore possibilities, and establish connections. These are exactly the sorts of issues that reflection addresses. Take the key concepts from your notes or from a chapter assignment, put them in ovals on a plain sheet of paper, and try numerous ways of arranging and connecting them. If you do, you will almost certainly learn something that wasn't clear to you when those concepts were merely isolated words on a page.

Combine Textbook and Lecture Notes

How do you combine textbook and lecture notes?

Although the classroom lectures you attend should presumably relate to your reading assignments, you won't always see the connections clearly until you can actually place notes from both side by side. Using the format shown in Figure 11.6, jot down the most important information from a textbook assignment in the middle column of the three-column note sheet. Then add any lecture notes that deal with the same topic in the right column, alongside the textbook notes they pertain to. Finally, just as you did with your original notes, use the Q System to arrive at a question for which the textbook note *and* any related information from the lecture is the answer. It's impossible to predict in advance what you'll learn from this experience, but by combining two sets of notes you'll almost certainly arrive at an answer that is greater than the sum of the parts. This is the essence of reflection.

FINAL WORDS

How do a scholar and a student differ?

There's a huge difference between proficiency and creativity. You can become proficient by studying your textbooks and lecture notes, but you will never be creative until you try to see beyond the facts, to leap mentally beyond the given. If your object is simply to tackle tests, pass your courses, and emerge from college with a degree and reasonably good prospects for employment, this book should serve you well. But if your aspirations aim higher, this book will serve you even better. The things that distinguish a scholar from a mere student are perpetual curiosity and an unquenchable thirst for learning. Reviewing and reciting should help you reach your modest goals. Reflection will enable you to reach for the stars.

www.cengage.com/success/Pauk/HowTOStudy10e

CHAPTER CHECKUP

SENTENCE COMPLETION

Complete the following sentences with one of the three words listed below each sentence.

1. You can bring forgetting almost to a standstill with _____.

    summaries   **recitation**   **questions**

2. Creativity comes only with _____.

    practice   **reflection**   **summaries**

3. Ideas in your notes that you have marked with an *S* can be _____.

    saved   **difficult**   **ignored**

MATCHING

In each blank space in the left column, write the letter preceding the phrase in the right column that matches the left item best.

_____ 1. Reflecting

_____ 2. Recitating

_____ 3. Split-level

_____ 4. Bookmark

_____ 5. Rereading

_____ 6. Silver Dollar

_____ 7. Reviewing

_____ 8. Writing

a. Method that summarizes an entire assignment as well as each page

b. System that allows you to reduce and reflect on your note sheets

c. Used as an alternative to the traditional method of reciting your notes

d. Using your innate curiosity to mull over ideas

e. Alternate Q System method when your textbook margins are too narrow

f. Provided when you add questions and summaries to your notes

g. Mistakenly thought to be an effective method of reviewing

h. Repeating key information from memory and in your own words

TRUE-FALSE

Circle T *beside the* true *statements and* F *beside the* false *statements.*

1. T   F   Most students review their notes by reading them over.

2. T   F   When using the Q System, try to come up with yes-or-no questions.

3. T   F   It's OK to abbreviate your Q System questions.

4. T   F   If your notes are in a computer file, you will be unable to recite them.

5. T   F   Although reciting by writing is slower than traditional reciting, it provides added benefits.

Turn Your Notes into Knowledge

MULTIPLE CHOICE *Choose the word or phrase that completes each sentence most accurately, and circle the letter that precedes it.*

1. The primary purpose of an immediate review is to
    a. cement your understanding.
    b. spot-check your notes.
    c. look up words or terms you don't know.
    d. make sure your notes are legible.

2. If your textbook's margins are too narrow for Q System questions, you can use
    a. the sticky note method.
    b. the bookmark method.
    c. separate notes.
    d. all of the above.

3. Adding summaries to your notes helps you
    a. zero in on key ideas.
    b. gain a broader perspective.
    c. anticipate multiple-choice questions.
    d. include questions you couldn't fit in the margins.

4. The traditional way to recite is
    a. out loud.
    b. in your own words.
    c. from memory.
    d. all of the above.

5. One strength and weakness of reflection is its
    a. cost.
    b. repetitiveness.
    c. flexibility.
    d. imagination

REFLECTION *Think about the ideas outlined in this chapter and then draw upon your own opinions and experiences to answer each question fully.*

1. Both the Q System and summaries help you master your notes but from two different perspectives. Which approach do you think will be easiest for you to adopt? Which approach will be the most valuable for you? Explain why in each case.

www.cengage.com/success/Pauk/HowTOStudy10e

2. Are you already in the habit of reciting your notes? If so, do you recite out loud or in writing? Explain your choice. If you haven't been reciting your notes up until now, why not? Has this chapter convinced you about the value of reciting?

3. Can you think of some specific examples where you already use the technique of reflection? If so, please explain. If not, suggest situations where you could use reflection in the future and mention a method of reflection that seems to best suit the way you learn and understand things.

IT'S YOUR Q

The Q System uses marginal questions to encourage active reading. You'll notice that most but not all paragraphs in this chapter are accompanied by marginal questions. Now it's your Q. Scan the chapter for any paragraph that is missing a question, reread the paragraph, establish the main idea, and then arrive at a question that elicits it. Use the questions in the surrounding paragraphs as models for your own marginal questions.

VOCABULARY IN ACTION

To expand the horizons of your understanding and to refine the precision of your thought, the three exercises that follow are designed to help you grow, strengthen, and maintain your own vocabulary.

SAY WHAT?

From the three choices beside each numbered item, select the one that most nearly expresses the meaning of the italicized word in the quote. Make a light check mark (√) next to your choice.

There are many examples of old, incorrect theories that stubbornly persisted, *sustained* only by the *prestige* of foolish but well-connected scientists. Many of these theories have been killed off only when some *decisive* experiment exposed their incorrectness.

—Michio Kaku (1947—) American theoretical physicist

1. *sustained*	suffered	prolonged	confirmed
2. *prestige*	reputation	charm	greatness
3. *decisive*	unmistakable	confident	conclusive

Turn Your Notes into Knowledge

Voting is the most precious right of every citizen, and we have a moral obligation to *ensure* the *integrity* of our voting process.

—Hillary Clinton (1947—), U.S. Secretary of State

4. *ensure*   underwrite   guarantee   pacify

5. *integrity*   reliability   honesty   morality

Part III: Retaining Information

VOCAB-U-LADDER

Use your knowledge of word synonyms and roots to connect the word at the top rung to the word at the bottom rung, using the words listed below.

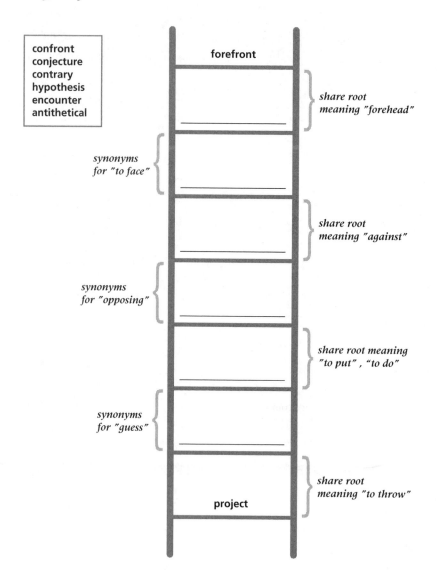

confront
conjecture
contrary
hypothesis
encounter
antithetical

forefront

*share root
meaning "forehead"*

*synonyms
for "to face"*

*share root
meaning "against"*

*synonyms
for "opposing"*

*share root meaning
"to put" , "to do"*

*synonyms
for "guess"*

*share root
meaning "to throw"*

project

Turn Your Notes into Knowledge

Here's the story behind a word that figures prominently in the chapter you've just read.

Cue Finding clues for cue leads to Q

cue kyōō *n.* 1. A signal, such as a word or action, used to prompt another event in a performance, such as an actor's speech or entrance, a change in lighting, or a sound effect. 2. a. A reminder or prompting. b. A hint or suggestion.*

Tracking down the story of a word isn't always easy. In fact, it can sometimes require quite a bit of detective work. Some words evolve naturally and often imperceptibly over time. As a result, when somebody finally steps back and asks "Hey, where did that word come from?" the answer may not be readily available. What's more, well-intentioned efforts to explain a word's origins can sometimes lead down the wrong path. For example, the word *queue,* which describes both a line of people and a pigtail, comes from the Old French word cue meaning "tail", the same source that gave us the word *curlicue.* So are the Q System cues you write in your Cornell-style columns related somehow to the French word for tail? That's doubtful, although some word experts have tried hard to make the connection. A more likely explanation comes from sixteenth century theater where actors would mark the margins of their scripts to indicate the places in the play where they were supposed to deliver their lines. Instead of drawing a line or an arrow, they would add the letter Q (or sometimes "qu") to the spots when it was their time to do the talking. Why a Q? Word detectives suggest that these marginal Qs were abbreviations for the Latin word *quando* meaning "when." And when the time came to refer to this Q mark in print, writers as well known as William Shakespeare and Henry Fielding started spelling it *cue.***

---

* Adapted from "cue." *The American Heritage Dictionary of the English Language,* 4th ed. Boston: Houghton Mifflin, 2000. http://dictionary.reference.com/browse/cue (accessed June 4, 2009).

** Based on information from "cue." *The American Heritage Dictionary of the English Language,* 4th ed. Boston: Houghton Mifflin, 2000. http://dictionary.reference.com/browse/cue (accessed June 4, 2009).;"cue." *Online Etymology Dictionary.* Douglas Harper, Historian. http://www.etymonline.com/index.php?search=cue (accessed June 4, 2009).; "cue, *n" Oxford English Dictionary,* 2nd ed. 20 vols. Oxford: Oxford University Press, 1989.; "cue, *n²" OED Online.* Oxford University Press. http://sc-www2.santacruzpl.org:2062/cgi/entry/50055417 (accessed Jun 4, 2009).